TODAY'S MORAL ISSUES

Classic and Contemporary Perspectives

Fourth Edition

DANIEL BONEVAC

University of Texas at Austin

Mc
Graw
Hill

Boston   Burr Ridge, IL   Dubuque, IA   Madison, WI   New York   San Francisco   St. Louis
Bangkok   Bogotá   Caracas   Kuala Lumpur   Lisbon   London   Madrid   Mexico City
Milan   Montreal   New Delhi   Santiago   Seoul   Singapore   Sydney   Taipei   Toronto

McGraw-Hill Higher Education
*A Division of The **McGraw-Hill** Companies*

1 2 3 4 5 6 7 8 9 0 BAH/BAH 0 9 8 7 6 5 4 3 2 1

Library of Congress Cataloging-in-Publication Data
Today's moral issues / [edited by] Daniel Bonevac.—4th ed.
     p.   cm.
   ISBN 0-7674-2020-9
   1. Ethical problems.   2. Applied ethics.   I. Bonevac, Daniel A.
BJ1031.T63   2001
170—dc21

Sponsoring editor, Kenneth King; production, Publishing Support Services; manuscript editor, April Wells-Hayes; design manager, Jean Mailander; text designer, Donna Davis; cover designer, Lisa Buckley; manufacturing manager, Randy Hurst. The text was set in 10/12 Berkeley Book by TBH Typecast, Inc., and printed on 45# Lighthouse Matte by The Banta Book Group.

Cover image: Paul Klee (1879–1940). *Scheidung abends,* 1922. Watercolor on paper. 33.5 × 23.3 cm. Klee family collection. © AKG London.

www.mhhe.com

For Joseph Horn

PREFACE

This book is a text for courses on contemporary moral issues. Such courses assume that philosophy has something important to contribute to contemporary moral problems. They try to bring philosophical theories to bear on practical questions. From one point of view, this seems difficult. Philosophy is in many ways the most abstract of all disciplines. The questions it addresses are very general: What is real? How do we know? What should we do? But philosophy is also the most practical of all disciplines. It aims at wisdom. Living wisely, displaying good judgment, understanding yourself and your surroundings—these offer immense benefits to all, no matter who they are, how they earn a living, or what kind of society they inhabit. Living wisely is a key to living well. For just that reason, Aristotle thought that philosophy was the highest human activity and that the contemplative life was the highest and happiest form of life possible for a human being.

Nevertheless, it is not always easy to bring theory and practice together in the classroom. Philosophical texts can be hard to read. Philosophers often write primarily for each other. And arguments about contemporary issues are rarely reflective; the underlying principles can be hard to discern.

Contemporary moral problems textbooks often amplify these difficulties. They contain mostly papers by professional philosophers written for a professional audience. They tend to either omit underlying theoretical approaches altogether or segregate them in a separate section of the book. The first strategy leaves students with no moral compass. Students have trouble abstracting ethical principles and methods from treatments of particular issues; even the best students flounder when faced with issues that have not been treated explicitly in class. The result is that students emerge with only the vaguest idea of what ethical thinking is. The second strategy divides courses into two parts that are hard to unify.

The theory usually strikes students as dry and irrelevant, while the practical part remains confusing or, at best, an exercise in applying theory.

This book tries to resolve the dilemma by tying theoretical and practical considerations together. *Today's Moral Issues* combines theoretical and practical readings on four general themes: first principles, liberty, rights and responsibilities, and justice. The theoretical readings relate closely to the contemporary readings that follow. I have found that using philosophical texts helps students connect theory and practice, for writers such as Locke and Mill tend to be more concrete and practical in outlook than most secondary discussions of their thought. Their motivations are not difficult for most students to understand. And I have edited the theoretical texts closely to bring students into direct contact with their chief motivations and arguments.

The classic and contemporary theoretical approaches constitute a foundation for thinking about contemporary issues. Combining these texts with discussions of contemporary problems lets students see the dialectic between theory and practice in ethics. Faced with practical dilemmas and disagreements, it is easy to see why ethical thinkers have sought to construct theories. And contemporary issues provide opportunities not only to apply theories but to test and evaluate them. Good students, I have found, attain not only a rich understanding of the theories, the issues, and how they relate, but also a real sense of what ethical thinking is all about.

Today's Moral Issues is unique in treating contemporary moral issues in the context of both political philosophy and ethics. Issues such as abortion, euthanasia, and the environment have political as well as personal dimensions. Others, such as freedom of speech, capital punishment, and economic, racial, sexual, and global equality, are almost entirely political. To treat them adequately, one must consider the proper ends of government and the bounds of state action.

New Features

This edition retains the virtues of earlier editions. It combines theoretical and practical treatments of ethical and political issues from a wide variety of perspectives and sources, including court cases, journalists, public figures, public policy researchers, and scientists as well as philosophers.

This edition also has some new virtues. It differs from earlier editions in some important ways:

1. The "Classic Texts" sections are now called "Theoretical Approaches." I have added a variety of new and, in many cases, contemporary readings to them, including Aquinas, Simone de Beauvoir, and Albert Camus. My goal has been to include continental and communitarian approaches that form a counterpoint to the readings from the Aristotelian, Kantian, utilitarian, and social contract traditions that remain from earlier editions, while also filling in gaps in the latter.

2. Part IV, Justice and Equality, is now organized around the theme of equality. There are sections on Economic, Racial, and Global Equality, with new readings (including *Brown* v. *Board of Education,* the Reverend Martin Luther King, Jr.'s, "I Have a Dream" speech, and Michael Walzer's communitarian argument for welfare programs as meeting needs) plus an entirely new section on Sexual Equality. These sections not only structure the discussion of the issues more clearly but give prominent place to feminist and communitarian perspectives. I have worked hard to maintain a balance of points of view from different parts of the political and philosophical spectrum.

3. The Privacy section has been revised extensively and moved to Part III, Rights and Responsibilities. It has important links to theoretical readings—including Kantian, utilitarian, continental, feminist, and communitarian ones—and to the abortion and euthanasia issues.

4. The Capital Punishment section has new readings to provide a richer historical perspective and to bring up to date the discussion of the deterrence effect of the death penalty and the possibility of executing the innocent.

5. The length of many readings has been reduced to make it easier for students to identify key concepts and arguments. I have retained court cases but have edited them more carefully to bring out their philosophical and practical significance more directly.

6. The reading selections, introductions, and discussion questions have been crafted carefully to stress the links between theoretical approaches and contemporary problems.

7. The Web page (*http://www.la.utexas.edu/ phl304db/tmi.html*) that accompanies the book has been expanded considerably. It includes many features to help both students and instructors, including

   a. sample course syllabi
   b. extensive class notes for all sections of the book, with links to relevant parts of philosophical texts (where they are public domain and available online)
   c. a study guide summarizing key points
   d. a comprehensive glossary of terms
   e. practice exams
   f. suggested readings
   g. relevant court cases
   h. Web links to other sources of information on contemporary issues
   i. a guide to writing philosophical essays
   j. tips on multimedia presentations

Acknowledgments

This book and the ideas behind it have evolved considerably during the twenty-four years I have been teaching contemporary moral issues courses at the University of Pittsburgh and the University of Texas at Austin. I am grateful to the many instructors, teaching assistants, and students who have used earlier versions and helped me refine them. I am particularly grateful to the nearly 10,000 students who have taken my contemporary moral problems course at the University of Texas at Austin. They have taught me much about what a course on moral issues ought to be.

I especially want to thank Nicholas Asher and Stephen Phillips, who have team-taught courses on contemporary moral problems with me. Their ideas have found expression here in more ways than I can distinguish. I am also grateful for the helpful criticism and advice I have received throughout the years from Randy Mayes, California State University, Sacramento; Bill Myers, Birmingham Southern College; David Bradshaw, University of Kentucky; and Jonathan Davis, University of Texas at Austin.

I would like to thank the reviewers whose comments have helped me clarify my own thinking and decide what issues and readings to include: for the first edition, L. E. Andrade, Illinois State University; Linda Bomstad, California State University, Sacramento; Karen Hanson, Indiana University; and Anita Silvers, San Francisco State University; for the second edition, Stephanie Beardman, Rutgers University; Ray Cebik, University of Tennessee, Knoxville; Deirdre Golash, American University; Patrick Lee, Franciscan University of Steubenville; Aaron Meskin, Rutgers University; Sharon Sytsma, Northern Illinois University; and Nathan Tierney, California Lutheran University; for the third edition, Naomi Azck, University of Albany, State University of New York; Stephen Carey, Virginia Commonwealth University; Scott Lehman, University of Connecticut; A. P. Roark, University of Washington; and Stewart Shapiro, Ohio State University at Newark; and, for the fourth edition, Abrol O. Fairweather, CSU, Hayward; A. R. Molina, University of Miami; Barbara Montero, NYU; Lawrence Pasternack, Oklahoma State University; Janice Staab, Southern Illinois University; and Lawrence Stark, State University of NY at Albany.

I am grateful to all of those at Mayfield Publishing Company who have supported this book and worked to make my ideas a reality. I want especially to thank my editors. Jim Bull was vital to the first two editions, and Ken King has been similarly vital to the next two. I am also grateful to Mayfield's Lynn Rabin Bauer and Vicki Moran of Publishing Support Services for their work in producing this book.

CONTENTS

PART III   RIGHTS AND RESPONSIBILITIES   251

PART IV   JUSTICE AND EQUALITY   417

MORAL ARGUMENTS
AND MORAL RELATIVISM

This is a book about moral issues. What are moral issues? To answer this question, we need to consider the definition of philosophy. If the word itself is any guide, philosophy is the love of wisdom. A simple definition of wisdom, in turn, is good judgment. Philosophy, then, is the love or pursuit of good judgment. Moral philosophy, or ethics, is the pursuit of good judgment about character and action—about what kind of person to be and about what to do. Ethics addresses questions about virtue and vice, good and bad, right and wrong.

Such questions, clearly, have varied answers; they are often the subject of controversy and debate. The moral issues considered in this book—abortion, euthanasia, pornography, capital punishment, affirmative action, and many others—are among the most controversial our society faces. Most of this book consists of moral arguments, in which a moral issue is considered and a particular position is supported or a particular conclusion is reached through reasoning.

How can we think through moral issues carefully and systematically? How do we develop arguments for ethical conclusions? These are questions that I attempt to answer in this introduction. I also consider an important objection to the idea of moral argument, namely, the view that different groups have different values and it is therefore impossible to argue logically about right and wrong. This position, known as *relativism,* is common today and poses a serious challenge to ethical thinking.

Relativism

Allan Bloom began his 1987 book *The Closing of the American Mind* with the statement, "There is one thing a professor can be absolutely certain of: Almost every student entering the university believes, or says he believes, that truth is relative."* This is especially so in philosophy courses and in ethics courses in particular. Ethics consists of principled reflection on questions such as, How should I live? and What should I do? It takes as its central tasks criticizing, justifying, and deciding on various answers to these questions. No one, of course, likes to be criticized; no one likes to think that his or her particular answer to the question, How should I live? is unjustified or just plain wrong. So it can be tempting to defang these questions by saying that truth in ethics is relative.

But relative to what? To an individual person? To a society, a culture, or the currently popular formulation, "interpretive community"? To humanity as a whole? The last, relativity to humanity, does not challenge the traditional project of ethics at all; Aristotle characterizes ethics as the search for the good life for man. Even the second, relativity to a society or a culture, has little effect on the discussions of contemporary issues in this book. The readings debate social problems in the context of affluent, technologically advanced societies such as those of the United States, Canada, and Europe. Problems such as welfare, abortion, and world hunger might look very different from the perspective of a poor developing nation. Relativity to a society or a culture does, however, have an impact on the theoretical discussions in the classic readings in this collection, which

---

* Allan Bloom, *The Closing of the American Mind* (New York: Simon & Schuster, 1987), 25.

generally purport to say something about what is good for all human beings, not just residents of the United States, Canada, or Europe. And relativity to an individual makes ethical thinking absurd; what is good for me may differ so completely from what is good for you that ethical reflection and argument make no sense.

To be more precise, let us say that an *ethical relativist* believes that fundamental ethical truth—the basic truth about how one should live and what one should do—is relative to a group smaller than humanity as a whole. Something may be fundamentally right for one group but fundamentally wrong for another. A *cultural relativist* holds that fundamental ethical truth is relative to a culture; an *individual relativist* holds that it is relative to each individual person.

These definitions depend on the idea of *fundamental* ethical truth. Certain answers to ethical questions presuppose other answers to more basic questions. An ethical truth is fundamental if it does not depend on facts and *derivative* if it does. Disagreement over fundamental ethical truths is thus purely ethical; it does not stem from a factual disagreement. To say that something may be fundamentally right for one group but fundamentally wrong for another is thus to say that there may be different answers to the questions of how to live and what to do for these groups, even though the factual circumstances and the groups' beliefs about the factual circumstances are exactly the same.

If we make no distinction between fundamental and derivative truths, individual relativism is obvious. Suppose that John has murdered someone and Mary has done no harm to anyone. Then John deserves to be punished and Mary does not. John should turn himself over to the police; Mary should not. John's obligations differ from Mary's because of the facts. Relativism is interesting only when it pertains to the most fundamental ethical truths, which are independent of facts. What these are, of course, is controversial. Different moral theories espouse different candidates. But it is at the level of fundamental truths—Maximize good, Treat others as ends, not merely as means, Treat others as you would want to be treated—that the issue must be decided.

Relativism is often motivated by toleration or openness. Since tolerance is a virtue, relativists see their own position as morally required. Bloom observes,

> That it is a moral issue for students is revealed by the character of their response when challenged—a combination of belief and indignation: "Are you an absolutist?," the only alternative they know, uttered in the same tone as "Are you a monarchist?" or "Do you really believe in witches?" This latter leads into the indignation, for someone who believes in witches might well be a witch-hunter or a Salem judge. The danger they have been taught to fear from absolutism is not error but intolerance.*

But tolerance and relativism are not the same thing. I may believe that I am right and you are wrong, while still tolerating your behavior and respecting your right to be wrong. The traditional belief in freedom of thought and freedom of speech requires just such an attitude.

Conversely, I may be a relativist, holding only that my opinion is right *for me,* yet show little tolerance for any deviation from my opinion. The intolerance of relativists is not only possible but common enough to have a label: *political correctness.* Friedrich Nietzsche predicted that the twentieth century would be a century of great wars, precisely because it would be a century of relativism. Without truth, Nietzsche understood, there is only power.

Bloom frets that his students cannot defend their opinions. But it is possible to think through issues in ethics, including ethical relativism, carefully and systematically, as mentioned earlier. This introduction provides you with some tools—the basic elements of reasoning—that will help you do this. It tells you how to recognize and evaluate arguments. The examples used are arguments for and against ethical relativism. At the end, you should not only know how to analyze an argument critically but also have greater insight into relativism.

Arguments

Arguments are bits of reasoning in language. Frequently, we think of arguments as conflicts. In that

---

* Bloom, *The Closing of the American Mind,* 25.

sense, this book presents a series of arguments about issues such as abortion, euthanasia, and affirmative action. But philosophers and logicians primarily use "argument" in the sense that one argues for a conclusion. An argument starts with some assertions and tries to justify a thesis.

Components of Arguments

The initial assertions of an argument are its *premises;* the thesis that the argument tries to justify is its *conclusion.* Arguments consist of *statements,* sentences that can be true or false. Almost every sentence in this book falls into this category. Statements are declarative, in the indicative mood; they say something about the way the world is, correctly or incorrectly.

Here, for example, is a simple argument that some have advanced in favor of cultural relativism:

(1) Societies differ in their fundamental ethical beliefs.
∴ Ethical truth is relative to culture.

(This format lists the premises in the order in which they are given and then gives the conclusion. The symbol ∴ means "therefore.")

How can we recognize arguments? The premises of an argument are meant to support the conclusion. We can recognize arguments, then, by recognizing when some statements are offered in support of others. We can do this most easily, in turn, if we can distinguish premises from conclusions. But how can we pick out the conclusion of an argument? In English, various words and phrases can signal the premises or the conclusion of an argument.

- *Conclusion Indicators:* therefore, thus, hence, consequently, it follows that, in conclusion, as a result, then, must, accordingly, this implies that, this entails that, we may infer that
- *Premise Indicators:* because, as, for, since, given that, for the reason that

Beware: These words and phrases have other uses as well.

Extended or *complex* arguments contain other arguments. *Simple* arguments do not. Because extended arguments are good only if the simple arguments within them are good, it is best to break extended arguments down into their simple components and analyze them separately.

Validity and Soundness

To evaluate arguments, we need to ask, What distinguishes good from bad arguments? What makes a good argument good?

A good argument links its premises to its conclusion in the right way. In a (deductively) *valid* argument, the truth of the premises guarantees the truth of the conclusion. If the premises are all true, then the conclusion has to be true. Or, equivalently, if the conclusion of a valid argument is false, at least one premise must also be false. Consider, for example, the argument:

(2) All promises ought to be kept.
Your promise to Joe is a promise.
∴ You ought to keep your promise to Joe.

In any circumstance in which the premises of this argument are true, the conclusion must be true as well. It is impossible to conceive of a state of affairs in which, while all promises ought to be kept, and your promise to Joe is a promise, you nevertheless should not keep your promise to Joe. If it is false that you should keep your promise to Joe, then either there are promises that shouldn't be kept, or your "promise" wasn't a real promise.

Valid arguments are only one species of good argument. Others are *inductively strong* (or *reliable*). The truth of the premises of such an argument does not guarantee the truth of its conclusion, but it does make the truth of the conclusion probable. Consider, for example, this argument:

(3) Every generous person I've ever known has also been kind.
∴ All generous people are kind.

It is possible for the premise to be true while the conclusion is false. There may be generous but nasty people I've never met. So the argument is invalid. Nevertheless, the premise lends some support to the conclusion. The argument is inductively strong; how strong depends on how many generous people I've known, among other things.

In general, good arguments not only are valid or inductively strong but also have true premises. A *sound* argument is a valid argument with true premises. In any valid argument, the truth of the premises guarantees the truth of the conclusion. So, a sound argument also has a true conclusion. A *cogent* argument is an inductively strong argument with true premises. In a cogent argument, the truth of the conclusion is likely but not guaranteed.

Evaluating Arguments: Three Arguments for Cultural Relativism

Logic develops precise ways of determining whether arguments are valid (although the most powerful ways of evaluating arguments are intuitive). An argument is valid if the truth of the premises guarantees the truth of the conclusion. To show that an argument is invalid, therefore, one needs to show that the premises could all be true while the conclusion is false.

There are two ways of showing that an argument is invalid. The first, the *direct* method, is simply to describe such a situation. That is, we can show an argument to be invalid by depicting a possible circumstance in which the premises were all true but the conclusion was false. Consider the argument with which we began:

(1) Societies differ in their fundamental ethical beliefs.
   ∴ Ethical truth is relative to culture.

To show that this is invalid, we might imagine a circumstance in which societies differ in fundamental ethical beliefs because one or both are wrong, not because ethical truth is relative.

The second way to show that an argument is invalid, devised by Aristotle, is based on the idea of *form* and is known as the method of *counterexamples*. To show that an argument is invalid using this method, we must produce another argument of the same form with true premises and a false conclusion. This introduction is too short to present a detailed discussion of form. But Aristotle's insight was that validity is *formal* in the sense that arguments can be classified into certain general patterns, or forms, of which individual arguments are instances. An argument form is valid if and only if every instance of it is valid. More to the point, an argument form is invalid

if and only if some instance of it is invalid. To show that an argument form is invalid, then, find an instance with true premises and a false conclusion. To show that an *individual argument* is invalid, find an argument with true premises and a false conclusion that shares the *specific form* of the original argument: the most explicit form we can devise, displaying the most structure.

Let's now consider and evaluate three arguments for cultural relativism: the argument from cultural variation, the argument from undecidability, and the argument from subjectivism.

The Argument from Cultural Variation

The argument from cultural variation is an extended argument consisting of several simple arguments in sequence:

(4) Ancient Greek society accepted infanticide.
   Contemporary American society does not.
   ∴ Societies differ in their fundamental ethical beliefs.
   Societies differ in their fundamental ethical beliefs.
   ∴ Ethical truth is relative to culture.

To apply the method of counterexamples to (1) (which is a key step in the argument from cultural variation), we need to find an argument with the same specific form but with true premises and a false conclusion:

(5) Societies differ in their fundamental astronomical beliefs.
   ∴ Astronomical truth is relative to culture.

Ancient Greeks believed that the sun revolves around the earth. We believe that the earth revolves around the sun. But nobody thinks that the truth of the matter is culturally relative; the earth and sun did not switch places at some point in the last 2000 years. Thus, the argument from cultural variation can be shown to be invalid.

The Argument from Undecidability

Another argument for cultural relativism is the argument from undecidability, which insists that there is no neutral ground on which one might judge competing ethical claims.

(6) Ancient Greeks could not neutrally judge which society is right.
 [Ancient Greeks will use their own society's standards.
 They will judge their own society to be right.
 Their use of their own standards biases them.
 ∴ They could not neutrally judge which society is right.]
 Contemporary Americans cannot neutrally judge which society is right.
 [Contemporary Americans will use their own society's standards.
 They will judge their own society to be right.
 Their use of their own standards biases them.
 ∴ They cannot neutrally judge which society is right.]
 Members of other societies cannot neutrally judge which society is right.
 [They will use their own society's standards.
 They will judge their own society to be right.
 Their use of their own standards biases them.
 ∴ They cannot neutrally judge which society is right.]
 ∴ No one can neutrally judge which society is right.

The argument from undecidability is an extended argument containing an overall argument (6)a and three subarguments, one for each premise, all having a similar form (6)b:

(6)a Ancient Greeks could not neutrally judge which society is right.
 Contemporary Americans cannot neutrally judge which society is right.
 Members of other societies cannot neutrally judge which society is right.
 ∴ No one can neutrally judge which society is right.

(6)b Members of society X will use X's standards.
 They will judge X to be right.
 Their use of X's standards biases them.
 ∴ They could not neutrally judge which society is right.

As long as everyone is a member of some society or other, (6)a is valid. And if all must use their own

societies' standards, which biases them, then none can neutrally judge which society is right, so (6)b is valid as well. One can certainly raise questions about the truth of its premises, of course. Remember that even if an argument is valid, it may not be sound; one or more premises may be false. Members of a society often use different standards, while people from different societies use similar standards, making the first premise of (6)b doubtful. Members of a society can judge their own society and its standards inadequate, even by its own standards; the standards themselves may contain norms of self-improvement. That casts doubt on the second premise. Finally, their use of their society's standards may not bias them, if there is significant overlap between those standards and those of the competing society. It may be possible to evaluate which society is right on the basis of standards that both accept.

Moreover, to use the argument from undecidability to support cultural relativism, one must make a further move:

(7) Nobody can neutrally judge which society's fundamental ethical beliefs are right.
 ∴ Ethical truths are relative to a culture.

We can combine the direct method and the method of counterexamples to show that this is not valid. Say that the Steelers and the Cowboys are about to play in the Super Bowl. Pittsburgh fans are convinced that the Steelers are the better team; Dallas fans feel similarly about the Cowboys. Before the game, there may be no way to tell who is right. But that doesn't mean that which team is better is relative to a group of fans. This argument with the same form, then, seems to have true premises but a false conclusion in such a situation:

(8) Nobody can neutrally judge which fans' beliefs are right.
 ∴ Which team is better is relative to a set of fans.

An even better example is this: Say that two groups of paleontologists have competing hypotheses about how a certain species evolved in the distant past. Suppose further that no fossil or other evidence favoring one over the other will become available. The groups, moreover, appeal to rather different standards of paleontological research. Then the premise of the following argument may be true:

(9) Nobody can neutrally judge which hypothesis
is right.
∴ How a certain species evolved is relative to a
group of paleontologists.

But this conclusion is absurd. The species evolved
however it evolved, no matter what contemporary
paleontologists think.

The problem with the arguments from cultural
variation and undecidability is that they support not
relativism but skepticism. (In fact, they are classic
arguments that skeptics have used to support the
conclusion that ethical knowledge is uncertain, unjustified, or impossible.) In short, they suggest at
best that there are problems about ethical *knowledge,*
not about ethical *truth.*

The Argument from Subjectivism

A third argument for cultural relativism is the argument from subjectivism, the view that ethical truth is
in the eye of the beholder. The argument from subjectivism is an extended argument consisting of a list
of premises followed by several conclusions stated at
once.

(10) Ethical truth depends on emotional reactions.
Emotional reactions depend on
socialization.
What depends on emotion is subjective.
Whatever results from socialization is relative
to culture.
∴ Ethical truth is subjective.
∴ Ethical truth depends on socialization.
∴ Ethical truth is relative to culture.

To evaluate this, we must distinguish three simple
arguments, one for each conclusion.

(11) Ethical truth depends on emotional reactions.
What depends on emotion is subjective.
∴ Ethical truth is subjective.

This argument certainly seems valid; it appears to
have the same form as "Socrates is a man; all men are
mortal; therefore, Socrates is mortal." But the appearance can be misleading, because the premises
are ambiguous. "X depends on Y" can mean that X
depends on Y among other things, or that X depends

on Y alone. It is tempting to read the first premise as
asserting that ethical truth depends on emotion,
among other things, but to read the second as asserting that what depends solely on emotion is subjective. In that interpretation, the argument is not valid
at all. Compare:

(12) Life depends on the pumping of the heart,
among other things.
What depends on nothing but the pumping of
the heart is circulatory.
∴ Life is circulatory.

So, we must distinguish two possible arguments:

(13) Ethical truth depends partly on emotional
reactions.
What depends partly on emotion is
subjective.
∴ Ethical truth is subjective.
(14) Ethical truth depends solely on emotional
reactions.
What depends solely on emotion is subjective.
∴ Ethical truth is subjective.

These arguments are valid. But are they sound? Are
the premises true?

Some philosophers, such as Hume, hold that ethical truth depends partly on emotional reactions;
others, such as Kant, Mill, and Rawls, think that ethical truth can be given a purely rational foundation.
This is a large issue that cannot be resolved in this
introduction. Suffice it to say that many philosophers have thought that ethical truth does not depend even partly on emotion; very few have held
that it depends entirely on emotion. The first
premise is dubious in (13), therefore, and even more
dubious in (14).

The second premise of (13) is also questionable.
Philosophers who have accepted the dependence of
ethical truth on emotion, among other things, have
often thought that people have an emotional "moral
sense" that tells them right from wrong in regular
ways by detecting and responding to real properties
of actions and circumstances. In such a view, moral
emotions are not arbitrary or subjective; they respond to real features of things.

The argument for the second conclusion appears
to be valid:

(15) Ethical truth depends on emotional reactions.
  Emotional reactions depend on socialization.
  ∴ Ethical truth depends on socialization.

Once again, however, these statements are ambiguous. If ethical truth depends on emotion, among other things, and emotion depends on socialization, among other things, then we can hardly conclude that ethical truth depends on nothing but socialization. So, we must distinguish two possible arguments:

(16) Ethical truth depends on emotional reactions, among other things.
  Emotional reactions depend on socialization, among other things.
  ∴ Ethical truth depends on socialization, among other things.
(17) Ethical truth depends solely on emotional reactions.
  Emotional reactions depend solely on socialization.
  ∴ Ethical truth depends solely on socialization.

These are valid. But are they sound?

As we have seen, the first premise is controversial in both arguments and is especially so in (17). The second premise of (17) is also questionable. Many philosophers have held that at least some emotional reactions are biological, products of nature rather than nurture. The ancient Chinese philosopher Mencius, for example, describes a situation in which an adult sees a child about to fall into a well. It is natural, Mencius says, for the adult to feel compassion and race to the child's rescue. Mencius does not deny that socialization has effects on emotion; it may develop or stunt one's natural reactions. But emotion depends at least as much on biology as on society— a point on which Mencius and contemporary biology agree.

The third argument is also ambiguous:

(18) Ethical truth depends on socialization.
  ∴ Ethical truth is relative to culture.

To evaluate it, we must isolate two interpretations:

(19) Ethical truth depends among other things on socialization.

  ∴ Ethical truth is relative to culture.
(20) Ethical truth depends solely on socialization.
  ∴ Ethical truth is relative to culture.

We have already noted that the premises are controversial. Turn, then, to the question of validity. One problem with (19) is brought out nicely by this argument, which shares its specific form:

(21) Combustion depends on a spark, among other things.
  ∴ Combustion is relative to a spark.

The problem is that, once a spark occurs, combustion proceeds independently; additional sparks don't matter. Tossing lit matches onto a fire has no appreciable effect on the fire. To apply the moral to (19): Socialization may be needed to activate and develop a person's moral sense, but it may be that the content of what is activated and developed is then independent of socialization.

Another problem is brought out by the following argument, which also has the specific form of (19):

(22) The properties of a triangle depend on its size, among other things.
  ∴ The properties of a triangle are relative to its size.

The point is that *some* properties depend on size, but some do not. Any triangle has three sides, for example, no matter how large it is. At best, then, (19) could show that *some* ethical truths are relative to culture, but not that *all* are.

Argument (20) may seem to be valid, though it has a dubious premise. But an argument with (20)'s specific form shows that this is not so:

(23) The design of a house solely depends on the architect.
  ∴ The design of a house is relative to the architect.

The problem this brings out affects (19) as well as (20). Even if the architect has total control over the design of a house, it may be that all houses have certain design functions in common, because architects are trying to solve similar problems with their designs. People need shelter; they need places to cook, eat, sleep, and so on. So, even if ethical truth depends on nothing but socialization, ethical truth may contain some universally accepted fundamental truths because socialization may have some universal features. Every society, after all, faces the same problem: how to raise its young to lead successful human lives.

Arguments against Cultural Relativism

We have been considering traditional arguments in favor of relativism. There are also traditional arguments against relativism. They are the argument from error, the argument from change, the argument from interaction, the argument from inconsistency, and the argument from intolerance.

The Argument from Error

The first argument against relativism is the argument from error, originally articulated by Plato:

> Protagoras . . . says that man is the measure of all things, and that things are to me as they appear to me, and that they are to you as they appear to you. . . . But if Protagoras is right, and the truth is that things are as they appear to anyone, how can some of us be wise and some of us foolish? (*Cratylus* 386a, c)*

The essence of Plato's argument appears to be:

(24) If ethical truth is relative to an individual, no way of living is better than any other.
But some ways of living are better than others.
∴ Ethical truth is not relative to an individual.

It is easy to adapt the argument to cultural relativism:

(25) If ethical truth is relative to a culture, no social standards of conduct are better than any others.
But some social standards of conduct are better than others.
∴ Ethical truth is not relative to a culture.

The key premise is the second, that some ways of living and some social codes of conduct are better than others. For Plato's argument to succeed, we must be justified in saying that some people and societies are wiser than others. It must be possible, in other words, for people and societies to make moral mistakes—to do wrong.

Can people make moral mistakes? The mind leaps to examples of moral horror: the Holocaust, in which 6 million Jews, a quarter of them children, were murdered; or Stalin's induced famine, which killed over 30 million Ukrainians; or the centuries-long enslavement of Africans in the New World. These are crimes so enormous that they are hard to comprehend. (As Judith Miller has said, "We must remind ourselves that the Holocaust was not six million. It was one plus one plus one.")† Easier to contemplate, perhaps, are individual acts of immorality—two teenagers raping and then murdering a young mother, for example, or a thug breaking into a house and killing the occupants. To suggest that no patterns of conduct are better than any others in the face of such examples seems itself an example of immorality.

The Argument from Change

The argument from error suggests a second argument, the one from *change*. People change their minds; societies reform. Sometimes these changes respond to changes in circumstances. But often people change because they come to think that their opinions are wrong. The abolition of slavery and the protection of civil rights exemplify this sort of moral reform on a social level. The relativist seems committed to saying that, relative to our society, discrimination used to be permissible but is now wrong. If the change was not in the situation but in our convictions, however, this sounds very strange. We changed our minds; discrimination did not change its moral character. Indeed, we now think not only that discrimination is wrong *now* but that it was wrong *then*.

The Argument from Interaction

A third argument is from *interaction*. Say that what is right is relative to the society under consideration.

---

* *The Dialogues of Plato,* translated by Benjamin Jowett (Oxford: Oxford University Press, 1892).

† Judith Miller, *One by One by One: Facing the Holocaust* (New York: Simon & Schuster, 1990), 287.

What happens when societies interact? Imagine yourself as Cortés, horrified by the spectacle of mass human sacrifice at an Aztec temple, or, to take an example of current significance, as an Ohio police chief who discovers that recent African immigrants in the community have been practicing female genital mutilation. Bloom asks a similar question: "If you had been a British administrator in India, would you have let the natives under your governance burn the widow at the funeral of a man who had died?"* Bloom complains that his students have no answer. Sidney Hook, in response, reports,

> My students would have replied, "Of course the administrator should have tried to stamp out the barbarous practice . . . but not if the attempt was to result in communal riots and violence by fanatics resulting in widespread loss of life. The timing is important and it might be better to work through the Hindu religious authorities, not all of whom approved of the practice, even when it was really voluntary. As it is, it took the British almost fifty years before declaring the practice illegal."†

In short, when cultures interact, complicated moral problems arise. It is far too simple to say that they should not try to impose their values on each other, but it is also too simple to say that they should, or even that one of them should. Imposition of certain moral beliefs might be unwarranted, while imposition of others might be vital. Tolerance is a primary motivation for relativism, but it is not always a virtue. There are things that should not be tolerated.

The argument from interaction might then be summarized,

(26) If ethical truth is relative to a culture, then, when cultures interact, one should not impose one's own values on people of the other culture.
But sometimes, when cultures interact, one should impose one's own values on people of another culture.
∴ Ethical truth is not relative to a culture.

The Argument from Inconsistency

This argument suggests another, the *argument from inconsistency.* Consider the first premise: "If ethical

truth is relative to a culture, then, when cultures interact, one *should* not impose one's own values on people of the other culture." To what is that "should" relative? Presumably, it is meant to hold no matter what cultures are under consideration. In short, if relativism is supposed to imply tolerance, there seems to be at least one universal moral prescription—tolerance itself. But that refutes relativism.

(27) If ethical truth is relative to a culture, there are no universal ethical truths.
If ethical truth is relative to a culture, then, when cultures interact, one should not impose one's own values on people of the other culture.
But the preceding premise expresses a universal ethical truth.
∴ Ethical truth is not relative to a culture.

The Argument from Intolerance

Finally, the argument from inconsistency suggests another, the *argument from intolerance.* Say that relativism does imply tolerance. Waive the point about inconsistency. Should one be willing to tolerate intolerance? There are intolerant people and societies. The Soviet Union had the Gulag Archipelago, a vast string of camps for political prisoners throughout Siberia; China has the *Laogai.* In only a few of the world's nations are political opponents and dissenters accorded rights. Relativism seems to imply that one should tolerate such intolerance, but that seems to violate the concern that motivated relativism in the first place.

(28) Some people and cultures are intolerant of dissent.
If ethical truth is relative to a culture, then, when cultures interact, one should not impose one's own values on people of the other culture.
When cultures interact, one should support tolerance for dissenters of the other culture.
∴ Ethical truth is not relative to a culture.

Making Moral Arguments

As we have seen, it is possible to attack an argument by showing that one of its premises is false. Even if

---

* Bloom, *The Closing of the American Mind,* 26.
† Sidney Hook, "The Closing of the American Mind: An Intellectual Best-Seller Revisited." *American Scholar* 58, 1 (Winter 1989): 128.

the argument is valid or strong, such an attack shows that it is not sound or cogent and undercuts its conclusion. To apply this to our initial argument, (1), one might contend that societies share the same fundamental ethical beliefs. This might seem implausible, given the diversity of the world's beliefs and practices. But there are striking similarities in moral codes across the globe. Prohibitions against killing, stealing, committing adultery, and lying are common to Judaism, Christianity, Islam, Hinduism, Buddhism, and other religions.

When societies appear to differ—on infanticide, for example—one could argue that the disagreement is not a matter of fundamental ethical truth but a matter of fact. Perhaps the Greeks thought that it was wrong to kill persons, for example, but that infants are not persons. Or perhaps the Greeks recognized that infanticide was wrong—they left deformed babies on mountaintops to die rather than killing them, so that the gods could save the infants and would share the blame if they did not—but that endangering others by devoting scarce resources to trying to save them was worse.

Behind this is a more general point. Moral arguments typically have both moral and factual premises. Some statements are *factual* or *descriptive*. They say how the world is. Other statements are *evaluative, prescriptive,* or *normative.* They say how the world ought to be; more generally, they evaluate how the world is, characterizing it as right or wrong, acceptable or unacceptable, delightful or dismal. They include specifically evaluative terms. A *moral argument* is an argument with an evaluative conclusion. People who reach opposite conclusions may differ in moral principles, but they may also differ in factual assumptions. One of the chief purposes of a contemporary moral problems course is to teach people how to disentangle moral from factual issues. The distinction matters, because factual and moral conclusions require different kinds of support.

Consider a simple example:

(29) You promised to sublet the apartment.
       You should keep your promises.
       ∴ You should sublet the apartment.

The first premise is factual. Whether you promised to sublet the apartment is a matter of fact. If it is disputed, we may ask about the facts: What exactly did

you say? Is there any agreement in writing? Did you sign anything? Was it really this apartment? The second premise, in contrast, is evaluative. It speaks of how things ought to be, not how they are. Consequently, no amount of inquiry into the facts can help us determine its truth or falsehood. To justify it, we must appeal to more general moral principles.

The general pattern of moral arguments for particular conclusions is thus:

(30) Factual premise(s)
       Moral premise(s)
       ∴ Moral conclusion

This is utterly familiar. You ought to return those books to the library. Why? You borrowed them (factual premise), they are due (factual premise), and you ought to return what you borrow when it is due (moral premise). Or, you may take vacation the last week of April. Why? It won't cause your coworkers any inconvenience (factual premise), and you may take vacation whenever it won't cause your coworkers any inconvenience (moral premise).

Arguing for a Moral Principle

(30) is a pattern for arguing to a particular moral conclusion. But how can one argue for general moral conclusions, such as the moral principles on which such arguments rely? How, in other words, does one support moral premises such as You ought to keep your promises, You ought to return what you borrow when it's due, or You may take vacation whenever it won't cause your coworkers any inconvenience?

In essence, there are two ways to argue for a moral generalization: from above and from below. To argue from above, appeal to a more general moral principle. John Stuart Mill, for example, would argue as follows for the generalization, You ought to keep your promises:

(31) You ought to follow the rules that will
        maximize human happiness.
       Following the rule You ought to keep your
        promises will maximize human
        happiness.
       ∴ You ought to keep your promises.

Immanuel Kant would justify it differently:

(32) You ought to treat others as ends, not merely as
means.

Keeping a promise to someone treats that
person as an end, but breaking one treats
him or her as a means to your ends.

∴ You ought to keep your promises.

Philosophers who prefer justifications from above
tend, like Mill and Kant, to search for a single,
very general moral principle that can justify other
principles.

Moral principles may also be justified from below,
by appeal to their instances. One could try to argue
that it is wrong to break promises, for example, by
generalizing from examples of particular situations:

(33) Say someone promises to marry you but
doesn't show up at the altar; that would be
wrong.

Say Frank borrows money from you, promising
insincerely to repay it, and then absconds;
that would be wrong.

Say the doctor makes an appointment to see
you and then goes to play golf instead; that
would be wrong.

Say Joan agrees to pay you $1,000 for land-
scaping her yard, you do the work, and she
refuses to pay; that would be wrong.

∴ Breaking promises is wrong.

or more specific kinds of situations:

(34) Someone who agrees to marry someone on
a particular day should show up for the
wedding.

Someone who borrows money ought to
repay it.

Someone who makes an appointment ought to
keep it.

Someone who signs a contract ought to fulfill it.

∴ Breaking promises is wrong.

These arguments are not valid, but they are inductively strong if the examples are numerous and diverse enough.

The readings in this book contain many arguments for moral principles, some from above, some
from below. Arguments from above are important,
for they say something about *why* the moral princi-

ple holds. Kant's argument for promise keeping, for
example, not only concludes that promises should
be kept but indicates that they should be kept because breaking them treats others as means to your
own ends. Mill's argument, similarly, indicates that
promise keeping is obligatory because it maximizes
human happiness. Arguments from below are also
important, for they link principles to particular cases
about which we have strong moral intuitions. The
more abstract and general a moral principle is, the
fewer intuitions we have about whether it is correct. Moral theories therefore rely on both kinds of
arguments.

Arguing against a Moral Principle

How does one argue *against* a moral principle? One
tries to find a counterexample: an instance in which
the principle seems to give the wrong result. Is it *always* right to keep promises, for instance? One can
try to find examples of promises that should not be
kept. Recall that, in a valid argument, the truth of the
premises guarantees the truth of the conclusion, or,
equivalently, the falsehood of the conclusion guarantees the falsehood of at least one premise. One can
construct a valid argument from the principle to a
false conclusion:

(35) One should always keep one's promises.

∴ If Herman promised to murder the entire
city council, he should do it.

The absurdity of the conclusion shows that there is
something wrong with the premise.

Many philosophers have objected to Kant's opinion that lying is always wrong by constructing a similar argument. Suppose that a distraught child runs
to you begging for help. A homicidal maniac is chas-
ing her. You hide her in a closet. The maniac bangs
on your door and asks whether you know where she
is. Surely you should not tell the truth.

Exceptions to Moral Principles

This example illustrates that most moral principles
have exceptions. Most moral principles are true *other
things being equal* (in Latin, *ceteris paribus*), but not
universally. Plato recognized this about promise
keeping and telling the truth:

. . . are we to say that justice or right is simply to speak the truth and to pay back any debt one may have contracted? Or are these same actions sometimes right and sometimes wrong? I mean this sort of thing, for example: everyone would surely agree that if a friend has deposited weapons with you when he was sane, and he asks for them when he is out of his mind, you should not return them. The man who returns them is not doing right, nor is one who is willing to tell the whole truth to a man in such a state. (*Republic,* 331c)*

Although Keep your promises and Tell the truth are good moral rules in general, they can be overridden or defeated by other moral considerations. For that reason, they are called *defeasible.* Normally, you ought to keep your promises. Normally, you ought to tell the truth. But sometimes there are good reasons to break a promise or to lie, and then you have a moral conflict.

Philosophers often analyze such situations of moral conflict in terms of *prima facie* duties. W. D. Ross defined "prima facie duty" as a "characteristic (quite distinct from that of being a duty proper) which an act has, in virtue of being of a certain kind (e.g., the keeping of a promise), of being an act which would be a duty proper if it were not at the same time of another kind which is morally significant."† A prima facie obligation, that is, holds under normal circumstances; it holds all other things being equal, becoming *actual*—an obligation all things considered, or, in Ross's terms, "a duty proper"—unless some other moral consideration intervenes.

Prima facie obligations offer a way to explain the force of rules while allowing for exceptions. The idea, in essence, is that a prima facie rule applies unless some other rule conflicts with it. John Stuart Mill's secondary principles are paradigms of prima facie principles: They dictate obligations unless they come into conflict. In that case, Mill stipulates, the principle of utility, the sole rule in his system that has an absolute rather than prima facie character, resolves the conflict. This indicates a key difference between actual and prima facie obligation: Prima facie obligations can conflict, whereas actual obligations cannot. If a homicidal maniac asks whether you know where an innocent child is hiding, there is a moral conflict: You have a prima facie obligation to tell the truth and another to tell a lie. Only one can be actual—what you ought actually to do in that situation, all things considered. Saving a life is more important than telling a lie, so your obligation to lie is actual, overriding your obligation to tell the truth.

Let's revisit Plato's puzzle about returning weapons to a friend who is out of his mind. Because unconditional statements of actual obligation *cannot* conflict, this pair is inconsistent:

(36) You have an actual obligation to return the weapons.
     You have an actual obligation not to return the weapons.

You cannot be obliged, actually, all things considered, both to return the weapons and not to return them.

Because unconditional prima facie obligations *can* conflict, this pair of statements is consistent:

(37) You have a prima facie obligation to return the weapons.
     You have a prima facie obligation not to return the weapons.

In general, you have a prima facie obligation to do something whenever the circumstances trigger a defeasible moral rule. In Plato's case, there are defeasible rules that you ought to keep your promises and that you ought to prevent harm. Your promise gives rise to the prima facie obligation to return the weapons; your friend's madness gives rise to the prima facie obligation not to return them.

Here are some basic reasoning patterns involving prima facie obligation and defeasible rules:

Default Modus Ponens. Inferences such as (38) count as acceptable if no other moral considerations apply.

(38) If you make a promise, you should keep it.
     You promised you would go.
     ∴ You should go.

They are not deductively valid, but they are induc-

---

* *Plato: The Republic,* translated by Paul Shorey (Cambridge, Mass.: Loeb Classical Library, 1930).
† W. D. Ross, *The Right and the Good* (Oxford: Oxford University Press, 1930), 19.

tively strong. They are legitimate default inferences; we may draw the conclusion if no other rules intervene. We may infer actual obligations from prima facie obligations in the absence of moral complications.

Conditional Conflict. In cases where conditional prima facie principles conflict, we can generally draw no conclusions. Consider Plato's puzzle:

(39) If you promised to return the weapons, you
        should return them.
      If returning them will cause mayhem, you
        should not return them.
      You did promise.
      Returning the weapons will cause mayhem.
      ∴ ??

Should you return the weapons? This is a substantive moral question; no obligation follows as a matter of logic. We must look at the situation and the importance of the conflicting considerations.

Specificity. More specific prima facie obligations take precedence over less specific ones. To return to Plato's puzzle: Add the premise that results from reflecting on the competing values at stake in the situation. Lives are more important than promises. It follows that you should not return the weapons.

(40) If you promised to return the weapons, you
        should return them.

If returning them will cause mayhem, you
    should not return them.
You did promise.
Returning the weapons will cause mayhem.
If you promised to return the weapons but do-
    ing so will cause mayhem, you should not
    return them.
∴ You should not return the weapons.

But it is important that the last premise requires independent moral reflection. We cannot infer it from the other premises. Indeed, moral conflicts such as those Plato describes have spurred philosophers to devise moral theories to help us compare different kinds of moral considerations and resolve conflicts generated by them.

Seeing that moral considerations can come into conflict helps to dissolve some of the motivation for relativism. In morality, it is often true that one person or culture sees things one way and another sees them quite differently. But even within the view of a single person and culture, there are many different perspectives, which it is the task of morality to relate, evaluate, and, in particular situations, reconcile. Reasonable people can differ on how to reconcile them. That is what makes a book like this both possible and important.

FIRST PRINCIPLES

Most of our moral judgments concern particular things. We judge certain actions and certain people good or bad. There are many gradations: Acts and people may be heroic, splendid, admirable, acceptable, indifferent, unsatisfactory, despicable, or horrible, to mention just a few moral adjectives. There are also many dimensions of moral consideration: Acts or people may be honest, kind, loyal, trustworthy, noble, brave, generous, self-controlled, gentle, friendly, witty, pleasant, helpful, effective, efficient, or considerate, to mention just a few positive attributes. Usually, we apply these to particular actions or to particular people.

When people disagree about a moral judgment, they try to justify their views. They do this by constructing an argument that appeals to moral principles. Suppose, for example, that Jennifer killed Michael by breaking a baseball bat over his head. And say that you and I disagree about the morality of the act. I think it was wrong; you think it was justifiable. I might try to justify my judgment by constructing a simple argument:

1. Jennifer's killing Michael was murder. (Fact)

2. Murder is always wrong. (Moral principle)

3. Therefore, Jennifer's killing Michael was wrong. (Moral conclusion)

An argument for a particular moral conclusion generally contains both factual and moral premises, just as this one does. The first premise is factual; it purports to describe the way the world is. The second premise, in contrast, is moral. It does not describe the world as it is but evaluates a general category of

action. Assertions like the first premise are often called *factual* or *descriptive*. Those like the second premise or the conclusion are often called *evaluative, prescriptive,* or *normative.*

The distinction between these kinds of assertion matters, for we resolve disagreements about them in very different ways. Suppose, for example, that you challenge my first premise. You deny, in other words, that Jennifer committed a murder. We might resolve our disagreement by clarifying our use of words and investigating the facts. If I defend my premise with further premises:

4. Murder is killing a human being with malice aforethought.

5. Jennifer killed Michael.

6. Michael was human.

7. Jennifer intended to do Michael harm.

you might challenge my definition of murder (4) or my description of the facts (5, 6, and 7). We might proceed to investigate whether Jennifer was really the killer and Michael really the victim; whether Jennifer intended to harm Michael or killed him accidentally; whether Michael was human or a robot; and whether my definition of murder is correct. All these issues concern definitions or matters of fact.

If you challenge my second premise, however, investigating matters of fact cannot resolve our disagreement. We differ not on how the world is but on how it ought to be. And, as David Hume stresses, there is no way to derive *ought* from *is;* no amount of factual information can determine how the world ought to be. To justify my premise, I must appeal to some broader moral principle—and ultimately, many philosophers have thought, to a first, most fundamental moral principle from which all others follow. The thinkers of the Enlightenment, especially, saw that if we could establish and agree upon a first principle of morality, all our disagreements would concern definitions and matters of fact and thus would be resolvable by investigation. Morality would lend itself to scientific inquiry as much as anything else.

The search for a first principle of morality has other sources. One stems from the great variety of things we call good. We say that certain actions, people, and even qualities (such as honesty) are good. What makes them all good? What do they have in common? Similarly, we call things as diverse as the Kennedy assassination, Hitler, deception, and cruelty wrong. What makes them all wrong? What do they have in common? To answer would be to give the first principle of morality. Why couldn't there be several such principles? Because we could raise the question, What makes *them* fundamental principles of morality? What do *they* all have in common?

To try to justify moral principles as well as particular moral judgments is to construct a moral theory. Moral theories are systematic attempts to provide and justify answers to questions such as, What should I do? and What kind of person should I be? Most modern moral theories take the former question as basic. They focus on action and try to distinguish right from wrong in principled ways. But some theories focus instead on the latter question and try to distinguish good character traits from bad. Good traits are *virtues;* bad traits, *vices.*

Aristotle develops the classic theory of virtue. He distinguishes *intrinsic* goods, which are desired for their own sake, from *instrumental* goods, which are desired as means to other things. To justify any answers to the above questions, we must appeal to intrinsic goods. Suppose that someone asks why you are reading this book. "Because it's required for my ethics course," you answer. "But why do what's required?" "I want to get a good grade." "Why do you want a good grade?" "I want to have a good GPA." "Why?" "It will help me get a job." "Why do you

want a job?' "I want money." "Why?" "I want things money can buy!" "Why do you want them?" To stop the chain of questions, you must appeal to something that is intrinsically good. Every time you appeal to an instrumental good, the questioner can ask in turn why you want *it.*

Aristotle contends that people desire only one thing for its own sake and never for the sake of something else: happiness. Any series of requests for justification leads eventually to the response, "Because I want to be happy!" If someone persists in asking why, there is nothing more to say; happiness is desirable for its own sake.

What is happiness? What is it to live well? Aristotle's answer relies on the idea that human beings have a function. Just as a good knife cuts well and a good teacher teaches well, a good person fulfills the function of a human being well. But what is the function of a person? It is what is most distinctive of human beings: to act rationally. A good person acts in accordance with virtue, and to act virtuously is to act rationally. A good person does the right thing at the right time, and in the right way, *for the right reason.* Virtue is thus a mean between extremes. The ability to find that mean Aristotle calls *practical wisdom.* To fear too much is cowardly, but to fear too little is rash. Courage is fearing what ought to be feared, when it ought to be feared, to the extent that it ought to be feared, and for the appropriate reason.

How does a person become virtuous? How, in other words, can someone become practically wise? Not by abstract thought, Aristotle says, but by doing virtuous things. Shakespeare's Polonius advised "Assume a virtue if you have it not"; Aristotle agrees. If you do brave things, for example—initially, by forcing yourself to do them, by pretending to be brave—you gradually develop the habit of doing brave things. When the habit is ingrained and automatic, to the point of being "second nature," you *are* brave. In general, people become good by doing good things. There is no rule for becoming good or for distinguishing good from bad, right from wrong; a person of practical wisdom has a highly refined ability to draw the right distinctions and tell right from wrong.

The Enlightenment produced two great and competing accounts of the foundations of morality. Immanuel Kant maintains that all of ethics reduces to a single principle, the categorical imperative. He articulates five versions of the principle, but he takes all to be equivalent. The two most important versions are

I. Act so that the maxim of your action might be willed as universal law.

II. Treat everyone as a end, not merely as a means.

The first means that you must act on the basis of principle; you cannot make an exception for yourself. You must act, in other words, in such a way that everyone could act on your principles. The second means that every human being deserves to be treated with respect, as an independent moral agent; you must not use people as means to your own ends.

Kant derives the categorical imperative from general considerations about morality. A first principle, he warns, must be necessarily true; it must hold no matter what the world is like, for as a moral assertion, it does not describe the world. It must be something we can know *a priori,* independently of experience. It must therefore be universal, applying to all rational agents capable of thinking and acting morally. And it must be categorical, of the form "Everyone always ought to . . . ," rather than hypothetical (of the form "If you want . . . , you ought to . . ."), for it must not depend on the goals we adopt for ourselves, even general goals such as happiness. What all hypothetical imperatives have in common is simply the form of law, that is, the idea of acting on principle as a moral agent. That leads to Kant's formulations of the categorical imperative. You must act on principle; you must respect yourself and others as moral agents.

The second great Enlightenment account of the foundations of morality rejects Kant's picture completely. Utilitarianism, a moral theory mentioned in Plato's dialogues, first advocated by Francis Hutcheson, and brought to full development by Jeremy Bentham and John Stuart Mill, can be summarized in two words: *Maximize good.* Utilitarians hold that all of ethics and political philosophy reduces to that one maxim, the principle of utility.

The principle seems simple but has a number of far-reaching consequences. First, utilitarians evaluate actions by the extent to which they maximize good. They evaluate actions, therefore, solely by examining their consequences. In determining whether an action or kind of action is right or wrong, we need to ask, Is it for the best? What effect does it have on the amount of good in the universe? Utilitarianism is thus a version of *consequentialism,* the view that the moral value of an action depends completely on its consequences.

Other moral philosophers contend that other features of actions are relevant to their moral value. Killing, for example, is generally a bad thing. But our judgment of a killer depends on other factors. Was the killing purely accidental, or did it result from negligence? Did it stem from a fit of rage, or was it premeditated? The prior actions, motives, intentions, and general state of mind of the agent, we think, make a moral difference. Utilitarians are committed to saying that all these things are irrelevant to evaluating the killing itself—but, they would say, they are highly relevant to evaluating the killer. Utilitarians need not banish motives, intentions, states of mind, and circumstances from ethics. But they must define their moral values ultimately in terms of the moral value of actions. We might say, for example, that an intention is good to the extent that it results in good actions, that a motive is good to the extent that it results in good intentions, that a character trait is good to the extent that it results in good motives, and so on.

Second, utilitarianism is a *universalist* theory: We must judge whether an action or kind of action maximizes the total amount of good in the universe. Thus, we must consider the consequences of the action on everyone it affects. We cannot consider ourselves alone, or just people in our community, or our fellow citizens; we must consider *everyone.* Most actions affect only a few people in any significant, identifiable way. Political decisions, however, often affect millions. In either case, we must be prepared to consider the effects on everyone affected.

Third, utilitarianism requires an independent theory of the good. The principle of utility tells us to maximize good, but it does not tell us what the good is. What, exactly, must we maximize? Bentham and Mill are *hedonists*: They believe that pleasure and pain are the only sources of value. The good, for both, is pleasure and the absence of pain. In the view of these philosophers, then, the principle of utility directs us to maximize the balance of pleasure over pain. Other utilitarians hold other theories of the good. Some, for example, identify the good with the satisfaction of desire. Some maintain that the good is indefinable and cannot be identified with anything else.

Whatever theory of the good a utilitarian holds, however, that theory must treat the good as a quantity to be maximized. The principle requires us to maximize good; good, therefore, must be the kind of thing that can be maximized. Certainly this means that we must be able to judge whether one circumstance contains more good than another. It probably also means that we must be able to quantify the amount of good in any given circumstance; that is, that we must be able to say how much good that circumstance contains—ideally, by assigning it a number.

Utilitarians tend to fall into two main categories. Some, called *act-utilitarians,* take the evaluation of individual actions as primary. They judge an action by the effects it has on the amount of good. Others, *rule-utilitarians,* take the evaluation of kinds of actions as primary. They judge rules by the effects of following them and then judge individual actions by appealing to the recommended rules. Bentham is an act-utilitarian; Mill appears to be a rule-utilitarian, although it is possible to interpret him as an act-utilitarian or even a *character-utilitarian,* one who takes the evaluation of character traits as primary and holds that one should develop the virtues that tend to maximize everyone's happiness.

In most cases, act- and rule-utilitarians agree in their moral evaluations of individual actions. They disagree, however, (a) when an action maximizes good while violating rules that usually—but not in a particular case—maximize good, and (b) when an action does not maximize good in a particular case but does follow those rules. Both situations involve a conflict between the principle of utility and a rule designed to maximize good in general. Act-utilitarians consider it bizarre to say that we should follow the rule instead of the principle of utility; according to rule-utilitarianism itself, the rule derives its force solely from the principle in the first place. But rule-utilitarians believe that rules are indispensable to moral thinking. We cannot calculate what to do in every individual case; we must think about kinds of actions, formulate rules that, if followed, maximize good, and then follow those rules.

Rule-utilitarians encounter a special difficulty: the rules justified by the principle of utility may come into conflict with each other. Among the good-maximizing rules, for example, are some commanding us to avoid murder and to save innocent lives. But there may be cases in which we can save lives only by committing a murder. Which rule takes precedence? Mill suggests that, in such cases, we appeal to the principle of utility itself. In his theory, then, the principle has two roles. It determines which rules we should adopt and resolves conflicts between them.

John Rawls justifies moral principles differently. Instead of seeking one fundamental principle that can justify others or seeking one intrinsic good that can justify all other goods, Rawls sketches a method for justifying moral principles (specifically, principles of justice). Imagine trying to design a society in which you would want to live. Setting up the rules and institutions of this society wisely would require a great deal of knowledge of human psychology, sociology, economics, politics, and so on. Imagine that you have all that knowledge. Now imagine, furthermore, that you are subject to what Rawls calls the *veil of ignorance:* you do not know where you will fit into the social order you create or even what kind of personality, character, or preferences you will have. What rules would you choose? The rules that rational agents would agree upon with unlimited general knowledge of social interaction but no particular knowledge of their own places or preferences—in short, in the *original position*—are legitimate moral principles. They are legitimate not because we have shown that they derive from a more fundamental principle or promote the highest good but because it would be rational to choose, under informed and fair circumstances, to live under them. Because, in Rawls's view, moral principles are legitimate if people would, in idealized circumstances, agree to enter into a contract to follow them, his position is a form of *contractualism*.

Rawls proposes another test, to check principles selected in the original position as well as any other proposed principles of morality. We test principles against our own considered judgments. We are convinced, for example, that torturing babies is evil and that rescuing innocent, drowning people is good. Any moral theory or principle that suggests otherwise should be rejected or revised. But we also test our judgments against the principles; sometimes we may reject our initial moral judgment as insufficiently considered or sensitive. We go back and forth in this way, proposing and revising principles, affirming and sometimes revising particular moral judgments, until the principles we accept match our considered (and in some cases reconsidered) judgments. At this point, we reach *reflective equilibrium:* "our principles and judgments coincide." Again, we affirm the principles not because we have deduced them from something more fundamental but because they are the outcome of a reasonable and fair procedure.

French philosopher Simone de Beauvoir, an existentialist and feminist, sees moral thinking very differently. Like Rawls, she holds that we choose not only how to act in particular situations but what principles to adopt in general. From her perspective, however, reason does not dictate those choices. Existence is ambiguous, she maintains, in that our lives have no fixed meaning; we give them meaning by making the free choices we do. "Ethics does not furnish recipes," she proclaims; there is no formula for leading a good life or making the right choice. Kant is right that we must recognize and promote the freedom of other moral agents. Utilitarians are right that we must promote the happiness of others. But what promotes freedom and happiness is often hard to discern. We find ourselves caught frequently in moral dilemmas, in which competing moral considerations pull us in different directions. There is no rule for reconciling these competing considerations. As in science or art, we must consider the meaning and the content of our acts, contemplating their internal consistency as well as their external effects. We must confront our own freedom and the ambiguity of the situations we face and work out our own solutions in context.

ARISTOTLE

from *Nicomachean Ethics*

Aristotle (384–322 B.C.E.), born in Stagira, was the son of Nicomachus, the court physician to Amyntas II, the king of Macedonia. Nicomachus died when Aristotle was a boy. After training in medicine, Aristotle entered Plato's Academy in Athens at the age of seventeen. He stayed twenty years, until Plato's death. In 342, he became the tutor of Alexander the Great, Amyntas's grandson, who was thirteen; Aristotle stayed at the Macedonian court as Alexander's teacher for three years, until Alexander was appointed regent. In 335, Aristotle returned to Athens to establish his own school, the Lyceum. When Alexander died in 323, Athenians became suspicious of Aristotle's links to Macedonia. Fearing that he might be executed, as Socrates had been, he fled Athens, "lest the Athenians sin twice against philosophy." He died a year later in Chalcis of chronic indigestion brought about by overwork.

Aristotle's influence on intellectual history has been immense. He wrote treatises on physics, biology, astronomy, psychology, logic, metaphysics, poetry, rhetoric, ethics, and politics. Through the Middle Ages, in Europe and the Islamic world, Aristotle was known simply as "the philosopher." His philosophy is still important; most Western and Islamic thought is to some degree Aristotelian. His scientific work, though now chiefly of historical interest, was remarkably sophisticated. It was not superseded for more than 1500 years.

The Nicomachean Ethics *addresses the basic questions of moral philosophy: What is the good? What is virtue? What is happiness? Aristotle believes that the good, for human beings— what humans properly desire for its own sake—is happiness, which he thinks has its highest form in contemplative activity. Aristotle holds that people can attain virtue and happiness, however, only in the context of a good state governed in the proper way. Aristotle thus believes that ethics and politics are intertwined. (Source: Reprinted by permission of the publishers from Aristotle's* Nicomachean Ethics, *translated by W. D. Ross. Oxford University Press, 1925. Most notes have been omitted.)*

BOOK I

4

Let us resume our inquiry and state, in view of the fact that all knowledge and every pursuit aims at some good, what it is that we say political science aims at and what is the highest of all goods achievable by action. Verbally there is very general agreement; for both the general run of men and people of superior refinement say that it is happiness, and identify living well and doing well with being happy; but with regard to what happiness is they differ, and the many do not give the same account as the wise. . . .

7

Let us again return to the good we are seeking, and ask what it can be. It seems different in different actions and arts; it is different in medicine, in strategy, and in the other arts likewise. What then is the good of each? Surely that for whose sake everything else is done. In medicine this is health, in strategy victory, in architecture a house, in any other sphere something else, and in every action and pursuit the end; for it is for the sake of this that all men do whatever else they do. Therefore, if there is an end for all that we do, this will be the good achievable by· action, and if there are more than one, these will be the goods achievable by action.

So the argument has by a different course reached the same point; but we must try to state this even more clearly. Since there are evidently more than one end, and we choose some of these (e.g. wealth, flutes, and in general instruments) for the sake of something else, clearly not all ends are final ends; but the chief good is evidently something final. Therefore, if there is only one final end, this will be what we are seeking, and if there are more than one, the most final of these will be what we are seeking. Now we call that which is in itself worthy of pursuit more final than that which is worthy of pursuit for the sake of something else, and that which is never desirable for the sake of something else more final than the things that are desirable both in themselves and for the sake of that other thing, and therefore we call final without qualification that which is always desirable in itself and never for the sake of something else.

Now such a thing happiness, above all else, is held to be; for this we choose always for itself and never for the sake of something else, but honour, pleasure, reason, and every virtue we choose indeed for themselves (for if nothing resulted from them we should still choose each of them), but we choose them also for the sake of happiness, judging that by means of them we shall be happy. Happiness, on the other hand, no one chooses for the sake of these, nor, in general, for anything other than itself. . . .

. . . Happiness, then, is something final and self-sufficient, and is the end of action.

Presumably, however, to say that happiness is the chief good seems a platitude, and a clearer account of what it is is still desired. This might perhaps be given, if we could first ascertain the function of man. For just as for a flute-player, a sculptor, or any artist, and, in general, for all things that have a function or activity, the good and the "well" is thought to reside in the function, so would it seem to be for man, if he has a function. Have the carpenter, then, and the tanner certain functions or activities, and has man

none? Is he born without a function? Or as eye, hand, foot, and in general each of the parts evidently has a function, may one lay it down that man similarly has a function apart from all these? What then can this be? Life seems to be common even to plants, but we are seeking what is peculiar to man. Let us exclude, therefore, the life of nutrition and growth. Next there would be a life of perception, but *it* also seems to be common even to the horse, the ox, and every animal. There remains, then, an active life of the element that has a rational principle; of this, one part has such a principle in the sense of being obedient to one, the other in the sense of possessing one and exercising thought. And, as "life of the rational element" also has two meanings, we must state that life in the sense of activity is what we mean; for this seems to be the more proper sense of the term. Now if the function of man is an activity of soul which follows or implies a rational principle, and if we say "a so-and-so" and "a good so-and-so" have a function which is the same in kind, e.g. a lyre-player and a good lyre-player, and so without qualification in all cases, eminence in respect of goodness being added to the name of the function (for the function of a lyre-player is to play the lyre, and that of a good lyre-player is to do so well): if this is the case, [and we state the function of man to be a certain kind of life, and this to be an activity or actions of the soul implying a rational principle, and the function of a good man to be the good and noble performance of these, and if any action is well performed when it is performed in accordance with the appropriate excellence: if this is the case,] human good turns out to be activity of soul in accordance with virtue, and if there are more than one virtue, in accordance with the best and most complete.

But we must add "in a complete life." For one swallow does not make a summer, nor does one day; and so too one day, or a short time, does not make a man blessed and happy. . . .

BOOK II

1

Virtue, then, being of two kinds, intellectual and moral, intellectual virtue in the main owes both its birth and its growth to teaching (for which reason it requires experience and time), while moral virtue comes about as a result of habit, whence also its name (ἠθική) is one that is formed by a slight variation from the word ἔθος (habit). From this it is also plain that none of the moral virtues arises in us by nature; for nothing that exists by nature can form a habit contrary to its nature. For instance the stone which by nature moves downwards cannot be habituated to move upwards, not even if one tries to train it by throwing it up ten thousand times; nor can fire be habituated to move downwards, nor can anything else that by nature behaves in one way be trained to behave in another. Neither by nature, then, nor contrary to nature do the virtues arise in us; rather we are adapted by nature to receive them, and are made perfect by habit.

Again, of all the things that come to us by nature we first acquire the potentiality and later exhibit the activity (this is plain in the case of the senses; for it was not by often seeing or often hearing that we got these senses, but on the contrary we had them before we used them, and did not come to have them by using them); but the virtues we get by first exercising them, as also happens in the case of the arts as well. For the things we have to learn before we can do them, we learn by doing them, e.g. men become builders by building and lyre-players by playing the lyre; so too we become just by doing just acts, temperate by doing temperate acts, brave by doing brave acts.

This is confirmed by what happens in states; for legislators make the citizens good by forming habits in them, and this is the wish of every legislator, and those who do not effect it miss their mark, and it is in this that a good constitution differs from a bad one.

Again, it is from the same causes and by the same means that every virtue is both produced and destroyed, and similarly every art; for it is from playing the lyre that both good and bad lyre-players are produced. And the corresponding statement is true of builders and of all the rest; men will be good or bad builders as a result of building well or badly. For if this were not so, there would have been no need of a teacher, but all men would have been born good or bad at their craft. This, then, is the case with the virtues also; by doing the acts that we do in our transactions with other men we become just or unjust, and by doing the acts that we do in the presence of danger, and being habituated to feel fear or confidence, we become brave or cowardly. The same is true of appetites and feelings of anger; some men become temperate and good-tempered, others self-indulgent and irascible, by behaving in one way or the other in the appropriate circumstances. Thus, in one word, states of character arise out of like activities. This is why the activities we exhibit must be of a certain kind; it is because the states of character correspond to the differences between these. It makes no small difference, then, whether we form habits of one kind or of another from our very youth; it makes a very great difference, or rather *all* the difference.

2

Since, then, the present inquiry does not aim at theoretical knowledge like the others (for we are inquiring not in order to know what virtue is, but in order to become good, since otherwise our inquiry would have been of no use), we must examine the nature of actions, namely how we ought to do them; for these determine also the nature of the states of character that are produced, as we have said. Now, that we must act according to the right rule is a common principle and must be assumed—it will be discussed later, i.e. both what the right rule is, and how it is related to the other virtues. But this must be agreed upon beforehand, that the whole account of matters of conduct must be given in outline and not precisely, as we said at the very beginning that the accounts we demand must be in accordance with the subject-matter; matters concerned with conduct and questions of what is good for us have no fixity, any more than matters of health. The general account being of this nature, the account of particular cases is yet more lacking in exactness; for they do not fall under any art or precept but the agents themselves must in each case consider what is appropriate to the occasion, as happens also in the art of medicine or of navigation.

But though our present account is of this nature we must give what help we can. First, then, let us consider this, that it is the nature of such things to be destroyed by defect and excess, as we see in the case of strength and of health (for to gain light on things imperceptible we must use the evidence of sensible things); both excessive and defective exercise destroys the strength, and similarly drink or food which is above or below a certain amount destroys the health, while that which is proportionate both produces and increases and preserves it. So too is it, then, in the case of temperance and courage and the other virtues. For the man who flies from and fears everything and does not stand his ground against anything becomes a coward, and the man who fears nothing at all but goes to meet every danger becomes rash; and similarly the man who indulges in every pleasure and abstains from none becomes self-indulgent, while the man who shuns every pleasure, as boors do, becomes in a way insensible; temperance and courage, then, are destroyed by excess and defect, and preserved by the mean.

But not only are the sources and causes of their origination and growth the same as those of their destruction, but also the sphere of their actualization will be the same; for this is also true of the things which are more evident to sense, e.g. of strength; it is produced by taking much food and undergoing much exertion, and it is the strong man that will be most able to do these things. So too is it with the virtues; by abstaining from pleasures we become temperate, and it is when we have become so that we are most able to abstain from them; and similarly too in the case of courage; for by being habituated to despise things that are terrible and to stand our ground against them we become brave, and it is when we have become so that we shall be most able to stand our ground against them. . . .

4

. . . Actions, then, are called just and temperate when they are such as the just or the temperate man would do; but it is not the man who does these that is just and temperate, but the man who also does them *as* just and temperate men do them. It is well said, then, that it is by doing just acts that the just man is produced, and by doing temperate acts the temperate man; without doing these no one would have even a prospect of becoming good. . . .

6

We must, however, not only describe virtue as a state of character, but also say what sort of state it is. We may remark, then, that every virtue or excellence both brings into good condition the thing of which it is the excellence and makes the work of that thing be done well; e.g. the excellence of the eye makes both the eye and its work good; for it is by the excellence of the eye that we see well. Similarly the excellence of the horse makes a horse both good in itself and good at running and at carrying its rider and at awaiting the attack of the enemy. Therefore, if this is true in every case, the virtue of man also will be the state of character which makes a man good and which makes him do his own work well.

How this is to happen we have stated already, but it will be made plain also by the following consideration of the specific nature of virtue. In everything that is continuous and divisible it is possible to take more, less, or an equal amount, and that either in terms of the thing itself or relatively to us; and the equal is an intermediate between excess and defect. By the intermediate in the object I mean that which is equidistant from each of the extremes, which is one and the same for all men; by the intermediate relatively to us that which is neither too much nor too little—and this is not one, nor the same for all. For instance, if ten is many and two is few, six is the intermediate, taken in terms of the object; for it exceeds and is exceeded by an equal amount; this is intermediate according to arithmetical proportion. But the intermediate relatively to us is not to be taken so; if ten pounds are too much for a particular person to eat and two too little, it does not follow that the trainer will order six pounds; for this also is perhaps too much for the person who is to take it, or too little—too little for Milo,* too much for the beginner in athletic exercises. The same is true of running and wrestling. Thus a master of any art avoids excess and defect, but seeks the intermediate and chooses this—the intermediate not in the object but relatively to us.

If it is thus, then, that every art does its work well—by looking to the intermediate and judging its

---

* A famous wrestler.

works by this standard (so that we often say of good works of art that it is not possible either to take away or to add anything, implying that excess and defect destroy the goodness of works of art, while the mean preserves it; and good artists, as we say, look to this in their work), and if, further, virtue is more exact and better than any art, as nature also is, then virtue must have the quality of aiming at the intermediate. I mean moral virtue; for it is this that is concerned with passions and actions, and in these there is excess, defect, and the intermediate. For instance, both fear and confidence and appetite and anger and pity and in general pleasure and pain may be felt both too much and too little, and in both cases not well; but to feel them at the right times, with reference to the right objects, towards the right people, with the right motive, and in the right way, is what is both intermediate and best, and this is characteristic of virtue. Similarly with regard to actions also there is excess, defect, and the intermediate. Now virtue is concerned with passions and actions, in which excess is a form of failure, and so is defect, while the intermediate is praised and is a form of success; and being praised and being successful are both characteristics of virtue. Therefore virtue is a kind of mean, since, as we have seen, it aims at what is intermediate.

Again, it is possible to fail in many ways (for evil belongs to the class of the unlimited, as the Pythagoreans conjectured, and good to that of the limited), while to succeed is possible only in one way (for which reason also one is easy and the other difficult—to miss the mark easy, to hit it difficult); for these reasons also, then, excess and defect are characteristic of vice, and the mean of virtue;

For men are good in but one way, but bad in many.

Virtue, then, is a state of character concerned with choice, lying in a mean, i.e. the mean relative to us, this being determined by a rational principle, and by that principle by which the man of practical wisdom would determine it. Now it is a mean between two vices, that which depends on excess and that which depends on defect; and again it is a mean because the vices respectively fall short of or exceed what is right in both passions and actions, while virtue both finds and chooses that which is intermediate. Hence in respect of its substance and the definition which states its essence virtue is a mean, with regard to what is best and right an extreme.

But not every action nor every passion admits of a mean; for some have names that already imply badness, e.g. spite, shamelessness, envy, and in the case of actions adultery, theft, murder; for all of these and suchlike things imply by their names that they are themselves bad, and not the excesses or deficiencies of them. It is not possible, then, ever to be right with regard to them; one must always be wrong. Nor does goodness or badness with regard to such things depend on committing adultery with the right woman, at the right time, and in the right way, but simply to do any of them is to go wrong. It would be equally absurd, then, to expect that in unjust, cowardly, and voluptuous action there should be a mean, an excess, and a deficiency; for at that rate there would be a mean of excess and of deficiency, and excess of excess, and a deficiency of deficiency. But as there is no excess and deficiency of temperance and courage because what is intermediate is in a sense an extreme, so too of the actions we have mentioned there is no mean nor any excess and deficiency, but however they are done they are wrong; for in general there is neither a mean of excess and deficiency, nor excess and deficiency of a mean. . . .

QUESTIONS FOR REFLECTION

1. How does Aristotle argue that happiness is the highest human good?

2. What is virtue, according to Aristotle?

3. How may a person become virtuous?

4. In what sense is virtue a mean between extremes?

5. What is it to be a good person, according to Aristotle? What does this mean for legislation?

ST. THOMAS AQUINAS

from *Summa Theologica* (1265–1273)

St. Thomas Aquinas (1224–1274), perhaps the greatest of all Catholic theologians and philosophers, was born in Roccasecca, Italy, and studied at Naples, Paris, and Cologne. At age thirty-two he was awarded a doctorate in theology at Paris; he joined the faculty there the next year. Starting in 1259 he spent a decade teaching at various Dominican monasteries near Rome, returning to Paris to teach in 1268. In 1272, at forty-eight, he joined the faculty in Naples and died just two years later.

Aquinas based his views on ethics and political philosophy on those of Aristotle. But he added many innovations, blending Aristotelian insights into a Christian worldview. He developed a comprehensive theory of natural law that remains influential today. Aquinas begins with Aristotle's idea that human good depends on human nature. To live well—to excel or flourish—is to fulfill one's function well. Just as an excellent knife cuts well and an excellent eye sees well, an excellent human being displays excellence in rational activity. As these examples suggest, different things have different functions. In general, the function of a thing depends on its nature. So, what something ought to do and be depends on its function, which in turn depends on its nature.

Aquinas adds God to this Aristotelian picture. God establishes the order of nature, determining the natures of things and their functions and their excellences. God thus indirectly establishes not only the physical laws that constitute the order of nature but also the natural laws *that free beings ought to obey. Since human nature is distinctively rational, law itself is essentially a matter of reason.*

Aquinas distinguishes several different kinds of law. Eternal law is the law of nature, established by God, that governs the entire universe. Everything in the universe obeys eternal law and does so necessarily. Science investigates eternal law and tries to describe it. Natural law is normative; it prescribes what things should do and be. Since a thing's nature determines its function and thus its virtue—what it ought to do and be—eternal law determines natural law. Natural law is the manifestation of eternal law in creatures capable of rational choice and activity. Natural law manifests the eternal law by way of "the light of natural reason." God imprints on us the natural ability to tell right from wrong.

Aquinas also distinguishes natural law from human law. Natural law is fully general and universal, but human law must apply to particular circumstances in specific ways. Natural law relates to human law as principles relate to conclusions drawn from them. One can think of natural law, then, as comprising the axioms of the moral law in general. Because natural law serves as an axiom of the moral law, it must be self-evident; it cannot be a conclusion from some other premise. Precepts of natural law must be both general and obvious. That might make it seem that natural law has little content. Pursue good; avoid evil. Everyone can agree to that. But what is good? What is evil?

Here, Aquinas appeals to human nature. As Aristotle argued, human excellence depends on our characteristic function, which depends in turn on our nature. This is true in two senses. What we are determines what we ought to do and be. And what we are tells us what we ought to do and be. The universe is ordered so that we naturally tend to pursue good and avoid evil. Our own dispositions thus provide a test. We are naturally disposed to pursue good and avoid evil. We have a natural tendency not only to have certain inclinations (toward food, drink, and sex, for example), but also to control them through the exercise of reason. If lust is natural, so are rationality, shame, and self-restraint.

Aquinas classifies the precepts of natural law into three groups: (1) laws of self-preservation, (2) laws of biological welfare, and (3) laws of reason.

Aquinas does not develop his theory of natural law into a comprehensive political philosophy. Nevertheless, several important theses follow from it.

First, human law aims at the common good. Second, the purpose of human law is to help people follow natural law, that is, to make them virtuous. Law is essentially paternalistic, restricting people's freedom for their own good. The law accomplishes this by training people to recognize right and wrong. Third, human law must be flexible. As Aristotle said, virtue is a mean; there is no strict rule for finding it. Human laws cannot take into account the full complexity of the world; they inevitably oversimplify. We must create law to regulate our behavior but also must allow for exceptions in those cases in which the law does not make sense. One might think that we may solve this problem by making law more specific. We might, for example, require people to return goods held in trust unless such return poses a risk to national security. But this only makes the problem worse. We are better off with general laws flexibly applied. Fourth, a law that is unjust or fails to promote the common good, in general or in a particular case, has no authority as law. It should not be obeyed.

Finally, just as people have a natural inclination to virtue, they have a natural inclination to live in certain social structures: in families, in communities, and in states. These social institutions are natural, not conventional; they thus have moral force. People are inherently social, as Aristotle observed. More specifically, they are naturally family members, members of communities, and citizens. Law, therefore, should serve to strengthen these natural institutions. (Source: Translated by the author from Summa Theologica *by Thomas Aquinas. [Rome: Ex typographica Senatus, 1886–1887. For English translations, see New York, Benziger Bros., 1947–48; Westminster: Christian Classics, 1948] I, II.)*

The law commands and forbids. But it belongs to reason to command. Therefore, law is something pertaining to reason.

Law is a certain rule and measure of acts that induces people to act or refrain from acting, for *lex* [law] comes from *ligare* [to bind], because it binds one to act. Now the rule and measure of human acts is reason, the first principle of human acts . . . since it belongs to reason to direct to the end, which is the first principle in all matters of action. . . .* Law, properly speaking, concerns first and foremost an ordering of the common good. . . .

Law, being a rule and measure, can be in someone in two ways: (a) as in him that rules and measures; (b) as in what is ruled and measured; a thing is ruled and measured to the extent that it partakes of a rule or measure. So, since all things subject to divine providence are ruled and measured by the eternal law, all things partake to some extent of the eternal law—to the extent, namely, that it is imprinted on them, they derive their inclinations to their proper acts and ends. Now the rational creature is subject to divine providence in a more excellent way than anything else, for it partakes of a share of providence, by being provident both for itself and for others. So, it has a share of the eternal reason, whereby it has a natural inclination to its proper act and end. This participation in the eternal law in the rational creature is called the *natural*

---

* Francisco Suárez disputes Aquinas's etymology, citing Cicero and Augustine, who contend that *lex* derives from *lectio* or *legendo*, whose root is *legere* [to read]. Modern scholarship supports Suárez, Cicero, and Augustine on this point.

law. Hence the Psalmist, after saying "offer up the sacrifice of justice," as though someone asked what the works of justice are, adds: "Many say, 'Who shows us good things?'" In answer, he says: "The light of your countenance, O Lord, is signed upon us." This implies that the light of natural reason, by which we discern what is good and what is evil, which pertains to the natural law, is nothing else than an imprint on us of the divine light. It is therefore evident that the natural law is nothing other than the rational creature's participation in the eternal law.

A law is a certain dictate of practical reason. Now evidently the same procedure takes place in practical and in speculative reason, for each goes from principles to conclusions. In speculative reason, we draw the conclusions of the various sciences from naturally known, indemonstrable principles. The knowledge of them is not imparted to us by nature but acquired by the efforts of reason. So too it is from the precepts of the natural law, as from general and indemonstrable principles, that human reason needs to proceed to certain particular determinations of the laws. These particular determinations, devised by human reason, are called human laws. . . .

The proper effect of law is to lead its subjects to their proper virtue. Since virtue is "what makes its subjects good," it follows that the proper effect of law is to make its subjects good, either simply or in some particular respect. A tyrannical law, through not being according to reason, is not a law, absolutely speaking, but rather a perversion of law. . . .

The precepts of the natural law are to practical reason what the first principles of demonstrations are to speculative reason, because both are self-evident principles. Consequently, the first principle in practical reason is one founded on the notion of good: namely, that good is what all things seek. Hence this is the first precept of law: Good is to be done and pursued, and evil is to be avoided. All other precepts of natural law are based on this. So, whatever practical reason naturally apprehends as man's good [or evil] belongs to the precepts of natural law as something to be done or avoided.

Good has the nature of an end, and evil the nature of a contrary. Hence, all those things to which people have a natural inclination are naturally apprehended by reason as being good and, consequently, as objects of pursuit. Their contraries are naturally apprehended as evil and objects of avoidance. So, the order of the precepts of natural law follows the order of natural inclinations.

First, people have an inclination to good in accordance with the nature they have in common with all substances. Every substance seeks the preservation of its own being according to its nature. By reason of this inclination, whatever preserves human life and wards off its obstacles belongs to the natural law. Second, people have an inclination to things that pertain to them more specially according to that nature which they have in common with other animals. In virtue of this inclination, those things are said to belong to the natural law "which nature has taught to all animals," such as sexual intercourse, the education of offspring, and so on. Third, people have an inclination to good according to the nature of their reason, which is proper to them. Thus, people have a natural inclination to know the truth about God and to live in society. In this respect, whatever pertains to this inclination belongs to natural law: for instance, to shun ignorance, to avoid offending those among whom one has to live, and other such things.

[St. John] Damascene says that "virtues are natural."* Therefore, virtuous acts are also a subject of natural law. . . . We may speak of virtuous acts in two ways: first, as being virtuous; second, as being such and such acts. If, then, we speak of acts of virtue considered as virtuous, all virtuous acts belong to natural law. For to natural law belongs everything to which people are naturally inclined. Now each thing inclines naturally to what is suitable to it according to its form. Thus, fire is inclined to give heat. So, since the rational soul is the proper form of a human being, people have a natural inclination to act according to reason. This is to act according to virtue. Consequently, considered in this way, all acts of virtue are prescribed by natural law, since each one's reason naturally dictates to him to act virtuously. But if we speak of virtuous acts considered in themselves, that is, in their proper

---

* St. John Damascene (700?–754?), *De fide orthodoxa* I, 5; in J. P. Migne (ed.), *Patrologia Latina* (Paris: Garnier fratres et J.-P. Migne successores, 1879) 32, 1228.

species, not all virtuous acts are prescribed by natural law; many things are done virtuously to which nature does not incline us at first, but which, through the inquiry of reason, we have found conducive to living well.

Practical reason concerns contingent matters, as do human actions. Consequently, though the general principles are necessary, the more we descend to matters of detail, the more frequently we encounter deviations. . . .

Thus, it is right and true for all to act according to reason. From this principle, it follows that goods entrusted to someone else should be restored to their owner. Now this is true for the majority of cases, but it may happen in a particular case that it would be harmful, and therefore unreasonable, to restore goods held in trust: for instance, if they are claimed for the purpose of fighting against one's country.

This principle will be found to fail more often as we descend further into detail: for example, if one were to say that goods held in trust should be restored with such and such a guarantee or in such and such a way. The greater the number of conditions added, the greater the number of ways in which the principle may fail, so that it is not right to restore or not to restore. . . .

People have a natural aptitude for virtue, but the perfection of virtue must be acquired by a kind of training. . . . Now, it is hard to see how a man could train himself, since the perfection of virtue consists chiefly in withdrawing him from undue pleasures, to which, above all, he is inclined. This is especially true of the young, who are more capable of being trained. Consequently, a man needs to receive this training from another to arrive at the perfection of virtue. Some young people are inclined to acts of virtue by their good natural disposition or by custom, or rather by the gift of God. For them, paternal training suffices, which is by warnings. But some are depraved, prone to vice, and not easily amenable to words. It is necessary for them to be restrained from evil by force and fear in order that they might at least desist from evildoing and leave others in peace. They themselves, by being habituated in this way, might be brought to do willingly

what they earlier did from fear and thus become virtuous. Now this kind of training, which compels through fear of punishment, is the discipline of laws.

Whatever is for an end should be proportioned to it. Now the end of law is the common good, because, as Isidore says, "Law should be framed not for any private benefit but for the common good of all the citizens."* Hence human laws should be proportioned to the common good. . . .

Every law is directed to the common welfare of people and derives the force and nature of law accordingly. But it has no power to oblige morally if it is not so directed. Hence the Jurist says: "By no reason of law or favor of equity may we interpret harshly and render burdensome those useful measures enacted for the welfare of man."† Now, often the observance of some point of law conduces to the common welfare in the majority of instances and yet in some cases is very harmful. Since, then, lawgivers cannot have in view every single case, they shape the law according to what happens most frequently, by directing their attention to the common good. So, if a case arises where the observance of that law would be harmful to the general welfare, it should not be observed. For instance, suppose that, in a city under siege, there is a law that the gates of the city must be kept closed. This is good for public welfare as a general rule. But if the enemy were in pursuit of certain citizens defending the city, it would be a great loss to the city if the gates were not opened to them. So, in that case, the gates ought to be opened, contrary to the letter of the law, in order to maintain the common welfare, which the lawgivers had in view.

---

* St. Isodore of Seville (560?–636), *Etymologiarum Libri* V, 21; in J. P. Migne (ed.), *Patrologia Latina* (Paris: Garnier fratres et J.-P. Migne successores, 1879) 82, 203.
† Domitian Ulpian (170?–228), *Digest* I, 3, 25; in P. Kruger (ed.), *Corpus Juris Civilis* (Berlin: Weidmannos, 1899, 1928), 34b.

QUESTIONS FOR REFLECTION

1. What is natural law? How does it relate to eternal law?

2. What role does natural law play in practical reason?

3. What is "the first precept of law"?

4. Explain the significance of natural inclinations for natural law.

5. What is virtue? How does it relate to inclination?

6. What is the goal of law? What is the status of laws that do not serve that goal?

7. Why, according to Aquinas, do many laws have exceptions?

DAVID HUME

from *A Treatise of Human Nature* (1739)

David Hume (1711–1776), Scottish philosopher and historian, was a contemporary of Voltaire, Rousseau, Handel, Bach, and fellow Scotsman Adam Smith. A prodigy, Hume entered the University of Edinburgh at age twelve. His family urged him to study law. He disliked it and opted for a business career but found that unsatisfying as well.

At age twenty-three, Hume gave up business and went to France, where he wrote A Treatise of Human Nature, *his greatest philosophical work. Hume argued for a skeptical empiricism, maintaining that all knowledge comes from sense experience and that therefore we can have no objective knowledge of anything beyond experience. The* Treatise *has been and continues to be immensely influential, but at the time it was ignored. Disappointed by the lack of response—"It fell stillborn from the press," he would later write—he turned to more popular works, such as* Essays Moral and Political *(1742). At thirty-one, he was rejected for a professorship at the University of Edinburgh because of his skeptical religious views. He returned to philosophy, writing* An Inquiry Concerning Human Understanding *(1748) and* An Inquiry Concerning the Principles of Morals *(1751) to set out his empiricism in more accessible form.*

At forty-one, Hume became librarian of the Advocates' Library in Edinburgh and began his six-volume History of England *(1754–1761), which earned him a substantial reputation as a man of letters in England and France as well as in Scotland. One of Hume's most important works,* Dialogues Concerning Natural Religion, *was published three years after his death at age sixty-five to avoid the controversy that he knew its criticisms of religious arguments would bring.*

In his writings on ethics, Hume stresses the importance of feeling as opposed to reason. There is a gulf, he argued, between is and ought; factual premises can never yield a moral conclusion on their own. Moreover, purely rational principles can never provide a motive for action. In morality, as in other areas where we seek to go beyond the data of sense experience, "reason is, and ought to be, the slave of the passions." (Source: From David Hume, A Treatise of Human Nature, *edited by Selby-Bigge [Oxford: Clarendon Press, 1888]. Footnotes have been omitted.)*

BOOK III / OF MORALS

Part I. Of Virtue and Vice in General.

SECTION I. *Moral Distinctions not deriv'd from Reason.*

. . . Those who affirm that virtue is nothing but a conformity to reason; that there are eternal fitnesses and unfitnesses of things, which are the same to every rational being that considers them; that the immutable measures of right and wrong impose an obligation, not only on human creatures, but also on the Deity himself: All these systems concur in the opinion, that morality, like truth, is discern'd merely by ideas, and by their juxtaposition and comparison. In order, therefore, to judge of these systems, we need only consider, whether it be possible, from reason alone, to distinguish betwixt moral good and evil, or whether there must concur some other principles to enable us to make that distinction.

If morality had naturally no influence on human passions and actions, 'twere in vain to take such pains to inculcate it; and nothing wou'd be more fruitless than that multitude of rules and precepts, with which all moralists abound. Philosophy is commonly divided into *speculative* and *practical;* and as morality is always comprehended under the latter division, 'tis supposed to influence our passions and actions, and to go beyond the calm and indolent judgments of the understanding. And this is confirm'd by common experience, which informs us, that men are often govern'd by their duties, and are deter'd from some actions by the opinion of injustice, and impell'd to others by that of obligation.

Since morals, therefore, have an influence on the actions and affections, it follows, that they cannot be deriv'd from reason; and that because reason alone, as we have already prov'd, can never have any such influence. Morals excite passions, and produce or prevent actions. Reason of itself is utterly impotent in this particular. The rules of morality, therefore, are not conclusions of our reason. . . .

Nor does this reasoning only prove, that morality consists not in any relations, that are the objects of science; but if examin'd, will prove with equal certainty, that it consists not in any *matter of fact,* which can be discover'd by the understanding. This is the *second* part of our argument; and if it can be made evident, we may conclude, that morality is not an object of reason. But can there be any difficulty in proving, that vice and virtue are not matters of fact, whose existence we can infer by reason? Take any action allow'd to be vicious: Wilful murder, for instance. Examine it in all lights, and see if you can find that matter of fact, or real existence, which you call *vice.* In whichever way you take it, you find only certain passions, motives, volitions and thoughts. There is no other matter of fact in the case. The vice entirely escapes you, as long as you consider the object. You never can find it, till you turn your reflexion into your own breast, and find a sentiment of disapprobation, which arises in you, towards this action. Here is a matter of fact; but 'tis the object of feeling, not of reason. It lies in yourself, not in the object. So that when you pronounce any action or

character to be vicious, you mean nothing, but that from the constitution of your nature you have a feeling or sentiment of blame from the contemplation of it. Vice and virtue, therefore, may be compar'd to sounds, colours, heat and cold, which, according to modern philosophy, are not qualities in objects, but perceptions in the mind: And this discovery in morals, like that other in physics, is to be regarded as a considerable advancement of the speculative sciences; tho', like that too, it has little or no influence on practice. Nothing can be more real, or concern us more, than our own sentiments of pleasure and uneasiness; and if these be favourable to virtue, and unfavourable to vice, no more can be requisite to the regulation of our conduct and behaviour.

I cannot forbear adding to these reasonings an observation, which may, perhaps, be found of some importance. In every system of morality, which I have hitherto met with, I have always remark'd, that the author proceeds for some time in the ordinary way of reasoning, and establishes the being of a God, or makes observations concerning human affairs; when of a sudden I am surpriz'd to find, that instead of the usual copulations of propositions, *is,* and *is not,* I meet with no proposition that is not connected with an *ought,* or an *ought not.* This change is imperceptible; but is, however, of the last consequence. For as this *ought,* or *ought not,* expresses some new relation or affirmation, 'tis necessary that it shou'd be observ'd and explain'd; and at the same time that a reason should be given, for what seems altogether inconceivable, how this new relation can be a deduction from others, which are entirely different from it. But as authors do not commonly use this precaution, I shall presume to recommend it to the readers; and am persuaded, that this small attention wou'd subvert all the vulgar systems of morality, and let us see, that the distinction of vice and virtue is not founded merely on the relations of objects, nor is perceiv'd by reason.

SECTION II. *Moral distinctions deriv'd from a moral sense.*

Thus the course of the argument leads us to conclude, that since vice and virtue are not discoverable merely by reason, or the comparison of ideas, it must be by means of some impression or sentiment they occasion, that we are able to mark the difference betwixt them. Our decisions concerning moral rectitude and depravity are evidently perceptions; and as all perceptions are either impressions or ideas, the exclusion of the one is a convincing argument for the other. Morality, therefore, is more properly felt than judg'd of; tho' this feeling or sentiment is commonly so soft and gentle, that we are apt to confound it with an idea, according to our common custom of taking all things for the same, which have any near resemblance to each other.

The next question is, Of what nature are these impressions, and after what manner do they operate upon us? Here we cannot remain long in suspense, but must pronounce the impression arising from virtue, to be agreeable, and that proceeding from vice to be uneasy. Every moment's experience must convince us of this. There is no spectacle so fair and beautiful as a noble and generous action; nor any which gives us more abhorrence than one that is cruel and treacherous. No enjoyment equals the satisfaction we receive from the company of those we love and esteem; as the greatest of all punishments is to be oblig'd to pass our lives with those we hate or contemn. A very play or romance may afford us instances of this pleasure, which virtue conveys to us; and pain, which arises from vice.

Now since the distinguishing impressions, by which moral good or evil is known, are nothing but *particular* pains or pleasures; it follows, that in all enquiries concerning these moral distinctions, it will be sufficient to shew the principles, which make us feel a satisfaction or uneasiness from the survey of any character, in order to satisfy us why the character is laudable or blameable. An action, or sentiment, or character is virtuous or vicious; why? because its view causes a pleasure or uneasiness of a particular kind. In giving a reason, therefore, for the pleasure or uneasiness, we sufficiently explain the vice or virtue. To have the sense of virtue, is nothing but to *feel* a satisfaction of a particular kind from the contemplation of a character. The very *feeling* constitutes our praise or admiration. We go no farther; nor do we enquire into the cause of the satisfaction. We do not infer a character to be virtuous, because it pleases: But in feeling that it pleases after such a particular manner, we in effect feel that it is virtuous. The case is the same as in our judgments concerning all kinds of beauty, and tastes, and sensations. Our approbation is imply'd in the immediate pleasure they convey to us. . . .

Thus we are still brought back to our first position, that virtue is distinguished by the pleasure, and vice by the pain, that any action, sentiment or character gives us by the mere view and contemplation. This decision is very commodious; because it reduces us to this simple question, *Why any action or sentiment upon the general view or survey, gives a certain satisfaction or uneasiness,* in order to shew the origin of its moral rectitude or depravity, without looking for any incomprehensible relations and qualities, which never did exist in nature, nor even in our imagination, by any clear and distinct conception. I flatter myself I have executed a great part of my present design by a state of the question, which appears to me so free from ambiguity and obscurity.

QUESTIONS FOR REFLECTION

1. Summarize Hume's arguments that "the rules of morality are not conclusions of our reason."

2. Why, according to Hume, are rational principles unable to motivate the will?

3. Where, according to Hume, do most moral arguments fail?

4. How, if at all, can one get from *is* to *ought?* How, that is, is it possible to justify a moral conclusion?

5. In what sense is Hume's position a critique of Aristotle?

6. Plato held that virtue is knowledge—and thus that vice results from ignorance or error. How does Hume argue against that position?

7. How do we distinguish vice from virtue, according to Hume?

IMMANUEL KANT

from *Fundamental Principles of the Metaphysics of Morals* (1785)

Immanuel Kant (1724–1804), a contemporary of Blake, Goethe, and Mozart, was born in Königsberg, in East Prussia (now Kaliningrad, part of the Russian republic). The son of a saddlemaker and grandson of a Scottish immigrant, Kant attended the University of Königsberg, from which he graduated at twenty-two. A year later he published his first philosophical work, a book on living forces. He was a private tutor for several years while continuing his studies. At twentynine, he received a master's degree and began teaching at Königsberg as a Privatdozent— roughly, an unpaid lecturer who collected fees from his students. He continued in that capacity for fifteen years. Finally, in 1770, he was appointed to a chair of logic and metaphysics at the University of Königsberg.

At the age of fifty-seven, Kant published the Critique of Pure Reason, *a work that earned him fame and that contemporary philosophers regard as one of the greatest works of the Western philosophical tradition. The decade that followed was extremely productive for Kant.* Prolegomena to Any Future Metaphysics *appeared in 1783;* Fundamental Principles of the Metaphysics of Morals *in 1785; the second edition of the* Critique of Pure Reason *in 1787; the* Critique of Practical Reason *in 1788; and the* Critique of Judgment *in 1790. Kant continued writing well into his seventies.*

Though known for his wit and conversational skill as well as for his intellect, Kant never married and never traveled more than a few miles from the place of his birth. His habits were so regular that, according to legend, neighbors would set their clocks by his afternoon walks.

Kant's Fundamental Principles of the Metaphysics of Morals *argues that only one thing is good intrinsically, that is, in itself: a good will. He argues that rational beings will recognize that they are subject to the moral law, which he formulates in several versions of what he takes to be single moral principle: the categorical imperative. From it stem human rights, human dignity, and everything else essential to morality. (Source: Reprinted by permission from* Fundamental Principles of the Metaphysics of Morals, *translated by Thomas Kingsmill Abbott. New York: Longmans, Green, 1926).*

Nothing can possibly be conceived in the world, or even out of it, which can be called good, without qualification, except a good will. Intelligence, wit, judgment, and the other talents of the mind, however they may be named, or courage, resolution, perseverance, as qualities of temperament, are undoubtedly good and desirable in many respects; but these gifts of nature may also become extremely bad and mischievous if the will which is to make use of them, and which, therefore, constitutes what is called character, is not good. It is the same with the gifts of fortune. Power, riches, honour, even health, and the general well-being and contentment with one's condition which is called happiness, inspire pride, and often presumption, if there is not a good will to correct the influence of these on the mind, and with this also to rectify the whole principle of acting and adapt it to its end. The sight of a being who is not adorned with a single feature of a pure and good will, enjoying unbroken prosperity, can never give pleasure to an impartial rational spectator. Thus a good will appears to constitute the indispensable condition even of being worthy of happiness.

[A good will,] like a jewel, . . . would still shine by its own light, as a thing which has its whole value in itself. Its usefulness or fruitfulness can neither add nor take away anything from this value. It would be, as it were, only the setting to enable us to handle it the more conveniently in common commerce, or to attract to it the attention of those who are not yet connoisseurs, but not to recommend it to true connoisseurs, or to determine its value.

The conception of an objective principle, in so far as it is obligatory for a will, is called a *command* (of reason), and the formula of the command is called an *imperative.*

All imperatives are expressed by the word *ought* [or *should*], and thereby indicate the relation of an objective law of reason to a will, which from its subjective constitution is not necessarily determined by it (an obligation). They say that something would be good to do or to forbear, but they say it to a will which does not always do a thing because it is conceived to be good to do it. That is practically good, however, which determines the will by means of the conceptions of reason, and consequently not from subjective causes, but objectively, that is, on principles which are valid for every rational being as such. It is distinguished from the pleasant, as that which influences the will only by means of sensation from merely subjective causes, valid only for the sense of this or that one, and not as a principle of reason, which holds for every one. . . .

Now all imperatives command either hypothetically or categorically. The former represent the practical necessity of a possible action as means to something else that is willed (or at least which one might possibly will). The categorical imperative would be that which represented an action as necessary of itself without reference to another end, i.e., as objectively necessary.

. . . If now the action is good only as a means to something else, then the imperative is hypothetical; if it is conceived as good in itself and consequently as being necessarily the principle of a will which of itself conforms to reason, then it is categorical. . . .

Accordingly the hypothetical imperative only says that the action is good for some purpose, possible or actual. . . . The categorical imperative . . . declares an action to be objectively necessary in itself without reference to any purpose, i.e., without any other end. . . .

There is one end, however, which may be assumed to be actually such to all rational beings (so far as imperatives apply to them, viz., as dependent beings), and, therefore, one purpose which they not merely may have, but which we may with certainty assume that they all actually have by a natural necessity, and this is happiness. The hypothetical imperative which expresses the practical necessity of an action as means to the advancement of happiness is assertorial. We are not to present it as necessary for an uncertain and merely possible purpose, but for a purpose which we may presuppose with certainty and a priori in every man, because it belongs to his being. Now skill in the choice of means to his own greatest well-being may be called prudence, in the narrowest sense. And thus the imperative which refers to the choice of means to one's own happiness, i.e., the precept of prudence, is still always hypothetical; the action is not commanded absolutely, but only as means to another purpose.

[Morality] concerns not the matter of the action, or its intended result, but its form and the principle of which it is itself a result; and what is essentially good in it consists in the mental disposition, let the consequence be what it may.

When I conceive a hypothetical imperative, in general I do not know beforehand what it will contain until I am given the condition. But when I conceive a categorical imperative, I know at once what it contains. For as the imperative contains besides the law only the necessity that the maxims shall conform to this law, while the law contains no conditions restricting it, there remains nothing but the general statement that the maxim of the action should conform to a universal law, and it is this conformity alone that the imperative properly represents as necessary.

There is therefore but one categorical imperative, namely, this: Act only on that maxim whereby thou canst at the same time will that it should become a universal law.

. . . Since the universality of the law according to which effects are produced constitutes what is properly called nature in the most general sense (as to form), that is, the existence of things so far as it is determined by general laws, the imperative of duty may be expressed thus: Act as if the maxim of thy action were to become by thy will a universal law of nature.

1. A man reduced to despair by a series of misfortunes feels wearied of life, but is still so far in possession of his reason that he can ask himself whether it would not be contrary to his duty to himself to take his own life. Now he inquires whether the maxim of his action could become a universal law of nature. His maxim is: "From self-love I adopt it as a principle to shorten my life when its longer duration is likely to bring more evil than satisfaction." It is asked then simply whether this principle founded on self-love can become a universal law of nature. Now we see at once that a system of nature of which it should be a law to destroy life by means of the very feeling whose special nature it is to impel to the improvement of life would contradict itself and, therefore, could not exist as a system of nature; hence that maxim cannot possibly exist as a universal law of nature and, consequently, would be wholly inconsistent with the supreme principle of all duty.

2. Another finds himself forced by necessity to borrow money. He knows that he will not be able to repay it, but sees also that nothing will be lent to him unless he promises stoutly to repay it in a definite time. He desires to make this promise, but he has still so much conscience as to ask himself: "Is it not unlawful and inconsistent with duty to get out of a difficulty in this way?" Suppose however that he resolves to do so: then the maxim of his action would be expressed thus: "When I think myself in want of money, I will borrow money and promise to repay it, although I know that I never can do so." Now this principle of self-love or of one's own advantage may perhaps be consistent with my whole future welfare; but the question now is, "Is it right?" I change then the suggestion of self-love into a universal law, and state the question thus: "How would it be if my maxim were a universal law?" Then I see at once that it could never hold as a universal law of nature, but would necessarily contradict itself. For supposing it to be a universal law that everyone when he thinks himself in a difficulty should be able to promise whatever he pleases, with the purpose of not keeping his promise, the promise itself would become impossible, as well as the end that one might have in view in it, since no one would consider that anything was promised to him, but would ridicule all such statements as vain pretenses.

3. A third finds in himself a talent which with the help of some culture might make him a useful man in many respects. But he finds himself in comfortable circumstances and prefers to indulge in pleasure rather than to take pains in enlarging and improving his happy natural capacities. He asks, however, whether his maxim of neglect of his natural gifts, besides agreeing with his inclination to indulgence, agrees also with what is called duty. He sees then that a system of nature could indeed subsist with such a universal law although men (like the South Sea islanders) should let their talents rest and resolve to devote their lives merely to idleness, amusement, and propagation of their species—in a word, to enjoyment; but he cannot possibly will that this should be a universal law of nature, or be implanted in us as such by a natural instinct. For, as a rational being, he necessarily wills that his faculties be developed, since they serve him and have been given him, for all sorts of possible purposes.

4. A fourth, who is in prosperity, while he sees that others have to contend with great wretchedness and that he could help them, thinks: "What concern is it of mine? Let everyone be as happy as Heaven pleases, or as he can make himself; I will take nothing from him nor even envy him, only I do not wish to contribute anything to his welfare or to his assistance in distress!" Now no doubt if such a mode of thinking

were a universal law, the human race might very well subsist and doubtless even better than in a state in which everyone talks of sympathy and good-will, or even takes care occasionally to put it into practice, but, on the other side, also cheats when he can, betrays the rights of men, or otherwise violates them. But although it is possible that a universal law of nature might exist in accordance with that maxim, it is impossible to will that such a principle should have the universal validity of a law of nature. For a will which resolved this would contradict itself, inasmuch as many cases might occur in which one would have need of the love and sympathy of others, and in which, by such a law of nature, sprung from his own will, he would deprive himself of all hope of the aid he desires. . . .

If now we attend to ourselves on occasion of any transgression of duty, we shall find that we in fact do not will that our maxim should be a universal law, for that is impossible for us; on the contrary, we will that the opposite should remain a universal law, only we assume the liberty of making an exception in our own favor or (just for this time only) in favor of our inclination. Consequently if we considered all cases from one and the same point of view, namely, that of reason, we should find a contradiction in our own will, namely, that a certain principle should be objectively necessary as a universal law, and yet subjectively should not be universal, but admit of exceptions. . . .

Supposing, however, that there were something whose existence has in itself an absolute worth, something which, being an end in itself, could be a source of definite laws; then in this and this alone would lie the source of a possible categorical imperative, i.e., a practical law.

Now I say: man and generally any rational being exists as an end in himself, not merely as a means to be arbitrarily used by this or that will, but in all his actions, whether they concern himself or other rational beings, must be always regarded at the same time as an end. All objects of the inclinations have only a conditional worth, for if the inclinations and the wants founded on them did not exist, then their object would be without value. . . . Beings whose exis-

tence depends not on our will but on nature's, have nevertheless, if they are irrational beings, only a relative value as means, and are therefore called things; rational beings, on the contrary, are called persons, because their very nature points them out as ends in themselves, that is, as something which must not be used merely as means, and so far therefore restricts freedom of action (and is an object of respect). These, therefore, are not merely subjective ends whose existence has a worth for us as an effect of our action, but objective ends, that is, things whose existence is an end in itself; an end moreover for which no other can be substituted, which they should subserve merely as means, for otherwise nothing whatever would possess absolute worth; but if all worth were conditioned and therefore contingent, then there would be no supreme practical principle of reason whatever.

. . . The foundation of this principle [the categorical imperative] is: rational nature exists as an end in itself. Man necessarily conceives his own existence as being so; so far, then, this is a subjective principle of human actions. But every other rational being regards its existence similarly, just on the same rational principle that holds for me: so that it is at the same time an objective principle, from which as a supreme practical law all laws of the will must be capable of being deduced. Accordingly the practical imperative will be as follows: So act as to treat humanity, whether in thine own person or in that of any other, in every case as an end withal, never as means only. . . .

Firstly, under the head of necessary duty to oneself: He who contemplates suicide should ask himself whether his action can be consistent with the idea of humanity as an end in itself. If he destroys himself in order to escape from painful circumstances, he uses a person merely as a means to maintain a tolerable condition up to the end of life. But a man is not a thing, that is to say, something which can be used merely as means, but must in all his actions be always considered as an end in himself. I cannot, therefore, dispose in any way of a man in my own person so as to mutilate him, to damage or kill him. (It belongs to ethics proper to define this principle more precisely, so as to avoid all misunderstanding, e.g., as to the amputation of the limbs in order to preserve myself, as to exposing my life to danger with a view to preserve it, etc. This question is therefore omitted here.)

Secondly, as regards necessary duties, or those of strict obligation, towards others: He who is thinking of making a lying promise to others will see at once that he would be using another man merely as a means, without the latter containing at the same time the end in himself. For he whom I propose by such a promise to use for my own purposes cannot possibly assent to my mode of acting towards him and, therefore, cannot himself contain the end of this action. This violation of the principle of humanity in other men is more obvious if we take in examples of attacks on the freedom and property of others. For then it is clear that he who transgresses the rights of men intends to use the person of others merely as a means, without considering that as rational beings they ought always to be esteemed also as ends, that is, as beings who must be capable of containing in themselves the end of the very same action.

Thirdly, as regards contingent (meritorious) duties to oneself: It is not enough that the action does not violate humanity in our own person as an end in itself, it must also harmonize with it. Now there are in humanity capacities of greater perfection, which belong to the end that nature has in view in regard to humanity in ourselves as the subject: to neglect these might perhaps be consistent with the maintenance of humanity as an end in itself, but not with the advancement of this end.

Fourthly, as regards meritorious duties towards others: The natural end which all men have is their own happiness. Now humanity might indeed subsist, although no one should contribute anything to the happiness of others, provided he did not intentionally withdraw anything from it; but after all this would only harmonize negatively not positively with humanity as an end in itself, if every one does not also endeavour, as far as in him lies, to forward the ends of others. For the ends of any subject which is an end in himself ought as far as possible to be my ends also, if that conception is to have its full effect with me. . . .

Looking back now on all previous attempts to discover the principle of morality, we need not wonder why they all failed. It was seen that man was bound to laws by duty, but it was not observed that the laws to which he is subject are only those of his own giving, though at the same time they are universal, and that he is only bound to act in conformity with his own will; a will, however, which is designed by nature to give universal laws. For when one has conceived man only as subject to a law (no matter what), then this law required some interest, either by way of attraction or constraint, since it did not originate as a law from his own will, but this will was according to a law obliged by something else to act in a certain manner. Now by this necessary consequence all the labour spent in finding a supreme principle of duty was irrevocably lost. For men never elicited duty, but only a necessity of acting from a certain interest. Whether this interest was private or otherwise, in any case the imperative must be conditional and could not by any means be capable of being a moral command. I will therefore call this the principle of autonomy of the will, in contrast with every other which I accordingly reckon as heteronomy. . . .

In the kingdom of ends everything has either value or dignity. Whatever has a value can be replaced by something else which is equivalent; whatever, on the other hand, is above all value, and therefore admits of no equivalent, has a dignity.

Whatever has reference to the general inclinations and wants of mankind has a market value; whatever, without presupposing a want, corresponds to a certain taste, that is to a satisfaction in the mere purposeless play of our faculties, has a fancy value; but that which constitutes the condition under which alone anything can be an end in itself, this has not merely a relative worth, i.e., value, but an intrinsic worth, that is, dignity.

Now morality is the condition under which alone a rational being can be an end in himself, since by this alone is it possible that he should be a legislating member in the kingdom of ends. Thus morality, and humanity as capable of it, is that which alone has dignity.

. . . Autonomy then is the basis of the dignity of human and of every rational nature. . . . although the conception of duty implies subjection to the law, we yet ascribe a certain dignity and sublimity to the person who fulfills all his duties. There is not, indeed, any sublimity in him, so far as he is subject to the moral law; but inasmuch as in regard to that very law he is likewise a legislator, and on that account alone subject to it, he has sublimity. We have also shown above that neither fear nor inclination, but simply respect for the law, is the spring which can give actions a moral worth. Our own will, so far as we suppose it to act only under the condition that its maxims are potentially universal laws, this ideal will which is possible to us is the proper object of respect; and the dignity of humanity consists just in this capacity of being universally legislative, though with the condition that it is itself subject to this same legislation.

QUESTIONS FOR REFLECTION

1. What is an imperative? What is the difference between hypothetical and categorical imperatives?

2. Why must a categorical imperative be established *a priori*, that is, independently of experience?

3. Kant gives several different formulations of the categorical imperative. What are they? Why does he take them to be equivalent?

4. Consider Kant's four examples. How does he apply the categorical imperative to each?

5. What is autonomy? How does it relate to dignity?

JOHN STUART MILL

from *Utilitarianism* (1861)

John Stuart Mill (1806–1873) was a contemporary of Darwin, Dickens, Marx, and Tolstoy. Born in London, he was the most influential philosopher of the English-speaking world during the nineteenth century. His father, James Mill (1773–1836), was the son of a Scottish shoemaker who had become a prominent supporter of philosophical radicalism, a school of thought that advocated representative democracy, universal suffrage, and a scientific approach to philosophy. The elder Mill had a highly unusual and ambitious plan for educating his son at home. Consequently, John Stuart Mill never attended any school or college. He learned to read Greek at three and Latin just a few years later; he was well read in classical literature and history by eight and studied philosophy, mathematics, and economics before reaching his teens. At seventeen, he became a clerk in the East India Company, which governed India under charter from the British government. He eventually became chief of his department and worked at the company until 1858. In that year, Harriet Taylor, Mill's wife of six years—whom in the dedication of On Liberty *he calls "the inspirer, and in part the author, of all that is best in my writings"—died while they were traveling together in France. Mill decided to devote his time fully to writing the works they had discussed together. The next few years saw the publication of Mill's most influential ethical works:* On Liberty *(1859),* Utilitarianism *(1861), and* On the Subjection of Women *(1869). In 1865, Mill won election to Parliament, despite his refusal to campaign or defend his views. (Source: Reprinted from John Stuart Mill,* Utilitarianism. *London: Longman's, 1907.)*

CHAPTER II / WHAT UTILITARIANISM IS

. . . The creed which accepts as the foundation of morals "utility" or the "greatest happiness principle" holds that actions are right in proportion as they tend to promote happiness; wrong as they tend to produce the reverse of happiness. By happiness is intended pleasure and the absence of pain; by unhappiness, pain and the privation of pleasure. To give a clear view of the moral standard set up by the theory, much more requires to be said; in particular, what things it includes in the ideas of pain and pleasure, and to what extent this is left an open question. But these supplementary explanations do not affect the theory of life on which this theory of morality is grounded—namely, that pleasure and freedom from pain are the only things desirable as ends; and that all desirable things (which are as numerous in the utilitarian as in any other scheme) are desirable either for pleasure inherent in themselves or as means to the promotion of pleasure and the prevention of pain.

Now such a theory of life excites in many minds, and among them some of the most estimable in feeling and purpose, inveterate dislike. To suppose that life has (as they express it) no higher end than pleasure—no better and nobler object of desire and pursuit—they designate as utterly mean and groveling, as a doctrine worthy only of swine, to whom the followers of Epicurus were, at a very early period, contemptuously likened; and modern holders of the doctrine are occasionally made the subject of equally polite comparison by its German, French, and English assailants.

When thus attacked, the Epicureans have always answered that it is not they, but their accusers, who represent human nature in a degrading light, since the accusation supposes human beings to be capable of no pleasures except those of which swine are capable. If this supposition were true, the charge could not be gainsaid, but would then be no longer an imputation; for if the sources of pleasure were precisely the same to human beings and to swine, the rule of life which is good enough for the one would be good enough for the other. The comparison of the Epicurean life to that of beasts is felt as degrading, precisely because a beast's pleasures do not satisfy a human being's conceptions of happiness. Human beings have faculties more elevated than the animal appetites and, when once made conscious of them, do not regard anything as happiness which does not include their gratification. I do not indeed, consider the Epicureans to have been by any means faultless in drawing out their scheme of consequences from the utilitarian principle. To do this in any sufficient manner, many Stoic, as well as Christian, elements require to be included. But there is no known Epicurean theory of life which does not assign to the pleasures of the intellect, of the feelings and imagination, and of the moral sentiments a much higher value as pleasures than to those of mere sensation. It must be admitted, however, that utilitarian writers in general have placed the superiority of mental over bodily pleasures chiefly in the greater permanency, safety, uncostliness, etc., of the former—that is, in their circumstantial advantages rather than in their intrinsic nature. And on all these points utilitarians have fully proved their case; but they might have taken the other and, as it may be called, higher ground with entire consistency. It is quite compatible with the principle of utility to recognize the fact that some kinds of pleasure are more desirable and more valuable than others. It would be absurd that, while in estimating all other things quality is considered as well as quantity, the estimation of pleasure should be supposed to depend on quantity alone.

If I am asked what I mean by difference of quality in pleasures, or what makes one pleasure more valuable than another, merely as a pleasure, except its being greater in amount, there is but one possible answer. Of two pleasures, if there be one to which all or almost all who have experience of both give a decided preference, irrespective of any feeling of moral obligation to prefer it, that is the more desirable pleasure. If one of the two is, by those who are competently acquainted with both, placed so far above the other that they prefer it, even though knowing it to be attended with a greater amount of discontent, and would not resign it for any quantity of the other pleasure which their nature is capable of, we are justified in ascribing to the preferred enjoyment a superiority in quality so far outweighing quantity as to render it, in comparison, of small account.

Now it is an unquestionable fact that those who are equally acquainted with and equally capable of appreciating and enjoying both do give a most marked preference to the manner of existence which employs their higher faculties. Few human creatures would consent to be changed into any of the lower animals for a promise of the fullest allowance of a beast's pleasures; no intelligent human being would consent to be a fool, no instructed person would be an ignoramus, no person of feeling and conscience would be selfish and base, even though they should be persuaded that the fool, the dunce, or the rascal is better satisfied with his lot than they are with theirs. They would not resign what they possess more than he for the most complete satisfaction of all the desires which they have in common with him. If they ever fancy they would, it is only in cases of unhappiness so extreme that to escape from it they would exchange their lot for almost any other, however undesirable in their own eyes. A being of higher faculties requires more to make him happy, is capable probably of more acute suffering, and certainly accessible to it at more points, than one of an inferior type; but in spite of these liabilities, he can never really wish to sink into what he feels to be a lower grade of existence.

We may give what explanation we please of this unwillingness; we may attribute it to pride, a name which is given indiscriminately to some of the most and to some of the least estimable feelings of which mankind are capable; we may refer it to the love of liberty and personal independence, an appeal to which was with the Stoics one of the most effective means for the inculcation of it; to the love of power or to the love of excitement, both of which do really enter into and contribute to it; but its most appropriate appellation is a sense of dignity, which all human beings possess in one form or other, and in some, though by no means in exact, proportion to their higher faculties, and which is so essential a part of the happiness of those in whom it is strong that nothing which conflicts with it could be otherwise than momentarily an object of desire to them. Whoever supposes that this preference takes place at a sacrifice of happiness—that the superior being, in anything like equal circumstances, is not happier than the inferior—confounds the two very different ideas of happiness and content. It is indisputable that the being whose capacities of enjoyment are low has the greatest chance of having them fully satisfied; and a highly endowed being will always feel that any happiness which he can look for, as the world is constituted, is imperfect. But he can learn to bear its imperfections, if they are at all bearable; and they will not make him envy the being who is indeed unconscious of the imperfections, but only because he feels not at all the good which those imperfections qualify. It is better to be a human being dissatisfied than a pig satisfied; better to be Socrates dissatisfied than a fool satisfied. And if the fool, or the pig, are of a different opinion, it is because they only know their own side of the question. The other party to the comparison knows both sides.

It may be objected that many who are capable of the higher pleasures occasionally, under the influence of temptation, postpone them to the lower. But this is quite compatible with a full appreciation of the intrinsic superiority of the higher. Men often, from infirmity of character, make their election for the nearer good, though they know it to be the less valuable; and this no less when the choice is between two bodily pleasures than when it is between bodily and mental. They pursue sensual indulgence to the injury of health, though perfectly aware that health is the greater good. It may be further objected that many who begin with youthful enthusiasm for everything noble, as they advance in years, sink into indolence and selfishness. But I do not believe that those who undergo this very common change voluntarily choose the lower description of pleasures in preference to the higher. I believe that, before they devote themselves exclusively to the one, they have already become incapable of the other. Capacity for the nobler feelings is in most natures a very tender plant, easily killed, not only by hostile influences, but by mere want of sustenance; and in the majority of young persons it speedily dies away if the occupations to which their position in life has devoted them, and the society into which it has thrown them, are not favorable to keeping that higher capacity in

exercise. Men lose their high aspirations as they lose their intellectual tastes, because they have not time or opportunity for indulging them; and they addict themselves to inferior pleasures, not because they deliberately prefer them, but because they are either the only ones to which they have access or the only ones which they are any longer capable of enjoying. It may be questioned whether anyone who has remained equally susceptible to both classes of pleasures ever knowingly and calmly preferred the lower, though many, in all ages, have broken down in an ineffectual attempt to combine both.

From this verdict of the only competent judges, I apprehend there can be no appeal. On a question which is the best worth having of two pleasures, or which of two modes of existence is the most grateful to the feelings, apart from its moral attributes, and from its consequences, the judgment of these who are qualified by knowledge of both, or, if they differ, that of the majority among them, must be admitted as final. And there needs be the less hesitation to accept this judgment respecting the quality of pleasures, since there is no other tribunal to be referred to even on the question of quantity. What means are there of determining which is the acutest of two pains, or the intensest of two pleasurable sensations, except the general suffrage of those who are familiar with both? Neither pains nor pleasures are homogeneous, and pain is always heterogeneous with pleasure. What is there to decide whether a particular pleasure is worth purchasing at the cost of a particular pain, except the feelings and judgment of the experienced? When, therefore, those feelings and judgment declare the pleasures derived from the higher faculties to be preferable *in kind,* apart from the question of intensity, to those of which the animal nature, disjoined from the higher faculties, is susceptible, they are entitled on this subject to the same regard.

I have dwelt on this point as being part of a perfectly just conception of utility or happiness considered as the directive rule of human conduct. But it is by no means an indispensable condition to the acceptance of the utilitarian standard; for that standard is not the agent's own greatest happiness, but the greatest amount of happiness altogether; and if it may possibly be doubted whether a noble character is always the happier for its nobleness, there can be no doubt that it makes other people happier, and that the world in general is immensely a gainer by it. Utilitarianism, therefore, could only attain its end by the general cultivation of nobleness of character, even if each individual were only benefited by the nobleness of others, and his own, so far as happiness is concerned, were a sheer deduction from the benefit. But the bare enunciation of such an absurdity as this last renders refutation superfluous.

According to the greatest happiness principle, as above explained, the ultimate end, with reference to and for the sake of which all other things are desirable—whether we are considering our own good or that of other people—is an existence exempt as far as possible from pain, and as rich as possible in enjoyments, both in point of quantity and quality; the test of quality and the rule for measuring it against quantity being the preference felt by those who, in their opportunities of experience, to which must be added their habits of self-consciousness and self-observation, are best furnished with the means of comparison. This, being according to the utilitarian opinion the end of human action, is necessarily also the standard of morality, which may accordingly be defined "the rules and precepts for human conduct," by the observance of which an existence such as has been described might be, to the greatest extent possible, secured to all mankind; and not to them only, but, so far as the nature of things admits, to the whole sentient creation. . . .

I must again repeat what the assailants of utilitarianism seldom have the justice to acknowledge, that the happiness which forms the utilitarian standard of what is right in conduct is not the agent's own happiness but that of all concerned. As between his own happiness and that of others, utilitarianism requires him to be as strictly impartial as a disinterested and benevolent spectator. In the golden rule of Jesus of Nazareth, we read the complete spirit of the ethics of utility. "To do as you would be done by," and "to love your neighbor as yourself," constitute the ideal perfection of utilitarian morality. As the means of making the nearest approach to this ideal, utility would enjoin, first, that laws and social arrangements should place the happiness or (as, speaking practically, it may be called) the interest of every individual as nearly as possible in harmony with the interest of the whole; and, secondly, that education and opinion, which have so vast a power over human character, should so use that power as

to establish in the mind of every individual an indissoluble association between his own happiness and the good of the whole, especially between his own happiness and the practice of such modes of conduct, negative and positive, as regard for the universal happiness prescribes; so that not only he may be unable to conceive the possibility of happiness to himself, consistently with conduct opposed to the general good, but also that a direct impulse to promote the general good may be in every individual one of the habitual motives of action, and the sentiments connected therewith may fill a large and prominent place in every human being's sentient existence. If the impugners of the utilitarian morality represented it to their own minds in this its true character, I know not what recommendations possessed by any other morality they could possibly affirm to be wanting to it; what more beautiful or more exalted developments of human nature any other ethical system can be supposed to foster, or what springs of action, not accessible to the utilitarian, such systems rely on for giving effect to their mandates.

The objectors to utilitarianism cannot always be charged with representing it in a discreditable light. On the contrary, those among them who entertain anything like a just idea of its disinterested character sometimes find fault with its standard as being too high for humanity. They say it is exacting too much to require that people shall always act from the inducement of promoting the general interest of society. But this is to mistake the very meaning of a standard of morals and confound the rule of action with the motive of it. It is the business of ethics to tell us what are our duties, or by what test we may know them; but no system of ethics requires that the sole motive of all we do shall be a feeling of duty; on the contrary, ninety-nine hundredths of all our actions are done from other motives, and rightly so done if the rule of duty does not condemn them. It is the more unjust to utilitarianism that this particular misapprehension should be made a ground of objection to it, inasmuch as utilitarian moralists have gone beyond almost all others in affirming that the motive has nothing to do with the morality of the action, though much with the worth of the agent. He who saves a fellow creature from drowning does what is morally right, whether his motive be duty or the hope of being paid for his trouble; he who betrays the friend that trusts him is guilty of a crime, even if his object be to serve another friend to whom he is under great obligations. But to speak only of actions done from the motive of duty, and in direct obedience to principle: it is a misapprehension of the utilitarian mode of thought to conceive it as implying that people should fix their minds upon so wide a generality as the world, or society at large. The great majority of good actions are intended not for the benefit of the world, but for that of individuals, of which the good of the world is made up; and the thoughts of the most virtuous man need not on these occasions travel beyond the particular persons concerned, except so far as is necessary to assure himself that in benefiting them he is not violating the rights, that is, the legitimate and authorized expectations, of anyone else. The multiplication of happiness is, according to the utilitarian ethics, the object of virtue: the occasions on which any person (except one in a thousand) has it in his power to do this on an extended scale—in other words, to be a public benefactor—are but exceptional; and on these occasions alone is he called on to consider public utility; in every other case, private utility, the interest or happiness of some few persons, is all he has to attend to. Those alone the influence of whose actions extends to society in general need concern themselves habitually about so large an object. In the case of abstinences indeed—of things which people forbear to do from moral considerations, though the consequences in the particular case might be beneficial—it would be unworthy of an intelligent agent not to be consciously aware that the action is of a class which, if practiced generally, would be generally injurious, and that this is the ground of the obligation to abstain from it. The amount of regard for the public interest implied in this recognition is no greater than is demanded by every system of morals, for they all enjoin to abstain from whatever is manifestly pernicious to society. . . .

Again, defenders of utility often find themselves called upon to reply to such objections as this—that there is not time, previous to action, for calculating and weighing the effects of any line of conduct on the general happiness. This is exactly as if anyone were to say that it is impossible to guide our conduct by Christianity because there is not time, on every occasion on which anything has to be done, to read through the Old and New Testaments. The answer to the objection is that there has been ample time, namely, the whole past duration of the human species. During all that time mankind have been learning by experience the tendencies of actions; on which experience all the prudence as well as all the morality of life are dependent. People talk as if the commencement of this course of experience had hitherto been put off, and as if, at the moment when some man feels tempted to meddle with the property or life of another, he had to begin considering for the first time whether murder and theft are injurious to human happiness. Even then I do not think that he would find the question very puzzling; but, at all events, the matter is now done to his hand.

It is truly a whimsical supposition that, if mankind were agreed in considering utility to be the test of morality, they would remain without any agreement as to what *is* useful, and would take no measures for having their notions on the subject taught to the young and enforced by law and opinion. There is no difficulty in proving any ethical standard whatever to work ill if we suppose universal idiocy to be conjoined with it; but on any hypothesis short of that, mankind must by this time have acquired positive beliefs as to the effects of some actions on their happiness; and the beliefs which have thus come down are the rules of morality for the multitude, and for the philosopher until he has succeeded in finding better. That philosophers might easily do this, even now, on many subjects; that the received code of ethics is by no means of divine right; and that mankind have still much to learn as to the effects of actions on the general happiness, I admit or rather earnestly maintain. The corollaries from the principle of utility, like the precepts of every practical art, admit of indefinite improvement, and, in a progressive state of the human mind, their improvement is perpetually going on. But to consider the rules of morality as improvable is one thing; to pass over the intermediate generalization entirely and endeavor to test each individual action directly by the first principle is another.

It is a strange notion that the acknowledgment of a first principle is inconsistent with the admission of secondary ones. To inform a traveler respecting the place of his ultimate destination is not to forbid the use of landmarks and direction-posts on the way. The proposition that happiness is the end and aim of morality does not mean that no road ought to be laid down to that goal, or that persons going thither should not be advised to take one direction rather than another. Men really ought to leave off talking a kind of nonsense on this subject, which they would neither talk nor listen to on other matters of practical concernment. Nobody argues that the art of navigation is not founded on astronomy because sailors cannot wait to calculate the Nautical Almanac. Being rational creatures, they go to sea with it ready calculated; and all rational creatures go out upon the sea of life with their minds made up on the common questions of right and wrong, as well as on many of the far more difficult questions of wise and foolish. And this, as long as foresight is a human quality, it is to be presumed they will continue to do. Whatever we adopt as the fundamental principle of morality, we require subordinate principles to apply it by; the impossibility of doing without them, being common to all systems, can afford no argument against any one in particular; but gravely to argue as if no such seondary principles could be had, and as if mankind had remained till now, and always must remain, without drawing any general conclusions from the experience of human life is as high a pitch, I think, as absurdity has ever reached in philosophical controversy.

The remainder of the stock arguments against utilitarianism mostly consist in laying to its charge the common infirmities of human nature, and the general difficulties which embarrass conscientious persons in shaping their course through life. We are told that a utilitarian will be apt to make his own particular case an exception to moral rules, and, when under temptation, will see a utility in the breach of a rule, greater than he will see in its observance. But is utility the only creed which is able to furnish us with excuses for evildoing and means of cheating our own conscience? They are afforded in abundance by all doctrines which recognize as a fact in morals the existence of conflicting considerations, which all doctrines do that have been believed by sane persons. It is not the fault of any creed, but of the complicated nature of human affairs, that rules of conduct cannot be so framed as to require no exceptions, and that hardly any kind of action can safely be laid down as either always obligatory or always condemnable. There is no ethical creed which does not temper the rigidity of its laws by giving a certain latitude, under the moral responsibility of the agent, for accommodation to peculiarities of circumstances; and under every creed, at the opening thus made, self-deception and dishonest casuistry get in. There exists no moral system under which there do not arise unequivocal cases of conflicting obligation. These are the real difficulties, the knotty points both in the theory of ethics and in the conscientious guidance of personal conduct. They are overcome practically, with greater or with less success, according to the intellect and virtue of the individual; but it can hardly be pretended that anyone will be the less qualified for dealing with them, from possessing an ultimate standard to which conflicting rights and duties can be referred. If utility is the ultimate source of moral obligations, utility may be invoked to decide between them when their demands are incompatible. Though the application of the standard may be difficult, it is better than none at all; while in other systems, the moral laws all claiming independent authority, there is no common umpire entitled to interfere between them; their claims to precedence one over another rest on little better than sophistry, and, unless determined, as they generally are, by the unacknowledged influence of consideration of utility, afford a free scope for the action of personal desires and partialities. We must remember that only in these cases of conflict between secondary principles is it requisite that first principles should be appealed to. There is no case of moral obligation in which some secondary principle is not involved; and if only one, there can seldom be any real doubt which one it is, in the mind of any person by whom the principle itself is recognized.

QUESTIONS FOR REFLECTION

1. What is Mill's principle of utility? What does he mean by "utility"?

2. Mill distinguishes qualities, as well as quantities, of pleasures. Why? How does Mill rank pleasures in terms of quality?

3. People sometimes choose pleasures of lower quality over those of higher quality. How does Mill explain this?

4. Some philosophers have held that Mill's distinction between qualities of pleasures confronts him with a dilemma. Either differences in quality can be measured in terms of differences in quantity, in which case the distinction does not seem very important, or they cannot be, in which case the idea of maximizing the general happiness seems to make little sense. How do you think Mill might respond to this dilemma?

5. What objections against utilitarianism does Mill consider? How does he respond to them?

6. What are the roles of tradition and conscience in Mill's theory?

7. What are secondary principles? What role do they play in Mill's theory? How do we decide which secondary principles to adopt? What happens when these principles conflict?

JOHN RAWLS

from *A Theory of Justice* (1970)

John Rawls is Professor Emeritus of Philosophy at Harvard University. (Source: Reprinted by permission of the publishers from A Theory of Justice *by John Rawls, Cambridge, Mass.: Harvard University Press. Copyright © 1971 by the President and Fellows of Harvard College.)*

CHAPTER I / JUSTICE AS FAIRNESS

1. The Role of Justice

Justice is the first virtue of social institutions, as truth is of systems of thought. A theory however elegant and economical must be rejected or revised if it is untrue; likewise laws and institutions no matter how efficient and well arranged must be reformed or abolished if they are unjust. Each person possesses an inviolability founded on justice that even the welfare of society as a whole cannot override. For this reason justice denies that the loss of freedom for some is made right by a greater good shared by others. It does not allow that the sacrifices imposed on a few are outweighed by the larger sum of advantages enjoyed by many. Therefore in a just society the liberties of equal citizenship are taken as settled; the rights secured by justice are not subject to political bargaining or to the calculus of social interests. The only thing that permits us to acquiesce in an erroneous theory is the lack of a better one; analogously, an injustice is tolerable only when it is necessary to avoid an even greater injustice. Being first virtues of human activities, truth and justice are uncompromising.

These propositions seem to express our intuitive conviction of the primacy of justice. No doubt they are expressed too strongly. In any event I wish to inquire whether these contentions or others similar to them are sound, and if so how they can be accounted for. To this end it is necessary to work out a theory of justice in the light of which these assertions can be interpreted and assessed. I shall begin by considering the role of the principles of justice. Let us assume, to fix ideas, that a society is a more or less self-sufficient association of persons who in their relations to one another recognize certain rules of conduct as binding and who for the most part act in accordance with them. Suppose further that these rules specify a system of cooperation designed to advance the good of those taking part in it. Then, although a society is a cooperative venture for mutual advantage, it is typically marked by a conflict as well as by an identity of interests. There is an identity of interests since social cooperation makes possible a better life for all than any would have if each were to live solely by his own efforts. There is a conflict of interests since persons are not indifferent as to how the greater benefits produced by their collaboration are distributed, for in order to pursue their ends they each prefer a larger to a lesser share. A set of principles is required for choosing among the various social arrangements which determine this division of advantages and for underwriting an agreement on the proper distributive shares. These principles are the principles of social justice: they provide a way of assigning rights and duties in the basic institutions of society and they define the appropriate distribution of the benefits and burdens of social cooperation. . . .

3. The Main Idea of the Theory of Justice

My aim is to present a conception of justice which generalizes and carries to a higher level of abstraction the familiar theory of the social contract as found, say, in Locke, Rousseau, and Kant. In order to do this we are not to think of the original contract as one to enter a particular society or to set up a particular form of government. Rather, the guiding idea is that the principles of justice for the basic structure of society are the object of the original agreement. They are the principles that free and rational persons concerned to further their own interests would accept in an initial position of equality as defining the fundamental terms of their association. These principles are to regulate all further agreements; they specify the kinds of social cooperation that can be entered into and the forms of government that can be established. This way of regarding the principles of justice I shall call justice as fairness.

Thus we are to imagine that those who engage in social cooperation choose together, in one joint act, the principles which are to assign basic rights and duties and to determine the division of social benefits. Men are to decide in advance how they are to regulate their claims against one another and what is to be the foundation charter of their society. Just as each person must decide by rational reflection what constitutes his good, that is, the system of ends which it is rational for him to pursue, so a group of persons must decide once and for all what is to count among them as just and unjust. The choice which rational men would make in this hypothetical situation of equal liberty, assuming for the present that this choice problem has a solution, determines the principles of justice.

In justice as fairness the original position of equality corresponds to the state of nature in the traditional theory of the social contract. This original position is not, of course, thought of as an actual historical state of affairs, much less as a primitive condition of culture. It is understood as a purely hypothetical situation characterized so as to lead to a certain conception of justice. Among the essential features of this situation is that no one knows his place in society, his class position or social status, nor does any one know his fortune in the distribution of natural assets and abilities, his intelligence, strength, and the like. I shall even assume that the parties do not know their conceptions of the good or their special psychological propensities. The principles of justice are chosen behind a veil of ignorance.

This ensures that no one is advantaged or disadvantaged in the choice of principles by the outcome of natural chance or the contingency of social circumstances. Since all are similarly situated and no one is able to design principles to favor his particular condition, the principles of justice are the result of a fair agreement or bargain. For given the circumstances of the original position, the symmetry of everyone's relations to each other, this initial situation is fair between individuals as moral persons, that is, as rational beings with their own ends and capable, I shall assume, of a sense of justice. The original position is, one might say, the appropriate initial status quo, and thus the fundamental agreements reached in it are fair. This explains the propriety of the name "justice as fairness": it conveys the idea that the principles of justice are agreed to in an initial situation that is fair. The name does not mean that the concepts of justice and fairness are the same, any more than the phrase "poetry as metaphor" means that the concepts of poetry and metaphor are the same.

Justice as fairness begins, as I have said, with one of the most general of all choices which persons might make together, namely, with the choice of the first principles of a conception of justice which is to regulate all subsequent criticism and reform of institutions. Then, having chosen a conception of justice, we can suppose that they are to choose a constitution and a legislature to enact laws, and so on, all in accordance with the principles of justice initially agreed upon. Our social situation is just if it is such that by this sequence of hypothetical agreements we would have contracted into the general system of rules which defines it. Moreover, assuming that the original position does determine a set of principles (that is, that a particular conception of justice would be chosen), it will then be true that whenever social institutions satisfy these principles those engaged in them can say to one another that they are cooperating on terms to which they would agree if they were free and equal persons whose relations with respect to one another were fair. They could all view their arrangements as meeting the stipulations which they would acknowledge in an initial situation that embodies widely accepted and reasonable constraints on the choice of principles. The general recognition of this fact would provide the basis for a public acceptance of the corresponding principles of justice.

No society can, of course, be a scheme of cooperation which men enter voluntarily in a literal sense; each person finds himself placed at birth in some particular position in some particular society, and the nature of this position materially affects his life prospects. Yet a society satisfying the principles of justice as fairness comes as close as a society can to being a voluntary scheme, for it meets the principles which free and equal persons would assent to under circumstances that are fair. In this sense its members are autonomous and the obligations they recognize self-imposed.

One feature of justice as fairness is to think of the parties in the initial situation as rational and mutually disinterested. This does not mean that the parties are egoists, that is, individuals with only certain kinds of interests, say in wealth, prestige, and domination. But they are conceived as not taking an interest in one another's interests. They are to presume that even their spiritual aims may be opposed, in the way that the aims of those of different religions may be opposed. Moreover, the concept of rationality must be interpreted as far as possible in the narrow sense, standard in economic theory, of taking the most effective means to given ends. I shall modify this concept to some extent, . . . but one must try to avoid introducing into it any controversial ethical elements. The initial situation must be characterized by stipulations that are widely accepted.

In working out the conception of justice as fairness one main task clearly is to determine which principles of justice would be chosen in the original position. To do this we must describe this situation in some detail and formulate with care the problem of choice which it presents. . . . It may be observed, however, that once the principles of justice are thought of as arising from an original agreement in a situation of equality, it is an open question whether the principle of utility would be acknowledged. Offhand it hardly seems likely that persons who view themselves as equals, entitled to press their claims upon one another, would agree to a principle which may require lesser life prospects for some simply for the sake of a greater sum of advantages enjoyed by others. Since each desires to protect his interests, his capacity to advance his conception of the good, no one has a reason to acquiesce in an enduring loss for himself in order to bring about a greater net balance of satisfaction. In the absence of strong and lasting benevolent impulses, a rational man would not accept a basic structure merely because it maximized the algebraic sum of advantages irrespective of its permanent effects on his own basic rights and interests. Thus it seems that the principle of utility is incompatible with the conception of social cooperation among equals for mutual advantage. It appears to be inconsistent with the idea of reciprocity implicit in the notion of a well-ordered society. Or, at any rate, so I shall argue.

I shall maintain instead that the persons in the initial situation would choose two rather different principles: the first requires equality in the assignment of basic rights and duties, while the second holds that social and economic inequalities, for example inequalities of wealth and authority, are just only if they result in compensating benefits for everyone, and in particular for the least advantaged members of society. These principles rule out justifying institutions on the grounds that the hardships of some are offset by a greater good in the aggregate. It may be expedient but it is not just that some should have less in order that others may prosper. But there is no injustice in the greater benefits earned by a few provided that the situation of persons not so fortunate is thereby improved. The intuitive idea is that since everyone's well-being depends upon a scheme of cooperation without which no one could have a satisfactory life, the division of advantages should be such as to draw forth the willing cooperation of everyone taking part in it, including those less well situated. Yet this can be expected only if reasonable terms are proposed. The two principles mentioned seem to be a fair agreement on the basis of which those better endowed, or more fortunate in their social position, neither of which we can be said to deserve, could expect the willing cooperation of others when some workable scheme is a necessary condition of the welfare of all. Once we decide to look for a conception of justice that nullifies the accidents of natural endowment and the contingencies of social circumstance as counters in quest for political and economic advantage, we are led to these principles. They express the result of leaving aside those aspects of the social world that seem arbitrary from a moral point of view.

The problem of the choice of principles, however, is extremely difficult. I do not expect the answer I shall suggest to be convincing to everyone. It is, therefore, worth noting from the outset that justice as fairness, like other contract views, consists of two parts: (1) an interpretation of the initial situation and of the problem of choice posed there, and (2) a set of principles which, it is argued, would be agreed to. One may accept the first part of the theory (or some variant thereof), but not the other, and conversely. The concept of the initial contractual situation may seem reasonable although the particular principles proposed are rejected. . . .

4. The Original Position and Justification

I have said that the original position is the appropriate initial status quo which ensures that the fundamental agreements reached in it are fair. This fact yields the name "justice as fairness." It is clear, then, that I want to say that one conception of justice is more reasonable than another, or justifiable with respect to it, if rational persons in the initial situation would choose its principles over those of the other for the role of justice. Conceptions of justice are to be ranked by their acceptability to persons so circumstanced. Understood in this way the question of justification is settled by working out a problem of deliberation: we have to ascertain which principles it would be rational to adopt given the contractual situation. This connects the theory of justice with the theory of rational choice. . . .

It seems reasonable to suppose that the parties in the original position are equal. That is, all have the same rights in the procedure for choosing principles; each can make proposals, submit reasons for their acceptance, and so on. Obviously the purpose of these conditions is to represent equality between human beings as moral persons, as creatures having a conception of their good and capable of a sense of justice. The basis of equality is taken to be similarity in these two respects. Systems of ends are not ranked in value; and each man is presumed to have the requisite ability to understand and to act upon whatever principles are adopted. Together with the veil of ignorance, these conditions define the principles of justice as those which rational persons concerned to advance their interests would consent to as equals when none are known to be advantaged or disadvantaged by social and natural contingencies.

There is, however, another side to justifying a particular description of the original position. This is to see if the principles which would be chosen match our considered convictions of justice or extend them in an acceptable way. We can note whether applying these principles would lead us to make the same judgments about the basic structure of society which we now make intuitively and in which we have the greatest confidence; or whether, in cases where our present judgments are in doubt and given with hesitation, these principles offer a resolution which we can affirm on reflection. There are questions which we feel sure must be answered in a certain way. For example, we are confident that religious intolerance and racial discrimination are unjust. We think that we have examined these things with care and have reached what we believe is an impartial judgment not likely to be distorted by an excessive attention to our own interests. These convictions are provisional fixed points which we presume any conception of justice must fit. But we have much less assurance as to what is the correct distribution of wealth and authority. Here we may be looking for a way to remove our doubts. We can check an interpretation of the initial situation, then, by the capacity of its principles to accommodate our firmest convictions and to provide guidance where guidance is needed.

In searching for the most favored description of this situation we work from both ends. We begin by describing it so that it represents generally shared and preferably weak conditions. We then see if these conditions are strong enough to yield a significant set of principles. If not, we look for further premises equally reasonable. But if so, and these principles match our considered convictions of justice, then so far well and good. But presumably there will be discrepancies. In this case we have a choice. We can either modify the account of the initial situation or we can revise our existing judgments, for even the judgments we take provisionally as fixed points are liable to revision. By going back and forth, sometimes altering the conditions of the contractual circumstances, at others withdrawing our judgments and conforming them to principle, I assume that eventually we shall find a description of the initial situation that both expresses reasonable conditions and yields principles which match our considered judgments duly pruned and adjusted. This state of affairs I refer to as reflective equilibrium. It is an equilibrium because at last our principles and judgments coincide; and it is reflective since we know to what principles our judgments conform and the premises of their derivation. At the moment everything is in order. But this equilibrium is not necessarily stable. It is liable to be upset by further examination of the conditions which should be imposed on the contractual situation and by particular cases which may lead us to revise our judgments. Yet for the time being we have done what we can to render coherent and to justify our convictions of social justice. We have reached a conception of the original position. . . .

QUESTIONS FOR REFLECTION

1. What is the original position? What is the role of the veil of ignorance?

2. What is reflective equilibrium? What is its significance for moral theory?

3. Why does Rawls believe that rational agents in the original position would reject the principle of utility?

SIMONE DE BEAUVOIR

from *The Ethics of Ambiguity* (1947)

French philosopher Simone de Beauvoir (1908–1986), contemporary of Bertrand Russell, John Rawls, and Jean-Paul Sartre, became one of the best-known women of the twentieth century. Her novels, her essays, and especially her book The Second Sex *(1949) earned her a reputation as an existentialist and a feminist. She wrote two philosophical works:* Pyrrhus and Cineas *(1944), on freedom, and* The Ethics of Ambiguity *(1947), which outlines an existentialist ethics.*

Sartre, her companion and intellectual collaborator, defined existentialism as the thesis that "existence precedes essence"; human beings exist but have no determinate essence. Life, that is, has no fixed meaning; humans have no fixed purpose or function. Thus, de Beauvoir argues, life is ambiguous. It can be interpreted in various ways. We assign our lives meaning by interpreting them as we do and making the choices that we do.

This might seem to grant us complete freedom from ethical constraints. Not so, argues de Beauvoir. The contents and meanings of our acts must be in harmony; our acts must be unified so that they can be assigned a coherent meaning. This is more difficult than it sounds, for we frequently encounter moral dilemmas. Competing moral considerations pull us in opposite directions. There is no rule that we can specify in advance for resolving these dilemmas. We must work out their resolutions in experience, constantly submitting our actions and our attitudes to moral scrutiny and valuing individuals over abstract rules and systems. De Beauvoir criticizes the "recourse to the serious," a person's identifying him- or herself with a fixed moral attitude and code of conduct. The method of ethics requires us to retain an attitude of questioning, never settling our ethical outlook once and for all. (Source: Reprinted by permission of the publishers from The Ethics of Ambiguity *by Simone de Beauvoir, New York: Carol Publishing Group. Copyright © 1948, 1976 by the Philosophical Library.)*

Ambiguity

The notion of ambiguity must not be confused with that of absurdity. To declare that existence is absurd is to deny that it can ever be given a meaning; to say that it is ambiguous is to assert that its meaning is never fixed, that it must be constantly won. Absurdity challenges every ethics; but also the finished rationalization of the real would leave no room for ethics; it is because man's condition is ambiguous that he seeks, through failure and outrageousness, to save his existence. Thus, to say that action has to be lived in its truth, that is, in the consciousness of the antinomies which it involves, does not mean that one has to renounce it. . . .

It is interesting to pursue this comparison; not that we are likening action to a work of art or a scientific theory, but because in any case human transcendence must cope with the same problem: it has to found itself, though it is prohibited from ever fulfilling itself. Now, we know that neither science nor art ever leaves it up to the future to justify its present existence. In no age does art consider itself as something which is paving the way for Art: so-called archaic art prepares for classicism only in the eyes of archaeologists; the sculptor who fashioned the Korai of Athens rightfully thought that he was producing a finished work of art; in no age has science considered itself as partial and lacunary; without believing itself to be definitive, it has however, always wanted to be a total expression of the world, and it is in its totality that in each age it again raises the question of its own validity. There we have an example of how man must, in any event, assume his finiteness: not by treating his existence as transitory or relative but by reflecting the infinite within it, that is, by treating it as absolute. There is an art only because at every moment art has willed itself absolutely; likewise there is a liberation of man only if, in aiming at itself, freedom is achieved absolutely in the very fact of aiming at itself. This requires that each action be considered as a finished form whose different moments, instead of fleeing toward the future in order to find there their justification, reflect and confirm one another so well that there is no longer a sharp separation between present and future, between means and ends.

But if these moments constitute a unity, there must be no contradiction among them. Since the liberation aimed at is not a *thing* situated in an unfamiliar time, but a movement which realizes itself by tending to conquer, it cannot attain itself if it denies itself at the start; action cannot seek to fulfill itself by means which would destroy its very meaning. So much so that in certain situations there will be no other issue for man than rejection. In what is called political realism there is no room for rejection because the present is considered as transitory; there is rejection only if man lays claim in the present to his existence as an absolute value; then he must absolutely reject what would deny this value. Today, more or less consciously in the name of such an ethics, we condemn a magistrate who handed over a communist to save ten hostages and along with him all the Vichyites who were trying "to make the best of things:" it was not a matter of rationalizing the present such as it was imposed by the German occupation, but of rejecting it unconditionally. The resistance did not aspire to a positive effectiveness; it was a negation, a revolt, a martyrdom; and in this negative movement freedom was positively and absolutely confirmed.

. . . We have seen that this recourse to the serious is a lie; it entails the sacrifice of man to the Thing, of freedom to the Cause. In order for the return to the

positive to be genuine it must involve negativity, it must not conceal the antinomies between means and end, present and future; they must be lived in a permanent tension; one must retreat from neither the outrage of violence nor deny it, or, which amounts to the same thing, assume it lightly. Kierkegaard has said that what distinguishes the pharisee from the genuinely moral man is that the former considers his anguish as a sure sign of his virtue; from the fact that he asks himself, "Am I Abraham?" he concludes, "I am Abraham;" but morality resides in the painfulness of an indefinite questioning. The problem which we are posing is not the same as that of Kierkegaard; the important thing to us is to know whether, in given conditions, Isaac must be killed or not. But we also think that what distinguishes the tyrant from the man of good will is that the first rests in the certainty of his aims, whereas the second keeps asking himself, "Am I really working for the liberation of men? Isn't this end contested by the sacrifices through which I aim at it?" In setting up its ends, freedom must put them in parentheses, confront them at each moment with that absolute end which it itself constitutes, and contest, in its own name, the means it uses to win itself.

It will be said that these considerations remain quite abstract. What must be done, practically? Which action is good? Which is bad? To ask such a question is also to fall into a naïve abstraction. We don't ask the physicist, "Which hypotheses are true?" Nor the artist, "By what procedures does one produce a work whose beauty is guaranteed?" Ethics does not furnish recipes any more than do science and art. One can merely propose methods. Thus, in science the fundamental problem is to make the idea adequate to its content and the law adequate to the facts; the logician finds that in the case where the pressure of the given fact bursts the concept which serves to comprehend it, one is obliged to invent another concept; but he can not define *a priori* the moment of invention, still less foresee it. Analogously, one may say that in the case where the content of the action falsifies its meaning, one must modify not the meaning, which is here willed absolutely, but the content itself; however, it is impossible to determine this relationship between meaning and content abstractly and universally: there must be a trial and decision in each case. But likewise just as the physicist finds it profitable to reflect on the conditions of scientific invention and the artist on those of artistic creation without expecting any ready-made solutions to come from these reflections, it is useful for the man of action to find out under what conditions his undertakings are valid. We are going to see that on this basis new perspectives are disclosed.

In the first place, it seems to us that the individual as such is one of the ends at which our action must aim. Here we are at one with the point of view of Christian charity, the Epicurean cult of friendship, and Kantian moralism which treats each man as an end. He interests us not merely as a member of a class, a nation, or a collectivity, but as an individual man. This distinguishes us from the systematic politician who cares only about collective destinies; and probably a tramp enjoying his bottle of wine, or a child playing with a balloon, or a Neapolitan *lazzarone* loafing in the sun in no way helps in the liberation of man; that is why the abstract will of the revolutionary scorns the concrete benevolence which occupies itself in satisfying desires which have no morrow. However, it must not be forgotten that there is a concrete bond between freedom and existence; to will man free is to will there to *be* being, it is to will the disclosure of being in the joy of existence; in order for the idea of liberation to have a concrete meaning, the joy of existence must be asserted in each one, at every instant; the movement toward freedom assumes its real, flesh-and-blood-figure in the world by thickening into pleasure, into happiness. If the satisfaction of an old man drinking a glass of wine counts for nothing, then production and wealth are only hollow myths; they have meaning only if they are capable of being retrieved in individual and living joy. The saving of time and the conquest of leisure have no meaning if we are not moved by the laugh of a child at play. If we do not love life on our own account and through others, it is futile to seek to justify it in any way.

However, politics is right in rejecting benevolence to the extent that the latter thoughtlessly sacrifices the future to the present. The ambiguity of freedom, which very often is occupied only in fleeing from itself, introduces a difficult equivocation into relationships with each individual taken one by one. Just what is meant by the expression "to love others"? What is meant by taking them as ends? In any event, it is evident that we are not going to decide to fulfill the will of every man. There are cases where a man

positively wants evil, that is, the enslavement of other men, and he must then be fought. It also happens that, without harming anyone, he flees from his own freedom, seeking passionately and alone to attain the being which constantly eludes him. If he asks for our help, are we to give it to him? We blame a man who helps a drug addict intoxicate himself or a desperate man commit suicide, for we think that rash behavior of this sort is an attempt of the individual against his own freedom; he must be made aware of his error and put in the presence of the real demands of his freedom. Well and good. But what if he persists? Must we then use violence? There again the serious man busies himself dodging the problem; the values of life, of health, and of moral conformism being set up, one does not hesitate to impose them on others. But we know that this pharisaism can cause the worst disasters: lacking drugs, the addict may kill himself. It is no more necessary to serve an abstract ethics obstinately than to yield without due consideration to impulses of pity or generosity; violence is justified only if it opens concrete possibilities to the freedom which I am trying to save; by practising it I am willy-nilly assuming an engagement in relation to others and to myself; a man whom I snatch from the death which he had chosen has the right to come and ask me for means and reasons for living; the tyranny practised against an invalid can be justified only by his getting better; whatever the purity of the intention which animates me, any dictatorship is a fault for which I have to get myself pardoned. Besides, I am in no position to make decisions of this sort indiscriminately; the example of the unknown person who throws himself in to the Seine and whom I hesitate whether or not to fish out is quite abstract; in the absence of a concrete bond with this desperate person my choice will never be anything but a contingent facticity. If I find myself in a position to do violence to a child, or to a melancholic, sick, or distraught person the reason is that I also find myself charged with his upbringing, his happiness, and his health: I am a parent, a teacher, a nurse, a doctor, or a friend. . . . So, by a tacit agreement, by the very fact that I am solicited, the strictness of my decision is accepted or even desired; the more seriously I accept my responsibilities, the more justified it is. That is why love authorizes severities which are not granted to indifference. What makes the problem so complex is that, on the one hand, one must not make himself an accomplice of that flight from freedom that is found in heedlessness, caprice, mania, and passion, and that, on the other hand, it is the abortive movement of man toward being which is his very existence, it is through the failure which he has assumed that he asserts himself as a freedom. To want to prohibit a man from error is to forbid him to fulfill his own existence, it is to deprive him of life. At the beginning of Claudel's *The Satin Shoe,* the husband of Dona Prouheze, the Judge, the Just, as the author regards him, explains that every plant needs a gardener in order to grow and that he is the one whom heaven has destined for his young wife; beside the fact that we are shocked by the arrogance of such a thought (for how does he know that he is this enlightened gardener? Isn't he merely a jealous husband?) this likening of a soul to a plant is not acceptable; for, as Kant would say, the value of an act lies not in its *conformity* to an external model, but in its internal truth. We object to the inquisitors who want to create faith and virtue from without; we object to all forms of fascism which seek to fashion the happiness of man from without; and also the paternalism which thinks that it has done something for man by prohibiting him from certain possibilities of temptation, whereas what is necessary is to give him reasons for resisting it.

Thus, violence is not immediately justified when it opposes willful acts which one considers perverted; it becomes inadmissible if it uses the pretext of ignorance to deny a freedom which, as we have seen, can be practised within ignorance itself. Let the "enlightened elites" strive to change the situation of the child, the illiterate, the primitive crushed beneath his superstitions; that is one of their most urgent tasks; but in this very effort they must respect a freedom which, like theirs, is absolute. They are always opposed, for example, to the extension of universal suffrage by adducing the incompetence of the masses, of women, of the natives in the colonies; but this forgetting that man always has to decide by himself in the darkness, that he must want beyond what he knows. If infinite knowledge were necessary (even supposing that it were conceivable), then the colonial administrator himself would not have the right to freedom; he is much further from perfect knowledge than the most backward savage is from him. . . .

Thus, we can set up point number one: the good

of an individual or a group of individuals requires that it be taken as an absolute end of our action; but we are not authorized to decide upon this end *a priori.* The fact is that no behavior is ever authorized to begin with, and one of the concrete consequences of existentialist ethics is the rejection of all the previous justifications which might be drawn from the civilization, the age, and the culture; it is the rejection of every principle of authority. To put it positively, the precept will be to treat the other (to the extent that he is the only one concerned, which is the moment that we are considering at present) as a freedom so that his end may be freedom; in using this conducting-wire one will have to incur the risk, in each case, of inventing an original solution. Out of disappointment in love a young girl takes an overdose of phenobarbital; in the morning friends find her dying, they call a doctor, she is saved; later on she becomes a happy mother of a family; her friends were right in considering her suicide as a hasty and heedless act and in putting her into a position to reject it or return to it freely. But in asylums one sees melancholic patients who have tried to commit suicide twenty times, who devote their freedom to seeking the means of escaping their jailers and of putting an end to their intolerable anguish; the doctor who gives them a friendly pat on the shoulder is their tyrant and their torturer. A friend who is intoxicated by alcohol or drugs asks me for money so that he can go and buy the poison that is necessary to him; I urge him to get cured, I take him to a doctor, I try to help him live; insofar as there is a chance of my being successful, I am acting correctly in refusing him the sum he asks for. But if circumstances prohibit me from doing anything to change the situation in which he is struggling, all I can do is give in; a deprivation of a few hours will do nothing but exasperate his torments uselessly; and he may have recourse to extreme means to get what I do not give him. That is also the problem touched on by Ibsen in *The Wild Duck.* An individual lives in a situation of falsehood; the falsehood is violence, tyranny: shall I tell the truth in order to free the victim? It would first be necessary to create a situation of such a kind that the truth might be bearable and that, though losing his illusions, the deluded individual might again find about him reasons for hoping. What makes the problem more complex is that the freedom of one man almost always concerns that of other individuals. Here is a married couple who persist in living in a hovel; if one does not succeed in giving them the desire to live in a more healthful dwelling, they must be allowed to follow their preferences; but the situation changes if they have children; the freedom of the parents would be the ruin of their sons, and as freedom and the future are on the side of the latter, these are the ones who must first be taken into account. The Other is multiple, and on the basis of this new questions arise.

. . . Contrary to the formal strictness of Kantianism for whom the more abstract the act is the more virtuous it is, generosity seems to us to be better grounded and therefore more valid the less distinction there is between the other and ourself and the more we fulfill ourself in taking the other as an end. That is what happens if I am engaged in relation to others. The Stoics impugned the ties of family, friendship, and nationality so that they recognized only the universal form of man. But man is man only through situations whose particularity is precisely a universal fact. There are men who expect help from certain men and not from others, and these expectations define privileged lines of action. It is fitting that the negro fight for the negro, the Jew for the Jew, the proletarian for the proletarian, and the Spaniard in Spain. But the assertion of these particular solidarities must not contradict the will for universal solidarity and each finite undertaking must also be open on the totality of men.

But it is then that we find in concrete form the conflicts which we have described abstractly; for the cause of freedom can triumph only through particular sacrifices. And certainly there are hierarchies among the goods desired by men: one will not hesitate to sacrifice the comfort, luxury, and leisure of certain men to assure the liberation of certain others;

but when it is a question of choosing among freedoms, how shall we decide?

Let us repeat, one can only indicate a method here. The first point is always to consider what genuine human interest fills the abstract form which one proposes as the action's end. Politics always puts forward Ideas: Nation, Empire, Union, Economy, etc. But none of these forms has value in itself; it has it only insofar as it involves concrete individuals. If a nation can assert itself proudly only to the detriment of its members, if a union can be created only to the detriment of those it is trying to unite, the nation or the union must be rejected. We repudiate all idealisms, mysticisms, etcetera which prefer a Form to man himself. But the matter becomes really agonizing when it is a question of a Cause which genuinely serves man. . . .

It is apparent that the method we are proposing, analogous in this respect to scientific or aesthetic methods, consists, in each case, of confronting the values realized with the values aimed at, and the meaning of the act with its content. . . . But an action which wants to serve man ought to be careful not to forget him on the way; if it chooses to fulfill itself blindly, it will lose its meaning or will take on an unforeseen meaning; for the goal is not fixed once and for all; it is defined all along the road which leads to it. Vigilance alone can keep alive the validity of the goals and the genuine assertion of freedom. Moreover, ambiguity cannot fail to appear on the scene; it is felt by the victim, and his revolt or his complaints also make it exist for his tyrant; the latter will then be tempted to put everything into question, to renounce, thus denying both himself and his ends; or, if he persists, he will continue to blind himself only by multiplying crimes and by perverting his original design more and more. . . .

QUESTIONS FOR REFLECTION

1. What does de Beauvoir mean in saying that existence is ambiguous? In what sense would Aristotle and Mill disagree with her claim?

2. In what sense must actions constitute a unity?

3. What is the "recourse to the serious"? Why does de Beauvoir object to it?

4. De Beauvoir maintains that "morality resides in the painfulness of an indefinite questioning." Explain.

5. If "ethics does not furnish recipes," what can it do?

6. In what sense must we take the individual as our aim? How does this constrain our actions?

7. Compare de Beauvoir's ethics to Kant's. Where do they agree? How does she criticize Kant?

8. What method is de Beauvoir recommending? How does it help us to understand moral dilemmas?

SEXUAL BEHAVIOR

Teenagers and young adults often think of "morals" and "sexual morals" as equivalent expressions. Throughout life, our sexual identities and relationships remain central to our happiness and our conceptions of ourselves. The social roles implicit in being a husband, wife, lover, father, or mother remain among the most important we adopt. Our actions in the context of sexual relationships can thus affect other people more profoundly than almost anything else we do. We can make someone happy or break someone's heart. We can even create someone. Sexual morality, for all these reasons, has special importance.

Bertrand Russell, one of the twentieth century's most renowned philosophers, argues for a liberalization of sexual morality. Russell finds traditional restrictions on sexual behavior to be part superstition and part response to social and biological conditions that no longer hold. He adopts the perspective of a rule-utilitarian—unsurprisingly, perhaps, since his godfather was John Stuart Mill!—asking "what moral rules are most likely to promote human happiness." He advocates the acceptance of premarital and even extramarital sexual relationships, stressing that the pursuit of pleasure is good, though it must of course be constrained by other moral concerns.

Thomas Mappes sees Kant's categorical imperative as providing the key, if not to all of morality, at least to sexual morality. Kant urged that we treat others as "ends in themselves," not as "means only." In other words, the categorical imperative insists that we not use people but, instead, treat them with the respect that we ourselves deserve as moral agents. Mappes contends, accordingly, that the cardinal principle of sexual behavior is "Don't use people." He discusses applications of the principle, pointing out that, while his theory is more permissive than traditional morality, it prohibits a variety of behaviors, from deception and harassment to rape.

Roger Scruton offers a justification of traditional sexual morality. He critiques utilitarian and Kantian points of view, arguing that only an Aristotelian approach to an ethics of character can provide an adequate account of human flourishing. The chief sexual virtue, Scruton believes, is chastity, which involves not abstaining from sexual behavior but restricting it to relationships of erotic love. The capacity to love is a virtue crucial to human flourishing, Scruton maintains, and must be cultivated carefully. Chastity is one aspect of that cultivation, for it is necessary for sexual integrity, that is, the union of one's sexuality with the rest of one's personality.

Sidney Callahan is a feminist. Sexual equality, she insists, does not require abandoning sexual intercourse. Nor does it require adopting an aggressive, "male," sexual attitude. Callahan examines traditionally feminine sex roles and identifies a number of virtues that protect women and the social structure at large. She rejects feminist demands for reproductive freedom as not, ultimately, in the best interests of women, men, or children.

BERTRAND RUSSELL

Our Sexual Ethics

Bertrand Russell (1872–1970), winner of the Nobel Prize for Literature in 1950, is arguably the greatest philosopher of the twentieth century. A Fellow of the Royal Society, Honorary Fellow of the British Academy, and winner of the Order of Merit, he taught at Trinity College, Cambridge; the University of Chicago; and the University of California at Los Angeles. (Source: The American Mercury 38 [May 1936].)

I

Sex, more than any other element in human life, is still viewed by many, perhaps by most, in an irrational way. Homicide, pestilence, insanity, gold and precious stones—all the things, in fact, that are the objects of passionate hopes or fears—have been seen, in the past, through a mist of magic or mythology; but the sun of reason has now dispelled the mist, except here and there. The densest cloud that remains is in the territory of sex, as is perhaps natural since sex is concerned in the most passionate part of most people's lives.

It is becoming apparent, however, that conditions in the modern world are working to effect a change in the public attitude toward sex. As to what change, or changes, this will bring about, no one can speak with any certainty; but it is possible to note some of the forces now at work, and to discuss what their results are likely to be upon the structure of society.

Insofar as human nature is concerned, it cannot be said to be *impossible* to produce a society in which there is very little sexual intercourse outside of marriage. The conditions necessary for this result, however, are such as are made almost unattainable by modern life. Let us, then, consider what they are.

The greatest influence toward effecting monogamy is immobility in a region containing few inhabitants. If a man hardly ever has occasion to leave home and seldom sees any woman but his wife, it is easy for him to be faithful; but if he travels without her or lives in a crowded urban community, the problem is proportionately more difficult. The next greatest assistance to monogamy is superstition: those who genuinely believe that "sin" leads to eternal punishment might be expected to avoid it, and to some extent they do so, although not to so great an extent as might be expected. The third support of virtue is public opinion. Where, as in agricultural societies, all that a man does is known to his neighbors, he has powerful motives for avoiding whatever convention condemns. But all these causes of correct behavior are much less potent than they used to be. Fewer people live in isolation; the belief in hell-fire is dying out; and in large towns no one knows what his neighbor does. It is, therefore, not surprising that both men and women are less monogamous than they were before the rise of modern industrialism.

Of course, it may be said that, while an increasing number of people fail to observe the moral law, that is no reason for altering our standards. Those who sin, we are sometimes told, should know and recognize that they sin, and an ethical code is none the worse for being difficult to live up to. But I should

57

reply that the question whether a code is good or bad is the same as the question whether or not it promotes human happiness. Many adults, in their hearts, still believe all that they were taught in childhood and feel wicked when their lives do not conform to the maxims of the Sunday school. The harm done is not merely to introduce a division between the conscious reasonable personality and the unconscious infantile personality; the harm lies also in the fact that the valid parts of conventional morality become discredited along with the invalid parts, and it comes to be thought that, if adultery is excusable, so are laziness, dishonesty, and unkindness. This danger is inseparable from a system which teaches the young, *en bloc,* a number of beliefs that they are almost sure to discard when they become mature. In the process of social and economic revolt, they are likely to throw over the good along with the bad.

The difficulty of arriving at a workable sexual ethic arises from the conflict between the impulse to jealousy and the impulse to polygamy. There is no doubt that jealousy, while in part instinctive, is to a very large degree conventional. In societies in which a man is considered a fit object for ridicule if his wife is unfaithful, he will be jealous where she is concerned, even if he no longer has any affection for her. Thus jealousy is intimately connected with the sense of property and is much less where this sense is absent. If faithfulness is no part of what is conventionally expected, jealousy is much diminished. But although there is more possibility of lessening jealousy than many people suppose, there are very definite limits so long as fathers have rights and duties. So long as this is the case, it is inevitable that men should desire some assurance that they are the fathers of their wives' children. If women are to have sexual freedom, fathers must fade out, and wives must no longer expect to be supported by their husbands. This may come about in time, but it will be a profound social change, and its effects, for good or ill, are incalculable.

In the meantime, if marriage and paternity are to survive as social institutions, some compromise is necessary between complete promiscuity and lifelong monogamy. To decide on the best compromise at any given moment is not easy; and the decision should vary from time to time, according to the habits of the population and the reliability of birth-control methods. Some things, however, can be said with some definiteness.

In the first place, it is undesirable, both physiologically and educationally, that women should have children before the age of twenty. Our ethics should, therefore be such as to make this a rare occurrence.

In the second place, it is unlikely that a person without previous sexual experience, whether man or woman, will be able to distinguish between mere physical attraction and the sort of congeniality that is necessary in order to make marriage a success. Moreover, economic causes compel men, as a rule, to postpone marriage, and it is neither likely that they will remain chaste in the years from twenty to thirty nor desirable psychologically that they should do so; but it is much better that, if they have temporary relations, they should not be with professionals but with girls of their own class, whose motive is affection rather than money. For both these reasons, young unmarried people should have considerable freedom, as long as children are avoided.

In the third place, divorce should be possible without blame to either party and should not be regarded as in any way disgraceful. A childless marriage should be terminable at the wish of one of the partners, and any marriage should be terminable by mutual consent—a year's notice being necessary in either case. Divorce should, of course, be possible on a number of other grounds—insanity, desertion, cruelty, and so on; but mutual consent should be the most usual ground.

In the fourth place, everything possible should be done to free sexual relations from the economic taint. At present, wives, just as much as prostitutes, live by the sale of their sexual charms; and even in temporary free relations the man is usually expected to bear all the joint expenses. The result is that there is a sordid entanglement of money with sex, and that women's motives not infrequently have a mercenary element. Sex, even when blessed by the church, ought not to be a profession. It is right that a woman should be paid for housekeeping or cooking or the care of children, but not merely for having sexual relations with a man. Nor should a woman who has once loved and been loved by a man be able to live ever after on alimony when his love and hers have ceased. A woman, like a man, should work for her living, and an idle wife is no more intrinsically worthy of respect than a gigolo.

II

Two very primitive impulses have contributed, though in very different degrees, to the rise of the currently accepted code of sexual behavior. One of these is modesty and the other, as mentioned above, is jealousy. Modesty, in some form and to some degree, is almost universal in the human race and constitutes a taboo which must only be broken in accordance with certain forms and ceremonies, or, at the least, in conformity with some recognized etiquette. Not everything may be seen, and not all facts may be mentioned. This is not, as some moderns suppose, an invention of the Victorian age; on the contrary, anthropologists have found the most elaborate forms of prudery among primitive savages. The conception of the obscene has its roots deep in human nature. We may go against it from a love of rebellion, or from loyalty to the scientific spirit, or from a wish to feel wicked, such as existed in Byron; but we do not thereby eradicate it from among our natural impulses. No doubt convention determines, in a given community, exactly what is to be considered indecent, but the universal existence of *some* convention of the kind is conclusive evidence of a source which is not merely conventional. In almost every human society, pornography and exhibitionism are reckoned as offenses, except when, as not infrequently occurs, they form part of religious ceremonies.

Asceticism—which may or may not have a psychological connection with modesty—is an impulse which seems to arise only where a certain level of civilization has been reached, but may then become powerful. It is not to be found in the earlier books of the Old Testament, but it appears in the later books, in the Apocrypha and in the New Testament. Similarly, among the Greeks there is little of it in early times, but more and more as time goes on. In India, it arose at a very early date and acquired great intensity. I will not attempt to give a psychological analysis of its origin, but I cannot doubt that it is a spontaneous sentiment, existing, to some slight extent, in almost all civilized human beings. Its faintest form is reluctance to imagine a revered individual—especially a person possessed of religious sanctity—engaged in lovemaking, which is felt to be scarcely compatible with the highest degree of dignity. The wish to free the spirit from bondage to the flesh has inspired many of the great religions of the world and is still powerful even among modern intellectuals.

But jealousy, I believe, has been the most potent single factor in the genesis of sexual morality. Jealousy instinctively rouses anger; and anger, rationalized, becomes moral disapproval. The purely instinctive motive must have been reinforced, at an early stage in the development of civilization, by the desire of males to be certain of paternity. Without security in this respect the patriarchal family would have been impossible, and fatherhood, with all its economic implications, could not have become the basis of social institutions. It was, accordingly, wicked to have relations with another man's wife but not even mildly reprehensible to have relations with an unmarried woman. There were excellent practical reasons for condemning the adulterer, since he caused confusion and very likely bloodshed. The siege of Troy was an extreme example of the upheavals due to disrespect for the rights of husbands, but something of the sort, though on a smaller scale, was to be expected even when the parties concerned were less exalted. There were, of course, in those days, no corresponding rights of wives; a husband had no duty to his wife, though he had the duty of respecting the property of other husbands. The old system of the patriarchal family, with an ethic based on the feelings that we have been considering, was, in a sense, successful: men, who dominated, had considerable liberty, and women, who suffered, were in such complete subjection that their unhappiness seemed not important. It is the claim of women to equality with men that has done most to make a new system necessary in the world today. Equality can be secured in two ways: either by exacting from men the same strict monogamy as was, in the past, exacted from women; or by allowing women, equally with men, a certain relaxation of the traditional code. The first of these ways was preferred by most of the pioneers of women's rights and is still preferred by the churches; but the second has many more adherents in practice, although most of them are in doubt as to the theoretical justifiability of their own behavior. And those who recognize that *some* new ethic is required find it difficult to know just what its precepts should be.

There is another source of novelty, and that is the effect of the scientific outlook in weakening the taboo on sexual knowledge. It has come to be understood that various evils—for example, venereal disease—cannot be effectivly combated unless they are spoken of much more openly than was formerly thought permissible; and it has also been found that reticence and ignorance are apt to have injurious effects upon the psychology of the individual. Both sociology and psychoanalysis have led serious students to deprecate the policy of silence in regard to sexual matters, and many practical educators, from experience with children, have adopted the same position. Those who have a scientific outlook on human behavior, moreover, find it impossible to label any action as "sin"; they realize that what we do has its origin in our heredity, our education, and our environment, and that is by control of these causes, rather than by denunciation, that conduct injurious to society is to be prevented.

In seeking a new ethic of sexual behavior, therefore, we must not ourselves be dominated by the ancient irrational passions which gave rise to the old ethic, though we should recognize that they may, by accident, have led to some sound maxims, and that, since they still exist, though perhaps in a weakened form, they are still among the data of our problem. What we have to do positively is to ask ourselves what moral rules are most likely to promote human happiness, remembering always that whatever the rules may be, they are not likely to be universally observed. That is to say, we have to consider the effect which the rules will in fact have, not that which they would have if they were completely effective.

III

Let us look at the next question of knowledge on sexual subjects, which arises at the earliest age and is the least difficult and doubtful of the various problems with which we are concerned. There is no sound reason, of any sort or kind, for concealing facts when talking to children. Their questions should be answered and their curiosity satisfied in exactly the same way in regard to sex as in regard to the habits of fishes, or any other subject that interests them. There should be no sentiment, because children cannot feel as adults do and see no occasion for high-flown talk. It is a mistake to begin with the loves of the bees and the flowers; there is no point in leading up to the facts of life by devious routes. The child who is told what he wants to know and allowed to see his parents naked will have no pruriency and no obsession of a sexual kind. Boys who are brought up in official ignorance think and talk much more about sex than boys who have always heard this topic treated on a level with any other. Official ignorance and actual knowledge teach them to be deceitful and hypocritical with their elders. On the other hand, real ignorance, when it is achieved, is likely to be a source of shock and anxiety, and to make adaptation to real life difficult. All ignorance is regrettable, but ignorance on so important a matter as sex is a serious danger.

When I say that children should be told about sex, I do not mean that they should be told only the bare physiological facts; they should be told whatever they wish to know. There should be no attempt to represent adults as more virtuous than they are, or sex as occurring only in marriage. There is no excuse for deceiving children. And when, as must happen in conventional families, they find that their parents have lied, they lose confidence in them and feel justified in lying to them. There are facts which I should not obtrude upon a child, but I would tell him anything sooner than say what is not true. Virtue which is based upon a false view of the facts is not real virtue. Speaking not only from theory but from practical experience, I am convinced that complete openness on sexual subjects is the best way to prevent children from thinking about them excessively, nastily, or unwholesomely, and also the almost indispensable preliminary to an enlightened sexual morality.

Where adult sexual behavior is concerned, it is by no means easy to arrive at a rational compromise between the antagonistic considerations that have each their own validity. The fundamental difficulty is, of course, the conflict between the impulse to jealousy and the impulse to sexual variety. Neither impulse, it is true, is universal: there are those (though they are few) who are never jealous, and there are those (among men as well as among women) whose affections never wander from the chosen partner. If either of these types could be made universal, it would be easy to devise a satisfactory code. It must be admitted, however, that either type can be made more common by conventions designed to that end.

Much ground remains to be covered by a complete sexual ethic, but I do not think we can say anything very positive until we have more experience, both of the effects of various systems and of the changes resulting from a rational education in matters of sex. It is clear that marriage, as an institution, should only interest the state because of children and should be viewed as a purely private matter so long as it is childless. It is clear, also, that, even where there are children, the state is only interested through the duties of fathers, which are chiefly financial. Where divorce is easy, as in Scandinavia, the children usually go with the mother, so that the pa-triarchal family tends to disappear. If, as is increasingly happening where wage earners are concerned, the state takes over the duties that have hitherto fallen upon fathers, marriage will cease to have any *raison d'être* and will probably be no longer customary except among the rich and the religious.

In the meantime, it would be well if men and women could remember, in sexual relations, in marriage, and in divorce, to practice the ordinary virtues of tolerance, kindness, truthfulness, and justice. Those who, by conventional standards, are sexually virtuous too often consider themselves thereby absolved from behaving like decent human beings. Most moralists have been so obsessed by sex that they have laid much too little emphasis on other more socially useful kinds of ethically commendable conduct.

QUESTIONS FOR REFLECTION

1. Why, according to Russell, is premarital sex almost inevitable in modern societies? Why is the same true for adultery, in his view?

2. What does Russell mean by saying, "an idle wife is no more intrinsically worthy of respect than a gigolo"? Do you agree?

3. Why does Russell think jealousy is bound to decline? What effect will this have on sexual morality? Is the effect beneficial, according to Russell?

4. Upholders of traditional morality often attacked Russell as an immoralist preaching free love. Is he?

5. In what ways is Russell's argument based on utilitarianism?

6. How might a utilitarian object to Russell's views?

7. How might a Kantian or contractualist object?

8. Are there, for Russell, any distinctively sexual virtues? If so, what are they?

THOMAS A. MAPPES

Sexual Morality
and the Concept of Using Another Person

Thomas A. Mappes is Professor of Philosophy at Frostburg State University, Maryland. (Source: From Thomas A. Mappes and Jane S. Zembaty (ed.), Social Ethics: Morality and Social Policy [New York: McGraw-Hill, 1992]. Notes have been omitted. Reprinted by permission of the author.)

The central tenet of *conventional* sexual morality is that nonmarital sex is immoral. A somewhat less restrictive sexual ethic holds that *sex without love* is immoral. If neither of these positions is philosophically defensible, and I would contend that neither is, it does not follow that there are no substantive moral restrictions on human sexual interaction. *Any* human interaction, including sexual interaction, may be judged morally objectionable to the extent that it transgresses a justified moral rule or principle. The way to construct a detailed account of sexual morality, it would seem, is simply to work out the implications of relevant moral rules or principles in the area of human sexual interaction.

As one important step in the direction of such an account, I will attempt to work out the implications of an especially relevant moral principle, the principle that it is wrong for one person to use another person. However ambiguous the expression "using another person" may seem to be, there is a determinate and clearly specifiable sense according to which using another person is morally objectionable. Once this morally significant sense of "using another person" is identified and explicated, the concept of using another person can play an important role in the articulation of a defensible account of sexual morality.

I. The Morally Significant Sense of "Using Another Person"

Historically, the concept of using another person is associated with the ethical system of Immanuel Kant. According to a fundamental Kantian principle, it is morally wrong for A to use B *merely as a means* (to achieve A's ends). Kant's principle does not rule out A using B as a means, only A using B *merely* as a means, that is, in a way incompatible with respect for B as a person. In the ordinary course of life, it is surely unavoidable (and morally unproblematic) that each of us in numerous ways uses others as a means to achieve our various ends. A college teacher uses students as a means to achieve his or her livelihood. A college student uses instructors as a means of gaining knowledge and skills. Such human interactions, presumably based on the voluntary participation of the respective parties, are quite compatible with the idea of respect for persons. But respect for persons entails that each of us recognize the rightful authority of other persons (as rational beings) to conduct their individual lives as they see fit. We may legitimately recruit others to participate in the satisfaction of our personal ends, but they are used merely as a means whenever we undermine the voluntary or informed character of their consent to interact with us in some desired way. A coerces B at knifepoint to

62

hand over $200. A uses B merely as a means. If A had requested of B a gift of $200, leaving B free to determine whether or not to make the gift, A would have proceeded in a manner compatible with respect for B as a person. C deceptively rolls back the odometer of a car and thereby manipulates D's decision to buy the car. C uses D merely as a means.

On the basis of these considerations, I would suggest that the morally significant sense of "using another person" is best understood by reference to the notion of *voluntary informed consent*. More specifically, A immorally uses B if and only if A intentionally acts in a way that violates the requirement that B's involvement with A's ends be based on B's voluntary informed consent. If this account is correct, using another person (in the morally significant sense) can arise in at least two important ways: via *coercion,* which is antithetical to voluntary consent, and via *deception,* which undermines the informed character of voluntary consent. . . .

II. Deception and Sexual Morality

. . . If we presume a state of affairs in which A desires some form of sexual interaction with B, we can say that this desired form of sexual interaction with B is A's end. Thus A sexually *uses* B if and only if A intentionally acts in a way that violates the requirement that B's sexual interaction with A be based on B's voluntary informed consent. It seems clear then that A may sexually use B in at least two distinctive ways, (1) via coercion and (2) via deception. However, before proceeding to discuss deception and then the more problematic case of coercion, one important point must be made. In emphasizing the centrality of coercion and deception as mechanisms for the sexual using of another person, I have in mind sexual interaction with a fully competent adult partner. We should also want to say, I think, that sexual interaction with a child inescapably involves the sexual using of another person. Even if a child "consents" to sexual interaction, he or she is, strictly speaking, incapable of *informed* consent. It's a matter of being *incompetent* to give consent. Similarly, to the extent that a mentally retarded person is rightly considered incompetent, sexual interaction with such a person amounts to the sexual using of that person, unless someone empow-

ered to give "proxy consent" has done so. (In certain circumstances, sexual involvement might be in the best interests of a mentally retarded person.) We can also visualize the case of an otherwise fully competent adult temporarily disordered by drugs or alcohol. To the extent that such a person is rightly regarded as temporarily incompetent, winning his or her "consent" to sexual interaction could culminate in the sexual using of that person.

There are a host of clear cases in which one person sexually uses another precisely because the former employs deception in a way that undermines the informed character of the latter's consent to sexual interaction. Consider this example. One person, A, has decided, as a matter of personal prudence based on past experience, not to become sexually involved outside the confines of a loving relationship. Another person, B, strongly desires a sexual relationship with A but does not love A. B, aware of A's unwillingness to engage in sex without love, professes love for A, thereby hoping to win A's consent to a sexual relationship. B's ploy is successful; A consents. When the smoke clears and A becomes aware of B's deception, it would be both appropriate and natural for A to complain, "I've been used."

In the same vein, here are some other examples. (1) Mr. A is aware that Ms. B will consent to sexual involvement only on the understanding that in time the two will be married. Mr. A has no intention of marrying Ms. B but says that he will. (2) Ms. C has herpes and is well aware that Mr. D will never consent to sex if he knows of her condition. When asked by Mr. D, Ms. C denies that she has herpes. (3) Mr. E knows that Ms. F will not consent to sexual intercourse in the absence of responsible birth control measures. Mr. E tells Ms. F that he has had a vasectomy, which is not the case. (4) Ms. G knows that Mr. H. would not consent to sexual involvement with a married woman. Ms. G is married but tells Mr. H that she is single. (5) Ms. I is well aware that Ms. J is interested in a stable lesbian relationship and will not consent to become sexually involved with someone who is bisexual. Ms. I tells Ms. J that she is exclusively homosexual, whereas the truth is that she is bisexual.

If one person's consent to sex is predicated on false beliefs that have been intentionally and deceptively inculcated by one's sexual partner in an effort to win the former's consent, the resulting sexual interaction involves one person sexually using another. In each of the above cases, one person explicitly *lies* to another. False information is intentionally conveyed to win consent to sexual interaction, and the end result is the sexual using of another person.

As noted earlier, however, lying is not the only form of deception. Under certain circumstances, the simple withholding of information can be considered a form of deception. Accordingly, it is possible to sexually use another person not only by (deceptively) lying about relevant facts but also by (deceptively) not disclosing relevant facts. If A has good reason to believe that B would refuse to consent to sexual interaction should B become aware of certain factual information, and if A withholds disclosure of this information in order to enhance the possibility of gaining B's consent, then, if B does consent, A sexually uses B via deception. One example will suffice. Suppose that Mr. A meets Ms. B in a singles bar. Mr. A realizes immediately that Ms. B is the sister of Ms. C, a woman that Mr. A has been sexually involved with for a long time. Mr. A, knowing that it is very unlikely that Ms. B will consent to sexual interaction if she becomes aware of Mr. A's involvement with her sister, decides not to disclose this information. If Ms. B eventually consents to sexual interaction, since her consent is the product of Mr. A's deception, it is rightly thought that she has been sexually used by him.

III. Coercion and Sexual Morality

We have considered the case of deception. The present task is to consider the more difficult case of coercion. Whereas deception functions to undermine the *informed* character of voluntary consent (to sexual interaction), coercion either obliterates consent entirely (the case of occurrent coercion) or undermines the voluntariness of consent (the case of dispositional coercion).

Forcible rape is the most conspicuous, and most brutal, way of sexually using another person via coercion. Forcible rape may involve either occurrent coercion or dispositional coercion. A man who rapes a woman by the employment of sheer physical force, by simply overpowering her, employs occurrent coercion. There is literally no sexual *interaction* in such a case; only the rapist performs an action. In no sense does the woman consent to or participate in sexual activity. She has no choice in what takes place, or rather, physical force results in her choice being simply beside the point. The employment of occurrent coercion for the purpose of rape "objectifies" the victim in the strongest sense of that term. She is treated like a physical object. One does not interact with physical objects; one acts upon them. In a perfectly ordinary (not the morally significant) sense of the term, we "use" physical objects. But when the victim of rape is treated as if she were a physical object, there we have one of the most vivid examples of the immoral using of another person.

Frequently, forcible rape involves not occurrent coercion (or not *only* occurrent coercion) but dispositional coercion. In dispositional coercion, the relevant factor is not physical force but the threat of harm. The rapist threatens his victim with immediate and serious bodily harm. For example, a man threatens to kill or beat a woman if she resists his sexual demands. She "consents," that is, she submits to his demands. He may demand only passive participation (simply not struggling against him) or he may demand some measure of active participation. Rape that employs dispositional coercion is surely just as wrong as rape that employs occurrent coercion, but there is a notable difference in the mechanism by which the rapist uses his victim in the two cases. With occurrent coercion, the victim's consent is entirely bypassed. With dispositional coercion, the victim's consent is not bypassed. It is coerced. Dispositional coercion undermines the *voluntariness* of consent. The rapist, by employing the threat of immediate and serious bodily harm, may succeed in bending the victim's will. He may gain the victim's "consent." But he uses another person precisely because consent is coerced.

The relevance of occurrent coercion is limited to the case of forcible rape. Dispositional coercion, a notion that also plays an indispensable role in an overall account of forcible rape, now becomes our central concern. Although the threat of immediate and serious bodily harm stands out as the most brutal way of coercing consent to sexual interaction, we must not neglect the employment of other kinds of threats to this same end. There are numerous ways in which one person can effectively harm, and thus effectively threaten, another. Accordingly, for example, consent to sexual interaction might be coerced by threatening to damage someone's reputation. If a person consents to sexual interaction to avoid a threatened harm, then that person has been sexually used (via dispositional coercion). In the face of a threat, of course, it remains possible that a person will refuse to comply with another's sexual demands. It is probably best to describe this sort of situation as a case not of coercion, which entails the *successful* use of threats to gain compliance, but of *attempted* coercion. Of course, the moral fault of an individual emerges with the *attempt* to coerce. A person who attempts murder is morally blameworthy even if the attempt fails. The same is true for someone who fails in an effort to coerce consent to sexual interaction.

Consider now each of the following cases:

Case 1   Mr. Supervisor makes a series of increasingly less subtle sexual overtures to Ms. Employee. These advances are consistently and firmly rejected by Ms. Employee. Eventually, Mr. Supervisor makes it clear that the granting of "sexual favors" is a condition of her continued employment.

Case 2   Ms. Debtor borrowed a substantial sum of money from Mr. Creditor, on the understanding that she would pay it back within one year. In the meantime, Ms. Debtor has become sexually attracted to Mr. Creditor, but he does not share her interest. At the end of the one-year period, Mr. Creditor asks Ms. Debtor to return the money. She says she will be happy to return the money so long as he consents to sexual interaction with her.

Case 3   Mr. Theatregoer has two tickets to the most talked-about play of the season. He is introduced to a woman whom he finds sexually attractive and who shares his interest in the theater. In the course of their conversation, she expresses disappointment that the play everyone is talking about is sold out; she would love to see it. At this point, Mr. Theatregoer suggests that she be his guest at the theater. "Oh, by the way," he says, "I always expect sex from my dates."

Case 4   Ms. Jetsetter is planning a trip to Europe. She has been trying for some time to develop a sexual relationship with a man who has shown little interest in her. She knows, however, that he has always wanted to go to Europe and that it is only lack of money that has deterred him. Ms. Jetsetter proposes that he come along as her traveling companion, all expenses paid, on the express understanding that sex is part of the arrangement.

Cases 1 and 2 involve attempts to sexually use another person whereas cases 3 and 4 do not. To see why this is so, it is essential to introduce a distinction between two kinds of proposals, viz., the distinction between *threats* and *offers*. The logical form of a threat differs from the logical form of an offer in the following way. Threat: "If you *do not* do what I am proposing you do, I will bring about an *undesirable consequence* for you." Offer: "If you *do* what I am proposing you do, I will bring about a *desirable consequence* for you." The person who makes a threat attempts to gain compliance by attaching an undesirable consequence to the alternative of noncompliance. This person attempts to *coerce* consent. The person who makes an offer attempts to gain compliance by attaching a desirable consequence to the alternative of compliance. This person attempts not to coerce but to *induce* consent.

Since threats are morally problematic in a way that offers are not, it is not uncommon for threats to be advanced in the language of offers. Threats are represented as if they were offers. An armed assailant might say, "I'm going to make you an *offer.* If you give me your money, I will allow you to go on living." Though this proposal on the surface has the logical form of an offer, it is in reality a threat. The underlying sense of the proposal is this: "If you do not give me your money, I will kill you." If, in a given case, it is initially unclear whether a certain proposal is to count as a threat or an offer, ask the following question. Does the proposal in question have the effect of making a person *worse off upon noncompliance?* The recipient of an offer, upon noncompliance, *is not worse off* than he or she was before the offer. In contrast, the recipient of a threat, upon noncompliance, *is worse off* than he or she was before the threat. Since the "offer" of our armed assailant has the effect, upon noncompliance, of rendering its recipient worse off (relative to the preproposal situation of the recipient), the recipient is faced with a threat, not an offer.

The most obvious way for a coercer to attach an undesirable consequence to the path of noncompliance is by threatening to render the victim of coercion materially worse off than he or she has heretofore been. Thus a person is threatened with loss of life, bodily injury, damage to property, damage to reputation, etc. It is important to realize, however, that a person can also be effectively coerced by being threatened with the withholding of something (in some cases, what we would call a "benefit") to which the person is entitled. Suppose that A is mired in quicksand and is slowly but surely approaching death. When B happens along, A cries out to B for assistance. All B need do is throw A a rope. B is quite willing to accommodate A, "provided you pay me $100,000 over the next ten years." Is B making A an offer? Hardly! B, we must presume, stands under a moral obligation to come to the aid of a person in serious distress, at least when such assistance entails no significant risk, sacrifice of time, etc. A is entitled to B's assistance. Thus, in reality, B attaches an undesirable consequence to A's noncompliance with the proposal that A pay B $100,000. A is undoubtedly better off that B has happened along, but A is not rendered better off *by B's proposal*. Before B's proposal, A legitimately expected assistance from B, "no strings attached." In attaching a very unwelcome string, B's proposal effectively renders A worse off. What B proposes, then, is not an offer of assistance. Rather, B threatens A with the withholding of something (assistance) that A is entitled to have from B.

Since threats have the effect of rendering a person worse off upon noncompliance, it is ordinarily the case that a person does not welcome (indeed, despises) them. Offers, on the other hand, are ordinarily welcome to a person. Since an offer provides no penalty for noncompliance with a proposal but only an inducement for compliance, there is *in principle* only potential advantage in being confronted with an offer. In real life, of course, there are numerous reasons why a person may be less than enthusiastic about being presented with an offer. Enduring the presentation of trivial offers does not warrant the necessary time and energy expenditures. Offers can be both annoying and offensive; certainly this is true of some sexual offers. A person might also be unsettled by an offer that confronts him or her with a difficult decision. All this, however, is compatible with the fact that an offer is fundamentally welcome to a

rational person in the sense that the *content* of an offer necessarily widens the field of opportunity and thus provides, in principle, only potential advantage.

With the distinction between threats and offers clearly in view, it now becomes clear why cases 1 and 2 do indeed involve attempts to sexually use another person whereas cases 3 and 4 do not. Cases 1 and 2 embody threats, whereas cases 3 and 4 embody offers. In case 1, Mr. Supervisor proposes sexual interaction with Ms. Employee and, in an effort to gain compliance, threatens her with the loss of her job. Mr. Supervisor thereby attaches an undesirable consequence to one of Ms. Employee's alternatives, the path of noncompliance. Typical of the threat situation, Mr. Supervisor's proposal has the effect of rendering Ms. Employee worse off upon noncompliance. Mr. Supervisor is attempting via (dispositional) coercion to sexually use Ms. Employee. The situation in case 2 is similar. Ms. Debtor, as *she* might be inclined to say, "offers" to pay Mr. Creditor the money she owes him *if* he consents to sexual interaction with her. In reality, Ms. Debtor is threatening Mr. Creditor, attempting to coerce his consent to sexual interaction, attempting to sexually use him. Though Mr. Creditor is not now in possession of the money Ms. Debtor owes him, he is *entitled* to receive it from her at this time. She threatens to deprive him of something to which he is entitled. Clearly, her proposal has the effect of rendering him worse off upon noncompliance. Before her proposal, he had the legitimate expectation, "no strings attached," of receiving the money in question.

Cases 3 and 4 embody offers; neither involves an attempt to sexually use another person. Mr. Theatregoer simply provides an inducement for the woman he has just met to accept his proposal of sexual interaction. He offers her the opportunity to see the play that everyone is talking about. In attaching a desirable consequence to the alternative of compliance, Mr. Theatregoer in no way threatens or attempts to coerce his potential companion. Typical of the offer situation, his proposal does not have the effect of rendering her worse off upon noncompliance. She now has a new opportunity; if she chooses to forgo this opportunity, she is no worse off. The situation in case 4 is similar. Ms. Jetsetter provides an inducement for a man that she is interested in to accept her proposal of sexual involvement. She offers him the opportunity to see Europe, without expense, as her traveling companion. Before Ms. Jetsetter's proposal, he had no prospect of a European trip. If he chooses to reject her proposal, he is no worse off than he has heretofore been. Ms. Jetsetter's proposal embodies an offer, not a threat. She cannot be accused of attempting to sexually use her potential traveling companion.

Consider now two further cases, 5 and 6, each of which develops in the following way. Professor Highstatus, a man of high academic accomplishment, is sexually attracted to a student in one of his classes. He is very anxious to secure her consent to sexual interaction. Ms. Student, confused and unsettled by his sexual advances, has begun to practice "avoidance behavior." To the extent that it is possible, she goes out of her way to avoid him.

Case 5   Professor Highstatus tells Ms. Student that, though her work is such as to entitle her to a grade of B in the class, she will be assigned a D unless she consents to sexual interaction.

Case 6   Professor Highstatus tells Ms. Student that, though her work is such as to entitle her to a grade of B, she will be assigned an A if she consents to sexual interaction.

It is clear that case 5 involves an attempt to sexually use another person. Case 6, however, at least at face value, does not. In case 5, Professor Highstatus *threatens* to deprive Ms. Student of the grade she deserves. In case 6, he *offers* to assign her a grade that is higher than she deserves. In case 5, Ms. Student would be worse off upon noncompliance with Professor Highstatus's proposal. In case 6, she would not be worse off upon noncompliance with his proposal. In saying that case 6 does not involve an attempt to sexually use another person, it is not being asserted that Professor Highstatus is acting in a morally legitimate fashion. In offering a student a higher grade than she deserves, he is guilty of abusing his institutional authority. He is under an obligation to assign the grades that students earn, as defined by the relevant course standards. In case 6, Professor Highstatus is undoubtedly acting in a morally reprehensible way, but in contrast to case 5, where it is fair to say that he both abuses his institutional authority *and* attempts to sexually use another person, we can plau-

sibly say that in case 6 his moral failure is limited to abuse of his institutional authority.

There remains, however, a suspicion that case 6 might after all embody an attempt to sexually use another person. There is no question that the literal content of what Professor Highstatus conveys to Ms. Student has the logical form of an offer and not a threat. Still, is it not the case that Ms. Student may very well feel threatened? Professor Highstatus, in an effort to secure consent to sexual interaction, has announced that he will assign Ms. Student a higher grade than she deserves. Can she really turn him down without substantial risk? Is he not likely to retaliate? If she spurns him, will he not lower her grade or otherwise make it harder for her to succeed in her academic program? He does, after all, have power over her. Will he use it to her detriment? Surely he is not above abusing his institutional authority to achieve his ends; this much is abundantly clear from his willingness to assign a grade higher than a student deserves.

Is Professor Highstatus naive to the threat that Ms. Student may find implicit in the situation? Perhaps. In such a case, if Ms. Student reluctantly consents to sexual interaction, we may be inclined to say that he has *unwittingly* used her. More likely, Professor Highstatus is well aware of the way in which Ms. Student will perceive his proposal. He knows that threats need not be verbally expressed. Indeed, it may even be the case that he consciously exploits his underground reputation. "Everyone knows what happens to the women who reject Professor Highstatus's little offers." To the extent, then, that Professor Highstatus intends to convey a threat in case 6, he is attempting via coercion to sexually use another person.

Many researchers "have pointed out the fact that the possibility of sanctions for noncooperation is implicit in all sexual advances across authority lines, as between teacher and student." I do not think that this consideration should lead us to the conclusion that a person with an academic appointment is obliged in all circumstances to refrain from attempting to initiate sexual involvement with one of his or her students. Still, since even "good faith" sexual advances may be ambiguous in the eyes of a student, it is an interesting question what precautions an instructor must take to avoid unwittingly coercing a student to consent to sexual interaction.

Much of what has been said about the professor/student relationship in an academic setting can be applied as well to the supervisor/subordinate relationship in an employment setting. A manager who functions within an organizational structure is required to evaluate fairly his or her subordinates according to relevant corporate or institutional standards. An unscrupulous manager, willing to abuse his or her institutional authority in an effort to win the consent of a subordinate to sexual interaction, can advance threats and/or offers related to the managerial task of employee evaluation. An employee whose job performance is entirely satisfactory can be threatened with an unsatisfactory performance rating, perhaps leading to termination. An employee whose job performance is excellent can be threatened with an unfair evaluation, designed to bar the employee from recognition, merit pay, consideration for promotion, etc. Such threats, when made in an effort to coerce employee consent to sexual interaction, clearly embody the attempt to sexually use another person. On the other hand, the manager who (abusing his or her institutional authority) offers to provide an employee with an inflated evaluation as an inducement for consent to sexual interaction does not, at face value, attempt to sexually use another person. Of course, all of the qualifications introduced in the discussion of case 6 above are applicable here as well.

QUESTIONS FOR REFLECTION

1. How does Mappes interpret Kant's prohibition on using another person as a means only?

2. Can you think of cases where someone gives voluntary informed consent but is nevertheless in some sense used?

3. Conversely, can you think of cases in which someone is treated as an end without voluntary informed consent?

4. How does Mappes distinguish threats from offers? What, in his view, is the moral significance of the distinction? Do you agree?

5. What implications does Mappes's view have for sexual harassment?

6. How might a utilitarian criticize Mappes's argument?

SIDNEY CALLAHAN

Abortion and the Sexual Agenda

Sidney Callahan is Professor of Psychology at Mercy College. (Source: From Commonweal [April 25, 1986], pp. 232–238. Copyright © 1986 by Commonweal, Inc. Reprinted by permissio n.)

. . . Pro-life feminists seek to expand and deepen the more communitarian, maternal elements of feminism—and move society from its male-dominated course. First and foremost, women have to insist upon a different, woman-centered approach to sex and reproduction. While Margaret Mead stressed the "womb envy" of males in other societies, it has been more or less repressed in our own. In our male-dominated world, what men don't do, doesn't count. Pregnancy, childbirth, and nursing have been characterized as passive, debilitating, animal-like. The disease model of pregnancy and birth has been entrenched. This female disease or impairment, with its attendant "female troubles," naturally handicaps women in the "real" world of hunting, war, and the corporate fast track. Many pro-choice feminists, deliberately childless, adopt the male perspective when they cite the "basic injustice that women have to bear the babies," instead of seeing the injustice in the fact that men cannot. Women's biologically unique capacity and privilege has been denied, despised, and suppressed under male domination; unfortunately, many women have fallen for the phallic fallacy.

Childbirth often appears in pro-choice literature as a painful, traumatic, life-threatening experience. Yet giving birth is accurately seen as an arduous but normal exercise of lifegiving power, a violent and ecstatic peak experience, which men can never know. Ironically, some pro-choice men and women think and talk of pregnancy and childbirth with the same repugnance that ancient ascetics displayed toward orgasms and sexual intercourse. The similarity may not be accidental. The obstetrician Niles Newton, herself a mother, has written of the extended three-fold sexuality of women, who can experience orgasm, birth, and nursing as passionate pleasure-giving experiences. All of these are involuntary processes of the female body. Only orgasm, which males share, has been glorified as an involuntary function that is nature's gift; the involuntary feminine processes of childbirth and nursing have been seen as bondage to biology.

Fully accepting our bodies as ourselves, what should women want? I think women will only flourish when there is a feminization of sexuality, very different from the current cultural trend toward masculinizing female sexuality. Women can never have the self-confidence and self-esteem they need to achieve feminist goals in society until a more holistic, feminine model of sexuality becomes the dominant cultural ethos. To say this affirms the view that men and women differ in the domain of sexual functioning, although they are more alike than different in other personality characteristics and competencies. For those of us committed to achieving sexual equality in the culture, it may be hard to accept the fact that sexual differences make it imperative to talk of distinct male and female models of sexuality. But if one wants to change sexual roles, one has to recognize pre-existing conditions. A great deal of evidence is accumulating which points to biological pressures for different male and female sexual functioning.

Males always and everywhere have been more physically aggressive and more likely to fuse sexuality with aggression and dominance. Females may be more variable in their sexuality, but since Masters and Johnson, we know that women have a greater capacity than men for repeated orgasm and a more tenuous path to arousal and orgasmic release. Most obviously, women also have a far greater sociobiological investment in the act of human reproduction. On the whole, women as compared to men possess a sexuality which is more complex, more intense, more extended in time, involving higher investment, risks, and psychosocial involvement.

Considering the differences in sexual functioning, it is not surprising that men and women in the same culture have often constructed different sexual ideals. In Western culture, since the nineteenth century at least, most women have espoused a version of sexual functioning in which sex acts are embedded within deep emotional bonds and secure long-term commitments. Within these committed "pair bonds" males assume parental obligations. In the idealized Victorian version of the Christian sexual ethic, culturally endorsed and maintained by women, the double standard was not countenanced. Men and women did not need to marry to be whole persons, but if they did engage in sexual functioning, they were to be equally chaste, faithful, responsible, loving, and parentally concerned. Many of the most influential women in the nineteenth-century women's movement preached and lived this sexual ethic, often by the side of exemplary feminist men. While the ideal has never been universally obtained, a culturally dominant demand for monogamy, self-control, and emotionally bonded and committed sex works well for women in every stage of their sexual life cycles. When love, chastity, fidelity, and commitment for better or worse are the ascendant cultural prerequisites for sexual functioning, young girls and women expect protection from rape and seduction, adult women justifiably demand male support in childrearing, and older women are more protected from abandonment as their biological attractions wane.

Of course, these feminine sexual ideals always coexisted in competition with another view. A more male-oriented model of erotic or amative sexuality endorses sexual permissiveness without long-term commitment or reproductive focus. Erotic sexuality emphasizes pleasure, play, passion, individual self-expression, and romantic games of courtship and conquest. It is assumed that a variety of partners and sexual experiences are necessary to stimulate romantic passion. This erotic model of the sexual life has often worked satisfactorily for men, both heterosexual and gay, and for certain cultural elites. But for the average woman, it is quite destructive. Women can only play the erotic game successfully when, like the "*Cosmopolitan* women," they are young, physically attractive, economically powerful, and fulfilled enough in a career to be willing to sacrifice family life. Abortion is also required. As our society increasingly endorses this male-oriented, permissive view of sexuality, it is all too ready to give women abortion on demand. Abortion helps a woman's body be more like a man's. It has been observed that *Roe v. Wade* removed the last defense women possessed against male sexual demands.

Unfortunately, the modern feminist movement made a mistaken move at a critical juncture. Rightly rebelling against patriarchy, unequal education, restricted work opportunities, and women's downtrodden political status, feminists also rejected the nineteenth-century feminine sexual ethic. Amative erotic, permissive sexuality (along with abortion rights) became symbolically identified with other struggles for social equality in education, work, and politics. This feminist mistake also turned off many potential recruits among women who could not deny the positive dimensions of their own traditional feminine roles, nor their allegiance to the older feminine sexual ethic of love and fidelity.

An ironic situation then arose in which many prochoice feminists preach their own double standard. In the world of work and career, women are urged to grow up, to display mature self-discipline and self-control; they are told to persevere in long-term commitments, to cope with unexpected obstacles by learning to tough out the inevitable sufferings and setbacks entailed in life and work. But this mature ethic of commitment and self-discipline, recommended as the only way to progress in the world of work and personal achievement, is discounted in the domain of sexuality.

In pro-choice feminism, a permissive, erotic view of sexuality is assumed to be the only option. Sexual intercourse with a variety of partners is seen as "inevitable" from a young age and as a positive growth experience to be managed by access to contraception and abortion. Unfortunately, the pervasive cultural conviction that adolescents, or their elders, cannot exercise sexual self-control, undermines the responsible use of contraception. When a pregnancy occurs, the first abortion is viewed in some pro-choice circles as a *rite de passage*. Responsibly choosing an abortion supposedly ensures that a young woman will take charge of her own life, make her own decisions, and carefully practice contraception. But the social dynamics of a permissive, erotic model of sexuality, coupled with permissive laws, work toward repeat abortions. Instead of being empowered by their abortion choices, young women having abortions are confronting the debilitating reality of *not* bringing a baby into the world; *not* being able to count on a committed male partner; *not* accounting oneself strong enough, or the master of enough resources, to avoid killing the fetus. Young women are hardly going to develop the self-esteem, self-discipline, and self-confidence necessary to confront a male-dominated society through abortion.

The male-oriented sexual orientation has been harmful to women and children. It has helped bring us epidemics of venereal disease, infertility, pornography, sexual abuse, adolescent pregnancy, divorce, displaced older women, and abortion. Will these signals of something amiss stimulate pro-choice feminists to rethink what kind of sex ideal really serves women's best interests? While the erotic model cannot encompass commitment, the committed model can—happily—encompass and encourage romance, passion, and playfulness. In fact, within the security of long-term commitments, women may be more likely to experience sexual pleasure and fulfillment.

The pro-life feminist position is not a return to the old feminine mystique. That espousal of "the eternal feminine" erred by viewing sexuality as so sacred that it cannot be humanly shaped at all. Woman's *whole* nature was supposed to be opposite to man's, necessitating complementary and radically different social roles. Followed to its logical conclusion, such a view presumes that reproductive and sexual experience is necessary for human fulfillment. But as the early feminists insisted, no woman has to marry or engage in sexual intercourse to be fulfilled,

nor does a woman have to give birth and raise children to be complete, nor must she stay home and function as an earth mother. But female sexuality does need to be deeply respected as a unique potential and trust. Since most contraceptives and sterilization procedures really do involve only the woman's body rather than destroying new life, they can be an acceptable and responsible moral option.

With sterilization available to accelerate the inevitable natural ending of fertility and childbearing, a woman confronts only a limited number of years in which she exercises her reproductive trust and may have to respond to an unplanned pregnancy. Responsible use of contraception can lower the probabilities even more. Yet abortion is not decreasing. The reason is the current permissive attitude embodied in the law, not the "hard cases" which constitute 3 percent of today's abortions. Since attitudes, the law, and behavior interact, pro-life feminists conclude that unless there is an enforced limitation of abortion, which currently confirms the sexual and social status quo, alternatives will never be developed. For women to get what they need in order to combine childbearing, education, and careers, society has to recognize that female bodies come with wombs. Women and their reproductive power, and the children women have, must be supported in new ways. Another and different round of feminist consciousness-raising is needed in which all of women's potential is accorded respect. This time, instead of humbly buying entrée by conforming to male lifestyles, women will demand that society accommodate to them.

New feminist efforts to rethink the meaning of sexuality, femininity, and reproduction are all the more vital as new techniques for artificial reproduction, surrogate motherhood, and the like present a whole new set of dilemmas. In the long run, the very long run, the abortion debate may be merely the opening round in a series of far-reaching struggles over the role of human sexuality and the ethics of reproduction. Significant changes in the culture, both positive and negative in outcome, may begin as local storms of controversy. We may be at one of those vaguely realized thresholds when we had best come to full attention. What kind of people are we going to be? Pro-life feminists pursue a vision for their sisters, daughters, and granddaughters. Will their great-granddaughters be grateful?

QUESTIONS FOR REFLECTION

1. How does Callahan distinguish masculine from feminine conceptions of sexuality?

2. How, according to Callahan, is the masculine conception of sexuality harmful for women and children? How is the feminine conception beneficial?

3. How, according to Callahan, should a feminist think of sexuality? Do you agree?

4. How does the abortion controversy relate to conceptions of sexuality, in Callahan's view?

ROGER SCRUTON

from *Sexual Desire*

Roger Scruton, British writer and philosopher, is the author of The Aesthetics of Architecture, Kant, The Meaning of Conservatism, Art and Imagination, The Politics of Culture, Untimely Tracts, The Aesthetics of Music, *and many other books on philosophy, politics, and art. (Source: Roger Scruton,* Sexual Desire *[London: Weidenfeld and Nicolson, 1986]. Notes have been omitted. Copyright © 1986 by Roger Scruton. Reprinted by permission.)*

SEXUAL MORALITY

We must now attempt to apply the Aristotelian strategy [here] and ask whether there is such a thing as sexual virtue, and, if so, what is it, and how is it acquired? Clearly, sexual desire, which is an interpersonal attitude with the most far-reaching consequences for those who are joined by it, cannot be morally neutral. On the contrary, it is in the experience of sexual desire that we are most vividly conscious of the distinction between virtuous and vicious impulses, and most vividly aware that, in the choice between them, our happiness is at stake.

The Aristotelian strategy enjoins us to ignore the actual conditions of any particular person's life, and to look only at the permanent features of human nature. We know that people feel sexual desire; that they feel erotic love, which may grow from desire; that they may avoid both these feelings, by dissipation or self-restraint. Is there anything to be said about desire, other than that it falls within the general scope of the virtue of temperance, which enjoins us to desire only what reason approves?

The first, and most important, observation to be made is that the capacity for love in general, and for erotic love in particular, is a virtue. . . . [E]rotic love involves an element of mutual self-enhancement; it generates a sense of the irreplaceable value, both of the other and of the self, and of the activities which bind them. To receive and to give this love is to achieve something of incomparable value in the process of self-fulfilment. It is to gain the most powerful of all interpersonal *guarantees;* in erotic love the subject becomes conscious of the full reality of his personal existence, not only in his own eyes, but in the eyes of another. Everything that he is and values gains sustenance from his love, and every project receives a meaning beyond the moment. All that exists for us as mere hope and hypothesis—the attachment to life and to the body—achieves under the rule of *erōs* the aspect of a radiant certainty. Unlike the cold glances of approval, admiration and pride, the glance of love sees value precisely in that which is the source of anxiety and doubt: in the merely contingent, merely "empirical," existence of the flesh, the existence which we did not choose, but to which we are condemned. It is the answer to man's fallen condition—to his *Geworfenheit.**

---

* Literally, "thrownness." German philosopher Martin Heidegger used this term for the human condition of being thrown into the midst of possibilities not of our own making.—ED.

To receive erotic love, however, a person must be able to give it: or if he cannot, the love of others will be a torment to him, seeking from him that which he cannot provide, and directing against him the fury of a disappointed right. It is therefore unquestionable that we have reason to acquire the capacity for erotic love, and, if this means bending our sexual impulses in a certain direction, that will be the direction of sexual virtue. Indeed, . . . the development of the sexual impulse towards love may be impeded: there are sexual habits which are vicious, precisely in neutralising the capacity for love. The first thing that can be said, therefore, is that we all have reason to avoid those habits and to educate our children not to possess them.

Here it may be objected that not every love is happy, that there are many—Anna Karenina, for example, or Phaedra—whose capacity for love was the cause of their downfall. But we must remind ourselves of the Aristotelian strategy. In establishing that courage or wisdom is a virtue, the Aristotelian does not argue that the possession of these virtues is in every particular circumstance bound to be advantageous. . . .

. . . We wish to know, in advance of any particular experience, which dispositions a person must have if he is successfully to express himself in sexual desire and to be fulfilled in his sexual endeavours. Love is the fulfilment of desire, and therefore love is its *telos*. A life of celibacy may also be fulfilled; but, assuming the general truth that most of us have a powerful, and perhaps overwhelming, urge to make love, it is in our interests to ensure that love—and not some other thing—is made.

Love, I have argued, is prone to jealousy, and the object of jealousy is defined by the thought of the beloved's desire. Because jealousy is one of the greatest of psychical catastrophes, involving the possible ruin of both partners, a morality based in the need for erotic love must forestall and eliminate jealousy. It is in the deepest human interest, therefore, that we form the habit of fidelity. This habit is natural and normal; but it is also easily broken, and the temptation to break it is contained in desire itself—in the element of generality which tempts us always to experiment, to verify, to detach ourselves from that which is too familiar in the interest of excitement and risk. Virtuous desire is faithful; but virtuous desire is also an artefact, made possible by

a process of moral education which we do not, in truth, understand in its complexity.

If that observation is correct, a whole section of traditional sexual morality must be upheld. The fulfilment of sexual desire defines the nature of desire: *to telos phuseis estin*. And the nature of desire gives us our standard of normality. There are enormous varieties of human sexual conduct, and of "common-sense" morality: some societies permit or encourage polygamy, others look with indifference upon premarital intercourse, or regard marriage itself as no more than an episode in a relation that pre-exists and perhaps survives it. But no society, and no "common-sense" morality—not even, it seems, the morality of Samoa—looks with favour upon promiscuity or infidelity, unless influenced by a doctrine of "emancipation" or "liberation" which is dependent for its sense upon the very conventions which it defies. Whatever the institutional forms of human sexual union, and whatever the range of permitted partners, sexual desire is itself inherently "nuptial"; it involves concentration upon the embodied existence of the other, leading through tenderness to the "vow" of erotic love. It is a telling observation that the civilisation which has most tolerated the institution of polygamy—the Islamic—has also, in its erotic literature, produced what are perhaps the intensest and most poignant celebrations of monogamous love, precisely through the attempt to capture, not the institution of marriage, but the human datum of desire.

The nuptiality of desire suggests, in its turn, a natural history of desire: a principle of development which defines the "normal course" of sexual education. "Sexual maturity" involves incorporating the sexual impulse into the personality, and so making sexual desire into an expression of the subject himself, even though it is, in the heat of action, a force which also overcomes him. If the Aristotelian approach to these things is as plausible as I think it is, the virtuous habit will also have the character of a "mean": it will involve the disposition to desire what is desirable, despite the competing impulses of animal lust (in which the intentionality of desire may be demolished) and timorous frigidity (in which the sexual impulse is impeded altogether). Education is directed towards the special kind of temperance which shows itself, sometimes as chastity, sometimes as fidelity, sometimes as passionate desire, according to the "right judgment" of the subject. In wanting what is judged to be desirable, the virtuous person wants what may also be loved, and what may therefore be obtained without hurt or humiliation.

Virtue is a matter of degree, rarely attained in its completion, but always admired. Because traditional sexual education has pursued sexual virtue, it is worthwhile summarising its most important features, in order to see the power of the idea that underlies and justifies it.

The most important feature of traditional sexual education is summarised in anthropological language as the "ethic of pollution and taboo." The child was taught to regard his body as sacred, and as subject to pollution by misperception or misuse. The sense of pollution is by no means a trivial side-effect of the "bad sexual encounter": it may involve a penetrating disgust, at oneself, one's body and one's situation, such as is experienced by the victim of rape. Those sentiments—which arise from our "fear of the obscene"—express the tension contained within the experience of embodiment. At any moment we can become "mere body," the self driven from its incarnation, and its habitation ransacked. The most important root idea of personal morality is that I am *in* my body, not (to borrow Descartes' image) as a pilot in a ship, but as an incarnate self. My body is identical with me, and sexual purity is the precious guarantee of this.

Sexual purity does not forbid desire: it simply ensures the status of desire as an interpersonal feeling. The child who learns "dirty habits" detaches his sex from himself, sets it outside himself as something curious and alien. His fascinated enslavement to the body is also a withering of desire, a scattering of erotic energy and a loss of union with the other. Sexual purity sustains the *subject* of desire, making him present as a self in the very act which overcomes him. . . .

The child was traditionally brought up to achieve sexual fulfilment only *through* chastity, which is the condition which surrounds him on his first entering the adult world—the world of commitments and obligations. At the same time, he was encouraged to ponder certain "ideal objects" of desire. These, presented to him under the aspect of an idealised physical beauty, were never *merely* beautiful, but also endowed with the moral

attributes that fitted them for love. This dual inculcation of "pure" habits and "ideal" love might seem, on the face of it, to be unworthy of the name of education. Is it not, rather, like the mere *training* of a horse or a dog, which arbitrarily forbids some things and fosters others, without offering the first hint of a reason why? And is it not the distinguishing mark of education that it engages with the rational nature of its recipient, and does not merely mould him indifferently to his own understanding of the process? Why, in short, is this moral education, rather than a transference into the sexual sphere—as Freud would have it—of those same processes of interdiction that train us to defecate, not in our nappies, but in a porcelain pot?

The answer is clear. The cult of innocence is an attempt to *generate* rational conduct, by incorporating the sexual impulse into the self-activity of the subject. It is an attempt to impede the impulse, until such a time as it may attach itself to the interpersonal project that leads to its fulfilment: the project of union with another person, who is wanted not merely for his body, but for the person who *is* this body. Innocence is the disposition to avoid sexual encounter, except with the person whom one may fully desire. Children who have lost their innocence have acquired the habit of gratification through the body alone, in a state of partial or truncated desire. Their gratification is detached from the conditions of personal fulfilment and wanders from object to object with no settled tendency to attach itself to any, pursued all the while by a sense of the body's obscene dominion. "Debauching of the innocent" was traditionally regarded as a most serious offence, and one that offered genuine *harm* to the victim. The harm in question was not physical, but moral: the undermining of the process which prepares the child to enter the world of *erōs*. (Thus Nabokov's Lolita, who passes with such rapidity from childish provocativeness to a knowing interest in the sexual act, finds, in the end, a marriage devoid of passion, and dies without knowledge of desire.)

The personal and the sexual can become divorced in many ways. The task of sexual morality is to unite them, to sustain thereby the intentionality of desire, and to prepare the individual for erotic love. Sexual morality is the morality of embodiment: the posture which strives to unite us with our bodies, precisely in those situations when our bodies are foremost in our thoughts. Without such a morality the human world is subject to a dangerous divide, a gulf between self and body, at the verge of which all our attempts at personal union falter and withdraw. Hence the prime focus of sexual morality is not the attitude to others, but the attitude to one's own body and its uses. Its aim is to safeguard the integrity of our embodiment. Only on that condition, it is thought, can we inculcate either innocence in the young or fidelity in the adult. . . .

Traditional sexual education was, despite its exaggerations and imbecilities, truer to human nature than the libertarian culture which has succeeded it. Through considering its wisdom and its shortcomings, we may understand how to resuscitate an idea of sexual virtue, in accordance with the broad requirements of the Aristotelian argument that I have, in this chapter, been presenting. The ideal of virtue remains one of "sexual integrity": of a sexuality that is entirely integrated into the life of personal affection, and in which the self and its responsibility are centrally involved and indissolubly linked to the pleasures and passions of the body. . . .

QUESTIONS FOR REFLECTION

1. What, according to Scruton, are the advantages of an Aristotelian approach to sexual ethics?

2. What is chastity, and why is it an important virtue, according to Scruton?

3. What is sexual integrity? How does it justify traditional sexual morality?

ANIMALS

Concern for the rights, interests, and welfare of animals is not new. In ancient India, Mahavira and the Buddha, founders of Jainism and Buddhism, respectively, taught that killing any sentient creature was wrong. The *Acaranga Sutra,* for example, proclaims, "All animals, living beings, organisms and sentient creatures should not be injured, governed, enslaved, tortured and killed." In the United States, Benjamin Franklin practiced vegetarianism for moral reasons. Eventually, he gave it up:

> I consider'd . . . the taking every fish as a kind of unprovoked murder, since none of them had, or ever could do us any injury that might justify the slaughter. All this seemed very reasonable. But I had formerly been a great lover of fish, and, when this came hot out of the frying-pan, it smelt admirably well. I balanc'd some time between principle and inclination, till I recollected that, when the fish were opened, I saw smaller fish taken out of their stomachs; then thought I, "If you eat one another, I don't see why we mayn't eat you." So I din'd upon cod very heartily, and continued to eat with other people, returning only now and then occasionally to a vegetable diet.*

Killing animals for meat or fur, using animals for research, factory farming, and other practices have become even more controversial in an affluent society in which few can be considered necessities of human survival.

Few people think that animals have no moral status. Someone who causes an animal gratuitous pain does something wrong. Yet to say that animals and humans are morally on a par also seems incorrect; for instance, someone who chooses to save a dog rather than a child from dying in a burning building surely makes a serious moral error. The difficulty is explaining what moral status animals do have, and why.

The International League of the Rights of Animals takes the extreme view that all animals have equal claims on life. That entails not only that killing animals for fur or meat, using animals in research, and so forth, are wrong, but also that organizations promoting the humane treatment of animals are wrong to euthanize unwanted animals; that pet-owners are wrong to spay, neuter, or confine their pets; and that zoos are immoral.

Peter Singer, a utilitarian, believes that all animals are equal in the sense that all suffering and all pleasure must be given moral weight, no matter who or what is suffering or feeling pleasure. From a utilitarian point of view, what matters is maximizing good. For a hedonistic utilitarian such as Bentham or Mill, the goal is maximizing the balance of pleasure over pain. Moral value depends solely on amounts of pleasure and pain; it makes no difference whether the pleasure or pain is felt by a human or an animal. This does not mean that it makes no moral difference whether one saves the life of a child or a dog, however, or that a hunter is the moral equivalent of a murderer. Just as Mill stresses that pleasures differ in quality—"It is better to be a human being dissatisfied than a pig satisfied"—Singer stresses that animals of different species have different capacities for pleasure and pain. Singer states that the same quantity of pain has the same moral value, no matter who feels it, but that humans are capable of greater suffering and greater happiness than animals are.

Tom Regan, a contractualist, also argues that animals deserve moral respect, but not solely because they have the capacity to suffer. Regan maintains that animals have rights just as humans do. Human life, we think, has inherent moral value; we would agree to that in the original position. Animal life, Regan says, also has inherent moral value, and any attempt to distinguish between degrees, levels, or kinds of inherent value to make human life more valuable faces serious difficulties. The distinction is bound to be arbitrary, Regan asserts, and also to imply that certain human lives are less valuable than others. We consider babies and people who are senile or comatose to have rights and to deserve full moral status, for we

---

* *Autobiography,* in *The Works of Benjamin Franklin,* Volume I (Boston: Hilliard Gray, and Company, 1840). p. 46.

realize, behind the veil of ignorance, that we might end up as one in the hypothetical society we are designing. We should assign animals full moral value as well, Regan says, for we should also recognize that we might enter the social order as an animal—not because transmigration of souls is possible, but because, behind the veil of ignorance, we should not know our own species.

Carl Cohen begins with Kant's idea that what makes human life morally valuable is its autonomy. We can form a conception of ourselves and our lives and act on principle. Animals cannot. Only humans, therefore, can be self-legislating members of the kingdom of ends. Only humans deserve full moral consideration. Drawing moral distinctions between humans and animals is anything but arbitrary; it is founded on the nature of humanity and the nature of the moral community. That is not to say that animals have no moral significance at all. We should avoid unnecessary harm to animals. But medical research on animals, for example, may be justified. We must balance the pain the animals experience against the expected benefits of the research to humans and other animals.

Peter Carruthers, like Regan, begins with Rawls's original position and asks what principles we would adopt behind the veil of ignorance. Unlike Regan, however, Carruthers finds no place for animals there. Our humanity is not something morally irrelevant that we must disregard in thinking about which rules to adopt. The whole idea of choosing principles from behind the veil of ignorance is to illustrate that morality is rational. To participate, then, one must be a moral agent capable of entering into an agreement in the original position. That excludes animals. So, Carruthers says, animals do not have the same moral status as humans. Why, then, take them to have any moral status at all? Carruthers's answer relies partly on a theory of virtue. Cruel acts are wrong, not because they violate an animal's rights, but because they exhibit a bad trait of character.

INTERNATIONAL LEAGUE OF THE RIGHTS OF ANIMALS

Universal Declaration of the Rights of Animals

(This declaration was adopted by the International League of the Rights of Animals and the affiliated national leagues in London, September 21–23, 1977. The declaration was solemnly proclaimed in Paris, October 15, 1978, at the House of the UNESCO. Detailed information on this declaration is available from Ligue Française des Droits de l'Animal.)

1. All animals are born with an equal claim on life and the same rights to existence.

2. All animals are entitled to respect. Man as an animal species shall not arrogate to himself the right to exterminate or inhumanely exploit other species. It is his duty to use his knowledge for the welfare of animals. All animals have the right to the attention, care, and protection of man.

3. No animals shall be ill-treated or be subject to cruel acts. If an animal has to be killed, this must be instantaneous and without distress.

4. All wild animals have the right to liberty in their natural environment, whether land, air, or water, and should be allowed to procreate. Deprivation of freedom, even for educational purposes, is an infringement of this right.

5. Animals of species living traditionally in a human environment have the right to live and grow at the rhythm and under the conditions of life and freedom peculiar to their species. Any interference by man with this rhythm or these conditions for purposes of gain is infringement of this right.

6. All companion animals have the right to complete their natural life span. Abandonment of an animal is a cruel and degrading act.

7. All working animals are entitled to a reasonable limitation of the duration and intensity of their work, to necessary nourishment, and to rest.

8. Animal experimentation involving physical or psychological suffering is incompatible with the rights of animals, whether it be for scientific, medical, commercial, or any other form of research. Replacement methods must be used and developed.

9. Where animals are used in the food industry they shall be reared, transported, lairaged, and killed without the infliction of suffering.

10. No animal shall be exploited for the amusement of man. Exhibitions and spectacles involving animals are incompatible with their dignity.

11. Any act involving the wanton killing of the animals is biocide, that is, a crime against life.

12. Any act involving the mass killing of wild animals is genocide, that is, a crime against the species. Pollution or destruction of the natural environment leads to genocide.

13. Dead animals shall be treated with respect. Scenes of violence involving animals shall be banned from cinema and television, except for human education.

14. Representatives of movements that defend animal rights should have an effective voice at all levels of government. The rights of animals, like human rights, should enjoy the protection of law.

QUESTIONS FOR REFLECTION

1. For each proposition in the declaration, name a common social practice that it would prohibit.

2. Animal welfare organizations sometimes euthanize unwanted animals. Is this practice acceptable, according to the declaration?

3. Animal welfare organizations often encourage spaying or neutering animals and sometimes spay or neuter populations of wild dogs or cats, for example. Is this practice acceptable, according to the declaration?

4. Darwin described nature as "red in tooth and claw," governed by scarcity and natural selection, "the survival of the fittest." Is that portrait of nature consistent with the declaration? Why or why not?

PETER SINGER

from *Animal Liberation*

Peter Singer is Professor of Philosophy and Director of the Center for Human Values at Princeton University. (Source: Reprinted from Animal Liberation *[New York Review of Books, 1975, 1990], by permission of the author. Copyright © 1975, 1990 by Peter Singer.)*

ALL ANIMALS ARE EQUAL . . .

"Animal Liberation" may sound more like a parody of other liberation movements than a serious objective. The idea of "The Rights of Animals" actually was once used to parody the case for women's rights. When Mary Wollstonecraft, a forerunner of today's feminists, published her *Vindication of the Rights of Women* in 1792, her views were widely regarded as absurd, and before long an anonymous publication appeared entitled *A Vindication of the Rights of Brutes.* The author of this satirical work (now known to have been Thomas Taylor, a distinguished Cambridge philosopher) tried to refute Mary Wollstonecraft's arguments by showing that they could be carried one stage further. If the argument for equality was sound when applied to women, why should it not be applied to dogs, cats, and horses? The reasoning seemed to hold for these "brutes" too; yet to hold that brutes had rights was manifestly absurd; therefore the reasoning by which this conclusion had been reached must be unsound, and if unsound when applied to brutes, it must also be unsound when applied to women, since the very same arguments had been used in each case.

In order to explain the basis of the case for the equality of animals, it will be helpful to start with an examination of the case for the equality of women. Let us assume that we wish to defend the case for women's rights against the attack by Thomas Taylor. How should we reply?

One way in which we might reply is by saying that the case for equality between men and women cannot validly be extended to nonhuman animals. Women have a right to vote, for instance, because they are just as capable of making rational decisions about the future as men are; dogs, on the other hand, are incapable of understanding the significance of voting, so they cannot have the right to vote. There are many other obvious ways in which men and women resemble each other closely, while humans and animals differ greatly. So, it might be said, men and women are similar beings and should have similar rights, while humans and nonhumans are different and should not have equal rights.

The reasoning behind this reply to Taylor's analogy is correct up to a point, but it does not go far enough. There *are* important differences between humans and other animals, and these differences must give rise to *some* differences in the rights that each have. Recognizing this obvious fact, however, is no barrier to the case for extending the basic principle of equality to nonhuman animals. The differences that exist between men and women are equally undeniable, and the supporters of Women's Liberation are aware that these differences may give rise to different rights. Many feminists hold that women have the right to an abortion on request. It does not follow that since these same feminists are campaigning for equality between men and women they must support the right of men to have abortions too. Since a man cannot have an abortion, it is meaningless to talk of his right to have one. Since a dog can't vote, it is meaningless to talk of its right to vote. There is no reason why either Women's Liberation or Animal Liberation should get involved in such nonsense. The extension of the basic principle of equality from one group to another does not imply that we must treat both groups in exactly the same way, or grant exactly the same rights to both groups. Whether we should do so will depend on the nature of the members of the two groups. The basic principle of equality does not require equal or identical *treatment;* it requires equal *consideration.* Equal consideration for different beings may lead to different treatment and different rights.

So there is a different way of replying to Taylor's attempt to parody the case for women's rights, a way that does not deny the obvious differences between humans and nonhumans but goes more deeply into the question of equality and concludes by finding nothing absurd in the idea that the basic principle of equality applies to so-called "brutes." At this point such a conclusion may appear odd; but if we examine more deeply the basis on which our opposition to discrimination on grounds of race or sex ultimately rests, we will see that we would be on shaky ground if we were to demand equality for blacks, women, and other groups of oppressed humans while denying equal consideration to nonhumans. To make this clear we need to see, first, exactly why racism and sexism are wrong.

When we say that all human beings, whatever their race, creed, or sex, are equal, what is it that we are asserting? Those who wish to defend hierarchical, inegalitarian societies have often pointed out that by whatever test we choose it simply is not true that all humans are created equal. Like it or not we must face the fact that humans come in different shapes and sizes; they come with different moral capacities, different intellectual abilities, different amounts of benevolent feeling and sensitivity to the needs of others, different abilities to communicate effectively, and different capacities to experience pleasure and pain. In short, if the demand for equality were based on the actual equality of all human beings, we would have to stop demanding equality.

Still, one might cling to the view that the demand for equality among human beings is based on the actual equality of the different races and sexes. Although, it may be said, humans differ as individuals, there are no differences between the races and sexes *as such.* From the mere fact that a person is black or a woman we cannot infer anything about that person's intellectual or moral capacities. This, it may be said, is why racism and sexism are wrong. The white racist claims that whites are superior to blacks, but this is false—although there are differences among individuals, some blacks are superior to some whites in all of the capacities and abilities that could conceivably be relevant. The opponent of sexism would say the same: a person's sex is no guide to his or her abilities, and this is why it is unjustifiable to discriminate on the basis of sex.

The existence of individual variations that cut across the lines of race or sex, however, provides us with no defense at all against a more sophisticated opponent of equality, one who proposes that, say, the interests of all those with IQ scores below 100 be given less consideration than the interests of those with ratings over 100. Perhaps those scoring below the mark would, in this society, be made the slaves of those scoring higher. Would a hierarchical society of this sort really be so much better than one based on race or sex? I think not. But if we tie the moral principle of equality to the factual equality of the different races or sexes, taken as a whole, our opposition to racism and sexism does not provide us with any basis for objecting to this kind of inegalitarianism.

There is a second important reason why we ought not to base our opposition to racism and sexism on any kind of factual equality, even the limited kind that asserts that variations in capacities and abilities are spread evenly between the different races and sexes: we can have no absolute guarantee that these capacities and abilities really are distributed evenly, without regard to race or sex, among human beings. So far as actual abilities are concerned there do seem to be certain measurable differences between both races and sexes. These differences do not, of course, appear in each case, but only when averages are taken. More important still, we do not yet know how much of these differences is really due to the different genetic endowments of the different races and sexes, and how much is due to poor schools, poor housing, and other factors that are the result of past and continuing discrimination. Perhaps all of the important differences will eventually prove to be environmental rather than genetic. Anyone opposed to racism and sexism will certainly hope that this will be so, for it will make the task of ending discrimination a lot easier; nevertheless it would be dangerous to rest the case against racism and sexism on the belief that all significant differences are environmental in origin. The opponent of, say, racism who takes this line will be unable to avoid conceding that *if* differences in ability do after all prove to have some genetic connection with race, racism would in some way be defensible.

Fortunately there is no need to pin the case for equality to one particular outcome of a scientific investigation. The appropriate response to those who claim to have found evidence of genetically based differences in ability between the races or sexes is not to stick to the belief that the genetic explanation must be wrong, whatever evidence to the contrary may turn up: instead we should make it quite clear that the claim to equality does not depend on intelligence, moral capacity, physical strength, or similar matters of fact. Equality is a moral idea, not an assertion of fact. There is no logicially compelling reason for assuming that a factual difference in ability between two people justifies any difference in the amount of consideration we give to their needs and interests. *The principle of the equality of human beings is not a description of an alleged actual equality among humans: it is a prescription of how we should treat humans.*

Jeremy Bentham, the founder of the reforming utilitarian school of moral philosophy, incorporated the essential basis of moral equality into his system of ethics by means of the formula: "Each to count for one and none for more than one." In other words, the interests of every being affected by an action are to be taken into account and given the same weight as the like interests of any other being. A later utilitarian, Henry Sidgwick, put the point in this way: "The good of any one individual is of no more importance, from the point of view (if I may say so) of the Universe, than the good of any other." More recently the leading figures in contemporary moral philosophy have shown a great deal of agreement in specifying as a fundamental presupposition of their moral theories some similar requirement which operates so as to give everyone's interests equal consideration—although these writers generally cannot agree on how this requirement is best formulated.

It is an implication of this principle of equality that our concern for others and our readiness to consider their interests ought not to depend on what they are like or on what abilities they may possess. Precisely what this concern or consideration requires us to do may vary according to the characteristics of those affected by what we do: concern for the well-being of a child growing up in America would require that we teach him to read; concern for the well-being of a pig may require no more than that we leave him alone with other pigs in a place where there is adequate food and room to run freely. But the basic element—the taking into account of the interests of the being, whatever those interests may be—must, according to the principle of equality, be extended to all beings, black or white, masculine or feminine, human or nonhuman.

Thomas Jefferson, who was responsible for writing the principle of the equality of men into the American Declaration of Independence, saw this point. It led him to oppose slavery even though he was unable to free himself fully from his slaveholding background. He wrote in a letter to the author of a book that emphasized the notable intellectual achievements of Negroes in order to refute the then common view that they had limited intellectual capacities:

> Be assured that no person living wishes more sincerely than I do, to see a complete refutation of the doubts I have myself entertained and expressed on the grade of understanding allotted to them by nature, and to find that they are on a par with ourselves . . . but whatever be their degree of talent it is no measure of their rights. Because Sir Isaac Newton was superior to others in understanding, he was not therefore lord of the property or person of others.

Similarly when in the 1850s the call for women's rights was raised in the United States a remarkable black feminist named Sojourner Truth made the same point in more robust terms at a feminist convention:

> . . . they talk about this thing in the head; what do they call it? ["Intellect," whispered someone near by.] That's it. What's that got to do with women's rights or Negroes' rights? If my cup won't hold but a pint and yours holds a quart, wouldn't you be mean not to let me have my little half-measure full?

It is on this basis that the case against racism and the case against sexism must both ultimately rest; and it is in accordance with this principle that the attitude that we may call "speciesism," by analogy with racism, must also be condemned. Speciesism—the word is not an attractive one, but I can think of no better term—is a prejudice or attitude of bias toward the interests of members of one's own species and against those members of other species. It should be obvious that the fundamental objections to racism and sexism made by Thomas Jefferson and Sojourner Truth apply equally to speciesism. If possessing a higher degree of intelligence does not entitle one human to use another for his own ends, how can it entitle humans to exploit nonhumans for the same purpose?

Many philosophers and other writers have proposed the principle of equal consideration of interests, in some form or other, as a basic moral principle; but not many of them have recognized that this principle applies to members of other species as well as to our own. Jeremy Bentham was one of the few who did realize this. In a forward-looking passage written at a time when black slaves had been freed by the French but in the British dominions were still being treated in the way we now treat animals, Bentham wrote:

> The day *may* come when the rest of the animal creation may acquire those rights which never could have been withholden from them but by the hand of tyranny. The French have already discovered that the blackness of the skin is no reason why a human being should be abandoned without redress to the caprice of a tormentor. It may one day come to be recognized that the number of the legs, the villosity of the skin, or the termination of the *os sacrum* are reasons equally insufficient for abandoning a sensitive being to the same fate. What else is it that should trace the insuperable line? Is it the faculty of reason, or perhaps the faculty of discourse? But a full-grown horse or dog is beyond comparison a more rational, as well as a more conversable animal, than an infant of a day or a week or even a month, old. But suppose they were otherwise, what would it avail? The question is not, Can they *reason*? nor Can they *talk*? but, Can they *suffer*?

In this passage Bentham points to the capacity for suffering as the vital characteristic that gives a being the right to equal consideration. The capacity for suffering—or more strictly, for suffering and/or enjoyment or happiness—is not just another characteristic like the capacity for language or higher mathematics.

Bentham is not saying that those who try to mark "the insuperable line" that determines whether the interests of a being should be considered happen to have chosen the wrong characteristic. By saying that we must consider the interests of all beings with the capacity for suffering or enjoyment Bentham does not arbitrarily exclude from consideration any interests at all—as those who draw the line with reference to the possession of reason or language do. The capacity for suffering and enjoyment is *a prerequisite for having interests at all,* a condition that must be satisfied before we can speak of interests in a meaningful way. It would be nonsense to say that it was not in the interests of a stone to be kicked along the road by a schoolboy. A stone does not have interests because it cannot suffer. Nothing that we can do to it could possibly make any difference to its welfare. A mouse, on the other hand, does have an interest in not being kicked along the road, because it will suffer if it is.

If a being suffers there can be no moral justification for refusing to take that suffering into consideration. No matter what the nature of the being, the principle of equality requires that its suffering be counted equally with the like suffering—in so far as rough comparisons can be made—of any other being. If a being is not capable of suffering, or of experiencing enjoyment or happiness, there is nothing to be taken into account. So the limit of sentience (using the term as a convenient if not strictly accurate shorthand for the capacity to suffer and/or experience enjoyment) is the only defensible boundary of concern for the interests of others. To mark this boundary by some other characteristic like intelligence or rationality would be to mark it in an arbitrary manner. Why not choose some other characteristic, like skin color?

The racist violates the principle of equality by giving greater weight to the interests of members of his own race when there is a clash between their interests and the interests of those of another race. The sexist violates the principle of equality by favoring the interests of his own sex. Similarly the speciesist allows the interests of his own species to override the greater interests of members of other species. The pattern is identical in each case.

Most human beings are speciesists. . . . [o]rdinary human beings, not a few exceptionally cruel or heartless humans, but the overwhelming majority of humans—take an active part in, acquiesce in, and allow their taxes to pay for practices that require the sacrifice of the most important interests of members of other species in order to promote the most trivial interests of our own species. . . .

Animals can feel pain. As we saw earlier, there can be no moral justification for regarding the pain (or pleasure) that animals feel as less important than the same amount of pain (or pleasure) felt by humans. But what exactly does this mean, in practical terms? To prevent misunderstanding I shall spell out what I mean a little more fully.

If I give a horse a hard slap across its rump with my open hand, the horse may start, but it presumably feels little pain. Its skin is thick enough to protect it against a mere slap. If I slap a baby in the same way, however, the baby will cry and presumably does feel pain, for its skin is more sensitive. So it is worse to slap a baby than a horse, if both slaps are administered with equal force. But there must be some kind of blow—I don't know exactly what it would be, but perhaps a blow with a heavy stick—that would cause the horse as much pain as we cause a baby by slapping it with our hand. That is what I mean by "the same amount of pain" and if we consider it wrong to inflict that much pain on a baby for no good reason then we must, unless we are speciesists, consider it equally wrong to inflict the same amount of pain on a horse for no good reason.

There are other differences between humans and animals that cause other complications. Normal adult human beings have mental capacities which will, in certain circumstances, lead them to suffer more than animals would in the same circumstances. If, for instance, we decided to perform extremely painful or lethal scientific experiments on normal adult humans, kidnaped at random from public parks for this purpose, every adult who entered a park would become fearful that he would be kidnaped. The resultant terror would be a form of suffering additional to the pain of the experiment. The same experiments performed on nonhuman animals would cause less suffering since the animals would not have the anticipatory dread of being kidnaped and experimented upon. This does not mean, of course, that it would be *right* to perform the experiment on animals, but only that there is a reason, which is *not* speciesist, for preferring to use animals rather than normal adult humans, if the experiment is to be done at all. It should be noted, however, that this same argument gives us a reason for preferring to use human infants—orphans perhaps—or retarded humans for experiments, rather than adults, since infants and retarded humans would also have no idea of what was going to happen to them. So far as this argument is concerned nonhuman animals and infants and retarded humans are in the same category; and if we use this argument to justify experiments on nonhuman animals we have to ask ourselves whether we are also prepared to allow experiments on human infants and retarded adults; and if we make a distinction between animals and these humans, on what basis can we do it, other than a bare-faced—and morally indefensible—preference for members of our own species?

There are many areas in which the superior mental powers of normal adult humans make a difference: anticipation, more detailed memory, greater knowledge of what is happening, and so on. Yet these differences do not all point to greater suffering on the part of the normal human being. Sometimes an animal may suffer more because of his more limited understanding. If, for instance, we are taking prisoners in wartime we can explain to them that while they must submit to capture, search, and confinement they will not otherwise be harmed and will be set free at the conclusion of hostilities. If we capture a wild animal, however, we cannot explain that we are not threatening its life. A wild animal cannot distinguish an attempt to overpower and confine from an attempt to kill; the one causes as much terror as the other.

It may be objected that comparisons of the sufferings of different species are impossible to make, and that for this reason when the interests of animals and humans clash the principle of equality gives no guidance. It is probably true that comparisons of suffering between members of different species cannot be made precisely, but precision is not essential. Even if we were to prevent the infliction of suffering on animals only when it is quite certain that the interests of humans will not be affected to anything like the extent that animals are affected, we would be forced to make radical changes in our treatment of animals that would involve our diet, the farming methods we use, experimental procedures in many fields of science, our approach to wildlife and to hunting, trapping and the wearing of furs, and areas of entertainment like circuses, rodeos, and zoos. As a result, a vast amount of suffering would be avoided.

So far I have said a lot about the infliction of suffering on animals, but nothing about killing them. This omission has been deliberate. The application of the principle of equality to the infliction of suffering is, in theory at least, fairly straightforward. Pain and suffering are bad and should be prevented or minimized, irrespective of the race, sex, or species of the being that suffers. How bad a pain is depends on how intense it is and how long it lasts, but pains of the same intensity and duration are equally bad, whether felt by humans or animals. . . .

The belief that human life, and only human life, is sacrosanct is a form of speciesism. To see this, consider the following example.

Assume that, as sometimes happens, an infant has been born with massive and irreparable brain damage. The damage is so severe that the infant can never be any more than a "human vegetable," unable to talk, recognize other people, act independently of others, or develop a sense of self-awareness. The parents of the infant, realizing that they cannot hope for any improvement in their child's condition and being in any case unwilling to spend, or ask the state to spend, the thousands of dollars that would be needed annually for proper care of the infant, ask the doctor to kill the infant painlessly.

Should the doctor do what the parents ask? Legally, he should not, and in this respect the law reflects the sanctity of life view. The life of every human being is sacred. Yet people who would say this about the infant do not object to the killing of non-human animals. How can they justify their different judgments? Adult chimpanzees, dogs, pigs, and many other species far surpass the brain-damaged infant in their ability to relate to others, act independently, be self-aware, and any other capacity that could reasonably be said to give value to life. With the most intensive care possible, there are retarded infants who can never achieve the intelligence level of a dog. Nor can we appeal to the concern of the infant's parents, since they themselves, in this imaginary example (and in some actual cases) do not want the infant kept alive.

The only thing that distinguishes the infant from the animal, in the eyes of those who claim it has a "right to life," is that it is, biologically, a member of the species *Homo sapiens*, whereas chimpanzees, dogs, and pigs are not. But to use *this* difference as the basis for granting a right to life to the infant and not to the other animals is, of course, pure speciesism. It is exactly the kind of arbitrary difference that the most crude and overt kind of racist uses in attempting to justify racial discrimination.

This does not mean that to avoid speciesism we must hold that it is as wrong to kill a dog as it is to kill a normal human being. The only position that is irredeemably speciesist is the one that tries to make the boundary of the right to life run exactly parallel to the boundary of our own species. Those who hold the sanctity of life view do this, because while distinguishing sharply between humans and other animals they allow no distinctions to be made within our own species, objecting to the killing of the severely retarded and the hopelessly senile as strongly as they object to the killing of normal adults.

To avoid speciesism we must allow that beings which are similar in all relevant respects have a similar right to life—and mere membership in our own biological species cannot be a morally relevant criterion for this right. Within these limits we could still hold that, for instance, it is worse to kill a normal adult human, with a capacity for self-awareness, and the ability to plan for the future and have meaningful relations with others, than it is to kill a mouse, which presumably does not share all of these characteristics; or we might appeal to the close family and other personal ties which humans have but mice do not have to the same degree; or we might think that it is the consequences for other humans, who will be put in fear of their own lives, that makes the crucial difference; or we might think it is some combination of these factors, or other factors altogether.

Whatever criteria we choose, however, we will have to admit that they do not follow precisely the boundary of our own species. We may legitimately hold that there are some features of certain beings which make their lives more valuable than those of other beings; but there will surely be some non-human animals whose lives, by any standards, are more valuable than the lives of some humans. A chimpanzee, dog, or pig, for instance, will have a higher degree of self-awareness and a greater capacity for meaningful relations with others than a severely retarded infant or someone in a state of advanced senility. So if we base the right to life on these characteristics we must grant these animals a right to life as good as, or better than, such retarded or senile humans.

Now this argument cuts both ways. It could be taken as showing that chimpanzees, dogs, and pigs, along with some other species, have a right to life and we commit a grave moral offense whenever we kill them, even when they are old and suffering and our intention is to put them out of their misery. Alternatively, one could take the argument as showing that the severely retarded and hopelessly senile have no right to life and may be killed for quite trivial reasons, as we now kill animals.

Since the focus [here] is on ethical questions concerning animals and not on the morality of euthanasia I shall not attempt to settle this issue finally. I think it is reasonably clear, though, that while both of the positions just described avoid speciesism, neither is entirely satisfactory. What we need is some middle position which would avoid speciesism but would not make the lives of the retarded and senile as cheap as the lives of pigs and dogs now are, nor make the lives of pigs and dogs so sacrosanct that we think it wrong to put them out of hopeless misery. What we must do is bring nonhuman animals within our sphere of moral concern and cease to treat their lives as expendable for whatever trivial purposes we may have. At the same time, once we realize that the fact that a being is a member of our own species is not in itself enough to make it always wrong to kill that being, we may come to reconsider our policy of preserving human lives at all costs, even when there is no prospect of a meaningful life or of existence without terrible pain.

I conclude, then, that a rejection of speciesism does not imply that all lives are of equal worth. While self-awareness, intelligence, the capacity for meaningful relations with others, and so on are not relevant to the question of inflicting pain—since pain is pain, whatever other capacities, beyond the capacity to feel pain, the being may have—these capacities may be relevant to the question of taking life. It is not arbitrary to hold that the life of a self-aware being, capable of abstract thought, of planning for the future, of complex acts of communication, and so on, is more valuable than the life of a being without these capacities. To see the difference between the issues of inflicting pain and taking life, consider how we would choose within our own species. If we had to choose to save the life of a normal human or a mentally defective human, we would probably choose to save the life of the normal human; but if we had to choose between preventing pain in the normal human or the mental defective—imagine that both have received painful but superficial injuries, and we only have enough painkiller for one of them—it is not nearly so clear how we ought to choose. The same is true when we consider other species. The evil of pain is, in itself, unaffected by the other characteristics of the being that feels the pain; the value of life is affected by these other characteristics.

Normally this will mean that if we have to choose between the life of a human being and the life of another animal we would choose to save the life of the human; but there may be special cases in which the reverse holds true, because the human being in question does not have the capacities of a normal human being. So this view is not speciesist, although it may appear to be at first glance. The preference, in normal cases, for saving a human life over the life of an animal when a choice *has* to be made is a preference based on the characteristics that normal humans have, and not on the mere fact that they are members of our own species. This is why when we consider members of our own species who lack the characteristics of normal humans we can no longer say that their lives are always to be preferred to those of other animals. . . .

QUESTIONS FOR REFLECTION

1. Why, according to Singer, are racism and sexism wrong?

2. Singer contends that speciesism is analogous to racism and sexism, and wrong for the same reasons. What is speciesism? How is it similar to racism and sexism? Are there important differences?

3. Singer credits Bentham with seeing "the capacity for suffering as the vital characteristic that gives a being the right to equal consideration." What does this mean? Suppose that a person for some reason lacked the ability to suffer. Would he or she then deserve no moral consideration?

4. Is killing animals wrong in the same way and to the same degree that killing humans is wrong, according to Singer? If not, why not?

5. Does Singer's position support all fourteen propositions of the Universal Declaration of the Rights of Animals?

TOM REGAN

The Case for Animal Rights

Tom Regan is Professor of Philosophy at North Carolina State University. (Source: Reprinted from "The Case for Animal Rights," in In Defense of Animals, *ed. Peter Singer [New York: Perennial Library, 1986; originally published by Blackwell, 1985]. Reprinted by permission of Blackwell Publishers.)*

I regard myself as an advocate of animal rights—as a part of the animal rights movement. That movement, as I conceive it, is committed to a number of goals, including:

the total abolition of the use of animals in science,

the total dissolution of commercial animal agriculture;

the total elimination of commercial and sport hunting and trapping.

There are, I know, people who profess to believe in animal rights but do not avow these goals. Factory farming, they say, is wrong—it violates animals' rights—but traditional animal agriculture is all right. Toxicity tests of cosmetics on animals violates their rights, but important medical research—cancer research, for example—does not. The clubbing of baby seals is abhorrent, but not the harvesting of adult seals. I used to think I understood this reasoning. Not any more. You don't change unjust institutions by tidying them up.

What's wrong—fundamentally wrong—with the way animals are treated isn't the details that vary from case to case. It's the whole system. The forlornness of the veal calf is pathetic, heartwrenching; the pulsing pain of the chimp with electrodes planted deep in her brain is repulsive; the slow, tortuous death of the raccoon caught in the leg-hold trap is agonizing. But what is wrong isn't the pain, isn't the suffering, isn't the deprivation. These compound what's wrong. Sometimes—often—they make it much, much worse. But they are not the fundamental wrong.

The fundamental wrong is the system that allows us to view animals as *our resources,* here for *us*—to be eaten, or surgically manipulated, or exploited for sport or money. Once we accept this view of animals—as our resources—the rest is as predictable as it is regrettable. Why worry about their loneliness, their pain, their death? Since animals exist for us, to benefit us in one way or another, what harms them really doesn't matter—or matters only if it starts to bother us, makes us feel a trifle uneasy when we eat our veal escalope, for example. So, yes, let us get veal calves out of solitary confinement, give them more space, a little straw, a few companions. But let us keep our veal escalope.

But a little straw, more space and a few companions won't eliminate—won't even touch—the basic wrong that attaches to our viewing and treating these animals as our resources. A veal calf killed to be eaten after living in close confinement is viewed and treated in this way: but so, too, is another who is raised (as they say) "more humanely." To right the wrong of our treatment of farm animals requires more than making rearing methods "more humane"; it requires the total dissolution of commercial animal agriculture. . . .

How to proceed? We begin by asking how the moral status of animals has been understood by thinkers who deny that animals have rights. Then we test the mettle of their ideas by seeing how well they stand up under the heat of fair criticism. If we start our thinking in this way, we soon find that some people believe that we have no duties directly to animals, that we owe nothing to them, that we can do nothing that wrongs them. Rather, we can do wrong acts that involve animals, and so we have duties regarding them, though none to them. Such views may be called indirect duty views. By way of illustration: suppose your neighbour kicks your dog. Then your neighbour has done something wrong. But not to your dog. The wrong that has been done is a wrong to you. After all, it is wrong to upset people, and your neighbour's kicking your dog upsets you. So you are the one who is wronged, not your dog. Or again: by kicking your dog your neighbour damages your property. And since it is wrong to damage another person's property, your neighbour has done something wrong—to you, of course, not to your dog. Your neighbour no more wrongs your dog than your car would be wronged if the windshield were smashed. Your neighbour's duties involving your dog are indirect duties to you. More generally, all of our duties regarding animals are indirect duties to one another—to humanity.

How could someone try to justify such a view? Someone might say that your dog doesn't feel anything and so isn't hurt by your neighbour's kick, doesn't care about the pain since none is felt, is as unaware of anything as is your windshield. Someone might say this, but no rational person will, since, among other considerations, such a view will commit anyone who holds it to the position that no human being feels pain either—that human beings don't care about what happens to them. A second possibility is that though both humans and your dog are hurt when kicked, it is only human pain that matters. But, again, no rational person can believe this. Pain is pain wherever it occurs. If your neighbour's causing you pain is wrong because of the pain that is caused, we cannot rationally ignore or dismiss the moral relevance of the pain that your dog feels.

Philosophers who hold indirect duty views—and many still do—have come to understand that they must avoid the two defects just noted: that is, both the view that animals don't feel anything as well as the idea that only human pain can be morally relevant. Among such thinkers the sort of view now favoured is one or other form of what is called *contractarianism*.

Here, very crudely, is the root idea: morality consists of a set of rules that individuals voluntarily agree to abide by, as we do when we sign a contract (hence the name contractarianism). Those who understand and accept the terms of the contract are covered directly; they have rights created and recognized by, and protected in, the contract. And these contractors can also have protection spelled out for others who, though they lack the ability to understand morality and so cannot sign the contract themselves, are loved or cherished by those who can. Thus young children, for example, are unable to sign contracts and lack rights. But they are protected by the contract none the less because of the sentimental interests of others, most notably their parents. So we have, then, duties involving these children, duties regarding them, but no duties to them. Our duties in their case are indirect duties to other human beings, usually their parents.

As for animals, since they cannot understand contracts, they obviously cannot sign; and since they cannot sign, they have no rights. Like children, however, some animals are the objects of the sentimental interest of others. You, for example, love your dog or cat. So those animals that enough people care about (companion animals, whales, baby seals, the American bald eagle), though they lack rights themselves, will be protected because of the sentimental interests of people. I have, then, according to contractarianism, no duty directly to your dog or any other animal, not even the duty not to cause them pain or suffering; my duty not to hurt them is a duty I have to those people who care about what happens to them. As for other animals, where no or little sentimental interest is present—in the case of farm animals, for example, or laboratory rats—what duties we have grow weaker and weaker, perhaps to vanishing point. The pain and death they endure, though real, are not wrong if no one cares about them.

When it comes to the moral status of animals, contractarianism could be a hard view to refute if it were an adequate theoretical approach to the moral status of human beings. It is not adequate in this latter respect, however, which makes the question of its adequacy in the former case, regarding animals, utterly moot. For consider: morality, according to the (crude) contractarian position before us, consists of rules that people agree to abide by. What people? Well, enough to make a difference—enough, that is, *collectively* to have the power to enforce the rules that are drawn up in the contract. That is very well and good for the signatories but not so good for anyone who is not asked to sign. And there is nothing in contractarianism of the sort we are discussing that guarantees or requires that everyone will have a chance to participate equally in framing the rules of morality. The result is that this approach to ethics could sanction the most blatant forms of social, economic, moral and political injustice, ranging from a repressive caste system to systematic racial or sexual discrimination. Might, according to this theory, does make right. Let those who are the victims of injustice suffer as they will. It matters not so long as no one else—no contractor, or too few of them—cares about it. Such a theory takes one's moral breath away . . . as if, for example, there would be nothing wrong with apartheid in South Africa if few white South Africans were upset by it. A theory with so little to recommend it at the level of the ethics of our treatment of our fellow humans cannot have anything more to recommend it when it comes to the ethics of how we treat our fellow animals.

The version of contractarianism just examined is, as I have noted, a crude variety, and in fairness to those of a contractarian persuasion it must be noted that much more refined, subtle and ingenious varieties are possible. For example, John Rawls, in his *A Theory of Justice*, sets forth a version of contractarianism that forces contractors to ignore the accidental features of being a human being—for example, whether one is white or black, male or female, a genius or of modest intellect. Only by ignoring such features, Rawls believes, can we ensure that the principles of justice that contractors would agree upon are not based on bias or prejudice. Despite the improvement a view such as Rawls's represents over the cruder forms of contractarianism, it remains deficient: it systematically denies that we have direct duties to those human beings who do not have a sense of justice—young children, for instance, and many mentally retarded humans. And yet it seems reasonably certain that, were we to torture a young child or a retarded elder, we would be doing something that wronged him or her, not something that would be wrong if (and only if) other humans with a sense of justice were upset. And since this is true in the case

of these humans, we cannot rationally deny the same in the case of animals.

Indirect duty views, then, including the best among them, fail to command our rational assent. Whatever ethical theory we should accept rationally, therefore, it must at least recognize that we have some duties directly to animals, just as we have some duties directly to each other. . . .

What to do? Where to begin anew? The place to begin, I think, is with the utilitarian's view of the value of the individual—or, rather, lack of value. In its place, suppose we consider that you and I, for example, do have value as individuals—what we'll call *inherent value*. To say we have such value is to say that we are something more than, something different from, mere receptacles. Moreover, to ensure that we do not pave the way for such injustices as slavery or sexual discrimination, we must believe that all who have inherent value have it equally, regardless of their sex, race, religion, birthplace and so on. Similarly to be discarded as irrelevant are one's talents or skills, intelligence and wealth, personality or pathology, whether one is loved and admired or despised and loathed. The genius and the retarded child, the prince and the pauper, the brain surgeon and the fruit vendor, Mother Teresa and the most unscrupulous used-car salesman—all have inherent value, all possess it equally, and all have an equal right to be treated with respect, to be treated in ways that do not reduce them to the status of things, as if they existed as resources for others. My value as an individual is independent of my usefulness to you. Yours is not dependent on your usefulness to me. For either of us to treat the other in ways that fail to show respect for the other's independent value is to act immorally, to violate the individual's rights.

Some of the rational virtues of this view—what I call the rights view—should be evident. Unlike (crude) contractarianism, for example, the rights view *in principle* denies the moral tolerability of any and all forms of racial, sexual and social discrimination; and unlike utilitarianism, this view *in principle* denies that we can justify good results by using evil means that violate an individual's rights—denies, for example, that it could be moral to kill my Aunt Bea to harvest beneficial consequences for others. That would be to sanction the disrespectful treatment of the individual in the name of the social good, something the rights view will not—categorically will not—ever allow.

The rights view, I believe, is rationally the most satisfactory moral theory. It surpasses all other theories in the degree to which it illuminates and explains the foundation of our duties to one another—the domain of human morality. On this score it has the best reasons, the best arguments, on its side. Of course, if it were possible to show that only human beings are included within its scope, then a person like myself, who believes in animal rights, would be obliged to look elsewhere.

But attempts to limit its scope to humans only can be shown to be rationally defective. Animals, it is true, lack many of the abilities humans possess. They can't read, do higher mathematics, build a bookcase or make *baba ghanoush*. Neither can many human beings, however, and yet we don't (and shouldn't) say that they (these humans) therefore have less inherent value, less of a right to be treated with respect, than do others. It is the *similarities* between those human beings who most clearly, most noncontroversially have such value (the people reading this, for example), not our differences, that matter most. And the really crucial, the basic similarity is simply this: we are each of us the experiencing subject of a life, a conscious creature having an individual welfare that has importance to us whatever our usefulness to others. We want and prefer things, believe and feel things, recall and expect things. And all these dimensions of our life, including our pleasure and pain, our enjoyment and suffering, our satisfaction and frustration, our continued existence or our untimely death—all make a difference to the quality of our life as lived, as experienced, by us as individuals. As the same is true of those animals that concern us: (the ones that are eaten and trapped, for example), they too must be viewed as the experiencing subjects of a life, with inherent value of their own.

Some there are who resist the idea that animals have inherent value. "Only humans have such value," they profess. How might this narrow view be defended? Shall we say that only humans have the requisite intelligence, or autonomy, or reason? But there are many, many humans who fail to meet these standards and yet are reasonably viewed as having value above and beyond their usefulness to others. Shall we claim that only humans belong to the right species, the species *Homo sapiens*? But this is blatant speciesism. Will it be said, then, that all—and only—humans have immortal souls? Then our opponents have their work cut out for them. I am myself not ill-disposed to the proposition that there are immortal souls. Personally, I profoundly hope I have one. But I would not want to rest my position on a controversial ethical issue on the even more controversial question about who or what has an immortal soul. That is to dig one's hole deeper, not to climb out. Rationally, it is better to resolve moral issues without making more controversial assumptions than are needed. The question of who has inherent value is such a question, one that is resolved more rationally without the introduction of the idea of immortal souls than by its use.

Well, perhaps some will say that animals have some inherent value, only less than we have. Once again, however, attempts to defend this view can be shown to lack rational justification. What could be the basis of our having more inherent value than animals? Their lack of reason, or autonomy, or intellect? Only if we are willing to make the same judgment in the case of humans who are similarly deficient. But it is not true that such humans—the retarded child, for example, or the mentally deranged—have less inherent value than you or I. Neither, then, can we rationally sustain the view that animals like them in being the experiencing subjects of a life have less inherent value. *All* who have inherent value have it *equally*, whether they be human animals or not.

Inherent value, then, belongs equally to those who are the experiencing subjects of a life. Whether it belongs to others—to rocks and rivers, trees and glaciers, for example—we do not know and may never know. But neither do we need to know, if we are to make the case for animal rights. We do not need to know, for example, how many people are eligible to vote in the next presidential election before we can know whether I am. Similarly, we do not need to know how many individuals have inherent value before we can know that some do. When it comes to the case for animal rights, then, what we need to know is whether the animals that, in our culture, are routinely eaten, hunted and used in our laboratories, for example, are like us in being subjects of a life. And we do know this. We do know that many —literally, billions and billions—of these animals are the subjects of a life in the sense explained and so have inherent value if we do. And since, in order to arrive at the best theory of our duties to one another, we must recognize our equal inherent value as individuals, reason—not sentiment, not emotion—reason compels us to recognize the equal inherent value of these animals and, with this, their equal right to be treated with respect. . . .

. . . I can now say why [the rights view's] implications for farming and science, among other fields, are both clear and uncompromising. In the case of the use of animals in science, the rights view is categorically abolitionist. Lab animals are not our tasters; we are not their kings. Because these animals are treated routinely, systematically as if their value were reducible to their usefulness to others, they are routinely, systematically treated with a lack of respect, and thus are their rights routinely, systematically violated. This is just as true when they are used in trivial, duplicative, unnecessary or unwise research as it is when they are used in studies that hold out real promise of human benefits. We can't justify harming or killing a human being (my Aunt Bea, for example) just for these sorts of reasons. Neither can we do so even in the case of so lowly a creature as a laboratory rat. It is not just refinement or reduction that is called for, not just larger, cleaner cages, not just more generous use of anaesthetic or the elimination of multiple surgery, not just tidying up the system. It is complete replacement. The best we can do when it comes to using animals in science is—not to use them. That is where our duty lies, according to the rights view.

As for commercial animal agriculture, the rights view takes a similar abolitionist position. The fundamental moral wrong here is not that animals are kept in stressful close confinement or in isolation, or that their pain and suffering, their needs and preferences are ignored or discounted. All these *are* wrong, of course, but they are not the fundamental wrong. They are symptoms and effects of the deeper, systematic wrong that allows these animals to be viewed and treated as lacking independent value, as resources for us—as, indeed, a renewable resource. Giving farm animals more space, more natural environments, more companions does not right the fundamental wrong, any more than giving lab animals more anaesthesia or bigger, cleaner cages would right the fundamental wrong in their case. Nothing less than the total dissolution of commercial animal agriculture will do this, just as, for similar reasons I won't develop at length here, morality requires nothing less than the total elimination of hunting and trapping for commercial and sporting ends. The rights view's implications, then, as I have said, are clear and uncompromising. . . .

QUESTIONS FOR REFLECTION

1. Do you agree with Regan that a position rejecting, for example, factory farming and cosmetics research on animals, but not animal husbandry or medical experimentation, is incoherent? Why or why not?

2. What is an indirect-duty view? Why does Regan reject it?

3. Regan claims that Rawls cannot explain why it is wrong to harm young children or a retarded elderly person. Is this true?

4. Why does Regan reject utilitarianism? How might Mill respond?

5. What is inherent value? How does Regan decide who or what has inherent value? How does he defend his assertion that animals have it?

6. Does Regan's position support all fourteen propositions of the Universal Declaration of the Rights of Animals?

CARL COHEN

The Case for the Use of Animals
in Biomedical Research

Carl Cohen is a professor at the University of Michigan Medical School, Ann Arbor. (Source: "The Case for the Use of Animals in Biomedical Research," The New England Journal of Medicine *314 [1986], 865–869. Notes have been omitted. Copyright © 1986, Massachusetts Medical Society. All rights reserved. Reprinted by permission of* The New England Journal of Medicine.)

Using animals as research subjects in medical investigations is widely condemned on two grounds: first, because it wrongly violates the rights of animals, and second, because it wrongly imposes on sentient creatures much avoidable suffering. Neither of these arguments is sound. The first relies on a mistaken understanding of rights; the second relies on a mistaken calculation of consequences. Both deserve definitive dismissal.

Why Animals Have No Rights

A right, properly understood, is a claim, or potential claim, that one party may exercise against another. The target against whom such a claim may be registered can be a single person, a group, a community, or (perhaps) all humankind. The content of rights claims also varies greatly: repayment of loans, nondiscrimination by employers, noninterference by the state, and so on. To comprehend any genuine right fully, therefore, we must know who holds the right, against whom it is held, and to what it is a right.

Alternative sources of rights add complexity. Some rights are grounded in constitution and law (e.g., the right of an accused to trial by jury); some rights are moral but give no legal claims (e.g., my right to your keeping the promise you gave me); and some rights (e.g., against theft or assault) are rooted both in morals and in law.

The differing targets, contents, and sources of rights, and their inevitable conflict, together weave a tangled web. Notwithstanding all such complications, this much is clear about rights in general: they are in every case claims, or potential claims, within a community of moral agents. Rights arise, and can be intelligibly defended, only among beings who actually do, or can, make moral claims against one another. Whatever else rights may be, therefore, they are necessarily human; their possessors are persons, human beings.

The attributes of human beings from which this moral capability arises have been described variously by philosophers, both ancient and modern: the inner consciousness of a free will (Saint Augustine); the grasp, by human reason, of the binding character of moral law (Saint Thomas); the self-conscious participation of human beings in an objective ethical order (Hegel); human membership in an organic moral community (Bradley); the development of the human self through the consciousness of other moral selves (Mead); and the underivative, intuitive cognition of the rightness of an action (Prichard). Most influential has been Immanuel Kant's emphasis on the universal human possession of a uniquely moral will and the autonomy its use entails. Humans confront choices that are purely moral; humans—but certainly not dogs or mice—lay down moral laws, for others and for themselves. Human beings are self-legislative, morally *autonomous.*

Animals (that is, nonhuman animals, the ordinary sense of that word) lack this capacity for free moral judgment. They are not beings of a kind capable of exercising or responding to moral claims. Animals therefore have no rights, and they can have none. This is the core of the argument about the alleged rights of animals. The holders of rights must have the capacity to comprehend rules of duty, governing all including themselves. In applying such rules, the holders of rights must recognize possible conflicts between what is in their own interest and what is just. Only in a community of beings capable of self-restricting moral judgments can the concept of a right be correctly invoked.

Humans have such moral capacities. They are in this sense self-legislative, are members of communities governed by moral rules, and do possess rights. Animals do not have such moral capacities. They are not morally self-legislative, cannot possibly be members of a truly moral community, and therefore cannot possess rights. In conducting research on animal subjects, therefore, we do not violate their rights, because they have none to violate.

To animate life, even in its simplest forms, we give a certain natural reverence. But the possession of rights presupposes a moral status not attained by the vast majority of living things. We must not infer, therefore, that a live being has, simply in being alive, a "right" to its life. The assertion that all animals, only because they are alive and have interests, also possess the "right to life" is an abuse of that phrase, and wholly without warrant.

It does not follow from this, however, that we are morally free to do anything we please to animals. Certainly not. In our dealings with animals, as in our dealings with other human beings, we have obligations that do not arise from claims against us based on rights. Rights entail obligations, but many of the things one ought to do are in no way tied to another's entitlement. Rights and obligations are not reciprocals of one another, and it is a serious mistake to suppose that they are.

Illustrations are helpful. Obligations may arise from internal commitments made: physicians have obligations to their patients not grounded merely in their patients' rights. Teachers have such obligations to their students, shepherds to their dogs, and cowboys to their horses. Obligations may arise from differences of status: adults owe special care when playing with young children, and children owe special care when playing with young pets. Obligations may arise from special relationships: the payment of my son's college tuition is something to which he may have no right, although it may be my obligation to bear the burden if I reasonably can; my dog has no right to daily exercise and veterinary care, but I do have the obligation to provide these things for her. Obligations may arise from particular acts or circumstances: one may be obliged to another for a special kindness done, or obliged to put an animal out of its misery in view of its condition—although neither the human benefactor nor the dying animal may have had a claim of right.

Plainly, the grounds of our obligations to humans and to animals are manifold and cannot be formulated simply. Some hold that there is a general obligation to do no gratuitous harm to sentient creatures (the principle of nonmaleficence); some hold that there is a general obligation to do good to sentient creatures when that is reasonably within one's power (the principle of beneficence). In our dealings with animals, few will deny that we are at least obliged to act humanely—that is, to treat them with the decency and concern that we owe, as sensitive human beings, to other sentient creatures. To treat animals humanely, however, is not to treat them as humans or as the holders of rights.

A common objection, which deserves a response, may be paraphrased as follows:

> If having rights requires being able to make moral claims, to grasp and apply moral laws, then many humans—the brain-damaged, the comatose, the senile—who plainly lack those capacities must be without rights. But that is absurd. This proves [the critic concludes] that rights do not depend on the presence of moral capacities.

This objection fails; it mistakenly treats an essential feature of humanity as though it were a screen for sorting humans. The capacity for moral judgment that distinguishes humans from animals is not a test to be administered to human beings one by one. Persons who are unable, because of some disability, to perform the full moral functions natural to human beings are certainly not for that reason ejected from the moral community. The issue is one of kind. Humans are of such a kind that they may be the subject of experiments only with their voluntary consent. The choices they make freely must be respected. Animals are of such a kind that it is impossible for them, in principle, to give or withhold voluntary consent or to make a moral choice. What humans retain when disabled, animals have never had.

A second objection, also often made, may be paraphrased as follows:

> Capacities will not succeed in distinguishing humans from the other animals. Animals also reason; animals also communicate with one another; animals also care passionately for their young; animals also exhibit desires and preferences. Features of moral relevance—rationality, interdependence, and love—are not exhibited uniquely by human beings. Therefore [this critic concludes], there can be no solid moral distinction between humans and other animals.

This criticism misses the central point. It is not the ability to communicate or to reason, or dependence on one another, or care for the young, or the exhibition of preference, or any such behavior that marks the critical divide. Analogies between human families and those of monkeys, or between human communities and those of wolves, and the like, are entirely beside the point. Patterns of conduct are not at issue. Animals do indeed exhibit remarkable behavior at times. Conditioning, fear, instinct, and intelligence all contribute to species survival. Membership in a community of moral agents nevertheless remains impossible for them. Actors subject to moral judgment must be capable of grasping the generality of an ethical premise in a practical syllogism. Humans act immorally often enough, but only they—never wolves or monkeys—can discern, by applying some moral rule to the facts of a case, that a given act ought or ought not to be performed. The moral restraints imposed by humans on themselves are thus highly abstract and are often in conflict with the self-interest of the agent. Communal behavior among animals, even when most intelligent and most endearing, does not approach autonomous morality in this fundamental sense.

Genuinely moral acts have an internal as well as an external dimension. Thus, in law, an act can be criminal only when the guilty deed, the *actus reus,* is done with a guilty mind, *mens rea.* No animal can ever commit a crime; bringing animals to criminal trial is the mark of primitive ignorance. The claims of moral right are similarly inapplicable to them. Does a lion have a right to eat a baby zebra? Does a baby zebra have a right not to be eaten? Such questions, mistakenly invoking the concept of right where it does not belong, do not make good sense. Those who condemn biomedical research because it violates "animal rights" commit the same blunder.

In Defense of "Speciesism"

Abandoning reliance on animal rights, some critics resort instead to animal sentience—their feelings of pain and distress. We ought to desist from the imposition of pain insofar as we can. Since all or nearly all experimentation on animals does impose pain and could be readily forgone, say these critics, it should be stopped. The ends sought may be worthy, but those ends do not justify imposing agonies on humans, and by animals the agonies are felt no less. The laboratory use of animals (these critics conclude) must therefore be ended—or at least very sharply curtailed.

Argument of this variety is essentially utilitarian, often expressly so; it is based on the calculation of the net product, in pains and pleasures, resulting from experiments on animals. Jeremy Bentham, comparing horses and dogs with other sentient creatures, is thus commonly quoted: "The question is not, Can they reason? nor Can they talk? but, Can they suffer?"

Animals certainly can suffer and surely ought not to be made to suffer needlessly. But in inferring, from these uncontroversial premises, that biomedical research causing animal distress is largely (or wholly) wrong, the critic commits two serious errors.

The first error is the assumption, often explicitly defended, that all sentient animals have equal moral standing. Between a dog and a human being, according to this view, there is no moral difference; hence the pains suffered by dogs must be weighed no differently from the pains suffered by humans. To deny such equality, according to this critic, is to give unjust preference to one species over another; it is "speciesism." The most influential statement of this moral equality of species was made by Peter Singer:

> The racist violates the principle of equality by giving greater weight to the interests of members of his own race when there is a clash between their interests and the interests of those of another race. The sexist violates the principle of equality by favoring the interests of his own sex. Similarly the speciesist allows the interests of his own species to override the greater interests of members of other species. The pattern is identical in each case.

This argument is worse than unsound; it is atrocious. It draws an offensive moral conclusion from a deliberately devised verbal parallelism that is utterly specious. Racism has no rational ground whatever. Differing degrees of respect or concern for humans for no other reason than that they are members of different races is an injustice totally without foundation in the nature of the races themselves. Racists, even if acting on the basis of mistaken factual beliefs, do grave moral wrong precisely because there is no morally relevant distinction among the races. The supposition of such differences has led to outright horror. The same is true of the sexes, neither sex being entitled by right to greater respect or concern than the other. No dispute here.

Between species of animate life, however—between (for example) humans on the one hand and cats or rats on the other—the morally relevant differences are enormous, and almost universally appreciated. Humans engage in moral reflection; humans are morally autonomous; humans are members of moral communities, recognizing just claims against their own interest. Human beings do have rights; theirs is a moral status very different from that of cats or rats.

I am a speciesist. Speciesism is not merely plausible; it is essential for right conduct, because those who will not make the morally relevant distinctions among species are almost certain, in consequence, to misapprehend their true obligations. The analogy between speciesism and racism is insidious. Every sensitive moral judgment requires that the differing natures of the beings to whom obligations are owed be considered. If all forms of animate life—or vertebrate animal life?—must be treated equally, and if therefore in evaluating a research program the pains of a rodent count equally with the pains of a human, we are forced to conclude (1) that neither humans nor rodents possess rights, or (2) that rodents possess all the rights that humans possess. Both alternatives are absurd. Yet one or the other must be swallowed if the moral equality of all species is to be defended.

Humans owe to other humans a degree of moral regard that cannot be owed to animals. Some humans take on the obligation to support and heal others, both humans and animals, as a principal duty in their lives; the fulfillment of that duty may require the sacrifice of many animals. If biomedical investigators abandon the effective pursuit of their professional objectives because they are convinced that they may not do to animals what the service of humans requires, they will fail, objectively, to do their duty. Refusing to recognize the moral differences among species is a sure path to calamity. (The largest animal rights group in the country is People for the Ethical Treatment of Animals; its co-director, Ingrid Newkirk, calls research using animal subjects "fascism" and "supremacism." "Animal liberationists do not separate out the human animal," she says, "so there is no rational basis for saying that a human being has special rights. A rat is a pig is a dog is a boy. They're all mammals.")

Those who claim to base their objection to the use of animals in biomedical research on their reckoning of the net pleasures and pains produced make a second error, equally grave. Even if it were true—as it is surely not—that the pains of all animate beings must be counted equally, a cogent utilitarian calculation requires that we weigh all the consequences of the use, and of the nonuse, of animals in laboratory research. Critics relying (however mistakenly) on animal rights may claim to ignore the beneficial results of such research, rights being trump cards to which interest and advantage must give way. But an argument that is explicitly framed in terms of interest and benefit for all over the long run must attend also to the disadvantageous consequences of not using animals in research, and to all the achievements attained and attainable only through their use.

The sum of the benefits of their use is utterly beyond quantification. The elimination of horrible disease, the increase of longevity, the avoidance of great pain, the saving of lives, and the improvement of the quality of lives (for humans and for animals) achieved through research using animals is so incalculably great that the argument of these critics, systematically pursued, establishes not their conclusion but its reverse: to refrain from using animals in biomedical research is, on utilitarian grounds, morally wrong.

When balancing the pleasures and pains resulting from the use of animals in research, we must not fail to place on the scales the terrible pains that would have resulted, would be suffered now, and would long continue had animals not been used. Every disease eliminated, every vaccine developed, every method of pain relief devised, every surgical procedure invented, every prosthetic device implanted—indeed, virtually every modern medical therapy—is due, in part or in whole, to experimentation using animals. Nor may we ignore, in the balancing process, the predictable gains in human (and animal) well-being that are probably achievable in the future but that will not be achieved if the decision is made now to desist from such research or to curtail it.

Medical investigators are seldom insensitive to the distress their work may cause animal subjects. Opponents of research using animals are frequently insensitive to the cruelty of the results of the restrictions they would impose. Untold numbers of human beings—real persons, although not now identifiable—would suffer grievously as the consequence of this well-meaning but short-sighted tenderness. If the morally relevant differences between humans and animals are borne in mind, and if all relevant considerations are weighed, the calculation of long-term consequences must give overwhelming support for biomedical research using animals.

Concluding Remarks

Substitution

The humane treatment of animals requires that we desist from experimenting on them if we can accomplish the same result using alternative methods—*in vitro* experimentation, computer simulation,

or others. Critics of some experiments using animals rightly make this point.

It would be a serious error to suppose, however, that alternative techniques could soon be used in most research now using live animal subjects. No other methods now on the horizon or perhaps ever to be available—can fully replace the testing of a drug, a procedure, or a vaccine, in live organisms. The flood of new medical possibilities being opened by the successes of recombinant DNA technology will turn to a trickle if testing on live animals is forbidden. When initial trials entail great risks, there may be no forward movement whatever without the use of live animal subjects. In seeking knowledge that may prove critical in later clinical applications, the unavailability of animals for inquiry may spell complete stymie. In the United States, federal regulations require the testing of new drugs and other products on animals, for efficacy and safety, before human beings are exposed to them. We would not want it otherwise.

Every advance in medicine—every new drug, new operation, new therapy of any kind—must sooner or later be tried on a living being for the first time. That trial, controlled or uncontrolled, will be an experiment. The subject of that experiment, if it is not an animal, will be a human being. Prohibiting the use of live animals in biomedical research, therefore, or sharply restricting it, must result either in the blockage of much valuable research or in the replacement of animal subjects with human subjects. These are the consequences—unacceptable to most reasonable persons—of not using animals in research.

Reduction

Should we not at least reduce the use of animals in biomedical research? No, we should increase it to avoid when feasible the use of humans as experimental subjects. Medical investigations putting human subjects at some risk are numerous and greatly varied. The risks run in such experiments are usually unavoidable, and (thanks to earlier experiments on animals) most such risks are minimal or moderate. But some experimental risks are substantial.

When an experimental protocol that entails substantial risk to humans comes before an institutional review board, what response is appropriate? The investigation, we may suppose, is promising and deserves support, so long as its human subjects are protected against unnecessary dangers. May not the investigators be fairly asked, Have you done all that you can to eliminate risk to humans by the extensive testing of that drug, that procedure, or that device on animals? To achieve maximal safety for humans we are right to require thorough experimentation on animal subjects before humans are involved.

Opportunities to increase human safety in this way are commonly missed, trials in which risks may be shifted from humans to animals are often not devised, sometimes not even considered. Why? For the investigator, the use of animals as subjects is often more expensive, in money and time, than the use of human subjects. Access to suitable human subjects is often quick and convenient, whereas access to appropriate animal subjects may be awkward, costly, and burdened with red tape. Physician-investigators have often had more experience working with human beings and know precisely where the needed pool of subjects is to be found and how they may be enlisted. Animals, and the procedures for their use, are often less familiar to these investigators. Moreover, the use of animals in place of humans is now more likely to be the target of zealous protests from without. The upshot is that humans are sometimes subjected to risks that animals could have borne, and should have borne, in their place. To maximize the protection of human subjects, I conclude, the wide and imaginative use of live animal subjects should be encouraged rather than discouraged. This enlargement in the use of animals is our obligation.

Consistency

Finally, inconsistency between the profession and the practice of many who oppose research using animals deserves comment. This frankly *ad hominem* observation aims chiefly to show that a coherent position rejecting the use of animals in medical research imposes costs so high as to be intolerable even to the critics themselves.

One cannot coherently object to the killing of animals in biomedical investigations while continuing to eat them. Anesthetics and thoughtful animal husbandry render the level of actual animal distress in the laboratory generally lower than that in the abattoir. So long as death and discomfort do not substantially differ in the two contexts, the consistent objector must not only refrain from all eating of animals but also protest as vehemently against others eating them as against others experimenting on them. No less vigorously must the critic object to the wearing of animal hides in coats and shoes, to employment in any industrial enterprise that uses animal parts, and to any commercial development that will cause death or distress to animals.

Killing animals to meet human needs for food, clothing, and shelter is judged entirely reasonable by most persons. The ubiquity of these uses and the virtual universality of moral support for them confront the opponent of research using animals with an inescapable difficulty. How can the many common uses of animals be judged morally worthy, while their use in scientific investigation is judged unworthy?

The number of animals used in research is but the tiniest fraction of the total used to satisfy assorted human appetites. That these appetites, often base and satisfiable in other ways, morally justify the far larger consumption of animals, whereas the quest for improved human health and understanding cannot justify the far smaller, is wholly implausible. Aside from the numbers of animals involved, the distinction in terms of worthiness of use, drawn with regard to any single animal, is not defensible. A given sheep is surely not more justifiably used to put lamb chops on the supermarket counter than to serve in testing a new contraceptive or a new prosthetic device. The needless killing of animals is wrong; if the common killing of them for our food or convenience is right, the less common but more humane uses of animals in the service of medical science are certainly not less right.

Scrupulous vegetarianism, in matters of food, clothing, shelter, commerce, and recreation, and in all other spheres, is the only fully coherent position the critic may adopt. At great human cost, the lives of fish and crustaceans must also be protected, with equal vigor, if speciesism has been forsworn. A very few consistent critics adopt this position. It is the *reductio ad absurdum* of the rejection of moral distinctions between animals and human beings.

Opposition to the use of animals in research is based on arguments of two different kinds—those relying on the alleged rights of animals and those relying on the consequences for animals. I have argued that arguments of both kinds must fail. We surely do have obligations to animals, but they have, and can have, no rights against us on which research can infringe. In calculating the consequences of animal research, we must weigh all the long-term benefits of the results achieved—to animals and to humans—and in that calculation we must not assume the moral equality of all animate species.

QUESTIONS FOR REFLECTION

1. What is morally distinctive about humans as opposed to animals, in Cohen's view?

2. Do we have any obligations to animals, in Cohen's opinion? If so, what is their source?

3. How does Cohen defend speciesism?

4. What are Cohen's utilitarian arguments in favor of animal experimentation?

5. Which propositions in the Universal Declaration of the Rights of Animals does Cohen's position contradict?

PETER CARRUTHERS

from *The Animals Issue*

Peter Carruthers is Professor of Philosophy and Head of the Department of Philosophy at the University of Sheffield. (Source: Peter Carruthers, The Animals Issue *[Cambridge: Cambridge University Press, 1992]. Notes have been omitted. Copyright © 1992 by Cambridge University Press. Reprinted by permission of Cambridge University Press.)*

. . . My view is that the case for the moral standing of animals is weak, and that the contrary case is, by contrast, very powerful. In fact, I regard the present popular concern with animal rights in our culture as a reflection of moral decadence. Just as Nero fiddled while Rome burned, many in the West agonise over the fate of seal pups and cormorants while human beings elsewhere starve or are enslaved. This reaction is, to a degree, understandable. For animal sufferers are always blameless, and the steps necessary to improve their situation are generally plain. Our response to human suffering, in contrast, is often complicated by the suspicion that the victims, or their political representatives, are at least partially responsible for their fate, and by knowledge of the fearsome complexity of the economic and social problems involved in such issues as famine relief. Whatever may have been true of Nero, our species of decadence may consist in a weakness for easy options, rather than in any failure of moral sensitivity. . . .

CHAPTER I / MORAL ARGUMENT AND MORAL THEORY

The Limits of Morality

It needs to be emphasised that our question about the moral standing of animals is not the same as the question whether animals *matter*. There are many things that matter to us which do not give rise to moral rights or duties (or at least not directly—I shall return to this point shortly). Ancient buildings, oak trees, and works of art matter greatly to many of us without, I think, having moral standing. It is hardly sensible to say that a medieval castle, the oak on the village green, or the *Mona Lisa* have a moral right to be preserved. Nor is it plausible to claim that we have moral duties with respect to these things—though some people may have professional duties to care for them, through their roles as museum curators or foresters.

Things that lack moral standing may nevertheless have indirect moral significance, giving rise to moral duties in a roundabout way. Thus, while medieval castles are not the kinds of thing that can have rights, and while we have no moral duties towards them as such, it is plainly of moral significance that many people care deeply about them. This may be sufficient to give rise to duties to preserve and protect. Even the legitimate owner of a medieval castle may be under a moral obligation not to destroy it, since this would deprive present and future generations of a source of wonder, and of attachment to the past. So even if we were to agree that animals lack moral standing, it would not follow that we can, with impunity, treat animals as we please. For there may still be indirect duties towards animals arising out of the legitimate concerns of animal lovers. All the same, much may depend on the question whether our duties towards animals are direct or indirect. . . .

Since our task is to investigate the relationship between moral theory and the question of the moral standing of animals, seeking a position of reflective equilibrium on the issue, it will be useful to have a rough idea at the outset of what our commonsense morality tells us about the status and appropriate treatment of animals. The general view seems to imply that animals have *partial* moral standing—their lives and experiences having direct moral significance, but much less than that of human beings. Most people hold that it is wrong to cause animals unnecessary suffering. Opinions will differ as to what counts as necessary. Some would say that the suffering caused by the testing of detergents is permissible. Others would allow suffering only in the course of genuine scientific experiments. Yet others would allow animals to suffer only in the course of important medical experiments. But all will agree that gratuitous suffering—suffering caused for no good reason—is wrong. To cause such suffering is generally recognised to be cruel. . . .

When it comes to killing, I think commonsense morality tells us that the killing of animals is not wrong, except for no good reason. Again, opinions will differ as to what counts as good reason. Some would allow that animals may be killed for sport (perhaps provided that the manner of the killing is not cruel). Others would allow them to be killed for the pleasure of eating their flesh. Yet others would allow them to be killed only to protect legitimate human interests, as when rabbits are shot to prevent crop damage. And others again will only allow animals to be killed where human lives are at stake, as when meat is the only available food. But all will agree that there is no question of weighing up animal lives against the lives of humans.

To see this last point, imagine that you arrive at a fire in a dogs' home to find Kenneth, the human owner, unconscious on the floor while the dogs are all locked in their cages. Your judgment is that you only have time to drag Kenneth to safety, or to unlock the cages to allow the dogs to escape, but not both. Here I think no one would maintain that you ought to place the lives of many dogs above the life of a single human. Whereas most would believe that, in an otherwise comparable situation in which only hu-mans were involved, the best thing to do would be to save as many lives as possible. This is always supposing, of course, that all else is equal. If Kenneth is known to be a mass murderer or child molester then many might feel differently about the case. The commonsense view seems to be that human beings can, by their own actions, forfeit their right to life, or cease to be worth rescuing.

It is worth stressing, since it will prove to be of some importance later, that our commonsense belief that human and animal lives cannot be weighed against one another appears to be particularly central to morality, or especially firmly held. For even those philosophers who have been most vociferous in promoting the rights of animals, such as Tom Regan and Peter Singer, go to considerable lengths to retain it. If we are to be forced to give up this aspect of commonsense morality, it will require, at the least, a theoretical argument that is very powerful indeed.

CHAPTER 5 /
CONTRACTUALISM AND ANIMALS

. . .

Regan's Reply

Regan has mounted an argument designed to show that contractualism cannot coherently withhold moral standing from animals, without also withholding it from those human beings who are not rational agents, such as severe mental defectives or senile old people. . . .

Regan claims that if agents behind the veil of ignorance are to be ignorant of such fundamental matters as their qualities of character, life-plans, and position within society, then there is no good reason why they should not also be ignorant of their species. But if the agents were to be ignorant of the species into which they would subsequently be incarnated, when selecting basic moral principles, then, plainly, they would choose rules protecting the interests of members of all species equally. So Rawls has simply begged the question against the moral standing of animals in the manner in which he sets up the apparatus of the veil of ignorance. Had he arranged the details of that device slightly differently, then animals would have been accorded the same basic rights as human beings within contractualism. . . .

The real line of reply to Regan is that his suggestion would destroy the theoretical coherence of Rawlsian contractualism. As Rawls has it, morality is, in fact, a human construction (in the absence, that is, of any other known species of rational agent). . . . Morality is viewed as constructed *by* human beings, in order to facilitate interactions *between* human beings, and to make possible a life of cooperative community. This is, indeed, an essential part of the governing conception of contractualism. . . . To suggest, now, that contractualism should be so construed as to accord equal moral standing to animals would be to lose our grip on where moral notions are supposed to come from, or why we should care about them when they arrive. . . .

A Problem for Reflective Equilibrium

. . . If animals are not accorded moral standing under contractualism, on the grounds that they are not rational agents, then it would seem that by the same token all those human beings who are not rational agents will also fail to have moral standing bestowed on them. In which case killing a baby or a senile human being would not violate their rights, since they would have no rights. Such killings would at most violate our duty to respect the feelings of those people who care about babies (or that particular baby) or the senile. This is, to say the least, counterintuitive.

In the case of babies there may be more that a contractualist can say to explain the wrongness of causing them suffering. For such suffering may be expected to have an effect on the rational agents they will one day become. Our actions may thus directly violate the rights of those future persons, and hence be wrong even when done in private so as to cause no distress to others. In the same way, contractualists may be able to explain the wrongness of killing babies, if they are prepared to accept the principle that it is wrong to prevent a rational agent from coming into existence. (What they say about this will clearly have implications for their attitude towards abortion and contraception.) But they cannot similarly ex-

plain the wrongness of killing or causing suffering to mental defectives or senile old people, since such human beings no longer have the potential, in general, to become rational agents.

To make the case as strong as possible, consider . . . the example of Astrid, the astronaut.* Suppose that Astrid has taken her grandfather with her, who becomes increasingly senile as the journey progresses. Would it not be very wrong of her to start using *him* as a dart-board to relieve her tedium, or to kill him because the sight of his dribbling offends her? Yet on what grounds can such actions be wrong, if only rational agents have moral standing? For no other person will ever be worried or upset at the suffering or death of her grandfather.

It appears that contractualism faces severe difficulties in accommodating our commonsense attitudes towards those living beings who are not rational agents. Since these attitudes are even more deeply entrenched in connection with nonrational human beings than they are in connection with animals, any attempt to brush commonsense beliefs aside, on the grounds of their conflict with the theory of contractualism, will be correspondingly weaker. For example, no one is going to accept the testing of detergents on the senile, or the hunting of mental defectives for sport. If we cannot find some other way of handling these examples within contractualism, it would appear that the latter is doomed as an acceptable moral theory. . . .

Slippery Slopes and Social Stability

There is a very different way in which contractualists, of whatever variety, can attempt to secure direct moral rights for all human beings. As with Rawls's suggestion, this one, too, will leave animals without moral standing. The strategy depends upon the fact that there are no sharp boundaries between a baby and an adult, between a not-very-intelligent adult and a severe mental defective, or between a normal old person and someone who is severely senile. The

---

* Astrid takes a spacecraft into deep space, never encountering or communicating with another human being—or alien, for that matter.—ED.

argument is then that the attempt to accord direct moral rights only to rational agents (normal adults) would be inherently dangerous and open to abuse.

This is, of course, a version of slippery slope argument. The suggestion is that if we try to deny moral rights to some human beings, on the grounds that they are not rational agents, we shall be launched on a slippery slope which may lead to all kinds of barbarisms against those who *are* rational agents. It is important to be clear about the level on which this argument is supposed to operate, however. For there is nothing to stop us, at the level of theory, from insisting that only rational agents have rights, leaving a large range of cases in which possession of rights would be indeterminate. Or we could insist that possession of rights itself should be a matter of degree, the killing of a human being becoming more and more serious, in terms of direct infringements of right, as a baby gradually advances into adulthood. There would be nothing incoherent in these theories as such. The claim must be that it is in the application of these theories in the real world that the danger lies. The idea is that such theories would be inherently susceptible to abuse by unscrupulous people, and ought therefore not to be adopted.

In contrast, there really is a sharp boundary between human beings and all other animals. Not necessarily in terms of intelligence or degree of rational agency, of course—a chimpanzee may be more intelligent than a mentally defective human, and a dolphin may be a rational agent to a higher degree than a human baby. But there is not the same practical threat to the welfare of rational agents in the suggestion that all animals should be excluded from the domain of direct moral concern. Someone who argues that since animals do not have rights, therefore babies do not have rights, therefore there can be no moral objection to the extermination of Jews, Gypsies, gays, and other so-called "deviants," is unlikely to be taken very seriously, even by those who share their evil aims.

This argument for according rights to all human beings does seem to have a good chance of success. For rational agents choosing moral principles to govern their behaviour should, of course, pay attention to the ways in which those principles might be distorted or abused. If the argument has a weakness, however, it lies in its empirical assumption—namely, that a rule according direct rights only to rational agents would be likely to be abused in such a way as to undermine itself. For provided that all understand the theoretical basis of the rules, they will be forearmed against abuse. Thus, suppose it were generally agreed that all rational agents have moral rights, and that those who are not fully rational agents have rights in proportion to the extent of their rational agency. Then the reply is obvious to anyone who tries to argue that since babies do not have direct rights, and since there is no clear boundary between infancy and normal adulthood, therefore there can be no direct moral objection to the Holocaust. It is that the gradual transition from infancy to adulthood is at the same time the transition from not bearing moral rights, to having them in full measure.

This attempt to undermine the argument from a slippery slope fails in its turn, however. For one of the facts that rational agents will know is that most people are not very deeply theoretical. They should therefore select moral principles that will provide a stable and easily understood framework within which ordinary people can debate questions of right and wrong. Seen in these terms, a rule that accorded rights in proportion to degree of rational agency *would* be wide open to creeping abuse. For to think and speak in terms that withhold moral rights from some human beings is to invite people to try to draw yet further distinctions—for example, withholding rights from those who are sexually or intellectually "deviant," or from those whose intelligence is low. So I conclude that our slippery slope argument is indeed successful in according rights to all human beings.

It is worth noting the differences between the argument sketched here, and Regan's superficially similar argument for treating human babies as if they had rights. Recall that for Regan, those who have moral rights are primarily those who are subjects-of-a-life—that is, who have a sense of their own future and their own past. He then realises that on such an account human babies, up to the age of one, at least, will not count as having rights. His reply is that we should, nevertheless, treat such babies *as if* they had the same rights as everyone else, by way of encouraging a moral climate in which the rights of individuals are taken seriously. The first point to make about Regan's proposal is that it does not succeed in according rights to human babies. To say that we should treat babies *as if* they had rights is not the same as saying that they *do* have rights. Yet it is this stronger conclusion that we were able to deliver by means of the slippery slope argument outlined above. The second point is that it is, in any case, by no means clear how Regan's argument is supposed to go. That is, it is far from clear how treating those who do not have rights as if they did have them would foster a climate in which the rights of individuals are taken seriously. The only obvious suggestion is that any moral system in which some human beings are denied moral rights is liable, by creeping abuse, to lead to a situation in which some of those who do have moral rights have their rights ignored. This is, in effect, our slippery slope argument, only shorn of its contractualist context. The very argument that for Regan leads to the conclusion that we should treat all humans *as if* they had rights, for a contractualist leads to the conclusion that they *do* have rights. This is, I think, to the advantage of the latter. . . .

In addition to the argument from a slippery slope outlined above, contractualists have available one further argument for according moral standing to all human beings. This is an argument from social stability. One thing that rational contractors should certainly consider, in framing a basic set of principles, is whether those principles would have the desired effect of facilitating a stable, cooperative community. In this they should have regard, among other things, to the known facts of human psychology. One such fact is that human beings are apt to care as intensely about their offspring as they care about anything, irrespective of age and intelligence. A rule withholding moral standing from those who are very young, very old, or mentally defective is thus likely to produce social instability, in that many people would find themselves psychologically incapable of living in compliance with it.

It might be replied that stability could equally well be achieved by a rule requiring us to respect the legitimate concerns of others. Then all those nonrational humans who are objects of love would receive protection after all, out of respect for the feelings of those who love them. But this is inadequate. It would only accord such humans the same protection as items of property. Just as I am obliged

not to damage or destroy your cherished Mercedes, so I should be obliged not to damage or destroy your child. But such obligations may be overridden in cases where more fundamental rights are at stake. Suppose, for example, that your Mercedes blocks the entrance to a mine shaft in which I have become imprisoned. You have become accustomed to use the entrance as a garage during the week, and I should face a five-day wait to get out. Then I may surely destroy the car if this is my only means of escape, no matter how much you may care about it, and even though my life may be in no danger. In these circumstances you would, surely, accept that I had acted reasonably. But no one could bring themselves to accept with equanimity the destruction of their child in a similar situation. The only way of framing rules that we can live with, then, is to accord all human beings the same basic rights—that is to say, moral standing. . . .

Reflective Equilibrium Attained

I believe that the account now sketched of our duties towards animals is sufficiently plausible to enable us to achieve reflective equilibrium overall. First, it can explain our commonsense belief that it is wrong to cause unnecessary suffering to an animal, where "unnecessary" means either "for no reason," "for trivial reasons," or "for its own sake." (In the next section I shall consider what the implications of the account may be for practices that are more controversial, such as hunting, factory farming, and animal experimentation.) Second, the present approach also retains our intuitive belief that there can be no question of weighing animal suffering against the suffering of a human being. Since animals are still denied moral standing, on this contractualist account, they make no direct moral claims upon us. There is therefore nothing *to* be weighed against the claims of a human being. Finally, the account can retain the intuition shared by many people (including some champions of animals like Singer . . .), that there need be nothing wrong with causing the painless death of an animal. Since the sort of sympathy that we should feel for the loss of a human life is only appropriate, in the first instance, in connection with the death of a rational agent, such actions may fail to manifest any degree of cruelty. (Some killings may, however, be *wasteful*, in the same sense that the motiveless cutting down of an oak tree may be.)

A further advantage of our account is that it can explain how people so easily come to be under the illusion, when they engage in theoretical reflection, that animal suffering has moral standing, mattering for its own sake. For those who have the right moral dispositions in this area will act for the sake of the animal when prompted by feelings of sympathy. Since right action requires that you act for the sake of the animal, it is then easy to see how one might slip into believing that the animal itself has moral standing. But this would be to miss the point that there may be a variety of different levels to moral thinking. On the one hand there is the level of thought that manifests our settled moral dispositions and attitudes (this is where sympathy for animal suffering belongs), but on the other hand there is the level of theoretical reflection upon those dispositions and attitudes, asking how they may be justified by an acceptable moral theory. It is at this level that we come to realise, as contractualists, that animals are without moral standing.

For similar reasons, the proposed character-expressive account of our duties towards animals is able to avoid the charge of absurdity often levelled at Kant's somewhat similar treatment of the issue. Kant is sometimes represented—unfairly—as claiming that those who perform acts of kindness towards animals are merely practising for kindness towards humans. As if anyone ever helped an animal with such an intention! But in fact he is best interpreted as presenting an account along the lines of that above, which distinguishes between the motives of those who act out of the sort of beneficent state of character they ought to have, and the theoretical explanation of the moral value that state possesses. It is only at the latter level that we may see the value of a sympathetic character as deriving from the way in which it manifests itself in our treatment of human beings.

It therefore looks as if the present proposal can account for every aspect of common sense. . . .

QUESTIONS FOR REFLECTION

1. What is the difference between having moral standing and mattering?

2. Why does Carruthers reject Regan's interpretation of the original position?

3. Can a contractualist explain why animals matter? How?

4. Summarize Carruthers's slippery slope argument. Do you find it convincing?

5. Summarize Carruthers's argument from social stability. What does it presuppose about human nature?

6. Which propositions in the Universal Declaration of the Rights of Animals does Carruthers's position contradict?

THE ENVIRONMENT

Every living thing interacts with its environment. Humans have no choice, therefore, but to change the natural world. But two factors have turned such changes into a significant public policy issue. First, the world's population has grown rapidly during the past several centuries, greatly amplifying humanity's impact on the environment. Second, the technological advances of the industrial revolution have not only increased our ability to affect our surroundings but have brought about new kinds of effects that, even today, we only partially understand.

Utilitarians look at environmental questions in terms of consequences, that is, in terms of costs and benefits. Whether cost-benefit analysis is adequate to environmental issues, however, is itself subject to debate. One might argue that the interdependency of ecosystems makes consequences very difficult to predict. Small effects on one part of a system may produce large effects on another. Moreover, cost-benefit analyses usually omit various environmental effects that are difficult to quantify but nevertheless ecologically significant.

Paul and Anne Ehrlich point to other difficulties with utilitarian analysis. Environmental questions force us to assess difficult tradeoffs between very different kinds of goods. How much money, for example, is a year of a human life worth? How much should society be willing to spend to keep, say, a hundred people from dying prematurely each year? Even this is too simple, for real-world issues involve questions of *risk* rather than cost. Actual tradeoff questions are more like this: What should society be willing to spend to lower the probability of the average person's dying this year by, say, .00004%? And what if our confidence in that estimate of risk is itself low? The Ehrlichs argue for a policy of increasing humanity's margin for error, recognizing that our risk-benefit analyses are themselves highly uncertain.

Aldo Leopold, Bill Devall, and George Sessions raise other objections to utilitarian analysis. The natural world, they contend, deserves respect; it is not merely a tool for producing human pleasure and avoiding human pain. Outlining a land ethic known as *deep ecology,* they argue that all forms of life deserve equal respect. Other beings and species have intrinsic moral worth. Kant says that everything has a dignity or a price. To put the thesis in Kantian terms, Leopold, Devall, and Sessions maintain that everything in the natural environment has a dignity. Utilitarian calculations go wrong by assigning everything—including human beings—a price. They conclude that humanity must undertake a sweeping reevaluation of its place in the environment.

William Baxter defends risk-benefit calculations, contending that environmental decisions must be made by assessing the effects of actions and policies on human beings. People, he contends, are more important than penguins, and nobody is in a position to speak for the penguins' interests. Dr. Seuss's Lorax, who speaks for the trees, is fictional; we have no reason to accept anyone as entitled to speak for the natural world.

Baxter sees environmental problems as arising not from misguided calculations but from what Garrett Hardin dubs *the tragedy of the commons.* Often, each party to a collective decision has reason to pursue his or her self-interest, given what the others are doing. If everyone pursues self-interest, however, everyone becomes worse off. Each possible polluter, for example, may believe that his or her additional pollution will make no significant difference to the environment but will yield substantial economic rewards. This may be true. Yet if each potential polluter reasons similarly and pollutes, the resulting environmental degradation may make everyone worse off than before.

This is a special case of what has become known as a *prisoners' dilemma.* Suppose that the police catch two criminals, Mug and Thug. They immediately separate them and interrogate them independently. Having caught them on a minor violation, but lacking the evidence to be confident of obtaining a conviction on a major charge, the police offer Mug a deal: "You can make it easy for us, and on yourself, or you can make it tough. If you confess, and your testimony against Thug lets us get him on the major charge, you walk out of here. We bargain on the small stuff; you get probation. If you don't confess, you do time. You know we have you on the small stuff. If you don't work with us, we don't cut any deals. You go to jail. And if we get you on the big one, you go to jail for a long time. What do you say?" They offer the same deal to Thug.

We can represent the situation in a simple table, where Mug and Thug must choose to confess or remain silent, and where the outcomes are pairs [effect on Mug, effect on Thug]:

		Thug	
		Confess	Remain Silent
Mug	Confess	[−2, −2]	[0, −5]
	Remain Silent	[−5, 0]	[−1, −1]

That is, if both remain silent, they each get a year in jail on minor charges. If both confess, the police cut a deal for cooperation, but both are convicted of the serious offense, so each gets two years. If one confesses and the other doesn't, the one who confesses goes free, but the one who remains silent is convicted of everything, without any deals, and gets five years.

Mug and Thug can't communicate, and they aren't sure, let's assume, what the other will do. Mug might reason as follows: "If Thug confesses, I'm better off confessing. I'll get only two years instead of five. If Thug doesn't confess, I'm still better off confessing; I walk instead of getting a year. So, no matter what Thug does, I'm better off confessing." Mug therefore confesses. Thug reasons similarly, of course, and also confesses. So each criminal spends two years in jail. Their reasoning appears impeccable. Yet, if they had both remained silent, they would have cut their sentences in half.

Here's how the prisoners' dilemma applies to environmental problems and leads to the tragedy of the commons. Imagine that, in place of Mug and Thug, we have two companies, Vanishing, Inc., and Roco Co. Each faces a choice between polluting and in-

stalling pollution control equipment. Each reasons that its pollution will have minor effects on overall air and water quality, but that installing control equipment will have a big impact on its bottom line. So, each pollutes. But the result may be a lower quality of life for everyone, and even economic harm to the companies themselves (through additional costs required to clean the water to be used in their industrial processes, for example, or to replace equipment more frequently, or to attract workers to such an unpleasant community, or to pay increased health care costs).

Again, we can represent the choice in a table where the pairs are [effect on Vanishing, Inc., effect on Roco Co.]:

		Roco Co.	
		Pollute	Control
Vanishing, Inc.	Pollute	[2, 2]	[4, 1]
	Control	[1, 4]	[3, 3]

Each company can reason that it is better off polluting, no matter what the other does. Suppose that you are the CEO of Vanishing, Inc. If Roco Co. pollutes, you are better off polluting; you have to put up with the disadvantages of their pollution anyway, and the control equipment is expensive. If they control their pollution, you are still better off polluting, because you save the costs of the control equipment, and you gain the benefits of their cleanup efforts. But Roco Co. faces the same situation and reasons similarly. So, you both pollute. But this is the worst possible outcome: a tragedy of the commons. You would have been better off, jointly and singly, if you had both controlled your pollution. The two of you taken together would have been better off if even one of you had done so.

So far, prisoners' dilemmas make the point that people or companies acting independently and rationally to promote their own self-interest can produce substantial and avoidable harm to the community as a whole. But the point applies to act-utilitarians as well as to self-interested agents. Suppose that Mug and Thug are utilitarians and that no one else is affected by what happens to them, so that they are seeking to maximize their combined welfare. Summing their individual utilities to compute the effects on the two taken together, their choice becomes:

		Thug	
		Confess	Remain Silent
Mug	Confess	−4	−5
	Remain Silent	−5	−2

Mug, the utilitarian, sees that he should do whatever Thug does. Thug, the utilitarian, recognizes this too. So, Mug and Thug satisfy the demands of act-utilitarianism if they both remain silent *or if they both confess*. This shows that act-utilitarianism is *indeterminate*—it may be satisfied by different patterns of behavior with different utilities for the community as a whole.

If our companies act as utilitarians in the case outlined above, they solve their problem: Each maximizes welfare overall by controlling pollution, achieving the best outcome. (Vanishing, Inc., sees that the community is better off if it controls its pollution, no matter what Roco Co. does.) But small changes in the effects on the two companies change this:

		Roco Co.	
		Pollute	Control
Vanishing, Inc.	Pollute	[2.1, 2.1]	[4, 0]
	Control	[0, 4]	[3, 3]

Now, the choice is just like Mug and Thug's. Each company can reason, as an act-utilitarian, that it should do what the other company does. But that means that both can be good act-utilitarians even while polluting and achieving less than the best overall outcome.

This points to an important limitation of act-utilitarian (that is, cost-benefit or risk-benefit) analyses made by independent parties: Even when they accurately assess risks and benefits, different patterns of behavior with different implications for the community's welfare can pass all such tests. Only by co-operating can the criminals or the companies achieve the best combined outcome.

This might seem to be an argument for rule-utilitarianism. But it too can lead to suboptimal outcomes. Suppose that Pig, Inc., and Poke Co. each pollute slightly less than some threshold harmful amount. Then, if both pollute, they together produce significant harms. But the pollution of just one produces no harm at all. They seem to face the choice:

		Poke Co.	
		Pollute	Control
Pig, Inc.	Pollute	[2, 2]	[4, 3]
	Control	[3, 4]	[3, 3]

Self-interest and act-utilitarianism imply that exactly one company should pollute. The polluting company does better economically without producing any environmental harm. Yet rule-utilitarianism tells each company to follow the rule that will produce the best outcome overall. If both follow the rule "Pollute," the overall utility is 4; if they follow the rule "Don't pollute," it is 6. So, if the companies act as rule-utilitarians, they will both install controls, producing less than the best outcome for the community.

This has important implications for environmental problems, which Stroup and Baden elaborate. The traditional model of government regulation of the environment is one of law enforcement: determining what kinds of actions are tolerably safe and what kinds are environmentally dangerous, then banning the latter and prosecuting those who violate the law. In essence, the model is rule-utilitarian, requiring people to follow the best rules. In some circumstances, this may not lead to the best outcome, for it imposes uniformity: Everyone must follow the same rules. Stroup and Baden thus argue against governmental solutions to environmental problems and defend market-based solutions instead. This is true even if the rules that the government specifies really are the best rules to follow. As Stroup and Baden argue, that may not be so. Government officials have incentives, just as anyone else does. And those incentives often do not promote the public interest. Moreover, the political process may be swayed in various ways by special interests. Even at its best, however, regulation increases the costs of transferring resources, leading to a net loss for society as a whole.

Karen Warren develops a view called *ecological feminism,* or "ecofeminism" for short. Arguments for the moral superiority of humans over the rest of nature, she holds, parallel arguments for the superiority of men over women. In both cases, we must reject suspect assumptions and recognize moral equality. We must reject the "logic of domination"—the attempt to justify subordinating a person or group by appealing to their moral inferiority—wherever it is used.

GARRETT HARDIN

from *The Tragedy of the Commons*

*Garrett Hardin is Professor Emeritus of Biology at the University of Califor-
nia at Santa Barbara. (Source: Excerpted with permission from Garrett
Hardin, "The Tragedy of the Commons," Science 162 [1968]: 1243–1248.
Copyright © 1968 American Association for the Advancement of Science.)*

. . . In economic affairs, *The Wealth of Nations* (1776) popularized the "invisible hand," the idea that an individual who "intends only his own gain" is, as it were, "led by an invisible hand to promote the public interest." Adam Smith did not assert that this was invariably true, and perhaps neither did any of his followers. But he contributed to a dominant tendency of thought that has ever since interfered with positive action based on rational analysis, namely, the tendency to assume that decisions reached individually will, in fact, be the best decisions for an entire society. . . .

Tragedy of Freedom in a Commons

The rebuttal to the invisible hand in population control is to be found in a scenario first sketched in a little-known pamphlet in 1833 by a mathematical amateur named William Forster Lloyd (1794–1852). We may well call it "the tragedy of the commons," using the word "tragedy" as the philosopher Whitehead used it: "The essence of dramatic tragedy is not unhappiness. It resides in the solemnity of the remorseless working of things." He then goes on to say, "This inevitableness of destiny can only be illustrated in terms of human life by incidents which in fact involve unhappiness. For it is only by them that the futility of escape can be made evident in the drama."

The tragedy of the commons develops in this way. Picture a pasture open to all. It is to be expected that each herdsman will try to keep as many cattle as possible on the commons. Such an arrangement may work reasonably satisfactorily for centuries because tribal wars, poaching, and disease keep the numbers of both man and beast well below the carrying capacity of the land. Finally, however, comes the day of reckoning, that is, the day when the long-desired goal of social stability becomes a reality. At this point, the inherent logic of the commons remorselessly generates tragedy.

As a rational being, each herdsman seeks to maximize his gain. Explicitly or implicitly, more or less consciously, he asks, "What is the utility to me of adding one more animal to my herd?" This utility has one negative and one positive component.

1. The positive component is a function of the increment of one animal. Since the herdsman receives all the proceeds from the sale of the additional animal, the positive utility is nearly +1.

2. The negative component is a function of the additional overgrazing created by one more animal. Since, however, the effects of overgrazing are shared by all the herdsmen, the negative utility for any particular decisionmaking herdsman is only a fraction of −1.

Adding together the component partial utilities, the rational herdsman concludes that the only sensible course for him to pursue is to add another animal to his herd. And another . . . But this is the conclusion reached by each and every rational herdsman sharing a commons. Therein is the tragedy. Each man is locked into a system that compels him to increase his herd without limit—in a world that is limited. Ruin is the destination toward which all men rush, each pursuing his own best interest in a society that believes in the freedom of the commons. Freedom in a commons brings ruin to all.

Some would say that this is a platitude. Would that it were! In a sense, it was learned thousands of years ago, but natural selection favors the forces of psychological denial. The individual benefits as an individual from his ability to deny the truth even though society as a whole, of which he is a part, suffers. Education can counteract the natural tendency to do the wrong thing, but the inexorable succession of generations requires that the basis for this knowledge be constantly refreshed.

A simple incident that occurred a few years ago in Leominster, Massachusetts, shows how perishable the knowledge is. During the Christmas shopping season the parking meters downtown were covered with plastic bags that bore tags reading: "Do not open until after Christmas. Free parking courtesy of the mayor and city council." In other words, facing the prospect of an increased demand for already scarce space, the city fathers reinstituted the system of the commons. (Cynically, we suspect that they gained more votes than they lost by this retrogressive act.)

In an approximate way, the logic of the commons has been understood for a long time, perhaps since the discovery of agriculture or the invention of private property in real estate. But it is understood mostly only in special cases which are not sufficiently generalized. Even at this late date, cattlemen leasing national land on the Western ranges demonstrate no more than an ambivalent understanding, in constantly pressuring federal authorities to increase the head count to the point where overgrazing produces erosion and weed-dominance. Likewise, the oceans of the world continue to suffer from the survival of the philosophy of the commons. Maritime nations still respond automatically to the shibboleth of the "freedom of the seas." Professing to believe in the "inexhaustible resources of the oceans," they bring species after species of fish and whales closer to extinction.

The National Parks present another instance of the working out of the tragedy of the commons. At present, they are open to all, without limit. The parks themselves are limited in extent—there is only one Yosemite Valley—whereas population seems to grow without limit. The values that visitors seek in the parks are steadily eroded. Plainly, we must soon cease to treat the parks as commons or they will be of no value to anyone.

What shall we do? We have several options. We might sell them off as private property. We might keep them as public property, but allocate the right to enter them. The allocation might be on the basis of wealth, by the use of an auction system. It might be on the basis of merit, as defined by some agreed-upon standards. It might be by lottery. Or it might be on a first-come, first-served basis, administered to long queues. These, I think, are all objectionable. But we must choose—or acquiesce in the destruction of the commons that we call our National Parks.

Pollution

In a reverse way, the tragedy of the commons reappears in problems of pollution. Here it is not a question of taking something out of the commons, but of putting something in—sewage, or chemical, radioactive, and heat wastes into water; noxious and dangerous fumes into the air; and distracting and unpleasant advertising signs into the line of sight. The calculations of utility are much the same as before. The rational man finds that his share of the cost of the wastes he discharges into the commons is less than the cost of purifying his wastes before releasing them. Since this is true for everyone, we are locked into a system of "fouling our own nest," so long as we behave only as independent, rational, free enterprisers.

The tragedy of the commons as a food basket is averted by private property, or something formally like it. But the air and waters surrounding us cannot readily be fenced, and so the tragedy of the commons as a cesspool must be prevented by different means, by coercive laws or taxing devices that make it cheaper for the polluter to treat his pollutants than to discharge them untreated. We have not progressed as far with the solution of this problem as we have with the first. Indeed, our particular concept of private property, which deters us from exhausting the positive resources of the earth, favors pollution. The owner of a factory on the bank of a stream—whose property extends to the middle of the stream—often has difficulty seeing why it is not his natural right to muddy the waters flowing past his door. The law, always behind the times, requires elaborate stitching and fitting to adapt it to this newly perceived aspect of the commons. . . .

QUESTIONS FOR REFLECTION

1. How does the tragedy of the commons refute the idea behind the "invisible hand"?

2. Why would declaring free parking downtown during Christmas season decrease total happiness?

3. How does the tragedy of the commons apply to the national park system, in Hardin's view? Which of the options he outlines would you favor? Why?

4. Could we avoid the tragedy of the commons if everyone acted as a utilitarian? As a Kantian?

RICHARD STROUP AND JOHN BADEN, WITH DAVID FRACTOR

Property Rights: The Real Issue

Richard Stroup is Professor of Economics at Montana State University and Senior Associate of the Political Economy Research Center. John Baden is founder and chairman of the Foundation for Research on Economics and the Environment. David Fractor is a partner of Phillips and Fractor, LLC. (Source: from Richard Stroup and John Baden with David Fractor, Natural Resources: Bureaucratic Myths and Environmental Management. *Copyright © 1983 by Pacific Research Institute for Public Policy. Reprinted by permission.)*

Property rights to a resource, whether a tract of land, a coal mine, or a spring creek, consist of having control over that resource. Such rights are most valuable when ownership is outright and when property can be easily exchanged for other goods and services. Although an important feature of a property right is the power to exclude others from using it, even limited command over access to a resource confers status and power to the holder. Governments typically exercise at least some discretionary command in this regard. As Douglass North wrote, "One cannot develop a useful analysis of the state divorced from property rights." Indeed, a theory of property rights can become a theory of the state.

It is a common misconception that every citizen benefits from his share of the public lands and the resources found thereon. Public ownership of many natural resources lies at the root of resource control conflicts. With public ownership resources are held in common; that is, they are owned by everyone and, therefore, can be used by everyone. But public ownership by no means guarantees public benefits. Individuals make decisions regarding resource use, not large groups or societies. Yet, with government control, it is not the owners who make decisions, but politicians and bureaucrats. The citizen as beneficiary is often a fiction.

It is useful to characterize an institutional arrangement by describing how it defines and defends property rights and makes them transferable. Over the past few years, economists and others have developed a property right paradigm that examines these institutional characteristics, making it possible to analyze events based on actual or proposed institutional changes.

The property rights paradigm provides important analytical leverage that is useful for understanding how individuals interact in institutional contexts. The paradigm helps us to understand history, to predict the consequences of modern institutions, and to compare the likely outcomes of alternative arrangements. Given the growing pressures from larger populations and from technologies that enable us to acquire and process more natural resources, such predictive and analytical capabilities take on increasing importance. We *must* manage with care. The costs of failure are increasing.

Property Rights and Allocation of Resources

Most economists begin their analyses by assuming that decision makers seek to maximize profits, income, or even wealth. Property rights theorists assume that the decision maker's goals or utility function must first be specified in each case. It is assumed that the decision maker will maximize his own utility—not that of some institution or state—in whatever situation he finds himself.

Individuals seek their own advantage within prevailing institutional arrangements. Nevertheless, they may attempt to change the "rules of the game" or the institutions themselves. When privately held property rights to urban land are attenuated by building height restrictions, for example, landowners may gain by changing the rules or by influencing their administration. Since others will fight these changes or seek similar advantages for themselves, the resulting competition may be a negative sum game. In such economic situations, the winners gain less than the losses suffered or investments made by their competitors. In effect, then, negative sum games result in a net economic loss to society.

Institutional rules always allow governmental officials some discretion in determining access to resources. Claimants, therefore, have an incentive to invest in activities that might produce administrative outcomes favorable to themselves. Under these circumstances, some corruption exists in every political system. Informational lobbying, potential shifts of campaign support, actual or threatened lawsuits, and even bribery can all be brought to bear—at a cost—by those who wish to gain favorable decisions from governmental policymakers who control the rights to resources.

Economic growth and efficiency are greatly affected by the way in which existing institutions allow property rights to be traded and allocated. When rights are both privately held and easily transferable, decision makers have easy access to information through bid and asked prices, as well as an incentive to move resources to higher-valued uses. But if a person can gain by blocking socially useful resource moves through governmental means, then his gain is society's loss. Similarly, if potential uses can gain access to the resource through government without paying the opportunity costs of the resource, then low-valued uses may dominate at the expense of more highly valued uses.

The Evolution of Property Rights to Natural Resources

In analyzing the effects of alternative institutional arrangements for resource allocation, it is useful to look at the evolution of those institutions that established and protected property rights to natural resources. As part of that effort, an examination of the western American frontier allows us to compare methods of defining and enforcing these property rights. Two basic themes in the evolution of natural resource property rights emerge from a reading of *The Frontier in American History* by Frederick Jackson Turner. First, American institutions were formed as pioneers ventured into the West and resource constraints changed. Second, opportunities provided by the frontier placed a lower limit on wages. In a general way, these observations help explain how property rights evolved as a response to changing resource prices.

We can theorize that as more information was obtained about natural resources and as their value rose, potential rents to the resources induced decision makers to develop them and thus to define and enforce the property rights governing them. Further, when voluntary associations of resource users developed and enforced these rights, a strong incentive arose to allocate the resource efficiently. Finally, as the geographic frontier closed and the number of unclaimed resources declined, individual options for increasing wealth became limited to increasing productivity, confiscating resources through legitimate or illegitimate means, or both.

History of Frontier Development

. . . Actual or potential owners have incentives to use their resources efficiently. In contrast, agents with no stake in the residuals of the bargaining process (e.g., a bureaucrat at the Environmental Protection Agency [EPA] or the attorney in a divorce suit) have no direct and personal interest in reducing the cost of that process. Of course, when such third parties are easily monitored *and* there is competition for their jobs, incentives do appear, but this seldom occurs in the public sector. On the American frontier, the first efforts to settle resource allocation claims emerged through the establishment of voluntary associations and the development of informal property rights to resources. Land clubs, claims associations, cattlemen's associations, wagon trains, and mining camps within which individuals grappled with the allocation of water, land, livestock, minerals, timber, and even personal property all represent attempts to mitigate the problems associated with common ownership.

The forms of voluntary association varied, but each sought to bring order to competing multiple claims before the formal claims process applied to the land. . . .

Throughout this period, these extralegal, voluntary associations economized on definition and enforcement techniques. They recognized that high bargaining costs consumed resources that they intuitively knew could be put to better use.

The Frontiersman versus the Law

The Easterner, with his background of forest and farm, could not always understand the man of the cattle kingdom. One went on foot, the other went on horseback; one carried his law in books, the other carried his strapped around his waist. One represented tradition, the other represented innovation; one responded to convention, the other responded to necessity and evolved his own conventions. Yet the man of the timber and the town made the law for the man of the plain; the plainsman, finding this law unsuited to his needs, broke it and was called lawless.

In the late nineteenth century, as statutory mandates dating from 1785 focused on the rapid disposition and transfer of government lands to private parties and the promotion of the family farm, the growing conservation movement began charging private enterprise and private ownership with exploitation. The movement to preserve the public lands intensified.

To the extent that initial disposal schemes recognized scarcities, efficiencies were realized. But the change in policy evidenced by the Homestead Act of 1862 reversed eight decades of relatively unfettered land disposal and minimal transaction costs by re-

quiring often economically unrealistic labor and capital expenditures to retain land ownership. This reversal, of course, produced economic inefficiency, considerable human suffering, and even death.

As third party agents, the government increasingly interfered in resource allocation, setting the stage for the blossoming and growth of transfer activity. It is this institutional setting, now matured, that dominates property rights considerations in natural resource development, allocation, sale, and preservation.

The Growth of Transfer Activity

When the rule of willing consent applies, the transfer (exchange) of property is expected to benefit both parties. In contrast, when the coercive power of government is employed to transfer property from one party to another, neither equity nor efficiency can be assumed. It was these politically determined transfers that disturbed Sitting Bull—with serious consequences for Custer and his party. Politically enforced transfers require the use of the coercive power of government to transfer rights from one individual or group to another. Since individual wealth is a direct function of the property rights held, an institutional environment that allows coercive transfer activity will greatly increase the marginal benefit of using resources to generate transfers.

The closing of the American frontier compounded the effect of increased returns from transfer activity. Whereas the frontier had permitted individuals to increase their wealth by establishing property rights to previously unclaimed resources, the closing of the frontier enhanced the benefits to be gained from expending resources for transfer activity. This is not the zero sum game claimed by many economists—that one's gain must come at a loss to another—but rather a negative sum game in which the resources spent by some in generating and by others in opposing transfer activity lead to a *net* loss. The private gain of one is more than offset by the other's loss coupled with the unproductive waste of resources used in the process.

Beginning with the Slaughterhouse cases (1873) and continuing through *Munn* v. *Illinois* (1877) and *Muller* v. *Oregon* (1908), the institutional setting of property rights definition began to change. Third parties were increasingly granted a "property right" in what had previously been another's exclusive resource. This historical foundation provides the context within which conflicts over the definition of current property rights regarding natural resources can be judged.

Rights, Markets, and Resource Management

Another common but mistaken belief is that without social regulation, resources will be managed for profit, not people. When a natural resource is privately owned, it is often thought that the owner has only his conscience to tell him to pay attention to the desires of others. Normally, however, it is the *absence* of private, transferable ownership that leads to the resource user's lack of concern for others' desires. Private ownership holds the individual owner responsible for allocating a resource to its highest valued use, whether or not the resource is used by others. If the buffalo is not mine until I kill it and I cannot sell my interest in the living animal to another, I have no incentive—beyond altruism—to investigate others' interest in it. I will do with it as I wish. But if the buffalo is mine and I may sell it, I am motivated to consider others' value estimates of the animal. I will misuse the buffalo only at my economic peril. How does this work?

Privately owned resources that are freely transferable generate decentralized decisions regarding resource uses. The market rations scarce resources and coordinates individual plans. For example, the owner of a copper mine receives information on the value of alternative uses, as well as the incentive to supply the highest valued use, through bids for copper ore or offers to buy the mine. The market enables the owner to minimize the social opportunity cost of exploiting his resource simply by minimizing his total costs. Bid and asked prices of resources provide owners with information as well as the incentives to use that information for allocating resources efficiently, thereby serving others. Similarly, consumers are informed by prices of the value *others* place on a given resource. In an open market, no one consumes or controls a good desired more by others, as measured by the size of the others' bids.

The benefits of diversity, individual freedom, adaptiveness to changing conditions, the production

of information, and even a certain equity derive from this market system. Diversity flourishes because there is no single, centralized decision maker. Instead, many asset owners and entrepreneurs, making their own individual decisions, compete over resource allocations. Those who correctly anticipate people's desires are rewarded the most. Those who envisioned a retail market for television in the 1930s and 1940s and acted on their vision, for example, may have been amply rewarded in the 1950s.

This system preserves individual freedom since those who support and wish to participate in each activity may do so on the basis of willing consent. If I want more logs for my log house, my neighbor need not be concerned. I must pay at least as much for the logs as anyone else would, and in so doing I give up purchasing power that could be used to buy other items. No shortage will result. Adaptiveness is encouraged in both management and consumer activities, since prices provide immediate information and incentives for action as soon as changes are seen. In the political arena any change in resource policy requires convincing a majority of the voters, or the bureaucracy, of the benefits such change would generate. The market system, however, permits individuals who envision scarcities or opportunities in the future to buy or sell resources and develop expertise that may redirect resource use. If their expectations about the future prove correct, they will profit. Losses from foolish diversions of resources, on the one hand, ultimately channel those resources away from inefficient or little-valued ventures. From this marvelous adaptive quality, we get both television and Edsels. Successes quickly draw imitators. Losers are quickly dropped, and unsuccessful planners are disciplined by losses.

Information, produced as a byproduct of bids offered and prices asked, is vital to the coordination of individuals plans. The market pricing system provides a tangible measure of how individuals evaluate a particular product or service relative to others that use the same resources. Without a market system of exchange such assessments are virtually impossible to make, thereby rendering rational management of nonmarketed activities difficult if not impossible. No manager can make productive resource allocation decisions without knowing input and output values, without knowing, for example, how much people are willing to sacrifice for a thousand board feet of lumber. When rights are privately held and transferable, prices yield the necessary information about the relative value of alternative resource uses—information that is concise, measurable, comparable, and largely devoid of distortion.

A management system based on private property rights also provides a certain equity by having those people who use a resource or who wish to reserve it pay for it by sacrificing some of their wealth. Where natural resources are publicly owned but used by only a few, the sale of those resources could provide a new measure of equity. The proceeds from the sale of assets now in the public domain could be distributed widely in cash or in lower taxes. Alternatively, they could be invested to reduce the national debt or used to cope with the actuarial deficit of the social security system. . . . In a market, those who use the resources would receive from sale proceeds their share of the wealth and would then be required to pay for resources they use, whether for recreation, timber harvest, or research.

Private and Transferable Property Rights

Markets can generate both equity and efficiency. Their very essence requires decentralized decision making that can promote flexibility and individual freedom, as well as the information from which rational management of resources is made possible. Yet these advantages will materialize only when property rights to each resource are privately held and easily transferable, ensuring that decision makers will have an incentive to identify the highest value of their resources, including their value to others. In the absence of such clearly defined and enforceable rights, resources may be utilized by individuals who need not compensate or outbid anyone for their use, resulting in substantial waste.

Private ownership of property rights alone is insufficient to secure efficient resource use. If rights are not easily transferable, owners may, for example, have little incentive to conserve resources for which others might be willing to pay if transfer were possible. Transferability ensures that a resource owner must reject all bids for the resource in order to continue ownership and use. Thus, if ownership is retained, the cost to others is made real and explicit.

Private and transferable property rights mandate consideration of alternative users' interests. Any failure to do so imposes economic penalties on the owner. On the other hand, nonprivate or nontransferable property rights often result in inefficiency and waste, as well as a potential indifference to others' interests. When rights are private and transferable, a decentralized market provides diversity, individual freedom, flexibility, information, and equity, since the interests of nonowners are unavoidably observed and respected. . . .

Whether in pursuit of greater equity or efficiency, many persons have increasingly turned to governmental institutions to achieve preferred allocation of natural resources. This search for government solutions persists despite the government's tarnished performance as a natural resource manager.

Public, Nontransferable Rights in a Governmental Setting

An activist government has been lauded as the last line of defense between the bulldozer and the bald eagle. A corollary to this belief contends that those involved with governmental regulation are motivated by incentives that are incorrectly analyzed by economists, whose theories apply only to a perfectly competitive market. It is thought that even though economic analysis and economic principles can explain behavior in markets, they have little bearing on governmental actions, since motives change when people enter government service. Yet these contentions are incorrect. Economic principles apply in all settings, including bureaucracies and among primitive tribes. . . .

Though current market systems allocate resources imperfectly, even many critics of markets agree that governmental efforts to correct market imperfections have ensured neither efficiency nor equity. Furthermore, there is a growing awareness that self-interest is not absent in the public sector and that economic analysis is applicable and even necessary if the actions and goals of the public sector are to be understood.

The pioneering contributions of Anthony Downs, James Buchanan and Gordon Tullock, Mancur Olson, and William Niskanen have led to a developing awareness of the problems of representative government. Their analyses show some promise of approaching the rigor and predictive capacity of the economic theory of the firm. While precise predictions regarding public-sector decision making may not be possible, some general statements may be made with confidence.

Using the property rights approach in which decision makers act to advance their own perceived interests, we observe that, as in market systems with imperfect property rights and transaction costs, public-sector decision makers are not held fully accountable for their actions.

The public sector provides no incentives for politicians and bureaucrats to resist pressures from special interests or to manage natural resources efficiently. On the contrary, such resistance may even hinder the public decision maker's career. Presumably, those turning to government to resolve natural resource problems earnestly seek more efficient and equitable management. Why, then, are public officials not held more accountable for managing resources accordingly?

Five factors tend to undermine that accountability. First, no citizen has either the time or the resources to analyze every policy issue. Nor is every citizen able personally to influence decisions regarding most complex public policy issues. Given these constraints, the intelligent citizen's ignorance about most public policy matters is understandable.

Second, although no individuals attempt to analyze or influence *all* government policies, some do attempt to influence specific policies in which they have a pronounced interest. The result is a medley of narrowly focused, highly self-interested groups that wield tremendous influence, each over its particular policy domain. These special interest groups are able to dominate a particular policy domain precisely because others with more diffuse interests regarding such policies have little incentive to articulate their views.

The system of political representation further limits the accountability of policymakers. Voters themselves have no direct input on individual issues. They merely elect representatives who, in turn, make the decisions regarding all policy issues. Such a system obviously records individual preferences imperfectly, if at all.

A congressman or senator votes on hundreds of issues each year. The message sent (the vote cast) by even a thoroughly informed, decisive voter is garbled. While the voter agrees with his favorite candidate on some important issues, there may be serious disagreement on many other issues that are judged less important by the voter. By contrast, in the private sector the citizen can "vote for" tires made by one company and toasters made by another. His choices in a market are precisely recorded.

A fourth factor further weakens the incentive for efficient natural resource management. Many resource issues have significant long-term implications for future generations. How and which resources are developed today will affect future generations. Yet precisely what those future costs and benefits might be are generally poorly understood, especially by the average citizen, who remains ill-informed about such issues. Thus, most individuals evaluate the performance of politicians and bureaucrats not according to how well they shepherd resources for the future, but according to whether or not their decisions have produced current *net* benefits.

A government decision maker can seldom gain political support by locking resources away from voters to benefit the unborn. Charitable instincts toward future resource users are unaided by (and are, in fact, countered by) self-interest if the resources are publicly owned. Charity toward others at the expense of voting constituents does not usually contribute to political survival. So we can expect governmental policy to be shortsighted, especially in comparison to the long time-frames necessary for carrying out many natural resource policies. Future benefits are more difficult to measure and future costs are easy to ignore. In addition, there is no "voice of the future" in government equivalent to the rising market price of an increasingly valuable resource. The wise public resource manager who forgoes current benefits cannot personally profit from doing so.

Yet another widespread—and incorrect—assumption is that governmental intervention in private markets can be expected to produce farsighted decisions, whereas actions taken to enlarge profits or individual wealth are normally shortsighted. This belief springs from the conviction that future generations have a property right in current resources; that is, there are transgenerational property right for the unborn. The major implication of this and similar thinking is that a market mechanism, unlike collective control, deprives future generations of resources. This belief arises in turn from the conviction that resources are being rapidly depleted, although prices for many natural minerals are in fact declining. This obvious inconsistency aside, let us assume that future generations are in some fashion granted a property right in this generation's available resources. Can the government protect the interests of these future generations better than the market?

Enter the speculator. Even though "speculator" is a term often used derisively, it merely describes a market participant who performs a service consistent with the desires of his harshest critics: He defers consumption and thereby saves for the future by paying a market price higher than any other bidder who seeks resources for present use. Indeed, exploitation will occur only when all speculative bids have been overcome.

In effect, farsighted outcomes are made possible through the activities of speculators who have an incentive to protect resources for future sale and use because such preservation may benefit them. For example, the owner of an Indiana woodlot may think that his old-growth white oak trees should be saved rather than harvested. Any concern he has for the future is powerfully influenced by how much he can gain by hoarding his resource, which is becoming scarce and valuable, and selling it later to other hoarders or speculators. The speculator thus acts as a middleman between the present and the future. His position is similar to that of another middleman, a broker of Florida oranges. By purchasing the oranges and shipping them to Montana, the fruit broker acts *as if* he cares about the desires of Montanans. He bids oranges away from Florida buyers in order to send them to Montana. The woodlot owner may act in the same way, taking wood off the market and "transporting" it into the future by failing to cut it. Since the property rights are transferable, the speculator can do well for himself while he does good for

future resource users. He can profit from the transaction if he has guessed correctly. This incentive to look to the future contrasts sharply with the incentives faced in the public sector.

Private ownership allows the owner to capture the full capital value of his resource, and thus economic incentive directs him to maintain its long-term capital value. The owner of the resource, be it a fishery, a mine, or a forest, wants to produce today, tomorrow, and ten years from now; and with a renewable resource he will attempt to maintain a sustained yield. Do farmers consume their seed corn or slaughter the last of their prime breeding cattle even when prices are especially high? In contrast, when a resource is owned by everyone, the only way in which individuals can capture its economic value is to exploit the resource before someone else does.

A final factor dictates against efficient resource management within the public sector: There is no tangible internal measure of efficiency. Private sector firms whose use of resources (as measured by cost) exceeds the value of what they produce (as measured by revenue) lose money and go out of business. Their failure benefits society by removing control of scarce resources from those who use them inefficiently. Eliminating this mechanism from the market system is probably the most significant cost of government bailouts of private firms.

Government decision makers operate without this internal check on efficiency. The funding for government bureaus derives not from profits resulting from efficient use of resources, but from federal treasury "bailouts" and budget allocations. Public sector decision makers operate with no concrete measure of efficiency because their survival does not depend on the difference between costs and benefits. Indeed, the incentive is to expand rather than to economize. An expanding bureau allows its administrators more opportunities for advancement and achievement, greater scope for power, and less need for unpleasant budget trimming and layoff decisions. . . .

QUESTIONS FOR REFLECTION

1. Why don't all citizens benefit from public lands and resources?

2. Why, according to Stroup and Baden, does regulation often lead to a net economic loss to society?

3. What are the strengths of the market's allocation of natural resources, according to Stroup and Baden?

4. What are the disadvantages of public control of natural resources?

PAUL R. EHRLICH AND ANNE H. EHRLICH

Risks, Costs, and Benefits

Paul R. Ehrlich is Professor of Biological Sciences and Director of the Center for Conservation Biology at Stanford University. Anne H. Ehrlich, his wife, has collaborated with him on many works, including Ecoscience, Extinction, *and* The End of Affluence. *(Source: From* Healing the Planet: Strategies for Resolving the Environmental Crisis, *[Reading, Mass.: Addison-Wesley Publishing Company, Inc.] Notes have been omitted. Copyright © 1991 by Paul R. Ehrlich and Anne H. Ehrlich. Reprinted by permission.)*

. . .

Our Values and Risk-Benefit Decisions by Society

We may be conservative in dealing with risks personally, but we are extremely conservative—that is, risk-averse—when considering the health of Earth's ecosystems. We believe great caution is called for when making potentially irreversible changes in humanity's only home or in taking chances with hundreds of millions or even billions of lives, including those of our own grandchildren. We don't agree with political scientist Aaron Wildavsky, who wrote in 1989 that "the secret of safety lies in danger." He sees the free market as an ideal mechanism for balancing risks and benefits. If an activity is too risky, he believes people will decide not to pay the costs and the activity will fade away. Wildavsky is very concerned about the possible risks of overestimating the dangers posed by new technologies (forgoing some or all of their potential benefits). He greatly downplays the risks that may be associated with the harm such technologies may do to people or ecosystems, basically claiming that rich nations can buy their way out of any unforeseen difficulties.

Wildavsky's predilections are widely shared in business and government, and even in some segments of the scientific community. It normally appears in the form of statements such as "If you can't *prove* that doing X will do serious harm to the environment, then we should go ahead and reap the vast benefits of doing X." Like the accused in our criminal justice system, technologies are innocent until proven guilty. In other words, wait until the existence of negative externalities is proven before taking action that would internalize them. That was the defense of the chemical industry, which managed to delay badly needed action on the ozone front for a decade and a half.

This type of reasoning applied to the pharmaceutical industry, for example, would change the standard for drug approval to one where the drug could be sold without testing until someone "proved" that it was deadly. It is not clear that we should have different standards for the health of the ecosphere than for human health. In either case, one needs to weigh the expected costs and benefits of any action, not simply apply either "zero tolerance" rules or laissez-faire.

Under a laissez-faire philosophy, it would have been folly to oppose the conversion of the United States to a nation dependent on the automobile for commuting. The technology provided the imperative; the market demanded it. Of course, automobile and tire manufacturers and oil companies lent the market a hand, but that is a detail. We have reaped the benefits in mobility, jobs, economic growth, and privacy on the way to work. It wasn't until the 1960s that some of the costs became apparent in the form of smog, loss of community, and traffic jams. While the potential of carbon dioxide for causing global warming had been known in the nineteenth century, the automobiles' contribution to the problem was not widely discussed until the 1980s. Now it is clear that allowing the automobile to dominate the structure of American society entailed many unforeseen costs, and the United States is faced with a potentially traumatic and extremely costly task of reversing its dependence on individual automotive transport.

The risk of global warming was anticipated but long ignored. One can imagine many ways to improve society's performance in dealing with such recognized risks. But what about risks that remain unknown long after the technologies generating them have been deployed? The time it takes for costs to appear after decisions are made can be impressive, as the history of CFCs clearly illustrates. Even when the risks are anticipated by a few people, they often remain unappreciated by decision makers for a long time, as in the cases of the AIDS epidemic and global warming.

Social Risk Assessments

"Societies" can't make the kinds of conscious risk assessments that informed individuals do. Instead, those decisions are made by small subsets of the society, with most individuals (including many leaders) unaware that they are being made. Furthermore, although questions of intergenerational equity do play a role in individual risk assessment (women will, for example, avoid consuming substances in pregnancy they think may later harm their children), we believe that it should play a much larger role in social risk-taking. Social systems have adapted to the consequences of inevitable individual deaths. But should our generation's "decision" to wipe out much of Earth's biodiversity be carried out, the consequences could plague our descendants for a hundred thousand generations or more.

The consequences of mistakes in social risk-taking can be therefore much more widespread and long-lasting than those of individual risk-taking. As has often been said about the extinction crisis, we are not just causing the deaths of many other organisms, we are causing an end to their births. To most people, the latter is a much grimmer consequence, be it for rhinos or for humanity. Since the probability of the extinction of many organisms is very high and the consequences are deemed very serious, the risk being run by not dealing effectively with the extinction crisis is gigantic.

Social risk-benefit decisions differ from personal ones in another important way. The kinds of risks one faces day to day tend to be familiar and easily perceived, as are the benefits. Most of us have seen many automobile accidents, if not in person, then on the evening news. The risks one runs in driving are part of everyday life, but so is the convenience of personal transportation. Virtually everyone over fifty has seen a friend or relative die miserably of cancer and has lost someone close from a heart attack. Costs that are thought to lie far in the future may be heavily discounted—the "getting lung cancer in my seventies is a small price to pay for the joy of smoking until then" syndrome. But easily perceived risks are often ignored if one values the benefits highly enough. Skydivers are in no doubt about the potential costs of the chute's not opening but know the exhilaration of the drop. Many regularly confront the zero-infinity dilemma of jumping out of an airplane for the fun of it and accept the risk.

In contrast, few people recognize the benefits of sharing Earth with millions of other organisms or think much about the importance of a reasonably stable climate. Furthermore, the most critical environmental risks are difficult to perceive. With the possible exception of a zoo keeper or someone else observing the death of Martha, the last passenger pigeon (or some other sole survivor) in captivity, no one has ever watched one species go extinct, let alone thousands. No one has ever observed the results of heating the planet by a half-dozen degrees over fifty years or so, either. The costs associated with individual risks are usually paid in minutes or months; those associated with environmental risks may be paid over millennia or more. The costs may be virtually infinite, but they are distant in time and amorphous, unlike those of hitting the ground at 100 miles an hour after your parachute has failed to open.

Environmental risks often do not present themselves in forms that are easily perceived by people. A car swerving toward our car or a snarling dog lunging at us are the sorts of stimuli that millions of years of biological and cultural evolution have prepared us to recognize as threats. But the gradually climbing zigzag line on Keeling's chart of the CO_2 concentration above Mauna Loa or statistics on habitat destruction are not. For most of human history, people could do nothing about environmental changes occurring over decades. People didn't cause them, and people couldn't stop them. Consequently, human beings evolved perceptual systems that were not good at focusing on gradual change in the environmental backdrop against which their lives were played out—in fact, they actually suppress detection of such change. With the background held constant, the sudden appearance of a hungry tiger or a tasty gazelle (or a speeding car) was all the more readily perceived and dealt with.

Despite all these difficulties in perception, society must constantly weigh risks and benefits. Suppose, as the Stanford computer study suggested, that very rapid climate change in the next century could result in hundreds of millions of premature human deaths? What costs should be incurred to slow that change if its probability were 1 percent? 5 percent? 25 percent? 50 percent? These are not easy questions to answer, and there is no *scientific* basis for answering them. Since most of the measures required to slow the warming, from greatly increasing energy efficiency to land reform in poor nations, would carry other great benefits, and since the probability of unprecedented change appears to be in the vicinity of 50 percent, a very large social effort, one incurring substantial costs, seems to us not simply justified but virtually mandatory. In our view, the delay in dealing with chemicals that attack the ozone layer was inexcusable when the principal costs to societies would have been those of a transition to substitutes, a move that could have brought out the best in industry's competitiveness and innovation. . . .

. . . Suppose the economists who claim that it would cost a trillion dollars ($10 billion per year) over the next century for the United States to do its part in slowing global warming are correct. Suppose that slowing global warming would save 1 billion lives over that period (10 million per year). In that case, the American contribution to saving each life would be $1,000. If other nations contributed in proportion to their GNPs, the rough price paid to save each life would be about $3,000. Expressing the value of human life in dollars is difficult. By most of the criteria that can be used, however, from our own subjective judgments or jury awards for wrongful death to evaluations of productivity lost by premature demise or the amounts society is willing to pay to save lives, $3,000 is a few percent of the monetary value of a human life—which should probably be valued at least at $100,000. Now let's suppose that the chances of global warming costing 1 billion lives over the next century were 50-50. Clearly, inaction in the face of the threat of global warming would be difficult to defend, since we would be avoiding an "expected" loss of 50 trillion dollars (1 billion lives × 0.50 probability × [say] $100,000 per life) for an investment of 1 trillion dollars—a great bargain in cost-benefit terms.

Of course, the steps envisioned in the trillion-dollar estimate to abate global warming would not deal with all other environmental problems—although they *would* help ameliorate many (toxic air and water pollution, for example). To be conservative, let's suppose that to assure our environmental security comprehensively and effectively would cost ten times as much as just tackling the warming. In that case, the cost would be $100 billion annually. Could that be afforded? We think so; it represents about a third of that spent on military security, an expense that almost everyone believes should decline in the future. And, of course, just as military expenditures provide subsidiary benefits such as jobs and the development of technologies that also have nonmilitary uses, so one would expect subsidiary benefits from expenditures on environmental security. They would include having a more pleasant (not just more secure) environment, better health, and lower health care costs. In short, even without being able to calculate risks, costs, and benefits exactly, rough estimates indicate that *we can afford to insure ourselves against environmental catastrophe.* Not to do so would be bizarre for a society that routinely insures lives, limbs, homes, automobiles, and businesses against risks whose probabilities of occurrence are much smaller than those, say, of unprecedented climate change due to global warming.

We believe it is important to take out that insurance for another reason. Not all risk decisions are as straightforward as those involved in abating ozone destruction or even global warming. Yet in both cases, the risk-benefit question and decisions are coming much too late—when the problems are entering the "probable-infinity" range and may have so much inertia that avoiding serious consequences is impossible. The lesson of the unexpected depletion of Antarctic ozone due to previously unknown chemistry in stratospheric ice clouds is an important one. Insurance should be taken out *before* engaging in risk-taking. Once the parachute has failed to open, it's too late to call your insurance broker.

So we are convinced that a more conservative approach is needed in the environmental risk philosophy of our society. A primary component of that philosophy should be to *increase humanity's margin for error.* And the basic way to accomplish that is to reduce the scale of human activities. Lacking crystal balls, analysts cannot accurately judge all the possible hazards of our activities, much as they may try. But we could move to a situation where even serious technological errors (like the manufacture of CFCs) would be unlikely to overwhelm the capacity of the planet to heal itself before they are detected and corrected. So once again, we see that reduction of scale is the principal challenge for the next stage of human evolution.

QUESTIONS FOR REFLECTION

1. What problems do the Ehrlichs see in applying risk-benefit analysis to environmental problems?

2. How do social risk-benefit analyses differ from individual risk-benefit analyses?

3. The Ehrlichs argue for increasing humanity's margin for error. Summarize the argument. Do you find it persuasive?

4. What do the Ehrlichs' conclusions imply about the application of utilitarianism to environmental issues?

ALDO LEOPOLD

The Land Ethic

Aldo Leopold (1887–1948), often considered the father of American wildlife conservation, was Professor of Game Management at the University of Wisconsin. (Source: from Aldo Leopold, "The Land Ethic," from A Sand County Almanac, with Other Essays on Conservation from Round River [Oxford: Oxford University Press, 1949]). Copyright © 1949, 1953, 1966, renewed 1977, 1981 by Oxford University Press, Inc. Reprinted by permission of Oxford University Press, Inc.)

. . .

The Community Concept

All ethics so far evolved rest upon a single premise: that the individual is a member of a community of interdependent parts. His instincts prompt him to compete for his place in that community, but his ethics prompt him also to cooperate (perhaps in order that there may be a place to compete for).

The land ethic simply enlarges the boundaries of the community to include soils, waters, plants, and animals, or collectively, the land.

This sounds simple: do we not already sing our love for and obligation to the land of the free and the home of the brave? Yes, but just what and whom do we love? Certainly not the soil, which we are sending helter-skelter downriver. Certainly not the waters, which we assume have no function except to turn turbines, float barges, and carry off sewage. Certainly not the plants, of which we exterminate whole communities without batting an eye. Certainly not the animals, of which we have already extirpated many of the largest and most beautiful species. A land ethic of course cannot prevent the alteration, management, and use of these "re-

sources," but it does affirm their right to continued existence, and, at least in spots, their continued existence in a natural state.

In short, a land ethic changes the role of *Homo sapiens* from conqueror of the land-community to plain member and citizen of it. It implies respect for his fellowmembers, and also respect for the community as such.

In human history, we have learned (I hope) that the conqueror role is eventually self-defeating. Why? Because it is implicit in such a role that the conqueror knows, *ex cathedra,* just what makes the community tick, and just what and who is valuable, and what and who is worthless, in community life. It always turns out that he knows neither, and this is why his conquests eventually defeat themselves.

In the biotic community, a parallel situation exists. Abraham knew exactly what the land was for: it was to drip milk and honey into Abraham's mouth. At the present moment, the assurance with which we regard this assumption is inverse to the degree of our education.

The ordinary citizen today assumes that science knows what makes the community clock tick; the scientist is equally sure that he does not. He knows that the biotic mechanism is so complex that its workings may never be fully understood. . . .

Substitutes for a Land Ethic

When the logic of history hungers for bread and we hand out a stone, we are at pains to explain how much the stone resembles bread. I now describe some of the stones which serve in lieu of a land ethic.

One basic weakness in a conservation system based wholly on economic motives is that most members of the land community have no economic value. Wildflowers and songbirds are examples. Of the 22,000 higher plants and animals native to Wisconsin, it is doubtful whether more than 5 percent can be sold, fed, eaten, or otherwise put to economic use. Yet these creatures are members of the biotic community, and if (as I believe) its stability depends on its integrity, they are entitled to continuance.

When one of these noneconomic categories is threatened, and if we happen to love it, we invent subterfuges to give it economic importance. At the beginning of the century songbirds were supposed to be disappearing. Ornithologists jumped to the rescue with some distinctly shaky evidence to the effect that insects would eat us up if birds failed to control them. The evidence had to be economic in order to be valid.

It is painful to read these circumlocutions today. We have no land ethic yet, but we have at least drawn nearer the point of admitting that birds should continue as a matter of biotic right, regardless of the presence or absence of economic advantage to us.

A parallel situation exists in respect of predatory mammals, raptorial birds, and fish-eating birds. Time was when biologists somewhat overworked the evidence that these creatures preserve the health of game by killing weaklings, or that they control rodents for the farmer, or that they prey only on "worthless" species. Here again, the evidence had to be economic in order to be valid. It is only in recent years that we hear the more honest argument that predators are members of the community, and that no special interest has the right to exterminate them for the sake of a benefit, real or fancied, to itself. . . .

Some species of trees have been "read out of the party" by economics-minded foresters because they grow too slowly, or have too low a sale value to pay as timber crops: white cedar, tamarack, cypress, beech, and hemlock are examples. In Europe, where forestry is ecologically more advanced, the noncommercial tree species are recognized as members of the native forest community, to be preserved as such, within reason. Moreover, some (like beech) have been found to have a valuable function in building up soil fertility. The interdependence of the forest and its constituent tree species, ground flora, and fauna is taken for granted.

Lack of economic value is sometimes a character not only of species or groups, but of entire biotic communities: marshes, bogs, dunes, and "deserts" are examples. Our formula in such cases is to relegate their conservation to government as refuges, monuments, or parks. The difficulty is that these communities are usually interspersed with more valuable private lands; the government cannot possibly own or control such scattered parcels. The net effect is that we have relegated some of them to ultimate extinction over large areas. . . .

To sum up: a system of conservation based solely on economic self-interest is hopelessly lopsided. It tends to ignore, and thus eventually to eliminate, many elements in the land community that lack commercial value, but that are (as far as we know) essential to its healthy functioning. It assumes, falsely, I think, that the economic parts of the biotic clock will function without the uneconomic parts. . . .

The Outlook

It is inconceivable to me that an ethical relation to land can exist without love, respect, and admiration for land, and a high regard for its value. By value, I of course mean something far broader than mere economic value; I mean value in the philosophical sense. . . .

The "key-log" which must be moved to release the evolutionary process for an ethic is simply this: quit thinking about decent land-use as solely an economic problem. Examine each question in terms of what is ethically and esthetically right, as well as what is economically expedient. A thing is right when it tends to preserve the integrity, stability, and beauty of the biotic community. It is wrong when it tends otherwise.

It of course goes without saying that economic feasibility limits the tether of what can or cannot be done for land. It always has and it always will. The fallacy the economic determinists have tied around our collective neck, and which we now need to cast off, is the belief that economics determines *all* land-use. This is simply not true. An innumerable host of actions and attitudes, comprising perhaps the bulk of all land relations, is determined by the land-user's tastes and predilections, rather than by his purse. The bulk of all land relations hinges on investments of time, forethought, skill, and faith rather than on investments of cash. As a land-user thinketh, so is he. . . .

QUESTIONS FOR REFLECTION

1. What is the land ethic?
2. Why, according to Leopold, is our current attitude about the environment self-defeating?
3. Why does Leopold object to an environmental ethic based on economic self-interest?
4. How does Leopold distinguish right from wrong action? Contrast his criterion with those of Kant and Mill.

WILLIAM F. BAXTER

from *People or Penguins*

William F. Baxter is William Benjamin Scott and Luna M. Scott Professor of Law at Stanford University. (Source: From People or Penguins: The Case for Optimal Pollution *[New York: Columbia University Press]. Copyright © 1974 by Columbia University Press. Reprinted by permission of the publisher.)*

. . . My criteria are oriented to people, not penguins. Damage to penguins, or sugar pines, or geological marvels is, without more, simply irrelevant. One must go further, by my criteria, and say: Penguins are important because people enjoy seeing them walk about rocks; and furthermore, the well-being of people would be less impaired by halting use of DDT than by giving up penguins. In short, my observations about environmental problems will be people-oriented, as are my criteria. I have no interest in preserving penguins for their own sake.

It may be said by way of objection to this position that it is very selfish of people to act as if each person represented one unit of importance and nothing else was of any importance. It is undeniably selfish. Nevertheless I think it is the only tenable starting place for analysis for several reasons. First, no other position corresponds to the way most people really think and act—i.e., corresponds to reality.

Second, this attitude does not portend any massive destruction of nonhuman flora and fauna, for people depend on them in many obvious ways, and they will be preserved because and to the degree that humans do depend on them.

Third, what is good for humans is, in many respects, good for penguins and pine trees—clean air for example. So that humans are, in these respects, surrogates for plant and animal life.

Fourth, I do not know how we could administer any other system. Our decisions are either private or collective. Insofar as Mr. Jones is free to act privately, he may give such preferences as he wishes to other forms of life: he may feed birds in winter and do with less himself, and he may even decline to resist an advancing polar bear on the ground that the bear's appetite is more important than those portions of himself that the bear may choose to eat. In short my basic premise does not rule out private altruism to competing life-forms. It does rule out, however, Mr. Jones' inclination to feed Mr. Smith to the bear, however hungry the bear, however despicable Mr. Smith.

Insofar as we act collectively, on the other hand, only humans can be afforded an opportunity to participate in the collective decisions. Penguins cannot vote now and are unlikely subjects for the franchise—pine trees more unlikely still. Again each individual is free to cast his vote so as to benefit sugar pines if that is his inclination. But many of the more extreme assertions that one hears from some conservationists amount to tacit assertions that they are specially appointed representatives of sugar pines, and hence that their preferences should be weighted more heavily than the preferences of other humans who do not enjoy equal rapport with "nature." The simplistic assertion that agricultural use of DDT must stop at once because it is harmful to penguins is of that type.

Fifth, if polar bears or pine trees or penguins, like men, are to be regarded as ends rather than means, if they are to count in our calculus of social organization, someone must tell me how much each one counts, and someone must tell me how these life-forms are to be permitted to express their preferences, for I do not know either answer. If the answer is that certain people are to hold their proxies, then I want to know how those proxy-holders are to be selected: self-appointment does not seem workable to me.

Sixth, and by way of summary of all the foregoing, let me point out that the set of environmental issues under discussion—although they raise very complex technical questions of how to achieve any objective—ultimately raise a normative question: what *ought* we to do. Questions of *ought* are unique to the human mind and world—they are meaningless as applied to a nonhuman situation.

I reject the proposition that we *ought* to respect the "balance of nature" or to "preserve the environment" unless the reason for doing so, express or implied, is the benefit of man.

I reject the idea that there is a "right" or "morally correct" state of nature to which we should return. The word "nature" has no normative connotation. Was it "right" or "wrong" for the earth's crust to heave in contortion and create mountains and seas? Was it "right" for the first amphibian to crawl up out of the primordial ooze? Was it "wrong" for plants to reproduce themselves and alter the atmospheric composition in favor of oxygen? For animals to alter the atmosphere in favor of carbon dioxide both by breathing oxygen and eating plants? No answers can be given to these questions because they are meaningless questions.

All this may seem obvious to the point of being tedious, but much of the present controversy over environment and pollution rests on tacit normative assumptions about just such nonnormative phenomena: that it is "wrong" to impair penguins with DDT, but not to slaughter cattle for prime rib roasts. That it is wrong to kill stands of sugar pines with industrial fumes, but not to cut sugar pines and build housing for the poor. Every man is entitled to his own preferred definition of Walden Pond, but there is no definition that has any moral superiority over another, except by reference to the selfish needs of the human race.

From the fact that there is no normative definition of the natural state, it follows that there is no normative definition of clean air or pure water—hence no definition of polluted air—or of pollution—except by reference to the needs of man. The "right" composition of the atmosphere is one which has some dust in it and some lead in it and some hydrogen sulfide in it—just those amounts that attend a sensibly organized society thoughtfully and knowledgeably pursuing the greatest possible satisfaction for its human members. . . .

QUESTIONS FOR REFLECTION

1. How does Baxter argue that only effects on humans should be counted in environmental calculations?

2. What is the problem of the commons?

3. What constraints should govern collective decisions about the environment, in Baxter's view?

4. How might Baxter respond to the Ehrlichs' claim that we must reinterpret risk-benefit analyses to increase humanity's margin of error?

BILL DEVALL AND GEORGE SESSIONS

from *Deep Ecology*

Bill Devall is Professor of Sociology at Humboldt State University. George Sessions is Professor of Humanities at Sierra College. (Source: From Deep Ecology *[Salt Lake City: Gibbs Smith]. Notes have been omitted. Copyright © 1985 by Gibbs M. Smith, Inc. Reprinted by permission.)*

The term *deep ecology* was coined by Arne Naess in his 1973 article, "The Shallow and the Deep, Long-Range Ecology Movements." Naess was attempting to describe the deeper, more spiritual approach to Nature exemplified in the writings of Aldo Leopold and Rachel Carson. He thought that this deeper approach resulted from a more sensitive openness to ourselves and nonhuman life around us. The essence of deep ecology is to keep asking more searching questions about human life, society, and Nature as in the Western philosophical tradition of Socrates. As examples of this deep questioning, Naess points out "that we ask why and how, where others do not. For instance, ecology as a science does not ask what kind of a society would be the best for maintaining a particular ecosystem—that is considered a question for value theory, for politics, for ethics." Thus deep ecology goes beyond the so-called factual scientific level to the level of self and Earth wisdom.

Deep ecology goes beyond a limited piecemeal shallow approach to environmental problems and attempts to articulate a comprehensive religious and philosophical worldview. The foundations of deep ecology are the basic intuitions and experiencing of ourselves and Nature which comprise ecological consciousness. Certain outlooks on politics and public policy flow naturally from this consciousness. . . .

Ecological consciousness and deep ecology are in sharp contrast with the dominant worldview of technocratic-industrial societies which regards humans as isolated and fundamentally separate from the rest of Nature, as superior to, and in charge of, the rest of creation. But the view of humans as separate and superior to the rest of Nature is only part of larger cultural patterns. For thousands of years, Western culture has become increasingly obsessed with the idea of *dominance:* with dominance of humans over nonhuman Nature, masculine over the feminine, wealthy and powerful over the poor, with the dominance of the West over non-Western cultures. Deep ecological consciousness allows us to see through these erroneous and dangerous illusions.

For deep ecology, the study of our place in the Earth household includes the study of ourselves as part of the organic whole. Going beyond a narrowly materialist scientific understanding of reality, the spiritual and the material aspects of reality fuse together. While the leading intellectuals of the dominant worldview have tended to view religion as "just superstition," and have looked upon ancient spiritual practice and enlightenment, such as found in Zen Buddhism, as essentially subjective, the search for deep ecological consciousness is the search for a more objective consciousness and state of being through an active deep questioning and meditative process and way of life.

Many people have asked these deeper questions and cultivated ecological consciousness within the context of different spiritual traditions—Christianity, Taoism, Buddhism, and Native American rituals, for example. While differing greatly in other regards, many in these traditions agree with the basic principles of deep ecology.

Warwick Fox, an Australian philosopher, has succinctly expressed the central intuition of deep ecology: "It is the idea that we can make no firm ontological divide in the field of existence: That there is no bifurcation in reality between the human and the nonhuman realms . . . to the extent that we perceive boundaries, we fall short of deep ecological consciousness."

From this most basic insight or characteristic of deep ecological consciousness, Arne Naess has developed two *ultimate norms* or intuitions which are themselves not derivable from other principles or intuitions. They are arrived at by the deep questioning process and reveal the importance of moving to the philosophical and religious level of wisdom. They cannot be validated, of course, by the methodology of modern science based on its usual mechanistic assumptions and its very narrow definition of data. These ultimate norms are *self-realization* and *biocentric equality*.

I. Self-Realization

In keeping with the spiritual traditions of many of the world's religions, the deep ecology norm of self-realization goes beyond the modern Western *self* which is defined as an isolated ego striving primarily for hedonistic gratification or for a narrow sense of individual salvation in this life or the next. This socially programmed sense of the narrow self or social self dislocates us, and leaves us prey to whatever fad or fashion is prevalent in our society or social reference group. We are thus robbed of beginning the search for our unique spiritual/biological personhood. Spiritual growth, or unfolding, begins when we cease to understand or see ourselves as isolated and narrow competing egos and begin to identify with other humans from our family and friends to, eventually, our species. But the deep ecology sense of self requires a further maturity and growth, an identification which goes beyond humanity to include the nonhuman world. We must see beyond our narrow contemporary cultural assumptions and values, and the conventional wisdom of our time and place, and this is best achieved by the meditative deep questioning process. Only in this way can we hope to attain full mature personhood and uniqueness.

A nurturing nondominating society can help in the "real work" of becoming a whole person. The "real work" can be summarized symbolically as the realization of "self-in-Self" where "Self" stands for organic wholeness. This process of the full unfolding of the self can also be summarized by the phrase, "No one is saved until we are all saved," where the phrase "one" includes not only me, an individual human, but all humans, whales, grizzly bears, whole rain forest ecosystems, mountains and rivers, the tiniest microbes in the soil, and so on.

II. Biocentric Equality

The intuition of biocentric equality is that all things in the biosphere have an equal right to live and blossom and to reach their own individual forms of unfolding and self-realization within the larger Self-realization. This basic intuition is that all organisms and entities in the ecosphere, as parts of the interrelated whole, are equal in intrinsic worth. Naess suggests that biocentric equality as an intuition is true in principle, although in the process of living, all species use each other as food, shelter, etc. Mutual predation is a biological fact of life, and many of the world's religions have struggled with the spiritual implications of this. Some animal liberationists who attempt to sidestep this problem by advocating vegetarianism are forced to say that the entire plant kingdom including rain forests have no right to their own existence. This evasion flies in the face of the basic intuition of equality. Aldo Leopold expressed this intuition when he said humans are "plain citizens" of the biotic community, not lord and master over all other species.

Biocentric equality is intimately related to the all-inclusive Self-realization in the sense that if we harm the rest of Nature then we are harming ourselves. There are no boundaries and everything is interrelated. But insofar as we perceive things as individual organisms or entities, the insight draws us to respect all human and nonhuman individuals in their own right as parts of the whole without feeling the need to set up hierarchies of species with humans at the top.

The practical implications of this intuition or norm suggest that we should live with minimum rather than maximum impact on other species and on the Earth in general. Thus we see another aspect

Dominant Worldview	Deep Ecology
Dominance over Nature	Harmony with Nature
Natural environment as resource for humans	All nature has intrinsic worth/biospecies equality
Material/economic growth for growing human population	Elegantly simple material needs (material goals serving the larger goal of self-realization)
Belief in ample resource reserves	Earth "supplies" limited
High technological progress and solutions	Appropriate technology; nondominating science
Consumerism	Doing with enough/recycling
National/centralized community	Minority tradition/bioregion

Figure 5-1

of our guiding principle: "simple in means, rich in ends." . . .

A fuller discussion of the biocentric norm as it unfolds itself in practice begins with the realization that we, as individual humans, and as communities of humans, have vital needs which go beyond such basics as food, water, and shelter to include love, play, creative expression, intimate relationships with a particular landscape (or Nature taken in its entirety) as well as intimate relationships with other humans, and the vital need for spiritual growth, for becoming a mature human being.

Our vital material needs are probably more simple than many realize. In technocratic-industrial societies there is overwhelming propaganda and advertising which encourages false needs and destructive desires designed to foster increased production and consumption of goods. Most of this actually diverts us from facing reality in an objective way and from beginning the "real work" of spiritual growth and maturity. . . .

As a brief summary of our position thus far, Figure 5-1 summarizes the contrast between the dominant worldview and deep ecology.

III. Basic Principles of Deep Ecology

. . .

Basic Principles

1. The well-being and flourishing of human and nonhuman Life on Earth have value in themselves (synonyms: intrinsic value, inherent value). These values are independent of the usefulness of the nonhuman world for human purposes.

2. Richness and diversity of life forms contribute to the realization of these values and are also values in themselves.

3. Humans have no right to reduce this richness and diversity except to satisfy *vital* needs.

4. The flourishing of human life and cultures is compatible with a substantial decrease of the human population. The flourishing of nonhuman life requires such a decrease.

5. Present human interference with the nonhuman world is excessive, and the situation is rapidly worsening.

6. Policies must therefore be changed. These policies affect basic economic, technological, and ideological structures. The resulting state of affairs will be deeply different from the present.

7. The ideological change is mainly that of appreciating *life quality* (dwelling in situations of inherent value) rather than adhering to an increasingly higher standard of living. There will be a profound awareness of the difference between big and great.

8. Those who subscribe to the foregoing points have an obligation directly or indirectly to try to implement the necessary changes.

Naess and Sessions Provide Comments on the Basic Principles:

RE (1). This formulation refers to the biosphere, or more accurately, to the ecosphere as a whole. This includes individuals, species, populations, habitat, as well as human and nonhuman cultures. From our current knowledge of all-pervasive intimate relationships, this implies a fundamental deep concern and respect. Ecological processes of the planet should, on the whole, remain intact. "The world environment should remain 'natural'" (Gary Snyder).

The term "life" is used here in a more comprehensive nontechnical way to refer also to what biologists classify as "nonliving"; rivers (watersheds), landscapes, ecosystems. For supporters of deep ecology, slogans such as "Let the river live" illustrate this broader usage so common in most cultures.

Inherent value as used in (1) is common in deep ecology literature. ("The presence of inherent value in a natural object is independent of any awareness, interest, or appreciation of it by a conscious being.")

RE (2). More technically, this is a formulation concerning diversity and complexity. From an ecological standpoint, complexity and symbiosis are conditions for maximizing diversity. So-called simple, lower, or primitive species of plants and animals contribute essentially to the richness and diversity of life. They have value in themselves and are not merely steps toward the so-called higher or rational life forms. The second principle presupposes that life itself, as a process over evolutionary time, implies an increase of diversity and richness. The refusal to acknowledge that some life forms have greater or lesser intrinsic value than others (see points 1 and 2) runs counter to the formulations of some ecological philosophers and New Age writers.

Complexity, as referred to here, is different from complication. Urban life may be more complicated than life in a natural setting without being more complex in the sense of multifaceted quality.

RE (3). The term "vital need" is left deliberately vague to allow for considerable latitude in judgment. Differences in climate and related factors, together with differences in the structures of societies as they now exist, need to be considered (for some Eskimos, snowmobiles are necessary today to satisfy vital needs).

People in the materially richest countries cannot be expected to reduce their excessive interference with the nonhuman world to a moderate level overnight. The stabilization and reduction of the human population will take time. Interim strategies need to be developed. But this in no way excuses the present complacency—the extreme seriousness of our current situation must first be realized. But the longer we wait the more drastic will be the measures needed. Until deep changes are made, substantial decreases in richness and diversity are liable to occur: the rate of extinction of species will be ten to one hundred times greater than any other period of earth history.

RE (4). The United Nations Fund for Population Activities in their State of World Population Report (1984) said that high human population growth rates (over 2.0 percent annum) in many developing countries "were diminishing the quality of life for many millions of people." During the decade 1974–1984, the world population grew by nearly 800 million—more than the size of India. "And we will be adding about one Bangladesh (population 93 million) per annum between now and the year 2000."

The report noted that "The growth rate of the human population has declined for the first time in human history. But at the same time, the number of people being added to the human population is bigger than at any time in history because the population base is larger."

Most of the nations in the developing world (including India and China) have as their official government policy the goal of reducing the rate of human population increase, but there are debates over the types of measures to take (contraception, abortion, etc.) consistent with human rights and feasibility.

The report concludes that if all governments set specific population targets as public policy to help alleviate poverty and advance the quality of life, the current situation could be improved.

As many ecologists have pointed out, it is also absolutely crucial to curb population growth in the so-called developed (i.e., overdeveloped) industrial societies. Given the tremendous rate of consumption and waste production of individuals in these societies, they represent a much greater threat and impact on the biosphere per capita than individuals in Second and Third World countries.

RE (5). This formulation is mild. For a realistic assessment of the situation, see the unabbreviated version of the I.U.C.N.'s *World Conservation Strategy*. There are other works to be highly recommended, such as Gerald Barney's *Global 2000 Report to the President of the United States*.

The slogan of "noninterference" does not imply that humans should not modify some ecosystems as do other species. Humans have modified the earth and will probably continue to do so. At issue is the nature and extent of such interference.

The fight to preserve and extend areas of wilderness or near-wilderness should continue and should focus on the general ecological functions of these areas (one such function: large wilderness areas are required in the biosphere to allow for continued evolutionary speciation of animals and plants). Most present designated wilderness areas and game preserves are not large enough to allow for such speciation.

RE (6). Economic growth as conceived and implemented today by the industrial states is incompatible with (1)–(5). There is only a faint resemblance between ideal sustainable forms of economic growth and present policies of the industrial societies. And "sustainable" still means "sustainable in relation to humans."

Present ideology tends to value things because they are scarce and because they have a commodity value. There is prestige in vast consumption and waste (to mention only several relevant factors).

Whereas "self-determination," "local community," and "think globally, act locally," will remain key terms in the ecology of human societies, nevertheless the implementation of deep changes requires increasingly global action—action across borders.

Governments in Third World countries (with the exception of Costa Rica and a few others) are uninterested in deep ecological issues. When the governments of industrial societies try to promote ecological measures through Third World governments, practically nothing is accomplished (e.g., with problems of desertification). Given this situation, support for global action through nongovernmental international organizations becomes increasingly important. Many of these organizations are able to act globally "from grassroots to grassroots," thus avoiding negative governmental interference.

Cultural diversity today requires advanced technology, that is, techniques that advance the basic goals of each culture. So-called soft, intermediate, and alternative technologies are steps in this direction.

RE (7). Some economists criticize the term "quality of life" because it is supposed to be vague. But on closer inspection, what they consider to be vague is actually the nonquantitative nature of the term. One cannot quantify adequately what is important for the quality of life as discussed here, and there is no need to do so.

RE (8). There is ample room for different opinions about priorities: what should be done first, what next? What is most urgent? What is clearly necessary as opposed to what is highly desirable but not absolutely pressing? . . .

QUESTIONS FOR REFLECTION

1. What is *deep ecology*? How does it differ from environmentalism in general?

2. What is *biocentric equality*? How do Devall and Sessions argue for it? What are its implications for environmental issues?

3. Do you accept the principle of biocentric equality? Why, or why not?

4. Do any basic principles of deep ecology contradict utilitarianism?

5. Analyze and critique the basic principles from a Kantian perspective.

KAREN J. WARREN

The Power and the Promise
of Ecological Feminism

Karen J. Warren is Professor of Philosophy at Macalester College. (Source: from Karen J. Warren, "The Power and the Promise of Ecological Feminism," Environmental Ethics 12 [1990]:125–144. Reprinted by permission of the author and the publisher.)

. . . [E]cological feminism is the position that there are important connections—historical, experiential, symbolic, theoretical—between the domination of women and the domination of nature, an understanding of which is crucial to both feminism and environmental ethics. I argue that the promise and power of ecological feminism is that *it provides a distinctive framework both for preconceiving feminism and for developing an environmental ethic which takes seriously connections between the domination of women and the domination of nature.* . . .

Feminism, Ecological Feminism, and Conceptual Frameworks

. . . For ecofeminism, that a logic of domination is explanatorily basic is important for at least three reasons. First, without a logic of domination, a description of similarities and differences would be just that—a description of similarities and differences. Consider the claim, "Humans are different from plants and rocks in that humans can (and plants and rocks cannot) consciously and radically reshape the communities in which they live; humans are similar to plants and rocks in that they are both members of an ecological community." Even if humans are "better" than plants and rocks with respect to the conscious ability of humans to radically transform communities, one does not *thereby* get any *morally* relevant distinction between humans and nonhumans, or an argument for the domination of plants and rocks by humans. To get *those* conclusions one needs to add at least two powerful assumptions, viz., (A2) and (A4) in argument A below:

(A1) Humans do, and plants and rocks do not, have the capacity to consciously and radically change the community in which they live.

(A2) Whatever has the capacity to consciously and radically change the community in which it lives is morally superior to whatever lacks this capacity.

(A3) Thus, humans are morally superior to plants and rocks.

(A4) For any X and Y, if X is morally superior to Y, then X is morally justified in subordinating Y.

(A5) Thus, humans are morally justified in subordinating plants and rocks.

Without the two assumptions that *humans are morally superior* to (at least some) nonhumans, (A2), and that *superiority justifies subordination,* (A4), all one has is some difference between humans and some nonhumans. This is true *even if* that difference is given in terms of superiority. Thus, it is the logic of domination, (A4), which is the bottom line in ecofeminist discussions of oppression.

Second, ecofeminists . . . claim that, historically, within at least the dominant Western culture, a patriarchal conceptual framework has sanctioned the following argument B:

(B1) Women are identified with nature and the realm of the physical; men are identified with the "human" and the realm of the mental.

(B2) Whatever is identified with nature and the realm of the physical is inferior to ("below") whatever is identified with the "human" and the realm of the mental; or, conversely, the latter is superior to ("above") the former.

(B3) Thus, women are inferior to ("below") men; or, conversely, men are superior to ("above") women.

(B4) For any X and Y, if X is superior to Y, then X is justified in subordinating Y.

(B5) Thus, men are justified in subordinating women.

If sound, argument B establishes *patriarchy*, i.e., the conclusion given at (B5) that the systematic domination of women by men is justified. But according to ecofeminists, (B5) is justified by just those three features of an oppressive conceptual framework identified earlier: value-hierarchical thinking, the assumption at (B2); value dualisms, the assumed dualism of the mental and the physical at (B1) and the assumed inferiority of the physical vis-à-vis the mental at (B2); and a logic of domination, the assumption at (B4), the same as the previous premise (A4). Hence, according to ecofeminists, insofar as an oppressive patriarchal conceptual framework has functioned historically (within at least dominant Western culture) to sanction the twin dominations of women and nature (argument B), both argument B and the patriarchal conceptual framework, from whence it comes, ought to be rejected.

Of course, the preceding does not identify which premises of B are false. What is the status of premises (B1) and (B2)? Most, if not all, feminists claim that (B1), and many ecofeminists claim that (B2), have been assumed or asserted within the dominant Western philosophical and intellectual tradition. As such, these feminists assert, as a matter of historical fact, that the dominant Western philosophical tradition has assumed the truth of (B1) and (B2). Ecofemi-

nists, however, either deny (B2) or do not affirm (B2). Furthermore, because some ecofeminists are anxious to deny any ahistorical identification of women with nature, some ecofeminists deny (B1) when (B1) is used to support anything other than a strictly historical claim about what has been asserted or assumed to be true within patriarchal culture—e.g., when (B1) is used to assert that women properly are identified with the realm of nature and the physical. Thus, from an ecofeminist perspective, (B1) and (B2) are properly viewed as problematic though historically sanctioned claims: they are problematic precisely because of the way they have functioned historically in a patriarchal conceptual framework and culture to sanction the dominations of women and nature.

What *all* ecofeminists agree about, then, is the way in which *the logic of domination* has functioned historically within patriarchy to sustain and justify the twin dominations of women and nature. Since *all* feminists (and not just ecofeminists) oppose patriarchy, the conclusion given at (B5), all feminists (including ecofeminists) must oppose at least the logic of domination, premise (B4), on which argument B rests—whatever the truth-value status of (B1) and (B2) *outside* of a patriarchal context.

That *all* feminists must oppose the logic of domination shows the breadth and depth of the ecofeminist critique of B: it is a critique not only of the three assumptions on which this argument for the domination of women and nature rests, viz., the assumptions at (B1), (B2), and (B4); it is also a critique of patriarchal conceptual frameworks generally, i.e., of those oppressive conceptual frameworks which put men "up" and women "down," allege some way in which women are morally inferior to men, and use that alleged difference to justify the subordination of women by men. Therefore, ecofeminism is necessary to *any* feminist critique of patriarchy, and, hence, necessary to feminism. . . .

Third, ecofeminism clarifies why the logic of domination, and any conceptual framework which gives rise to it, must be abolished in order both to make possible a meaningful notion of difference which does not breed domination and to prevent feminism from becoming a "support" movement based primarily on shared experiences. In contemporary society, there is no one "woman's voice," no *woman* (or *human*) *simpliciter:* every woman (or human) is a woman (or human) of some race, class, age, affectional orientation, marital status, regional or national background, and so forth. Because there are no "monolithic experiences" that all women share, feminism must be a "solidarity movement" based on shared beliefs and interests rather than a "unity in sameness" movement based on shared experiences and shared victimization. In the words of Maria Lugones, "Unity—not to be confused with solidarity—is understood as conceptually tied to domination."

Ecofeminists insist that the sort of logic of domination used to justify the domination of humans by gender, racial or ethnic, or class status is also used to justify the domination of nature. Because eliminating a logic of domination is part of a feminist critique—whether a critique of patriarchy, white supremacist culture, or imperialism—ecofeminists insist that *naturism* is properly viewed as an integral part of any feminist solidarity movement to end sexist oppression and the logic of domination which conceptually grounds it. . . .

Ecofeminism as a Feminist and Environmental Ethic

. . . [A]n ecofeminist ethic involves a reconception of what it means to be human, and in what human ethical behavior consists. Ecofeminism denies abstract individualism. Humans are who we are in large part by virtue of the historical and social contexts and the relationships we are in, including our relationships with nonhuman nature. Relationships are not some-thing extrinsic to who we are, not an "add on" feature of human nature; they play an essential role in shaping what it is to be human. Relationships of humans to the nonhuman environment are, in part, constitutive of what it is to be a human.

By making visible the interconnections among the dominations of women and nature, ecofeminism shows that both are feminist issues and that explicit acknowledgement of both is vital to any responsible environmental ethic. Feminism *must* embrace ecological feminism if it is to end the domination of women because the domination of women is tied conceptually and historically to the domination of nature.

A responsible environmental ethic also *must* embrace feminism. Otherwise, even the seemingly most revolutionary, liberational, and holistic ecological ethic will fail to take seriously the interconnected dominations of nature and women that are so much a part of the historical legacy and conceptual framework that sanctions the exploitation of nonhuman nature. Failure to make visible these interconnected, twin dominations results in an inaccurate account of how it is that nature has been and continues to be dominated and exploited and produces an environmental ethic that lacks the depth necessary to be truly *inclusive* of the realities of persons who at least in dominant Western culture have been intimately tied with that exploitation, viz., women. Whatever else can be said in favor of such holistic ethics, a failure to make visible ecofeminist insights into the common denominators of the twin oppressions of women and nature is to perpetuate, rather than overcome, the source of that oppression. . . .

QUESTIONS FOR REFLECTION

1. What is ecological feminism?
2. What role does a logic of domination play in ecofeminism? What assumptions do those who draw moral distinctions between humans and nonhumans need to make?
3. What connects the domination of nature to the domination of women?
4. How does ecological feminism seek to overcome the domination of nature?
5. Baxter and Warren disagree sharply about a number of issues. Which disagreements are fundamental? How might Baxter critique Warren's view?
6. Compare ecofeminism to Leopold's land ethic and to deep ecology. How are they similar? Where do they diverge?

PART II

LIBERTY

The central problem of political philosophy is the relation between people and their governments—between the rulers and the ruled. When rulers acquire power through force or inheritance, they have little need to take the interests of the people into account. In a democracy, however, the rulers acquire power through elections and therefore must consider the interests of the people to some degree. But even if the rulers follow the will of the majority perfectly, the possibility of conflict remains. Rule by the people, as John Stuart Mill points out, is really rule of each by all the rest. Nothing in the concept of democracy itself protects the minority from the majority's power. As a joke has it, sometimes democracy is like three wolves and a sheep voting on what to have for dinner. Edmund Burke therefore warned of the "oppression of the minority"; Alexis de Tocqueville similarly foresaw "the tyranny of the majority." Both generalize Aristotle's worry that "If justice is the will of the majority, . . . they will unjustly confiscate the property of the wealthy minority" (*Politics* VI, 3).

Two kinds of issues arise here. First, certain distinct and unpopular or disadvantaged groups may consistently lose elections to a more powerful majority. Democracy, unembellished, does little to protect their rights. Second, individuals have little protection from the majority's power. Voters out of step with the majority may find themselves without any rights at all.

The Bill of Rights—the first ten amendments to the United States Constitution—attempts to protect people from the unfettered power of undemocratic minorities and democratic majorities. By delineating

people's rights, it carves out a sphere of individual liberty that government may not transgress. Philosophers such as John Stuart Mill seek to distinguish a sphere of personal liberty in a different way. A law is *paternalistic* if it restricts a person's liberty for his or her own good. Mill argues, with some important qualifications, that such laws are illegitimate. Mill's *harm principle* asserts that government may restrict a person's liberty only to prevent harm to others. To restrict liberty to prevent people from harming themselves or to promote their own good, Mill contends, goes beyond the proper bounds of government authority.

Many countries have a wide variety of paternalistic laws. They tend to fall into three categories:

1. *Laws promoting morality:* Laws regulating religious practices, diet, and various forms of sexual behavior—adultery, polygamy, polyandry, sodomy, prostitution, premarital sex, and pornography.

2. *Laws promoting health and safety:* Laws regulating alcohol, drugs (both medical and recreational), suicide, self-mutilation, voluntary euthanasia, working conditions, and the use of motorcycle helmets and seat belts.

3. *Laws promoting economic welfare:* Laws regulating wages, working hours, shopping hours (for example, "blue laws"), gambling, investments, and retirement (for example, Social Security).

Few people would accept all laws of this kind as legitimate, but just as few would find all objectionable. How can we distinguish legitimate from illegitimate paternalistic laws?

One way incorporates Mill's distinction between *self-regarding* and *other-regarding* actions. Roughly, a self-regarding action affects only the agent or agents of the action; an other-regarding action affects others. Mill's harm principle, in these terms, rules out government restriction of self-regarding actions.

There are several complications. Some self-regarding actions involve only a single agent—taking a drug or failing to wear a seat belt, for example. Others involve a group of agents; it takes at least two agents to indulge in prostitution, sodomy, gambling, or employment, for example. In either case, Mill says, we can consider the act self-regarding only if several conditions are satisfied. First, every agent must be acting freely; there must be no coercion. Everyone involved must consent to the action. We can treat ordinary, consensual sexual activity as self-regarding, but rape is clearly other-regarding. Second, every agent must be acting voluntarily. If any participant is in any way incapable of choosing—if he or she is a child, for example, or mentally incapacitated, drugged, or insane—then the action is other-regarding. Third, every agent must be reasonably well informed about the action. There must be no ignorance or deception about any important and relevant matters. Someone taking a dangerous drug while believing it to be aspirin is not exercising liberty in any meaningful sense. If any participant is ignorant or deceived about an important feature of the action, then, it counts as other-regarding. The harm principle protects from government intrusion only those actions that are undertaken freely and voluntarily by informed agents and that affect nobody but themselves.

Mill's harm principle has met with wide acceptance in certain realms, but it has also met serious objections. Aristotle, for example, holds a completely opposed view of liberty. He contends that the best government is that which produces the best citizens. The chief task of government, in his view, is to promote the good of its citizens by helping to educate and guide them. Edmund Burke and others take a more moderate view. They maintain that individual liberty is only one among many important and competing values. A society should value the individual liberty of its citizens, these philosophers charge, but it should also value harmony, order, justice, and equality, among others. These various values often come into conflict, both in our individual lives and in the political arena. The harm principle tries to resolve all such conflicts in favor of liberty. But, Burke holds, it is not obvious that any value wins out all of the time. Politics, in his view, is an art of balancing values, reconciling them when possible, seeking compromises between them when possible, and, if all else fails, resolving conflicts between them by appeal to analogy and the wisdom we have accumulated from the past.

The Supreme Court and various political philosophers of the twentieth century have responded to Mill's principle by distinguishing civil from economic liberties. Civil liberties—in the original sense of the term, liberties granted by society—have been interpreted as liberties relating in some way to a person's sense of identity or to the political process. It is not clear whether this distinction makes sense. In what category, for example, is the freedom to place an advertisement or produce a commercial in favor of a certain political position? Whatever the answer, Mill means his principle to apply to both civil and economic liberties. Some twentieth-century thinkers, however, have sought to apply it only to civil liberties, contending that liberty does take precedence over other values in such matters, whereas justice, equality, and other concerns often take precedence over liberty in economic matters.

Questions concerning freedom of speech have a central place in democratic societies. Democracies depend on informed and involved citizens. Citizens can be informed, however, only if they have access to information. Political argument and the supporting information it requires therefore need protection. Types of speech that have little in common with political discussion and debate, however, provoke greater controversy. Some issues concerning freedom of speech—pornography, for example—fall under the general topic of paternalism, for both speaker and listener are voluntary, informed, consenting adults. Other kinds of speech do not.

John Milton advances an early and sophisticated argument for freedom of the press. In brief, he contends that restrictions on publishing and printing interfere with the search for truth, inevitably fail to restrict what they are meant to restrict because of practical difficulties, insult citizens and prevent them from developing their own powers of judgment, and are in any case unnecessary, for truth will conquer falsehood in a free contest of ideas. John Stuart Mill adds to the arguments of Milton. An opinion may be true or contain some elements of truth. Even if it is false, only by battling such falsehoods can the truth remain vibrant and meaningful. Mill thus concludes that the content of an opinion can never justify suppressing it. Nor, he contends, can its manner of expression. Only circumstances in which an utterance might cause serious harm (for example, start a riot) can justify prohibiting it in those circumstances.

PLATO

from *The Republic*

Socrates (470–399 B.C.E.) was a contemporary of the great Greek playwrights Sophocles, Euripedes, and Aristophanes, as well as the historians Thucydides and Herodotus. He is in many ways the central figure of Western philosophy. Socrates was the first person in the West to advance philosophical arguments. As his student Plato (427–347 B.C.E.) portrays him, Socrates put forward no particular theories of his own—indeed, he wrote nothing—but used arguments to clarify, investigate, and, usually, refute the views of others.

Socrates is the central character of many of Plato's works. Unlike most later philosophers, Plato wrote dialogues rather than essays or treatises. He never speaks in his own voice. In the early dialogues, Socrates asks what some virtue (for example, piety, self-control, courage, or friendship) is. Someone answers. Socrates analyzes the proposed definition and begins asking questions, leading the parties to the conversation to see that the definition cannot be right. Sometimes, the definition is unclear; sometimes, it includes too much; sometimes, it does not include enough. Someone then proposes another definition, and the process continues. This constitutes the Socratic method (also called dialectic). The early dialogues end with at least some of the participants leaving discouraged, embarrassed, or irritated at being unable to give a good definition. Socrates himself takes no position. In fact, he maintains that he knows only that he knows nothing.

In Plato's Republic, Socrates and other characters of the dialogue discuss the question, What is justice? Socrates goes beyond criticizing the views of others and outlines the ideal state. He advocates a sweeping censorship. Those who are to be leaders—the guardians—must be brought up to be virtuous. That requires that they hear and read only what ennobles their characters. Anything that would debase them must be banned. (Source: Plato, Republic, *translated by Benjamin Jowett, from* The Dialogues of Plato *[Oxford: Oxford University Press, 1892].)*

(Socrates, Adeimantus.)

Then we have found the desired natures; and now that we have found them, how are they [the guardians, that is, the leaders of the state] to be reared and educated? Is not this an inquiry which may be expected to throw light on greater inquiry which is our final end—How do justice and injustice grow up in States? for we do not want either to omit what is to the point or to draw out the argument to an inconvenient length.

Adeimantus thought that the inquiry would be of great service to us.

Then, I said, my dear friend, the task must not be given up, even if somewhat long.

Certainly not.

Come then, and let us pass a leisure hour in storytelling, and our story shall be the education of our heroes.

By all means.

And what shall be their education? . . .

You know also that the beginning is the most important part of any work, especially in the case of a young and tender thing; for that is the time at which the character is being formed and the desired impression is more readily taken.

Quite true.

And shall we just carelessly allow children to hear any casual tales which may be devised by casual persons, and to receive into their minds ideas for the most part the very opposite of those which we should wish them to have when they are grown up?

We cannot.

Then the first thing will be to establish a censorship of the writers of fiction, and let the censors receive any tale of fiction which is good, and reject the bad; and we will desire mothers and nurses to tell their children the authorized ones only. Let them fashion the mind with such tales, even more fondly than they mould the body with their hands; but most of those which are now in use must be discarded.

Of what tales are you speaking? he said.

You may find a model of the lesser in the greater, I said; for they are necessarily of the same type, and there is the same spirit in both of them.

Very likely, he replied; but I do not as yet know what you would term the greater.

Those, I said, which are narrated by Homer and Hesiod, and the rest of the poets, who have ever been the great storytellers of mankind.

But which stories do you mean, he said; and what fault do you find with them?

A fault which is most serious, I said; the fault of telling a lie, and, what is more, a bad lie.

But when is this fault committed?

Whenever an erroneous representation is made of the nature of gods and heroes—as when a painter paints a portrait not having the shadow of a likeness to the original.

Yes, he said, that sort of thing is certainly very blamable; but what are the stories which you mean?

First of all, I said, there was that greatest of all lies in high places, which the poet told about Uranus, and which was a bad lie too—I mean what Hesiod says that Uranus did, and how Cronus retaliated on him. The doings of Cronus, and the sufferings which in turn his son inflicted upon him, even if they were true, ought certainly not to be lightly told to young and thoughtless persons; if possible, they had better be buried in silence. But if there is an absolute necessity for their mention, a chosen few might hear them

in a mystery, and they should sacrifice not a common pig, but some huge and unprocurable victim; and then the number of the hearers will be very few indeed.

Why, yes, said he, those stories are extremely objectionable.

Yes, Adeimantus, they are stories not to be repeated in our State; the young man should not be told that in committing the worst of crimes he is far from doing anything outrageous; and that even if he chastises his father when he does wrong, in whatever manner, he will only be following the example of the first and greatest among the gods.

I entirely agree with you, he said; in my opinion those stories are quite unfit to be repeated.

Neither, if we mean our future guardians to regard the habit of quarreling among themselves as of all things the basest, should any word be said to them of the wars in heaven, and of the plots and fightings of the gods against one another, for they are not true. No, we shall never mention the battles of the giants, or let them be embroidered on garments; and we shall be silent about the innumerable other quarrels of gods and heroes with their friends and relatives. If they would only believe us we would tell them that quarreling is unholy, and that never up to this time has there been any quarrel between citizens; this is what old men and old women should begin by telling children; and when they grow up, the poets also should be told to compose them in a similar spirit. But the narrative of Hephaestus binding Hera his mother, or how on another occasion Zeus sent him flying for taking her part when she was being beaten, and all the battles of the gods in Homer—these tales must not be admitted into our State, whether they are supposed to have an allegorical meaning or not. For a young person cannot judge what is allegorical and what is literal; anything that he receives into his mind at that age is likely to become indelible and unalterable; and therefore it is most important that the tales which the young first hear should be models of virtuous thoughts.

There you are right, he replied; but if anyone asks where are such models to be found and of what tales are you speaking—how shall we answer him?

I said to him, You and I, Adeimantus, at this moment are not poets, but founders of a State: now the founders of a State ought to know the general forms in which poets should cast their tales, and the limits which must be observed by them, but to make the tales is not their business.

Very true, he said; but what are these forms of theology which you mean?

Something of this kind, I replied: God is always to be represented as he truly is, whatever be the sort of poetry, epic, lyric, or tragic, in which the representation is given.

Right.

And is he not truly good? and must he not be represented as such?

Certainly.

And no good thing is hurtful?

No, indeed.

And that which is not hurtful hurts not?

Certainly not.

And that which hurts not does no evil?

No.

And can that which does no evil be a cause of evil?

Impossible.

And the good is advantageous?

Yes.

And therefore the cause of well-being?

Yes.

It follows, therefore, that the good is not the cause of all things, but of the good only?

Assuredly.

Then God, if he be good, is not the author of all things, as the many assert, but he is the cause of a few things only, and not of most things that occur to men. For few are the goods of human life, and many are the evils, and the good is to be attributed to God alone; of the evils the causes are to be sought elsewhere, and not in him.

That appears to me to be most true, he said.

Then we must not listen to Homer or to any other poet who is guilty of the folly of saying that two casks

Lie at the threshold of Zeus, full of lots, one of good, the other of evil lots,

and that he to whom Zeus gives a mixture of the two

Sometimes meets with evil fortune, at other times with good but that he to whom is given the cup of unmingled ill, Him wild hunger drives o'er the beauteous earth.

And again—

Zeus, who is the dispenser of good and evil to us.

And if anyone asserts that the violation of oaths and treaties, which was really the work of Pandarus, was brought about by Athena and Zeus, or that the strife and contention of the gods were instigated by Themis and Zeus, he shall not have our approval; neither will we allow our young men to hear the words of AEschylus, that

God plants guilt among men when he desires utterly to destroy a house.

And if a poet writes of the sufferings of Niobe—the subject of the tragedy in which these iambic verses occur—or of the house of Pelops, or of the Trojan War or on any similar theme, either we must not permit him to say that these are the works of God, or if they are of God, he must devise some explanation of them such as we are seeking: he must say that God did what was just and right, and they were the better for being punished; but that those who are punished are miserable, and that God is the author of their misery—the poet is not to be permitted to say; though he may say that the wicked are miserable because they require to be punished, and are benefited by receiving punishment from God; but that God being good is the author of evil to anyone is to be strenuously denied, and not to be said or sung or heard in verse or prose by anyone whether old or young in any well-ordered commonwealth. Such a fiction is suicidal, ruinous, impious.

I agree with you, he replied, and am ready to give my assent to the law.

Let this then be one of our rules and principles concerning the gods, to which our poets and reciters will be expected to conform—that God is not the author of all things, but of good only.

That will do, he said. . . .

BOOK III / THE ARTS IN EDUCATION

(Socrates, Adeimantus.)

Such, then, I said, are our principles of theology— some tales are to be told, and others are not to be told to our disciples from their youth upward, if we mean them to honor the gods and their parents, and to value friendship with one another.

Yes; and I think that our principles are right, he said.

But if they are to be courageous, must they not learn other lessons beside these, and lessons of such a kind as will take away the fear of death? Can any man be courageous who has the fear of death in him?

Certainly not, he said.

And can he be fearless of death, or will he choose death in battle rather than defeat and slavery, who believes the world below to be real and terrible?

Impossible.

Then we must assume a control over the narrators of this class of tales as well as over the others, and beg them not simply to revile, but rather to commend the world below, intimating to them that their descriptions are untrue, and will do harm to our future warriors.

That will be our duty, he said.

Then, I said, we shall have to obliterate many obnoxious passages, beginning with the verses

I would rather be a serf on the land of a poor and portionless man than rule over all the dead who have come to naught. . . .

And we must beg Homer and the other poets not to be angry if we strike out these and similar passages, not because they are unpoetical, or unattractive to the popular ear, but because the greater the poetical charm of them, the less are they meet for the ears of boys and men who are meant to be free, and who should fear slavery more than death.

Undoubtedly.

Also we shall have to reject all the terrible and appalling names which describe the world below— Cocytus and Styx, ghosts under the earth, and sapless shades, and any similar words of which the very mention causes a shudder to pass through the inmost soul of him who hears them. I do not say that these horrible stories may not have a use of some kind; but there is a danger that the nerves of our guardians may be rendered too excitable and effeminate by them.

There is a real danger, he said.

Then we must have no more of them.

True.

Another and a nobler strain must be composed and sung by us.

Clearly.

And shall we proceed to get rid of the weepings and wailings of famous men?

They will go with the rest.

But shall we be right in getting rid of them? Reflect: our principle is that the good man will not consider death terrible to any other good man who is his comrade.

Yes; that is our principle.

And therefore he will not sorrow for his departed friend as though he had suffered anything terrible?

He will not.

Such an one, as we further maintain, is sufficient for himself and his own happiness, and therefore is least in need of other men.

True, he said.

And for this reason the loss of a son or brother, or the deprivation of fortune, is to him of all men least terrible.

Assuredly.

And therefore he will be least likely to lament, and will bear with the greatest equanimity any misfortune of this sort which may befall him.

Yes, he will feel such a misfortune far less than another. . . .

For if, my sweet Adeimantus, our youth seriously listen to such unworthy representations of the gods, instead of laughing at them as they ought, hardly will any of them deem that he himself, being but a man, can be dishonored by similar actions; neither will he rebuke any inclination which may arise in his mind to say and do the like. And instead of having any shame or self-control, he will be always whining and lamenting on slight occasions.

Yes, he said, that is most true.

Yes, I replied; but that surely is what ought not to be, as the argument has just proved to us; and by that proof we must abide until it is disproved by a better.

It ought not to be.

Neither ought our guardians to be given to laughter. For a fit of laughter which has been indulged to excess almost always produces a violent reaction.

So I believe.

Then persons of worth, even if only mortal men, must not be represented as overcome by laughter, and still less must such a representation of the gods be allowed.

Still less of the gods, as you say, he replied. . . .

Again, truth should be highly valued; if, as we were saying, a lie is useless to the gods, and useful only as a medicine to men, then the use of such medicines should be restricted to physicians; private individuals have no business with them.

Clearly not, he said.

Then if anyone at all is to have the privilege of lying, the rulers of the State should be the persons; and they, in their dealings either with enemies or with their own citizens, may be allowed to lie for the public good. But nobody else should meddle with anything of the kind; and although the rulers have this privilege, for a private man to lie to them in return is to be deemed a more heinous fault than for the patient or the pupil of a gymnasium not to speak the truth about his own bodily illnesses to the physician or to the trainer, or for a sailor not to tell the captain what is happening about the ship and the rest of the crew, and how things are going with himself or his fellow sailors.

Most true, he said.

If, then, the ruler catches anybody beside himself lying in the State,

Any of the craftsmen, whether he be priest or physician or carpenter,

he will punish him for introducing a practice which is equally subversive and destructive of ship or State.

Most certainly, he said, if our idea of the State is ever carried out.

In the next place our youth must be temperate?

Certainly.

Are not the chief elements of temperance, speaking generally, obedience to commanders and self-control in sensual pleasures?

True.

Then we shall approve such language as that of Diomede in Homer,

Friend sit still and obey my word,

and the verses which follow,

The Greeks marched breathing prowess,
. . . in silent awe of their leaders.

and other sentiments of the same kind.

We shall.

What of this line,

O heavy with wine, who hast the eyes of a dog and the heart of a stag,

and of the words which follow? Would you say that these, or any similar impertinences which private individuals are supposed to address to their rulers, whether in verse or prose, are well or ill spoken?

They are ill spoken.

They may very possibly afford some amusement, but they do not conduce to temperance. And therefore they are likely to do harm to our young men—you would agree with me there?

Yes. . . .

In the next place, we must not let them be receivers of gifts or lovers of money.

Certainly not.

Neither must we sing to them of

Gifts persuading gods, and persuading reverend kings.

Neither is Phoenix, the tutor of Achilles, to be approved or deemed to have given his pupil good counsel when he told him that he should take the gifts of the Greeks and assist them; but that without a gift he should not lay aside his anger. Neither will we believe or acknowledge Achilles himself to have been such a lover of money that he took Agamemnon's gifts, or that when he had received payment he restored the dead body of Hector, but that without payment he was unwilling to do so.

Undoubtedly, he said, these are not sentiments which can be approved. . . .

And what shall we say about men? That is clearly the remaining portion of our subject.

Clearly so.

But we are not in a condition to answer this question at present, my friend.

Why not?

Because, if I am not mistaken, we shall have to say that about men; poets and storytellers are guilty of making the gravest misstatements when they tell us that wicked men are often happy, and the good miserable; and that injustice is profitable when undetected, but that justice is a man's own loss and another's gain—these things we shall forbid them to utter, and command them to sing and say the opposite.

To be sure we shall, he replied.

But if you admit that I am right in this, then I shall maintain that you have implied the principle for which we have been all along contending.

I grant the truth of your inference.

That such things are or are not to be said about men is a question which we cannot determine until we have discovered what justice is, and how naturally advantageous to the possessor, whether he seem to be just or not.

Most true, he said. . . .

QUESTIONS FOR REFLECTION

1. How would Socrates decide which religious stories and texts should be banned?

2. Which stories about heroes would Socrates censor? Why?

3. Why would Socrates punish liars? What kind of lies do we punish by law today? Would it be good to extend punishment to all lies, in your view?

4. Think of some well-known fairy tales. Which would Socrates censor? Why?

5. Are there well-known (a) Shakespeare plays; (b) movies; or (c) Bible stories that Socrates would ban? Which, and why?

5. Socrates moves from the relatively uncontroversial thesis that young children should not hear or read certain kinds of stories to the controversial position that those stories should be banned. How might he argue for this move?

ARISTOTLE

from *Nicomachean Ethics*

(Source: Reprinted from Aristotle's Nicomachean Ethics, *translated by W. D. Ross, 1925, by permission of Oxford University Press.)*

BOOK X

9

. . . Surely, as the saying goes, where there are things to be done the end is not to survey and recognize the various things, but rather to do them; with regard to virtue, then, it is not enough to know, but we must try to have and use it, or try any other way there may be of becoming good. Now if arguments were in themselves enough to make men good, they would justly, as Theognis says, have won very great rewards, and such rewards should have been provided; but as things are, while they seem to have power to encourage and stimulate the generous-minded among our youth, and to make a character which is gently born, and a true lover of what is noble, ready to be possessed by virtue, they are not able to encourage the many to nobility and goodness. For these do not by nature obey the sense of shame, but only fear, and do not abstain from bad acts because of their baseness but through fear of punishment; living by passion they pursue their own pleasures and the means to them, and avoid the opposite pains, and have not even a conception of what is noble and truly pleasant, since they have never tasted it. What argument would remould such people? It is hard, if not impossible, to remove by argument the traits that have long since been incorporated in the character; and perhaps we must be content if, when all the influences by which we are thought to become good are present, we get some tincture of virtue.

Now some think that we are made good by nature, others by habituation, others by teaching. Nature's part evidently does not depend on us, but as a result of some divine causes is present in those who are truly fortunate; while argument and teaching, we may suspect, are not powerful with all men, but the soul of the student must first have been cultivated by means of habits for noble joy and noble hatred, like earth which is to nourish the seed. For he who lives as passion directs will not hear argument that dissuades him, nor understand it if he does; and how can we persuade one in such a state to change his ways? And in general passion seems to yield not to argument but to force. The character, then, must somehow be there already with a kinship to virtue, loving what is noble and hating what is base.

But it is difficult to get . . . a right training for virtue if one has not been brought up under right laws; for to live temperately and hardily is not pleasant to most people, especially when they are young. For this reason their nurture and occupations should be fixed by law; for they will not be painful when they have become customary. But it is surely not enough that when they are young they should get the right nurture and attention; since they must, even when they are grown up, practise and be habituated to them, we shall need laws for this as well, and generally speaking to cover the whole of life; for most people obey necessity rather than argument, and punishments rather than the sense of what is noble.

This is why some think that legislators ought to stimulate men to virtue and urge them forward by the motive of the noble, on the assumption that those who have been well advanced by the formation of habits will attend to such influences; and that punishments and penalties should be imposed on those who disobey and are of inferior nature, while the incurably bad should be completely banished. A good man (they think), since he lives with his mind fixed on what is noble, will submit to argument, while a bad man, whose desire is for pleasure, is corrected by pain like a beast of burden. This is, too, why they say the pains inflicted should be those that are most opposed to the pleasures such men love.

However that may be, if (as we have said) the man who is to be good must be well trained and habituated, and go on to spend his time in worthy occupations and neither willingly nor unwillingly do bad actions, and if this can be brought about if men live in accordance with a sort of reason and right order, provided this has force—if this be so, the paternal command indeed has not the required force or compulsive power (nor in general has the command of one man, unless he be a king or something similar), but the law *has* compulsive power, while it is at the same time a rule proceeding from a sort of practical wisdom and reason. And while people hate *men* who oppose their impulses, even if they oppose them rightly, the law in its ordaining of what is good is not burdensome.

In the Spartan state alone, or almost alone, the legislator seems to have paid attention to questions of nurture and occupations; in most states such matters have been neglected, and each man lives as he pleases, Cyclops-fashion, "to his own wife and children dealing law." Now it is best that there should be a public and proper care for such matters; but if they are neglected by the community it would seem right for each man to help his children and friends towards virtue, and that they should have the power, or at least the will, to do this.

It would seem from what has been said that he can do this better if he makes himself capable of legislating. For public control is plainly effected by laws, and good control by good laws; whether written or unwritten would seem to make no difference, nor whether they are laws providing for the education of individuals or of groups—any more than it does in the case of music or gymnastics and other such pursuits. For as in cities laws and prevailing types of character have force, so in households do the injunctions and the habits of the father, and these have even more because of the tie of blood and the benefits he confers; for the children start with a natural affection and disposition to obey. Further, private education has an advantage over public, as private medical treatment has; for while in general rest and abstinence from food are good for a man in a fever, for a particular man they may not be; and a boxer presumably does not prescribe the same style of fighting to all his pupils. It would seem, then, that the detail is worked out with more precision if the control is private; for each person is more likely to get what suits his case.

But the details can be best looked after, one by one, by a doctor or gymnastic instructor or any one else who has the general knowledge of what is good for every one or for people of a certain kind (for the sciences both are said to be, and are, concerned with what is universal); not but what some particular detail may perhaps be well looked after by an unscientific person, if he has studied accurately in the light of experience what happens in each case, just as some people seem to be their own best doctors, though they could give no help to any one else. Nonetheless, it will perhaps be agreed that if a man does wish to become master of an art or science he must go to the universal, and come to know it as well as possible; for, as we have said, it is with this that the sciences are concerned.

And surely he who wants to make men, whether many or few, better by his care must try to become capable of legislating, if it is through laws that we can become good. For to get any one whatever—any one who is put before us—into the right condition is not for the first chance comer; if any one can do it, it is the man who knows, just as in medicine and all other matters which give scope for care and prudence. . . .

QUESTIONS FOR REFLECTION

1. "Some think that we are made good by nature, others by habituation, others by teaching." How does Aristotle react to each of these suggestions?

2. What role does law play in making people good?

3. Are there limits on the power of law to guide character?

4. What does Aristotle's view imply about the acceptability of paternalistic laws?

EDMUND BURKE

from *Reflections on the Revolution in France* (1790)

Edmund Burke (1729–1797) was born in Ireland to a Protestant family of modest means that had recently converted from Catholicism. Educated at a Quaker school and at Trinity College, Dublin, he took a first-class honors degree in classics, and proceeded to study law in London. He did not, however, practice law. Instead, he became a "man of letters": he edited the Annual Register *(a political journal) and belonged to Samuel Johnson's literary club. Burke's first two books appeared when he was twenty-seven; at thirty-seven, he became a member of the House of Commons. Eventually, he became paymaster-general.*

Burke was sixty when the French Revolution began in 1789. King Louis XVI, an absolute monarch, had summoned the largely advisory States General, had lost control of it, and had seen it transform itself into the National Assembly. That body had abolished feudalism, seized the lands of the French church, and inspired the capture and imprisonment of the royal family. A young Frenchman, Charles-François Depont, wrote Burke to ask his opinion of the Revolution. His response was Reflections on the Revolution in France, *which has become a classic of European political thought. The book is sharply critical of the Revolution. Burke's worries about the extremism of the revolutionaries were soon justified. The Reign of Terror led to the execution of thousands, including the king, his family, and much of the French aristocracy.*

Burke is a thoroughly practical thinker. He rejects the Enlightenment view that a change in the social or political order can perfect human nature and society. More fundamentally, he rejects all attempts to analyze human problems in terms of a few basic principles. Profoundly skeptical of philosophical theorizing, Burke stresses the complexity of real ethical problems. Solving a moral or political problem, he believes, involves balancing various moral considerations—various kinds of goods and evils—in light of features of the particular situation giving rise to it. Liberty, in Burke's view, is one kind of good, but there are many others; liberty does not always take precedence. There is no theory, method, or set of rules for achieving a proper balance between liberty and other goods. Instead, Burke urges, we should reason by analogy, clinging to social mechanisms that have stood the test of time. (Source: Edmund Burke, Reflections on the Revolution in France *[London: J. Dodsley, 1790].)*

. . . I flatter myself that I love a manly, moral, regulated liberty as well as any gentleman of that society, be he who he will; and perhaps I have given as good proofs of my attachment to that cause in the whole course of my public conduct. . . . But I cannot stand forward and give praise or blame to anything which relates to human actions, and human concerns, on a simple view of the object, as it stands stripped of every relation, in all the nakedness and solitude of metaphysical abstraction. Circumstances (which with some gentlemen pass for nothing) give in reality to every political principle its distinguishing color and discriminating effect. The circumstances are what render every civil and political scheme beneficial or noxious to mankind. Abstractedly speaking, government, as well as liberty, is good; yet could I, in common sense, ten years ago, have felicitated France on her enjoyment of a government (for she then had a government) without inquiry what the nature of that government was, or how it was administered? Can I now congratulate the same nation upon its freedom? Is it because liberty in the abstract may be classed amongst the blessings of mankind, that I am seriously to felicitate a madman, who has escaped from the protecting restraint and wholesome darkness of his cell, on his restoration to the enjoyment of light and liberty? Am I to congratulate a highwayman and murderer who has broke prison upon the recovery of his natural rights? This would be to act over again the scene of the criminals condemned to the galleys, and their heroic deliverer, the metaphysic Knight of the Sorrowful Countenance.*

When I see the spirit of liberty in action, I see a strong principle at work; and this, for a while, is all I can possibly know of it. The wild *gas,* the fixed air, is plainly broke loose; but we ought to suspend our judgment until the first effervescence is a little subsided, till the liquor is cleared, and until we see something deeper than the agitation of a troubled and frothy surface. I must be tolerably sure, before I venture publicly to congratulate men upon a blessing, that they have really received one. Flattery corrupts both the receiver and the giver, and adulation is not of more service to the people than to kings. I should, therefore, suspend my congratulations on the new liberty of France until I was informed how it had been combined with government, with public force, with the discipline and obedience of armies, with the collection of an effective and well-distributed revenue, with morality and religion, with the solidity of property, with peace and order, with civil and social manners. All these (in their way) are good things, too, and without them liberty is not a benefit whilst it lasts, and is not likely to continue long. The effect of liberty to individuals is that they may do what they please; we ought to see what it will please them to do, before we risk congratulations which may be soon turned into complaints. Prudence

would dictate this in the case of separate, insulated, private men, but liberty, when men act in bodies, is *power.* Considerate people, before they declare themselves, will observe the use which is made of *power,* and particularly of so trying a thing as *new* power in *new* persons of whose principles, tempers, and dispositions they have little or no experience, and in situations where those who appear the most stirring in the scene may possibly not be the real movers. . . .

. . . The Revolution was made to preserve our *ancient,* indisputable laws and liberties and that *ancient* constitution of government which is our only security for law and liberty. If you are desirous of knowing the spirit of our constitution and the policy which predominated in that great period which has secured it to this hour, pray look for both in our histories, in our records, in our acts of parliament, and journals of parliament, and not in the sermons of the Old Jewry† and the after-dinner toasts of the Revolution Society. In the former you will find other ideas and another language. Such a claim is as ill-suited to our temper and wishes as it is unsupported by any appearance of authority. The very idea of the fabrication of a new government is enough to fill us with disgust and horror. We wished at the period of the Revolution, and do now wish, to derive all we possess as *an inheritance from our forefathers.* Upon that body and stock of inheritance we have taken care not to inoculate any cyon‡ alien to the nature of the original plant. All the reformations we have hitherto made have proceeded upon the principle of reverence to antiquity; and I hope, nay, I am persuaded, that all those which possibly may be made hereafter will be carefully formed upon analogical precedent, authority, and example. . . .

You will observe that from Magna Carta to the Declaration of Right it has been the uniform policy of our constitution to claim and assert our liberties as an *entailed inheritance* derived to us from our forefathers, and to be transmitted to our posterity—as an estate specially belonging to the people of this kingdom, without any reference whatever to any other more general or prior right. By this means our constitution preserves a unity in so great a diversity of its

---

* A reference to Don Quixote, who set criminals free only to be beaten by them. —ED.

† The courthouse, so-called because it was built on the site of a former synagogue.—ED.

‡ A shoot, twig, or graft; old form of *scion.* —ED.

parts. We have an inheritable crown, an inheritable peerage, and a House of Commons and a people inheriting privileges, franchises, and liberties from a long line of ancestors.

This policy appears to me to be the result of profound reflection, or rather the happy effect of following nature, which is wisdom without reflection, and above it. A spirit of innovation is generally the result of a selfish temper and confined views. People will not look forward to posterity, who never look backward to their ancestors. Besides, the people of England well know that the idea of inheritance furnishes a sure principle of conservation and a sure principle of transmission, without at all excluding a principle of improvement. It leaves acquisition free, but it secures what it acquires. Whatever advantages are obtained by a state proceeding on these maxims are locked fast as in a sort of family settlement, grasped as in a kind of mortmain* forever. By a constitutional policy, working after the pattern of nature, we receive, we hold, we transmit our government and our privileges in the same manner in which we enjoy and transmit our property and our lives. The institutions of policy, the goods of fortune, the gifts of providence are handed down to us, and from us, in the same course and order. Our political system is placed in a just correspondence and symmetry with the order of the world and with the mode of existence decreed to a permanent body composed of transitory parts, wherein, by the disposition of a stupendous wisdom, molding together the great mysterious incorporation of the human race, the whole, at one time, is never old or middle-aged or young, but, in a condition of unchangeable constancy, moves on through the varied tenor of perpetual decay, fall, renovation, and progression. Thus, by preserving the method of nature in the conduct of the state, in what we improve we are never wholly new; in what we retain we are never wholly obsolete. By adhering in this manner and on those principles to our forefathers, we are guided not by the superstition of antiquarians, but by the spirit of philosophic analogy. In this choice of inheritance we have given to

our frame of polity the image of a relation in blood, binding up the constitution of our country with our dearest domestic ties, adopting our fundamental laws into the bosom of our family affections, keeping inseparable and cherishing with the warmth of all their combined and mutually reflected charities our state, our hearths, our sepulchres, and our altars.

Through the same plan of a conformity to nature in our artificial institutions, and by calling in the aid of her unerring and powerful instincts to fortify the fallible and feeble contrivances of our reason, we have derived several other, and those no small, benefits from considering our liberties in the light of an inheritance. Always acting as if in the presence of canonized forefathers, the spirit of freedom, leading in itself to misrule and excess, is tempered with an awful gravity. This idea of a liberal descent inspires us with a sense of habitual native dignity which prevents that upstart insolence almost inevitably adhering to and disgracing those who are the first acquirers of any distinction. By this means our liberty becomes a noble freedom. It carries an imposing and majestic aspect. It has a pedigree and illustrating ancestors. It has its bearings and its ensigns armorial. It has its gallery of portraits, its monumental inscriptions, its records, evidences, and titles. We procure reverence to our civil institutions on the principle upon which nature teaches us to revere individual men: on account of their age and on account of those from whom they are descended. All your sophisters cannot produce anything better adapted to preserve a rational and manly freedom than the course that we have pursued, who have chosen our nature rather than our speculations, our breasts rather than our inventions, for the great conservatories and magazines of our rights and privileges. . . .

. . . These opposed and conflicting interests which you considered as so great a blemish in your old and in our present constitution interpose a salutary check to all precipitate resolutions. They render deliberation a matter, not of choice, but of necessity; they make all change a subject of *compromise,* which naturally begets moderation; they produce *temperaments* preventing the sore evil of harsh, crude, unqualified reformations, and rendering all the headlong exertions of arbitrary power, in the few or in the many, for ever impracticable. Through that diversity of members and interests, general liberty had

---

* Literally "dead hand," a legal device to make a corporation possess something in perpetuity; or, the condition of lands held in perpetuity. —ED.

as many securities as there were separate views in the several orders. . . .

. . . I reprobate no form of government merely upon abstract principles. There may be situations in which the purely democratic form will become necessary. There may be some (very few, and very particularly circumstanced) where it would be clearly desirable. This I do not take to be the case of France or of any other great country. Until now, we have seen no examples of considerable democracies. The ancients were better acquainted with them. Not being wholly unread in the authors who had seen the most of those constitutions, and who best understood them, I cannot help concurring with their opinion that an absolute democracy, no more than absolute monarchy, is not to be reckoned among the legitimate forms of government. They think it rather the corruption and degeneracy than the sound constitution of a republic. If I recollect rightly, Aristotle observes that a democracy has many striking points of resemblance with a tyranny. Of this I am certain, that in a democracy the majority of the citizens is capable of exercising the most cruel oppressions upon the minority whenever strong divisions prevail in that kind of polity, as they often must; and that oppression of the minority will extend to far greater numbers and will be carried on with much greater fury than can almost ever be apprehended from the dominion of a single scepter. In such a popular persecution, individual sufferers are in a much more deplorable condition than in any other. Under a cruel prince they have the balmy compassion of mankind to assuage the smart of their wounds; they have the plaudits of the people to animate their generous constancy under their sufferings; but those who are subjected to wrong under multitudes are deprived of all external consolation. They seem deserted by mankind, overpowered by a conspiracy of their whole species. . . .

. . . A brave people will certainly prefer liberty accompanied with a virtuous poverty to a depraved and wealthy servitude. But before the price of comfort and opulence is paid, one ought to be pretty sure it is real liberty which is purchased, and that she is to be purchased at no other price. I shall always, however, consider that liberty as very equivocal in her appearance which has not wisdom and justice for her companions and does not lead prosperity and plenty in her train. . . .

The effects of the incapacity shown by the popular leaders in all the great members of the commonwealth are to be covered with the "all-atoning name" of liberty. In some people I see great liberty indeed; in many, if not in the most, an oppressive, degrading servitude. But what is liberty without wisdom and without virtue? It is the greatest of all possible evils; for it is folly, vice, and madness, without tuition or restraint. Those who know what virtuous liberty is cannot bear to see it disgraced by incapable heads on account of their having high-sounding words in their mouths. Grand, swelling sentiments of liberty I am sure I do not despise. They warm the heart; they enlarge and liberalize our minds; they animate our courage in time of conflict. Old as I am, I read the fine raptures of Lucan and Corneille with pleasure. Neither do I wholly condemn the little arts and devices of popularity. They facilitate the carrying of many points of moment; they keep the people together; they refresh the mind in its exertions; and they diffuse occasional gaiety over the severe brow of moral freedom. Every politician ought to sacrifice to the graces, and to join compliance with reason. But in such an undertaking as that in France, all these subsidiary sentiments and artifices are of little avail. To make a government requires no great prudence. Settle the seat of power, teach obedience, and the work is done. To give freedom is still more easy. It is not necessary to guide; it only requires to let go the rein. But to form a *free government,* that is, to temper together these opposite elements of liberty and restraint in one consistent work, requires much thought, deep reflection, a sagacious, powerful, and combining mind. This I do not find in those who take the lead in the National Assembly. Perhaps they are not so miserably deficient as they appear. I rather believe it. It would put them below the common level of human understanding. But when the leaders choose to make themselve bidders at an auction of popularity, their talents, in the construction of the state, will be of no service. They will become flatterers instead of legislators, the instruments, not the guides, of the people. If any of them should happen to propose a scheme of liberty, soberly limited and defined with proper qualifications, he will be immediately outbid by his competitors who will produce something more splendidly popular. Suspicions will be raised of his fidelity to his cause. Moderation will be stigmatized as the virtue of cowards, and compromise as the prudence of traitors, until, in hopes of preserving the credit which may enable him to temper and moderate, on some occasions, the popular leader is obliged to become active in propagating doctrines and establishing powers that will afterwards defeat any sober purpose at which he ultimately might have aimed. . . .

. . . I wish my countrymen rather to recommend to our neighbors the example of the British constitution than to take models from them for the improvement of our own. In the former, they have got an invaluable treasure. They are not, I think, without some causes of apprehension and complaint, but these they do not owe to their constitution but to their own conduct. I think our happy situation owing to our constitution, but owing to the whole of it, and not to any part singly, owing in a great measure to what we have left standing in our several reviews and reformations as well as to what we have altered or superadded. Our people will find employment enough for a truly patriotic, free, and independent spirit in guarding what they possess from violation. I would not exclude alteration neither, but even when I changed, it should be to preserve. I should be led to my remedy by a great grievance. In what I did, I should follow the example of our ancestors. I would make the reparation as nearly as possible in the style of the building. A politic caution, a guarded circumspection, a moral rather than a complexional timidity were among the ruling principles of our forefathers in their most decided conduct. Not being illuminated with the light of which the gentlemen of France tell us they have got so abundant a share, they acted under a strong impression of the ignorance and fallibility of mankind. He that had made them thus fallible rewarded them for having in their conduct attended to their nature. Let us imitate their caution if we wish to deserve their fortune or to retain their bequests. Let us add, if we please, but let us preserve what they have left; and, standing on the firm ground of the British constitution, let us be satisfied to admire rather than attempt to follow in their desperate flights the aeronauts of France. . . .

QUESTIONS FOR REFLECTION

1. What does Burke mean by a "manly, moral, regulated liberty"?

2. Burke is a pluralist—he believes that there are fundamentally different kinds of moral value. What are some of these kinds? What kind of value is liberty? Is it unequivocally good?

3. Burke points out that "liberty, when men act in bodies, is *power.*" What does he deduce from this?

What, in your view, does Burke's observation imply about liberty?

4. Burke thinks that it is very important "to derive all we possess as *an inheritance from our forefathers.*" Why does Burke place such an emphasis on tradition?

5. Burke worries that democracy allows the "oppression of the minority." Why? What can be done to guard against it?

JOHN STUART MILL

from *On Liberty* (1859)

On Liberty is a classic statement of the importance of individual liberty. Its chapter "Of the Liberty of Thought and Discussion" is probably the most famous and influential defense of freedom of speech ever written. Mill was a staunch advocate of democracy but saw that majority rule, in itself, could allow the oppression of the minority. Mill wrote On Liberty *to outline a realm of freedom that not even democratic majorities may transgress. (Source: London: Parker, 1859.)*

CHAPTER I / INTRODUCTORY

. . . The object of this essay is to assert one very simple principle, as entitled to govern absolutely the dealings of society with the individual in the way of compulsion and control, whether the means used be physical force in the form of legal penalties or the moral coercion of public opinion. That principle is that the sole end for which mankind are warranted, individually or collectively, in interfering with the liberty of action of any of their number is self-protection. That the only purpose for which power can be rightfully exercised over any member of a civilized community, against his will, is to prevent harm to others. His own good, either physical or moral, is not a sufficient warrant. He cannot rightfully be compelled to do or forbear because it will be better for him to do so, because it will make him happier, because, in the opinions of others, to do so would be wise or even right. These are good reasons for remonstrating with him, or reasoning with him, or persuading him, or entreating him, but not for compelling him or visiting him with any evil in case he do otherwise. To justify that, the conduct from which it is desired to deter him must be calculated to produce evil to someone else. The only part of the conduct of anyone for which he is amenable to society is that which concerns others. In the part which merely concerns himself, his independence is, of right, absolute. Over himself, over his own body and mind, the individual is sovereign.

It is, perhaps, hardly necessary to say that this doctrine is meant to apply only to human beings in the maturity of their faculties. We are not speaking of children or of young persons below the age which the law may fix as that of manhood or womanhood. Those who are still in a state to require being taken care of by others must be protected against their own actions as well as against external injury. . . . But as soon as mankind have attained the capacity of being guided to their own improvement by conviction or persuasion (a period long since reached in all nations with whom we need here concern ourselves), compulsion, either in the direct form or in that of pains and penalties for noncompliance, is no longer admissible as a means to their own good, and justifiable only for the security of others.

It is proper to state that I forgo any advantage which could be derived to my argument from the idea of abstract right as a thing independent of utility. I regard utility as the ultimate appeal on all ethical questions; but it must be utility in the largest sense, grounded on the permanent interests of man as a progressive being. Those interests, I contend, authorize the subjection of individual spontaneity to external control only in respect to those actions of each which concern the interest of other people.

If anyone does an act hurtful to others, there is a *prima facie* case for punishing him by law or, where legal penalties are not safely applicable, by general disapprobation. There are also many positive acts for the benefit of others which he may rightfully be compelled to perform, such as to give evidence in a court of justice, to bear his fair share in the common defense or in any other joint work necessary to the interest of the society of which he enjoys the protection, and to perform certain acts of individual beneficence, such as saving a fellow creature's life or interposing to protect the defenseless against ill usage—things which whenever it is obviously a man's duty to do he may rightfully be made responsible to society for not doing. A person may cause evil to others not only by his actions but by his inaction, and in either case he is justly accountable to them for the injury. The latter case, it is true, requires a much more cautious exercise of compulsion than the former. To make anyone answerable for doing evil to others is the rule; to make him answerable for not preventing evil is, comparatively speaking, the exception. Yet there are many cases clear enough and grave enough to justify that exception. In all things which regard the external relations of the individual, he is *de jure* amenable to those whose interests are concerned, and, if need be, to society as their protector. There are often good reasons for not holding him to the responsibility; but these reasons must arise from the special expediencies of the case: either because it is a kind of case in which he is on the whole likely to act better when left to his own discretion than when controlled in any way in which society have it in their power to control him; or because the attempt to exercise control would produce other evils, greater than those which it would prevent. When such reasons as these preclude the enforcement of responsibility, the conscience of the agent himself should step into the vacant judgment seat and protect those interests of others which have no external protection; judging himself all the more rigidly, because the case does not admit of his being made accountable to the judgment of his fellow creatures.

But there is a sphere of action in which society, as distinguished from the individual, has, if any, only an indirect interest: comprehending all that portion of a person's life and conduct which affects only himself or, if it also affects others, only with their free, voluntary, and undeceived consent and participation. When I say only himself, I mean directly and in the first instance; for whatever affects himself may affect others through himself: and the objection which may be grounded on this contingency will receive consideration in the sequel. This, then, is the appropriate region of human liberty. It comprises, first, the inward domain of consciousness, demanding liberty of conscience in the most comprehensive sense, liberty of thought and feeling, absolute freedom of opinion and sentiment on all subjects, practical or speculative, scientific, moral, or theological. The liberty of expressing and publishing opinions may seem to fall under a different principle, since it belongs to that part of the conduct of an individual which concerns other people, but, being almost of as much importance as the liberty of thought itself and resting in great part on the same reasons, is practically inseparable from it. Secondly, the principle requires liberty of tastes and pursuits, of framing the plan of our life to suit our own character, of doing as we like, subject to such consequences as may follow, without impediment from our fellow creatures, so long as what we do does not harm them, even though they should think our conduct foolish, perverse, or wrong. Thirdly, from this liberty of each individual follows the liberty, within the same limits, of combination among individuals; freedom to unite for any purpose not involving harm to others: the persons combining being supposed to be of full age and not forced or deceived.

No society in which these liberties are not, on the whole, respected is free, whatever may be its form of government; and none is completely free in which they do not exist absolute and unqualified. The only freedom which deserves the name is that of pursuing our own good in our own way, so long as we do not attempt to deprive others of theirs or impede their efforts to obtain it. Each is the proper guardian of his own health, whether bodily *or* mental and spiritual. Mankind are greater gainers by suffering each other to live as seems good to themselves than by compelling each to live as seems good to the rest. . . .

QUESTIONS FOR REFLECTION

1. What is the "one very simple principle"—usually called the *harm principle*—that Mill's essay aims to assert? What does it mean? What conditions and qualifications does Mill place on it? How does it counteract the "tyranny of the majority"?

2. Later philosophers have often stated Mill's harm principle in terms of a distinction between self-regarding and other-regarding actions. How might this distinction be drawn? How can Mill's principle be stated in terms of that distinction?

CHAPTER II / OF THE LIBERTY OF THOUGHT AND DISCUSSION

. . . Let us suppose . . . that the government is entirely at one with the people, and never thinks of exerting any power of coercion unless in agreement with what it conceives to be their voice. But I deny the right of the people to exercise such coercion, either by themselves or by their government. The power itself is illegitimate. The best government has no more title to it than the worst. It is as noxious, or more noxious, when exerted in accordance with public opinion than when in opposition to it. If all mankind minus one were of one opinion, mankind would be no more justified in silencing that one person than he, if he had the power, would be justified in silencing mankind. Were an opinion a personal possession of no value except to the owner, if to be obstructed in the enjoyment of it were simply a private injury, it would make some difference whether the injury was inflicted only on a few persons or on many. But the peculiar evil of silencing the expression of an opinion is that it is robbing the human race, posterity as well as the existing generation—those who dissent from the opinion, still more than those who hold it. If the opinion is right, they are deprived of the opportunity of exchanging error for truth; if wrong, they lose, what is almost as great a benefit, the clearer perception and livelier impression of truth produced by its collision with error.

It is necessary to consider separately these two hypotheses, each of which has a distinct branch of the argument corresponding to it. We can never be sure that the opinion we are endeavoring to stifle is a false opinion; and if we were sure, stifling it would be an evil still.

First, the opinion which it is attempted to suppress by authority may possibly be true. Those who desire to suppress it, of course, deny its truth; but they are not infallible. They have no authority to decide the question for all mankind and exclude every other person from the means of judging. To refuse a hearing to an opinion because they are sure that it is false is to assume that *their* certainty is the same thing as *absolute* certainty. All silencing of discussion is an assumption of infallibility. . . .

The objection likely to be made to this argument would probably take some such form as the following. There is no greater assumption of infallibility in forbidding the propagation of error than in any other thing which is done by public authority on its own judgment and responsibility. Judgment is given to men that they may use it. Because it may be used erroneously, are men to be told that they ought not to use it at all? To prohibit what they think pernicious is not claiming exemption from error, but fulfilling the duty incumbent on them, although fallible, of acting on their conscientious conviction. If we were never to act on our opinions, because those opinions may be wrong, we should leave all our interests uncared for, and all our duties unperformed. An objection which applies to all conduct can be no valid objection to any conduct in particular. It is the duty of governments, and of individuals, to form the truest opinions they can; to form them carefully, and never impose them upon others unless they are quite sure of being right. But when they are sure (such reasoners may say), it is not conscientiousness but cowardice to shrink from acting on their opinions and allow doctrines which they honestly think dangerous to the welfare of mankind, either in this life or in another, to be scattered abroad without restraint, because other people, in less enlightened times, have persecuted opinions now believed to be true. Let us take care, it may be said, not to make the same mistake; but governments and nations have made mistakes in other things which are not denied to be fit subjects for the exercise of authority: they have laid on bad taxes, made unjust wars. Ought we therefore to lay on no taxes and, under whatever provocation, make no wars? Men and governments must act to the best of their ability. There is no such thing as absolute certainty, but there is assurance sufficient for the purposes of human life. We may, and must, assume our opinion to be true for the guidance of our own conduct; and it is assuming no more when we forbid bad men to pervert society by the propagation of opinions which we regard as false and pernicious.

I answer, that it is assuming very much more. There is the greatest difference between presuming an opinion to be true because, with every opportunity for contesting it, it has not been refuted, and assuming its truth for the purpose of not permitting its refutation. Complete liberty of contradicting and disproving our opinion is the very condition which justifies us in assuming its truth for purposes of action; and on no other terms can a being with human faculties have any rational assurance of being right.

When we consider either the history of opinion or the ordinary conduct of human life, to what is it to be ascribed that the one and the other are no worse than they are? Not certainly to the inherent force of the human understanding, for on any matter not self-evident there are ninety-nine persons totally incapable of judging of it for one who is capable; and the capacity of the hundredth person is only comparative, for the majority of the eminent men of every past generation held many opinions now known to be erroneous, and did or approved numerous things which no one will now justify. Why is it, then, that there is on the whole a preponderance among mankind of rational opinions and rational conduct? If there really is this preponderance—which there must be unless human affairs are, and have always been, in an almost desperate state—it is owing to a quality of the human mind, the source of everything respectable in man either as an intellectual or as a moral being, namely, that his errors are corrigible. He is capable of rectifying his mistakes by discussion and experience. Not by experience alone. There must be discussion to show how experience is

to be interpreted. Wrong opinions and practices gradually yield to fact and argument; but facts and arguments, to produce any effect on the mind, must be brought before it. Very few facts are able to tell their own story, without comments to bring out their meaning. The whole strength and value, then, of human judgment depending on the one property, that it can be set right when it is wrong, reliance can be placed on it only when the means of setting it right are kept constantly at hand. In the case of any person whose judgment is really deserving of confidence, how has it become so? Because he has kept his mind open to criticism of his opinions and conduct. Because it has been his practice to listen to all that could be said against him; to profit by as much of it as was just, and to expound to himself, and upon occasion to others, the fallacy of what was fallacious. Because he has felt that the only way in which a human being can make some approach to knowing the whole of a subject is by hearing what can be said about it by persons of every variety of opinion, and studying all modes in which it can be looked at by every character of mind. No wise man ever acquired his wisdom in any mode but this; nor is it in the nature of human intellect to become wise in any other manner. The steady habit of correcting and completing his own opinion by collating it with those of others, so far from causing doubt and hesitation in carrying it into practice, is the only stable foundation for a just reliance on it; for, being cognizant of all that can, at least obviously, be said against him and having taken up his position against all gainsayers—knowing that he has sought for objections and difficulties instead of avoiding them, and has shut out no light which can be thrown upon the subject from any quarter—he has a right to think his judgment better than that of any person, or any multitude, who have not gone through a similar process. . . .

Let us now pass to the second division of the argument, and dismissing the supposition that any of the received opinions may be false, let us assume them to be true and examine into the worth of the manner in which they are likely to be held when their truth is not freely and openly canvassed. However unwillingly a person who has a strong opinion may admit the possibility that his opinion may be false, he ought to be moved by the consideration that, however true it may be, if it is not fully, frequently, and fearlessly discussed, it will be held as a dead dogma, not a living truth.

There is a class of persons (happily not quite so numerous as formerly) who think it enough if a person assents undoubtingly to what they think true, though he has no knowledge whatever of the grounds of the opinion and could not make a tenable defense of it against the most superficial objections. Such persons, if they can once get their creed taught from authority, naturally think that no good, and some harm, comes of its being allowed to be questioned. Where their influence prevails, they make it nearly impossible for the received opinion to be rejected wisely and considerately, though it may still be rejected rashly and ignorantly; for to shut out discussion entirely is seldom possible, and when it once gets in, beliefs not grounded on conviction are apt to give way before the slightest semblance of an argument. Waiving, however, this possibility—assuming that the true opinion abides in the mind, but abides as a prejudice, a belief independent of, and proof against, argument—this is not the way in which truth ought to be held by a rational being. This is not knowing the truth. Truth, thus held, is but one superstition the more, accidentally clinging to the words which enunciate a truth. . . .

If, however, the mischievous operation of the absence of free discussion, when the received opinions are true, were confined to leaving men ignorant of the grounds of those opinions, it might be thought that this, if an intellectual, is no moral evil and does not affect the worth of the opinions, regarded in their influence on the character. The fact, however, is that not only the grounds of the opinion are forgotten in the absence of discussion, but too often the meaning of the opinion itself. The words which convey it cease to suggest ideas, or suggest only a small portion of those they were originally employed to communicate. Instead of a vivid conception and a living belief, there remain only a few phrases retained by rote; or, if any part, the shell and husk only of the meaning is retained, the finer essence being lost. The great chapter in human history which this fact occupies and fills cannot be too earnestly studied and meditated on.

It is illustrated in the experience of almost all ethical doctrines and religious creeds: They are all full of meaning and vitality to those who originate them, and to the direct disciples of the originators. Their meaning continues to be felt in undiminished strength, and is perhaps brought out into even fuller consciousness, so long as the struggle lasts to give the doctrine or creed an ascendancy over other creeds. At last it either prevails and becomes the general opinion, or its progress stops; it keeps possession of the ground it has gained, but ceases to spread further. When either of these results has become apparent, controversy on the subject flags, and gradually dies away. The doctrine has taken its place, if not as a received opinion, as one of the admitted sects or divisions of opinion; those who hold it have generally inherited, not adopted it; and conversion from one of these doctrines to another, being now an exceptional fact, occupies little place in the thoughts of their professors. Instead of being, as at first, constantly on the alert either to defend themselves against the world or to bring the world over to them, they have subsided into acquiescence and neither listen, when they can help it, to arguments against their creed, nor trouble dissentients (if there be such) with arguments in its favor. From this time may usually be dated the decline in the living power of the doctrine. . . .

. . . There are many reasons, doubtless, why doctrines which are the badge of a sect retain more of their vitality than those common to all recognized sects, and why more pains are taken by teachers to keep their meaning alive; but one reason certainly is that the peculiar doctrines are more questioned and have to be oftener defended against open gainsayers. Both teachers and learners go to sleep at their post as soon as there is no enemy in the field. . . .

It still remains to speak of one of the principal causes which make diversity of opinion advantageous, and will continue to do so until mankind shall have entered a stage of intellectual advancement which at present seems at an incalculable distance. We have hitherto considered only two possibilities: that the received opinion may be false, and some other opinion, consequently, true; or that, the received opinion being true, a conflict with the opposite error is essential to a clear apprehension and deep feeling of its truth. But there is a commoner case than either of these: when the conflicting doctrines, instead of being one true and the other false, share the truth between them, and the nonconforming opinion is needed to supply the remainder of the truth of which the received doctrine embodies only a part. Popular opinions, on subjects not palpable to sense, are often true, but seldom or never the whole truth. They are a part of the truth, sometimes a greater, sometimes a smaller part, but exaggerated, distorted, and disjointed from the truths by which they ought to be accompanied and limited. Heretical opinions, on the other hand, are generally some of these suppressed and neglected truths, bursting the bonds which kept them down, and either seeking reconciliation with the truth contained in the common opinion, or fronting it as enemies, and setting themselves up, with similar exclusiveness, as the whole truth. The latter case is hitherto the most frequent, as, in the human mind, one-sidedness has always been the rule, and many-sidedness the exception. Hence, even in revolutions of opinion, one part of the truth usually sets while another rises. Even progress, which ought to superadd, for the most part only substitutes one partial and incomplete truth for another; improvement consisting chiefly in this, that the new fragment of truth is more wanted, more adapted to the needs of the time than that which it displaces. Such being the partial character of prevailing opinions, even when resting on a true foundation, every opinion which embodies somewhat of the portion of truth which the common opinion omits ought to be considered precious, with whatever amount of error and confusion that truth may be blended. No sober judge of human affairs will feel bound to be indignant because those who force on our notice truths which we should otherwise have overlooked, overlook some of those which we see. Rather, he will think that so long as popular truth is one-sided, it is more desirable than otherwise that unpopular truth should have one-sided assertors, too, such being usually the most energetic and the most likely to compel reluctant attention to the fragment of wisdom which they proclaim as if it were the whole. . . .

. . . only through diversity of opinion is there, in the existing state of human intellect, a chance of fair play to all sides of the truth. When there are persons to be found who form an exception to the apparent unanimity of the world on any subject, even if the world is in the right, it is always probable that dissentients have something worth hearing to say for

themselves, and that truth would lose something by their silence. . . .

We have now recognized the necessity to the mental well-being of mankind (on which all their other well-being depends) of freedom of opinion, and freedom of the expression of opinion, on four distinct grounds, which we will now briefly recapitulate:

First, if any opinion is compelled to silence, that opinion may, for aught we can certainly know, be true. To deny this is to assume our own infallibility.

Secondly, though the silenced opinion be an error, it may, and very commonly does, contain a portion of truth; and since the general or prevailing opinion on any subject is rarely or never the whole truth, it is only by the collision of adverse opinions that the remainder of the truth has any chance of being supplied.

Thirdly, even if the received opinion be not only true, but the whole truth; unless it is suffered to be, and actually is, vigorously and earnestly contested, it will, by most of those who receive it, be held in the manner of a prejudice, with little comprehension or feeling of its rational grounds. And not only this, but, fourthly, the meaning of the doctrine itself will be in danger of being lost or enfeebled, and deprived of its vital effect on the character and conduct: the dogma becoming a mere formal profession, inefficacious for good, but cumbering the ground and preventing the growth of any real and heartfelt conviction from reason or personal experience. . . .

CHAPTER III / OF INDIVIDUALITY, AS ONE OF THE ELEMENTS OF WELL-BEING

. . . No one pretends that actions should be as free as opinions. On the contrary, even opinions lose their immunity when the circumstances in which they are expressed are such as to constitute their expression a positive instigation to some mischievous act. An opinion that corn dealers are starvers of the poor, or that private property is robbery, ought to be unmolested when simply circulated through the press, but may justly incur punishment when delivered orally to an excited mob assembled before the house of a corn dealer, or when handed about among the same mob in the form of a placard. Acts of whatever kind, which without justifiable cause do harm to others may be, and in the more important cases absolutely require to be, controlled by the unfavorable sentiments, and, when needful, by the active interference of mankind. The liberty of the individual must be thus far limited; he must not make himself a nuisance to other people. But if he refrains from molesting others in what concerns them, and merely acts according to his own inclination and judgment in things which concern himself, the same reasons which show that opinion should be free prove also that he should be allowed, without molestation, to carry his opinions into practice at his own cost. . . .

QUESTIONS FOR REFLECTION

1. How does Mill's defense of freedom of thought and discussion fit into the overall scheme of *On Liberty*? Is speech self-regarding or other-regarding? Is his defense an application of the harm principle or an extension of it?

2. "All silencing of discussion is an assumption of infallibility," Mill contends. How does he argue for this claim? Do you agree?

3. Why does Mill think that the expression even of obviously false opinions should be protected?

4. Some contemporary advocates of controlling certain forms of expression argue that although the government cannot ban the expression of certain views, it can ban certain ways of expressing them—ways involving pornography, say, or the use of racial epithets. What is Mill's view about such restrictions? What arguments does he advance in support of his position? Do you find his arguments persuasive?

5. Mill mentions one exception to freedom of speech: inciting a mob to violence. What general principle lies behind this exception? What other exceptions might Mill be willing to accept?

CHAPTER IV / OF THE LIMITS TO THE AUTHORITY OF SOCIETY OVER THE INDIVIDUAL

What, then, is the rightful limit to the sovereignty of the individual over himself? Where does the authority of society begin? How much of human life should be assigned to individuality, and how much to society?

Each will receive its proper share if each has that which more particularly concerns it. To individuality should belong the part of life in which it is chiefly the individual that is interested; to society, the part which chiefly interests society.

Though society is not founded on a contract, and though no good purpose is answered by inventing a contract in order to deduce social obligations from it, everyone who receives the protection of society owes a return for the benefit, and the fact of living in society renders it indispensable that each should be bound to observe a certain line of conduct toward the rest. This conduct consists, first, in not injuring the interests of one another, or rather certain interests which, either by express legal provision or by tacit understanding, ought to be considered as rights; and secondly, in each person's bearing his share (to be fixed on some equitable principle) of the labors and sacrifices incurred for defending the society or its members from injury and molestation. These conditions society is justified in enforcing at all costs to those who endeavor to withhold fulfillment. Nor is this all that society may do. The acts of an individual may be hurtful to others or wanting in due consideration for their welfare, without going to the length of violating any of their constituted rights. The offender may then be justly punished by opinion, though not by law. As soon as any part of a person's conduct affects prejudicially the interests of others, society has jurisdiction over it, and the question whether the general welfare will or will not be promoted by interfering with it becomes open to discussion. But there is no room for entertaining any such question when a person's conduct affects the interests of no persons besides himself, or needs not affect them unless they like (all the persons concerned being of full age and the ordinary amount of understanding). In all such cases, there should be perfect freedom, legal and social, to do the action and stand the consequences. . . .

The distinction here pointed out between the part of a person's life which concerns only himself and that which concerns others, many persons will refuse to admit. How (it may be asked) can any part of the conduct of a member of society be a matter of indifference to the other members? No person is an entirely isolated being; it is impossible for a person to do anything seriously or permanently hurtful to himself without mischief reaching at least to his near connections, and often far beyond them. If he injures his property, he does harm to those who directly or indirectly derived support from it, and usually diminishes, by a greater or less amount, the general resources of the community. If he deteriorates his bodily or mental faculties, he not only brings evil upon all who depended upon him for any portion of their happiness, but disqualifies himself for rendering the services which he owes to his fellow creatures generally, perhaps becomes a burden on their affection or benevolence; and if such conduct were very frequent hardly any offense that is committed would detract more from the general sum of good. Finally, if by his vices or follies a person does no direct harm to others, he is nevertheless (it may be said) injurious by his example, and ought to be compelled to control himself for the sake of those whom the sight or knowledge of his conduct might corrupt or mislead.

And even (it will be added) if the consequences of misconduct could be confined to the vicious or thoughtless individual, ought society to abandon to their own guidance those who are manifestly unfit for it? If protection against themselves is confessedly due to children and persons under age, is not society equally bound to afford it to persons of mature years who are equally incapable of self-government? If gambling, or drunkenness, or incontinence, or idleness, or uncleanliness are as injurious to happiness, and as great a hindrance to improvement, as many or most of the acts prohibited by law, why (it may be asked) should not law, so far as is consistent with practicability and social convenience, endeavor to repress these also? And as a supplement to the unavoidable imperfections of law, ought not opinion at least to organize a powerful police against these vices and visit rigidly with social penalties those who are known to practice them? There is no question here (it may be said) about restricting individuality, or impeding the trial of new and original experiments in living. The only things it is sought to prevent are things which have been tried and condemned from the beginning of the world until now—things which experience has shown not to be useful or suitable to any person's individuality. There must be some length of time and amount of experience after which a moral or prudential truth may be regarded as established; and it is merely desired to prevent generation after generation from falling over the same precipice which has been fatal to their predecessors.

I fully admit that the mischief which a person does to himself may seriously affect, both through their sympathies and their interests, those nearly connected with him and, in a minor degree, society at large. When, by conduct of this sort, a person is led to violate a distinct and assignable obligation to any other person or persons, the case is taken out of the self-regarding class and becomes amenable to moral disapprobation in the proper sense of the term. If, for example, a man, through intemperance or extravagance, becomes unable to pay his debts, or, having undertaken the moral responsibility of a family, becomes from the same cause incapable of supporting or educating them, he is deservedly reprobated and might be justly punished; but it is for the breach of duty to his family or creditors, not for the extravagance. If the resources which ought to have been devoted to them had been diverted from them for the most prudent investment, the moral culpability would have been the same. George Barnwell murdered his uncle to get money for his mistress, but if he had done it to set himself up in business, he would equally have been hanged. Again, in the frequent case of a man who causes grief to his family by addiction to bad habits, he deserves reproach for his unkindness or ingratitude; but so he may for cultivating habits not in themselves vicious, if they are painful to those with whom he passes his life, or who from personal ties are dependent on him for their comfort. Whoever fails in the consideration generally due to the interests and feelings of others, not being compelled by some more imperative duty, or justified by allowable self-preference, is a subject of moral disapprobation for that failure, but not for the cause of it, nor for the errors, merely personal to himself, which may have remotely led to it. In like manner, when a person disables himself, by conduct purely self-regarding, from the performance of some definite duty incumbent on him to the public, he is guilty of a social offense. No person ought to be punished simply for being drunk; but a soldier or policeman should be punished for being drunk on duty. Whenever, in short, there is a definite damage, or a definite risk of damage, either to an individual or to the public, the case is taken out of the province of liberty and placed in that of morality or law.

But with regard to the merely contingent or, as it may be called, constructive injury which a person causes to society by conduct which neither violates any specific duty to the public, nor occasions perceptible hurt to any assignable individual except himself, the inconvenience is one which society can afford to bear, for the sake of the greater good of human freedom. . . .

But the strongest of all the arguments against the interference of the public with purely personal conduct is that, when it does interfere, the odds are that it interferes wrongly and in the wrong place. On questions of social morality, of duty to others, the opinion of the public, that is, of an overruling majority, though often wrong, is likely to be still oftener right, because on such questions they are only required to judge of their own interests, of the manner in which some mode of conduct, if allowed to be practiced, would affect themselves. But the opinion of a similar majority, imposed as a law on the minority, on questions of self-regarding conduct is quite as likely to be wrong as right, for in these cases public opinion means, at the best, some people's opinion of what is good or bad for other people, while very often it does not even mean that—the public, with the most perfect indifference, passing over the pleasure or convenience of those whose conduct they censure and considering only their own preference. There are many who consider as an injury to themselves any conduct which they have a distaste for, and resent it as an outrage to their feelings; as a religious bigot, when charged with disregarding the religious feelings of others, has been known to retort that they disregard his feelings by persisting in their abominable worship or creed. But there is no parity between the feeling of a person for his own opinion and the feeling of another who is offended at his holding it, no more than between the desire of a thief to take a purse and the desire of the right owner to keep it. And a person's taste is as much his own peculiar concern as his opinion or his purse. It is easy for anyone to imagine an ideal public which leaves the freedom and choice of individuals in all uncertain matters undisturbed and only requires them to abstain from modes of conduct which universal experience has condemned. But where has there been seen a public which set any such limit to its censorship? Or when does the public trouble itself about universal experience? In its interferences with personal conduct it is seldom thinking of anything but the enormity of acting or feeling differently from itself; and this standard of judgment, thinly disguised, is held up to mankind as the dictate of religion and philosophy by nine-tenths of all moralists and speculative writers. These teach that things are right because they are right; because we feel them to be so. They tell us to search in our own minds and hearts for laws of conduct binding on ourselves and on all others. What can the poor public do but apply these instructions and make their own personal feelings of good and evil, if they are tolerably unanimous in them, obligatory on all the world? . . .

QUESTIONS FOR REFLECTION

1. To what extent may people be punished by the opinions or behavior of others, independent of any legal coercion? Is Mill's view compatible with his analysis of the social stigma attending the expression of unpopular opinions?

2. Mill admits that distinguishing self-regarding from other-regarding actions is a matter of degree, for virtually every action affects someone other than the agent who performs it. What is Mill's criterion for determining whether an act affects others enough to count as other-regarding and, so, to be subject to government interference?

3. What arguments does Mill advance in this section in favor of the harm principle?

CHAPTER V / APPLICATIONS

Again, trade is a social act. Whoever undertakes to sell any description of goods to the public does what affects the interest of other persons, and of society in general; and thus his conduct, in principle, comes within the jurisdiction of society; accordingly, it was once held to be the duty of governments, in all cases which were considered of importance, to fix prices and regulate the process of manufacture. But it is now recognized, though not till after a long struggle, that both the cheapness and the good quality of commodities are most effectually provided for by leaving the producers and sellers perfectly free, under the sole check of equal freedom to the buyers for supplying themselves elsewhere. This is the so-called doctrine of "free trade," which rests on grounds different from, though equally solid with, the principle of individual liberty asserted in this essay. Restrictions on trade, or on production for purposes of trade, are indeed restraints; and all restraint, *qua* restraint, is an evil; but the restraints in question affect only that part of conduct which society is competent to restrain, and are wrong solely because they do not really produce the results which it is desired to produce by them. As the principle of individual liberty is not involved in the doctrine of free trade, so neither is it in most of the questions which arise respecting the limits of that doctrine, as, for example, what amount of public control is admissible for the prevention of fraud by adulteration; how far sanitary precautions, or arrangements to protect workpeople employed in dangerous occupations, should be enforced on employers. Such questions involve considerations of liberty only in so far as leaving people to themselves is better, *ceteris paribus,* than controlling them; but that they may be legitimately controlled for these ends is in principle undeniable. On the other hand, there are questions relating to interference with trade which are essentially questions of liberty, such as the Maine Law, already touched upon: the prohibition of the importation of opium into China; the restriction of the sale of poisons—all cases, in short, where the object of the interference is to make it impossible or difficult to obtain a particular commodity. These interferences are objectionable, not as infringements on the liberty of the producer or seller, but on that of the buyer.

One of these examples, that of the sale of poisons, opens a new question: the proper limits of what may be called the functions of police; how far liberty may legitimately be invaded for the prevention of crime, or of accident. It is one of the undisputed functions of government to take precautions against crime before it has been committed, as well as to detect and punish it afterwards. The preventive function of government, however, is far more liable to be abused, to the prejudice of liberty, than the punitory function; for there is hardly any part of the legitimate freedom of action of a human being which would not admit of being represented, and fairly, too, as increasing the facilities for some form or other of delinquency. Nevertheless, if a public authority, or even a private person, sees anyone evidently preparing to commit a crime, they are not bound to look on inactive until the crime is committed, but may interfere to prevent it. If poisons were never bought or used for any purpose except the commission of murder, it would be right to prohibit their manufacture and sale. They may, however, be wanted not only for innocent but for useful purposes, and restrictions cannot be imposed in the one case without operating in the other. Again, it is a proper office of public authority to guard against accidents. If either a public officer or anyone else saw a person attempting to cross a bridge which had been ascertained to be unsafe, and there were no time to warn him of his danger, they might seize him and turn him back, without any real infringement of his liberty; for liberty consists in doing what one desires, and he does not desire to fall into the river. Nevertheless, when there is not a certainty, but only a danger of mischief, no one but the person himself can judge of the sufficiency of the motive which may prompt him to incur the risk; in this case, therefore (unless he is a child, or delirious, or in some state of excitement or absorption incompatible with the full use of the reflecting faculty), he ought, I conceive, to be only warned of the danger; not forcibly prevented from exposing himself to it. Similar considerations, applied to such a question as the sale of poisons, may enable us to decide which among the possible modes of regulation are or are not contrary to principle. Such a precaution, for example, as that of labeling the drug with some word expressive of its dangerous character may be enforced without violation of liberty: the buyer cannot wish not to know that the thing he possesses has poisonous qualities. . . .

The right inherent in society to ward off crimes against itself by antecedent precautions suggests the obvious limitations to the maxim that purely self-regarding misconduct cannot properly be meddled with in the way of prevention or punishment. Drunkenness, for example, in ordinary cases, is not a fit subject for legislative interference, but I should deem it perfectly legitimate that a person who had once been convicted of any act of violence to others under the influence of drink should be placed under a special legal restriction, personal to himself; that if he were afterwards found drunk, he should be liable to a penalty, and that if, when in that state, he committed another offense, the punishment to which he would be liable for that other offense should be increased in severity. The making himself drunk, in a person whom drunkenness excites to do harm to others, is a crime against others. So, again, idleness, except in a person receiving support from the public, or except when it constitutes a breach of contract, cannot without tyranny be made a subject of legal punishment; but if, either from idleness or from any other avoidable cause, a man fails to perform his legal duties to others, as for instance to support his children, it is no tyranny to force him to fulfill that obligation by compulsory labor if no other means are available.

Again, there are many acts which, being directly injurious only to the agents themselves, ought not to be legally interdicted, but which, if done publicly, are a violation of good manners and, coming thus within the category of offenses against others, may rightly be prohibited. Of this kind are offenses against decency; on which it is unnecessary to dwell, the rather as they are only connected indirectly with our subject, the objection to publicity being equally strong in the case of many actions not in themselves condemnable, nor supposed to be so. . . .

A further question is whether the State, while it permits, should nevertheless indirectly discourage conduct which it deems contrary to the best interests of the agent; whether, for example, it should take measures to render the means of drunkenness more costly, or add to the difficulty of procuring them by limiting the number of the places of sale. On this, as on most other practical questions, many distinctions require to be made. To tax stimulants for the sole purpose of making them more difficult to be obtained is a measure differing only in degree from their entire prohibition, and would be justifiable only if that were justifiable. Every increase of cost is a prohibition to those whose means do not come up to the augmented price; and to those who do, it is a penalty laid on them for gratifying a particular taste. Their choice of pleasures and their mode of expending their income, after satisfying their legal and moral obligations to the State and to individuals, are their own concern and must rest with their own judgment. These considerations may seem at first sight to condemn the selection of stimulants as special subjects of taxation for purposes of revenue. But it must be remembered that taxation for fiscal purposes is absolutely inevitable; that in most countries it is necessary that a considerable part of that taxation should be indirect; that the State, therefore, cannot help imposing penalties, which to some persons may be prohibitory, on the use of some articles of consumption. It is hence the duty of the State to consider, in the imposition of taxes, what commodities the consumers can best spare; and *a fortiori,* to select in preference those of which it deems the use, beyond a very moderate quantity, to be positively injurious. Taxation, therefore, of stimulants up to the point which produces the largest amount of revenue (supposing that the State needs all the revenue which it yields) is not only admissible, but to be approved of. . . .

It was pointed out in an early part of this essay that the liberty of the individual, in things wherein the individual is alone concerned, implies a corresponding liberty in any number of individuals to regulate by mutual agreement such things as regard them jointly, and regard no persons but themselves. This question presents no difficulty so long as the will of all the persons implicated remains unaltered; but since that will may change it is often necessary, even in things in which they alone are concerned, that they should enter into engagements with one another; and when they do, it is fit, as a general rule, that those engagements should be kept. Yet, in the laws, probably, of every country, this general rule has some exceptions. Not only are persons not held to engagements which violate the rights of third parties, but it is sometimes considered a sufficient reason for releasing them from an engagement that it is injurious to themselves. In this and most other civilized countries, for example, an engagement by which a person should sell himself, or allow himself to be sold, as a slave would be null and void, neither enforced by law nor by opinion. The ground for thus limiting his power of voluntarily disposing of his own lot in life is apparent, and is very clearly seen in this extreme case. The reason for not interfering, unless for the sake of others, with a person's voluntary acts is consideration for his liberty. His voluntary choice is evidence that what he so chooses is desirable, or at least endurable, to him, and his good is on the whole best provided for by allowing him to take his own means of pursuing it. But by selling himself for a slave, he abdicates his liberty; he forgoes any future use of it beyond that single act. He therefore defeats, in his own case, the very purpose which is the justification of allowing him to dispose of himself. He is no longer free, but is thenceforth in a position which has no longer the presumption in its favor that would be afforded by his voluntarily remaining in it. The principle of freedom cannot require that he should be free not to be free. It is not freedom to be allowed to alienate his freedom. These reasons, the force of which is so conspicuous in this peculiar case, are evidently of far wider application, yet a limit is everywhere set to them by the necessities of life, which continually require, not indeed that we should resign our freedom, but that we should consent to this and the other limitation of it.

The principle, however, which demands uncontrolled freedom of action in all that concerns only the agents themselves requires that those who have become bound to one another, in things which concern no third party, should be able to release one another from the engagement; and even without such voluntary release there are perhaps no contracts or engagements, except those that relate to money or money's worth, of which one can venture to say that there ought to be no liberty whatever of retraction. Baron Wilhelm von Humboldt . . . states it as his conviction that engagements which involve personal relations or services should never be legally binding beyond a limited duration of time; and that the most important of these engagements, marriage, having the peculiarity that its objects are frustrated unless the feelings of both the parties are in harmony with it, should require nothing more than the declared will of either party to dissolve it. This subject is too important and too complicated to be discussed in a parenthesis, and I touch on it only so far as is necessary for purposes of illustration. If the conciseness and generality of Baron Humboldt's dissertation had not obliged him in this instance to content himself with enunciating his conclusion without discussing the premises, he would doubtless have recognized that the question cannot be decided on grounds so simple as those to which he confines himself. When a person, either by express promise or by conduct, has encouraged another to rely on his continuing to act in a certain way—to build expectations and calculations, and stake any part of his plan of life upon that supposition—a new series of moral obligations arises on his part toward that person, which may possibly be overruled, but cannot be ignored. And again, if the relation between two contracting parties has been followed by consequences to others; if it has placed third parties in any peculiar position, or, as in the case of marriage, has even called third parties into existence, obligations arise on the part of both the contracting parties toward those third persons, the fulfillment of which, or at all events the mode of fulfillment, must be greatly affected by the continuance or disruption of the relation between the original parties to the contract. It does not follow, nor can I admit, that these obligations extend to requiring the fulfillment of the contract at all costs to the happiness of the reluctant party; but they are a necessary element in the question; and, even if, as von Humboldt maintains, they ought to make no difference in the *legal* freedom of the parties to release themselves from the engagement (and I also hold that they ought not to make *much* difference), they necessarily make a great difference in the *moral* freedom. A person is bound to take all these circumstances into account before resolving on a step which may affect such important interests of others; and if he does not allow proper weight to those interests, he is morally responsible for the wrong. . . .

QUESTIONS FOR REFLECTION

1. Between 1905 and 1937, a period known as the *Lochner* era, the U.S. Supreme Court used a form of the harm principle to strike down laws regulating economic activity: laws setting a minimum wage, for example, or regulating working hours and conditions. Does the harm principle, in Mill's view, apply to economic transactions? How does the harm principle relate to what he calls the doctrine of "free trade"?

2. What is the point of Mill's example of someone about to cross an unsafe bridge? What does it indicate about the harm principle?

3. The United States, like many other countries, regulates advertising. Is such regulation compatible with Mill's position in *On Liberty*? What kinds of regulation, if any, might Mill be willing to accept?

4. Many governments impose "sin taxes" on items such as alcohol and cigarettes. What is Mill's criterion for determining whether such taxes are acceptable?

5. Mill insists that voluntary slavery ought to be prohibited, although it might appear to fall into the realm of individual liberty. Why? Is Mill's support for this prohibition consistent with the harm principle?

DRUG LEGALIZATION

Over the past several decades, drug use has grown from a fashion among a small collection of bohemian artists and musicians into a major social problem. The use of illegal and seriously harmful drugs can be found in almost any high school, college, or university in the United States; scores of cities routinely witness drug-related shootings and other forms of violence. Several times the government has declared a "war on drugs," but the result has seemed, at best, a stalemate. Frustration with this state of affairs has led some to call for the legalization of drugs.

Drug use may appear to be a self-regarding act that may harm the drug user but that has little effect on anyone else. Few contemporary advocates of legalization, however, have rested their case solely on Mill's harm principle. Many writers on both sides of the issue believe that nonusers suffer significant harms that must be taken into account; they have debated whether criminal penalties reduce or add to the harms to nonusers. Moreover, addictive drugs pose problems related to those Mill confronts in discussing voluntary slavery; people may initially choose, freely and voluntarily, to take an addictive drug, but their freedom does not last long. As Mill asks, do people have the freedom to surrender their freedom? Many contemporary writers share Mill's conviction that they do not and thus include harms to users of addictive drugs as morally relevant. This does not mean, however, that philosophical attitudes toward liberty are unrelated to discussions of the drug problem. Some writers clearly presuppose something akin to Mill's harm principle. Others assume the opposed principle of moral paternalism, holding that a government should promote the moral well-being of its citizens. Still others treat harms to users and harms to nonusers as morally equivalent, in effect denying the significance of the distinction between self-regarding and other-regarding actions.

Milton Friedman, a respected economist, argues that the war on drugs has been a costly failure. He urges decriminalization of drugs, that is, removing criminal penalties against their sale and use. He advocates treating drugs much as we now treat alcohol and cigarettes—as substances that should be regulated and whose users should be treated rather than jailed.

William Bennett, "drug czar" under Presidents Reagan and Bush, maintains that Friedman's proposal is flawed and even reckless. Bennett defends criminal penalties for drug use by arguing that they reduce harms both to drug users and to others. He contends that "government has a responsibility to craft and uphold laws that help educate citizens about right and wrong."

Ethan Nadelmann argues Friedman's case in greater detail. He holds that drug legalization would produce significant economic benefits, reduce crime, and revitalize the inner cities. Douglas Husak argues, from a more theoretical perspective, that laws against drug use violate fundamental liberties. James Q. Wilson further articulates Bennett's case, contending that the war on drugs is justifiable and moderately successful. He holds that enforcing criminal penalties has helped to confine the drug problem to a relatively small portion of the population while sheltering most people from harms associated with the drug trade. Legalization, he believes, would greatly increase drug use and the attendant harms to users and nonusers alike.

MILTON FRIEDMAN

An Open Letter to Bill Bennett

Milton Friedman is Senior Research Fellow at the Hoover Institution at Stanford University and Professor Emeritus of Economics at the University of Chicago. He was awarded the Nobel Prize in economics in 1976. (Source: Reprinted from The Wall Street Journal, *September 7, 1989, p. A14. Copyright © 1989 by Dow Jones and Company, Inc.)*

DEAR BILL:

In Oliver Cromwell's eloquent words, "I beseech you, in the bowels of Christ, think it possible you may be mistaken" about the course you and President Bush urge us to adopt to fight drugs. The path you propose of more police, more jails, use of the military in foreign countries, harsh penalties for drug users, and a whole panoply of repressive measures can only make a bad situation worse. The drug war cannot be won by those tactics without undermining the human liberty and individual freedom that you and I cherish.

You are not mistaken in believing that drugs are a scourge that is devastating our society. You are not mistaken in believing that drugs are tearing asunder our social fabric, ruining the lives of many young people, and imposing heavy costs on some of the most disadvantaged among us. You are not mistaken in believing that the majority of the public share your concerns. In short, you are not mistaken in the end you seek to achieve.

Your mistake is failing to recognize that the very measures you favor are a major source of the evils you deplore. Of course the problem is demand, but it is not only demand, it is demand that must operate through repressed and illegal channels. Illegality creates obscene profits that finance the murderous tactics of the drug lords; illegality leads to the corruption of law enforcement officials; illegality monopolizes the efforts of honest law forces so that they are starved for resources to fight the simpler crimes of robbery, theft and assault.

Drugs are a tragedy for addicts. But criminalizing their use converts that tragedy into a disaster for society, for users and non-users alike. Our experience with the prohibition of drugs is a replay of our experience with the prohibition of alcoholic beverages.

I append excerpts from a column that I wrote in 1972 on "Prohibition and Drugs." The major problem then was heroin from Marseilles; today, it is cocaine from Latin America. Today, also, the problem is far more serious than it was 17 years ago: more addicts, more innocent victims; more drug pushers, more law enforcement officials; more money spent to enforce prohibition, more money spent to circumvent prohibition.

Had drugs been decriminalized 17 years ago, "crack" would never have been invented (it was invented because the high cost of illegal drugs made it profitable to provide a cheaper version) and there would today be far fewer addicts. The lives of thousands, perhaps hundreds of thousands of innocent victims would have been saved, and not only in the U.S. The ghettos of our major cities would not be drug-and-crime-infested no-man's lands. Fewer people would be in jails, and fewer jails would have been built.

Colombia, Bolivia and Peru would not be suffering from narco-terror, and we would not be distorting our foreign policy because of narco-terror. Hell would not, in the words with which Billy Sunday welcomed Prohibition, "be forever for rent," but it would be a lot emptier.

Decriminalizing drugs is even more urgent now than in 1972, but we must recognize that the harm done in the interim cannot be wiped out, certainly not immediately. Postponing decriminalization will only make matters worse, and make the problem appear even more intractable.

Alcohol and tobacco cause many more deaths in users than do drugs. Decriminalization would not prevent us from treating drugs as we now treat alcohol and tobacco: prohibiting sales of drugs to minors, outlawing the advertising of drugs and similar measures. Such measures could be enforced, while outright prohibition cannot be. Moreover, if even a small fraction of the money we now spend on trying to enforce drug prohibition were devoted to treatment and rehabilitation, in an atmosphere of compassion not punishment, the reduction in drug usage and in the harm done to the users could be dramatic.

This plea comes from the bottom of my heart. Every friend of freedom, and I know you are one, must be as revolted as I am by the prospect of turning the United States into an armed camp, by the vision of jails filled with casual drug users and of an army of enforcers empowered to invade the liberty of citizens on slight evidence. A country in which shooting down unidentified planes "on suspicion" can be seriously considered as a drug-war tactic is not the kind of United States that either you or I want to hand on to future generations.

Milton Friedman
Senior Research Fellow
Hoover Institution
Stanford University

Flashback

This is a truncated version of a column by Mr. Friedman in Newsweek's *May 1, 1972, issue, as President Nixon was undertaking an earlier "drug war":*

"The reign of tears is over. The slums will soon be only a memory. We will turn our prisons into factories and our jails into storehouses and corncribs. Men will walk upright now, women will smile, and the children will laugh. Hell will be forever for rent."

That is how Billy Sunday, the noted evangelist and leading crusader against Demon Rum, greeted the onset of Prohibition in early 1920.

We know now how tragically his hopes were doomed.

Prohibition is an attempted cure that makes matters worse—for both the addict and the rest of us.

Consider first the addict. Legalizing drugs might increase the number of addicts, but it is not clear that it would. Forbidden fruit is attractive, particularly to the young. More important, many drug addicts are deliberately made by pushers, who give likely prospects that first few doses free. It pays the pusher to do so because, once hooked, the addict is a captive customer. If drugs were legally available, any possible profit from such inhumane activity would disappear, since the addict could buy from the cheapest source.

Whatever happens to the number of addicts, the individual addict would clearly be far better off if drugs were legal. Addicts are driven to associate with criminals to get the drugs, become criminals themselves to finance the habit, and risk constant danger of death and disease.

Consider next the rest of us. The harm to us from the addiction of others arises almost wholly from the fact that drugs are illegal. It is estimated that addicts commit one third to one half of all street crime in the U.S.

Legalize drugs, and street crime would drop dramatically.

Moreover, addicts and pushers are not the only ones corrupted. Immense sums are at stake. It is inevitable that some relatively low-paid police and other government officials—and some high-paid ones as well—will succumb to the temptation to pick up easy money.

Legalizing drugs would simultaneously reduce the amount of crime and raise the quality of law enforcement. Can you conceive of any other measure that would accomplish so much to promote law and order?

In drugs, as in other areas, persuasion and example are likely to be far more effective than the use of force to shape others in our image.

QUESTIONS FOR REFLECTION

1. Asserting that government prohibition of drug use is illegitimate in itself differs from asserting that it is a bad idea in practice. Certainly Friedman asserts the latter. How does he argue for this position? Does he also assert the former?

2. Friedman claims that the drug war undermines "human liberty and individual freedom." What is Friedman's conception of liberty? Is Friedman's argument compatible with Mill's harm principle?

WILLIAM J. BENNETT

A Response to Milton Friedman

William J. Bennett is Research Fellow at the American Enterprise Institute. He has served as Director of the Office of National Drug Control Policy and as U.S. Secretary of Education. (Source: Reprinted by permission from The Wall Street Journal, *September 19, 1989, p. A30. Copyright © 1989 by Dow Jones and Company, Inc.)*

DEAR MILTON:

There was little, if anything, new in your open letter to me calling for the legalization of drugs (*The Wall Street Journal,* Sept. 7). As the excerpt from your 1972 article made clear, the legalization argument is an old and familiar one, which has recently been revived by a small number of journalists and academics who insist that the only solution to the drug problem is no solution at all. What surprises me is that you would continue to advocate so unrealistic a proposal without pausing to consider seriously its consequences.

If the argument for drug legalization has one virtue it is its sheer simplicity. Eliminate laws against drugs, and street crime will disappear. Take the profit out of the black market through decriminalization and regulation, and poor neighborhoods will no longer be victimized by drug dealers. Cut back on drug enforcement, and use the money to wage a public health campaign against drugs, as we do with tobacco and alcohol.

Counting Costs

The basic premise of all these propositions is that using our nation's laws to fight drugs is too costly. To be sure, our attempts to reduce drug use do carry with them enormous costs. But the question that must be asked—and which is totally ignored by the legalization advocates—is what are the costs of *not* enforcing laws against drugs?

In my judgment, and in the judgment of virtually every serious scholar in this field, the potential costs of legalizing drugs would be so large as to make it a public policy disaster.

Of course, no one, including you, can say with certainty what would happen in the U.S. if drugs were suddenly to become a readily purchased product. We do know, however, that wherever drugs have been cheaper and more easily obtained, drug use—and addiction—has skyrocketed. In opium and cocaine-producing countries, addiction is rampant among the peasants involved in drug production.

Professor James Q. Wilson tells us that during the years in which heroin could be legally prescribed by doctors in Britain, the number of addicts increased forty-fold. And after the repeal of Prohibition—an analogy favored but misunderstood by legalization advocates—consumption of alcohol soared by 350%.

Could we afford such dramatic increases in drug use? I doubt it. Already the toll of drug use on American society—measured in lost productivity, in rising health insurance costs, in hospitals flooded with drug overdose emergencies, in drug-caused accidents, and in premature death—is surely more than we would like to bear.

You seem to believe that by spending just a little more money on treatment and rehabilitation, the costs of increased addiction can be avoided. That hope betrays a basic misunderstanding of the problems facing drug treatment. Most addicts don't suddenly decide to get help. They remain addicts either because treatment isn't available or because they don't seek it out. The National Drug Control Strategy announced by President Bush on Sept. 5 goes a long way in making sure that more treatment slots are available. But the simple fact remains that many drug users won't enter treatment until they are forced to— often by the very criminal justice system you think is the source of the problem.

As for the connection between drugs and crime, your unswerving commitment to a legalization solution prevents you from appreciating the complexity of the drug market. Contrary to your claim, most addicts do not turn to crime to support their habit. Research shows that many of them were involved in criminal activity before they turned to drugs. Many former addicts who have received treatment continue to commit crimes during their recovery. And even if drugs were legal, what evidence do you have that the habitual drug user wouldn't continue to rob and steal to get money for clothes, food or shelter? Drug addicts always want more drugs than they can afford, and no legalization scheme has yet come up with a way of satisfying that appetite.

The National Drug Control Strategy emphasizes the importance of reclaiming the streets and neighborhoods where drugs have wrought havoc because, I admit, the price of having drug laws is having criminals who will try to subvert them. Your proposal might conceivably reduce the amount of gang- and dealer-related crime, but it is fanciful to suggest that it would make crime vanish. Unless you are willing to distribute drugs freely and widely, there will always be a black market to undercut the regulated one. And as for the potential addicts, for the school children and for the pregnant mothers, all of whom would find drugs more accessible and legally condoned, your proposal would offer nothing at all.

So I advocate a larger criminal justice system to take drug users off the streets and deter new users from becoming more deeply involved in so hazard-

ous an activity. You suggest that such policies would turn the country "into an armed camp." Try telling that to the public housing tenants who enthusiastically support plans to enhance security in their buildings, or to the residents who applaud police when a local crack house is razed. They recognize that drug use is a threat to the individual liberty and domestic tranquility guaranteed by the Constitution.

I remain an ardent defender of our nation's laws against illegal drug use and our attempts to enforce them because I believe drug use is wrong. A true friend of freedom understands that government has a responsibility to craft and uphold laws that help educate citizens about right and wrong. That, at any rate, was the Founders' view of our system of government.

Liberal Ridicule

Today this view is much ridiculed by liberal elites and entirely neglected by you. So while I cannot doubt the sincerity of your opinion on drug legalization, I find it difficult to respect. The moral cost of legalizing drugs is great, but it is a cost that apparently lies outside the narrow scope of libertarian policy prescriptions.

I do not have a simple solution to the drug problem. I doubt that one exists. But I am committed to fighting the problem on several fronts through imaginative policies and hard work over a long period of time. As in the past, some of these efforts will work and some won't. Your response, however, is to surrender and see what happens. To my mind that is irresponsible and reckless public policy. At a time when national intolerance for drug use is rapidly increasing, the legalization argument is a political anachronism. Its recent resurgence is, I trust, only a temporary distraction from the genuine debate on national drug policy.

William J. Bennett
Director
Office of National Drug Control Policy

QUESTIONS FOR REFLECTION

1. Bennett contends that legalizing drugs would increase harms to nonusers. How does he argue this position?

2. Part of Bennett's case rests on his view that enforcing criminal penalties against drug use decreases harms done by drugs to drug users themselves. What is his argument? Is Bennett's use of this argument compatible with Mill's harm principle?

3. Friedman claims that the drug war undermines "human liberty and individual freedom." How does Bennett respond to this allegation, if at all? What does this indicate about Bennett's conception of freedom and of the proper bounds of government authority?

4. In what sense is Bennett's position Aristotelian?

5. To what extent might Burke's views lend support to Bennett's position?

ETHAN A. NADELMANN

The Case for Legalization

Ethan A. Nadelmann is Assistant Professor of Politics and Public Affairs at the Woodrow Wilson School of Public and International Affairs at Princeton University. (Source: Public Interest 92 [Summer 1988]. Notes have been omitted. Copyright © 1988 by National Interest, Inc. Reprinted by permission.)

What can be done about the "drug problem"? Despite frequent proclamations of war and dramatic increases in government funding and resources in recent years, there are many indications that the problem is not going away and may even be growing worse. During the past year alone, more than thirty million Americans violated the drug laws on literally billions of occasions. Drug-treatment programs in many cities are turning people away for lack of space and funding. In Washington, D.C., drug-related killings, largely of one drug dealer by another, are held responsible for a doubling in the homicide rate over the past year. In New York and elsewhere, courts and prisons are clogged with a virtually limitless supply of drug-law violators. In large cities and small towns alike, corruption of policemen and other criminal-justice officials by drug traffickers is rampant. . . .

If there were a serious public debate on this issue, far more attention would be given to one policy option that has just begun to be seriously considered but that may well prove more successful than anything currently being implemented or proposed: legalization. . . .

There is, of course, no single legalization strategy. At one extreme is the libertarian vision of virtually no government restraints on the production and sale of drugs or any psychoactive substances, except perhaps around the fringes, such as prohibiting sales to children. At the other extreme is total government control over the production and sale of these goods. In between lies a strategy that may prove more successful than anything yet tried in stemming the problems of drug abuse and drug-related violence, corruption, sickness, and suffering. It is one in which government makes most of the substances that are now banned legally available to competent adults, exercises strong regulatory powers over all large-scale production and sale of drugs, makes drug-treatment programs available to all who need them, and offers honest drug-education programs to children. This strategy, it is worth noting, would also result in a net benefit to public treasuries of at least ten billion dollars a year, and perhaps much more.

There are three reasons why it is important to think about legalization scenarios, even though most Americans remain hostile to the idea. First, current drug-control policies have failed, are failing, and will continue to fail, in good part because they are fundamentally flawed. Second, many drug-control efforts are not only failing but also proving highly costly and counterproductive; indeed, many of the drug-related evils that Americans identify as part and parcel of the "drug problem" are in fact caused by our drug-prohibition policies. Third, there is good reason to believe that repealing many of the drug laws would not lead, as many people fear, to a dramatic rise in drug abuse. In this essay I expand on each of these reasons for considering the legalization option. Government efforts to deal with the drug problem will succeed only if the rhetoric and crusading mentality that now dominate drug policy are replaced by reasoned and logical analysis.

Why Current Drug Policies Fail

Most proposals for dealing with the drug problem today reflect a desire to point the finger at those most removed from one's home and area of expertise. New York Mayor Ed Koch, Florida Congressman Larry Smith, and Harlem Congressman Charles Rangel, who recognize government's inability to deal with the drug problem in the cities, are among the most vocal supporters of punishing foreign drug-producing countries and stepping up interdiction efforts. Foreign leaders and U.S. State Department and drug-enforcement officials stationed abroad, on the other hand, who understand all too well why it is impossible to crack down successfully on illicit drug production outside the United States, are the most vigorous advocates of domestic enforcement and demand-reduction efforts within the United States. In between, those agencies charged with drug interdiction, from the Coast Guard and U.S. Customs Service to the U.S. military, know that they will never succeed in capturing more than a small percentage of the illicit drugs being smuggled into the United States. Not surprisingly, they point their fingers in both directions. The solution, they promise, lies in greater source-control efforts abroad and greater demand-reduction efforts at home.

Trying to pass the buck is always understandable. But in each of these cases, the officials are half right and half wrong—half right in recognizing that they can do little to affect their end of the drug problem, given the suppositions and constraints of current drug-control strategies; half wrong (if we assume that their finger pointing is sincere) in expecting that the solution lies elsewhere. It would be wrong, however, to assume that the public posturing of many officials reflects their real views. Many of them privately acknowledge the futility of all current drug-control strategies and wonder whether radically different options, such as legalization, might not

prove more successful in dealing with the drug problem. The political climate pervading this issue is such, however, that merely to ask that alternatives to current policies be considered is to incur a great political risk.

By most accounts, the dramatic increase in drug-enforcement efforts over the past few years has had little effect on the illicit drug market in the United States. The mere existence of drug-prohibition laws, combined with a minimal level of law-enforcement resources, is sufficient to maintain the price of illicit drugs at a level significantly higher than it would be if there were no such laws. Drug laws and enforcement also reduce the availability of illicit drugs, most notably in parts of the United States where demand is relatively limited to begin with. Theoretically, increases in drug-enforcement efforts should result in reduced availability, higher prices, and lower purity of illegal drugs. That is, in fact, what has happened to the domestic marijuana market (in at least the first two respects). But in general the illegal drug market has not responded as intended to the substantial increases in federal, state, and local drug-enforcement efforts.

Cocaine has sold for about a hundred dollars a gram at the retail level since the beginning of the 1980s. The average purity of that gram, however, has increased from 12 to 60 percent. Moreover, a growing number of users are turning to "crack," a potent derivative of cocaine that can be smoked; it is widely sold in ghetto neighborhoods now for five to ten dollars per vial. Needless to say, both crack and the 60 percent pure cocaine pose much greater threats to users than did the relatively benign powder available eight years ago. Similarly, the retail price of heroin has remained relatively constant even as the average purity has risen from 3.9 percent in 1983 to 6.1 percent in 1986. Throughout the southwestern part of the United States, a particularly potent form of heroin known as "black tar" has become increasingly prevalent. And in many cities, a powerful synthetic opiate, Dilaudid, is beginning to compete with heroin as the preferred opiate. The growing number of heroin-related hospital emergencies and deaths is directly related to these developments.

All of these trends suggest that drug-enforcement efforts are not succeeding and may even be backfiring. There are numerous indications, for instance, that a growing number of marijuana dealers in both the producer countries and the United States are switching to cocaine dealing, motivated both by the promise of greater profits and by government drug-enforcement efforts that place a premium on minimizing the bulk of the illicit product (in order to avoid detection). It is possible, of course, that some of these trends would be even more severe in the absence of drug laws and enforcement. At the same time, it is worth observing that the increases in the potency of illegal drugs have coincided with decreases in the potency of legal substances. Motivated in good part by health concerns, cigarette smokers are turning increasingly to lower-tar and lower-nicotine tobacco products, alcohol drinkers from hard liquor to wine and beer, and even coffee drinkers from regular to decaffeinated coffee. This trend may well have less to do with the nature of the substances than with their legal status. It is quite possible, for instance, that the subculture of illicit-drug use creates a bias or incentive in favor of riskier behavior and more powerful psychoactive effects. If this is the case, legalization might well succeed in reversing today's trend toward more potent drugs and more dangerous methods of consumption.

The most "successful" drug-enforcement operations are those that succeed in identifying and destroying an entire drug-trafficking organization. Such operations can send dozens of people to jail and earn the government millions of dollars in asset forfeitures. Yet these operations have virtually no effect on the availability or price of illegal drugs throughout much of the United States. During the past few years, some urban police departments have devoted significant manpower and financial resources to intensive crackdowns on street-level drug dealing in particular neighborhoods. Code-named Operation Pressure Point, Operation Clean Sweep, and so on, these massive police efforts have led to hundreds, even thousands, of arrests of low-level dealers and drug users and have helped improve the quality of life in the targeted neighborhoods. In most cases, however, drug dealers have adapted relatively easily by moving their operations to nearby neighborhoods. In the final analysis, the principal accomplishment of most domestic drug-enforcement efforts is not to reduce the supply or availability of illegal drugs, or even to raise their price; it is to punish the drug dealers who are apprehended, and cause minor disruptions in established drug markets.

The Failure of International Drug Control

Many drug-enforcement officials and urban leaders recognize the futility of domestic drug-enforcement efforts and place their hopes in international control efforts. Yet these too are doomed to fail—for numerous reasons. First, marijuana and opium can be grown almost anywhere, and the coca plant, from which cocaine is derived, is increasingly being cultivated successfully in areas that were once considered inhospitable environments. Wherever drug-eradication efforts succeed, other regions and countries are quick to fill the void; for example, Colombian marijuana growers rapidly expanded production following successful eradication efforts in Mexico during the mid-1970s. Today, Mexican growers are rapidly taking advantage of recent Colombian government successes in eradicating marijuana in the Guajira peninsula. Meanwhile, Jamaicans and Central Americans from Panama to Belize, as well as a growing assortment of Asians and Africans, do what they can to sell their own marijuana in American markets. And within the United States, domestic marijuana production is believed to be a multi-billion-dollar industry, supplying between 15 and 50 percent of the American market. . . .

Beyond the push-down/pop-up factor, international source-control efforts face a variety of other obstacles. In many countries, governments with limited resources lack the ability to crack down on drug production in the hinterlands and other poorly policed regions. In some countries, ranging from Colombia and Peru to Burma and Thailand, leftist insurgencies are involved in drug production for either financial or political profit and may play an important role in hampering government drug-control efforts. With respect to all three of the illicit crops, poor peasants with no comparable opportunities to earn as much money growing legitimate produce are prominently involved in the illicit business. In some cases, the illicit crop is part of a traditional, indigenous culture. Even where it is not, peasants typically perceive little or nothing immoral about taking advantage of the opportunity to grow the illicit crops. Indeed, from their perspective their moral obligation is not to protect the foolish American consumer of their produce but to provide for their families' welfare. And even among those who do perceive participation in the illicit drug market as somewhat unethical, the temptations held out by the drug traffickers often prove overwhelming.

No illicit drug is as difficult to keep out of the United States as heroin. The absence of geographical limitations on where it can be cultivated is just one minor obstacle. American heroin users consume an estimated 6 tons of heroin each year. The 60 tons of opium required to produce that heroin represent just 2 or 3 percent of the estimated 2,000 to 3,000 tons of illicit opium produced during each of the past few years. Even if eradication efforts combined with what often proves to be the opium growers' principal nemesis—bad weather—were to eliminate three-fourths of that production in one year, the U.S. market would still require just 10 percent of the remaining crop. Since U.S. consumers are able and willing to pay more than any others, the chances are good that they would still obtain their heroin. In any event, the prospects for such a radical reduction in illicit opium production are scanty indeed.

As Peter Reuter argues, interdiction, like source control, is largely unable to keep illicit drugs out of the United States. Moreover, the past twenty years' experience has demonstrated that even dramatic increases in interdiction and source-control efforts have little or no effect on the price and purity of drugs. The few small successes, such as the destruction of the Turkish-opium "French Connection" in the early 1970s and the crackdown on Mexican marijuana and heroin in the late 1970s, were exceptions to the rule. The elusive goal of international drug control since then has been to replicate those unusual successes. It is a strategy that is destined to fail, however, as long as millions of Americans continue to demand the illicit substances that foreigners are willing and able to supply.

The Costs of Prohibition

The fact that drug-prohibition laws and policies cannot eradicate or even significantly reduce drug abuse is not necessarily a reason to repeal them. They do, after all, succeed in deterring many people from trying drugs, and they clearly reduce the availability and significantly increase the price of illegal drugs. These accomplishments alone might warrant retaining the drug laws, were it not for the fact that these same laws are also responsible for much of what Americans identify as the "drug problem." Here the analogies to alcohol and tobacco are worth noting. There is little question that we could reduce the health costs associated with use and abuse of alcohol and tobacco if we were to criminalize their production, sale, and possession. But no one believes that we could eliminate their use and abuse, that we could create an "alcohol-free" or "tobacco-free" country. Nor do most Americans believe that criminalizing the alcohol and tobacco markets would be a good idea. Their opposition stems largely from two beliefs: that adult Americans have the right to choose what substances they will consume and what risks they will take and that the costs of trying to coerce so many Americans to abstain from those substances would be enormous. It was the strength of these two beliefs that ultimately led to the repeal of Prohibition, and it is partly due to memories of that experience that criminalizing either alcohol or tobacco has little support today.

Consider the potential consequences of criminalizing the production, sale, and possession of all tobacco products. On the positive side, the number of people smoking tobacco would almost certainly decline, as would the health costs associated with tobacco consumption. Although the "forbidden fruit" syndrome would attract some people to cigarette smoking who would not otherwise have smoked, many more would likely be deterred by the criminal sanction, the moral standing of the law, the higher cost and unreliable quality of the illicit tobacco, and the difficulties involved in acquiring it. Non-smokers would rarely if ever be bothered by the irritating habits of their fellow citizens. The anti-tobacco laws would discourage some people from ever starting to smoke and would induce others to quit.

On the negative side, however, millions of Americans, including both tobacco addicts and recreational users, would no doubt defy the law, generating a massive underground market and billions in profits for organized criminals. Although some to-

bacco farmers would find other work, thousands more would become outlaws and continue to produce their crops covertly. Throughout Latin America, farmers and gangsters would rejoice at the opportunity to earn untold sums of gringo greenbacks, even as U.S. diplomats pressured foreign governments to cooperate with U.S. laws. Within the United States, government helicopters would spray herbicides on illicit tobacco fields; people would be rewarded by the government for informing on their neighbors who grow, sell, and smoke tobacco; urine tests would be employed to identify violators of the anti-tobacco laws; and a Tobacco Enforcement Administration (the T.E.A.) would employ undercover agents, informants, and wiretaps to uncover tobacco-law violators. Municipal, state, and federal judicial systems would be clogged with tobacco traffickers and "abusers." "Tobacco-related murders" would increase dramatically as criminal organizations competed with one another for turf and markets. Smoking would become an act of youthful rebellion, and no doubt some users would begin to experiment with more concentrated, potent, and dangerous forms of tobacco. Tobacco-related corruption would infect all levels of government, and respect for the law would decline noticeably. Government expenditures on tobacco-law enforcement would climb rapidly into the billions of dollars, even as budget balancers longingly recalled the almost ten billion dollars per year in tobacco taxes earned by the federal and state governments prior to prohibition. Finally, the state of North Carolina might even secede again from the Union.

This seemingly far-fetched tobacco-prohibition scenario is little more than an extrapolation based on the current situation with respect to marijuana, cocaine, and heroin. In many ways, our predicament resembles what actually happened during Prohibition. Prior to Prohibition, most Americans hoped that alcohol could be effectively banned by passing laws against its production and supply. During the early years of Prohibition, when drinking declined but millions of Americans nonetheless continued to drink, Prohibition's supporters placed their faith in tougher laws and more police and jails. After a few more years, however, increasing numbers of Americans began to realize that laws and policemen were unable to eliminate the smugglers, bootleggers, and

illicit producers, as long as tens of millions of Americans continued to want to buy alcohol. At the same time, they saw that more laws and policemen seemed to generate more violence and corruption, more crowded courts and jails, wider disrespect for government and the law, and more power and profits for the gangsters. Repeal of Prohibition came to be seen not as a capitulation to Al Capone and his ilk but as a means of both putting the bootleggers out of business and eliminating most of the costs associated with the prohibition laws.

Today, Americans are faced with a dilemma similar to that confronted by our forebears sixty years ago. Demand for illicit drugs shows some signs of abating but no signs of declining significantly. Moreover, there are substantial reasons to doubt that tougher laws and policing have played an important role in reducing consumption. Supply, meanwhile, has not abated at all. Availability of illicit drugs, except for marijuana in some locales, remains high. Prices are dropping, even as potency increases. And the number of drug producers, smugglers, and dealers remains sizable, even as jails and prisons fill to overflowing. As was the case during Prohibition, the principal beneficiaries of current drug policies are the new and old organized-crime gangs. The principal victims, on the other hand, are not the drug dealers but the tens of millions of Americans who are worse off in one way or another as a consequence of the existence and failure of the drug-prohibition laws.

All public policies create beneficiaries and victims, both intended and unintended. When a public policy results in a disproportionate magnitude of unintended victims, there is good reason to reevaluate the assumptions and design of the policy. In the case of drug-prohibition policies, the intended beneficiaries are those individuals who would become drug abusers but for the existence and enforcement of the drug laws. The intended victims are those who traffic in illicit drugs and suffer the legal consequences. The unintended beneficiaries, conversely, are the drug producers and traffickers who profit handsomely from the illegality of the market, while avoiding arrest by the authorities and the violence perpetrated by other criminals. The unintended victims of drug-prohibition policies are rarely recognized as such, however. Viewed narrowly, they are the thirty million

Americans who use illegal drugs, thereby risking loss of their jobs, imprisonment, and the damage done to health by ingesting illegally produced drugs; viewed broadly, they are all Americans, who pay the substantial costs of our present ill-considered policies, both as taxpayers and as the potential victims of crime. These unintended victims are generally thought to be victimized by the unintended beneficiaries (i.e., the drug dealers), when in fact it is the drug-prohibition policies themselves that are primarily responsible for their plight.

If law-enforcement efforts could succeed in significantly reducing either the supply of illicit drugs or the demand for them, we would probably have little need to seek alternative drug-control policies. But since those efforts have repeatedly failed to make much of a difference and show little indication of working better in the future, at this point we must focus greater attention on their costs. Unlike the demand and supply of illicit drugs, which have remained relatively indifferent to legislative initiatives, the costs of drug-enforcement measures can be affected—quite dramatically—by legislative measures. What tougher criminal sanctions and more police have failed to accomplish, in terms of reducing drug-related violence, corruption, death, and social decay, may well be better accomplished by legislative repeal of the drug laws and adoption of less punitive but more effective measures to prevent and treat substance abuse.

Costs to the Taxpayer

Since 1981, federal expenditures on drug enforcement have more than tripled—from less than one billion dollars a year to about three billion. According to the National Drug Enforcement Policy Board, the annual budgets of the Drug Enforcement Administration (DEA) and the Coast Guard have each risen during the past seven years from about $220 million to roughly $500 million. During the same period, FBI resources devoted to drug enforcement have increased from $8 million a year to over $100 million, U.S. Marshals resources from $26 million to about $80 million, U.S. Attorney resources from $20 million to about $100 million, State Department resources from $35 million to $100 mil-

lion, U.S. Customs resources from $180 million to over $400 million, and Bureau of Prison resources from $77 million to about $300 million. Expenditures on drug control by the military and the intelligence agencies are more difficult to calculate, although by all accounts they have increased by at least the same magnitude and now total hundreds of millions of dollars per year. Even greater are the expenditures at lower levels of government. In a 1987 study for the U.S. Customs Service by Wharton Econometrics, state and local police were estimated to have devoted 18 percent of their total investigative resources, or close to five billion dollars, to drug-enforcement activities in 1986. This represented a 19 percent increase over the previous year's expenditures. All told, 1987 expenditures on all aspects of drug enforcement, from drug eradication in foreign countries to imprisonment of drug users and dealers in the United States, totaled at least ten billion dollars.

Of course, even ten billion dollars a year pales in comparison with expenditures on military defense. Of greater concern than the actual expenditures, however, has been the diversion of limited resources—including the time and energy of judges, prosecutors, and law-enforcement agents, as well as scarce prison space—from the prosecution and punishment of criminal activities that harm far more innocent victims than do violations of the drug laws. Drug-law violators account for approximately 10 percent of the roughly 800,000 inmates in state prisons and local jails and more than one-third of the 44,000 federal prison inmates. These proportions are expected to increase in coming years, even as total prison populations continue to rise dramatically. Among the 40,000 inmates in New York State prisons, drug-law violations surpassed first-degree robbery in 1987 as the number one cause of incarceration, accounting for 20 percent of the total prison population. The U.S. Sentencing Commission has estimated that, largely as a consequence of the Anti-Drug Act passed by Congress in 1986, the proportion of federal inmates incarcerated for drug violations will rise from one-third of the 44,000 prisoners sentenced to federal-prison terms today to one-half of the 100,000 to 150,000 federal prisoners anticipated in fifteen years. The direct costs of building and maintaining enough prisons to house this

growing population are rising at an astronomical rate. The opportunity costs, in terms of alternative social expenditures forgone and other types of criminals not imprisoned, are perhaps even greater.

During each of the last few years, police made about 750,000 arrests for violations of the drug laws. Slightly more than three-quarters of these have not been for manufacturing or dealing drugs but solely for possession of an illicit drug, typically marijuana. (Those arrested, it is worth noting, represent little more than 2 percent of the thirty million Americans estimated to have used an illegal drug during the past year.) On the one hand, this has clogged many urban criminal-justice systems: in New York City, drug-law violations last year accounted for more than 40 percent of all felony indictments—up from 25 percent in 1985; in Washington, D.C., the figure was more than 50 percent. On the other hand, it has distracted criminal-justice officials from concentrating greater resources on violent offenses and property crimes. In many cities, law enforcement has become virtually synonymous with drug enforcement.

Drug laws typically have two effects on the market in illicit drugs. The first is to restrict the general availability and accessibility of illicit drugs, especially in locales where underground drug markets are small and isolated from the community. The second is to increase, often significantly, the price of illicit drugs to consumers. Since the costs of producing most illicit drugs are not much different from the costs of alcohol, tobacco, and coffee, most of the price paid for illicit substances is in effect a value-added tax created by their criminalization, which is enforced and supplemented by the law-enforcement establishment but collected by the drug traffickers. A report by Wharton Econometrics for the President's Commission on Organized Crime identified the sale of illicit drugs as the source of more than half of all organized-crime revenues in 1986, with the marijuana and heroin business each providing over seven billion dollars and the cocaine business over thirteen billion. By contrast, revenues from cigarette bootlegging, which persists principally because of differences among the states in their cigarette-tax rates, were estimated at 290 million dollars. If the marijuana, cocaine, and heroin markets were legal, state and federal governments would collect billions of dollars annually in tax revenues. Instead, they ex-

pend billions on what amounts to a subsidy of organized crime and unorganized criminals.

Drugs and Crime

The drug/crime connection is one that continues to resist coherent analysis, both because cause and effect are so difficult to distinguish and because the role of the drug-prohibition laws in causing and labeling "drug-related crime" is so often ignored. There are four possible connections between drugs and crime, at least three of which would be much diminished if the drug-prohibition laws were repealed. First, producing, selling, buying, and consuming strictly controlled and banned substances are crimes that occur billions of times each year in the United States alone. In the absence of drug-prohibition laws, these activities would obviously cease to be crimes. Selling drugs to children would, of course, continue to be criminal, and other evasions of government regulation of a legal market would continue to be prosecuted; but by and large the drug/crime connection that now accounts for all of the criminal-justice costs noted above would be severed.

Second, many illicit-drug users commit crimes such as robbery and burglary, as well as drug dealing, prostitution, and numbers running, to earn enough money to purchase the relatively high-priced illicit drugs. Unlike the millions of alcoholics who can support their habits for relatively modest amounts, many cocaine and heroin addicts spend hundreds and even thousands of dollars a week. If the drugs to which they are addicted were significantly cheaper—which would be the case if they were legalized—the number of crimes committed by drug addicts to pay for their habits would, in all likelihood, decline dramatically. Even if a legal-drug policy included the imposition of relatively high consumption taxes in order to discourage consumption, drug prices would probably still be lower than they are today.

The third drug/crime connection is the commission of crimes—violent crimes in particular—by people under the influence of illicit drugs. This connection seems to have the greatest impact upon the popular imagination. Clearly, some drugs do "cause" some people to commit crimes by reducing normal

inhibitions, unleashing aggressive and other anti-social tendencies, and lessening the sense of responsibility. Cocaine, particularly in the form of crack, has gained such a reputation in recent years, just as heroin did in the 1960s and 1970s and marijuana did in the years before that. Crack's reputation for inspiring violent behavior may or may not be more deserved than those of marijuana and heroin; reliable evidence is not yet available. No illicit drug, however, is as widely associated with violent behavior as alcohol. According to Justice Department statistics, 54 percent of all jail inmates convicted of violent crimes in 1983 reported having used alcohol just prior to committing their offense. The impact of drug legalization on this drug/crime connection is the most difficult to predict. Much would depend on overall rates of drug abuse and changes in the nature of consumption, both of which are impossible to predict. It is worth noting, however, that a shift in consumption from alcohol to marijuana would almost certainly contribute to a decline in violent behavior.

The fourth drug/crime link is the violent, intimidating, and corrupting behavior of the drug traffickers. Illegal markets tend to breed violence—not only because they attract criminally minded individuals but also because participants in the market have no resort to legal institutions to resolve their disputes. During Prohibition, violent struggles between bootlegging gangs and hijackings of booze-laden trucks and sea vessels were frequent and notorious occurrences. Today's equivalents are the booby traps that surround some marijuana fields, the pirates of the Caribbean looking to rip off drug-laden vessels en route to the shores of the United States, and the machine-gun battles and executions carried out by drug lords—all of which occasionally kill innocent people. Most law-enforcement officials agree that the dramatic increases in urban murder rates during the past few years can be explained almost entirely by the rise in drug-dealer killings.

Perhaps the most unfortunate victims of the drug-prohibition policies have been the law-abiding residents of America's ghettos. These policies have largely proven futile in deterring large numbers of ghetto dwellers from becoming drug abusers, but they do account for much of what ghetto residents identify as the drug problem. In many neighborhoods, it often seems to be the aggressive gun-toting drug dealers who upset law-abiding residents far more than the addicts nodding out in doorways. Other residents, however, perceive the drug dealers as heroes and successful role models. In impoverished neighborhoods, they often stand out as symbols of success to children who see no other options. At the same time, the increasingly harsh criminal penalties imposed on adult drug dealers have led to the widespread recruitment of juveniles by drug traffickers. Formerly, children started dealing drugs only after they had been using them for a while; today the sequence is often reversed: many children start using illegal drugs now only after working for older drug dealers. And the juvenile-justice system offers no realistic options for dealing with this growing problem.

The conspicuous failure of law-enforcement agencies to deal with this drug/crime connection is probably most responsible for the demoralization of neighborhoods and police departments alike. Intensive police crackdowns in urban neighborhoods do little more than chase the menace a short distance away to infect new areas. By contrast, legalization of the drug market would drive the drug-dealing business off the streets and out of apartment buildings and into legal, government-regulated, tax-paying stores. It would also force many of the gun-toting dealers out of business and would convert others into legitimate businessmen. Some, of course, would turn to other types of criminal activities, just as some of the bootleggers did following Prohibition's repeal. Gone, however, would be the unparalleled financial temptations that lure so many people from all sectors of society into the drug-dealing business.

The Costs of Corruption

All vice-control efforts are particularly susceptible to corruption, but none so much as drug enforcement. When police accept bribes from drug dealers, no victim exists to complain to the authorities. Even when police extort money and drugs from traffickers and dealers, the latter are in no position to report the corrupt officers. What makes drug enforcement especially vulnerable to corruption are the tremendous amounts of money involved in the business. Today, many law-enforcement officials believe that police corruption is more pervasive than at any time since Prohibition. In Miami, dozens of law-enforcement

officials have been charged with accepting bribes, stealing from drug dealers, and even dealing drugs themselves. Throughout many small towns and rural communities in Georgia, where drug smugglers en route from Mexico, the Caribbean, and Latin America drop their loads of cocaine and marijuana, dozens of sheriffs have been implicated in drug-related corruption. In New York, drug-related corruption in one Brooklyn police precinct has generated the city's most far-reaching police-corruption scandal since the 1960s. More than a hundred cases of drug-related corruption are now prosecuted each year in state and federal courts. Every one of the federal law-enforcement agencies charged with drug-enforcement responsibilities has seen an agent implicated in drug-related corruption.

It is not difficult to explain the growing pervasiveness of drug-related corruption. The financial temptations are enormous relative to other opportunities, legitimate or illegitimate. Little effort is required. Many police officers are demoralized by the scope of the drug traffic, their sense that many citizens are indifferent, and the fact that many sectors of society do not even appreciate their efforts—as well as the fact that many of the drug dealers who are arrested do not remain in prison. Some police also recognize that enforcing the drug laws does not protect victims from predators so much as it regulates an illicit market that cannot be suppressed but can be kept underground. In every respect, the analogy to Prohibition is apt. Repealing the drug-prohibition laws would dramatically reduce police corruption. By contrast, the measures currently being proposed to deal with the growing problem, including better funded and more aggressive internal investigations, offer relatively little promise.

Among the most difficult costs to evaluate are those that relate to the widespread defiance of the drug-prohibition laws: the effects of labeling as criminals the tens of millions of people who use drugs illicitly, subjecting them to the risks of criminal sanction, and obligating many of these same people to enter into relationships with drug dealers (who may be criminals in many more senses of the word) in order to purchase their drugs; the cynicism that such laws generate toward other laws and the law in general; and the sense of hostility and suspicion that many otherwise law-abiding individuals feel toward law-enforcement officials. It was costs such as these that strongly influenced many of Prohibition's more conservative opponents.

Physical and Moral Costs

Perhaps the most paradoxical consequence of the drug laws is the tremendous harm they cause to the millions of drug users who have not been deterred from using illicit drugs in the first place. Nothing resembling an underground Food and Drug Administration has arisen to impose quality control on the illegal drug market and provide users with accurate information on the drugs they consume. Imagine that Americans could not tell whether a bottle of wine contained 6 percent, 30 percent, or 90 percent alcohol, or whether an aspirin tablet contained 5 or 500 grams of aspirin. Imagine, too, that no controls existed to prevent winemakers from diluting their product with methanol and other dangerous impurities and that vineyards and tobacco fields were fertilized with harmful substances by ignorant growers and sprayed with poisonous herbicides by government agents. Fewer people would use such substances, but more of those who did would get sick. Some would die.

The above scenario describes, of course, the current state of the illicit drug market. Many marijuana smokers are worse off for having smoked cannabis that was grown with dangerous fertilizers, sprayed with the herbicide paraquat, or mixed with more dangerous substances. Consumers of heroin and the various synthetic substances sold on the street face even severer consequences, including fatal overdoses and poisonings from unexpectedly potent or impure drug supplies. More often than not, the quality of a drug addict's life depends greatly upon his or her access to reliable supplies. Drug-enforcement operations that succeed in temporarily disrupting supply networks are thus a double-edged sword: they encourage some addicts to seek admission into drug-treatment programs, but they oblige others to seek out new and hence less reliable suppliers; the result is that more, not fewer, drug-related emergencies and deaths occur.

Today, over 50 percent of all people with AIDS in New York City, New Jersey, and many other parts of the country, as well as the vast majority of AIDS-infected heterosexuals throughout the country, have contracted the disease directly or indirectly through illegal intravenous drug use. Reports have emerged of drug dealers' beginning to provide clean syringes together with their illegal drugs. But even as other governments around the world actively attempt to limit the spread of AIDS by and among drug users by instituting free syringe-exchange programs, state and municipal governments in the United States resist following suit, arguing that to do so would "encourage" or "condone" the use of illegal drugs. Only in January 1988 did New York City approve such a program on a very limited and experimental basis. At the same time, drug-treatment programs remain notoriously underfunded, turning away tens of thousands of addicts seeking help, even as billions of dollars more are spent to arrest, prosecute, and imprison illegal drug sellers and users. In what may represent a sign of shifting priorities, the President's Commission on AIDS, in its March 1988 report, emphasized the importance of making drug-treatment programs available to all in need of them. In all likelihood, however, the criminal-justice agencies will continue to receive the greatest share of drug-control funds.

Most Americans perceive the drug problem as a moral issue and draw a moral distinction between use of the illicit drugs and use of alcohol and tobacco. Yet when one subjects this distinction to reasoned analysis, it quickly disintegrates. The most consistent moral perspective of those who favor drug laws is that of the Mormons and the Puritans, who regard as immoral any intake of substances to alter one's state of consciousness or otherwise cause pleasure: they forbid not only the illicit drugs and alcohol but also tobacco, caffeine, and even chocolate. The vast majority of Americans are hardly so consistent with respect to the propriety of their pleasures. Yet once one acknowledges that there is nothing immoral about drinking alcohol or smoking tobacco for non-medicinal purposes, it becomes difficult to condemn the consumption of marijuana, cocaine, and other substances on moral grounds. The "moral" condemnation of some substances and not others proves to be little more than a prejudice in favor of some drugs and against others.

The same false distinction is drawn with respect to those who provide the psychoactive substances to users and abusers alike. If degrees of immorality were measured by the levels of harm caused by one's products, the "traffickers" in tobacco and alcohol would be vilified as the most evil of all substance purveyors. That they are perceived instead as respected members of our community, while providers of the no more dangerous illicit substances are punished with long prison sentences, says much about the prejudices of most Americans with respect to psychoactive substances but little about the morality or immorality of purveyors' activities.

Much the same is true of gun salesmen. Most of the consumers of their products use them safely; a minority, however, end up shooting either themselves or someone else. Can we hold the gun salesman morally culpable for the harm that probably would not have occurred but for his existence? Most people say no, except perhaps where the salesman clearly knew that his product would be used to commit a crime. Yet in the case of those who sell illicit substances to willing customers, the providers are deemed not only legally guilty but also morally reprehensible. The law does not require any demonstration that the dealer knew of a specific harm to follow; indeed, it does not require any evidence at all of harm having resulted from the sale. Rather, the law is predicated on the assumption that harm will inevitably follow. Despite the patent falsity of that assumption, it persists as the underlying justification for the drug laws.

Although a valid moral distinction cannot be drawn between the licit and the illicit psychoactive substances, one can point to a different kind of moral justification for the drug laws: they arguably reflect a paternalistic obligation to protect those in danger of succumbing to their own weaknesses. If drugs were legally available, most people would either abstain from using them or would use them responsibly and in moderation. A minority without self-restraint, however, would end up harming themselves if the substances were more readily available. Therefore, the majority has a moral obligation to deny itself legal access to certain substances because of the plight of the minority. This obligation is presumably greatest when children are included among the minority.

At least in principle, this argument seems to provide the strongest moral justification for the drug laws. But ultimately the moral quality of laws must be judged not by how those laws are intended to work in principle but by how they function in practice. When laws intended to serve a moral end inflict great damage on innocent parties, we must rethink our moral position.

Because drug-law violations do not create victims with an interest in notifying the police, drug-enforcement agents rely heavily on undercover operations, electronic surveillance, and information provided by informants. These techniques are indispensable to effective law enforcement, but they are also among the least palatable investigative methods employed by the police. The same is true of drug testing: it may be useful and even necessary for determining liability in accidents, but it also threatens and undermines the right of privacy to which many Americans believe they are entitled. There are good reasons for requiring that such measures be used sparingly.

Equally disturbing are the increasingly vocal calls for people to inform not only on drug dealers but also on neighbors, friends, and even family members who use illicit drugs. Government calls on people not only to "just say no" but also to report those who have not heeded the message. Intolerance of illicit-drug use and users is heralded not only as an indispensable ingredient in the war against drugs but also as a mark of good citizenship. Certainly every society requires citizens to assist in the enforcement of criminal laws. But societies—particularly democratic and pluralistic ones—also rely strongly on an ethic of tolerance toward those who are different but do no harm to others. Overzealous enforcement of the drug laws risks undermining that ethic and encouraging the creation of a society of informants. This results in an immorality that is far more dangerous in its own way than that associated with the use of illicit drugs.

The Benefits of Legalization

Repealing the drug-prohibition laws promises tremendous advantages. Between reduced government expenditures on enforcing drug laws and new tax revenue from legal drug production and sales, public treasuries would enjoy a net benefit of at least ten billion dollars a year, and possibly much more. The quality of urban life would rise significantly. Homicide rates would decline. So would robbery and burglary rates. Organized criminal groups, particularly the newer ones that have yet to diversify out of drugs, would be dealt a devastating setback. The police, prosecutors, and courts would focus their resources on combatting the types of crimes that people cannot walk away from. More ghetto residents would turn their backs on criminal careers and seek out legitimate opportunities instead. And the health and quality of life of many drug users—and even drug abusers—would improve significantly. . . .

QUESTIONS FOR REFLECTION

1. Why, according to Nadelmann, have current drug policies failed?

2. In Nadelmann's view, what harms does drug prohibition produce?

3. How does Nadelmann relate drug use and drug prohibition to crime? Do you find his analysis persuasive? Why or why not?

JAMES Q. WILSON

Against the Legalization of Drugs

James Q. Wilson is Collins Professor of Management and Public Policy at the University of California at Los Angeles. (Source: Reprinted from Commentary *[February 1990], by permission; all rights reserved.)*

In 1972, the President appointed me chairman of the National Advisory Council for Drug Abuse Prevention. Created by Congress, the Council was charged with providing guidance on how best to coordinate the national war on drugs. (Yes, we called it a war then, too.) In those days, the drug we were chiefly concerned with was heroin. When I took office, heroin use had been increasing dramatically. Everybody was worried that this increase would continue. Such phrases as "heroin epidemic" were commonplace.

That same year, the eminent economist Milton Friedman published an essay in *Newsweek* in which he called for legalizing heroin. His argument was on two grounds: as a matter of ethics, the government has no right to tell people not to use heroin (or to drink or to commit suicide); as a matter of economics, the prohibition of drug use imposes costs on society that far exceed the benefits. Others, such as the psychoanalyst Thomas Szasz, made the same argument.

We did not take Friedman's advice. (Government commissions rarely do.) I do not recall that we even discussed legalizing heroin, though we did discuss (but did not take action on) legalizing a drug, cocaine, that many people then argued was benign. Our marching orders were to figure out how to win the war on heroin, not to run up the white flag of surrender.

That was 1972. Today, we have the same number of heroin addicts that we had then—half a million, give or take a few thousand. Having that many heroin addicts is no trivial matter; these people deserve our attention. But not having had an increase in that number for over fifteen years is also something that deserves our attention. What happened to the "heroin epidemic" that many people once thought would overwhelm us?

The facts are clear: a more or less stable pool of heroin addicts had been getting older, with relatively few new recruits. In 1976 the average age of heroin users who appeared in hospital emergency rooms was about twenty-seven; ten years later it was thirty-two. More than two-thirds of all heroin users appearing in emergency rooms are now over the age of thirty. Back in the early 1970's, when heroin got onto the national political agenda, the typical heroin addict was much younger, often a teenager. Household surveys show the same thing—the rate of opiate use (which includes heroin) has been flat for the better part of two decades. More fine-grained studies of inner-city neighborhoods confirm this. John Boyle and Ann Brunswick found that the percentage of young blacks in Harlem who used heroin fell from 8 percent in 1970–71 to about 3 percent in 1975–76.

Why did heroin lose its appeal for young people? When the young blacks in Harlem were asked why they stopped, more than half mentioned "trouble with the law" or "high cost" (and high cost is, of course, directly the result of law enforcement). Two-thirds said that heroin hurt their health; nearly all said they had had a bad experience with it. We need not rely, however, simply on what they said. In New York City in 1973–75, the street price of heroin rose dramatically and its purity sharply declined, probably as a result of the heroin shortage caused by the success of the Turkish government in reducing the supply of opium base and of the French government in closing down heroin-processing laboratories located in and around Marseilles. These were short-lived gains for, just as Friedman predicted, alternative sources of supply—mostly in Mexico—quickly emerged. But the three-year heroin shortage interrupted the easy recruitment of new users.

Health and related problems were no doubt part of the reason for the reduced flow of recruits. Over the preceding years, Harlem youth had watched as more and more heroin users died of overdoses, were poisoned by adulterated doses, or acquired hepatitis from dirty needles. The word got around: heroin can kill you. By 1974 new hepatitis cases and drug-overdose deaths had dropped to a fraction of what they had been in 1970.

Alas, treatment did not seem to explain much of the cessation in drug use. Treatment programs can and do help heroin addicts, but treatment did not explain the drop in the number of *new* users (who by definition had never been in treatment) nor even much of the reduction in the number of experienced users.

No one knows how much of the decline to attribute to personal observation as opposed to high prices or reduced supply. But other evidence suggests strongly that price and supply played a large role. In 1972 the National Advisory Council was especially worried by the prospect that U.S. servicemen returning to this country from Vietnam would bring their heroin habits with them. Fortunately, a brilliant study by Lee Robins of Washington University in St. Louis put that fear to rest. She measured drug use of Vietnam veterans shortly after they had returned home. Though many had used heroin regularly while in Southeast Asia, most gave up the habit when back in the United States. The reason: here, heroin was less available and sanctions on its use were more pronounced. Of course, if a veteran had been willing to pay enough—which might have meant traveling to another city and would certainly have meant making an illegal contact with a disreputable dealer in a threatening neighborhood in order to acquire a (possibly) dangerous dose—he could have sustained his drug habit. Most veterans

were unwilling to pay this price, and so their drug use declined or disappeared.

Reliving the Past

Suppose we had taken Friedman's advice in 1972. What would have happened? We cannot be entirely certain, but at a minimum we would have placed the young heroin addicts (and, above all, the prospective addicts) in a very different position from the one in which they actually found themselves. Heroin would have been legal. Its price would have been reduced by 95 percent (minus whatever we chose to recover in taxes). Now that it could be sold by the same people who make aspirin, its quality would have been assured—no poisons, no adulterants. Sterile hypodermic needles would have been readily available at the neighborhood drugstore, probably at the same counter where the heroin was sold. No need to travel to big cities or unfamiliar neighborhoods—heroin could have been purchased anywhere, perhaps by mail order.

There would no longer have been any financial or medical reason to avoid heroin use. Anybody could have afforded it. We might have tried to prevent children from buying it, but as we have learned from our efforts to prevent minors from buying alcohol and tobacco, young people have a way of penetrating markets theoretically reserved for adults. Returning Vietnam veterans would have discovered that Omaha and Raleigh had been converted into the pharmaceutical equivalent of Saigon.

Under these circumstances, can we doubt for a moment that heroin use would have grown exponentially? Or that a vastly larger supply of new users would have been recruited? Professor Friedman is a Nobel Prize–winning economist whose understanding of market forces is profound. What did he think would happen to consumption under his legalized regime? Here are his words: "Legalizing drugs might increase the number of addicts, but it is not clear that it would. Forbidden fruit is attractive, particularly to the young."

Really? I suppose that we should expect no increase in Porsche sales if we cut the price by 95 percent, no increase in whiskey sales if we cut the price by a comparable amount—because young people only want fast cars and strong liquor when they are "forbidden." Perhaps Friedman's uncharacteristic lapse from the obvious implications of price theory can be explained by a misunderstanding of how drug users are recruited. In his 1972 essay he said that "drug addicts are deliberately made by pushers, who give likely prospects their first few doses free." If drugs were legal it would not pay anybody to produce addicts, because everybody would buy from the cheapest source. But as every drug expert knows, pushers do not produce addicts. Friends or acquaintances do. In fact, pushers are usually reluctant to deal with non-users because a non-user could be an undercover cop. Drug use spreads in the same way any fad or fashion spreads: somebody who is already a user urges his friends to try, or simply shows already-eager friends how to do it.

But we need not rely on speculation, however plausible, that lowered prices and more abundant supplies would have increased heroin usage. Great Britain once followed such a policy and with almost exactly those results. Until the mid-1960's, British physicians were allowed to prescribe heroin to certain classes of addicts. (Possessing these drugs without a doctor's prescription remained a criminal offense.) For many years this policy worked well enough because the addict patients were typically middle-class people who had become dependent on opiate painkillers while undergoing hospital treatment. There was no drug culture. The British system worked for many years, not because it prevented drug abuse, but because there was no problem of drug abuse that would test the system.

All that changed in the 1960's. A few unscrupulous doctors began passing out heroin in wholesale amounts. One doctor prescribed almost 600,000 heroin tablets—that is, over thirteen pounds—in just one year. A youthful drug culture emerged with a demand for drugs far different from that of the older addicts. As a result, the British government required doctors to refer users to government-run clinics to receive their heroin.

But the shift to clinics did not curtail the growth in heroin use. Throughout the 1960's the number of addicts increased—the late John Kaplan of Stanford estimated by fivefold—in part as a result of the diversion of heroin from clinic patients to new users on the streets. An addict would bargain with the clinic doctor over how big a dose he would receive.

The patient wanted as much as he could get, the doctor wanted to give as little as was needed. The patient had an advantage in this conflict because the doctor could not be certain how much was really needed. Many patients would use some of their "maintenance" dose and sell the remaining part to friends, thereby recruiting new addicts. As the clinics learned of this, they began to shift their treatment away from heroin and toward methadone, an addictive drug that, when taken orally, does not produce a "high" but will block the withdrawal pains associated with heroin abstinence.

Whether what happened in England in the 1960's was a mini-epidemic or an epidemic depends on whether one looks at numbers or at rates of change. Compared to the United States, the numbers were small. In 1960 there were 68 heroin addicts known to the British government; by 1968 there were 2,000 in treatment and many more who refused treatment. (They would refuse in part because they did not want to get methadone at a clinic if they could get heroin on the street.) Richard Hartnoll estimates that the actual number of addicts in England is five times the number officially registered. At a minimum, the number of British addicts increased by thirtyfold in ten years; the actual increase may have been much larger.

In the early 1980's the numbers began to rise again, and this time nobody doubted that a real epidemic was at hand. The increase was estimated to be 40 percent a year. By 1982 there were thought to be 20,000 heroin users in London alone. Geoffrey Pearson reports that many cities—Glasgow, Liverpool, Manchester, and Sheffield among them—were now experiencing a drug problem that once had been largely confined to London. The problem, again, was supply. The country was being flooded with cheap, high-quality heroin, first from Iran and then from Southeast Asia.

The United States began the 1960's with a much larger number of heroin addicts and probably a bigger at-risk population than was the case in Great Britain. Even though it would be foolhardy to suppose that the British system, if installed here, would have worked the same way or with the same results, it would be equally foolhardy to suppose that a combination of heroin available from leaky clinics and from street dealers who faced only minimal law-enforcement risks would not have produced a much greater increase in heroin use than we actually experienced. My guess is that if we had allowed either doctors or clinics to prescribe heroin, we would have had far worse results than were produced in Britain, if for no other reason than the vastly larger number of addicts with which we began. We would have had to find some way to police thousands (not scores) of physicians and hundreds (not dozens) of clinics. If the British civil service found it difficult to keep heroin in the hands of addicts and out of the hands of recruits when it was dealing with a few hundred people, how well would the American civil service have accomplished the same tasks when dealing with tens of thousands of people?

Back to the Future

Now cocaine, especially in its potent form, crack, is the focus of attention. Now as in 1972 the government is trying to reduce its use. Now as then some people are advocating legalization. Is there any more reason to yield to those arguments today than there was almost two decades ago?

I think not. If we had yielded in 1972 we almost certainly would have had today a permanent population of several million, not several hundred thousand, heroin addicts. If we yield now we will have a far more serious problem with cocaine.

Crack is worse than heroin by almost any measure. Heroin produces a pleasant drowsiness and, if hygienically administered, has only the physical side effects of constipation and sexual impotence. Regular heroin use incapacitates many users, especially poor ones, for any productive work or social responsibility. They will sit nodding on a street corner, helpless, but at least harmless. By contrast, regular cocaine use leaves the user neither helpless nor harmless. When smoked (as with crack) or injected, cocaine produces instant, intense, and short-lived euphoria. The experience generates a powerful desire to repeat it. If the drug is readily available, repeat use will occur. Those people who progress to "bingeing" on cocaine become devoted to the drug and its effects to the exclusion of almost all other considerations—job, family, children, sleep, food, even sex. Dr. Frank Gawin at Yale and Dr. Everett Ellinwood at Duke report that a substantial percentage of all high-dose, binge users become uninhibited, impulsive, hypersexual, compulsive, irritable, and hyperactive. Their moods vac-

illate dramatically, leading at times to violence and homicide.

Women are much more likely to use crack than heroin, and if they are pregnant, the effects on their babies are tragic. Douglas Besharov, who has been following the effects of drugs on infants for twenty years, writes that nothing he learned about heroin prepared him for the devastation of cocaine. Cocaine harms the fetus and can lead to physical deformities or neurological damage. Some crack babies have for all practical purposes suffered a disabling stroke while still in the womb. The long-term consequences of this brain damage are lowered cognitive ability and the onset of mood disorders. Besharov estimates that about 30,000 to 50,000 such babies are born every year, about 7,000 in New York City alone. There may be ways to treat such infants, but from everything we now know the treatment will be long, difficult, and expensive. Worse, the mothers who are most likely to produce crack babies are precisely the ones who, because of poverty or temperament, are least able and willing to obtain such treatment. In fact, anecdotal evidence suggests that crack mothers are likely to abuse their infants.

The notion that abusing drugs such as cocaine is a "victimless crime" is not only absurd but dangerous. Even ignoring the fetal drug syndrome, crack-dependent people are, like heroin addicts, individuals who regularly victimize their children by neglect, their spouses by improvidence, their employers by lethargy, and their coworkers by carelessness. Society is not and could never be a collection of autonomous individuals. We all have a stake in ensuring that each of us displays a minimal level of dignity, responsibility, and empathy. We cannot, of course, coerce people into goodness, but we can and should insist that some standards must be met if society itself—on which the very existence of the human personality depends—is to persist. Drawing the line that defines those standards is difficult and contentious, but if crack and heroin use do not fall below it, what does?

The advocates of legalization will respond by suggesting that my picture is overdrawn. Ethan Nadelmann of Princeton argues that the risk of legalization is less than most people suppose. Over 20 million Americans between the ages of eighteen and twenty-five have tried cocaine (according to a government survey), but only a quarter million use it daily. From this Nadelmann concludes that at most 3 percent of all young people who try cocaine develop a problem with it. The implication is clear: make the drug legal and we only have to worry about 3 percent of our youth.

The implication rests on a logical fallacy and a factual error. The fallacy is this: the percentage of occasional cocaine users who become binge users *when the drug is illegal* (and thus expensive and hard to find) tells us nothing about the percentage who will become dependent when the drug is legal (and thus cheap and abundant). Drs. Gawin and Ellinwood report, in common with several other researchers, that controlled or occasional use of cocaine changes to compulsive and frequent use "when access to the drug increases" or when the user switches from snorting to smoking. More cocaine more potently administered alters, perhaps sharply, the proportion of "controlled" users who become heavy users.

The factual error is this: the federal survey Nadelmann quotes was done in 1985, *before* crack had become common. Thus the probability of becoming dependent on cocaine was derived from the responses of users who snorted the drug. The speed and potency of cocaine's action increases dramatically when it is smoked. We do not yet know how greatly the advent of crack increases the risk of dependency, but all the clinical evidence suggests that the increase is likely to be large.

It is possible that some people will not become heavy users even when the drug is readily available in its most potent form. So far there are no scientific grounds for predicting who will and who will not become dependent. Neither socioeconomic background nor personality traits differentiate between casual and intensive users. Thus, the only way to settle the question of who is correct about the effect of easy availability on drug use, Nadelmann or Gawin and Ellinwood, is to try it and see. But that social experiment is so risky as to be no experiment at all, for if cocaine is legalized and if the rate of its abusive use increases dramatically, there is no way to put the genie back in the bottle, and it is not a kindly genie.

Have We Lost?

Many people who agree that there are risks in legalizing cocaine or heroin still favor it because, they think, we have lost the war on drugs. "Nothing we have done has worked" and the current federal policy is just "more of the same." Whatever the costs of greater drug use, surely they would be less than the costs of our present, failed efforts.

That is exactly what I was told in 1972—and heroin is not quite as bad a drug as cocaine. We did not surrender and we did not lose. We did not win, either. What the nation accomplished then was what most efforts to save people from themselves accomplish: the problem was contained and the number of victims minimized, all at a considerable cost in law enforcement and increased crime. Was the cost worth it? I think so, but others may disagree. What are the lives of would-be addicts worth? I recall some people saying to me then, "Let them kill themselves." I was appalled. Happily, such views did not prevail.

Have we lost today? Not at all. High-rate cocaine use is not commonplace. The National Institute of Drug Abuse (NIDA) reports that less than 5 percent of high-school seniors used cocaine within the last thirty days. Of course this survey misses young people who have dropped out of school and miscounts those who lie on the questionnaire, but even if we inflate the NIDA estimate by some plausible percentage, it is still not much above 5 percent. Medical examiners reported in 1987 that about 1,500 died from cocaine use; hospital emergency rooms reported about 30,000 admissions related to cocaine abuse.

These are not small numbers, but neither are they evidence of a nationwide plague that threatens to engulf us all. Moreover, cities vary greatly in the proportion of people who are involved with cocaine. To get city-level data we need to turn to drug tests carried out on arrested persons, who obviously are more likely to be drug users than the average citizen. The National Institute of Justice, through its Drug Use Forecasting (DUF) project, collects urinalysis data on arrests in 22 cities. As we have already seen, opiate (chiefly heroin) use has been flat or declining in most of these cities over the last decade. Cocaine use has gone up sharply, but with great variation among cities. New York, Philadelphia, and Washington, D.C., all report that two-thirds or more of their arrestees tested positive for cocaine, but in Portland, San Antonio, and Indianapolis the percentage was one-third or less.

In some neighborhoods, of course, matters have reached crisis proportions. Gangs control the streets, shootings terrorize residents, and drug-dealing occurs in plain view. The police seem barely able to contain matters. But in these neighborhoods—unlike at Palo Alto cocktail parties—the people are not calling for legalization, they are calling for help. And often not much help has come. Many cities are willing to do almost anything about the drug problem except spend more money on it. The federal government cannot change that; only local voters and politicians can. It is not clear that they will.

It took about ten years to contain heroin. We have had experience with crack for only about three or four years. Each year we spend perhaps $11 billion on law enforcement (and some of that goes to deal with marijuana) and perhaps $2 billion on treatment. Large sums, but not sums that should lead anyone to say, "We just can't afford this any more."

The illegality of drugs increases crime, partly because some users turn to crime to pay for their habits, partly because some users are stimulated by certain drugs (such as crack or PCP) to act more violently or ruthlessly than they otherwise would, and partly because criminal organizations seeking to control drug supplies use force to manage their markets. These also are serious costs, but no one knows how much they would be reduced if drugs were legalized. Addicts would no longer steal to pay black-market prices for drugs, a real gain. But some, perhaps a great deal, of that gain would be offset by the great increase in the number of addicts. These people, nodding on heroin or living in the delusion-ridden high of cocaine, would hardly be ideal employees. Many would steal simply to support themselves, since snatch-and-grab, opportunistic crime can be managed even by people unable to hold a regular job or plan an elaborate crime. Those British addicts who get their supplies from government clinics are not models of law-abiding decency. Most are in crime, and though their per-capita rate of criminality may be lower thanks to the cheapness of their drugs, the total volume of crime they produce may be quite large. Of course, society could decide to support all unemployable addicts on welfare, but that would mean that gains from lowered rates of crime would have to be offset by large increases in welfare budgets.

Proponents of legalization claim that the costs of having more addicts around would be largely if not entirely offset by having more money available with which to treat and care for them. The money would come from taxes levied on the sale of heroin and cocaine.

To obtain this fiscal dividend, however, legalization's supporters must first solve an economic dilemma. If they want to raise a lot of money to pay for welfare and treatment, the tax rate on the drugs will have to be quite high. Even if they themselves do not want a high rate, the politicians' love of "sin taxes" would probably guarantee that it would be high anyway. But the higher the tax, the higher the price of the drug, and the higher the price the greater the likelihood that addicts will turn to crime to find the money for it and that criminal organizations will be formed to sell tax-free drugs at below-market rates. If we managed to keep taxes (and thus prices) low, we would get that much less money to pay for welfare and treatment and more people could afford to become addicts. There may be an optimal tax rate for drugs that maximizes revenue while minimizing crime, bootlegging, and the recruitment of new addicts, but our experience with alcohol does not suggest that we know how to find it.

The Benefits of Illegality

The advocates of legalization find nothing to be said in favor of the current system except, possibly, that it keeps the number of addicts smaller than it would otherwise be. In fact, the benefits are more substantial than that.

First, treatment. All the talk about providing "treatment on demand" implies that there is a demand for treatment. That is not quite right. There are some drug-dependent people who genuinely want treatment and will remain in it if offered; they should receive it. But there are far more who want only short-term help after a bad crash; once stabilized and bathed, they are back on the street again, hustling. And even many of the addicts who enroll in a program honestly wanting help drop out after a short while when they discover that help takes time and commitment. Drug-dependent people have very short time horizons and a weak capacity for commitment. These two groups—those looking for a quick fix and those unable to stick with a long-term fix—are not easily helped. Even if we increase the number of treatment slots—as we should—we would have to do something to make treatment more effective.

One thing that can often make it more effective is compulsion. Douglas Anglin of UCLA, in common with many other researchers, has found that the longer one stays in a treatment program, the better the chances of a reduction in drug dependency. But he, again like most other researchers, has found that drop-out rates are high. He has also found, however, that patients who enter treatment under legal compulsion stay in the program longer than those not subject to such pressure. His research on the California civil-commitment program, for example, found that heroin users involved with its required drug-testing program had over the long term a lower rate of heroin use than similar addicts who were free of such constraints. If for many addicts compulsion is a useful component of treatment, it is not clear how compulsion could be achieved in a society in which purchasing, possessing, and using the drug were legal. It could be managed, I suppose, but I would not want to have to answer the challenge from the American Civil Liberties Union that it is wrong to compel a person to undergo treatment for consuming a legal commodity.

Next, education. We are now investing substantially in drug-education programs in the schools. Though we do not yet know for certain what will work, there are some promising leads. But I wonder how credible such programs would be if they were aimed at dissuading children from doing something perfectly legal. We could, of course, treat drug education like smoking education: inhaling crack and inhaling tobacco are both legal, but you should not do it because it is bad for you. That tobacco is bad for you is easily shown; the Surgeon General has seen to that. But what do we say about crack? It is pleasurable, but devoting yourself to so much pleasure is not a good idea (though perfectly legal)? Unlike tobacco, cocaine will not give you cancer or emphysema, but it will lead you to neglect your duties to family, job, and neighborhood? Everybody is doing cocaine, but you should not?

Again, it might be possible under a legalized regime to have effective drug-prevention programs, but their effectiveness would depend heavily, I think, on first having decided that cocaine use, like tobacco use, is purely a matter of practical consequences; no fundamental moral significance attaches to either. But if we believe—as I do—that dependency on certain mind-altering drugs *is* a moral issue and that

their illegality rests in part on their immorality, then legalizing them undercuts, if it does not eliminate altogether, the moral message.

That message is at the root of the distinction we now make between nicotine and cocaine. Both are highly addictive; both have harmful physical effects. But we treat the two drugs differently, not simply because nicotine is so widely used as to be beyond the reach of effective prohibition, but because its use does not destroy the user's essential humanity. Tobacco shortens one's life, cocaine debases it. Nicotine alters one's habits, cocaine alters one's soul. The heavy use of crack, unlike the heavy use of tobacco, corrodes those natural sentiments of sympathy and duty that constitute our human nature and make possible our social life. To say, as does Nadelmann, that distinguishing morally between tobacco and cocaine is "little more than a transient prejudice" is close to saying that morality itself is but a prejudice.

The Alcohol Problem

Now we have arrived where many arguments about legalizing drugs begin: is there any reason to treat heroin and cocaine differently from the way we treat alcohol?

There is no easy answer to that question because, as with so many human problems, one cannot decide simply on the basis either of moral principles or of individual consequences; one has to temper any policy by a common-sense judgment of what is possible. Alcohol, like heroin, cocaine, PCP, and marijuana, is a drug—that is, a mood-altering substance—and consumed to excess it certainly has harmful consequences: auto accidents, barroom fights, bedroom shootings. It is also, for some people, addictive. We cannot confidently compare the addictive powers of these drugs, but the best evidence suggests that crack and heroin are much more addictive than alcohol.

Many people, Nadelmann included, argue that since the health and financial costs of alcohol abuse are so much higher than those of cocaine or heroin abuse, it is hypocritical folly to devote our efforts to preventing cocaine or drug use. But as Mark Kleiman of Harvard has pointed out, this comparison is quite misleading. What Nadelmann is doing is showing that a *legalized* drug (alcohol) produces greater social harm than *illegal* ones (cocaine and heroin). But of course. Suppose that in the 1920's we had made heroin and cocaine legal and alcohol illegal. Can anyone doubt that Nadelmann would now be writing that it is folly to continue our ban on alcohol because cocaine and heroin are so much more harmful?

And let there be no doubt about it—widespread heroin and cocaine use are associated with all manner of ills. Thomas Bewley found that the mortality rate of British heroin addicts in 1968 was 28 times as high as the death rate of the same age group of non-addicts, even though in England at the time an addict could obtain free or low-cost heroin and clean needles from British clinics. Perform the following mental experiment: suppose we legalized heroin and cocaine in this country. In what proportion of auto fatalities would the state police report that the driver was nodding off on heroin or recklessly driving on a coke high? In what proportion of spouse-assault and child-abuse cases would the local police report that crack was involved? In what proportion of industrial accidents would safety investigators report that the forklift or drill-press operator was in a drug-induced stupor or frenzy? We do not know exactly what the proportion would be, but anyone who asserts that it would not be much higher than it is now would have to believe that these drugs have little appeal except when they are illegal. And that is nonsense.

An advocate of legalization might concede that social harm—perhaps harm equivalent to that already produced by alcohol—would follow from making cocaine and heroin generally available. But at least, he might add, we would have the problem "out in the open" where it could be treated as a matter of "public health." That is well and good, *if* we knew how to treat—that is, cure—heroin and cocaine abuse. But we do not know how to do it for all the people who would need such help. We are having only limited success in coping with chronic alcoholics. Addictive behavior is immensely difficult to change, and the best methods for changing it—living in drug-free therapeutic communities, becoming faithful members of Alcoholics Anonymous or Narcotics Anonymous—require great personal commitment, a quality that is, alas, in short supply among the very persons—young people, disadvantaged people—who are often most at risk for addiction.

Suppose that today we had, not 15 million alcohol abusers, but half a million. Suppose that we already knew what we have learned from our long experience with the widespread use of alcohol. Would we make whiskey legal? I do not know, but I suspect there would be a lively debate. The Surgeon General would remind us of the risks alcohol poses to pregnant women. The National Highway Traffic Safety Administration would point to the likelihood of more highway fatalities caused by drunk drivers. The Food and Drug Administration might find that there is a nontrivial increase in cancer associated with alcohol consumption. At the same time the police would report great difficulty in keeping illegal whiskey out of our cities, officers being corrupted by bootleggers, and alcohol addicts often resorting to crime to feed their habits. Libertarians, for their part, would argue that every citizen has a right to drink anything he wishes and that drinking is, in any event, a "victimless crime."

However the debate might turn out, the central fact would be that the problem was still, at that point, a small one. The government cannot legislate away the addictive tendencies in all of us, nor can it remove completely even the most dangerous addictive substances. But it can cope with harms when the harms are still manageable.

Science and Addiction

One advantage of containing a problem while it is still containable is that it buys time for science to learn more about it and perhaps to discover a cure. Almost unnoticed in the current debate over legalizing drugs is that basic science has made rapid strides in identifying the underlying neurological processes involved in some forms of addiction. Stimulants such as cocaine and amphetamines alter the way certain brain cells communicate with one another. That alteration is complex and not entirely understood, but in simplified form it involves modifying the way in which a neurotransmitter called dopamine sends signals from one cell to another.

When dopamine crosses the synapse between two cells, it is in effect carrying a message from the first cell to activate the second one. In certain parts of the brain that message is experienced as pleasure. After the message is delivered, the dopamine returns to the first cell. Cocaine apparently blocks this return, or "reuptake," so that the excited cell and others nearby continue to send pleasure messages. When the exaggerated high produced by cocaine-influenced dopamine finally ends, the brain cells may (in ways that are still a matter of dispute) suffer from an extreme lack of dopamine, thereby making the individual unable to experience any pleasure at all. This would explain why cocaine users often feel so depressed after enjoying the drug. Stimulants may also affect the way in which other neurotransmitters, such as serotonin and noradrenaline, operate.

Whatever the exact mechanism may be, once it is identified it becomes possible to use drugs to block either the effect of cocaine or its tendency to produce dependency. There have already been experiments using desipramine, imipramine, bromocriptine, carbamazepine, and other chemicals. There are some promising results.

Tragically, we spend very little on such research, and the agencies funding it have not in the past occupied very influential or visible posts in the federal bureaucracy. If there is one aspect of the "war on drugs" metaphor that I dislike, it is its tendency to focus attention almost exclusively on the troops in the trenches, whether engaged in enforcement or treatment, and away from the research-and-development efforts back on the home front where the war may ultimately be decided.

I believe that the prospects of scientists in controlling addiction will be strongly influenced by the size and character of the problem they face. If the problem is a few hundred thousand chronic, high-dose users of an illegal product, the chances of making a difference at a reasonable cost will be much greater than if the problem is a few million chronic users of legal substances. Once a drug is legal, not only will its use increase but many of those who then use it will prefer the drug to the treatment: they will want the pleasure, whatever the cost to themselves or their families, and they will resist—probably successfully—any effort to wean them away from experiencing the high that comes from inhaling a legal substance.

If I Am Wrong . . .

No one can know what our society would be like if we changed the law to make access to cocaine, heroin, and PCP easier. I believe, for reasons given, that the result would be a sharp increase in use, a more widespread degradation of the human personality, and a greater rate of accidents and violence.

I may be wrong. If I am, then we will needlessly have incurred heavy costs in law enforcement and some forms of criminality. But if I am right, and the legalizers prevail anyway, then we will have consigned millions of people, hundreds of thousands of infants, and hundreds of neighborhoods to a life of oblivion and disease. To the lives and families destroyed by alcohol we will have added countless more destroyed by cocaine, heroin, PCP, and whatever else a basement scientist can invent.

Human character is formed by society; indeed, human character is inconceivable without society, and good character is less likely in a bad society. Will we, in the name of an abstract doctrine of radical individualism, and with the false comfort of suspect predictions, decide to take the chance that somehow individual decency can survive amid a more general level of deregulation?

I think not. The American people are too wise for that, whatever the academic essayists and cocktail-party pundits may say. But if Americans today are less wise than I suppose, then Americans at some future time will look back on us now and wonder, what kind of people were they that they could have done such a thing?

QUESTIONS FOR REFLECTION

1. Wilson contends that the war on drugs has been successful. What evidence does he adduce in support of this claim?

2. Wilson believes that legalizing drugs would increase drug use significantly, and he supports his view with an economic argument. What is that argument? Do you find it persuasive?

3. Wilson talks about heroin and cocaine, but not marijuana. Which of his arguments would apply to marijuana, in your view? Which would not?

4. Wilson rejects the view that cocaine use is a "victimless crime," that is, a self-regarding act. Why?

5. Wilson does not accept Mill's harm principle; he advocates a rather different conception of individual liberty and societal responsibility. What is Wilson's conception? What role does it play in his argument? Compare Wilson's conception to that of Burke.

6. Many advocates of legalization recommend treatment over incarceration. Wilson, however, is skeptical of drug treatment, at least in the absence of laws outlawing drug use. Why? Do you find his arguments persuasive?

DOUGLAS HUSAK

from *Drugs and Rights*

Douglas Husak is Associate Professor of Philosophy at Rutgers University. (Source: From Drugs and Rights, *Cambridge University Press, 1992. Copyright © 1992 by Cambridge University Press. Reprinted by permission. Notes have been omitted.)*

DRUGS AND HARM TO USERS

. . . The paternalistic case for LAD* can be compared and contrasted with the paternalistic case for other recreational activities that pose significant risks to adults who engage in them. These activities include boxing, mountain climbing, race car driving, skiing, eating fatty foods, playing football, driving a car with or without a seat belt, riding a motorcycle with or without a helmet, sunbathing, playing "Russian roulette," consuming saccharin, participating in rodeos, bungee-jumping, and a host of others. At present, some but not all of these activities are and ought to be prohibited by law. Does the principle of autonomy apply to and protect the decision to engage in any of these risky behaviors? If so, defenders of LAD can be asked to point to a morally relevant difference between drug use and the recreational activities that autonomy protects. But if the principle of autonomy does not apply to or protect the decision to engage in any of these risky behaviors, this strategy fails to offer much insight into the justifiability of LAD. All analogical arguments are limited in this respect. . . . .

Perhaps the most familiar reason that will be given to differentiate the use of illegal drugs from many other recreational activities is that drug use is *more* risky than members of the comparison class that are and ought to be permitted. . . .

A common standard to compare the extent of risk of very different kinds of activities is not easily constructed. Some risky activities result in broken bones that usually heal; others cause a deterioration in mental functions that may or may not be reversed; still others progressively damage soft tissue. No single statistic can reduce the extent of risk to a common denominator, and I do not pretend to do so here.

Yet insight can be gained by a quick comparison of the fatality records for legal and illegal drugs. These data, long available, should surprise only those who have succumbed to drug hysteria without bothering to examine the empirical evidence. There seems to be no correlation (except perhaps an inverse one) between the illegality of a drug and the likelihood that it will cause death. Nicotine causes many more deaths (between 350,000 and 430,000 annually) than all other drugs combined, both legal and illegal, and the toll is still rising. Next highest in number of fatalities is alcohol (between 50,000 and 200,000 annual deaths). These data become only slightly less alarming when adjusted for the fact that nicotine and alcohol are used more widely than illegal drugs. When the risk of a given drug is expressed as a ratio of the number of fatalities per weekly users, nicotine (83.3 deaths per 10,000 weekly users) is still far and away the most deadly drug. About 25 percent of all adolescents who smoke a pack of cigarettes daily lose, on average, ten to fifteen years of

---

* LAD stands for "laws against drugs."—ED.

their lives. Illegal drugs seem benign by comparison, although the data on their long-term effects are less reliable. Significantly, no known fatalities have ever been attributed to the consumption of marijuana, despite its use by 51 million Americans in the past fifteen years. Cocaine, even when smoked in the form of crack, was cited as the primary cause of death in only 2,496 cases in 1989, and there is reason to suspect that this figure may be exaggerated. Since 862,000 Americans reported using cocaine weekly in 1988, the number of deaths per 10,000 weekly users is about 29. This figure is roughly comparable to alcohol (perhaps 20.6 deaths per 10,000 weekly users).

If the rationale for LAD is to prevent persons from killing themselves, it seems apparent that the state has made the wrong recreational drugs illegal. Any number of commentators have concluded that "the data demonstrate that for the population as a whole, the health problems caused by the currently legal recreational drugs are far more serious than those caused by the currently illegal recreational drugs."

It is unlikely that anyone would react to these statistics by demanding that the use of both nicotine and alcohol should be punished. Even though some historical revisionists have begun to pronounce the country's past experiment with the prohibition of alcohol as "a success," no leading figure has recommended a return to that era. What is less clear is whether the universal unwillingness to reinstate the prohibition of alcohol is based on the perception that the experiment "failed" as social policy or is due to the conviction that adults have a moral right to drink. Many theorists would adopt both positions. After all, a constitutional amendment was required to ban alcohol in 1919, suggesting that prohibition could not be implemented by ordinary democratic procedures.

When placed in perspective, illegal drug use is not an extraordinarily dangerous recreational activity. The risk of fatality encountered by users of illegal recreational drugs is not unlike that faced in many permitted recreational pursuits. About 4,200 Americans died in motorcycle accidents in 1987, even though there are fewer motorcycles than cocaine users. The risk of recreational drug use may be roughly comparable to that of mountain climbing in general, but it is far smaller than the risk of an assault on the Himalayas in particular (which killed 47 of the 1,609 non-Nepalese who attempted it). Furthermore, illegal drug use is probably a good deal less hazardous than race car driving or boxing. . . .

Addiction, Slavery, and Autonomy

Prohibitions of addictive substances that give rise to severe withdrawal symptoms are not the only instances in which philosophers have argued that the need to protect autonomy justifies paternalistic interference. John Stuart Mill denied that a voluntary agreement to sell oneself into slavery should be enforceable, because it would involve a total forfeiture of autonomy. Mill concluded that

> by selling himself for a slave, [the individual] abdicates his liberty. . . . He therefore defeats, in his own case, the very purpose which is the justification of allowing him to dispose of himself. . . . The principle of freedom cannot require that he should be free not to be free. It is not freedom, to be allowed to alienate his freedom. These reasons, the force of which is so conspicuous in this peculiar case, are evidently of far wider application.

Mill's example of voluntary slavery has generated far more theoretical discussion than is warranted by its practical significance. To the best of my knowledge, no one has ever attempted to enforce such a bizarre agreement. Yet this example is important because it is "of far wider application." Even the most confirmed critics of paternalism might balk at enforcing this agreement. If paternalistic interference with a voluntary choice is ever justified to protect autonomy, it is justified here.

For present purposes, voluntary slavery agreements are significant because of their alleged affinities with decisions to use addictive drugs. According to Goodin,

> If the product is truly addictive, then we have no more reason to respect a person's voluntary choice (however well-informed) to abandon his future volition than we have for respecting a person's voluntary choice (however well-informed) to sell himself into slavery.

Goodin concludes that the desirability of safeguarding autonomy provides no reason to protect either decision.

In this section I will argue that the case for prohibiting the use of addictive drugs is much weaker than the case for prohibiting voluntary slavery. If I am correct, those who are persuaded by Mill's example might still reject LAD, in virtue of their several differences. And those who are unpersuaded by Mill's example should be even more resistant to LAD.

It is helpful to make the examples that I will contrast more believable. First, suppose that a wealthy Legree offers Smith one million dollars to become his slave. Smith, a person of moderate means, is inclined to accept this offer because of his beneficence and generosity; he would like to provide a first-rate education and upscale life-style for each of his several children. If it is clear that Smith is sane and that his consent is truly voluntary, should the state prevent him from binding himself for his own good? The second example, to be contrasted with the first, is more familiar. Jones would like to use an addictive recreational drug. If he is sane and his consent is truly voluntary, should the state prevent him from using the drug for his own good? . . .

Feinberg notes two significant differences between the slavery example and *any* instance of criminal paternalism. First, the slavery example does not involve criminal penalties. Neither Smith nor Legree is punished for having made their agreement. Instead, the state simply refuses to enforce their promise in the event of a breach. Jones, in contrast, is punished for his choice. Surely a much higher standard of justification is required to warrant the use of the penal sanction than to make contractual remedies unavailable. Second, the failure of the state to enforce their agreement does not prevent either Smith or Legree from acting according to his preferences by establishing a de facto arrangement of slavery. Smith is free to obey Legree's orders, and Legree is free to command him. However, the state will not compel Smith to continue as a slave should he change his mind. Jones, in contrast, is prohibited by LAD from acting according to his preferences.

Other important differences between these two examples are not common to each instance of criminal paternalism. I will explore six of these differences

at greater length. The first difference has already been discussed, and I will only summarize it here. Many of the evils of addiction that invite comparisons with slavery are a product of the illegality of drugs and not of their pharmacology. Persons addicted to illegal drugs deplete their bank accounts to pay for their supplies, go to extraordinary lengths to locate dealers, and avoid whatever medical treatment they might need for fear that their condition will come to the attention of authorities. If drugs were readily available, no one would think of addicts as enslaved to them.

The second significant difference between these examples is that the decision to sell oneself into voluntary slavery involves an *immediate* surrender of autonomy. In other words, autonomy is lost at the instant the agreement becomes effective. Smith is not given the opportunity to experiment with slavery for a while and postpone his final decision about whether to become enslaved. If Smith were afforded this opportunity, and allowed to enter into slavery gradually, there would be somewhat less reason not to enforce his agreement.

But addiction is not similarly instantaneous. Jones will not become addicted upon his initial use of a drug. This point is both conceptual and empirical. Many criteria of addiction (or of the "dependence syndrome") as construed in the preceding section cannot be satisfied by a single incidence of drug use. A drug user cannot "desire to stop drug use in the face of continued use," or display "a relatively stereotyped pattern of drug-taking behavior," or "[reinstate] the syndrome after a period of abstinence" by using a drug for the first time. A person might exhibit a few of the remaining criteria of addiction after a single exposure to a drug. Jones might immediately acquire a tolerance, afford drugs a psychological centrality relative to his other interests, or experience withdrawal after the effects of the drug recede. He would probably be unaware that he has developed a tolerance, or is prepared to make great sacrifices to obtain the drug again, or is undergoing withdrawal. Nonetheless, each of these criteria might be satisfied.

I have argued that most of the criteria of addiction that can be present after a single episode of drug use are irrelevant to the question of how the use of an addictive drug affects autonomy. The phenomena of tolerance and psychological dependence are not grounds for concluding that behavior is nonautonomous. However, there is no conceptual reason why the pain of withdrawal could not be so severe after a single incident that persons would be powerless to resist further use. If so, addiction would be immediate.

As a matter of fact, however, no existing recreational drug creates such extreme withdrawal symptoms so quickly. I have already expressed doubts that withdrawal symptoms from drugs that have been used over long periods of time are sufficiently severe to warrant the judgment that continued use is nonautonomous. Withdrawal symptoms after a single episode of drug use are practically nonexistent. If a new drug were created that triggered terrible withdrawal symptoms after a single use, the case for prohibiting Jones from taking it would be comparable, *ceteris paribus,* to the case for not enforcing Smith's agreement. However, existing recreational drugs addict persons much more slowly.

Many persons try drugs and conclude that they do not want to try them again. Some persons do not enjoy their experience enough to repeat it. Others have satisfied their curiosity and have no further motive to persist. Still others abstain from additional experimentation because they enjoyed their initial exposure too much and do not want to run the risk of addiction. But whatever their motives for failing to continue, no comparable opportunity is available to Smith.

Goodin appears to recognize this difference between Jones's choice and Smith's agreement. He concedes that the initial decision of the recreational drug user might be autonomous. Subsequent decisions, however, are said not to be comparable. Goodin contends: "The real force of the addiction findings . . . is to undercut the claim that there is any *continuing* consent to the risks involved. . . . Once you were hooked, you lost the capacity to consent in any meaningful sense on a continuing basis."

But Goodin has overlooked a crucial series of points. Admittedly, Smith and Jones are similarly situated at the time that they decide whether to take their initial steps. Suppose also that their positions are comparable after Smith has become enslaved and Jones has become "hooked." But what about the intermediary stages, when Jones decides whether to

use a drug for a second, ninth, or twentieth time? Notice that the same question cannot be raised about Smith; there *are* no intermediary stages to examine. One simply cannot compare the beginning point, at which the agent contemplates becoming a slave or using an addictive substance, with the end point, at which he has become a slave or an addict, and conclude that there are no important differences between the two. The crucial difference is that there are any number of intermediate points in the drug example but not in the slavery case.

A third important difference between LAD and the prohibition of voluntary slavery is that Smith's decision is *irrevocable.* This fact is crucial to the unwillingness to enforce his promise. If Smith were able to reconsider his decision and resume a normal life, reservations about allowing him to be enslaved would all but vanish.

Addiction, however, can be temporary. Although addictions are notoriously difficult to break, persons can and do overcome them every day. Few individuals who are addicted to an illegal drug remain addicts for the duration of their lives. Many heroin addicts permanently give up heroin after a relatively brief period of addiction. Even the most committed heroin users frequently "mature out" of addiction after a few years. Many crack addicts quit because they do not want to lose their jobs, alienate their friends, neglect their children, or ruin their social status.

The fact that many addicts "kick" their habits is well-known. Why, then, would anyone compare addiction to a permanent state of slavery? Perhaps there are misconceptions about the difficulty in overcoming addiction. It might be thought that just as slaves can be emancipated, so too can addiction be overcome, but only with the help of treatment.

This preconception cannot withstand empirical scrutiny, however. Because of their concern with health, the importance of a personal relationship, or their perception that they have "hit bottom," large numbers of addicts succeed in quitting even the most addictive drugs. Many persons "revoke" their addiction without the benefit of a treatment program. "Spontaneous" recoveries from addiction to opiates, alcohol, tobacco, and cocaine are well documented. Some of the more spectacular examples were provided by Vietnam War veterans who had been heroin addicts during the war. The vast majority of these addicts did not continue their use of heroin upon returning home, and only a handful required treatment to quit. In addition, only a tiny percentage of hospital patients who regularly receive more powerful doses of opiates than those available on the streets ever become addicted or remain addicted after release. Quite simply, addiction need not be a permanent condition.

A fourth important difference between slavery and addiction involves the probability of the undesirable outcome in each example. The use of addictive substances does not create a certainty of addiction. Many studies have shown that persons (sometimes called "chippers") are able to use addictive drugs over long periods of time in a controlled, non-abusive way, without ever becoming addicted. Although the percentages differ for various drugs, most users of what are generally considered to be the most addictive and dangerous substances do not become addicts. A majority of the persons who have ever tried *any* illegal drug have stopped using it. Perhaps these facts have not been widely publicized because of a fear that knowledge among prospective users would reduce their inhibitions against experimentation.

Consider cocaine. Empirical studies indicate that most persons control their intake, using cocaine during leisure hours or on special occasions. Statistics reinforce this finding. Few of the 21 to 25 million Americans who have tried cocaine have become addicts. Although 8 million people reported using cocaine at least once in 1988, only 862,000 used the drug at least once a week, and a mere 320,000 reported using it daily. Thus, daily users of cocaine constitute less than 5 percent of all persons who use it annually and less than 2 percent of persons who have ever tried it. These are not the statistics one would expect if cocaine addicted everyone who sampled it.

These figures do not seem to differ radically when cocaine is smoked in the form of crack. According to one estimate, approximately one of every six persons who tries crack becomes a crack addict. According to another survey, about 9 percent of current crack users (persons who have used crack in the last month) are heavy users (persons who have used crack twenty or more times in the last month). Some theorists contend that at any given time about 10 percent of cocaine and heroin users can be classified

as addicts, that is, about the same percentage as drinkers of alcohol who can be classified as alcoholics. Nicotine is the drug with the highest percentage of current users who are addicts; the figure may be as high as 90 percent. The exact ratio of addicts to users, however, is less important than the general conclusion to be drawn from this figure. The use of addictive recreational drugs creates only a possibility, not a probability, and clearly not a certainty, that addiction will result.

Mark Kleiman and Aaron Saiger reach a more pessimistic conclusion from these same data. They maintain that the ratio of one crack addict for every six users is "about as bad as it could be." They reason that if the ratio were higher, fewer persons would experiment and run the risk of addiction; if the ratio were lower, crack would be less socially disruptive. But whether this figure is "as bad as it could be" depends on the argumentative purpose for which it is employed. A ratio of one to six is not so bad in the context of comparing crack use to slavery. The comparable ratio in the slavery example is six times worse: Every person who enters into a slavery agreement becomes enslaved. Smith's consent does not merely create a possibility that Legree will enslave him; it creates a certainty.

Opinions about the legitimacy of the slavery example might change if it were modified to reflect this fact. Suppose that Smith were offered one million dollars in exchange for a 5 percent or 10 percent chance that he would become enslaved. This gamble appears more rational, and less repugnant. I am unclear about whether this modification is persuasive in allowing Legree to enforce his agreement, but surely it is a relevant factor.

A fifth difference is that Smith's agreement subjects him to a *continuous* state of slavery. His status as a slave is uninterrupted. Had Smith negotiated permission from Legree to take several extended vacations, his agreement would seem less objectionable. He might have agreed to become a slave only on weekends or holidays, otherwise leading a relatively normal life. Again, I am unclear about how much of a difference this modification makes to the judgment about whether Smith's agreement should be enforceable, but I am confident that it has importance.

Addiction, by way of contrast, is seldom continuous. Heroin addicts commonly undergo periods of semivoluntary abstinence. Less than one-half of the addicts on the street for a year will have used an opiate daily throughout that period. Sometimes addicts interrupt their heroin use to lower their tolerance, so that they can eventually resume consumption at a lower, cheaper, and more euphoric level. This behavior has no analogue in the case of slavery.

A sixth and final difference between these two examples contrasts the plight of the slave with that of the addict. Slavery is a dreadful state. We are loathe to allow Legree to enslave Smith because we imagine that slavery may include torture, humiliation, and working conditions that no person should be made to endure. After all, Smith has given Legree carte blanche to subject him to every kind of indignity. If we could be assured that Legree's treatment of Smith would be humane, involving working conditions no more terrible than those in typical factories, we would become more willing to enforce their agreement.

Comparisons between addiction and enslavement to a sadistic Legree become apt only when the horrors of addiction are grossly exaggerated. The zombielike image of the addict has been perpetuated by our government. Time and time again, the judiciary has presented a parody of the drug addict. Perhaps the most extreme example is the caricature described by Justice Douglas in 1962:

> To be a confirmed drug addict is to be one of the walking dead. . . . The teeth have rotted out; the appetite is lost and the stomach and intestines don't function properly. . . . Good traits of character disappear and bad ones emerge. Sex organs become affected. Veins collapse and livid purplish scars remain. Boils and abscesses plague the skin; gnawing pain racks the body. Nerves snap; vicious twitching develops. Imaginary and fantastic fears blight the mind and sometimes complete insanity results. Often times, too, death comes— much too early in life. . . . Such is the torment of being a drug addict; such is the plague of being one of the walking dead.

Small wonder that the Court concluded that punishment for such a condition was tantamount to punishment for a disease and thus was unconstitutional according to the Eighth Amendment's prohibition of cruel and unusual punishment. If typical cases of drug addiction conformed to this pathetic description, sympathies for paternalistic restrictions on drug use would be overwhelming.

Media portrayals of heavy drug users reinforce this dreadful stereotype. Television and movie depictions of recreational drug use follow a predictable script. Users initially believe that drugs are "cool," are confident that they can quit anytime, become helplessly addicted, squander their fortunes, turn to crime, abandon their loved ones, and either die a miserable death or are miraculously saved by heroic efforts. These case histories exist. But no effort is made to inform the public that these scenarios are atypical. No media exposure is afforded to moderate, successful, long-term drug users. This media bias is not inadvertent. Lorne Michaels, the producer of the irreverent "Saturday Night Live," admits that "the policy of NBC now is that the only references to drugs must be negative."

Even so, the public has ample reason to abandon this exaggerated stereotype of drug addiction. Many professional athletes have been exposed as drug addicts, and few remind anyone of a zombie. No one can know whether George Rogers was realizing his full potential during the football season in which his staggering cocaine habit came to the attention of the press. But his opponents did not confuse him with one of the walking dead while Rogers led the National Football League in rushing that year.

Empirical research simply does not support this terrible stereotype of drug addiction. Most drug addicts lead relatively normal lives. According to the U.S. Department of Labor, 77 percent of "serious cocaine users" are regularly employed. Bennett has cited this statistic to urge business leaders to join the "front" in the "fight" against drugs. But this statistic can also be used to undermine the dreadful portrayal of drug addiction. It is hard to imagine how the caricature of the drug addict described by Justice Douglas could be gainfully employed.

QUESTIONS FOR REFLECTION

1. Evaluate Husak's analogy between drug use and other recreational activities.

2. How does Husak argue that addiction does not undermine autonomy?

3. Husak rejects voluntary slavery as a model for addiction. Why? Do you agree?

PORNOGRAPHY

Most philosophers defend freedom of thought, of speech, and of the press. Some, like Milton and Mill, are strongly committed to these freedoms; others, like Burke, acknowledge that they are goods, but believe that they must be balanced against other goods. Nevertheless, virtually no one believes that these freedoms are completely unrestricted. Slander, libel, false advertising, harassment, inciting to riot, and public endangerment—shouting "Fire!" in a crowded theater, for example—have often been held up as exceptions. Thus the problem of determining the proper limits of these freedoms arises.

Pornography raises especially difficult questions about limits on freedom of thought, speech, and the press. The exceptions mentioned above are often thought to be exceptions because they risk or cause harm that outweighs their values as communications. Many people believe pornography to be harmful and base their opposition to it on that ground. But any harms caused by pornography are subtler and harder to detect than those of inciting to riot, for example. Consequently, the question of whether pornography is harmful has become an important focus of debate.

Also, the harm done by a speaker is usually weighed against the value of the communication. It is harder to slander a public official than a private citizen, for example, because the public's need for information about officials of government is much greater than its need for information about you or me; communication about the beliefs and behavior of public officials has greater value than communications about the rest of us. But what does pornography communicate? Often, it is hard to discern any message at all. Is pornography ever communication? These problems make weighing the value of a piece of pornography against its harmful effects very difficult.

Moreover, most of the arguments that Milton and Mill advance in favor of free speech rest on the supposition that speech communicates something that might be true or false. Mill argues that an opinion might be true; that, even if false, it might contain part of the truth; and that, even if totally false, its combat with the truth helps keep the truth alive. This argument makes sense for opinions, for propositions or bits of information that might be true or false. But does it make any sense applied to *Sex Orgies Illustrated?* Or *Deep Throat?* Or a *Playboy* centerfold? If not, on what does the case for freedom of pornographic speech rest?

The United States Supreme Court, in *Miller* v. *California,* decided that the government may regulate pornographic materials, banning those that are obscene. The Court moreover proposed criteria for determining whether something is obscene: (a) it must, judged by the average person applying contemporary community standards, appeal to a prurient (that is, arousing and unwholesome) interest in sex; (b) it must depict or describe sexual conduct in a patently offensive way; and (c) it must lack serious literary, artistic, political, or scientific value. The first two criteria pertain to harm; the third, to lack of any positive communicative value that might balance the harm.

Dissenters to the decisions have argued that sexual expression deserves protection against government interference. Some hold that such an expression may have positive value for individuals that outweighs any harm it causes; some claim that freedoms of thought, speech, and the press are all forms of freedom of expression, which is what properly defines the limits of government authority. Others believe that there is no fair and accurate way to distinguish obscene from nonobscene materials.

A recent and particularly crucial freedom of expression case is *Reno* v. *ACLU,* in which the Supreme Court struck down the Communications Decency Act as unconstitutional. The act regulated and provided criminal penalties for transmitting obscene or indecent "patently offensive" messages on the Internet. Justice John Paul Stevens, writing for the majority, found that the act abridged the freedom of speech guaranteed by the First Amendment. It made no mention of serious artistic or literary value, thus ignoring any positive value of a message that might balance its offensive or harmful aspects. More seriously, it went far beyond limiting offense by regulating the time, place, and manner of speech; it sought to regulate speech on the basis of its content.

Catharine MacKinnon asserts that pornography is a practice of sex discrimination and thus a violation of women's civil rights. She argues for the morality and constitutionality of ordinances that prohibit pornography. The Attorney General's Commission on Pornography argues at length that certain kinds of pornography, particularly those involving violence, are harmful and ought to be restricted. The commission argues that these forms of pornography harm not only the "users," the viewers of the material, but also others with whom the users come into contact. The commission holds, however, that other forms of pornography seem relatively harmless and should escape any government restrictions.

Wendy McElroy argues that feminism has exactly the opposite implications. Women who choose to produce or consume pornography are exercising freedom; MacKinnon's restrictions on pornography thus restrict the liberty of women. In general, censorship on grounds of sex discrimination treats women as children whose interests must be protected by law because they are incapable of taking responsibility for their own actions.

Nadine Strossen similarly argues that pornography does not harm women—that, in fact, women enjoy higher status in times and places in which pornography is tolerated. She rejects the contentions of MacKinnon and the Attorney General's Commission that pornography causes increased violence against women, and she points out that many great works of literature, including the Bible and many feminist works, would count as pornographic under MacKinnon's definition. In any event, Strossen argues, censorship would do little to reduce people's exposure to sexist, violent imagery, both because censorship is ineffective and because the mainstream media brims with such images.

CATHARINE MacKINNON

Pornography, Civil Rights, and Speech

Catharine MacKinnon is Professor of Law at the University of Michigan. (*Source: Reprinted by permission of the* Harvard Civil Rights/Civil Liberties Law Review. *Copyright © 1985 by the President and Fellows of Harvard College.*)

. . . There is a belief that this is a society in which women and men are basically equals. Room for marginal corrections is conceded, flaws are known to exist, attempts are made to correct what are conceived as occasional lapses from the basic condition of sex equality. Sex discrimination law has concentrated most of its focus on these occasional lapses. It is difficult to overestimate the extent to which this belief in equality is an article of faith for most people, including most women, who wish to live in self-respect in an internal universe, even (perhaps especially) if not in the world. It is also partly an expression of natural law thinking: if we are inalienably equal, we can't "really" be degraded.

This is a world in which it is worth trying. In this world of presumptive equality, people make money based on their training or abilities or diligence or qualifications. They are employed and advanced on the basis of merit. In this world of just deserts, if someone is abused, it is thought to violate the basic rules of the community. If it doesn't, victims are seen to have done something they could have chosen to do differently, by exercise of will or better judgment. Maybe such people have placed themselves in a situation of vulnerability to physical abuse. Maybe they have done something provocative. Or maybe they were just unusually unlucky. In such a world, if such a person has an experience, there are words for it. When they speak and say it, they are listened to. If they write about it, they will be published. If certain experiences are never spoken about, if certain people or issues are seldom heard from, it is supposed that silence has been chosen. The law, including much of the law of sex discrimination and the First Amendment, operates largely within the realm of these beliefs.

Feminism is the discovery that women do not live in this world, that the person occupying this realm is a man, so much more a man if he is white and wealthy. This world of potential credibility, authority, security, and just rewards, recognition of one's identity and capacity, is a world that some people do inhabit as a condition of birth, with variations among them. It is not a basic condition accorded humanity in this society, but a prerogative of status, a privilege, among other things, of gender.

I call this a discovery because it has not been an assumption. Feminism is the first theory, the first practice, the first movement, to take seriously the situation of all women from the point of view of all women, both on our situation and on social life as a whole. The discovery has therefore been made that the implicit social content of humanism, as well as the standpoint from which legal method has been designed and injuries have been defined, has not been women's standpoint. Defining feminism in a way that connects epistemology with power as the politics of women's point of view, this discovery can be summed up by saying that women live in another world: specifically, a world of *not* equality, a world of inequality. . . .

205

. . . In pornography, there it is, in one place, all of the abuses that women had to struggle so long even to begin to articulate, all the *unspeakable* abuse: the rape, the battery, the sexual harassment, the prostitution, and the sexual abuse of children. Only in the pornography it is called something else: sex, sex, sex, sex, and sex, respectively. Pornography sexualizes rape, battery, sexual harassment, prostitution, and child sexual abuse; it thereby celebrates, promotes, authorizes, and legitimizes them. More generally, it eroticizes the dominance and submission that is the dynamic common to them all. It makes hierarchy sexy and calls that "the truth about sex" or just a mirror of reality. Through this process pornography constructs what a woman is as what men want from sex. This is what the pornography means.

Pornography constructs what a woman is in terms of its view of what men want sexually, such that acts of rape, battery, sexual harassment, prostitution, and sexual abuse of children become acts of sexual equality. Pornography's world of equality is a harmonious and balanced place. Men and women are perfectly complementary and perfectly bipolar. . . .

. . . There, women substantively desire dispossession and cruelty. We desperately want to be bound, battered, tortured, humiliated, and killed. Or, to be fair to the soft core, merely taken and used. This is erotic to the male point of view. Subjection itself, with self-determination ecstatically relinquished, is the content of women's sexual desire and desirability. Women are there to be violated and possessed, men to violate and possess us, either on screen or by camera or pen on behalf of the consumer. On a simple descriptive level, the inequality of hierarchy, of which gender is the primary one, seems necessary for sexual arousal to work. Other added inequalities identify various pornographic genres or subthemes, although they are always added through gender: age, disability, homosexuality, animals, objects, race (including anti-Semitism), and so on. Gender is never irrelevant.

What pornography *does* goes beyond its content: it eroticizes hierarchy, it sexualizes inequality. It makes dominance and submission into sex. Inequality is its central dynamic; the illusion of freedom coming together with the reality of force is central to its working. Perhaps because this is a bourgeois culture, the victim must look free, appear to be freely acting. Choice is how she got there. Willing is what she is when she is being equal. It seems equally important that then and there she actually be forced and that forcing be communicated on some level, even if only through still photos of her in postures of receptivity and access, available for penetration. Pornography in this view is a form of forced sex, a practice of sexual politics, an institution of gender inequality.

From this perspective, pornography is neither harmless fantasy nor a corrupt and confused misrepresentation of an otherwise natural and healthy sexual situation. It institutionalizes the sexuality of male supremacy, fusing the erotization of dominance and submission with the social construction of male and female. To the extent that gender is sexual, pornography is part of constituting the meaning of that sexuality. Men treat women as who they see women as being. Pornography constructs who that is. Men's power over women means that the way men see women defines who women can be. Pornography is that way. Pornography is not imagery in some relation to a reality elsewhere constructed. It is not a distortion, reflection, projection, expression, fantasy, representation, or symbol either. It is a sexual reality.

. . . Pornography *participates* in its audience's eroticism through creating an accessible sexual object, the possession and consumption of which is male sexuality, as socially constructed; to be consumed and possessed as which, *is* female sexuality, as socially constructed; pornography is a process that constructs it that way.

The object world is constructed according to how it looks with respect to its possible uses. Pornography defines women by how we look according to how we can be sexually used. Pornography codes how to look at women, so you know what you can do with one when you see one. Gender is an assignment made visually, both originally and in everyday life. A sex object is defined on the basis of its looks, in terms of its usability for sexual pleasure, such that both the looking—the quality of the gaze, including its point of view—and the definition according to use become eroticized as part of the sex itself. This is what the feminist concept "sex object" means. In this sense, sex in life is no less mediated than it is in art. Men have sex with their image of a woman. It is not that life and art imitate each other; in this sexuality, they *are* each other.

To give a set of rough epistemological translations, to defend pornography as consistent with the equality of the sexes is to defend the subordination of women to men as sexual equality. What in the pornographic view is love and romance looks a great deal like hatred and torture to the feminist. Pleasure and eroticism become violation. Desire appears as lust for dominance and submission. The vulnerability of women's projected sexual availability, that acting we are allowed (that is, asking to be acted upon), is victimization. Play conforms to scripted roles. Fantasy expresses ideology, is not exempt from it. Admiration of natural physical beauty becomes objectification. Harmlessness becomes harm. Pornography is a harm of male supremacy made difficult to see because of its pervasiveness, potency, and, principally, because of its success in making the world a pornographic place. Specifically, its harm cannot be discerned, and will not be addressed, if viewed and approached neutrally, because it *is* so much of "what is." In other words, to the extent pornography succeeds in constructing social reality, it becomes invisible as harm. If we live in a world that pornography creates through the power of men in a male-dominated situation, the issue is not what the harm of pornography is, but how that harm is to become visible.

Obscenity law provides a very different analysis and conception of the problem of pornography. In 1973 the legal definition of obscenity became that which the average person, applying contemporary community standards, would find that, taken as a whole, appeals to the prurient interest; that which depicts or describes in a patently offensive way—you feel like you're a cop reading someone's *Miranda* rights—sexual conduct specifically defined by the applicable state law; and that which, taken as a whole, lacks serious literary, artistic, political or scientific value. Feminism doubts whether the average person gender-neutral exists; has more questions about the content and process of defining what community standards are than it does about deviations from them; wonders why prurience counts but powerlessness does not and why sensibilities are better protected from offense than women are from exploitation; defines sexuality, and thus its violation and expropriation, more broadly than does state law; and questions why a body of law that has not in practice been able to tell rape from intercourse should, without further guidance, be entrusted with telling pornography from anything less. Taking the work "as a whole" ignores that which the victims of pornography have long known: legitimate settings diminish the perception of injury done to those whose trivialization and objectification they contextualize. Besides, and this is a heavy one, if a woman is subjected, why should it matter that the work has other value? Maybe what redeems the work's value is what enhances its injury to women, not to mention that existing standards of literature, art, science, and politics, examined in a feminist light, are remarkably consonant with pornography's mode, meaning, and message. And finally—first and foremost, actually—although the subject of these materials is overwhelmingly women, their contents almost entirely made up of women's bodies, our invisibility has been such, our equation as a sex *with* sex has been such, that the law of obscenity has never even considered pornography a women's issue.

Obscenity, in this light, is a moral idea, an idea about judgments of good and bad. Pornography, by contrast, is a political practice, a practice of power and powerlessness. Obscenity is ideational and abstract; pornography is concrete and substantive. The two concepts represent two entirely different things. Nudity, excess of candor, arousal or excitement, prurient appeal, illegality of the acts depicted, and unnaturalness or perversion are all qualities that bother obscenity law when sex is depicted or portrayed. Sex forced on real women so that it can be sold at a profit and forced on other real women; women's bodies trussed and maimed and raped and made into things to be hurt and obtained and accessed, and this presented as the nature of women in a way that is acted on and acted out, over and over; the coercion that is visible and the coercion that has become invisible—this and more bothers feminists about pornography. Obscenity as such probably does little harm. Pornography is integral to attitudes and behaviors of violence and discrimination that define the treatment and status of half the population. . . .

QUESTIONS FOR REFLECTION

1. What is feminism, according to MacKinnon?

2. Why, in MacKinnon's view, is pornography discriminatory?

3. What are MacKinnon's arguments against the *Miller* decision? How might a defender of *Miller* respond?

4. How does MacKinnon distinguish obscenity from pornography?

5. To what extent is MacKinnon's position compatible with Mill's harm principle? With Kant's categorical imperative?

THE ATTORNEY GENERAL'S COMMISSION ON PORNOGRAPHY

The Question of Harm

(Source: From the United States Attorney General's Commission on Pornography, Attorney General's Commission on Pornography: Final Report *[Washington: U.S. Department of Justice, 1986].)*

5.1.2 What Counts as a Harm?

What is a harm? And why focus on harm at all? We do not wish in referring repeatedly to "harm" to burden ourselves with an unduly narrow conception of harm. To emphasize in different words what we said in the previous section, the scope of identifiable harms is broader than the scope of that with which government can or should deal. We refuse to truncate our consideration of the question of harm by defining harms in terms of possible government regulation. And we certainly reject the view that the only noticeable harm is one that causes physical or financial harm to identifiable individuals. An environment, physical, cultural, moral, or aesthetic, can be harmed, and so can a community, organization, or group be harmed independent of identifiable harms to members of that community.

Most importantly, although we have emphasized in our discussion of harms the kinds of harms that can most easily be observed and measured, the idea of harm is broader than that. To a number of us, the most important harms must be seen in moral terms, and the act of moral condemnation of that which is immoral is not merely important but essential. From this perspective there are acts that need be seen not only as causes of immorality but as manifestations of it. Issues of human dignity and human decency, no less real for their lack of scientific measurability, are for many of us central to thinking about the question

of harm. And when we think about harm in this way, there are acts that must be condemned not because the evils of the world will thereby be eliminated, but because conscience demands it.

We believe it useful in thinking about harms to note the distinction between harm and offense. Although the line between the two is hardly clear, most people can nevertheless imagine things that offend them, or offend others, that still would be hard to describe as harms. . . .

In thinking about harms, it is useful to draw a rough distinction between primary and secondary harms. Primary harms are those in which the alleged harm is commonly taken to be intrinsically harmful, even though the precise way in which the harm is harmful might yet be further explored. Nevertheless, murder, rape, assault, and discrimination on the basis of race and gender are all examples of primary harms in this sense. We treat these acts as harms not because of where they will lead, but simply because of what they are.

In other instances, however, the alleged harm is secondary, not in the sense that it is in any way less important, but in the sense that the concern is not with what the act is, but where it will lead. Curfews are occasionally imposed not because there is anything wrong with people being out at night, but because in some circumstances it is thought that being out at night in large groups may cause people to commit other crimes. Possession of "burglar tools" is often prohibited because of what those tools may be used for. Thus, when it is urged that pornography is harmful because it causes some people to commit acts of sexual violence, because it causes promiscuity, because it encourages sexual relations outside of marriage, because it promotes so-called "unnatural" sexual practices, or because it leads men to treat women as existing solely for the sexual satisfaction of men, the alleged harms are secondary, again not in any sense suggesting that the harms are less important. The harms are secondary here because the allegation of harm presupposes a causal link between the act and the harm, a causal link that is superfluous if, as in the case of primary harms, the act quite simply *is* the harm.

Thus we think it important, with respect to every area of possible harm, to focus on whether the allegation relates to a harm that comes from the sexually explicit material itself, or whether it occurs *as a result* of something the material does. If it is the former, then the inquiry can focus directly on the nature of the alleged harm. But if it is the latter, then there must be a two-step inquiry. First it is necessary to determine if some hypothesized result is in fact harmful. In some cases, where the asserted consequent harm is unquestionably a harm, this step of the analysis is easy. With respect to claims that certain sexually explicit material increases the incidence of rape or other sexual violence, for example, no one could plausibly claim that such consequences were not harmful, and the inquiry can then turn to whether the causal link exists. In other cases, however, the harmfulness of the alleged harm is often debated. With respect to claims, for example, that some sexually explicit material causes promiscuity, encourages homosexuality, or legitimizes sexual practices other than vaginal intercourse, there is serious societal debate about whether the consequences themselves are harmful.

Thus, the analysis of the hypothesis that pornography causes harm must start with the identification of hypothesized harms, proceed to the determination of whether those hypothesized harms are indeed harmful, and then conclude with the examination of whether a causal link exists between the material and the harm. When the consequences of exposure to sexually explicit material are not harmful, or when there is no causal relationship between exposure to sexually explicit material and some harmful consequence, then we cannot say that the sexually explicit material is harmful. But if sexually explicit material of some variety is causally related to, or increases the incidence of, some behavior that *is* harmful, then it is safe to conclude that the material is harmful. . . .

5.2.1 Sexually Violent Material

The category of material on which most of the evidence has focused is the category of material featuring actual or unmistakably simulated or unmistakably threatened violence presented in sexually explicit fashion with a predominant focus on the sexually explicit violence. Increasingly, the most prevalent forms of pornography, as well as an increasingly prevalent body of less sexually explicit material, fit this description. Some of this material involves sado-masochistic themes, with the standard accoutrements of the genre, including whips, chains, devices of torture, and so on. But another theme of some of this material is not sado-masochistic, but involves instead the recurrent theme of a man making some sort of sexual advance to a woman, being rebuffed, and then raping the woman or in some other way violently forcing himself on the woman. In almost all of this material, whether in magazine or motion picture form, the woman eventually becomes aroused and ecstatic about the initially forced sexual activity, and usually is portrayed as begging for more. There is also a large body of material, more "mainstream" in its availability, that portrays sexual activity or sexually suggestive nudity coupled with extreme violence, such as disfigurement or murder. The so-called "slasher" films fit this description, as does some material, both in films and in magazines, that is less or more sexually explicit than the prototypical "slasher" film. . . .

When clinical and experimental research has focused particularly on sexually violent material, the conclusions have been virtually unanimous. In both clinical and experimental settings, exposure to sexually violent materials has indicated an increase in the likelihood of aggression. More specifically, the research . . . shows a causal relationship between exposure to material of this type and aggressive behavior towards women.

Finding a link between aggressive behavior towards women and sexual violence, whether lawful or unlawful, requires assumptions not found exclusively in the experimental evidence. We see no reason, however, not to make these assumptions. The assumption that increased aggressive behavior towards women is causally related, for an aggregate population, to increased sexual violence is significantly supported by the clinical evidence, as well as by much of the less scientific evidence. They are also to all of us assumptions that are plainly justified by our own common sense. This is not to say that all people with heightened levels of aggression will commit acts of sexual violence. But it is to say that over a sufficiently large number of cases we are confident in asserting that an increase in aggressive behavior directed at women will cause an increase in the level of sexual violence directed at women.

Thus we reach our conclusions by combining the results of the research with highly justifiable assumptions about the generalizability of more limited research results. Since the clinical and experimental evidence supports the conclusion that there is a causal relationship between exposure to sexually violent materials and an increase in aggressive behavior directed towards women, and since we believe that an increase in aggressive behavior towards women will in a population increase the incidence of sexual violence in that population, we have reached the conclusion, unanimously and confidently, that the available evidence strongly supports the hypothesis that substantial exposure to sexually violent materials as described here bears a causal relationship to antisocial acts of sexual violence and, for some subgroups, possibly to unlawful acts of sexual violence.

Although we rely for this conclusion on significant scientific empirical evidence, we feel it worthwhile to note the underlying logic of the conclusion. The evidence says simply that the images that people are exposed to bears a causal relationship to their behavior. This is hardly surprising. What would be surprising would be to find otherwise, and we have not so found. We have not, of course, found that the images people are exposed to are a greater cause of sexual violence than all or even many other possible causes the investigation of which has been beyond our mandate. Nevertheless, it would be strange indeed if graphic representations of a form of behavior, especially in a form that almost exclusively portrays such behavior as desirable, did not have at least some effect on patterns of behavior.

Sexual violence is not the only negative effect reported in the research to result from substantial exposure to sexually violent materials. The evidence is also strongly supportive of significant attitudinal changes on the part of those with substantial exposure to violent pornography. These attitudinal changes are numerous. Victims of rape and other forms of sexual violence are likely to be perceived by people so exposed as more responsible for the assault, as having suffered less injury, and as having been less degraded as a result of the experience. Similarly, people with a substantial exposure to violent pornography are likely to see the rapist or other sexual offender as less responsible for the act and as deserving of less stringent punishment.

These attitudinal changes have been shown experimentally to include a larger range of attitudes than those just discussed. The evidence also strongly supports the conclusion that substantial exposure to violent sexually explicit material leads to a greater acceptance of the "rape myth" in its broader sense— that women enjoy being coerced into sexual activity, that they enjoy being physically hurt in sexual context, and that as a result a man who forces himself on a woman sexually is in fact merely acceding to the "real" wishes of the woman, regardless of the extent to which she seems to be resisting. The myth is that a woman who says "no" really means "yes," and that men are justified in acting on the assumption that the "no" answer is indeed the "yes" answer. We have little trouble concluding that this attitude is both pervasive and profoundly harmful, and that any stimulus reinforcing or increasing the incidence of this attitude is for that reason alone properly designated as harmful.

Two vitally important features of the evidence supporting the above conclusions must be mentioned here. The first is that all of the harms discussed here, including acceptance of the legitimacy of sexual violence against women but not limited to it, are more pronounced when the sexually violent materials depict the woman as experiencing arousal, orgasm, or other form of enjoyment as the ultimate result of the sexual assault. This theme, unfortunately very common in the materials we have examined, is likely to be the major, albeit not the only, component of what it is in the materials in this category that causes the consequences that have been identified.

The second important clarification of all of the above is that the evidence lends some support to the conclusion that the consequences we have identified here *do not vary with the extent of sexual explicitness so long as the violence is presented in an undeniably sexual context.* Once a threshold is passed at which sex and violence are plainly linked, increasing the sexual explicitness of the material, or the bizarreness of the sexual activity, seems to bear little relationship to the extent of the consequences discussed here. Although it is unclear whether sexually violent material makes a substantially greater causal contribution to sexual violence itself than does material containing violence alone, it appears that increasing the amount of violence after the threshold of connecting sex with violence is more related to increase in the incidence or severity of harmful consequences than is increasing the amount of sex. As a result, the so-called "slasher" films, which depict a great deal of violence connected with an undeniably sexual theme but less sexual explicitness than materials that are truly pornographic, are likely to produce the consequences discussed here to a greater extent than most of the materials available in "adults only" pornographic outlets.

Although we have based our findings about material in this category primarily on evidence presented by professionals in the behavioral sciences, we are confident that it is supported by the less scientific evidence we have consulted, and we are each personally confident on the basis of our own knowledge and experiences that the conclusions are justified. None of us has the least doubt that sexual violence is harmful, and that general acceptance of the view that "no" means "yes" is a consequence of the most serious proportions. We have found a causal relationship between sexually explicit materials featuring violence and these consequences, and thus conclude that the class of such materials, although not necessarily every individual member of that class, is on the whole harmful to society.

5.2.2 Nonviolent Materials Depicting Degradation, Domination, Subordination, or Humiliation

Current research has rather consistently separated out violent pornography, the class of materials we have just discussed, from other sexually explicit materials. With respect to further subdivision the process has been less consistent. A few researchers have made further distinctions, while most have merely classed everything else as "non-violent." We have concluded that more subdivision than that is necessary. Our examination of the variety of sexually explicit materials convinces us that once again the category of "non-violent" ignores significant distinctions within this category, and thus combines classes of material that are in fact substantially different.

The subdivision we adopt is one that has surfaced in some of the research. And it is also one that might explain a significant amount of what would otherwise seem to be conflicting research results. Some researchers have found negative effects from non-violent material, while others report no such negative effects. But when the stimulus material these researchers have used is considered, there is some suggestion that the presence or absence of negative effects from non-violent material might turn on the non-violent material being considered "degrading," a term we shall explain shortly. It appears that effects similar to although not as extensive as that involved with violent material can be identified with respect to such degrading material, but that these effects are likely absent when neither degradation nor violence is present.

An enormous amount of the most sexually explicit material available, as well as much of the material that is somewhat less sexually explicit, is material that we would characterize as "degrading," the term we use to encompass the undeniably linked characteristics of degradation, domination, subordination, and humiliation. The degradation we refer to is degradation of people, most often women, and here we are referring to material that, although not violent, depicts people, usually women, as existing solely for the sexual satisfaction of others, usually men, or that depicts people, usually women, in decidedly subordinate roles in their sexual relations with others, or that depicts people engaged in sexual practices that would to most people be considered humiliating. Indeed, forms of degradation represent the largely predominant proportion of commercially available pornography.

With respect to material of this variety, our conclusions are substantially similar to those with respect to violent material, although we make them with somewhat less confidence and our making of them requires more in the way of assumption than was the case with respect to violent material. The evidence, scientific and otherwise, is more tentative, but supports the conclusion that the material we describe as degrading bears some causal relationship to the attitudinal changes we have previously identified. That is, substantial exposure to material of this variety is likely to increase the extent to which those exposed will view rape or other forms of sexual violence as less serious than they otherwise would have, will view the victim of rape and other forms of sexual violence as significantly more responsible, and will view the offenders as significantly less responsible. We also conclude that the evidence supports the conclusion that substantial exposure to material of this type will increase acceptance of the proposition that women like to be forced into sexual practices, and, once again, that the woman who says "no" really means "yes."

With respect to material of this type, there is less evidence causally linking the material with sexual aggression, but this may be because this is a category that has been isolated in only a few studies, albeit an increasing number. The absence of evidence should by no means be taken to deny the existence of the causal link. But because the causal link is less the subject of experimental studies, we have been required to think more carefully here about the assumptions necessary to causally connect increased acceptance of rape myths and other attitudinal changes with increased sexual aggression and sexual violence. And on the basis of all the evidence we have considered, from all sources, and on the basis of our own insights and experiences, we believe we are justified in drawing the following conclusion: Over a large enough sample a population that believes that many women like to be raped, that believes that sexual violence or sexual coercion is often desired or appropriate, and that believes that sex offenders are less responsible for their acts, will commit more acts of sexual violence or sexual coercion than would a population holding these beliefs to a lesser extent.

We should make clear what we have concluded here. We are not saying that everyone exposed to material of this type had his attitude about sexual violence changed. We are saying only that the evidence supports the conclusion that substantial exposure to degrading material increases the likelihood for an individual and the incidence over a large population that these attitudinal changes will occur. And we are not saying that everyone with these atti-

tudes will commit an act of sexual violence or sexual coercion. We are saying that such attitudes will increase the likelihood for an individual and the incidence for a population that acts of sexual violence, sexual coercion, or unwanted sexual aggression will occur. Thus, we conclude that substantial exposure to materials of this type bears some causal relationship to the level of sexual violence, sexual coercion, or unwanted sexual aggression in the population so exposed.

We need mention as well that our focus on these more violent or more coercive forms of actual subordination of women should not diminish what we take to be a necessarily incorporated conclusion: Substantial exposure to materials of this type bears some causal relationship to the incidence of various non-violent forms of discrimination against or subordination of women in our society. To the extent that these materials create or reinforce the view that women's function is disproportionately to satisfy the sexual needs of men, then the materials will have pervasive effects on the treatment of women in society far beyond the incidence of identifiable acts of rape or other sexual violence. We obviously cannot here explore fully all of the forms in which women are discriminated against in contemporary society. Nor can we explore all of the causes of that discrimination against women. But we feel confident in concluding that the view of women as available for sexual domination is one cause of that discrimination, and we feel confident as well in concluding that degrading material bears a causal relationship to the view that women ought to subordinate their own desires and beings to the sexual satisfaction of men.

Although the category of the degrading is one that has only recently been isolated in some research, in the literature generally, and in public discussion of the issue, it is not a small category. If anything, it constitutes somewhere between the predominant and the overwhelming portion of what is currently standard fare heterosexual pornography, and is a significant theme in a broader range of materials not commonly taken to be sexually explicit enough to be pornographic. But as with sexually violent materials, the extent of the effect of these degrading materials may not turn substantially on the amount of sexual explicitness once a threshold of undeniable sexual content is surpassed. The category therefore includes a great deal of what would now be considered to be pornographic, and includes a great deal of what would now be held to be legally obscene, but it includes much more than that. Since we are here identifying harms for a class, rather than identifying harms caused by every member of that class, and since we are here talking about the identification of harm rather than making recommendations for legal control, we are not reluctant to identify harms for a class of material considerably wider than what is or even should be regulated by law.

5.2.3 Non-Violent and Non-Degrading Materials

Our most controversial category has been the category of sexually explicit materials that are not violent and are not degrading as we have used that term. They are materials in which the participants appear to be fully willing participants occupying substantially equal roles in a setting devoid of actual or apparent violence or pain. This category is in fact quite small in terms of currently available materials. There is some, to be sure, and the amount may increase as the division between the degrading and the non-degrading becomes more accepted, but we are convinced that only a small amount of currently available highly sexually explicit material is neither violent nor degrading. We thus talk about a small category, but one that should not be ignored. . . .

. . . Although the social science evidence is far from conclusive, we are on the current state of the evidence persuaded that material of this type does not bear a causal relationship to rape and other acts of sexual violence. . . .

A larger issue is the very question of promiscuity. Even to the extent that the behavior depicted is not inherently condemned by some or any of us, the manner of presentation almost necessarily suggests that the activities are taking place outside of the context of marriage, love, commitment, or even affection. Again, it is far from implausible to hypothesize that materials depicting sexual activity without marriage, love, commitment, or affection bear some causal relationship to sexual activity without marriage, love, commitment, or affection. There are undoubtedly many causes for what used to be called the "sexual revolution," but it is absurd to sup-

pose that depictions or descriptions of uncommitted sexuality were not among them. Thus, once again our disagreements reflect disagreements in society at large, although not to as great an extent. Although there are many members of this society who can and have made affirmative cases for uncommitted sexuality, none of us believes it to be a good thing. A number of us, however, believe that the level of commitment in sexuality is a matter of choice among those who voluntarily engage in the activity. Others of us believe that uncommitted sexual activity is wrong for the individuals involved and harmful to society to the extent of its prevalence. Our view of the ultimate harmfulness of much of this material, therefore, is reflective of our individual views about the extent to whether sexual commitment is purely a matter of individual choice.

Even insofar as sexually explicit material of the variety being discussed here is not perceived as harmful for the messages it carries or the symbols it represents, the very publicness of what is commonly taken to be private is cause for concern. Even if we hypothesize a sexually explicit motion picture of a loving married couple engaged in mutually pleasurable and procreative vaginal intercourse, the depiction of that act on a screen or in a magazine may constitute a harm in its own right (a "primary harm" in the terminology introduced earlier in this Chapter) solely by virtue of being shown. Here the concern is with the preservation of sex as an essentially private act, in conformity with the basic privateness of sex long recognized by this and all other societies. The alleged harm here, therefore, is that as soon as sex is put on a screen or put in a magazine it changes its character, regardless of what variety of sex is portrayed. And to the extent that the character of sex as public rather than private is the consequence here, then that to many would constitute a harm. . . .

A number of witnesses have testified about the effects on their own sexual relations, usually with their spouses, of the depiction on the screen and in magazines of sexual practices in which they had not previously engaged. A number of these witnesses, *all women,* have testified that men in their lives have used such material to strongly encourage, or coerce, them into engaging in sexual practices in which they do not choose to engage. To the extent that such implicit or explicit coercion takes place as a result of these materials, we all agree that it is a harm. There has been other evidence, however, about the extent to which such material might for some be a way of revitalizing their sex lives, or, more commonly, simply constituting a part of a mutually pleasurable sexual experience for both partners. On this we could not agree. For reasons relating largely to the question of publicness in the first sense discussed above, some saw this kind of use as primarily harmful. Others saw it as harmless and possibly beneficial in contexts such as this. Some professional testimony supported this latter view, but we have little doubt that professional opinion is also divided on the issue. . . .

QUESTIONS FOR REFLECTION

1. In answering the question "What is a harm?" the commission distinguishes primary from secondary harm. Explain this distinction. What, according to the commission, is its moral significance?

2. Why does the commission believe that sexually violent material is harmful?

3. The commission holds that nonviolent but degrading material is also harmful. What is "degrading" material? Why is it harmful?

4. What is the commission's opinion of nonviolent, nondegrading pornography? Is it harmful in any way? Should the government attempt to restrict access to such material, according to the commission? Do you agree?

5. Does the test for obscenity in *Miller* correspond to the distinction the commission makes between harmful and (largely) harmless pornography? If not, how might the test be revised to make it correspond?

WENDY McELROY

from *Sexual Correctness*

Wendy McElroy is the author of several libertarian critiques of feminism, including The Reasonable Woman *and* XXX: A Woman's Right to Pornography. *(Source: Reprinted from* Sexual Correctness: The Gender-Feminist Attack on Women. *[Jefferson, NC: McFarland and Company, Inc., 1996]. Notes have been omitted. Copyright © 1996 by Wendy McElroy. Reprinted by permission of the publisher.)*

CHAPTER THREE / A FEMINIST DEFENSE OF PORNOGRAPHY

Pornography is haunting feminists, who make such bald and insupportable statements as "pornography is the theory: rape is the practice." Women who work in the porn industry, who consume pornography, or who simply disagree are all considered to be brainwashed victims of patriarchy. In other words, they are sick and need not be taken seriously. This chapter attacks the ideology and strategy behind the crusade to limit women's sexual choices. It denies that pornography degrades women.

Gender Feminists and Conservatives: An Unholy Alliance

Pornography has been a traditional battleground between conservatives, who advocate family values, and liberals, who champion freedom of expression. The political makeup of contemporary feminism is overwhelmingly liberal; the more extreme feminists—called radical or gender feminist—are socialist. Nevertheless since the mid-eighties there has been a startling sight. Feminists have been standing alongside conservatives to demand legislation against pornography. Antipornography feminists have even joined hands with fundamentalists in a common cause.

This alliance makes some feminists nervous. Lisa Duggan, Nan Hunter and Carole S. Vance, in, their essay *False Promises,* summarized the amazement with which many liberal feminists view these recent events: "One is tempted to ask in astonishment, how can this be happening? . . . But in fact this new development is not as surprising as it at first seems. Pornography has come to be seen as a central cause of women's oppression by a significant number of feminists." They also expressed great concern about the future consequences of standing side by side with conservatives: "This analysis takes feminism very close—indeed far too close to measures that will ultimately support conservative, antisex, procensorship forces in American society for it is with these forces that women have formed alliances."

Gender feminists dismiss the dangers of this alliance. They discount the possibility that the legislation they seek could backlash against the feminist movement. Gender feminist Catharine MacKinnon obviated the question of whether or not to trust the law by observing: "We do not trust medicine, yet we insist it respond to women's needs. We do not trust theology, but we claim spirituality as more than a male preserve. We do not abdicate the control of technology because it was not invented by women."

MacKinnon concludes by dismissing those who question using patriarchy to protect women: "If women are to restrict our demands for change to spheres we can trust, spheres we already control, there will not be any."

The unlikely alliance between feminists and conservatives, and the split within feminism itself, has led to strange spectacles. For example, when an antipornography ordinance was proposed in Indianapolis, the law was supported by the Moral Majority—even though it had been drafted by gender feminists. Within the local feminist community, however, the ordinance found no support. The issue of pornography is turning feminist against feminist.

The Drift within Feminism on Pornography

The current antipornography crusade within feminism is something new on the political scene. It is new in at least two important ways: (1) it signals a break in feminism from its liberal insistence on freedom of speech and (2) it offers a revolutionary definition of pornography. The battle over pornography has shifted to new ground.

Pornography is the *bête noire* of gender feminism. To them, pornography is gender violence and a violation of the civil rights of women. It victimizes not merely women who work in the industry or who are exposed to magazines and films; pornography damages *all* women because it contributes to the general degradation of women that is prevalent in our society. Indeed, some theorists go so far as to claim that pornography is *the* source of society's unhealthy attitude toward women. Pornography is considered to be so damaging that it is linked, in a cause and effect relationship, to violent crimes such as rape. Thus, eliminating this form of expression is viewed as self-defense, not censorship.

The legal theorist Catharine MacKinnon has been a key voice in the antipornography campaign. In her book *Feminism Unmodified,* MacKinnon defined the object of attack: "Pornography, in the feminist view, is a form of forced sex, a practice of sexual politics, an institution of gender inequality." MacKinnon claims that pornography is not just a form of expres-

sion; pornographic material is—in and of itself—an act of violence: "Pornography not only teaches the reality of male dominance. It is one way its reality is imposed as well as experienced. It is a way of seeing and treating women."

MacKinnon further erases the line between attitude and behavior, image and action:

> Male power makes authoritative a way of seeing and treating women, so that when a man looks at a pornographic picture—pornographic meaning that the woman is defined as to be acted upon, a sexual object, a sexual thing—the *viewing* is an *act,* an act of male supremacy. [Emphasis in the original.]

The wholesale condemnation of pornography is new in feminism. Since its revival in the early 1960s the movement has been dominated by socialists and liberals; both these traditions advocated freedom of speech. Moreover, pornography tended to be viewed as part of a larger trend toward sexual liberation—a liberation that feminists applauded because it ushered in such things as birth control and the unveiling of women's sexuality.

Lisa Duggan, Nan Hunter, and Carole S. Vance typified this attitude in acknowledging the possible benefits pornography offered to women. They note that pornography has "served to flout conventional sexual mores, to ridicule sexual hypocrisy and to underscore the importance of sexual needs." In short, pornography has liberated women from the status quo by transmitting many messages:

> It advocates sexual adventure, sex outside of marriage, sex for pleasure, casual sex, illegal sex, anonymous sex, public sex, voyeuristic sex. Some of these ideas appeal to women . . . who may interpret some images as legitimating their own sense of sexual urgency or desire to be sexually aggressive.

Pornography and feminism have much in common. Both deal with women as sexual beings and both attempt to bring this sexuality out into the open. Moreover, pornography and feminism share a history of being targeted by obscenity laws. In particular, the Comstock Laws of the 1870s were used not only against pornographic material but also against birth control information. Feminist material—especially lesbian material—has always suffered under laws regulating sexual expression.

Gender Feminists: The New Puritans

By the late 1970s sexual liberation was being viewed with suspicion by feminists. Pornography was being redefined as an enemy of women. In her book, *Our Blood*, gender feminist Andrea Dworkin spells this out: "In pornography, sadism is the means by which men establish their dominance. Sadism is the authentic exercise of power which confirms manhood; and the first characteristic of manhood is that its existence is based on the negation of the female." Dworkin explains that manhood requires the destruction of women's bodies and will. Why? Dworkin explains this as well:

> The sexual sadism actualizes male identity. . . . The common erotic project of destroying women makes it possible for men to unite into a brotherhood; this project is the only firm and trustworthy groundwork for cooperation among males and all male bonding is based on it.

Antiporn Strategy

The feminist attack on pornography is not merely another cry for censorship from those who hate sex. It is more sophisticated than that. Feminists are using a strategy that has proved successful with other issues, such as affirmative action. Pornography is being defined as a violation of women's civil rights. Thus, instead of advocating criminal proceedings against pornographers, feminists restrict themselves to civil suits. This approach avoids sticky constitutional questions; in particular, it avoids the First Amendment. It also turns the entire discussion of pornography on its head. Conventional arguments for and against pornography simply do not apply.

Traditional obscenity laws have focused on the connection between pornography and moral harm. One of the standard tests of obscenity came from Supreme Court Justice Brennan in his ruling on *Memoirs* v. *Massachusetts:*

> (a) The dominant theme of the material taken as a whole appeals to the prurient interest in sex; (b) the material is patently offensive because it affronts contemporary community standards relating to the de-

scription or representation of sexual matters; and (c) the material is utterly without redeeming social value.

Antipornography feminists dwell on the connection between pornography and political harm —namely, the oppression of women. Consider MacKinnon's presentation of how pornography differs from obscenity. She argues that obscenity is concerned with morality—white male morality. Pornography is concerned with politics—the politics of women's subjugation. She further distinguishes between the two: "Morality here means good and evil; politics means power and powerlessness. Obscenity is a moral idea; pornography is a political practice. Obscenity is abstract; pornography is concrete. The two concepts represent two entirely different things."

In the mid-eighties, gender feminists launched a campaign to pass antipornography ordinances on a city by city basis. By localizing the issue, they bypassed the problem of obtaining a national consensus, which had proven so difficult with the ERA. The first ordinance—drafted by MacKinnon and Dworkin—served as the model for future ones. This was the Minneapolis Ordinance of 1983. In addressing the Minneapolis City Council, MacKinnon declared the key theme of gender feminism's attack on pornography: namely, that pornography was a violation of civil rights—an act of discrimination against women:

> We are proposing . . . a statutory scheme that will situate pornography as a central practice in the subordination of women. . . . The understanding and the evidence which we will present to you today to support defining pornography as a practice of discrimination on the basis of sex is a new idea.

Further, pornography was now placed at the heart of how men oppress women: "Pornography conditions and determines the way in which men actually treat women . . . and we will show that it is central to the way in which women remain second-class citizens."

Under the ordinance's provisions, a woman who had worked in pornography—a *Playboy* centerfold, for example—could bring a civil lawsuit against her employers for having coerced her into a "pornographic performance." Laws and remedies already existed for fraud or for contracts signed under duress. The purpose of the ordinance was to make "coercion" into a civil matter.

The definition of coercion was all-important. The ordinance was clear. Coercion was deemed to be present even if the woman was of age, fully understood the nature of the performance, signed a contract and release, agreed to it before witnesses, was under no threat, and was fully paid. None of these factors provided evidence of consent.

In essence, consent was not possible. In principle, the woman could not be treated as a consenting adult. By definition, coercion was always present in a pornographic act.

MacKinnon later explained: "In the context of unequal power (between the sexes), one needs to think about the meaning of consent—whether it is a meaningful concept at all." Gloria Steinem, in her introduction to Linda Lovelace's exposé *Out of Bondage,* agreed: "The question is free will: Are the subjects of pornography there by choice, or by coercion, *economic* or physical." (Emphasis added.)

In other words, if the woman needed or wanted the money offered, this would constitute economic coercion. The politics of society made it impossible for women to fully consent to a pornographic act. Women who thought they had agreed were mistaken. Such women had been so damaged by a male dominated culture that they were not able to give true consent. Lisa Duggan, Nan Hunter, and Carole S. Vance observe: "Advocates of the ordinance effectively assume that women have been so conditioned by the pornographic world view that if their own experiences of the sexual acts . . . are not subordinating, then they must simply be victims of false consciousness."

My Background as a Defender of Pornography

Several years ago, antipornography feminists attempted to pass an ordinance in Los Angeles. I was among the feminists who went down to city hall to argue against the ordinance. The arguments I decided *not* to use are almost as revealing as the ones I settled on.

I decided not to argue that pornography is undefinable and, therefore, not appropriate for a legal system that requires a clear point of enforcement. The ordinance had defined what it meant by pornography in excruciating—if subjective—detail. To focus on definitions would be to divert the debate into the bogs of what constitutes "dehumanization" or "exploitation." I simply accepted the rule of thumb offered by Supreme Court Justice Potter Stewart in his ruling on *Jacobellis* v. *Ohio,* 1964: "I know it when I see it." I assumed that everyone was talking about the same thing.

I also abandoned appeals to the First Amendment. Antipornography feminists had a tangled web of counterarguments, which would require more time to answer than I would be allotted. MacKinnon's arguments are typical. She begins by attacking the Constitution as a "white male" document: "The First Amendment essentially presumes some level of social equality among people and hence essentially equal social access to the means of expression. In a context of inequality between the sexes, we cannot presume that that is accurate."

MacKinnon then adds the dual claims: freedom of speech is not necessary for human fulfillment and pornography is an act of violence, not a form of speech: "The First Amendment also presumes that for the mind to be free to fulfill itself, speech must be free and open . . . Pornography amounts to terrorism and promotes not freedom but silence. Rather, it promotes freedom for men and enslavement and silence for women." If pornography was an act of violence, then the First Amendment was irrelevant.

I also avoided a discussion of privacy rights. Supreme Court Justice Thurgood Marshall (*Stanley* v. *Georgia,* 1969) had maintained: "If the First Amendment means anything, it means that a state has no business telling a man, sitting alone in his own house, what books he may read or what films he must watch." But, again, if pornography was violence, the issue of committing it in private was beside the point.

The only way to effectively challenge the new attack was to answer gender feminists in their own terms. The debate on pornography had been shifted to new ground. Thus, the key questions were: Are all women coerced into pornography? and How does pornography relate to violence against women? Everything seemed to return to the basic contention of feminists: pornography is an act of violence. It is an act committed upon and against unconsenting women. This is the level on which the assault on pornography must be addressed.

A Feminist Defense of Pornography

To begin with, I divided women into two categories: women who were directly involved with pornography—either in production or consumption and women who had no direct exposure. The first category is the litmus test. If women are degraded by pornography, surely the women closest to it would be the most deeply affected. At the heart of this question is the problem of pinning down subjective terms such as "degrading."

It was not possible to ask every woman who was involved in pornography whether or not she felt degraded by it. This left only one way to judge the matter. Namely, did women freely chose to work in the porn industry or to consume pornography?

The answer is clear: pornographic models and actresses sign contracts. Women who produce pornography, such as Ms. Hefner at *Playboy* or Candida Royalle at *Femme Films*, do so willingly. Women shopkeepers who stock pornography choose to fill in the order forms. Women who consume pornography—including me—pay money to do so.

However, gender feminists insist, no "healthy" woman would consent to the humiliation of pornography. Therefore, women who make this choice are so psychologically damaged by a male-dominated culture that they are incapable of true consent. In Indianapolis, the ordinance explicitly argued that women, like children, need special protection under the law.

Pause with me for a moment. Consider how insulting this is to women who have made an "unacceptable" choice with their bodies—that is, women who work in pornography. Antipornography feminists label these women as psychologically sick because they have made nonfeminist choices. These women are called victims of their culture.

But gender feminists were raised in the same culture. Presumably, these "enlightened" women wish us to believe that their choices are based on reason and knowledge; somehow, they have risen above the culture in which they were raised. They are unwilling, however, to grant such a courteous assumption to any woman who disagrees with them.

Gender feminists are adamant that women involved in the production of pornography cannot be held legally responsible for their actions because they are psychologically impaired by cultural influence. Their arguments need not be taken seriously, their contracts need not be respected. They are psychologically impaired. If a woman enjoys consuming pornography, it is not because she comes from another background, has a different emotional makeup, or has reasoned from different facts. No, it is because she is mentally incompetent. Like any three-year-old, she is unable to give informed consent regarding her own body.

The touchstone principle of feminism used to be, "a woman's body, a woman's right." Regarding date rape, feminists still declare, "No means no." The logical corollary of this is, "Yes means yes." Now, modern feminists are declaring that "yes" means nothing. It is difficult to believe that any form of pornography could be more degrading to women than this attitude.

As to whether cultural pressure has influenced women's decisions—of course it has. The culture we live in impacts on every choice we make. But to say that women who participate in pornography cannot make a choice because of cultural pressure, is to eliminate the possibility of choice in any realm. Because every choice of every person is made in the presence of cultural pressure—including the choice to become a feminist.

The Right to Pose Is the Right to Contract

The antipornography ordinances were intended to protect women from the consequences of their own actions. But what legal implications does this have for women's contracts—a right for which past generations fought hard? In the nineteenth century, women battled to become the legal equal of men, to have their consent taken seriously in the form of contracts, and to have control of their own bodies legally recognized. After the antipornography crusade, who will take a woman's consent seriously? When the Fifteenth Amendment was proposed in a form that enfranchised black men while ignoring women, the pioneering feminist Susan B. Anthony protested: "We have stood with the black man in the Constitution over a half a century. . . . Enfranchise him and we are left outside with lunatics, idiots and criminals."

To deprive women of the right to make their own contracts is to place them, once again, outside the constitution with lunatics, idiots, and criminals. Gender feminists are reducing a woman's consent to a legal triviality. Women are being granted the protection of no longer being taken seriously when they sign contracts. This is not a step toward dignity or freedom for women.

But what of the women who do not choose to be involved in pornography? What of the women who are offended by it? The simplistic answer is that they should not buy or consume it. Moreover, they should use any and all peaceful means to persuade others that pornography is not a proper form of expression.

The Bias of Researchers

The argument runs that whether or not women are directly exposed to pornography, they are still victimized. Pornography is the first step of a slippery slope that leads to explicit violence against women, such as rape. Thus, *every* woman is a victim, because every woman is in danger. This argument assumes: (1) that pornography impacts on men's behavior, (2) that the impact can be measured objectively, and (3) that it can be correlated with sexual violence.

Pornography probably does impact on people's behavior, but it is next to impossible to objectively measure that impact. Human psychology is extremely complex, especially in the area of sexual response. Moreover, the standard of measurement and the conclusions drawn from data usually depend on the bias of the researchers or of those who commission the research.

For example, in 1983 the Metropolitan Toronto Task Force on Violence against Women commissioned Thelma McCormack to study pornography's connection with sexual aggression. Her research did not support the assumption that there was one. Indeed, McCormack's study indicated that the effect of pornography might be cathartic. It might reduce the incidence of rape.

Her report, *Making Sense of Research on Pornography*, was discarded. The study was reassigned to David Scott, a nonfeminist committed to antipornography. Scott found a clear connection between pornography and sexual aggression. Students, journalists, and researchers who tried to obtain a copy of McCormack's paper were told that it was unavailable.

Statistics almost always contain assumptions and biases. Sometimes the bias is obvious and acknowledged. For example, a researcher who believes that sexual aggression is a learned behavior will naturally ask different questions than someone who believes aggression is an instinct. Other forms of bias are not so obvious.

However, for the sake of argument, let's assume that a correlation exists between pornography and rape. What would such a correlation prove? If a society with more pornography tended to have more rape, what would this say? A correlation is not a cause and effect relationship. It is a logical fallacy to assume that if A is correlated with B, then A causes B. Both might be caused by a totally separate factor, C. For example, there is a high correlation between the number of doctors in a city and the amount of alcohol consumed there. One does not cause the other. Both result from a third factor, the size of the city's population.

Similarly, a correlation between pornography and rape may indicate nothing more than a common cause for both, namely, that we live in a sexually repressed society. To further repress sex by restricting pornography might well increase the incidence of rape. Opening up the area of pornography might well diffuse sexual violence by making it more understandable.

Conclusion

There is great irony in the spectacle of gender feminists aligning themselves with their two greatest ideological enemies: conservatives and the patriarchal state. In using ordinances, antipornography feminists are legitimizing a system they themselves condemn as patriarchy. It is a strange leap of faith. After all, once a law is on the books, it is the state bureaucracy, not NOW, who will enforce it. In *Our Blood*, Andrea Dworkin excoriated patriarchal bureaucracy:

Under patriarchy, no woman is safe to live her life, or to love, or to mother children. Under patriarchy, every woman is a victim, past, present, and future. Under patriarchy, every woman's daughter is a victim, past, present, and future. Under patriarchy, every woman's son is her potential betrayer and also the inevitable rapist or exploiter of another woman.

Now feminists are appealing to this same state as a protector.

The final irony is that it is the state—not free speech—that has been the oppressor of women. It was the state, not pornography, that burned women as witches. It was eighteenth-century law, not pornography, that defined women as chattel. Nineteenth-century laws allowed men to commit wayward women to insane asylums, to claim their wives' earnings, and to beat them with impunity.

Twentieth-century laws refuse to recognize rape within marriage and sentence the sexes differently for the same crime. The state, not pornography, has raised barriers against women. And censorship, not freedom, will keep the walls intact.

One of the most important questions confronting feminism at the turn of this century is whether or not women's liberation can embrace sexual liberation. Can the freedom of women and freedom of speech become fellow travelers once more?

The feminist Myrna Kostash answered this question well: "To paraphrase Albert Camus, freedom to publish and read does not necessarily assure a society of justice and peace, but without these freedoms it has no assurance at all."

QUESTIONS FOR REFLECTION

1. How, according to McElroy, do restrictions on pornography harm women who neither produce nor consume pornography?

2. What is McElroy's chief argument against MacKinnon and the antipornography ordinances that she supports?

3. Apply Mill's harm principle to pornography. Does it generally agree or disagree with McElroy's position?

4. Apply Kant's categorical imperative to pornography. Does it generally agree or disagree with McElroy's position?

NADINE STROSSEN

from *Defending Pornography*

Nadine Strossen is Executive Director of the American Civil Liberties Union. (Source: Reprinted from Defending Pornography. *[New York: Scribner]. Notes have been omitted. Copyright © 1995 by Nadine Strossen. Reprinted by permission.)*

The only thing pornography is known to cause directly is the solitary act of masturbation. As for corruption, the only immediate victim is English prose.
—Gore Vidal, writer

Most of this book has aimed to illuminate the legal flaws and misconceptions of MacKinnon-Dworkin–style antipornography laws, to show how any such law undermines rather than advances important women's rights and human rights causes, and to paint a picture of the suppressed society that this type of law would produce when put in practice. Especially given recently renewed interest in MacKinnon-Dworkinite laws, they—and their chilling consequences—are my immediate concern. I have accordingly exposed the overwhelming problems that are inherent in all such laws. But, for the sake of argument, let's make the purely hypothetical assumption that we could fix those problems: let's pretend we could wave a magic wand that would miraculously make the laws do what they are supposed to without trampling on rights that are vital to everyone, and without stifling speech that serves women.

Even in this "Never-Never Land," where we could neutralize its negative side effects, would censorship "cure"—or at least reduce—the discrimination and violence against women allegedly caused by pornography? That is the assumption that underlies the feminist procensorship position, fueling the argument that we should trade in our free speech rights

to promote women's safety and equality rights. In fact, though, the hoped-for benefits of censorship are as hypothetical as our exercise in wishing away the evils of censorship. I will show this by examining the largely unexamined assumption that censorship would reduce sexism and violence against women. This assumption rests, in turn, on three others:

- that exposure to sexist, violent imagery leads to sexist, violent behavior;
- that the effective suppression of pornography would significantly reduce exposure to sexist, violent imagery; and
- that censorship would effectively suppress pornography.

To justify censoring pornography on the rationale that it would reduce violence or discrimination against women, one would have to provide actual support for all three of these assumptions. Each presupposes the others. Yet the only one of them that has received substantial attention is the first—that exposure to sexist, violent imagery leads to sexist, violent behavior—and, as I show later in this chapter, there is no creditable evidence to bear it out. Even feminist advocates of censoring pornography have acknowledged that this asserted causal connection cannot be proven, and therefore fall back on the argument that it should be accepted "on faith." Catharine MacKinnon has well captured this fallback position through her defensive double negative . . .

"There is no evidence that pornography does no harm."

Of course, given the impossibility of proving that there is *no* evidence of *no* harm, we would have no free speech, and indeed no freedom of any kind, were such a burden of proof actually to be imposed on those seeking to enjoy their liberties. To appreciate this, just substitute for the word "pornography" in MacKinnon's pronouncement any other type of expression or any other human right. We would have to acknowledge that "there is no evidence" that television does no harm, or that editorials criticizing government officials do no harm, or that religious sermons do no harm, and so forth. There certainly is no evidence that feminist writing in general, or MacKinnon's in particular, does no harm.

In its 1992 *Butler* decision, accepting the antipornography feminist position, the Canadian Supreme Court also accepted this dangerous intuitive approach to limiting sexual expression, stating:

> It might be suggested that proof of actual harm should be required . . . [I]t is sufficient . . . for Parliament to have a reasonable basis for concluding that harm will result and this requirement does not demand actual proof of harm.

Even if we were willing to follow the Canadian Supreme Court and procensorship feminists in believing, without evidence, that exposure to sexist, violent imagery does lead to sexist, violent behavior, we still should not accept their calls for censorship. Even if we assumed that *seeing* pornography leads to committing sexist and violent actions, it still would not follow that *censoring* pornography would reduce sexism or violence, due to flaws in the remaining two assumptions: we still would have to prove that pornography has a corner on the sexism and violence market, and that pornography is in fact entirely suppressible.

Even if pornography could be completely suppressed, the sexist, violent imagery that pervades the mainstream media would remain untouched. Therefore, if exposure to such materials caused violence and sexism, these problems would still remain with us. But no censorship regime could completely suppress pornography. It would continue to exist underground. In this respect, censorship would bring us the worst of both worlds. On one hand, . . . suppressive laws make it difficult to obtain a wide range of sexually oriented materials, so that most people would not have access to those materials. On the other hand, though, some such materials would continue to be produced and consumed no matter what. Every governmental effort to prohibit any allegedly harmful material has always caused this kind of "double trouble." Witness the infamous "Prohibition" of alcohol earlier in this century, for example.

Let's now examine in more detail the fallacies in each of the three assumptions underlying the feminist procensorship stance. And let's start with the single assumption that has been the focus of discussion—the alleged causal relationship between exposure to sexist, violent imagery and sexist, violent behavior.

Monkey See, Monkey Do?

Aside from the mere fear that sexual expression might cause discrimination or violence against women, advocates of censorship attempt to rely on four types of evidence concerning this alleged causal link: laboratory research data concerning the attitudinal effects of showing various types of sexually explicit materials to volunteer subjects, who are usually male college students; correlational data concerning availability of sexually oriented materials and antifemale discrimination or violence; anecdotal data consisting of accounts by sex offenders and their victims concerning any role that pornography may have played in the offenses; and studies of sex offenders, assessing factors that may have led to their crimes.

As even some leading procensorship feminists have acknowledged, along with the Canadian Supreme Court in *Butler,* none of these types of "evidence" prove that pornography harms women. Rather than retracing the previous works that have reviewed this evidence and reaffirmed its failure to substantiate the alleged causal connection, I will simply summarize their conclusions.

Laboratory Experiments

The most comprehensive recent review of the social science data is contained in Marcia Pally's 1994 book *Sex and Sensibility: Reflections on Forbidden Mirrors and the Will to Censor.* It exhaustively canvasses laboratory studies that have evaluated the impact of exposing experimental subjects to sexually explicit expression of many varieties, and concludes that no credible evidence substantiates a clear causal connection between any type of sexually explicit material and any sexist or violent behavior. The book also draws the same conclusion from its thorough review of field and correlational studies, as well as sociological surveys, in the U.S., Canada, Europe, and Asia.

Numerous academic and governmental surveys of the social science studies have similarly rejected the purported link between sexual expression and aggression. The National Research Council's Panel on Understanding and Preventing Violence concluded, in 1993: "Demonstrated empirical links between pornography and sex crimes in general are weak or absent." . . .

Since the feminist censorship proposals aim at sexually explicit material that allegedly is "degrading" to women, it is especially noteworthy that research data show no link between exposure to "degrading" sexually explicit material and sexual aggression.

Even two research literature surveys that were conducted for the Meese Commission, one by University of Calgary professor Edna Einseidel and the other by then–Surgeon General C. Everett Koop, also failed to find any link between "degrading" pornography and sex crimes or aggression. Surgeon General Koop's survey concluded that only two reliable generalizations could be made about the impact of exposure to "degrading" sexual material on its viewers: it caused them to think that a variety of sexual practices were more common than they had previously believed, and it caused them to more accurately estimate the prevalence of varied sexual practices.

Experiments also fail to establish any link between women's exposure to such materials and their development of negative self-images. Carol Krafka found that, in comparison with other women, women who were exposed to sexually "degrading" materials did not engage in more sex-role stereotyping; nor did they experience lower self-esteem, have less satisfaction with their body image, accept more anti-woman myths about rape, or show greater acceptance of violence against women. Similar conclusions have been reached by Donnerstein, Linz, and Penrod.

Correlational Data

Both the Meese Commission and procensorship feminists have attempted to rely on studies that allegedly show a correlation between the availability of sexually explicit materials and sexual offense rates. Of course, though, a positive correlation between two phenomena does not prove that one causes the other. Accordingly, even if the studies did consistently show a positive correlation between the prevalence of sexual materials and sexual offenses—which they do not—they still would not establish that exposure to the materials *caused* the rise in offenses. The same correlation could also reflect the opposite causal chain—if, for example, rapists relived their violent acts by purchasing sexually violent magazines or videotapes.

Any correlation between the availability of sexual materials and the rate of sex offenses could also reflect an independent factor that causes increases in both. Cynthia Gentry's correlational studies have identified just such an independent variable in geographical areas that have high rates of both the circulation of sexually explicit magazines and sexual violence: namely, a high population of men between the ages of eighteen and thirty-four. Similarly, Larry Baron and Murray Straus have noted that areas where both sexual materials and sexual aggression are prevalent are characterized by a "hypermasculated or macho culture pattern," which may well be the underlying causal agent. Accordingly, Joseph Scott and Loretta Schwalm found that communities with higher rape rates experienced stronger sales not only of porn magazines, but also of *all* male-oriented magazines, including *Field and Stream*.

Even more damning to the attempt to rest the "porn-causes-rape-or-discrimination" theory on alleged correlations is that there simply are no consistent correlations. While the asserted correlation would not be *sufficient* to prove the claimed causal connection, it is *necessary* to prove that connection. Therefore, the existence of the alleged causal relationship is conclusively refuted by the fact that levels of violence and discrimination against women are often *inversely* related to the availability of sexually explicit materials, including violent sexually explicit materials. This inverse relationship appears in various kinds of comparisons: between different states within the United States; between different countries; and between different periods within the same country.

Within the United States, the Baron and Straus research has shown no consistent pattern between the availability of sexual materials and the number of rapes from state to state. Utah is the lowest-ranking state in the availability of sexual materials but twenty-fifth in the number of rapes, whereas New Hampshire ranks ninth highest in the availability of sexual materials but only forty-fourth in the number of rapes.

The lack of a consistent correlation between pornography consumption and violence against women is underscored by one claim of the procensorship feminists themselves: they maintain that the availability and consumption of pornography, including violent pornography, have been increasing throughout the United States. At the same time, though, the rates of sex crimes have been decreasing or remaining steady. The Bureau of Justice Statistics reports that between 1973 and 1987, the national rape rate remained steady and the attempted rape rate decreased. Since these data were gathered from household surveys rather than from police records, they are considered to be the most accurate measures of the incidence of crimes. These data also cover the period during which feminists helped to create a social, political, and legal climate that should have encouraged higher percentages of rape victims to report their assaults. Thus, the fact that rapes reported to the Bureau of Justice Statistics have not increased provokes serious questions about the procensorship feminists' theories of pornography-induced harm. Similar questions are raised by data showing a decrease in wife battery between 1975 and 1985, again despite changes that should have encouraged the increased reporting of this chronically underreported crime.

Noting that "[t]he mass-market pornography . . . industr[y] took off after World War II," Marcia Pally has commented:

> In the decades since the 1950s, with the marketing of sexual material . . . , the country has seen the greatest advances in sensitivity to violence against women and children. Before the . . . mass publication of sexual images, no rape or incest hot lines and battered women's shelters existed; date and marital rape were not yet phrases in the language. Should one conclude that the presence of pornography . . . has inspired public outrage at sexual crimes?

Pally's rhetorical question underscores the illogicality of presuming that just because two phenomena happen to coexist, they therefore are causally linked. I have already shown that any correlation that might exist between the increased availability of pornography and *increased* misogynistic discrimination or violence could well be explained by other factors. The same is true for any correlation that might exist between the increased availability of pornography and *decreased* misogynistic discrimination or violence.

In a comparative state-by-state analysis, Larry Baron and Murray Straus have found a positive correlation between the circulation of pornographic magazines and the state's "index of gender equality," a composite of twenty-four indicators of economic, political, and legal equality. As the researchers have observed, these findings may suggest that both sexually explicit material and gender equality flourish in tolerant climates with fewer restrictions on speech. . . .

Anecdotes and Suspicions

As Seventh Circuit Court of Appeals Judge Richard Posner observed about MacKinnon's book *Only Words:*

> MacKinnon's treatment of the central issue of pornography as she herself poses it—the harm that pornography does to women—is shockingly casual. Much of her evidence is anecdotal, and in a nation of 260 million people, anecdotes are a weak form of evidence.

Many procensorship advocates attempt to rest their case on self-serving "porn-made-me-do-it" claims by sexual offenders, as well as on statements by victims or police officers that sexual offenders had sexually explicit materials in their possession at the time they committed their crimes.

The logical fallacy of relying on anecdotes to establish a general causal connection between exposure to sexual materials and violence against women was aptly noted by journalist Ellen Willis: "Anti-porn activists cite cases of sexual killers who were also users of pornography, but this is no more logical than arguing that marriage causes rape because some rapists are married."

Even assuming that sexual materials really were the triggering factors behind some specific crimes, that could not justify restrictions on such materials. As former Supreme Court Justice William O. Douglas wrote: "The First Amendment demands more than a horrible example or two of the perpetrator of a crime of sexual violence, in whose pocket is found a pornographic book, before it allows the Nation to be saddled with a regime of censorship." If we attempted to ban all words or images that had ever been blamed for inspiring or instigating particular crimes by some aberrant or antisocial individual, we would end up with little left to read or view. Throughout history and around the world, criminals have regularly blamed their conduct on a sweeping array of words and images in books, movies, and television. . . .

The countless expressive works that have been blamed for crimes include many that convey pro-feminist messages. Therefore, an anecdotal, image-blaming rationale for censorship would condemn many feminist works. For example, the television movie *The Burning Bed,* which told the true story of a battered wife who set fire to her sleeping husband, was blamed for some "copycat" crimes, as well as for some acts of violence by men against women. The argument that such incidents would justify suppres-

sion would mark the end of any films or other works depicting—and deploring—the real violence that plagues the lives of too many actual women.

Under a censorship regime that permits anecdotal, book-blaming "evidence," all other feminist materials would be equally endangered, not "just" works that depict the violence that has been inflicted on women. That is because, as feminist writings themselves have observed, some sexual assaults are committed by men who feel threatened by the women's movement. Should feminist works therefore be banned on the theory that they might well motivate a man to act out his misogynistic aggression? . . .

. . . .Even assuming for the sake of argument that there were a causal link between pornography and anti-female discrimination and violence, the insignificant contribution that censorship might make to reducing them would not outweigh the substantial damage that censorship would do to feminist goals. From the lack of actual evidence to substantiate the alleged causal link, the conclusion follows even more inescapably: *Censoring pornography would do women more harm than good.*

QUESTIONS FOR REFLECTION

1. What would an advocate of censorship have to show, according to Strossen, to justify the claim that censorship would reduce discrimination and violence against women?

2. Why, in Strossen's view, would censorship have little effect on people's exposure to sexist, violent imagery?

3. Summarize the research Strossen cites in support of her contention that pornography does not increase tendencies to violence. Do you find it convincing?

4. Summarize Strossen's argument that pornography does not increase discrimination against women. Do you find it convincing?

OFFENSIVE SPEECH AND BEHAVIOR

In response to racial incidents, colleges and universities across the country have been enacting speech codes to limit what can be said on campus. Some are narrow, proscribing only repeated harassment of individuals; others are broad, prohibiting "insensitive" speech and behavior. At least one restriction has been struck down by a court as unconstitutional. Off campus, legal scholars have proposed new rules for civil lawsuits related to racial insults, and complaints and lawsuits concerning sexual harassment have become commonplace. Many companies now have sexual harassment policies and complaint procedures. Many states have passed laws giving stiffer penalties to criminals motivated by prejudice.

Advocates of these changes point to equality, the protection of rights, and the benefits of a more inclusive social environment. Critics, however, see restrictions on speech that are hard to justify.

Freedoms of thought, speech, and the press have well-recognized exceptions. One may not slander a person, incite a mob to riot, or shout "Fire!" in a crowded theater that is not on fire. In Mill's words, "Acts, of whatever kind, which without justifiable cause do harm to others may be, and in the more important cases absolutely require to be, controlled by the unfavorable sentiments, and, when needful, by the active interference of mankind." In cases of the kinds just mentioned, the harm done to particular people outweighs any possible value the speech possesses.

Is that true of racial insults, sexual harassment, and other offensive speech? Undoubtedly, harassment of various kinds can cause harm. But often offensive speech is just that—offensive. If someone insults me, or makes lewd remarks to me, or makes an obscene gesture toward me, I am probably going to be offended. But it is not so clear that I will suffer harm. There seems to be a big difference between an obscene gesture and a punch in the nose. The childhood rhyme says "Sticks and stones will break my bones, but words will never hurt me." This seems wrong—words can hurt—but it nevertheless makes an important point: There are differences between offense and harm.

In *R.A.V. v. St. Paul,* the Supreme Court struck down the city's "hate crimes" ordinance. R.A.V., a juvenile, allegedly burned a cross on a black family's lawn. He was charged with a hate crime under the city ordinance and was convicted. He appealed on the ground that he was being punished for the content of his opinions. The Court decided in his favor, arguing that the First Amendment protects even highly offensive expressions of opinion.

Stanley Fish argues that speech is never really free; all defenses of freedom of speech make exceptions. The exceptions, Fish contends, are based not on principle but on politics. Deciding what speech to allow is deciding what will be politically favored. Fish concludes by defending speech codes and other restrictions, maintaining that they produce social benefits.

Jonathan Rauch sees in arguments such as Fish's a humanitarian threat to freedom. People restrict offensive speech for good, humanitarian reasons—to protect people from offense and harm. But, Rauch thinks, the restrictions threaten the entire institution of liberal science. Seeking the truth requires not only free inquiry but free intellectual battle, which may sometimes include offensive speech and behavior. Liberal science, Rauch insists, is the best method we have for determining truth. And it punishes those who are wrong by ridiculing them and their ideas. This is not an unfortunate accident, Rauch believes; it is essential to the scientific process.

JUSTICE ANTONIN SCALIA

Majority Opinion in *R.A.V.* v. *City of St. Paul, Minnesota*

(Source: R.A.V. v. St. Paul, 505 U.S. 377, 112 S. Ct. 2 [1992]. Most legal references have been omitted.)

[Mr.] Justice Scalia delivered the opinion of the Court.

In the predawn hours of June 21, 1990, petitioner and several other teenagers allegedly assembled a crudely made cross by taping together broken chair legs. They then allegedly burned the cross inside the fenced yard of a black family that lived across the street from the house where petitioner was staying. Although this conduct could have been punished under any of a number of laws, one of the two provisions under which respondent city of St. Paul chose to charge petitioner (then a juvenile) was the St. Paul Bias-Motivated Crime Ordinance, St. Paul, Minn. Legis. Code § 292.02 (1990), which provides:

> "Whoever places on public or private property a symbol, object, appellation, characterization or graffiti, including, but not limited to, a burning cross or Nazi swastika, which one knows or has reasonable grounds to know arouses anger, alarm or resentment in others on the basis of race, color, creed, religion or gender commits disorderly conduct and shall be guilty of a misdemeanor."

Petitioner moved to dismiss this count on the ground that the St. Paul ordinance was substantially overbroad and impermissibly content based and therefore facially invalid under the First Amendment. . . .

I

In construing the St. Paul ordinance, we are bound by the construction given to it by the Minnesota court. Accordingly, we accept the Minnesota Supreme Court's authoritative statement that the ordinance reaches only those expressions that constitute "fighting words" within the meaning of *Chaplinsky*. Petitioner and his amici urge us to modify the scope of the *Chaplinsky* formulation, thereby invalidating the ordinance as "substantially overbroad." We find it unnecessary to consider this issue. Assuming, arguendo, that all of the expression reached by the ordinance is proscribable under the "fighting words" doctrine, we nonetheless conclude that the ordinance is facially unconstitutional in that it prohibits otherwise permitted speech solely on the basis of the subjects the speech addresses.

The First Amendment generally prevents government from proscribing speech, see, e.g., *Cantwell* v. *Connecticut* (1940), or even expressive conduct, see, e.g., *Texas* v. *Johnson* (1989), because of disapproval of the ideas expressed. Content-based regulations are presumptively invalid. From 1791 to the present, however, our society, like other free but civilized societies, has permitted restrictions upon the content of speech in a few limited areas, which are "of such slight social value as a step to truth that any benefit that may be derived from them is clearly outweighed by the social interest in order and morality." *Chaplinsky*. We have recognized that "the freedom of speech" referred to by the First Amendment does not include a freedom to disregard these traditional limitations. Our decisions since the 1960's have narrowed the scope of the traditional categorical exceptions for

229

defamation, but a limited categorical approach has remained an important part of our First Amendment jurisprudence.

We have sometimes said that these categories of expression are "not within the area of constitutionally protected speech," or that the "protection of the First Amendment does not extend" to them. Such statements must be taken in context, however, and are no more literally true than is the occasionally repeated shorthand characterizing obscenity "as not being speech at all." What they mean is that these areas of speech can, consistently with the First Amendment, be regulated because of their constitutionally proscribable content (obscenity, defamation, etc.)—not that they are categories of speech entirely invisible to the Constitution, so that they may be made the vehicles for content discrimination unrelated to their distinctively proscribable content. Thus, the government may proscribe libel; but it may not make the further content discrimination of proscribing only libel critical of the government. We recently acknowledged this distinction in *Ferber,* where, in upholding New York's child pornography law, we expressly recognized that there was no "question here of censoring a particular literary theme. . . ." See also id. (O'Connor, J., concurring) ("As drafted, New York's statute does not attempt to suppress the communication of particular ideas").

Our cases surely do not establish the proposition that the First Amendment imposes no obstacle whatsoever to regulation of particular instances of such proscribable expression, so that the government "may regulate [them] freely" (White, J., concurring in judgment). That would mean that a city council could enact an ordinance prohibiting only those legally obscene works that contain criticism of the city government or, indeed, that do not include endorsement of the city government. Such a simplistic, all-or-nothing-at-all approach to First Amendment protection is at odds with common sense and with our jurisprudence as well. It is not true that "fighting words" have at most a "*de minimis*" expressive content, or that their content is in all respects "worthless and undeserving of constitutional protection"; sometimes they are quite expressive indeed. We have not said that they constitute "no part of the expression of ideas," but only that

they constitute "no *essential** part of any exposition of ideas." *Chaplinsky* (emphasis added).

The proposition that a particular instance of speech can be proscribable on the basis of one feature (e.g., obscenity) but not on the basis of another (e.g., opposition to the city government) is commonplace, and has found application in many contexts. We have long held, for example, that nonverbal expressive activity can be banned because of the action it entails, but not because of the ideas it expresses—so that burning a flag in violation of an ordinance against outdoor fires could be punishable, whereas burning a flag in violation of an ordinance against dishonoring the flag is not. Similarly, we have upheld reasonable "time, place, or manner" restrictions, but only if they are "justified without reference to the content of the regulated speech." And just as the power to proscribe particular speech on the basis of a noncontent element (e.g., noise) does not entail the power to proscribe the same speech on the basis of a content element; so also, the power to proscribe it on the basis of one content element (e.g., obscenity) does not entail the power to proscribe it on the basis of other content elements.

In other words, the exclusion of "fighting words" from the scope of the First Amendment simply means that, for purposes of that Amendment, the unprotected features of the words are, despite their verbal character, essentially a "nonspeech" element of communication. Fighting words are thus analogous to a noisy sound truck: Each is, as Justice Frankfurter recognized, a "mode of speech," *Niemotko* v. *Maryland* (1951); both can be used to convey an idea; but neither has, in and of itself, a claim upon the First Amendment. As with the sound truck, however, so also with fighting words: The government may not regulate use based on hostility—or favoritism—towards the underlying message expressed. Compare *Frisby* v. *Schultz* (1988) (upholding, against facial challenge, a content-neutral ban on targeted residential picketing) with *Carey* v. *Brown* (1980) (invalidating a ban on residential picketing that exempted labor picketing).

The concurrences describe us as setting forth a new First Amendment principle that prohibition of

---

* Italics mine.—ED.

constitutionally proscribable speech cannot be "underinclusiv[e]," a First Amendment "absolutism" whereby "within a particular 'proscribable' category of expression, . . . a government must either proscribe all speech or no speech at all." That easy target is of the concurrences' own invention. In our view, the First Amendment imposes not an "underinclusiveness" limitation but a "content discrimination" limitation upon a State's prohibition of proscribable speech. There is no problem whatever, for example, with a State's prohibiting obscenity (and other forms of proscribable expression) only in certain media or markets, for although that prohibition would be "underinclusive," it would not discriminate on the basis of content.

Even the prohibition against content discrimination that we assert the First Amendment requires is not absolute. It applies differently in the context of proscribable speech than in the area of fully protected speech. The rationale of the general prohibition, after all, is that content discrimination "rais[es] the specter that the Government may effectively drive certain ideas or viewpoints from the marketplace." But content discrimination among various instances of a class of proscribable speech often does not pose this threat.

When the basis for the content discrimination consists entirely of the very reason the entire class of speech at issue is proscribable, no significant danger of idea or viewpoint discrimination exists. Such a reason, having been adjudged neutral enough to support exclusion of the entire class of speech from First Amendment protection, is also neutral enough to form the basis of distinction within the class. To illustrate: A State might choose to prohibit only that obscenity which is the most patently offensive in its prurience, i.e., that which involves the most lascivious displays of sexual activity. But it may not prohibit, for example, only that obscenity which includes offensive political messages. And the Federal Government can criminalize only those threats of violence that are directed against the President, see 18 U.S.C. § 871—since the reasons why threats of violence are outside the First Amendment (protecting individuals from the fear of violence, from the disruption that fear engenders, and from the possibility that the threatened violence will occur) have special force when applied to the person of the Pres-

ident. See *Watts* v. *United States* (1969) (upholding the facial validity of § 871 because of the "overwhelmin[g] interest in protecting the safety of [the] Chief Executive and in allowing him to perform his duties without interference from threats of physical violence"). But the Federal Government may not criminalize only those threats against the President that mention his policy on aid to inner cities. And to take a final example (one mentioned by Justice Stevens, post, at 2563-2564), a State may choose to regulate price advertising in one industry but not in others, because the risk of fraud (one of the characteristics of commercial speech that justifies depriving it of full First Amendment protection, is in its view greater there. But a State may not prohibit only that commercial advertising that depicts men in a demeaning fashion, . . .

Another valid basis for according differential treatment to even a content defined subclass of proscribable speech is that the subclass happens to be associated with particular "secondary effects" of the speech, so that the regulation is "justified without reference to the content of the . . . speech," *Renton* v. *Playtime Theatres, Inc.* (1986). A State could, for example, permit all obscene live performances except those involving minors. Moreover, since words can in some circumstances violate laws directed not against speech but against conduct (a law against treason, for example, is violated by telling the enemy the nation's defense secrets), a particular content based subcategory of a proscribable class of speech can be swept up incidentally within the reach of a statute directed at conduct rather than speech. Thus, for example, sexually derogatory "fighting words," among other words, may produce a violation of Title VII's general prohibition against sexual discrimination in employment practices. Where the government does not target conduct on the basis of its expressive content, acts are not shielded from regulation merely because they express a discriminatory idea or philosophy.

These bases for distinction refute the proposition that the selectivity of the restriction is "even arguably 'conditioned upon the sovereign's agreement with what a speaker may intend to say.'" *Metromedia, Inc.* v. *San Diego* (1981). There may be other such bases as well. Indeed, to validate such selectivity (where totally proscribable speech is at issue) it may not even be necessary to identify any particular "neutral" basis, so long as the nature of the content discrimination is such that there is no realistic possibility that official suppression of ideas is afoot. (We cannot think of any First Amendment interest that would stand in the way of a State's prohibiting only those obscene motion pictures with blue-eyed actresses.) Save for that limitation, the regulation of "fighting words," like the regulation of noisy speech, may address some offensive instances and leave other, equally offensive, instances alone.

II

Applying these principles to the St. Paul ordinance, we conclude that, even as narrowly construed by the Minnesota Supreme Court, the ordinance is facially unconstitutional. Although the phrase in the ordinance, "arouses anger, alarm or resentment in others," has been limited by the Minnesota Supreme Court's construction to reach only those symbols or displays that amount to "fighting words," the remaining, unmodified terms make clear that the ordinance applies only to "fighting words" that insult, or provoke violence, "on the basis of race, color, creed, religion or gender." Displays containing abusive invective, no matter how vicious or severe, are permissible unless they are addressed to one of the specified disfavored topics. Those who wish to use "fighting words" in connection with other ideas—to express hostility, for example, on the basis of political affiliation, union membership, or homosexuality—are not covered. The First Amendment does not permit St. Paul to impose special prohibitions on those speakers who express views on disfavored subjects.

In its practical operation, moreover, the ordinance goes even beyond mere content discrimination, to actual viewpoint discrimination. Displays containing some words—odious racial epithets, for example—would be prohibited to proponents of all views. But "fighting words" that do not themselves invoke race, color, creed, religion, or gender—aspersions upon a person's mother, for example—would seemingly be usable *ad libitum* in the placards of those arguing in favor of racial, color, etc., tolerance and equality, but could not be used by that speaker's opponents. One could hold up a sign say-

ing, for example, that all "anti-Catholic bigots" are misbegotten; but not that all "papists" are, for that would insult and provoke violence "on the basis of religion." St. Paul has no such authority to license one side of a debate to fight freestyle, while requiring the other to follow Marquis of Queensbury Rules.

What we have here, it must be emphasized, is not a prohibition of fighting words that are directed at certain persons or groups (which would be facially valid if it met the requirements of the Equal Protection Clause); but rather, a prohibition of fighting words that contain (as the Minnesota Supreme Court repeatedly emphasized) messages of "bias-motivated" hatred and in particular, as applied to this case, messages "based on virulent notions of racial supremacy." One must wholeheartedly agree with the Minnesota Supreme Court that "[i]t is the responsibility, even the obligation, of diverse communities to confront such notions in whatever form they appear," but the manner of that confrontation cannot consist of selective limitations upon speech. St. Paul's brief asserts that a general "fighting words" law would not meet the city's needs because only a content-specific measure can communicate to minority groups that the "group hatred" aspect of such speech "is not condoned by the majority." The point of the First Amendment is that majority preferences must be expressed in some fashion other than silencing speech on the basis of its content.

Despite the fact that the Minnesota Supreme Court and St. Paul acknowledge that the ordinance is directed at expression of group hatred, Justice Stevens suggests that this "fundamentally misreads" the ordinance. It is directed, he claims, not to speech of a particular content, but to particular "injur[ies]" that are "qualitatively different" from other injuries. This is word play. What makes the anger, fear, sense of dishonor, etc., produced by violation of this ordinance distinct from the anger, fear, sense of dishonor, etc., produced by other fighting words is nothing other than the fact that it is caused by a distinctive idea, conveyed by a distinctive message. The First Amendment cannot be evaded that easily. It is obvious that the symbols which will arouse "anger, alarm or resentment in others on the basis of race, color, creed, religion or gender" are those symbols that communicate a message of hostility based on one of these characteristics. St. Paul concedes in its brief that the ordinance applies only to "racial, religious, or gender-specific symbols" such as "a burning cross, Nazi swastika or other instrumentality of like import." Indeed, St. Paul argued in the Juvenile Court that "[t]he burning of a cross does express a message and it is, in fact, the content of that message which the St. Paul Ordinance attempts to legislate."

The content-based discrimination reflected in the St. Paul ordinance comes within neither any of the specific exceptions to the First Amendment prohibition we discussed earlier, nor within a more general exception for content discrimination that does not threaten censorship of ideas. It assuredly does not fall within the exception for content discrimination based on the very reasons why the particular class of speech at issue (here, fighting words) is proscribable. As explained earlier, the reason why fighting words are categorically excluded from the protection of the First Amendment is not that their content communicates any particular idea, but that their content embodies a particularly intolerable (and socially unnecessary) mode of expressing whatever idea the speaker wishes to convey. St. Paul has not singled out an especially offensive mode of expression—it has not, for example, selected for prohibition only those fighting words that communicate ideas in a threatening (as opposed to a merely obnoxious) manner. Rather, it has proscribed fighting words of whatever manner that communicate messages of racial, gender, or religious intolerance. Selectivity of this sort creates the possibility that the city is seeking to handicap the expression of particular ideas. That possibility would alone be enough to render the ordinance presumptively invalid, but St. Paul's comments and concessions in this case elevate the possibility to a certainty.

St. Paul argues that the ordinance comes within another of the specific exceptions we mentioned, the one that allows content discrimination aimed only at the "secondary effects" of the speech, see *Renton v. Playtime Theatres, Inc.* (1986). According to St. Paul, the ordinance is intended, "not to impact on [sic] the right of free expression of the accused," but rather to "protect against the victimization of a person or persons who are particularly vulnerable because of their membership in a group that historically has been discriminated against." Even assuming that an ordi-

nance that completely proscribes, rather than merely regulates, a specified category of speech can ever be considered to be directed only to the secondary effects of such speech, it is clear that the St. Paul ordinance is not directed to secondary effects within the meaning of *Renton*. As we said in *Boos v. Barry* (1988), "[l]isteners' reactions to speech are not the type of 'secondary effects' we referred to in *Renton*." "The emotive impact of speech on its audience is not a 'secondary effect.'"

It hardly needs discussion that the ordinance does not fall within some more general exception permitting all selectivity that for any reason is beyond the suspicion of official suppression of ideas. The statements of St. Paul in this very case afford ample basis for, if not full confirmation of, that suspicion.

Finally, St. Paul and its amici defend the conclusion of the Minnesota Supreme Court that, even if the ordinance regulates expression based on hostility towards its protected ideological content, this discrimination is nonetheless justified because it is narrowly tailored to serve compelling state interests. Specifically, they assert that the ordinance helps to ensure the basic human rights of members of groups that have historically been subjected to discrimination, including the right of such group members to live in peace where they wish. We do not doubt that these interests are compelling, and that the ordinance can be said to promote them. But the "danger of censorship" presented by a facially content-based statute requires that that weapon be employed only where it is "necessary to serve the asserted [compelling] interest," *Burson v. Freeman* (1992) (emphasis added). The existence of adequate content-neutral alternatives thus "undercut[s] significantly" any defense of such a statute, *Boos v. Barry,* casting considerable doubt on the government's protestations that "the asserted justification is in fact an accurate description of the purpose and effect of the law," *Burson*. The dispositive question in this case, therefore, is whether content discrimination is reasonably necessary to achieve St. Paul's compelling interests; it plainly is not. An ordinance not limited to the favored topics, for example, would have precisely the same beneficial effect. In fact the only interest distinctively served by the content limitation is that of displaying the city council's special hostility towards the particular biases thus singled out. That is precisely what the First Amendment forbids. The politicians of St. Paul are entitled to express that hostility—but not through the means of imposing unique limitations upon speakers who (however benightedly) disagree.

Let there be no mistake about our belief that burning a cross in someone's front yard is reprehen-

sible. But St. Paul has sufficient means at its disposal to prevent such behavior without adding the First Amendment to the fire.

The judgment of the Minnesota Supreme Court is reversed, and the case is remanded for proceedings not inconsistent with this opinion.

QUESTIONS FOR REFLECTION

1. Why, according to Justice Scalia, is the ordinance facially unconstitutional?

2. Could Mill's arguments for freedom of speech be used against the St. Paul ordinance? Why or why not?

3. Why does the Court reject St. Paul's claim that offensive expressions may be banned because of their secondary effects? Do you agree?

STANLEY FISH

from *There's No Such Thing as Free Speech, and It's a Good Thing, Too*

Stanley Fish is Professor of English at Duke University. (Source: There's No Such Thing as Free Speech, and It's a Good Thing, Too *[New York: Oxford, 1994]. Copyright © 1994 by Stanley Fish. Reprinted by permission of Oxford University Press, Inc.)*

Nowadays the First Amendment is the First Refuge of Scoundrels.

— *S. Johnson and S. Fish*

Lately, many on the liberal and progressive left have been disconcerted to find that words, phrases, and concepts thought to be their property and generative of their politics have been appropriated by the forces of neoconservatism. This is particularly true of the concept of free speech, for in recent years First Amendment rhetoric has been used to justify policies and actions the left finds problematical if not abhorrent: pornography, sexist language, campus hate speech. How has this happened? The answer I shall give in this essay is that abstract concepts like free speech do not have any "natural" content but are filled with whatever content and direction one can manage to put into them. "Free speech" is just the name we give to verbal behavior that serves the substantive agendas we wish to advance; and we give our preferred verbal behaviors *that* name when we can, when we have the power to do so, because in the rhetoric of American life, the label "free speech" is the one you want your favorites to wear. Free speech, in short, is not an independent value but a political prize, and if that prize has been captured by a politics opposed to yours, it can no longer be invoked in ways that further your purposes, for it is now an obstacle to those purposes. This is some-

thing that the liberal left has yet to understand, and what follows is an attempt to pry its members loose from a vocabulary that may now be a disservice to them.

Not far from the end of his *Areopagitica,* and after having celebrated the virtues of toleration and unregulated publication in passages that find their way into every discussion of free speech and the First Amendment, John Milton catches himself up short and says, of course I didn't mean Catholics, them we exterminate:

> I mean not tolerated popery, and open superstition, which as it extirpates all religious and civil supremacies, so itself should be extirpated . . . that also which is impious or evil absolutely against faith or manners no law can possibly permit that intends not to unlaw itself.

Notice that Milton is not simply stipulating a single exception to a rule generally in place; the kinds of utterance that might be regulated and even prohibited on pain of trial and punishment constitute an open set; popery is named only as a particularly perspicuous instance of the advocacy that cannot be tolerated. No doubt there are other forms of speech and action that might be categorized as "open superstitions" or as subversive of piety, faith, and manners, and presumably these too would be candidates for "extirpation." Nor would Milton think himself culpable for having failed to provide a list of unprotected utterances. The list will fill itself out as utterances are put to the test implied by his formulation: Would this form of speech or advocacy, if permitted to flourish, tend to undermine the very purposes for which our society is constituted? One cannot answer this question with respect to a particular utterance in advance of its emergence on the world's stage; rather, one must wait and ask the question in the full context of its production and (possible) dissemination. It might appear that the result would be *ad hoc* and unprincipled, but for Milton the principle inheres in the core values in whose name individuals of like mind came together in the first place. Those values, which include the search for truth and the promotion of virtue, are capacious enough to accommodate a diversity of views. But at some point—again impossible of advance specification—capaciousness will threaten to become shapelessness, and at that point fidelity to the original values will demand acts of extirpation.

I want to say that all affirmations of freedom of expression are like Milton's, dependent for their force on an exception that literally carves out the space in which expression can then emerge. I do not mean that expression (saying something) is a realm whose integrity is sometimes compromised by certain restrictions but that restriction, in the form of an underlying articulation of the world that necessarily (if silently) negates alternatively possible articulations, is constitutive of expression. Without restriction, without an inbuilt sense of what it would be meaningless to say or wrong to say, there could be no assertion and no reason for asserting it. The exception to unregulated expression is not a negative restriction but a positive hollowing out of value—we are for *this,* which means we are against *that*—in relation to which meaningful assertion can then occur. It is in reference to that value—constituted as all values are by an act of exclusion—that some forms of speech will be heard as (quite literally) intolerable. Speech, in short, is never a value in and of itself but is always produced within the precincts of some assumed conception of the good to which it must yield in the event of conflict. When the pinch comes (and sooner or later it will always come) and the institution (be it church, state, or university) is confronted by behavior subversive of its core rationale, it will respond by declaring "of course we mean not tolerated———, that we extirpate," not because an excep-

tion to a general freedom has suddenly and contradictorily been announced, but because the freedom has never been general and has always been understood against the background of an originary exclusion that gives it meaning.

This is a large thesis, but before tackling it directly I want to buttress my case with another example, taken not from the seventeenth century but from the charter and case law of Canada. Canadian thinking about freedom of expression departs from the line usually taken in the United States in ways that bring that country very close to the *Areopagitica* as I have expounded it. The differences are fully on display in a recent landmark case, *R. v. Keegstra.* James Keegstra was a high school teacher in Alberta who, it was established by evidence, "systematically denigrated Jews and Judaism in his classes." He described Jews as treacherous, subversive, sadistic, money loving, power hungry, and child killers. He declared them "responsible for depressions, anarchy, chaos, wars and revolution" and required his students "to regurgitate these notions in essays and examinations." Keegstra was indicted under Section 319(2) of the Criminal Code and convicted. The Court of Appeal reversed, and the Crown appealed to the Supreme Court, which reinstated the lower court's verdict.

Section 319(2) reads in part, "Every one who, by communicating statements other than in private conversation, willfully promotes hatred against any identifiable group is guilty of . . . an indictable offense and is liable to imprisonment for a term not exceeding two years." In the United States, this provision of the code would almost certainly be struck down because, under the First Amendment, restrictions on speech are apparently prohibited without qualification. To be sure, the Canadian charter has its own version of the First Amendment, in Section 2(b): "Everyone has the following fundamental freedoms . . . (b) freedom of thought, belief, opinion, and expression, including freedom of the press and other media of communication." But Section 2(b), like every other section of the charter, is qualified by Section 1: "The Canadian Charter of Rights and Freedoms guarantees the rights and freedoms set out in it subject only to such reasonable limits prescribed by law as can be demonstrably justified in a free and democratic society." Or in other words, every right and freedom herein granted can be trumped if its exercise is found to be in conflict with the principles that underwrite the society.

This is what happens in *Keegstra* as the majority finds that Section 319(2) of the Criminal Code does in fact violate the right of freedom of expression guaranteed by the charter but is nevertheless a *permissible* restriction because it accords with the principles proclaimed in Section 1. There is, of course, a dissent that reaches the conclusion that would have been reached by most, if not all, U.S. courts; but even in dissent the minority is faithful to Canadian ways of reasoning. "The question," it declares, "is always one of balance," and thus even when a particular infringement of the charter's Section 2(b) has been declared unconstitutional, as it would have been by the minority, the question remains open with respect to the next case. In the United States the question is presumed closed and can only be pried open by special tools. In our legal culture as it is now constituted, if one yells "free speech" in a crowded courtroom and makes it stick, the case is over.

Of course, it is not that simple. Despite the apparent absoluteness of the First Amendment, there are any number of ways of getting around it, ways that are known to every student of the law. In general, the preferred strategy is to manipulate the distinction, essential to First Amendment jurisprudence, between speech and action. The distinction is essential because no one would think to frame a First Amendment that began "Congress shall make no law abridging freedom of action," for that would amount to saying "Congress shall make no law," which would amount to saying "There shall be no law," only actions uninhibited and unregulated. If the First Amendment is to make any sense, have any bite, speech must be declared not to be a species of action, or to be a special form of action lacking the aspects of action that cause it to be the object of regulation. The latter strategy is the favored one and usually involves the separation of speech from consequences. This is what Archibald Cox does when he assigns to the First Amendment the job of protecting "expressions separable from conduct harmful to other individuals and the community." The difficulty of managing this segregation is well known: speech always seems to be crossing the line into action, where it becomes, at least potentially, consequential. In the face of this categorical instability, First Amendment theorists and jurists fashion a distinc-

tion within the speech/action distinction: some forms of speech are not really speech because their purpose is to incite violence or because they are, as the court declares in *Chaplinsky* v. *New Hampshire* (1942), "fighting words," words "likely to provoke the average person to retaliation, and thereby cause a breach of the peace."

The trouble with this definition is that it distinguishes not between fighting words and words that remain safely and merely expressive but between words that are provocative to one group (the group that falls under the rubric "average person") and words that might be provocative to other groups, groups of persons not now considered average. And if you ask what words are likely to be provocative to those nonaverage groups, what are likely to be *their* fighting words, the answer is anything and everything, for as Justice Holmes said long ago (in *Gitlow* v. *New York*), every idea is an incitement to somebody, and since ideas come packaged in sentences, in words, every sentence is potentially, in some situation that might occur tomorrow, a fighting word and therefore a candidate for regulation.

This insight cuts two ways. One could conclude from it that the fighting words exception is a bad idea because there is no way to prevent clever and unscrupulous advocates from shoveling so many forms of speech into the excepted category that the zone of constitutionally protected speech shrinks to nothing and is finally without inhabitants. Or, alternatively, one could conclude that there was never anything in the zone in the first place and that the difficulty of limiting the fighting words exception is merely a particular instance of the general difficulty of separating speech from action. And if one opts for this second conclusion, as I do, then a further conclusion is inescapable: insofar as the point of the First Amendment is to identify speech separable from conduct and from the consequences that come in conduct's wake, there is no such speech and therefore nothing for the First Amendment to protect. Or, to make the point from the other direction, when a court invalidates legislation because it infringes on protected speech, it is not because the speech in question is without consequences but because the consequences have been discounted in relation to a good that is judged to outweigh them. Despite what they say, courts are never in the business of protecting speech per se, "mere" speech (a nonexistent animal); rather, they are in the business of classifying speech (as protected or regulatable) in relation to a value—the health of the republic, the vigor of the economy, the maintenance of the status quo, the undoing of the status quo—that is the true, if unacknowledged, object of their protection.

But if this is the case, a First Amendment purist might reply, why not drop the charade along with the malleable distinctions that make it possible, and declare up front that total freedom of speech is our primary value and trumps anything else, no matter what? The answer is that freedom of expression would only be a primary value if it didn't matter what was said, didn't matter in the sense that no one gave a damn but just liked to hear talk. There are contexts like that, a Hyde Park corner or a call-in talk show where people get to sound off for the sheer fun of it. These, however, are special contexts, artificially bounded spaces designed to assure that talking is not taken seriously. In ordinary contexts, talk is produced with the goal of trying to move the world in one direction rather than another. In these contexts—the contexts of everyday life—you go to the trouble of asserting that X is Y only because you suspect that some people are wrongly asserting that X is Z or that X doesn't exist. You assert, in short, because you give a damn, not about assertion—as if it were a value in and of itself—but about what your assertion is about. It may seem paradoxical, but free expression could only be a primary value if what you are valuing is the right to make noise; but if you are engaged in some purposive activity in the course of which speech happens to be produced, sooner or later you will come to a point when you decide that some forms of speech do not further but endanger that purpose.

Take the case of universities and colleges. Could it be the purpose of such places to encourage free expression? If the answer were "yes," it would be hard to say why there would be any need for classes, or examinations, or departments, or disciplines, or libraries, since freedom of expression requires nothing but a soapbox or an open telephone line. The very fact of the university's machinery—of the events, rituals, and procedures that fill its calendar—argues for some other, more substantive purpose. In relation to that purpose (which will be realized differently in different kinds of institutions), the flourishing of free expression will in almost all circumstances be an obvious good; but in some circumstances, freedom of expression may pose a threat to that purpose, and at that point it may be necessary to discipline or regulate speech, lest, to paraphrase Milton, the institution sacrifice itself to one of its *accidental* features.

Interestingly enough, the same conclusion is reached (inadvertently) by Congressman Henry Hyde, who is addressing these very issues in a recently offered amendment to Title VI of the Civil Rights Act. The first section of the amendment states its purpose, to protect "the free speech rights of college students" by prohibiting private as well as public educational institutions from "subjecting any student to disciplinary sanctions solely on the basis of conduct that is speech." The second section enumerates the remedies available to students whose speech rights may have been abridged; and the third, which is to my mind the nub of the matter, declares as an exception to the amendment's jurisdiction any "educational institution that is controlled by a religious organization," on the reasoning that the application of the amendment to such institutions "would not be consistent with the religious tenets of such organizations." In effect, what Congressman Hyde is saying is that at the heart of these colleges and universities is a set of beliefs, and it would be wrong to require them to tolerate behavior, including speech behavior, inimical to those beliefs. But insofar as this logic is persuasive, it applies across the board, for all educational institutions rest on some set of beliefs—no institution is "just there" independent of any purpose—and it is hard to see why the rights of an institution to protect and preserve its basic "tenets" should be restricted only to those that are religiously controlled. Read strongly, the third section of the amendment undoes sections one and two—the exception becomes, as it always was, the rule—and points us to a balancing test very much like that employed in Canadian law: given that any college or university is informed by a core rationale, an administrator faced with complaints about offensive speech should ask whether damage to the core would be greater if the speech were tolerated or regulated.

The objection to this line of reasoning is well known and has recently been reformulated by Benno Schmidt, former president of Yale University. According to Schmidt, speech codes on campuses constitute "well-intentioned but misguided efforts to give values of community and harmony a higher place than freedom" (*Wall Street Journal,* May 6, 1991). "When the goals of harmony collide with freedom of expression," he continues, "freedom must be the paramount obligation of an academic community." The flaw in this logic is on display in the phrase "academic community," for the phrase recognizes what Schmidt would deny, that expression only occurs in communities—if not in an academic community, then in a shopping mall community or a dinner party community or an airplane ride community or an office community. In these communities and in any others that could be imagined (with the possible exception of a community of major league baseball fans), limitations on speech in relation to a defining and deeply assumed purpose are inseparable from community membership.

Indeed, "limitations" is the wrong word because it suggests that expression, as an activity and a value, has a pure form that is always in danger of being compromised by the urgings of special interest communities; but independently of a community context informed by interest (that is, purpose), expression would be at once inconceivable and unintelligible. Rather than being a value that is threatened by limitations and constraints, expression, in any form worth worrying about, is a *product* of limitations and constraints, of the already-in-place presuppositions that give assertions their very particular point. Indeed, the very act of thinking of something to say (whether or not it is subsequently regulated) is already constrained—rendered impure, and because impure, communicable—by the background context within which the thought takes its shape. (The analysis holds too for "freedom," which in Schmidt's vision is an entirely empty concept referring to an urge without direction. But like expression, freedom is a coherent notion only in relation to a goal or good that limits and, by limiting, shapes its exercise.)

Arguments like Schmidt's only get their purchase by first imagining speech as occurring in no context whatsoever, and then stripping particular speech acts of the properties conferred on them by contexts. The trick is nicely illustrated when Schmidt urges protection for speech "no matter how obnoxious in content." "Obnoxious" at once acknowledges the reality of speech-related harms and trivializes them by suggesting that they are *surface* injuries that any large-minded ("liberated and humane") person should be able to bear. The possibility that speech-related in-

juries may be grievous and *deeply* wounding is carefully kept out of sight, and because it is kept out of sight, the fiction of a world of weightless verbal exchange can be maintained, at least within the confines of Schmidt's carefully denatured discourse.

To this Schmidt would no doubt reply, as he does in his essay, that harmful speech should be answered not by regulation but by more speech; but that would make sense only if the effects of speech could be canceled out by additional speech, only if the pain and humiliation caused by racial or religious epithets could be ameliorated by saying something like "So's your old man." What Schmidt fails to realize at every level of his argument is that expression is more than a matter of proffering and receiving propositions, that words do work in the world of a kind that cannot be confined to a purely cognitive realm of "mere" ideas.

It could be said, however, that I myself mistake the nature of the work done by freely tolerated speech because I am too focused on short-run outcomes and fail to understand that the good effects of speech will be realized, not in the present, but in a future whose emergence regulation could only inhibit. This line of reasoning would also weaken one of my key points, that speech in and of itself cannot be a value and is only worth worrying about if it is in the service of something with which it cannot be identical. My mistake, one could argue, is to equate the something in whose service speech is with some locally espoused value (e.g., the end of racism, the empowerment of disadvantaged minorities), whereas in fact we should think of that something as a now-inchoate shape that will be given firm lines only by time's pencil. That is why the shape now receives such indeterminate characterizations (e.g., true self-fulfillment, a more perfect polity, a more capable citizenry, a less partial truth); we cannot now know it, and therefore we must not prematurely fix it in ways that will bind successive generations to error.

This forward-looking view of what the First Amendment protects has a great appeal, in part because it continues in a secular form the Puritan celebration of millenarian hopes, but it imposes a requirement so severe that one would expect more justification for it than is usually provided. The requirement is that we endure whatever pain racist and hate speech inflicts for the sake of a future whose emergence we can only take on faith. In a specifically religious vision like Milton's, this makes perfect sense (it is indeed the whole of Christianity), but in the context of a politics that puts its trust in the world and not in the Holy Spirit, it raises more questions than it answers and could be seen as the second of two strategies designed to delegitimize the complaints of victimized groups. The first strategy, as I have noted, is to define speech in such a way as to render it inconsequential (on the model of "sticks and stones will break my bones, but . . ."); the second strategy is to acknowledge the (often grievous) consequences of speech but declare that we must suffer them in the name of something that cannot be named. The two strategies are denials from slightly different directions of the *present* effects of racist speech; one confines those effects to a closed and safe realm of pure mental activity; the other imagines the effects of speech spilling over into the world but only in an ever-receding future for whose sake we must forever defer taking action.

I find both strategies unpersuasive, but my own skepticism concerning them is less important than the fact that in general they seem to have worked; in the parlance of the marketplace (a parlance First Amendment commentators love), many in the society seemed to have bought them. Why? The answer, I think, is that people cling to First Amendment pieties because they do not wish to face what they correctly take to be the alternative. That alternative is *politics,* the realization (at which I have already hinted) that decisions about what is and is not protected in the realm of expression will rest not on principle or firm doctrine but on the ability of some persons to interpret—recharacterize or rewrite— principle and doctrine in ways that lead to the protection of speech they want heard and the regulation of speech they want silenced. (That is how George Bush can argue *for* flag-burning statutes and *against* campus hate-speech codes.) When the First Amendment is successfully invoked, the result is not a victory for free speech in the face of a challenge from politics but a *political victory* won by the party that has managed to wrap its agenda in the mantle of free speech.

It is from just such a conclusion—a conclusion that would put politics *inside* the First Amendment—that commentators recoil, saying things like "This could render the First Amendment a dead let-

ter," or "This would leave us with no normative guidance in determining when and what speech to protect," or "This effaces the distinction between speech and action," or "This is incompatible with any viable notion of freedom of expression." To these statements (culled more or less at random from recent law review pieces) I would reply that the First Amendment has always been a dead letter if one understood its "liveness" to depend on the identification and protection of a realm of "mere" expression distinct from the realm of regulatable conduct; the distinction between speech and action has always been effaced in principle, although in practice it can take whatever form the prevailing political conditions mandate; we have never had any normative guidance for marking off protected from unprotected speech; rather, the guidance we have has been fashioned (and refashioned) in the very political struggles over which it then (for a time) presides. In short, the name of the game has always been politics, even when (indeed, especially when) it is played by stigmatizing politics as the area to be avoided.

In saying this, I would not be heard as arguing either for or against regulation and speech codes as a matter of general principle. Instead my argument turns away from general principle to the pragmatic (anti)principle of considering each situation as it emerges. The question of whether or not to regulate will always be a local one, and we cannot rely on abstractions that are either empty of content or filled with the content of some partisan agenda to generate a "principled" answer. Instead we must consider in every case what is at stake and what are the risks and gains of alternative courses of action. In the course of this consideration many things will be of help, but among them will not be phrases like "freedom of speech" or "the right of individual expression," because, as they are used now, these phrases tend to obscure rather than clarify our dilemmas. Once they are deprived of their talismanic force, once it is no longer strategically effective simply to invoke them in the act of walking away from a problem, the conversation could continue in directions that are now blocked by a First Amendment absolutism that has only been honored in the breach anyway. To the student reporter who complains that in the wake of the promulgation of a speech code at the University of Wisconsin there is now something in the back of his mind as he writes, one could reply, "There was always something in the back of your mind, and perhaps it might be better to have this code in the back of your mind than whatever was in there before." And when someone warns about the slippery slope and predicts mournfully that if you restrict one form of speech, you never know what will be restricted next, one could reply, "Some form of speech is always being restricted, else there could be no meaningful assertion; we have always and already slid down the slippery slope; someone is always going to be restricted next, and it is your job to make sure that the someone is not you." And when someone observes, as someone surely will, that antiharassment codes chill speech, one could reply that since speech only becomes intelligible against the background of what isn't being said, the background of what has already been silenced, the only question is the political one of which speech is going to be chilled, and, all things considered, it seems a good thing to chill speech like "nigger," "cunt," "kike," and "faggot." And if someone then says, "But what happened to free-speech principles?" one could say what I have now said a dozen times, free-speech principles don't exist except as a component in a bad argument in which such principles are invoked to mask motives that would not withstand close scrutiny. . . .

Let me be clear. I am not saying that First Amendment principles are inherently bad (they are *inherently* nothing), only that they are not always the appropriate reference point for situations involving the production of speech, and that even when they are the appropriate reference point, they do not constitute a politics-free perspective because the shape in which they are invoked will always be political, will always, that is, be the result of having drawn the relevant line (between speech and action, or between high-value speech and low-value speech, or between words essential to the expression of ideas and fighting words) in a way that is favorable to some interests and indifferent or hostile to others. This having been said, the moral is not that First Amendment talk should be abandoned, for even if the standard First Amendment formulas do not and could not perform the function expected of them (the elimination of political considerations in decisions about speech), they still serve a function that is not at all negligible: they slow down outcomes in an area in which the fear of overhasty outcomes is justified by a long record of abuses of power. It is often said that history shows (itself a formula) that even a minimal restriction on the right of expression too easily leads to ever-larger restrictions; and to the extent that this is an empirical fact (and it is a question one could debate), there is some comfort and protection to be found in a procedure that requires you to jump through hoops—do a lot of argumentative work—before a speech regulation will be allowed to stand.

I would not be misunderstood as offering the notion of "jumping through hoops" as a new version of the First Amendment claim to neutrality. A hoop must have a shape—in this case the shape of whatever binary distinction is representing First Amendment "interests"—and the shape of the hoop one is asked to jump through will in part determine what kinds of jumps can be regularly made. Even if they are only mechanisms for slowing down outcomes, First Amendment formulas by virtue of their substantive content (and it is impossible that they be without content) will slow down some outcomes more easily than others, and that means that the form they happen to have at the present moment will favor some interests more than others. Therefore, even with a reduced sense of the effectivity of First Amendment rhetoric (it can not assure any particular result), the counsel with which I began remains relevant: so long as so-called free-speech principles have been fashioned by your enemy (so long as it is *his* hoops you have to jump through), contest their relevance to the issue at hand; but if you manage to refashion them in line with your purposes, urge them with a vengeance.

It is a counsel that follows from the thesis that there is no such thing as free speech, which is not, after all, a thesis as startling or corrosive as may first have seemed. It merely says that there is no class of utterances separable from the world of conduct and that therefore the identification of some utterances as members of that nonexistent class will always be evidence that a political line has been drawn rather than a line that denies politics entry into the forum of public discourse. It is the job of the First Amendment to mark out an area in which competing views can be considered without state interference; but if the very marking out of that area is itself an interference (as it always will be), First Amendment jurisprudence is inevitably self-defeating and subversive of its own aspirations. That's the bad news. The good news is that precisely *because* speech is never "free" in the two senses required—free of consequences and free from state pressure—speech always matters, is always doing work; because everything we say impinges on the world in ways indistinguishable from the effects of physical action, we must take responsibility for our verbal performances—*all* of them—and not assume that they are being taken care of by a clause in the Constitution. Of course, with responsibility comes risks, but they have always been our risks, and no doctrine of free speech has ever insulated us from them. They are the risks, respectively, of permitting speech that does obvious harm and of shutting off speech in ways that might deny us the benefit of Joyce's *Ulysses* or Lawrence's *Lady Chatterly's Lover* or Titian's paintings. Nothing, I repeat, can insulate us from those risks. (If there is no normative guidance in determining when and what speech to protect, there is no normative guidance in determining what is art—like free speech a

category that includes everything and nothing—and what is obscenity.) Moreover, nothing can provide us with a principle for deciding which risk in the long run is the best to take. I am persuaded that at the present moment, right now, the risk of not attending to hate speech is greater than the risk that by regulating it we will deprive ourselves of valuable voices and insights or slide down the slippery slope toward tyranny. This is a judgment for which I can offer reasons but no guarantees. All I am saying is that the judgments of those who would come down on the other side carry no guarantees either. They urge us to put our faith in apolitical abstractions, but the abstractions they invoke—the marketplace of ideas, speech alone, speech itself—only come in political guises, and therefore in trusting to them we fall (unwittingly) under the sway of the very forces we wish to keep at bay. It is not that there are no choices to make or means of making them; it is just that the choices as well as the means are inextricable from the din and confusion of partisan struggle. There is no safe place.

QUESTIONS FOR REFLECTION

1. Why, according to Fish, does freedom of speech always have exceptions?

2. Fish rejects the distinction between speech and action. Why? Do you agree?

3. How does Fish defend campus speech codes?

4. What does Fish mean when he says, "There's no such thing as free speech"? Why does he think "it's a good thing, too"?

JONATHAN RAUCH

Kindly Inquisitors:
The New Attacks on Free Thought

Jonathan Rauch is a Fellow of the Cato Institute. (Source: From Kindly Inquisitors: The New Attacks on Free Thought. *Chicago: University of Chicago Press, 1993. Notes have been omitted. Copyright © 1993 by Jonathan Rauch. Reprinted by permission.)*

As knowledge-making regimes go, nothing is as successful or as respectful of diversity or as humane as liberal science. The trouble is that liberal science often does not look very humane. It uses sticks as well as carrots. The carrots are the respectability, frequent use, and public credit that it bestows on the opinions that it validates; the sticks are the disrespect and the silent treatment that it inflicts on the opinions that fail. Those sticks are nonviolent, true. But it is unconscionable not to admit that denying respectability is a very serious matter indeed. It causes pain and outrage. . . . Here is where the door opens to the most formidable attack on the liberal science—the humanitarian attack.

"Well," goes the argument, "we must, it appears, have intellectual standards. But what should our standards be? Obviously it is desirable to have standards that minimize pain. And a lot of beliefs cause pain (that is, they hurt people's feelings). Racist beliefs cause pain. Anti-Semitic and sexist and homophobic beliefs cause pain. So do anti-American and anti-religious beliefs. So do beliefs which proclaim one ethnic group or culture to be better than another, or different from others in some way which carries social disapproval. If we're going to have a social system for weeding out beliefs, it should start by weeding out beliefs which cause pain. Thus it should weed out racist and anti-Semitic and ethnocentric and sexist beliefs. The first criterion for sorting wor-

thy from unworthy beliefs should be: Cause no pain, and allow none to be caused—especially not to the politically vulnerable. Intellectuals should be like doctors. They should first do no harm."

The empathetic spirit from which that line of thinking springs is admirable. But the principle to which it leads is nothing but dreadful. The right principle, and the only one consonant with liberal science, is, Cause no pain solely in order to hurt. The wrong principle, but the one that has increasingly taken the place of the right one, is, Allow no pain to be caused.

The social system does not and never can exist which allows no harm to come to anybody. Conflict of impulse and desire is an inescapable fact of human existence, and where there is conflict there will always be losers and wounds. Utopian systems premised on a world of loving harmony—communism, for instance—fail because in the attempt to obliterate conflict they obliterate freedom. The chore of a social regime is not to obliterate conflict but to manage it, so as to put it to good use while causing a minimum of hurt and abuse. Liberal systems, although far from perfect, have at least two great advantages: they can channel conflict rather than obliterate it, and they give a certain degree of protection from centrally administered abuse. The liberal intellectual system is no exception. It causes pain to people whose views are criticized, still more to those whose views fail to check out and so are rejected. But there are two important consolations. First, no one gets to run the system to his own advantage or stay in charge for long. Whatever you can do to me, I can do to you. Those who are criticized may give as good as they get. Second, the books are never closed, and the game is never over. Sometimes rejected ideas (continental drift, for one) make sensational comebacks.

Humanitarians, though, remain unsatisfied. Their hope, which is no less appealing for being futile, is that somehow the harm can be prevented in the first place. Their worry is that the harm may emanate in two directions, one social and the other individual.

Social harm accrues to society as a whole from the spread of bad ideas; held to be especially vulnerable are minorities or groups seen as lacking power. "AIDS comes from homosexuals," "Jews fabricated the Holocaust," "Blacks are less intelligent than whites"—those ideas and others like them can do real mischief.

Though the special concern for minorities as groups is a new twist, this argument is an old and highly principled one. It was used, in all good conscience, by the Inquisition. The heretic, in those days, endangered the peace and stability of the whole society by challenging the rightful authority of the Church. The Inquisition was a policing action. But by its own lights it was a humanitarian action, too. The heretic endangered the faith of believers, and so threatened to drag others with him to an eternity of suffering in perdition; not least of all, he threw away his own soul. To allow such a person to destroy souls seemed at least as indecent as allowing racist hate speech seems today. "It is an error to think of the persecution of heretics as being forced by the Church upon unwilling or indifferent laity. The heretic was an unpopular person in the Middle Ages. There are, in fact, instances in the late eleventh century and early twelfth century of heretics being lynched by an infuriated mob, who regarded the clergy as too lenient." If you cared about the good of society and about the souls of your neighbors and friends, then you believed that the Inquisition's mission was at bottom humane, even if the inquisitorial methods sometimes were not.

Humane motives, however, could not save the Inquisition from the same problem that faces humani-

tarians today: although allowing mistakes is risky, suppressing them is much riskier, because then a "mistake" becomes whatever it is that the authorities don't like to hear. Suppressing offensiveness, too, comes at a high cost, since offensiveness is not the same thing as wrongness—often just the contrary. Sometimes patently "offensive" verbiage turns out to be telling the unpopular truth. As I am hardly the first to point out, practically all knowledge of any importance began as a statement which offended someone. "All the durable truths that have come into the world within historic times," said Mencken, "have been opposed as bitterly as if they were so many waves of smallpox." Many people were appalled by the notion that the earth was not at the center of the universe (to say so was hate speech—hateful of God), many other people by the proposition that man was created last rather than first, and still others by the exploding of the common "knowledge" that white people were inherently more intelligent than people of all other races.

Will someone's belief, if accepted, destroy society? Maybe. But more likely not. "Throughout history, scientists have been urged to suppress their views about nature for the sake of the public welfare," wrote David Hull. That the solar system is heliocentric, that species evolve, that genes influence mental traits—at one time or another people feared that those ideas and many others would destroy society if they became widely accepted. "Thus far, however, those who have urged the suppression of new views for the 'good of the people' have underestimated the ability of both societies and individual people to survive successive challenges to their conceptions of the world and how it works." So often have those who warned us about "dangerous" ideas been wrong, and so often have they abused whatever restraining power they possessed, that I have no hesitation in saying: it is better in every case to let critical public inquiry run its course than to try to protect society from it. If we have anything to learn from the progress of knowledge in the last few centuries, it is that to Peirce's injunction, "Do not block the way of inquiry," must be added, "And by no means should inquiry be blocked to 'save' society."

The other, and much newer, strand of intellectual humanitarianism is intuitively more appealing and emotionally harder to resist. It says that wrong-headed opinions and harsh words are hurtful, if not necessarily to society as a whole, then to *individuals*. And here liberal science has been put squarely on the defensive, for the first time in more than a hundred years; for here you have, not the cold-blooded public censor raising bureaucratic objections on behalf of "society," but an identifiable person saying "*I am hurt*" and speaking for his own dignity. In today's world the second kind of claim, like all human-rights claims, seems compelling. Facing it means owning up to the truth about knowledge and about the system which best produces it.

So let us be frank, once and for all: creating knowledge is painful, for the same reason that it can also be exhilarating. Knowledge does not come free to any of us; we have to suffer for it. We have to stand naked before the court of critical checkers and watch our most cherished beliefs come under fire. Sometimes we have to watch while our notion of evident truth gets tossed in the gutter. Sometimes we feel we are treated rudely, even viciously. As others prod and test and criticize our ideas, we feel angry, hurt, embarrassed.

We would all like to think that knowledge could be separated from hurt. We would all like to think that painful but useful and thus "legitimate" criticism is objectively distinguishable from criticism which is merely ugly and hurtful. Surely criticism is one thing, and "Hitler should have finished the job" is another. But what we would like to think is not so: the only such distinction is in the eye of the beholder. The fact is that even the most "scientific" criticism can be horribly hurtful, devastatingly so. The physicist Ludwig Boltzmann was so depressed by the harshness of F. W. Ostwald's and Ernst Mach's attacks on his ideas that he committed suicide. "And Georg Cantor, the originator of the modern theory of sets of points and of the orders of infinity, lost his mind because of the hatred and animosity against him and his ideas by his teacher Leopold Kronecker: he was confined to a mental hospital for many years at the end of his life." The medical researcher Robert Gallo wrote vividly about the pain and shock of what he believed to be viciously harsh criticism.

What surprised me were not the findings—as I say, I was already developing my own doubts—but the vehemence with which they were delivered. More than one speaker used our misfortune to ridicule the very idea of a human retrovirus. . . . Even now I have difficulty thinking back to that day. I would be subjected to far more extensive, personal, and even vicious attacks years later when I entered AIDS research. . . . But nothing compared with the feelings that passed over me as I sat that day in Hershey, Pennsylvania, hearing not just HL-23 but much of my life's work—the search for tumor-causing RNA viruses in humans—systematically and disdainfully dismissed. . . . I was too old to cry, but it hurt too much to laugh.

I am certainly not saying that we should all go out and be offensive or inflammatory just for the sake of it. Please don't paint swastikas on the synagogue and say I gave my blessing. I am against offending people for fun. But I am also only too well aware that in the pursuit of knowledge many people—probably most of us at one time or another—will be hurt, and that this is a reality which no amount of wishing or regulating can ever change. It is not good to offend people, but it is necessary. A no-offense society is a no-knowledge society. . . .

A liberal society stands on the proposition that we should all take seriously the idea that we might be wrong. That means we must place no one, including ourselves, beyond the reach of criticism (no final say); it means that we must allow people to err, even where the error offends and upsets, as it often will. But we also are not supposed to claim we have knowledge except where belief is checked by no one in particular (no personal authority).

In other words, liberal science is built on two pillars. One is the right to offend in pursuit of truth. The other is the responsibility to check and be checked. Here, and here alone, is the social morality which finds error as fast as possible while keeping hurt to a minimum: intellectual license checked by intellectual discipline. . . .

And what should we require be done to assuage the feelings of people who have been offended, to recompense them for their hurt and punish their tormentors? This and only this: *absolutely nothing.* Nothing at all.

The standard answer to people who say they are offended should be: "Is there any casualty other than your feelings? Are you or others being threatened with violence or vandalism? No? Then it's a shame your feelings are hurt, but that's too bad. You'll live." If one is going to enjoy the benefits of living in a liberal society without being shamelessly hypocritical, one must try to be thick-skinned, since the way we make knowledge is by rubbing against one another. In a liberal culture, this is a matter of positive moral obligation. In practical terms, it means that people who get righteously offended twice every day before breakfast should learn to count to a hundred—granted, that takes discipline—and say to themselves, "Well, it's just that fellow's opinion," before they charge out the door crying for justice. (A sense of humor would help.) And it means that people receiving the complaints of the offended should count to a thousand before rushing out to do something about them. The alternative is to reward people for being upset. And as soon as people learn they can get something if they raise Cain about being offended, they go into the business of professional offendedness. Some people believe that the Russians are reading their minds with microwaves; other people fret about French classes that might inadvertently upset balding men. In a liberal society, the initial presumption ought to be that neither kind of concern deserves any better than to be politely ignored.

If that sounds callous, remember that the establishment of a right not to be offended would lead not to a more civil culture but to a lot of shouting matches over who was being offensive to whom, and who could claim to be more offended. All we will do that way is to shut ourselves up. The doctrine of Never Offend is the biggest reason so many Western intellectuals had so little to say when Khomeini went after Rushdie. The fundamentalists offended us, but one of our writers offended them first, so who's to blame? "We understand that the book itself has been found deeply offensive by people of the Muslim faith. It is a book that is offensive in many other ways as well. We can understand why it could be criticized," and so on.

In one sense the rise of intellectual humanitarianism represents an advance of honesty: it drops the pretense that liberal science is a painless and purely mechanistic process, like doing crossword puzzles. But the conclusion which the humanitarians draw—that the hurting must be stopped—is all wrong. Impelling them toward their wrong conclusion is a dreadful error: the notion that hurtful words are a form of violence. Offensive speech hurts, say the humanitarians; it constitutes "words that wound" (writes one law professor); it does "real harm to real people" who deserve protection and redress (writes another law professor). When a law student at Georgetown University published an article charging that the academic credentials of white and black students accepted at Georgetown were "dramatically unequal," a number of students demanded that the writer be punished. And note carefully the terms of the condemnation: "I think the article is assaultive. People were injured. I think that kind of speech is outrageous." The notion of "assaultive speech" is no rarity today. Stanley Fish, a professor at Duke University, has said that "the speech that is being assaulted [on college campuses] is itself assaultive speech."

A University of Michigan law professor said: "To me, racial epithets are not speech. They are bullets." This, finally, is where the humanitarian line leads: to the erasure of the distinction, in principle and ultimately also in practice, between discussion and bloodshed. My own view is that words are words and bullets are bullets, and that it is important to keep this straight. For you do not have to be Kant to see what comes after "offensive words are bullets": if you hurt me with words, I reply with bullets, and the exchange is even. Rushdie hurt fundamentalist Muslims with words; his book was every bit as offensive to them as any epithet or slogan you can imagine. So they set out to hurt him back. Words are bullets; fair is fair.

If you are inclined to equate verbal offense with physical violence, think again about the logic of your position. If hurtful opinions are violence, then painful criticism is violence. In other words, on the humanitarian premise, *science itself is a form of violence.* What do you do about violence? You establish policing authorities—public or private—to stop it and to punish the perpetrators. You set up authorities empowered to weed out hurtful ideas and speech. In other words: an inquisition. . . .

And how are restraints on offensive opinion justified? With arguments that are appealing on the surface but alarming down below. Trace their logic and you find that they all lead back to the same conclusion: freewheeling criticism (thus liberal science) is dangerous or hurtful and must be regulated by right-thinking people.

"Why tolerate bigotry?" A classic argument, framed today in terms like this: "Prohibiting racially and religiously bigoted speech is praiseworthy because it seeks to elevate, not to degrade, because it draws from human experience, not from woolly dogmas or academic slogans, because it salutes reason as the backbone of freedom and tolerance."

That kind of rhetoric, besides being almost completely empty of meaning, glides right around the important question: just who is supposed to decide what speech is "bigoted" and what speech is merely "critical"? What about the student at Michigan who was summoned to a disciplinary hearing for saying that homosexuality is a disease treatable with therapy? Why is that a "bigoted" suggestion rather than an unpopular opinion? What's the difference? And who is to say? . . .

The anti-bigotry people never approach the question directly, because doing so would show them up. The answer is: *we,* the right-thinking, are the ones who will say who is and isn't bigoted.

Whenever anyone says that bigoted or offensive or victimizing or oppressing or vicious opinions should be suppressed, all he is really saying is, "Opinions which *I* hate should be suppressed." In other words, he is doing the same thing Plato did when he claimed that the philosopher (i.e., himself) should rule for the good of society: he is making a power grab. He wants to be the pope, the ayatollah, the philosopher-king.

The answer to the question "Why tolerate hateful or misguided opinions?" has been the same ever since Plato unveiled his ghastly utopia: because the alternative is worse.

"We don't want to block criticism and inquiry, just hate and intimidation." The trouble is the same: one person's hate speech is another person's sincerest criticism ("The Holocaust is an Israeli fabrication"). So who is to draw the line? Let's make up some examples. It is hard to see any redeeming social value in someone's saying "Niggers are stupid." But what about "On average, blacks are less intelligent than whites"? Should people who say that be punished? Then what about "Blacks display less aptitude for math, on average, than Asians"? If you clamp down on the first of those opinions, what do you do when

someone complains about the next, and the next? Who will draw the fine distinctions? . . .

Suppose, for argument's sake, that someone managed to discover a distinction separating hate talk from criticism as definitively as zero separates negative numbers from positive ones. Even that would be no guarantee of anything. The distinction might (or might not) satisfy philosophers, but in the political world ambitious activists would have every reason to smudge the line, stretch it, blur it, erase it, move it, or cross over it outright. And if they had support in the voting booths or in the student senate or in the streets, they would succeed. In politics the only distinction, finally, is between what you can get away with and what you can't. . . .

The unhappy reality is that some people are always going to say gross and vicious things to hurt other people. If they don't destroy property or do violence, ignore them or criticize them. But do not set up an authority to punish them. Any guidelines elaborate enough to distinguish vicious opinions from unpopular ones will be too elaborate to work. In practice, the distinction will be between the opinions which the political authorities find congenial and those which they find inconvenient.

"In practice, we can distinguish verbal harassment from legitimate criticism by the hurtful intent of the speaker." No. In the first place, even the most "legitimate" criticism may be intended to hurt or discredit its target, as Robert Gallo, among many other scientists, knows well. In the second place, and more important: authorities that seek to punish the "intent" of criticism are even more dangerous than ones that seek to punish criticism itself. To establish the intent of words you must put the speaker's mind on trial. When the Michigan student said that homosexuality was a curable disease, did he intend to upset gay students, or not? That is the Inquisition indeed. . . .

"Real people are being hurt, and so protective action is morally imperative." That people's *feelings* are hurt is undeniable. But one of the glaring failings of the never-offend movement—the same failing that the anti-pornography movement always has to finesse—is its absolute inability to show any concrete, objective damage which offensive speech and opinions have actually done beyond damage to feelings. Nor have they been able to define how seriously one's feelings must be hurt to qualify one as verbally

"wounded," or how to tell whether the victim of wounding words is really as badly hurt as he claims to be. How do you distinguish words that wound from words that annoy? . . .

When pressed on this, humanitarians retreat to rhetoric about the way bigoted or vicious ideas are deeply repugnant, damage people's self-esteem, are a form of oppression, and the like. They argue that even to speak of hurtful words as "obnoxious" or "offensive" is to slight the words' damage. "'Obnoxious' suggests that the injury or offense is a surface one that a large-minded ('liberated and humane') person should be able to tolerate if not embrace," writes Stanley Fish. "The idea that the effects of speech can penetrate to the core—either for good or for ill—is never entertained; everything is kept on the level of weightless verbal exchange; there is no sense of the lacerating harms that speech of certain kinds can inflict." Note the retreat to the violence metaphor ("lacerating"). Note also the circularity: true, words "of certain kinds" *can* "penetrate to the core," but the whole question is *which* kinds and *which* words, and how do you tell, and how deep into the core is too deep? If we had an offendedness meter, then we might be able to solve that problem; as it is, the complaint that "real people are being hurt" does not begin to tell us who is being hurt, when, how badly, or how much is too much. Even if such a meter did exist, we would still have a problem: what about *true* words that "penetrate to the core"? What about useful but harsh criticisms that "penetrate to the core"? Suppose a creationist collapses in tears and drops out of college after a biology teacher declares that Darwin was right? Is that a "laceration"? Should it be stopped?

By and large, the humanitarians never even reach those questions, much less answer them. Beyond the rhetoric, all they are saying is this: "These ideas or words are very upsetting to me and to some others." Yes, they are upsetting. But if everyone has a right not to be upset, then all criticism, and therefore all scientific inquiry, is at best morally hazardous and at worst impossible. Even joking becomes impossible.

Faced with this problem, very often the humanitarians retreat to the position that *some* people—historically oppressed groups—have a special right not to be upset. That answer is no better. In the first place, it throws liberal science out the window, because it junks the empirical rule that anyone is allowed to criticize anyone, regardless of race or ethnic history or whatever. The fact that you're oppressed doesn't make you right. In the second place, who is going to decide who is allowed to upset whom? The only possible answer: a centralized political authority.

"It is hardly reasonable to justify here-and-now pain in the name of abstract principles or of knowledge which may or may not ever be produced." This is another humanitarian standby: hurting people in the name of abstract or future "freedom" or "knowledge" is like torturing people in the name of "God's word" or "your future salvation." "The requirement is that we endure whatever pain racist and hate speech inflicts for the sake of a future whose emergence we can only take on faith," writes Fish. "In a specifically religious vision like Milton's this makes perfect sense (it is indeed the whole of Christianity), but in the context of a politics that puts trust in the world and not in the Holy Spirit, it raises more questions than it answers and could be seen as the other prong of a strategy designed to de-legitimize the complaints of victimized groups." In effect, abstract principles are all too often smoke screens for attacks on minorities.

Maybe they are; but we are not, in fact, talking about abstract principles or vague future gains. The trouble with the argument that real pain outweighs airy abstractions is that it leaves out one whole side of the equation: the pain is very real and very concrete for the "offensive" speaker who is sentenced by political authorities to prison, privation, or, as in Salman Rushdie's case, death. The whole point of liberal science is that it *substitutes* criticism for force and violence. That is to say, it substitutes the power of critics to select worthy ideas verbally for the power of political authorities to select "worthy" ideas forcibly. The false choice presented by humanitarians is between wounding people with words and not wounding people with words. The real choice is between hurtful words and billy clubs, jail cells, or worse. If you think that the right to offend is a mere "abstraction," ask Rushdie.

"We're making the intellectual climate more free, not less free." The conventional wisdom now in many American universities seems to be that you can't have free thought or free speech where people, especially members of minority groups, feel intimidated, harassed, upset. Thus, if you get rid of talk which upsets or intimidates, you add to intellectual freedom. . . .

Leave aside, for now, the question of whether you actually can get rid of "intimidating" speech by slapping controls on it. Look instead at the premise of the argument: that you can only do science where people feel good about each other, where they feel secure and unharassed—in other words, where they are exempt from upsetting criticism. Of course, that is dead wrong. A lot of researchers and theorists hate each other. The history of science is full of bitter criticism and hard feelings; there is simply no way around it. If you insist on an unhostile or nonoffensive environment, then you belong in a monastery, not a university. . . .

QUESTIONS FOR REFLECTION

1. What are the basic features of liberal science, according to Rauch?

2. What is the fundamental argument for restrictions on speech? How does Rauch reply?

3. Which of the arguments outlined by Rauch do you find most persuasive? Evaluate his response to it.

PART III

RIGHTS
AND RESPONSIBILITIES

We find it hard to talk for very long about ethics or politics without talking about rights. But talk of rights is young by philosophical standards. Rights first made their appearance in Western moral discourse about 340 years ago, in the writings of Thomas Hobbes. Hobbes and many later writers present rights in the context of a general theory of government. To understand their conceptions of rights, therefore, we must consider their overall political theories.

Hobbes revives an ancient idea: that a government is legitimate if people, given a choice, would voluntarily opt to be subject to its dominion. Facing this choice requires us to consider what life would be like without government, in what Hobbes calls the state of nature. Hobbes provides a brief but stunning glimpse of the state of nature where, in his view, life would be "solitary, poor, nasty, brutish, and short." Even the strongest and smartest would be vulnerable to the tricks and physical force of groups of others. No one would be safe; people would routinely fight each other to survive. To gain security, therefore, people would choose to form a government. They would be willing to sacrifice much of their freedom to gain relief from the brutality of the state of nature. The resulting compact among competing individuals underlies the legitimacy of government. Hobbes's account is thus a version of *social contract theory*.

Rights emerge at two levels of Hobbes's theory. First, people have some rights even in the state of

nature. There are *natural* rights that do not depend on government. Second, people have rights bestowed by government, which they acquire through the social contract. These are *social,* or *civil,* rights. These kinds of rights rest on different foundations. Hobbes believes that natural rights must underlie civil rights, for civil rights are founded on a contract. That contract can bind the contracting parties only if they already recognize an obligation to keep promises and, correlatively, a right to have promises kept. This kind of right and obligation must be prior to civil rights, depending not on a social contract but on the nature of human beings.

In any version of social contract theory, we can ask two questions that determine much about the theory of government that results: (1) What do the parties hope to gain by entering into the social contract? (2) What are they willing to give up to achieve it? In Hobbes's theory, the parties hope to gain security, which, for them, is a matter of life and death. They are willing to give up much for the protection of government. As a result, in Hobbes's theory, there are few limitations on the government, which Hobbes calls by the name of a monster, *Leviathan.* People are willing to sacrifice even their natural rights in order to survive.

John Locke presents a very different social contract theory. He, too, considers government legitimate only if it would be chosen over the state of nature. But Locke's state of nature is far tamer than Hobbes's. Precisely because everyone is vulnerable to everyone else's revenge, few would commit crimes, and those few would meet severe punishment. In the state of nature, we would have natural rights of life, liberty, and property, which would give us the right to punish anyone who violated those rights. The chief danger Locke sees in this condition is that punishment, often at the hands of the people wronged or those closely associated with them, would tend to be harsh, indiscriminate, and unfair. Consequently, people would feel the need for an impartial judge who could enforce the law of nature. People would therefore contract to form a government to serve as impartial arbitrator of their disputes. What do they hope to gain? Impartiality. This is important, but not a matter of life and death, as in Hobbes, except in extreme cases. What, therefore, are people willing to give up? A limited amount, according to Locke. They would give up their right to enforce the laws of nature by themselves. But they would retain their natural rights to life, liberty, and property, as long as they did not violate the rights of others. And they would gain civil rights to impartial treatment as well. Stemming from Locke's conception of the social contract is a limited view of government, which has little role other than enforcement and arbitration.

Jean-Jacques Rousseau provides a third version of contract theory, in which people are willing to give up everything in order to regain everything. Rousseau sees the state of nature as inconvenient and difficult; people would band together, entering the social contract to overcome these difficulties through cooperation. Because cooperation is their major motivation, they would be willing to surrender everything they have to the community to help others and also would expect the entire community to help them. For Rousseau, there are no natural rights; all rights—and all questions—arise from the social contract. All rights, for him, are civil rights. Government, according to Rousseau, has only one constraint: that it act in accord with the general will, that is, for the best of the whole community.

Rights are fundamental to our modern conception of ethics and political philosophy. But they give rise to a serious problem. Rights frequently seem to come into conflict. Abortion, capital punishment, and many other public problems can be seen as involving conflicts of rights. How are such conflicts to be resolved? Social contract theory in itself provides little help.

Some philosophers have maintained that conflicts cannot arise, because rights stem from a single, underlying moral principle: the categorical imperative, the principle of utility, or the law of nature, for example. But Edmund Burke maintains that there is no such principle. There are fundamentally different kinds of moral considerations, Burke contends; there is no theory that can take all into account and tell us, in every particular case, which considerations ought to take precedence. What is right or wrong depends on the circumstances, Burke says, and those may be extremely complex, involving many different kinds of values. The best we can do is to seek the right balance between those values. For that purpose, moral sensitivity and practical experience matter more than moral theories or talk of rights.

Finally, John Stuart Mill explains a utilitarian theory of rights. Many obligations are general, allowing us to choose how and when to fulfill them. We ought to give to charity, for example, but we can choose how much to give to whom. No one else has a right to our charity. Other, *perfect* obligations permit us no such choice and do correspond to other people's rights. We ought to pay the rent, for example, but have no choice about how much to pay or to whom. The landlord has a right to the rent money. A right, then, is simply a perfect obligation that ought to be enforced by society to maximize happiness.

THOMAS HOBBES

from *Leviathan* (1651)

Thomas Hobbes (1588–1679), a contemporary of Descartes, Milton, Galileo, and Rembrandt, was born prematurely in Malmesbury, Wiltshire, England, when his mother heard of the approach of the Spanish Armada. "Fear and I were born twins," he later quipped. He was raised by an uncle after his father, a vicar, was involved in a fistfight outside the door of his church. Hobbes attended Magdalen Hall, Oxford, at fourteen, completing his degree five years later. He became tutor to an earl's son, a position that provided him a good library and the means to travel. He became a member of an intellectual circle in France that included Mersenne, Gassendi, and Descartes. In 1636, he met Galileo. In 1640, when King Charles I dissolved Parliament, Hobbes fled England for Paris.

Over the next decade, while in his fifties, Hobbes wrote a series of notable works: Human Nature, De Corpore Politico (On the Body Politic), De Cive (On the State), *and several works on optics. In 1646–1647, he tutored the future King Charles II in Paris. In 1651, Hobbes published* Leviathan, *probably his greatest work, in which he argued for absolute and undivided sovereignty in the state. Hobbes there gave the first modern defense of social contract theory, which, despite our contemporary distaste for monarchy, continues to be influential.*

When Charles II was restored to the throne in 1660, Hobbes returned to England. He was seventy-two, but still an avid tennis player. The king, in gratitude for Hobbes's tutoring and for his public defense of monarchy, granted him a government pension. In 1665, however, came the great plague; the great fire of London followed a year later. Parliament, taking these events as signs of divine displeasure, investigated anyone who was suspected of atheism. Hobbes's Leviathan *made him a target; he was forbidden to publish any further writings. Still vigorous, however, Hobbes continued to write, completing several major works while in his eighties. (Source: Reprinted from Thomas Hobbes,* Leviathan. *Oxford: Clarendon Press, 1909. Spelling and punctuation have been modernized for clarity.)*

PART I, CHAPTER XIII / OF THE NATURAL CONDITION OF MANKIND AS CONCERNING THEIR FELICITY AND MISERY

Nature has made men so equal in the faculties of body and mind, as that though there be found one man sometimes manifestly stronger in body, or of quicker mind than another; yet when all is reckoned together, the difference between man and man is not so considerable, as that one man can thereupon claim to himself any benefit to which another may not pretend as well as he. For as to the strength of body, the weakest has strength enough to kill the strongest, either by secret machination or by confederacy with others, that are in the same danger with himself.

And as to the faculties of the mind (setting aside the arts grounded upon words, and especially that skill of proceeding upon general and infallible rules, called science; which very few have, and but in few things; as being not a native faculty, born with us;

nor attained, [as prudence] while we look after somewhat else), I find yet a greater equality amongst men than that of strength. For prudence is but experience; which equal time equally bestows on all men in those things they equally apply themselves unto. That which may perhaps make such equality incredible is but a vain conceit of one's own wisdom which almost all men think they have in a greater degree than the vulgar; that is, than all men but themselves and a few others, whom by fame, or for concurring with themselves, they approve. For such is the nature of men, that howsoever they may acknowledge many others to be more witty, or more eloquent, or more learned; yet they will hardly believe there be many so wise as themselves: For they see their own wit at hand, and other men's at a distance. But this proves rather that men are in that point equal, than unequal. For there is not ordinarily a greater sign of the equal distribution of anything, than that every man is contented with his share.

From this equality of ability arises equality of hope in the attaining of our ends. And therefore if any two men desire the same thing, which nevertheless they cannot both enjoy, they become enemies; and in the way to their end (which is principally their own conservation, and sometimes their delectation only) endeavour to destroy or subdue one another. And from hence it comes to pass, that where an invader has no more to fear than another man's single power; if one plant, sow, build, or possess a convenient seat, others may probably be expected to come prepared with forces united to dispossess and deprive him not only of the fruit of his labour, but also of his life or liberty. And the invader again is in the like danger of another.

And from this diffidence of one another, there is no way for any man to secure himself, so reasonable, as anticipation; that is, by force or wiles to master the persons of all men he can, so long, till he see no other power great enough to endanger him: And this is no more than his own conservation requires and is generally allowed. Also because there be some, that taking pleasure in contemplating their own power in the acts of conquest, which they pursue farther than their security requires; if others, that otherwise would be glad to be at ease within modest bounds, should not by invasion increase their power, they would not be able, long time, by standing only on their defence, to subsist. And by consequence, such augmentation of dominion over men, being necessary to a man's conservation . . . ought to be allowed him.

Again, men have no pleasure (but on the contrary a great deal of grief) in keeping company where there is no power able to over-awe them all. For every man looks that his companion should value him at the same rate he sets upon himself: And upon all signs of contempt or undervaluing naturally endeavours, as far as he dares (which amongst them that have no common power to keep them in quite is far enough to make them destroy each other) to extort a greater value from his condemners, by damage; and from others, by the example.

So that in the nature of man, we find three principal causes of quarrel. First, competition; secondly, diffidence; thirdly, glory.

The first makes men invade for gain; the second, for safety; and the third, for reputation. The first use violence to make themselves masters of other men's persons, wives, children, and cattle; the second, to defend them; the third, for trifles, as a word, a smile, a different opinion, and any other sign of undervalue, either direct in their persons, or by reflexion in their kindred, their friends, their nation, their profession, or their name.

Hereby it is manifest that during the time men live without a common power to keep them all in awe, they are in that condition which is called war; and such a war as is of every man against every man. For war consists not in battle only, or the act of fighting; but in a tract of time, wherein the will to contend by battle is sufficiently known: and therefore the notion of *time* is to be considered in the nature of war, as it is in the nature of weather. For as the nature of foul weather lies not in a shower or two of rain, but in an inclination thereto of many days together; So the nature of war consisteth not in actual fighting, but in the known disposition thereto during all the time there is no assurance to the contrary. All other time is peace.

Whatsoever therefore is consequent to a time of war, where every man is enemy to every man; the same is consequent to the time wherein men live without other security than what their own strength and their own invention shall furnish them withall.

In such condition, there is no place for industry; because the fruit thereof is uncertain: and consequently no culture of the earth, no navigation, nor use of the commodities that may be imported by sea; no commodious building; no instruments of moving, and removing such things as require much force; no knowledge of the face of the earth; no account of time; no arts; no letters; no society; and which is worst of all, continual fear and danger of violent death; And the life of man, solitary, poor, nasty, brutish, and short.

It may seem strange to some man that has not well weighed these things that nature should thus dissociate and render man apt to invade and destroy one another: and he may therefore, not trusting to this inference made from the passions, desire perhaps to have the same confirmed by experience. Let him therefore consider with himself, when taking a journey, he arms himself and seeks to go well accompanied; when going to sleep, he locks his doors; when even in his house he locks his chests; and this when he knows there be laws and public officers armed to revenge all injuries shall be done him; what opinion he has of his fellow subjects, when he rides armed; of his fellow citizens, when he locks his doors; and of his children and servants when he locks his chests. Does he not there as much accuse mankind by his actions, as I do by my words? But neither of us accuse man's nature in it. The desires, and other passions of man, are in themselves no sin. No more are the actions, that proceed from those passions, till they know a law that forbids them: which till laws be made they cannot know: nor can any law be made, till they have agreed upon the person that shall make it.

It may peradventure be thought, there was never such a time, nor condition of war as this; and I believe it was never generally so, over all the world; but there are many places, where they live so now. For the savage people in many places of *America,* except the government of small families, that concord whereof depends on natural lust, have no government at all; and live at this day in that brutish manner, as I said before. Howsoever, it may be perceived what manner of life there would be where there were no common power to fear; by the manner of life, which men that have formerly lived under a peaceful government, use to degenerate into, in a civil war.

But though there had never been any time wherein particular men were in a condition of war one against another, yet in all times kings, and persons of sovereign authority, because of their independence, are in continual jealousies and in the state and posture of gladiators, having their weapons pointing and their eyes fixed on one another; that is, their forts, garrisons, and guns, upon the frontiers of their kingdoms and continual spies upon their neighbours; which is a posture of war. But because they uphold thereby the industry of their subjects, there does not follow it that misery which accompanies the liberty of particular men.

To this war of every man against every man, this also is consequent; that nothing can be unjust. The notions of right and wrong, justice and injustice have no place. Where there is no common power, there is no law: where no law, no injustice. Force and fraud are in war, and two cardinal virtues. Justice and injustice are none of the faculties neither of the body nor mind. If they were, they might be in a man that were alone in the world, as well as his senses and passions. They are qualities that relate to men in society, not in solitude. It is consequent also to the same condition, that there be no propriety, no dominion, no *mine* and *thine* distinct; but only that to be every man's, that he can get; and for so long as he can keep it. And thus much for the ill condition, which man by mere nature is actually placed in; though with a possibility to come out of it, consisting partly in the passions, partly in his reason.

The passions that incline men to peace are fear of death, desire of such things as are necessary to commodious living, and a hope by their industry to obtain them. And reason suggests convenient articles of peace, upon which men may be drawn to agreement. These articles are they, which otherwise are called the laws of nature, whereof I shall speak more particularly in the following chapters.

CHAPTER XIV / OF THE FIRST AND SECOND NATURAL LAWS AND OF CONTRACTS

The right of nature, which writers commonly call *jus naturale,* is the liberty each man has to use his own power, as he wills himself, for the preservation of his own nature; that is to say, of his own life; and consequently, of doing anything which in his own judgment and reasons he shall conceive to be the aptest means thereunto.

By liberty is understood, according to the proper signification of the word, the absence of external impediments: which impediments may oft take away part of a man's power to do what he would but cannot hinder him from using the power left him, according as his judgment and reason shall dictate to him.

A law of nature (*lex naturalis*) is a precept, or general rule, found out by reason, by which a man is forbidden to do that which is destructive of his life or takes away the means of preserving the same and to omit that by which he thinks it may be best preserved. For though they that speak of this subject used to confound *jus,* and *lex, right* and *law;* yet they ought to be distinguished, because right, consists in liberty to do or to forbear, whereas law determines and binds to one of them: so that law and right differ as much as obligation and liberty, which in one and the same matter are inconsistent.

And because the condition of man (as has been declared in the precedent chapter) is a condition of war of everyone against everyone, in which case everyone is governed by his own reason; and there is nothing he can make use of that may not be a help unto him in preserving his life against his enemies; it follows that in such a condition, every man has a right to everything; even to one another's body. And therefore, as long as this natural right of every man to every thing endures, there can be no security to any man (how strong or wise soever he be) of living out the time which nature ordinarily allows men to live. And consequently it is a precept or general rule of reason, *That every man ought to endeavour peace, as far as he has hope of obtaining it; and when he cannot obtain it, that he may seek, and use, all helps and advantages of war.* The first branch of which rule contains the first and fundamental law of nature; which is *to seek peace and follow it.* The second, the sum of the right of nature, which is by *all means we can, to defend ourselves.*

From this fundamental law of nature, by which men are commanded to endeavour peace, is derived this second law: *That a man be willing, when others are so too, as far-forth, as for peace and defence of himself he shall think it necessary to lay down this right to all things and be contented with so much liberty against other men as he would allow other men against himself.* For as long as every man holds this right of doing any thing he likes, so long are all men in the condition of war. But if other men will not lay down their right, as well as he, then there is no reason for anyone to divest himself of his: For that were to expose himself to prey (which no man is bound to) rather than to dispose himself to peace. This is that law of the gospel: *Whatsoever you require that others should do to you, that do ye to them.* And that law of all men, *Quod tibi fieri non vis, alteri ne feceris.**

To *lay down* a man's *right* to any thing is to divest himself of the *liberty* of hindering another of the benefit of his own right to the same. For he that renounces or passes away his right gives not to any other man a right which he had not before; because there is nothing to which every man had not right by nature; but only stands out of his way, that he may enjoy his own original right without hindrance from him; not without hindrance from another. So that the effect which redounds to one man by another man's defect of right is but so much diminution of impediments to the use of his own right original. . . .

---

* "What you do not want done to yourself, do not do to others."
—Ed.

QUESTIONS FOR REFLECTION

1. What is Hobbes's conception of the state of nature? Why would a person's life in that state be "solitary, poor, nasty, brutish, and short"?

2. What, for Hobbes, is liberty? What is a law of nature? How does Hobbes distinguish law from right?

3. What are the first three laws of nature, according to Hobbes? How does he derive them from the state of nature?

4. What motivates us, in the state of nature, to contract to form associations and governments?

What are we willing to give up? What do we hope to gain?

5. Why, according to Hobbes, are we obliged to fulfill contracts, even when doing so is not in our best interest?

6. "Whatsoever is done to a man conformable to his own will, signified to the doer, is no injury to him." This is Hobbes's statement of a traditional principle: "To the willing no injustice is done." How does Hobbes argue for this? How does this principle relate to Mill's harm principle?

JOHN LOCKE

from *Second Treatise of Government* (1690)

John Locke (1632–1704), a contemporary of Boyle, Leibniz, and Newton, was born in Wrington, Somerset, England. The son of an attorney, he was raised in a liberal Puritan family. At the age of fourteen, he entered Westminster School, where he studied the classics, Hebrew, and Arabic. At twenty, he entered Christ's Church, Oxford, where he earned a B.A. in 1656. After receiving an M.A., he was appointed censor of moral philosophy at Oxford.

When his father died in 1661, Locke received a small inheritance. He began studying for a medical degree, and in 1667 became personal physician to the earl of Shaftesbury. Locke received his medical degree in 1674; while completing his studies, he wrote the first two drafts of his Essay Concerning Human Understanding, *was appointed a fellow of the Royal Society, and was named secretary to the Council of Trade and Plantations.*

Locke spent several years in France, returning in 1679. Because of his ties to Shaftesbury, who had been implicated in a plot against the king, Locke was placed under surveillance; he fled to Holland in 1683. There he became an adviser to William of Orange, published a series of works, and wrote the third draft of the Essay. *The Glorious Revolution of 1688 enabled him to return to England in the company of the future queen, Mary. In 1689 and 1690, Locke published the philosophical work that made him internationally famous: the* Essay *and the* Two Treatises of Government. *He became commissioner of the Board of Trade and Plantations, where he served with great distinction until failing health forced him to retire.*

Locke's Second Treatise *presents a classically liberal theory of government. People in the state of nature would choose to sacrifice a portion of their liberty for the impartial judgment the government can provide. The people nevertheless retain most of their natural rights, which place limits on the power of government. In addition, they receive social rights from the government itself. The government's purpose is the protection of life, liberty, and property; it can act only with the consent of the governed. (Source: Reprinted from John Locke,* Two Treatises of Government. *London: Printed for Awnsham Churchill, 1690. Spelling and punctuation have been modernized for clarity.)*

CHAPTER II / OF THE STATE OF NATURE

§. 4. To understand political power right and derive it from its original, we must consider what state all men are naturally in, and that is a state of perfect freedom to order their actions and dispose of their possessions and persons, as they think fit, within the bounds of the law of nature, without asking leave or depending upon the will of any other man.

A state also of equality, wherein all the power and jurisdiction is reciprocal, no one having more than another; there being nothing more evident than that creatures of the same species and rank, promiscuously born to all the same advantages of nature and the use of the same faculties should also be equal one amongst another without subordination or subjection, unless the lord and master of them all should, by any manifest declaration of his will, set one above another and confer on him, by an evident and clear appointment, an undoubted right to dominion and sovereignty.

§. 5. This equality of men by nature the judicious Hooker* looks upon as so evident in itself and beyond all question that he makes it the foundation of that obligation to mutual love amongst men, on which he builds the duties they owe one another and from whence he derives the great maxims of justice and charity. His words are,

> The like natural inducement has brought men to know that it is no less their duty to love others than themselves; for seeing those things which are equal must needs all have one measure; if I cannot but wish to receive good, even as much at every man's hands as any man can wish unto his own soul, how should I look to have any part of my desire herein satisfied, unless myself be careful to satisfy the like desire, which is undoubtedly in other men, being of one and the same nature? To have anything offered them repugnant to this desire must needs in all respects grieve them as much as me; so that if I do harm, I must look to suffer, there being no reason that others should show greater measure of love to me than they have by me shown unto them: my desire therefore to be loved of my equals in nature, as much as possible may be, imposes upon me a natural duty of bearing to them fully the like affection; from which relation of equality between ourselves and them that are as ourselves, what several rules and canons natural reason has drawn for direction of life no man is ignorant, *Eccl. Pol. Lib.* i.

§. 6. But though this be a state of liberty, yet it is not a state of license: though man in that state have an uncontrollable liberty to dispose of his person or possessions, yet he has not liberty to destroy himself or so much as any creature in his possession, but where some nobler use than its bare preservation calls for it. The state of nature has a law of nature to govern it, which obliges every one: and reason, which is that law, teaches all mankind who will but consult it that being all equal and independent, no one ought to harm another in his life, health, liberty, or possessions: for men being all the workmanship of one omnipotent and infinitely wise maker, all the servants of one sovereign master, sent into the world by his order and about his business; they are his property, whose workmanship they are, made to last during his, not one another's pleasure: and being furnished with like faculties, sharing all in one community of nature, there cannot be supposed any such subordination among us that may authorize us to destroy one another, as if we were made for one another's uses, as the inferior ranks of creatures are for ours. Every one, as he is bound to preserve himself and not to quit his station wilfully, so by the like reason, when his own preservation comes not in competition, ought he as much as he can to preserve the rest of mankind and may not, unless it be to do justice on an offender, take away or impair the life or what tends to the preservation of the life, the liberty, health, limb, or goods of another.

§. 7. And that all men may be restrained from invading others' rights and from doing hurt to one another, and the law of nature be observed which wills the peace and preservation of all mankind, the execution of the law of nature is, in that state, put into every man's hands, whereby everyone has a right to punish the transgressors of that law to such a degree as may hinder its violation: for the law of nature would, as all other laws that concern men in this world, be in vain if there were no body that in the state of nature had a power to execute that law and thereby preserve the innocent and restrain offenders. And if any one in the state of nature may punish another for any evil he has done, every one may do so: for in that state of perfect equality, where naturally there is no superiority or jurisdiction of one over another, what any may do in prosecution of that law everyone must needs have a right to do.

§. 8. And thus, in the state of nature, one man comes by a power over another; but yet no absolute or arbitrary power to use a criminal, when he has got him in his hands, according to the passionate heats, or boundless extravagancy of his own will; but only to retribute to him, so far as calm reason and conscience dictate, what is proportionate to his

---

* Richard Hooker (1553–1600), English theologian and political philosopher, wrote *The Laws of Ecclesiastical Polity,* which focuses on reason and natural law as foundations of the state. —Ed.

transgression, which is so much as may serve for reparation and restraint: for these two are the only reasons why one man may lawfully do harm to another, which is that we call punishment. In transgressing the law of nature, the offender declares himself to live by another rule than that of reason and common equity, which is that measure God has set to the actions of men for their mutual security; and so he becomes dangerous to mankind, the tie which is to secure them from injury and violence being slighted and broken by him. Which being a trespass against the whole species and the peace and safety of it provided for by the law of nature, every man upon this score, by the right he has to preserve mankind in general, may restrain or, where it is necessary, destroy things noxious to them and so may bring such evil on anyone who has transgressed that law, as may make him repent the doing of it and thereby deter him, and by his example others, from doing the like mischief. And in the case, and upon this ground, every man has a right to punish the offender and be executioner of the law of nature.

§. 9. I doubt not but this will seem a very strange doctrine to some men: but before they condemn it, I desire them to resolve me, by what right any prince or state can put to death or punish an alien for any crime he commits in their country. It is certain their laws, by virtue of any sanction they receive from the promulgated will of the legislative, reach not a stranger: they speak not to him, nor, if they did, is he bound to hearken to them. The legislative authority, by which they are in force over the subjects of that commonwealth, has no power over him. Those who have the supreme power of making laws in England, France or Holland are to an Indian but like the rest of the world, men without authority: and therefore, if by the law of nature every man has not a power to punish offences against it as he soberly judges the case to require, I see not how the magistrates of any community can punish an alien of another country; since, in reference to him, they can have no more power than what every man naturally may have over another.

§. 10. Besides the crime which consists in violating the law and varying from the right rule of reason, whereby a man so far becomes degenerate and declares himself to quit the principles of human nature and to be a noxious creature, there is commonly injury done to some person or other, and some other man receives damage by his transgression: in which case he who has received any damage has, besides the right of punishment common to him with other men, a particular right to seek reparation from him that has done it: and any other person who finds it just may also join with him that is injured and assist him in recovering from the offender so much as may make satisfaction for the harm he has suffered.

§. 11. From these two distinct rights, the one of punishing the crime for restraint and preventing the like offence, which right of punishing is in everybody; the other of taking reparation, which belongs only to the injured party, comes it to pass that the magistrate, who by being magistrate has the common right of punishing put into his hands, can often, where the public good demands not the execution of the law, remit the punishment of criminal offenses by his own authority, but yet cannot remit the satisfaction due to any private man for the damage he has received. That he who has suffered the damage has a right to demand in his own name, and he alone can remit: the damnified person has this power of appropriating to himself the goods or service of the offender by right of self-preservation, as every man has a power to punish the crime to prevent its being committed again, by the right he has of preserving all mankind and doing all reasonable things he can in order to that end: and thus it is that every man in the state of nature has a power to kill a murderer, both to deter others from doing the like injury, which no reparation can compensate, by the example of the punishment that attends it from everybody, and also to secure men from the attempts of a criminal, who having renounced reason, the common rule and measure God has given to mankind, has by the unjust violence and slaughter he has committed upon one, declared war against all mankind and therefore may be destroyed as a lion or a tiger, one of those wild savage beasts with whom men can have no society nor security: and upon this is grounded that great law of nature, *Whoso sheddeth man's blood, by man shall his blood be shed.* And Cain was so fully convinced that every one had a right to destroy such a criminal that after the murder of his brother, he cries out, *Every one that findeth me, shall slay me;* so plain was it writ in the hearts of all mankind.

§. 12. By the same reason may a man in the state of nature punish the lesser breaches of that law. It will perhaps be demanded, with death? I answer, each transgression may be punished to that degree and with so much severity as will suffice to make it an ill bargain to the offender, give him cause to repent, and terrify others from doing the like. Every offence that can be committed in the state of nature may in the state of nature be also punished equally, and as far forth as it may, in a commonwealth: for though it would be besides my present purpose to enter here into the particulars of the law of nature or its measures of punishment, yet, it is certain there is such a law, and that too as intelligible and plain to a rational creature and a studier of that law as the positive laws of commonwealths; nay, possibly plainer, as much as reason is easier to be understood than the fancies and intricate contrivances of men following contrary and hidden interests put into words; for so truly are a great part of the municipal laws of countries, which are only so far right as they are founded on the law of nature, by which they are to be regulated and interpreted.

§. 13. To this strange doctrine, *viz.* That in the state of nature every one has the executive power of the law of nature, I doubt not but it will be objected that it is unreasonable for men to be judges in their own cases, that self-love will make men partial to themselves and their friends, and, on the other side, that ill nature, passion and revenge will carry them too far in punishing others; and hence nothing but confusion and disorder will follow and that therefore God has certainly appointed government to restrain the partiality and violence of men. I easily grant that civil government is the proper remedy for the inconveniences of the state of nature, which must certainly be great where men may be judges in their own case, since it is easy to be imagined that he who was so unjust as to do his brother an injury will scarce be so just as to condemn himself for it: but I shall desire those who make this objection to remember that absolute monarchs are but men; and if government is to be the remedy of those evils which necessarily follow from men's being judges in their own cases and the state of nature is therefore not to be endured, I desire to know what kind of government that is and how much better it is than the state of nature, where one man commanding a multitude has the liberty to be judge in his own case and may do to all his subjects whatever he pleases, without the least liberty to anyone to question or control those who execute his pleasure? and in whatsoever he does, whether led by reason, mistake or passion, must be submitted to? Much better it is in the state of nature, where men are not bound to submit to the unjust will of another, and if he that judges judges amiss in his own or any other case, he is answerable for it to the rest of mankind.

§. 14. It is often asked as a mighty objection, where are, or ever were there, any men in such a state of nature? To which it may suffice as an answer at present that since all princes and rulers of independent governments all through the world are in a state of nature, it is plain the world never was, nor ever will be, without numbers of men in that state. I have named all governors of independent communities, whether they are or are not in league with others: for it is not every compact that puts an end to the state of nature between men, but only this one of agreeing together mutually to enter into the community and make one body politic; other promises and compacts men may make one with another and yet still be in the state of nature. The promises and bargains for truck, &c. between the two men in the desert island, mentioned by Garcilasso de la Vega in his history of Peru, or between a Swiss and an Indian in the woods of America are binding to them, though they are perfectly in a state of nature in reference to one another: for truth and keeping of faith belongs to men as men and not as members of society.

§. 15. To those that say there were never any men in the state of nature, I will not only oppose the authority of the judicious Hooker, *Eccl. Pol. lib.* i. *sect.* 10. where he says, *The laws which have been hitherto mentioned,* i.e. the laws of nature, *do bind men absolutely, even as they are men, although they have never any settled fellowship, never any solemn agreement amongst themselves what to do, or not to do: but forasmuch as we are not by ourselves sufficient to furnish ourselves with competent store of things, needful for such a life as our nature doth desire, a life fit for the dignity of man; therefore to supply those defects and imperfections which are in us, as living single and solely by ourselves, we are naturally induced to seek communion and fellowship with others: this was the cause of men's uniting themselves at first in politic societies.* But I moreover affirm that all men are naturally in that state and remain so until by their own consents they make themselves members of some politic society; and I doubt not in the sequel of this discourse, to make it very clear.

CHAPTER III / OF THE STATE OF WAR

§. 16. The state of war is a state of enmity and destruction: and therefore declaring by word or action, not a passionate and hasty, but a sedate settled design upon another man's life, puts him in a state of war with him against whom he has declared such an intention, and so has exposed his life to the other's power to be taken away by him or any one that joins with him in his defence and espouses his quarrel; it being reasonable and just, I should have a right to destroy that which threatens me with destruction: for by the fundamental law of nature, man being to be preserved as much as possible, when all cannot be preserved, the safety of the innocent is to be preferred: and one may destroy a man who makes war upon him or has discovered an enmity to his being, for the same reason that he may kill a wolf or a lion; because such men are not under the ties of the common law of reason, have no other rule but that of force and violence, and so may be treated as beasts of prey those dangerous and noxious creatures that will be sure to destroy him whenever he falls into their power.

§. 17. And hence it is that he who attempts to get another man into his absolute power does thereby put himself into a state of war with him, it being to be understood as a declaration of a design upon his life: for I have reason to conclude that he who would get me into his power without my consent would use me as he pleased when he had got me there and destroy me too when he had a fancy to it; for nobody can desire to have me in his absolute power, unless it be to compel me by force to that which is against the right of my freedom, i.e. make me a slave. To be free from such force is the only security of my preservation, and reason bids me look on him, as an enemy to my preservation, who would take away that freedom which is the fence to it; so that he who makes

an attempt to enslave me thereby puts himself into a state of war with me. He that in the state of nature would take away the freedom that belongs to anyone in that state must necessarily be supposed to have a design to take away every thing else, that freedom being the foundation of all the rest; as he that in the state of society would take away the freedom belonging to those of that society or commonwealth must be supposed to design to take away from them everything else and so be looked on as in a state of war.

§. 18. This makes it lawful for a man to kill a thief who has not in the least hurt him nor declared any design upon his life any farther than by the use of force so to get him in his power, as to take away his money, or what he pleases, from him; because using force where he has no right to get me into his power, let his pretence be what it will, I have no reason to suppose that he who would take away my liberty would not, when he had me in his power, take away everything else. And therefore it is lawful for me to treat him as one who has put himself into a state of war with me, i.e. kill him if I can; for to that hazard does he justly expose himself, whoever introduces a state of war and is aggressor in it.

§. 19. And here we have the plain difference between the state of nature and the state of war, which however some men have confounded, are as far distant as a state of peace, good will, mutual assistance and preservation and a state of enmity, malice, violence and mutual destruction are one from another. Men living together according to reason, without a common superior on earth with authority to judge between them, is properly the state of nature. But force, or a declared design of force, upon the person of another, where there is no common superior on earth to appeal to for relief, is the state of war: and it is the want of such an appeal gives a man the right of war even against an aggressor, though he be in society and a fellow subject. Thus a thief, whom I cannot harm but by appeal to the law for having stolen all that I am worth, I may kill when he sets on me to rob me but of my horse or coat; because the law, which was made for my preservation where it cannot interpose to secure my life from present force, which, if lost, is capable of no reparation, permits me my own defence and the right of war, a liberty to kill the aggressor, because the aggressor allows not time to appeal to our common judge nor the decision of the law for remedy in a case where the mischief may be irreparable. Want of a common judge with authority puts all men in a state of nature: force without right upon a man's person makes a state of war, both where there is and is not a common judge.

§. 20. But when the actual force is over, the state of war ceases between those that are in society and are equally on both sides subjected to the fair determination of the law; because then there lies open the remedy of appeal for the past injury and to prevent future harm: but where no such appeal is, as in the state of nature, for want of positive laws and judges with authority to appeal to, the state of war once begun continues, with a right to the innocent party to destroy the other whenever he can until the aggressor offers peace and desires reconciliation on such terms as may repair any wrongs he has already done and secure the innocent for the future; nay, where an appeal to the law and constituted judges lies open, but the remedy is denied by a manifest perverting of justice and a barefaced wresting of the laws to protect or indemnify the violence or injuries of some men or party of men, there it is hard to imagine anything but a state of war: for wherever violence is used and injury done, though by hands appointed to administer justice, it is still violence and injury, however coloured with the name, pretences, or forms of law, the end whereof being to protect and redress the innocent by an unbiased application of it to all who are under it; wherever that is not *bona fide* done, war is made upon the sufferers, who, having no appeal on earth to right them, they are left to the only remedy in such cases, an appeal to heaven.

§. 21. To avoid this state of war (wherein there is no appeal but to heaven, and wherein every the least difference is apt to end where there is no authority to decide between the contenders) is one great reason of men's putting themselves into society and quitting the state of nature: for where there is an authority, a power on earth from which relief can be had by appeal there the continuance of the state of war is excluded, and the controversy is decided by that power. Had there been any such court, any superior jurisdiction on earth, to determine the right between Jephtha and the Ammonities, they had never come to a state of war: but we see he was forced to appeal to heaven. *The Lord the Judge* (says he) *be judge this day between the children of* Israel *and the children of* Ammon, *Judg.* xi. 27. and then prosecuting and relying on his appeal, he leads out his army to battle: and therefore in such controversies, where the question is put, *who shall be judge?* It cannot be meant, who shall decide the controversy; everyone knows what Jephtha here tells us, that the Lord the Judge shall judge. Where there is no judge on earth, the appeal lies to God in heaven. That question then cannot mean, who shall judge whether another has put himself in a state of war with me and whether I may, as Jephtha did, appeal to heaven in it? of that I myself can only be judge in my own conscience, as I will answer it, at the great day, to the supreme judge of all men.

CHAPTER IV/OF SLAVERY

§. 22. The natural liberty of man is to be free from any superior power on earth and not to be under the will or legislative authority of man, but to have only the law of nature for his rule. The liberty of man in society is to be under no other legislative power but that established by consent in the commonwealth, nor under the dominion of any will or restraint of any law but what that legislative shall enact according to the trust put in it. Freedom then is not what Sir Robert Filmer tells us, *Observations,* A. 55. *a liberty for every one to do what he lists, to live as he pleases, and not to be tied by any laws:* but *freedom of men under government* is to have a standing rule to live by, common to every one of that society and made by the legislative power erected in it; a liberty to follow my own will in all things, where the rule prescribes not; and not to be subject to the inconstant, uncertain, unknown, arbitrary will of another man: as freedom of nature is to be under no other restraint but the law of nature.

§. 23. This freedom from absolute, arbitrary power is so necessary to and closely joined with a man's preservation that he cannot part with it, but by what forfeits his preservation and life together: for a man, not having the power of his own life, cannot by compact or his own consent enslave himself to anyone nor put himself under the absolute, arbitrary power of another to take away his life when he pleases. Nobody can give more power than he has himself; and he that cannot take away his own life cannot give another power over it. Indeed, having by his fault forfeited his own life by some act that deserves death, he to whom he has forfeited it may (when he has him in his power) delay to take it and make use of him to his own service, and he does him no injury by it: for whenever he finds the hardship of his slavery outweigh the value of his life, it is in his power, by resisting the will of his master, to draw on himself the death he desires. . . .

QUESTIONS FOR REFLECTION

1. In what sense is the state of nature a state of equality?

2. How does Locke distinguish liberty from license? Why is the state of nature characterized only by the former?

3. How does Locke argue for capital punishment?

4. What motivates us, in the state of nature, to contract to form a government? What are we willing to give up? What do we hope to gain?

5. Hobbes describes the state of nature as a "war of every man against every man." Locke, however, finds the state of nature different from a state of war. In what ways?

6. What, for Locke, is natural liberty? Liberty in society? Liberty under government?

EDMUND BURKE

from *Reflections on the Revolution in France* (1790)

(Source: Reprinted from Edmund Burke, Reflections on the Revolution in France. *London: Printed for J. Dodsley, 1790.)*

. . . [I]t is vain to talk to them of the practice of their ancestors, the fundamental laws of their country, the fixed form of a constitution whose merits are confirmed by the solid test of long experience and an increasing public strength and national prosperity. They despise experience as the wisdom of unlettered men; and as for the rest, they have wrought underground a mine that will blow up, at one grand explosion, all examples of antiquity, all precedents, charters, and acts of parliament. They have "the rights of men." Against these there can be no prescription, against these no agreement is binding; these admit no temperament and no compromise; anything withheld from their full demand is so much of fraud and injustice. Against these their rights of men let no government look for security in the length of its continuance, or in the justice and lenity of its administration. The objections of these speculatists, if its forms do not quadrate with their theories, are as valid against such an old and beneficent government as against the most violent tyranny or the greenest usurpation. . . .

Far am I from denying in theory, full as far is my heart from withholding in practice (if I were of power to give or to withhold) the *real* rights of men. In denying their false claims of right, I do not mean to injure those which are real, and are such as their pretended rights would totally destroy. If civil society be made for the advantage of man, all the advantages for which it is made become his right. It is an institution of beneficence; and law itself is only beneficence acting by a rule. Men have a right to live by that rule; they have a right to do justice, as between their fellows, whether their fellows are in public function or in ordinary occupation. They have a right to the fruits of their industry and to the means of making their industry fruitful. They have a right to the acquisitions of their parents, to the nourishment and improvement of their offspring, to instruction in life, and to consolation in death. Whatever each man can separately do, without trespassing upon others, he has a right to do for himself; and he has a right to a fair portion of all which society, with all its combinations of skill and force, can do in his favor. In this partnership all men have equal rights, but not to equal things. He that has but five shillings in the partnership has as good a right to it as he that has five hundred pounds has to his larger proportion. But he has not a right to an equal dividend in the product of the joint stock; and as to the share of power, authority, and direction which each individual ought to have in the management of the state, that I must deny to be amongst the direct original rights of man in civil society; for I have in my contemplation the civil social man, and no other. It is a thing to be settled by convention.

If civil society be the offspring of convention, that convention must be its law. That convention must limit and modify all the descriptions of constitution which are formed under it. Every sort of legislative, judicial, or executory power are its creatures. They can have no being in any other state of things; *and how can any man claim under the conventions of civil rights which do not so much as suppose its existence— rights which are absolutely repugnant to it?* One of the first motives to civil society, and which becomes one of its fundamental rules, is *that no man should be judge in his own cause.* By this each person has at once divested himself of the first fundamental right of uncovenanted man, that is, to judge for himself and to assert his own cause. He abdicates all right to be his own governor. He inclusively, in a great measure, abandons the right of self-defense, the first law of nature. Men cannot enjoy the rights of an uncivil and of a civil state together. That he may obtain justice, he gives up his right of determining what it is in points the most essential to him. That he may secure some liberty, he makes a surrender in trust of the whole of it.

Government is not made in virtue of natural rights, which may and do exist in total independence of it, and exist in much greater clearness and in a much greater degree of abstract perfection; but their abstract perfection is their practical defect. By having a right to everything they want everything. Government is a contrivance of human wisdom to provide for human *wants.* Men have a right that these wants should be provided for by this wisdom. Among these wants is to be reckoned the want, out of civil society, of a sufficient restraint upon their passions. Society requires not only that the passions of individuals should be subjected, but that even in the mass and body, as well as in the individuals, the inclinations of men should frequently be thwarted, their will controlled, and their passions brought into subjection. This can only be done *by a power out of themselves,* and not, in the exercise of its function, subject to that will and to those passions which it is its office to bridle and subdue. In this sense the restraints on men, as well as their liberties, are to be reckoned among their rights. But as the liberties and the restrictions vary with times and circumstances and admit to infinite modifications, they cannot be settled upon any abstract rule; and nothing is so foolish as to discuss them upon that principle.

The moment you abate anything from the full rights of men, each to govern himself, and suffer any artificial, positive limitation upon those rights, from that moment the whole organization of government becomes a consideration of convenience. This it is which makes the constitution of a state and the due distribution of its powers a matter of the most delicate and complicated skill. It requires a deep knowledge of human nature and human necessities, and of the things which facilitate or obstruct the various ends which are to be pursued by the mechanism of civil institutions. The state is to have recruits to its strength, and remedies to its distempers. What is the use of discussing a man's abstract right to food or medicine? The question is upon the method of procuring and administering them. In that deliberation I shall always advise to call in the aid of the farmer and the physician rather than the professor of metaphysics.

The science of constructing a commonwealth, or renovating it, or reforming it, is, like every other experimental science, not to be taught *a priori.* Nor is it a short experience that can instruct us in that practical science, because the real effects of moral causes are not always immediate; but that which in the first instance is prejudicial may be excellent in its remoter operation, and its excellence may arise even from the ill effects it produces in the beginning. The reverse also happens: and very plausible schemes, with very pleasing commencements, have often shameful and lamentable conclusions. In states there are often some obscure and almost latent causes, things which appear at first view of little moment, on which a very great part of its prosperity or adversity may most essentially depend. The science of government being therefore so practical in itself and intended for such practical purposes—a matter which requires experience, and even more experience than any person can gain in his whole life, however sagacious and observing he may be—it is with infinite caution that any man ought to venture upon pulling down an edifice which has answered in any tolerable degree for ages the common purposes of society, or on building it up again without having models and patterns of approved utility before his eyes.

These metaphysic rights entering into common life, like rays of light which pierce into a dense medium, are by the laws of nature refracted from their straight line. Indeed, in the gross and complicated mass of human passions and concerns the primitive rights of men undergo such a variety of refractions and reflections that it becomes absurd to talk of them as if they continued in the simplicity of their original direction. The nature of man is intricate; the objects of society are of the greatest possible complexity; and, therefore, no simple disposition or direction of power can be suitable either to man's nature or to the quality of his affairs. When I hear the simplicity of contrivance aimed at and boasted of in any new political constitutions, I am at no loss to decide that the artificers are grossly ignorant of their trade or totally negligent of their duty. The simple governments are fundamentally defective, to say no worse of them. If you were to contemplate society in but one point of view, all these simple modes of polity are infinitely captivating. In effect each would answer its single end much more perfectly than the more complex is able to attain all its complex purposes. But it is better that the whole should be imperfectly and anomalously answered than that, while some parts are provided for with great exactness, others might be totally neglected or perhaps materially injured by the over-care of a favorite member.

The pretended rights of these theorists are all extremes; and in proportion as they are metaphysically true, they are morally and politically false. The rights of men are in a sort of *middle,* incapable of definition, but not impossible to be discerned. The rights of men in governments are their advantages; and these are often in balances between differences of good, in compromises sometimes between good and evil, and sometimes between evil and evil. Political reason is a computing principle: adding, subtracting, multiplying, and dividing, morally and not metaphysically or mathematically, true moral denominations. . . .

You see, Sir, that in this enlightened age I am bold enough to confess that we are generally men of untaught feelings, that, instead of casting away all our old prejudices, we cherish them to a very considerable degree, and, to take more shame to ourselves, we cherish them because they are prejudices; and the longer they have lasted and the more generally they have prevailed, the more we cherish them. We are afraid to put men to live and trade each on his own private stock of reason, because we suspect that this stock in each man is small, and that the individuals would do better to avail themselves of the general bank and capital of nations and of ages. Many of our men of speculation, instead of exploding general prejudices, employ their sagacity to discover the latent wisdom which prevails in them. If they find what they seek, and they seldom fail, they think it more wise to continue the prejudice, with the reason involved, than to cast away the coat of prejudice and to leave nothing but the naked reason; because prejudice, with its reason, has a motive to give action to that reason, and an affection which will give it permanence. Prejudice is of ready application in the emergency; it previously engages the mind in a steady course of wisdom and virtue and does not leave the man hesitating in the moment of decision skeptical, puzzled, and unresolved. Prejudice renders a man's virtue his habit, and not a series of unconnected acts. Through just prejudice, his duty becomes a part of his nature. . . .

. . . Rage and frenzy will pull down more in half an hour than prudence, deliberation, and foresight can build up in a hundred years. The errors and defects of old establishments are visible and palpable. It calls for little ability to point them out; and where absolute power is given, it requires but a word wholly to abolish the vice and the establishment together. The same lazy but restless disposition which loves sloth and hates quiet directs the politicians when they come to work for supplying the place of what they have destroyed. To make everything the reverse of what they have seen is quite as easy as to destroy. No difficulties occur in what has never been tried. Criticism is almost baffled in discovering the defects of what has not existed; and eager enthusiasm and cheating hope have all the wide field of imagination in which they may expatiate with little or no opposition.

At once to preserve and to reform is quite another thing. When the useful parts of an old establishment are kept, and what is superadded is to be fitted to what is retained, a vigorous mind, steady, persevering attention, various powers of comparison and combination, and the resources of an understanding fruitful in expedients are to be exercised; they are to be exercised in a continued conflict with the combined force of opposite vices, with the obstinacy that rejects all improvement and the levity that is fatigued and disgusted with everything of which it is in possession. But you may object—"A process of this kind is slow. It is not fit for an assembly which glories in performing in a few months the work of ages. Such a mode of reforming, possibly, might take up many years." Without question it might; and it ought. It is one of the excellences of a method in which time is amongst the assistants, that its operation is slow and in some cases almost imperceptible. If circumspection and caution are a part of wisdom when we work only upon inanimate matter, surely they become a part of duty, too, when the subject of our demolition and construction is not brick and timber but sentient beings, by the sudden alteration of whose state, condition, and habits multitudes may be rendered miserable. But it seems as if it were the prevalent opinion in Paris that an unfeeling heart and an undoubting confidence are the sole qualifications for a perfect legislator. Far different are my ideas of that high office. The true lawgiver ought to have a heart full of sensibility. He ought to love and respect his kind, and to fear himself. It may be allowed to his temperament to catch his ultimate object with an intuitive glance, but his movements toward it ought to be deliberate. Political arrangement, as it is a work for social ends, is to be only wrought by social means. There mind must conspire with mind. Time is required to produce that union of minds which alone can produce all the good we aim at. Our patience will achieve more than our force. If I might venture to appeal to what is so much out of fashion in Paris, I mean to experience, I should tell you that in my course I have known and, according to my measure, have co-operated with great men; and I have never yet seen any plan which has not been mended by the observation of those who were much inferior in understanding to the person who took the lead in the business. By a slow but well-sustained progress the effect of each step is watched; the good or ill success of the first gives light to us in the second; and so, from light to light, we are conducted with safety through the whole series. We see that the parts of the system do not clash. The evils latent in the most promising contrivances are provided for as they arise. One advantage is as little as possible sacrificed to another. We compensate, we reconcile, we balance. We are enabled to unite into a consistent whole the various anomalies and contending principles that are found in the minds and affairs of men. From hence arises, not an excellence in simplicity, but one far superior, an excellence in composition. Where the great interests of mankind are concerned through a long succession of generations, that succession ought to be admitted into some share in the councils which are so deeply to affect them. If justice requires this, the work itself requires the aid of more minds than one age can furnish. It is from this view of things that the best legislators have been often satisfied with the establishment of some sure, solid, and ruling principle in government—a power like that which some of the philosophers have called a plastic nature; and having fixed the principle, they have left it afterwards to its own operation. . . .

QUESTIONS FOR REFLECTION

1. How does Burke distinguish "real rights" from pretenders?

2. What real rights, in Burke's opinion, do people have? On what are these rights based?

3. What, according to Burke, is the purpose of government? Why does this lead Burke to claim that "the restraints on men, as well as their liberties, are to be reckoned among their rights"?

4. Why does reform require "infinite caution," in Burke's view? Why does Burke stress the importance of tradition?

5. What is the role of "natural feeling" and prejudice in Burke's theory?

6. How do we resolve conflicts between rights, according to Burke?

JOHN STUART MILL

from *Utilitarianism*

(Source: Reprinted from John Stuart Mill, Utilitarianism. London: Longman's, 1907)

. . . We do not call anything wrong unless we mean to imply that a person ought to be punished in some way or other for doing it—if not by law, by the opinion of his fellow creatures; if not by opinion, by the reproaches of his own conscience. This seems the real turning point of the distinction between morality and simple expediency. It is a part of the notion of duty in every one of its forms that a person may rightfully be compelled to fulfil it. Duty is a thing which may be *exacted* from a person, as one exacts a debt. Unless we think that it may be exacted from him, we do not call it his duty. Reasons of prudence, or the interest of other people, may militate against actually exacting it, but the person himself, it is clearly understood, would not be entitled to complain. There are other things, on the contrary, which we wish that people should do, which we like or admire them for doing, perhaps dislike or despise them for not doing, but yet admit that they are not bound to do; it is not a case of moral obligation; we do not blame them, that is, we do not think that they are proper objects of punishment. How we come by these ideas of deserving and not deserving punishment will appear, perhaps, in the sequel; but I think there is no doubt that this distinction lies at the bottom of the notions of right and wrong; that we call any conduct wrong, or employ, instead, some other term of dislike or disparagement, according as we think that the person ought, or ought not, to be punished for it; and we say it would be right to do so and so, or merely that it would be desirable or laudable, according as we would wish to see the person whom it concerns compelled, or only persuaded and exhorted, to act in that manner.

This, therefore, being the characteristic difference which marks off, not justice, but morality in general from the remaining provinces of expediency and worthiness, the character is still to be sought which distinguishes justice from other branches of morality. Now it is known that ethical writers divide moral duties into two classes, denoted by the ill-chosen expressions, duties of perfect and of imperfect obligation; the latter being those in which, though the act is obligatory, the particular occasions of performing it are left to our choice, as in the case of charity or beneficence, which we are indeed bound to practice but not towards any definite person, nor at any prescribed time. In the more precise language of philosophic jurists, duties of perfect obligation are those duties in virtue of which a correlative *right* resides in some person or persons; duties of imperfect obligation are those moral obligations which do not give birth to any right. I think it will be found that this distinction exactly coincides with that which exists between justice and the other obligations of morality. In our survey of the various popular acceptations of justice, the term appeared generally to involve the idea of a personal right—a claim on the part of one or more individuals, like that which the law gives when it confers a proprietary or other legal right. Whether the injustice consists in depriving a person of a possession, or in breaking faith with him, or in treating him worse than he deserves, or worse than other people who have no greater claims—in each case the supposition implies two things: a wrong done, and some assignable person who is wronged. Injustice may also be done by treating a person better than others; but the wrong in this case is to his competitors, who are also assignable persons. It seems to me that this feature in the case—a right in some person, correlative to the moral obligation—constitutes the specific difference between justice and generosity of beneficence. Justice implies something which it is not only right to do, and wrong not to do, but which some individual person can claim from us as his moral right. No one has a moral right to our generosity or beneficence because we are not morally bound to practice those virtues towards any given individual. And it will be found with respect to this as to every correct definition that the instances which seem to conflict with it are those which most confirm it. For if a moralist attempts, as some have done, to make out that mankind generally, though not any given individual, have a right to all the good we can do them, he at once, by that thesis, includes generosity and beneficence within the category of justice. He is obliged to say that our utmost exertions are *due* to our fellow creatures, thus assimilating them to a debt; or that nothing less can be a sufficient *return* for what society does for us, thus classing the case as one of gratitude; both of which are acknowledged cases of justice, and not of the virtue of beneficence; and whoever does not place the distinction between justice and morality in general, where we have now placed it, will be found to make no distinction between them at all, but to merge all morality in justice. . . .

. . . It is common enough, certainly, though the reverse of commendable, to feel resentment merely because we have suffered pain; but a person whose resentment is really a moral feeling, that is, who considers whether an act is blamable before he allows himself to resent it—such a person, though he may not say expressly to himself that he is standing up for the interest of society, certainly does feel that he is asserting a rule which is for the benefit of others as well as for his own. If he is not feeling this—if he is regarding the act solely as it affects him individually—he is not consciously just; he is not concerning himself about the justice of his actions. This is admitted even by anti-utilitarian moralists. When Kant (as before remarked) propounds as the fundamental principle of morals, "So act that thy rule of conduct might be adopted as a law by all rational beings," he virtually acknowledges that the interest of mankind collectively, or at least of mankind indiscriminately, must be in the mind of the agent when conscien-

tiously deciding on the morality of the act. Otherwise he uses words without a meaning; for that a rule even of utter selfishness could not *possibly* be adopted by all rational beings—that there is any insuperable obstacle in the nature of things to its adoption—cannot be even plausibly maintained. To give any meaning to Kant's principle, the sense put upon it must be that we ought to shape our conduct by a rule which all rational beings might adopt *with benefit to their collective interest.*

To recapitulate: the idea of justice supposes two things—a rule of conduct and a sentiment which sanctions the rule. The first must be supposed common to all mankind and intended for their good. The other (the sentiment) is a desire that punishment may be suffered by those who infringe the rule. There is involved, in addition, the conception of some definite person who suffers by the infringement, whose rights (to use the expression appropriated to the case) are violated by it. And the sentiment of justice appears to me to be the animal desire to repel or retaliate a hurt or damage to oneself or to those with whom one sympathises, widened so as to include all persons, by the human capacity of enlarged sympathy and the human conception of intelligent self-interest. From the latter elements the feeling derives its morality; from the former, its peculiar impressiveness and energy of self-assertion.

I have, throughout, treated the idea of a *right* residing in the injured person and violated by the injury, not as a separate element in the composition of the idea and sentiment, but as one of the forms in which the other two elements clothe themselves. These elements are a hurt to some assignable person or persons, on the one hand, and a demand for punishment, on the other. An examination of our own minds, I think, will show that these two things include all that we mean when we speak of violation of a right. When we call anything a person's right, we mean that he has a valid claim on society to protect him in the possession of it, either by the force of law or by that of education and opinion. If he has what we consider a sufficient claim, on whatever account, to have something guaranteed to him by society, we say that he has a right to it. If we desire to prove that anything does not belong to him by right, we think this done as soon as it is admitted that society ought not to take measures for securing it to him, but should leave him to chance or to his own exertions.

Thus a person is said to have a right to what he can earn in fair professional competition, because society ought not to allow any other person to hinder him from endeavouring to earn in that manner as much as he can. But he has not a right to three hundred a year, though he may happen to be earning it; because society is not called on to provide that he shall earn that sum. On the contrary, if he owns ten thousand pounds three-per-cent stock, he *has* a right to three hundred a year because society has come under an obligation to provide him with an income of that amount.

To have a right, then, is, I conceive, to have something which society ought to defend me in the possession of. If the objector goes on to ask why it ought, I can give him no other reason than general utility. If that expression does not seem to convey a sufficient feeling of the strength of the obligation, nor to account for the peculiar energy of the feeling, it is because there goes to the composition of the sentiment, not a rational only but also an animal element—the thirst for retaliation; and this thirst derives its intensity, as well as its moral justification, from the extraordinarily important and impressive kind of utility which is concerned. The interest involved is that of security, to everyone's feelings the most vital of all interests. All other earthly benefits are needed by one person, not needed by another; and many of them can, if necessary, be cheerfully foregone or replaced by something else; but security no human being can possibly do without; on it we depend for all our immunity from evil and for the whole value of all and every good, beyond the passing moment since nothing but the gratification of the instant could be of any worth to us if we could be deprived of everything the next instant by whoever was momentarily stronger than ourselves. Now this most indispensable of all necessaries, after physical nutriment, cannot be had unless the machinery for providing it is kept unintermittedly in active play. Our notion, therefore, of the claim we have on our fellow creatures to join in making safe for us the very groundwork of our existence gathers feelings around it so much more intense than those concerned in any of the more common cases of utility that the difference in degree (as is often the case in psychology) becomes a real difference in kind. The claim assumes that character of absoluteness, that apparent infinity and incommensurability with all other considerations which constitute the distinction between the feeling of right and wrong and that of ordinary expediency and inexpediency. The feelings concerned are so powerful, and we count so positively on finding a responsive feeling in others (all being alike interested), that *ought* and *should* grow into *must,* and recognized indispensability becomes a moral necessity, analogous to physical, and often not inferior to it in binding force.

QUESTIONS FOR REFLECTION

1. Distinguish perfect from imperfect duties. Which corresponds to rights?

2. "To treat someone unjustly is to violate their rights." Does Mill agree? Do you?

3. What is a right, according to Mill? Explain, in these terms, what rights to life, liberty, and property are.

4. How does Mill's conception of rights differ from that of Locke? Of Rousseau?

PRIVACY

Philosophers have been concerned with liberty and rights for hundreds of years. Concern with privacy, in contrast, is more recent, a product of denser living conditions, faster and more widely available means of transportation and communication, a more active press, and technological advances that make it possible to amass large amounts of information about people in one place and then transmit it across the globe almost instantaneously.

Samuel Warren and Louis Brandeis first focused attention on the right to privacy in 1890, when they wrote an influential article defending it as "the right to be let alone." Locke saw the law of nature as giving everyone rights to life, health, liberty, and property. All these stem from a right to self-preservation. All, moreover, are rights to protection—from theft, confiscation, imprisonment, slavery, injury, and death. But people can be injured in more intangible ways as well. In particular, they may be harmed through exposure. Others may try to see or know what you are doing. The government may insist upon gathering information about your activities (employment or stock trading, for example). It may require you to reveal your activities (by filing a tax return, for example) or even observe your activities (by tapping your telephone, say, or by other forms of surveillance). Other people may try to peek through your windows, listen to your conversations, track your purchases or car trips, read your mail, and discuss or even publish intimate details of your personal life. All of these attempts seek to expose you or your activities and thus restrict your privacy. Some are legitimate; others violate your rights. We need an account of the right to privacy to distinguish them. Warren and Brandeis argue for a very broad right to be let alone to "protect the privacy of private life."

Richard Posner argues that Warren and Brandeis omit half the picture. Your right to privacy restricts the freedom of others. To protect you from exposure in some respect, we must restrict the ability of others to gather information about you in that respect (at least, without your consent). As always, protecting the liberty or rights of one requires restricting the liberty of others. So, Posner contends, we must weigh the benefits of protecting privacy against the cost of losing information. Sometimes—as with the tax code, for instance—we find that the cost of losing information outweighs the costs of exposure. Applying a utilitarian calculation, Posner finds many similar situations. People usually try to hide information from others to benefit themselves and deceive or manipulate others. But we are all better off when people can make decisions on the basis of good information. Preventing people from learning about others can thus impose serious costs on society. Juvenile criminal records, for example, are private. That may prevent some unfair discrimination, but it can also prevent potential associates and employers from making reasonable decisions. An eighteen-year-old with a long history of theft, for example, should probably not be hired as a bank teller. But keeping juvenile criminal records private prevents a bank from knowing that history. This is not to say that all exposure is good and all protection of privacy bad. Posner finds that many things, including much business activity, should be protected from exposure. But my privacy is a loss of information for you, so we must circumscribe the right to privacy carefully.

Jeffrey Reiman offers a Kantian defense of privacy. He asks us to consider Jeremy Bentham's ideal prison, the panopticon, where every prisoner can be observed from a central location. Regardless of whether anyone is actually watching, the possibility of observation changes one's behavior and severely restricts freedom. Consider the proposed Intelligent Vehicle Highway System (IVHS), which would track each automobile in the country. This would be useful in many ways, helping to prevent accidents, plan and manage traffic patterns, and detect criminal activity. But it would also change the nature of driving. It would be impossible simply to go somewhere; one would have to go there *and* leave a record of the trip in the central database. Reiman thus observes that rights to privacy, freedom, and autonomy extend beyond traditional bounds. Driving is not something one does in private. It is publicly observable. But having records of it in one place—the idea of the panopticon—threatens privacy and liberty nonetheless. To track someone's car trips now requires great effort and expense. The IVHS would make it easy. The same is true for government and private databases that track economic transactions. Gathering information about your income and expenditures used to be difficult; now it is a matter of typing a number on a keyboard.

Rita Manning defends privacy from a communitarian point of view. Like Edmund Burke, she maintains that the good of society as a whole is not just a function of the good of the individuals in it. In deciding how to define the limits of the right to privacy, we need to think not just about benefits and costs to individuals, or even about freedom and autonomy, but also about what kind of community we are creating. Giving everyone a right to privacy over everything might make community impossible. But insisting on the exposure of all activities also imposes serious costs, eroding trust and self-respect while discouraging frankness and honesty.

Finally, Mayes and Alfino defend Warren and Brandeis's original conception of privacy as a right to be let alone. They note, however, that such a conception leads to a surprising view of privacy. Many violations of rights are also violations of privacy. Moreover, the right to privacy understood in this sense does not entail a right to protect personal information from exposure. Mayes and Alfino defend an Aristotelian/Kantian conception of rationality as underlying our right to protection. Something violates our right to privacy if it violates our ability to act rationally. By that criterion, some exposure violates our rights, for it interferes with a person's rational conduct. I may find myself unable to act reasonably—unable to think—if I realize that everything I do is being broadcast on national television. But a peeping Tom's glimpsing me changing clothes in my own room without my being aware of it may have no effect at all on my ability to think or act rationally.

SAMUEL WARREN
AND LOUIS D. BRANDEIS

The Right to Privacy

Samuel Warren was a prominent Boston attorney. Louis D. Brandeis (1856–1941), his law partner, served as Justice of the United States Supreme Court from 1916 to 1938. [Source: Harvard Law Review *4 (1890).]*

It could be done only on principles of private justice, moral fitness, and public convenience, which, when applied to a new subject, make common law without a precedent; much more when received and approved by usage.
—Willes, J., in *Millar v. Taylor*, 4 Burr, 2303, 2312

That the individual shall have full protection in person and in property is a principle as old as the common law; but it has been found necessary from time to time to define anew the exact nature and extent of such protection. Political, social, and economic changes entail the recognition of new rights, and the common law, in its eternal youth, grows to meet the demands of society. Thus, in very early times, the law gave a remedy only for physical interference with life and property, for trespasses *vi et armis.* Then the "right to life" served only to protect the subject from battery in its various forms; liberty meant freedom from actual restraint; and the right to property secured to the individual his lands and his cattle. Later, there came a recognition of man's spiritual nature, of his feelings and his intellect. Gradually the scope of these legal rights broadened; and now the right to life has come to mean the right to enjoy life—the right to be let alone, the right to liberty secures the exercise of extensive civil privileges; and the term "property" has grown to comprise every form of possession—intangible, as well as tangible.

Thus, with the recognition of the legal value of sensations, the protection against actual bodily injury was extended to prohibit mere attempts to do such injury; that is, the putting another in fear of such injury. From the action of battery grew that of assault. Much later there came a qualified protection of the individual against offensive noises and odors, against dust and smoke, and excessive vibration. The law of nuisance was developed. So regard for human emotions soon extended the scope of personal immunity beyond the body of the individual. His reputation, the standing among his fellow men, was considered, and the law of slander and libel arose. Man's family relations became a part of the legal conception of his life, and the alienation of a wife's affections was held remediable. Occasionally the law halted—as in its refusal to recognize the intrusion by seduction upon the honor of the family. But even here the demands of society were met. A mean fiction, the action *per quod servitium amisit,* was resorted to, and by allowing damages for injury to the parents' feelings, an adequate remedy was ordinarily afforded. Similar to the expansion of the right to life was the growth of the legal conception of property. From corporeal property arose the incorporeal rights issuing out of it; and then there opened the wide realm of intangible property, in the products and processes of the mind, as works of literature and art, good will, trade secrets, and trademarks.

This development of the law was inevitable. The intense intellectual and emotional life, and the heightening of sensations which came with the advance of civilization, made it clear to man that only a part of the pain, pleasure, and profit of life lay in physical things. Thoughts, emotions, and sensations demanded legal recognition, and the beautiful capacity for growth which characterizes the common law enabled the judges to afford the requisite protection, without the interposition of the legislature.

Recent inventions and business methods call attention to the next step which must be taken for the protection of the person, and for securing to the individual what Judge Cooley calls the right "to be let alone." Instantaneous photographs and newspaper enterprise have invaded the sacred precincts of private and domestic life; and numerous mechanical devices threaten to make good the prediction that "what is whispered in the closet shall be proclaimed from the house-tops." For years there has been a feeling that the law must afford some remedy for the unauthorized circulation of portraits of private persons; and the evil of the invasion of privacy by the newspapers, long keenly felt, has been but recently discussed by an able writer. The alleged facts of a somewhat notorious case brought before an inferior tribunal in New York a few months ago directly involved the consideration of the right of circulating portraits; and the question whether our law will recognize and protect the right to privacy in this and in other respects must soon come before our courts for consideration.

Of the desirability—indeed of the necessity—of some such protection, there can, it is believed, be no doubt. The press is overstepping in every direction the obvious bounds of propriety and of decency. Gossip is no longer the resource of the idle and of the vicious, but has become a trade, which is pursued with industry as well as effrontery. To satisfy a prurient taste the details of sexual relations are spread broadcast in the columns of the daily papers. To occupy the indolent, column upon column is filled with idle gossip, which can only be procured by intrusion upon the domestic circle. The intensity and complexity of life, attendant upon advancing civilization, have rendered necessary some retreat from the world, and man, under the refining influence of culture, has become more sensitive to publicity, so that solitude and privacy have become more essential to the individual; but modern enterprise and invention have, through invasions upon his privacy, subjected him to mental pain and distress, far greater than could be inflicted by mere bodily injury.

Nor is the harm wrought by such invasions confined to the suffering of those who may be made the subjects of journalistic or other enterprise. In this, as in other branches of commerce, the supply creates the demand. Each crop of unseemly gossip, thus harvested, becomes the seed of more, and, in direct proportion to its circulation, results in a lowering of social standards and of morality. Even gossip apparently harmless, when widely and persistently circulated, is potent for evil. It both belittles and perverts. It belittles by inverting the relative importance of things, thus dwarfing the thoughts and aspirations of a people. When personal gossip attains the dignity of print, and crowds the space available for matters of real interest to the community, what wonder that the ignorant and thoughtless mistake its relative importance. Easy of comprehension, appealing to that weak side of human nature which is never wholly cast down by the misfortunes and frailties of our neighbors, no one can be surprised that it usurps the place of interest in brains capable of other things. Triviality destroys at once robustness of thought and delicacy of feeling. No enthusiasm can flourish, no generous impulse can survive under its blighting influence.

It is our purpose to consider whether the existing law affords a principle which can properly be invoked to protect the privacy of the individual; and, if it does, what the nature and extent of such protection is.

Owing to the nature of the instruments by which privacy is invaded, the injury inflicted bears a superficial resemblance to the wrongs dealt with by the law of slander and of libel, while a legal remedy for such injury seems to involve the treatment of mere wounded feelings, as a substantive cause of action. The principle on which the law of defamation rests, covers, however, a radically different class of effects from those for which attention is now asked. It deals only with damage to reputation, with the injury done to the individual in his external relations to the community, by lowering him in the estimation of his fellows. The matter published of him, however widely circulated, and however unsuited to publicity, must, in order to be actionable, have a direct tendency to injure him in his intercourse with others, and even if in writing or in print, must subject him to the hatred, ridicule, or contempt of his fellow men—the effect of the publication upon his estimate of himself and upon his own feelings not forming an essential element in the cause of action. In short, the wrongs and correlative rights recognized by the law of slander and libel are in their nature material rather than spiritual. That branch of the law simply extends the protection surrounding physical property to certain of the conditions necessary or helpful to worldly prosperity. On the other hand, our law recognizes no principle upon which compensation can be granted for mere injury to the feelings. However painful the mental effects upon another of an act, though purely wanton or even malicious, yet if the act itself is otherwise lawful, the suffering inflicted is *damnum absque injuria*. Injury of feelings may indeed be taken account of, in ascertaining the amount of damages when attending what is recognized as a legal injury; but our system, unlike the Roman law, does not afford a remedy even for mental suffering which results from mere contumely and insult, from an intentional and unwarranted violation of the "honor" of another.

It is not, however, necessary, in order to sustain the view that the common law recognizes and upholds a principle applicable to cases of invasion of privacy, to invoke the analogy, which is but superficial, to injuries sustained, either by an attack upon reputation or by what the civilians called a violation of honor; for the legal doctrines relating to infractions of what is ordinarily termed the common-law right to intellectual and artistic property are, it is believed, but instances and applications of a general right to privacy, which properly understood afford a remedy for the evils under consideration.

The common law secures to each individual the right of determining, ordinarily, to what extent his thoughts, sentiments, and emotions shall be communicated to others. Under our system of government, he can never be compelled to express them (except when upon the witness stand); and even if he has chosen to give them expression, he generally retains the power to fix the limits of the publicity which shall be given them. The existence of this right does not depend upon the particular method of expression adopted. It is immaterial whether it be by word or by signs, in painting, by sculpture, or in music. Neither does the existence of the right depend upon the nature or value of the thought or emotion, nor upon the excellence of the means of expression. The same protection is accorded to a casual letter or an entry in a diary and to the most valuable poem or essay, to a botch or daub and to a masterpiece. In every such case the individual is entitled to decide whether that which is his shall be given to the public. No other has the right to publish his productions in any form, without his consent. This right is wholly independent of the material on which, or the means by which, the thought, sentiment, or emotion is expressed. It may exist independently of any corporeal being, as in words spoken, a song sung, a drama acted. Or if expressed on any material, as a poem in writing, the author may have parted with the paper, without forfeiting any proprietary right in the composition itself. The right is lost only when the author himself communicates his production to the public—in other words, publishes it. It is entirely independent of the copyright laws, and their extension into the domain of art. The aim of those statutes is to secure to the author, composer, or artist the entire profits arising from publication; but the common-law protection enables him to control absolutely the act of publication, and in the exercise of his own discretion, to decide whether there shall be any publication at all. The stautory right is of no value, *unless* there is a publication; the common-law right is lost *as soon as* there is a publication.

What is the nature, the basis, of this right to prevent the publication of manuscripts or works of art? It is stated to be the enforcement of a right of property; and no difficulty arises in accepting this view, so long as we have only to deal with the reproduction of literary and artistic compositions. They certainly possess many of the attributes of ordinary property: they are transferable; they have a value; and publication or reproduction is a use by which that value is realized. But where the value of the production is found not in the right to take the profits arising from publication, but in the peace of mind or the relief afforded by the ability to prevent any publication at all, it is difficult to regard the right as one of property, in the common acceptation of that term. A man records in a letter to his son, or in his diary, that he did not dine with his wife on a certain day. No one into whose hands those papers fall could publish them to the world, even if possession of the documents had been obtained rightfully and the prohibition would not be confined to the publication of a copy of the letter itself, or of the diary entry; the restraint extends also to a publication of the contents. What is the thing which is protected? Surely, not the intellectual act of recording the fact that the husband did not dine with his wife, but that fact itself. It is not the intellectual product, but the domestic occurrence. A man writes a dozen letters to different people. No person would be permitted to publish a list of the letters written. If the letters or the contents of the diary were protected as literary compositions, the scope of the protection afforded should be the same secured to a published writing under the copyright law. But the copyright law would not prevent an enumeration of the letters, or the publication of some of the facts contained therein. The copyright of a series of paintings or etchings would prevent a reproduction of the paintings as pictures; but it would not prevent a publication of a list or even a description of them. Yet in the famous case of *Prince Albert* v. *Strange* the court held that the common-law rule prohibited not merely the reproduction of the etchings which the plaintiff and Queen Victoria had made for their own pleasure, but also "'the publishing (at least by printing or writing) though not by copy or resemblance, a description of them, whether more or less limited or summary, whether in the form of a catalogue or otherwise." Likewise, an unpublished collection of news possessing no element of a literary nature is protected from piracy.

That this protection cannot rest upon the right to literary or artistic property in any exact sense appears the more clearly when the subject matter for which protection is invoked is not even in the form of intellectual property but has the attributes of ordinary tangible property. Suppose a man has a collection of gems or curiosities which he keeps private: it would hardly be contended that any person could publish a catalogue of them, and yet the articles enumerated are certainly not intellectual property in the legal sense, any more than a collection of stoves or of chairs.

The belief that the idea of property in its narrow sense was the basis of the protection of unpublished manuscripts led an able court to refuse, in several cases, injunctions against the publication of private letters, on the ground that "letters not possessing the attributes of literary compositions are not property entitled to protection"; and that it was "evident the plaintiff could not have considered the letters as of any value whatever as literary productions, for a let-

ter cannot be considered of value to the author which he never would consent to have published." But these decisions have not been followed, and it may now be considered settled that the protection afforded by the common law to the author of any writing is entirely independent of its pecuniary value, its intrinsic merits, or of any intention to publish the same, and, of course, also, wholly independent of the material, if any, upon which, or the mode in which, the thought or sentiment was expressed.

Although the courts have asserted that they rested their decisions on the narrow grounds of protection to property, yet there are recognitions of a more liberal doctrine. Thus in the case of *Prince Albert* v. *Strange,* already referred to, the opinions both of the Vice-Chancellor and of the Lord Chancellor, on appeal, show a more or less clearly defined perception of a principle broader than those which were mainly discussed, and on which they both placed their chief reliance. Vice-Chancellor Knight Bruce referred to publishing of a man that he had "written to particular persons or on particular subjects" as an instance of possibly injurious disclosures as to private matters, that the courts would in a proper case prevent; yet it is difficult to perceive how, in such a case, any right of property, in the narrow sense, would be drawn in questions, or why, if such a publication would be restrained when it threatened to expose the victim not merely to sarcasm, but to ruin, it should not equally be enjoined, if it threatened to embitter his life. To deprive a man of the potential profits to be realized by publishing a catalogue of his gems cannot *per se* be a wrong to him. The possibility of future profits is not a right of property which the law ordinarily recognizes; it must, therefore, be an infraction of other rights which constitutes the wrongful act, and that infraction is equally wrongful, whether its results are to forestall the profits that the individual himself might secure by giving the matter a publicity obnoxious to him, or to gain an advantage at the expense of his mental pain and suffering. If the fiction of property in a narrow sense must be preserved, it is still true that the end accomplished by the gossip-monger is attained by the use of that which is another's, the facts relating to his private life, which he has seen fit to keep private. Lord Cottenham stated that a man "is entitled to be protected in the exclusive use and enjoyment of that which is exclusively his," and cited with approval the opinion of Lord Eldon, as reported in a manuscript note of the case of *Wyatt v. Wilson,* in 1820, respecting an engraving of George the Third during his illness, to the effect that "if one of the late king's physicians had kept a diary of what he heard and saw, the court would not, in the king's lifetime, have permitted him to print and publish it"; and Lord Cottenham declared, in respect to the acts of the defendants in the case before him, that "privacy is the right invaded." But if privacy is once recognized as a right entitled to legal protection, the interposition of the courts cannot depend on the particular nature of the injuries resulting.

These considerations lead to the conclusion that the protection afforded to thoughts, sentiments, and emotions, expressed through the medium of writing or of the arts, so far as it consists in preventing publication, is merely an instance of the enforcement of the more general right of the individual to be let alone. It is like the right not to be assaulted or beaten, the right not to be imprisoned, the right not to be maliciously prosecuted, the right not to be defamed. In each of these rights, as indeed in all other rights recognized by the law, there inheres the quality of being owned or possessed—and (as that is the distinguishing attribute of property) there may be some propriety in speaking of those rights as property. But, obviously, they bear little resemblance to what is ordinarily comprehended under that term. The principle which protects personal writings and all other personal productions, not against theft and physical appropriation, but against publication in any form, is in reality not the principle of private property, but that of an inviolate personality.

If we are correct in this conclusion, the existing law affords a principle which may be invoked to protect the privacy of the individual from invasion either by the too-enterprising press, the photographer, or the possessor of any other modern device for recording or reproducing scenes or sounds. For the protection afforded is not confined by the authorities to those cases where any particular medium or form of expression has been adopted, nor to products of the intellect. The same protection is afforded to emotions and sensations expressed in a musical composition or other work of art as to a literary composition; and words spoken, a pantomime acted, a sonata performed, is no less entitled to protection than if each had been reduced to writing. The circumstance that

a thought or emotion has been recorded in a permanent form renders its identification easier and hence may be important from the point of view of evidence, but it has no significance as a matter of substantive right. If, then, the decisions indicate a general right to privacy for thoughts, emotions, and sensations, these should receive the same protection, whether expressed in writing, in conduct, in conversation, in attitudes, or in facial expression.

It may be urged that a distinction should be taken between the deliberate expression of thoughts and emotions in literary or artistic compositions and the casual and often involuntary expression given to them in the ordinary conduct of life. In other words, it may be contended that the protection afforded is granted to the conscious products of labor, perhaps as an encouragement effort. This contention, however plausible, has, in fact, little to recommend it. If the amount of labor involved be adopted as the test, we might well find that the effort to conduct oneself properly in business and in domestic relations had been far greater than that involved in painting a picture or writing a book; one would find that it was far easier to express lofty sentiments in a diary than in the conduct of a noble life. If the test of deliberateness of the act be adopted, much casual correspondence which is now accorded full protection would be excluded from the beneficent operation of existing rules. After the decisions denying the distinction attempted to be made between those literary productions which it was intended to publish and those which it was not, all considerations of the amount of labor involved, the degree of deliberation, the value of the product, and the intention of publishing must be abandoned, and no basis is discerned upon which the right to restrain publication and reproduction of such so-called literary and artistic works can be rested, except the right to privacy, as a part of the more general right to the immunity of the person— the right to one's personality.

It should be stated that, in some instances where protection has been afforded against wrongful publication, the jurisdiction has been asserted, not on the ground of property, or at least not wholly on that ground, but upon the ground of an alleged breach of an implied contract or of a trust or confidence.

Thus, in *Abernethy v. Hutchinson,* 3 L. J. Ch. 209 (1825), where the plaintiff, a distinguished surgeon, sought to restrain the publication in the *Lancet* of unpublished lectures which he had delivered at St. Bartholomew's Hospital in London, Lord Eldon doubted whether there could be property in lectures which had not been reduced to writing, but granted the injunction on the ground of breach of confidence, holding "that when persons were admitted as pupils or otherwise, to hear these lectures, although they were orally delivered, and although the parties might go to the extent, if they were able to do so, of putting down the whole by means of shorthand, yet they could do that only for the purposes of their own information, and could not publish, for profit, that which they had not obtained the right of selling."

In *Prince Albert v. Strange,* 1 McN. & G. 25 (1849), Lord Cottenham, on appeal, while recognizing a right of property in the etchings which of itself would justify the issuance of the injunction, stated, after discussing the evidence, that he was bound to assume that the possession of the etchings by the defendant had "its foundation in a breach of trust, confidence, or contract," and that upon such ground also the plaintiff's title to the injunction was fully sustained.

In *Tuck v. Priester,* 19 Q. B. D. 639 (1887), the plaintiffs were owners of a picture and employed the defendant to make a certain number of copies. He did so, and made also a number of other copies for himself, and offered them for sale in England at a lower price. Subsequently, the plaintiffs registered their copyright in the picture, and then brought suit for an injunction and damages. The Lords Justices differed as to the application of the copyright acts to the case but held unanimously that, independently of those acts, the plaintiffs were entitled to an injunction and damages for breach of contract.

In *Pollard v. Photographic Co.,* 40 Ch. Div. 345 (1888), a photographer who had taken a lady's photograph under the ordinary circumstances was restrained from exhibiting it, and also from selling copies of it, on the ground that it was a breach of an implied term in the contract, and also that it was a breach of confidence. Mr. Justice North interjected in the argument of the plaintiff's counsel the inquiry: "Do you dispute that if the negative likeness were taken on the sly, the person who took it might exhibit copies?" and counsel for the plaintiff answered: "In that case there would be no trust or consideration to support a contract." Later, the defendant's counsel argued that "a person has no property in his own features; short of doing what is libelous or otherwise illegal, there is no restriction on the photographer's using his negative." But the court, while expressly finding a breach of contract and of trust sufficient to justify its interposition, still seems to have felt the necessity of resting the decision also upon a right of property in order to bring it within the line of those cases which were relied upon as precedents.

This process of implying a term in a contract, or of implying a trust (particularly where the contract is written, and where there is no established usage or custom), is nothing more nor less than a judicial declaration that public morality, private justice, and general convenience demand the recognition of such a rule, and that the publication under similar circumstances would be considered an intolerable abuse. So long as these circumstances happen to present a contract upon which such a term can be engrafted by the judicial mind, or to supply relations upon which a trust or confidence can be erected, there may be no objection to working out the desired protection through the doctrines of contract or of trust. But the court can hardly stop there. The narrower doctrine may have satisfied the demands of society at a time when the abuse to be guarded against could rarely have arisen without violating a contract or a special confidence; but now that modern devices afford abundant opportunities for the perpetration of such wrongs without any participation by the injured party, the protection granted by the law must be placed upon a broader foundation. While, for instance, the state of the photographic art was such that one's picture could seldom be taken without his consciously "sitting" for the purpose, the law of contract or of trust might afford the prudent man sufficient safeguards against the improper circulation of his portrait; but since the latest advances in photographic art have rendered it possible to take pictures surreptitiously, the doctrines of contract and of trust are inadequate to support the required protection, and the law of tort must be resorted to. The right of property in its widest sense, including all possession, including all rights and privileges, and hence embracing the right to an inviolate personality, affords alone that broad basis upon which the protection which the individual demands can be rested.

Thus, the courts, in searching for some principle upon which the publication of private letters could be enjoined, naturally came upon the ideas of a breach of confidence, and of an implied contract; but it required little consideration to discern that this doctrine could not afford all the protection required, since it would not support the court in granting a remedy against a stranger; and so the theory of property in the contents of letters was adopted. Indeed, it is difficult to conceive on what theory of the law the casual recipient of a letter, who proceeds to publish it is guilty of a breach of contract, express or implied, or of any breach of trust, in the ordinary acceptation of that term. Suppose a letter has been addressed to him without his solicitation. He opens it and reads. Surely, he has not made any contract; he has not accepted any trust. He cannot, by opening and reading the letter, have come under any obligation save what the law declares; and, however expressed, that obligation is simply to observe the legal right of the sender, whatever it may be, and whether it be called his right of property in the contents of the letter, or his right to privacy.

A similar groping for the principle upon which a wrongful publication can be enjoined is found in the law of trade secrets. There, injunctions have generally been granted on the theory of a breach of contract or of an abuse of confidence. It would, of course, rarely happen that anyone would be in the possession of a secret unless confidence had been reposed in him. But can it be supposed that the court would hesitate to grant relief against one who had obtained his knowledge by an ordinary trespass—for instance, by wrongfully looking into a book in which the secret was recorded, or by eavesdropping? Indeed, in *Yovatt v. Winyard,* 1 J. & W. 394 (1820), where an injunction was granted against making any use of or communicating certain recipes for veterinary medicine, it appeared that the defendant, while in the plaintiff's employ, had surreptitiously got access to his book of recipes, and copied them. Lord Eldon "granted the injunction, upon the ground of there having been a breach of trust and confidence"; but it would seem to be difficult to draw any sound legal distinction between such a case and one where a mere stranger wrongfully obtained access to the book.

We must therefore conclude that the rights, so protected, whatever their exact nature, are not rights arising from contract or from special trust, but are rights as against the world; and, as above stated, the principle which has been applied to protect these rights is in reality not the principle of private property, unless that word be used in an extended and unusual sense. The principle which protects personal writings and any other productions of the intellect or of the emotions is the right to privacy, and the law has no new principle to formulate when it extends this protection to the personal appearance, sayings, acts, and to personal relations, domestic or otherwise.

If the invasion of privacy constitutes a legal *injuria,* the elements for demanding redress exist, since already the value of mental suffering, caused by an act wrongful in itself, is recognized as a basis for compensation.

The right of one who has remained a private individual, to prevent his public portraiture, presents the simplest case for such extension; the right to protect one's self from pen portraiture, from a discussion by the press of one's private affairs, would be a more important and far-reaching one. If casual and unimportant statements in a letter, if handiwork, however inartistic and valueless, if possessions of all sorts are protected not only against reproduction, but against description and enumeration, how much more should the acts and sayings of a man in his social and domestic relations be guarded from ruthless publicity. If you may not reproduce a woman's face photographically without her consent, how much less should be tolerated the reproduction of her face, her form, and her actions, by graphic descriptions colored to suit a gross and depraved imagination.

The right to privacy, limited as such right must necessarily be, has already found expression in the law of France.

It remains to consider what are the limitations of this right to privacy, and what remedies may be granted for the enforcement of the right. To determine in advance of experience the exact line at which the dignity and convenience of the individual must yield to the demands of the public welfare or of private justice would be a difficult task; but the more general rules are furnished by the legal analogies already developed in the law of slander and libel, and in the law of literary and artistic property.

First. The right to privacy does not prohibit any publication of matter which is of public or general interest.

In determining the scope of this rule, aid would be afforded by the analogy, in the law of libel and slander, of cases which deal with the qualified privilege of comment and criticism on matters of public and general interest. There are of course difficulties in applying such a rule; but they are inherent in the subject matter and are certainly no greater than those which exist in many other branches of the law—for instance, in that large class of cases in which the reasonableness or unreasonableness of an act is made the test of liability. The design of the law must be to protect those persons with whose affairs the community has no legitimate concern from being dragged into an undesirable and undesired publicity and to protect all persons, whatsoever their position or station, from having matters which they may properly prefer to keep private, made public against their will. It is the unwarranted invasion of individual privacy which is reprehended, and to be, so far as possible, prevented. The distinction, however, noted in the above statement is obvious and fundamental. There are persons who may reasonably claim as a right, protection from the notoriety entailed by being made the victims of journalistic enterprise. There are others who, in varying degrees, have renounced the right to live their lives screened from public observation. Matters which men of the first class may justly contend concern themselves alone, may in those of the second be the subject of legitimate interest to their fellow citizens. Peculiarities of manner and person, which in the ordinary individual should be free from comment, may acquire a public importance if found in a candidate for political office. Some further discrimination is necessary, therefore, than to class facts or deeds as public or private according to a standard to be applied to the fact or deed *per se*. To publish of a modest and retiring individual that he suffers from an impediment in his speech or that he cannot spell correctly is an unwarranted, if not an unexampled, infringement of his rights, while to state and comment on the same characteristics found in a would-be congressman could not be regarded as beyond the pale of propriety.

The general object in view is to protect the privacy of private life, and to whatever degree and in whatever connection a man's life has ceased to be private, before the publication under consideration has been made, to that extent the protection is to be withdrawn. Since, then, the propriety of publishing the very same facts may depend wholly upon the person concerning whom they are published, no

fixed formula can be used to prohibit obnoxious publications. Any rule of liability adopted must have in it an elasticity which shall take account of the varying circumstances of each case—a necessity which unfortunately renders such a doctrine not only more difficult of application but also to a certain extent uncertain in its operation and easily rendered abortive. Besides, it is only the more flagrant breaches of decency and propriety that could in practice be reached, and it is not perhaps desirable even to attempt to repress everything which the nicest taste and keenest sense of the respect due to private life would condemn.

In general, then, the matters of which the publication should be repressed may be described as those which concern the private life, habits, acts, and relations of an individual, and have no legitimate connection with his fitness for a public office which he seeks or for which he is suggested, or for any public quasi-public position which he seeks or for which he is suggested, and have no legitimate relation to or bearing upon any act done by him in a public or quasi-public capacity. The foregoing is not designed as a wholly accurate or exhaustive definition, since that which must ultimately in a vast number of cases become a question of individual judgment and opinion is incapable of such definition; but it is an attempt to indicate broadly the class of matters referred to. Some things all men alike are entitled to keep from popular curiosity, whether in public life or not, while others are only private because the persons concerned have not assumed a position which makes their doings legitimate matters of public investigation.

Second. The right to privacy does not prohibit the communication of any matter, though in its nature private, when the publication is made under circumstances which would render it a privileged communication according to the law of slander and libel.

Under this rule, the right to privacy is not invaded by any publication made in a court of justice, in legislative bodies, or the committees of those bodies; in municipal assemblies, or the committee of such assemblies, or practically by any communication made in any other public body, municipal or parochial, or in any body quasi-public, like the large voluntary associations formed for almost every purpose of benevolence, business, or other general interest; and (at least in many jurisdictions) reports of any such proceedings would in some measure be accorded a like privilege. Nor would the rule prohibit any publication made by one in the discharge of some public or private duty, whether legal or moral, or in conduct of one's own affairs, in matters where his own interest is concerned.

Third. The law would probably not grant any redress for the invasion of privacy by oral publication in the absence of special damage.

The same reasons exist for distinguishing between oral and written publications of private matters, as is afforded in the law of defamation by the restricted liability for slander as compared with the liability for libel. The injury resulting from such oral communications would ordinarily be so trifling that the law might well, in the interest of free speech, disregard it altogether.

Fourth. The right to privacy ceases upon the publication of the facts by the individual, or with his consent.

This is but another application of the rule which has become familiar in the law of literary and artistic property. The cases there decided established also what should be deemed a publication—the important principle in this connection being that a private communication or circulation for a restricted purpose is not a publication within the meaning of the law.

Fifth. The truth of the matter published does not afford a defense.

Obviously this branch of the law should have no concern with the truth or falsehood of the matters published. It is not for injury to the individual's character that redress or prevention is sought, but for injury to the right of privacy. For the former, the law of slander and libel provides perhaps a sufficient safeguard. The latter implies the right not merely to prevent inaccurate portrayal of private life but to prevent its being depicted at all.

Sixth. The absence of "malice" in the publisher does not afford a defense.

Personal ill will is not an ingredient of the offense, any more than in an ordinary case of trespass to person or to property. Such malice is never necessary to be shown in any action for libel or slander at common law, except in rebuttal of some defense, e.g., that the occasion rendered the communication privileged, or, under the statutes in this state and elsewhere, that the statement complained of was true. The invasion of the privacy that is to be protected is

causally complete and equally injurious, whether the motives by which the speaker or writer was actuated are, taken by themselves, culpable or not; just as the damage to character, and to some extent the tendency to provoke a breach of the peace, is equally the result of defamation without regard to the motives leading to its publication. Viewed as a wrong to the individual, this rule is the same pervading the whole law of torts, by which one is held responsible for his intentional acts, even though they are committed with no sinister intent; and viewed as a wrong to society, it is the same principle adopted in a large category of statutory offenses.

The remedies for an invasion of the right of privacy are also suggested by those administered in the law of defamation and in the law of literary and artistic property, namely:

1. An action of tort for damages in all cases. Even in the absence of special damages, substantial compensation could be allowed for injury to feelings as in the action of slander and libel.

2. An injunction, in perhaps a very limited class of cases.

It would doubtless be desirable that the privacy of the individual should receive the added protection of the criminal law, but for this, legislation would be required. Perhaps it would be deemed proper to bring the criminal liability for such publication within narrower limits; but that the community has an interest in preventing such invasions of privacy, sufficiently strong to justify the introduction of such a remedy, cannot be doubted. Still, the protection of society must come mainly through a recognition of the rights of the individual. Each man is responsible for his own acts and omissions only. If he condones what he reprobates, with a weapon at hand equal to his defense, he is responsible for the results. If he resists, public opinion will rally to his support. Has he then such a weapon? It is believed that the common law provides him with one, forged in the slow fire of the centuries and today fitly tempered to his hand. The common law has always recognized a man's house as his castle, impregnable, often even to its own officers engaged in the execution of its commands. Shall the courts thus close the front entrance to constituted authority, and open wide the back door to idle or prurient curiosity?

QUESTIONS FOR REFLECTION

1. Why, according to Warren and Brandeis, does privacy need protection?

2. What, in their view, is the right to privacy?

3. Can we subsume the right to privacy under the general umbrella of the right to property? Why or why not?

4. How does the right to privacy relate to the right not to be beaten? To the right not to be maliciously defamed?

5. Why should we not draw a distinction between the publication of literary works and the disclosure of personal information, according to Warren and Brandeis? Do you agree?

6. What limits do Warren and Brandeis place upon the right to privacy?

7. Can one derive from the thought of Hobbes, Locke, Rousseau, or Mill any general "right to be let alone"?

8. Suppose we monitor Jones's movements and speech electronically without her being aware of it. Have we violated her rights, in Warren and Brandeis's view?

RICHARD POSNER

from *The Economics of Justice*

*Richard Posner is Chief Judge of the U.S. Court of Appeals, Seventh Circuit.
(Source: Richard Posner,* The Economics of Justice, *Cambridge, MA:
Harvard University Press, 1981. Most notes have been omitted. Reprinted by
permission.)*

The Economics of Private Information and Communications

Concealment of Personal Facts

The question whether and to what extent people
should have a legally protected right to conceal personal information arises only because some people
want to uncover such information about others—to
pry, in a word. The first question I address, therefore,
is why people want to pry. Is it a matter purely of
idle or prurient curiosity, or is a functional, that is to
say an economic, explanation possible?

I believe such an explanation is possible, most
clearly where an actual or potential relationship,
whether business or personal, creates opportunities
to profit (monetarily or not) from possessing information about someone else. This is what motivates
the demand for personal information by the tax collector, fiancé, partner, creditor, and competitor. Less
obviously, much of the casual prying (a term used
here without any pejorative connotation) into the
private lives of friends and colleagues, such a common feature of social life, may also be motivated by
rational considerations of self-interest. Prying enables one to form a more accurate picture of a friend
or colleague, and the knowledge gained is useful in
social or professional dealings with him. For example, in choosing a friend one wants to know whether
he will be discreet or indiscreet, selfish or generous,
and these qualities are not always apparent on initial

acquaintance. Even a pure altruist needs to know the
approximate wealth of a prospective beneficiary of
his altruism in order to gauge the value of a transfer
to him.

The other side of the coin is that social, like business, dealings present opportunities for exploitation
through misrepresentation. Psychologists and sociologists have pointed out—what everyone knows—
that even in everyday life people frequently resort to
misrepresentation (of their income, prospects, opinions, and so forth) in order to manipulate other people's opinion of them. The "wish for privacy expresses a desire . . . to control others' perceptions
and beliefs vis-à-vis the self-concealing person."*
Even the strongest defenders of privacy describe the
individual's right to privacy as the right to "control
the flow of information about him,"† and it is only
fair to add that this may be information concerning
past or present criminal activity, or moral conduct at
variance with the individual's professed moral standards, and that often the motive for concealment is
to mislead those with whom he transacts. Other private information that people wish to conceal, while

---

* Signey M. Jourard, "Some Psychological Aspects of Privacy," 31
Law & Contemp. Prob. 307 (1966).
† Geoffrey R. Stone, "The Scope of the Fourth Amendment: Privacy and the Police Use of Spies, Secret Agents and Informers,"
1976 *Am. Bar Found. Research J.* 1193, 1207. See also references
cited there, and Edward A. Shils, *The Torment of Secrecy: The Background and Consequences of American Security Policies* 26 (1956).

not discreditable in a moral sense, would if revealed correct misapprehensions that the individual is trying to exploit, as when a worker conceals a serious health problem from his employer, or a prospective husband conceals his sterility from his fiancée. It is not clear why society should assign the property right in such information to the individual to whom it pertains; the common law, as we shall see, generally does not. (A separate question, to which I return later, is whether the decision to assign the property right away from the possessor of guilty secrets implies that the law should countenance any and all methods of uncovering those secrets.)

We would think it wrong (and inefficient) if the law permitted a seller in hawking his wares to make false or incomplete representations of their quality. But people "sell" themselves as well as their goods by professing high standards of behavior to induce others to engage in advantageous social or business dealings with them, while concealing facts that these acquaintances need in order to evaluate their character. There are practical reasons for not imposing a general legal duty of full and frank disclosure of one's material personal shortcomings. But shouldn't a person be allowed to protect himself from disadvantageous transactions by ferreting out concealed facts about individuals which are material to the implicit or explicit representations that those individuals make concerning their moral qualities? It is no answer that people have "the right to be let alone,"* for few people want to be let alone. Rather, they want to manipulate the world around them by selective disclosure of facts about themselves.

To be sure, some private information that people desire to conceal is not discreditable. In our culture, for example, most people do not like to be seen naked, quite apart from any discreditable fact that such observation might reveal. Since this reticence, unlike concealment of discreditable facts, is not a source of social costs, and since transaction costs are low, there is an economic case for assigning the

property right in this area of private information to the individual; and this is what the law does. But few people have a *general* reticence that makes them want to conceal nondiscrediting personal information. Anyone who has sat next to a stranger on an airplane or a ski lift knows the delight most people take in talking about themselves to complete strangers. Reticence is more likely in speaking to friends, relatives, acquaintances, or business associates who might use a personal disclosure to gain an advantage (or avoid being disadvantaged) in a business or social transaction.

People's reluctance to reveal their incomes may seem a good example of a desire for privacy that cannot be explained in purely instrumental terms. But I think that people conceal an unexpectedly *low* income mainly because being thought to have a high income has value in credit markets and elsewhere, and they conceal an unexpectedly *high* income to avoid the attention of tax collectors, kidnappers, and thieves; fend off solicitations from charities and family members; and preserve a reputation for generosity that might be impaired if others knew what fraction of their income they gave away. (The first and second points may explain anonymous gifts to charity.) One must distinguish, however, between concealing one's income from kidnappers and other criminals, on the one hand, and from the tax collector, family members, and creditors, on the other; the former concealment serves a perfectly legitimate self-protective function.

To my argument that people conceal facts about themselves in order to mislead others, one could reply that such concealment may on balance foster efficient transactions, because many of the facts that people conceal (homosexuality, ethnic origins, aversions, sympathy toward communism or fascism, minor mental illnesses, early scrapes with the law, marital discord, nose picking) would if revealed provoke irrational reactions by prospective employers, friends, creditors, lovers, and so on. This objection overlooks the opportunity costs of shunning people for stupid reasons, or, stated otherwise, the gains from dealing with someone whom others shun irrationally. If ex-convicts are good workers but most employers do not know this, employers who do know will be able to hire them at a below-average wage because of their depressed job opportunities and will thereby obtain a competitive advantage over

---

* *Olmstead* v. *United States,* 277 U.S. 438, 478 (1928), dissenting opinion of Justice Brandeis. It is a good answer if the question is whether people should have a right to be free from unwanted solicitations, noisy sound trucks, or obscene telephone calls. These invade a privacy interest different from the one discussed in this chapter, since they involve no effort to obtain information.

the bigots. In a diverse, decentralized, and competitive society, irrational shunning will be weeded out over time.

A commercial analogy will help to bring out this point. For many years the Federal Trade Commission required importers of certain products, especially those made in Japan, to label the product's country of origin. The reason was a widespread belief, whose rationality the commission was not prepared to confirm or deny, that certain foreign (especially Japanese) goods were inferior. It was also believed that there was some residual anger over Pearl Harbor. But as is well known, Japanese products proved themselves in the marketplace, the prejudice against them waned and eventually disappeared, and today Japanese origin is a proudly displayed sign of quality and good value. This is an example of how competition can, over time, dispel prejudice. A similar example, that of Japanese-American people rather than Japanese products, illustrates the competitive process at work in the realm of employment and personal relationships.

The different treatment of past criminal conduct in the law of torts and the law of evidence provides further insight into this point. Except in California, there is no right of action against someone who publicizes an individual's criminal record, no matter how far in the past the crime occurred; but the use of past crimes to impeach the testimony of a witness in a criminal trial is limited (in the judge's discretion) to relatively recent crimes. In both cases, it is arguable that people can be trusted to discount negative personal information by its recency. But in the tort case the people doing the discounting—friends, creditors, employers, and other actual and potential transactors—pay a price, in the form of lost opportunities for advantageous transactions, if they attach excessive weight to information about the remote past. They thus have an incentive not to react irrationally to such information. Jurors, in contrast, incur no cost from behaving irrationally; the market analogy therefore fails, and a paternalistic approach to the question of the rationality of their decisions may be warranted.

Irrational prejudices, which a market system tends to weed out, must not be confused with acting on incomplete information. The rational individual or firm will stop searching for a social or business partner at the point where the marginal gain in knowledge from additional search is just equal to the marginal cost in time or money. Consequently, if the value of transacting with one individual rather than another is small or the cost of additional information great, the process of rational search may end at what some would consider a very early stage. If exconvicts have on average poor employment records, if the cost is high of correcting this average judgment for the individual exconvict applying for a job, and if substitute employees without criminal records are available at not much higher wages, it may be rational for an employer to adopt a flat rule of not employing anyone who has a criminal record.*

There is no evidence that people are in general less rational about how far to carry their search for employees, spouses, and friends than they are in traditional market activities (of which employment is one). A growing empirical literature on nonmarket behavior, including marriage, procreation, and crime, finds that people behave as rationally in these areas as do firms and consumers in explicit markets. These findings argue for allowing people to make their own determinations of how much weight to attach to discreditable facts that other people try to conceal. This "free market" approach suggests that whatever rules governing fraud are optimal in ordinary product markets ought, as a first approximation, to govern labor markets, credit markets, and "markets" for purely personal relationships as well. Thus, if economic analysis would deem it fraudulent to refuse to disclose a particular type of fact in the market for goods, such refusal should equally be deemed fraudulent when made by someone seeking a job, a personal loan, or a wife. Annulment of a marriage because of fraud is thus a strict analogue to rescision of a fraudulent commercial contract. Of course, in many areas of personal relations the costs of fraud are too slight to warrant formal legal remedies. And in some where they are high, notably marriage, alternative remedies are available. Courtship provides a period in which

---

* Notice how minimum-wage laws retard the process by which members of different groups obtain access to the employment market. This observation invites the familiar argument that public intervention is warranted to correct the consequences of a previous ill-advised intervention. But the new intervention may turn out to be ill advised too. For this reason, government's previous failures provide an insufficient basis for urging additional public intervention.

prospective spouses can learn enough about each other to cure any misrepresentations. This may be why evidence of more serious fraud is required in annulment cases than in cases seeking rescision of ordinary commercial contracts.

I have suggested that much of the demand for private information about others is really a form of self-protection. But self-protection does not explain the demand, supplied by newspaper gossip columns, to learn about the private lives of complete strangers. Gossip columns provide valuable information of a different sort, however. They recount the personal lives of wealthy and successful people whose tastes and habits offer models to the ordinary person in making consumption, career, and other decisions. The models are not always edifying. The story of Howard Hughes, for example, is a morality play warning of the pitfalls of success. Tales of the notorious and the criminal—of a Profumo or a Leopold—have a similar function.

Why is there less curiosity about the lives of the poor, as measured, for example, by the frequency with which poor people are central characters in novels, than about those of the rich?* The reason, I conjecture, is that the lives of the poor do not provide as much useful information in patterning our own lives. What interest there is in the poor is focused on people who are (or were) affluent but who become poor, rather than on those who were always poor; the cautionary function of such information should be evident.

Warren and Brandeis, in a famous article on privacy, attributed the rise of curiosity about people's lives to the excesses of the press.† The economist does not believe, however, that supply creates demand.‡ A more persuasive explanation for the rise of the gossip column is the secular increase in personal incomes. There is little privacy in most poor societies, and consequently people can easily observe at first hand the intimate lives of others. Personal surveillance is costlier in wealthier societies, both because people have greater privacy and because the value (and hence opportunity cost) of time is greater—too great to make it worthwhile to allot a generous amount of time to watching neighbors. In societies where the costs of obtaining information have become too great for the Nosy Parker, the press provides, among its other functions, specialization in prying. The press also unmasks the misrepresentations that people employ to deceive others into transacting with them on advantageous terms. I use "transaction" in a broad sense to include, for example, the individual who wants to be vice-president without disclosing his history of mental illness (Thomas Eagleton in 1972).

The idea that gossip columns have an informational function is one of the most strongly resisted implications of the economic analysis of privacy. But how else is one to explain why "prurient" interest in the private lives of the wealthy and celebrated apparently is positively correlated with physical privacy? Gossip columns and movie magazines flourish more in the United States than in Europe, where there is less physical privacy (space, anonymity) than in the United States. And although gossip columns, movie magazines, and other vehicles of public gossip are considered the province of the vulgar and uneducated, their rise in popularity in this country coincides with a rising level of education—because, I suggest, the growth of physical privacy has shut off direct observation of how strangers live.

The element of misrepresentation in the concealment of personal information is important, but there are other elements: First, concealment sometimes promotes rather than impedes the transmittal of accurate information. At any moment one's mind is likely to be brimming over with vagrant, half-formed, and ill-considered thoughts that, if revealed to others, would provide less information about one's intentions and capacities than the thoughts one chooses to express in speech. Concealing one's "inner thoughts" is just the other side of selecting certain thoughts for utterance and thus communicating one's intentions and values. Similarly, wearing

---

* Surely not because writers know the lives of the rich more intimately than those of the poor: Shakespeare's protagonists are kings and nobles, but he was not an aristocrat.

† "The press is overstepping in every direction the obvious bounds of propriety and of decency. Gossip is no longer the resource of the idle and of the vicious, but has become a trade, which is pursued with industry as well as effrontery . . . To occupy the indolent, column upon column is filled with idle gossip, which can only be procured by intrusion upon the domestic circle." Samuel D. Warren and Louis D. Brandeis, "The Right to Privacy," 4 *Harv. L. Rev.* 193, 196 (1890).

‡"In this, as in other branches of commerce, the supply creates the demand." *Id.*

clothes serves not merely to protect one against the elements but also to make a public statement about one's values and tastes. If we went around naked, babbling the first thing that came into our minds, we would be revealing less of ourselves than we do by dressing carefully and speaking with reticence. This is not the point that hypocrisy is the essential lubricant of social relations, which has no obvious economic interpretation. The point is, rather, that if A values B as a potential business associate, telling B he looks like a frog will obscure rather than elucidate A's sincere view of B—which is that he values him as a potential business associate.* (The borderland between concealment as information and as misrepresentation is illustrated by the dyeing of hair. The purpose may be to communicate something about the kind of person one is, or it may be to conceal one's age, or it may be both.)

That clothing, adornment, cosmetics, accent, and the like serve not only to communicate but also to misrepresent may conceivably explain some of the sporadic efforts to regulate luxury in dress. In the fourteenth century,

> nothing was more resented by the hereditary nobles than the imitation of their clothes and manners by the upstarts, thus obscuring the lines between the eternal orders of society. Magnificence in clothes was considered a prerogative of nobles, who should be identifiable by modes of dress foribidden to others. In the effort to establish this principle as law and prevent "outrageous and excessive apparel of diverse people against their estate and degree," sumptuary laws were repeatedly announced, attempting to fix what kinds of clothes people might wear and how much they might spend.†

A second qualification of the analysis is that the competitive provision of information may lead to its overproduction from an efficiency standpoint. A firm's advertising serves partly to offset a rival firm's advertising, and the same point can be made of truthful signaling through dress, manners, and other forms of self-advertising. Even where the signal is true, the effort of each individual to signal loud and clear may result in producing more information about personal characteristics than is optimal, in the sense that if transaction costs were zero, all would be better off agreeing to signal less. The dress codes occasionally found in business firms and private schools, though ostensibly intended to raise the standard of dress, may sometimes have the opposite result, to reduce the level and costs of dress. And this may be the real intention; limiting variety in dress reduces the amount of resources devoted to this form of self-advertising.

Secrecy and Innovation

The most important qualifications of the view of privacy as manipulation or misrepresentation involve innovative ideas and private conversations. The public character of information makes its prompt appropriation by others easy. But such appropriation prevents the original producer of the information from recouping his investment in its production and thereby reduces the incentive to make such investments. Two methods of overcoming this problem are compatible with a market system as usually understood. The first is the explicit creation of property rights in information, as in the patent and copyright laws. The second is secrecy, meaning that the information is used by the producer but not disclosed until he has had a chance to profit from his exclusive possession.

The choice between these methods depends on a weighing of relative costs and benefits in particular circumstances. On the benefit side, compare statutory and common law copyright. The former gives the author a property right in his work; no one may copy it without his authorization. Common law copyright used the method of secrecy: so long as the author did not publish his manuscript, the law would protect him against unauthorized dissemination by others. Obviously, the method of secrecy would be self-defeating if an author wanted to publish his work or if the practice of an invention would immediately disclose the embodied innovation. And even where secrecy would afford some protection (a

---

* If the above analysis is correct, efforts to improve social interactions through nudism, extreme frankness of speech, and other fashionable techniques of group therapy are fundamentally confused. On clothes as signals see Irwin Altman, *The Environment and Social Behavior: Privacy, Personal Space, Territory, Crowding* 36–37 (1975).

† Barbara W. Tuchman, *A Distant Mirror: The Calamitous 14th Century* 19 (1978).

publisher might earn substantial revenues before a pirate edition could be printed and distributed), it might be extremely costly. It might entail, for example, accelerated, secretive book publication at higher costs than if the publisher had a property right in the published work. Or a secret process might have valuable applications in another industry, yet the owner of the process would be afraid to sell it because the secret might get out to his competitors.

On the other hand, the costs of enforcing a property right in information would often be disproportionate to the value of the information to be protected: the patent system could not be used to protect a popular host's dinner recipes. And often the costs of tracing information to its origin preclude reliance on a property-rights system: if ideas as such, as distinct from the sorts of concretely embodied ideas protected by the patent and copyright laws, could be patented or copyrighted, the scope of, and difficulty of determining, infringement would be excessive. Consequently, secrecy is an important social instrument for encouraging the production of information, especially in settings where the formal rights system in intellectual property is undeveloped. Thus the law does not require the shrewd bargainer to disclose to the other party the bargainer's true opinion of its value. By a "shrewd bargainer" we mean, in part at least, someone who invests resources in acquiring information about the true values of things. Were he forced to share this information with potential sellers, he would obtain no return on his investment, and the transfer of goods by voluntary exchange into successively more valuable uses would be impaired. So he is not forced to do so, even though the resulting lack of candor in the bargaining process deprives it of some of its "voluntary" character. Similarly, the law does not punish the large purchaser of some company's stock who places a lot of small orders under false names so that his activity will not inform the sellers that they have undervalued the stock. Secrecy is the indispensable method not only of protecting the speculator's investment in obtaining information vital to the prompt adjustment of markets to changed conditions, but also of protecting the investment in information of the great chef or of the housewife who "buys" the esteem of friends with her imaginative cooking. Similarly, the attorney-work-product doctrine is, I think, best understood as the use of secrecy to protect the lawyer's

(and hence client's) investment in research and analysis of a case.

I have thus far been speaking as if any information should be the inviolable property of its creator. But this is not what economic theory implies. The purpose of a property right, or of according legal protection to secrecy as a surrogate for an explicit property right, is to create an incentive to invest in the creation of information. Where information is not a product of a significant investment, the case for protection is weakened. This is an important consideration in drawing the line between socially desirable and fraudulent nondisclosure. It may explain why the common law often requires the owner of a house to disclose latent, that is, nonobvious, defects to a purchaser. The ownership and maintenance of a house are productive activities, costly to engage in, but the owner acquires knowledge of the defects in his house costlessly (or nearly so). Hence requiring him to disclose those defects will not lead him to forgo expending to discover them.

Privacy of Communications

A communication (letter, phone call, face-to-face conversation, or whatever) is a medium by which facts are disclosed. It might seem that if the facts are the sort for which secrecy is desired in order to foster innovation, the communication should be privileged, and if they are discrediting, it should not be. But this approach is too simple. Besides revealing facts about the speaker or listener, a communication may refer to a third party. If that party were privy to it, the speaker would modify the communication. The modification would be costly both in time for deliberation and in reduction of clarity of the communication. For example, if A in conversation with B disparages C, and C overhears the conversation, C is likely to be angry or upset. If A does not want to engender this reaction in C, because he likes C or because C may retaliate for the disparagement, then, knowing that C might be listening, he will avoid the disparagement. He will choose his words more carefully, and the added deliberateness and obliqueness of the conversation will reduce its communication value and increase its cost. To be sure, there is an offsetting benefit if the disparagement is false and damaging to C. But there is no reason to believe that on average more false than true disparagements are made in private conversations, and the true are as likely to be suppressed by the prospect of publicity as the false. If A derives no substantial benefit from correctly observing to B that C is a liar, but stands only to incur C's wrath, the knowledge that C might overhear the conversation may induce A to withhold information that would be valuable to B. This is the reason for, among other things, the practice of according anonymity to referees of articles submitted to scholarly journals.

This analysis implies that eavesdropping is not an efficient way of finding out facts. If the danger of eavesdropping is known, conversations will be modified, at some social cost, in order to reduce their informational content for third parties. The parallel in nonconversational information would be the man who, having a criminal record that the law does not entitle him to conceal, goes to great lengths to avoid its discovery, by changing his name, his place of work and residence, and perhaps even his physical appearance. If the principal effect of refusing to recognize property rights in discrediting information about the individual were simply to call forth an expenditure on some costly but effective method of covering one's tracks, the gains to society would be small and could be negative. But probably that would not be the principal effect. When Thomas Eagleton was nominated for vice-president on the Democratic party ticket in 1972, he could not have concealed his history of mental illness, but he could have concealed his opinions of third parties, given conversational privacy.*

Some evidence in support of the above analysis is provided by the experience, well known to every academic administrator, under the Buckley Amendment. This statute gives students access to letters of recommendation written about them unless they waive in advance their right of access. Almost all students execute such waivers, because they know that the information value of a letter of recommendation to which the subject has access is much less than that of a private letter.

Additional evidence for my analysis of conversational privacy is the fact that discourse becomes less formal as society evolves. . . . the languages of primitive peoples are more elaborate, more ceremonious, and more courteous than the language of twentieth-century Americans. One reason may be the lack of privacy in primitive societies. Few really private conversations take place, because third parties are normally present and the effects on them of the conversation must be taken into account. (Even today, people speak more formally when there are more people present.) The growth of privacy has facilitated private conversation and thereby enabled us to economize on communication—to speak with a brevity and informality apparently rare among primitive peoples.* Allowing eavesdropping would undermine this valuable economy of communication.†

---

* Clifford Geertz writes: "In Java people live in small, bamboo-walled houses, each of which almost always contains a single nuclear family . . . There are no walls or fences around them, the house walls are thinly and loosely woven, and there are commonly not even doors. Within the house people wander freely just about any place any time, and even outsiders wander in fairly freely almost any time during the day and early evening. In brief, privacy in our terms is about as close to nonexistent as it can get . . . Relationships even within the household are very restrained; people speak softly, hide their feelings and even in the bosom of a Javanese family you have the feeling that you are in the public square and must behave with appropriate decorum. Javanese shut people out with a wall of etiquette (patterns of politeness are very highly developed), with emotional restraint, and with a general lack of candor in both speech and behavior . . . Thus there is really no sharp break between public and private in Java: people behave more or less the same in private as they do in public—in a manner we would call stuffy at best."

Additional evidence of the relationship between linguistic formality and publicity is that written speech is usually more decorous, grammatical, and formal than spoken speech. In part this is because speaking involves additional levels of meaning—gesture and intonation—which allow the speaker to achieve the same clarity with less semantic and grammatical precision. But in part it is because the audience for spoken speech is typically smaller and more intimate than that for written speech, which makes the costs of ambiguity lower and hence lowers the cost-justified investment in achieving precision through the various formal resources of language. This potential for ambiguity is one reason why people who speak to large audiences normally do so from a prepared text.

† To be sure, some communication, as among criminal conspirators, may not be related to socially productive activity. In these cases, where limited eavesdropping is indeed permitted, its effect in reducing communication is, from society's standpoint, not an

---

* An intermediate case is the impact of pretrial discovery on corporate record-retention policies. Fewer and less candid records are kept, but an organization (especially a large one) cannot function without keeping *some* documents.

The analysis can readily be extended to any efforts to obtain other people's notes, letters, and other private papers; these efforts inhibit communication. One purpose of common law copyright was in fact to protect the secrecy of diaries and correspondence. The case for privacy against photographic surveillance—for example, of the interior of a person's home—is also strong. Privacy enables a person to dress and otherwise disport himself in his home without regard to the effect on third parties. This informality, which conserves resources, would be lost if the interior of the home were in the public domain. People dress not merely because of the effect on others but also because of the reticence, remarked earlier, concerning nudity; that reticence is an additional reason for giving people a privacy right with regard to places in which it would be costly to avoid occasional nudity.

Legislative Trends in the Privacy Area

Recent years have witnessed a spate of state and federal statutes relating to privacy. . . . Here I want only to note an irony in the legislative movement.

My economic analysis implies that privacy of business information should receive greater legal protection, in general, than privacy of personal information. Secrecy is an important method for the entrepreneur to appropriate the social benefits he creates, but in private life secrecy is more likely to operate simply to conceal discreditable facts. And communications within business and other private organizations (the case of government is special . . .) seem entitled to as much protection as communications among individuals; in either case the effect of publicity would be to encumber and retard communication. Yet with some exceptions . . . the legislative trend, state and federal, has been to give individuals more and more legal protection of the privacy of both facts and communications, and to give business firms and other private organizations less and less. While facts about individuals— arrest record, health, credit-worthiness, marital status, sexual proclivities—increasingly are protected from involuntary disclosure, facts concerning business corporations increasingly are thrust into public view by the expansive disclosure requirements of the federal securities laws (to the point where some firms are "going private" to secure greater confidentiality for their plans and operations), civil rights laws, line of business reporting, and other regulations.

The trend toward elevating personal and downgrading organizational privacy is mysterious from an economic standpoint. The economic case for privacy of communications is unrelated to whether the communicator is a private individual or the employee of a university or corporation; and concerning privacy of information, the case for protecting business privacy is stronger than that for individual privacy. . . .

Other Privacy Theories

A brief and perhaps partisan review of some other theories of privacy will place the economic theory in perspective. I begin with the most famous theory, that of Warren and Brandeis, who wrote:

> The press is overstepping in every direction the obvious bounds of propriety and of decency. Gossip is no longer the resource of the idle and of the vicious, but has become a trade, which is pursued with industry as well as effrontery. To satisfy a prurient taste the details of sexual relations are spread broadcast in the columns of the daily papers. To occupy the indolent, column upon column is filled with idle gossip, which can only be procured by intrusion upon the domestic circle. The intensity and complexity of life, attendant upon advancing civilization, have rendered necessary some retreat from the world, and man, under the refining influence of culture, has become more sensitive to publicity, so that solitude and privacy have become more essential to the individual; but modern enterprise and invention have, through invasions upon his privacy, subjected him to mental pain and distress, far greater than could be inflicted by mere bodily injury. Nor is the harm wrought by such invasions confined to the suffering of those who may be made the subjects of journalistic or other enterprise. In this, as in other branches of commerce, the supply creates the demand. Each crop of unseemly gossip, thus harvested, becomes

---

objection but an advantage, because it makes the criminal activity more costly.

the seed of more, and, in direct proportion to its circulation, results in a lowering of social standards and of morality.*

Narrowly focused on justifying a right not to be talked about in a newspaper gossip column, the Warren-Brandeis analysis is based on a series of unsupported and implausible empirical propositions: (1) newspapers deliberately try to debase their readers' tastes; (2) the gossip they print harms the people gossiped about far more seriously than bodily injury could; (3) the more gossip the press supplies, the more the readers will demand; (4) reading gossip columns impairs intelligence and morality.†

Edward Bloustein is representative of those theorists who relate privacy to individuality:

> The man who is compelled to live every minute of his life among others and whose every need, thought, desire, fancy or gratification is subject to public scrutiny, has been deprived of his individuality and human dignity. Such an individual merges with the mass. His opinions, being public, tend never to be different; his aspirations, being known, tend always to be conventionally accepted ones; his feelings, being openly exhibited, tend to lose their quality of unique personal warmth and to become the feelings of every man. Such a being, although sentient, is fungible; he is not an individual.‡

At one level, Bloustein is saying that if people had no privacy, they would behave more in accordance with customary norms of behavior. That is (to oversimplify slightly), people would be better behaved if they had less privacy. This result he considers objectionable, apparently because greater conformity to socially accepted patterns of behavior would produce (by definition) more conformists, a type he dislikes for reasons he must consider self-evident since he does not attempt to explain them.

Bloustein does suggest that publicity reduces not only deviations from accepted moral standards but also creative departures from conventional thought and behavior. While the possession of some privacy may indeed be a precondition to intellectual creativity, these qualities have flourished in societies, including ancient Greece, Renaissance Italy, and Elizabethan England, that had much less privacy than people in the United States have today.

Charles Fried argues that privacy is indispensable to the fundamental values of love, friendship, and trust; love and friendship are inconceivable "without the intimacy of shared private information," and trust presupposes an element of ignorance about what the trusted one is up to: if all is known, there is nothing to take on trust. But rather than being something valued for itself and therefore missed where full information makes it unnecessary, trust is an imperfect substitute for information. And love and friendship flourish in societies where there is little privacy. The privacy theories of Bloustein and Fried are ethnocentric.

Even within our own culture, some people question whether privacy is more supportive than destructive of treasured values. If ignorance is a prerequisite to trust, it is equally true that knowledge, which privacy thwarts, is a prerequisite to forgiveness. The alleged anomie, impersonality, and lack of communal feeling of modern society may, to the extent that it is real, be related to the high level of privacy our society has achieved.

Fried is explicit in not wanting to ground the right of privacy on utilitarian considerations, but the quest for nonutilitarian grounds has thus far failed. It is doubtful whether the kind of analysis that seeks to establish rights on nonutilitarian or noneconomic grounds can even be applied to privacy. It makes no sense to treat reputation as a "right." Reputation is what others think of us, and we have no right to control other people's thoughts. Equally we have no

---

* Warren and Brandeis.

† This last point is elaborated in a passage of Victorian prissiness: "Even gossip apparently harmless, when widely and persistently circulated, is potent for evil. It both belittles and perverts. It belittles by inverting the relative importance of things, thus dwarfing the thoughts and aspirations of a people. When personal gossip attains the dignity of print, and crowds the space available for matters of real interest to the community, what wonder that the ignorant and thoughtless mistake its relative importance. Easy of comprehension, appealing to that weak side of human nature which is never wholly cast down by the misfortunes and frailties of our neighbors, no one can be surprised that it usurps the place of interest in brains capable of other things. Triviality destroys at once robustness of thought and delicacy of feeling. No enthusiasm can flourish, no generous impulse can survive under its blighting influence."

‡ Edward J. Bloustein. "Privacy as an Aspect of Human Dignity: An Answer to Dean Prosser," 39 *N.Y.U. L. Rev.* 962, 1003 (1964).

right, by controlling the information that is known about us, to manipulate the opinions that other people hold of us. Yet it is just this control that is sought in the name of privacy.

Greenawalt and Noam mention additional grounds for valuing privacy: the "fresh start" and "mental health." The first holds that people who have committed crimes or otherwise transgressed the moral standards of society have a right to a fresh start, which requires that they be allowed to conceal their past misdeeds. The second states as a fact of human psychology that people cannot function effectively unless they have some private area where they can behave very differently, often scandalously differently, from their public self; an example is the waiters who curse in the kitchen the patrons on whom they fawn in the dining room. The first point rests on the popular but unsubstantiated assumption that people do not evaluate past criminal acts ratio-

nally; only if they irrationally refused to accept evidence of rehabilitation could one argue that society has unfairly denied the former miscreant a fresh start. The second point has some intuitive appeal but seems exaggerated and ethnocentric and is offered as pure assertion; . . . the evidence is against it.

Similarly unsupported is Steven Shavell's suggestion that people operating behind a Rawlsian "veil of ignorance" might agree to the concealment of discreditable personal facts, not knowing whether they *would* do discreditable things but wanting some insurance against the consequences if they should. It is possible that people would make that choice, but without futher specification of the preference functions of people in the original position and the alternative forms of private and social insurance, one cannot conclude that such an agreement is a likely outcome of choice in that position.

QUESTIONS FOR REFLECTION

1. What is privacy, according to Posner?

2. Why does privacy conflict with liberty?

3. What are the costs of protecting privacy of personal information, according to Posner?

4. Why will markets weed out irrational prejudices?

5. How does Posner explain the interest in gossip about the rich and famous?

6. Why is privacy of the home justified, in Posner's view?

7. Why does Posner hold that privacy of business information is more worthy of protection than privacy of personal information?

JEFFREY H. REIMAN

Driving to the Panopticon:
A Philosophical Exploration of the Risks
to Privacy Posed by the Information
Technology of the Future

Jeffrey H. Reiman is William Fraser McDowell Professor of Philosophy, American University, Washington, D.C. (Source: Reprinted by permission from Santa Clara Computer and High Technology Law Journal *11 [1995]: 27–44. Most notes have been omitted. Copyright © 1995 by Jeffrey H. Reiman.)*

> *. . . the major effect of the Panopticon [is] to induce in the inmate a state of conscious and permanent visibility that assures the automatic functioning of power.*
> —Michel Foucault

> *If we can never be sure whether or not we are being watched and listened to, all our actions will be altered and our very character will change.*
> —Hubert Humphrey

> *Experience should teach us to be most on our guard to protect liberty when the government's purposes are beneficent.*
>
> —Louis Brandeis

According to the IVHS AMERICA Legal Issues Committee, "IVHS [Intelligent Vehicle Highway Systems] information systems [will] contain information on where travelers go, the routes they use, and when they travel. This information could be used to disadvantage individuals, and should be secure." This is from a list of what the Privacy Task Group of the Legal Issues Committee calls, interestingly, "'Strawman' Privacy Principles." I hope that my title, "Driving to the Panopticon," indicates to you that I don't regard the threat to privacy posed by Intelligent Vehicle Highway Systems as a strawman at all. Nor do I think that vague reference to use of information to individuals' disadvantage does anymore than begin to hint at the nature of that threat.

The Panopticon was Jeremy Bentham's plan for a prison in which large numbers of convicts could be kept under surveillance by very few guards. The idea was to build the prison cells in a circle around the guard post. All the prisoners would be silhouetted against light coming into the cells from windows on the outside of the circle. Their movements would be visible to a single guard in the center. The French philosopher Michel Foucault used Bentham's Panopticon as an ominous metaphor for the mechanisms of large-scale social control that characterize the modern world. He contended that it became, perhaps subconsciously, the model for institutions in nineteenth-century Europe and America. "Is it surprising," asked Foucault, "that prisons resemble factories, schools, barracks, hospitals, which all resemble prisons?"

As Bentham realized and Foucault emphasized, the system works even if there is no one in the guard house. The very fact of general visibility—being see-*able* more than being seen—will be enough to produce effective social control. Indeed, awareness of being visible makes people the agents of their own subjection. Writes Foucault,

> He who is subjected to a field of visibility, and who knows it, assumes responsibility for the constraints of power; he makes them play spontaneously upon himself; he inscribes in himself the power relation in which he simultaneously plays both roles; he becomes the principle of his own subjection.

Foucault went on to stretch the panopticon metaphor beyond architecture to characterize the practices of conventional medicine, psychology and sex education, all of which he thought subject us to increasing social control because they create a world in which the details of our lives become symptoms exposed to a clinical gaze—even if no one is actually looking. I want to stretch the panopticon metaphor yet further, to emphasize not just the way it makes people visible, but the way that it makes them visible *from a single point.*

An intriguing and illuminating feature of the suspicion about the threat to privacy posed by IVHS is that the information that would be accumulated by it is public. Wherever we drive, we drive in the public world, and thus normally subject to unobjectionable public observation. Courts have held that normal observation by police officers in or from public places does not intrude on a person's private affairs. And this has been specifically applied to "the following of an automobile on public streets and highways," even when the following was done by tracking a beeper planted on an object in the driver's possession. In *U.S. v. Knotts,* the Supreme Court held that "While in [their] vehicles on public roads . . . , [t]he defendants had no privacy interest in what could have been visually observed in these public places."

If there is a threat to privacy from IVHS, it comes from the fact that—as readers of detective fiction well know—by accumulating a lot of disparate pieces of public information, you can construct a fairly detailed picture of a person's private life. You can find out who her friends are, what she does for fun or profit, and from such facts others can be in-

ferred, whether she is punctual, whether she is faithful, and so on. Richard Wasserstrom observes, in an article first published in 1978, that the information already collected in data banks at that time, if gathered together, could produce a "picture of how I had been living and what I had been doing . . . that is fantastically more detailed, accurate, and complete than the one I could supply from my own memory."

There is, then, something to learn about privacy from the sort of threat that IVHS represents: namely, that privacy results not only from locked doors and closed curtains, but also from the way our publicly observable activities are dispersed over space and time. If we direct our privacy-protection efforts at reinforcing our doors and curtains, we may miss the way in which modern means of information collection threaten our privacy by gathering up the pieces of our public lives and making them visible from a single point. This is why the panopticon is a more fitting metaphor for the new threat to privacy than, for example, that old staple, the fishbowl.

But a threat to privacy is only worrisome insofar as privacy is valuable or protects other things that are valuable. No doubt privacy is valuable to people who have mischief to hide, but that is not enough to make it generally worth protecting. However, it is enough to remind us that whatever value privacy has, it also has costs. The more privacy we have, the more difficult it is to get the information that society needs to stop or punish wrongdoers. Moreover, the curtain of privacy that is traditionally brought down around the family has often provided cover for the subjugation and abuse of women and children. Privacy is not a free lunch. To believe, as I do, that privacy is essential to a free society is to believe that it is worth its costs. But then freedom, itself, is not a free lunch. A free society is a dangerous and often chaotic one. Let us then look at the value of privacy.

By *privacy,* I understand the condition in which other people are deprived of access to either some information about you or some experience of you. For the sake of economy, I will shorten this and say that *privacy is the condition in which others are deprived of access to you.* I include experience alongside information under access, since I think that privacy is about more than information. Your ability to take a shower unwatched is part of your privacy even though watchers may gain no information about you that they didn't already get in their high school biology course. Or, if you think that they might after all gain some information about your particular physiognomy, I would say that it is a matter of privacy that you are able to keep your body unobserved even by people who have already seen it and thus who already have that particular information. This said, I shall primarily speak of the value of privacy regarding information, since it is information about us that will be collected by IVHS.

Note that I have defined privacy in terms of the condition of others' lack of access to you. Some philosophers, for example Charles Fried, have claimed that it is your *control* over who has access to you that is essential to privacy. According to Fried, it would be ironic to say that a person alone on an island had privacy. I don't find this ironic at all. But more importantly, including control as part of privacy leads to anomalies. For example, Fried writes that "in our culture the excretory functions are shielded by more or less absolute privacy, so much so that situations in which this privacy is violated are experienced as extremely distressing." But, in our culture one does not have control over who gets to observe one's performance of the excretory functions, since it is generally prohibited to execute them in public. Since prying on someone in the privy is surely a violation of privacy, privacy must be a condition independent of the issue of control.

It's easy to get confused here since there are some private matters in which control is of great importance. For example, we don't simply want to restrict access to our naked bodies, we want to be able to decide who gets to see or touch them. The privy should remind us, however, that cases like these do not exhaust our interest in privacy. To include control in the definition of privacy would restrict our understanding of the value of privacy to only that part of privacy in which control is important—which is precisely the result in Fried's case. He ends up taking privacy to be a value because it gives us a kind of scarce resource (access to ourselves) to distribute. And he claims that our ability to distribute this resource is the key to our ability to have intimate relations. I think that Fried is wrong about intimate relations, since I think that intimate relations are a function of how much people care about each other, not how much they know about each other. One may have an intensely intimate relationship with

someone without—or at least before—sharing a lot of private information with them; and one can share private information with one's shrink or priest or even with a stranger on an airplane without thereby having an intimate relationship with them.

If we include control in the definition of privacy we will find the value of the sort of privacy we want in the bedroom, but not of the sort we want in the bathroom. In our bedrooms, we want to have power over who has access to us; in our bathrooms, we just want others deprived of that access. But notice here that the sort of privacy we want in the bedroom presupposes the sort we want in the bathroom. We cannot have discretion over who has access to us in the bedroom unless others lack access at their discretion. In the bathroom, that is all we want. In the bedroom, we want additionally the power to decide at our discretion who does have access. What is common to both sorts of privacy interests, then, is that others not have access to you at their discretion. If we are to find the value of privacy generally, then it will have to be the value of this restriction on others. Sometimes its value will lie precisely in the fact that the restriction leaves room for our own control. But other times it will lie just in that others lack the access. And this is important for our purposes, since the information that IVHS systems will gather is not the sort which it will be terribly important for us to be able to give out at our discretion. It will be information that we simply do not want others to have.

From the definition of privacy just given follows a specific conception of the *right to* privacy. The right to privacy is not my right to control access to me—it is my right that others be deprived of that access.* In some cases, though not all, having this right will protect my ability to control access to me.

Having privacy is not the same thing as having a right to privacy. I can have either without the other. I can have privacy without the right to privacy, say,

---

* It might be objected that, if I have a right that others be deprived of access to me, then I can waive that right, and thus effectively I would have the right to grant individuals access to me. This would bring control back in, not back into the definition of privacy, but into the definition of the right to privacy. But, there are rights that people have but cannot waive in the sense here needed. For example, my right to life is not generally taken as one that I can waive and thereby have a right to stop living; and my right to not be enslaved is not generally taken as one that I can waive and thereby have a right to sell myself into slavery.

when I successfully conceal my criminal activities. And, I can have a right to privacy and not have privacy, say, when others successfully violate the right.

For there to be a right to privacy, there must be some valid norm that specifies that some personal information about, or experience of, individuals should be kept out of other people's reach. Such norms may be legal. I've already quoted some of the legal norms governing the right to privacy in the United States. If, however, we think that people ought to have others deprived of access to some of their personal affairs whether or not a law says so, then we think that there is (something like) a moral right to privacy. And we will want our laws to protect this moral right by backing it up with an effective legal right. Since I think that IVHS threatens our privacy in ways that go beyond current legal rights, I am concerned to defend a moral right to privacy.

To say that someone has a moral right to privacy doesn't say much unless we know what the scope of that right is, what things or activities a person has a right to keep out of other people's view. For anyone who doesn't live in a cave or in a desert, a completely private life is impossible. Normally, we will think that some things are rightly within the scope of a person's privacy (say, their religious beliefs), and other things (say, the color of their eyes) are not. Often, as cases like *Roe* v. *Wade* and *Bowers* v. *Hardwick* show, precisely what should or should not come under the scope of the right to privacy is controversial. As these cases testify, some will argue that citizens of a free society should have as extensive a right to privacy as is compatible with reasonably safe social coexistence, while others will argue that only certain specific areas of people's lives (for example, bodily processes, intimate relationships, activities relating to the formation of political opinions and plans) should be protected. And, as the tension between current law and fears about IVHS shows, there is disagreement over whether the accumulation of bits of public information should come under the scope of privacy.

To resolve such disagreements, we must get clear on the value of privacy. If we know why having privacy, or, equivalently, having an effective right to privacy, is an especially important and good thing for human beings, we will be able to determine what must come under the scope of privacy for that value to be realized.

To do this, I propose that we imagine together the world in which the full IVHS project is completed, and then see what losses we might suffer as a result of the information about us that would then be gathered. Here it is of great importance that a fully developed IVHS will not exist in an informational vacuum. IVHS's information will exist alongside that provided by other developments already in existence and likely to grow, such as computerization of census and IRS information, computer records of people's credit-card purchases, their bank transactions, their credit histories generally, their telephone calls, their medical conditions, their education and employment histories, and of course the records of their brushes with the law, even of arrests that end in acquittal. Add to this the so-called "information highway" on which we will all soon be riding, with its automatic recording of all interactions, not to mention the FBI's desire to keep it eternally wiretappable. It has been observed, by the way, that as people conduct the business of their daily lives more and more via digital communications, mere knowledge of who people call—knowledge now readily available to police agencies—"would give law enforcers extensive access to people's habits and daily activities."

It is this whole complex of information-gathering that I think threatens us. It is this whole complex that, in its potential to make our lives as a whole visible from a single point, brings to mind the panopticon. Accordingly, it is as helping to bring about this whole complex that I shall consider the threat posed by IVHS.

It might seem unfair to IVHS to consider it in light of all this other accumulated information—but I think, on the contrary, that it is the only way to see the threat accurately. The reason is this: We have privacy when we can keep personal things out of the public view. Information-gathering in any particular realm may not seem to pose a very grave threat precisely because it is generally possible to preserve one's privacy by escaping into other realms. Consequently, as we look at each kind of information-gathering in isolation from the others, each may seem relatively benign. However, as each is put into practice, its effect is to close off yet another escape route from public access, so that when the whole complex is in place, its overall effect on privacy will be greater than the sum of the effects of the parts.

What we need to know is IVHS's role in bringing about this overall effect, and it plays that role by contributing to the establishment of the whole complex of information-gathering modalities.

I call this whole complex of which IVHS will be a part the *informational panopticon*. It is the risks posed to privacy by the informational panopticon as a whole that I shall explore.

Ride with me, then, into the informational panopticon and consider what we stand to lose if our lives become generally visible. I think that we can characterize the potential risks under four headings: *First,* the risk of extrinsic loss of freedom; *second,* the risk of intrinsic loss of freedom; *third,* symbolic risks; and, *fourth,* risk of psychopolitical metamorphosis. All these strange titles will become clear in due course. I have given the last category a particularly unwieldy and ugly title precisely because it is the one that I regard as least familiar, most speculative and most ominous. The reference to Kafka is intentional. This said, I should add that these headings are not put forth as airtight metaphysical divisions. They are meant simply to get unruly ideas under control. Like many philosophical categories, they will crumble if pressed too hard. If, however, we see them for what they are, they will give us an orderly picture of the risks that IVHS and the rest of the informational panopticon pose to privacy. But, more, this picture will be just a negative image of the value of privacy.

I. The Risk of Extrinsic Loss of Freedom

By extrinsic loss of freedom, I mean all those ways in which lack of privacy makes people vulnerable to having their behavior controlled by others. Most obviously, this refers to the fact that people who want to do unpopular or unconventional actions may be subject to social pressure in the form of denial of certain benefits, jobs or promotions or membership in formal or informal groups, or even blackmail, if their actions are known to others. And even if they have reason to believe that their actions *may* be known to others and that those others *may* penalize them, this is likely to have a chilling effect on them that will constrain the range of their freedom to act. Remember, it is by inducing the consciousness of visibility

that the panopticon, in Foucault's words, "assures the automatic functioning of power."

Ruth Gavison writes, "Privacy . . . prevents interference, pressures to conform, ridicule, punishment, unfavorable decisions, and other forms of hostile reaction. To the extent that privacy does this, it functions to promote liberty of action, removing the unpleasant consequences of certain actions and thus increasing the liberty to perform them." This is not just a matter of the freedom to do immoral or illegal acts. It applies equally to unpopular political actions which have nothing immoral or illegal about them.

Moreover, in a free society, there are actions thought immoral by many or even a majority of citizens that a significant minority thinks are morally acceptable. The preservation of freedom requires that, wherever possible, the moral status of these actions be left to individuals to decide for themselves, and thus that not everything that a majority of citizens thinks is immoral be made illegal. (Think here of pornography, gambling, drunkenness, homosexual or pre- or extramarital heterosexual sex.) If it would be wrong to force people legally to conform to the majority's views on such issues, it will be equally wrong to use harsh social pressure to accomplish the same effect. For this reason, Mill argued in *On Liberty* against both legal enforcement of morality and its informal social enforcement by stigmatization or ostracism.

Mill was not, by the way, against people trying to persuade one another about what is moral. Actually, he thought we should do more of that than we normally do. He distinguished, however, between appeals to reason and appeals to force or its equivalent, harsh informal social penalties. Trying to persuade the minority by making arguments and producing evidence can be done in public forums without pointing fingers, and thus without putting any particular person at risk. Most importantly, it leaves the members of the minority free to make up their own minds. Threatening the minority with stigmatization or ostracism works like force because it changes people's actions by attaching painful consequences to them, without changing their minds at all. Privacy protects people from the operation of this force, and thus preserves their freedom.

Some may wonder whether the idea that people need privacy to act freely is based on too dim a view of human character. Those who raise this doubt think that people with strong characters will be able to resist social pressure, and thus only those with weak characters need dark private corners in order to act freely. In different ways, this objection can be raised against all the risks to privacy that I shall describe, and so I want to give a general answer to it. The answer has three parts:

First, laws and social practices generally have to be designed for the real people that they will govern, not for some ideal people that we would like to see or be. Just as Madison observed that if people were angels we wouldn't need government at all, so we might add that if people were heroes we wouldn't need privacy at all. Since people are neither angels nor (except in a few instances) heroes, we need both government and privacy.

Second, just because people are not angels, some will be tempted to penalize those who act unconventionally. Even if people should ideally be able to withstand social pressure in the form of stigmatization or ostracism, it remains unjust that they should suffer these painful fates simply for acting in unpopular or unconventional ways. In any actual society we will need privacy to prevent this injustice.

Third, suppose we wanted to make our citizens into the sorts of strong-willed people who could resist social pressures. We would still have to give them experience in formulating their own judgments and in acting upon those judgments. And this experience will have to be given to them before they have the strong characters we hope them to attain. They will have to be sheltered from the pressures toward social conformity while they are still vulnerable, in order to become the sorts of people who are not vulnerable. They will need privacy in order to become the sorts of people who don't need it. Much as Mill felt that liberty was a school for character, so too is privacy. And, since this school must provide continuing education for adults as well as for children, we will need privacy as an abiding feature of the society. In short, the vast majority of actual people need privacy for free action, and those who do not will need privacy to become that way. With or without heroes, we will need privacy.

II. The Risk of Intrinsic Loss of Freedom

By intrinsic loss of freedom, I point to ways in which denial of privacy limits people's freedom directly,

independently of the ways in which it makes them susceptible to social pressure or penalties. Put differently, I want here to suggest that privacy is not just a means of protecting freedom, it is itself constitutive of freedom in a number of important ways.

To start, recall the discussion about the place of control in the definition of privacy. I concluded there that control is not part of privacy, but in some cases it is part of what privacy makes possible. For me to be able to decide who touches my body, or who knows the details of my personal history, those things must be generally not accessible to others at their discretion. That means that if those things are not shielded by privacy, I am automatically denied certain important choices. This is what I mean by an intrinsic loss of freedom. I am not here denied the choices by fear of certain consequences; I am denied them directly because privacy is the condition of their being choices for me in the first place.

Another intrinsic loss of freedom is the following. A number of writers have emphasized the ways in which some actions have a different nature when they are observed than they do when they are not. This is clearest in cases that are distant from IVHS: Criticizing an individual in front of others is a different act than uttering the same critical words to him in private. And, of course, making love before an audience is something quite different from the same act done in private. In the case of our informational panopticon the alteration is more subtle. Every act, say, driving to destination X at time T, is now a more complex event: It now becomes driving to X at T and *creating a record of driving to X at T.* These differ from one another as leaving a message on someone's answering machine differs from rehearsing the same words in one's imagination. If my every driving act (not to mention all the other acts visible in the information panopticon) is also the depositing of a record, not only are my acts changed, but my freedom is limited: I am no longer free to do the act of simply driving to X at T *without leaving a record.*

With this, I lose as well the freedom of acting spontaneously. In a society which collected data on all of an individual's transactions, Richard Wasserstrom writes,

> one would be both buying a tank of gas and leaving a part of a systematic record of where one was on that particular date. One would not just be applying for life

insurance; one would also be recording in a permanent way one's health on that date and a variety of other facts about oneself. No matter how innocent one's intentions and actions at any given moment . . . persons would think more carefully before they did things that would become part of the record. Life would to this degree become less spontaneous and more measured.*

When you know you are being observed, you naturally identify with the outside observer's viewpoint, and add that alongside your own viewpoint on your action. This double vision makes your act different, whether the act is making love or taking a drive. The targets of the panopticon know and feel the eye of the guard on them, making their actions different than if they were done in private. Their repertoire of possible actions diminishes as they lose those choices whose intrinsic nature depends on privacy.

III. Symbolic Risks

Elsewhere I have argued that privacy is a social ritual by which we show one another that we regard each person as the owner of herself, her body, her thoughts. It is for this reason that privacy is generally absent from organizations like monasteries, armies, communist cells and madhouses, where individuals are thought to belong to some larger whole or greater purpose. This is also why invasions of privacy are wrong even when they don't pose any risk to reputation or freedom, even when the invader will not use what he observes in any harmful way, even when the individual is unaware that her privacy is being invaded. Aside from any harms that invasions of privacy threaten, such invasions are, in addition, *insults*. They slight an individual's ownership of himself, and thus insult him by denying his special dignity. The peeping Tom treats his prey with unmerited, and thus unjust, contempt.

Privacy conveys to the individual his self-ownership precisely by the knowledge that the individual gains of his ability and his authority to withdraw himself from the scrutiny of others. Those who lose this ability and authority are thereby told

that they don't belong to themselves; they are specimens belonging to those who would investigate them.† They are someone else's data. It is no accident that the panopticon was a design for a prison, an institution which in effect suspends a person's ownership of himself because he committed a crime. And since our informational panopticon effectively suspends self-ownership though no crime has been committed, it conveys an unmerited, and thus unjust, insult.

I said earlier that I wanted to emphasize the way in which the panopticon makes our lives visible from a single point. Here it is worth noting that that point is outside of us, where the guardian stands. The panopticon symbolizes a kind of draining of our individual sovereignty away and outside of us into a single center. We become its data to observe at its will—our outsides belong to its inside rather than to our own.

I have called this a symbolic risk because it affects us as a kind of message, a message inscribed in an institutional structure. We are not deprived of our self-ownership in the way that slaves are deprived permanently or the way that prisoners are deprived temporarily. Rather, the arrangement of the institution broadcasts an image of us, to us, as beings lacking the authority to withdraw ourselves from view. It conveys the loss of self-ownership to us by announcing that our every move is fitting data for observation by others. As a symbolic message, it insults rather than injures.

But, of course, what is symbolic is almost never merely symbolic. By such symbols do we come to acquire our self-conceptions. They shape the way we identify ourselves to ourselves and to one another, and thus they shape our identities themselves. Growing up in the informational panopticon, people will be less likely to acquire selves that think of themselves as owning themselves. They will say *mine* with less authority, and *yours* with less

---

* Wasserstrom, "Privacy: Some Arguments and Assumptions," in Ferdinand Schoeman (ed.), *Philosophical Dimensions of Privacy.*

---

† "A man whose home my be entered at the will of another, whose conversation may be overheard at the will of another, whose marital and familial intimacies may be overseen at the will of another, is less of a man, has less human dignity, on that account." Edward J. Bloustein, *Privacy As an Aspect of Human Dignity: An Answer to Dean Prosser,* in Ferdinand Schoeman (ed.), *Philosophical Dimensions of Privacy.*

respect. And I think that selves that think of themselves as owning themselves are precisely what we understand as "moral selves". They are selves that naturally accept ownership of their actions and thus responsibility for them. They naturally insist on ownership of their destinies and thus on the right to choose their own way. Here the loss of privacy threatens an incalculable loss. What will it be worth if a man should gain the world but lose his soul?

IV. The Risk of Psycho-Political Metamorphosis

The risk just discussed is not that we shall lose something we now enjoy, but that we will become something different than we currently are, something less noble, less interesting, less worthy of respect. This is the fear expressed in the quote from Hubert Humphrey. What I shall say now continues in this vein.

The film *Demolition Man* portrays a future society characterized by widespread information gathering, including a full IVHS system. However, to me, the most interesting feature of the film is that the denizens of the society depicted there speak, and thus seem to think, in a way that can only be described as childish. They have an oversimplified way of labeling things and experiences, and appear to have a repertoire of responses that is limited in number and nuance. Their emotional lives are, you might say, reduced to the primary colors, without shade or tone, disharmony or ambiguity. I want to suggest that this is a product of the informational panopticon in which they live. Total visibility infantilizes people. It impoverishes their inner life and makes them more vulnerable to oppression from without.

There is already a widely recognized correlation between privacy and adulthood. But it is normally understood in the reverse direction: The less mature a person is the less privacy he gets, and he gets more privacy as he moves toward adulthood. I want to suggest that this is a two-way street. The deprivation of privacy stunts maturity, keeps people suspended in a childish state.

How does this happen? Consider the words of Edward Bloustein, President of Rutgers University:

The man who is compelled to live every minute of his life among others and whose every need, thought, desire, fancy or gratification is subject to public scrutiny, has been deprived of his individuality and human dignity. Such an individual merges with the mass. His opinions, being public, tend always to be conventionally accepted ones; his feelings, being openly exhibited, tend to lose their quality of unique personal warmth and to become the feelings of every man. Such a being, although sentient, is fungible; he is not an individual.

But this is only the beginning. Consider the process and where it leads: To the extent that a person experiences himself as subject to public observation, he naturally experiences himself as subject to public review. As a consequence, he will tend to act in ways that are publicly acceptable. People who are shaped to act in ways that are publicly acceptable will tend to act in safe ways, to hold and express and manifest the most widely accepted views, indeed, the lowest common denominator of conventionality. (Think here of the pressure that TV sponsors exercise against anything unconventional, in their fear of offending any segment of the purchasing population.) But, thought and feeling follow behavior. (Pascal said: "Kneel down, move your lips in prayer, and you will believe.") Trained by society to act conventionally at all times, people will come so to think and so to feel. Their inner lives will be impoverished to the extent that their outer lives are subject to observation. Infiltrated by social convention, their emotions and reactions will become simpler, safer, more predictable, less nuanced, more interchangeable. This much is noted by Bloustein, but I think the process goes further.

As the inner life that is subject to social convention grows, the still deeper inner life that is separate from social convention contracts and, given little opportunity to develop, remains primitive. Likewise, as more and more of your inner life is made sense of from without, the need to make your own sense out of your inner life shrinks. You lose both the practice of making your own sense out of your deepest and most puzzling longings, and the potential for self-discovery and creativity that lurk within a rich inner life. Your inner emotional life is impoverished, and your capacity for evaluating and shaping it is stunted.

Thus will be lost—and this is the most ominous possibility of all—the inner personal core that is the source of criticism of convention, of creativity, rebellion and renewal. To say that people who suffer this loss will be easy to oppress doesn't say enough. They won't have to be oppressed, since there won't be anything in them that is tempted to drift from the beaten path or able to see beyond it. They will be the "one-dimensional men" that Herbert Marcuse feared. The art of such people will be insipid decoration, and their politics fascist.

Here, I think, we reach something deep and rarely noted about the liberal vision—something that shows the profound link between liberalism and privacy, and between those two and democracy. The liberal vision is guided by the ideal of the autonomous individual, the one who acts on principles which she has accepted after critical review rather than simply absorbing them unquestioned from outside. Moreover, the liberal stresses the importance of people making sense of their own lives, and of having authority over the sense of those lives. All this requires a kind of space in which to reflect on and entertain beliefs, and to experiment with them—*a private space*.

Deeper still, however, the liberal vision has an implicit trust in the transformational and ameliorative possibilities of private inner life. Without this, neither democracy nor individual freedom have worth. Unless people can form their own views, democratic voting becomes mere ratification of conventionality, and individual freedom mere voluntary conformity. And, unless, in forming their own views, people can find within themselves the resources for better views, neither democracy nor individualism can be expected to improve human life.

This concludes my catalogue of the risks posed by loss of privacy. As I suggested earlier, the risks give us a negative image of the value to us of maintaining privacy. I can sum up that value as: the protection of freedom, moral personality, and a rich and critical inner life. If IVHS endangers these values, then we will have to bring the heretofore public information about travel on public streets under the scope of privacy.

But that is just the beginning of what is necessary. Here we should remember Bentham's and Foucault's recognition that the panopticon works even if no one is in the guard house. The risks that are posed by the informational panopticon come not from being seen, but from the knowledge that one is visible. And this means that protecting ourselves from the risks I have described will be harder than we might imagine.

Consider that privacy can be protected in two ways, which I shall call, respectively, the formal conditions of privacy and the material conditions. By the *formal* conditions of privacy, I mean generally the rules that either specifically give one a right to privacy or that have a similar effect (such as conventions of modesty or reserve, of appropriate levels of curiosity or prying). Such rules might be legal or customary or moral, or some combination of these. By the *material* conditions of privacy, I mean physical realities that hinder others in gathering information about or experiences of you, things like locks, fences, doors, curtains, isolation and distance.

It should be clear that one might have formal conditions without the material, and that the formal conditions might be effective without the material being in place. For example, people packed like sardines in a rush-hour subway train have a way of respecting each other's privacy even though they have, materially, extensive access to one another's bodies. On the other hand, one can have the material conditions of privacy without the formal, and the material conditions might be effective without the formal being in place. For example, after my students are duly shocked by Hobbes' defense of absolute political authority, I remind them that, when Hobbes wrote, it took about a week to travel from the west coast of England to the east coast, and about two weeks from north coast to south. An absolute sovereign in Hobbes' time, without any formal constraints, surely had less actual ability to invade his subjects' lives than, say, a contemporary U.S. president, even with all our constitutional safeguards.

That constitutional safeguards can be and have been ignored by the powerful bears a lesson for us: Material conditions of privacy more reliably prevent invasions of privacy than formal conditions can. Material conditions have a kind of toughness that the formal condtions never can match. Thus, formal conditions of privacy can never fully guarantee protection of privacy when the material conditions for invading privacy are at hand. The material conditions for invading privacy are a kind of power, and power is always tempting, often corrupting, and, to paraphrase Lord Acton, the more power there is the more corrupting it is likely to be.

This is important because the accumulation of detailed information about people's goings and comings is a material condition for invading privacy. What's more, the continued and increasing amassing of this and all the other sorts of information that make up the informational panopticon seems to me to be inevitable. This is for the simple reason that, as with IVHS, all of the elements of the informational panopticon serve good purposes and can and will be put in place with the best of intentions. Here we should remember Louis Brandeis's warning, quoted at the outset, and watch out for threats of liberty dressed in beneficent intentions. The existence of all this collected information and of the technical ability to bring these different records together will add up to an enormous capacity to amass detailed portraits of people's lives—in short, material conditions for invasion of privacy on unheard-of scale. One has to be very optimistic indeed about the power of rules, to think that formal guarantees of privacy will protect us. And, to the extent that we are not so opti-

mistic, we will experience ourselves as visible even if we are not being observed, which will bring in its train all the risks earlier described.

To the extent that the material conditions for our virtually total visibility come ineluctably into place in the years ahead, we will need not only to prevent the misuse of information *but to prevent the fear that it is being misused.* That is the lesson of the Panopticon. We will have to protect people not only from being seen but from feeling visible. Thus, we will need more than ever before to teach and explain the importance of privacy, so that respect for it becomes second nature, and violation of it repugnant. And, of course, we will need more than ever to make sure that our fellows are complying with the formal rules that protect privacy. If we are going to protect privacy in the informational panopticon, we're really going to have to keep an eye on one another!

QUESTIONS FOR REFLECTION

1. How does Reiman define privacy?

2. How does privacy relate to liberty?

3. How does a large database like IVHS affect individual liberty?

4. What is the informational panopticon? Why does it worry Reiman?

5. What is the link between autonomy and privacy?

6. How might Reiman respond to Posner's charge that claiming a right to privacy is in effect claiming a right to control the thoughts of others?

RITA C. MANNING

Liberal and Communitarian Defenses of Workplace Privacy

Rita Manning is Professor of Philosophy at San Jose State University. (Source: from the Journal of Business Ethics 16 [1997]. *Copyright © 1997 by Kluwer Academic Publishers. Reprinted by permission.)*

. . . I want to defend a communitarianism . . . which is committed to the intrinsic value of the individual and the instrumental value of the community. On my view, the individual is essentially a communal creature who defines him- or herself at least in part by appeal to the communal aims and values, and communally defined and assigned roles. Hence, even if we assign intrinsic value to individuals and merely instrumental value to communities, we shall have to be very concerned with the good of communities because the good of individuals is intimately connected with the good of communities. . . .

Communitarian Defenses of Privacy

The concept of privacy is a notoriously difficult one, in large part because it is both a normative and a descriptive notion. I don't intend to settle the issue of the correct analysis of privacy here. What I shall do instead is to list the kinds of invasions of privacy which occur in the workplace and see if we can sort them out in some reasonable way. The current list of workplace invasions of privacy include drug testing, polygraphs, visual surveillance, computer surveillance and auditory surveillance. All of these techniques involve the loss of control about whether and

how information about oneself is to be made public. In addition, polygraphs and drug testing might be said to involve an invasion of bodily integrity. Some drug testing involves the public performance of an act which we are culturally conditioned to view as essentially private. I don't want to rehearse all the liberal arguments against these invasions of privacy, but rather to focus on one invasion that is not satisfactorily accounted for by liberalism. The practice I am interested in here is electronic surveillance, either by listening in to a worker's calls or by computer. Service employees who spend a great deal of time on the phone are often subject to surveillance. A supervisor can listen in to the worker's calls. The stated reason for such surveillance is to ensure that the customer's problem is handled correctly and that the customer is treated with respect. Computer monitoring allows a supervisor to measure the amount of work done, the speed at which it is done, and the time the worker spends on the terminal.

I now turn to a communitarian defense of protecting workers against these kinds of intrusions. On the communitarian view, I am not an individual who just happens to be working for company X. I am, at least in part, defined by my role as a worker for company X. This is not just the way company X sees me; to a certain extent, I share this view. True, I am also defined by my membership in other communities, and these other roles also help to define who I am.

The communitarian is not committed to the view that we must simply accept the given roles that society assigns because the communitarian realizes that roles can be oppressive. Sandel, for example, argues that we can critique communities and communally assigned roles by appeal to an account of human flourishing. What communitarianism is committed to is the importance of roles to my self-identity and self-esteem. I shall confess at the outset that communitarianism invites a certain amount of scepticism about the value of privacy. The liberal who believes that we are all free to choose or reject ends is less likely to see roles as oppressive. For example, family roles are seen by liberals as voluntarily accepted by the adult members of the family, and family matters are often seen as intrinsically private. James Fitzjames Stephen included among matters firmly within the private sphere "internal affairs of a family, the relationships of love or friendship." The communitarian who doesn't see us as separate from our ends or able to freely choose them, but as created in part by the roles we inhabit, would deny that the internal affairs of a family should be totally private. Similarly, the relationships of love or friendship are in part created by complex social roles. It doesn't follow that the law should intervene in every oppressive family or relationship, but we should be leery of attempts to protect all these relationships. We should also be willing to admit that the choices made within relationships are not totally free. This is the meaning of the feminist slogan, "the personal is the political."

I want now to return to the claim offered by Rachels and Fried that privacy ought to be protected because it is required for my participation in a society in which individuals play a variety of roles. I suspect that a communitarian would be sympathetic to part of this thesis. They would agree that societies are often structured in such a way that I gain my self-identity, if not totally, at least in part, through my performance of various socially defined roles. If playing these various roles requires the selective disclosure of information, then we have a reason for protecting individuals from at least some disclosures of information. The communitarian would part company with Rachels and Fried here. They would agree

with Jeffrey Reiman's point that intimate relationships are characterized by mutual caring and not by widespread sharing of information. The communitarian would point out that the sharing of information is merely a consequence of the trust and caring which is a part of intimate relationships. The disclosure of such shared information places the relationship at risk only if the disclosure was made by one of the parties without the consent of the other. Here, the intimacy is threatened by the loss of trust, not by the loss of information available only to the parties to the relationship.

To return to the issue of surveillance in the workplace, the communitarian would point out that such surveillance is not a violation of the real self who is hidden behind all the roles I play, but a violation of my self *qua* worker. If, as a worker in company X, I am not considered trustworthy or competent enough to do my job without surveillance, my sense of myself is diminished. To see how invasions of privacy in the workplace undermine my sense of self, consider the following example. Imagine that I. M. Curious owned company X and that she were an eccentric collector of trivia. Suppose that she wanted to see if there was a correlation between wearing blue clothing and bull markets. As part of her research, she mounted cameras to surreptitiously monitor the color clothing worn by the workers in company X. My guess is that this kind of surveillance would be tolerated by the workers precisely because it did not imply that they were deficient as workers. In addition, few of us have an identity that is connected to the color clothes we wear, so we would not be so offended by surveillance designed to discover facts about color preferences in clothing.

There is another difference between liberalism and communitarianism that is derived from the difference in pictures of the self that is relevant here. The liberal is concerned about the community in a secondary way, as a place for the flourishing of individuals. The community plays a much more central role for the communitarian. My sense of self is derived from the communities I inhabit and the roles which I play in those communities. Hence, even if the individual were the sole focus of moral concern, a concern for the good of the community would be central. When we look at the workplaces in which surveillance is common, we see communities in trouble. What is missing in these communities is trust. Managers might argue that surveillance is designed to promote trust, but such managers are confused about what trust is. Trust would exist, on their view, if the behavior of the workers was predictable and if it conformed to certain norms. This is the kind of trust that I can have in a car, for example, but it is a poor substitute for the trust that can exist in human relationships. I trust people in this wider sense if I believe that they respect and care about me and will treat me appropriately. If people trust each other in this sense, then their interaction will be predictable and will conform to certain norms, not as a result of being watched, but as a result of the care and respect which are part of the communal fabric.

So there are two intuitions about invasions of privacy in the workplace that can be better captured by a communitarian analysis. The first is that the harm is to the worker *qua* worker and not to the separate individual who just happens to hold a particular job. Communitarianism explains this by pointing out that self-identity is in part a function of the roles we inhabit. The second is that the harm is not just to the individuals, but to the community. Communitarianism explains this by pointing out that the trust which is required for stable and successful communities is eroded by such invasions.

QUESTIONS FOR REFLECTION

1. In what sense does electronic surveillance violate privacy?

2. What is communitarianism? How does communitarianism entail respect for individuals, according to Manning?

3. Why are self-respect and self-identity important for understanding issues of privacy?

4. Where might liberals and communitarians disagree about the right to privacy?

5. How does Manning delimit the right to privacy in the workplace?

6. Contrast Manning's account of privacy with the analysis of Posner or Reiman. On what issues might they disagree?

G. RANDOLPH MAYES AND MARK ALFINO

Rationality and the Right to Privacy

G. Randolph Mayes is Lecturer in Philosophy at California State University, Sacramento. Mark Alfino is Associate Professor of Philosophy at Gonzaga University. This paper was written especially for this volume.

1. Introduction

When tennis fan Jane Bronstein attended the 1995 U.S. Open, she probably knew there was a remote chance her image would end up on television screens around the world. But she surely did not know she was at risk of becoming the object of worldwide attention on the *David Letterman Show*. As it happened, Letterman spotted an unflattering clip from the U.S. Open showing a heavyset Bronstein with peach juice dripping down her chin. Not only did he show the footage six times that fall, but he ridiculed her on his "Top 10 List," calling her a "seductive temptress," even paying to put the clip on the Sony Jumbotron electronic billboard at Times Square. Ms. Bronstein sued David Letterman's production company under New York civil rights law for violating her privacy.

At the time, Ms. Bronstein was fifty-four years old and suffering from the effects of childhood polio, two spinal fusions, and a thyroid condition. Letterman surely added insult to injury. But does it really make sense to claim that he violated her *privacy*? Bronstein chose to go to a *public* event, which she knew would be televised. Letterman's right to ridicule others is guaranteed by the First Amendment, but there are other plausible ways of characterizing the harm he did to Bronstein. For example, if Letterman made unfair commercial use of Bronstein's image, then her property rights may have been violated. If he unfairly ridiculed her, causing damage to her reputation and severe emotional dis-

tress, this may have been an adequate basis for a tort case against him. But why would anyone suggest that Letterman's actions violated Bronstein's privacy?

We believe there is an answer to this question, and it begins as follows: Certainly, when we enter the public sphere, we give up a large measure of privacy. We can not legitimately complain about people noticing us as we cross the quad or speaking to others about what they see. Still, it is rude to stare or threaten to follow too closely, and downright illegal to eavesdrop as we punch out our PIN at the ATM. All such actions occur in the public sphere, but they are legitimately construed as violations of privacy even so. So there is really nothing incoherent about the claim that Letterman violated Bronstein's privacy, even in the radically public setting of a televised sporting event. What's interesting, however, is that there is no generally adequate theory of privacy that validates this claim. In this paper we attempt to provide just such a theory.

2. The Right to Be Let Alone

In 1890 a prominent Boston attorney named Samuel Warren, together with his friend, future Supreme Court justice Louis Brandeis, co-authored a *Harvard Law Review* article entitled "The Right to Privacy." In it they argued that individuals have a right to an "inviolate personality," which entails, among other things, "a right to be let alone." This essay is widely acknowledged as the first and most influential ever written in defense of a distinct identifiable right to privacy. Today, however, it is also the most casually dismissed.

Two serious problems with the Warren and Brandeis theory of privacy are commonly noted. First, it appears to be too broad. This means that it counts as violations of privacy things that intuitively are not. As Judith Thomson observes:

> If I hit Jones on the head with a brick, I have not let him alone. Yet, while hitting Jones on the head with a brick is surely violating some right of Jones's, doing it should surely not turn out to violate his right to privacy. Else, where is this to end? Is every violation of a right a violation of the right to privacy?*

In other respects, however, the theory appears to be too narrow. This means that it fails to count as violations of privacy things that intuitively are. Thomson again writes:

> The police might say, "We grant that we used a special X-ray device on Smith, we grant we trained an amplifying device on him so as to be able to hear everything he said; but we let him strictly alone, we didn't even go near him—our devices operate at a distance."†

Today almost all philosophers who write on the topic of privacy agree that the Warren and Brandeis view is fundamentally flawed, but they offer very different analyses of its failings. These analyses can be roughly divided into two types. One we will call the *reductionist* analysis. The other we will call the *intuitionist* analysis.

According to the reductionist analysis, it is a mistake to characterize privacy as a *distinct* right. Thomson subscribes to this view. She argues that the so-called right to privacy is actually the core of a cluster of rights (including the rights to life, liberty, and property) all of which protect an individual's private life from unwarranted public intrusion. This way of thinking about privacy preserves the breadth of the Warren and Brandeis view while rejecting their suggestion that privacy is a unique moral concern.

The intuitionist analysis, on the other hand, holds that privacy really is a distinct right. The problem with the Warren and Brandeis view is that it generalizes on a common but purely accidental feature of privacy violations. People may wish to be let alone for any number of reasons that have nothing essentially to do with privacy, e.g., to get some sleep, to get some work done, or to get to where they are going. The aim in these cases is to restrict access to the person. The desire for privacy, many intuitionists claim, is best understood more narrowly as the desire to *restrict access to personal information*. To establish a degree of privacy is to prevent certain people from knowing certain things about you. Since undetected spying is the paradigm case of illicit access to personal information, this approach easily deals with the second objection above, *viz.*, that the Warren and Brandeis view does not account for the evil of spying.

These two alternatives offer a clear choice. On the one hand, we could choose to continue to invoke the "right to privacy" in a broad range of circumstances so long as we agree that privacy is not a distinct right but just a useful way of referring to a cluster of other distinct rights. On the other hand, we could speak meaningfully of a distinct right to privacy as long as we understand that it applies to a far narrower range of circumstances than is usually assumed. Either way, it seems that for the sake of clarity we must reject the common intuition that the right to privacy is a general and distinct right to be let alone.

In this essay we reinstate the abandoned option. We believe that it is possible to preserve a clear sense in which the right to privacy consists in a general and distinct right to be let alone. We show below that this right can be derived in a surprisingly standard way, i.e., through an analysis of the conditions needed to establish and maintain personal autonomy. The analysis we provide is highly intuitive at one level, for it fits comfortably within the liberal tradition and extends the right to privacy in useful ways. At another level, however, the analysis is shocking, for it secures no basic right to control personal information. Indeed, our view of the right to privacy is logically compatible with the existence of a transparent society in which the most intimate details of one's life are easily known to all.

---

*Judith Jarvis Thomson, "The Right to Privacy," *Philosophy and Public Affairs*, 4.4 (1975):295.

† Judith Jarvis Thomson, "The Right to Privacy," p. 295.

3. Privacy, Autonomy, and Personal Space

We begin by taking seriously the common assumption that privacy is a *fundamental moral right*. Let's be clear about what this means. All three terms are essential. First, privacy is a right to which people are entitled, rather than a mere good that any person might strive to achieve. Second, privacy is a *moral* right, rather than just a constitutional or legal right. Third, privacy is a *fundamental* right, rather than one that can be explicated in terms of other fundamental rights like life, liberty or property.

The assumption that there are fundamental moral rights of any sort makes sense only within the liberal tradition, which emphasizes the inherent capacity of individuals to be "self-legislating" or autonomous. As we noted above, most philosophers who argue that we have a moral right to privacy have not attempted to show that privacy is a fundamental right. Warren and Brandeis, for example, argued that the right to privacy follows from the right to life. Others have attempted to derive a right to privacy from the right to property or liberty. Our view, by contrast, is that the right to privacy is a fundamental right because privacy is an essential and independent requirement of personal autonomy.

Perhaps the most widely used metaphor in describing the violation of privacy is that it consists in a violation of "personal space." Indeed, the idea of personal space is more than just a metaphor. To be autonomous, people need in some sense to "own" the physical space around them. After all, how can a person enjoy any liberty or protection from harm if he may be routinely ejected from the space he occupies at any given time? But the idea of personal space can be extended along a different axis as well. Physical space, after all, is just the space inhabited by physical objects. But persons are not your ordinary physical objects. Persons are thinking, reasoning objects, and this activity requires a space of a different kind.

Philosophers from Aristotle to the present have consistently identified the capacity for rational deliberation and planning as the distinguishing feature of personhood. Kant, in an effort to comprehend how autonomous physical objects can exist at all, argued that there must be more than one kind of law operating in the universe. If the laws of nature determine the motion of physical bodies through physical space, then there are also laws of rationality for the self-determination of persons in moral space.

This analogy between physical and moral space is a commonplace of privacy discussions. Privacy theorists almost always use spatial metaphors, such as "domains," to explicate their notion of privacy. Disputes about privacy rights can often be articulated in terms of how far to extend the "domain of privacy" surrounding the individual. On the other hand, theories of privacy often go wrong precisely by confusing the moral space of this domain with physical space. They move too easily from the well-founded view that individuals need some control of their physical environment to the conclusion that some physical space like the home or some type of personal information must be a sacrosanct domain of privacy.

Our suggestion, then, is that personal space is not only completely real but also logically distinct from physical space. It is the space inhabited by persons and essential to the exercise of their nature as autonomous agents. To violate a person's privacy is to interfere in some important way with the exercise of a person's rationality. To interfere with a person's rationality is to interfere in the most fundamental way possible with a person's capacity for self-government. Hence, we suggest that to assert a right to privacy is to assert a *right to exercise our rationality without undue interference from others*.

We understand that many will find it strange at first to speak of a right to exercise our rationality without interference. It sounds odd, and you certainly will not find it in the Bill of Rights. (Of course, you won't find the right to privacy there either.) We do not think this is a serious objection, however. As we noted above, respect for the rationality of persons is at the absolute core of the liberal tradition. In the Kantian system the absolute duty of all persons is to respect the rationality of others. If we have not customarily spoken of reason as a right, it has been for lack of need, not lack of justification.

4. Squaring with Intuitions

Let's test this view first by looking at how it stands up to the criticisms of Warren and Brandeis. Recall that their view of privacy as "the right to be let alone" is generally regarded as being too broad in some ways and too narrow in others. It is too broad because it implies that hitting someone in the head with a brick is a violation of privacy. It is too narrow because it implies that undetected spying is not.

We want to be clear that our view of privacy is best understood as a refined version of the right to be let alone. We fail to let the physical *human being* alone when we hit him on the head with a brick, but we fail to let the *person* alone only when we interfere with the exercise of his rationality. Now this distinction may seem entirely academic. After all, hitting a human being in the head with a brick will inevitably interfere with his rationality. So aren't we still stuck with the absurdity that it is a violation of privacy to do so? The answer is that we are stuck with the conclusion, but it is no longer an absurdity. The Warren and Brandeis view is justifiably criticized as too broad, not because it implies that hitting someone on the head with a brick will violate her privacy, but because it cannot distinguish between a threat to a person's life and a threat to her privacy. Our view does make that distinction and explains why it is a threat to both. There is, of course, no absurdity in assuming that multiple harms can be done by the same event. If I hit you in the head with a brick from your garden, I violate your right to life. I also violate your liberty, property, and privacy. These are just not your primary concerns.

Our approach also seems to preserve the undesirable narrowness of the Warren and Brandeis view. How does undetected spying constitute interference with a person's rationality? Our answer is that it doesn't. Unlike Warren and Brandeis, who clearly intended their theory to apply to such cases, in our view no fundamental moral rights are violated by the simple act of observing others. We understand that this is contentious. Most people think of spying as the very epitome of a violation of privacy. To many there is something fundamentally corrupt and loathsome about surreptitious observation of any sort. But we do not share this feeling. We regard casual curiosity about the private lives of others as a universal and largely benign human compulsion. Of course, we agree that anyone who commits substantial personal resources to spying on others is morally suspect. He may be plotting some evil; he may just need to get a

life. But whatever the potential harms of spying, the act of observation itself cannot be one of them.

The reason for this is simple. Within the liberal tradition, respect for personal autonomy is matched only by respect for knowledge. There can be nothing in the world that it is intrinsically wrong to know, for knowledge is itself an intrinsic good, and acquiring it is one of the essential activities of the autonomous agent. Hence, any restriction we place on the acquisition of knowledge must be justified by the overriding harm that results either in the process or as a result of acquiring it. Clearly the potential for such harm is sometimes extraordinary, and in many cases it will be plausible to argue that the mere act of acquiring it is a clear indication of the intention to do such harm. Such is often the case with sensitive personal information like medical records, credit card numbers, and video rental logs. But it is important to understand that the proper justification of such restrictions *cannot* be that people have a fundamental moral right to control personal information. For this would imply that others have a fundamental moral obligation to not know these things, and this can only be true if there are certain things that it is fundamentally wrong to know.

Even though knowing personal information does not itself constitute a violation of privacy, in our view there are certainly ways in which spying can result in such a violation. We currently protect certain forms of personal information in the interest of preventing theft, assuring personal safety, ensuring access to medical care, and providing due process of law. But we can also justify protecting personal information in the interest of privacy, i.e., in preventing undue interference with the exercise of rationality. (Notice that in our view of privacy this actually means something. If the right to privacy were just the right to control personal information, it would be a perfectly vacuous statement.) Clearly, it would be impossible to make rational plans for the future if we had no control over our basic resources, and it is control of our resources that we relinquish when others have access to the information needed to take them.

There is another interesting way in which the simple act of observing others can interfere with the exercise of rationality. Consider for a moment what happens when we become conscious of the fact that we are being observed. Anyone who has ever interviewed for a job, performed for an audience, or endured the piercing stare of a stranger knows that this experience can induce a kind of mental paralysis. Sometimes we are afraid that the observers intend to harm us in some way, but this needn't be the case. Even a friend looking over your shoulder as you attempt to read or compose a letter can utterly derail your rationality. It seems that the simple fact of knowing that we are the object of another person's attention can cause us to be so consumed by the point of view of the observer that we lose touch with that unique internal perspective upon which clear thinking and reasoning depend. Although we learn to endure casual public observation as well as occasional intense scrutiny, for most of us the demands of autonomy require that we be able to secure a personal space in which we are free to think and reason without interference from other minds.

5. Some Implications

Our theory of privacy clearly doesn't justify the instant outrage that many people feel upon learning how much is known about their private lives. In the information age our shopping preferences are recorded and analyzed, our movements are followed by surveillance cameras, our credit, medical, and employment histories are all easily acquired by those who want to know. Even our charge records and internet surfing habits are easily tracked. Some of these may be unreasonably invasive, but it is important to realize that technologies and practices that give people access to our personal information also give them the ability to protect and improve our lives. That, after all, is how liars, adulterers, and criminals are caught. In the "transparent society," social relations in general, not just law enforcement efforts, are characterized by the easy availability of personal information.

Often those who favor a simple notion of privacy as "control of personal information" have not thought carefully about the harms that can result from strengthening such control. In addition to holding people to their agreements and enforcing the law, many contemporary disciplines depend upon easy access to personal information. Epidemiologists and urban planners, for example, need information about incidence of disease, traffic, and consumer preferences. Gathering data often compromises individual control of personal information, but the value to society can be enormous.

Our theory of privacy may be too weak for the guardians of personal information, but it may also be too strong for the guardians of personal liberty. One interesting aspect of our approach is that it provides a novel way to understand the moral dimension of acts that the liberal tradition has always required us to discount as merely rude or offensive. Because things like staring, talking too loudly, and interrupting are all legitimately characterized as interfering with a person's rationality, we can now see that they are not beyond moral criticism.

More significant perhaps are offensive forms of communication (racial invective, pornography) and conduct (public lewdness, flag burning). Many people, including some philosophers, have become impatient with the requirement that we tolerate such things in the name of personal liberty. They claim that it shows not strength but a lack of moral courage when we shrink from legislating against such activity. We believe that the right to privacy has an essential role in this debate. Speech offensive enough to compromise a person's rationality, whether in public or in private, is now legitimately construed as a violation of privacy. Indeed, the "fighting words" proviso on constitutionally protected free speech makes implicit use of this criterion. Those who respond violently to fighting words are forgiven, not because they were acting in self-defense, but because the words compromised their ability to maintain rational control of their behavior.

Our analysis of privacy extends to other morally repugnant activities the harm of which can be quite difficult to characterize. Brainwashing, blackmailing people with the truth, white lies, all may be fairly characterized as interfering with the exercise of rationality. This actually raises a skeptical question. What *isn't* a possible violation of privacy in our model? After all, exceptional ugliness, unrequited affection, and peculiar habits can all drive a person to distraction under the right circumstances. Are they therefore to be counted as violations of the right to privacy? This is a fair question, but the answer is not particularly difficult. My very presence in the world restricts your liberty, but it does not restrict your *right* to liberty. Similarly, my strange appearance or habits may violate your privacy without violating your *right* to privacy. Moral rights are universal, but what constitutes a violation of any particular right will depend on certain inherently cultural standards of behavior.

This actually helps to explain our earlier claim that the right to privacy is compatible with the existence of a perfectly transparent society. In partial support of our view we noted above that people can find it very difficult to function rationally when being observed. This is true of most people in our culture, but it is hardly a law of nature. Performers and politicians thrive on public attention. Those forced to live in close quarters with strangers get used to it. So, while our view of privacy does not advocate for the transparent society, neither does it counsel against it. It is perfectly possible that at some point in the future the social value of transparency will largely eliminate the fears that now underlie our need for secrecy. In any case, no theory of privacy should decide this issue on *a priori* grounds.

Finally, what of Jan Bronstein? Did David Letterman violate her privacy? Of course. What (besides a blow to the head with a brick) could interfere more with a person's rationality than to be ridiculed on international television? But was Bronstein's *right* to privacy violated? This is less clear. Our public figures are routinely required to suffer such indignities. (Compare, for instance, Bronstein's plight to that of President Clinton and Monica Lewinsky during the Oval Office imbroglio.) One can plausibly argue that insofar as Bronstein knowingly participated in a televised event, she consented to these conditions. But there may be a question of degree. Most people would agree that someone who holds public office must accept a greater degree of public scrutiny than a private citizen. (Indeed, it is partly the ability to function rationally under such exposure that convinces us of a person's fitness for public office.) But it may be plausibly argued that Letterman respected this distinction by limiting his use of Bronstein to her voluntary behavior and appearance at a public event. In the end, whether Bronstein's right to privacy was violated depends on subtle distinction of degree, distinctions which must be made by human judges, not theories. The theory supplies the criterion of judgment, however, and for privacy matters, the proper criterion is the degree of interference with rationality.

QUESTIONS FOR REFLECTION

1. What objections do philosophers commonly raise against the Warren and Brandeis view of the right to privacy?

2. What is the difference between reductionist and intuitionist analyses of privacy?

3. What do Mayes and Alfino mean in saying that privacy is a fundamental moral right? Who might disagree?

4. What do Mayes and Alfino mean by "personal space"?

5. What, in their analysis, is the right to privacy?

6. How do Mayes and Alfino defend the claim that surveillance does not violate the right to privacy?

7. Why is the right to privacy compatible with a perfectly transparent society, in their view? Do you agree?

ABORTION

Abortion raises notoriously difficult ethical problems. At root, these problems seem to revolve around rights. Opponents of abortion speak of the right to life of the fetus; pro-choice advocates speak of a woman's right to choose. Obviously, these two putative rights come into conflict over abortion. One cannot respect both the right to life of the fetus and the woman's right to choose if the woman chooses to abort. Consequently, the abortion issue seems to call for some neutral or well-grounded way of deciding when some rights take precedence over others.

Of course, not everyone grants the rights in question. Some argue that the fetus is not a person and, indeed, is sufficiently unlike a person that it has no rights. Others argue that the woman may have obligations toward a fetus inside her even if it is there through no choice of her own. They deny that, at least in some cases, a woman has a right to choose abortion. The abortion problem thus raises two other very difficult issues: (1) What kinds of beings have rights? Fetuses, severely ill or injured people, and animals all share many basic human characteristics but lack others common to typical, healthy adults. Which characteristics, if any, are essential to having rights? In general, how do we decide the boundaries of our moral categories? (2) What kinds of obligations do we have toward others? Under what circumstances do other people have rights against us—rights to have us do certain things to help them and to refrain from doing things to harm them? To what extent do such obligations depend on our willingness to assume them? These questions are crucial to the abortion issue and, moreover, reach far beyond it.

Abortion had been illegal in most areas of the United States until 1973, when the Supreme Court decided, in *Roe* v. *Wade,* that the Constitution guarantees a right to privacy, implying that the state may not restrict abortions in the first trimester (the first three months of pregnancy). The Court backed away from any decision about the ultimate moral status of the fetus; it treated fetuses as "potential people," having value if not rights. (Opponents of the decision contend that this failure to decide the status of the fetus is itself a decision, since the Court does not take the rights of fetuses into account.) Instead, the Court based its decision on the medical fact that first-trimester abortions are less risky than carrying a child to term, whereas later abortions are riskier. The government's interest in preserving the health and safety of the mother thus gives the government reason to restrict abortions, but only after the first trimester. The value of the fetus also gives the government reason to restrict abortions, but only after the fetus becomes "viable"—that is, able to survive outside the mother's body. Until then, the mother's right to privacy takes precedence. The Court's decision in *Roe* v. *Wade* raises profound constitutional questions and analogous moral questions: Is there a right to privacy? If so, what is it? How far does it extend? How does it relate to other rights? What obligations does it place on others? . . .

Judith Jarvis Thomson contends that the unacceptability of abortion does not follow automatically from the right to life of the fetus. She grants, for the sake of argument, that the fetus has such a right. She then maintains that under many circumstances, a woman nevertheless has no obligation to carry a child to term. She distinguishes some important conceptions of our obligations to others and argues that only on a very (and, she thinks, unacceptably) strong conception does the woman generally have an obligation not to abort.

Mary Anne Warren rejects Thomson's argument. If the fetus were a person with a right to life, Warren believes, abortion would generally be immoral. But Warren rejects the premise. A fetus, she contends, is at best a potential person, for it lacks basic defining features of personhood: consciousness, reasoning, self-motivated activity, communicative ability, and self-awareness. Since the rights of actual people take precedence over the rights (if there are any) of potential people, abortion is therefore permissible.

Jane English argues that both conservative and liberal positions on abortion are mistaken. She contends moreover that questions of personhood and rights are not as important to the moral issues surrounding abortion as many believe. Even if fetuses are persons with rights to life, she maintains, abortion is sometimes justifiable. And even if fetuses are not persons and have no rights, abortion is sometimes wrong. She concludes that we cannot resolve the abortion issue by reflecting on rights alone; we must reflect generally on our obligations to others.

Don Marquis contends that abortion is immoral for the same reason that murdering an adult human is immoral—it deprives something that would have had a human life of its future. Marquis does not argue, as many anti-abortionists have, that the fetus has a right to life or that abortion is murder; he argues instead that it is *like* murder in that it deprives something that would have gone on to experience a human life of that very opportunity.

JUSTICE HARRY BLACKMUN

Majority Opinion in *Roe* v. *Wade* (1973)

(Source: Roe v. Wade *410 U.S. 113 [1973]. Most legal references have been omitted.)*

Mr. Justice Blackmun delivered the opinion of the Court. . . .

I

The Texas statutes that concern us here are Arts. 1191-1194 and 1196 of the State's Penal Code. These make it a crime to "procure an abortion," as therein defined, or to attempt one, except with respect to "an abortion procured or attempted by medical advice for the purpose of saving the life of the mother." Similar statutes are in existence in a majority of the States. . . .

II

Jane Roe, a single woman who was residing in Dallas County, Texas, instituted this federal action in March 1970 against the District Attorney of the county. She sought a declaratory judgment that the Texas criminal abortion statutes were unconstitutional on their face and an injunction restraining the defendant from enforcing the statutes.

Roe alleged that she was unmarried and pregnant; that she wished to terminate her pregnancy by an abortion "performed by a competent, licensed physician, under safe, clinical conditions"; that she was unable to get a "legal" abortion in Texas because her life did not appear to be threatened by the continuation of her pregnancy; and that she could not afford to travel to another jurisdiction in order to secure a legal abortion under safe conditions. She claimed that the Texas statutes were unconstitutionally vague and that they abridged her right of personal privacy, protected by the First, Fourth, Fifth, Ninth, and Fourteenth Amendments. By an amendment to her complaint Roe purported to sue "on behalf of herself and all other women" similarly situated. . . .

VIII

The Constitution does not explicitly mention any right of privacy. In a line of decisions, however, going back perhaps as far as *Union Pacific R. Co.* v. *Botsford* (1891), the Court has recognized that a right of personal privacy, or a guarantee of certain areas or zones of privacy, does exist under the Constitution. . . . The decisions make it clear that only personal rights that can be deemed "fundamental" or "implicit in the concept of ordered liberty" are included in this guarantee of personal privacy. They also make it clear that the right has some extension to activities relating to marriage, procreation, contraception, family relationships, and child rearing and education.

This right of privacy, whether it be founded in the Fourteenth Amendment's concept of personal liberty and restrictions upon state action, as we feel it is, or, as the District Court determined, in the Ninth Amendment's reservation of rights to the people, is broad enough to encompass a woman's decision whether or not to terminate her pregnancy. The detriment that the State would impose upon the pregnant woman by denying this choice altogether is apparent. Specific and direct harm medically diagnosable even in early pregnancy may be involved. Maternity, or additional offspring, may force upon the woman a distressful life and future. Psychological harm may be imminent. Mental and physical health may be taxed by child care. There is also the distress, for all concerned, associated with the unwanted child, and there is the problem of bringing a child into a family already unable, psychologically and otherwise, to care for it. In other cases, as in this one, the additional difficulties and continuing stigma of unwed motherhood may be involved. All these are factors the woman and her responsible physician necessarily will consider in consultation.

On the basis of elements such as these, appellant and some *amici* argue that the woman's right is absolute and that she is entitled to terminate her pregnancy at whatever time, in whatever way, and for whatever reason she alone chooses. With this we do not agree. Appellant's arguments that Texas either has no valid interest at all in regulating the abortion decision, or no interest strong enough to support any limitation upon the woman's sole determination, are unpersuasive. The Court's decisions recognizing a right of privacy also acknowledge that some state regulation in areas protected by that right is appropriate. As noted above, a State may properly assert important interests in safeguarding health, in maintaining medical standards, and in protecting potential life. At some point in pregnancy, these respective interests become sufficiently compelling to sustain regulation of the factors that govern the abortion decision. The privacy right involved, therefore, cannot be said to be absolute. In fact, it is not clear to us that the claim asserted by some *amici* that one has an unlimited right to do with one's body as one pleases bears a close relationship to the right of privacy previously articulated in the Court's decisions. The Court has refused to recognize an unlimited right of this kind in the past.

We, therefore, conclude that the right of personal privacy includes the abortion decision, but that this right is not unqualified and must be considered against important state interests in regulation. . . .

IX

The District Court held that the appellee failed to meet his burden of demonstrating that the Texas statute's infringement upon Roe's rights was necessary to support a compelling state interest, and that, although the appellee presented "several compelling justifications for state presence in the area of abortions," the statutes outstripped these justifications and swept "far beyond any areas of compelling state interest." Appellant and appellee both contest that holding. Appellant, as has been indicated, claims an absolute right that bars any state imposition of criminal penalties in the area. Appellee argues that the State's determination to recognize and protect prenatal life from and after conception constitutes a compelling state interest. As noted above, we do not agree fully with either formulation.

A. The appellee and certain *amici* argue that the fetus is a "person" within the language and meaning of the Fourteenth Amendment. In support of this, they outline at length and in detail the well-known facts of fetal development. If this suggestion of personhood is established, the appellant's case, of course, collapses, for the fetus' right to life would then be guaranteed specifically by the Amendment. The appellant conceded as much on reargument. On the other hand, the appellee conceded on reargument that no case could be cited that holds that a fetus is a person within the meaning of the Fourteenth Amendment.

The Constitution does not define "person" in so many words. Section 1 of the Fourteenth Amendment contains three references to "person." The first, in defining "citizens," speaks of "persons born or naturalized in the United States." The word also appears both in the Due Process Clause and in the Equal Protection Clause. "Person" is used in other places in the Constitution. . . . But in nearly all these instances, the use of the word is such that it has application only postnatally. None indicates, with any assurance, that it has any possible prenatal application.

All this, together with our observation that throughout the major portion of the 19th century prevailing legal abortion practices were far freer than they are today, persuades us that the word "person," as used in the Fourteenth Amendment, does not include the unborn. This is in accord with the results reached in those few cases where the issue has been squarely presented. Indeed, our decision in *United States* v. *Vuitch* (1971), inferentially is to the same effect, for we there would not have indulged in statutory interpretation favorable to abortion in specified circumstances if the necessary consequence was the termination of life entitled to Fourteenth Amendment protection.

This conclusion, however, does not of itself fully answer the contentions raised by Texas, and we pass on to other considerations.

B. The pregnant woman cannot be isolated in her privacy. She carries an embryo and, later, a fetus, if one accepts the medical definitions of the developing young in the human uterus. . . . The situation therefore is inherently different from marital intimacy, or bedroom possession of obscene material, or marriage, or procreation, or education, with which *Eisenstadt* and *Griswold, Stanley, Loving, Skinner,* and *Pierce* and *Meyer* were respectively concerned. As we have intimated above, it is reasonable and appropriate for a State to decide that at some point in time another interest, that of health of the mother or that of potential human life, becomes significantly involved. The woman's privacy is no longer sole and any right of privacy she possesses must be measured accordingly.

Texas urges that, apart from the Fourteenth Amendment, life begins at conception and is present throughout pregnancy, and that, therefore, the State has a compelling interest in protecting that life from and after conception. We need not resolve the difficult question of when life begins. When those trained in the respective disciplines of medicine, philosophy, and theology are unable to arrive at any consensus, the judiciary, at this point in the development of man's knowledge, is not in a position to speculate as to the answer.

It should be sufficient to note briefly the wide divergence of thinking on this most sensitive and difficult question. There has always been strong support for the view that life does not begin until live birth. This was the belief of the Stoics. It appears to be the predominant, though not the unanimous, attitude of the Jewish faith. It may be taken to represent also the position of a large segment of the Protestant community, insofar as that can be ascertained; organized groups that have taken a formal position on the abortion issue have generally regarded abortion as a matter for the conscience of the individual and her

family. As we have noted, the common law found greater significance in quickening. Physicians and their scientific colleagues have regarded that event with less interest and have tended to focus either upon conception, upon live birth, or upon the interim point at which the fetus becomes "viable," that is, potentially able to live outside the mother's womb, albeit with artificial aid. Viability is usually placed at about seven months (28 weeks) but may occur earlier, even at 24 weeks. The Aristotelian theory of "mediate animation," that held sway throughout the Middle Ages and the Renaissance in Europe, continued to be official Roman Catholic dogma until the 19th century, despite opposition to this "ensoulment" theory from those in the Church who would recognize the existence of life from the moment of conception. The latter is now, of course, the official belief of the Catholic Church. As one brief *amicus* discloses, this is a view strongly held by many non-Catholics as well, and by many physicians. Substantial problems for precise definition of this view are posed, however, by new embryological data that purport to indicate that conception is a "process" over time, rather than an event, and by new medical techniques such as menstrual extraction, the "morning-after" pill, implantation of embryos, artificial insemination, and even artificial wombs.

In areas other than criminal abortion, the law has been reluctant to endorse any theory that life, as we recognize it, begins before live birth or to accord legal rights to the unborn except in narrowly defined situations and except when the rights are contingent upon live birth. For example, the traditional rule of tort law denied recovery for prenatal injuries even though the child was born alive. That rule has been changed in almost every jurisdiction. In most States, recovery is said to be permitted only if the fetus was viable, or at least quick, when the injuries were sustained, though few courts have squarely so held. In a recent development, generally opposed by the commentators, some States permit the parents of a stillborn child to maintain an action for wrongful death because of prenatal injuries. Such an action, however, would appear to be one to vindicate the parents' interest and is thus consistent with the view that the fetus, at most, represents only the potentiality of life. Similarly, unborn children have been recognized as acquiring rights or interests by way of inheritance or other devolution of property, and have been represented by guardians *ad litem*. Perfection of the interests involved, again, has generally been contingent upon live birth. In short, the unborn have never been recognized in the law as persons in the whole sense.

X

In view of all this, we do not agree that, by adopting one theory of life, Texas may override the rights of the pregnant woman that are at stake. We repeat, however, that the State does have an important and legitimate interest in preserving and protecting the health of the pregnant woman, whether she be a resident of the State or a nonresident who seeks medical consultation and treatment there, and that it has still *another* important and legitimate interest in protecting the potentiality of human life. These interests are separate and distinct. Each grows in substantiality as the woman approaches term and, at a point during pregnancy, each becomes "compelling."

With respect to the State's important and legitimate interest in the health of the mother, the "compelling" point, in the light of present medical knowledge, is at approximately the end of the first trimester. This is so because of the now-established medical fact . . . that until the end of the first trimester mortality in abortion may be less than mortality in normal childbirth. It follows that, from and after this point, a State may regulate the abortion procedure to the extent that the regulation reasonably relates to the preservation and protection of maternal health. Examples of permissible state regulation in this area are requirements as to the qualifications of the person who is to perform the abortion; as to the licensure of that person; as to the facility in which the procedure is to be performed, that is, whether it must be a hospital or may be a clinic or some other place of less-than-hospital status; as to the licensing of the facility; and the like.

This means, on the other hand, that, for the period of pregnancy prior to this "compelling" point, the attending physician, in consultation with his patient, is free to determine, without regulation by the State, that, in his medical judgment, the patient's pregnancy should be terminated. If that decision is reached, the judgment may be effectuated by an abortion free of interference by the State.

With respect to the State's important and legitimate interest in potential life, the "compelling" point is at viability. This is so because the fetus then presumably has the capability of meaningful life outside the mother's womb. State regulation protective of fetal life after viability thus has both logical and biological justifications. If the State is interested in protecting fetal life after viability, it may go so far as to proscribe abortion during that period, except when it is necessary to preserve the life or health of the mother.

Measured against these standards, Art. 1196 of the Texas Penal Code, in restricting legal abortions to those "procured or attempted by medical advice for the purpose of saving the life of the mother," sweeps too broadly. The statute makes no distinction between abortions performed early in pregnancy and those performed later, and it limits to a single reason, "saving" the mother's life, the legal justification for the procedure. The statute, therefore, cannot survive the constitutional attack made upon it here. . . .

XI

To summarize and to repeat:

1. A state criminal abortion statute of the current Texas type, that excepts from criminality only a *life-saving* procedure on behalf of the mother, without regard to pregnancy stage and without recognition of the other interests involved, is violative of the Due Process Clause of the Fourteenth Amendment.

   a. For the stage prior to approximately the end of the first trimester, the abortion decision and its effectuation must be left to the medical judgment of the pregnant woman's attending physician.

   b. For the stage subsequent to approximately the end of the first trimester, the State, in promoting its interest in the health of the mother, may, if it chooses, regulate the abortion procedure in ways that are reasonably related to maternal health.

c. For the stage subsequent to viability, the State in promoting its interest in the potentiality of human life may, if it chooses, regulate, and even proscribe, abortion except where it is necessary, in appropriate medical judgment, for the preservation of the life or health of the mother.

2. The State may define the term "physician," as it has been employed in the preceding paragraphs of this Part XI of this opinion, to mean only a physician currently licensed by the State, and may proscribe any abortion by a person who is not a physician as so defined. . . .

QUESTIONS FOR REFLECTION

1. What, according to the majority, are the chief interests of the state in making a decision about abortion?

2. The majority bases its decision on the right of privacy. What is this right? How does the majority argue for it? What are its limitations?

3. The majority contends that the "compelling point" for balancing the rights and interests involved is viability. What is viability? Why does the majority settle on it as the compelling point? Do you find the argument convincing?

JUDITH JARVIS THOMSON

A Defense of Abortion

Judith Jarvis Thomson is Professor of Philosophy at the Massachusetts Institute of Technology. (*Source: From* Philosophy and Public Affairs, *Vol. I, No. 1 [Fall 1971], pp. 47–66. Copyright © 1971 by Princeton University Press. Reprinted by permission of Princeton University Press.*)

Most opposition to abortion relies on the premise that the fetus is a human being, a person, from the moment of conception. The premise is argued for, but, as I think, not well. Take, for example, the most common argument. We are asked to notice that the development of a human being from conception through birth into childhood is continuous; then it is said that to draw a line, to choose a point in this development and say "before this point the thing is not a person, after this point it is a person" is to make an arbitrary choice, a choice for which in the nature of things no good reason can be given. It is concluded that the fetus is, or anyway that we had better say it is, a person from the moment of conception. But this conclusion does not follow. Similar things might be said about the development of an acorn into an oak tree, and it does not follow that acorns are oak trees, or that we had better say they are. Arguments of this form are sometimes called "slippery slope arguments"—the phrase is perhaps self-explanatory— and it is dismaying that opponents of abortion rely on them so heavily and uncritically.

I am inclined to agree, however, that the prospects for "drawing a line" in the development of the fetus look dim. I am inclined to think also that we shall probably have to agree that the fetus has already become a human person well before birth. Indeed, it comes as a surprise when one first learns how early in its life it begins to acquire human characteristics. By the tenth week, for example, it already has a face, arms and legs, fingers and toes; it has in-

ternal organs, and brain activity is detectable. On the other hand, I think that the premise is false, that the fetus is not a person from the moment of conception. A newly fertilized ovum, a newly implanted clump of cells, is no more a person than an acorn is an oak tree. But I shall not discuss any of this. For it seems to me to be of great interest to ask what happens if, for the sake of argument, we allow the premise. How, precisely, are we supposed to get from there to the conclusion that abortion is morally impermissible? Opponents of abortion commonly spend most of their time establishing that the fetus is a person, and hardly any time explaining the step from there to the impermissibility of abortion. Perhaps they think the step too simple and obvious to require much comment. Or perhaps instead they are simply being economical in argument. Many of those who defend abortion rely on the premise that the fetus is not a person, but only a bit of tissue that will become a person at birth; and why pay out more arguments than you have to? Whatever the explanation, I suggest that the step they take is neither easy nor obvious, that it calls for closer examination than it is commonly given, and that when we do give it this closer examination we shall feel inclined to reject it.

I propose, then, that we grant that the fetus is a person from the moment of conception. How does the argument go from here? Something like this, I take it. Every person has a right to life. So the fetus has a right to life. No doubt the mother has a right to decide what shall happen in and to her body; everyone would grant that. But surely a person's right to life is stronger and more stringent than the mother's right to decide what happens in and to her body, and so outweighs it. So the fetus may not be killed; an abortion may not be performed.

It sounds plausible. But now let me ask you to imagine this. You wake up in the morning and find yourself back to back in bed with an unconscious violinist. A famous unconscious violinist. He has been found to have a fatal kidney ailment, and the Society of Music Lovers has canvassed all the available medical records and found that you alone have the right blood type to help. They have therefore kidnapped you, and last night the violinist's circulatory system was plugged into yours, so that your kidneys can be used to extract poisons from his blood as well as your own. The director of the hospital now tells you, "Look, we're sorry the Society of Music Lovers did this to you—we would never have permitted it if we had known. But still, they did it, and the violinist now is plugged into you. To unplug you would be to kill him. But never mind, it's only for nine months. By then he will have recovered from his ailment, and can safely be unplugged from you." Is it morally incumbent on you to accede to this situation? No doubt it would be very nice of you if you did, a great kindness. But do you *have* to accede to it? What if it were not nine months, but nine years? Or longer still? What if the director of the hospital says, "Tough luck, I agree, but you've now got to stay in bed, with the violinist plugged into you, for the rest of your life. Because remember this. All persons have a right to life, and violinists are persons. Granted you have a right to decide what happens in and to your body, but a person's right to life outweighs your right to decide what happens in and to your body. So you cannot ever be unplugged from him." I imagine you would regard this as outrageous, which suggests that something really is wrong with that plausible-sounding argument I mentioned a moment ago.

In this case, of course, you were kidnapped; you didn't volunteer for the operation that plugged the violinist into your kidneys. Can those who oppose abortion on the ground I mentioned make an exception for a pregnancy due to rape? Certainly. They can say that persons have a right to life only if they didn't come into existence because of rape; or they can say that all persons have a right to life, but that some

have less of a right to life than others, in particular, that those who came into existence because of rape have less. But these statements have a rather unpleasant sound. Surely the question of whether you have a right to life at all, or how much of it you have, shouldn't turn on the question of whether or not you are the product of a rape. And in fact the people who oppose abortion on the ground I mentioned do not make this distinction, and hence do not make an exception in case of rape.

Nor do they make an exception for a case in which the mother has to spend the nine months of her pregnancy in bed. They would agree that would be a great pity, and hard on the mother; but all the same, all persons have a right to life, the fetus is a person, and so on. I suspect, in fact, that they would not make an exception for a case in which, miraculously enough, the pregnancy went on for nine years, or even the rest of the mother's life.

Some won't even make an exception for a case in which continuation of the pregnancy is likely to shorten the mother's life; they regard abortion as impermissible even to save the mother's life. Such cases are nowadays very rare, and many opponents of abortion do not accept this extreme view. All the same, it is a good place to begin: a number of points of interest come out in respect to it.

1. Let us call the view that abortion is impermissible even to save the mother's life "the extreme view." I want to suggest first that it does not issue from the argument I mentioned earlier without the addition of some fairly powerful premises. Suppose a woman has become pregnant, and now learns that she has a cardiac condition such that she will die if she carries the baby to term. What may be done for her? The fetus, being a person, has a right to life, but as the mother is a person too, so has she a right to life. Presumably they have an equal right to life. How is it supposed to come out that an abortion may not be performed? If mother and child have an equal right to life, shouldn't we perhaps flip a coin? Or should we add to the mother's right to life her right to decide what happens in and to her body, which everybody seems to be ready to grant—the sum of her rights now outweighing the fetus' right to life?

The most familiar argument here is the following. We are told that performing the abortion would be directly killing the child, whereas doing nothing would not be killing the mother, but only letting her die. Moreover, in killing the child, one would be killing an innocent person, for the child has committed no crime, and is not aiming at his mother's death. And then there are a variety of ways in which this might be continued. (1) But as directly killing an innocent person is always and absolutely impermissible, an abortion may not be performed. Or, (2) as directly killing an innocent person is murder, and murder is always and absolutely impermissible, an abortion may not be performed. Or, (3) as one's duty to refrain from directly killing an innocent person is more stringent than one's duty to keep a person from dying, an abortion may not be performed. Or, (4) if one's only options are directly killing an innocent person or letting a person die, one must prefer letting the person die, and thus an abortion may not be performed.

Some people seem to have thought that these are not further premises which must be added if the conclusion is to be reached, but that they follow from the very fact that an innocent person has a right to life. But this seems to me to be a mistake, and perhaps the simplest way to show this is to bring out that while we must certainly grant that innocent persons have a right to life, the theses in (1) through (4) are all false. Take (2), for example. If directly killing an innocent person is murder, and thus is impermissible, then the mother's directly killing the innocent person inside her is murder, and thus is impermissible. But it cannot seriously be thought to be murder if the mother performs an abortion on herself to save her life. It cannot seriously be said that she *must* refrain, that she *must* sit passively by and wait for her death. Let us look again at the case of you and the violinist. There you are, in bed with the violinist, and the director of the hospital says to you, "It's all most distressing, and I deeply sympathize, but you see this is putting an additional strain on your kidneys, and you'll be dead within the month. But you *have* to stay where you are all the same. Because unplugging you would be directly killing an innocent violinist, and that's murder, and that's impermissible." If anything in the world is true, it is that you do not commit murder, you do not do what is impermissible, if you reach around to your back and unplug yourself from that violinist to save your life.

The main focus of attention in writings on abortion has been on what a third party may or may not

do in answer to a request from a woman for an abortion. This is in a way understandable. Things being as they are, there isn't much a woman can safely do to abort herself. So the question asked is what a third party may do, and what the mother may do, if it is mentioned at all, is deduced, almost as an afterthought, from what it is concluded that third parties may do. But it seems to me that to treat the matter in this way is to refuse to grant to the mother that very status of person which is so firmly insisted on for the fetus. For we cannot simply read off what a person may do from what a third party may do. Suppose you find yourself trapped in a tiny house with a growing child. I mean a very tiny house, and a rapidly growing child—you are already up against the wall of the house and in a few minutes you'll be crushed to death. The child on the other hand won't be crushed to death; if nothing is done to stop him from growing he'll be hurt, but in the end he'll simply burst open the house and walk out a free man. Now I could well understand it if a bystander were to say, "There's nothing we can do for you. We cannot choose between your life and his, we cannot be the ones to decide who is to live, we cannot intervene." But it cannot be concluded that you too can do nothing, that you cannot attack it to save your life. However innocent the child may be, you do not have to wait passively while it crushes you to death. Perhaps a pregnant woman is vaguely felt to have the status of house, to which we don't allow the right of self-defense. But if the woman houses the child, it should be remembered that she is a person who houses it.

I should perhaps stop to say explicitly that I am not claiming that people have a right to do anything whatever to save their lives. I think, rather, that there are drastic limits to the right of self-defense. If someone threatens you with death unless you torture someone else to death, I think you have not the right, even to save your life, to do so. But the case under consideration here is very different. In our case there are only two people involved, one whose life is threatened, and one who threatens it. Both are innocent: the one who is threatened is not threatened because of any fault, the one who threatens does not threaten because of any fault. For this reason we may feel that we bystanders cannot intervene. But the person threatened can.

In sum, a woman surely can defend her life against the threat to it posed by the unborn child, even if doing so involves its death. And this shows not merely that the theses in (1) through (4) are false; it shows also that the extreme view of abortion is false, and so we need not canvass any other possible ways of arriving at it from the argument I mentioned at the outset.

2. The extreme view could of course be weakened to say that while abortion is permissible to save the mother's life, it may not be performed by the third party, but only by the mother herself. But this cannot be right either. For what we have to keep in mind is that the mother and the unborn child are not like two tenants in a small house which has, by an unfortunate mistake, been rented to both: the mother *owns* the house. The fact that she does adds to the offensiveness of deducing that the mother can do nothing from the supposition that third parties can do nothing. But it does more than this: it casts a bright light on the supposition that third parties can do nothing. Certainly it lets us see that a third party who says "I cannot choose between you" is fooling himself if he thinks this is impartiality. If Jones has found and fastened on a certain coat, which he needs to keep him from freezing, but which Smith also needs to keep him from freezing, then it is not impartiality that says "I cannot choose between you" when Smith owns the coat. Women have said again and again "This body is *my* body!" and they have reason to feel angry, reason to feel that it has been like shouting into the wind. Smith, after all, is hardly likely to bless us if we say to him, "Of course it's your coat, anybody would grant that it is. But no one may choose between you and Jones who is to have it."

We should really ask what it is that says "no one may choose" in the face of the fact that the body that houses the child is the mother's body. It may be simply a failure to appreciate this fact. But it may be something more interesting, namely the sense that one has a right to refuse to lay hands on people, even where it would be just and fair to do so, even where justice seems to require that somebody do so. Thus justice might call for somebody to get Smith's coat back from Jones, and yet you have a right to refuse to be the one to lay hands on Jones, a right to refuse to do physical violence to him. This, I think, must be granted. But then what should be said is not "no one may choose," but only "I cannot choose," and indeed not even this, but "I will not *act*," leaving it open that somebody else can or should, and in particular that anyone in a position of authority, with the job of securing people's rights, both can and should. So this is no difficulty. I have not been arguing that any given third party must accede to the mother's request that he perform an abortion to save her life, but only that he may.

I suppose that in some views of human life the mother's body is only on loan to her, the loan not being one which gives her any prior claim to it. One who held this view might well think it impartiality to say "I cannot choose." But I shall simply ignore this possibility. My own view is that if a human being has any just, prior claim to anything at all, he has a just, prior claim to his own body. And perhaps this needn't be argued for here anyway, since, as I mentioned, the arguments against abortion we are looking at do grant that the woman has a right to decide what happens in and to her body.

But although they do grant it, I have tried to show that they do not take seriously what is done in granting it. I suggest the same thing will reappear even more clearly when we turn away from cases in which the mother's life is at stake, and attend, as I propose we now do, to the vastly more common cases in which a woman wants an abortion for some less weighty reason than preserving her own life.

3. Where the mother's life is not at stake, the argument I mentioned at the outset seems to have a much stronger pull. "Everyone has a right to life, so the unborn person has a right to life." And isn't the child's right to life weightier than anything other than the mother's own right to life, which she might put forward as ground for an abortion?

This argument treats the right to life as if it were unproblematic. It is not, and this seems to me to be precisely the source of the mistake.

For we should now, at long last, ask what it comes to, to have a right to life. In some views having a right to life includes having a right to be given at least the bare minimum one needs for continued life. But suppose that what in fact *is* the bare minimum a man needs for continued life is something he has no right at all to be given? If I am sick unto death, and the only thing that will save my life is the touch of Henry Fonda's cool hand on my fevered brow, then all the same, I have no right to be given the touch of Henry Fonda's cool hand on my fevered brow. It would be frightfully nice of him to fly in from the West Coast to provide it. It would be less nice, though no doubt well meant, if my friends flew out to the West Coast and carried Henry Fonda back with them. But I have no right at all against anybody that he should do this for me. Or again, to return to the story I told earlier, the fact that for continued life that violinist needs the continued use of your kidneys does not establish that he has a right to be given the continued use of your kidneys. He certainly has no right against you that *you* should give him continued use of your kidneys. For nobody has any right to use your kidneys unless you give him such a right; and nobody has the right against you that you shall give him this right—if you do allow him to go on using your kidneys, this is kindness on your part, and not something he can claim from you as his due. Nor has he any right against anybody else that *they* should give him continued use of your kidneys. Certainly he had no right against the Society of Music Lovers that they should plug him into you in the first place. And if you now start to unplug yourself, having learned that you will otherwise have to spend nine years in bed with him, there is nobody in the world who must try to prevent you, in order to see to it that he is given something he has a right to be given.

Some people are rather stricter about the right to life. In their view, it does not include the right to be given anything, but amounts to, and only to, the right not to be killed by anybody. But here a related difficulty arises. If everybody is to refrain from killing that violinist, then everybody must refrain from doing a great many different sorts of things. Everybody must refrain from slitting his throat, everybody must refrain from shooting him—and everybody must refrain from unplugging you from him. But does he have a right against everybody that they shall refrain from unplugging you from him? To refrain from doing this is to allow him to continue to use your kidneys. It could be argued that he has a right against us that *we* should allow him to continue to use your kidneys. That is, while he had no right against us that we should give him the use of your kidneys, it might be argued that he anyway has a right against us that we shall not now intervene and deprive him of the use of your kidneys. I shall come back to third-party interventions later. But certainly the violinist has no right against you that *you* shall al-

low him to continue to use your kidneys. As I said, if you do allow him to use them, it is a kindness on your part, and not something you owe him.

The difficulty I point to here is not peculiar to the right to life. It reappears in connection with all the other natural rights; and it is something which an adequate account of rights must deal with. For present purposes it is enough just to draw attention to it. But I would stress that I am not arguing that people do not have a right to life—quite to the contrary, it seems to me that the primary control we must place on the acceptability of an account of rights is that it should turn out in that account to be a truth that all persons have a right to life. I am arguing only that having a right to life does not guarantee having either a right to be given the use of or a right to be allowed continued use of another person's body—even if one needs it for life itself. So the right to life will not serve the opponents of abortion in the very simple and clear way in which they seem to have thought it would.

4. There is another way to bring out the difficulty. In the most ordinary sort of case, to deprive someone of what he has a right to is to treat him unjustly. Suppose a boy and his small brother are jointly given a box of chocolates for Christmas. If the older boy takes the box and refuses to give his brother any of the chocolates, he is unjust to him, for the brother has been given a right to half of them. But suppose that, having learned that otherwise it means nine years in bed with that violinist, you unplug yourself from him. You surely are not being unjust to him, for you gave him no right to use your kidneys, and no one else can have given him any such right. But we have to notice that in unplugging yourself, you are killing him; and violinists, like everybody else, have a right to life, and thus in the view we were considering just now, the right not to be killed. So here you do what he supposedly has a right you shall not do, but you do not act unjustly to him in doing it.

The emendation which may be made at this point is this: the right to life consists not in the right not to be killed, but rather in the right not to be killed unjustly. This runs a risk of circularity, but never mind: it would enable us to square the fact that the violinist has a right to life with the fact that you do not act unjustly toward him in unplugging yourself, thereby killing him. For if you do not kill him unjustly, you do not violate his right to life, and so it is no wonder you do him no injustice.

But if this emendation is accepted, the gap in the argument against abortion stares us plainly in the face: it is by no means enough to show that the fetus is a person, and to remind us that all persons have a right to life—we need to be shown also that killing the fetus violates its right to life, i.e., that abortion is unjust killing. And is it?

I suppose we may take it as a datum that in a case of pregnancy due to rape the mother has not given the unborn person a right to the use of her body for food and shelter. Indeed, in what pregnancy could it be supposed that the mother has given the unborn person such a right? It is not as if there were unborn persons drifting about the world, to whom a woman who wants a child says "I invite you in."

But it might be argued that there are other ways one can have acquired a right to the use of another person's body than by having been invited to use it by that person. Suppose a woman voluntarily indulges in intercourse, knowing of the chance it will issue in pregnancy, and then she does become pregnant; is she not in part responsible for the presence, in fact the very existence, of the unborn person inside her? No doubt she did not invite it in. But doesn't her partial responsibility for its being there itself give it a right to the use of her body? If so, then her aborting it would be more like the boy's taking away the chocolates, and less like your unplugging yourself from the violinist—doing so would be depriving it of what it does have a right to, and thus would be doing it an injustice.

And then, too, it might be asked whether or not she can kill it even to save her own life: If she voluntarily called it into existence, how can she now kill it, even in self-defense?

The first thing to be said about this is that it is something new. Opponents of abortion have been so concerned to make out the independence of the fetus, in order to establish that it has a right to life, just as its mother does, that they have tended to overlook the possible support they might gain from making out that the fetus is *dependent* on the mother, in order to establish that she has a special kind of responsibility for it, a responsibility that gives it rights against her which are not possessed by any independent person—such as an ailing violinist who is a stranger to her.

On the other hand, this argument would give the unborn person a right to its mother's body only if her pregnancy resulted from a voluntary act, undertaken in full knowledge of the chance a pregnancy might result from it. It would leave out entirely the unborn person whose existence is due to rape. Pending the availability of some further argument, then, we would be left with the conclusion that unborn persons whose existence is due to rape have no right to the use of their mothers' bodies, and thus that aborting them is not depriving them of anything they have a right to and hence is not unjust killing.

And we should also notice that it is not at all plain that this argument really does go even as far as it purports to. For there are cases and cases, and the details make a difference. If the room is stuffy, and I therefore open a window to air it, and a burglar climbs in, it would be absurd to say, "Ah, now he can stay, she's given him a right to the use of her house—for she is partially responsible for his presence there, having voluntarily done what enabled him to get in, in full knowledge that there are such things as burglars, and that burglars burgle." It would be still more absurd to say this if I had had bars installed outside my windows, precisely to prevent burglars from getting in, and a burglar got in only because of a defect in the bars. It remains equally absurd if we imagine it is not a burglar who climbs in, but an innocent person who blunders or falls in. Again, suppose it were like this: people-seeds drift about in the air like pollen, and if you open your windows, one may drift in and take root in your carpets or upholstery. You don't want children, so you fix up your windows with fine mesh screens, the very best you can buy. As can happen, however, and on very, very rare occasions does happen, one of the screens is defective; and a seed drifts in and takes root. Does the person-plant who now develops have a right to the use of your house? Surely not—despite the fact that you voluntarily opened your windows, you knowingly kept carpets and upholstered furniture, and you knew that screens were sometimes defective. Someone may argue that you are responsible for its rooting, that it does have a right to your house, because after all you *could* have lived out your life with bare floors and furniture, or with sealed windows and doors. But this won't do—for by the same token anyone can avoid a pregnancy due to rape by having a hysterectomy, or anyway by never leaving home without a (reliable!) army.

It seems to me that the argument we are looking at can establish at most that there are *some* cases in which the unborn person has a right to the use of its mother's body, and therefore *some* cases in which abortion is unjust killing. There is room for much discussion and argument as to precisely which, if any. But I think we should sidestep this issue and leave it open, for at any rate the argument certainly does not establish that all abortion is unjust killing.

5. There is room for yet another argument here, however. We surely must all grant that there may be cases in which it would be morally indecent to detach a person from your body at the cost of his life. Suppose you learn that what the violinist needs is not nine years of your life, but only one hour: all you need do to save his life is to spend one hour in that bed with him. Suppose also that letting him use your kidneys for that one hour would not affect your health in the slightest. Admittedly you were kidnapped. Admittedly you did not give anyone permission to plug him into you. Nevertheless it seems to me plain you *ought* to allow him to use your kidneys for that hour—it would be indecent to refuse.

Again, suppose pregnancy lasted only an hour, and constituted no threat to life or health. And suppose that a woman becomes pregnant as a result of rape. Admittedly she did not voluntarily do anything to bring about the existence of a child. Admittedly she did nothing at all which would give the unborn person a right to the use of her body. All the same it might well be said, as in the newly emended violinist story, that she *ought* to allow it to remain for that hour—that it would be indecent in her to refuse.

Now some people are inclined to use the term "right" in such a way that it follows from the fact that you ought to allow a person to use your body for the hour he needs, that he has a right to use your body for the hour he needs, even though he has not been given that right by any person or act. They may say that it follows also that if you refuse, you act unjustly toward him. This use of the term is perhaps so common that it cannot be called wrong; nevertheless it seems to me to be an unfortunate loosening of what we would do better to keep a tight rein on. Suppose that box of chocolates I mentioned earlier had not been given to both boys jointly, but was given only to the older boy. There he sits, stolidly eating his way through the box, his small brother watching enviously. Here we are likely to say "You ought not to be so mean. You ought to give your brother some of those chocolates." My own view is that it just does not follow from the truth of this that the brother has any right to any of the chocolates. If the boy refuses to give his brother any, he is greedy, stingy, callous—but not unjust. I suppose that the people I have in mind will say it does follow that the brother has a right to some of the chocolates, and thus that the boy does act unjustly if he refuses to give his brother any. But the effect of saying this is to obscure what we should keep distinct, namely the difference between the boy's refusal in this case and the boy's refusal in the earlier case, in which the box was given to both boys jointly, and in which the small brother thus had what was from any point of view clear title to half.

A further objection to so using the term "right" that from the fact that A ought to do a thing for B, it follows that B has a right against A that A do it for him, is that it is going to make the question of whether or not a man has a right to a thing turn on how easy it is to provide him with it; and this seems not merely unfortunate, but morally unacceptable. Take the case of Henry Fonda again. I said earlier that I had no right to the touch of his cool hand on my fevered brow, even though I needed it to save my life. I said it would be frightfully nice of him to fly in from the West Coast to provide me with it, but that I had no right against him that he should do so. But suppose he isn't on the West Coast. Suppose he has only to walk across the room, place a hand briefly on my brow—and lo, my life is saved. Then surely he ought to do it, it would be indecent to refuse. Is it to be said "Ah, well, it follows that in this case she has a right to the touch of his hand on her brow, and so it would be an injustice in him to refuse"? So that I have a right to it when it is easy for him to provide it, though no right when it's hard? It's rather a shocking idea that anyone's rights should fade away and disappear as it gets harder and harder to accord them to him.

So my own view is that even though you ought to let the violinist use your kidneys for the one hour he needs, we should not conclude that he has a right to do so—we would say that if you refuse, you are, like the boy who owns all the chocolates and will give none away, self-centered and callous, indecent in fact, but not unjust. And similarly, that even suppos-ing a case in which a woman pregnant due to rape ought to allow the unborn person to use her body for the hour he needs, we should not conclude that he has a right to do so; we should conclude that she is self-centered, callous, indecent, but not unjust, if she refuses. The complaints are no less grave; they are just different. However, there is no need to insist on this point. If anyone does wish to deduce "he has a right" from "you ought," then all the same he must surely grant that there are cases in which it is not morally required of you that you allow that violinist to use your kidneys, and in which he does not have a right to use them, and in which you do not do him an injustice if you refuse. And so also for mother and unborn child. Except in such cases as the unborn person has a right to demand it—and we were leav-ing open the possibility that there may be such cases—nobody is morally *required* to make large sac-rifices, of health, of all other interests and concerns, of all other duties and commitments, for nine years, or even for nine months, in order to keep another person alive.

6. We have in fact to distinguish between two kinds of Samaritan: the Good Samaritan and what we might call the Minimally Decent Samaritan. The story of the Good Samaritan, you will remember, goes like this:

> A certain man went down from Jerusalem to Jericho, and fell among thieves, which stripped him of his raiment, and wounded him, and departed, leaving him half dead.
>
> And by chance there came down a certain priest that way; and when he saw him, he passed by on the other side.
>
> And likewise a Levite, when he was at the place, came and looked on him, and passed by on the other side.
>
> But a certain Samaritan, as he journeyed, came where he was; and when he saw him he had compas-sion on him.
>
> And went to him, and bound up his wounds, pour-ing in oil and wine, and set him on his own beast, and brought him to an inn, and took care of him.
>
> And on the morrow, when he departed, he took out two pence, and gave them to the host, and said unto him, "Take care of him; and whatsoever thou spendest more, when I come again, I will repay thee."
>
> (Luke 10:30–35)

The Good Samaritan went out of his way, at some cost to himself, to help one in need of it. We are not told what the options were, that is, whether or not the priest and the Levite could have helped by doing less than the Good Samaritan did, but assuming they could have, then the fact they did nothing at all shows they were not even Minimally Decent Samari-tans, not because they were not Samaritans, but be-cause they were not even minimally decent.

These things are a matter of degree, of course, but there is a difference, and it comes out perhaps most clearly in the story of Kitty Genovese, who, as you will remember, was murdered while thirty-eight people watched or listened, and did nothing at all to help her. A Good Samaritan would have rushed out to give di-rect assistance against the murderer. Or perhaps we had better allow that it would have been a Splendid Samaritan who did this, on the ground that it would have involved a risk of death for himself. But the thirty-eight not only did not do this, they did not even trouble to pick up a phone to call the police. Mini-mally Decent Samaritanism would call for doing at least that, and their not having done it was monstrous.

After telling the story of the Good Samaritan, Je-sus said "Go, and do thou likewise." Perhaps he meant that we are morally required to act as the Good Samaritan did. Perhaps he was urging people to do more than is morally required of them. At all events it seems plain that it was not morally required of any of the thirty-eight that he rush out to give di-rect assistance at the risk of his own life, and that it is not morally required of anyone that he give long stretches of his life—nine years or nine months—to sustaining the life of a person who has no special right (we were leaving open the possibility of this) to demand it.

Indeed, with one rather striking class of excep-tions, no one in any country in the world is *legally* required to do anywhere near as much as this for anyone else. The class of exceptions is obvious. My main concern here is not the state of the law in re-spect to abortion, but it is worth drawing attention to the fact that in no state in this country is any man compelled by law to be even a Minimally Decent Samaritan to any person; there is no law under which charges could be brought against the thirty-eight who stood by while Kitty Genovese died. By contrast, in most states in this country women are compelled by law to be not merely Minimally Decent

Samaritans, but Good Samaritans to unborn persons inside them. This doesn't by itself settle anything one way or the other, because it may well be argued that there should be laws in this country—as there are in many European countries—compelling at least Minimally Decent Samaritanism. But it does show that there is a gross injustice in the existing state of the law. And it shows also that the groups currently working against liberalization of abortion laws, in fact working toward having it declared unconstitutional for a state to permit abortion, had better start working for the adoption of Good Samaritan laws generally, or earn the charge that they are acting in bad faith.

I should think, myself, that Minimally Decent Samaritan laws would be one thing, Good Samaritan laws quite another, and in fact highly improper. But we are not here concerned with the law. What we should ask is not whether anybody should be compelled by law to be a Good Samaritan, but whether we must accede to a situation in which somebody is being compelled—by nature, perhaps—to be a Good Samaritan. We have, in other words, to look now at third-party interventions. I have been arguing that no person is morally required to make large sacrifices to sustain the life of another who has no right to demand them, and this even where the sacrifices do not include life itself; we are not morally required to be Good Samaritans or anyway Very Good Samaritans to one another. But what if a man cannot extricate himself from such a situation? What if he appeals to us to extricate him? It seems to me plain that there are cases in which we can, cases in which a Good Samaritan would extricate him. There you are, you were kidnapped, and nine years in bed with that violinist lie ahead of you. You have your own life to lead. You are sorry, but you simply cannot see giving up so much of your life to the sustaining of his. You cannot extricate yourself, and ask us to do so. I should have thought that—in light of his having no right to the use of your body—it was obvious that we do not have to accede to your being forced to give up so much. We can do what you ask. There is no injustice to the violinist in our doing so.

7. Following the lead of the opponents of abortion, I have throughout been speaking of the fetus merely as a person, and what I have been asking is whether or not the argument we began with, which

proceeds only from the fetus' being a person, really does establish its conclusion. I have argued that it does not.

But of course there are arguments and arguments, and it may be said that I have simply fastened on the wrong one. It may be said that what is important is not merely the fact that the fetus is a person, but that it is a person for whom the woman has a special kind of responsibility issuing from the fact that she is its mother. And it might be argued that all my analogies are therefore irrelevant—for you do not have that special kind of responsibility for that violinist, Henry Fonda does not have that special kind of responsibility for me. And our attention might be drawn to the fact that men and women both *are* compelled by law to provide support for their children.

I have in effect dealt (briefly) with this argument in section 4 above; but a (still briefer) recapitulation now may be in order. Surely we do not have any such "special responsibility" for a person unless we have assumed it, explicitly or implicitly. If a set of parents do not try to prevent pregnancy, do not obtain an abortion, and then at the time of birth of the child do not put it out for adoption, but rather take it home with them, then they have assumed responsibility for it, they have given it rights, and they cannot *now* withdraw support from it at the cost of its life because they now find it difficult to go on providing for it. But if they have taken all reasonable precautions against having a child, they do not simply by virtue of their biological relationship to the child who comes into existence have a special responsibility for it. They may wish to assume responsibility for it, or they may not wish to. And I am suggesting that if assuming responsibility for it would require large sacrifices, then they may refuse. A Good Samaritan would not refuse—or anyway, a Splendid Samaritan, if the sacrifices that had to be made were enormous. But then so would a Good Samaritan assume responsibility for that violinist; so would Henry Fonda, if he is a Good Samaritan, fly in from the West Coast and assume responsibility for me.

8. My argument will be found unsatisfactory on two counts by many of those who want to regard abortion as morally permissible. First, while I do argue that abortion is not impermissible, I do not argue that it is always permissible. There may well be

cases in which carrying the child to term requires only Minimally Decent Samaritanism of the mother, and this is a standard we must not fall below. I am inclined to think it a merit of my account precisely that it does *not* give a general yes or a general no. It allows for and supports our sense that, for example, a sick and desperately frightened fourteen-year-old schoolgirl, pregnant due to rape, may *of course* choose abortion, and that any law which rules this out is an insane law. And it also allows for and supports our sense that in other cases resort to abortion is even positively indecent. It would be indecent in the woman to request an abortion, and indecent in a doctor to perform it, if she is in her seventh month, and wants the abortion just to avoid the nuisance of postponing a trip abroad. The very fact that the arguments I have been drawing attention to treat all cases of abortion, or even all cases of abortion in which the mother's life is not at stake, as morally on a par ought to have made them suspect at the outset.

Secondly, while I am arguing for the permissibility of abortion in some cases, I am not arguing for the right to secure the death of the unborn child. It is easy to confuse these two things in that up to a certain point in the life of the fetus it is not able to survive outside the mother's body; hence removing it from her body guarantees its death. But they are importantly different. I have argued that you are not morally required to spend nine months in bed, sustaining the life of that violinist; but to say this is by no means to say that if, when you unplug yourself, there is a miracle and he survives, you then have a right to turn round and slit his throat. You may detach yourself even if this costs him his life; you have no right to be guaranteed his death, by some other means, if unplugging yourself does not kill him. There are some people who will feel dissatisfied by this feature of my argument. A woman may be utterly devastated by the thought of a child, a bit of herself, put out for adoption and never seen or heard of again. She may therefore want not merely that the child be detached from her, but more, that it die. Some opponents of abortion are inclined to regard this as beneath contempt—thereby showing insensitivity to what is surely a powerful source of despair. All the same, I agree that the desire for the child's death is not one which anybody may gratify, should it turn out to be possible to detach the child alive.

At this place, however, it should be remembered that we have only been pretending throughout that the fetus is a human being from the moment of conception. A very early abortion is surely not the killing of a person, and so is not dealt with by anything I have said here.

QUESTIONS FOR REFLECTION

1. What conclusions does Thomson draw from the violinist example? Do you agree with her interpretation of the example?

2. Do your feelings about the violinist case change if you add that the violinist is your own child?

3. How does Thomson argue against what she calls "the extreme view"?

4. What is a right to life, for Thomson? Why does she reject other accounts of this right?

5. What is Good Samaritanism? Minimally Decent Samaritanism? Which, according to Thomson, is required of us? What does this imply for the morality of abortion?

6. Some philosophers have found Thomson's view on the violinist example inconsistent with her view that you do not have the right to torture someone, even to save your own life. Are these consistent? Explain.

MARY ANNE WARREN

On the Moral and Legal Status of Abortion

Mary Anne Warren teaches at San Francisco State University. (Source: From "On the Moral and Legal Status of Abortion," The Monist, vol. 57, no. 1 [January 1973], p. 43–51. Notes have been omitted. Reprinted with permission from The Monist and Dr. Mary Anne Warren, San Francisco State University.)

We will be concerned with both the moral status of abortion, which for our purposes we may define as the act which a woman performs in voluntarily terminating, or allowing another person to terminate, her pregnancy, and the legal status which is appropriate for this act. I will argue that, while it is not possible to produce a satisfactory defense of a woman's right to obtain an abortion without showing that a fetus is not a human being, in the morally relevant sense of that term, we ought not to conclude that the difficulties involved in determining whether or not a fetus is human make it impossible to produce any satisfactory solution to the problem of the moral status of abortion. For it is possible to show that, on the basis of intuitions which we may expect even the opponents of abortion to share, a fetus is not a person, and hence not the sort of entity to which it is proper to ascribe full moral rights.

Of course, while some philosophers would deny the possibility of any such proof, others will deny that there is any need for it, since the moral permissibility of abortion appears to them to be too obvious to require proof. But the inadequacy of this attitude should be evident from the fact that both the friends and the foes of abortion consider their position to be morally self-evident. Because pro-abortionists have never adequately come to grips with the conceptual issues surrounding abortion, most if not all, of the arguments which they advance in opposition to laws restricting access to abortion fail to refute or even weaken the traditional antiabortion argument, i.e., that a fetus is a human being, and therefore abortion is murder.

These arguments are typically one of two sorts. Either they point to the terrible side effects of the restrictive laws, e.g., the deaths due to illegal abortions, and the fact that it is poor women who suffer the most as a result of these laws, or else they state that to deny a woman access to abortion is to deprive her of her right to control her own body. Unfortunately, however, the fact that restricting access to abortion has tragic side effects does not, in itself, show that the restrictions are unjustified, since murder is wrong regardless of the consequences of prohibiting it; and the appeal to the right to control one's body, which is generally construed as a property right, is at best a rather feeble argument for the permissibility of abortion. Mere ownership does not give me the right to kill innocent people whom I find on my property, and indeed I am apt to be held responsible if such people injure themselves while on my property. It is equally unclear that I have any moral right to expel an innocent person from my property when I know that doing so will result in his death.

Furthermore, it is probably inappropriate to describe a woman's body as her property, since it seems natural to hold that a person is something distinct from her property, but not from her body. Even those who would object to the identification of a person with his body, or with the conjunction of his body and his mind, must admit that it would be very odd to describe, say, breaking a leg, as damaging one's property, and much more appropriate to describe it as injuring one*self*. Thus it is probably a mistake to argue that the right to obtain an abortion is in any way derived from the right to own and regulate property.

But however we wish to construe the right to abortion, we cannot hope to convince those who consider abortion a form of murder of the existence of any such right unless we are able to produce a clear and convincing refutation of the traditional antiabortion argument, and this has not, to my knowledge, been done. With respect to the two most vital issues which that argument involves, i.e., the humanity of the fetus and its implication for the moral status of abortion, confusion has prevailed on both sides of the dispute.

Thus, both proabortionists and antiabortionists have tended to abstract the question of whether abortion is wrong to that of whether it is wrong to destroy a fetus, just as though the rights of another person were not necessarily involved. This mistaken abstraction has led to the almost universal assumption that if a fetus is a human being, with a right to life, then it follows immediately that abortion is wrong (except perhaps when necessary to save the woman's life), and that it ought to be prohibited. It has also been generally assumed that unless the question about the status of the fetus is answered, the moral status of abortion cannot possibly be determined.

Two recent papers, one by B. A. Brody, and one by Judith Thomson, have attempted to settle the question of whether abortion ought to be prohibited apart from the question of whether or not the fetus is human. Brody examines the possibility that the following two statements are compatible: (1) that abortion is the taking of innocent human life, and therefore wrong; and (2) that nevertheless it ought not to be prohibited by law, at least under the present circumstances. Not surprisingly, Brody finds it impossible to reconcile these two statements, since, as he rightly argues, none of the unfortunate side effects of the prohibition of abortion is bad enough to justify legalizing the *wrongful* taking of human life. He is mistaken, however, in concluding that the incompatibility of (1) and (2), in itself, shows that "the legal problem about abortion cannot be resolved independently of the status of the fetus problem. . . ."

What Brody fails to realize is that (1) embodies the questionable assumption that if a fetus is a human being, then of course abortion is morally wrong, and that an attack on *this* assumption is more promising, as a way of reconciling the humanity of the fetus with the claim that laws prohibiting abortion are unjustified, than is an attack on the assumption that if abortion is the wrongful killing of innocent human beings then it ought to be prohibited. He thus overlooks the possibility that a fetus may have a right to life and abortion still be morally permissible, in that the right of a woman to terminate an unwanted pregnancy might override the right of the fetus to be kept alive. The immorality of abortion is no more demonstrated by the humanity of the fetus, in itself, than the immorality of killing in self-defense is demonstrated by the fact that the assailant is a human being. Neither is it demonstrated by the *innocence* of the fetus, since there may be situations in which the killing of innocent human beings is justified.

It is perhaps not surprising that Brody fails to spot this assumption, since it has been accepted with little or no argument by nearly everyone who has written on the morality of abortion. John Noonan is correct in saying that "the fundamental question in the long history of abortion is, How do you determine the humanity of a being?" He summarizes his own antiabortion argument, which is a version of the official position of the Catholic Church, as follows:

> . . . it is wrong to kill humans, however poor, weak, defenseless, and lacking in opportunity to develop their potential they may be. It is therefore morally wrong to kill Biafrans. Similarly, it is morally wrong to kill embryos.

Noonan bases his claim that fetuses are human upon what he calls the theologians' criterion of humanity: that whoever is conceived of human beings is human. But although he argues at length for the appropriateness of this criterion, he never questions the assumption that if a fetus is human then abortion is wrong for exactly the same reason that murder is wrong.

Judith Thomson is, in fact, the only writer I am aware of who has seriously questioned this assumption; she has argued that, even if we grant the antiabortionist his claim that a fetus is a human being, with the same right to life as any other human being, we can still demonstrate that, in at least some and perhaps most cases, a woman is under no moral obligation to complete an unwanted pregnancy. Her argument is worth examining, since if it holds up it may enable us to establish the moral permissibility of abortion without becoming involved in problems about what entitles an entity to be considered human, and accorded full moral rights. To be able to do this would be a great gain in the power and simplicity of the proabortion position, since, although I will argue that these problems can be solved at least as decisively as can any other moral problem, we should certainly be pleased to be able to avoid having to solve them as part of the justification of abortion.

On the other hand, even if Thomson's argument does not hold up, her insight, i.e., that it requires *argument* to show that if fetuses are human then abortion is properly classified as murder, is an extremely valuable one. The assumption she attacks is particularly invidious, for it amounts to the decision that it is appropriate, in deciding the moral status of abortion, to leave the rights of the pregnant woman out of consideration entirely, except possibly when her life is threatened. Obviously, this will not do; determining what moral rights, if any, a fetus possesses is only the first step in determining the moral status of abortion. Step two, which is at least equally essential, is finding a just solution to the conflict between whatever rights the fetus may have, and the rights of the woman who is unwillingly pregnant. While the historical error has been to pay far too little attention to the second step, Ms. Thomson's suggestion is that if we look at the second step first we may find that a woman has a right to obtain an abortion *regardless* of what rights the fetus has.

Our own inquiry will also have two stages. In Section I, we will consider whether or not it is possible to establish that abortion is morally permissible even on the assumption that a fetus is an entity with a full-fledged right to life. I will argue that in fact this cannot be established, at least not with the conclusiveness which is essential to our hopes of convincing those who are skeptical about the morality of abortion, and that we therefore cannot avoid dealing with the question of whether or not a fetus really does have the same right to life as a (more fully developed) human being.

In Section II, I will propose an answer to this question, namely, that a fetus cannot be considered a member of the moral community, the set of beings with full and equal moral rights, for the simple reason that it is not a person, and that it is personhood, and not genetic humanity, i.e., humanity as defined by Noonan, which is the basis for membership in this community. I will argue that a fetus, whatever its stage of development, satisfies none of the basic criteria of personhood, and is not even enough *like* a person to be accorded even some of the same rights on the basis of this resemblance. Nor, as we will see, is a fetus's *potential* personhood a threat to the morality of abortion, since, whatever the rights of potential people may be, they are invariably overridden in any conflict with the moral rights of actual people.

I

We turn now to Professor Thomson's case for the claim that even if a fetus has full moral rights, abortion is still morally permissible, at least sometimes, and for some reasons other than to save the woman's life. Her argument is based upon a clever, but I think faulty, analogy. She asks us to picture ourselves waking up one day, in bed with a famous violinist. Imagine that you have been kidnapped, and your bloodstream hooked up to that of the violinist, who happens to have an ailment which will certainly kill him unless he is permitted to share your kidneys for a period of nine months. No one else can save him, since you alone have the right type of blood. He will be unconscious all that time, and you will have to stay in bed with him, but after the nine months are over he may be unplugged, completely cured; that is, provided that you have cooperated.

Now then, she continues, what are your obligations in this situation? The antiabortionist, if he is consistent, will have to say that you are obligated to stay in bed with the violinist: for all people have a right to life, and violinists are people, and therefore it would be murder for you to disconnect yourself from him and let him die. . . . But this is outrageous, and so there must be something wrong with the same argument when it is applied to abortion. It would certainly be commendable of you to agree to save the violinist, but it is absurd to suggest that your refusal to do so would be murder. His right to life does not obligate you to do whatever is required to keep him alive; nor does it justify anyone else in forcing you to do so. A law which required you to stay in bed with the violinist would clearly be an unjust law, since it is no proper function of the law to force unwilling people to make huge sacrifices for the sake of other people toward whom they have no such prior obligation.

Thomson concludes that, if this analogy is an apt one, then we can grant the antiabortionist his claim that a fetus is a human being, and still hold that it is at least sometimes the case that a pregnant woman has the right to refuse to be a Good Samaritan towards the fetus, i.e., to obtain an abortion. For there is a great gap between the claim that x has a right to life, and the claim that y is obligated to do whatever is necessary to keep x alive, let alone that he ought to be forced to do so. It is y's duty to keep x alive only if he has somehow contracted a *special* obligation to do so; and a woman who is unwillingly pregnant, e.g., who was raped, has done nothing which obligates her to make the enormous sacrifice which is necessary to preserve the conceptus.

This argument is initially quite plausible, and in the extreme case of pregnancy due to rape it is probably conclusive. Difficulties arise, however, when we try to specify more exactly the range of cases in which abortion is clearly justifiable even on the assumption that the fetus is human. Professor Thomson considers it a virtue of her argument that it does not enable us to conclude that abortion is *always* permissible. It would, she says, be "indecent" for a woman in her seventh month to obtain an abortion just to avoid having to postpone a trip to Europe. On the other hand, her argument enables us to see that "a sick and desperately frightened [. . .] schoolgirl pregnant due to rape may *of course* choose abortion, and that any law which rules this out is an insane law." . . . So far, so good; but what are we to say about the woman who becomes pregnant not through rape but as a result of her own carelessness, or because of contraceptive failure, or who gets pregnant intentionally and then changes her mind about wanting a child? With respect to such cases, the violinist analogy is of much less use to the defender of the woman's right to obtain an abortion.

Indeed, the choice of a pregnancy due to rape, as an example of a case in which abortion is permissible even if a fetus is considered a human being, is extremely significant; for it is only in the case of pregnancy due to rape that the woman's situation is adequately analogous to the violinist case for our intuitions about the latter to transfer convincingly. The crucial difference between a pregnancy due to rape and the *normal* case of an unwanted pregnancy is that in the normal case we cannot claim that the woman is in no way responsible for her predicament; she could have remained chaste, or taken her pills more faithfully, or abstained on dangerous days, and so on. If, on the other hand, you are kidnapped by strangers, and hooked up to a strange violinist, then you are free of any shred of responsibility for the situation, on the basis of which it could be argued that you are obligated to keep the violinist alive. Only when her pregnancy is due to rape is a woman clearly just as nonresponsible.

Consequently, there is room for the antiabortionist to argue that in the normal case of unwanted pregnancy a woman has, by her own actions, assumed responsibility for the fetus. For if x behaves in a way which he could have avoided, and which he knows involves, let us say, a 1 percent chance of bringing into existence a human being, with a right to life, and does so knowing that if this should happen then that human being will perish unless x does certain things to keep him alive, then it is by no means clear that when it does happen x is free of any obligation to what he knew in advance would be required to keep that human being alive.

The plausibility of such an argument is enough to show that the Thomson analogy can provide a clear and persuasive defense of a woman's right to obtain an abortion only with respect to those cases in which the woman is in no way responsible for her pregnancy, e.g., where it is due to rape. In all other cases, we would almost certainly conclude that it was necessary to look carefully at the particular circumstances in order to determine the extent of the woman's responsibility, and hence the extent of her obligation. This is an extremely unsatisfactory outcome, from the viewpoint of the opponents of restrictive abortion laws, most of whom are convinced that a woman has a right to obtain an abortion regardless of how and why she got pregnant.

Of course a supporter of the violinist analogy might point out that it is absurd to suggest that forgetting her pill one day might be sufficient to obligate a woman to complete an unwanted pregnancy. And indeed it is absurd to suggest this. As we will see, the moral right to obtain an abortion is not in the least dependent upon the extent to which the woman is responsible for her pregnancy. But unfortunately, once we allow the assumption that a fetus has full moral rights, we cannot avoid taking this absurd suggestion seriously. Perhaps we can make this point more clear by altering the violinist story just enough to make it more analogous to a normal unwanted pregnancy and less to a pregnancy due to rape, and then seeing whether it is still obvious that you are not obligated to stay in bed with the fellow.

Suppose, then, that violinists are peculiarily prone to the sort of illness the only cure for which is the use of someone else's bloodstream for nine months, and that because of this there has been formed a society of music lovers who agree that whenever a violinist is stricken they will draw lots and the loser will, by some means, be made the one and only person capable of saving him. Now then, would you be obligated to cooperate in curing the violinist if you had voluntarily joined this society, knowing the possible consequences, and then your name had been drawn and you had been kidnapped? Admittedly, you did not promise ahead of time that you would, but you did deliberately place yourself in a position in which it might happen that a human life would be lost if you did not. Surely this is at least a *prima facie* reason for supposing that you have an obligation to stay in bed with the violinist. Suppose that you had gotten your name drawn deliberately; surely *that* would be quite a strong reason for thinking that you had such an obligation.

It might be suggested that there is one important disanalogy between the modified violinist case and the case of an unwanted pregnancy, which makes the woman's responsibility significantly less, namely, the fact that the fetus *comes into existence* as the result of the woman's actions. This fact might give her a right to refuse to keep it alive, whereas she would not have had this right had it existed previously, independently, and then as a result of her actions become dependent upon her for its survival.

My own intuition, however, is that x has no more right to bring into existence, either deliberately or as a foreseeable result of actions he could have avoided, a being with full moral rights (y), and then refuse to do what he knew beforehand would be required to keep that being alive, than he has to enter into an agreement with an existing person, whereby he may be called upon to save that person's life, and then refuse to do so when so called upon. Thus, x's responsibility for y's existence does not seem to lessen his obligation to keep y alive, if he is also responsible for y's being in a situation in which only he can save him.

Whether or not this intuition is entirely correct, it brings us back once again to the conclusion that once we allow the assumption that a fetus has full moral rights, it becomes an extremely complex and difficult question whether and when abortion is justifiable. Thus the Thomson analogy cannot help us produce a clear and persuasive proof of the moral permissibility of abortion. Nor will the opponents of the restrictive laws thank us for anything less; for their conviction (for the most part) is that abortion is obviously *not* a morally serious and extremely unfortunate, even though sometimes justified act, comparable to killing in self-defense or to letting the violinist die, but rather is closer to being a morally neutral act, like cutting one's hair.

The basis of this conviction, I believe, is the realization that a fetus is not a person, and thus does not have a full-fledged right to life. Perhaps the reason why this claim has been so inadequately defended is that it seems self-evident to those who accept it. And so it is, insofar as it follows from what I take to be perfectly obvious claims about the nature of personhood, and about the proper grounds for ascribing moral rights, claims which ought, indeed, to be obvious to both the friends and foes of abortion. Nevertheless, it is worth examining these claims, and showing how they demonstrate the moral innocuousness of abortion, since this apparently has not been adequately done before.

II

The question which we must answer in order to produce a satisfactory solution to the problem of the moral status of abortion is this: How are we to define the moral community, the set of beings with full and equal moral rights, such that we can decide whether a human fetus is a member of this community or not? What sort of entity, exactly, has the inalienable rights to life, liberty, and the pursuit of happiness? Jefferson attributed these rights to all *men,* and it may or may not be fair to suggest that he intended to attribute them *only* to men. Perhaps he ought to have attributed them to all human beings. If so, then we arrive, first, at Noonan's problem of defining what makes a being human, and, second, at the equally vital question which Noonan does not consider, namely, What reason is there for identifying the moral community with the set of all human beings, in whatever way we have chosen to define that term?

On the Definition of "Human"

One reason why this vital second question is so frequently overlooked in the debate over the moral status of abortion is that the term "human" has two distinct, but not often distinguished, senses. This fact results in a slide of meaning, which serves to conceal the fallaciousness of the traditional argument that since (1) it is wrong to kill innocent human beings, and (2) fetuses are innocent human beings, then (3) it is wrong to kill fetuses. For if "human" is used in the same sense in both (1) and (2) then, which ever of the two senses is meant, one of these premises is question-begging. And if it is used in two different senses then of course the conclusion doesn't follow.

Thus, (1) is a self-evident moral truth, and avoids begging the question about abortion, only if "human being" is used to mean something like "a full-fledged member of the moral community." (It may or may not also be meant to refer exclusively to members of the species *Homo sapiens.*) We may call this the *moral* sense of "human." It is not to be confused with what we will call the *genetic* sense, i.e., the sense in which *any* member of the species is a human being, and no member of any other species could be. If (1) is acceptable only if the moral sense is intended, (2) is non-question-begging only if what is intended is the genetic sense.

In "Deciding Who Is Human," Noonan argues for the classification of fetuses with human beings by pointing to the presence of the full genetic code, and the potential capacity for rational thought. . . . It is clear that what he needs to show, for his version of the traditional argument to be valid, is that fetuses are human in the moral sense, the sense in which it is analytically true that all human beings have full moral rights. But, in the absence of any argument showing that whatever is genetically human is also morally human, and he gives none, nothing more than genetic humanity can be demonstrated by the presence of the human genetic code. And, as we will see, the *potential* capacity for rational thought can at most show that an entity has the potential for *becoming* human in the moral sense.

Defining the Moral Community

Can it be established that genetic humanity is sufficient for moral humanity? I think that there are very good reasons for not defining the moral community in this way. I would like to suggest an alternative way of defining the moral community, which I will argue for only to the extent of explaining why it is, or should be, self-evident. The suggestion is simply that the moral community consists of all and only *people,* rather than all and only human beings; and probably the best way of demonstrating its self-evidence is by considering the concept of personhood, to see what sorts of entity are and are not persons, and what the decision that a being is or is not a person implies about its moral rights.

What characteristics entitle an entity to be considered a person? This is obviously not the place to attempt a complete analysis of the concept of personhood, but we do not need such a full adequate analysis just to determine whether and why a fetus is or isn't a person. All we need is a rough and approximate list of the most basic criteria of personhood, and some idea of which, or how many, of these an entity must satisfy in order to properly be considered a person.

In searching for such criteria, it is useful to look beyond the set of people with whom we are acquainted, and ask how we would decide whether a totally alien being was a person or not. (For we have no right to assume that genetic humanity is necessary for personhood.) Imagine a space traveler who lands on an unknown planet and encounters a race of beings utterly unlike any he has ever seen or heard of. If he wants to be sure of behaving morally toward these beings, he has to somehow decide whether they are people, and hence have full moral rights, or whether they are the sort of thing which he need not feel guilty about treating as, for example, a source of food.

How should he go about making this decision? If he has some anthropological background, he might look for such things as religion, art, and the manufacturing of tools, weapons, or shelters, since these factors have been used to distinguish our human from our prehuman ancestors, in what seems to be closer to the moral than the genetic sense of "human." And no doubt he would be right to consider the presence of such factors as good evidence that the alien beings were people, and morally human. It would, however, be overly anthropocentric of him to take the absence of these things as adequate evidence that they were not, since we can imagine people who have progressed beyond, or evolved without ever developing, these cultural characteristics.

I suggest that the traits which are most central to the concept of personhood, or humanity in the moral sense, are, very roughly, the following:

1. consciousness (of objects and events external and/or internal to the being), and in particular the capacity to feel pain;

2. reasoning (the *developed* capacity to solve new and relatively complex problems);

3. self-motivated activity (activity which is relatively independent of either genetic or direct external control);

4. the capacity to communicate, by whatever means, messages of an indefinite variety of types, that is, not just with an indefinite number of possible contents, but on indefinitely many possible topics;

5. the presence of self-concepts, and self-awareness, either individual or racial, or both.

Admittedly, there are apt to be a great many problems involved in formulating precise definitions of these criteria, let alone in developing universally valid behavioral criteria for deciding when they apply. But I will assume that both we and our explorer know approximately what (1)–(5) mean, and that he is also able to determine whether or not they apply. How, then, should he use his findings to decide whether or not the alien beings are people? We needn't suppose that an entity must have *all* of these attributes to be properly considered a person; (1) and (2) alone may well be sufficient for personhood, and quite probably (1)–(3) are sufficient. Neither do we need to insist that any one of these criteria is *necessary* for personhood, although once again (1) and (2) look like fairly good candidates for necessary conditions, as does (3), if "activity" is construed so as to include the activity of reasoning.

All we need to claim, to demonstrate that a fetus is not a person, is that any being which satisfies *none* of (1)–(5) is certainly not a person. I consider this claim to be so obvious that I think anyone who denied it, and claimed that a being which satisfied none of (1)–(5) was a person all the same, would thereby demonstrate that he had no notion at all of what a person is—perhaps because he had confused the concept of a person with that of genetic humanity. If the opponents of abortion were to deny the appropriateness of these five criteria, I do not know what further arguments would convince them. We would probably have to admit that our conceptual schemes were indeed irreconcilably different, and that our dispute could not be settled objectively.

I do not expect this to happen, however, since I think that the concept of a person is one which is very nearly universal (to people), and that it is common to both proabortionists and antiabortionists, even though neither group has fully realized the relevance of this concept to the resolution of their dispute. Furthermore, I think that on reflection even the antiabortionists ought to agree not only that (1)–(5) are central to the concept of personhood, but also that it is a part of this concept that all and only people have full moral rights. The concept of a person is in part a moral concept; once we have admitted that x is a person we have recognized, even if we have not agreed to respect, x's right to be treated as a member of the moral community. It is true that the claim that x is a *human being* is more commonly voiced as part of an appeal to treat x decently than is the claim that x is a person, but this is either because "human being" is here used in the sense which implies personhood, or because the genetic and moral senses of "human" have been confused.

Now if (1)–(5) are indeed the primary criteria of personhood, then it is clear that genetic humanity is neither necessary nor sufficient for establishing that an entity is a person. Some human beings are not people, and there may well be people who are not human beings. A man or woman whose consciousness has been permanently obliterated but who remains alive is a human being which is no longer a person; defective human beings, with no appreciable mental capacity, are not and presumably never will be people: and a fetus is a human being which is not yet a person, and which therefore cannot coherently be said to have full moral rights. Citizens of the next century should be prepared to recognize highly advanced, self-aware robots or computers, should such be developed, and intelligent inhabitants of other worlds, should such be found, as people in the fullest sense, and to respect their moral rights. But to ascribe full moral rights to an entity which is not a person is as absurd as to ascribe moral obligations and responsibilities to such an entity.

Fetal Development and the Right to Life

Two problems arise in the application of these suggestions for the definition of the moral community to the determination of the precise moral status of a human fetus. Given that the paradigm example of a person is a normal adult human being, then (1) How like this paradigm, in particular how far advanced since conception, does a human being need to be before it begins to have a right to life by virtue, not of being fully a person as of yet, but of being *like* a person? and (2) To what extent, if any, does the fact that a fetus has the *potential* for becoming a person endow it with some of the same rights? Each of these questions requires some comment.

In answering the first question, we need not attempt a detailed consideration of the moral rights of organisms which are not developed enough, aware enough, intelligent enough, etc., to be considered people, but which resemble people in some respects. It does seem reasonable to suggest that the more like a person, in the relevant respects, a being is, the stronger is the case for regarding it as having a right to life, and indeed the stronger its right to life is. Thus we ought to take seriously the suggestion that, insofar as "the human individual develops biologically in a continuous fashion . . . the rights of a human person might develop in the same way." But we must keep in mind that the attributes which are relevant in determining whether or not an entity is enough like a person to be regarded as having some

of the same moral rights are no different from those which are relevant to determining whether or not it is full a person—i.e., are no different from (1)–(5)— and that being genetically human, or having recognizably human facial and other physical features, or detectable brain activity, or the capacity to survive outside the uterus, are simply not among these relevant attributes.

Thus it is clear that even though a seven- or eight-month fetus has features which make it apt to arouse in us almost the same powerful protective instinct as is commonly aroused by a small infant, nevertheless it is not significantly more personlike than is a very small embryo. It is *somewhat* more personlike; it can apparently feel and respond to pain, and it may even have a rudimentary form of consciousness, insofar as its brain is quite active. Nevertheless, it seems safe to say that it is not fully conscious, in the way that an infant of a few months is, and that it cannot reason, or communicate messages of indefinitely many sorts, does not engage in self-motivated activity, and has no self-awareness. Thus, in the *relevant* respects, a fetus, even a fully developed one, is considerably less personlike than is the average fish. And I think that a rational person must conclude that if the right to life of a fetus is to be based upon its resemblance to a person, then it cannot be said to have any more right to life than, let us say, a newborn guppy (which also seems to be capable of feeling pain), and that a right of that magnitude could never override a woman's right to obtain an abortion, at any stage of her pregnancy.

There may, of course, be other arguments in favor of placing legal limits upon the stage of pregnancy in which an abortion may be performed. Given the relative safety of the new techniques of artificially inducing labor during the third trimester, the danger to the woman's life or health is no longer such an argument. Neither is the fact that people tend to respond to the thought of abortion in the later stages of pregnancy with emotional repulsion, since mere emotional responses cannot take the place of moral reasoning in determining what ought to be permitted. Nor, finally, is the frequently heard argument that legalizing abortion, especially late in the pregnancy, may erode the level of respect for human life, leading, perhaps, to an increase in unjustified euthanasia and other crimes. For this threat, if it is a threat, can be better met by educating people to the kinds of moral distinctions which we are making here than by limiting access to abortion (which limitation may, in its disregard for the rights of women, be just as damaging to the level of respect for human rights).

Thus, since the fact that even a fully developed fetus is not personlike enough to have any significant right to life on the basis of its personlikeness shows that no legal restrictions upon the stage of pregnancy in which an abortion may be performed can be justified on the grounds that we should protect the rights of the older fetus; and since there is no other apparent justification for such restrictions, we may conclude that they are entirely unjustified. Whether or not it would be *indecent* (whatever that means) for a woman in her seventh month to obtain an abortion just to avoid having to postpone a trip to Europe, it would not, in itself, be *immoral,* and therefore it ought to be permitted.

Potential Personhood and the Right to Life

We have seen that a fetus does not resemble a person in any way which can support the claim that it has even some of the same rights. But what about its *potential,* the fact that if nurtured and allowed to develop naturally it will very probably become a person? Doesn't that alone give it at least some right to life? It is hard to deny that the fact that an entity is a potential person is a strong *prima facie* reason for not destroying it; but we need not conclude from this that a potential person has a right to life, by virtue of that potential. It may be that our feeling that it is better, other things being equal, not to destroy a potential person is better explained by the fact that potential people are still (felt to be) an invaluable resource, not to be lightly squandered. Surely, if every speck of dust were a potential person, we would be much less apt to conclude that every potential person has a right to become actual.

Still, we do not need to insist that a potential person has no right to life whatever. There may well be something immoral, and not just imprudent, about wantonly destroying potential people, when doing so isn't necessary to protect anyone's rights. But even if a potential person does have some *prima facie* right to life, such a right could not possibly outweigh the right of a woman to obtain an abortion, since the rights of any actual person invariably outweigh those of any potential person, whenever the two conflict. Since this may not be immediately obvious in the case of a human fetus, let us look at another case.

Suppose that our space explorer falls into the hands of an alien culture whose scientists decide to create a few hundred thousand or more human beings, by breaking his body into its component cells, and using these to create fully developed human beings, with, of course, his genetic code. We may imagine that each of these newly created men will have all of the original man's abilities, skills, knowledge, and so on, and also have an individual self-concept, in short that each of them will be a bona fide (though hardly unique) person. Imagine that the whole project will take only seconds, and that its chances of success are extremely high, and that our explorer knows all of this, and also knows that these people will be treated fairly. I maintain that in such a situation he would have every right to escape if he could, and thus to deprive all of these potential people of their potential lives; for his right to life outweighs all of theirs together, in spite of the fact that they are all genetically human, all innocent, and all have a very high probability of becoming people very soon, if only he refrains from acting.

Indeed, I think he would have a right to escape even if it were not his life which the alien scientists planned to take, but only a year of his freedom, or, indeed, only a day. Nor would he be obligated to stay if he had gotten captured (thus bringing all these people-potentials into existence) because of his own carelessness, or even if he had done so deliberately, knowing the consequences. Regardless of how he got captured he is not morally obligated to remain in captivity for *any* period of time for the sake of permitting any number of potential people to come into actuality, so great is the margin by which one actual person's right to liberty outweighs whatever right to life even a hundred thousand potential people have. And it seems reasonable to conclude that the rights of a woman will outweigh by a similar margin whatever right to life a fetus may have by virtue of its potential personhood.

Thus, neither a fetus's resemblance to a person, nor its potential for becoming a person provides any basis whatever for the claim that it has any significant right to life. Consequently, a woman's right to protect her health, happiness, freedom, and even her life, by terminating an unwanted pregnancy, will always override whatever right to life it may be appropriate to ascribe to a fetus, even a fully developed one. And thus, in the absence of any overwhelming social need for every possible child, the laws which restrict the right to obtain an abortion, or limit the period of pregnancy during which an abortion may be performed, are a wholly unjustified violation of a woman's most basic moral and constitutional rights.

Postscript on Infanticide

Since the publication of this article, many people have written to point out that my argument appears to justify not only abortion but infanticide as well. For a newborn infant is not significantly more personlike than an advanced fetus, and consequently it would seem that if the destruction of the latter is permissible, so too must be that of the former. Inasmuch as most people, regardless of how they feel about the morality of abortion, consider infanticide a form of murder, this might appear to represent a serious flaw in my argument.

Now, if I am right in holding that it is only people who have a full-fledged right to life, and who can be murdered, and if the criteria of personhood are as I have described them, then it obviously follows that killing a newborn infant isn't murder. It does *not* follow, however, that infanticide is permissible, for two reasons. In the first place, it would be wrong, at least in this country and in this period of history, and other things being equal, to kill a newborn infant, because even if its parents do not want it and would not suffer from its destruction, there are other people who would like to have it, and would, in all probability, be deprived of a great deal of pleasure by its destruction. Thus, infanticide is wrong for reasons analogous to those which make it wrong to wantonly destroy natural resources, or great works of art.

Secondly, most people, at least in this country, value infants, and would much prefer that they be preserved, even if foster parents are not immediately available. Most of us would rather be taxed to support orphanages than allow unwanted infants to be destroyed. So long as there are people who want an infant preserved, and who are willing and able to provide the means of caring for it, under reasonably humane conditions, it is, *ceteris paribus,* wrong to destroy it.

But, it might be replied, if this argument shows that infanticide is wrong, at least at this time and in this country, doesn't it also show that abortion is wrong? After all, many people value fetuses, are disturbed by their destruction, and would much prefer that they be preserved, even at some cost to themselves. Furthermore, as a potential source of pleasure to some foster family, a fetus is just as valuable as an infant. There is, however, a crucial difference between the two cases: so long as the fetus is unborn, its preservation, contrary to the wishes of the pregnant woman, violates her rights to freedom, happiness, and self-determination. Her rights override the rights of those who would like the fetus preserved, just as if someone's life or limb is threatened by a wild animal, his right to protect himself by destroying the animal overrides the rights of those who would prefer that the animal not be harmed.

The minute the infant is born, however, its preservation no longer violates any of its mother's rights, even if she wants it destroyed, because she is free to put it up for adoption. Consequently, while the moment of birth does not mark any sharp discontinuity in the degree to which an infant possesses the right to life, it does mark the end of its mother's right to determine its fate. Indeed, if abortion could be performed without killing the fetus, she would never possess the right to have the fetus destroyed, for the same reasons that she has no right to have an infant destroyed.

On the other hand, it follows from my argument that when an unwanted or defective infant is born into a society which cannot afford and/or is not willing to care for it, then its destruction is permissible. This conclusion will, no doubt, strike many people as heartless and immoral; but remember that the very existence of people who feel this way, and who are willing and able to provide care for unwanted infants, is reason enough to conclude that they should be preserved.

QUESTIONS FOR REFLECTION

1. Explain Warren's criticisms of Thomson.

2. Why does Warren reject the traditional pro-life and pro-choice arguments?

3. Distinguish the genetic and moral senses of "human." Noonan argues for their equivalence. Why does Warren reject it?

4. What are the central features of personhood, according to Warren? To what extent does a fetus have them? When are they acquired?

5. How does Warren respond to the charge that her view implies that infanticide is permissible? Do you find her response convincing?

6. Warren says that the rights of a potential person can never outweigh those of an actual person. Do you agree? Why or why not?

JANE ENGLISH

Abortion and the Concept of a Person

Jane English was Associate Professor of Philosophy at the University of North Carolina when she died in 1978. (Source: Reprinted by permission from The Canadian Journal of Philosophy 5, 2 [October 1975], pp. 233–243. Copyright © 1975 by the Canadian Journal of Philosophy.)

The abortion debate rages on. Yet the two most popular positions seem to be clearly mistaken. Conservatives maintain that a human life begins at conception and that therefore abortion must be wrong because it is murder. But not all killings of humans are murders. Most notably, self-defense may justify even the killing of an innocent person.

Liberals, on the other hand, are just as mistaken in their argument that, since a fetus does not become a person until birth, a woman may do whatever she pleases in and to her own body. First, you cannot do as you please with your own body if it affects other people adversely. Second, if a fetus is not a person, that does not imply that you can do to it anything you wish. Animals, for example, are not persons, yet to kill or torture them for no reason at all is wrong.

At the center of the storm has been the issue of just when it is between ovulation and adulthood that a person appears on the scene. Conservatives draw the line at conception, liberals at birth. In this paper I first examine our concept of a person and conclude that no single criterion can capture the concept of a person and no sharp line can be drawn. Next I argue that if a fetus is a person, abortion is still justifiable in many cases; and if a fetus is not a person, killing it is still wrong in many cases. To a large extent, these two solutions are in agreement. I conclude that our concept of a person cannot and need not bear the weight that the abortion controversy has thrust upon it.

I

The several factions in the abortion argument have drawn battle lines around various proposed criteria for determining what is and what is not a person. For example, Mary Anne Warren lists five features (capacities for reasoning, self-awareness, complex communication, etc.) as her criteria for personhood and argues for the permissibility of abortion because a fetus falls outside this concept. Baruch Brody uses brain waves. Michael Tooley picks having-a-concept-of-self as his criterion and concludes that infanticide and abortion are justifiable, while the killing of adult animals is not. On the other side, Paul Ramsey claims a certain gene structure is the defining characteristic. John Noonan prefers conceived-of-humans and presents counterexamples to various other candidate criteria. For instance, he argues against viability as the criterion because the newborn and infirm would then be non-persons, since they cannot live without the aid of others. He rejects any criterion that calls upon the sorts of sentiments a being can evoke in adults on the grounds that this would allow us to exclude other races as non-persons if we could just view them sufficiently unsentimentally.

These approaches are typical: foes of abortion propose sufficient conditions for personhood which fetuses satisfy, while friends of abortion counter with necessary conditions for personhood which fetuses lack. But these both presuppose that the concept of a person can be captured in a straitjacket of necessary and/or sufficient conditions. Rather, "person" is a cluster of features, of which rationality, having a self concept and being conceived of humans are only part.

What is typical of persons? Within our concept of a person we include, first, certain biological factors: descended from humans, having a certain genetic makeup, having a head, hands, arms, eyes, capable of locomotion, breathing, eating, sleeping. There are psychological factors: sentience, perception, having a concept of self and of one's own interests and desires, the ability to use tools, the ability to use language or symbol systems, the ability to joke, to be angry, to doubt. There are rationality factors: the ability to reason and draw conclusions, the ability to generalize and to learn from past experience, the ability to sacrifice present interests for greater gains in the future. There are social factors: the ability to work in groups and respond to peer pressures, the ability to recognize and consider as valuable the interests of others, seeing oneself as one among "other minds," the ability to sympathize, encourage, love, the ability to evoke from others the responses of sympathy, encouragement, love, the ability to work with others for mutual advantage. Then there are legal factors: being subject to the law and protected by it, having the ability to sue and enter contracts, being counted in the census, having a name and citizenship, the ability to own property, inherit, and so forth.

Now the point is not that this list is incomplete, or that you can find counterinstances to each of its points. People typically exhibit rationality, for instance, but someone who was irrational would not thereby fail to qualify as a person. On the other hand, something could exhibit the majority of these features and still fail to be a person, as an advanced robot might. There is no single core of necessary and sufficient features which we can draw upon with the assurance that they constitute what really makes a person; there are only features that are more or less typical.

This is not to say that no necessary or sufficient conditions can be given. Being alive is a necessary condition for being a person, and being a U.S. Senator is sufficient. But rather than falling inside a sufficient condition or outside a necessary one, a fetus lies in the penumbra region where our concept of a person is not so simple. For this reason I think a conclusive answer to the question whether a fetus is a person is unattainable.

Here we might note a family of simple fallacies that proceed by stating a necessary condition for personhood and showing that a fetus has that characteristic. This is a form of the fallacy of affirming the consequent. For example, some have mistakenly reasoned from the premise that a fetus is human (after all, it is a human fetus rather than, say, a canine fetus), to the conclusion that it is *a* human. Adding an equivocation on "being," we get the fallacious argument that since a fetus is something both living and human, it is a human being.

Nonetheless, it does seem clear that a fetus has very few of the above family of characteristics, whereas a newborn baby exhibits a much larger proportion of them—and a two-year-old has even more. Note that one traditional anti-abortion argument has centered on pointing out the many ways in which a fetus resembles a baby. They emphasize its development ("It already has ten fingers. . . .") without mentioning its dissimilarities to adults (it still has gills and a tail). They also try to evoke the sort of sympathy on our part that we only feel toward other persons ("Never to laugh . . . or feel the sunshine?"). This all seems to be a relevant way to argue, since its purpose is to persuade us that a fetus satisfies so many of the important features on the list that it ought to be treated as a person. Also note that a fetus near the time of birth satisfies many more of these factors than a fetus in the early months of development. This could provide reason for making distinctions among the different stages of pregnancy, as the U.S. Supreme Court has done.

Historically, the time at which a person has been said to come into existence has varied widely. Muslims date personhood from fourteen days after conception. Some medievals followed Aristotle in placing ensoulment at forty days after conception for a male fetus and eighty days for a female fetus. In European common law since the Seventeenth Century, abortion was considered the killing of a person only after quickening, the time when a pregnant woman first feels the fetus move on its own. Nor is this variety of opinions surprising. Biologically, a human being develops gradually. We shouldn't expect there to be any specific time or sharp dividing point when a person appears on the scene.

For these reasons I believe our concept of a person is not sharp or decisive enough to bear the weight of a solution to the abortion controversy. To use it to solve that problem is to clarify *obscurum per obscurius*.

II

Next let us consider what follows if a fetus is a person after all. Judith Jarvis Thomson's landmark article, "A Defense of Abortion," correctly points out that some additional argumentation is needed at this point in the conservative argument to bridge the gap between the premise that a fetus is an innocent person and the conclusion that killing it is always wrong. To arrive at this conclusion, we would need the additional premise that killing an innocent person is always wrong. But killing an innocent person is sometimes permissible, most notably in self-defense. Some examples may help draw out our intuitions or ordinary judgments about self-defense.

Suppose a mad scientist, for instance, hypnotized innocent people to jump out of the bushes and attack innocent passers-by with knives. If you are so attacked, we agree you have a right to kill the attacker in self defense, if killing him is the only way to protect your life or to save yourself from serious injury. It does not seem to matter here that the attacker is not malicious but himself an innocent pawn, for your killing of him is not done in a spirit of retribution but only in self-defense.

How severe an injury may you inflict in self-defense? In part this depends upon the severity of the injury to be avoided: you may not shoot someone merely to avoid having your clothes torn. This might lead one to the mistaken conclusion that the defense may only equal the threatened injury in severity; that to avoid death you may kill, but to avoid a black eye you may only inflict a black eye or the equivalent. Rather, our laws and customs seem to say that you may create an injury somewhat, but not enormously, greater than the injury to be avoided. To fend off an attack whose outcome would be as serious as rape, a severe beating or the loss of a finger, you may shoot; to avoid having your clothes torn, you may blacken an eye.

Aside from this, the injury you may inflict should only be the minimum necessary to deter or inca-pacitate the attacker. Even if you know he intends to kill you, you are not justified in shooting him if you could equally well save yourself by the simple expedient of running away. Self-defense is for the purpose of avoiding harms rather than equalizing harms.

Some cases of pregnancy present a parallel situation. Though the fetus is itself innocent, it may pose a threat to the pregnant woman's well-being, life prospects or health, mental or physical. If the pregnancy presents a slight threat to her interests, it seems self-defense cannot justify abortion. But if the threat is on a par with a serious beating or the loss of a finger, she may kill the fetus that poses such a threat, even if it is an innocent person. If a lesser harm to the fetus could have the same defensive effect, killing it would not be justified. It is unfortunate that the only way to free the woman from the pregnancy entails the death of the fetus (except in very late stages of pregnancy). Thus a self-defense model supports Thomson's point that the woman has a right only to be freed from the fetus, not a right to demand its death.

The self-defense model is most helpful when we take the pregnant woman's point of view. In the pre-Thomson literature, abortion is often framed as a question for a third party: do you, a doctor, have a right to choose between the life of the woman and that of the fetus? Some have claimed that if you were a passer-by who witnessed a struggle between the innocent hypnotized attacker and his equally innocent victim, you would have no reason to kill either in defense of the other. They have concluded that the self-defense model implies that a woman may attempt to abort herself, but that a doctor should not assist her. I think the position of the third party is somewhat more complex. We do feel some inclination to intervene on behalf of the victim rather than the attacker, other things equal. But if both parties are innocent, other factors come into consideration. You would rush to the aid of your husband whether he was attacker or attackee. If a hypnotized famous violinist were attacking a skid row bum, we would try to save the individual who is of more value to society. These considerations would tend to support abortion in some cases.

But suppose you are a frail senior citizen who wishes to avoid being knifed by one of these innocent hypnotics, so you have hired a bodyguard to accompany you. If you are attacked, it is clear we believe that the bodyguard, acting as your agent, has a right to kill the attacker to save you from a serious beating. Your rights of self-defense are transferred to your agent. I suggest that we should similarly view the doctor as the pregnant woman's agent in carrying out a defense she is physically incapable of accomplishing herself.

Thanks to modern technology, the cases are rare in which pregnancy poses as clear a threat to a woman's bodily health as an attacker brandishing a switchblade. How does self-defense fare when more subtle, complex and long-range harms are involved?

To consider a somewhat fanciful example, suppose you are a highly trained surgeon when you are kidnapped by the hypnotic attacker. He says he does not intend to harm you but to take you back to the mad scientist who, it turns out, plans to hypnotize you to have a permanent mental block against all your knowledge of medicine. This would automatically destroy your career, which would in turn have a serious adverse impact on your family, your personal relationships, and your happiness. It seems to me that if the only way you can avoid this outcome is to shoot the innocent attacker, you are justified in so doing. You are defending yourself from a drastic injury to your life prospects. I think it is no exaggeration to claim that unwanted pregnancies (most obviously among teenagers) often have such adverse lifelong consequences as the surgeon's loss of livelihood.

Several parallels arise between various views on abortion and the self-defense model. Let's suppose further that these hypnotized attackers only operate at night, so that it is well known that they can be avoided completely by the considerable inconvenience of never leaving your house after dark. One view is that since you could stay home at night, therefore if you go out and are selected by one of these hypnotized people, you have no right to defend yourself. This parallels the view that abstinence is the only acceptable way to avoid pregnancy. Others might hold that you ought to take along some defense such as Mace which will deter the hypnotized person without killing him, but that if this defense fails, you are obliged to submit to the resulting injury, no matter how severe it is. This parallels the view that contraception is all right but abortion is always wrong, even in cases of contraceptive failure.

A third view is that you may kill the hypnotized person only if he will actually kill you, but not if he will only injure you. This is like the position that abortion is permissible only if it is required to save a woman's life. Finally we have the view that it is all right to kill the attacker, even if only to avoid a very slight inconvenience to yourself and even if you knowingly walked down the very street where all these incidents have been taking place without taking along any Mace or protective escort. If we assume that a fetus is a person, this is the analogue of the view that abortion is always justifiable, "on demand."

The self-defense model allows us to see an important difference that exists between abortion and infanticide, even if a fetus is a person from conception. Many have argued that the only way to justify abortion without justifying infanticide would be to find some characteristic of personhood that is acquired at birth. Michael Tooley, for one, claims infanticide is justifiable because the really significant characteristics of a person are acquired some time after birth. But all such approaches look to characteristics of the developing human and ignore the relation between the fetus and the woman. What if, after birth, the presence of an infant or the need to support it posed a grave threat to the woman's sanity or life prospects? She could escape this threat by the simple expedient of running away. So a solution that does not entail the death of the infant is available. Before birth, such solutions are not available because of the biological dependence of the fetus on the woman. Birth is the crucial point not because of any characteristics the fetus gains, but because after birth the woman can defend herself by a means less drastic than killing the infant. Hence self-defense can be used to justify abortion without necessarily thereby justifying infanticide.

III

On the other hand, supposing a fetus is not after all a person, would abortion always be morally permissible? Some opponents of abortion seem worried that if a fetus is not a full-fledged person, then we are justified in treating it in any way at all. However, this does not follow. Non-persons do get some consideration in our moral code, though of course they do not have the same rights as persons have (and in general they do not have moral responsibilities), and though their interests may be overridden by the interests of persons. Still, we cannot just treat them in any way at all.

Treatment of animals is a case in point. It is wrong to torture dogs for fun or to kill wild birds for no reason at all. It is wrong period, even though dogs and birds do not have the same rights persons do. However, few people think it is wrong to use dogs as experimental animals, causing them considerable suffering in some cases, provided that the resulting research will probably bring discoveries of great benefit to people. And most of us think it all right to kill birds for food or to protect our crops. People's rights are different from the consideration we give to animals, then, for it is wrong to experiment on people, even if others might later benefit a great deal as a result of their suffering. You might volunteer to be a subject, but this would be supererogatory; you certainly have a right to refuse to be a medical guinea pig.

But how do we decide what you may or may not do to non-persons? This is a difficult problem, one for which I believe no adequate account exists. You do not want to say, for instance, that torturing dogs is all right whenever the sum of its effects on people is good—when it doesn't warp the sensibilities of the torturer so much that he mistreats people. If that were the case, it would be all right to torture dogs if you did it in private, or if the torturer lived on a desert island or died soon afterward, so that his actions had no effect on people. This is an inadequate account, because whatever moral consideration animals get, it has to be indefeasible, too. It will have to be a general proscription of certain actions, not merely a weighing of the impact on people on a case-by-case basis.

Rather, we need to distinguish two levels on which consequences of actions can be taken into account in moral reasoning. The traditional objections to Utilitarianism focus on the fact that it operates solely on the first level, taking all the consequences into account in particular cases only. Thus Utilitarianism is open to "desert island" and "lifeboat" counterexamples because these cases are rigged to make the consequences of actions severely limited.

Rawls' theory could be described as a teleological sort of theory, but with teleology operating on a higher level. In choosing the principles to regulate society from the original position, his hypothetical choosers make their decision on the basis of the total consequences of various systems. Furthermore,

they are constrained to choose a general set of rules which people can readily learn and apply. An ethical theory must operate by generating a set of sympathies and attitudes toward others which reinforces the functioning of that set of moral principles. Our prohibition against killing people operates by means of certain moral sentiments including sympathy, compassion and guilt. But if these attitudes are to form a coherent set, they carry us further: we tend to perform supererogatory actions, and we tend to feel similar compassion toward person-like non-persons.

It is crucial that psychological facts play a role here. Our psychological constitution makes it the case that for our ethical theory to work, it must prohibit certain treatment of non-persons which are significantly person-like. If our moral rules allowed people to treat some person-like non-persons in ways we do not want people to be treated, this would undermine the system of sympathies and attitudes that makes the ethical system work. For this reason, we would choose in the original position to make mistreatment of some sorts of animals wrong in general (not just wrong in the cases with public impact), even though animals are not themselves parties in the original position. Thus it makes sense that it is those animals whose appearance and behavior are most like those of people that get the most consideration in our moral scheme.

It is because of "coherence of attitudes," I think, that the similarity of a fetus to a baby is very significant. A fetus one week before birth is so much like a newborn baby in our psychological space that we cannot allow any cavalier treatment of the former while expecting full sympathy and nurturative support for the latter. Thus, I think that anti-abortion forces are indeed giving their strongest arguments when they point to the similarities between a fetus and a baby, and when they try to evoke our emotional attachment to and sympathy for the fetus. An early horror story from New York about nurses who were expected to alternate between caring for six-week premature infants and disposing of viable 24-week aborted fetuses is just that—a horror story. These beings are so much alike that no one can be asked to draw a distinction and treat them so very differently.

Remember, however, that in the early weeks after conception, a fetus is very much unlike a person. It is hard to develop these feelings for a set of genes which doesn't yet have a head, hands, beating heart, response to touch or the ability to move by itself. Thus it seems to me that the alleged "slippery slope" between conception and birth is not so very slippery. In the early stages of pregnancy, abortion can hardly be compared to murder for psychological reasons, but in the latest stages it is psychologically akin to murder.

Another source of similarity is the bodily continuity between fetus and adult. Bodies play a surprisingly central role in our attitudes toward persons. One has only to think of the philosophical literature on how far physical identity suffices for personal identity or Wittgenstein's remark that the best picture of the human soul is the human body. Even after death, when all agree the body is no longer a person, we still observe elaborate customs of respect for the human body; like people who torture dogs, necrophiliacs are not to be trusted with people. So it is appropriate that we show respect to a fetus as the body continuous with the body of a person. This is a degree of resemblance to persons that animals cannot rival.

Michael Tooley also utilizes a parallel with animals. He claims that it is always permissible to drown newborn kittens and draws conclusions about infanticide. But it is only permissible to drown kittens when their survival would cause some hardship. Perhaps it would be a burden to feed and house six more cats or to find other homes for them. The alternative of letting them starve produces even more suffering than the drowning. Since the kittens get their rights second-hand, so to speak, *via* the need for coherence in our attitudes, their interests are often overridden by the interests of fullfledged persons. But if their survival would be no inconvenience to people at all, then it is wrong to drown them, *contra* Tooley.

Tooley's conclusions about abortion are wrong for the same reason. Even if a fetus is not a person, abortion is not always permissible, because of the resemblance of a fetus to a person. I agree with Thomson that it would be wrong for a woman who is seven months pregnant to have an abortion just to avoid having to postpone a trip to Europe. In the early months of pregnancy when the fetus hardly resembles a baby at all, then, abortion is permissible whenever it is in the interests of the pregnant woman or her family. The reasons would only need to outweigh the pain and inconvenience of the abortion itself. In the middle months, when the fetus comes to resemble a person, abortion would be justifiable only when the continuation of the pregnancy or the birth of the child would cause harms—physical, psychological, economic or social—to the woman. In the late months of pregnancy, even on our current assumption that a fetus is not a person, abortion seems to be wrong except to save a woman from significant injury or death.

The Supreme Court has recognized similar gradations in the alleged slippery slope stretching between conception and birth. To this point, the present paper has been a discussion of the moral status of abortion only, not its legal status. In view of the great physical, financial and sometimes psychological costs of abortion, perhaps the legal arrangement most compatible with the proposed moral solution would be the absence of restrictions, that is, so-called abortion "on demand."

So I conclude, first, that application of our concept of a person will not suffice to settle the abortion issue. After all, the biological development of a human being is gradual. Second, whether a fetus is a person or not, abortion is justifiable early in pregnancy to avoid modest harms and seldom justifiable late in pregnancy except to avoid significant injury or death.

QUESTIONS FOR REFLECTION

1. English argues that "our concept of a person is not sharp or decisive enough" to resolve the abortion controversy. How does she reach this conclusion?

2. What is the point of English's arguments concerning self-defense? What do you think they show?

3. How does English distinguish abortion from infanticide?

4. Why, according to English, are some abortions impermissible?

DON MARQUIS

Why Abortion Is Immoral

Don Marquis is Associate Professor of Philosophy at the University of Kansas. (Source: Reprinted from The Journal of Philosophy *LXXXVI, 4 [April 1989]: 183–202, with permission of the author and* The Journal of Philosophy. *Copyright © 1989 by the Journal of Philosophy, Inc.)*

The view that abortion is, with rare exceptions, seriously immoral has received little support in the recent philosophical literature. No doubt most philosophers affiliated with secular institutions of higher education believe that the anti-abortion position is either a symptom of irrational religious dogma or a conclusion generated by seriously confused philosophical argument. The purpose of this essay is to undermine this general belief. This essay sets out an argument that purports to show, as well as any argument in ethics can show, that abortion is, except possibly in rare cases, seriously immoral, that it is in the same moral category as killing an innocent adult human being.

The argument is based on a major assumption. Many of the most insightful and careful writers on the ethics of abortion—such as Joel Feinberg, Michael Tooley, Mary Anne Warren, H. Tristram Engelhardt, Jr., L. W. Sumner, John T. Noonan, Jr., and Philip Devine—believe that whether or not abortion is morally permissible stands or falls on whether or not a fetus is the sort of being whose life it is seriously wrong to end. The argument of this essay will assume, but not argue, that they are correct.

Also, this essay will neglect issues of great importance to a complete ethics of abortion. Some anti-abortionists will allow that certain abortions, such as abortion before implantation or abortion when the life of a woman is threatened by a pregnancy or abortion after rape, may be morally permissible. This essay will not explore the casuistry of these hard cases.

The purpose of this essay is to develop a general argument for the claim that the overwhelming majority of deliberate abortions are seriously immoral.

I

A sketch of standard anti-abortion and pro-choice arguments exhibits how those arguments possess certain symmetries that explain why partisans of those positions are so convinced of the correctness of their own positions, why they are not successful in convincing their opponents, and why, to others, this issue seems to be unresolvable. An analysis of the nature of this standoff suggests a strategy for surmounting it.

Consider the way a typical anti-abortionist argues. She will argue or assert that life is present from the moment of conception or that fetuses look like babies or that fetuses possess a characteristic such as a genetic code that is both necessary and sufficient for being human. Anti-abortionists seem to believe that (1) the truth of all of these claims is quite obvious, and (2) establishing any of these claims is sufficient to show that abortion is morally akin to murder.

A standard pro-choice strategy exhibits similarities. The pro-choicer will argue or assert that fetuses are not persons or that fetuses are not rational agents or that fetuses are not social beings. Pro-choicers seem to believe that (1) the truth of any of these claims is quite obvious, and (2) establishing any of these claims is sufficient to show that an abortion is not a wrongful killing.

In fact, both the pro-choice and the anti-abortion claims do seem to be true, although the "it looks like a baby" claim is more difficult to establish the earlier the pregnancy. We seem to have a standoff. How can it be resolved?

As everyone who has taken a bit of logic knows, if any of these arguments concerning abortion is a good argument, it requires not only some claim characterizing fetuses, but also some general moral principle that ties a characteristic of fetuses to having or not having the right to life or to some other moral characteristic that will generate the obligation or the lack of obligation not to end the life of a fetus. Accordingly, the arguments of the anti-abortionist and the pro-choicer need a bit of filling in to be regarded as adequate.

Note what each partisan will say. The anti-abortionist will claim that her position is supported by such generally accepted moral principles as "It is always *prima facie* seriously wrong to take a human life" or "It is always *prima facie* seriously wrong to end the life of a baby." Since these are generally accepted moral principles, her position is certainly not obviously wrong. The pro-choicer will claim that her position is supported by such plausible moral principles as "Being a person is what gives an individual intrinsic moral worth" or "It is only seriously *prima facie* wrong to take the life of a member of the human community." Since these are generally accepted moral principles, the pro-choice position is certainly not obviously wrong. Unfortunately, we have again arrived at a standoff.

Now, how might one deal with this standoff? The standard approach is to try to show how the moral principles of one's opponent lose their plausibility under analysis. It is easy to see how this is possible. On the one hand, the anti-abortionist will defend a moral principle concerning the wrongness of killing which tends to be broad in scope in order that even fetuses at an early stage of pregnancy will fall under it. The problem with broad principles is that they often embrace too much. In this particular instance, the principle "It is always *prima facie* wrong to take a human life" seems to entail that it is wrong to end the existence of a living human cancer-cell culture, on the grounds that the culture is both living and

human. Therefore, it seems that the anti-abortionist's favored principle is too broad.

On the other hand, the pro-choicer wants to find a moral principle concerning the wrongness of killing which tends to be narrow in scope in order that fetuses will *not* fall under it. The problem with narrow principles is that they often do not embrace enough. Hence, the needed principles such as "It is *prima facie* seriously wrong to kill only persons" or "It is *prima facie* wrong to kill only rational agents" do not explain why it is wrong to kill infants or young children or the severely retarded or even perhaps the severely mentally ill. Therefore, we seem again to have a standoff. The anti-abortionist charges, not unreasonably, that pro-choice principles concerning killing are too narrow to be acceptable; the pro-choicer charges, not unreasonably, that anti-abortionist principles concerning killing are too broad to be acceptable.

Attempts by both sides to patch up the difficulties in their positions run into further difficulties. The anti-abortionist will try to remove the problem in her position by reformulating her principle concerning killing in terms of human beings. Now we end up with: "It is always *prima facie* seriously wrong to end the life of a human being." This principle has the advantage of avoiding the problem of the human cancer-cell culture counterexample. But this advantage is purchased at a high price. For although it is clear that a fetus is both human and alive, it is not at all clear that a fetus is a human *being*. There is at least something to be said for the view that something becomes a human being only after a process of development, and that therefore first-trimester fetuses and perhaps all fetuses are not yet human beings. Hence, the anti-abortionist, by this move, has merely exchanged one problem for another.

The pro-choicer fares no better. She may attempt to find reasons why killing infants, young children, and the severely retarded is wrong which are independent of her major principle that is supposed to explain the wrongness of taking human life, but which will not also make abortion immoral. This is no easy task. Appeals to social utility will seem satisfactory only to those who resolve not to think of the enormous difficulties with a utilitarian account of the wrongness of killing and the significant social costs of preserving the lives of the unproductive. A pro-choice strategy that extends the definition of "person" to infants or even to young children seems just as arbitrary as an anti-abortion strategy that extends the definition of "human being" to fetuses. Again, we find symmetries in the two positions and we arrive at a standoff.

There are even further problems that reflect symmetries in the two positions. In addition to counterexample problems, or the arbitrary application problems that can be exchanged for them, the standard anti-abortionist principle "It is *prima facie* seriously wrong to kill a human being," or one of its variants, can be objected to on the grounds of ambiguity. If "human being" is taken to be a *biological* category, then the anti-abortionist is left with the problem of explaining why a merely biological category should make a moral difference. Why, it is asked, is it any more reasonable to base a moral conclusion on the number of chromosomes in one's cells than on the color of one's skin? If "human being," on the other hand, is taken to be a *moral* category, then the claim that a fetus is a human being cannot be taken to be a premise in the anti-abortion argument, for it is precisely what needs to be established. Hence, either the anti-abortionist's main category is a morally irrelevant, merely biological category, or it is of no use to the anti-abortionist in establishing (noncircularly, of course) that abortion is wrong.

Although this problem with the anti-abortionist position is often noticed, it is less often noticed that the pro-choice position suffers from an analogous problem. The principle "Only persons have the right to life" also suffers from an ambiguity. The term "person" is typically defined in terms of psychological characteristics, although there will certainly be disagreement concerning which characteristics are most important. Supposing that this matter can be settled, the pro-choicer is left with the problem of explaining why *psychological* characteristics should make a *moral* difference. If the pro-choicer should attempt to deal with this problem by claiming that an explanation is not necessary, that in fact we do treat such a cluster of psychological properties as having moral significance, the sharp-witted anti-abortionist should have a ready response. We do treat being both living and human as having moral significance. If it is legitimate for the pro-choicer to demand that the anti-abortionist provide an explanation of the connection between the biological character of being a human being and the wrongness of being killed (even

though people accept this connection), then it is legitimate for the anti-abortionist to demand that the pro-choicer provide an explanation of the connection between psychological criteria for being a person and the wrongness of being killed (even though that connection is accepted).

Feinberg has attempted to meet this objection (he calls psychological personhood "commonsense personhood"):

> The characteristics that confer commonsense personhood are not arbitrary bases for rights and duties, such as race, sex or species membership; rather they are traits that make sense out of rights and duties and without which those moral attributes would have no point or function. It is because people are conscious; have a sense of their personal identities; have plans, goals, and projects; experience emotions; are liable to pains, anxieties, and frustrations; can reason and bargain, and so on—it is because of these attributes that people have values and interests, desires and expectations of their own, including a stake in their own futures, and a personal well-being of a sort we cannot ascribe to unconscious or nonrational beings. Because of their developed capacities they can assume duties and responsibilities and can have and make claims on one another. Only because of their sense of self, their life plans, their value hierarchies, and their stakes in their own futures can they be ascribed fundamental rights. There is nothing arbitrary about these linkages.

The plausible aspects of this attempt should not be taken to obscure its implausible features. There is a great deal to be said for the view that being a psychological person under some description is a necessary condition for having duties. One cannot have a duty unless one is capable of behaving morally, and a being's capability of behaving morally will require having a certain psychology. It is far from obvious, however, that having rights entails consciousness or rationality, as Feinberg suggests. We speak of the rights of the severely retarded or the severely mentally ill, yet some of these persons are not rational. We speak of the rights of the temporarily unconscious. The New Jersey Supreme Court based their decision in the Quinlan case on Karen Ann Quinlan's right to privacy, and she was known to be permanently unconscious at that time. Hence, Feinberg's claim that having rights entails being conscious is, on its face, obviously false.

Of course, it might not make sense to attribute rights to a being that would never in its natural history have certain psychological traits. This modest connection between psychological personhood and moral personhood will create a place for Karen Ann Quinlan and the temporarily unconscious. But then it makes a place for fetuses also. Hence, it does not serve Feinberg's pro-choice purposes. Accordingly, it seems that the pro-choicer will have as much difficulty bridging the gap between psychological personhood and personhood in the moral sense as the anti-abortionist has bridging the gap between being a biological human being and being a human being in the moral sense.

Furthermore, the pro-choicer cannot any more escape her problem by making person a purely moral category than the anti-abortionist could escape by the analogous move. For if person is a moral category, then the pro-choicer is left without the resources for establishing (noncircularly, of course) the claim that a fetus is not a person, which is an essential premise in her argument. Again, we have both a symmetry and a standoff between pro-choice and anti-abortion views.

Passions in the abortion debate run high. There are both plausibilities and difficulties with the standard positions. Accordingly, it is hardly surprising that partisans of either side embrace with fervor the moral generalizations that support the conclusions they preanalytically favor, and reject with disdain the moral generalizations of their opponents as being subject to inescapable difficulties. It is easy to believe that the counterexamples to one's own moral principles are merely temporary difficulties that will dissolve in the wake of further philosophical research, and that the counterexamples to the principles of one's opponents are as straightforward as the contradiction between *A* and *O* propositions in traditional logic. This might suggest to an impartial observer (if there are any) that the abortion issue is unresolvable.

There is a way out of this apparent dialectical quandary. The moral generalizations of both sides are not quite correct. The generalizations hold for the most part, for the usual cases. This suggests that they are all *accidental* generalizations, that the moral claims made by those on both sides of the dispute do not touch on the *essence* of the matter.

This use of the distinction between essence and accident is not meant to invoke obscure metaphysical categories. Rather, it is intended to reflect the rather atheoretical nature of the abortion discussion. If the generalization a partisan in the abortion dispute adopts were derived from the reason why ending the life of a human being is wrong, then there could not be exceptions to that generalization unless some special case obtains in which there are even more powerful countervailing reasons. Such generalizations would not be merely accidental generalizations; they would point to, or be based upon, the essence of the wrongness of killing, what it is that makes killing wrong. All this suggests that a necessary condition of resolving the abortion controversy is a more theoretical account of the wrongness of killing. After all, if we merely believe, but do not understand, why killing adult human beings such as ourselves is wrong, how could we conceivably show that abortion is either immoral or permissible?

II

In order to develop such an account, we can start from the following unproblematic assumption concerning our own case: it is wrong to kill us. Why is it wrong? Some answers can be easily eliminated. It might be said that what makes killing us wrong is that a killing brutalizes the one who kills. But the brutalization consists of being inured to the performance of an act that is hideously immoral; hence, the brutalization does not explain the immorality. It might be said that what makes killing us wrong is the great loss others would experience due to our absence. Although such hubris is understandable, such an explanation does not account for the wrongness of killing hermits, or those whose lives are relatively independent and whose friends find it easy to make new friends.

A more obvious answer is better. What primarily makes killing wrong is neither its effect on the murderer nor its effect on the victim's friends and relatives, but its effect on the victim. The loss of one's life is one of the greatest losses one can suffer. The loss of one's life deprives one of all the experiences, activities, projects, and enjoyments that would otherwise have constituted one's future. Therefore, killing someone is wrong, primarily because the killing inflicts (one of) the greatest possible losses on the victim. To describe this as the loss of life can be misleading, however. The change in my biological state does not by itself make killing me wrong. The effect of the loss of my biological life is the loss to me of all those activities, projects, experiences, and enjoyments which would otherwise have constituted my future personal life. These activities, projects, experiences, and enjoyments are either valuable for their own sakes or are means to something else that is valuable for its own sake. Some parts of my future are not valued by me now, but will come to be valued by me as I grow older and as my values and capacities change. When I am killed, I am deprived both of what I now value which would have been part of my future personal life, but also what I would come to value. Therefore, when I die, I am deprived of all of the value of my future. Inflicting this loss on me is ultimately what makes killing me wrong. This being the case, it would seem that what makes killing *any* adult human being *prima facie* seriously wrong is the loss of his or her future.

How should this rudimentary theory of the wrongness of killing be evaluated? It cannot be faulted for deriving an "ought" from an "is," for it does not. The analysis assumes that killing me (or you, reader) is *prima facie* seriously wrong. The point of the analysis is to establish which natural property ultimately explains the wrongness of the killing, given that it is wrong. A natural property will ultimately explain the wrongness of killing, only if (1) the explanation fits with our intuitions about the matter and (2) there is no other natural property that provides the basis for a better explanation of the wrongness of killing. This analysis rests on the intuition that what makes killing a particular human or animal wrong is what it does to that particular human or animal. What makes killing wrong is some natural effect or other of the killing. Some would deny this. For instance, a divine-command theorist in ethics would deny it. Surely this denial is, however, one of those features of divine-command theory which renders it so implausible.

The claim that what makes killing wrong is the loss of the victim's future is directly supported by two considerations. In the first place, this theory explains why we regard killing as one of the worst of crimes. Killing is especially wrong, because it deprives the victim of more than perhaps any other crime. In the second place, people with AIDS or cancer who know they are dying believe, of course, that dying is a very bad thing for them. They believe that the loss of a future to them that they would otherwise have experienced is what makes their premature death a very bad thing for them. A better theory of the wrongness of killing would require a different natural property associated with killing which better fits with the attitudes of the dying. What could it be?

The view that what makes killing wrong is the loss to the victim of the value of the victim's future gains additional support when some of its implications are examined. In the first place, it is incompatible with the view that it is wrong to kill only beings who are biologically human. It is possible that there exists a different species from another planet whose members have a future like ours. Since having a future like that is what makes killing someone wrong, this theory entails that it would be wrong to kill members of such a species. Hence, this theory is opposed to the claim that only life that is biologically human has great moral worth, a claim which many anti-abortionists have seemed to adopt. This opposition, which this theory has in common with personhood theories, seems to be a merit of the theory.

In the second place, the claim that the loss of one's future is the wrong-making feature of one's being killed entails the possibility that the futures of some actual nonhuman mammals on our own planet are sufficiently like ours that it is seriously wrong to kill them also. Whether some animals do have the same right to life as human beings depends on adding to the account of the wrongness of killing some additional account of just what it is about my future or the futures of other adult human beings which makes it wrong to kill us. No such additional account will be offered in this essay. Undoubtedly, the provision of such an account would be a very difficult matter. Undoubtedly, any such account would be quite controversial. Hence, it surely should not reflect badly on this sketch of an elementary theory of the wrongness of killing that it is indeterminate with respect to some very difficult issues regarding animal rights.

In the third place, the claim that the loss of one's future is the wrong-making feature of one's being killed does not entail, as sanctity of human life theories do, that active euthanasia is wrong. Persons who are severely and incurably ill, who face a future of pain and despair, and who wish to die will not have suffered a loss if they are killed. It is, strictly speaking, the value of a human's future which makes killing wrong in this theory. This being so, killing does not necessarily wrong some persons who are sick and dying. Of course, there may be other reasons for a prohibition of active euthanasia, but that is another matter. Sanctity-of-human-life theories seem to hold that active euthanasia is seriously wrong even in an individual case where there seems to be good reason for it independently of public policy considerations. This consequence is most implausible, and it is a plus for the claim that the loss of a future of value is what makes killing wrong that it does not share this consequence.

In the fourth place, the account of the wrongness of killing defended in this essay does straightforwardly entail that it is *prima facie* seriously wrong to kill children and infants, for we do presume that they have futures of value. Since we do believe that it is wrong to kill defenseless little babies, it is important that a theory of the wrongness of killing easily account for this. Personhood theories of the wrongness of killing, on the other hand, cannot straightforwardly account for the wrongness of killing infants and young children. Hence, such theories must add special ad hoc accounts of the wrongness of killing the young. The plausibility of such ad hoc theories seems to be a function of how desperately one wants such theories to work. The claim that the primary wrong-making feature of a killing is the loss to the victim of the value of its future accounts for the wrongness of killing young children and infants directly; it makes the wrongness of such acts as obvious as we actually think it is. This is a further merit of this theory. Accordingly, it seems that this value of a future-like-ours theory of the wrongness of killing shares strengths of both sanctity-of-life and personhood accounts while avoiding weaknesses of both. In addition, it meshes with a central intuition concerning what makes killing wrong.

The claim that the primary wrong-making feature of a killing is the loss to the victim of the value of its future has obvious consequences for the ethics of abortion. The future of a standard fetus includes a set of experiences, projects, activities, and such which are identical with the futures of adult human beings and are identical with the futures of young children. Since the reason that is sufficient to explain why it is wrong to kill human beings after the time of birth is a reason that also applies to fetuses, it follows that abortion is *prima facie* seriously morally wrong.

This argument does not rely on the invalid inference that, since it is wrong to kill persons, it is wrong to kill potential persons also. The category that is morally central to this analysis is the category of having a valuable future like ours; it is not the category of personhood. The argument to the conclusion that abortion is *prima facie* seriously morally wrong proceeded independently of the notion of person or potential person or any equivalent. Someone may wish to start with this analysis in terms of the value of a human future, conclude that abortion is, except perhaps in rare circumstances, seriously morally wrong, infer that fetuses have the right to life, and then call fetuses "persons" as a result of their having the right to life. Clearly, in this case, the category of person is being used to state the *conclusion* of the analysis rather than to generate the *argument* of the analysis.

The structure of this anti-abortion argument can be both illuminated and defended by comparing it to what appears to be the best argument for the wrongness of the wanton infliction of pain on animals. This latter argument is based on the assumption that it is *prima facie* wrong to inflict pain on me (or you, reader). What is the natural property associated with the infliction of pain which makes such infliction wrong? The obvious answer seems to be that the infliction of pain causes suffering and that suffering is a misfortune. The suffering caused by the infliction of pain is what makes the wanton infliction of pain on me wrong. The wanton infliction of pain on other adult humans causes suffering. The wanton infliction of pain on animals causes suffering. Since causing suffering is what makes the wanton infliction of pain wrong and since the wanton infliction of pain on animals causes suffering, it follows that the wanton infliction of pain on animals is wrong.

This argument for the wrongness of the wanton infliction of pain on animals shares a number of structural features with the argument for the serious *prima facie* wrongness of abortion. Both arguments start with an obvious assumption concerning what it is wrong to do to me (or you, reader). Both then look for the characteristic or the consequence of the wrong action which makes the action wrong. Both recognize that the wrong-making feature of these immoral actions is a property of actions sometimes directed at individuals other than postnatal human beings. If the structure of the argument for the wrongness of the wanton infliction of pain on animals is sound, then the structure of the argument for the *prima facie* serious wrongness of abortion is also sound, for the structure of the two arguments is the same. The structure common to both is the key to the explanation of how the wrongness of abortion can be demonstrated without recourse to the category of person. In neither argument is that category crucial.

This defense of an argument for the wrongness of abortion in terms of a structurally similar argument for the wrongness of the wanton infliction of pain on animals succeeds only if the account regarding animals is the correct account. Is it? In the first place, it seems plausible. In the second place, its major competition is Kant's account. Kant believed that we do not have direct duties to animals at all, because they are not persons. Hence, Kant had to explain and justify the wrongness of inflicting pain on animals on the grounds that "he who is hard in his dealings with animals becomes hard also in his dealing with men." The problem with Kant's account is that there seems to be no reason for accepting this latter claim unless Kant's account is rejected. If the alternative to Kant's account is accepted, then it is easy to understand why someone who is indifferent to inflicting pain on animals is also indifferent to inflicting pain on humans, for one is indifferent to what makes inflicting pain wrong in both cases. But, if Kant's account is accepted, there is no intelligible reason why one who is hard in his dealings with animals (or crabgrass or stones) should also be hard in his dealings with men. After all, men are persons: animals are no more persons than crabgrass or stones. Persons are Kant's crucial moral category. Why, in short, should a Kantian accept the basic claim in Kant's argument?

Hence, Kant's argument for the wrongness of inflicting pain on animals rests on a claim that, in a world of Kantian moral agents, is demonstrably false. Therefore, the alternative analysis, being more plausible anyway, should be accepted. Since this alternative analysis has the same structure as the anti-abortion argument being defended here, we have further support for the argument for the immorality of abortion being defended in this essay.

Of course, this value of a future-like-ours argument, if sound, shows only that abortion is *prima facie* wrong, not that it is wrong in any and all circumstances. Since the loss of the future to a standard fetus, if killed, is, however, at least as great a loss as the loss of the future to a standard adult human being who is killed, abortion, like ordinary killing, could be justified only by the most compelling reasons. The loss of one's life is almost the greatest misfortune that can happen to one. Presumably abortion could be justified in some circumstances, only if the loss consequent on failing to abort would be at least as great. Accordingly, morally permissible abortions will be rare indeed unless, perhaps, they occur so early in pregnancy that a fetus is not yet definitely an individual. Hence, this argument should be taken as showing that abortion is presumptively very seriously wrong, where the presumption is very strong —as strong as the presumption that killing another adult human being is wrong.

III

How complete an account of the wrongness of killing does the value of a future-like-ours account have to be in order that the wrongness of abortion is a consequence? This account does not have to be an account of the necessary conditions for the wrongness of killing. Some persons in nursing homes may lack valuable human futures, yet it may be wrong to kill them for other reasons. Furthermore, this account does not obviously have to be the sole reason killing is wrong where the victim did have a valuable future. This analysis claims only that, for any killing where the victim did have a valuable future like ours, having that future by itself is sufficient to create the strong presumption that the killing is seriously wrong.

One way to overturn the value of a future-like-ours argument would be to find some account of the wrongness of killing which is at least as intelligible and which has different implications for the ethics of abortion. Two rival accounts possess at least some degree of plausibility. One account is based on the obvious fact that people value the experience of living and wish for that valuable experience to continue. Therefore, it might be said, what makes killing wrong is the discontinuation of that experience for the victim. Let us call this the *discontinuation account.* Another rival account is based upon the obvious fact that people strongly desire to continue to live. This suggests that what makes killing us so wrong is that it interferes with the fulfillment of a strong and fundamental desire, the fulfillment of which is necessary for the fulfillment of any other desires we might have. Let us call this the *desire account*.

Consider first the desire account as a rival account of the ethics of killing which would provide the basis for rejecting the anti-abortion position. Such an account will have to be stronger than the value of a future-like-ours account of the wrongness of abortion if it is to do the job expected of it. To entail the wrongness of abortion, the value of a future-like-ours account has only to provide a sufficient, but not a necessary, condition for the wrongness of killing. The desire account, on the other hand, must provide us also with a necessary condition for the wrongness of killing in order to generate a pro-choice conclusion on abortion. The reason for this is that presumably the argument from the desire account moves from the claim that what makes killing wrong is interference with a very strong desire to the claim that abortion is not wrong because the fetus lacks a strong desire to live. Obviously, this inference fails if someone's having the desire to live is not a necessary condition of its being wrong to kill that individual.

One problem with the desire account is that we do regard it as seriously wrong to kill persons who have little desire to live or who have no desire to live or, indeed, have a desire not to live. We believe it is seriously wrong to kill the unconscious, the sleeping, those who are tired of life, and those who are suicidal. The value-of-a-human-future account renders standard morality intelligible in these cases; these cases appear to be incompatible with the desire account.

The desire account is subject to a deeper difficulty. We desire life because we value the goods of this life. The goodness of life is not secondary to our desire for it. If this were not so, the pain of one's own premature death could be done away with merely by an appropriate alteration in the configuration of one's desires. This is absurd. Hence, it would seem that it is the loss of the goods of one's future, not the interference with the fulfillment of a strong desire to live, which accounts ultimately for the wrongness of killing.

It is worth noting that, if the desire account is modified so that it does not provide a necessary, but only a sufficient, condition for the wrongness of killing, the desire account is compatible with the value of a future-like-ours account. The combined accounts will yield an anti-abortion ethic. This suggests that one can retain what is intuitively plausible about the desire account without a challenge to the basic argument of this paper.

It is also worth noting that, if future desires have moral force in a modified desire account of the wrongness of killing, one can find support for an anti-abortion ethic even in the absence of a value of a future-like-ours account. If one decides that a morally relevant property, the possession of which is sufficient to make it wrong to kill some individual, is the desire at some future time to live—one might decide to justify one's refusal to kill suicidal teenagers on these grounds, for example—then, since typical fetuses will have the desire in the future to live, it is wrong to kill typical fetuses. Accordingly, it does not seem that a desire account of the wrongness of killing can provide a justification of a pro-choice ethic of abortion which is nearly as adequate as the value of a human-future justification on an anti-abortion ethic.

The discontinuation account looks more promising as an account of the wrongness of killing. It seems just as intelligible as the value of a future-like-ours account, but it does not justify an anti-abortion position. Obviously, if it is the continuation of one's activities, experiences, and projects, the loss of which makes killing wrong, then it is not wrong to kill fetuses for that reason, for fetuses do not have experiences, activities, and projects to be continued or discontinued. Accordingly, the discontinuation account does not have the anti-abortion consequences that the value of a future-like-ours account has. Yet, it seems as intelligible as the value of a future-like-ours account, for when we think of what would be wrong with our being killed, it does seem as if it is the discontinuation of what makes our lives worthwhile which makes killing us wrong.

Is the discontinuation account just as good an account as the value of a future-like-ours account? The discontinuation account will not be adequate at all, if it does not refer to the *value* of the experience that may be discontinued. One does not want the discontinuation account to make it wrong to kill a patient who begs for death and who is in severe pain that cannot be relieved short of killing. (I leave open the question of whether it is wrong for other reasons.) Accordingly, the discontinuation account must be more than a bare discontinuation account. It must make some reference to the positive value of the patient's experiences. But, by the same token, the value of a future-like-ours account cannot be a bare future account either. Just having a future surely does not itself rule out killing the above patient. This account must make some reference to the value of the patient's future experiences and projects also. Hence, both accounts involve the value of experiences, projects, and activities. So far we still have symmetry between the accounts.

The symmetry fades, however, when we focus on the time period of the value of the experiences, etc., which has moral consequences. Although both accounts leave open the possibility that the patient in our example may be killed, this possibility is left open only in virtue of the utterly bleak future for the patient. It makes no difference whether the patient's immediate past contains intolerable pain, or consists in being in a coma (which we can imagine is a situation of indifference), or consists in a life of value. If the patient's future is a future of value, we want our account to make it wrong to kill the patient. If the patient's future is intolerable, whatever his or her immediate past, we want our account to allow killing the patient. Obviously, then, it is the value of that patient's future which is doing the work in rendering the morality of killing the patient intelligible.

This being the case, it seems clear that whether one has immediate past experiences or not does no work in the explanation of what makes killing wrong. The addition the discontinuation account makes to the value of a human future account is otiose. Its addition to the value-of-a-future account plays no role at all in rendering intelligible the wrongness of killing. Therefore, it can be discarded with the discontinuation account of which it is a part.

IV

The analysis of the previous section suggests that alternative general accounts of the wrongness of killing are either inadequate or unsuccessful in getting around the anti-abortion consequences of the value of a future-like-ours argument. A different strategy for avoiding these anti-abortion consequences involves limiting the scope of the value of a future argument. More precisely, the strategy involves arguing that fetuses lack a property that is essential for the value-of-a-future argument (or for any anti-abortion argument) to apply to them.

One move of this sort is based upon the claim that a necessary condition of one's future being valuable is that one values it. Value implies a valuer. Given this one might argue that, since fetuses cannot value their futures, their futures are not valuable to them. Hence, it does not seriously wrong them deliberately to end their lives.

This move fails, however, because of some ambiguities. Let us assume that something cannot be of value unless it is valued by someone. This does not entail that my life is of no value unless it is valued by me. I may think, in a period of despair, that my future is of no worth whatsoever, but I may be wrong because others rightly see value—even great value—in it. Furthermore, my future can be valuable to me even if I do not value it. This is the case when a young person attempts suicide, but is rescued and goes on to significant human achievements. Such young people's futures are ultimately valuable to them, even though such futures do not seem to be valuable to them at the moment of attempted suicide. A fetus's future can be valuable to it in the same way. Accordingly, this attempt to limit the anti-abortion argument fails.

Another similar attempt to reject the anti-abortion position is based on Tooley's claim that an entity cannot possess the right to life unless it has the capacity to desire its continued existence. It follows that, since fetuses lack the conceptual capacity to desire to continue to live, they lack the right to life. Accordingly, Tooley concludes that abortion cannot be seriously *prima facie* wrong. . . .

What could be the evidence for Tooley's basic claim? Tooley once argued that individuals have a *prima facie* right to what they desire and that the lack of the capacity to desire something undercuts the basis of one's right to it. . . . This argument plainly will not succeed in the context of the analysis of this essay, however, since the point here is to establish the fetus's right to life on other grounds. Tooley's argument assumes that the right to life cannot be established in general on some basis other than the desire for life. This position was considered and rejected in the preceding section of this paper.

One might attempt to defend Tooley's basic claim on the grounds that, because a fetus cannot apprehend continued life as a benefit, its continued life cannot be a benefit or cannot be something it has a right to or cannot be something that is in its interest. This might be defended in terms of the general proposition that, if an individual is literally incapable of caring about or taking an interest in some *X*, then one does not have a right to *X* or *X* is not a benefit or *X* is not something that is in one's interest.

Each member of this family of claims seems to be open to objections. As John C. Stevens has pointed out, one may have a right to be treated with a certain medical procedure (because of a health insurance policy one has purchased), even though one cannot conceive of the nature of the procedure. And, as Tooley himself has pointed out, persons who have been indoctrinated, or drugged, or rendered temporarily unconscious may be literally incapable of caring about or taking an interest in something that is in their interest or is something to which they have a right, or is something that benefits them. Hence, the Tooley claim that would restrict the scope of the value of a future-like-ours argument is undermined by counterexamples.

Finally, Paul Bassen has argued that, even though the prospects of an embryo might seem to be a basis for the wrongness of abortion, an embryo cannot be a victim and therefore cannot be wronged. An embryo cannot be a victim, he says, because it lacks sentience. His central argument for this seems to be that, even though plants and the permanently unconscious are alive, they clearly cannot be victims. What is the explanation of this? Bassen claims that the explanation is that their lives consist of mere metabolism and mere metabolism is not enough to ground victimizability. Mentation is required.

The problem with this attempt to establish the absence of victimizability is that both plants and the permanently unconscious clearly lack what Bassen calls "prospects" or what I have called "a future life like ours." Hence, it is surely open to one to argue that the real reason we believe plants and the permanently unconscious cannot be victims is that killing them cannot deprive them of a future life like ours; the real reason is not their absence of present mentation.

Bassen recognizes that his view is subject to this difficulty, and he recognizes that the case of children seems to support this difficulty, for "much of what

we do for children is based on prospects." He argues, however, that, in the case of children and in other such cases, "potentiality comes into play only where victimizability has been secured on other grounds". . . .

Bassen's defense of his view is patently question-begging, since what is adequate to secure victimizability is exactly what is at issue. His examples do not support his own view against the thesis of this essay. Of course, embryos can be victims: when their lives are deliberately terminated, they are deprived of their futures of value, their prospects. This makes them victims, for it directly wrongs them.

The seeming plausibility of Bassen's view stems from the fact that paradigmatic cases of imagining someone as a victim involve empathy, and empathy requires mentation of the victim. The victims of flood, famine, rape, or child abuse are all persons with whom we can empathize. That empathy seems to be part of seeing them as victims.

In spite of the strength of these examples, the attractive intuition that a situation in which there is victimization requires the possibility of empathy is subject to counterexamples. Consider a case that Bassen himself offers: "Posthumous obliteration of an author's work constitutes a misfortune for him only if he had wished his work to endure". . . . The conditions Bassen wishes to impose upon the possibility of being victimized here seem far too strong. Perhaps this author, due to his unrealistic standards of excellence and his low self-esteem, regarded his work as unworthy of survival, even though it possessed genuine literary merit. Destruction of such work would surely victimize its author. In such a case, empathy with the victim concerning the loss is clearly impossible.

Of course, Bassen does not make the possibility of empathy a necessary condition of victimizability; he requires only mentation. Hence, on Bassen's actual view, this author, as I have described him, can be a victim. The problem is that the basic intuition that renders Bassen's view plausible is missing in the author's case. In order to attempt to avoid counterexamples, Bassen has made his thesis too weak to be supported by the intuitions that suggested it.

Even so, the mentation requirement on victimizability is still subject to counterexamples. Suppose a severe accident renders me totally unconscious for a month, after which I recover. Surely killing me while I am unconscious victimizes me, even though I am incapable of mentation during that time. It follows that Bassen's thesis fails. Apparently, attempts to restrict the value of a future-like-ours argument so that fetuses do not fall within its scope do not succeed.

V

In this essay, it has been argued that the correct ethic of the wrongness of killing can be extended to fetal life and used to show that there is a strong presumption that any abortion is morally impermissible. If the ethic of killing adopted here entails, however, that contraception is also seriously immoral, then there would appear to be a difficulty with the analysis of this essay.

But this analysis does not entail that contraception is wrong. Of course, contraception prevents the actualization of a possible future of value. Hence, it follows from the claim that futures of value should be maximized that contraception is *prima facie* immoral. This obligation to maximize does not exist, however; furthermore, nothing in the ethics of killing in this paper entails that it does. The ethics of killing in this essay would entail that contraception is wrong only if something were denied a human future of value by contraception. Nothing at all is denied such a future by contraception, however.

Candidates for a subject of harm by contraception fall into four categories: (1) some sperm or other, (2) some ovum or other, (3) a sperm and an ovum separately, and (4) a sperm and an ovum together. Assigning the harm to some sperm is utterly arbitrary, for no reason can be given for making a sperm the subject of harm rather than an ovum. Assigning the harm to some ovum is utterly arbitrary, for no reason can be given for making an ovum the subject of harm rather than a sperm. One might attempt to avoid these problems by insisting that contraception deprives both the sperm and the ovum separately of a valuable future like ours. On this alternative, too many futures are lost. Contraception was supposed to be wrong, because it deprived us of one future of value, not two. One might attempt to avoid this problem by holding that contraception deprives the combination of sperm and ovum of a valuable future like ours. But here the definite article misleads. At the time of contraception, there are hundreds of millions of sperm, one (released) ovum and millions of possible combinations of all of these. There is no actual combination at all. Is the subject of the loss to be a merely possible combination? Which one? This alternative does not yield an actual subject of harm either. Accordingly, the immorality of contraception is not entailed by the loss of a future-like-ours argument simply because there is no nonarbitrarily identifiable subject of the loss in the case of contraception.

VI

The purpose of this essay has been to set out an argument for the serious presumptive wrongness of abortion subject to the assumption that the moral permissibility of abortion stands or falls on the moral status of the fetus. Since a fetus possesses a property, the possession of which in adult human beings is sufficient to make killing an adult human being wrong, abortion is wrong. This way of dealing with the problem of abortion seems superior to other approaches to the ethics of abortion, because it rests on an ethics of killing which is close to self-evident, because the crucial morally relevant property clearly applies to fetuses, and because the argument avoids the usual equivocations on "human life," "human being," or "person." The argument rests neither on religious claims nor on Papal dogma. It is not subject to the objection of "speciesism." Its soundness is compatible with the moral permissibility of euthanasia and contraception. It deals with our intuitions concerning young children.

Finally, this analysis can be viewed as resolving a standard problem—indeed, *the* standard problem—concerning the ethics of abortion. Clearly, it is wrong to kill adult human beings. Clearly, it is not wrong to end the life of some arbitrarily chosen single human cell. Fetuses seem to be like arbitrarily chosen human cells in some respects and like adult humans in other respects. The problem of the ethics of abortion is the problem of determining the fetal property that settles this moral controversy. The thesis of this essay is that the problem of the ethics of abortion, so understood, is solvable.

QUESTIONS FOR REFLECTION

1. Marquis argues that usual anti-abortion and pro-choice arguments have symmetric problems and so are at a standoff. Review his reasoning. Do you agree?

2. Why, according to Marquis, is it wrong to kill an adult human being?

3. Marquis argues that it is wrong to kill a fetus for just the same reason that it is wrong to kill an adult. How does his argument go? Do you find it convincing?

4. Marquis compares his argument to one for the wrongness of the wanton infliction of pain on animals. Do you find the arguments analogous?

5. What are the discontinuation and desire accounts? Why does Marquis reject them?

EUTHANASIA AND PHYSICIAN-ASSISTED SUICIDE

Euthanasia, or mercy killing, presents some very difficult and painful dilemmas for doctors, patients, family members, and moral philosophers. Sometimes a patient's condition is so poor and holds so little hope of future recovery that death seems better than life. Is it ever morally justifiable to allow such patients to die by withholding treatment that would otherwise be given? Is it ever justifiable to kill them?

Clearly, this topic concerns both rights and liberty. The patient has a right to life and perhaps a right to die. The patient may also have the liberty to make certain fundamental decisions about whether to continue treatment. Frequently, however, euthanasia becomes a serious issue only after the patient is comatose or otherwise incapable of making a competent decision. Moreover, many factors seem to be morally relevant to the decision between life and death. Is the patient conscious? Suffering? If so, how much? What are the prospects for improvement? Is the patient terminally ill? What kind of life can the patient hope to lead, and for how long? The course of action being contemplated may also matter: Cessation of "heroic" lifesaving efforts? Withdrawal of food and water? A lethal injection?

The Supreme Court of New Jersey, in a much-publicized case, decided in 1976 to allow the parents of Karen Ann Quinlan to remove her from a respirator. She was comatose and diagnosed as having no chance of regaining consciousness. The court decided that Quinlan's right of privacy gave her or her guardian the right to decide the course of her treatment, since a respirator, which might be deemed ordinary for a curable patient, should count as extraordinary for someone with her poor prognosis.

Eight years later, the Supreme Court of Missouri reached the opposite verdict in a related case. Nancy Cruzan, after an automobile accident, was "in a persistent vegetative state." She was nevertheless not terminally ill and not reliant on a respirator or other extraordinary machinery for support. However, she did require a feeding tube. Her guardians requested that fluids and nutrition be withdrawn. The court found no justification for granting that request, arguing that Cruzan's condition was significantly different from Quinlan's and that the relevant state interest is life, not the quality of life, as the *Quinlan* court seemed to suggest.

The United States Supreme Court upheld that decision, saying that although a competent person might make an informed and voluntary choice to have hydration and nutrition withdrawn, the state has an interest in preserving life and demanding clear and convincing evidence of the patient's wishes.

J. Gay-Williams argues that euthanasia is invariably wrong. It is, he contends, contrary to everyone's natural inclination to continue living. Moreover, it is extremely dangerous for several reasons. First, we can never know that death is really preferable to continued life. Second, people may choose death out of ignorance, a temporary feeling of hopelessness, or consideration for their families. Finally, euthanasia would lead to a lowered respect for life that could have serious consequences for medical care and society's treatment of the infirm.

James Rachels offers two arguments for the permissibility of euthanasia. First, he contends that mercy sometimes requires mercy killing. The pain involved in terminal illness may be so great that death is better than continued life. Second, he argues that the Golden Rule similarly indicates that euthanasia is sometimes acceptable, for we would be willing to be killed to escape extreme pain.

Closely related to the question of euthanasia is that of physician-assisted suicide. Dr. Jack Kevorkian has become famous for traveling the country assisting in the suicides of desperate patients. In 1997 two cases before the Supreme Court, *Vacco* v. *Quill* and *Washington* v. *Glucksberg,* raised the issue of a right to physician-assisted suicide. Six of America's best-respected philosophers—Ronald Dworkin, Thomas Nagel, Robert Nozick, John Rawls, Thomas Scanlon, and Judith Jarvis Thomson—filed an *amici curiae* (friend of the Court) brief in favor of a right to assisted suicide. They contended that the right to liberty entails the freedom to make fundamental decisions, such as the decision to die, without governmental interference. The Supreme Court unanimously rejected their reasoning in both cases, contending instead that tradition and a concern for human life give the state sufficient reason to restrict or prohibit physician-assisted suicide.

Matter of Quinlan (1976)

(*Source:* Matter of Quinlan *70 N.J. 10, 355 A. 2d. 647 [1976]. Most legal references have been omitted.*)

The Litigation

The central figure in this tragic case is Karen Ann Quinlan, a New Jersey resident. At the age of 22, she lies in a debilitated and allegedly moribund state at Saint Clare's Hospital in Denville, New Jersey. The litigation has to do, in final analysis, with her life—its continuance or cessation—and the responsibilities, rights and duties, with regard to any fateful decision concerning it, of her family, her guardian, her doctors, the hospital, the State through its law enforcement authorities, and finally the courts of justice.

Due to extensive physical damage fully described in the able opinion of the trial judge, Judge Muir, supporting that judgment, Karen allegedly was incompetent. Joseph Quinlan sought the adjudication of that incompetency. He wished to be appointed guardian of the person and property of his daughter. It was proposed by him that such letters of guardianship, if granted, should contain an express power to him as guardian to authorize the discontinuance of all extraordinary medical procedures now allegedly sustaining Karen's vital processes and hence her life, since these measures, he asserted, present no hope of her eventual recovery. A guardian *ad litem* was appointed by Judge Muir to represent the interest of the alleged incompetent.

The Factual Base

On the night of April 15, 1975, for reasons still unclear, Karen Quinlan ceased breathing for at least two 15-minute periods. She received some ineffectual mouth-to-mouth resuscitation from friends. She was taken by ambulance to Newton Memorial Hospital. There she had a temperature of 100 degrees, her pupils were unreactive, and she was unresponsive even to deep pain. The history at the time of her admission to that hospital was essentially incomplete and uninformative.

Three days later, Dr. Morse examined Karen at the request of the Newton admitting physician, Dr. McGee. He found her comatose with evidence of decortication, a condition relating to derangement of the cortex of the brain causing a physical posture in which the upper extremities are flexed and the lower extremities are extended. She required a respirator to assist her breathing. Dr. Morse was unable to obtain an adequate account of the circumstances and events leading up to Karen's admission to the Newton Hospital. Such initial history or etiology is crucial in neurological diagnosis. Relying as he did upon the Newton Memorial records and his own examination, he concluded that prolonged lack of oxygen in the bloodstream, anoxia, was identified with her condition as he saw it upon first observation. When she was later transferred to Saint Clare's Hospital she was still unconscious, still on a respirator, and a tracheotomy had been performed. On her arrival Dr. Morse conducted extensive and detailed examinations. An electroencephalogram (EEG) measuring electrical rhythm of the brain was performed, and Dr. Morse characterized the result as "abnormal but it showed some activity and was consistent with her clinical state." Other significant neurological tests, including a brain scan, an angiogram, and a lumbar puncture were normal in result. Dr. Morse testified that Karen has been in a state of coma, lack of consciousness, since he began treating her. He explained that there are basically two types of coma, sleep-like unresponsiveness and awake unresponsiveness. Karen was originally in a sleep-like unresponsive condition but soon developed "sleep-wake" cycles, apparently a normal improvement for comatose patients occurring within three to four weeks. In the awake cycle she blinks, cries out and does things of that sort but is still totally unaware of anyone or anything around her.

Dr. Morse and other expert physicians who examined her characterized Karen as being in a "chronic persistent vegetative state." Dr. Fred Plum, one of such expert witnesses, defined this as a "subject who remains with the capacity to maintain the vegetative parts of neurological function but who . . . no longer has any cognitive function." . . .

It seemed to be the consensus not only of the treating physicians but also of the several qualified experts who testified in the case, that removal from the respirator would not conform to medical practices, standards and traditions.

The further medical consensus was that Karen in addition to being comatose is in a chronic and persistent "vegetative" state, having no awareness of anything or anyone around her and existing at a primitive reflex level. Although she does have some brain stem function (ineffective for respiration) and has other reactions one normally associates with being alive, such as moving, reacting to light, sound and noxious stimuli, blinking her eyes, and the like, the quality of her feeling impulses is unknown. She grimaces, makes stereotyped cries and sounds and has chewing motions. Her blood pressure is normal.

Karen is described as emaciated, having suffered a weight loss of at least 40 pounds, and undergoing a continuing deteriorative process. Her posture is described as fetal-like and grotesque; there is extreme flexion-rigidity of the arms, legs and related muscles and her joints are severely rigid and deformed.

From all of this evidence, and including the whole testimonial record, several basic findings in the physical area are mandated. Severe brain and associated damage, albeit of uncertain etiology, has left Karen in a chronic and persistent vegetative state. No form of treatment which can cure or improve that condition is known or available. As nearly as may be determined, considering the guarded area of remote uncertainties characteristic of most medical science predictions, she can *never* be restored to cognitive or sapient life. Even with re-

gard to the vegetative level and improvement therein (if such it may be called) the prognosis is extremely poor and the extent unknown if it should in fact occur.

She is debilitated and moribund and although fairly stable at the time of argument before us (no new information having been filed in the meanwhile in expansion of the record), no physician risked the opinion that she could live more than a year and indeed she may die much earlier. Excellent medical and nursing care so far has been able to ward off the constant threat of infection, to which she is peculiarly susceptible because of the respirator, the tracheal tube, and other incidents of care in her vulnerable condition. Her life accordingly is sustained by the respirator and tubal feeding, and removal from the respirator would cause her death soon, although the time cannot be stated with more precision.

It is from this factual base that the Court confronts and responds to three basic issues:

1. Was the trial court correct in denying the specific relief requested by plaintiff, i.e., authorization for termination of the life-supporting apparatus, on the case presented to him? Our determination on that question is in the affirmative.

2. Was the court correct in withholding letters of guardianship from the plaintiff and appointing in his stead a stranger? On that issue our determination is in the negative.

3. Should this Court, in the light of the foregoing conclusions, grant declaratory relief to the plaintiff? On that question our Court's determination is in the affirmative.

This brings us to a consideration of the constitutional and legal issues underlying the foregoing determinations.

Constitutional and Legal Issues

The Right of Privacy

It is the issue of the constitutional right of privacy that has given us most concern, in the exceptional circumstances of this case. Here a loving parent, *qua* parent and raising the rights of his incompetent and profoundly damaged daughter, probably irreversibly doomed to no more than a biologically vegetative remnant of life, is before the court. He seeks authorization to abandon specialized technological procedures which can only maintain for a time a body having no potential for resumption or continuance of other than a "vegetative" existence.

We have no doubt, in these unhappy circumstances, that if Karen were herself miraculously lucid for an interval (not altering the existing prognosis of the condition to which she would soon return) and perceptive of her irreversible condition, she could effectively decide upon discontinuance of the life-support apparatus, even if it meant the prospect of natural death. . . .

We have no hesitancy in deciding . . . that no external compelling interest of the State could compel Karen to endure the unendurable, only to vegetate a few measurable months with no realistic possibility of returning to any semblance of cognitive or sapient life. We perceive no thread of logic distinguishing between such a choice on Karen's part and a similar choice which, under the evidence in this case, could be made by a competent patient terminally ill, riddled by cancer and suffering great pain; such a patient would not be resuscitated or put on a respirator . . . and *a fortiori* would not be kept *against his will* on a respirator.

Although the Constitution does not explicitly mention a right of privacy, Supreme Court decisions have recognized that a right of personal privacy exists and that certain areas of privacy are guaranteed under the Constitution. . . .

The court in *Griswold* found the unwritten constitutional right of privacy to exist in the penumbra of specific guarantees of the Bill of Rights "formed by emanations from those guarantees that help give them life and substance." Presumably this right is broad enough to encompass a patient's decision to decline medical treatment under certain circumstances, in much the same way as it is broad enough to encompass a woman's decision to terminate pregnancy under certain conditions. . . .

The claimed interests of the State in this case are essentially the preservation and sanctity of human life and defense of the right of the physician to administer medical treatment according to his best judgment. In this case the doctors say that removing Karen from the respirator will conflict with their professional judgment. The plaintiff answers that

Karen's present treatment serves only a maintenance function; that the respirator cannot cure or improve her condition but at best can only prolong her inevitable slow deterioration and death; and that the interests of the patient, as seen by her surrogate, the guardian, must be evaluated by the court as predominant, even in the face of an opinion *contra* by the present attending physicians. Plaintiff's distinction is significant. The nature of Karen's care and the realistic chances of her recovery are quite unlike those of the patients discussed in many of the cases where treatments were ordered. In many of those cases the medical procedure required (usually a transfusion) constituted a minimal bodily invasion and the chances of recovery and return to functioning life were very good. We think that the State's interest *contra* weakens and the individual's right to privacy grows as the degree of bodily invasion increases and the prognosis dims. Ultimately there comes a point at which the individual's rights overcome the State interest. It is for that reason that we believe Karen's choice, if she were competent to make it, would be vindicated by the law. Her prognosis is extremely poor—she will never resume cognitive life. And the bodily invasion is very great—she requires 24 hour intensive nursing care, antibiotics, the assistance of a respirator, a catheter and feeding tube.

Our affirmation of Karen's independent right of choice, however, would ordinarily be based upon her competency to assert it. The sad truth, however, is that she is grossly incompetent and we cannot discern her supposed choice based on the testimony of her previous conversations with friends, where such testimony is without sufficient probative weight. . . . Nevertheless we have concluded that Karen's right of privacy may be asserted on her behalf by her guardian under the peculiar circumstances here present.

If a putative decision by Karen to permit this non-cognitive, vegetative existence to terminate by natural forces is regarded as a valuable incident of her right of privacy, as we believe it to be, then it should not be discarded solely on the basis that her condition prevents her conscious exercise of the choice. The only practical way to prevent destruction of the right is to permit the guardian and family of Karen to render their best judgment, subject to the qualifications hereinafter stated, as to whether she would exercise it in these circumstances. If their conclusion is in the affirmative, this decision should be accepted by a society the overwhelming majority of whose members would, we think, in similar circumstances, exercise such a choice in the same way for themselves or for those closest to them. It is for this reason that we determine that Karen's right of privacy may be asserted in her behalf, in this respect, by her guardian and family under the particular circumstances presented by this record.

Regarding Mr. Quinlan's right of privacy, we agree with Judge Muir's conclusion that there is no parental constitutional right that would entitle him to a grant of relief *in propria persona*. . . . Insofar as a parental right of privacy has been recognized, it has been in the context of determining the rearing of infants and, as Judge Muir put it, involved "continuing life styles." . . . Karen Quinlan is a 22-year-old adult. Her right of privacy in respect of the matter before the court is to be vindicated by Mr. Quinlan as guardian, as hereinabove determined.

The Medical Factor

. . . We glean from the record here that physicians distinguish between curing the ill and comforting and easing the dying; that they refuse to treat the curable as if they were dying or ought to die, and that they have sometimes refused to treat the hopeless and dying as if they were curable. In this sense, as we were reminded by the testimony of Drs. Korein and Diamond, many of them have refused to inflict an undesired prolongation of the process of dying on a patient in irreversible condition when it is clear that such "therapy" offers neither human nor humane benefit. We think these attitudes represent a balanced implementation of a profoundly realistic perspective on the meaning of life and death and that they respect the whole Judeo-Christian tradition of regard for human life. No less would they seem consistent with the moral matrix of medicine, "to heal," very much in the sense of the endless mission of the law, "to do justice."

Yet this balance, we feel, is particularly difficult to perceive and apply in the context of the development by advanced technology of sophisticated and artificial life-sustaining devices. For those possibly curable, such devices are of great value, and, as ordinary medical procedures, are essential. Consequently, as pointed out by Dr. Diamond, they are necessary because of the ethic of medical practice. But in light of the situation in the present case (while the record here is somewhat hazy in distinguishing between "ordinary" and "extraordinary" measures), one would have to think that the use of the same respirator or life support could be considered "ordinary" in the context of the possibly curable patient but "extraordinary" in the context of the forced sustaining by cardiorespiratory processes of an irreversibly doomed patient. . . .

The evidence in this case convinces us that the focal point of decision should be the prognosis as to the reasonable possibility of return to cognitive and sapient life, as distinguished from the forced continuance of that biological vegetative existence to which Karen seems to be doomed.

In summary of the present Point of this opinion, we conclude that the state of the pertinent medical standards and practices which guided the attending physicians in this matter is not such as would justify this Court in deeming itself bound or controlled thereby in responding to the case for declaratory relief established by the parties on the record before us. . . .

Declaratory Relief

. . . [W]e herewith declare the following affirmative relief on behalf of the plaintiff. Upon the concurrence of the guardian and family of Karen, should the responsible attending physicians conclude that there is no reasonable possibility of Karen's ever emerging from her present comatose condition to a cognitive, sapient state and that the life-support apparatus now being administered to Karen should be discontinued, they shall consult with the hospital "Ethics Committee" or like body of the institution in which Karen is then hospitalized. If that consultative body agrees that there is no reasonable possibility of Karen's ever emerging from her present comatose condition to a cognitive, sapient state, the present life-support system may be withdrawn and said action shall be without any civil or criminal liability therefor on the part of any participant, whether guardian, physician, hospital or others. We herewith specifically so hold.

QUESTIONS FOR REFLECTION

1. Which features of Karen Ann Quinlan's condition did the court find relevant to reaching a decision? Do you agree that these are all the relevant factors?

2. How did the court justify its decision? Do you find the justification persuasive?

3. In fact, when Karen Ann Quinlan was disconnected from life-support machinery after this decision, she did not die. If the court had known she would survive without the equipment, would the justification the court offered be weakened?

J. GAY-WILLIAMS

The Wrongfulness of Euthanasia

(Source: Reprinted from Ronald Munson [ed.], Intervention and Reflection: Basic Issues in Medical Ethics. *Belmont, CA: Wadsworth Publishing Company. Copyright © 1992 by Ronald Munson. Reprinted with permission.)*

My impression is that euthanasia—the idea, if not the practice—is slowly gaining acceptance within our society. Cynics might attribute this to an increasing tendency to devalue human life, but I do not believe this is the major factor. The acceptance is much more likely to be the result of unthinking sympathy and benevolence. Well-publicized, tragic stories like that of Karen Quinlan elicit from us deep feelings of compassion. We think to ourselves, "She and her family would be better off if she were dead." It is an easy step from this very human response to the view that if someone (and others) would be better off dead, then it must be all right to kill that person. Although I respect the compassion that leads to this conclusion, I believe the conclusion is wrong. I want to show that euthanasia is wrong. It is inherently wrong, but it is also wrong judged from the standpoints of self-interest and of practical effects.

Before presenting my arguments to support this claim, it would be well to define "euthanasia." An essential aspect of euthanasia is that it involves taking a human life, either one's own or that of another. Also, the person whose life is taken must be someone who is believed to be suffering from some disease or injury from which recovery cannot reasonably be expected. Finally, the action must be deliberate and intentional. Thus, euthanasia is intentionally taking the life of a presumably hopeless person. Whether the life is one's own or that of another, the taking of it is still euthanasia.

It is important to be clear about the deliberate and intentional aspect of the killing. If a hopeless person is given an injection of the wrong drug by mistake and this causes his death, this is wrongful killing but not euthanasia. The killing cannot be the result of accident. Furthermore, if the person is given an injection of a drug that is believed to be necessary to treat his disease or better his condition and the person dies as a result, then this is neither wrongful killing nor euthanasia. The intention was to make the patient well, not kill him. Similarly, when a patient's condition is such that it is not reasonable to hope that any medical procedures or treatments will save his life, a failure to implement the procedures or treatments is not euthanasia. If the person dies, this will be as a result of his injuries or disease and not because of his failure to receive treatment.

The failure to continue treatment after it has been realized that the patient has little chance of benefitting from it has been characterized by some as "passive euthanasia." This phrase is misleading and mistaken. In such cases, the person involved is not killed (the first essential aspect of euthanasia), nor is the death of the person intended by the withholding of additional treatment (the third essential aspect of euthanasia). The aim may be to spare the person additional and unjustifiable pain, to save him from the indignities of hopeless manipulations, and to avoid increasing the financial and emotional burden on his family. When I buy a pencil it is so that I can use it to write, not to contribute to an increase in the gross national product. This may be the unintended consequence of my action, but it is not the aim of my action. So it is with failing to continue the treatment of a dying person. I intend his death no more than I intend to reduce the GNP by not using medical supplies. His is an unintended dying, and so-called "passive euthanasia" is not euthanasia at all.

1. The Argument from Nature

Every human being has a natural inclination to continue living. Our reflexes and responses fit us to fight attackers, flee wild animals, and dodge out of the way of trucks. In our daily lives we exercise the caution and care necessary to protect ourselves. Our bodies are similarly structured for survival right down to the molecular level. When we are cut, our capillaries seal shut, our blood clots, and fibrogen is produced to start the process of healing the wound. When we are invaded by bacteria, antibodies are produced to fight against the alien organisms, and their remains are swept out of the body by special cells designed for clean-up work.

Euthanasia does violence to this natural goal of survival. It is literally acting against nature because all the processes of nature are bent towards the end of bodily survival. Euthanasia defeats these subtle mechanisms in a way that, in a particular case, disease and injury might not.

It is possible, but not necessary, to make an appeal to revealed religion in this connection. Man as trustee of his body acts against God, its rightful possessor, when he takes his own life. He also violates the commandment to hold life sacred and never to take it without just and compelling cause. But since this appeal will persuade only those who are prepared to accept that religion has access to revealed truths, I shall not employ this line of argument.

It is enough, I believe, to recognize that the organization of the human body and our patterns of behavioral responses make the continuation of life a natural goal. By reason alone, then, we can recognize that euthanasia sets us against our own nature. Furthermore, in doing so, euthanasia does violence to our dignity. Our dignity comes from seeking our ends. When one of our goals is survival, and actions are taken that eliminate that goal, then our natural dignity suffers. Unlike animals, we are conscious through reason of our nature and our ends. Euthanasia involves acting as if this dual nature—incli-

nation towards survival and awareness of this as an end—did not exist. Thus, euthanasia denies our basic human character and requires that we regard ourselves or others as something less than fully human.

2. The Argument from Self-Interest

The above arguments are, I believe, sufficient to show that euthanasia is inherently wrong. But there are reasons for considering it wrong when judged by standards other than reason. Because death is final and irreversible, euthanasia contains within it the possibility that we will work against our own interest if we practice it or allow it to be practiced on us.

Contemporary medicine has high standards of excellence and a proven record of accomplishment, but it does not possess perfect and complete knowledge. A mistaken diagnosis is possible, and so is a mistaken prognosis. Consequently, we may believe that we are dying of a disease when, as a matter of fact, we may not be. We may think that we have no hope of recovery when, as a matter of fact, our chances are quite good. In such circumstances, if euthanasia were permitted, we would die needlessly. Death is final and the chance of error too great to approve the practice of euthanasia.

Also, there is always the possibility that an experimental procedure or a hitherto untried technique will pull us through. We should at least keep this option open, but euthanasia closes it off. Furthermore, spontaneous remission does occur in many cases. For no apparent reason, a patient simply recovers when those all around him, including his physicians, expected him to die. Euthanasia would just guarantee their expectations and leave no room for the "miraculous" recoveries that frequently occur.

Finally, knowing that we can take our life at any time (or ask another to take it) might well incline us to give up too easily. The will to live is strong in all of us, but it can be weakened by pain and suffering and feelings of hopelessness. If during a bad time we allow ourselves to be killed, we never have a chance to reconsider. Recovery from a serious illness requires that we fight for it, and anything that weakens our determination by suggesting that there is an easy way out is ultimately against our own interest. Also, we may be inclined towards euthanasia because of our concern for others. If we see our sickness and suffering as an emotional and financial burden on our family, we may feel that to leave our life is to make their lives easier. The very presence of the possibility of euthanasia may keep us from surviving when we might.

3. The Argument from Practical Effects

Doctors and nurses are, for the most part, totally committed to saving lives. A life lost is, for them, almost a personal failure, an insult to their skills and knowledge. Euthanasia as a practice might well alter this. It could have a corrupting influence so that in any case that is severe doctors and nurses might not try hard enough to save the patient. They might decide that the patient would simply be "better off dead" and take the steps necessary to make that come about. This attitude could then carry over to their dealings with patients less seriously ill. The result would be an overall decline in the quality of medical care.

Finally, euthanasia as a policy is a slippery slope. A person apparently hopelessly ill may be allowed to take his own life. Then he may be permitted to deputize others to do it for him should he no longer be able to act. The judgment of others then becomes the ruling factor. Already at this point euthanasia is not personal and voluntary, for others are acting "on behalf of" the patient as they see fit. This may well incline them to act on behalf of other patients who have not authorized them to exercise their judgment. It is only a short step, then, from voluntary euthanasia (self-inflicted or authorized), to directed euthanasia administered to a patient who has given no authorization, to involuntary euthanasia conducted as part of a social policy. Recently many psychiatrists and sociologists have argued that we define as "mental illness" those forms of behavior that we disapprove of. This gives us license then to lock up those who display the behavior. The category of the "hopelessly ill" provides the possibility of even worse abuse. Embedded in a social policy, it would give society or its representatives the authority to eliminate all those who might be considered too "ill" to function normally any longer. The dangers of euthanasia are too great to all to run the risk of approving it in any form. The first slippery step may well lead to a serious and harmful fall.

I hope that I have succeeded in showing why the benevolence that inclines us to give approval of euthanasia is misplaced. Euthanasia is inherently wrong because it violates the nature and dignity of human beings. But even those who are not convinced by this must be persuaded that the potential personal and social dangers inherent in euthanasia are sufficient to forbid our approving it either as a personal practice or as a public policy.

Suffering is surely a terrible thing, and we have a clear duty to comfort those in need and to ease their suffering when we can. But suffering is also a natural part of life with values for the individual and for others that we should not overlook. We may legitimately seek for others and for ourselves an easeful death. Euthanasia, however, is not just an easeful death. It is a wrongful death. Euthanasia is not just dying. It is killing.

QUESTIONS FOR REFLECTION

1. Why does Gay-Williams object to the phrase "passive euthanasia"?

2. Gay-Williams argues that euthanasia is unnatural. In what way? How does this argument lead to the moral conclusion that euthanasia is wrong?

3. Can euthanasia ever be in a patient's self-interest, according to Gay-Williams? Do you agree?

4. What is Gay-Williams's "slippery slope" argument? How persuasive is it?

JAMES RACHELS

The Morality of Euthanasia

James Rachels is Professor of Philosophy at the University of Alabama at Birmingham. (Source: From The End of Life: The Morality of Euthanasia. *Oxford: Oxford University Press. Copyright © 1986 by James Rachels. Reprinted by permission.)*

An Absolute Rule?

The late Franz Ingelfinger, who was editor of the *New England Journal of Medicine,* observed that

> This is the heyday of the ethicist in medicine. He delineates the rights of patients, of experimental subjects, of fetuses, of mothers, of animals, and even of doctors. (And what a far cry it is from the days when medical "ethics" consisted of condemning economic improprieties such as fee splitting and advertising!) With impeccable logic—once certain basic assumptions are granted—and with graceful prose, the ethicist develops his arguments . . . Yet his precepts are essentially the products of armchair exercise and remain abstract and idealistic until they have been tested in the laboratory of experience.

One problem with such armchair exercises, he complained, is that in spite of the impeccable logic and the graceful prose, the result is often an absolutist ethic that is unsatisfactory when applied to particular cases, and that is therefore of little use to the practising physician. Unlike some absolutist philosophers (and theologians), "the practitioner appears to prefer the principles of individualism. As there are few atheists in foxholes, there tend to be few absolutists at the bedside."

Dr. Ingelfinger was right to be suspicious of absolute rules. However, despite his picture of the flexible physician, there are some rules that doctors do tend to regard as absolute. One such rule is the prohibition of mercy-killing. From the time of Hippocrates, whose oath has doctors pledge "not to give a deadly drug," they have held firm to this absolute "at the bedside" as well as in the seminar room. The "principles of individualism" have made little headway against it.

Are the doctors right? The arguments I have already presented, especially those concerning the sanctity of life and the two senses of "life," suggest that in fact euthanasia is morally acceptable, at least in some circumstances. As in the other matters, there is no need here to be an "absolutist at the bedside." But there are other arguments that demand attention before we can be confident of this conclusion.

. . . [W]e will examine some other arguments that are commonly advanced for and against euthanasia. We will be concerned with the morality of killing in what we might call the "standard case" of euthanasia—that is, the case of the suffering terminal patient who, while rational, requests to be killed as an alternative to a slow, lingering death. Moreover, we will be concerned with the morality of *individual acts* of killing in such cases: considered separately, are they morally wrong? This is slightly different from asking whether euthanasia ought to be illegal, in the way that questions of individual morality are often different from questions of social policy. . . .

The Argument from Mercy

The most common argument in support of euthanasia is one that we may call "the argument from mercy." It is an exceptionally simple argument, at least in its main idea, which makes one uncomplicated point. Terminal patients sometimes suffer pain so horrible that it can hardly be comprehended by those who have not actually experienced it. Their suffering can be so terrible that we do not like even to read about it or think about it; we recoil even from its description. The argument from mercy says: euthanasia is justified because it puts an end to *that*.

The great Irish satirist Jonathan Swift took eight years to die while, in the words of Joseph Fletcher, "His mind crumbled to pieces." At times the pain in his blinded eyes was so intense he had to be restrained from tearing them out. Knives and other potential instruments of suicide were kept from him. For the last three years of his life, he could do nothing but drool; and when he finally died it was only after convulsions that lasted thirty-six hours.

Swift died in 1745. Since then, doctors have learned how to eliminate much of the pain that accompanies terminal illness, but the victory has been far from complete. Here is a more recent example. Stewart Alsop was a respected journalist who died in 1975 of a rare form of cancer. Before he died, he wrote movingly of his experiences as a terminal patient. Although he had not thought much about euthanasia before, he came to approve of it after sharing a room briefly with someone he called Jack:

> The third night that I roomed with Jack in our tiny double room in the solid-tumor ward of the cancer clinic of the National Institutes of Health in Bethesda, Md., a terrible thought occurred to me.
>
> Jack had a melanoma in his belly, a malignant solid tumor that the doctors guessed was about the size of a softball. The cancer had started a few months before with a small tumor in his left shoulder, and there had been several operations since. The doctors planned to remove the softball-sized tumor, but they knew Jack would soon die. The cancer had metastasized—it had spread beyond control.
>
> Jack was good-looking, about 28, and brave. He was in constant pain, and his doctor had prescribed an intravenous shot of a synthetic opiate—a pain-killer, or analgesic—every four hours. His wife spent many of the daylight hours with him, and she would sit or lie on his bed and pat him all over, as one pats a child, only more methodically, and this seemed to help control the pain. But at night, when his pretty wife had left (wives cannot stay overnight at the NIH clinic) and darkness fell, the pain would attack without pity.
>
> At the prescribed hour, a nurse would give Jack a shot of the synthetic analgesic, and this would control the pain for perhaps two hours or a bit more. Then he would begin to moan, or whimper, very low, as though he didn't want to wake me. Then he would begin to howl, like a dog.
>
> When this happened, either he or I would ring for a nurse, and ask for a pain-killer. She would give him some codeine or the like by mouth, but it never did any real good—it affected him no more than half an aspirin might affect a man who had just broken his arm. Always the nurse would explain as encouragingly as she could that there was not long to go before the next intravenous shot—"Only about 50 minutes now." And always poor Jack's whimpers and howls would become more loud and frequent until at last the blessed relief came.
>
> The third night of this routine, the terrible thought occurred to me. "If Jack were a dog," I thought, "what would be done with him?" The answer was obvious: the pound, and chloroform. No human being with a spark of pity could let a living thing suffer so, to no good end.

I have discussed this case with some physicians who were indignant that Jack was not given larger doses of the pain-killing drug more often. They suggest that modern medicine can deal better with this type of pain. But it is worth noting that the NIH clinic is one of the best-equipped modern facilities we have; it is not as though Jack's suffering was caused by neglect in some backward rural hospital. Few of us could expect better care, were we in Jack's position. Moreover, the moral issue regarding euthanasia is not affected by whether more could have been done for Jack. The moral issue is whether mercy-killing is permissible *if* it is the only alternative to this kind of torment. We may readily grant that in any particular case where suffering can be eliminated, the argument for euthanasia will be weaker. But we will still need to know what is morally permissible in those cases in which, for whatever reason, suffering cannot, or will not, be eliminated.

I have quoted Alsop at length not for the sake of indulging in gory details but to give a clear idea of the kind of suffering we are talking about. We should not gloss over these facts with euphemistic language, or squeamishly avert our eyes from them. For only by keeping them firmly and vividly in mind can we appreciate the full force of the argument from mercy: if a person prefers—and even begs for—death as an alternative to lingering on *in this kind of torment,* only to die anyway after a while, then surely it is not immoral to help this person die sooner. As Alsop put it, "No human being with a spark of pity could let a living thing suffer so, to no good end."

Utilitarianism

The basic idea of the argument from mercy is clear enough; but how is it to be developed into a rigorous argument? Among philosophers, the utilitarians attempted to do this. They held that actions should be judged right or wrong according to whether they cause happiness or misery; and they argued that when judged by this standard, euthanasia turns out to be morally acceptable. The classic utilitarian version of the argument may be elaborated like this:

1. Any action is morally right if it serves to increase the amount of happiness in the world or to decrease the amount of misery. Conversely, an action is morally wrong if it serves to decrease happiness or increase misery.

2. Killing a hopelessly ill patient, who is suffering great pain, at his own request, would decrease the amount of misery in the world. ·

3. Therefore, such an action would be morally right.

The first premise of this argument states the principle of utility, the basic utilitarian assumption. Today most philosophers think this principle is unacceptable, because they think the promotion of happiness and the avoidance of misery are not the *only* morally important things. To take one example: People *might* be happier if there were no freedom of religion; for, if everyone adhered to the same religious beliefs, there would be greater harmony among people. There would be no unhappiness caused by Jewish girls marrying Catholic boys; the religious element of conflicts such as in Northern

Ireland would be removed; and so forth. Moreover, if people were brainwashed well enough, no one would mind not having freedom of choice. Thus happiness might be increased. But, the argument continues, even if happiness *could* be increased in this way, it would be wrong to do so, because people should be allowed to make their own choices. Therefore, the argument concludes, the principle of utility is unacceptable.

There is a related difficulty for utilitarianism, which connects more directly with euthanasia. Suppose a person is leading a miserable life—full of more unhappiness than happiness—but does not want to die. This person thinks a miserable life is better than none at all. Now I assume we would all agree that this person should not be killed; that would be plain, unjustifiable murder. Yet it *would* decrease the amount of misery in the world if we killed him—and so it is hard to see how, on strictly utilitarian grounds, it could be wrong. Again, the principle of utility seems to be an inadequate guide for determining right and wrong.

Such arguments have led many philosophers to reject this moral theory. Yet contemporary utilitarians have an easy answer. In the first place, in so far as euthanasia is concerned, the classical utilitarian argument retains considerable force, even if it is faulty. For even if the promotion of happiness and the avoidance of misery are not the *only* morally important things, they are still very important. So, when an action would decrease misery, that is *a* very strong reason in its favour. The utilitarian argument in favour of euthanasia might therefore be decisive, even if the general complaints about the principle of utility are sound.

Moreover, utilitarianism may also be defended against the general complaints. Classical utilitarianism, as set out by Bentham and Mill, is a combination of three ideas. The first is that actions are to be judged right or wrong entirely according to their *consequences.* Nothing else matters—actions are not good or bad "in themselves," and moral "rules" have no independent importance. Right actions are, simply, the ones that have the best results. The second idea is that good and evil are to be measured in terms of happiness and unhappiness—nothing else is ultimately valuable. Material goods, art and ideas, friendship, and so on, are good only *because* they contribute to happiness. Thus, right actions are said to be those that produce the most happiness, or prevent the most misery. Third, and finally, classical utilitarianism includes the idea of equality—each individual's happiness is counted as equally important.

The difficulties we noted for utilitarianism all may be traced to its narrow identification of good and evil with happiness and unhappiness. . . . All that is necessary to save it, therefore, is to adopt a broader conception of individual welfare. The basic idea of the theory is that actions are right or wrong as they increase or decrease welfare. So, suppose we substitute a better conception of welfare: rather than speaking of maximizing *happiness,* let us speak of maximizing *interests*—let the principle of utility say that actions are right if they satisfy as many interests as possible. Such a broader principle will still be "utilitarian" in that it still sees the rightness of actions as consisting in their effects on the welfare of the creatures affected by them. But the new principle avoids the problems that plagued the old one: if it is in a person's best interests to have freedom of choice in religion, or in choosing to remain alive, then the principle will not countenance taking away that freedom or that life. Armed with this better version of the principle of utility, we may then offer this improved argument concerning euthanasia:

1. If an action promotes the best interests of everyone concerned, then that action is morally acceptable.

2. In at least some cases, euthanasia promotes the best interests of everyone concerned.

3. Therefore, in at least some cases euthanasia is morally acceptable.

It would have been in everyone's best interests if euthanasia had been employed in the case of Stewart Alsop's roommate Jack. First, and most important, it would have been in Jack's own interests, since it would have provided him with an easier death, without additional pain. Moreover, it would have been best for his wife. Her misery, helplessly watching him suffer, was second only to his. Third, the hospital staff's interests would have been served, since if Jack's dying had not been prolonged, they could have turned their attention to other patients whom they could have helped. Fourth, other patients would have benefited since medical resources would no longer have been used in the sad, pointless maintenance of Jack's physical existence. Finally, if Jack

himself requested to be killed, the act would not have violated his rights. Considering all this, how can euthanasia be wrong?

Two additional comments are necessary before we leave the argument from mercy. First, I have discussed the utilitarians in connection with this argument, but one does not have to accept a general utilitarian theory of ethics to find it persuasive. There are other possible theories that one might prefer. However, no matter what ethical theory one accepts, the consequences of one's actions—whether they do or do not promote people's interests, or cause happiness or misery—must be among the matters considered important. An ethical theory that did *not* have an important place for this would have no credibility at all. And, to the extent that these matters *are* seen as important, the argument from mercy will be compelling.

Second, it should be noted that the argument does *not* imply that euthanasia is justified *whenever* a patient says he can no longer endure pain. Suppose the doctor, or the family, knows that the painful condition can be cured, and that the patient's request to die is only a temporary irrational reaction, which he will later repudiate. It is entirely reasonable for them to take this into account, and to refuse the irrational request. The argument from mercy does not say otherwise; in such circumstances euthanasia would not promote his best interests, and would hardly be "merciful" at all. This should not be taken to mean, however, that such requests are always irrational, or that pain always destroys a patient's ability to make sensible choices. Sadly, some requests to die, in circumstances such as those of Stewart Alsop's roommate, are all too rational.

The Argument from the Golden Rule

"Do unto others as you would have them do unto you" is one of the oldest and most familiar moral maxims. Stated in just that way, it is not a very good maxim: suppose a sexual pervert, with fantasies of being raped, started treating others as he would like to be treated. We might not be happy with the results. Nevertheless, the idea behind the Golden Rule is a good one. Moral rules apply to everyone alike. You cannot say that you are justified in treating someone else in a certain way unless you are willing to admit that that person would be justified in treating *you* in that way if your positions were reversed.

Kant's moral philosophy is usually regarded as the major historical alternative to utilitarianism. Like the utilitarians, Kant sought to express all of morality in a single principle. Kant's principle may be viewed as a sophisticated version of the Golden Rule. He argued that we should act only on rules that we are willing to have applied universally; that is, we should behave as we would be willing to have *everyone* behave. Thus, the one supreme principle of morality, which he called the "Categorical Imperative," says:

> Act only according to that maxim which you can at the same time will to become a universal law.

What does this mean? When we are trying to decide whether to do a certain action, we must first ask what general rule we would be following if we did it. Then, we ask whether we would be willing for everyone to follow that rule, in similar circumstances. (This determines whether "the maxim of the act"— the rule we would be following—can be "willed" to be a "universal law.") If we would not be willing for the rule to be followed universally, then we should not follow it ourselves. Thus, if we are not willing for others to apply the rule to *us,* we ought not apply it to *them.*

In the eighteenth chapter of St. Matthew's gospel there is a story that perfectly illustrates this point. A man is owed money by another, who cannot pay, and so he has the debtor thrown into prison. But he himself owes money to the King and begs that *his* debt be forgiven. At first the King forgives the debt. However, when the King hears how this man has treated the one who owed him, he changes his mind and "delivers him unto the tormentors" until he can pay. The moral is clear: If you do not think that others should apply the rule "Don't forgive debts!" to *you,* then you should not apply it to others.

The application of this to the question of euthanasia is fairly obvious. Each of us is going to die some day, although most of us do not know when or how, and will probably have little choice in the matter. But suppose you were given a choice: suppose you were told that you would die in one of two ways, and were asked to choose between them. First, you could die quietly, and without pain, at the

age of eighty, from a fatal injection. Or second, you could choose to die at the age of eighty-plus-a-few-days of an affliction so painful that for those few days before death you would be reduced to howling like a dog, with your family standing helplessly by. It is hard to believe that anyone would choose to have a rule applied that would force upon him or her the second option—if, that is, they were making a choice based upon *their own preferences.* And if we would not want such a rule, which excludes euthanasia, applied to us, then we should not apply such a rule to others.

The contemporary British philosopher R. M. Hare has made the same point in a slightly different way. Hare tells the following (true) story:

> The driver of a petrol lorry was caught in an accident in which his tanker overturned and immediately caught fire. He himself was trapped in the cab and could not be freed. He therefore besought the bystanders to kill him by hitting him on the head, so that he would not roast to death. I think that somebody did this, but I do not know what happened in the courts afterwards.
>
> Now will you please all ask yourselves, as I have many times asked myself, what you wish that men should do to you if you were in the situation of that driver. I cannot believe that anybody who considered the matter seriously, as if he himself were going to be in that situation and had now to give instructions as to what rule the bystanders should follow, would say that the rule should be one ruling out euthanasia absolutely.

There is a considerable irony here. Kant was personally opposed to mercy-killing; he thought it contrary to reason. Yet his own Categorical Imperative seems to sanction it. The larger irony, however, is for those in the Christian Church who have for centuries opposed euthanasia. The article written by Professor Hare, from which the story of the lorry driver is taken, has the title "Euthanasia: A Christian View." According to the New Testament accounts, Jesus himself promulgated the Golden Rule as the supreme moral principle—"This is the Law and the Prophets," he said. But, as Hare points out, if this is the supreme principle of morality, then how can euthanasia be absolutely wrong? This seems to be another one of those instances in which the historical Church has strayed from the principles laid down by its founder. . . .

The Possibility of Unexpected Cures

Euthanasia may also be opposed on the grounds that we cannot really tell when a patient's condition is hopeless. There are cases in which patients have recovered even after doctors have given up hope; if those patients had been killed, it would have been tragic, for they would have been deprived of many additional years of life. According to this argument, euthanasia is unacceptable because we never know for certain that a patient's situation is hopeless. *Any so-called hopeless patient might defy the odds and recover.*

The argument has two sources: first, it draws some plausibility from the fact that doctors have sometimes made mistakes; and second, it trades on a naive view of the possibilities of medical research.

It must be admitted, of course, that doctors have sometimes made mistakes in labelling cases "hopeless," and so we should be cautious in any given instance before saying there is no chance of recovery. But it does not follow from the fact that physicians have *sometimes* been mistaken that they can *never* know for sure that a case is hopeless. That would be like saying that since some people have confused a Rolls-Royce with a Mercedes, no one can ever be certain which is which. In fact, doctors do sometimes know for sure that a patient cannot recover. There may be spontaneous remissions of cancer, for example, at a relatively early stage of the disease. But after the cancer has spread throughout the body and reached an advanced stage of development, there may truly be no hope whatever. Although there may be some doubt about some cases—and where there is doubt, perhaps euthanasia should not be considered—no one with the slightest medical knowledge could have had any doubt about Jack. He was going to die of that cancer, and that is all there is to it. No one has ever recovered from *that* condition, and doctors can explain exactly why this is so.

The argument from the possibility of unexpected cures sometimes takes a slightly different form, and appeals to a naive view of medical research. According to this view, researchers are continually exploring new possibilities of treating disease; and we never know when a new "miracle cure" for a previously untreatable disease might be discovered. Thus, if we grant a dying patient's request for euthanasia, we run the risk that the next day a cure for his condition might be discovered—"If only we had waited, he could have been saved," it may be said.

This argument will have little appeal to those more familiar with the realities of medical research. Progress in treating disease comes, not with the sudden and unexpected discovery of magical remedies, but from slow and painstaking investigation. Whether it is reasonable to hope for a "cure" depends on the particular case in question. In the case of some diseases, investigators may have promising results from some lines of inquiry; here, it may be reasonable to hold out some hope for a dying patient, *if* death can be postponed long enough. In other cases, we may be dealing with a disease that is getting very little attention from researchers, or the researchers investigating it may obviously be very far from achieving any impressive results. Here, it may be simply dishonest to tell a patient with only a short time to live that there is hope. Or again, it may be that even if a cure is found, it will do a particular patient no good because in him the disease is so far advanced that the "cure" would not help *him* even if it were found.

What, then, are we to conclude? We may certainly conclude that extreme care should be taken so as to avoid declaring a patient "hopeless" when there really is a chance of recovery; and we may perhaps conclude that in any case where there is the slightest doubt, euthanasia should not be considered. However, we may *not* conclude that doctors *never* know that a case is hopeless. Nor may we always hold out the hope of a "miracle cure." Sadly, we know that in some cases there is no hope, and in those cases the possibility of an unexpected cure cannot be offered as an objection to euthanasia.

QUESTIONS FOR REFLECTION

1. Summarize and evaluate Rachels's utilitarian argument from mercy.

2. How does Rachels use the Golden Rule to argue for the permissibility of euthanasia? Do you think he succeeds?

3. Why does Rachels reject the argument from unexpected cures?

4. Does it make any difference, from the perspective of any of Rachels's arguments, whether a patient is sentient or comatose? Whether a patient consents or does not consent? Whether a patient is terminal or not? Whether the doctor withholds potentially life-prolonging treatment, assists the patient in committing suicide, or kills the patient outright? Should it make any difference?

RONALD DWORKIN, THOMAS NAGEL, ROBERT NOZICK, JOHN RAWLS, THOMAS SCANLON, AND JUDITH JARVIS THOMSON

The Brief of the Amici Curiae

Ronald Dworkin and Thomas Nagel are Professors of Philosophy at New York University. Robert Nozick, John Rawls, and Thomas Scanlon are Professors of Philosophy at Harvard University. Judith Jarvis Thomson is Professor of Philosophy at the Massachusetts Institute of Technology. (Source: Reprinted from an amicus curiae ["friend of the Court"] brief submitted to the United States Supreme Court in the cases Washington v. Glucksberg *and* Vacco v. Quill, *1997. Notes have been omitted.)*

Argument

I. The Liberty Interest Asserted Here Is Protected by the Due Process Clause

Certain decisions are momentous in their impact on the character of a person's life—decisions about religious faith, political and moral allegiance, marriage, procreation, and death, for example. Such deeply personal decisions pose controversial questions about how and why human life has value. In a free society, individuals must be allowed to make those decisions for themselves, out of their own faith, conscience, and convictions. This Court has insisted, in a variety of contexts and circumstances, that this great freedom is among those protected by the Due Process Clause as essential to a community of "ordered liberty." *Palko* v. *Connecticut* (1937). In its recent decision in *Planned Parenthood* v. *Casey* (1992), the Court offered a paradigmatic statement of that principle:

> matters involving the most intimate and personal choices a person may make in a lifetime, choices central to a person's dignity and autonomy, are central to the liberty protected by the Fourteenth Amendment.

That declaration reflects an idea underlying many of our basic constitutional protections. As the Court explained in *West Virginia State Board of Education* v. *Barnette* (1943):

> If there is any fixed star in our constitutional constellation, it is that no official . . . can prescribe what shall be orthodox in politics, nationalism, religion, or other matters of opinion or force citizens to confess by word or act their faith therein.

A person's interest in following his own convictions at the end of life is so central a part of the more general right to make "intimate and personal choices" for himself that a failure to protect that particular interest would undermine the general right altogether. Death is, for each of us, among the most significant events of life. As the Chief Justice said in *Cruzan* v. *Missouri* (1990), "[t]he choice between life and death is a deeply personal decision of obvious and overwhelming finality." Most of us see death—whatever we think will follow it—as the final act of life's drama, and we want that last act to reflect our own convictions, those we have tried to live by, not the convictions of others forced on us in our most vulnerable moment.

Different people, of different religious and ethical beliefs, embrace very different convictions about which way of dying confirms and which contradicts the value of their lives. Some fight against death with every weapon their doctors can devise. Others will do nothing to hasten death even if they pray it will come soon. Still others, including the patient-plaintiffs in these cases, want to end their lives when they think that living on, in the only way they can, would disfigure rather than enhance the lives they had created. Some people make the latter choice not just to escape pain. Even if it were possible to eliminate all pain for a dying patient—and frequently that is not possible—that would not end or even much alleviate the anguish some would feel at remaining alive, but intubated, helpless, and often sedated near oblivion.

None of these dramatically different attitudes about the meaning of death can be dismissed as irrational. None should be imposed, either by the pressure of doctors or relatives or by the fiat of government, on people who reject it. Just as it would be intolerable for government to dictate that doctors never be permitted to try to keep someone alive as long as possible, when that is what the patient wishes, so it is intolerable for government to dictate that doctors may never, under any circumstances, help someone to die who believes that further life means only degradation. The Constitution insists that people must be free to make these deeply personal decisions for themselves and must not be forced to end their lives in a way that appalls them, just because that is what some majority thinks proper. . . .

III. State Interests Do Not Justify a Categorical Prohibition on All Assisted Suicide

The Solicitor General concedes that "a competent, terminally ill adult has a constitutionally cognizable liberty interest in avoiding the kind of suffering experienced by the plaintiffs in this case." He agrees that this interest extends not only to avoiding pain, but to avoiding an existence the patient believes to be one of intolerable indignity or incapacity as well. The Solicitor General argues, however, that states nevertheless have the right to "override" this liberty interest altogether, because a state could reasonably conclude that allowing doctors to assist in suicide, even under the most stringent regulations and procedures that could be devised, would unreasonably endanger the lives of a number of patients who might ask for death in circumstances when it is plainly not in their interests to die or when their consent has been improperly obtained.

This argument is unpersuasive, however, for at least three reasons. *First,* in *Cruzan,* this Court noted that its various decisions supported the recognition of a general liberty interest in refusing medical treatment, even when such refusal could result in death. The various risks described by the Solicitor General apply equally to those situations. For instance, a patient kept alive only by an elaborate and disabling life-support system might well become depressed, and doctors might be equally uncertain whether the depression is curable: such a patient might decide for death only because he has been advised that he will die soon anyway or that he will never live free of the burdensome apparatus, and either diagnosis might conceivably be mistaken. Relatives or doctors might subtly or crudely influence that decision, and state provision for the decision may (to the same degree in this case as if it allowed assisted suicide) be thought to encourage it.

Yet there has been no suggestion that states are incapable of addressing such dangers through regulation. In fact, quite the opposite is true. In *McKay* v. *Bergstedt* (1990), for example, the Nevada Supreme Court held that "competent adult patients desiring to refuse or discontinue medical treatment" must be examined by two non-attending physicians to determine whether the patient is mentally competent, understands his prognosis and treatment options, and appears free of coercion or pressure in making his decision. See also: *id.* (in the case of terminally ill patients with natural life expectancy of less than six months, [a] patient's right of self-determination shall be deemed to prevail over state interests, whereas [a] non-terminal patient's decision to terminate life-support systems must first be weighed against relevant state interests by trial judge); [and] *In re Farrell*

(1987) ([which held that a] terminally-ill patient requesting termination of life-support must be determined to be competent and properly informed about [his] prognosis, available treatment options and risks, and to have made the decision voluntarily and without coercion). Those protocols served to guard against precisely the dangers that the Solicitor General raises. The case law contains no suggestion that such protocols are inevitably insufficient to prevent deaths that should have been prevented.

Indeed, the risks of mistake are overall greater in the case of terminating life support. *Cruzan* implied that a state must allow individuals to make such decisions through an advance directive stipulating either that life support be terminated (or not initiated) in described circumstances when the individual was no longer competent to make such a decision himself, or that a designated proxy be allowed to make that decision. All the risks just described are present when the decision is made through or pursuant to such an advance directive, and a grave further risk is added: that the directive, though still in force, no longer represents the wishes of the patient. The patient might have changed his mind before he became incompetent, though he did not change the directive, or his proxy may make a decision that the patient would not have made himself if still competent. In *Cruzan,* this Court held that a state may limit these risks through reasonable regulation. It did not hold—or even suggest—that a state may avoid them through a blanket prohibition that, in effect, denies the liberty interest altogether.

Second, nothing in the record supports the [Solicitor General's] conclusion that no system of rules and regulations could adequately reduce the risk of mistake. As discussed above, the experience of states in adjudicating requests to have life-sustaining treatment removed indicates the opposite. The Solicitor General has provided no persuasive reason why the same sort of procedures could not be applied effectively in the case of a competent individual's request for physician-assisted suicide.

Indeed, several very detailed schemes for regulating physician-assisted suicide have been submitted to the voters of some states and one has been enacted. In addition, concerned groups, including a group of distinguished professors of law and other professionals, have drafted and defended such schemes. Such draft statutes propose a variety of protections and review procedures designed to insure against mistakes, and neither Washington nor New York attempted to show that such schemes would be porous or ineffective. Nor does the Solicitor General's brief: it relies instead mainly on flat and conclusory statements. It cites a New York Task Force report, written before the proposals just described were drafted, whose findings have been widely disputed and were implicitly rejected in the opinion of the Second Circuit below. The weakness of the Solicitor General's argument is signaled by his strong reliance on the experience in the Netherlands which, in effect, allows assisted suicide pursuant to published guidelines. The Dutch guidelines are more permissive than the proposed and model American statutes, however. The Solicitor General deems the Dutch practice of ending the lives of people like neonates who cannot consent particularly noteworthy, for example, but that practice could easily and effectively be made illegal by any state regulatory scheme without violating the Constitution.

The Solicitor General's argument would perhaps have more force if the question before the Court were simply whether a state has any rational basis for an absolute prohibition; if that were the question, then it might be enough to call attention to risks a state might well deem not worth running. But as the Solicitor General concedes, the question here is a very different one: whether a state has interests sufficiently compelling to allow it to take the extraordinary step of altogether refusing the exercise of a liberty interest of constitutional dimension. In those circumstances, the burden is plainly on the state to demonstrate that the risk of mistakes is very high, and that no alternative to complete prohibition would adequately and effectively reduce those risks. Neither of the Petitioners has made such a showing.

Nor could they. The burden of proof on any state attempting to show this would be very high. Consider, for example, the burden a state would have to meet to show that it was entitled altogether to ban public speeches in favor of unpopular causes because it could not guarantee, either by regulations short of an outright ban or by increased police protection, that such speeches would not provoke a riot that would result in serious injury or death to an innocent party. Or that it was entitled to deny those accused of crime the procedural rights that the Constitution guarantees, such as the right to a jury trial, because the security risk those rights would impose on the community would be too great. One can posit extreme circumstances in which some such argument would succeed. See, e.g., *Korematsu* v. *United States* (1944) (permitting United States to detain individuals of Japanese ancestry during wartime). But these circumstances would be extreme indeed, and the *Korematsu* ruling has been widely and severely criticized.

Third, it is doubtful whether the risks the Solicitor General cites are even of the right character to serve as justification for an absolute prohibition on the exercise of an important liberty interest. The risks fall into two groups. The first is the risk of medical mistake, including a misdiagnosis of competence or terminal illness. To be sure, no scheme of regulation, no matter how rigorous, can altogether guarantee that medical mistakes will not be made. But the Constitution does not allow a state to deny patients a great variety of important choices, for which informed consent is properly deemed necessary, just because the information on which the consent is given may, in spite of the most strenuous efforts to avoid mistake, be wrong. Again, these identical risks are present in decisions to terminate life support, yet they do not justify an absolute prohibition on the exercise of the right.

The second group consists of risks that a patient will be unduly influenced by considerations that the state might deem it not in his best interests to be swayed by, for example, the feelings and views of close family members. But what a patient regards as proper grounds for such a decision normally reflects exactly the judgments of personal ethics—of why his life is important and what affects its value—that patients have a crucial liberty interest in deciding for themselves. Even people who are dying have a right to hear and, if they wish, act on what others might wish to tell or suggest or even hint to them, and it would be dangerous to suppose that a state may prevent this on the ground that it knows better than its citizens when they should be moved by or yield to particular advice or suggestion in the exercise of their right to make fateful personal decisions for themselves. It is not a good reply that some people may not decide as they really wish—as they would decide, for example, if free from the "pressure" of others. That possibility could hardly justify the most serious pressure of all—the criminal law which tells

them that they may not decide for death if they need the help of a doctor in dying, no matter how firmly they wish it.

There is a fundamental infirmity in the Solicitor General's argument. He asserts that a state may reasonably judge that the risk of "mistake" to some persons justifies a prohibition that not only risks but ensures and even aims at what would undoubtedly be a vastly greater number of "mistakes" of the opposite kind—preventing many thousands of competent people who think that it disfigures their lives to continue living, in the only way left to them, from escaping that—to them—terrible injury. A state grievously and irreversibly harms such people when it prohibits that escape. The Solicitor General's argument may seem plausible to those who do not agree that individuals are harmed by being forced to live on in pain and what they regard as indignity. But many other people plainly do think that such individuals are harmed, and a state may not take one side in that essentially ethical or religious controversy as its justification for denying a crucial liberty.

Of course, a state has important interests that justify regulating physician-assisted suicide. It may be legitimate for a state to deny an opportunity for assisted suicide when it acts in what it reasonably judges to be the best interests of the potential suicide, and when its judgment on that issue does not rest on contested judgments about "matters involving the most intimate and personal choices a person may make in a lifetime, choices central to personal dignity and autonomy." *Casey.* A state might assert, for example, that people who are not terminally ill, but who have formed a desire to die, are, as a group, very likely later to be grateful if they are prevented from taking their own lives. It might then claim that it is legitimate, out of concern for such people, to deny any of them a doctor's assistance [in taking their own lives].

This Court need not decide now the extent to which such paternalistic interests might override an individual's liberty interest. No one can plausibly claim, however—and it is noteworthy that neither Petitioners nor the Solicitor General does claim—that any such prohibition could serve the interests of any significant number of terminally ill patients. On the contrary, any paternalistic justification for an absolute prohibition of assistance to such patients would of necessity appeal to a widely contested religious or ethical conviction many of them, including the patient-plaintiffs, reject. Allowing *that* justification to prevail would vitiate the liberty interest.

Even in the case of terminally ill patients, a state has a right to take all reasonable measures to ensure that a patient requesting such assistance has made an informed, competent, stable and uncoerced decision. It is plainly legitimate for a state to establish procedures through which professional and administrative judgments can be made about these matters, and to forbid doctors to assist in suicide when its reasonable procedures have not been satisfied. States may be permitted considerable leeway in designing such procedures. They may be permitted, within reason, to err on what they take to be the side of caution. But they may not use the bare possibility of error as justification for refusing to establish any procedures at all and relying instead on a flat prohibition.

Conclusion

Each individual has a right to make the "most intimate and personal choices central to personal dignity and autonomy." That right encompasses the right to exercise some control over the time and manner of one's death.

The patient-plaintiffs in these cases were all mentally competent individuals in the final phase of terminal illness and died within months of filing their claims.

Jane Doe described how her advanced cancer made even the most basic bodily functions such as swallowing, coughing, and yawning extremely painful and that it was "not possible for [her] to reduce [her] pain to an acceptable level of comfort and to retain an alert state." Faced with such circumstances, she sought to be able to "discuss freely with [her] treating physician [her] intention of hastening [her] death through the consumption of drugs prescribed for that purpose." *Quill* v. *Vacco* (2d Cir. 1996).

George A. Kingsley, in advanced stages of AIDS which included, among other hardships, the attachment of a tube to an artery in his chest which made even routine functions burdensome and the development of lesions on his brain, sought advice from his doctors regarding prescriptions which could hasten his impending death.

Jane Roe, suffering from cancer since 1988, had been almost completely bedridden since 1993 and experienced constant pain which could not be alleviated by medication. After undergoing counseling for herself and her family, she desired to hasten her death by taking prescription drugs. *Compassion in Dying* v. *Washington* (1994).

John Doe, who had experienced numerous AIDS-related ailments since 1991, was "especially cognizant of the suffering imposed by a lingering terminal illness because he was the primary caregiver for his long-term companion who died of AIDS" and sought prescription drugs from his physician to hasten his own death after entering the terminal phase of AIDS.

James Poe suffered from emphysema which caused him "a constant sensation of suffocating" as well as a cardiac condition which caused severe leg pain. Connected to an oxygen tank at all times but unable to calm the panic reaction associated with his feeling of suffocation even with regular doses of morphine, Mr. Poe sought physician-assisted suicide.

A state may not deny the liberty claimed by the patient-plaintiffs in these cases without providing them an opportunity to demonstrate, in whatever way the state might reasonably think wise and necessary, that the conviction they expressed for an early death is competent, rational, informed, stable, and uncoerced.

Affirming the decisions by the Courts of Appeals would establish nothing more than that there is such a constitutionally protected right in principle. It would establish only that some individuals, whose decisions for suicide plainly cannot be dismissed as irrational or foolish or premature, must be accorded a reasonable opportunity to show that their decision for death is informed and free. It is not necessary to decide precisely which patients are entitled to that opportunity. If, on the other hand, this Court reverses the decisions below, its decision could only be justified by the momentous proposition—a proposition flatly in conflict with the spirit and letter of the Court's past decisions—that an American citizen does not, after all, have the right, even in principle, to live and die in the light of his own religious and ethical beliefs, his own convictions about why his life is valuable and where its value lies.

QUESTIONS FOR REFLECTION

1. How do the philosophers argue that denying a right to physician-assisted suicide would undermine the general right to make "intimate and personal choices"? Do you find their argument convincing?

2. Would Mill's view in *On Liberty* support or contradict the philosophers' view on physician-assisted suicide? Explain.

3. Why do the philosophers find the possibility of error incapable of supporting a ban on euthanasia?

4. Many have alleged that allowing physician-assisted suicide would endanger the lives of patients who do not want to die. How do the philosophers respond to this argument?

5. Would Kant agree with the philosophers that facing death on something other than your own terms is an indignity? How would he view physician-assisted suicide?

CHIEF JUSTICE WILLIAM REHNQUIST

Majority Opinion in *Washington et al.*
v. *Glucksberg et al.* (1997)

(Source: 117 S.Ct. 2258 [1997]. Most legal references have been omitted.)

Chief Justice Rehnquist delivered the opinion of the Court.

The question presented in this case is whether Washington's prohibition against "caus[ing]" or "aid[ing]" a suicide offends the Fourteenth Amendment to the United States Constitution. We hold that it does not.

It has always been a crime to assist a suicide in the State of Washington. In 1854, Washington's first Territorial Legislature outlawed "assisting another in the commission of self-murder." Today, Washington law provides: "A person is guilty of promoting a suicide attempt when he knowingly causes or aids another person to attempt suicide." "Promoting a suicide attempt" is a felony, punishable by up to five years' imprisonment and up to a $10,000 fine. At the same time, Washington's Natural Death Act, enacted in 1979, states that the "withholding or withdrawal of life-sustaining treatment" at a patient's direction "shall not, for any purpose, constitute a suicide." . . .

I

We begin, as we do in all due-process cases, by examining our Nation's history, legal traditions, and practices. In almost every State—indeed, in almost every western democracy—it is a crime to assist a suicide. The States' assisted-suicide bans are not innovations. Rather, they are longstanding expressions of the States' commitment to the protection and preservation of all human life. *Cruzan* ("[T]he States —indeed, all civilized nations—demonstrate their commitment to life by treating homicide as a serious crime. Moreover, the majority of States in this country have laws imposing criminal penalties on one who assists another to commit suicide"); see *Stanford v. Kentucky* (1989) ("[T]he primary and most reliable indication of [a national] consensus is . . . the pattern of enacted laws"). Indeed, opposition to and condemnation of suicide—and, therefore, of assisting suicide—are consistent and enduring themes of our philosophical, legal, and cultural heritages.

More specifically, for over 700 years, the Anglo-American common-law tradition has punished or otherwise disapproved of both suicide and assisting suicide. *Cruzan* (Scalia, J., concurring). In the 13th century, Henry de Bracton, one of the first legal-treatise writers, observed that "[j]ust as a man may commit felony by slaying another so may he do so by slaying himself." The real and personal property of one who killed himself to avoid conviction and punishment for a crime were forfeit to the king; however, thought Bracton, "if a man slays himself in weariness of life or because he is unwilling to endure further bodily pain . . . [only] his movable goods [were] confiscated." Thus, "[t]he principle that suicide of a sane person, for whatever reason, was a punishable felony was . . . introduced into English common law." Centuries later, Sir William Blackstone, whose *Commentaries on the Laws of England* not only provided a definitive summary of the common law but was also a primary legal authority for 18th and 19th-century

American lawyers, referred to suicide as "self-murder" and "the pretended heroism, but real cowardice, of the Stoic philosophers, who destroyed themselves to avoid those ills which they had not the fortitude to endure. . . ." Blackstone emphasized that "the law has . . . ranked [suicide] among the highest crimes," *ibid,* although, anticipating later developments, he conceded that the harsh and shameful punishments imposed for suicide "borde[r] a little upon severity."

For the most part, the early American colonies adopted the common-law approach. . . .

That suicide remained a grievous, though nonfelonious, wrong is confirmed by the fact that colonial and early state legislatures and courts did not retreat from prohibiting assisting suicide. . . .

The earliest American statute explicitly to outlaw assisting suicide was enacted in New York in 1828, and many of the new States and Territories followed New York's example. Between 1857 and 1865, a New York commission led by Dudley Field drafted a criminal code that prohibited "aiding" a suicide and, specifically, "furnish[ing] another person with any deadly weapon or poisonous drug, knowing that such person intends to use such weapon or drug in taking his own life." By the time the Fourteenth Amendment was ratified, it was a crime in most States to assist a suicide. . . .

Though deeply rooted, the States' assisted-suicide bans have in recent years been reexamined and, generally, reaffirmed. Because of advances in medicine and technology, Americans today are increasingly likely to die in institutions, from chronic illnesses. Public concern and democratic action are therefore sharply focused on how best to protect dignity and independence at the end of life, with the result that there have been many significant changes in state laws and in the attitudes these laws reflect. Many States, for example, now permit "living wills," surrogate health-care decisionmaking, and the withdrawal or refusal of life-sustaining medical treatment. At the same time, however, voters and legislators continue for the most part to reaffirm their States' prohibitions on assisting suicide.

The Washington statute at issue in this case was enacted in 1975 as part of a revision of that State's criminal code. Four years later, Washington passed its Natural Death Act, which specifically stated that the "withholding or withdrawal of life-sustaining treatment . . . shall not, for any purpose, constitute a suicide" and that "[n]othing in this chapter shall be construed to condone, authorize, or approve mercy killing . . . ." In 1991, Washington voters rejected a ballot initiative which, had it passed, would have permitted a form of physician-assisted suicide. Washington then added a provision to the Natural Death Act expressly excluding physician-assisted suicide.

California voters rejected an assisted-suicide initiative similar to Washington's in 1993. On the other hand, in 1994, voters in Oregon enacted, also through ballot initiative, that State's "Death with Dignity Act," which legalized physician-assisted suicide for competent, terminally ill adults. Since the Oregon vote, many proposals to legalize assisted suicide have been and continue to be introduced in the States' legislatures, but none has been enacted. And just last year, Iowa and Rhode Island joined the overwhelming majority of States explicitly prohibiting assisted suicide. Also, on April 30, 1997, President Clinton signed the Federal Assisted Suicide Funding Restriction Act of 1997, which prohibits the use of federal funds in support of physician-assisted suicide.

Thus, the States are currently engaged in serious, thoughtful examinations of physician-assisted suicide and other similar issues. For example, New York State's Task Force on Life and the Law—an ongoing, blue-ribbon commission composed of doctors, ethicists, lawyers, religious leaders, and interested laymen—was convened in 1984 and commissioned with "a broad mandate to recommend public policy on issues raised by medical advances." Over the past decade, the Task Force has recommended laws relating to end-of-life decisions, surrogate pregnancy, and organ donation. After studying physician-assisted suicide, however, the Task Force unanimously concluded that "[l]egalizing assisted suicide and euthanasia would pose profound risks to many individuals who are ill and vulnerable. . . . [T]he potential dangers of this dramatic change in public policy would outweigh any benefit that might be achieved."

Attitudes toward suicide itself have changed since Bracton, but our laws have consistently condemned, and continue to prohibit, assisting suicide. Despite changes in medical technology and notwithstanding an increased emphasis on the importance of end-of-life decisionmaking, we have not retreated from this prohibition. Against this backdrop of history, tradition, and practice, we now turn to respondents' constitutional claim.

II

The Due Process Clause guarantees more than fair process, and the "liberty" it protects includes more than the absence of physical restraint. The Clause also provides heightened protection against government interference with certain fundamental rights and liberty interests. In a long line of cases, we have held that, in addition to the specific freedoms protected by the Bill of Rights, the "liberty" specially protected by the Due Process Clause includes the rights to marry, to have children, to direct the education and upbringing of one's children, to marital privacy, to use contraception, to bodily integrity, and to abortion. We have also assumed, and strongly suggested, that the Due Process Clause protects the traditional right to refuse unwanted lifesaving medical treatment.

But we "ha[ve] always been reluctant to expand the concept of substantive due process because guideposts for responsible decisionmaking in this unchartered area are scarce and open-ended." By extending constitutional protection to an asserted right or liberty interest, we, to a great extent, place the matter outside the arena of public debate and legislative action. We must therefore "exercise the utmost care whenever we are asked to break new ground in this field," lest the liberty protected by the Due Process Clause be subtly transformed into the policy preferences of the members of this Court.

Our established method of substantive-due-process analysis has two primary features: First, we have regularly observed that the Due Process Clause specially protects those fundamental rights and liberties which are, objectively, "deeply rooted in this Nation's history and tradition," and "implicit in the concept of ordered liberty," such that "neither liberty nor justice would exist if they were sacrificed," *Palko v. Connecticut* (1937). Second, we have required in substantive-due-process cases a "careful description" of the asserted fundamental liberty interest. Our Nation's history, legal traditions, and practices thus provide the crucial "guideposts for responsible decisionmaking," that direct and restrain our exposition of the Due Process Clause. As we stated recently in *Flores,* the Fourteenth Amendment "forbids the government to infringe . . . 'fundamental' liberty interests at all, no matter what process is provided, unless the infringement is narrowly tailored to serve a compelling state interest."

Justice Souter, relying on Justice Harlan's dissenting opinion in *Poe v. Ullman,* would largely abandon this restrained methodology, and instead ask "whether [Washington's] statute sets up one of those 'arbitrary impositions' or 'purposeless restraints' at odds with the Due Process Clause of the Fourteenth Amendment." In our view, however, the development of this Court's substantive-due-process jurisprudence, described briefly above, has been a process whereby the outlines of the "liberty" specially protected by the Fourteenth Amendment—never fully clarified, to be sure, and perhaps not capable of being fully clarified—have at least been carefully refined by concrete examples involving fundamental rights found to be deeply rooted in our legal tradition. This approach tends to rein in the subjective elements that are necessarily present in due-process judicial review. In addition, by establishing a threshold requirement—that a challenged state action implicate a fundamental right—before requiring more than a reasonable relation to a legitimate state interest to justify the action, it avoids the need for complex balancing of competing interests in every case.

Turning to the claim at issue here, the Court of Appeals stated that "[p]roperly analyzed, the first issue to be resolved is whether there is a liberty interest in determining the time and manner of one's death," or, in other words, "[i]s there a right to die?" Similarly, respondents assert a "liberty to choose how to die" and a right to "control of one's final days," and describe the asserted liberty as "the right to choose a humane, dignified death," and "the liberty to shape death." As noted above, we have a tradition of carefully formulating the interest at stake in substantive-due-process cases. For example, although *Cruzan* is often described as a "right to die" case, we were, in fact, more precise: we assumed that the Constitution granted competent persons a "constitutionally protected right to refuse lifesaving hydration and nutrition." *Cruzan* (O'Connor, J., concurring) ("[A] liberty interest in refusing unwanted medical treatment may be inferred from our prior decisions"). The Washington statute at issue in this case prohibits "aid[ing] another person to attempt suicide," and, thus, the question before us is whether the "liberty" specially protected by the Due Process Clause includes a right to commit suicide which itself includes a right to assistance in doing so.

We now inquire whether this asserted right has any place in our Nation's traditions. Here, as discussed above, we are confronted with a consistent and almost universal tradition that has long rejected the asserted right, and continues explicitly to reject it today, even for terminally ill, mentally competent adults. To hold for respondents, we would have to reverse centuries of legal doctrine and practice, and strike down the considered policy choice of almost every State. . . .

The history of the law's treatment of assisted suicide in this country has been and continues to be one of the rejection of nearly all efforts to permit it. That being the case, our decisions lead us to conclude that the asserted "right" to assistance in committing suicide is not a fundamental liberty interest protected by the Due Process Clause. The Constitution also requires, however, that Washington's assisted-suicide ban be rationally related to legitimate government interests. This requirement is unquestionably met here. As the court below recognized, Washington's assisted-suicide ban implicates a number of state interests.

First, Washington has an "unqualified interest in the preservation of human life." *Cruzan.* The State's prohibition on assisted suicide, like all homicide laws, both reflects and advances its commitment to this interest. This interest is symbolic and aspirational as well as practical:

> While suicide is no longer prohibited or penalized, the ban against assisted suicide and euthanasia shores up the notion of limits in human relationships. It reflects the gravity with which we view the decision to take one's own life or the life of another, and our reluctance to encourage or promote these decisions.—New York Task Force.

Respondents admit that "[t]he State has a real interest in preserving the lives of those who can still contribute to society and enjoy life." The Court of Appeals also recognized Washington's interest in protecting life, but held that the "weight" of this interest depends on the "medical condition and the wishes of the person whose life is at stake." Washington, however, has rejected this sliding-scale approach and, through its assisted-suicide ban, insists that all persons' lives, from beginning to end, regardless of physical or mental condition, are under the full protection of the law. As we have previously affirmed, the States "may properly decline to make judgments about the 'quality' of life that a particular individual may enjoy," *Cruzan.* This remains true, as *Cruzan* makes clear, even for those who are near death.

Relatedly, all admit that suicide is a serious public-health problem, especially among persons in otherwise vulnerable groups. The State has an interest in preventing suicide, and in studying, identifying, and treating its causes.

Those who attempt suicide—terminally ill or not—often suffer from depression or other mental disorders. Research indicates, however, that many people who request physician-assisted suicide withdraw that request if their depression and pain are treated. The New York Task Force, however, expressed its concern that, because depression is difficult to diagnose, physicians and medical professionals often fail to respond adequately to seriously ill patients' needs. Thus, legal physician-assisted suicide could make it more difficult for the State to protect depressed or mentally ill persons, or those who are suffering from untreated pain, from suicidal impulses.

The State also has an interest in protecting the integrity and ethics of the medical profession. In contrast to the Court of Appeals' conclusion that "the integrity of the medical profession would [not] be threatened in any way by [physician-assisted suicide]," the American Medical Association, like many other medical and physicians' groups, has concluded that "[p]hysician-assisted suicide is fundamentally incompatible with the physician's role as healer." And physician-assisted suicide could, it is argued, undermine the trust that is essential to the doctor-patient relationship by blurring the time-honored line between healing and harming.

Next, the State has an interest in protecting vulnerable groups—including the poor, the elderly, and disabled persons—from abuse, neglect, and mistakes. The Court of Appeals dismissed the State's concern that disadvantaged persons might be pressured into physician-assisted suicide as "ludicrous on its face." We have recognized, however, the real risk of subtle coercion and undue influence in end-of-life situations. *Cruzan*. Similarly, the New York Task Force warned that "[l]egalizing physician-assisted suicide would pose profound risks to many individuals who are ill and vulnerable. . . . The risk of harm is greatest for the many individuals in our society whose autonomy and well-being are already compromised by poverty, lack of access to good medical care, advanced age, or membership in a stigmatized social group." If physician-assisted suicide were permitted, many might resort to it to spare their families the substantial financial burden of end-of-life health-care costs.

The State's interest here goes beyond protecting the vulnerable from coercion; it extends to protecting disabled and terminally ill people from prejudice, negative and inaccurate stereotypes, and "societal indifference." The State's assisted-suicide ban reflects and reinforces its policy that the lives of terminally ill, disabled, and elderly people must be no less valued than the lives of the young and healthy, and that a seriously disabled person's suicidal impulses should be interpreted and treated the same way as anyone else's.

Finally, the State may fear that permitting assisted suicide will start it down the path to voluntary and perhaps even involuntary euthanasia. The Court of Appeals struck down Washington's assisted-suicide ban only "as applied to competent, terminally ill adults who wish to hasten their deaths by obtaining medication prescribed by their doctors." Washington insists, however, that the impact of the court's decision will not and cannot be so limited. If suicide is protected as a matter of constitutional right, it is argued, "every man and woman in the United States must enjoy it." The Court of Appeals' decision, and its expansive reasoning, provide ample support for the State's concerns. The court noted, for example, that the "decision of a duly appointed surrogate decision maker is for all legal purposes the decision of the patient himself"; that "in some instances, the patient may be unable to self-administer the drugs and . . . administration by the physician . . . may be the only way the patient may be able to receive them"; and that not only physicians, but also family members and loved ones, will inevitably participate in assisting suicide. Thus, it turns out that what is couched as a limited right to "physician-assisted suicide" is likely, in effect, a much broader license, which could prove extremely difficult to police and contain. Washington's ban on assisting suicide prevents such erosion.

This concern is further supported by evidence about the practice of euthanasia in the Netherlands. The Dutch government's own study revealed that in 1990, there were 2,300 cases of voluntary euthanasia (defined as "the deliberate termination of another's life at his request"), 400 cases of assisted suicide, and more than 1,000 cases of euthanasia without an explicit request. In addition to these latter 1,000 cases, the study found an additional 4,941 cases where physicians administered lethal morphine overdoses without the patients' explicit consent. This study suggests that, despite the existence of various reporting procedures, euthanasia in the Netherlands has not been limited to competent, terminally ill adults who are enduring physical suffering, and that regulation of the practice may not have prevented abuses in cases involving vulnerable persons, including severely disabled neonates and elderly persons suffering from dementia. The New York Task Force, citing the Dutch experience, observed that "assisted suicide and euthanasia are closely linked," and concluded that the "risk of . . . abuse is neither speculative nor distant." Washington, like most other States, reasonably ensures against this risk by banning, rather than regulating, assisting suicide.

We need not weigh exactly the relative strengths of these various interests. They are unquestionably important and legitimate, and Washington's ban on assisted suicide is at least reasonably related to their promotion and protection. We therefore hold that Wash. Rev. Code §9A.36.060(1) (1994) does not violate the Fourteenth Amendment, either on its face or "as applied to competent, terminally ill adults who wish to hasten their deaths by obtaining medication prescribed by their doctors."

Throughout the Nation, Americans are engaged in an earnest and profound debate about the morality, legality, and practicality of physician-assisted suicide. Our holding permits this debate to continue, as it should in a democratic society. The decision of the *en banc* Court of Appeals is reversed, and the case is remanded for further proceedings consistent with this opinion.

QUESTIONS FOR REFLECTION

1. How is the history of prohibition on suicide and assisted suicide relevant to the Court's decision?

2. What philosophical view of rights would most closely correspond to the attitude the Court adopts?

3. What rationales does the Court find for prohibiting physician-assisted suicide?

4. How does the Court's decision respond to the philosophers' argument that people have the right to make "intimate and personal choices?"

5. Does the Court's decision depend on the distinction between killing and letting die?

CAPITAL PUNISHMENT

Ordinarily, we think that people have a right to life and that governments, if they have any obligations at all, are obliged to protect that right. But many people believe that the government is nevertheless justified in putting certain kinds of criminals to death. Generally, they believe that the government needs to deprive some people of the right to life in order to protect that right for others—indeed, for the vast majority of its citizens. From this belief arises the issue of capital punishment: Can the government be justified in putting someone to death?

The death penalty raises important questions about the origin, status, and extent of the right to life. Most people believe that they have the right to defend themselves against an assailant. They believe, in particular, that they have the right to kill an attacker if their own lives are in danger. Some philosophers have extended this reasoning to the state as a whole. The murderer, for example, can be seen as attacking society; society is justified in using lethal force to defend itself. Of course, once apprehended, the murderer no longer threatens society in quite the same way. But if murderers are likely to murder again, the self-protection argument may apply. This strategy argues that the right to life is limited so that those who threaten death to others lose their own right to life or, at least, deserve to have it overridden by the rights of others.

Other philosophers have argued in favor of a right to revenge. Society, having suffered a serious harm, has the right to take retribution by punishing the offender. Moreover, the punishment that seems appropriate for causing death is suffering death. They have thus maintained that justice sometimes requires the death penalty.

Still others have stressed deterrence as a justification for capital punishment. Putting a criminal to death, in this view, deters others from committing similar crimes. Enforcing the death penalty thus promotes the good of society; it may save more lives than it costs. Statistical studies of the effects of capital punishment tend to be inconclusive; it is not clear whether the death penalty actually has this effect. But some studies report that each execution saves several lives by deterring prospective murderers.

These arguments raise large issues beyond those involving the right to life itself. What rights does society have to defend itself against criminal activity? What is the moral justification for punishment? When can the interests of a larger group justify violating the rights of an individual? Under what circumstances does a person lose or surrender rights? In each case, arguments for and against capital punishment take or presuppose controversial stands.

In *Furman* v. *Georgia,* in 1972, the Supreme Court held that a Georgia capital punishment law was unconstitutional. The Court found that the death penalty, under the circumstances of its application there, was incompatible with human dignity and violated the Eighth Amendment prohibiting "cruel and unusual" punishment. Some members of the Court argued that the death penalty was in itself objectionable. The majority, however, concluded simply that its application was too haphazard, unprincipled, and unjust to count as constitutional.

In *Gregg* v. *Georgia,* four years later, the Court upheld Georgia's revision of its capital punishment law. Under that revision, the jury receives detailed instructions about the appropriateness of the death penalty. Certain kinds of circumstances are aggravating, tending to justify the death penalty; others are mitigating, tending to justify an alternative sentence. The Court decided that the death penalty, administered in this way, is constitutionally acceptable.

Strictly speaking, these decisions rest on legal rather than moral grounds. They are not, however, morally irrelevant. Cruel and unusual punishments are ethically as well as legally objectionable. Consequently, the legal arguments of the justices in these cases parallel moral arguments about the permissibility of capital punishment.

Hugo Adam Bedau advances several different arguments against the death penalty. He affirms the *Furman* Court's arguments that capital punishment is cruel, arbitrary, discriminatory, incompatible with human dignity, and ineffective as a deterrent. The changes wrought by *Gregg* do not alter these points. In addition, he contends that the death penalty is wrong for just the same reason that murder itself is wrong: It demonstrates disrespect for human life. When the government shows such disrespect, the consequences for society are far worse than when an individual does so.

Albert Camus also argues that the death penalty fails to deter crime. He adds, moreover, that no one deserves it; no victims are imprisoned for months or years before finally being murdered. He doubts that any government ought to be trusted with the decision to put some people to death.

William Tucker, in contrast, argues that the death penalty does deter murder—specifically felony or stranger murder. Without capital punishment, it is rational for a thief or rapist to kill the victim, who is also the chief witness to the crime.

Ernest van den Haag goes beyond typical defenses of capital punishment in at least two ways. First, he argues that deterrence provides an argument for the death penalty, even if we cannot determine whether it succeeds in deterring or not. If there is a chance that it does, he contends, then we place innocent lives at risk by failing to carry it out. Second, he argues that certain special cases justify capital punishment, even if it is unacceptable in most cases. Thus, we may be justified in executing war criminals and criminals who murder in prison while already serving life terms, even if we are not justified in executing most murderers.

ALBERT CAMUS

from *Reflections on the Guillotine*

Albert Camus was born in Algeria but lived most of his life in France. His essays, novels, and philosophical works established him as a leader of the existentialist movement. (Source: from Albert Camus, "Reflections on the Guillotine," in Reason, Rebellion, and Death [New York: Knopf, 1961]. Copyright © 1960 by Alfred A. Knopf. Reprinted by permission.)

. . .We all know that the great argument of those who defend capital punishment is the exemplary value of the punishment. Heads are cut off not only to punish but to intimidate, by a frightening example, any who might be tempted to imitate the guilty. Society is not taking revenge; it merely wants to forestall. It waves the head in the air so that potential murderers will see their fate and recoil from it.

This argument would be impressive if we were not obliged to note:

1. that society itself does not believe in the exemplary value it talks about;

2. that there is no proof that the death penalty ever made a single murderer recoil when he had made up his mind, whereas clearly it had no effect but one of fascination on thousands of criminals;

3. that, in other regards, it constitutes a repulsive example, the consequences of which cannot be foreseen.

To begin with, society does not believe in what it says. If it really believed what it says, it would exhibit the heads. Society would give executions the benefit of the publicity it generally uses for national bond issues or new brands of drinks. But we know that executions in our country, instead of taking place publicly, are now perpetrated in prison courtyards before a limited number of specialists. . . .

But, after all, why should society believe in that example when it does not stop crime, when its effects, if they exist, are invisible? To begin with, capital punishment could not intimidate the man who doesn't know that he is going to kill, who makes up his mind to it in a flash and commits his crime in a state of frenzy or obsession, nor the man who, going to an appointment to have it out with someone, takes along a weapon to frighten the faithless one or the opponent and uses it although he didn't want to or didn't think he wanted to. In other words, it could not intimidate the man who is hurled into crime as if into a calamity. This is tantamount to saying that it is powerless in the majority of cases. It is only fair to point out that in our country capital punishment is rarely applied in such cases. But the word "rarely" itself makes one shudder.

Does it frighten at least that race of criminals on whom it claims to operate and who live off crime? Nothing is less certain. We can read in Koestler that at a time when pickpockets were executed in England, other pickpockets exercised their talents in the crowd surrounding the scaffold where their colleague was being hanged. Statistics drawn up at the beginning of the century in England show that out of 250 who were hanged, 170 had previously attended one or more executions. And in 1886, out of 167 condemned men who had gone through Bristol prison, 164 had witnessed at least one execution. . . .

. . .For centuries the death penalty, often accompanied by barbarous refinements, has been trying to hold crime in check; yet crime persists. Why? Because the instincts that are warring in man are not, as the law claims, constant forces in a state of equilibrium. They are variable forces constantly waxing and waning, and their repeated lapses from equilibrium nourish the life of the mind as electrical oscillations, when close enough, set up a current. Just imagine the series of oscillations, from desire to lack of appetite, from decision to renunciation, through which each of us passes in a single day, multiply these variations infinitely, and you will have an idea of psychological proliferation. Such lapses from equilibrium are generally too fleeting to allow a single force to dominate the whole being. But it may happen that one of the soul's forces breaks loose until it fills the whole field of consciousness; at such a moment no instinct, not even that of life, can oppose the tyranny of that irresistible force. For capital punishment to be really intimidating, human nature would have to be different; it would have to be as stable and serene as the law itself. But then human nature would be dead.

It is not dead. This is why, however surprising this may seem to anyone who has never observed or directly experienced human complexity, the murderer, most of the time, feels innocent when he kills. Every criminal acquits himself before he is judged. He considers himself, if not within his right, at least excused by circumstances. He does not think nor foresee; when he thinks, it is to foresee that he will be forgiven altogether or in part. How could he fear what he considers highly improbable? He will fear death after the verdict but not before the crime. Hence the law, to be intimidating, should leave the murderer no chance, should be implacable in advance and particularly admit no extenuating circumstance. But who among us would dare ask this?

If anyone did, it would still be necessary to take into account another paradox of human nature. If the instinct to live is fundamental, it is no more so than another instinct of which the academic psychologists do not speak: the death instinct, which at certain moments calls for the destruction of oneself and of others. It is probable that the desire to kill often coincides with the desire to die or to annihilate oneself.* Thus, the instinct for self-preservation is matched, in variable proportions, by the instinct for destruction. The latter is the only way of explaining altogether the various perversions which, from alcoholism to drugs, lead an individual to his death while he knows full well what is happening. Man wants to live, but it is useless to hope that this desire will dictate all his actions. He also wants to be nothing; he wants the irreparable, and death for its own sake. So it happens that the criminal wants not only the crime but the suffering that goes with it, even (one might say, especially) if that suffering is exceptional. When that odd desire grows and becomes dominant, the prospect of being put to death not only fails to stop the criminal, but probably even adds to the vertigo in which he swoons. Thus, in a way, he kills in order to die.

Such peculiarities suffice to explain why a penalty that seems calculated to frighten normal minds is in reality altogether unrelated to ordinary psychology. All statistics without exception, those concerning countries that have abolished execution as well as the others, show that there is no connection between the abolition of the death penalty and criminality.† Criminal statistics neither increase nor decrease. The guillotine exists, and so does crime; between the two there is no other apparent connection than that of the law. All we can conclude from the figures, set down at length in statistical tables, is this: for centuries crimes other than murder were punished with death, and the supreme punishment, repeated over and over again, did not do away with any of those crimes. For centuries now, those crimes have no longer been punished with death. Yet they have not increased; in fact, some of them have decreased. Similarly, murder has been punished with execution for centuries and yet the race of Cain has not disappeared. Finally, in the thirty-three nations that have abolished the death penalty or no longer use it, the number of murders has not increased. Who could

---

* It is possible to read every week in the papers of criminals who originally hesitated between killing themselves and killing others.
† Report of the English Select Committee of 1930 and of the English Royal Commission that recently resumed the study: "All the statistics we have examined confirm the fact that abolition of the death penalty has not provoked an increase in the number of crimes."

deduce from this that capital punishment is really intimidating?

Conservatives cannot deny these facts or these figures. Their only and final reply is significant. They explain the paradoxical attitude of a society that so carefully hides the executions it claims to be exemplary. "Nothing proves, indeed," say the conservatives, "that the death penalty is exemplary; as a matter of fact, it is certain that thousands of murderers have not been intimidated by it. But there is no way of knowing those it has intimidated; consequently, nothing proves that it is not exemplary." Thus, the greatest of punishments, the one that involves the last dishonor for the condemned and grants the supreme privilege to society, rests on nothing but an unverifiable possibility. Death, on the other hand, does not involve degrees or probabilities. It solidifies all things, culpability and the body, in a definitive rigidity. Yet it is administered among us in the name of chance and a calculation. Even if that calculation were reasonable, should there not be a certainty to authorize the most certain of deaths? However, the condemned is cut in two, not so much for the crime he committed but by virtue of all the crimes that might have been and were not committed, that can be and will not be committed. The most sweeping uncertainty in this case authorizes the most implacable certainty.

I am not the only one to be amazed by such a dangerous contradiction. Even the State condemns it, and such bad conscience explains in turn the contradiction of its own attitude. The State divests its executions of all publicity because it cannot assert, in the face of facts, that they ever served to intimidate criminals. The State cannot escape the dilemma Beccaria described when he wrote: "If it is important to give the people proofs of power often, then executions must be frequent; but crimes will have to be frequent too, and this will prove that the death penalty does not make the complete impression that it should, whence it results that it is both useless and necessary." What can the State do with a penalty that is useless and necessary, except to hide it without abolishing it? The State will keep it then, a little out of the way, not without embarrassment, in the blind hope that one man at least, one day at least, will be stopped from his murderous gesture by thought of the punishment and, without anyone's ever knowing it, will justify a law that has neither reason nor expe-

rience in its favor. In order to continue claiming that the guillotine is exemplary, the State is consequently led to multiply very real murders in the hope of avoiding a possible murder which, as far as it knows or ever will know, may never be perpetuated. An odd law, to be sure, which knows the murder it commits and will never know the one it prevents. . . .

A punishment that penalizes without forestalling is indeed called revenge. It is a quasi-arithmetical reply made by society to whoever breaks its primordial law. That reply is as old as man; it is called the law of retaliation. Whoever has done me harm must suffer harm; whoever has put out my eye must lose an eye; and whoever has killed must die. This is an emotion, and a particularly violent one, not a principle. Retaliation is related to nature and instinct, not to law. Law, by definition, cannot obey the same rules as nature. If murder is in the nature of man, the law is not intended to imitate or reproduce that nature. It is intended to correct it. . . .

Let us leave aside the fact that the law of retaliation is inapplicable and that it would seem just as excessive to punish the incendiary by setting fire to his house as it would be insufficient to punish the thief by deducting from his bank account a sum equal to his theft. Let us admit that it is just and necessary to compensate for the murder of the victim by the death of the murderer. But beheading is not simply death. It is just as different, in essence, from the privation of life as a concentration camp is from prison. It is a murder, to be sure, and one that arithmetically pays for the murder committed. But it adds to death a rule, a public premeditation known to the future victim, an organization, in short, which is in itself a source of moral sufferings more terrible than death. Hence there is no equivalence. Many laws consider a premeditated crime more serious than a crime of pure violence. But what then is capital punishment but the most premeditated of murders, to which no criminal's deed, however calculated it may be, can be compared? For there to be equivalence, the death penalty would have to punish a criminal who had warned his victim of the date at which he would inflict a horrible death on him and who, from that moment onward, had confined him at his mercy for months. Such a monster is not encountered in private life.

There, too, when our official jurists talk of putting to death without causing suffering, they don't know what they are talking about and, above all, they lack imagination. The devastating, degrading fear that is imposed on the condemned for months or years is a punishment more terrible than death, and one that was not imposed on the victim. Even in the fright caused by the mortal violence being done to him, most of the time the victim is hastened to his death without knowing what is happening to him. The period of horror is counted out with his life, and hope of escaping the madness that has swept down upon that life probably never leaves him. On the other hand, the horror is parceled out to the man who is condemned to death. Torture through hope alternates with the pangs of animal despair. The lawyer and chaplain, out of mere humanity, and the jailers, so that the condemned man will keep quiet, are unanimous in assuring him that he will be reprieved. He believes this with all his being and then he ceases to believe it. He hopes by day and despairs of it by night. As the weeks pass, hope and despair increase and become equally unbearable. According to all accounts, the color of the skin changes, fear acting like an acid. "Knowing that you are going to die is nothing," said a condemned man in Fresnes. "But not knowing whether or not you are going to live, that's terror and anguish." Cartouche said of the supreme punishment: "Why, it's just a few minutes that have to be lived through." But it is a matter of months, not of minutes. Long in advance the condemned man knows that he is going to be killed and that the only thing that can save him is a reprieve, rather similar, for him, to the decrees of heaven. In any case, he cannot intervene, make a plea himself, or convince. Everything goes on outside of him. He is no longer a man but a thing waiting to be handled by the executioners. He is kept as if he were inert matter, but he still has a consciousness which is his chief enemy. . . .

In relation to crime, how can our civilization be defined? The reply is easy: for thirty years now, State crimes have been far more numerous than individual crimes. I am not even speaking of wars, general or localized, although bloodshed too is an alcohol that eventually intoxicates like the headiest of wines. But the number of individuals killed directly by the State has assumed astronomical proportions and infinitely outnumbers private murders. There are fewer and fewer condemned by common law and more and more condemned for political reasons. The proof is that each of us, however honorable he may be, can foresee the possibility of being someday condemned to death, whereas that eventuality would have seemed ridiculous at the beginning of the century. Alphonse Karr's witty remark: "Let the noble assassins begin" has no meaning now. Those who cause the most blood to flow are the same ones who believe they have right, logic, and history on their side.

Hence our society must now defend herself not so much against the individual as against the State. . . .

QUESTIONS FOR REFLECTION

1. Why does Camus reject the argument from deterrence?

2. How might Locke or van den Haag respond to Camus's arguments?

3. Why, according to Camus, does carrying out the death penalty trap the State in a contradiction?

4. Why is execution a more severe harm than a typical murder, according to Camus? Do you agree?

5. Camus does not trust the State to make decisions about life and death. Why?

JUSTICE WILLIAM BRENNAN

Concurring Opinion in *Furman* v. *Georgia* (1972)

William Brennan was Justice of the United States Supreme Court from 1956 to 1990. (Source: Furman v. Georgia *408 U.S. 238 [1972]. Most legal references have been omitted.)*

. . . Mr. Justice Brennan, concurring.

The question presented in these cases is whether death is today a punishment for crime that is "cruel and unusual" and consequently, by virtue of the Eighth and Fourteenth Amendments, beyond the power of the State to inflict. . . .

III

. . . The question, then, is whether the deliberate infliction of death is today consistent with the command of the Clause that the State may not inflict punishments that do not comport with human dignity. I will analyze the punishment of death in terms of the principles set out above and the cumulative test to which they lead: It is a denial of human dignity for the State arbitrarily to subject a person to an unusually severe punishment that society has indicated it does not regard as acceptable, and that cannot be shown to serve any penal purpose more effectively than a significantly less drastic punishment. Under these principles and this test, death is today a "cruel and unusual" punishment.

Death is a unique punishment in the United States. In a society that so strongly affirms the sanctity of life, not surprisingly the common view is that death is the ultimate sanction. This natural human feeling appears all about us. There has been no national debate about punishment, in general or by imprisonment, comparable to the debate about the punishment of death. No other punishment has been so continuously restricted, nor has any State yet abolished prisons, as some have abolished this punishment. And those States that still inflict death reserve it for the most heinous crimes. Juries, of course, have always treated death cases differently, as have governors exercising their commutation powers. Criminal defendants are of the same view. "As all practicing lawyers know, who have defended persons charged with capital offenses, often the only goal possible is to avoid the death penalty." Some legislatures have required particular procedures, such as two-stage trials and automatic appeals, applicable only in death cases. "It is the universal experience in the administration of criminal justice that those charged with capital offenses are granted special considerations." This Court, too, almost always treats death cases as a class apart. And the unfortunate effect of this punishment upon the functioning of the judicial process is well known; no other punishment has a similar effect.

The only explanation for the uniqueness of death is its extreme severity. Death is today an unusually severe punishment, unusual in its pain, in its finality, and in its enormity. No other existing punishment is comparable to death in terms of physical and mental suffering. Although our information is not conclusive, it appears that there is no method available that guarantees an immediate and painless death. Since the discontinuance of flogging as a constitutionally permissible punishment, death remains as the only punishment that may involve the conscious infliction of physical pain. In addition, we know that mental pain is an inseparable part of our practice of punishing criminals by death, for the prospect of pending execution exacts a frightful toll during the inevitable long wait between the imposition of sentence and the actual infliction of death. As the California Supreme Court pointed out, "the process of carrying out a verdict of death is often so degrading and brutalizing to the human spirit as to constitute psychological torture." Indeed, as Mr. Justice Frankfurter noted, "the onset of insanity while awaiting execution of a death sentence is not a rare phenomenon." The "fate of ever-increasing fear and distress" to which the expatriate is subjected can only exist to a greater degree for a person confined in prison awaiting death.

The unusual severity of death is manifested most clearly in its finality and enormity. Death, in these respects, is in a class by itself. Expatriation, for example, is a punishment that "destroys for the individual the political existence that was centuries in the development," that "strips the citizen of his status in the national and international political community," and that puts "[h]is very existence" in jeopardy. Expatriation thus inherently entails "the total destruction of the individual's status in organized society." "In short, the expatriate has lost the right to have rights." Yet, demonstrably, expatriation is not "a fate worse than death." Although death, like expatriation, destroys the individual's "political existence" and his "status in organized society," it does more, for, unlike expatriation, death also destroys "[h]is very existence." There is, too, at least the possibility that the expatriate will in the future regain "the right to have rights." Death forecloses even that possibility.

Death is truly an awesome punishment. The calculated killing of a human being by the State involves, by its very nature, a denial of the executed person's humanity. The contrast with the plight of a person punished by imprisonment is evident. An individual in prison does not lose "the right to have rights." A prisoner retains, for example, the constitutional rights to the free exercise of religion, to be free of cruel and unusual punishments, and to treatment as a "person" for purposes of due process of law and the equal protection of the laws. A prisoner remains a member of the human family. Moreover, he retains the right of access to the courts. His punishment is not irrevocable. Apart from the common charge, grounded upon the recognition of human fallibility, that the punishment of death must inevitably be inflicted upon innocent men, we know that death has been the lot of men whose convictions were unconstitutionally secured in view of later, retroactively applied, holdings of this Court. The punishment itself may have been unconstitutionally inflicted, yet the finality of death precludes relief. An executed person has indeed "lost the right to have rights." As one 19th century proponent of punishing criminals by death declared, "When a man is hung, there is an end of our relations with him. His execution is a way of saying, 'You are not fit for this world, take your chance elsewhere.'"

In comparison to all other punishments today, then, the deliberate extinguishment of human life by the State is uniquely degrading to human dignity. . . .

QUESTIONS FOR REFLECTION

1. Justice Brennan offers some principles for determining whether a punishment "comports with human dignity." Explain them.

2. Why, in Justice Brennan's view, is capital punishment incompatible with human dignity? Would Kant agree?

3. How is human dignity connected to the "right to have rights," in Justice Brennan's view?

4. What is the moral significance of the rare application and seeming arbitrariness of the death penalty?

5. How, according to Justice Brennan, does the death penalty differ from imprisonment? What is the moral significance of those differences?

6. Suppose someone were to argue, "Everything Justice Brennan says about death at the hands of the state is also true of death resulting from a terminal illness." But it is absurd to conclude that death from natural causes is unconstitutional or morally unacceptable. So his reasoning must be flawed. How would you respond?

JUSTICES STEWART, POWELL, AND STEVENS

Majority Opinion in *Gregg* v. *Georgia* (1976)

(Source: Gregg v. Georgia 428 U.S. 153 [1976]. Most legal references have been omitted.)

Judgment of the Court, and opinion of Mr. Justice Stewart, Mr. Justice Powell, and Mr. Justice Stevens, announced by Mr. Justice Stewart. . . .

III

. . . The Court on a number of occasions has both assumed and asserted the constitutionality of capital punishment. In several cases that assumption provided a necessary foundation for the decision, as the Court was asked to decide whether a particular method of carrying out a capital sentence would be allowed to stand under the Eighth Amendment. But until *Furman* v. *Georgia,* the Court never confronted squarely the fundamental claim that the punishment of death always, regardless of the enormity of the offense or the procedure followed in imposing the sentence, is cruel and unusual punishment in violation of the Constitution. Although this issue was presented and addressed in *Furman,* it was not resolved by the Court. Four Justices would have held that capital punishment is not unconstitutional *per se;* two Justices would have reached the opposite conclusion; and three Justices, while agreeing that the statutes then before the Court were invalid as applied, left open the question whether such punishment may ever be imposed. We now hold that the punishment of death does not invariably violate the Constitution. . . .

C

. . . The imposition of the death penalty for the crime of murder has a long history of acceptance both in the United States and in England. The common-law rule imposed a mandatory death sentence on all convicted murderers. And the penalty continued to be used into the 20th century by most American States, although the breadth of the common-law rule was diminished, initially by narrowing the class of murders to be punished by death and subsequently by widespread adoption of laws expressly granting juries the discretion to recommend mercy.

It is apparent from the text of the Constitution itself that the existence of capital punishment was accepted by the Framers. At the time the Eighth Amendment was ratified, capital punishment was a common sanction in every State. Indeed, the First Congress of the United States enacted legislation providing death as the penalty for specified crimes. The Fifth Amendment, adopted at the same time as the Eighth, contemplated the continued existence of the capital sanction by imposing certain limits on the prosecution of capital cases:

"No person shall be held to answer for a capital, or otherwise infamous crime, unless on a presentment or indictment of a Grand Jury . . . ; nor shall any person be subject for the same offense to be twice put in jeopardy of life or limb; . . . nor be deprived of life, liberty, or property, without due process of law. . . ."

And the Fourteenth Amendment, adopted over three-quarters of a century later, similarly contemplates the existence of the capital sanction in providing that no State shall deprive any person of "life, liberty, or property" without due process of law.

For nearly two centuries, this Court, repeatedly and often expressly, has recognized that capital punishment is not invalid *per se.* . . .

The death penalty is said to serve two principal social purposes: retribution and deterrence of capital crimes by prospective offenders.

In part, capital punishment is an expression of society's moral outrage at particularly offensive conduct. This function may be unappealing to many, but it is essential in an ordered society that asks its citizens to rely on legal processes rather than self-help to vindicate their wrongs.

"The instinct for retribution is part of the nature of man, and channeling that instinct in the administration of criminal justice serves an important purpose in promoting the stability of a society governed by law. When people begin to believe that organized society is unwilling or unable to impose upon criminal offenders the punishment they 'deserve,' then there are sown the seeds of anarchy—of self-help, vigilante justice, and lynch law." *Furman* v. *Georgia* (Stewart, J., concurring).

"Retribution is no longer the dominant objective of the criminal law," but neither is it a forbidden objective nor one inconsistent with our respect for the dignity of men. Indeed, the decision that capital punishment may be the appropriate sanction in extreme cases is an expression of the community's belief that certain crimes are themselves so grievous an affront to humanity that the only adequate response may be the penalty of death.

Statistical attempts to evaluate the worth of the death penalty as a deterrent to crimes by potential offenders have occasioned a great deal of debate. The results simply have been inconclusive. As one opponent of capital punishment has said:

"[A]fter all possible inquiry, including the probing of all possible methods of inquiry, we do not know, and for systematic and easily visible reasons cannot know, what the truth about this 'deterrent' effect may be. . . .

"The inescapable flaw is . . . that social conditions in any state are not constant through time, and that social conditions are not the same in any two states. If an effect were observed (and the observed effects, one way or another, are not large) then one could not at all tell whether any of this effect is attributable to the presence or absence of capital punishment. A 'scientific'—that is to say, a soundly based—conclusion is simply impossible, and no methodological path out of this tangle suggests itself."

Although some of the studies suggest that the death penalty may not function as a significantly greater deterrent than lesser penalties, there is no convincing empirical evidence either supporting or refuting this view. We may nevertheless assume safely that there are murderers, such as those who act in passion, for whom the threat of death has little or no deterrent effect. But for many others, the death penalty undoubtedly is a significant deterrent. There are carefully contemplated murders, such as murder for hire, where the possible penalty of death may well enter into the cold calculus that precedes the decision to act. And there are some categories of murder, such as murder by a life prisoner, where other sanctions may not be adequate.

The value of capital punishment as a deterrent of crime is a complex factual issue the resolution of which properly rests with the legislatures, which can evaluate the results of statistical studies in terms of their own local conditions and with a flexibility of approach that is not available to the courts. Indeed, many of the post-*Furman* statutes reflect just such a responsible effort to define those crimes and those criminals for which capital punishment is most probably an effective deterrent.

In sum, we cannot say that the judgment of the Georgia Legislature that capital punishment may be necessary in some cases is clearly wrong. Considerations of federalism, as well as respect for the ability of a legislature to evaluate, in terms of its particular State, the moral consensus concerning the death penalty and its social utility as a sanction, require us to conclude, in the absence of more convincing evidence, that the infliction of death as a punishment for murder is not without justification and thus is not unconstitutionally severe.

Finally, we must consider whether the punishment of death is disproportionate in relation to the crime for which it is imposed. There is no question that death as a punishment is unique in its severity and irrevocability. When a defendant's life is at stake, the Court has been particularly sensitive to ensure that every safeguard is observed. But we are concerned here only with the imposition of capital punishment for the crime of murder, and when a life has been taken deliberately by the offender, we cannot say that the punishment is invariably disproportionate to the crime. It is an extreme sanction, suitable to the most extreme of crimes.

We hold that the death penalty is not a form of punishment that may never be imposed, regardless of the circumstances of the offense, regardless of the character of the offender, and regardless of the procedure followed in reaching the decision to impose it.

IV

. . .

B

We now turn to consideration of the constitutionality of Georgia's capital-sentencing procedures. In the wake of *Furman,* Georgia amended its capital punishment statute, but chose not to narrow the scope of its murder provisions. Thus, now as before *Furman,* in Georgia "[a] person commits murder when he unlawfully and with malice aforethought, either express or implied, causes the death of another human being." All persons convicted of murder "shall be punished by death or by imprisonment for life."

Georgia did act, however, to narrow the class of murderers subject to capital punishment by specifying 10 statutory aggravating circumstances, one of which must be found by the jury to exist beyond a reasonable doubt before a death sentence can ever be imposed. In addition, the jury is authorized to consider any other appropriate aggravating or mitigating circumstances. The jury is not required to find any mitigating circumstances in order to make a recom-

mendation of mercy that is binding on the trial court, but it must find a *statutory* aggravating circumstance before recommending a sentence of death.

These procedures require the jury to consider the circumstances of the crime and the criminal before it recommends sentence. No longer can a Georgia jury do as *Furman's* jury did: reach a finding of the defendant's guilt and then, without guidance or direction, decide whether he should live or die. Instead, the jury's attention is directed to the specific circumstances of the crime: Was it committed in the course of another capital felony? Was it committed for money? Was it committed upon a peace officer or judicial officer? Was it committed in a particularly heinous way or in a manner that endangered the lives of many persons? In addition, the jury's attention is focused on the characteristics of the person who committed the crime: Does he have a record of prior convictions for capital offenses? Are there any special facts about this defendant that mitigate against imposing capital punishment (*e.g.,* his youth, the extent of his cooperation with the police, his emotional state at the time of the crime)? As a result, while some jury discretion still exists, "the discretion to be exercised is controlled by clear and objective standards so as to produce non-discriminatory application."

As an important additional safeguard against arbitrariness and caprice, the Georgia statutory scheme provides for automatic appeal of all death sentences to the State's Supreme Court. That court is required by statute to review each sentence of death and determine whether it was imposed under the influence of passion or prejudice, whether the evidence supports the jury's finding of a statutory aggravating circumstance, and whether the sentence is disproportionate compared to those sentences imposed in similar cases.

In short, Georgia's new sentencing procedures require as a prerequisite to the imposition of the death penalty, specific jury findings as to the circumstances of the crime or the character of the defendant. Moreover, to guard further against a situation comparable to that presented in *Furman,* the Supreme Court of Georgia compares each death sentence with the sentences imposed on similarly situated defendants to ensure that the sentence of death in a particular case is not disproportionate. On their face these procedures seem to satisfy the concerns of *Furman.* No longer should there be "no meaningful basis for distinguishing the few cases in which [the death penalty] is imposed from the many cases in which it is not." . . .

V

The basic concern of *Furman* centered on those defendants who were being condemned to death capriciously and arbitrarily. Under the procedures before the Court in that case, sentencing authorities were not directed to give attention to the nature or circumstances of the crime committed or to the character or record of the defendant. Left unguided, juries imposed the death sentence in a way that could only be called freakish. The new Georgia sentencing procedures, by contrast, focus the jury's attention on the particularized nature of the crime and the particular-ized characteristics of the individual defendant. While the jury is permitted to consider any aggravating or mitigating circumstances, it must find and identify at least one statutory aggravating factor before it may impose a penalty of death. In this way the jury's discretion is channeled. No longer can a jury wantonly and freakishly impose the death sentence; it is always circumscribed by the legislative guidelines. In addition, the review function of the Supreme Court of Georgia affords additional assurance that the concerns that prompted our decision in *Furman* are not present to any significant degree in the Georgia procedure applied here.

For the reasons expressed in this opinion, we hold that the statutory system under which Gregg was sentenced to death does not violate the Constitution. Accordingly, the judgment of the Georgia Supreme Court is affirmed. . . .

QUESTIONS FOR REFLECTION

1. The majority argues that the death penalty is sometimes justified. What are the majority's chief arguments?
2. In *Furman* v. *Georgia,* Justice Brennan outlined arguments that the death penalty is incompatible with human dignity. Does the majority in *Gregg* v. *Georgia* accept those arguments? Does it present arguments that the death penalty is compatible with, or even required by, human dignity?

ERNEST VAN DEN HAAG

from *The Death Penalty: A Debate*

Ernest van den Haag is Professor of Jurisprudence and Public Policy at Ford-ham University. (Source: Excerpts from Ernest van den Haag and Joseph P. Conrad, The Death Penalty: A Debate *[Plenum Press, 1983]. Copyright © 1983 by Plenum Publishing Corporation.)*

CHAPTER 4 / MORE ON THE DETERRENT EFFECT OF THE DEATH PENALTY

. . . Does capital punishment deter more than life imprisonment?

Science, logic, or statistics often have been unable to prove what common sense tells us to be true. Thus, the Greek philosopher Zeno some 2000 years ago found that he could not show that motion is possible; indeed, his famous paradoxes appear to show that motion is impossible. Though nobody believed them to be true, nobody succeeded in showing the fallacy of these paradoxes until the rise of mathematical logic less than a hundred years ago. But meanwhile, the world did not stand still. Indeed, nobody argued that motion should stop because it had not been shown to be logically possible. There is no more reason to abolish the death penalty than there was to abolish motion simply because the death penalty has not been, and perhaps cannot be, shown statistically to be a deterrent over and above other penalties. Indeed, there are two quite satisfactory, if nonstatistical, indications of the marginal deterrent effect of the death penalty.

In the first place, our experience shows that the greater the threatened penalty, the more it deters. *Ceteris paribus,* the threat of 50 lashes deters more than the threat of 5; a $1000 fine deters more than a $10 fine; 10 years in prison deter more than 1 year in prison—just as, conversely, the promise of a $1000 reward is a greater incentive than the promise of a $10 reward, etc. There may be diminishing returns. Once a reward exceeds, say, $1 million, the additional attraction may diminish. Once a punishment exceeds, say, 10 years in prison (net of parole), there may be little additional deterrence in threatening additional years. We know hardly anything about diminishing returns of penalties. It would still seem likely, however, that the threat of life in prison deters more than any other term of imprisonment.

The threat of death may deter still more. For it is a mistake to regard the death penalty as though it were of the same kind as other penalties. If it is not, then diminishing returns are unlikely to apply. And death differs significantly, in kind, from any other penalty. Life in prison is still life, however unpleasant. In contrast, the death penalty does not just threaten to make life unpleasant—it threatens to take life altogether. This difference is perceived by those affected. We find that when they have the choice between life in prison and execution, 99% of all prisoners under sentence of death prefer life in prison. By means of appeals, pleas for commutation, indeed by all means at their disposal, they indicate that they prefer life in prison to execution.

From this unquestioned fact a reasonable conclusion can be drawn in favor of the superior deterrent effect of the death penalty. Those who have the choice in practice, those whose choice has actual and immediate effects on their life and death, fear death more than they fear life in prison or any other available penalty. If they do, it follows that the threat of the death penalty, all other things equal, is likely to deter more than the threat of life in prison. One is most deterred by what one fears most. From which it follows that whatever statistics fail, or do not fail, to show, the death penalty is likely to be more deterrent than any other.

Suppose now one is not fully convinced of the superior deterrent effect of the death penalty. I believe I can show that even if one is genuinely uncertain as to whether the death penalty adds to deterrence, one should still favor it, from a purely deterrent viewpoint. For if we are not sure, we must choose either to (1) trade the certain death, by execution, of a convicted murderer for the probable survival of an indefinite number of murder victims whose future murder is less likely (whose survival is more likely)—if the convicted murderer's execution deters prospective murderers, as it might, or to (2) trade the certain survival of the convicted murderer for the probable loss of the lives of future murder victims more likely to be murdered because the convicted murderer's nonexecution might not deter prospective murderers, who could have been deterred by executing the convicted murderer.

To restate the matter: If we were quite ignorant about the marginal deterrent effects of execution, we would have to choose—like it or not—between the certainty of the convicted murderer's death by execution and the likelihood of the survival of future victims of other murderers on the one hand, and on the other his certain survival and the likelihood of the death of new victims. I'd rather execute a man convicted of having murdered others than put the lives of innocents at risk. I find it hard to understand the opposite choice.

However, I doubt that those who insist that the death penalty has not been demonstrated to be more deterrent than other penalties really believe that it is not. Or that it matters. I am fairly certain that the deterrent effect of the death penalty, or its absence, is not actually important to them. Rather, I think, they use the lack of statistical demonstration of a marginal deterrent effect to rationalize an opposition to the death penalty that has nonrational sources yet to be examined. In fact, although they use the alleged inconclusiveness of statistical demonstrations of deterrence as an argument to dissuade others from the death penalty, it can be shown that most abolitionists are not quite serious about the relevance of their own argument from insufficient deterrence.

In numerous discussions I have asked those who oppose capital punishment because, in their opinion, it will not deter capital crimes enough, whether they would favor the death penalty if it could be shown to deter more than life imprisonment does. My question usually led to some embarrassment and to attempts to dodge it by saying that additional deterrence has not been shown. However, when I persisted, conceding as much but asking abolitionists to give a hypothetical answer to a hypothetical question, they would admit that they would continue to oppose the death penalty—even if it were shown to deter more than life imprisonment. Which is to say that the argument based on the alleged lack of superior deterrence is factitious.

At times I have pursued the question. I would ask: "Suppose it were shown that every time we execute a person convicted of murder, ten fewer homicides are committed annually than were otherwise expected—would you still favor abolition?" The answer has been "yes" in all cases I can recall. I would persist: "Suppose every time we execute a convicted murderer, 500 fewer persons are murdered than otherwise would be expected to be murdered; suppose that, by executing the convicted murderer, we so much more deter others, who are not deterred by the threat of life imprisonment, that 500 victims will be spared?" After some hesitation, such staunch abolitionists as Professor Hugo Adam Bedau (Tufts University); Ramsey Clark, attorney general of the United States under President Johnson; Professor Charles Black (Yale); and Mr. Henry Schwarzchild, capital punishment project director of the American Civil Liberties Union, admitted that if they had the choice, they would rather see 500 innocents murdered than execute one convict found guilty of murder. This leads me to doubt the sincerity of abolitionist arguments based on the alleged lack of significant additional deterrent effect of capital punishment.

I also wonder why anyone would hold more precious the life of a convicted murderer than that of 500 innocents, if by executing him he could save them. . . .

CHAPTER 10 / SPECIAL CASES

There are some special cases—special because the threat of the death penalty is the only threat that may deter the crime. We do not know that it will. We do know that in these cases no other threat can.

Unless threatened with the death penalty, prisoners serving life sentences without parole can murder fellow prisoners or guards with impunity. Without the death penalty we give effective immunity, we promise impunity, to just those persons who are most likely to need deterrent threats if they are to be restrained. From a moral viewpoint one may add that if a prisoner already convicted of a crime sufficient to send him to prison for life commits a murder, the death penalty seems likely to be well deserved. At any rate, without the death penalty his fellow prisoners and the correctional officers can and will be victimized with impunity should he decide to murder them. To avoid threatening the convict with the only punishment available to restrain him, their lives are put at risk. This seems hard to justify.

The matter is all too well illustrated by the following:

Two hard-case inmates apparently wangled their way into the warden's offices and stabbed the warden and his deputy to death with sharpened mess-hall knives.

. . . investigators said that the death mission had been specifically ordered the night before at a meeting of Muslim inmates because Fromhold had resisted their demands "once too often." Fromhold was stabbed thirteen times in the back and chest; Warden Patrick Curran, 47, who dashed into his deputy's first-floor office, was stabbed three times in the back.

Neither inmate had much to lose. Burton was doing life in the cold-blooded execution of a Philadelphia police sergeant, and Bowen was awaiting trial in another cop-killing and the shooting of an elderly couple.*

I can think of no reason for giving permanent immunity to homicidal life prisoners, thereby victimizing guards and other prisoners.

Outside prison, too, the threat of the death penalty is the only threat that is likely to restrain some criminals. Without the death penalty an offender

having committed a crime that leads to imprisonment for life has nothing to lose if he murders the arresting officer. By murdering the officer or, for that matter, witnesses to their crimes, such criminals increase their chances of escape, without increasing the severity of the punishment they will suffer if caught. This is the case for all criminals likely to be given life imprisonment if caught who commit an additional crime such as murdering the arresting officer. Only the death penalty could rationally restrain them.

In some states the death penalty is threatened to those who murder a police officer in the performance of his duties. Thus, special protection is extended to police officers, who, after all, are specially exposed. They deserve that extra protection. But it seems to me that everyone deserves the protection against murder that the death penalty can provide.

There are still other cases in which the death penalty alone is likely to be perceived as the threat that may deter from the crime. Thus, there is little point in imprisoning a spy in wartime: He expects his side to win, to be liberated by it, and to become a hero. On the other hand, if he had to fear immediate execution, the victory of his side would help the spy little. This may deter some people from becoming spies. It may not deter the man who does not mind becoming a patriotic martyr, but it may deter a man who does his spying for money.

A deserter, too, afraid of the risk of death on the battlefield, afraid enough to desert, is not going to be restrained by the threat of a prison sentence. But he may be afraid of certain death by firing squad. So may be anyone who deserts for any reason whatsoever.

Even the death penalty cannot restrain certain crimes. Once a man has committed a first murder for which, if convicted, he would be punished by execution, he can commit additional murders without fear of additional punishment. The range of punishments is limited. The range of crimes is not. The death penalty is the most severe punishment we can impose. It is reserved for the most serious crimes. But we can add nothing for still more serious crimes such as multiple murders or torture murders.

Unlike death, which we will all experience, torture is repulsive to us. Thus, we will not apply it even to those who richly deserve it. It is, moreover, most unlikely that anyone not deterred by death

---

* *Newsweek*, 11 June 1973.

would be deterred by torture or that death with torture would be more deterrent than death without. Thus, there is little point in trying to extend the range of punishment upward, beyond death.

Unfortunately, criminals can and sometimes do torture victims. They also can and sometimes do murder more than one person. The law cannot threaten more than death. But at least it should not threaten less. Although the threat of the death penalty may not restrain the second murder, it may restrain the first. . . .

CHAPTER 16 / THE ADVOCATE ADVOCATES

There are two basic arguments for the death penalty; they are independent of, yet consistent with, one another.

The first argument is moral: The death penalty is just; it is deserved for certain crimes. One can explain why one feels that certain crimes deserve the death penalty. But as usual with moral arguments, one cannot show this conviction to be *factually* correct (or, for that matter, incorrect) since moral arguments rest not on facts but on our evaluation of them. My evaluation leads me to believe that, e.g., premeditated murder or treason (a fact) is so grave and horrible a crime (an evaluation) as to deserve nothing less than the death penalty, that only the death penalty (a fact) is proportionate to the gravity of the crime (an evaluation).

My widely shared view is opposed by abolitionists, who claim that the death penalty is unjust for any crime, and inconsistent with human dignity. . . . Since most abolitionists believe, as I do, that punishments should be proportionate to the perceived gravity of crimes, the abolitionist claim seems to me logically precarious. It implies either that murder is not so horrible after all—not horrible enough, at any rate, to deserve death—or that the death penalty is too harsh a punishment for it, and indeed for any conceivable crime. I find it hard to believe that one can hold either view seriously, let alone both. . . .

I must confess that I have never understood the assorted arguments claiming that the death penalty is inconsistent with human dignity or that, somehow, society has no right to impose it. One might as well claim that death generally, or at least death from illness, is inconsistent with human dignity, or that birth is, or any suffering or any undesirable social condition. Most of these are unavoidable. At least death by execution can be avoided by not killing someone else, by not committing murder. One can preserve one's dignity in this respect if one values it. Incidentally, execution may be physically less humiliating and painful than death in a hospital. It is, however, morally more humiliating and meant to be: It indicates the extreme blame we attach to the crime of murder by deliberately expelling the murderer from among the living.

As for the dignity of society, it seems to me that by executing murderers it tries to keep its promise to secure the lives of innocents, to vindicate the law, and to impose retribution on those who so horribly violate it. To do anything less would be inconsistent with the dignity of society. . . .

QUESTIONS FOR REFLECTION

1. Van den Haag argues that we should accept the deterrent value of the death penalty, despite the inconclusive results of most statistical studies. What are his arguments?

2. In what special circumstances, according to van den Haag, is capital punishment justified, even if it is unacceptable in most cases? Do you agree?

3. Why, in van den Haag's view, is the death penalty compatible with human dignity?

HUGO ADAM BEDAU

The Case against the Death Penalty

Introduction

. . .

Despite the Supreme Court's 1976 ruling in *Gregg v. Georgia,* the ACLU continues to oppose capital punishment on moral and practical, as well as on constitutional, grounds:

- Capital punishment is cruel and unusual. It is a relic of the earliest days of penology, when slavery, branding, and other corporal punishments were commonplace. Like those other barbaric practices, executions have no place in a civilized society.

- Opposition to the death penalty does not arise from misplaced sympathy for convicted murderers. On the contrary, murder demonstrates a lack of respect for human life. For this very reason, murder is abhorrent, and any policy of state-authorized killings is immoral.

- Capital punishment denies due process of law. Its imposition is arbitrary and irrevocable. It forever deprives an individual of benefits of new evidence or new law that might warrant the reversal of a conviction or the setting aside of a death sentence.

- The death penalty violates the constitutional guarantee of the equal protection of the laws. It is applied randomly at best and discriminatorily at worst. It is imposed disproportionately upon those whose victims are white, on offenders who are people of color, and on those who are themselves poor and uneducated.

- The defects in death-penalty laws, conceded by the Supreme Court in the early 1970s, have not been appreciably altered by the shift from unfettered discretion to "guided discretion." These changes in death sentencing have proved to be largely cosmetic. They merely mask the impermissible arbitrariness of a process that results in an execution.

- Executions give society the unmistakable message that human life no longer deserves respect when it is useful to take it and that homicide is legitimate when deemed justified by pragmatic concerns.

- Reliance on the death penalty obscures the true causes of crime and distracts attention from the social measures that effectively contribute to its control. Politicians who preach the desirability of executions as a weapon of crime control deceive the public and mask their own failure to support anti-crime measures that will really work.

- Capital punishment wastes resources. It squanders the time and energy of courts, prosecuting attorneys, defense counsel, juries, and courtroom and correctional personnel. It unduly burdens the system of criminal justice, and it is therefore counterproductive as an instrument for society's control of violent crime. It epitomizes the tragic inefficacy and brutality of the resort to violence rather than reason for the solution of difficult social problems.

- A decent and humane society does not deliberately kill human beings. An execution is a dramatic, public spectacle of official, violent homicide that teaches the permissibility of killing people to solve social problems—the worst possible example to set for society. In this century, governments have too often attempted to justify their lethal fury by the benefits such killing would bring to the rest of society. The bloodshed is real and deeply destructive of the common decency of the community; the benefits are illusory.

Two conclusions buttress our entire case: Capital punishment does not deter crime, and the death penalty is uncivilized in theory and unfair and inequitable in practice.

Deterrence

The argument most often cited in support of capital punishment is that the threat of executions deters capital crimes more effectively than imprisonment. This claim is plausible, but the facts do not support it. The death penalty fails as a deterrent for several reasons.

1. Any punishment can be an effective deterrent only if it is consistently and promptly employed. Capital punishment cannot be administered to meet these conditions.

   Only a small proportion of first-degree murderers is sentenced to death, and even fewer are executed. Although death sentences since 1980 have increased in number to about 250 per year, this is still only 1 percent of all homicides known to the police. Of all those convicted on a charge of criminal homicide, only 2 percent—about 1 in 50—are eventually sentenced to death.

   The possibility of increasing the number of convicted murderers sentenced to death and executed by enacting mandatory death penalty laws was ruled unconstitutional in 1976 (*Woodson v. North Carolina*).

   Considerable delay in carrying out the death sentence is unavoidable, given the procedural safeguards required by the courts in capital cases. Starting with empaneling the trial jury, murder trials take far longer when the death penalty is involved. Post-conviction appeals in death-penalty cases are far more frequent as well. All these factors increase the time and cost of administering criminal justice.

   The sobering lesson is that we can reduce such delay and costs only by abandoning the procedural safeguards and constitutional rights of suspects, defendants, and convicts, with the attendant high risk of convicting the wrong person and executing the innocent.

2. Persons who commit murder and other crimes of personal violence either premeditate them or they do not. If the crime is premeditated, the criminal ordinarily concentrates on escaping detection, arrest, and conviction. The threat of even the severest punishment will not deter those who expect to escape detection and arrest. If the crime is not premeditated, then it is impossible to imagine how the threat of any punishment could deter it. Most capital crimes are committed during moments of great emotional stress or under the influence of drugs or alcohol, when logical thinking has been suspended. Impulsive or expressive violence is inflicted by persons heedless of the consequences to themselves as well as to others.

   Gangland killings, air piracy, drive-by shootings, and kidnapping for ransom are among the graver felonies that continue to be committed because some individuals think they are too clever to get caught. Political terrorism is usually committed in the name of an ideology that honors its martyrs; trying to cope with it by threatening death for terrorists is futile. Such threats leave untouched the underlying causes and ignore the many political and diplomatic sanctions (such as treaties against asylum for international terrorists) that could appreciably lower the incidence of terrorism.

   The attempt to reduce murders in the illegal drug trade by the threat of severe punishment ignores this fact: Anyone trafficking in illegal drugs is already betting his life in violent competition with other dealers. It is irrational to think that the death penalty—a remote threat at best—will deter murders committed in drug turf wars or by street-level dealers.

3. If, however, severe punishment can deter crime, then long-term imprisonment is severe enough to cause any rational person not to commit violent crimes. The vast preponderance of the evidence shows that the death penalty is no more effective than imprisonment in deterring murder and that it may even be an incitement to criminal violence in certain cases.

a. Death-penalty states as a group do not have lower rates of criminal homicide than non–death-penalty states. During the 1980s, death-penalty states averaged an annual rate of 7.5 criminal homicides per 100,000 population; abolitionist states averaged a rate of 7.4.

b. Use of the death penalty in a given state may increase the subsequent rate of criminal homicide in that state. In New York, for example, between 1907 and 1964, 692 executions were carried out. On the average, over this 57-year period, one or more executions in a given month aided a net increase of two homicides to the total committed in the next month.

c. In neighboring states—one with the death penalty and the others without it—the one with the death penalty does not show a consistently lower rate of criminal homicide. For example, between 1972 and 1990, the homicide rate in Michigan (which has no death penalty) was generally as low as or lower than the neighboring state of Indiana, which restored the death penalty in 1973 and since then has sentenced 70 persons to death and carried out 2 executions.

d. Police officers on duty do not suffer a higher rate of criminal assault and homicide in states that have abolished the death penalty than they do in death-penalty states. Between 1973 and 1984, for example, lethal assaults against police were not significantly more or less frequent in abolition states than in death-penalty states. There is "no support for the view that the death penalty provides a more effective deterrent to police homicides than alternative sanctions. Not for a single year was evidence found that police are safer in jurisdictions that provide for capital punishment."

e. Prisoners and prison personnel do not suffer a higher rate of criminal assault and homicide from life-term prisoners in abolition states than they do in death-penalty states. Between 1984 and 1989, seventeen prison staff were murdered by prisoners in ten states; of these murders, 88 percent (15 of 17) occurred in death-penalty jurisdictions—just as about 88 percent of all the prisoners in those ten states were in death-penalty jurisdictions. Evidently, the threat of the death penalty "does not even exert an incremental deterrent effect over the threat of a lesser punishment in the abolitionist state."

Actual experience establishes these conclusions beyond a reasonable doubt. No comparable body of evidence contradicts them.

Three investigations since *Furman,* using methods pioneered by economists, reported findings in the opposite direction. Subsequently, several qualified investigators have independently examined these claims, and all have rejected them. The National Academy of Sciences, in its thorough report on the effects of criminal sanctions on crime rates, concluded: "It seems unthinkable to us to base decisions on the use of the death penalty" on such "fragile" and "uncertain" results. "We see too many plausible explanations for [these] findings . . . other than the theory that capital punishment deters murder."

Furthermore, cases have been clinically documented where the death penalty actually incited the capital crimes it was supposed to deter. These include instances of the so-called suicide-by-execution syndrome—persons who wanted but feared to take their own life and committed murder so that society would kill them.

It must, of course, be conceded that inflicting the death penalty guarantees that the condemned person will commit no further crimes. This is an incapacitative, not a deterrent, effect of executions. Furthermore, it is too high a price to pay when studies show that very few convicted murderers ever commit another crime of violence. A recent study examined the prison and post-release records of 533 prisoners on death row in 1972 whose sentences were reduced to life by the Supreme Court's ruling in *Furman.* The research showed that 6 had committed another murder. But the same study showed that in 4 other cases, an innocent man had been sentenced to death.

Recidivism among murderers does occasionally happen. But it happens less frequently than most people believe; the media rarely distinguish between a paroled murderer who murders again and other murderers who have a previous criminal record but not for homicide.

There is no way to predict which convicted murderers will kill again. Repeat murders could be prevented only by executing all those convicted of criminal homicide. Such a policy is too inhumane and brutal to be taken seriously. Society would never tolerate dozens of executions daily, yet nothing less would suffice. Equally effective but far less inhumane is a policy of life imprisonment without the possibility of parole.

Unfairness

Constitutional due process as well as elementary justice require that the judicial functions of trial and sentencing be conducted with fundamental fairness, especially where the irreversible sanction of the death penalty is involved. In murder cases (since 1930, 99 percent of all executions have been for this crime), there has been substantial evidence to show that courts have been arbitrary, racially biased, and unfair in the way in which they have sentenced some persons to prison but others to death.

Racial discrimination was one of the grounds on which the Supreme Court relied in *Furman* in ruling the death penalty unconstitutional. Half a century ago, Gunnar Myrdal, in his classic *American Dilemma* (1944), reported that "the South makes the widest application of the death penalty, and Negro criminals come in for much more than their share of the executions." Statistics confirm this discrimination, only it is not confined to the South. Between 1930 and 1990, 4,016 persons were executed in the United States. Of these, 2,129 (or 53 percent) were black. For the crime of murder, 3,343 were executed; 1,693 (or 51 percent) were black. During these years African-Americans were about 12 percent of the nation's population.

The nation's death rows have always had a disproportionately large population of African-Americans, relative to their fraction of the total population. Over the past century, black offenders, as compared with white, were often executed for crimes less often receiving the death penalty, such as rape and burglary. (Between 1930 and 1976, 455 men were executed for rape, of whom 405 [or 90 percent] were black.) A higher percentage of the blacks who were executed were juveniles; and

blacks were more often executed than were whites without having their conviction reviewed by any higher court.

In recent years, it has been widely believed that such flagrant discrimination is a thing of the past. Since the revival of the death penalty in the mid-1970s, about half of those on death row at any given time have been black—a disproportionately large fraction given the black/white ratio of the total population, but not so obviously unfair if judged by the fact that roughly 50 percent of all those arrested for murder were also black. Nevertheless, when those under death sentence are examined more closely, it turns out that race is a decisive factor after all.

An exhaustive statistical study of racial discrimination in capital cases in Georgia, for example, showed that "the average odds of receiving a death sentence among all indicted cases were 4.3 times higher in cases with white victims." In 1987 these data were placed before the Supreme Court in *McCleskey* v. *Kemp* and the Court did not dispute the statistical evidence. The Court did hold, however, that the evidence failed to show that there was "a constitutionally significant risk of racial bias. . . ."

In 1990, the U.S. General Accounting Office reported to the Congress the results of its review of empirical studies on racism and the death penalty. The GAO concluded: "Our synthesis of the 28 studies shows a pattern of evidence indicating racial disparities in the charging, sentencing, and imposition of the death penalty after the *Furman* decision" and that "race of victim influence was found at all stages of the criminal justice system process. . . ."

These results cannot be explained away by relevant non-racial factors (such as prior criminal record or type of crime), and they lead to a very unsavory conclusion: In the trial courts of this nation, even at the present time, the killing of a white is treated much more severely than the killing of a black. Of the 168 persons executed between January 1977 and April 1992, only 29 had been convicted of the killing of a non-white, and only one of these 29 was himself white. Where the death penalty is involved, our criminal justice system essentially reserves the death penalty for murderers (regardless of their race) who kill white victims.

Both sex and socioeconomic class are also factors that enter into determining who receives a death sentence and who is executed. During the 1980s and 1990s, only about 1 percent of all those on death row were women, even though women commit about 15 percent of all criminal homicides. A third or more of the women under death sentence were guilty of killing men who had victimized them with years of violent abuse. Since 1930, only 33 women (12 of them black) have been executed in the United States.

Discrimination against the poor (and in our society racial minorities are disproportionately poor) is also well established. "Approximately ninety percent of those on death row could not afford to hire a lawyer when they were tried." A defendant's poverty, lack of firm social roots in the community, inadequate legal representation at trial or on appeal—all these have been common factors among death-row populations. As Justice William O. Douglas noted in *Furman,* "One searches our chronicles in vain for the execution of any member of the affluent strata in this society."

The demonstrated inequities in the actual administration of capital punishment should tip the balance against it in the judgment of fair-minded and impartial observers. "Whatever else might be said for the use of death as a punishment, one lesson is clear from experience: this is a power that we cannot exercise fairly and without discrimination."

Justice John Marshall Harlan, writing for the Court, noted: ". . . the history of capital punishment for homicides . . . reveals continual efforts, uniformly unsuccessful, to identify before the fact those homicides for which the slayer should die. . . . Those who have come to grips with the hard task of actually attempting to draft means of channeling capital sentencing discretion have confirmed the lesson taught by history. . . . To identify before the fact those characteristics of criminal homicides and their perpetrators which call for the death penalty, and to express these characteristics in language which can be fairly understood and applied by the sentencing authority, appears to be tasks which are beyond present human ability." (*McGautha* v. *California* [1971])

Yet in the *Gregg* decision, the majority of the Supreme Court abandoned the wisdom of Justice Harlan and ruled as though the new guided-discretion statutes could accomplish the impossible. The truth is that death statutes approved by the Court "do not effectively restrict the discretion of juries by any real standards. They never will. No society is going to kill everybody who meets certain preset verbal requirements, put on the statute books without awareness of coverage of the infinity of special factors the real world can produce."

Even if these statutes were to succeed in guiding the jury's choice of sentence, a vast reservoir of unfettered discretion remains: the prosecutor's decision to prosecute for a capital or lesser crime, the court's willingness to accept or reject a guilty plea, the jury's decision to convict for second-degree murder or manslaughter rather than capital murder, the determination of the defendant's sanity, the final decision by the governor on clemency.

Discretion in the criminal-justice system is unavoidable. The history of capital punishment in American society clearly shows the desire to mitigate the harshness of this penalty by narrowing its scope. Discretion, whether authorized by statutes or by their silence, has been the main vehicle to this end. But when discretion is used, as it always has been, to mark for death the poor, the friendless, the uneducated, the members of racial minorities, and the despised, then discretion becomes injustice.

Thoughtful citizens, who in contemplating capital punishment in the abstract might support it, must condemn it in actual practice.

Inevitability of Error

Unlike all other criminal punishments, the death penalty is uniquely irrevocable. Speaking to the French Chamber of Deputies in 1830, years after the excesses of the French Revolution, which he had witnessed, the Marquis de Lafayette said, "I shall ask for the abolition of the punishment of death until I have the infallibility of human judgment demonstrated to me." Although some proponents of capital punishment would argue that its merits are worth the occasional execution of innocent people, most would also insist that there is little likelihood of the innocent being executed. Yet a large body of evidence shows that innocent people are often convicted of crimes, including capital crimes, and that some of them have been executed.

Since 1900, in this country, there have been on the average more than four cases per year in which an entirely innocent person was convicted of murder. Scores of these persons were sentenced to death. In many cases, a reprieve or commutation arrived just hours, or even minutes, before the scheduled execution. These erroneous convictions have occurred in virtually every jurisdiction from one end of the nation to the other. Nor have they declined in recent years, despite the new death-penalty statutes approved by the Supreme Court. Consider this handful of representative cases:

- In 1975, only a year before the Supreme Court affirmed the constitutionality of capital punishment, two African-American men in Florida, Freddie Pitts and Wilbert Lee, were released from prison after twelve years awaiting execution for the murder of two white men. Their convictions were the result of coerced confessions, erroneous testimony of an alleged eyewitness, and incompetent defense counsel. Though a white man eventually admitted his guilt, a nine-year legal battle was required before the governor would grant Pitts and Lee a pardon. Had their execution not been stayed while the constitutional status of the death penalty was argued in the courts, these two innocent men probably would not be alive today.

- Just months after Pitts and Lee were released, authorities in New Mexico were forced to admit they had sentenced to death four white men—motorcyclists from Los Angeles—who were innocent. The accused offered a documented alibi at their trial, but the prosecution dismissed it as an elaborate ruse. The jury's verdict was based mainly on what was later revealed to be perjured testimony (encouraged by the police) from an alleged eyewitness. Thanks to persistent investigation by newspaper reporters and the confession of the real killer, the error was exposed and the defendants were released after eighteen months on death row.

- In Georgia in 1975, Earl Charles was convicted of murder and sentenced to death. A surviving victim of the crime erroneously identified Charles as the gunman; her testimony was supported by a jail-house informant who claimed he had heard Charles confess. Incontrovertible alibi evidence,

showing that Charles was in Florida at the very time of the crime, eventually established his innocence—but not until he had spent more than three years under death sentence. His release was owing largely to his mother's unflagging efforts.

- In 1989, Texas authorities decided not to retry Randall Dale Adams after the appellate court reversed his conviction for murder. Adams had spent more than three years on death row for the murder of a Dallas police officer. He was convicted on the perjured testimony of a 16-year-old youth who was the real killer. Adams's plight was vividly presented in the 1988 docudrama, *The Thin Blue Line,* which convincingly told the true story of the crime and exposed the errors that resulted in his conviction.

- Another case in Texas from the 1980s tells an even more sordid story. In 1980, a black high school janitor, Clarence Brandley, and his white co-worker found the body of a missing 15-year-old white schoolgirl. Interrogated by the police, they were told, "One of you two is going to hang for this." Looking at Brandley, the officer said, "Since you're the nigger, you're elected." In a classic case of rush to judgment, Brandley was tried, convicted, and sentenced to death. The circumstantial evidence against him was thin, other leads were ignored by the police, and the courtroom atmosphere reeked of racism. In 1986, Centurion Ministries—a volunteer group devoted to freeing wrongly convicted prisoners—came to Brandley's aid. Evidence had meanwhile emerged that another man had committed the murder for which Brandley was awaiting execution. Brandley was not released until 1990.

Each of these five stories told above has a reassuring ending: The innocent prisoner is saved from execution and is released. But when prisoners are executed, no legal forum exists in which unanswered questions about their guilt can be resolved. In May 1992, Roger Keith Coleman was executed in Virginia despite widely publicized doubts surrounding his guilt and evidence that pointed to another person as the murderer—evidence that was never submitted at his trial. Not until late in the appeal process did anyone take seriously the possibility that the state was about to kill an innocent man, and then efforts to delay or nullify his execution failed. Was Coleman really innocent? At the time of his execution, his case was marked with many of the features found in other cases where the defendant was eventually cleared. Were Coleman still in prison, his friends and attorneys would have a strong incentive to resolve these questions. But with Coleman dead, further inquiry into the facts of the crime for which he was convicted is unlikely.

Overzealous prosecution, mistaken or perjured testimony, faulty police work, coerced confessions, the defendant's previous criminal record, inept defense counsel, seemingly conclusive circumstantial evidence, community pressure for a conviction—such factors help explain why the judicial system cannot guarantee that justice will never miscarry. And when it does miscarry, volunteers outside the criminal justice system—newspaper reporters, for example—and not the police or prosecutors are the ones who rectify the errors. To retain the death penalty in the face of the demonstrable failures of the system is unacceptable, especially as there are no strong counterbalancing factors in favor of the death penalty. . . .

Financial Costs

It is sometimes suggested that abolishing capital punishment is unfair to the taxpayer, as though life imprisonment were obviously more expensive than executions. If one takes into account all the relevant costs, the reverse is true. "The death penalty is not now, nor has it ever been, a more economical alternative to life imprisonment."

A murder trial normally takes much longer when the death penalty is at issue than when it is not. Litigation costs—including the time of judges, prosecutors, public defenders, and court reporters, and the high costs of briefs—are all borne by the taxpayer.

A 1982 study showed that were the death penalty to be reintroduced in New York, the cost of the capital trial alone would be more than double the cost of a life term in prison.

In Maryland, a comparison of capital trial costs with and without the death penalty for the years 1979–1984 concluded that a death penalty case costs "approximately 42 percent more than a case resulting in a non-death sentence." In 1988 and 1989 the Kansas legislature voted against reinstating the death penalty after it was informed that reintroduction would involve a first-year cost of "more than $11 million." Florida, with one of the nation's largest death rows, has estimated that the true cost of each execution is approximately $3.2 million, or approximately six times the cost of a life-imprisonment sentence.

The only way to make the death penalty a "better buy" than imprisonment is to weaken due process and curtail appellate review, which are the defendant's (and society's) only protections against the grossest miscarriages of justice. The savings in dollars would be at the cost of justice: In nearly half of the death-penalty cases given review under federal habeas corpus, the conviction is overturned.

QUESTIONS FOR REFLECTION

1. How does Bedau argue against the deterrent effect of the death penalty? Do you find his arguments convincing?

2. Which of Bedau's arguments are based on utility? On a concept of rights?

3. How would Bedau answer Locke's charge that a murderer has given up his right to life?

4. Suppose that Bedau's arguments are correct. Could imposing the death penalty ever be justifiable?

WILLIAM TUCKER

Why the Death Penalty Works

William J. Tucker is the New York correspondent for The American Specta-tor *and the CEO of TheElevator.com. (Source: from* The American Specta-tor *33 [October 2000]. Copyright © 2000 by* The American Spectator, Inc. *Reprinted by permission.)*

. . . The death penalty works. You can prove this yourself. Just go to two Websites: www.ojp.usdoj. gov/bjs/homicide/homtrnd.htm and http://www.ojp. usdoj.gov/bjs/glance/exe.txt. There you will find graphs showing the rate of murder per capita over the last 50 years and the annual number of execu-tions over the past 50 years. Superimpose these two graphs upon each other (I know of no crime expert who has ever bothered to do this), and you get the graph below.

Now statistics may prove nothing—or, alterna-tively, anything you like. Undoubtedly, some criminol-ogist somewhere will argue that these figures illustrate the death penalty actually *encourages* murder. But here is the interpretation I would put upon them.

During the 1930s, murders hit an all-time high—probably as a result of Prohibition. Executions also peaked in 1935. In those distant days, people were executed fairly routinely, and the number of execu-tions generally tracked the number of murders.

Over the next 30 years, both the murder rate and the number of executions declined. This could be in-terpreted two ways: murder declined because of some external reason (the end of Prohibition) and the number of executions fell accordingly; or the high number of executions pushed down the murder rate. Both explanations would work for the pre-1963 portion of the graph.

But after 1963, something entirely new hap-pened. Executions ceased altogether—not because murders had ceased but because of an entirely extra-neous factor—the U.S. Supreme Court. In the early 1960s, the Court began its wholesale review of state capital cases, imposing various exclusionary rules for confessions and search-and-seizure and creating the lengthy—almost endless—appeals process. The im-mediate result was that executions virtually ended after 1964. In 1971 the justices declared all existing death penalties to be unconstitutional. This ban was not lifted until 1978. Only after a painful legislative reformation did more than half the states impose the death penalty on murderers by the 1990s.

What was the impact on murder? The results are plain to see. Beginning at almost the exact point when executions ended, murder soared to unprece-dented heights. The murder rate tied the 1933 record in 1973, broke it in 1974, broke it again in 1980, and peaked a third time in 1990–92. Then suddenly it plummeted, so that by 1999 we were once again back to the levels of 1966 when murder first began its upward sweep.

What does all this prove? Well, on the surface, the answer seems obvious. Executions deter murder. When we stop executing people, murders soar. When we resume executing people, murders decline.

But don't think for a minute that professional criminologists will accept this. Criminologists are a peculiar breed, worthy of a sociological study them-selves. They are the only people in the world who believe that punishment does not deter crime. In-stead, they have one simple, uniform explanation for all kinds of crime: It is the result of population

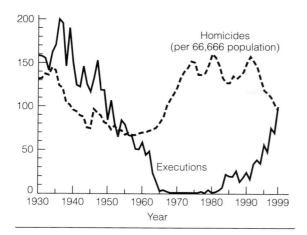

Executions vs. Homicides, 1930–1999

trends, specifically the number of "crime-prone" young men (ages 16–25) in the population. Most crimes are committed, so the argument goes, by this particular cohort of young men. When this portion of the population bulges, crime will go up. When it shrinks, crime will go down. It's like charting the weather. Trends in law enforcement, efficient policing, the number of people in jail—nothing has any effect. Pick up any newspaper article announcing a crime trend, up or down, and you will find a criminologist saying it is the result of demographic shifts in the population. I have seen crime trends from the past *six months* explained in this manner.

In fact, the size of the crime-prone population tracks murders only marginally. There is the same dip in the 1950s, followed by the maturation of the baby boom in the late 1960s and 1970s. But the adolescent population dropped off sharply in the 1980s while crime remained high. Some other explanation is required, perhaps the rearing of a whole generation of potential criminals who never even heard of the death penalty.

So capital punishment does deter murder. But is there anything more specific we can say about how this deterrent effect works? There is. This is because the rise and eventual fall in murder rates over the past 35 years was not an undifferentiated phenomenon. Rather, it was an explosion of a very particular kind of homicide—"felony" or "stranger" murder.

There are actually two types of murder. The first is called a "crime of passion." This evolves from arguments between friends, lovers, married couples, blood relatives, or people who are at least casually acquainted (opponents in a card game, for example). A dispute erupts and eventually escalates into a homicide. (Murder by a husband, ex-husband, or boyfriend is still the most common cause of homicidal death among women.)

Historically, the vast majority of murders have been crimes of passion. As the gangland killings of the 1930s and 40s subsided, acquaintance murder became the most common form of homicide. By 1960, *90 percent* of all murders involved people who knew each other. This became one of the conerstone arguments of death penalty opponents. Executions could do nothing to deter these "crimes of passion," since "people don't think of the consequences" (or so the defense attorneys said). Therefore it was "barbaric" to continue executing people when it couldn't produce any results.

Of course, this shallow argument missed the most important point—the number of murders that *were* being deterred by the death penalty. Once capital punishment was effectively abolished, these murders returned with a vengeance.

Almost the entire run-up of homicide from 1965 to 1995 was in one specific category—felony or stranger murders. These are murders committed in the course of *another* crime. While felony murders constituted only 10 percent of a low crime rate in 1960, by 1990 they constituted *half* the murder rate, which was itself twice as high. The rate of acquaintance murder has barely changed over the last 40 years. Almost the entire increase in homicide has been among felony and stranger murders. (Note: The category "stranger murder" did not even exist in 1960. It is used today to describe a situation where a dead body is found in a public place for no apparent reason. Robbery is the presumed motive, although the category can also include cases where people are murdered entirely at random.)

Why should felony and stranger murders be particularly affected by the death penalty? The answer is transparently simple—although very difficult to discuss in public debate. Criminologists and death penalty opponents willfully refuse to talk about it. The average person doesn't like to think about it.

Only criminals know it in their bones. The reason is this: All things being equal, it pays to kill your victim.

When you are engaged in a felonious crime—armed robbery, burglary, rape—your victim also is the *principal witness* to that crime. He or she can testify against you to the police or in court. That testimony is the most likely evidence that will put you in jail. It is hard to rape or rob someone without letting them see some identifying feature of yourself.

The execution of the victim does not have to be planned (although often it is). Many times it is impulsive. Youthful and amateur criminals are particularly susceptible. A young hoodlum pulls a carjacking or "push-in" robbery and suddenly realizes that the victim has had a good look at him. One common scenario is the "surprised burglar." A neighborhood youth breaks into your home. You come home unexpectedly and discover him. You may know the burglar by sight or even be casually acquainted with him. What possible avenue does the burglar have for avoiding your identification and testimony? Murder is the only rational alternative.

For this reason, societies have always felt compelled to draw a bright line between felonies—robbery, burglary, and rape—and felony *murder*—the execution of the victim of the crime. Or rather, societies have felt compelled when they were thinking straight. Traditionally, societies made the mistake of *over*utilizing the death penalty by applying it to noncapital crimes. This created a situation that actually encouraged felony murder. Reformers of the Enlightenment were quick to point this out. In *The Spirit of the Laws* (1748), Montesquieu wrote:

> It is a great abuse among us to condemn to the same punishment a person what only robs on the highway and another who robs and murders. Surely, for the public security, some difference should be made in the punishment.
>
> In China, those who add murder to robbery are cut in pieces: but not so the others; to this difference it is owing that though they rob in that country they never murder.
>
> In Russia, where the punishment of robbery and murder is the same, they always murder. The dead, they say, tell no tales.

Over the next two centuries, reformers succeeded almost completely in eliminating this dangerous ambiguity. (But they did not eliminate it entirely. As late as the 1960s, North Carolina and Georgia were still executing people for rape and "chronic burglary." The Supreme Court had half a case.) But by abolishing the death penalty, however, we only recreated the dilemma. Now the differential between armed robber and murder is only jail time and maybe a little more jail time after that. By 1990, the average armed robber was serving three years in jail; the average murderer was serving eleven. Meanwhile, less than *half* the felony and stranger murders in the country were being solved. Was there any real risk in murdering your victim? Until the recent revival of capital punishment, was there any rational deterrent?

So both homicides and executions are now headed in the right direction. Will the trend continue? Execution rates will remain high for some time, even as murder rates decline. In the 1930s, murderers were often executed within months of committing a crime. In 1999, the median murderer was executed for a crime committed in 1988. Despite hand-wringing about the imaginary "rush to judgment," five percent of death row inmates are there for crimes committed in the 1970s. Yet the costs of such delays are apparent. Had executions remained at the same reasonable level they were in the early 1960s, 450,000 Americans probably would have avoided being murdered over the next 35 years.

George W. Bush has been among the leaders in stemming what had become the nation's most alarming public health epidemic. Homicide has been traditionally high in Texas, Oklahoma, Louisiana, and Arkansas. However, these four states now account for half the nation's executions, and murder rates have dropped more precipitously there than anywhere else in the country. In regions such as New England, where there are no executions, murder rates, although traditionally low, have fallen hardly at all.

Carrying out public executions is not a pleasant task. In addition to the inevitable protestations of innocence—the jailhouse girlfriend who swears the murderer is a changed man, the outright falsehoods put out by death penalty opponents and reported as whole truths by the press—there is the moral burden of taking responsibility for ending someone's life. But that is part of the burden of public office—putting the greater good of society above one's personal qualms and preferences.

© *The American Spectator*

QUESTIONS FOR REFLECTION

1. What is Tucker's evidence that the death penalty works?

2. How do criminologists usually explain changes in the murder rate? How does Tucker respond to their explanations?

3. Why is the distinction between stranger murder and acquaintance murder important, according to Tucker?

4. How might opponents of the death penalty respond to Tucker's arguments? How persuasive do you find them to be?

PART IV

JUSTICE AND EQUALITY

Aristotle distinguishes several different senses of justice. He identifies one sense of justice with virtue as a whole, but specifically in relation to other people. Another sense of justice pertains to rectification—setting right previous wrongs. This section concerns distributive justice: the problem of distributing goods and obligations among the members of a society.

Aristotle holds a simple but extremely powerful theory of distributive justice. He believes that both goods and obligations ought to be distributed according to merit. He considers a group of people who have somehow obtained a flute. Who in the group should get the flute? The best flute player, Aristotle answers. Similarly, goods ought to go to those who deserve them—that is, those who can make the best use of them. This answer has very strong intuitive appeal. How should a professor assign grades? The top grades should go to those with the most merit, those who have performed best. Who should receive a Grammy award? Those who have produced the best music. Who should receive political power? Those who have the most political virtue, Aristotle answers—the people with the greatest ability to bring about good government.

Aristotle's theory is an end-state theory of justice. It says that people should receive goods of a certain kind to the extent that they have merit of that kind. Thus, it answers the question of distributive justice in terms of who has what other characteristics now or at some other definite time. Jean-Jacques Rousseau, Karl Marx, Friedrich Engels, and John Rawls all propose very different theories of justice, but all are similarly end-state; all specify who should get what in terms of who has what now or at some other time.

Rousseau's analysis of distributive justice is somewhat vague. He makes clear that no one should have too much and no one too little. Within the bounds this principle establishes, however, the general will rules. Recall that according to Rousseau's conception of the social contract, we would agree to form a government because we hope to gain from the cooperation it makes possible. We are willing to commit everything we have in the interests of cooperation and expect to receive in return our share of everything that anyone else has. Distribution, then, is in the hands of the community as a whole. Rousseau treats the community as a body with its own interests. He characterizes limits on the community's behavior in terms of the general will. Roughly, the community can legitimately do only what accords with the general will—that is, with the community's own self-interest. This seems to imply that a just distribution is one that accords with the interests of the community as a whole. What this distribution is, of course, is an empirical matter. But Rousseau feels confident enough to say that the multitude should not lack necessities and that the fortunate should not be able to pursue luxuries.

Marx and Engels take Rousseau's position to a more definite conclusion. They analyze social structures in terms of class struggle. They see moral language as little more than a tool in class struggle; consequently, they are reluctant to offer a general theory of justice. But Marx does provide a slogan that embodies such a theory: "From each according to his abilities, to each according to his needs!" This, too, is a patterned theory. It determines who should receive what by considering who has what abilities and needs. Note that Marx's theory has something in common with Aristotle's; both agree that responsibilities are functions of ability. Aristotle, however, believes that rewards should also be proportionate to ability; Marx believes that they should go to those in need, regardless of merit or contribution.

Marx holds that all people have a positive right to have their needs met, even if this restricts the general rights and thus the freedom of others. What good is freedom if you have no bread? Albert Camus provides an answer: Your bread depends in part on your freedom. Political and economic liberty go hand in hand. The Marxist asks that we restrict freedom now for the sake of justice and greater liberty later. But the promised end never arrives, and the loss of freedom, serious in itself, merely leads to further losses of freedom.

John Rawls offers another development of Rousseau's approach. Imagine being in the state of nature, choosing whether or not to submit to a government. To determine principles of justice, Rawls says, we must imagine that we make the choice based not on any contingent features of our own characters, but on the basis of what we share with all other human beings. Rawls thus imagines us making the choice from behind the veil of ignorance, in which we know everything we need to know about economics, political science, sociology, and so on, but know nothing about our own position in the social structure. What principles, Rawls asks, would we choose from behind the veil of ignorance? What institutions would be rational choices? He concludes that we would choose to minimize risk and so opt for a system that would make the least well off in society as well off as possible; that is, we would choose to maximize the welfare of the least advantaged. We would not choose to maximize good overall, as a utilitarian would, for we would fear coming out a loser in the social order. We would not choose absolute equality, for we have no reason to object to inequality as long as it does not disadvantage us, no matter where we might end up in the resulting society. Rawls thus advocates two principles of justice. The first is a principle of liberty, that each person should have the most liberty compatible with an equal liberty for all. The second has two parts: (a) inequalities should be to everyone's advantage (that is, those who receive less would be even worse off if others weren't receiving more) and (b) the positions to which benefits attach should be open to everyone. Part (a) is often called the *difference principle*; part (b) is a principle of equal opportunity. The difference principle, by far, has stirred the most controversy concerning Rawls's theory.

Rawls's approach to distributive justice is also an end-state theory. We determine whether a set of institutions is just by looking at the distribution they produce—not now, perhaps, but at some point in the future when the distribution stabilizes. John Locke and Robert Nozick offer a very different theory of justice. How do we determine whether people hold their possessions justly? Locke and Nozick deny that any sort of structural account can provide an answer. Do you, for example, possess this book justly? To answer that question, in their view, we need to ask, not about your abilities or your needs or your total wealth or whether your possession of the book benefits everyone, but about how you obtained it. Did you steal it? Did you buy it from someone who had the right to sell it? Locke takes property as a fundamental natural and civil right. The purpose of government, Locke insists, is to preserve property. Consequently, government cannot consider every good in society its own and reflect abstractly on how to distribute it. People acquire goods justly from nature. They buy and sell them justly. When an injustice occurs, they try to compensate for it. To determine whether a distribution is just, according to Locke and Nozick, we must see how it came about. Were the initial acquisitions just? Were subsequent transfers just? Were any injustices sufficiently rectified? If we can answer yes to these questions, then, Locke and Nozick believe, the distribution is just. Their theories are thus *historical* theories: whether a distribution is just depends on how it came about.

ARISTOTLE

from *Nicomachean Ethics*

(Source: Aristotle's Nichomachean Ethics, *translated by W. D. Ross [1925], by permission of Oxford University Press. Notes have been omitted, and punctuation has been modernized for clarity.)*

Book V

2

. . . Of particular justice and that which is just in the corresponding sense, (A) one kind is that which is manifested in distributions of honour or money or the other things that fall to be divided among those who have a share in the constitution (for in these it is possible for one man to have a share either unequal or equal to that of another), and (B) one is that which plays a rectifying part in transactions between man and man. Of this there are two divisions; of transactions (1) some are voluntary and (2) others involuntary—voluntary such transactions as sale, purchase, loan for consumption, pledging, loan for use, depositing, letting (they are called voluntary because the origin of these transactions is voluntary), while of the involuntary (a) some are clandestine, such as theft, adultery, poisoning, procuring, enticement of slaves, assassination, false witness, and (b) others are violent, such as assault, imprisonment, murder, robbery with violence, mutilation, abuse, insult.

3

(A) We have shown that both the unjust man and the unjust act are unfair or unequal; now it is clear that there is also an intermediate between the two unequals involved in either case. And this is the equal; for in any kind of action in which there is a more and a less, there is also what is equal. If, then, the unjust is unequal, the just is equal, as all men

suppose it to be, even apart from argument. And since the equal is intermediate, the just will be an intermediate. Now equality implies at least two things. The just, then, must be both intermediate and equal and relative (i.e., for certain persons). And *qua* intermediate it must be between certain things (which are respectively greater and less); *qua* equal, it involves *two* things; *qua* just, it is for certain people. The just, therefore, involves at least four terms; for the persons for whom it is in fact just are two, and the things in which it is manifested, the objects distributed, are two. And the same equality will exist between the persons and between the things concerned; for as the latter—the things concerned—are related, so are the former; if they are not equal, they will not have what is equal, but this is the origin of quarrels and complaints—when either equals have and are awarded unequal shares, or unequals equal shares. Further, this is plain from the fact that awards should be "according to merit"; for all men agree that what is just in distribution must be according to merit in some sense, though they do not all specify the same sort of merit, but democrats identify it with the status of freeman, supporters of oligarchy with wealth (or with noble birth), and supporters of aristocracy with excellence.

The just, then, is a species of the proportionate (proportion being not a property only of the kind of number which consists of abstract units, but of number in general). For proportion is equality of ratios, and involves four terms at least (that discrete proportion involves four terms is plain, but so does continuous proportion, for it uses one term as two and mentions it twice; e.g., "as the line A is to the line B, so is the line B to the line C"; the line B, then, has been mentioned twice, so that if the line B be assumed twice, the proportional terms will be four); and the just, too, involves at least four terms, and the ratio between one pair is the same as that between the other pair; for there is a similar distinction between the persons and between the things. As the term A, then, is to B, so will C be to D, and therefore, *alternando,* as A is to C, B will be to D. Therefore also the whole is in the same ratio to the whole; and this coupling the distribution effects, and, if the terms are so combined, effects justly. The conjunction, then, of the term A with C and of B with D is what is just in distribution, and this species of the just is intermediate, and the unjust is what violates the proportion; for the proportional is intermediate, and the just is proportional. (Mathematicians call this kind of proportion geometrical; for it is in geometrical proportion that it follows that the whole is to the whole as either part is to the corresponding part.) This proportion is not continuous; for we cannot get a single term standing for a person and a thing.

This, then, is what the just is—the proportional; the unjust is what violates the proportion. Hence one term becomes too great, the other too small, as indeed happens in practice; for the man who acts unjustly has too much, and the man who is unjustly treated too little, of what is good. In the case of evil the reverse is true; for the lesser evil is reckoned a good in comparison with the greater evil, since the lesser evil is rather to be chosen than the greater, and what is worthy of choice is good, and what is worthier of choice a greater good. . . .

QUESTIONS FOR REFLECTION

1. How does Aristotle argue for his assertion that justice is equality?

2. What is merit? Which interpretations of it does he discuss?

3. What particular kinds of justice does Aristotle discuss? Explain each.

4. According to Aristotle's theory of distributive justice, the just is the proportional. What does this mean? What should be proportional to what?

ARISTOTLE

from *Politics*

(*Source:* The Works of Aristotle, *Vol. X [Oxford: Clarendon Press, 1921], translated by Benjamin Jowett. Notes have been omitted, and punctuation has been modernized for clarity.*)

Book III

Section 12

In all sciences and arts the end is a good, and the greatest good and in the highest degree a good in the most authoritative of all—this is the political science of which the good is justice, in other words, the common interest. All men think justice to be a sort of equality; and to a certain extent they agree in the philosophical distinctions which have been laid down by us about Ethics. For they admit that justice is a thing and has a relation to persons, and that equals ought to have equality. But there still remains a question: equality or inequality of what? Here is a difficulty which calls for political speculation. For very likely some persons will say that offices of state ought to be unequally distributed according to superior excellence, in whatever respect, of the citizen, although there is no other difference between him and the rest of the community; for that those who differ in any one respect have different rights and claims. But, surely, if this is true, the complexion or height of a man, or any other advantage, will be a reason for his obtaining a greater share of political rights. The error here lies upon the surface, and may be illustrated from the other arts and sciences. When a number of flute-players are equal in their art, there is no reason why those of them who are better born should have better flutes given to them; for they will not play any better on the flute, and the superior instrument should be reserved for him who is the superior artist. If what I am saying is still obscure, it will be made clearer as we proceed. For if there were

a superior flute-player who was far inferior in birth and beauty, although either of these may be a greater good than the art of flute-playing, and may excel flute-playing in a greater ratio than he excels the others in his art, still he ought to have the best flutes given to him, unless the advantages of wealth and birth contribute to excellence in flute-playing, which they do not. Moreover, upon this principle any good may be compared with any other. For if a given height may be measured against wealth and against freedom, height in general may be so measured. Thus if A excels in height more than B in virtue, even if virtue in general excels height still more, all goods will be commensurable; for if a certain amount is better than some other, it is clear that some other will be equal. But since no such comparison can be made, it is evident that there is good reason why in politics men do not ground their claim to office on every sort of inequality any more than in the arts. For if some be slow, and others swift, that is no reason why the one should have little and the others much; it is in gymnastic contests that such excellence is rewarded. Whereas the rival claims of candidates for office can only be based on the possession of elements which enter into the composition of a state. And therefore the noble, or freeborn, or rich, may with good reason claim office; for holders of offices must be freemen and taxpayers: a state can be no more composed entirely of poor men than entirely of slaves. But if wealth and freedom are necessary elements, justice and valor are equally so; for without the former qualities a state cannot exist at all, without the latter not well. . . .

QUESTIONS FOR REFLECTION

1. According to Aristotle's theory of distributive justice, the just is the proportional. What does this mean? What should be proportional to what?

2. Aristotle denies that "any good may be compared with any other." Why? What is the significance of his denial?

JOHN LOCKE

from *Second Treatise of Government* (1690)

(Source: Reprinted from John Locke, Two Treatises of Government. *London: Printed for Awnsham Churchill, 1690. Spelling and punctuation have been modernized for clarity.)*

CHAPTER V / OF PROPERTY

§. 25. Whether we consider natural reason, which tells us that men, being once born, have a right to their preservation and consequently to meat and drink and such other things as nature affords for their subsistence, or revelation, which gives us an account of those grants God made of the world to Adam and to Noah and his sons, it is very clear that God, as King David says, Psal. cxv. 16., has given the earth to the children of men: given it to mankind in common. But this being supposed, it seems to some a very great difficulty how anyone should ever come to have a property in any thing: I will not content myself to answer that if it be difficult to make out property upon a supposition that God gave the world to Adam and his posterity in common, it is impossible that any man, but one universal monarch, should have any property upon a supposition that God gave the world to Adam and his heirs in succession, exclusive of all the rest of his posterity. But I shall endeavour to show how men might come to have a property in several parts of that which God gave to mankind in common, and that without any express compact of all the commoners.

§. 26. God, who has given the world to men in common, has also given them reason to make use of it to the best advantage of life and convenience. The earth and all that is therein is given to men for the support and comfort of their being. And though all the fruits it naturally produces and beasts it feeds belong to mankind in common, as they are produced by the spontaneous hand of nature, and nobody has originally a private dominion exclusive of the rest of mankind, in any of them, as they are thus in their natural state; yet being given for the use of men, there must of necessity be a means to appropriate them some way or other before they can be of any use or at all beneficial to any particular man. The fruit or venison which nourishes the wild Indian, who knows no inclosure and is still a tenant in common, must be his, and so his, *i.e.*, a part of him, that another can no longer have any right to it before it can do him any good for the support of his life.

§. 27. Though the earth and all inferior creatures be common to all men, yet every man has a property in his own person: this no body has any right to but himself. The labor of his body and the work of his hands, we may say, are properly his. Whatsoever then he removes out of the state that nature has provided, and left in it, he has mixed his labor with and joined to it something that is his own and thereby makes it his property. It being by him removed from the common state nature has placed it in, it has by this labor something annexed to it that excludes the common right of other men: for this labor being the unquestionable property of the laborer, no man but he can have a right to what that is once joined to, at least where there is enough, and as good, left in common for others.

§. 28. He that is nourished by the acorns he picked up under an oak or the apples he gathered from the trees in the wood has certainly appropriated them to himself. Nobody can deny but the nourishment is his. I ask then, when did they begin to be his? When he digested? Or when he ate? Or when he boiled? Or when he brought them home? Or when he picked them up? And it is plain, if the first gathering made them not his, nothing else could. That labor put a distinction between them and common: that added something to them more than nature, the common mother of all, had done; and so they became his private right. And will anyone say he had no right to those acorns or apples he thus appropriated, because he had not the consent of all mankind to make them his? Was it a robbery thus to assume to himself what belonged to all in common? If such a consent as that was necessary, man had starved, notwithstanding the plenty God had given him. We see in commons, which remain so by compact, that it is the taking any part of what is common and removing it out of the state nature leaves it in, which begins the property, without which the common is of no use. And the taking of this or that part does not depend on the express consent of all the commoners. Thus the grass my horse has bit, the turfs my servant has cut, and the ore I have digged in any place where I have a right to them in common with others became my property, without the assignation or consent of any body. The labor that was mine, removing them out of that common state they were in, has fixed my property to them.

§. 29. By making an explicit consent of every commoner necessary to anyone's appropriating to himself any part of what is given in common, children or servants could not cut the meat which their father or master had provided for them in common without assigning to everyone his peculiar part. Though the water running in the fountain be everyone's, yet who can doubt but that in the pitcher is his only who drew it out? His labor has taken it out of the hands of nature, where it was common and belonged equally to all her children, and has thereby appropriated it to himself.

§. 30. Thus this law of reason makes the deer that Indian's who has killed it; it is allowed to be his goods, who has bestowed his labor upon it, though before it was the common right of everyone. And amongst those who are counted the civilized part of mankind, who have made and multiplied positive laws to determine property, this original law of nature, for the beginning of property, in what was before common, still takes place; and by virtue thereof, what fish anyone catches in the ocean, that great and still remaining common of mankind, or what ambergris anyone takes up here, is by the labor that removes it out of that common state nature left it in made his property, who takes that pains about it. And even amongst us, the hare that anyone is hunting is thought his who pursues her during the chase: for being a beast that is still looked upon as common and no man's private possession, whoever has employed so much labor about any of that kind as to find and pursue her has thereby removed her from the state of nature, wherein she was common, and has begun a property.

§. 31. It will perhaps be objected to this, that if gathering the acorns, or other fruits of the earth, etc., makes a right to them, then any one may ingross as much as he will. To which I answer, Not so. The same law of nature that does by this means give us property does also bound that property too. *God has given us all things richly*, 1 Tim. vi. 12., is the voice of reason confirmed by inspiration. But how far has he given it us? To enjoy. As much as anyone can make use of to any advantage of life before it spoils, so much he may by his labor fix a property in: whatever is beyond this is more than his share and belongs to others. Nothing was made by God for man to spoil or destroy. And thus, considering the plenty of natural provisions there was a long time in the world and the few spenders and to how small a part of that provision the industry of one man could extend itself and ingross it to the prejudice of others, especially keeping within the bounds, set by reason, of what might serve for his use, there could be then little room for quarrels or contentions about property so established.

§. 32. But the chief matter of property being now not the fruits of the earth and the beasts that subsist on it, but the earth itself, as that which takes in and carries with it all the rest; I think it is plain that property in that too is acquired as the former. As much land as a man tills, plants, improves, cultivates, and can use the product of, so much is his property. He by his labor does, as it were, enclose it from the common. Nor will it invalidate his right to say everybody else has an equal title to it and therefore he cannot appropriate, he cannot enclose, without the consent of all his fellow-commoners, all mankind. God, when he gave the world in common to all mankind, commanded man also to labor, and the penury of his condition required it of him. God and his reason commanded him to subdue the earth, *i.e.,* improve it for the benefit of life, and therein lay out something upon it that was his own, his labor. He that in obedience to this command of God, subdued, tilled and sowed any part of it thereby annexed to it something that was his property, which another had no title to nor could without injury take from him.

§. 33. Nor was this appropriation of any parcel of land, by improving it, any prejudice to any other man, since there was still enough and as good left; and more than the yet unprovided could use. So that, in effect, there was never the less left for others because of his enclosure for himself: for he that leaves as much as another can make use of does as good as take nothing at all. Nobody could think himself injured by the drinking of another man, though he took a good draught, who had a whole river of the same water left him to quench his thirst; and the case of land and water, where there is enough of both, is perfectly the same. . . .

§. 37. This is certain, that in the beginning, before the desire of having more than man needed had altered the intrinsic value of things, which depends only on their usefulness to the life of man or had agreed that a little piece of yellow metal which would keep without wasting or decay should be worth a great piece of flesh or a whole heap of corn; though men had a right to appropriate by their labor each one of himself as much of the things of nature as he could use, yet this could not be much, nor to the prejudice of others, where the same plenty was still left to those who would use the same industry. To which let me add, that he who appropriates land to himself by his labor does not lessen, but increases the common stock of mankind; for the provisions serving to the support of human life produced by one acre of enclosed and cultivated land are (to speak much within compass) ten times more than those which are yielded by an acre of land of an equal richness lying waste in common. And therefore he that encloses land and has a greater plenty of the conveniencies of life from ten acres than he

could have from a hundred left to nature may truly be said to give ninety acres to mankind: for his labor now supplies him with provisions out of ten acres which were but the product of a hundred lying in common. I have here rated the improved land very low in making its product but as ten to one, when it is much nearer a hundred to one; for I ask whether in the wild woods and uncultivated waste of America, left to nature, without any improvement, tillage or husbandry, a thousand acres yield the needy and wretched inhabitants as many conveniencies of life as ten acres of equally fertile land do in Devonshire, where they are well cultivated?

Before the appropriation of land, he who gathered as much of the wild fruit, killed, caught, or tamed as many of the beasts as he could; he that so employed his pains about any of the spontaneous products of nature as any way to alter them from the state which nature put them in, by placing any of his labor on them, did thereby acquire a propriety in them: but if they perished in his possession, without their due use; if the fruits rotted or the venison putrified before he could spend it, he offended against the common law of nature and was liable to be punished; he invaded his neighbour's share, for he had no right farther than his use called for any of them, and they might serve to afford him conveniencies of life. . . .

§. 44. From all which it is evident that though the things of nature are given in common, yet man, by being master of himself, and proprietor of his own person and the actions or labor of it had still in himself the great foundation of property; and that which made up the great part of what he applied to the support or comfort of his being, when invention and arts had improved the conveniencies of life, was perfectly his own and did not belong in common to others. . . .

§. 46. The greatest part of things really useful to the life of man, and such as the necessity of subsisting made the first commoners of the world look after, as it does the Americans now, are generally things of short duration such as, if they are not consumed by use, will decay and perish of themselves; gold, silver and diamonds are things that fancy or agreement has put the value on, more than real use and the necessary support of life. Now of those good things which nature has provided in common, everyone had a right (as has been said) to as much as he could use, and property in all that he could effect with his labor; all that his industry could extend to, to alter from the state nature had put in it, was his. He that gathered a hundred bushels of acorns or apples had thereby a property in them; they were his goods as soon as gathered. He was only to look that he used them before they spoiled, else he took more than his share and robbed others. And indeed it was a foolish thing, as well as dishonest, to hoard up more than he could make use of. If he gave away a part to any body else, so that it perished not uselessly in his possession, these he also made use of. And if he also bartered away plums that would have rotted in a week for nuts that would last good for his eating a whole year, he did no injury; he wasted not the common stock, destroyed no part of the portion of goods that belonged to others, so long as nothing perished uselessly in his hands. Again, if he would give his nuts for a piece of metal, pleased with its colour; or exchange his sheep for shells, or wool for a sparkling pebble or a diamond, and keep those by him all his life, he invaded not the right of others; he might heap up as much of these durable things as he pleased, the exceeding of the bounds of his just property not lying in the largeness of his possession, but the perishing of any thing uselessly in it.

§. 47. And thus came in the use of money, some lasting thing that men might keep without spoiling and that by mutual consent men would take in exchange for the truly useful but perishable supports of life.

§. 48. And as different degrees of industry were apt to give men possessions in different proportions, so this invention of money gave them the opportunity to continue and enlarge them: for supposing an island, separate from all possible commerce with the rest of the world, wherein there were but a hundred families, but there were sheep, horses and cows, with other useful animals, wholesome fruits, and land enough for corn for a hundred thousand times as many, but nothing in the island, either because of its commonness or perishableness fit to supply the place of money; what reason could any one have there to enlarge his possessions beyond the use of his family and a plentiful supply to its consumption, either in what their own industry produced or they could barter for like perishable, useful commodities with others? Where there is not something both last-

ing and scarce and so valuable to be hoarded up, there men will not be apt to enlarge their possessions of land, were it never so rich, never so free for them to take: for I ask, what would a man value ten thousand or a hundred thousand acres of excellent land, ready cultivated and well stocked too with cattle, in the middle of the inland parts of America, where he had no hopes of commerce with other parts of the world, to draw money to him by the sale of the product? It would not be worth the enclosing, and we should see him give up again to the wild common of nature whatever was more than would supply the conveniencies of life to be had there for him and his family.

§. 49. Thus in the beginning all the world was America, and more so than that is now; for no such thing as money was any where known. Find out something that has the use and value of money amongst his neighbors; you shall see the same man will begin presently to enlarge his possessions.

§. 50. But since gold and silver, being little useful to the life of man in proportion to food, raiment, and carriage, has its value only from the consent of men, whereof labor yet makes in great part the measure, it is plain that men have agreed to a disproportionate and unequal possession of the earth, they having by a tacit and voluntary consent found out a way how a man may fairly possess more land than he himself can use the product of, by receiving in exchange for the overplus gold and silver which may be hoarded up without injury to anyone, these metals not spoiling or decaying in the hands of the possessor. This partage of things in an inequality of private possessions, men have made practicable out of the bounds of society, and without compact, only by putting a value on gold and silver and tacitly agreeing in the use of money; for in governments, the laws regulate the right of property, and the possession of land is determined by positive constitutions.

§. 51. And thus, I think, it is very easy to conceive, without any difficulty, how labor could at first begin a title of property in the common things of nature and how the spending it upon our uses bounded it. So that there could then be no reason of quarreling about title nor any doubt about the largeness of possession it gave. Right and convenience went together; for as a man had a right to all he could employ his labor upon, so he had no temptation to labor for more than he could make use of. This left no room for controversy about the title, nor for encroachment on the right of others; what portion a man carved to himself was easily seen; and it was useless, as well as dishonest, to carve himself too much or take more than he needed.

CHAPTER VIII / OF THE BEGINNING OF POLITICAL SOCIETIES

§. 95. Men being, as has been said, by nature all free, equal, and independent, no one can be put out of this estate and subjected to the political power of another without his own consent. The only way whereby any one divests himself of his natural liberty and puts on the bonds of civil society is by agreeing with other men to join and unite into a community for their comfortable, safe, and peaceable living one amongst another, in a secure enjoyment of their properties and a greater security against any that are not of it. This any number of men may do, because it injures not the freedom of the rest; they are left as they were in the liberty of the state of nature. When any number of men have so consented to make one community or government, they are thereby presently incorporated and make one body politic, wherein the majority have a right to act and conclude the rest.

§. 96. For when any number of men have, by the consent of every individual, made a community, they have thereby made that community one body, with a power to act as one body, which is only by the will and determination of the majority: for that which acts any community, being only the consent of the individuals of it, and it being necessary to that which is one body to move one way, it is necessary the body should move that way whither the greater force carries it, which is the consent of the majority; or else it is impossible it should act or continue one body, one community, which the consent of every individual that united into it agreed that it should; and so everyone is bound by that consent to be concluded by the majority. And therefore we see that in assemblies empowered to act by positive laws, where no number is set by that positive law which empowers them, the act of the majority passes for the act of

the whole and of course determines as having, by the law of nature and reason, the power of the whole.

§. 97. And thus every man, by consenting with others to make one body politic under one government, puts himself under an obligation to everyone of that society to submit to the determination of the majority and to be concluded by it; or else this original compact, whereby he with others incorporated into one society, would signify nothing and be no compact if he be left free and under no other ties than he was in before in the state of nature. For what appearance would there be of any compact? what new engagement if he were no farther tied by any decrees of the society than he himself thought fit and did actually consent to? This would be still as great a liberty as he himself had before his compact, or anyone else in the state of nature has, who may submit himself and consent to any acts of it if he thinks fit.

§. 98. For if the consent of the majority shall not, in reason, be received as the act of the whole and conclude every individual, nothing but the consent of every individual can make anything to be the act of the whole: but such a consent is next to impossible ever to be had, if we consider the infirmities of health and avocations of business, which in a number, though much less than that of a commonwealth, will necessarily keep many away from the public assembly. To which if we add the variety of opinions and contrariety of interest which unavoidably happen in all collections of men, the coming into society upon such terms would be only like Cato's coming into the theatre only to go out again. Such a constitution as this would make the mighty Leviathan of a shorter duration than the feeblest creatures and not let it outlast the day it was born in, which cannot be supposed until we can think that rational creatures should desire and constitute societies only to be dissolved, for where the majority cannot conclude the rest, there they cannot act as one body and consequently will be immediately dissolved again.

§. 99. Whosoever therefore out of a state of nature unite into a community must be understood to give up all the power necessary to the ends for which they unite into society to the majority of the community, unless they expressly agreed in any number greater than the majority. And this is done by barely agreeing to unite into one political society, which is all the compact that is, or needs be, between the individuals that enter into or make up a commonwealth. And thus that which begins and actually constitutes any political society is nothing but the consent of any number of freemen capable of a majority to unite and incorporate into such a society. And this is that, and that only, which did or could give beginning to any lawful government in the world. . . .

CHAPTER IX / OF THE ENDS OF POLITICAL SOCIETY AND GOVERNMENT

§. 123. If man in the state of nature be so free, as has been said; if he be absolute lord of his own person and possessions, equal to the greatest and subject to nobody, why will he part with his freedom? why will he give up this empire and subject himself to the dominion and control of any other power? To which it is obvious to answer that though in the state of nature he hath such a right, yet the enjoyment of it is very uncertain and constantly exposed to the invasion of others; for all being kings as much as he, every man his equal, and the greater part no strict observers of equity and justice, the enjoyment of the property he has in this state is very unsafe, very unsecure. This makes him willing to quit a condition which, however free, is full of fears and continual dangers; and it is not without reason that he seeks out and is willing to join in society with others who are already united, or have a mind to unite, for the mutual preservation of their lives, liberties and estates, which I call by the general name *property*.

§. 124. The great and chief end, therefore, of men's uniting into commonwealths, and putting themselves under government is the preservation of their property. To which in the state of nature there are many things wanting.

First, there wants an established, settled, known law, received and allowed by common consent to be the standard of right and wrong, and the common measure to decide all controversies between them; for though the law of nature be plain and intelligible to all rational creatures, yet men being biased by their interest, as well as ignorant for want of study of

it, are not apt to allow of it as a law binding to them in the application of it to their particular cases.

§. 125. *Secondly,* in the state of nature there wants a known and indifferent judge with authority to determine all differences according to the established law; for everyone in that state being both judge and executioner of the law of nature, men being partial to themselves, passion and revenge is very apt to carry them too far and with too much heat in their own cases, as well as negligence and unconcernedness to make them too remiss in other men's.

§. 126. *Thirdly,* in the state of nature there often wants power to back and support the sentence when right and to give it due execution. They who by any injustice offended will seldom fail where they are able by force to make good their injustice; such resistance many times makes the punishment dangerous and frequently destructive to those who attempt it.

§. 127. Thus mankind, notwithstanding all the privileges of the state of nature, being but in an ill condition while they remain in it, are quickly driven into society. Hence it comes to pass that we seldom find any number of men live any time together in this state. The inconveniences that they are therein exposed to by the irregular and uncertain exercise of the power every man has of punishing the transgressions of others make them take sanctuary under the established laws of government and therein seek the preservation of their property. It is this makes them so willingly give up every one his single power of punishing, to be exercised by such alone as shall be appointed to it amongst them and by such rules as the community, or those authorized by them to that purpose, shall agree on. And in this we have the original right and rise of both the legislative and executive power, as well as of the governments and societies themselves.

§. 128. For in the state of nature, to omit the liberty he has of innocent delights, a man has two powers.

The first is to do whatsoever he thinks fit for the preservation of himself and others within the permission of the law of nature, by which law, common to them all, he and all the rest of mankind are one community, make up one society, distinct from all other creatures. And were it not for the corruption and viciousness of degenerate men, there would be no need of any other, no necessity that men should separate from this great and natural community and by positive agreements combine into smaller and divided associations.

The other power a man has in the state of nature is the power to punish the crimes committed against that law. Both these he gives up when he joins in a private, if I may so call it, or particular politic society and incorporates into any commonwealth separate from the rest of mankind.

§. 129. The first power, *viz.,* of doing whatsoever he thought for the preservation of himself and the rest of mankind, he gives up to be regulated by laws made by the society, so far forth as the preservation of himself and the rest of that society shall require; which laws of the society in many things confine the liberty he had by the law of nature.

§. 130. Secondly, the power of punishing he wholly gives up and engages his natural force (which he might before employ in the execution of the law of nature, by his own single authority, as he thought fit) to assist the executive power of the society, as the law thereof shall require; for being now in a new state, wherein he is to enjoy many conveniencies from the labor, assistance, and society of others in the same community, as well as protection from its whole strength, he is to part also with as much of his natural liberty in providing for himself as the good, prosperity, and safety of the society shall require; which is not only necessary, but just, since the other members of the society do the like.

§. 131. But though men, when they enter into society, give up the equality, liberty, and executive power they had in the state of nature, into the hands of the society to be so far disposed of by the legislative as the good of the society shall require, yet, it being only with an intention in everyone the better to preserve himself, his liberty and property (for no rational creature can be supposed to change his condition with an intention to be worse), the power of the society, or legislative constituted by them, can never be supposed to extend farther than the common good but is obliged to secure everyone's property by providing against those three defects above mentioned that made the state of nature so unsafe and uneasy. And so whoever has the legislative or supreme power of any commonwealth is bound to govern by established standing laws promulgated and known to the people, and not by extemporary

decrees; by indifferent and upright judges, who are to decide controversies by those laws and to employ the force of the community at home only in the execution of such laws or abroad to prevent or redress foreign injuries and secure the community from inroads and invasion. And all this to be directed to no other end but the peace, safety, and public good of the people.

CHAPTER XI / OF THE EXTENT OF THE LEGISLATIVE POWER

§. 134. The great end of men's entering into society, being the enjoyment of their properties in peace and safety, and the great instrument and means of that being the laws established in that society, the first and fundamental positive law of all commonwealths is the establishing of the legislative power; as the first and fundamental natural law, which is to govern even the legislative itself, is the preservation of the society and (as far as will consist with the public good) of every person in it. This legislative is not only the supreme power of the commonwealth, but sacred and unalterable in the hands where the community have once placed it; nor can any edict of anybody else, in what form soever conceived or by what power soever backed, have the force and obligation of a law which has not its sanction from that legislative which the public has chosen and appointed; for without this the law could not have that which is absolutely necessary to its being a law, the consent of the society, over whom no body can have a power to make laws but by their own consent and by authority received from them; and therefore all the obedience, which by the most solemn ties anyone can be obliged to pay, ultimately terminates in this supreme power and is directed by those laws which it enacts; nor can any oaths to any foreign power whatsoever or any domestic subordinate power discharge any member of the society from his obedience to the legislative acting pursuant to their trust, nor oblige him to any obedience contrary to the laws so enacted or farther than they do allow, it being ridiculous to imagine one can be tied ultimately to obey any power in the society which is not the supreme.

§. 135. Though the legislative, whether placed in one or more, whether it be always in being or only by intervals, though it be the supreme power in every commonwealth; yet,

First, it is not nor can possibly be absolutely arbitrary over the lives and fortunes of the people; for it being but the joint power of every member of the society given up to that person, or assembly which is legislator, it can be no more than those persons had in a state of nature before they entered into society and gave up to the community; for nobody can transfer to another more power than he has in himself, and nobody has an absolute arbitrary power over himself or over any other to destroy his own life or take away the life or property of another. A man, as has been proved, cannot subject himself to the arbitrary power of another; and having in the state of nature no arbitrary power over the life, liberty, or possession of another, but only so much as the law of nature gave him for the preservation of himself and the rest of mankind, this is all he does, or can give up to the commonwealth, and by it to the legislative power, so that the legislative can have no more than this. Their power, in the utmost bounds of it, is limited to the public good of the society. It is a power that has no other end but preservation and therefore can never have a right to destroy, enslave, or designedly to impoverish the subjects. The obligations of the law of nature cease not in society, but only in many cases are drawn closer and have by human laws known penalties annexed to them to enforce their observation. Thus the law of nature stands as an eternal rule to all men, legislators as well as others. The rules that they make for other men's actions, must, as well as their own and other men's actions, be conformable to the law of nature, i.e., to the will of God, of which that is a declaration, and the fundamental law of nature being the preservation of mankind, no human sanction can be good or valid against it.

§. 136. *Secondly,* the legislative, or supreme authority, cannot assume to itself a power to rule by extemporary arbitrary decrees, but is bound to dispense justice and decide the rights of the subject by promulgated standing laws and known authorized judges; for the law of nature being unwritten and so nowhere to be found but in the minds of men, they who through passion or interest shall miscite or misapply it cannot so easily be convinced of their mistake where there is no established judge; and so it serves not, as it ought, to determine the rights and fence the properties of those that live under it, especially where everyone is judge, interpreter, and executioner of it too, and that in his own case; and he that has right on his side, having ordinarily but his own single strength, has not force enough to defend himself from injuries or to punish delinquents. To avoid these inconveniences, which disorder men's properties in the state of nature, men unite into societies that they may have the united strength of the whole society to secure and defend their properties and may have standing rules to bound it, by which everyone may know what is his. To this end it is that men give up all their natural power to the society which they enter into, and the community put the legislative power into such hands as they think fit, with this trust, that they shall be governed by declared laws, or else their peace, quiet, and property will still be at the same uncertainty as it was in the state of nature.

§. 137. Absolute arbitrary power, or governing without settled standing laws, can neither of them consist with the ends of society and government, which men would not quit the freedom of the state of nature for, and tie themselves up under, were it not to preserve their lives, liberties and fortunes, and by stated rules of right and property to secure their peace and quiet. It cannot be supposed that they should intend, had they a power so to do, to give to anyone, or more, an absolute arbitrary power over their persons and estates and put a force into the magistrate's hand to execute his unlimited will arbitrarily upon them. This were to put themselves into a worse condition than the state of nature, wherein they had a liberty to defend their right against the injuries of others and were upon equal terms of force to maintain it, whether invaded by a single man or many in combination. Whereas by supposing they have given up themselves to the absolute arbitrary power and will of a legislator, they have disarmed themselves and armed him to make a prey of them when he pleases; he being in a much worse condition, who is exposed to the arbitrary power of one man who has the command of 100,000, than he that is exposed to the arbitrary power of 100,000 single men; nobody being secure, that his will, who has such a command, is better than that of other men, though his force be 100,000 times stronger. And therefore, whatever form the commonwealth is under, the ruling power ought to govern by declared and received laws, and not by extemporary dictates and undetermined resolutions: for then mankind will be in a far worse conditon than in the state of nature, if they shall have armed one, or a few men with the joint power of a multitude, to force them to obey at pleasure the exorbitant and unlimited decrees of their sudden thoughts or unrestrained, and until that moment unknown wills, without having any measures set down which may guide and justify their actions; for all the power the government has, being only for the good of the society, as it ought not to be arbitrary and at pleasure, so it ought to be exercised by established and promulgated laws that both the people may know their duty and be safe and secure within the limits of the law and the rulers too kept within their bounds and not be tempted by the power they have in their hands to employ it to such purposes and by such measures as they would not have known and own not willingly.

§. 138. *Thirdly,* the supreme power cannot take from any man any part of his property without his own consent; for the preservation of property being the end of government and that for which men enter into society, it necessarily supposes and requires that the people should have property, without which they must be supposed to lose that, by entering into society, which was the end for which they entered into it; too gross an absurdity for any man to own. Men therefore in society having property, they have such a right to the goods which by the law of the community are theirs, that nobody has a right to take their substance or any part of it from them without their own consent: without this they have no property at all; for I have truly no property in that which another can by right take from me when he pleases against my consent. Hence it is a mistake to think that the supreme or legislative power of any commonwealth can do what it will and dispose of the estates of the subject arbitrarily or take any part of them at pleasure. This is not much to be feared in governments where the legislative consists, wholly or in part, in assemblies which are variable, whose members upon the dissolution of the assembly are subjects under the common laws of their country equally with the rest. But in governments, where the legislative is in one lasting assembly always in being, or in one man, as in absolute monarchies, there is danger still that

they will think themselves to have a distinct interest from the rest of the community and so will be apt to increase their own riches and power by taking what they think fit from the people; for a man's property is not at all secure, though there be good and equitable laws to set the bounds of it between him and his fellow subjects, if he who commands those subjects have power to take from any private man what part he pleases of his property and use and dispose of it as he thinks good.

§. 139. But government, into whatsoever hands it is put, being, as I have before shown, entrusted with this condition and for this end, that men might have and secure their properties, the prince or senate, however it may have power to make laws for the regulating of property between the subjects one amongst another, yet can never have a power to take to themselves the whole or any part of the subjects' property without their own consent: for this would be in effect to leave them no property at all. And to let us see that even absolute power, where it is necessary, is not arbitrary by being absolute but is still limited by that reason and confined to those ends which required it in some cases to be absolute, we need look no farther than the common practice of martial discipline: for the preservation of the army, and in it of the whole commonwealth, requires an absolute obedience to the command of every superior officer, and it is justly death to disobey or dispute the most dangerous or unreasonable of them; but yet we see that neither the sergeant that could command a soldier to march up to the mouth of a cannon or stand in a breach where he is almost sure to perish can command that soldier to give him one penny of his money; nor the general that can condemn him to death for deserting his post or for not obeying the most desperate orders can yet, with all his absolute power of life and death, dispose of one farthing of that soldier's estate or seize one jot of his goods, whom yet he can command anything, and hang for the least disobedience; because such a blind obedience is necessary to that end for which the commander has his power, *viz.,* the preservation of the rest, but the disposing of his goods has nothing to do with it.

§. 140. It is true, governments cannot be supported without great charge, and it is fit everyone who enjoys his share of the protection should pay out of his estate his proportion for the maintenance of it.

But still it must be with his own consent, *i.e.,* the consent of the majority, giving it either by themselves or their representatives chosen by them; for if any one shall claim a power to lay and levy taxes on the people by his own authority and without such consent of the people, he thereby invades the fundamental law of property and subverts the end of government: for what property have I in that which another may be right to take when he pleases to himself?

§. 141. *Fourthly,* the legislative cannot transfer the power of making laws to any other hands, for it being but a delegated power from the people, they who have it cannot pass it over to others. The people alone can appoint the form of the commonwealth, which is by constituting the legislative and appointing in whose hands that shall be. And when the people have said, We will submit to rules and be governed by laws made by such men and in such forms, nobody else can say other men shall make laws for them; nor can the people be bound by any laws but such as are enacted by those whom they have chosen and authorized to make laws for them. The power of the legislative, being derived from the people by a positive voluntary grant and institution, can be no other than what that positive grant conveyed, which being only to make laws and not to make legislators, the legislative can have no power to transfer their authority to making laws and place it in other hands.

§. 142. These are the bounds which the trust that is put in them by the society and the law of God and nature have set to the legislative power of every commonwealth, in all forms of government.

First, they are to govern by promulgated established laws, not to be varied in particular cases, but to have one rule for rich and poor, for the favourite at court, and the country man at plough.

Secondly, these laws also ought to be designed for no other end ultimately but the good of the people.

Thirdly, they must not raise taxes on the property of the people without the consent of the people, given by themselves or their deputies. And this properly concerns only such governments where the legislative is always in being, or at least where the people have not reserved any part of the legislative to deputies, to be from time to time chosen by themselves.

Fourthly, the legislative neither must nor can transfer the power of making laws to any body else or place it anywhere but where the people have.

QUESTIONS FOR REFLECTION

1. Locke takes the right to property as natural. Why? What allows me to appropriate things I find in nature? Are there limits to my right of appropriation?

2. What, for Locke, justifies allowing a person to appropriate more than he or she needs?

3. How does money affect principles of property, in Locke's view?

4. What, for Locke, is the chief end of government? How does it limit government action?

5. Why, according to Locke, is the minority bound to follow the majority's decision?

JEAN-JACQUES ROUSSEAU

from *Discourse on the Origin of Inequality*

(*Source:* The Social Contract and Discourses, *translated by G. D. H. Cole. London: J. M. Dent & Sons, Ltd., 1913.*)

The Second Part

The first man who, having enclosed a piece of ground, bethought himself of saying *This is mine,* and found people simple enough to believe him, was the real founder of civil society. From how many crimes, wars and murders, from how many horrors and misfortunes might not any one have saved mankind, by pulling up the stakes, or filling up the ditch, and crying to his fellows, "Beware of listening to this impostor; you are undone if you once forget that the fruits of the earth belong to us all, and the earth itself to nobody." But there is great probability that things had then already come to such a pitch, that they could no longer continue as they were; for the idea of property depends on many prior ideas, which could only be acquired successively, and cannot have been formed all at once in the human mind. Mankind must have made very considerable progress, and acquired considerable knowledge and industry which they must also have transmitted and increased from age to age, before they arrived at this last point of the state of nature. Let us then go farther back, and endeavour to unify under a single point of view that slow succession of events and discoveries in the most natural order.

Man's first feeling was that of his own existence, and his first care that of self-preservation. The produce of the earth furnished him with all he needed, and instinct told him how to use it. Hunger and other appetites made him at various times experience various modes of existence; and among these was one which urged him to propagate his species—a blind propensity that, having nothing to do with the heart, produced a merely animal act. The want once gratified, the two sexes knew each other no more; and even the offspring was nothing to its mother, as soon as it could do without her. . . .

Other men, it is true, were not then to him what they now are to us, and he had no greater intercourse with them than with other animals; yet they were not neglected in his observations. The conformities, which he would in time discover between them, and between himself and his female, led him to judge of others which were not then perceptible; and finding that they all behaved as he himself would have done in like circumstances, he naturally inferred that their manner of thinking and acting was altogether in conformity with his own. This important truth, once deeply impressed on his mind, must have induced him, from an intuitive feeling more certain and much more rapid than any kind of reasoning, to pursue the rules of conduct, which he had best observe towards them, for his own security and advantage.

Taught by experience that the love of well-being is the sole motive of human actions, he found himself in a position to distinguish the few cases, in which mutual interest might justify him in relying upon the assistance of his fellows; and also the still fewer cases in which a conflict of interests might give cause to suspect them. In the former case, he joined in the same herd with them, or at most in some kind of loose association, that laid no restraint on its members, and lasted no longer than the transitory occasion that formed it. In the latter case, every one sought his own private advantage, either by open force, if he thought himself strong enough, or by address and cunning, if he felt himself the weaker. . . .

As ideas and feelings succeeded one another, and heart and head were brought into play, men continued to lay aside their original wildness; their private connections became every day more intimate as their limits extended. They accustomed themselves to assemble before their huts round a large tree; singing and dancing, the true offspring of love and leisure, became the amusement, or rather the occupation, of men and women thus assembled together with nothing else to do. Each one began to consider the rest, and to wish to be considered in turn; and thus a value came to be attached to public esteem. Whoever sang or danced best, whoever was the handsomest, the strongest, the most dexterous, or the most eloquent, came to be of most consideration; and this was the first step towards inequality, and at the same time towards vice. From these first distinctions arose on the one side vanity and contempt and on the other shame and envy: and the fermentation caused by these new leavens ended by producing combinations fatal to innocence and happiness.

As soon as men began to value one another, and the idea of consideration had got a footing in the mind, every one put in his claim to it, and it became impossible to refuse it to any with impunity. Hence arose the first obligations of civility even among savages; and every intended injury became an affront; because, besides the hurt which might result from it, the party injured was certain to find in it a contempt for his person, which was often more insupportable than the hurt itself.

Thus, as every man punished the contempt shown him by others, in proportion to his opinion of himself, revenge became terrible, and men bloody and cruel. This is precisely the state reached by most of the savage nations known to us: and it is for want of having made a proper distinction in our ideas, and seen how very far they already are from the state of nature, that so many writers have hastily concluded that man is naturally cruel, and requires civil institutions to make him more mild; whereas nothing is more gentle than man in his primitive state, as he is placed by nature at an equal distance from the stupidity of brutes, and the fatal ingenuity of civilised man. Equally confined by instinct and reason to the sole care of guarding himself against the mischiefs which threaten him, he is restrained by natural compassion from doing any injury to others, and is not led to do such a thing even in return for injuries received. For, according to the axiom of the wise Locke, *There can be no injury, where there is no property.*

But it must be remarked that the society thus formed, and the relations thus established among men, required of them qualities different from those which they possessed from their primitive constitution. Morality began to appear in human actions, and every one, before the institution of law, was the only judge and avenger of the injuries done him, so that the goodness which was suitable in the pure state of nature was no longer proper in the newborn state of society. Punishments had to be made more severe, as opportunities of offending became more frequent, and the dread of vengeance had to take the place of the rigour of the law. Thus, though men had become less patient, and their natural compassion had already suffered some diminution, this period of expansion of the human faculties, keeping a just mean between the indolence of the primitive state and the petulant activity of our egoism, must have been the happiest and most stable of epochs. The more we reflect on it, the more we shall find that this state was the least subject to revolutions, and altogether the very best man could experience; so that he can have departed from it only through some fatal accident, which, for the public good, should never have happened. The example of savages, most of whom have been found in this state, seems to prove that men were meant to remain in it, that it is the real youth of the world, and that all subsequent advances have been apparently so many steps towards the perfection of the individual, but in reality towards the decrepitude of the species.

So long as men remained content with their rustic huts, so long as they were satisfied with clothes made of the skins of animals and sewn together with thorns and fishbones, adorned themselves only with feathers and shells, and continued to paint their bodies different colours, to improve and beautify their bows and arrows and to make with sharp-edged stones fishing boats or clumsy musical instruments; in a word, so long as they undertook only what a single person could accomplish, and confined themselves to such arts as did not require the joint labor of several hands, they lived free, healthy, honest and happy lives, so long as their nature allowed, and as they continued to enjoy the pleasures of mutual and independent intercourse. But from the moment one man began to stand in need of the help of another; from the moment it appeared advantageous to any one man to have enough provisions for two, equality disappeared, property was introduced, work became indispensable, and vast forests became smiling fields, which man had to water with the sweat of his brow, and where slavery and misery were soon seen to germinate and grow up with the crops.

Metallurgy and agriculture were the two arts which produced this great revolution. The poets tell us it was gold and silver, but, for the philosophers, it was iron and corn, which first civilised men, and ruined humanity. Thus both were unknown to the savages of America, who for that reason are still savage: the other nations also seem to have continued in a state of barbarism while they practised only one of these arts. One of the best reasons, perhaps, why Europe has been, if not longer, at least more constantly and highly civilised than the rest of the world, is that it is at once the most abundant in iron and the most fertile in corn. . . .

The cultivation of the earth necessarily brought about its distribution; and property, once recognised, gave rise to the first rules of justice; for, to secure each man his own, it had to be possible for each to have something. Besides, as men began to look forward to the future, and all had something to lose, every one had reason to apprehend that reprisals would follow any injury he might do to another. This origin is so much the more natural, as it is impossible to conceive how property can come from anything but manual labor: for what else can a man add to things which he does not originally create, so as to make them his own property? It is the husbandman's labor alone that, giving him a title to the produce of the ground he has tilled, gives him a claim also to the land itself, at least till harvest; and so, from year to year, a constant possession which is easily transformed into property. When the ancients, says Grotius, gave to Ceres* the title of Legislatrix, and to a festival celebrated in her honour the name of Thesmophoria, they meant by that that the distribution of lands had produced a new kind of right:

that is to say, the right of property, which is different from the right deducible from the law of nature.

In this state of affairs, equality might have been sustained, had the talents of individuals been equal, and had, for example, the use of iron and the consumption of commodities always exactly balanced each other; but, as there was nothing to preserve this balance, it was soon disturbed; the strongest did most work; the most skilful turned his labor to best account; the most ingenious devised methods of diminishing his labor: the husbandman wanted more iron, or the smith more corn, and, while both labored equally, the one gained a great deal by his work, while the other could hardly support himself. Thus natural inequality unfolds itself insensibly with that of combination, and the difference between men, developed by their different circumstances, becomes more sensible and permanent in its effects, and begins to have an influence, in the same proportion, over the lot of individuals.

Matters once at this pitch, it is easy to imagine the rest. I shall not detain the reader with a description of the successive invention of other arts, the development of language, the trial and utilisation of talents, the inequality of fortunes, the use and abuse of riches, and all the details connected with them which the reader can easily supply for himself. I shall confine myself to a glance at mankind in this new situation.

Behold then all human faculties developed, memory and imagination in full play, egoism interested, reason active, and the mind almost at the highest point of its perfection. Behold all the natural qualities in action, the rank and condition of every man assigned him; not merely his share of property and his power to serve or injure others, but also his wit, beauty, strength or skill, merit or talents: and these being the only qualities capable of commanding respect, it soon became necessary to possess or to affect them.

It now became the interest of men to appear what they really were not. To be and to seem became two totally different things; and from this distinction sprang insolent pomp and cheating trickery, with all the numerous vices that go in their train. On the other hand, free and independent as men were before, they were now, in consequence of a multiplicity of new wants, brought into subjection, as it were, to all nature, and particularly to one another; and each became in some degree a slave even in becoming the

---

* Ceres was the goddess of agriculture.—ED.

master of other men: if rich, they stood in need of the services of others; if poor, of their assistance; and even a middle condition did not enable them to do without one another. Man must now, therefore, have been perpetually employed in getting others to interest themselves in his lot, and in making them, apparently at least, if not really, find their advantage in promoting his own. Thus he must have been sly and artful in his behaviour to some, and imperious and cruel to others; being under a kind of necessity to ill use all the persons of whom he stood in need, when he could not frighten them into compliance, and did not judge it his interest to be useful to them. Insatiable ambition, the thirst of raising their respective fortunes, not so much from real want as from the desire to surpass others, inspired all men with a vile propensity to injure one another, and with a secret jealousy, which is the more dangerous, as it puts on the mask of benevolence, to carry its point with greater security. In a word, there arose rivalry and competition on the one hand, and conflicting interests on the other, together with a secret desire on both of profiting at the expense of others. All these evils were the first effects of property, and the inseparable attendants of growing inequality.

Before the invention of signs to represent riches, wealth could hardly consist in anything but lands and cattle, the only real possessions men can have. But, when inheritances so increased in number and extent as to occupy the whole of the land, and to border on one another, one man could aggrandise himself only at the expense of another; at the same time the supernumeraries, who had been too weak or too indolent to make such acquisitions, and had grown poor without sustaining any loss, because, while they saw everything change around them, they remained still the same, were obliged to receive their subsistence, or steal it, from the rich; and this soon bred, according to their different characters, dominion and slavery, or violence and rapine. The wealthy, on their part, had no sooner begun to taste the pleasure of command, than they disdained all others, and, using their old slaves to acquire new, thought of nothing but subduing and enslaving their neighbours; like ravenous wolves, which, having once tasted human flesh, despise every other food and thenceforth seek only men to devour.

Thus, as the most powerful or the most miserable considered their might or misery as a kind of right to the possessions of others, equivalent, in their opinion, to that of property, the destruction of equality was attended by the most terrible disorders. Usurpations by the rich, robbery by the poor, and the unbridled passions of both, suppressed the cries of natural compassion and the still feeble voice of justice, and filled men with avarice, ambition and vice. Between the title of the strongest and that of the first occupier, there arose perpetual conflicts, which never ended but in battles and bloodshed. The newborn state of society thus gave rise to a horrible state of war; men thus harassed and depraved were no longer capable of retracing their steps or renouncing the fatal acquisitions they had made, but, laboring by the abuse of the faculties which do them honor, merely to their own confusion, brought themselves to the brink of ruin.

Attonitus novitate mali, divesque miserque,
Effugere optat opes; et quæ modo voverat odit. *

It is impossible that men should not at length have reflected on so wretched a situation, and on the calamities that overwhelmed them. The rich, in particular, must have felt how much they suffered by a constant state of war, of which they bore all the expense; and in which, though all risked their lives, they alone risked their property. Besides, however speciously they might disguise their usurpations, they knew that they were founded on precarious and false titles; so that, if others took from them by force what they themselves had gained by force, they would have no reason to complain. Even those who had been enriched by their own industry, could hardly base their proprietorship on better claims. It was in vain to repeat, "I built this well; I gained this spot by my industry." Who gave you your standing, it might be answered, and what right have you to demand payment of us for doing what we never asked you to do? Do you not know that numbers of your fellow creatures are starving, for want of what you have too much of? You ought to have had the express and universal consent of mankind, before appropriating more of the common subsistence than you needed for your own maintenance. Destitute of

---

* [Ovid, Metamorphoses xi, 127.
    Both rich and poor, shocked at their new-found ills,
    Would fly from wealth, and lose what they had sought.]

valid reasons to justify and sufficient strength to defend himself, able to crush individuals with ease, but easily crushed himself by a troop of bandits, one against all, and incapable, on account of mutual jealousy, of joining with his equals against numerous enemies united by the common hope of plunder, the rich man, thus urged by necessity, conceived at length the profoundest plan that ever entered the mind of man: this was to employ in his favour the forces of those who attacked him, to make allies of his adversaries, to inspire them with different maxims, and to give them other institutions as favourable to himself as the law of nature was unfavourable.

With this view, after having represented to his neighbours the horror of a situation which armed every man against the rest, and made their possessions as burdensome to them as their wants, and in which no safety could be expected either in riches or in poverty, he readily devised plausible arguments to make them close with his design. "Let us join," said he, "to guard the weak from oppression, to restrain the ambitious, and secure to every man the possession of what belongs to him: let us institute rules of justice and peace, to which all without exception may be obliged to conform; rules that may in some measure make amends for the caprices of fortune, by subjecting equally the powerful and the weak to the observance of reciprocal obligations. Let us, in a word, instead of turning our forces against ourselves, collect them in a supreme power which may govern us by wise laws, protect and defend all the members of the association, repulse their common enemies, and maintain eternal harmony among us."

Far fewer words to this purpose would have been enough to impose on men so barbarous and easily seduced; especially as they had too many disputes among themselves to do without arbitrators, and too much ambition and avarice to go long without masters. All ran headlong to their chains, in hopes of securing their liberty; for they had just wit enough to perceive the advantages of political institutions, without experience enough to enable them to foresee the dangers. The most capable of foreseeing the dangers were the very persons who expected to benefit by them; and even the most prudent judged it not inexpedient to sacrifice one part of their freedom to ensure the rest; as a wounded man has his arm cut off to save the rest of his body.

Such was, or may well have been, the origin of society and law, which bound new fetters on the poor, and gave new powers to the rich; which irretrievably destroyed natural liberty, eternally fixed the law of property and inequality, converted clever usurpation into unalterable right, and, for the advantage of a few ambitious individuals, subjected all mankind to perpetual labor, slavery and wretchedness. It is easy to see how the establishment of one community made that of all the rest necessary, and how, in order to make head against united forces, the rest of mankind had to unite in turn. Societies soon multiplied and spread over the face of the earth, till hardly a corner of the world was left in which a man could escape the yoke, and withdraw his head from beneath the sword which he saw perpetually hanging over him by a thread. Civil right having thus become the common rule among the members of each community, the law of nature maintained its place only between different communities, where, under the name of the right of nations, it was qualified by certain tacit conventions, in order to make commerce practicable, and serve as a substitute for natural compassion, which lost, when applied to societies, almost all the influence it had over individuals, and survived no longer except in some great cosmopolitan spirits, who, breaking down the imaginary barriers that separate different peoples, follow the example of our Sovereign Creator, and include the whole human race in their benevolence.

But bodies politic, remaining thus in a state of nature among themselves, presently experienced the inconveniences which had obliged individuals to forsake it; for this state became still more fatal to these great bodies than it had been to the individuals of whom they were composed. Hence arose national wars, battles, murders, and reprisals, which shock nature and outrage reason; together with all those horrible prejudices which class among the virtues the honor of shedding human blood. The most distinguished men hence learned to consider cutting each other's throats a duty; at length men massacred their fellow creatures by thousands without so much as knowing why, and committed more murders in a single day's fighting, and more violent outrages in the sack of a single town, than were committed in the state of nature during whole ages over the whole earth. Such were the first effects which we can see to have followed the division of mankind into different communities. . . .

If we follow the progress of inequality in these various revolutions, we shall find that the establishment of laws and of the right of property was its first term, the institution of magistracy the second, and the conversion of legitimate into arbitrary power the third and last; so that the condition of rich and poor was authorized by the first period; that of powerful and weak by the second; and only by the third that of master and slave, which is the last degree of inequality, and the term at which all the rest remain, when they have got so far, till the government is either entirely dissolved by new revolutions, or brought back again to legitimacy.

To understand this progress as necessary we must consider not so much the motives for the establishment of the body politic, as the forms it assumes in actuality, and the faults that necessarily attend it: for the flaws which make social institutions necessary are the same as make the abuse of them unavoidable. . . .

This is the last term of inequality, the extreme point that closes the circle, and meets that from which we set out. Here all private persons return to their first equality, because they are nothing; and, subjects having no law but the will of their master, and their master no restraint but his passions, all notions of good and all principles of equity again vanish. There is here a complete return to the law of the strongest, and so to a new state of nature, differing from that we set out from; for the one was a state of nature in its first purity, while this is the consequence of excessive corruption. There is so little difference between the two states in other respects, and the contract of government is so completely dissolved by despotism, that the despot is master only so long as he remains the strongest; as soon as he can be expelled, he has no right to complain of violence. The popular insurrection that ends in the death or deposition of a Sultan is as lawful an act as those by which he disposed, the day before, of the lives and fortunes of his subjects. As he was maintained by force alone, it is force alone that overthrows him. Thus everything takes place according to the natural order; and, whatever may be the result of such frequent and precipitate revolutions, no one man has reason to complain of the injustice of another, but only of his own ill fortune or indiscretion.

If the reader thus discovers and retraces the lost and forgotten road, by which man must have passed from the state of nature to the state of society; if he carefully restores, along with the intermediate situations which I have just described, those which want of time has compelled me to suppress, or my imagination has failed to suggest, he cannot fail to be struck by the vast distance which separates the two states. It is in tracing this slow succession that he will find the solution of a number of problems of politics and morals, which philosophers cannot settle. He will feel that, men being different in different ages, the reason why Diogenes could not find a man was that he sought among his contemporaries a man of an earlier period. He will see that Cato died with Rome and liberty, because he did not fit the age in which he lived; the greatest of men served only to astonish a world which he would certainly have ruled, had he lived five hundred years sooner. In a word, he will explain how the soul and the passions of men insensibly change their very nature; why our wants and pleasures in the end seek new objects; and why, the original man having vanished by degrees, society offers to us only an assembly of artificial men and factitious passions, which are the work of all these new relations, and without any real foundation in nature. We are taught nothing on this subject, by reflection, that is not entirely confirmed by observation. The savage and the civilized man differ so much in the bottom of their hearts and in their inclinations, that what constitutes the supreme happiness of one would reduce the other to despair. The former breathes only peace and liberty; he desires only to live and be free from labor; even the *ataraxia* of the Stoic falls far short of his profound indifference to every other object. Civilized man, on the other hand, is always moving, sweating, toiling and racking his brains to find still more laborious occupations: he goes on in drudgery to his last moment, and even seeks death to put himself in a position to live, or renounces life to acquire immortality. He pays his court to men in power, whom he hates, and to the wealthy, whom he despises; he stops at nothing to have the honour of serving them; he is not ashamed to value himself on his own meanness and their protection; and, proud of his slavery, he speaks with disdain of those, who have not the honor of sharing it. What a sight would the perplexing and envied labors of a European minister of State present to the eyes of a Carib[b]ean! How many cruel deaths would not this indolent savage prefer to the horrors of such a life, which is seldom even sweetened by the pleasure of doing good! But, for him to see into the motives of all this solicitude, the words *power* and *reputation,* would have to bear some meaning in his mind; he would have to know that there are men who set a value on the opinion of the rest of the world; who can be made happy and satisfied with themselves rather on the testimony of other people than on their own. In reality, the source of all these differences is, that the savage lives within himself, while social man lives constantly outside himself, and only knows how to live in the opinion of others, so that he seems to receive the consciousness of his own existence merely from the judgment of others concerning him. It is not to my present purpose to insist on the indifference to good and evil which arises from this disposition, in spite of our many fine works on morality, or to show how, everything being reduced to appearances, there is but art and mummery in even honor, friendship, virtue, and often vice itself, of which we at length learn the secret of boasting; to show, in short, how, always asking others what we are, and never daring to ask ourselves, in the midst of so much philosophy, humanity and civilisation, and of such sublime codes of morality, we have nothing to show for ourselves but a frivolous and deceitful appearance, honor without virtue, reason without wisdom, and pleasure without happiness. It is sufficient that I have proved that this is not by any means the original state of man, but that it is merely the spirit of society, and the inequality which society produces, that thus transform and alter all our natural inclinations.

I have endeavoured to trace the origin and progress of inequality, and the institution and abuse of political societies, as far as these are capable of being deduced from the nature of man merely by the light of reason, and independently of those sacred dogmas which give the sanction of divine right to sovereign authority. It follows from this survey that, as there is hardly any inequality in the state of nature, all the inequality which now prevails owes its strength and growth to the development of our faculties and the advance of the human mind, and becomes at last permanent and legitimate by the establishment of property and laws. Secondly, it follows that moral inequality, authorised by positive right alone, clashes with natural right, whenever it is not proportionate to physical inequality; a distinction which sufficiently determines what we ought to think of that species of inequality which prevails in all civilised countries; since it is plainly contrary to the law of nature, however defined, that children should command old men, fools wise men, and that the privileged few should gorge themselves with superfluities, while the starving multitude are in want of the bare necessities of life.

QUESTIONS FOR REFLECTION

1. What is Rousseau's conception of the state of nature in the *Discourse on the Origin of Inequality*? Does it differ from that of *On the Social Contract*?

2. Why, in Rousseau's view, does property give rise to deception?

3. How does Rousseau criticize the right to property?

4. What stages of inequality does Rousseau discuss? What is the final stage?

JEAN-JACQUES ROUSSEAU

from *On the Social Contract*

(*Source:* The Social Contract and Discourses, *translated by G. D. H. Cole. London: J. M. Dent & Sons, Ltd., 1913.*)

Book I

CHAPTER IX / REAL PROPERTY

Each member of the community gives himself to it, at the moment of its foundation, just as he is, with all the resources at his command, including the goods he possesses. This act does not make possession, in changing hands, change its nature, and become property in the hands of the Sovereign; but, as the forces of the city are incomparably greater than those of an individual, public possession is also, in fact, stronger and more irrevocable, without being any more legitimate, at any rate from the point of view of foreigners. For the State, in relation to its members, is master of all their goods by the social contract, which, within the State, is the basis of all rights; but, in relation to other powers, it is so only by the right of the first occupier, which it holds from its members.

The right of the first occupier, though more real than the right of the strongest, becomes a real right only when the right of property has already been established. Every man has naturally a right to everything he needs; but the positive act which makes him proprietor of one thing excludes him from everything else. Having his share, he ought to keep to it, and can have no further right against the community. This is why the right of the first occupier, which in the state of nature is so weak, claims the respect of every man in civil society. In this right we are respecting not so much what belongs to another as what does not belong to ourselves.

In general, to establish the right of the first occupier over a plot of ground, the following conditions are necessary: first, the land must not yet be inhabited; secondly, a man must occupy only the amount he needs for his subsistence; and, in the third place, possession must be taken, not by an empty ceremony, but by labour and cultivation, the only sign of proprietorship that should be respected by others, in default of a legal title. . . .

It may also happen that men begin to unite one with another before they possess anything, and that, subsequently occupying a tract of country which is enough for all, they enjoy it in common, or share it out among themselves, either equally or according to a scale fixed by the Sovereign. However the acquisition be made, the right which each individual has to his own estate is always subordinate to the right which the community has over all: without this, there would be neither stability in the social tie, nor real force in the exercise of Sovereignty.

I shall end this chapter and this book by remarking on a fact on which the whole social system should rest: *i.e.*, that, instead of destroying natural inequality, the fundamental compact substitutes, for such physical inequality as nature may have set up between men, an equality that is moral and legitimate, and that men, who may be unequal in strength or intelligence, become every one equal by convention and legal right.*

---

* Under bad governments, this equality is only apparent and illusory: it serves only to keep the pauper in his poverty and the rich man in the position he has usurped. In fact, laws are always of use to those who possess and harmful to those who have nothing: from which it follows that the social state is advantageous to men only when all have something and none too much.

Book II

CHAPTER III / WHETHER THE GENERAL WILL IS FALLIBLE

It follows from what has gone before that the general will is always right and tends to the public advantage; but it does not follow that the deliberations of the people are always equally correct. Our will is always for our own good, but we do not always see what that is; the people is never corrupted, but it is often deceived, and on such occasions only does it seem to will what is bad.

There is often a great deal of difference between the will of all and the general will; the latter considers only the common interest, while the former takes private interest into account, and is no more than a sum of particular wills: but take away from these same wills the pluses and minuses that cancel one another, and the general will remains as the sum of the differences.

If, when the people, being furnished with adequate information, held its deliberations, the citizens had no communication one with another, the grand total of the small differences would always give the general will, and the decision would always be good. But when factions arise, and partial associations are formed at the expense of the great association, the will of each of these associations becomes general in relation to its members, while it remains particular in relation to the State: it may then be said that there are no longer as many votes as there are men, but only as many as there are associations. The differences become less numerous and give a less general result. Lastly, when one of these associations is so great as to prevail over all the rest, the result is no longer a sum of small differences, but a single difference; in this case there is no longer a general will, and the opinion which prevails is purely particular.

It is therefore essential, if the general will is to be able to express itself, that there should be no partial society within the State, and that each citizen should think only his own thoughts. . . . But if there are partial societies, it is best to have as many as possible and to prevent them from being unequal. . . . These precautions are the only ones that can guarantee that the general will shall be always enlightened, and that the people shall in no way deceive itself.

CHAPTER IV / THE LIMITS OF THE SOVEREIGN POWER

If the State is a moral person whose life is in the union of its members, and if the most important of its cares is the care for its own preservation, it must have a universal and compelling force, in order to move and dispose each part as may be most advantageous to the whole. As nature gives each man absolute power over all his members, the social compact gives the body politic absolute power over all its members also; and it is this power which, under the direction of the general will, bears, as I have said, the name of Sovereignty. . . .

Each man alienates, I admit, by the social compact, only such part of his powers, goods and liberty as it is important for the community to control; but it must also be granted that the Sovereign is sole judge of what is important.

Every service a citizen can render the State he ought to render as soon as the Sovereign demands it; but the Sovereign, for its part, cannot impose upon its subjects any fetters that are useless to the community, nor can it even wish to do so; for no more by the law of reason than by the law of nature can anything occur without a cause.

The undertakings which bind us to the social body are obligatory only because they are mutual; and their nature is such that in fulfilling them we cannot work for others without working for ourselves. Why is it that the general will is always in the right, and that all continually will the happiness of each one, unless it is because there is not a man who does not think of "each" as meaning him, and consider himself in voting for all? This proves that equality of rights and the idea of justice which such equality creates originate in the preference each man gives to himself, and accordingly in the very nature of man. . . .

It should be seen from the foregoing that what makes the will general is less the number of voters than the common interest uniting them; for, under this system, each necessarily submits to the conditions he imposes on others: and this admirable agreement between interest and justice gives to the common deliberations an equitable character which at once vanishes when any particular question is discussed, in the absence of a common interest to unite and identify the ruling of the judge with that of the party.

From whatever side we approach our principle, we reach the same conclusion, that the social compact sets up among the citizens an equality of such a kind, that they all bind themselves to observe the same conditions and should therefore all enjoy the same rights. Thus, from the very nature of the compact, every act of Sovereignty, *i.e.,* every authentic act of the general will, binds or favors all the citizens equally; so that the Sovereign recognizes only the body of the nation, and draws no distinctions between those of whom it is made up. What, then, strictly speaking, is an act of Sovereignty? It is not a convention between a superior and an inferior, but a convention between the body and each of its members. It is legitimate, because based on the social contract, and equitable, because common to all; useful, because it can have no other object than the general good, and stable, because guaranteed by the public force and the supreme power. So long as the subjects have to submit only to conventions of this sort, they obey no one but their own will; and to ask how far the respective rights of the Sovereign and the citizens extend, is to ask up to what point the latter can enter into undertakings with themselves, each with all, and all with each.

We can see from this that the sovereign power, absolute, sacred and inviolable as it is, does not and cannot exceed the limits of general conventions, and that every man may dispose at will of such goods and liberty as these conventions leave him; so that the Sovereign never has a right to lay more charges on one subject than on another, because, in that case, the question becomes particular, and ceases to be within its competency.

When these distinctions have once been admitted, it is seen to be so untrue that there is, in the social contract, any real renunciation on the part of the individuals, that the position in which they find themselves as a result of the contract is really preferable to that in which they were before. Instead of a renunciation, they have made an advantageous exchange: instead of an uncertain and precarious way of living they have got one that is better and more secure; instead of natural independence they have got liberty, instead of the power to harm others security for themselves, and instead of their strength, which others might overcome, a right which social union makes invincible. Their very life, which they have devoted to the State, is by it constantly protected; and when they risk it in the State's defence, what more are they doing than giving back what they have received from it? What are they doing that they would not do more often and with greater danger in the state of nature, in which they would inevitably have to fight battles at the peril of their lives in defence of that which is the means of their preservation? All have indeed to fight when their country needs them; but then no one has ever to fight for himself. Do we not gain something by running, on behalf of what gives us our security, only some of the risks we should have to run for ourselves, as soon as we lost it? . . .

CHAPTER XI / THE VARIOUS SYSTEMS OF LEGISLATION

If we ask in what precisely consists the greatest good of all, which should be the end of every system of legislation, we shall find it reduce itself to two main objects, liberty and equality—liberty, because all particular dependence means so much force taken from the body of the State, and equality, because liberty cannot exist without it.

I have already defined civil liberty; by equality, we should understand, not that the degrees of power and riches are to be absolutely identical for everybody; but that power shall never be great enough for violence, and shall always be exercised by virtue of rank and law; and that, in respect of riches, no citizen shall ever be wealthy enough to buy another, and none poor enough to be forced to sell himself:*

---

* If the object is to give the State consistency, bring the two extremes as near to each other as possible; allow neither rich men nor beggars. These two estates, which are naturally inseparable, are equally fatal to the common good; from the one come the friends of tyranny, and from the other tyrants. It is always between them that public liberty is put up to auction: the one buys, and the other sells.

which implies, on the part of the great, moderation in goods and position, and, on the side of the common sort, moderation in avarice and covetousness.

Such equality, we are told, is an unpractical ideal that cannot actually exist. But if its abuse is inevitable, does it follow that we should not at least make regulations concerning it? It is precisely because the force of circumstances tends continually to destroy equality that the force of legislation should always tend to its maintenance. . . .

QUESTIONS FOR REFLECTION

1. What is Rousseau's conception of the state of nature in *On the Social Contract?* Does it differ from that of *Discourse on the Origin of Inequality?*

2. What principles of distributive justice does Rousseau advocate? Are they compatible with one another?

3. According to Rousseau, are there any limits on government power? If so, what are they?

KARL MARX AND FRIEDRICH ENGELS

from *Manifesto of the Communist Party* (1848)

Karl Marx (1818–1883) was born in Treves, in the German Rhineland, to a Jewish family that had converted to Lutheranism. He earned his doctorate at Jena in 1841 and edited a newspaper in Cologne. Friedrich Engels (1820–1895), born in Barmen, also in the Rhineland, was the son of a textile manufacturer. He worked for his father in a cotton mill in Manchester, England, as a clerk, manager, and part owner. He met Marx in Cologne in 1842 and again in Paris in 1844. In 1848, a year that brought revolution to Paris as well as to Berlin, Vienna, Venice, Milan, and Parma, they collaborated to write The Communist Manifesto.*

Though a vision of justice lies behind much of their work, Marx and Engels wrote little about it. The Communist Manifesto *contains some of their most explicit comments about distributive justice and details the theory of class struggle. (Source: Karl Marx and Friedrich Engels,* Manifesto of the Communist Party, *New York: International Publishers, 1932.)*

I. Bourgeois and Proletarians*

The history of all hitherto existing society is the history of class struggles.

Freeman and slave, patrician and plebeian, lord and serf, guild-master and journeyman, in a word, oppressor and oppressed, stood in constant opposition to one another, carried on an uninterrupted, now hidden, now open fight, a fight that each time ended, either in a revolutionary reconstitution of society at large, or in the common ruin of the contending classes. . . .

. . . Society as a whole is more and more splitting up into two great hostile camps, into two great classes directly facing each other: Bourgeoisie and Proletariat. . . .

The bourgeoisie, historically, has played a most revolutionary part.

The bourgeoisie, wherever it has got the upper hand, has put an end to all feudal, patriarchal, idyllic relations. It has pitilessly torn asunder the motley feudal ties that bound man to his "natural superiors," and has left remaining no other nexus between man and man than naked self-interest, than callous "cash payment." It has drowned the most heavenly ecstasies of religious fervour, of chivalrous enthusiasm, of philistine sentimentalism, in the icy water of egotistical calculation. It has resolved personal worth into exchange value, and in place of the numberless indefeasible chartered freedoms, has set up that single, unconscionable freedom—Free Trade. In one word, for exploitation, veiled by religious and political illusions, it has substituted naked, shameless, direct, brutal exploitation.

The bourgeoisie has stripped of its halo every occupation hitherto honoured and looked up to with reverent awe. It has converted the physician, the lawyer, the priest, the poet, the man of science, into its paid wage-laborers.

---

* By bourgeoisie is meant the class of modern Capitalists, owners of the means of social production and employers of wage-labor. By proletariat, the class of modern wage-laborers who, having no means of production of their own, are reduced to selling their labor-power in order to live.

The bourgeoisie has torn away from the family its sentimental veil, and has reduced the family relation to a mere money relation. . . .

The bourgeoisie cannot exist without constantly revolutionising the instruments of production, and thereby the relations of production, and with them the whole relations of society. Conservation of the old modes of production in unaltered form, was, on the contrary, the first condition of existence for all earlier industrial classes. Constant revolutionising of production, uninterrupted disturbance of all social conditions, everlasting uncertainty and agitation distinguish the bourgeois epoch from all earlier ones. All fixed, fast-frozen relations, with their train of ancient and venerable prejudices and opinions, are swept away, all new-formed ones become antiquated before they can ossify. All that is solid melts into air, all that is holy is profaned, and man is at last compelled to face with sober senses, his real conditions of life, and his relations with his kind.

The need of a constantly expanding market for its products chases the bourgeoisie over the whole surface of the globe. It must nestle everywhere, settle everywhere, establish connections everywhere.

The bourgeoisie has through its exploitation of the world-market given a cosmopolitan character to production and consumption in every country. To the great chagrin of Reactionists, it has drawn from under the feet of industry the national ground on which it stood. All old-established national industries have been destroyed or are daily being destroyed. They are dislodged by new industries, whose introduction becomes a life and death question for all civilized nations, by industries that no longer work up indigenous raw material, but raw material drawn from the remotest zones; industries whose products are consumed, not only at home, but in every quarter of the globe. In place of the old wants, satisfied by the productions of the country, we find new wants, requiring for their satisfaction the products of distant lands and climes. In place of the old local and national seclusion and self-sufficiency, we have intercourse in every direction, universal interdependence of nations. And as in material, so also in intellectual production. The intellectual creations of individual nations become common property. National one-sidedness and narrow-mindedness become more and more impossible, and from the numerous national and local literatures, there arises a world literature.

The bourgeoisie, by the rapid improvement of all instruments of production, by the immensely facilitated means of communication, draws all, even the most barbarian, nations into civilisation. The cheap prices of its commodities are the heavy artillery with which it batters down all Chinese walls, with which it forces the barbarians' intensely obstinate hatred of foreigners to capitulate. It compels all nations, on pain of extinction, to adopt the bourgeois mode of production; it compels them to introduce what it calls civilisation into their midst, *i.e.*, to become bourgeois themselves. In one word, it creates a world after its own image.

The bourgeoisie has subjected the country to the rule of the towns. It has created enormous cities, has greatly increased the urban population as compared with the rural, and has thus rescued a considerable part of the population from the idiocy of rural life. Just as it has made the country dependent on the towns, so it has made barbarian and semi-barbarian countries dependent on the civilised ones, nations of peasants on nations of bourgeois, the East on the West.

The bourgeoisie keeps more and more doing away with the scattered state of the population, of the means of production, and of property. It has agglomerated population, centralized means of production, and has concentrated property in a few hands. The necessary consequence of this was political centralization. Independent, or but loosely connected provinces, with separate interests, laws, government and systems of taxation, became lumped together into one nation, with one government, one code of laws, one national class-interest, one frontier and one customs-tariff. . . .

. . . Modern bourgeois society with its relations of production, of exchange and of property, a society that has conjured up such gigantic means of production and of exchange, is like the sorcerer, who is no longer able to control the powers of the nether world whom he has called up by his spells. For many a decade past the history of industry and commerce is but the history of the revolt of modern productive forces against modern conditions of production, against the property relations that are the conditions for the existence of the bourgeoisie and of its rule. It is enough to mention the commercial crises that by their periodical return put on its trial, each time more threateningly, the existence of the entire bourgeois society. In these crises a great part not only of the existing products, but also of the previously created productive forces, are periodically destroyed. In these crises there breaks out an epidemic that, in all earlier epochs, would have seemed an absurdity—the epidemic of overproduction. Society suddenly finds itself put back into a state of momentary barbarism; it appears as if a famine, a universal war of devastation had cut off the supply of every means of subsistence; industry and commerce seem to be destroyed; and why? Because there is too much civilisation, too much means of subsistence, too much industry, too much commerce. The productive forces at the disposal of society no longer tend to further the development of the conditions of bourgeois property; on the contrary, they have become too powerful for these conditions, by which they are fettered, and so soon as they overcome these fetters, they bring disorder into the whole of bourgeois society, endanger the existence of bourgeois property. The conditions of bourgeois society are too narrow to comprise the wealth created by them. And how does the bourgeoisie get over these crises? On the one hand by enforced destruction of a mass of productive forces; on the other, by the conquest of new markets, and by the more thorough exploitation of the old ones. That is to say, by paving the way for more extensive and more destructive crises, and by diminishing the means whereby crises are prevented.

The weapons with which the bourgeoisie felled feudalism to the ground are now turned against the bourgeoisie itself.

But not only has the bourgeoisie forged the weapons that bring death to itself; it has also called into existence the men who are to wield those weapons—the modern working class—the proletarians.

In proportion as the bourgeoisie, *i.e.,* capital, is developed, in the same proportion is the proletariat, the modern working class, developed—a class of laborers, who live only so long as they find work, and who find work only so long as their labor increases capital. These laborers, who must sell themselves piecemeal, are a commodity, like every other article of commerce, and are consequently exposed to all the vicissitudes of competition, to all the fluctuations of the market.

Owing to the extensive use of machinery and to division of labor, the work of the proletarians has lost all individual character, and consequently, all charm for the workman. He becomes an appendage of the machine, and it is only the most simple, most monotonous, and most easily acquired knack, that is required of him. Hence, the cost of production of a workman is restricted, almost entirely, to the means of subsistence that he requires for his maintenance, and for the propagation of his race. But the price of a commodity, and therefore also of labor, is equal to its cost of production. In proportion, therefore, as the repulsiveness of the work increases, the wage decreases. Nay more, in proportion as the use of machinery and division of labor increases, in the same proportion the burden of toil also increases, whether by prolongation of the working hours, by increase of the work exacted in a given time or by increased speed of the machinery, etc.

Modern industry has converted the little workshop of the patriarchal master into the great factory of the industrial capitalist. Masses of laborers, crowded into the factory, are organised like soldiers. As privates of the industrial army they are placed under the command of a perfect hierarchy of officers and sergeants. Not only are they slaves of the bourgeois class, and of the bourgeois State; they are daily and hourly enslaved by the machine, by the overlooker, and, above all, by the individual bourgeois manufacturer himself. The more openly this despotism proclaims gain to be its end and aim, the more petty, the more hateful and the more embittering it is.

The less the skill and exertion of strength implied in manual labor, in other words, the more modern industry becomes developed, the more is the labor of men superseded by that of women. Differences of age and sex have no longer any distinctive social validity for the working class. All are instruments of labor, more or less expensive to use, according to their age and sex. . . .

Hitherto, every form of society has been based, as we have already seen, on the antagonism of oppressing and oppressed classes. But in order to oppress a class, certain conditions must be assured to it under which it can, at least, continue its slavish existence. The serf, in the period of serfdom, raised himself to membership in the commune, just as the petty bourgeois, under the yoke of feudal absolutism, managed to develop into a bourgeois. The modern laborer, on the contrary, instead of rising with the progress of industry, sinks deeper and deeper below the conditions of existence of his own class. He becomes a pauper, and pauperism develops more rapidly than population and wealth. And here it becomes evident, that the bourgeoisie is unfit any longer to be the ruling class in society, and to impose its conditions of existence upon society as an overriding law. It is unfit to rule because it is incompetent to assure an existence to its slave within his slavery, because it cannot help letting him sink into such a state, that it has to feed him, instead of being fed by him. Society can no longer live under this bourgeoisie, in other words, its existence is no longer compatible with society.

The essential condition for the existence, and for the sway of the bourgeois class, is the formation and augmentation of capital; the condition for capital is wage-labor. Wage-labor rests exclusively on competition between the laborers. The advance of industry, whose involuntary promoter is the bourgeoisie, replaces the isolation of the laborers, due to competition, by their revolutionary combination, due to association. The development of Modern Industry, therefore, cuts from under its feet the very foundation on which the bourgeoisie produces and appropriates products. What the bourgeoisie, therefore, produces, above all, is its own grave-diggers. Its fall and the victory of the proletariat are equally inevitable.

II. Proletarians and Communists

. . .

The distinguishing feature of Communism is not the abolition of property generally, but the abolition of bourgeois property. But modern bourgeois private property is the final and most complete expression of the system of producing and appropriating products, that is based on class antagonisms, on the exploitation of the many by the few.

In this sense, the theory of the Communists may be summed up in the single sentence: Abolition of private property. . . .

You are horrified at our intending to do away with private property. But in your existing society, private property is already done away with for nine-tenths of the population; its existence for the few is solely due to its non-existence in the hands of those nine-tenths. You reproach us, therefore, with intending to do away with a form of property, the necessary condition for whose existence is the nonexistence of any property for the immense majority of society.

In one word, you reproach us with intending to do away with your property. Precisely so; that is just what we intend.

From the moment when labor can no longer be converted into capital, money, or rent, into a social power capable of being monopolised, *i.e.,* from the moment when individual property can no longer be transformed into bourgeois property, into capital, from that moment, you say, individuality vanishes.

You must, therefore, confess that by "individual" you mean no other person than the bourgeois, than the middle-class owner of property. This person must, indeed, be swept out of the way, and made impossible.

Communism deprives no man of the power to appropriate the products of society; all that it does is to deprive him of the power to subjugate the labor of others by means of such appropriation.

It has been objected that upon the abolition of private property all work will cease, and universal laziness will overtake us.

According to this, bourgeois society ought long ago to have gone to the dogs through sheer idleness; for those of its members who work, acquire nothing, and those who acquire anything, do not work. The whole of this objection is but another expression of the tautology: that there can no longer be any wage-labor when there is no longer any capital.

All objections urged against the Communistic mode of producing and appropriating material products, have, in the same way, been urged against the Communistic modes of producing and appropriating intellectual products. Just as, to the bourgeois, the disappearance of class property is the disappearance of production itself, so the disappearance of class culture is to him identical with the dissappearance of all culture.

That culture, the loss of which he laments, is, for the enormous majority, a mere training to act as a machine.

But don't wrangle with us so long as you apply, to our intended abolition of bourgeois property, the standard of your bourgeois notions of freedom, culture, law, etc. Your very ideas are but the outgrowth of the conditions of your bourgeois production and bourgeois property, just as your jurisprudence is but the will of your class made into a law for all, a will, whose essential character and direction are determined by the economical conditions of existence of your class. . . .

Does it require deep intuition to comprehend that man's ideas, views and conceptions, in one word, man's consciousness, changes with every change in the conditions of his material existence, in his social relations and in his social life?

What else does the history of ideas prove, than that intellectual production changes its character in proportion as material production is changed? The ruling ideas of each age have ever been the ideas of its ruling class. . . .

We have seen above, that the first step in the revolution by the working class, is to raise the proletariat to the position of ruling class, to win the battle of democracy.

The proletariat will use its political supremacy to wrest, by degrees, all capital from the bourgeoisie, to centralise all instruments of production in the hands of the State, *i.e.,* of the proletariat organized as the ruling class; and to increase the total of productive forces as rapidly as possible.

Of course, in the beginning, this cannot be effected except by means of despotic inroads on the rights of property, and on the conditions of bourgeois production; by means of measures, therefore, which appear economically insufficient and untenable, but which, in the course of the movement, outstrip themselves, necessitate further inroads upon the old social order, and are unavoidable as a means of entirely revolutionising the mode of production.

These measures will of course be different in different countries.

Nevertheless in the most advanced countries, the following will be pretty generally applicable.

1. Abolition of property in land and application of all rents of land to public purposes.

2. A heavy progressive or graduated income tax.

3. Abolition of all right of inheritance.

4. Confiscation of the property of all emigrants and rebels.

5. Centralisation of credit in the hands of the State, by means of a national bank with State capital and an exclusive monopoly.

6. Centralisation of the means of communication and transport in the hands of the State.

7. Extention of factories and instruments of production owned by the State; the bringing into cultivation of wastelands, and the improvement of the soil generally in accordance with a common plan.

8. Equal liability of all to labor. Establishment of industrial armies, especially for agriculture.

9. Combination of agriculture with manufacturing industries; gradual abolition of the distinction between town and country, by a more equable distribution of the population over the country.

10. Free education for all children in public schools. Abolition of children's factory labor in its present form. Combination of education with industrial production, etc., etc.

When, in the course of development, class distinctions have disappeared, and all production has been concentrated in the hands of a vast association of the whole nation, the public power will lose its political character. Political power, properly so called, is merely the organised power of one class for oppressing another. If the proletariat during its contest with the bourgeoisie is compelled, by the force of circumstances, to organise itself as a class, if, by means of a revolution, it makes itself the ruling class, and, as such, sweeps away by force the old conditions of production, then it will, along with these conditions, have swept away the conditions for the existence of class antagonisms and of classes generally, and will thereby have abolished its own supremacy as a class.

In place of the old bourgeois society, with its classes and class antagonisms, we shall have an association, in which the free development of each is the condition for the free development of all.

IV. Position of the Communists in Relation to the Various Existing Opposition Parties

. . . In short, the Communists everywhere support every revolutionary movement against the existing social and political order of things.

In all these movements they bring to the front, as the leading question in each, the property question, no matter what its degree of development at the time.

Finally, they labor everywhere for the union and agreement of the democratic parties of all countries.

The Communists disdain to conceal their views and aims. They openly declare that their ends can be attained only by the forcible overthrow of all existing social conditions. Let the ruling classes tremble at a Communistic revolution. The proletarians have nothing to lose but their chains. They have a world to win.

WORKING MEN OF ALL COUNTRIES, UNITE!

QUESTIONS FOR REFLECTION

1. What is the bourgeoisie? What is the proletariat?

2. Why, according to Marx and Engels, are the bourgeoisie and the proletariat in conflict?

3. What arguments do Marx and Engels advance for the abolition of private property? What objections might be raised against that program?

4. What practical measures do Marx and Engels advocate? How do they relate to the primary aim of communism?

ALBERT CAMUS

Bread and Freedom

. . .Yes, the great event of the twentieth century was the forsaking of the values of freedom by the revolutionary movement, the progressive retreat of socialism based on freedom before the attacks of a Caesarian and military socialism. Since that moment a certain hope has disappeared from the world and a solitude has begun for each and every free man.

When, after Marx, the rumor began to spread and gain strength that freedom was a bourgeois hoax, a single word was misplaced in that definition, and we are still paying for that mistake through the convulsions of our time. For it should have been said merely that bourgeois freedom was a hoax—and not all freedom. It should have been said simply that bourgeois freedom was not freedom or, in the best of cases, was not yet freedom. But that there were liberties to be won and never to be relinquished again. It is quite true that there is no possible freedom for the man tied to his lathe all day long who, when evening comes, crowds into a single room with his family. But this fact condemns a class, a society and the slavery it assumes, not freedom itself, without which the poorest among us cannot get along. For even if society were suddenly transformed and became decent and comfortable for all, it would still be a barbarous state unless freedom triumphed. And because bourgeois society talks about freedom without practicing it, must the world of workers also give up practicing it and boast merely of not talking about it? Yet the confusion took place and in the revolutionary movement freedom was gradually condemned because bourgeois society used it as a hoax. From a justifiable and healthy distrust of the way that bourgeois society prostituted freedom, people came to distrust freedom itself. At best, it was postponed to the end of time, with the request that meanwhile it be not talked about. The contention was that we needed justice first and that we would come to freedom later on, as if slaves could ever hope to achieve justice. And forceful intellectuals announced to the worker that bread alone interested him rather than freedom, as if the worker didn't know that his bread depends in part on his freedom. . . .

How then can this infernal circle be broken? Obviously, it can be done only by reviving at once, in ourselves and in others, the value of freedom—and by never again agreeing to its being sacrificed, even temporarily, or separated from our demand for justice. The current motto for all of us can only be this: without giving up anything on the plane of justice, yield nothing on the plane of freedom. In particular, the few democratic liberties we still enjoy are not unimportant illusions that we can allow to be taken from us without a protest. They represent exactly what remains to us of the great revolutionary conquests of the last two centuries. Hence they are not, as so many clever demagogues tell us, the negation of true freedom. There is no ideal freedom that will someday be given us all at once, as a pension comes at the end of one's life. There are liberties to be won painfully, one by one, and those we still have are stages—most certainly inadequate, but stages nevertheless—on the way to total liberation. If we agree to suppress them, we do not progress nonetheless. On the contrary, we retreat, we go backward, and someday we shall have to retrace our steps along that road, but that new effort will once more be made in the sweat and blood of men. . . .

Choosing freedom is not, as we are told, choosing against justice. On the other hand, freedom is chosen today in relation to those who are everywhere suffering and fighting, and this is the only freedom that counts. It is chosen at the same time as justice, and, to tell the truth, henceforth we cannot choose one without the other. If someone takes away your bread, he suppresses your freedom at the same time. But if someone takes away your freedom, you may be sure that your bread is threatened, for it depends no longer on you and your struggle but on the whim of a master. Poverty increases insofar as freedom retreats throughout the world, and vice versa. And if this cruel century has taught us anything at all, it has taught that the economic revolution must be free just as liberation must include the economic. The oppressed want to be liberated not only from their hunger but also from their masters. They are well aware that they will be effectively freed of hunger only when they hold their masters, all their masters, at bay. . . .

. . . The way ahead of us is long. Yet if war does not come and mingle everything in its hideous confusion, we shall have time at last to give a form to the justice and freedom we need. But to achieve that we must henceforth categorically refuse, without anger but irrevocably, the lies with which we have been stuffed. No, freedom is not founded on concentration camps, or on the subjugated peoples of the colonies, or on the workers' poverty! No, the doves of peace do not perch on gallows! No, the forces of freedom cannot mingle the sons of the victims with the executioners of Madrid and elsewhere! Of that, at least, we shall henceforth be sure, as we shall be sure that freedom is not a gift received from a State or a leader but a possession to be won every day by the effort of each and the union of all.

QUESTIONS FOR REFLECTION

1. Why, according to Camus, is freedom vital even for the poor?
2. How should we think about the relation between justice and freedom, in Camus's view?
3. Why does the restriction of freedom increase poverty?
4. Summarize Camus's critique of Marxism. How might a Marxist respond? Do you find those responses persuasive?

JOHN RAWLS

from *A Theory of Justice* (1970)

John Rawls is Professor of Philosophy at Harvard University. (Source: Reprinted by permission of the publishers from A Theory of Justice *by John Rawls. Cambridge, Mass.: Harvard University Press. Copyright © 1971 by the President and Fellows of Harvard College.)*

CHAPTER I / JUSTICE AS FAIRNESS

11. Two Principles of Justice

I shall now state in a provisional form the two principles of justice that I believe would be chosen in the original position. In this section I wish to make only the most general comments, and therefore the first formulation of these principles is tentative. . . .

The first statement of the two principles reads as follows.

First: each person is to have an equal right to the most extensive basic liberty compatible with a similar liberty for others.

Second: social and economic inequalities are to be arranged so that they are both (a) reasonably expected to be to everyone's advantage, and (b) attached to positions and offices open to all. . . .

By way of general comment, these principles primarily apply, as I have said, to the basic structure of society. They are to govern the assignment of rights and duties and to regulate the distribution of social and economic advantages. As their formulation suggests, these principles presuppose that the social structure can be divided into two more or less distinct parts, the first principle applying to the one, the second to the other. They distinguish between those aspects of the social system that define and secure the equal liberties of citizenship and those that specify and establish social and economic inequalities. The basic liberties of citizens are, roughly speaking, political liberty (the right to vote and to be eligible for public office) together with freedom of speech and assembly; liberty of conscience and freedom of thought; freedom of the person along with the right to hold (personal) property; and freedom from arbitrary arrest and seizure as defined by the concept of the rule of law. These liberties are all required to be equal by the first principle, since citizens of a just society are to have the same basic rights.

The second principle applies, in the first approximation, to the distribution of income and wealth and to the design of organizations that make use of differences in authority and responsibility, or chains of command. While the distribution of wealth and income need not be equal, it must be to everyone's advantage, and at the same time, positions of authority and offices of command must be accessible to all. One applies the second principle by holding positions open, and then, subject to this constraint, arranges social and economic inequalities so that everyone benefits.

These principles are to be arranged in a serial order with the first principle prior to the second. This ordering means that a departure from the institutions of equal liberty required by the first principle cannot be justified by, or compensated for, by greater social and economic advantages. The distribution of wealth and income, and the hierarchies of authority, must be consistent with both the liberties of equal citizenship and equality of opportunity.

It is clear that these principles are rather specific in their content, and their acceptance rests on certain assumptions that I must eventually try to explain and justify. A theory of justice depends upon a theory of society in ways that will become evident as we proceed. For the present, it should be observed that the two principles (and this holds for all formulations) are a special case of a more general conception of justice that can be expressed as follows.

All social values—liberty and opportunity, income and wealth, and the bases of self-respect—are to be distributed equally unless an unequal distribution of any, or all, of these values is to everyone's advantage.

Injustice, then, is simply inequalities that are not to the benefit of all. Of course, this conception is extremely vague and requires interpretation.

As a first step, suppose that the basic structure of society distributes certain primary goods, that is, things that every rational man is presumed to want. These goods normally have a use whatever a person's rational plan of life. For simplicity, assume that the chief primary goods at the disposition of society are rights and liberties, powers and opportunities, income and wealth. . . . These are the social primary goods. Other primary goods such as health and vigor, intelligence and imagination, are natural goods; although their possession is influenced by the basic structure, they are not so directly under its control. Imagine, then, a hypothetical initial arrangement in which all the social primary goods are equally distributed: everyone has similar rights and duties, and income and wealth are evenly shared. This state of affairs provides a benchmark for judging improvements. If certain inequalities of wealth and organizational powers would make everyone better off than in this hypothetical starting situation, then they accord with the general conception. . . .

QUESTIONS FOR REFLECTION

1. Explain Rawls's first principle. Give an example of something ruled out by the principle.

2. How does Rawls's first principle differ from Mill's harm principle? From Hobbes's law of nature?

3. Explain Rawls's second principle. Give an example of something ruled out by each part of the principle.

4. Rawls justifies his principles by saying that rational agents in the original position would agree to them. Do you agree?

5. Describe a situation in which Rawls's second principle would disagree with (a) the principle of utility, (b) the historical theory of Locke and Nozick, (c) Aristotle's meritocratic theory, (d) the maxim of Marx and Engels, and (e) Rousseau's conception of justice. In each case, do you find Rawls's theory more or less plausible than its competitor? Why?

ROBERT NOZICK

from *Anarchy, State, and Utopia* (1974)

Robert Nozick is Professor of Philosophy at Harvard University. (Source: From Anarchy, State, and Utopia *by Robert Nozick. Copyright © 1974 by Basic Books, Inc.; reprinted by permission of Basic Books, a division of HarperCollins Publishers Inc.)*

CHAPTER 7 / DISTRIBUTIVE JUSTICE

The minimal state is the most extensive state that can be justified. Any state more extensive violates people's rights. Yet many persons have put forth reasons purporting to justify a more extensive state. . . . In this chapter we consider the claim that a more extensive state is justified, because necessary (or the best instrument) to achieve distributive justice.

The term "distributive justice" is not a neutral one. Hearing the term "distribution," most people presume that some thing or mechanism uses some principle or criterion to give out a supply of things. Into this process of distributing shares some error may have crept. So it is an open question, at least, whether *redistribution* should take place; whether we should do again what has already been done once, though poorly. However, we are not in the position of children who have been given portions of pie by someone who now makes last minute adjustments to rectify careless cutting. There is no *central* distribution, no person or group entitled to control all the resources, jointly deciding how they are to be doled out. What each person gets, he gets from others who give to him in exchange for something, or as a gift. In a free society, diverse persons control different resources, and new holdings arise out of the voluntary exchanges and actions of persons. There is no more a distributing or distribution of shares than there is a distributing of mates in a society in which persons choose whom they shall marry. The total result is the product of many individual decisions which the different individuals involved are entitled to make. Some uses of the term "distribution," it is true, do not imply a previous distributing appropriately judged by some criterion (for example, "probability distribution"); nevertheless, despite the title of this chapter, it would be best to use a terminology that clearly is neutral. We shall speak of people's holdings; a principle of justice in holdings describes (part of) what justice tells us (requires) about holdings. I shall state first what I take to be the correct view about justice in holdings, and then turn to the discussion of alternate views.

Section I

The Entitlement Theory

The subject of justice in holdings consists of three major topics. The first is the *original acquisition of holdings,* the appropriation of unheld things. This includes the issues of how unheld things may come to be held, the process, or processes, by which unheld things may come to be held, the things that may come to be held by these processes, the extent of what comes to be held by a particular process, and so on. We shall refer to the complicated truth about this topic, which we shall not formulate here, as the principle of justice in acquisition. The second topic concerns the *transfer of holdings* from one person to another. By what processes may a person transfer holdings to another? How may a person acquire a holding from another who holds it? Under this topic come general descriptions of voluntary exchange, and gift and (on the other hand) fraud, as well as reference to particular conventional details fixed upon in a given society. The complicated truth about this subject (with placeholders for conventional details) we shall call the principle of justice in transfer. (And we shall suppose it also includes principles governing how a person may divest himself of a holding, passing it into an unheld state.)

If the world were wholly just, the following inductive definition would exhaustively cover the subject of justice in holdings.

1. A person who acquires a holding in accordance with the principle of justice in acquisition is entitled to that holding.

2. A person who acquires a holding in accordance with the principle of justice in transfer, from someone else entitled to the holding, is entitled to the holding.

3. No one is entitled to a holding except by (repeated) applications of 1 and 2.

The complete principle of distributive justice would say simply that a distribution is just if everyone is entitled to the holdings they possess under the distribution.

A distribution is just if it arises from another just distribution by legitimate means. The legitimate means of moving from one distribution to another are specified by the principle of justice in transfer. The legitimate first "moves" are specified by the principle of justice in acquisition. Whatever arises from a just situation by just steps is itself just. The means of change specified by the principle of justice in transfer preserve justice. As correct rules of inference are truth-preserving, and any conclusion deduced via repeated application of such rules from only true premises is itself true, so the means of transition from one situation to another specified by the principle of justice in transfer are justice-preserving, and any situation actually arising from repeated transitions in accordance with the principle from a just situation is itself just. The parallel between justice-preserving transformations and truth-preserving transformations illuminates where it fails as well as where it holds. That a conclusion could have been deduced by truth-preserving means from premises that are true suffices to show its truth. That from a just situation a situation *could* have arisen via justice-preserving means does not suffice to show its justice. The fact that a thief's victims voluntarily *could* have presented him with gifts does not entitle the thief to his ill-gotten gains. Justice in holdings is historical; it depends upon what actually has happened. We shall return to this point later.

Not all actual situations are generated in accordance with the two principles of justice in holdings: the principle of justice in acquisition and the principle of justice in transfer. Some people steal from others, or defraud them, or enslave them, seizing their product and preventing them from living as they choose, or forcibly exclude others from competing in exchanges. None of these are permissible modes of transition from one situation to another. And some persons acquire holdings by means not sanctioned by the principle of justice in acquisition. The existence of past injustice (previous violations of the first two principles of justice in holdings) raises the third major topic under justice in holdings: the rectification of injustice in holdings. If past injustice has shaped present holdings in various ways, some identifiable and some not, what now, if anything, ought to be done to rectify these injustices? What obligations do the performers of injustice have toward those whose position is worse than it would have been had the injustice not been done? Or, than it would have been had compensation been paid promptly? How, if at all, do things change if the beneficiaries and those made worse off are not the direct parties in the act of injustice, but, for example, their descendants? Is an injustice done to someone whose holding was itself based upon an unrectified injustice? How far back must one go in wiping clean the historical slate of injustices? What may victims of injustice permissibly do in order to rectify the injustices being done to them, including the many injustices done by persons acting through their government? I do not know of a thorough or theoretically sophisticated treatment of such issues. Idealizing greatly, let us suppose theoretical investigation will produce a principle of rectification. This principle uses historical information about previous situations and injustices done in them (as defined by the first two principles of justice and rights against interference), and information about the actual course of events that flowed from these injustices, until the present, and it yields a description (or descriptions) of holdings in the society. The principle of rectification presumably will make use of its best estimate of subjunctive information about what would have occurred (or a probability distribution over what might have occurred, using the expected value) if the injustice had not taken place. If the actual description of holdings turns out not to be one of the descriptions yielded by the principle, then one of the descriptions yielded must be realized.

The general outlines of the theory of justice in holdings are that the holdings of a person are just if he is entitled to them by the principles of justice in acquisition and transfer, or by the principle of rectification of injustice (as specified by the first two principles). If each person's holdings are just, then the total set (distribution) of holdings is just. To turn these general outlines into a specific theory we would have to specify the details of each of the three principles of justice in holdings: the principle of acquisition of holdings, the principle of transfer of holdings, and the principle of rectification of violations of the first two principles. I shall not attempt that task here. (Locke's principle of justice in acquisition is discussed below.)

Historical Principles and End-Result Principles

The general outlines of the entitlement theory illuminate the nature and defects of other conceptions of distributive justice. The entitlement theory of justice in distribution is *historical;* whether a distribution is just depends upon how it came about. In contrast, *current time-slice principles* of justice hold that the justice of a distribution is determined by how things are distributed (who has what) as judged by some *structural* principle(s) of just distribution. A utilitarian who judges between any two distributions by seeing which has the greater sum of utility and, if the sums tie, applies some fixed equality criterion to choose the more equal distribution, would hold a current time-slice principle of justice. As would someone who had a fixed schedule of trade-offs between the sum of happiness and equality. According to a current time-slice principle, all that needs to be looked at, in judging the justice of a distribution, is who ends up with what; in comparing any two distributions one need look only at the matrix present-

ing the distributions. No further information need be fed into a principle of justice. It is a consequence of such principles of justice that any two structurally identical distributions are equally just. (Two distributions are structurally identical if they present the same profile, but perhaps have different persons occupying the particular slots. My having ten and your having five, and my having five and your having ten are structurally identical distributions.) Welfare economics is the theory of current time-slice principles of justice. The subject is conceived as operating on matrices representing only current information about distribution. This, as well as some of the usual conditions (for example, the choice of distribution is invariant under relabeling of columns), guarantees that welfare economics will be a current time-slice theory, with all of its inadequacies.

Most persons do not accept current time-slice principles as constituting the whole story about distributive shares. They think it relevant in assessing the justice of a situation to consider not only the distribution it embodies, but also how that distribution came about. If some persons are in prisons for murder or war crimes, we do not say that to assess the justice of the distribution in the society we must look only at what this person has, and that person has, and that person has, . . . at the current time. We think it relevant to ask whether someone did something so that he *deserved* to be punished, deserved to have a lower share. Most will agree to the relevance of further information with regard to punishments and penalties. Consider also desired things. One traditional socialist view is that workers are entitled to the produce and full fruits of their labor; they have earned it; a distribution is unjust if it does not give the workers what they are entitled to. Such entitlements are based upon some past history. No socialist holding this view would find it comforting to be told that because the actual distribution A happens to coincide structurally with the one he desires D, A therefore is no less just than D; it differs only in that the "parasitic" owners of capital receive under A what the workers are entitled to under D, and the workers receive under A what the owners are entitled to under D, namely very little. This socialist rightly, in my view, holds onto the notions of earning, producing, entitlement, desert, and so forth, and he rejects current time-slice principles that look only to the structure of the resulting set of holdings. (The set of holdings resulting from what? Isn't it implausible that how holdings are produced and come to exist has no effect at all on who should hold what?) His mistake lies in his view of what entitlements arise out of what sorts of productive processes.

We construe the position we discuss too narrowly by speaking of *current* time-slice principles. Nothing is changed if structural principles operate upon a time sequence of current time-slice profiles and, for example, give someone more now to counterbalance the less he has had earlier. A utilitarian or an egalitarian or any mixture of the two over time will inherit the difficulties of his more myopic comrades. He is not helped by the fact that *some* of the information others consider relevant in assessing a distribution is reflected, unrecoverably, in past matrices. Henceforth, we shall refer to such unhistorical principles of distributive justice, including the current time-slice principles, as *end-result principles* or *end-state principles*.

In contrast to end-result principles of justice, *historical principles* of justice hold that past circumstances or actions of people can create differential entitlements or differential deserts to things. An injustice can be worked by moving from one distribution to another structurally identical one, for the second, in profile the same, may violate people's entitlements or deserts; it may not fit the actual history.

Patterning

The entitlement principles of justice in holdings that we have sketched are historical principles of justice. To better understand their precise character, we shall distinguish them from another subclass of the historical principles. Consider, as an example, the principle of distribution according to moral merit. This principle requires that total distributive shares vary directly with moral merit; no person should have a greater share than anyone whose moral merit is greater. (If moral merit could be not merely ordered but measured on an interval or ratio scale, stronger principles could be formulated.) Or consider the principle that results by substituting "usefulness to society" for "moral merit" in the previous principle. Or instead of "distribute according to moral merit," or "distribute according to usefulness to society," we might consider "distribute according to the weighted sum of moral merit, usefulness to society, and need," with the weights of the different dimensions equal.

Let us call a principle of distribution *patterned* if it specifies that a distribution is to vary along with some natural dimension, weighted sum of natural dimensions, or lexicographic ordering of natural dimensions. And let us say a distribution is patterned if it accords with some patterned principle. (I speak of natural dimensions, admittedly without a general criterion for them, because for any set of holdings some artificial dimensions can be gimmicked up to vary along with the distribution of the set.) The principle of distribution in accordance with moral merit is a patterned historical principle, which specifies a patterned distribution. "Distribute according to I.Q." is a patterned principle that looks to information not contained in distributional matrices. It is not historical, however, in that it does not look to any past actions creating differential entitlements to evaluate a distribution; it requires only distributional matrices whose columns are labeled by I.Q. scores. The distribution in a society, however, may be composed of such simple patterned distributions, without itself being simply patterned. Different sectors may operate different patterns, or some combination of patterns may operate in different proportions across a society. A distribution composed in this manner, from a small number of patterned distributions, we also shall term "patterned." And we extend the use of "pattern" to include the overall designs put forth by combinations of end-state principles.

Almost every suggested principle of distributive justice is patterned: to each according to his moral merit, or needs, or marginal product, or how hard he tries, or the weighted sum of the foregoing, and so on. The principle of entitlement we have sketched is *not* patterned. There is no one natural dimension or weighted sum or combination of a small number of natural dimensions that yields the distributions generated in accordance with the principle of entitlement. The set of holdings that results when some persons receive their marginal products, others win at gambling, others receive a share of their mate's income, others receive gifts from foundations, others receive interest on loans, others receive gifts from admirers, others receive returns on investment, others make for themselves much of what they have, others find things, and so on, will not be patterned. Heavy strands of patterns will run through it; significant portions of the variance in holdings will be accounted for by pattern-variables. If most people most of the time choose to transfer some of their entitlements to others only in exchange for something from them, then a large part of what many people hold will vary with what they held that others wanted. More details are provided by the theory of marginal productivity. But gifts to relatives, charitable donations, bequests to children, and the like, are not best conceived, in the first instance, in this manner. Ignoring the strands of pattern, let us suppose for the moment that a distribution actually arrived at by the operation of the principle of entitlement is random with respect to any pattern. Though the resulting set of holdings will be unpatterned, it will not be incomprehensible, for it can be seen as arising from the operation of a small number of principles. These principles specify how an initial distribution may arise (the principle of acquisition of holdings) and how distributions may be transformed into others (the principle of transfer of holdings). The process whereby the set of holdings is generated will be intelligible, though the set of holdings itself that results from this process will be unpatterned.

The writings of F. A. Hayek focus less than is usually done upon what patterning distributive justice requires. Hayek argues that we cannot know enough about each person's situation to distribute to each according to his moral merit (but would justice demand we do so if we did have this knowledge?); and he goes on to say, "our objection is against all attempts to impress upon society a deliberately chosen pattern of distribution, whether it be an order of equality or of inequality." However, Hayek concludes that in a free society there will be distribution in accordance with value rather than moral merit; that is, in accordance with the perceived value of a person's actions and services to others. Despite his rejection of a patterned conception of distributive justice, Hayek himself suggests a pattern he thinks justifiable: distribution in accordance with the perceived benefits given to others, leaving room for the complaint that a free society does not realize exactly this pattern. Stating this patterned strand of a free capitalist society more precisely, we get "To each according to how much he benefits others who have the resources for benefiting those who benefit them." This will seem arbitrary unless some acceptable initial set of holdings is specified, or unless it is held that the operation of the system over time washes out any significant effects from the initial set of holdings. As an example of the latter, if almost anyone would have bought a car from Henry Ford, the supposition that it was an arbitrary matter who held the money then (and so bought) would not place Henry Ford's earnings under a cloud. In any event, *his* coming to hold it is not arbitrary. Distribution according to benefits to others is a major patterned strand in a free capitalist society, as Hayek correctly points out, but it is only a strand and does not constitute the whole pattern of a system of entitlements (namely, inheritance, gifts for arbitrary reasons, charity, and so on) or a standard that one should insist a society fit. Will people tolerate for long a system yielding distributions that they believe are unpatterned? No doubt people will not long accept a distribution they believe is *unjust*. People want their society to be and to look just. But must the look of justice reside in a resulting pattern rather than in the underlying generating principles? We are in no position to conclude that the inhabitants of a society embodying an entitlement conception of justice in holdings will find it unacceptable. Still, it must be granted that were people's reasons for transferring some of their holdings to others always irrational or arbitrary, we would find this disturbing. (Suppose people always determined what holdings they would transfer, and to whom, by using a random device.) We feel more comfortable upholding the justice of an entitlement system if most of the transfers under it are done for reasons. This does not mean necessarily that all deserve what holdings they receive. It means only that there is a purpose or point to someone's transferring a holding to one person rather than to another; that usually we can see what the transferrer thinks he's gaining, what cause he thinks he's serving, what goals he thinks he's helping to achieve, and so forth. Since in a capitalist society people often transfer holdings to others in accordance with how much they perceive these others benefiting them, the fabric constituted by the individual transactions and transfers is largely reasonable and intelligible. (Gifts to loved ones, bequests to children, charity to the needy also are nonarbitrary components of the fabric.) In stressing the large strand of distribution in accordance with benefit to others, Hayek shows the point of many transfers, and so shows that the system of transfer of entitlements is not just spinning its gears aimlessly. The system of entitlements is defensible when constituted by the individual aims of individual transactions. No overarching aim is needed, no distributional pattern is required.

To think that the task of a theory of distributive justice is to fill in the blank in "to each according to his _____" is to be predisposed to search for a pattern; and the separate treatment of "from each according to his _____" treats production and distribution as two separate and independent issues. On an entitlement view these are *not* two separate questions. Whoever makes something, having bought or contracted for all other held resources used in the process (transferring some of his holdings for these cooperating factors), is entitled to it. The situation is *not* one of something's getting made, and there being an open question of who is to get it. Things come into the world already attached to people having entitlements over them. From the point of view of the historical entitlement conception of justice in holdings, those who start afresh to complete "to each according to his _____" treat objects as if they appeared from nowhere, out of nothing. A complete theory of justice might cover this limit case as well; perhaps here is a use for the usual conceptions of distributive justice.

So entrenched are maxims of the usual form that perhaps we should present the entitlement conception as a competitor. Ignoring acquisition and rectification, we might say:

> From each according to what he chooses to do, to each according to what he makes for himself (perhaps with the contracted aid of others) and what others choose to do for him and choose to give him of what they've been given previously (under this maxim) and haven't yet expended or transferred.

This, the discerning reader will have noticed, has its defects as a slogan. So as a summary and great simplification (and not as a maxim with any independent meaning) we have:

> *From each as they choose, to each as they are chosen.*

How Liberty Upsets Patterns

It is not clear how those holding alternative conceptions of distributive justice can reject the entitlement conception of justice in holdings. For suppose a distribution favored by one of these nonentitlement conceptions is realized. Let us suppose it is your favorite one and let us call this distribution D_1; perhaps everyone has an equal share, perhaps shares vary in accordance with some dimension you treasure. Now suppose that Wilt Chamberlain is greatly in demand by basketball teams, being a great gate attraction. (Also suppose contracts run only for a year, with players being free agents.) He signs the following sort of contract with a team: In each home game, twenty-five cents from the price of each ticket of admission goes to him. (We ignore the question of whether he is "gouging" the owners, letting them look out for themselves.) The season starts, and people cheerfully attend his team's games; they buy their tickets, each time dropping a separate twenty-five cents of their admission price into a special box with Chamberlain's name on it. They are excited about seeing him play; it is worth the total admission price to them. Let us suppose that in one season one million persons attend his home games, and Wilt Chamberlain winds up with $250,000, a much larger sum than the average income and larger even than anyone else has. Is he entitled to this income? Is this new distribution D_2, unjust? If so, why? There is *no* question about whether each of the people was entitled to the control over the resources they held in D_1; because that was the distribution (your favorite) that (for the purposes of argument) we assumed was acceptable. Each of these persons *chose* to give twenty-five cents of their money to Chamberlain. They could have spent it on going to the movies, or on candy bars, or on copies of *Dissent* magazine, or of *Monthly Review*. But they all, at least one million of them, converged on giving it to Wilt Chamberlain in exchange for watching him play basketball. If D_1 was a just distribution, and people voluntarily moved from it to D_2, transferring parts of their shares they were given under D_1 (what was it for if not to do something with?), isn't D_2 also just? If the people were entitled to dispose of the resources to which they were entitled (under D_1), didn't this include their being entitled to give it to, or exchange it with, Wilt Chamberlain? Can anyone else complain on grounds of justice? Each other person already has his legitimate share under D_1. Under D_1, there is nothing that anyone has that anyone else has a claim of justice against. After someone transfers something to Wilt Chamberlain, third parties *still* have their legitimate shares; *their* shares are not changed. By what process could such a transfer among two persons give rise to a legitimate claim of distributive justice on a portion of what was transferred, by a third party who had no claim of justice on any holding of the others *before* the transfer? To cut off objections irrelevant here, we might imagine the exchanges occurring in a socialist society, after hours. After playing whatever basketball he does in his daily work, or doing whatever other daily work he does, Wilt Chamberlain decides to put in *overtime* to earn additional money. (First his work quota is set; he works time over that.) Or imagine it is a skilled juggler people like to see, who puts on shows after hours.

Why might someone work overtime in a society in which it is assumed their needs are satisfied? Perhaps because they care about things other than needs. I like to write in books that I read, and to have easy access to books for browsing at odd hours. It would be very pleasant and convenient to have the resources of Widener Library in my back yard. No society, I assume, will provide such resources close to each person who would like them as part of his regular allotment (under D_1). Thus, persons either must do without some extra things that they want, or be allowed to do something extra to get some of these things. On what basis could the inequalities that would eventuate be forbidden? Notice also that small factories would spring up in a socialist society, unless forbidden. I melt down some of my personal possessions (under D_1) and build a machine out of the material. I offer you, and others, a philosophy lecture once a week in exchange for your cranking the handle on my machine, whose products I exchange for yet other things, and so on. (The raw materials used by the machine are given to me by others who possess them under D_1, in exchange for hearing lectures.) Each person might participate to gain things over and above their allotment under D_1. Some persons even might want to leave their job in socialist industry and work full time in this private sector. . . . Here I wish merely to note how private property even in means of production would occur in a socialist society that did not forbid people to use as they wished some of the resources they are given under the socialist distribution D_1. The socialist soci-

ety would have to forbid capitalist acts between consenting adults.

The general point illustrated by the Wilt Chamberlain example and the example of the entrepreneur in a socialist society is that no end-state principle or distributional patterned principle of justice can be continuously realized without continuous interference with people's lives. Any favored pattern would be transformed into one unfavored by the principle, by people choosing to act in various ways; for example, by people exchanging goods and services with other people, or giving things to other people, things the transferrers are entitled to under the favored distributional pattern. To maintain a pattern one must either continually interfere to stop people from transferring resources as they wish to, or continually (or periodically) interfere to take from some persons resources that others for some reason chose to transfer to them. (But if some time limit is to be set on how long people may keep resources others voluntarily transfer to them, why let them keep these resources for *any* period of time? Why not have immediate confiscation?) It might be objected that all persons voluntarily will choose to refrain from actions which would upset the pattern. This presupposes unrealistically (1) that all will most want to maintain the pattern (are those who don't, to be "reeducated" or forced to undergo "self-criticism"?), (2) that each can gather enough information about his own actions and the ongoing activities of others to discover which of his actions will upset the pattern, and (3) that diverse and far-flung persons can coordinate their actions to dovetail into the pattern. Compare the manner in which the market is neutral among persons' desires, as it reflects and transmits widely scattered information via prices, and coordinates persons' activities.

It puts things perhaps a bit too strongly to say that every patterned (or end-state) principle is liable to be thwarted by the voluntary actions of the individual parties transferring some of their shares they receive under the principle. For perhaps some *very* weak patterns are not so thwarted. Any distributional pattern with any egalitarian component is overturnable by the voluntary actions of individual persons over time; as is every patterned condition with sufficient content so as actually to have been proposed as presenting the central core of distributive justice. Still, given the possibility that some weak conditions or patterns may not be unstable in this way, it would be better to formulate an explicit description of the kind of interesting and contentful patterns under discussion, and to prove a theorem about their instability. Since the weaker the patterning, the more likely it is that the entitlement system itself satisfies it, a plausible conjecture is that any patterning either is unstable or is satisfied by the entitlement system. . . .

QUESTIONS FOR REFLECTION

1. Outline Nozick's entitlement theory. What principles would be required, if the world were perfect? What principle is needed because it is not?

2. How do historical principles differ from end-result principles?

3. What is a patterned theory of justice? Is Nozick's theory patterned? Can a theory be both patterned and historical?

4. Why, according to Nozick, are patterned theories of justice incompatible with liberty?

ECONOMIC EQUALITY

The central problem of distributive justice is how goods should be allotted to members of a society. In many societies, the prevailing methods of allotment leave some people with very little. Some may not have enough to eat; some may have inadequate housing or no housing at all. Some may lack basic medical care. Some may receive no, or very poor, education. How should society respond to these problems?

Clearly, this question raises two major issues. One is philosophical: What are the proper principles of distribution? What, in other words, is the correct theory of distributive justice? The other is practical: Given a set of principles of distribution, how can we devise policies to bring about distributions in accord with them? Answering the first question defines our obligations to help others; answering the second defines a way of fulfilling them in practice. The first question is prior. Only if we know what we are trying to accomplish can we judge how well various policies accomplish it.

These questions go to the root of our conception of political and economic organization. A society that alters its laws about capital punishment, abortion, or pornography, for example, may bring about significant changes by doing so, but it does not fundamentally change the way it is organized. Changing one's conception of distribution, however, can change social organization. Socialism, capitalism, communism, and other forms of economic organization aim at satisfying different principles of distribution. Within each system arise important questions about policies for satisfying them.

Kai Nielsen defends egalitarianism—the view that everyone is entitled to equality. Almost all moral philosophers agree that people ought to be treated equally in some respects. The formal principle of justice, which requires that similar cases receive similar treatment, commands nearly universal assent. Nielsen argues for a more substantive entitlement to equality, one which, he argues, requires fundamental changes in social organization.

Philosopher John Hospers argues in favor of libertarianism, the view that the government may act only to prevent harm to others. Taking Mill's harm principle and applying it broadly, Hospers finds little justification for any government action concerning distribution. The government may of course enforce laws against stealing, for example, because that involves direct harm to others. But nothing justifies government action to take from A and give to B simply because B has less than A. Hospers argues that all other conceptions of government and of distributive justice give people rights over the lives of others—rights that, in his view, they do not have.

Ronald Dworkin defends liberalism. He argues that liberals do not merely assign a greater weight to equality, and a smaller weight to liberty, than conservatives. Instead, liberals share the belief that government ought to be neutral on the question of what the good is. Neutrality leads the government to protect liberty in the sphere of civil rights but to promote equal opportunity in economic matters. That, he maintains, provides a justification for welfare programs.

Michael Walzer goes further. He finds welfare essential, not to provide equal opportunity but to meet people's needs. Communities exist to provide spheres of security and welfare; their members owe each other what they need. The social contract does not demand equality, but it does demand redistribution to meet individual and collective needs. What do people need? That, Walzer says, is for communities to decide. He advocates a version of Marx's principle: "From each according to his ability (or his resources); and to each according to his socially recognized needs."

Social theorist Charles Murray addresses the practical problem of welfare. He assumes that government is justified in attempting to eliminate poverty, homelessness, and other social problems, but asks how it can do so. Murray draws several laws about social programs, which imply that such programs inevitably do more harm than good. Murray concludes that a society without any welfare programs at all would be better off than one in which government expends a great deal of energy and money trying to redistribute income and other goods. If Murray is right, there is a sense in which the practical problem of welfare policy may be prior to the question of distributive justice: perhaps no policies can achieve anything worth achieving—on any plausible conception of justice—without doing even greater harm. If so, then what conception of justice is correct makes no difference for social policy, for no combination of welfare programs could bring about a just distribution.

Michael Tanner and Stephen Moore show how much government welfare programs have varied. In many states, welfare has paid better than work; in some, it has paid better than the average job. Tanner and Moore argue that this not only provides perverse incentives but violates basic notions of fairness.

KAI NIELSEN

Egalitarian Justice:
Equality as a Goal and Equality as a Right

Kai Nielsen is Professor of Philosophy at the University of Calgary. (Source: From Kai Nielsen, Equality and Liberty, *[Totowa, New Jersey: Rowman & Allenheld, 1985]. Notes have been omitted. Copyright © 1985 by Rowman & Allenheld, Publishers. Reprinted by permission.)*

I

The argument in this chapter will attempt to show that justice should be linked closely to equality and that, so construed, it is not, as conservatives and even some liberals think, the mortal enemy of liberty. I shall also argue that equality, in an important reading, should be regarded as a goal—indeed as a fundamental human good. Moreover, it is something which is both instrumentally and intrinsically good. There is also a reading—a compatible but distinct reading from the reading mentioned above—in which equality is a right. I shall elucidate and also argue for that reading but I shall principally be concerned with arguing for equality as a fundamental goal, a goal essential for justice, which a perfectly just society would realize. In our class societies, and indeed in our dark times, such justice is not in the immediate offing. It is not the sort of thing we are going to achieve in the next decade or so. But such a conception of justice should remain a heuristic ideal in our emancipatory struggles. . . .

VI

I want now to consider equality as a goal, though this is not to say that some equalities are not rights, though

how this can be needs, of course, to be elucidated. As a goal, as an ideal state of affairs to be obtained, an egalitarian is committed to trying to provide the social basis for an equality of *condition* for all human beings. The ideal, putting it minimally as a first step, is to provide the social basis for an equality of life prospects such that there cannot be anything like the vast disparities in whole life prospects that exist now.

Suppose we ask, "Why should this be thought to be desirable?" We are, I believe, so close to bedrock here that it is difficult to know what to say. That such a condition is desirable gives expression, to speak autobiographically for a moment, to a root pre-analytical (pre-theoretical) conception of a central element in a good society and to my pre-analytic (pre-theoretical) conception of what fairness between persons comes to. Vis-à-vis fairness/unfairness, I have in mind the sense of unfairness which goes with the acceptance, where something non-catastrophic could be done about it, of the existence of very different life prospects of equally talented, equally energetic children from very different social backgrounds: say the children of a successful businessman and a dishwasher. Their whole life prospects are very unequal indeed and, given the manifest quality of that difference, that this should be so seems to me very unfair. It conflicts sharply with my sense of justice.

My egalitarian ideal is a generalization of that. I can understand someone saying that the existence of such disparities is unfortunate, that life itself in that respect is not fair, but to try to do something about it would be still worse for it would entail an onslaught on the family, the undermining of liberty, the violation of individual rights and the like. That being so, we must just live with these disparities in life prospects. Here we have something we can reason about in a common universe of discourse. But what I do not see, what indeed seems both incredible and morally monstrous, is someone who would honestly think that if none of these consequences obtained, with regard to the family, liberty, rights, and so on, they would *still* not see that there is any unfairness in a society, particularly an abundant society, so structured. There is nothing wrong, they seem at least to think, with such people having such radically unequal life prospects even when something could be done about it without violating anyone's rights or causing a social catastrophe. If someone sees no unfairness here, nothing that, other things being equal, should be corrected in the direction of equality, then I do not know where to turn. It is almost like a situation in which someone says that he sees nothing wrong with racial bigotry, religious intolerance or torturing people to get them to confess to petty crimes. It seems that there are very basic considered judgments (moral intuitions, if you will) being appealed to here and that there is little likelihood of getting back of them to something more fundamental or evident. It seems to me to be an intrinsic good that fair relations obtain between people and that it is intrinsically desirable that at least between equally deserving people there obtain, if that is reasonably possible, an equality of life conditions. Equality seems to me to be an intrinsic good, though surely not the sole intrinsic good.

VII

However, and perhaps more importantly, equality is also a very important instrumental good. Where there are extensive differences in life prospects between people, at least within a single society, where their condition is markedly unequal, where there are extensive income differentials, the better off people in this respect tend to gain a predominance of power and control in society. It is as evident as anything can be that there is a close correlation between wealth and power. If we are reasonably clear-headed, and if we prize liberty and autonomy, and if we prize democracy, we will also be egalitarians. With those inequalities of power and control, liberty and democracy must suffer. Equality, liberty, autonomy, democracy and justice, I shall argue, come as a packaged deal. To have any of them in any secure or extensive manner we must have all of them.

VIII

I also want to argue that a certain kind of equality is a right. That everyone, where this is reasonably possible, is to have his or her needs equally met is an egalitarian *goal;* that people be treated as equals, that in the design of our institutions people have an equal right to respect, that none be treated as a means only, are natural *rights.* That kind of equality is something we have by right. (By a "natural right" I mean nothing more arcane than rights which need not be legal rights or rights which must be conventionally acknowledged.) It is not that I am saying that a right is a goal. What I am saying is that *a certain condition of equality* is a goal that we should strive toward and that, quite independently of its attainment, there are certain rights that we all have, the covering formula for which is the claim that we all are to be treated as moral equals. This is something that could obtain now, though it is certainly not observed, and it is something that we could and should claim as a right, while the egalitarian goal I speak of is something for the future when the productive forces are more developed and when the productive relations and parallel political and legal formations have been transformed.

The link between such rights-talk and such goals-talk is this: if we believe that we human beings have an equal right to respect and that our institutions should be designed so as to achieve and sustain this, we are also very likely, when we think about what this comes to, to say that all human beings also have an equal right to concern on the part of society. By this we mean that our social institutions should be impartially concerned with all human beings under their jurisdiction. We cannot allow any playing of favorites here. If we get this far, it is a very short step, or so at least we are going to be naturally inclined to believe, to the belief that we must not construct our lives together in such a way that the needs of any human being are simply ignored. Beyond that we will also be inclined to believe that there must be an equal concern on the part of society for the satisfaction of the needs of all human beings. (I am, of course, talking about situations of plenty where this is possible.) No one in such a circumstance can be treated as being simply expendable. Rather, all needs and all interests must, as far as that is possible, be equally considered. What starts as a goal—what in some historical circumstances is little more than a heuristic ideal—turns into a right when the goal can realistically be achieved. And a just social order, if such is ever to come into existence, must have these egalitarian commitments.

It is not likely that a condition of moral equality between human beings can be stably sustained where there is not something approaching a rough equality of condition. Where people do not stand in that condition, one person is very likely to have, in various ways, some subtle and some not so subtle, greater power than another. Because of this, it will be the case that in some ways at least some will gain control over others or at least will be in a position to exercise control or partial control, and that in turn limits the autonomy of some and works to undermine their self-respect. If we want a world of moral equals, we also need a world in which people stand to each other in a rough equality of condition. To have a world in which a condition of equal respect and concern obtain, we need, where a person's whole lifetime is the measure, a rough equality of resources. If equality as a right is to be secure; that is, if that is a right that people actually can securely exercise, we must attain the goal of equality of condition. That, of course, is something we are not within a country mile of attaining. To think about justice seriously is to think about what must be done to be on our way to attaining it. . . .

QUESTIONS FOR REFLECTION

1. What is the formal principle of justice? What implications does it have for equality?

2. What is the difference between treating equality as a goal and treating it as a right, in Nielsen's view?

3. What is the difference between positive and negative rights?

4. Why does Nielsen advocate a right to conditions of equality? Do you find the argument convincing?

5. Compare Nielsen's view of equality to Rawls's.

JOHN HOSPERS

What Libertarianism Is

John Hospers is Professor Emeritus of Philosophy at the University of Southern California. He ran for president on the Libertarian Party ticket in 1972. (Source: Reprinted by permission from Tibor R. Machan [ed.], The Libertarian Alternative: Essays in Social and Political Philosophy. *[Chicago: Nelson-Hall, 1974]. Copyright © 1974 by Nelson-Hall, Inc.)*

The political philosophy that is called libertarianism (from the Latin *libertas,* liberty) is the doctrine that every person is the owner of his own life, and that no one is the owner of anyone else's life; and that consequently every human being has the right to act in accordance with his own choices, unless those actions infringe on the equal liberty of other human beings to act in accordance with *their* choices.

There are several other ways of stating the same libertarian thesis:

1. *No one is anyone else's master, and no one is anyone else's slave.* Since I am the one to decide how my life is to be conducted, just as you decide about yours, I have no right (even if I had the power) to make you my slave and be your master, nor have you the right to become the master by enslaving me. Slavery is *forced* servitude, and since no one owns the life of anyone else, no one has the right to enslave another. Political theories past and present have traditionally been concerned with who should be the master (usually the king, the dictator, or government bureaucracy) and who should be the slaves, and what the extent of the slavery should be. Libertarianism holds that no one has the right to use force to enslave the life of another, or any portion or aspect of that life.

2. *Other men's lives are not yours to dispose of.* I enjoy seeing operas; but operas are expensive to produce. Opera-lovers often say, "The state (or the city, etc.) should subsidize opera, so that we can all see it.

Also it would be for people's betterment, cultural benefit, etc." But what they are advocating is nothing more or less than legalized plunder. They can't pay for the productions themselves, and yet they want to see opera, which involves a large number of people and their labor; so what they are saying in effect is, "Get the money through legalized force. Take a little bit more out of every worker's paycheck every week to pay for the operas we want to see." But I have no right to take by force from the workers' pockets to pay for what I want.

Perhaps it would be better if he *did* go to see opera—then I should try to convince him to go voluntarily. But to take the money from him forcibly, because in my opinion it would be good for *him,* is still seizure of his earnings, which is plunder.

Besides, if I have the right to force him to help pay for my pet projects, hasn't he equally the right to force me to help pay for his? Perhaps he in turn wants the government to subsidize rock-and-roll, or his new car, or a house in the country? If I have the right to milk him, why hasn't he the right to milk me? If I can be a moral cannibal, why can't he too?

We should beware of the inventors of utopias. They would remake the world according to their vision—with the lives and fruits of the labor of *other* human beings. Is it someone's utopian vision that others should build pyramids to beautify the landscape? Very well, then other men should provide the labor; and if he is in a position of political power, and he can't get men to do it voluntarily, then he must *compel* them to "cooperate"—i.e., he must enslave them.

A hundred men might gain great pleasure from beating up or killing just one insignificant human being; but other men's lives are not theirs to dispose of. "In order to achieve the worthy goals of the next five-year-plan, we must forcibly collectivize the peasants . . ."; but other men's lives are not theirs to dispose of. Do you want to occupy, rent-free, the mansion that another man has worked for twenty years to buy? But other men's lives are not yours to dispose of. Do you want operas so badly that everyone is forced to work harder to pay for their subsidization through taxes? But other men's lives are not yours to dispose of. Do you want to have free medical care at the expense of other people, whether they wish to provide it or not? But this would require them to work longer for you whether they want to or not, and other men's lives are not yours to dispose of.

> The freedom to engage in any type of enterprise, to produce, to own and control property, to buy and sell on the free market, is derived from the rights to life, liberty, and property . . . which are stated in the Declaration of Independence . . . [but] when a government guarantees a "right" to an education or parity on farm products or a guaranteed annual income, it is staking a claim on the property of one group of citizens for the sake of another group. In short, it is violating one of the fundamental rights it was instituted to protect.*

3. *No human being should be a nonvoluntary mortgage on the life of another.* I cannot claim your life, your work, or the products of your efforts as mine. The fruit of one man's labor should not be fair game for every freeloader who comes along and demands it as his own. The orchard that has been carefully grown, nurtured, and harvested by its owner should not be ripe for the plucking for any bypasser who has a yen for the ripe fruit. The wealth that some men have produced should not be fair game for looting by government, to be used for whatever purposes its representatives determine, no matter what their motives in so doing may be. The theft of your money by a robber is not justified by the fact that he used it to help his injured mother.

It will already be evident that libertarian doctrine is embedded in a view of the rights of man. Each human being has the right to live his life as he chooses, compatibly with the equal right of all other human beings to live their lives as they choose.

All man's rights are implicit in the above statement. Each man has the right to life: any attempt by others to take it away from him, or even to injure him, violates this right, through the use of coercion against him. Each man has the right to liberty: to conduct his life in accordance with the alternatives open to him without coercive action by others. And every man has the right to property: to work to sustain his life (and the lives of whichever others he chooses to sustain, such as his family) and to retain the fruits of his labor.

People often defend the rights of life and liberty but denigrate property rights, and yet the right to property is as basic as the other two; indeed, without property rights no other rights are possible. Depriving you of property is depriving you of the means by which you live.

> . . . All that which an individual possesses by right (including his life and property) are morally his to use, dispose of and even destroy, as he sees fit. If I own my life, then it follows that I am free to associate with whom I please and not to associate with whom I please. If I own my knowledge and services, it follows that I may ask any compensation I wish for providing them for another, or I may abstain from providing them at all, if I so choose. If I own my house, it follows that I may decorate it as I please and live in it with whom I please. If I control my own business, it follows that I may charge what I please for my products or services, hire whom I please and not hire whom I please. All that which I own in fact, I may dispose of as I choose to in reality. For anyone to attempt to limit my freedom to do so is to violate my rights.
>
> Where do my rights end? Where yours begin. I may do anything I wish with my own life, liberty and property without your consent; but I may do nothing with your life, liberty and property without your consent. If we recognize the principle of man's rights, it follows

---

* William W. Bayes, "What Is Property?" *The Freeman*, July 1970, p. 348.

that the individual is sovereign of the domain of his own life and property, and is sovereign of no other domain. To attempt to interfere forcibly with another's use, disposal or destruction of his own property is to initiate force against him and to violate his rights.

I have no right to decide how *you* should spend your time or your money. I can make that decision for myself, but not for you, my neighbor. I may deplore your choice of life-style, and I may talk with you about it provided you are willing to listen to me. But I have no right to use force to change it. Nor have I the right to decide how you should spend the money you have earned. I may appeal to you to give it to the Red Cross, and you may prefer to go to prizefights. But that is your decision, and however much I may chafe about it I do not have the right to interfere forcibly with it, for example by robbing you in order to use the money in accordance with *my* choices. (If I have the right to rob you, have you also the right to rob me?)

When I claim a right, I carve out a niche, as it were, in my life, saying in effect, "This activity I must be able to perform without interference from others. For you and everyone else, this is off limits." And so I put up a "no trespassing" sign, which marks off the area of my right. Each individual's right is his "no trespassing" sign in relation to me and others. I may not encroach upon his domain any more than he upon mine, without my consent. Every right entails a duty, true—but the duty is only that of *forbearance*—that is, of *refraining* from violating the other person's right. If you have a right to life, I have no right to take your life; if you have a right to the products of your labor (property), I have no right to take it from you without your consent. The non-violation of these rights will not guarantee you protection against natural catastrophes such as floods and earthquakes, but it will protect you against the aggressive activities *of other men.* And rights, after all, have to do with one's relations to other human beings, not with one's relations to physical nature.

Nor were these rights created by government; governments—some governments, obviously not all —*recognize* and *protect* the rights that individuals already have. Governments regularly forbid homicide and theft; and, at a more advanced stage, protect individuals against such things as libel and breach of contract. . . .

Government is the most dangerous institution known to man. Throughout history it has violated the rights of men more than any individual or group of individuals could do: it has killed people, enslaved them, sent them to forced labor and concentration camps, and regularly robbed and pillaged them of the fruits of their expended labor. Unlike individual criminals, government has the power to arrest and try; unlike individual criminals, it can surround and encompass a person totally, dominating every aspect of one's life, so that one has no recourse from it but to leave the country (and in totalitarian nations even that is prohibited). Government throughout history has a much sorrier record than any individual, even that of a ruthless mass murderer. The signs we see on bumper stickers are chillingly accurate: "Beware: the Government is Armed and Dangerous."

The only proper role of government, according to libertarians, is that of the protector of the citizen against aggression by other individuals. The government, of course, should never initiate aggression; its proper role is as the embodiment of the *retaliatory* use of force against anyone who initiates its use.

If each individual had constantly to defend himself against possible aggressors, he would have to spend a considerable portion of his life in target practice, karate exercises, and other means of self-defenses, and even so he would probably be helpless against groups of individuals who might try to kill, maim, or rob him. He would have little time for cultivating those qualities which are essential to civilized life, nor would improvements in science, medicine, and the arts be likely to occur. The function of government is to take this responsibility off his shoulders: the government undertakes to defend him against aggressors and to punish them if they attack him. When the government is effective in doing this, it enables the citizen to go about his business unmolested and without constant fear for his life. To do this, of course, government must have physical power—the police, to protect the citizen from aggression within its borders, and the armed forces, to protect him from aggressors outside. Beyond that, the government should not intrude upon his life, either to run his business, or adjust his daily activities, or prescribe his personal moral code.

Government, then, undertakes to be the individual's protector; but historically governments have gone far beyond this function. Since they already have the physical power, they have not hesitated to use it for purposes far beyond that which was entrusted to them in the first place. Undertaking initially to protect its citizens against aggression, it has often itself become an aggressor—a far greater aggressor, indeed, than the criminals against whom it was supposed to protect its citizens. Governments have done what no private citizens can do: arrest and imprison individuals without a trial and send them to slave labor camps. Government must have power in order to be effective—and yet the very means by which alone it can be effective make it vulnerable to the abuse of power, leading to managing the lives of individuals and even inflicting terror upon them.

What then should be the function of government? In a word, the *protection of human rights*.

1. *The right to life:* Libertarians support all such legislation as will protect human beings against the use of force by others, for example, laws against killing, attempted killing, maiming, beating, and all kinds of physical violence.

2. *The right to liberty:* There should be no laws compromising in any way freedom of speech, of the press, and of peaceable assembly. There should be no censorship of ideas, books, films, or of anything else by government.

3. *The right to property:* Libertarians support legislation that protects the property rights of individuals against confiscation, nationalization, eminent domain, robbery, trespass, fraud and misrepresentation, patent and copyright, libel and slander.

Someone has violently assaulted you. Should he be legally liable? Of course. He has violated one of your rights. He has knowingly injured you, and since he has initiated aggression against you he should be made to expiate.

Someone has negligently left his bicycle on the sidewalk where you trip over it in the dark and injure yourself. He didn't do it intentionally; he didn't mean you any harm. Should he be legally liable? Of course; he has, however unwittingly, injured you, and since the injury is caused by him and you are the victim, he should pay.

Someone across the street is unemployed. Should you be taxed extra to pay for his expenses? Not at all. You have not injured him, you are not responsible for the fact that he is unemployed (unless you are a senator or bureaucrat who agitated for further curtailing of business, which legislation passed, with the result that your neighbor was laid off by the curtailed business). You may voluntarily wish to help him out, or better still, try to get him a job to put him on his feet again; but since you have initiated no aggressive act against him, and neither purposely nor accidentally injured him in any way, you should not be legally penalized for the fact of his unemployment. (Actually, it is just such penalties that increase unemployment.)

One man, A, works hard for years and finally earns a high salary as a professional man. A second man, B, prefers not to work at all, and to spend wastefully what money he has (through inheritance), so that after a year or two he has nothing left. At the end of this time he has a long siege of illness and lots of medical bills to pay. He demands that the bills be paid by the government—that is, by the taxpayers of the land, including Mr. A.

But of course B has no such right. He chose to lead his life in a certain way—that was his voluntary decision. One consequence of that choice is that he must depend on charity in case of later need. Mr. A chose not to live that way. (And if everyone lived like Mr. B, on whom would he depend in case of later need?) Each has a right to live in the way he pleases, but each must live with the consequences of his own decision (which, as always, fall primarily on himself). He cannot, in time of need, claim A's beneficence as his right. . . .

Laws may be classified into three types: (1) laws protecting individuals against themselves, such as laws against fornication and other sexual behavior, alcohol, and drugs; (2) laws protecting individuals against aggressions by other individuals, such as laws against murder, robbery, and fraud; (3) laws requiring people to help one another; for example, all laws which rob Peter to pay Paul, such as welfare.

Libertarians reject the first class of laws totally. Behavior which harms no one else is strictly the individual's own affair. Thus, there should be no laws against becoming intoxicated, since whether or not to become intoxicated is the individual's own decision; but there should be laws against driving while intoxicated, since the drunken driver is a threat to every other motorist on the highway (drunken driving falls into type 2). Similarly, there should be no laws against drugs (except the prohibition of sale of drugs to minors) as long as the taking of these drugs poses no threat to anyone else. Drug addiction is a psychological problem to which no present solution exists. Most of the social harm caused by addicts, other than to themselves, is the result of thefts which they perform in order to continue their habit—and then the *legal* crime is the theft, not the addiction. The actual cost of heroin is about ten cents a shot; if it were legalized, the enormous traffic in illegal sale and purchase of it would stop, as well as the accompanying proselytization to get new addicts (to make more money for the pusher) and the thefts performed by addicts who often require eighty dollars a day just to keep up the habit. Addiction would not stop, but the crimes would: it is estimated that 75 percent of the burglaries in New York City today are performed by addicts, and all these crimes could be wiped out at one stroke through the legalization of drugs. (Only when the taking of drugs could be shown to constitute a threat to *others* should it be prohibited by law. It is only laws protecting people against *themselves* that libertarians oppose.)

Laws should be limited to the second class only: aggression by individuals against other individuals. These are laws whose function is to protect human beings against encroachment by others; and this, as we have seen, is (according to libertarianism) the sole function of government.

Libertarians also reject the third class of laws totally: no one should be forced by law to help others, not even to tell them the time of day if requested, and certainly not to give them a portion of one's weekly paycheck. Governments, in the guise of humanitarianism, have given to some by taking from others (charging a "handling fee" in the process, which, because of the government's waste and inefficiency, sometimes is several hundred percent). And in so doing they have decreased incentive, violated the rights of individuals, and lowered the standard of living of almost everyone.

All such laws constitute what libertarians call *moral cannibalism*. A cannibal in the physical sense is a person who lives off the flesh of other human be-

ings. A *moral* cannibal is one who believes he has a right to live off the "spirit" of other human beings— who believes that he has a moral claim on the productive capacity, time, and effort expended by others.

It has become fashionable to claim virtually everything that one needs or desires as one's *right.* Thus, many people claim that they have a right to a job, the right to free medical care, to free food and clothing, to a decent home, and so on. Now if one asks, apart from any specific context, whether it would be desirable if everyone had these things, one might well say yes. But there is a gimmick attached to each of them: *At whose expense?* Jobs, medical care, education, and so on, don't grow on trees. These are goods and services *produced only by men.* Who, then, is to provide them, and under what conditions?

If you have a right to a job, who is to supply it? Must an employer supply it even if he doesn't want to hire you? What if you are unemployable, or incurably lazy? (If you say "the government must supply it," does that mean that a job must be created for you which no employer needs done, and that you must be kept in it regardless of how much or little you work?) If the employer is forced to supply it at his expense even if he doesn't need you, then isn't *he* being enslaved to that extent? What ever happened to *his* right to conduct his life and his affairs in accordance with his choices?

If you have a right to free medical care, then, since medical care doesn't exist in nature as wild apples do, some people will have to supply it to you for free: that is, they will have to spend their time and money and energy taking care of you whether they want to or not. What ever happened to *their* right to conduct their lives as they see fit? Or do you have a right to violate theirs? Can there be a right to violate rights?

All those who demand this or that as a "free service" are consciously or unconsciously evading the fact that there is in reality no such thing as free services. All man-made goods and services are the result of human expenditure of time and effort. There is no such thing as "something for nothing" in this world. If you demand something free, you are demanding that other men give their time and effort to you without compensation. If they voluntarily choose to do this, there is no problem; but if you demand that they be *forced* to do it, you are interfering with their right not to do it if they so choose. "Swimming in this pool ought to be free!" says the indignant passerby. What he means is that others should build a pool, others should provide the materials, and still others should run it and keep it in functioning order, so that *he* can use it without fee. But what right has he to the expenditure of *their* time and effort? To expect something "for free" is to expect it *to be paid for by others* whether they choose to or not.

Many questions, particularly about economic matters, will be generated by the libertarian account of human rights and the role of government. Should government have no role in assisting the needy, in providing social security, in legislating minimum wages, in fixing prices and putting a ceiling on rents, in curbing monopolies, in erecting tariffs, in guaranteeing jobs, in managing the money supply? To these and all similar questions the libertarian answers with an unequivocal no.

"But then you'd let people go hungry!" comes the rejoinder. This, the libertarian insists, is precisely what would not happen; with the restrictions removed, the economy would flourish as never before. With the controls taken off business, existing enterprises would expand and new ones would spring into existence satisfying more and more consumer needs; millions more people would be gainfully employed instead of subsisting on welfare, and all kinds of research and production, released from the stranglehold of government, would proliferate, fulfilling man's needs and desires as never before. It has always been so whenever government has permitted men to be free traders on a free market. . . .

QUESTIONS FOR REFLECTION

1. How does Hospers define libertarianism?

2. What conception of rights emerges from Hospers's analysis?

3. What, according to Hospers, is the proper function of government? How does his view compare to Mill's? To Locke's?

4. How does Hospers respond to the charge that libertarianism fails to respond to real human needs? Do you find his answer convincing?

RONALD DWORKIN

Liberalism

Ronald Dworkin is Professor of Jurisprudence at Oxford University, Professor of Law at New York University, and Professor-at-Large at Cornell University. (Source: From A Matter of Principle *[Cambridge: Harvard University Press, 1985]. Notes have been omitted. Copyright © 1985 by Ronald M. Dworkin. Reprinted by permission of Cambridge University Press. Portions originally published in Stuart Hampshire [ed.],* Public and Private Morality, *Cambridge, Cambridge University Press. Copyright © 1978 by Cambridge University Press. Reprinted by permission.)*

. . .

What does it mean for the government to treat its citizens as equals? That is, I think, the same question as the question of what it means for the government to treat all its citizens as free, or as independent, or with equal dignity. In any case, it is a question that has been central to political theory at least since Kant.

It may be answered in two fundamentally different ways. The first supposes that government must be neutral on what might be called the question of the good life. The second supposes that government cannot be neutral on that question, because it cannot treat its citizens as equal human beings without a theory of what human beings ought to be. I must explain that distinction further. Each person follows a more-or-less articulate conception of what gives value to life. The scholar who values a life of contemplation has such a conception; so does the television-watching, beer-drinking citizen who is fond of saying "This is the life," though he has thought less about the issue and is less able to describe or defend his conception.

The first theory of equality supposes that political decisions must be, so far as is possible, independent of any particular conception of the good life, or of what gives value to life. Since the citizens of a society differ in their conceptions, the government does not treat them as equals if it prefers one conception to another, either because the officials believe that one is intrinsically superior, or because one is held by the more numerous or more powerful group. The second theory argues, on the contrary, that the content of equal treatment cannot be independent of some theory about the good for man or the good of life, because treating a person as an equal means treating him the way the good or truly wise person would wish to be treated. Good government consists in fostering or at least recognizing good lives; treatment as an equal consists in treating each person as if he were desirous of leading the life that is in fact good, at least so far as this is possible. . . .

I now define a liberal as someone who holds the first, or liberal, theory of what equality requires. Suppose that a liberal is asked to found a new state. He is required to dictate its constitution and fundamental institutions. He must propose a general theory of political distribution, that is, a theory of how whatever the community has to assign, by way of goods or resources or opportunities, should be assigned. He will arrive initially at something like this principle of rough equality: resources and opportunities should be distributed, so far as possible, equally, so that roughly the same share of whatever is available is devoted to satisfying the ambitions of each. Any other general aim of distribution will assume either that the fate of some people should be of greater concern than that of others, or that the ambitions or talents of some are more worthy, and should be supported more generously on that account.

Someone may object that this principle of rough equality is unfair because it ignores the fact that people have different tastes, and that some of these are more expensive to satisfy than others, so that, for example, the man who prefers champagne will need more funds if he is not to be frustrated than the man satisfied with beer. But the liberal may reply that tastes as to which people differ are, by and large, not afflictions, like diseases, but are rather cultivated, in accordance with each person's theory of what his life should be like. The most effective neutrality, therefore, requires that the same share be devoted to each, so that the choice between expensive and less expensive tastes can be made by each person for himself, with no sense that his overall share will be enlarged by choosing a more expensive life, or that, whatever he chooses, his choice will subsidize those who have chosen more expensively.

But what does the principle of rough equality of distribution require in practice? If all resources were distributed directly by the government through grants of food, housing, and so forth; if every opportunity citizens have were provided directly by the government through the provisions of civil and criminal law; if every citizen had exactly the same talents; if every citizen started his life with no more than what any other citizen had at the start; and if every citizen had exactly the same theory of the good life and hence exactly the same scheme of preferences as every other citizen, including preferences between productive activity of different forms and leisure, then the principle of rough equality of treatment could be satisfied simply by equal distributions of everything to be distributed and by civil and criminal laws of universal application. Government would arrange for production that maximized the mix of goods, including jobs and leisure, that everyone favored, distributing the product equally.

Of course, none of these conditions of similarity holds. But the moral relevance of different sorts of diversity are very different, as may be shown by the following exercise. Suppose all the conditions of similarity I mentioned did hold except the last: citizens have different theories of the good and hence

different preferences. They therefore disagree about what product the raw materials and labor and savings of the community should be used to produce, and about which activities should be prohibited or regulated so as to make others possible or easier. The liberal, as lawgiver, now needs mechanisms to satisfy the principles of equal treatment in spite of these disagreements. He will decide that there are no better mechanisms available, as general political institutions, than the two main institutions of our own political economy: the economic market, for decisions about what goods shall be produced and how they shall be distributed, and representative democracy, for collective decisions about what conduct shall be prohibited or regulated so that other conduct might be made possible or convenient. Each of these familiar institutions may be expected to provide a more egalitarian division than any other general arrangement. The market, if it can be made to function efficiently, will determine for each product a price that reflects the cost in resources of material, labor, and capital that might have been applied to produce something different that someone else wants. That cost determines, for anyone who consumes that product, how much his account should be charged in computing the egalitarian division of social resources. It provides a measure of how much more his account should be charged for a house than a book, and for one book rather than another. The market will also provide, for the laborer, a measure of how much should be credited to his account for his choice of productive activity over leisure, and for one activity rather than another. It will tell us, through the price it puts on his labor, how much he should gain or lose by his decision to pursue one career rather than another. These measurements make a citizen's own distribution a function of the personal preferences of others as well as of his own, and it is the sum of these personal preferences that fixes the true cost to the community of meeting his own preferences for goods and activities. The egalitarian distribution, which requires that the cost of satisfying one person's preferences should as far as is possible be equal to the cost of satisfying another's, cannot be enforced unless those measurements are made.

We are familiar with the anti-egalitarian consequences of free enterprise in practice; it may therefore seem paradoxical that the liberal as lawgiver should choose a market economy for reasons of equality rather than efficiency. But, under the special condition that people differ only in preferences for goods and activities, the market is more egalitarian than any alternative of comparable generality. The most plausible alternative would be to allow decisions of production, investment, price, and wage to be made by elected officials in a socialist economy. But what principles should officials use in making those decisions? The liberal might tell them to mimic the decisions that a market would make if it was working efficiently under proper competition and full knowledge. This mimicry would be, in practice, much less efficient than an actual market would be. In any case, unless the liberal had reason to think it would be much more efficient, he would have good reason to reject it. Any minimally efficient mimicking of a hypothetical market would require invasions of privacy to determine what decisions individuals would make if forced actually to pay for their investment, consumption, and employment decisions at market rates, and this information gathering would be, in many other ways, much more expensive than an actual market. Inevitably, moreover, the assumptions officials make about how people would behave in a hypothetical market reflect the officials' own beliefs about how people should behave. So there would be, for the liberal, little to gain and much to lose in a socialist economy in which officials were asked to mimic a hypothetical market.

But any other instructions would be a direct violation of the liberal theory of what equality requires, because if a decision is made to produce and sell goods at a price below the price a market would fix, then those who prefer those goods are, *pro tanto,* receiving more than an equal share of the resources of the community at the expense of those who would prefer some other use of the resources. Suppose the limited demand for books, matched against the demand for competing uses for wood pulp, would fix the price of books at a point higher than the socialist managers of the economy will charge; those who want books are having less charged to their account than the egalitarian principle would require. It might be said that in a socialist economy books are simply valued more, because they are inherently more worthy uses of social resources, quite apart from the popular demand for books. But the liberal theory of equality rules out that appeal to the inherent value of one theory of what is good in life.

In a society in which people differed only in preferences, then, a market would be favored for its egalitarian consequences. Inequality of monetary wealth would be the consequence only of the fact that some preferences are more expensive than others, including the preference for leisure time rather than the most lucrative productive activity. But we must now return to the real world. In the actual society for which the liberal must construct political institutions, there are all the other differences. Talents are not distributed equally, so the decision of one person to work in a factory rather than a law firm, or not to work at all, will be governed in large part by his abilities rather than his preferences for work or between work and leisure. The institutions of wealth, which allow people to dispose of what they receive by gift, means that children of the successful will start with more wealth than the children of the unsuccessful. Some people have special needs, because they are handicapped; their handicap will not only disable them from the most productive and lucrative employment, but will incapacitate them from using the proceeds of whatever employment they find as efficiently, so that they will need more than those who are not handicapped to satisfy identical ambitions.

These inequalities will have great, often catastrophic, effects on the distribution that a market economy will provide. But, unlike differences in preferences, the differences these inequalities make are indefensible according to the liberal conception of equality. It is obviously obnoxious to the liberal conception, for example, that someone should have more of what the community as a whole has to distribute because he or his father had superior skill or luck. The liberal lawgiver therefore faces a difficult task. His conception of equality requires an economic system that produces certain inequalities (those that reflect the true differential costs of goods and opportunities) but not others (those that follow from differences in ability, inheritance, and so on). The market produces both the required and the forbidden inequalities, and there is no alternative system that can be relied upon to produce the former without the latter.

The liberal must be tempted, therefore, to a reform of the market through a scheme of redistribution that leaves its pricing system relatively intact but sharply limits, at least, the inequalities in welfare that his initial principle prohibits. No solution will seem perfect. The liberal may find the best answer in a scheme of welfare rights financed through redistributive income and inheritance taxes of the conventional sort, which redistributes just to the Rawlsian point, that is, to the point at which the worst-off group would be harmed rather than benefited by further transfers. In that case, he will remain a reluctant capitalist, believing that a market economy so reformed is superior, from the standpoint of his conception of equality, to any practical socialist alternative. Or he may believe that the redistribution that is possible in a capitalist economy will be so inadequate, or will be purchased at the cost of such inefficiency, that it is better to proceed in a more radical way, by substituting socialist for market decisions over a large part of the economy, and then relying on the political process to ensure that prices are set in a manner at least roughly consistent with his conception of equality. In that case he will be a reluctant socialist, who acknowledges the egalitarian defects of socialism but counts them as less severe than the practical alternatives. In either case, he chooses a mixed economic system—either redistributive capitalism or limited socialism—not in order to compromise antagonistic ideals of efficiency and equality, but to achieve the best practical realization of the demands of equality itself. . . .

. . . So liberalism as based on equality justifies the traditional liberal principle that government should not enforce private morality of this sort. But it has an economic as well as a social dimension. It insists on an economic system in which no citizen has less than an equal share of the community's resources just in order that others may have more of what he lacks. I do not mean that liberalism insists on what is often called "equality of result," that is, that citizens must each have the same wealth at every moment of their lives. A government bent on the latter ideal must constantly redistribute wealth, eliminating whatever inequalities in wealth are produced by market transactions. But this would be to devote *unequal* resources to different lives. Suppose that two people have very different bank accounts, in the middle of their careers, because one decided not to work, or not to work at the most lucrative job he could have found, while the other single-mindedly worked for gain. Or because one was willing to assume especially demanding or responsible work, for example, which the other declined. Or because one took larger risks which might have been disastrous but which were in fact successful, while the other invested conservatively. The principle that people must be treated as equals provides no good reason for redistribution in these circumstances; on the contrary, it provides a good reason *against* it.

For treating people as equals requires that each be permitted to use, for the projects to which he devotes his life, no more than an equal share of the resources available for all, and we cannot compute how much any person has consumed, on balance, without taking into account the resources he has contributed as well as those he has taken from the economy. The choices people make about work and leisure and investment have an impact on the resources of the community as a whole, and this impact must be reflected in the calculation equality demands. If one person chooses work that contributes less to other people's lives than different work he might have chosen, then, although this might well have been the right choice for him, given his personal goals, he has nevertheless added less to the resources available for others, and this must be taken into account in the egalitarian calculation. If one person chooses to invest in a productive enterprise rather than spend his funds at once, and if his investment is successful because it increases the stock of goods or services other people actually want, without coercing anyone, his choice has added more to social resources than the choice of someone who did not invest, and this, too, must be reflected in any calculation of whether he has, on balance, taken more than his share.

This explains, I think, why liberals have in the past been drawn to the idea of a market as a method of allocating resources. An efficient market for investment, labor, and goods works as a kind of auction in which the cost to someone of what he consumes, by way of goods and leisure, and the value of what he adds, through his productive labor or decisions, is fixed by the amount his use of some resource costs others, or his contributions benefit them, in each case measured by their willingness to pay for it. Indeed, if the world were very different from what it is, a liberal could accept the results of an efficient market as *defining* equal shares of community resources. If people start with equal amounts of wealth, and have roughly equal levels of raw skill, then a market allocation would ensure that no one could properly complain that he had less than others, over his whole life. He could have had the same as they if he had made the decisions to consume, save, or work that they did.

But in the real world people do not start their lives on equal terms; some begin with marked advantages of family wealth or of formal and informal education. Others suffer because their race is despised. Luck plays a further and sometimes devastating part in deciding who gains or keeps jobs everyone wants. Quite apart from these plain inequities, people are not equal in raw skill or intelligence or other native capacities; on the contrary, they differ greatly, through no choice of their own, in the various capacities that the market tends to reward. So some people who are perfectly willing, even anxious, to make exactly the choices about work and consumption and savings that other people make end up with fewer resources, and no plausible theory of equality can accept this as fair. This is the defect of the ideal fraudulently called "equality of opportunity": fraudulent because in a market economy people do not have equal opportunity who are less able to produce what others want.

So a liberal cannot, after all, accept the market results as defining equal shares. His theory of economic justice must be complex, because he accepts two principles which are difficult to hold in the administration of a dynamic economy. The first requires that people have, at any point in their lives, different amounts of wealth insofar as the genuine choices they have made have been more or less expensive or beneficial to the community, measured by what other people want for their lives. The market seems indispensable to this principle. The second requires that people not have different amounts of wealth just because they have different inherent capacities to produce what others want, or are differently favored by chance. This means that market allocations must be corrected in order to bring some people closer to the share of resources they would have had but for these various differences of initial advantage, luck, and inherent capacity.

Obviously any practical program claiming to respect both these principles will work imperfectly and will inevitably involve speculation, compromise, and arbitrary lines in the face of ignorance. For it is impossible to discover, even in principle, exactly which aspects of any person's economic position flow from his choices and which from advantages or disadvantages that were not matters of choice; and even if we could make this determination for particular people, one by one, it would be impossible to develop a tax system for the nation as a whole that would leave the first in place and repair only the second. There is therefore no such thing as the perfectly just program of redistribution. We must be content to choose whatever programs we believe bring us closer to the complex and unattainable ideal of equality, all things considered, than the available alternatives, and be ready constantly to reexamine that conclusion when new evidence or new programs are proposed.

Nevertheless, in spite of the complexity of that ideal, it may sometimes be apparent that a society falls far short of any plausible interpretation of its requirements. It is, I think, apparent that the United States falls far short now. A substantial minority of Americans are chronically unemployed or earn wages below any realistic "poverty line" or are handicapped in various ways or burdened with special needs; and most of these people would do the work necessary to earn a decent living if they had the opportunity and capacity. Equality of resources would require more rather than less redistribution than we now offer.

This does not mean, of course, that we should discontinue past liberal programs, however inefficient these have proved to be, or even that we should insist on "targeted" programs of the sort some liberals have favored—that is, programs that aim to provide a particular opportunity or resource, like education or medicine, to those who need it. Perhaps a more general form of transfer, like a negative income tax, would prove on balance more efficient and fairer, in spite of the difficulties in such schemes. And whatever devices are chosen for bringing distribution closer to equality of resources, some aid undoubtedly goes to those who have avoided rather than sought jobs. This is to be regretted, because it offends one of the two principles that together make up equality of resources. But we come closer to that ideal by tolerating this inequity than by denying aid to the far greater number who would work if they could. If equality of resources were our only goal, therefore, we could hardly justify the present retreat from redistributive welfare programs.

QUESTIONS FOR REFLECTION

1. What is liberalism, according to Dworkin?

2. Why, in Dworkin's view, can we not think of liberalism and conservatism as assigning different weights to equality and liberty as competing values? Do you agree?

3. Why would a liberal choose a market economy, according to Dworkin? What would be a proper role for government in the economy?

4. Because most conservatives would also choose a market economy, where would they disagree with Dworkin's liberals about the role of government in economic matters?

5. What does liberalism imply about the goals of welfare policies, in Dworkin's view, and in your view?

MICHAEL WALZER

Welfare, Membership and Need

Michael Walzer is UPS Foundation Professor of Social Science at the Institute for Advanced Study. (Source: from Spheres of Justice. *New York: Basic Books. Copyright © 1983 by Basic Books, Inc. Reprinted by permission.)*

Membership is important because of what the members of a political community owe to one another and to no one else, or to no one else in the same degree. And the first thing they owe is the communal provision of security and welfare. This claim might be reversed: communal provision is important because it teaches us the value of membership. If we did not provide for one another, if we recognized no distinction between members and strangers, we would have no reason to form and maintain political communities. "How shall men love their country," Rousseau asked, "if it is nothing more for them than for strangers, and bestows on them only that which it can refuse to none?" Rousseau believed that citizens ought to love their country and therefore that their country ought to give them particular reasons to do so. Membership (like kinship) is a special relation. It's not enough to say, as Edmund Burke did, that "to make us love our country, our country ought to be lovely." The crucial thing is that it be lovely for us—though we always hope that it will be lovely for others (we also love its reflected loveliness).

Political community for the sake of provision, provision for the sake of community: the process works both ways, and that is perhaps its crucial feature. Philosophers and political theorists have been too quick to turn it into a simple calculation. Indeed, we are rationalists of everyday life; we come together, we sign the social contract or reiterate the signing of it, in order to provide for our needs. And we value the contract insofar as those needs are met.

But one of our needs is community itself: culture, religion, and politics. It is only under the aegis of these three that all the other things we need become *socially recognized needs,* take on historical and determinate form. The social contract is an agreement to reach decisions together about what goods are necessary to our common life, and then to provide those goods for one another. The signers owe one another more than mutual aid, for that they owe or can owe to anyone. They owe mutual provision of all those things for the sake of which they have separated themselves from mankind as a whole and joined forces in a particular community. *Amour social* is one of those things; but though it is a distributed good—often unevenly distributed—it arises only in the course of other distributions (and of the political choices that the other distributions require). Mutual provision breeds mutuality. So the common life is simultaneously the prerequisite of provision and one of its products.

Men and women come together because they literally cannot live apart. But they can live together in many different ways. Their survival and then their well-being require a common effort: against the wrath of the gods, the hostility of other people, the indifference and malevolence of nature (famine, flood, fire, and disease), the brief transit of a human life. Not army camps alone, as David Hume wrote, but temples, storehouses, irrigation works, and burial grounds are the true mothers of cities. As the list suggests, origins are not singular in character.

Cities differ from one another, partly because of the natural environments in which they are built and the immediate dangers their builders encounter, partly because of the conceptions of social goods that the builders hold. They recognize but also create one another's needs and so give a particular shape to what I will call the "sphere of security and welfare." The sphere itself is as old as the oldest human community. Indeed, one might say that the original community is a sphere of security and welfare, a system of communal provision, distorted, no doubt, by gross inequalities of strength and cunning. But the system has, in any case, no natural form. Different experiences and different conceptions lead to different patterns of provision. Though there are some goods that are needed absolutely, there is no good such that once we see it, we know how it stands *vis-à-vis* all other goods and how much of it we owe to one another. The nature of a need is not self-evident. . . .

The Extent of Provision

Distributive justice in the sphere of welfare and security has a twofold meaning: it refers, first to the recognition of need and, second, to the recognition of members. Goods must be provided to needy members because of their neediness, but they must also be provided in such a way as to sustain their membership. It's not the case, however, that members have a claim on any specific set of goods. Welfare rights are fixed only when a community adopts some program of mutual provision. There are strong arguments to be made that, under given historical conditions, such-and-such a program should be adopted. But these are not arguments about individual rights; they are arguments about the character of a particular political community. No one's rights were violated because the Athenians did not allocate public funds for the education of children. Perhaps they believed, and perhaps they were right, that the public life of the city was education enough.

The right that members can legitimately claim is of a more general sort. It undoubtedly includes some version of the Hobbesian right to life, some claim on communal resources for bare subsistence. No community can allow its members to starve to death when there is food available to feed them; no gov-

ernment can stand passively by at such a time—not if it claims to be a government of or by or for the community. The indifference of Britain's rulers during the Irish potato famine in the 1840s is a sure sign that Ireland was a colony, a conquered land, no real part of Great Britain. This is not to justify the indifference—one has obligations to colonies and to conquered peoples—but only to suggest that the Irish would have been better served by a government, virtually any government, of their own. Perhaps Burke came closest to describing the fundamental right that is at stake here when he wrote: "Government is a contrivance of human wisdom to provide for human wants. Men have a right that these wants should be provided for by this wisdom." It only has to be said that the wisdom in question is the wisdom not of a ruling class, as Burke seems to have thought, but of the community as a whole. Only its culture, its character, its common understandings, can define the "wants" that are to be provided for. But culture, character, and common understandings are not givens; they don't operate automatically; at any particular moment, the citizens must argue about the extent of mutual provision.

They argue about the meaning of the social contract, the original and reiterated conception of the sphere of security and welfare. This is not a hypothetical or an ideal contract of the sort John Rawls has described. Rational men and women in the original position, deprived of all particular knowledge of their social standing and cultural understanding, would probably opt, as Rawls has argued, for an equal distribution of whatever goods they were told they needed. But this formula doesn't help very much in determining what choices people will make, or what choices they should make, once they know who and where they are. In a world of particular cultures, competing conceptions of the good, scarce resources, elusive and expansive needs, there isn't going to be a single formula, universally applicable. There isn't going to be a single universally approved path that carries us from a notion like, say, "fair shares" to a comprehensive list of the goods to which that notion applies. Fair share of what?

Justice, tranquility, defense, welfare, and liberty: that is the list provided by the United States Constitution. One could construe it as an exhaustive list, but the terms are vague; they provide at best a starting point for public debate. The standard appeal in that debate is to a larger idea: the Burkeian general right, which takes on determinate force only under determinate conditions and requires different sorts of provision in different times and places. The idea is simply that we have come together, shaped a community, in order to cope with difficulties and dangers that we could not cope with alone. And so whenever we find ourselves confronted with difficulties and dangers of that sort, we look for communal assistance. As the balance of individual and collective capacity changes, so the kinds of assistance that are looked for change, too.

The history of public health in the West might usefully be told in these terms. Some minimal provision is very old, as the Greek and Jewish examples suggest; the measures adopted were a function of the community's sense of danger and the extent of its medical knowledge. Over the years, living arrangements on a larger scale bred new dangers, and scientific advance generated a new sense of danger and a new awareness of the possibilities of coping. And then groups of citizens pressed for a wider program of communal provision, exploiting the new science to reduce the risks of urban life. That, they might rightly say, is what the community is for. A similar argument can be made in the case of social security. The very success of general provision in the field of public health has greatly extended the span of a normal human life and then also the span of years during which men and women are unable to support themselves, during which they are physically but most often not socially, politically, or morally incapacitated. Once again, support for the disabled is one of the oldest and most common forms of particular provision. But now it is required on a much larger scale than ever before. Families are overwhelmed by the costs of old age and look for help to the political community. Exactly what ought to be done will be a matter of dispute. Words like *health, danger, science,* even *old age,* have very different meanings in different cultures; no external specification is possible. But this is not to say that it won't be clear enough to the people involved that something —some particular set of things—ought to be done.

Perhaps these examples are too easy. Disease is a general threat; old age, a general prospect. Not so unemployment and poverty, which probably lie beyond the ken of many well-to-do people. The poor can always be isolated, locked into ghettos, blamed and punished for their own misfortune. At this point, it might be said, provision can no longer be defended by invoking anything like the "meaning" of the social contract. But let us look more closely at the easy cases; for, in fact, they involve all the difficulties of the difficult ones. Public health and social security invite us to think of the political community, in T. H. Marshall's phrase, as a "mutual benefit club." All provision is reciprocal; the members take turns providing and being provided for, much as Aristotle's citizens take turns ruling and being ruled. This is a happy picture, and one that is really understandable in contractualist terms. It is not only the case that rational agents, knowing nothing of their specific situation, would agree to these two forms of provision; the real agents, the ordinary citizens, of every modern democracy have in fact agreed to them. The two are, or so it appears, equally in the interests of hypothetical and of actual people. Coercion is only necessary in practice because some minority of actual people don't understand, or don't consistently understand, their real interests. Only the reckless and the improvident need to be forced to contribute—and it can always be said of them that they joined in the social contract precisely in order to protect themselves against their own recklessness and improvidence. In fact, however, the reasons for coercion go much deeper than this; the political community is something more than a mutual benefit club; and the extent of communal provision in any given case—what it is and what it should be—is determined by conceptions of need that are more problematic than the argument thus far suggests.

Consider again the case of public health. No communal provision is possible here without the constraint of a wide range of activities profitable to individual members of the community but threatening to some larger number. Even something so simple, for example, as the provision of uncontaminated milk to large urban populations requires extensive public control; and control is a political achievement, the result (in the United States) of bitter struggles, over many years, in one city after another. When the farmers or the middlemen of the dairy industry defended free enterprise, they were certainly acting rationally in their own interests. The same thing can be said of other entrepreneurs who defend themselves against the constraints of inspection, regulation, and enforcement. Public activities of these sorts may be of the highest value to the rest of us; they are not of the highest value to all of us. Though I have taken public health as an example of general provision, it is provided only at the expense of some members of the community. Moreover, it benefits most the most vulnerable of the others: thus, the special importance of the building code for those who live in crowded tenements, and of anti-pollution laws for those who live in the immediate vicinity of factory smokestacks or water drains. Social security, too, benefits the most vulnerable members, even if, for reasons I have already suggested, the actual payments are the same for everyone. For the well-to-do can, or many of them think they can, help themselves even in time of trouble and would much prefer not to be forced to help anyone else. The truth is that every serious effort at communal provision (insofar as the income of the community derives from the wealth of its members) is redistributive in character. The benefits it provides are not, strictly speaking, mutual.

Once again, rational agents ignorant of their own social standing would agree to such a redistribution. But they would agree too easily, and their agreement doesn't help us understand what sort of a redistribution is required: How much? For what purposes? In practice, redistribution is a political matter, and the coercion it involves is foreshadowed by the conflicts that rage over its character and extent. Every particular measure is pushed through by some coalition of particular interests. But the ultimate appeal in these conflicts is not to the particular interests, not even to a public interest conceived as their sum, but to collective values, shared understandings of membership, health, food and shelter, work and leisure. The conflicts themselves are often focused, at least overtly, on questions of fact; the understandings are assumed. Thus the entrepreneurs of the dairy industry denied as long as they could the connection between contaminated milk and tuberculosis. But once that connection was established, it was difficult for them to deny that milk should be inspected: *caveat emptor* was not, in such a case, a plausible doctrine. Similarly, in the debates over old-age pensions in Great Britain, politicians mostly agreed on the tradi-

tional British value of self-help but disagreed sharply about whether self-help was still possible through the established working-class friendly societies. These were real mutual-benefit clubs organized on a strictly voluntary basis, but they seemed about to be overwhelmed by the growing numbers of the aged. It became increasingly apparent that the members simply did not have the resources to protect themselves and one another from poverty in old age. And few British politicians were prepared to say that they should be left unprotected.

Here, then, is a more precise account of the social contract: it is an agreement to redistribute the resources of the members in accordance with some shared understanding of their needs, subject to ongoing political determination in detail. The contract is a moral bond. It connects the strong and the weak, the lucky and the unlucky, the rich and the poor, creating a union that transcends all differences of interest, drawing its strength from history, culture, religion, language, and so on. Arguments about communal provision are, at the deepest level interpretations of that union. The closer and more inclusive it is, the wider the recognition of needs, the greater the number of social goods that are drawn into the sphere of security and welfare. I don't doubt that many political communities have redistributed resources on very different principles, not in accordance with the needs of the members generally but in accordance with the power of the wellborn or the wealthy. But that, as Rousseau suggested in his *Discourse on Inequality,* makes a fraud of the social contract. In any community, where resources are taken away from the poor and given to the rich, the rights of the poor are being violated. The wisdom of the community is not engaged in providing for their wants. Political debate about the nature of those wants will have to be repressed, else the fraud will quickly be exposed. When all the members share in the business of interpreting the social contract, the result will be a more or less extensive system of communal provision. If all states are in principle welfare states, democracies are most likely to be welfare states in practice. Even the imitation of democracy breeds welfarism, as in the "people's democracies," where the state protects the people against every disaster except those that it inflicts on them itself.

So democratic citizens argue among themselves and opt for many different sorts of security and welfare, extending far beyond my "easy" examples of public health and old-age pensions. The category of socially recognized needs is open-ended. For the people's sense of what they need encompasses not only life itself but also the good life, and the appropriate balance between these two is itself a matter of dispute. The Athenian drama and the Jewish academies were both financed with money that could have been spent on housing, say, or on medicine. But drama and education were taken by Greeks and Jews to be not merely enhancements of the common life but vital aspects of communal welfare. I want to stress again that these are not judgments that can easily be called incorrect.

An American Welfare State

What sort of communal provision is appropriate in a society like our own? It's not my purpose here to anticipate the outcomes of democratic debate or to stipulate in detail the extent or the forms of provision. But it can be argued, I think, that the citizens of a modern industrial democracy owe a great deal to one another, and the argument will provide a useful opportunity to test the critical force of the principles I have defended up until now: that every political community must attend to the needs of its members as they collectively understand those needs; that the goods that are distributed must be distributed in proportion to need; and that the distribution must recognize and uphold the underlying equality of membership. These are very general principles; they are meant to apply to a wide range of communities —to any community, in fact, where the members are each other's equals (before God or the law), or where it can plausibly be said that, however they are treated in fact, they ought to be each other's equals. The principles probably don't apply to a community organized hierarchically, as in traditional India, where the fruits of the harvest are distributed not according

to need but according to caste—or rather, as Louis Dumont has written, where "the needs of each are conceived to be different, depending on [his] caste." Everyone is guaranteed a share, so Dumont's Indian village is still a welfare state, "a sort of cooperative where the main aim is to ensure the subsistence of everyone in accordance with his social function," but not a welfare state or a cooperative whose principles we can readily understand. (But Dumont does not tell us how food is supposed to be distributed in time of scarcity. If the subsistence standard is the same for everyone, then we are back in a familiar world.)

Clearly, the three principles apply to the citizens of the United States; and they have considerable force here because of the affluence of the community and the expansive understanding of individual need. On the other hand the United States currently maintains one of the shabbier systems of communal provision in the Western world. This is so for a variety of reasons: the community of citizens is loosely organized; various ethnic and religious groups run welfare programs of their own; the ideology of self-reliance and entrepreneurial opportunity is widely accepted; and the movements of the left, particularly the labor movement, are relatively weak. Democratic decision-making reflects these realities, and there is nothing in principle wrong with that. Nevertheless, the established pattern of provision doesn't measure up to the internal requirements of the sphere of security and welfare, and the common understandings of the citizens point toward a more elaborate pattern. . . .

So change is always a matter of political argument, organization, and struggle. All that the philosopher can do is to describe the basic structure of the arguments and the constraints they entail. Hence the three principles, which can be summed up in a revised version of Marx's famous maxim: From each according to his ability (or his resources); to each according to his socially recognized needs. This, I think, is the deepest meaning of the social contract. It only remains to work out the details— but in everyday life, the details are everything.

QUESTIONS·FOR REFLECTION

1. Why, according to Walzer, do we owe something to other members of our community?

2. What, specifically, do we owe them?

3. What is Walzer's conception of the social contract? How does it compare to that of Locke, Rousseau, or Rawls?

4. In what ways does Walzer's view of justice resemble Marx's? How do they differ?

5. What is a sphere of security and welfare? Why is it important?

6. Walzer cites Burke several times. In what sense is Walzer's view Burkean?

CHARLES MURRAY

from *Losing Ground:*
American Social Policy, 1950–1980

*Charles Murray is Bradley Fellow at the Manhattan Institute for Policy
Research. (Source: From* Losing Ground: American Social Policy,
1950–1980 *by Charles Murray. Copyright © 1984 by Charles Murray.
Reprinted by permission of Basic Books, a division of HarperCollins Publishers Inc.)*

CHAPTER 16 / THE CONSTRAINTS ON HELPING

Laws of Social Programs

. . . Let me suggest some characteristics . . . that occur so widely and for such embedded reasons that they suggest laws. That is, no matter how ingenious the design of a social transfer program may be, we cannot—in a free society—design programs that escape their influence. . . .

#1. The Law of Imperfect Selection. Any objective rule that defines eligibility for a social transfer program will irrationally exclude some persons.

It can always be demonstrated that some persons who are excluded from the Food Stamps program are in greater need than some persons who receive Food Stamps. It can always be demonstrated that someone who is technically ineligible for Medicaid really "ought" to be receiving it, given the intent of the legislation.

These inequities, which are observed everywhere, are not the fault of inept writers of eligibility rules, but an inescapable outcome of the task of rule-writing. Eligibility rules must convert the concept of "true need" into objectified elements. The rules constructed from these bits and pieces are necessarily subject to what Herbert Costner has called "epistemic error"—the inevitable gap between quantified measures and the concept they are intended to capture. We have no way of defining "truly needy" precisely—not those who truly need to stop smoking, nor those truly in need of college scholarships or subsidized loans or disability insurance. Any criterion we specify will inevitably include a range of people, some of whom are unequivocally the people we intended to help, others of whom are less so, and still others of whom meet the letter of the eligibility requirement but are much less needy than some persons who do not.

Social welfare policy in earlier times tended to deal with this problem by erring in the direction of exclusion—better to deny help to some truly needy persons than to let a few slackers slip through. Such attitudes depended, however, on the assumption that the greater good was being served. Moral precepts had to be upheld. Whenever a person was inappropriately given help, it was bad for the recipient (undermining his character) and a bad example to the community at large.

When that assumption is weakened or dispensed with altogether, it follows naturally that the Law of Imperfect Selection leads to programs with constantly broadening target populations. If persons are not to blame for their plight, no real harm is done by giving them help they do not fully "need." No moral cost is incurred by permitting some undeserving into the program. A moral cost is incurred by excluding a deserving person. No one has a scalpel sharp enough to excise only the undeserving. Therefore it is not just a matter of political expedience to add a new layer to the eligible population rather than to subtract one (though that is often a factor in the actual decision-making process). It is also the morally correct thing to do, given the premises of the argument.

#2. The Law of Unintended Rewards. Any social transfer increases the net value of being in the condition that prompted the transfer.

A deficiency is observed—too little money, too little food, too little academic achievement—and a social transfer program tries to fill the gap—with a welfare payment, Food Stamps, a compensatory education program. An unwanted behavior is observed—drug addiction, crime, unemployability—and the program tries to change that behavior to some other, better behavior—through a drug rehabilitation program, psychotherapy, vocational training. In each case, the program, however unintentionally, *must* be constructed in such a way that it increases the net value of being in the condition that it seeks to change—either by increasing the rewards or by reducing the penalties.

For some people in some circumstances, it is absurd to think in terms of "net value," because they so clearly have no choice at all about the fix they are in or because the net value is still less desirable than virtually any alternative. Paraplegics receiving Medicaid cannot easily be seen as "rewarded" for becoming paraplegics by the existence of free medical care. Poor children in Head Start cannot be seen as rewarded for being poor. Persons who are in the unwanted condition *completely involuntarily* are not affected by the existence of the reward.

But the number of such pure examples is very small. Let us return to the case of the middle-aged worker who loses his job, wants desperately to work, but can find nothing. He receives Unemployment Insurance, hating every penny of it. He would seem to be "completely involuntarily" in his situation and his search for a job unaffected by the existence of Unemployment Insurance. In fact, however, his behavior (unless he is peculiarly irrational) is affected by the existence of the Unemployment

Insurance. For example, the cushion provided by Unemployment Insurance may lead him to refuse to take a job that requires him to move to another town, whereas he would take the job and uproot his home if he were more desperate. Most people (including me) are glad that his behavior is so affected, that he does not have to leave the home and friends of a lifetime, that he can wait for a job opening nearby. But he is not "completely involuntarily" unemployed in such a case, and the reason he is not is that the Unemployment Insurance has made the condition of unemployment more tolerable.

Our paraplegic anchors one end of the continuum labeled "Degree of Voluntarism in the Conditions that Social Policy Seeks to Change or Make Less Painful," and our unemployed worker is only slightly to one side of him—but he is to one side, not in the same place. The apparent unattractiveness of most of the conditions that social policy seeks to change must not obscure the continuum involved. No one chooses to be a paraplegic, and perhaps no one chooses to be a heroin addict. But the distinction remains: very few heroin addicts developed their addiction by being tied down and forcibly injected with heroin. They may not have chosen to become addicts, but they *did* choose initially to take heroin.

Let us consider the implications in terms of the archetypical social program for helping the chronic unemployed escape their condition, the job-training program.

Imagine that a program is begun that has the most basic and benign inducement of all, the chance to learn a marketable skill. It is open to everybody. By opening it to all, we have circumvented (for the time being) the Law of Unintended Rewards. All may obtain the training, no matter what their job history, so no unintended reward is being given for the condition of chronic unemployment.

On assessing the results, we observe that the ones who enter the program, stick with it, and learn a skill include very few of the hardcore unemployed whom we most wanted to help. The typical "success" stories from our training program are persons with a history of steady employment who wanted to upgrade their earning power. This is admirable. But what about the hardcore unemployed? A considerable number entered the program, but almost all of them dropped out or failed to get jobs once they left. Only a small proportion used the training opportunity as we had hoped. The problem of the hardcore unemployed remains essentially unchanged.

We may continue to circumvent the Law of Unintended Rewards. All we need do is continue the job-training program unchanged. It will still be there, still available to all who want to enroll, but we will do nothing to entice participation. Our theory (should we adopt this stance) is that, as time goes on, we will continue to help at least a few of the hardcore unemployed who are in effect skimmed from the top of the pool. We may even hope that the number skimmed from the top will be larger than the number who enter the pool, so that, given enough time, the population of hardcore unemployed will diminish. But this strategy is a gradualist one and relies on the assumption that other conditions in society are not creating more hardcore unemployed than the program is skimming off.

The alternative is to do something to get more of the hardcore unemployed into the program, and to improve the content so that more of them profit from the training. And once this alternative is taken, the program planner is caught in the trap of unintended rewards. Because we cannot "draft" people into the program or otherwise coerce their participation, our only alternative is to make it more attractive by changing the rules a bit.

Suppose, for example, we find that the reason many did not profit from the earlier program was that they got fired from (or quit) their new jobs within a few days of getting them, and that the reason they did so had to do with the job-readiness problem. The ex-trainee was late getting to work, the boss complained, the ex-trainee reacted angrily and was fired. We observe this to be a common pattern. We know the problem is not that the ex-trainee is lazy or unmotivated, but that he has never been socialized into the discipline of the workplace. He needs more time, more help, more patience than other workers until he develops the needed work habits. Suppose that we try to compensate—for example, by placing our trainees with employers who are being subsidized to hire such persons. The employer accepts lower productivity and other problems in return for a payment to do so (such plans have been tried frequently, with mixed results). Given identical work at identical pay, the ex-trainee is being rewarded for his "credential" of hardcore unemployment. He can get away with behavior that an ordinary worker cannot get away with.

May we still assume that the program is making progress in preparing its trainees for the real-world marketplace? Will the hardcore unemployed modify their unreliable behavior? What will be the effect on morale and self-esteem among those trainees who were succeeding in the program before the change of rules? It is tempting to conclude that the program has already ceased to function effectively for anyone anymore, that the change in rules has done more harm than good. But my proposition is for the moment a more restricted one: The reward for unproductive behavior (both past and present) now exists.

What of the case of a drug addict who is chronically unemployed because (let us assume) of the addiction? It might seem that the unintended reward in such a case is innocuous; it consists of measures to relieve the addict of his addiction, measures for which the nonaddict will have no need or use. If we were dealing with an involuntary disability—our paraplegic again—the argument would be valid. But in the case of drug addiction (or any other behavior that has its rewards), a painless cure generally increases the attractiveness of the behavior. Imagine, for example, a pill that instantly and painlessly relieved dependence on heroin, and the subsequent effects on heroin use.

Thus we are faced with the problem we observed in the thought experiment. The program that seeks to change behavior must offer an inducement that unavoidably either adds to the attraction of, or reduces the penalties of engaging in, the behavior in question. The best-known example in real life is the thirty-and-a-third rule for AFDC recipients. It becomes more advantageous financially to hold a job than not to hold a job (the intended inducement for AFDC recipients to work), but it also becomes more advantageous to be on AFDC (the unintended reward to nonrecipients).

We are now ready to tackle the question of when a social program can reasonably be expected to accomplish net good and when it can reasonably be expected to produce net harm. Again let us think in terms of a continuum. All social programs, I have argued, provide an unintended reward for being in the condition that the program is trying to change or make more tolerable. But some of these unintended rewards are so small that they are of little practical importance. Why then can we not simply bring a bit of care to the design of such programs, making sure that the unintended reward is *always* small? The reason we are not free to do so lies in the third law of social programs:

> **#3. The Law of Net Harm**. The less likely it is that the unwanted behavior will change voluntarily, the more likely it is that a program to induce change will cause net harm.

A social program that seeks to change behavior must do two things. It must induce participation by the persons who are to benefit, as described under the Law of Unintended Rewards. Then it must actually produce the desired change in behavior. It must succeed, and success depends crucially on one factor above all others: The price that the participant is willing to pay.

The more that the individual is willing to accept whatever needs to be done in order to achieve the desired state of affairs, the broader the discretion of the program designers. Thus, expensive health resorts can withhold food from their guests, hospitals can demand that their interns work inhuman schedules, and elite volunteer units in the armed forces can ask their trainees to take risks in training exercises that seem (to the rest of us) suicidal. Such programs need offer no inducement at all except the "thing in itself" that is the *raison d'être* of the program—a shapelier body, a career as a physician, membership in the elite military unit. Similarly, the drug addict who is prepared to sign over to a program a great of deal of control over his own behavior may very well be successful—witness the sometimes impressive success rates of private treatment clinics.

The smaller the price that the participant is willing to pay, the greater the constraints on program design. It makes no difference to an official running a training program for the hardcore unemployed that (for example) the Marine Corps can instill exemplary work habits in recruits who come to the Corps no more "job-ready" than the recruits to the job-training program. If the training program tried for one day to use the techniques that the Marine Corps uses, it would lose its participants. Boot camp was not part of the bargain the job trainees struck with the government when they signed on. Instead, the training program must not only induce persons to join the program (which may be fairly easy). It must also in-

duce them to stay in the program, induce them to cooperate with its curriculum, and induce them, finally, to adopt major changes in outlook, habits, and assumptions. The program content must be almost entirely carrot.

There is nothing morally reprehensible in approaches that are constrained to use only positive inducements. The objections are practical.

First, it is guaranteed that success rates will be very low. The technology of changing human behavior depends heavily on the use of negative reinforcement in conjunction with positive reinforcement. The more deeply engrained the behavior to be changed and the more attractions it holds for the person whose behavior is involved, the more important it is that the program have both a full tool kit available to it *and* the participant's willingness to go along with whatever is required. The Marine Corps has both these assets. Social programs to deal with the hardcore unemployed, teenaged mothers, delinquents, and addicts seldom do.

Second, as inducements become large—as they must, if the program is dealing with the most intractable problems—the more attractive they become to people who were not in need of help in the first place. We do not yet know how large they must finally become. We do know from experience, however, that quite generous experimental programs have provided extensive counseling, training, guaranteed jobs, and other supports—and failed. We can only guess at what would be enough—perhaps a matter of years of full-time residential training, followed by guaranteed jobs at double or triple the minimum wage; we do not know. Whatever they are, however, consider their effects on the people not in the program. At this point, it appears that any program that would succeed in helping large numbers of the hardcore unemployed will make hardcore unemployment a highly desirable state to be in.

The conditions that combine to produce net harm are somewhat different in the theoretical and the practical cases, but they come to the same thing. Theoretically, any program that mounts an intervention with sufficient rewards to sustain participation and an effective result will generate so much of the unwanted behavior (in order to become eligible for the program's rewards) that the net effect will be to increase the incidence of the unwanted behavior. In practice, the programs that deal with the most intractable behavior problems have included a package of rewards large enough to induce participation, but not large enough to produce the desired result.

My conclusion is that social programs in a democratic society tend to produce net harm in dealing with the most difficult problems. They will inherently tend to have enough of an inducement to produce bad behavior and not enough of a solution to stimulate good behavior; and the more difficult the problem, the more likely it is that this relationship will prevail. The lesson is not that we can do no good at all, but that we must pick our shots.

CHAPTER 17 / CHOOSING A FUTURE

A Proposal for Public Welfare

I begin with the proposition that it is within our resources to do enormous good for some people quickly. We have available to us a program that would convert a large proportion of the younger generation of hardcore unemployed into steady workers making a living wage. The same program would drastically reduce births to single teenage girls. It would reverse the trendline in the breakup of poor families. It would measurably increase the upward socioeconomic mobility of poor families. These improvements would affect some millions of persons.

All these are results that have eluded the efforts of the social programs installed since 1965, yet, from everything we know, there is no real question about whether they would occur under the program I propose. A wide variety of persuasive evidence from our own culture and around the world, from experimental data and longitudinal studies, from theory and practice, suggests that the program would achieve such results.

The proposed program, our final and most ambitious thought experiment, consists of scrapping the entire federal welfare and income-support structure for working-aged persons, including AFDC, Medicaid, Food Stamps, Unemployment Insurance, Worker's Compensation, subsidized housing, disability insurance, and the rest. It would leave the working-aged person with no recourse whatsoever except the job market, family members, friends, and public or private locally funded services. It is the Alexandrian solution: cut the knot, for there is no way to untie it.

It is difficult to examine such a proposal dispassionately. Those who dislike paying for welfare are for it without thinking. Others reflexively imagine bread lines and people starving in the streets. But as a means of gaining fresh perspective on the problem of effective reform, let us consider what this hypothetical society might look like.

A large majority of the population is unaffected. A surprising number of the huge American middle and working classes go from birth to grave without using any social welfare benefits until they receive their first Social Security check. Another portion of the population is technically affected, but the change in income is so small or so sporadic that it makes no difference in quality of life. A third group comprises persons who have to make new arrangements and behave in different ways. Sons and daughters who fail to find work continue to live with their parents or relatives or friends. Teenaged mothers have to rely on support from their parents or the father of the child and perhaps work as well. People laid off from work have to use their own savings or borrow from others to make do until the next job is found. All these changes involve great disruption in expectations and accustomed roles.

Along with the disruptions go other changes in behavior. Some parents do not want their young adult children continuing to live off their income, and become quite insistent about their children learning skills and getting jobs. This attitude is most prevalent among single mothers who have to depend most critically on the earning power of their offspring.

Parents tend to become upset at the prospect of a daughter's bringing home a baby that must be entirely supported on an already inadequate income. Some become so upset that they spend considerable parental energy avoiding such an eventuality. Potential fathers of such babies find themselves under more pressure not to cause such a problem, or to help with its solution if it occurs.

Adolescents who were not job-ready find they are job-ready after all. It turns out that they can work for low wages and accept the discipline of the workplace if the alternative is grim enough. After a few years, many—not all, but many—find that they have acquired salable skills, or that they are at the right place at the right time, or otherwise find that the original entry-level job has gradually been transformed into a secure job paying a decent wage. A few—not a lot, but a few—find that the process leads to affluence.

Perhaps the most rightful, deserved benefit goes to the much larger population of low-income families who have been doing things right all along and have been punished for it: the young man who has taken responsibility for his wife and child even though his friends with the same choice have called him a fool; the single mother who has worked full time and forfeited her right to welfare for very little extra money; the parents who have set an example for their children even as the rules of the game have taught their children that the example is outmoded. For these millions of people, the instantaneous result is that no one makes fun of them any longer. The longer-term result will be that they regain the status that is properly theirs. They will not only be the bedrock upon which the community is founded (which they always have been), they will be recognized as such. The process whereby they regain their position is not magical, but a matter of logic. When it becomes highly dysfunctional for a person to be dependent, status will accrue to being independent, and in fairly short order. Noneconomic rewards will once again reinforce the economic rewards of being a good parent and provider.

The prospective advantages are real and extremely plausible. In fact, if a government program of the traditional sort (one that would "do" something rather than simply get out of the way) could *as plausibly* promise these advantages, its passage would be a foregone conclusion. Congress, yearning for programs that are not retreads of failures, would be prepared to spend billions. Negative side-effects (as long as they were the traditionally acceptable negative side-effects) would be brushed aside as trivial in return for the benefits. For let me be quite clear: I am not suggesting that we dismantle income support for the working-aged to balance the budget or punish welfare cheats. I am hypothesizing, with the advantage of powerful collateral evidence, that the lives of large numbers of poor people would be radically changed for the better.

There is, however, a fourth segment of the population yet to be considered, those who are pauperized by the withdrawal of government supports and unable to make alternate arrangements: the teenaged mother who has no one to turn to; the incapacitated or the inept who are thrown out of the house; those to whom economic conditions have brought long periods in which there is no work to be had; those with illnesses not covered by insurance. What of these situations?

The first resort is the network of local services. Poor communities in our hypothetical society are still dotted with storefront health clinics, emergency relief agencies, employment services, legal services. They depend for support on local taxes or local philanthropy, and the local taxpayers and philanthropists tend to scrutinize them rather closely. But, by the same token, they also receive considerably more resources than they formerly did. The dismantling of the federal services has poured tens of billions of dollars back into the private economy. Some of that money no doubt has been spent on Mercedes and summer homes on the Cape. But some has been spent on capital investments that generate new jobs. And some has been spent on increased local services to the poor, voluntarily or as decreed by the municipality. In many cities, the coverage provided by this network of agencies is more generous, more humane, more wisely distributed, and more effective in its results than the services formerly subsidized by the federal government.

But we must expect that a large number of people will fall between the cracks. How might we go about trying to retain the advantages of a zero-level welfare system and still address the residual needs?

As we think about the nature of the population still in need, it becomes apparent that their basic problem in the vast majority of the cases is the lack of a job, and this problem is temporary. What they need is something to tide them over while finding a new place in the economy. So our first step is to reinstall the Unemployment Insurance program in more or less its previous form. Properly administered, unemployment insurance makes sense. Even if it is restored with all the defects of current practice, the negative effects of Unemployment Insurance *alone* are relatively minor. Our objective is not to wipe out chicanery or to construct a theoretically unblemished system, but to meet legitimate human needs without doing more harm than good. Unemployment Insurance is one of the least harmful ways of contributing to such ends. Thus the system has been amended to take care of the victims of short-term swings in the economy.

Who is left? We are now down to the hardest of the hard core of the welfare-dependent. They have no jobs. They have been unable to find jobs (or have not tried to find jobs) for a longer period of time than the unemployment benefits cover. They have no families who will help. They have no friends who will help. For some reason, they cannot get help from local services or private charities except for the soup kitchen and a bed in the Salvation Army hall.

What will be the size of this population? We have never tried a zero-level federal welfare system under conditions of late-twentieth-century national wealth, so we cannot do more than speculate. But we may speculate. Let us ask of whom the population might consist and how they might fare.

For any category of "needy" we may name, we find ourselves driven to one of two lines of thought. Either the person is in a category that is going to be at the top of the list of services that localities vote for themselves, and at the top of the list of private services, or the person is in a category where help really is not all that essential or desirable. The burden of the conclusion is not that every single person will be taken care of, but that the extent of resources to deal with needs is likely to be very great—not based on wishful thinking, but on extrapolations from reality.

To illustrate, let us consider the plight of the stereotypical welfare mother—never married, no skills, small children, no steady help from a man. It is safe to say that, now as in the 1950s, there is no one who has less sympathy from the white middle class, which is to be the source of most of the money for the private and local services we envision. Yet this same white middle class is a soft touch for people trying to make it on their own, and a soft touch for "deserving" needy mothers—AFDC was one of the most widely popular of the New Deal welfare measures, intended as it was for widows with small children. Thus we may envision two quite different scenarios.

In one scenario, the woman is presenting the local or private service with this proposition: "Help me find a job and day-care for my children, and I will take care of the rest." In effect, she puts herself into the same category as the widow and the deserted wife—identifies herself as one of the most obviously deserving of the deserving poor. Welfare mothers who want to get into the labor force are

likely to find a wide range of help. In the other scenario, she asks for an outright and indefinite cash grant—in effect, a private or local version of AFDC—so that she can stay with the children and not hold a job. In the latter case, it is very easy to imagine situations in which she will not be able to find a local service or a private philanthropy to provide the help she seeks. The question we must now ask is: What's so bad about that? If children were always better off being with their mother all day and if, by the act of giving birth, a mother acquired the inalienable right to be with the child, then her situation would be unjust to her and injurious to her children. Neither assertion can be defended, however—especially not in the 1980s, when more mothers of all classes work away from the home than ever before, and even more especially not in view of the empirical record for the children growing up under the current welfare system. Why should the mother be exempted by the system from the pressures that must affect everyone else's decision to work?

As we survey these prospects, important questions remain unresolved. The first of these is why, if federal social transfers are treacherous, should locally mandated transfers be less so? Why should a municipality be permitted to legislate its own AFDC or Food Stamp program if their results are so inherently bad?

Part of the answer lies in conceptions of freedom. I have deliberately avoided raising them—the discussion is about how to help the disadvantaged, not about how to help the advantaged cut their taxes, to which arguments for personal freedom somehow always get diverted. Nonetheless, the point is valid: Local or even state systems leave much more room than a federal system for everyone, donors and recipients alike, to exercise freedom of choice about the kind of system they live under. Laws are more easily made and changed, and people who find them unacceptable have much more latitude in going somewhere more to their liking.

But the freedom of choice argument, while legitimate, is not necessary. We may put the advantages of local systems in terms of the Law of Imperfect Selection. A federal system must inherently employ very crude, inaccurate rules for deciding who gets what kind of help, and the results are as I outlined them in Chapter 16. At the opposite extreme—a neighbor helping a neighbor, a family member helping another family member—the law loses its validity nearly altogether. Very fine-grained judgments based on personal knowledge are being made about specific people and changing situations. In neighborhoods and small cities, the procedures can still bring much individualized information to bear on decisions. Even systems in large cities and states can do much better than a national system; a decaying industrial city in the Northeast and a booming sunbelt city of the same size can and probably should adopt much different rules about who gets what and how much.

A final and equally powerful argument for not impeding local systems is diversity. We know much more in the 1980s than we knew in the 1960s about what does not work. We have a lot to learn about what *does* work. Localities have been a rich source of experiments. Marva Collins in Chicago gives us an example of how a school can bring inner-city students up to national norms. Sister Falaka Fattah in Philadelphia shows us how homeless youths can be rescued from the streets. There are numberless such lessons waiting to be learned from the diversity of local efforts. By all means, let a hundred flowers bloom, and if the federal government can play a useful role in lending a hand and spreading the word of successes, so much the better.

The ultimate unresolved question about our proposal to abolish income maintenance for the working-aged is how many people will fall through the cracks. In whatever detail we try to foresee the consequences, the objection may always be raised: We cannot be *sure* that everyone will be taken care of in the degree to which we would wish. But this observation by no means settles the question. If one may point in objection to the child now fed by Food Stamps who would go hungry, one may also point with satisfaction to the child who would have an entirely different and better future. Hungry children should be fed; there is no argument about that. It is no less urgent that children be allowed to grow up in a system free of the forces that encourage them to remain poor and dependent. If a strategy reasonably promises to remove those forces, after so many attempts to "help the poor" have failed, it is worth thinking about.

But that rationale is too vague. Let me step outside the persona I have employed and put the issue in terms of one last intensely personal hypothetical example. Let us suppose that you, a parent, could

know that tomorrow your own child would be made an orphan. You have a choice. You may put your child with an extremely poor family, so poor that your child will be badly clothed and will indeed sometimes be hungry. But you also know that the parents have worked hard all their lives, will make sure your child goes to school and studies, and will teach your child that independence is a primary value. Or you may put your child with a family with parents who have never worked, who will be incapable of overseeing your child's education—but who have plenty of food and good clothes, provided by others. If the choice about where one would put one's own child is as clear to you as it is to me, on what grounds does one justify support of a system that, indirectly but without doubt, makes the other choice for other children? The answer that "What we really want is a world where that choice is not forced upon us" is no answer. We have tried to have it that way. We failed. Everything we know about why we failed tells us that more of the same will not make the dilemma go away.

The Ideal of Opportunity

Billions for equal opportunity, not one cent for equal outcome—such is the slogan to inscribe on the banner of whatever cause my proposals constitute. Their common theme is to make it possible to get as far as one can go on one's merit, hardly a new ideal in American thought.

The ideal itself has never lapsed. What did lapse was the recognition that practical merit exists. Some people are better than others. They deserve more of society's rewards, of which money is only one small part. A principal function of social policy is to make sure they have the opportunity to reap those rewards. Government cannot identify the worthy, but it can protect a society in which the worthy can identify themselves.

I am proposing triage of a sort, triage by self-selection. In triage on the battlefield, the doctor makes the decision—this one gets treatment, that one waits, the other one is made comfortable while waiting to die. In our social triage, the decision is left up to the patient. The patient always has the right to say "I can do X" and get a chance to prove it. Society always has the right to hold him to that pledge. The patient always has the right to fail. Society always has the right to let him.

There is in this stance no lack of compassion but a presumption of respect. People—all people, black or white, rich or poor—may be unequally responsible for what has happened to them in the past, but all are equally responsible for what they do next. Just as in our idealized educational system a student can come back a third, fourth, or fifth time to a course, in our idealized society a person can fail repeatedly and always be qualified for another chance—to try again, to try something easier, to try something different. The options are always open. Opportunity is endless. There is no punishment for failure, only a total absence of rewards. Society—or our idealized society—should be preoccupied with making sure that achievement is rewarded.

There is no shortage of people to be rewarded. Go into any inner-city school and you will find students of extraordinary talent, kept from knowing how good they are by rules we imposed in the name of fairness. Go into any poor community, and you will find people of extraordinary imagination and perseverance, energy and pride, making tortured ac-commodations to the strange world we created in the name of generosity. The success stories of past generations of poor in this country are waiting to be repeated.

There is no shortage of institutions to provide the rewards. Our schools know how to educate students who want to be educated. Our industries know how to find productive people and reward them. Our police know how to protect people who are ready to cooperate in their own protection. Our system of justice knows how to protect the rights of individuals who know what their rights are. Our philanthropic institutions know how to multiply the effectiveness of people who are already trying to help themselves. In short, American society is very good at reinforcing the investment of an individual in himself. For the affluent and for the middle-class, these mechanisms continue to work about as well as they ever have, and we enjoy their benefits. Not so for the poor. American government, in its recent social policy, has been ineffectual in trying to stage-manage the decision to invest, and it has been unintentionally punitive toward those who would make the decision on their own. It is time to get out of the way. . . .

QUESTIONS FOR REFLECTION

1. Explain Murray's three laws.

2. Are you convinced that Murray's laws are true? Why or why not?

3. What benefits would accrue, according to Murray, if welfare programs were eliminated altogether?

4. Who might be harmed by eliminating welfare programs, in Murray's view? In your view?

5. Is Murray committed to any particular theory of justice?

MICHAEL TANNER AND STEPHEN MOORE

Why Welfare Pays

Michael Tanner is director of health and welfare studies and Stephen Moore is director of fiscal policy studies at the Cato Institute in Washington, D.C. (Source: The Wall Street Journal [September 25, 1995]. Copyright © 1995 by Dow Jones, Inc. Reprinted by permission.)

While most of official Washington congratulates itself on having "ended welfare as we know it," the reality is that current welfare reform legislation may do relatively little to move families from welfare to work. Despite the bill's good intentions, Congress has once again failed to deal with one of the most important underlying flaws of our welfare system: Welfare pays better than work.

One of the most enduring myths about the modern-day welfare state is the notion that "welfare doesn't pay." This myth pervades the current debate on Capitol Hill.

Where the Money Is

Liberal defenders of current public assistance policies argue that the average Aid to Families with Dependent Children benefits of about $400 a month barely provide a subsistence level-income to the needy and are therefore hardly an attractive substitute for work. Republicans who would cut these meager benefits are decried as uncaring and even cruel.

The fallacy of this argument is that the modern-day social safety net encompasses far more than just AFDC. There are now an estimated 77 means-tested welfare programs. State, county, and municipal governments often operate additional benefit programs. Obviously, no one collects benefits from all of these programs, but if we examine the benefit levels of just the six most common types of welfare assistance—

AFDC, food stamps, Medicaid, housing, nutrition assistance and energy assistance—we find that welfare is a much more financially attractive way of life than is conventionally believed in Washington.

In a new Cato Institute study, we calculated the state-by-state value of this typical welfare package for a mother with two children. In eight states—Hawaii, Alaska, Connecticut, Massachusetts, New York, New Jersey, Rhode Island, California and Washington, D.C.—these six programs alone provide an annual benefit worth more than $20,000 a year. The value of the welfare package in a medium-level welfare state is $17,500.

But to assess how these benefit levels would compare with the economic alternative of finding a job and working 40 hours a week, we have to remember that welfare benefits are not taxed, whereas wages are. So next, we calculated the amount of money a welfare recipient receiving these six benefits would have to earn in pretax income if she took a job and left the welfare rolls. We computed the federal income tax, the state income tax and the FICA payroll taxes that would have to be paid on the wage income. We also took into account the federal earned income tax credit, which provides a financial incentive for work to families making the transition from welfare to a job.

The results, summarized in the accompanying table, lead to the inescapable conclusion that welfare pays very well. The value of benefits for a mother and two children ranged from a high of $36,400 in

WHY WORK?			
Hourly wage equivalent of welfare			
Hawaii	$17.50	Indiana	$9.13
Alaska	15.45	Iowa	9.13
Massachusetts	14.66	New Mexico	8.94
Connecticut	14.23	Florida	8.75
Washington, D.C.	13.99	Idaho	8.65
New York	13.13	Oklahoma	8.51
New Jersey	12.74	Kansas	8.46
Rhode Island	12.55	North Dakota	8.46
California	11.59	Georgia	8.37
Virginia	11.11	Ohio	8.37
Maryland	10.96	South Dakota	8.32
New Hampshire	10.96	Louisiana	8.17
Maine	10.38	Kentucky	8.08
Delaware	10.34	North Carolina	8.08
Colorado	10.05	Montana	7.84
Vermont	10.05	South Carolina	7.79
Minnesota	10.00	Nebraska	7.64
Washington	9.95	Texas	7.31
Nevada	9.71	West Virginia	7.31
Utah	9.57	Missouri	7.16
Michigan	9.47	Arizona	6.78
Pennsylvania	9.47	Tennessee	6.59
Illinois	9.33	Arkansas	6.35
Wisconsin	9.33	Alabama	6.25
Oregon	9.23	Mississippi	5.53
Wyoming	9.18		

SOURCE: Cato Institute

more than a $12-an-hour job—or 2½ times the minimum wage.

How does welfare compare with the salaries of conventional jobs? In eight states and the District of Columbia, welfare pays more than the national average first-year salary for a teacher. In 28 states and the District of Columbia, welfare is more generous than the starting salary for a secretary. In 46 states and the District of Columbia, welfare recipients make more than full-time janitors.

The situation is worse in many large cities, where benefits are often more generous and the tax burden for working is more punitive, because of an extra layer of city income taxes. Welfare provides the pre-tax income equivalent of a $14.75-an-hour job in New York City, $12.45 in Philadelphia and $10.90 in Detroit. Not surprisingly, welfare dependency has reached very high rates in all of these cities. Generous benefit levels and abnormally high tax rates on even low levels of income conspire to plunge residents into a welfare trap, often permanently.

Our results suggest that many of the conventional welfare reforms sponsored by both Democrats and Republicans on Capitol Hill may be futile as long as welfare remains a financially attractive alternative to work. Indeed, the results probably explain why the policy prescriptions championed by liberals (such as job training and child care) and conservatives (such as workfare) have produced disappointing results in terms of ending hard-core dependency. They also may explain why surveys have found that nearly 70% of welfare recipients are not currently looking for work. It is simply an economic reality that the typical untrained, uneducated welfare mother is not likely to find a job that pays $10 to $12 an hour. But for her to take a job for less than this salary range often would result in a financial loss. Thus staying on welfare is in many cases an economically prudent decision.

These results also underscore the fundamental unfairness of the modern-day welfare system. Today, millions of working, moderate-income American families are paying taxes to support a public assistance system that provides a higher living standard than they themselves achieve through work and sacrifice. In 12 states and the District of Columbia, welfare recipients receive benefits worth more than 90% of the mean area wage. Incredibly, there are four

Hawaii to a low of $11,500 in Mississippi. In 39 states and the District of Columbia, welfare pays more than an $8-an-hour job. In 16 states and the District of Columbia, the welfare package is more generous than a $10-an-hour job. In Hawaii, Alaska, Massachusetts, Connecticut, New York, New Jersey, Rhode Island, and Washington, D.C., welfare pays states—Hawaii, Rhode Island, Massachusetts, and Alaska—where the average worker received less compensation than the average welfare recipient after taxes.

A Rational Choice

Of course, not every welfare recipient meets our profile, and many who meet our profile do not receive all the benefits listed. (On the other hand, some receive even more.) Still, what is undeniable is that for many recipients—particularly the "long-term" dependents—welfare pays substantially more than an entry level job. By not working, welfare recipients are simply responding rationally to the incentive systems our public policy makers have established for them.

The welfare reform proposals just passed by the Senate, and the earlier House version, are designed to reduce "hard-core" welfare dependency, discourage illegitimacy, and reward work. But we believe the most critical public policy implication of our findings is that ultimately these goals can be accomplished only by cutting benefit levels substantially. Unless or until this is done, Congress will have failed to end welfare as we know it.

QUESTIONS FOR REFLECTION

1. Why, according to Tanner and Moore, are welfare programs often ineffective in decreasing dependency?

2. How might the effects of welfare in high-benefit states differ from its effects in low-benefit states? What does this imply about appropriate benefit levels?

3. What assumptions about justice underlie Tanner and Moore's argument that, in some states, at least, welfare programs are unfair?

4. How do Tanner and Moore's assumptions relate to classic theories of justice, in particular, the theories of Aristotle, Locke, Nozick, and Rawls?

RACIAL EQUALITY

The United States, like many other countries, has a history of racial and sexual discrimination. Unlike many other countries, it also has a history of slavery. Discrimination and slavery have long been recognized as evils. Discrimination, for example, might be defined as making a judgment or decision on the basis of irrelevant factors. Race and sex are almost always irrelevant to decisions about whom to hire, whom to fire, whom to admit to a college or university, and other similar decisions. Kant's categorical imperative requires that we judge similar cases similarly—that we judge a case as if our judgment were universal law. To discriminate is to judge similar cases differently, depending on some irrelevant factor such as race or sex. Discrimination thus directly violates Kant's imperative.

The obligation to eliminate discrimination, therefore, is not controversial. What its elimination requires is. In a landmark case, *Brown* v. *Board of Education,* the Supreme Court held that segregation is a form of discrimination and so must be eliminated. It took a long series of subsequent cases, however, to spell out exactly what that requires. It is wrong to separate students of different race as a matter of law. But is it acceptable to assign students to the nearest school without regard to race, even if, due to housing patterns, some schools fill up with students of a single race? What other changes must occur in society if discrimination is to be ended? Rev. Martin Luther King, Jr., painted a dramatic and powerfully influential picture of those changes in his speech, "I Have a Dream."

Agreement about the goal of racial equality leaves room for disagreement about the means to that goal. Racial or sexual discrimination, as a violation of Kant's principle, is by its very nature unfair. So, we might think that justice requires making decisions about hiring, firing, admissions, and other matters of economic and political significance in a "color-blind" way, without regard for race, sex, or other irrelevant factors. From another perspective, however, this apparent even-handedness is only apparent, for some

of the players in the economic and political game have been harmed by prior discrimination. Setting things right requires, from this point of view, giving those players an advantage to balance the disadvantages they suffer as a result of past injustices. On this conception, then, race, sex, and perhaps other characteristics are no longer irrelevant. The history of discrimination has turned them into relevant factors.

From this perspective have sprung "affirmative-action" programs: programs that give preferences to some people because of their race, sex, ethnic background, or other characteristic. Generally, these programs try to "level the playing field" by granting preference to those who have suffered from prior discrimination or are otherwise disadvantaged. Sometimes, the preference is general, of the form "all other things being equal, we prefer people with the following characteristics"; in other cases, there are explicit quotas for people of different groups. Affirmative-action programs have been a source of controversy. In the United States, they have provoked arguments and lawsuits. In other countries, they have provoked riots and bloodshed.

The University of California operated a quota system at its medical school at Davis. It reserved sixteen of the one hundred places in each class at the medical school for members of minority groups. Alan Bakke, a white male, applied and was rejected. He learned, however, that his grades and test scores were higher than those of many students admitted under the minority quota. Bakke sued, claiming that he had been discriminated against on account of his race. In 1978, the Supreme Court decided in Bakke's favor. The Court stopped short of declaring that taking race and similar qualities into account is unacceptable. The Court did, however, decide that quota systems like that operating at the University of California were unconstitutional, amounting themselves to a form of discrimination. Dissenters on the Court decried the decision, maintaining that there is a great moral difference between using a racial classification against a disadvantaged group and using it to benefit that group. In short, the dissenters insisted that race, sex, and other factors are not irrelevant in themselves, though there is a strong presumption of their irrelevance. Prior discrimination and economic disadvantage may, they claimed, make these factors relevant and even require that they be taken into account in decision making.

Following *Bakke* was a series of decisions on affirmative action in various contexts: education, industry, unions, state government, and others. These decisions are extremely complex. They agree, however, that affirmative-action programs, to be constitutional, must pass strict scrutiny; that is, they must be necessary to achieve a compelling state interest. Racial equality is a compelling state interest, so the crucial question has been, Is this program necessary to achieve it? In the Court's jargon, Is it *narrowly tailored?* The Court has upheld several voluntary race-conscious affirmative-action plans, and even some court-imposed quota systems in cases where there appeared to be ongoing discrimination.

Antonin Scalia and Ronald Dworkin react to the *Bakke* decision in opposite ways: Scalia arguing that the decision makes no sense, and Dworkin arguing that racial preference is justified. In a recent case, *Hopwood* v. *Texas,* the Fifth Circuit U.S. Court of Appeals rejected the reasoning of *Bakke* and struck down racial preferences at the University of Texas Law School, holding its admission procedures to be neither narrowly tailored nor serving a compelling state interest.

Bernard Boxill argues in favor of affirmative action on two grounds. First, past injustice requires compensation. African Americans have been subjected to slavery and then to decades of legal and extralegal discrimination. Affirmative action is needed, Boxill argues, to rectify inequalities resulting from that injustice. Second, affirmative action programs have advantages for the future, producing greater equality and enabling people whose talents would otherwise be overlooked to exercise their abilities to everyone's benefit.

Thomas Sowell, an economist, argues that affirmative action brings about far more harm than good. He traces the history of affirmative action in many societies around the world, contending that it uniformly increases racial tensions. Advocates argue that affirmative-action plans are temporary repairs of harm brought about by prior discrimination. Sowell argues that there is no way to determine how much of the economic position of an individual or a group is due to prior discrimination. Consequently, there is no way to tell when the effects of prior discrimination have been eliminated. Once instituted, therefore, preferences never go away; indeed, they expand to more groups, few of whose claims can be founded on prior discrimination.

Finally, William Bowen and Derek Bok argue that affirmative action programs in higher education have achieved their goals without producing the negative side effects that critics such as Sowell have alleged. Studying the progress of minority students admitted to elite colleges and universities, they find that most were able to succeed both in college and in a career. Without affirmative action programs, they argue, there would be many fewer minority college graduates and professionals.

CHIEF JUSTICE EARL WARREN

Majority Opinion in *Brown* v. *Board of Education*

(*Source:* Brown v. Board of Education *347 U.S. 483 [1954].*)

Mr. Chief Justice Warren delivered the opinion of the Court.

These cases come to us from the States of Kansas, South Carolina, Virginia, and Delaware. They are premised on different facts and different local conditions, but a common legal question justifies their consideration together in this consolidated opinion.

In each of the cases, minors of the Negro race, through their legal representatives, seek the aid of the courts in obtaining admission to the public schools of their community on a nonsegregated basis. In each instance, they had been denied admission to schools attended by white children under laws requiring or permitting segregation according to race. This segregation was alleged to deprive the plaintiffs of the equal protection of the laws under the Fourteenth Amendment. In each of the cases other than the Delaware case, a three-judge federal district court denied relief to the plaintiffs on the so-called "separate but equal" doctrine announced by this Court in *Plessy* v. *Ferguson.* Under that doctrine, equality of treatment is accorded when the races are provided substantially equal facilities, even though these facilities be separate. In the Delaware case, the Supreme Court of Delaware adhered to that doctrine, but ordered that the plaintiffs be admitted to the white schools because of their superiority to the Negro schools.

The plaintiffs contend that segregated public schools are not "equal" and cannot be made "equal," and that hence they are deprived of the equal protection of the laws. . . .

In the first cases in this Court construing the Fourteenth Amendment, decided shortly after its adoption, the Court interpreted it as proscribing all state-imposed discriminations against the Negro race. The doctrine of "separate but equal" did not make its appearance in this Court until 1896 in the case of *Plessy* v. *Ferguson,* involving not education but transportation. American courts have since labored with the doctrine for over half a century. In this Court, there have been six cases involving the "separate but equal" doctrine in the field of public education. In *Cumming* v. *County Board of Education* and *Gong Lum* v. *Rice,* the validity of the doctrine itself was not challenged. In more recent cases, all on the graduate school level, inequality was found in that specific benefits enjoyed by white students were denied to Negro students of the same educational qualifications. In none of these cases was it necessary to re-examine the doctrine to grant relief to the Negro plaintiff. And in *Sweatt* v. *Painter,* the Court expressly reserved decision on the question whether *Plessy* v. *Ferguson* should be held inapplicable to public education.

In the instant cases, that question is directly presented. Here, unlike *Sweatt* v. *Painter,* there are findings below that the Negro and white schools involved have been equalized, or are being equalized, with respect to buildings, curricula, qualifications and salaries of teachers, and other "tangible" factors. Our decision, therefore, cannot turn on merely a comparison of these tangible factors in the

Negro and white schools involved in each of the cases. We must look instead to the effect of segregation itself on public education.

In approaching this problem, we cannot turn the clock back to 1868 when the Amendment was adopted, or even to 1896 when *Plessy* v. *Ferguson* was written. We must consider public education in the light of its full development and its present place in American life throughout the nation. Only in this way can it be determined if segregation in public schools deprives these plaintiffs of the equal protection of the laws.

Today, education is perhaps the most important function of state and local governments. Compulsory school attendance laws and the great expenditures for education both demonstrate our recognition of the importance of education to our democratic society. It is required in the performance of our most basic public responsibilities, even service in the armed forces. It is the very foundation of good citizenship. Today it is a principal instrument in awakening the child to cultural values, in preparing him for later professional training, and in helping him to adjust normally to his environment. In these days, it is doubtful that any child may reasonably be expected to succeed in life if he is denied the opportunity of an education. Such an opportunity, where the state has undertaken to provide it, is a right which must be made available to all on equal terms.

We come then to the question presented: Does segregation of children in public schools solely on the basis of race, even though the physical facilities and other "tangible" factors may be equal, deprive the children of the minority group of equal educational opportunities? We believe that it does.

In *Sweatt* v. *Painter,* in finding that a segregated law school for Negroes could not provide them equal educational opportunities, this Court relied in large part on "those qualities which are incapable of objective measurement but which make for greatness in a law school." In *McLaurin* v. *Oklahoma State Regents,* the Court, in requiring that a Negro admitted to a white graduate school be treated like all other students, again resorted to intangible considerations: ". . . his ability to study, to engage in discussions and exchange views with other students, and, in general, to learn his profession." Such considerations apply with added force to children in grade and high schools. To separate them from others of similar age and qualifications solely because of their race generates a feeling of inferiority as to their status in the community that may affect their hearts and minds in a way unlikely ever to be undone. The effect of this separation on their educational opportunities was well stated by a finding in the Kansas case by a court which nevertheless felt compelled to rule against the Negro plaintiffs:

"Segregation of white and colored children in public schools has a detrimental effect upon the colored children. The impact is greater when it has the sanction of the law; for the policy of separating the races is usually interpreted as denoting the inferiority of the Negro group. A sense of inferiority affects the motivation of a child to learn. Segregation with the sanction of law, therefore, has a tendency to [retard] the educational and mental development of Negro children and to deprive them of some of the benefits they would receive in a racial[ly] integrated school system."

Whatever may have been the extent of psychological knowledge at the time of *Plessy* v. *Ferguson,* this finding is amply supported by modern authority. Any language in *Plessy* v. *Ferguson* contrary to this finding is rejected.

We conclude that in the field of public education the doctrine of "separate but equal" has no place. Separate educational facilities are inherently unequal. Therefore, we hold that the plaintiffs and others similarly situated for whom the actions have been brought are, by reason of the segregation complained of, deprived of the equal protection of the laws guaranteed by the Fourteenth Amendment. This disposition makes unnecessary any discussion whether such segregation also violates the Due Process Clause of the Fourteenth Amendment.

Because these are class actions, because of the wide applicability of this decision, and because of the great variety of local conditions, the formulation of decrees in these cases presents problems of considerable complexity. On reargument, the consideration of appropriate relief was necessarily subordinated to the primary question—the constitutionality of segregation in public education. We have now announced that such segregation is a denial of the equal protection of the laws.

QUESTIONS FOR REFLECTION

1. What is the "separate but equal" doctrine?

2. Why does the Court find it unconstitutional?

3. How does the Court justify a right to education? What does it entail?

4. What role do psychological considerations play in the Court's argument?

5. Robert Bork, among others, has argued that psychological considerations are irrelevant and that the Court should have found segregation unconstitutional even if schools for children of different races really were equal in quality and segregation produced no feelings of inferiority. Do you agree? If so, how might such an argument go?

MARTIN LUTHER KING, JR.

"I Have a Dream"

The Reverend Martin Luther King, Jr., was the nation's foremost civil rights leader until his assassination in 1968. He gave this speech at a 1963 March on Washington for Jobs and Freedom, from the steps of the Lincoln Memorial, to an audience of about 250,000 people. (Source: Reprinted by arrangement with the Heirs to the Estate of Martin Luther King, Jr., c/o Writers House, Inc. as agent for the proprietor. Copyright © 1963 by Martin Luther King, Jr., renewed 1991 by Coretta Scott King.)

I am happy to join with you today in what will go down in history as the greatest demonstration for freedom in the history of our nation.

Five score years ago, a great American, in whose symbolic shadow we stand today, signed the Emancipation Proclamation. This momentous decree came as a great beacon light of hope to millions of Negro slaves who had been seared in the flames of withering injustice. It came as a joyous daybreak to end the long night of their captivity.

But 100 years later, the Negro still is not free. One hundred years later, the life of the Negro is still sadly crippled by the manacles of segregation and the chains of discrimination. One hundred years later, the Negro lives on a lonely island of poverty in the midst of a vast ocean of material prosperity. One hundred years later, the Negro is still languishing in the corners of American society and finds himself an exile in his own land. And so we've come here today to dramatize a shameful condition.

In a sense we've come to our nation's capital to cash a check. When the architects of our republic wrote the magnificent words of the Constitution and the Declaration of Independence, they were signing a promissory note to which every American was to fall heir. This note was a promise that all men—yes, black men as well as white men—would be guaranteed the unalienable rights of life, liberty, and the pursuit of happiness.

It is obvious today that America has defaulted on this promissory note insofar as her citizens of color are concerned. Instead of honoring this sacred obligation, America has given the Negro people a bad check, a check that has come back marked "insufficient funds."

But we refuse to believe that the bank of justice is bankrupt. We refuse to believe that there are insufficient funds in the great vaults of opportunity of this nation. And so we've come to cash this check, a check that will give us upon demand the riches of freedom and security of justice. We have also come to his hallowed spot to remind America of the fierce urgency of now. This is no time to engage in the luxury of cooling off or to take the tranquilizing drug of gradualism. Now is the time to make real the promises of democracy. Now is the time to rise from the dark and desolate valley of segregation to the sunlit path of racial justice. Now is the time to lift our nation from the quicksands of racial injustice to the solid rock of brotherhood. Now is the time to make justice a reality for all of God's children.

It would be fatal for the nation to overlook the urgency of the moment. This sweltering summer of the Negro's legitimate discontent will not pass until there is an invigorating autumn of freedom and equality. Nineteen sixty-three is not an end but a beginning. Those who hoped that the Negro needed to blow off steam and will now be content will have a rude awakening if the nation returns to business as usual. There will be neither rest nor tranquility in America until the Negro is granted his citizenship rights. The whirlwinds of revolt will continue to shake the foundations of our nation until the bright day of justice emerges.

But there is something that I must say to my people who stand on the warm threshold which leads into the palace of justice. In the process of gaining our rightful place we must not be guilty of wrongful deeds. Let us not seek to satisfy our thirst for freedom by drinking from the cup of bitterness and hatred. We must forever conduct our struggle on the high plane of dignity and discipline. We must not allow our creative protest to degenerate into physical violence. Again and again we must rise to the majestic heights of meeting physical force with soul force. The marvelous new militancy which has engulfed the Negro community must not lead us to a distrust of all white people, for many of our white brothers, as evidenced by their presence here today, have come to realize that their destiny is tied up with our destiny. And they have come to realize that their freedom is inextricably bound to our freedom. We cannot walk alone.

And as we walk, we must make the pledge that we shall always march ahead. We cannot turn back. There are those who are asking the devotees of civil rights, "When will you be satisfied?" We can never be satisfied as long as the Negro is the victim of the unspeakable horrors of police brutality. We can never be satisfied as long as our bodies, heavy with the fatigue of travel, cannot gain lodging in the motels of the highways and the hotels of the cities. We cannot be satisfied as long as the Negro's basic mobility is from a smaller ghetto to a larger one. We can never be satisfied as long as our children are stripped of their selfhood and robbed of their dignity by signs stating "for whites only." We cannot be satisfied as long as a Negro in Mississippi cannot vote and a Negro in New York believes he has nothing for which to vote. No, no, we are not satisfied and we will not be satisfied until justice rolls down like waters and righteousness like a mighty stream.

I am not unmindful that some of you have come here out of great trials and tribulations. Some of you have come fresh from narrow jail cells. Some of you have come from areas where your quest for freedom left you battered by storms of persecution and staggered by the winds of police brutality. You have been the veterans of creative suffering. Continue to work with the faith that unearned suffering is redemptive.

Go back to Mississippi, go back to Alabama, go back to South Carolina, go back to Georgia, go back to Louisiana, go back to the slums and ghettos of our northern cities, knowing that somehow this situation can and will be changed.

Let us not wallow in the valley of despair. I say to you today my friends—so even though we face the difficulties of today and tomorrow, I still have a dream. It is a dream deeply rooted in the American dream.

I have a dream that one day this nation will rise up and live out the true meaning of its creed: "We hold these truths to be self-evident, that all men are created equal."

I have a dream that one day on the red hills of Georgia the sons of former slaves and the sons of former slave owners will be able to sit down together at the table of brotherhood.

I have a dream that one day even the state of Mississippi, a state sweltering with the heat of injustice, sweltering with the heat of oppression, will be transformed into an oasis of freedom and justice.

I have a dream that my four little children will one day live in a nation where they will not be judged by the color of their skin but by the content of their character.

I have a dream today.

I have a dream that one day down in Alabama, with its vicious racists, with its governor having his lips dripping with the words of interposition and nullification—one day right there in Alabama little black boys and black girls will be able to join hands with little white boys and white girls as sisters and brothers.

I have a dream today.

I have a dream that one day every valley shall be exalted, and every hill and mountain shall be made low, the rough places will be made plain, and the crooked places will be made straight, and the glory of the Lord shall be revealed and all flesh shall see it together.

This is our hope. This is the faith that I go back to the South with. With this faith we will be able to hew out of the mountain of despair a stone of hope.

With this faith we will be able to transform the jangling discords of our nation into a beautiful symphony of brotherhood. With this faith we will be able to work together, to pray together, to struggle together, to go to jail together, to stand up for freedom together, knowing that we will be free one day.

This will be the day, this will be the day when all of God's children will be able to sing with new meaning "My country 'tis of thee, sweet land of liberty, of thee I sing. Land where my fathers died, land of the Pilgrim's pride, from every mountainside, let freedom ring!"

And if America is to be a great nation, this must become true. And so let freedom ring from the prodigious hilltops of New Hampshire. Let freedom ring from the mighty mountains of New York. Let freedom ring from the heightening Alleghenies of Pennsylvania.

Let freedom ring from the snow-capped Rockies of Colorado. Let freedom ring from the curvaceous slopes of California.

But not only that; let freedom ring from Stone Mountain of Georgia.

Let freedom ring from Lookout Mountain of Tennessee.

Let freedom ring from every hill and molehill of Mississippi—from every mountainside.

Let freedom ring. And when this happens, and when we allow freedom to ring—when we let it ring from every village and every hamlet, from every state and every city, we will be able to speed up that day when all of God's children—black men and white men, Jews and Gentiles, Protestants and Catholics—will be able to join hands and sing in the words of the old Negro spiritual: "Free at last! Free at last! Thank God Almighty, we are free at last!"

QUESTIONS FOR REFLECTION

1. What is the "shameful condition" that Reverend King seeks to change?

2. To what rights does Reverend King appeal?

3. What moral constraints does Reverend King place on the quest for justice?

4. What signs does Reverend King cite that show that we have not yet achieved racial justice?

5. How does Reverend King's dream elaborate the goal of racial equality?

JUSTICE LEWIS POWELL

Majority Opinion in
Regents of the University of California v.
Bakke (1978)

(*Source:* Regents of the University of California v. Bakke *438 U.S. 265 [1978]. Most legal references have been omitted.*)

. . . Mr. Justice Powell announced the judgment of the Court. . . .

I

The Medical School of the University of California at Davis opened in 1968 with an entering class of 50 students. In 1971, the size of the entering class was increased to 100 students, a level at which it remains. No admissions program for disadvantaged or minority students existed when the school opened, and the first class contained three Asians but no blacks, no Mexican-Americans, and no American Indians. Over the next two years, the faculty devised a special admissions program to increase the representation of "disadvantaged" students in each Medical School class. The special program consisted of a separate admissions system operating in coordination with the regular admissions process. . . .

The special admissions program operated with a separate committee, a majority of whom were members of minority groups. On the 1973 application form, candidates were asked to indicate whether they wished to be considered as "economically and/or educationally disadvantaged" applicants; on the 1974 form the question was whether they wished to be considered as members of a "minority group," which the Medical School apparently viewed

as "Blacks," "Chicanos," "Asians," and "American Indians." If these questions were answered affirmatively, the application was forwarded to the special admissions committee. No formal definition of "disadvantaged" was ever produced, but the chairman of the special committee screened each application to see whether it reflected economic or educational deprivation. Having passed this initial hurdle, the applications then were rated by the special committee in a fashion similar to that used by the general admissions committee, except that special candidates did not have to meet the 2.5 grade point average cutoff applied to regular applicants. About one-fifth of the total number of special applicants were invited for interviews in 1973 and 1974. Following each interview, the special committee assigned each special applicant a benchmark score. The special committee then presented its top choices to the general admissions committee. The latter did not rate or compare the special candidates against the general applicants, but could reject recommended special candidates for failure to meet course requirements or other specific deficiencies. The special committee continued to recommend special applicants until a number prescribed by faculty vote were admitted. While the overall class size was still 50, the prescribed number was 8; in 1973 and 1974, when the class size had doubled to 100, the prescribed number of special admissions also doubled, to 16.

From the year of the increase in class size—1971 —through 1974, the special program resulted in the admission of 21 black students, 30 Mexican-Americans, and 12 Asians, for a total of 63 minority students. Over the same period, the regular admissions program produced 1 black, 6 Mexican-Americans, and 37 Asians, for a total of 44 minority students. Although disadvantaged whites applied to the special program in large numbers, none received an offer of admission through that process. Indeed, in 1974, at least, the special committee explicitly considered only "disadvantaged" special applicants who were members of one of the designated minority groups.

Allan Bakke is a white male who applied to the Davis Medical School in both 1973 and 1974. In both years Bakke's application was considered under the general admissions program, and he received an interview. His 1973 interview was with Dr. Theodore C. West, who considered Bakke "a very desirable applicant to [the] medical school." Despite a strong benchmark score of 468 out of 500, Bakke was rejected. His application had come late in the year, and no applicants in the general admissions process with scores below 470 were accepted after Bakke's application was completed. There were four special admissions slots unfilled at that time, however, for which Bakke was not considered. After his 1973 rejection, Bakke wrote to Dr. George H. Lowrey, Associate Dean and Chairman of the Admissions Committee, protesting that the special admissions program operated as a racial and ethnic quota.

Bakke's 1974 application was completed early in the year. His student interviewer gave him an overall rating of 94, finding him "friendly, well tempered, conscientious and delightful to speak with." His faculty interviewer was, by coincidence, the same Dr. Lowrey to whom he had written in protest of the special admissions program. Dr. Lowrey found Bakke "rather limited in his approach" to the problems of the medical profession and found disturbing Bakke's "very definite opinions which were based more on his personal viewpoints than upon a study of the total problem." Dr. Lowrey gave Bakke the lowest of his six ratings, an 86; his total was 549 out of 600. Again, Bakke's application was rejected. In neither year did the chairman of the admissions committee, Dr. Lowrey, exercise his discretion to place Bakke on the waiting list. In both years, applicants were admitted under the special program with grade point averages, MCAT scores, and benchmark scores significantly lower than Bakke's. The table on page 621 compares Bakke's science grade point average, overall grade point average, and MCAT scores with the average scores of regular admittees and of special admittees in both 1973 and 1974.

After the second rejection, Bakke filed the instant suit in the Superior Court of California. He sought mandatory, injunctive, and declaratory relief compelling his admission to the Medical School. He alleged that the Medical School's special admissions program operated to exclude him from the school on the basis of his race, in violation of his rights under the Equal Protection Clause of the Fourteenth Amendment, Art. I, *1/8* 21, of the California Constitution, and *1/8* 601 of Title VI of the Civil Rights Act of 1964. The University cross-complained for a declaration that its special admissions program was lawful. . . .

III

A

. . . The guarantees of the Fourteenth Amendment extend to all persons. Its language is explicit: "No State shall . . . deny to any person within its jurisdiction the equal protection of the laws." It is settled beyond question that the "rights created by the first section of the Fourteenth Amendment are, by its terms, guaranteed to the individual. The rights established are personal rights." The guarantee of equal protection cannot mean one thing when applied to one individual and something else when applied to a person of another color. If both are not accorded the same protection, then it is not equal.

Nevertheless, petitioner argues that the court below erred in applying strict scrutiny to the special admissions program because white males, such as respondent, are not a "discrete and insular minority" requiring extraordinary protection from the majoritarian political process. This rationale, however, has never been invoked in our decisions as a prerequisite to subjecting racial or ethnic distinctions to strict scrutiny. Nor has this Court held that discreteness

CLASS ENTERING IN 1973

	SGPA	OGPA	MCAT Percentiles			
			Verbal	Quantitative	Science	General Information
Bakke	3.44	3.46	96	94	97	72
Average of regular admittees	3.51	3.49	81	76	83	69
Average of special admittees	2.62	2.88	46	24	35	33

CLASS ENTERING IN 1974

	SGPA	OGPA	MCAT Percentiles			
			Verbal	Quantitative	Science	General Information
Bakke	3.44	3.46	96	94	97	72
Average of regular admittees	3.36	3.29	69	67	82	72
Average of special admittees	2.42	2.62	34	30	37	18

Applicants admitted under the special program also had benchmark scores significantly lower than many students, including Bakke, rejected under the general admissions program, even though the special rating system apparently gave credit for overcoming "disadvantage."

and insularity constitute necessary preconditions to a holding that a particular classification is invidious. These characteristics may be relevant in deciding whether or not to add new types of classifications to the list of "suspect" categories or whether a particular classification survives close examination. Racial and ethnic classifications, however, are subject to stringent examination without regard to these additional characteristics. We declared as much in the first cases explicitly to recognize racial distinctions as suspect:

> Distinctions between citizens solely because of their ancestry are by their very nature odious to a free people whose institutions are founded upon the doctrine of equality.
>
> [A]ll legal restrictions which curtail the civil rights of a single racial group are immediately suspect. That is not to say that all such restrictions are unconstitutional. It is to say that courts must subject them to the most rigid scrutiny.

The Court has never questioned the validity of those pronouncements. Racial and ethnic distinctions of any sort are inherently suspect and thus call for the most exacting judicial examination.

B

This perception of racial and ethnic distinctions is rooted in our Nation's constitutional and demographic history. The Court's initial view of the Fourteenth Amendment was that its "one pervading purpose" was "the freedom of the slave race, the security and firm establishment of that freedom, and the protection of the newly-made freeman and citizen from the oppressions of those who had formerly exercised dominion over him." *Slaughter-House Cases* (1873). The Equal Protection Clause, however, was "[v]irtually strangled in infancy by post-Civil-War judicial reactionism." It was relegated to decades of relative desuetude while the Due Process Clause of the Fourteenth Amendment, after a short germinal period, flourished as a cornerstone in the Court's defense of property and liberty of contract. In that cause, the Fourteenth Amendment's "one pervading purpose" was displaced. It was only as the era of substantive due process came to a close that the Equal Protection Clause began to attain a genuine measure of vitality.

By that time it was no longer possible to peg the guarantees of the Fourteenth Amendment to the struggle for equality of one racial minority. During the dormancy of the Equal Protection Clause, the United States had become a Nation of minorities. Each had to struggle—and to some extent struggles still—to overcome the prejudices not of a monolithic majority, but of a "majority" composed of various minority groups of whom it was said—perhaps unfairly in many cases—that a shared characteristic was a willingness to disadvantage other groups. As the Nation filled with the stock of many lands, the reach of the Clause was gradually extended to all ethnic groups seeking protection from official discrimination. The guarantees of equal protection, said the Court in *Yick Wo,* "are universal in their application, to all persons within the territorial jurisdiction, without regard to any differences of race, of color, or of nationality; and the equal protection of the laws is a pledge of the protection of equal laws."

Although many of the Framers of the Fourteenth Amendment conceived of its primary function as bridging the vast distance between members of the Negro race and the white "majority," the Amendment itself was framed in universal terms, without reference to color, ethnic origin, or condition of prior servitude. As this Court recently remarked in interpreting the 1866 Civil Rights Act to extend to claims of racial discrimination against white persons, "the 39th Congress was intent upon establishing in the federal law a broader principle than would have been necessary simply to meet the particular and immediate plight of the newly freed Negro slaves." And that legislation was specifically broadened in 1870 to ensure that "all persons," not merely "citizens," would enjoy equal rights under the law. Indeed, it is not unlikely that among the Framers were many who would have applauded a reading of the Equal Protection Clause that states a principle of universal application and is responsive to the racial, ethnic, and cultural diversity of the Nation.

Over the past 30 years, this Court has embarked upon the crucial mission of interpreting the Equal Protection Clause with the view of assuring to all persons "the protection of equal laws," in a Nation confronting a legacy of slavery and racial discrimi-

nation. Because the landmark decisions in this area arose in response to the continued exclusion of Negroes from the mainstream of American society, they could be characterized as involving discrimination by the "majority" white race against the Negro minority. But they need not be read as depending upon that characterization for their results. It suffices to say that "[o]ver the years, this Court has consistently repudiated '[d]istinctions between citizens solely because of their ancestry' as being 'odious to a free people whose institutions are founded upon the doctrine of equality.'"

Petitioner urges us to adopt for the first time a more restrictive view of the Equal Protection Clause and hold that discrimination against members of the white "majority" cannot be suspect if its purpose can be characterized as "benign."* The clock of our liberties, however, cannot be turned back to 1868. It is far too late to argue that the guarantee of equal protection to *all* persons permits the recognition of special wards entitled to a degree of protection greater than that accorded others.† "The Fourteenth

---

* In the view of Mr. Justice Brennan, Mr. Justice White, Mr. Justice Marshall, and Mr. Justice Blackmun, the pliable notion of "stigma" is the crucial element in analyzing racial classifications. The Equal Protection Clause is not framed in terms of "stigma." Certainly the word has no clearly defined constitutional meaning. It reflects a subjective judgment that is standardless. *All* state-imposed classifications that rearrange burdens and benefits on the basis of race are likely to be viewed with deep resentment by the individuals burdened. The denial to innocent persons of equal rights and opportunities may outrage those so deprived and therefore may be perceived as invidious. These individuals are likely to find little comfort in the notion that the deprivation they are asked to endure is merely the price of membership in the dominant majority and that its imposition is inspired by the supposedly benign purpose of aiding others. One should not lightly dismiss the inherent unfairness of, and the perception of mistreatment that accompanies, a system of allocating benefits and privileges on the basis of skin color and ethnic origin. Moreover, Mr. Justice Brennan, Mr. Justice White, Mr. Justice Marshall, and Mr. Justice Blackmun offer no principle for deciding whether preferential classifications reflect a benign remedial purpose or a malevolent stigmatic classification, since they are willing in this case to accept mere *post hoc* declarations by an isolated state entity—a medical school faculty —unadorned by particularized findings of past discrimination, to establish such a remedial purpose.

† Professor Bickel noted the self-contradiction of that view:

"The lesson of the great decisions of the Supreme Court and the lesson of contemporary history have been the same for at least a generation: discrimination on the basis of race is illegal, immoral, unconstitutional, inherently wrong, and destructive of

Amendment is not directed solely against discrimination due to a 'two-class theory'—that is, based upon differences between 'white' and Negro."

Once the artificial line of a "two-class theory" of the Fourteenth Amendment is put aside, the difficulties entailed in varying the level of judicial review according to a perceived "preferred" status of a particular racial or ethnic minority are intractable. The concepts of "majority" and "minority" necessarily reflect temporary arrangements and political judgments. As observed above, the white "majority" itself is composed of various minority groups, most of which can lay claim to a history of prior discrimination at the hands of the State and private individuals. Not all of these groups can receive preferential treatment and corresponding judicial tolerance of distinctions drawn in terms of race and nationality, for then the only "majority" left would be a new minority of white Anglo-Saxon Protestants. There is no principled basis for deciding which groups would merit "heightened judicial solicitude" and which would not. Courts would be asked to evaluate the extent of the prejudice and consequent harm suffered by various minority groups. Those whose societal injury is thought to exceed some arbitrary level of tolerability then would be entitled to preferential classifications at the expense of individuals belonging to other groups. Those classifications would be free from exacting judicial scrutiny. As these preferences began to have their desired effect, and the consequences of past discrimination were undone, new judicial rankings would be necessary. The kind of variable sociological and political analysis necessary to produce such rankings simply does not lie within the judicial competence—even if they otherwise were politically feasible and socially desirable.

Moreover, there are serious problems of justice connected with the idea of preference itself. First, it may not always be clear that a so-called preference is in fact benign. Courts may be asked to validate burdens imposed upon individual members of a particular group in order to advance the group's general interest. Nothing in the Constitution supports the notion that individuals may be asked to suffer otherwise impermissible burdens in order to enhance the societal standing of their ethnic groups. Second, preferential programs may only reinforce common stereotypes holding that certain groups are unable to achieve success without special protection based on a factor having no relationship to individual worth. Third, there is a measure of inequity in forcing innocent persons in respondent's position to bear the burdens of redressing grievances not of their making.

By hitching the meaning of the Equal Protection Clause to these transitory considerations, we would be holding, as a constitutional principle, that judicial scrutiny of classifications touching on racial and ethnic background may vary with the ebb and flow of political forces. Disparate constitutional tolerance of such classifications well may serve to exacerbate racial and ethnic antagonisms rather than alleviate them. Also, the mutability of a constitutional principle, based upon shifting political and social judgments, undermines the chances for consistent application of the Constitution from one generation to the next, a critical feature of its coherent interpretation. In expounding the Constitution, the Court's role is to discern "principles sufficiently absolute to give them roots throughout the community and continuity over significant periods of time, and to lift them above the level of the pragmatic political judgments of a particular time and place."

If it is the individual who is entitled to judicial protection against classifications based upon his racial or ethnic background because such distinctions impinge upon personal rights, rather than the individual only because of his membership in a particular group, then constitutional standards may be applied consistently. Political judgments regarding the necessity for the particular classification may be weighed in the constitutional balance, but the standard of justification will remain constant. This is as it should be, since those political judgments are the product of rough compromise struck by contending groups within the democratic process. When they touch upon an individual's race or ethnic background, he is entitled to a judicial determination that the burden he is asked to bear on that basis is precisely tailored to serve a compelling governmental interest. The Constitution guarantees

democratic society. Now this is to be unlearned and we are told that this is not a matter of fundamental principle but only a matter of whose ox is gored. Those for whom racial equality was demanded are to be more equal than others. Having found support in the Constitution for equality, they now claim support for inequality under the same Constitution." A. Bickel, *The Morality of Consent* 133 (1975).

that right to every person regardless of his background. . . .

IV

We have held that in "order to justify the use of a suspect classification, a State must show that its purpose or interest is both constitutionally permissible and substantial, and that its use of the classification is 'necessary . . . to the accomplishment' of its purpose or the safeguarding of its interest." The special admissions program purports to serve the purposes of: (i) "reducing the historic deficit of traditionally disfavored minorities in medical schools and in the medical profession," (ii) countering the effects of societal discrimination; (iii) increasing the number of physicians who will practice in communities currently underserved; and (iv) obtaining the educational benefits that flow from an ethnically diverse student body. It is necessary to decide which, if any, of these purposes is substantial enough to support the use of a suspect classification.

A

If petitioner's purpose is to assure within its student body some specified percentage of a particular group merely because of its race or ethnic origin, such a preferential purpose must be rejected not as insubstantial but as facially invalid. Preferring members of any one group for no reason other than race or ethnic origin is discrimination for its own sake. This the Constitution forbids.

B

The State certainly has a legitimate and substantial interest in ameliorating, or eliminating where feasible, the disabling effects of identified discrimination. The line of school desegregation cases, commencing with *Brown,* attests to the importance of this state goal and the commitment of the judiciary to affirm all lawful means toward its attainment. In the school cases, the States were required by court order to redress the wrongs worked by specific instances of racial discrimination. That goal was far more focused than the remedying of the effects of "societal discrimination," an amorphous concept of injury that may be ageless in its reach into the past.

We have never approved a classification that aids persons perceived as members of relatively victimized groups at the expense of other innocent individuals in the absence of judicial, legislative, or administrative findings of constitutional or statutory violations. After such findings have been made, the governmental interest, in preferring members of the injured groups at the expense of others is substantial, since the legal rights of the victims must be vindicated. In such a case, the extent of the injury and the consequent remedy will have been judicially, legislatively, or administratively defined. Also, the remedial action usually remains subject to continuing oversight to assure that it will work the least harm possible to other innocent persons competing for the benefit. Without such findings of constitutional or statutory violations, it cannot be said that the government has any greater interest in helping one individual than in refraining from harming another. Thus, the government has no compelling justification for inflicting such harm. . . .

Hence, the purpose of helping certain groups whom the faculty of the Davis Medical School perceived as victims of "societal discrimination" does not justify a classification that imposes disadvantages upon persons like respondent, who bear no responsibility for whatever harm the beneficiaries of the special admissions program are thought to have suffered. To hold otherwise would be to convert a remedy heretofore reserved for violations of legal rights into a privilege that all institutions throughout the Nation could grant at their pleasure to whatever groups are perceived as victims of societal discrimination. That is a step we have never approved.

C

Petitioner identifies, as another purpose of its program, improving the delivery of health-care services to communities currently underserved. It may be assumed that in some situations a State's interest in facilitating the health care of its citizens is sufficiently compelling to support the use of a suspect classification. But there is virtually no evidence in the record indicating that petitioner's special admissions program is either needed or geared to promote that goal. The court below addressed this failure of proof:

The University concedes it cannot assure that minority doctors who entered under the program, all of whom expressed an "interest" in practicing in a disadvantaged community, will actually do so. It may be correct to assume that some of them will carry out this intention, and that it is more likely they will practice in minority communities than the average white doctor. Nevertheless, there are more precise and reliable ways to identify applicants who are genuinely interested in the medical problems of minorities than by race. An applicant of whatever race who has demonstrated his concern for disadvantaged minorities in the past and who declares that practice in such a community is his primary professional goal would be more likely to contribute to alleviation of the medical shortage than one who is chosen entirely on the basis of race and disadvantage. In short, there is no empirical data to demonstrate that any one race is more selflessly socially oriented or by contrast that another is more selfishly acquisitive.

Petitioner simply has not carried its burden of demonstrating that it must prefer members of particular ethnic groups over all other individuals in order to promote better health-care delivery to deprived citizens. Indeed, petitioner has not shown that its preferential classification is likely to have any significant effect on the problem.

D

The fourth goal asserted by petitioner is the attainment of a diverse student body. This clearly is a constitutionally permissible goal for an institution of higher education. Academic freedom, though not a specifically enumerated constitutional right, long has been viewed as a special concern of the First Amendment. The freedom of a university to make its own judgments as to education includes the selection of its student body. Mr. Justice Frankfurter summarized the "four essential freedoms" that constitute academic freedom:

'It is the business of a university to provide that atmosphere which is most conducive to speculation, experiment and creation. It is an atmosphere in which there prevail "the four essential freedoms" of a university—to determine for itself on academic grounds who may teach, what may be taught, how it shall be taught, and who may be admitted to study.'

Our national commitment to the safeguarding of these freedoms within university communities was emphasized in *Keyishian* v. *Board of Regents* (1967):

Our Nation is deeply committed to safeguarding academic freedom which is of transcendent value to all of us and not merely to the teachers concerned. That freedom is therefore a special concern of the First Amendment. . . . The Nation's future depends upon leaders trained through wide exposure to that robust exchange of ideas which discovers truth "out of a multitude of tongues, [rather] than through any kind of authoritative selection."

The atmosphere of "speculation, experiment and creation"—so essential to the quality of higher education—is widely believed to be promoted by a diverse student body. As the Court noted in *Keyishian,* it is not too much to say that the "nation's future depends upon leaders trained through wide exposure" to the ideas and mores of students as diverse as this Nation of many peoples.

Thus, in arguing that its universities must be accorded the right to select those students who will contribute the most to the "robust exchange of ideas," petitioner invokes a countervailing constitutional interest, that of the First Amendment. In this light, petitioner must be viewed as seeking to achieve a goal that is of paramount importance in the fulfillment of its mission.

It may be argued that there is greater force to these views at the undergraduate level than in a medical school where the training is centered primarily on professional competency. But even at the graduate level, our tradition and experience lend support to the view that the contribution of diversity is substantial. In *Sweatt* v. *Painter,* the Court made a similar point with specific reference to legal education:

The law school, the proving ground for legal learning and practice, cannot be effective in isolation from the individuals and institutions with which the law interacts. Few students and no one who has practiced law would choose to study in an academic vacuum, removed from the interplay of ideas and the exchange of views with which the law is concerned.

Physicians serve a heterogeneous population. An otherwise qualified medical student with a particular background—whether it be ethnic, geographic, culturally advantaged or disadvantaged—may bring to a professional school of medicine experiences, outlooks, and ideas that enrich the training of its student body and better equip its graduates to render with understanding their vital service to humanity.

Ethnic diversity, however, is only one element in a range of factors a university properly may consider in attaining the goal of a heterogeneous student body. Although a university must have wide discretion in making the sensitive judgments as to who should be admitted, constitutional limitations protecting individual rights may not be disregarded. Respondent urges—and the courts below have held —that petitioner's dual admissions program is a racial classification that impermissibly infringes his rights under the Fourteenth Amendment. As the interest of diversity is compelling in the context of a university's admissions program, the question remains whether the program's racial classification is necessary to promote this interest.

V

A

It may be assumed that the reservation of a specified number of seats in each class for individuals from the preferred ethnic groups would contribute to the attainment of considerable ethnic diversity in the student body. But petitioner's argument that this is the only effective means of serving the interest of diversity is seriously flawed. In a most fundamental sense the argument misconceives the nature of the state interest that would justify consideration of race or ethnic background. It is not an interest in simple ethnic diversity, in which a specified percentage of the student body is in effect guaranteed to be members of selected ethnic groups, with the remaining percentage an undifferentiated aggregation of students. The diversity that furthers a compelling state interest encompasses a far broader array of qualifications and characteristics of which racial or ethnic origin is but a single though important element. Petitioner's special admissions program, focused *solely* on ethnic diversity, would hinder rather than further attainment of genuine diversity. . . .

B

In summary, it is evident that the Davis special admissions program involves the use of an explicit racial classification never before countenanced by this Court. It tells applicants who are not Negro, Asian, or Chicano that they are totally excluded from a specific percentage of the seats in an entering class. No matter how strong their qualifications, quantitative and extracurricular, including their own potential for contribution to educational diversity, they are never afforded the chance to compete with applicants from the preferred groups for the special admissions seats. At the same time, the preferred applicants have the opportunity to compete for every seat in the class.

The fatal flaw in petitioner's preferential program is its disregard of individual rights as guaranteed by the Fourteenth Amendment. Such rights are not absolute. But when a State's distribution of benefits or imposition of burdens hinges on ancestry or the color of a person's skin, that individual is entitled to a demonstration that the challenged classification is necessary to promote a substantial state interest. Petitioner has failed to carry this burden. For this reason, that portion of the California court's judgment holding petitioner's special admissions program invalid under the Fourteenth Amendment must be affirmed. . . .

QUESTIONS FOR REFLECTION

1. Justice Powell argues that the University of California's racial classification should not simply be viewed as "benign." Why?

2. How did the University of California try to justify its affirmative-action program? Why does Justice Powell reject those arguments?

3. What sort of affirmative-action program does Justice Powell find acceptable? How does it differ from the University of California program?

Hopwood v. Texas (1996)

(*Source:* Hopwood v. State of Texas 78 F.3d 932 [5th Cir. 1996] Most legal references have been omitted.)

With the best of intentions, in order to increase the enrollment of certain favored classes of minority students, the University of Texas School of Law ("the law school") discriminates in favor of those applicants by giving substantial racial preferences in its admissions program. The beneficiaries of this system are blacks and Mexican Americans, to the detriment of whites and non-preferred minorities. The question we decide today . . . is whether the Fourteenth Amendment permits the school to discriminate in this way.

We hold that it does not. The law school has presented no compelling justification, under the Fourteenth Amendment or Supreme Court precedent, that allows it to continue to elevate some races over others, even for the wholesome purpose of correcting perceived racial imbalance in the student body. "Racial preferences appear to 'even the score' . . . only if one embraces the proposition that our society is appropriately viewed as divided into races, making it right that an injustice rendered in the past to a black man should be compensated for by discriminating against a white." *City of Richmond v. J. A. Croson Co.* (1989) (Scalia, J., concurring in the judgment).

As a result of its diligent efforts in this case, the district court concluded that the law school may continue to impose racial preferences. . . . [w]e reverse and remand, concluding that the law school may not use race as a factor in law school admissions. . . .

I

A

The University of Texas School of Law is one of the nation's leading law schools, consistently ranking in the top twenty. Accordingly, admission to the law school is fiercely competitive, with over 4,000 applicants a year competing to be among the approximately 900 offered admission to achieve an entering class of about 500 students. Many of these applicants have some of the highest grades and test scores in the country.

Numbers are therefore paramount for admission. In the early 1990's, the law school largely based its initial admissions decisions upon an applicant's so-called Texas Index (TI) number, a composite of undergraduate grade point average (GPA) and Law School Aptitude Test (LSAT) score. The law school used this number as a matter of administrative convenience in order to rank candidates and to predict, roughly, one's probability of success in law school. Moreover, the law school relied heavily upon such numbers to estimate the number of offers of admission it needed to make in order to fill its first-year class.

Of course, the law school did not rely upon numbers alone. The admissions office necessarily exercised judgment in interpreting the individual scores of applicants, taking into consideration factors such as the strength of a student's undergraduate education, the difficulty of his major, and significant trends in his own grades and the undergraduate grades at his respective college (such as grade inflation). Admissions personnel also considered what qualities each applicant might bring to his law school class. Thus, the law school could consider an applicant's background, life experiences, and outlook. Not surprisingly, these hard-to-quantify factors were especially significant for marginal candidates.

Because of the large number of applicants and potential admissions factors, the TI's administrative usefulness was its ability to sort candidates. For the class entering in 1992—the admissions group at issue in this case—the law school placed the typical applicant in one of three categories according to his TI scores: "presumptive admit," "presumptive deny," or a middle "discretionary zone." An applicant's TI category determined how extensive a review his application would receive.

Most, but not all, applicants in the presumptive admit category received offers of admission with little review. Professor Stanley Johanson, the Chairman of the Admissions Committee, or Dean Laquita Hamilton, the Assistant Dean for Admissions, reviewed these files and downgraded only five to ten percent to the discretionary zone because of weaknesses in their applications, generally a noncompetitive major or a weak undergraduate education.

Applicants in the presumptive denial category also received little consideration. Similarly, these files would be reviewed by one or two professors, who could upgrade them if they believed that the TI score did not adequately reflect potential to compete at the law school. Otherwise, the applicant was rejected.

Applications in the middle range were subjected to the most extensive scrutiny. For all applicants other than blacks and Mexican Americans, the files were bundled into stacks of thirty, which were given to admissions subcommittees consisting of three members of the full admissions committee. Each subcommittee member, in reviewing the thirty files, could cast a number of votes—typically from nine to eleven—among the thirty files. Subject to the chairman's veto, if a candidate received two or three votes, he received an offer; if he garnered one vote, he was put on the waiting list; those with no votes were denied admission.

Blacks and Mexican Americans were treated differently from other candidates, however. First, compared to whites and non-preferred minorities, the TI ranges that were used to place them into the three admissions categories were lowered to allow the law school to consider and admit more of them. In March 1992, for example, the presumptive TI admission score for resident whites and non-preferred minorities was 199. Mexican Americans and blacks needed a TI of only 189 to be presumptively admitted. The difference in the presumptive-deny ranges is even more striking. The presumptive denial score

for "nonminorities" was 192; the same score for blacks and Mexican Americans was 179.

While these cold numbers may speak little to those unfamiliar with the pool of applicants, the results demonstrate that the difference in the two ranges was dramatic. According to the law school, 1992 resident white applicants had a *mean* GPA of 3.53 and an LSAT of 164. Mexican Americans scored 3.27 and 158; blacks scored 3.25 and 157. The category of "other minority" achieved a 3.56 and 160.

These disparate standards greatly affected a candidate's chance of admission. For example, by March 1992, because the presumptive *denial* score for whites was a TI of 192 or lower, and the presumptive *admit* TI for minorities was 189 or higher, a minority candidate with a TI of 189 or above almost certainly would be *admitted,* even though his score was considerably below the level at which a white candidate almost certainly would be *rejected.* Out of the pool of resident applicants who fell within this range (189–192 inclusive), 100% of blacks and 90% of Mexican Americans, but only 6% of whites, were offered admission.

The stated purpose of this lowering of standards was to meet an "aspiration" of admitting a class consisting of 10% Mexican Americans and 5% blacks, proportions roughly comparable to the percentages of those races graduating from Texas colleges. The law school found meeting these "goals" difficult, however, because of uncertain acceptance rates and the variable quality of the applicant pool. In 1992, for example, the entering class contained 41 blacks and 55 Mexican Americans, respectively 8% and 10.7% of the class.

In addition to maintaining separate presumptive TI levels for minorities and whites, the law school ran a segregated application evaluation process. Upon receiving an application form, the school color-coded it according to race. If a candidate failed to designate his race, he was presumed to be in a nonpreferential category. Thus, race was always an overt part of the review of any applicant's file.

The law school reviewed minority candidates within the applicable discretionary range differently from whites. Instead of being evaluated and compared by one of the various discretionary zone subcommittees, black and Mexican American applicants' files were reviewed by a minority subcommittee of three, which would meet and discuss every minority candidate. Thus, each of these candidates' files could get extensive review and discussion. And while the minority subcommittee reported summaries of files to the admissions committee as a whole, the minority subcommittee's decisions were "virtually final."

Finally, the law school maintained segregated waiting lists, dividing applicants by race and residence. Thus, even many of those minority applicants who were not admitted could be set aside in "minority-only" waiting lists. Such separate lists apparently helped the law school maintain a pool of potentially acceptable, but marginal, minority candidates.

B

Cheryl Hopwood, Douglas Carvell, Kenneth Elliott, and David Rogers (the "plaintiffs") applied for admission to the 1992 entering law school class. All four were white residents of Texas and were rejected.

The plaintiffs were considered as discretionary zone candidates. Hopwood, with a GPA of 3.8 and an LSAT of 39 (equivalent to a three-digit LSAT of 160), had a TI of 199, a score barely within the presumptive-admit category for resident whites, which was 199 and up. She was dropped into the discretionary zone for resident whites (193 to 198), however, because Johanson decided her educational background overstated the strength of her GPA. Carvell, Elliott, and Rogers had TI's of 197, at the top end of that discretionary zone. Their applications were reviewed by admissions subcommittees, and each received one or no vote. . . .

III

The central purpose of the Equal Protection Clause "is to prevent the States from purposefully discriminating between individuals on the basis of race." *Shaw* v. *Reno* (1993) (citing *Washington* v. *Davis* [1976]). It seeks ultimately to render the issue of race irrelevant in governmental decisionmaking. See *Palmore* v. *Sidoti* (1984) ("A core purpose of the Fourteenth Amendment was to do away with all governmentally imposed discrimination").

Accordingly, discrimination based upon race is highly suspect. "Distinctions between citizens solely because of their ancestry are by their very nature odious to a free people whose institutions are founded upon the doctrine of equality," and "racial discriminations are in most circumstances irrelevant and therefore prohibited. . . ." *Hirabayashi* v. *United States* (1943). Hence, "[p]referring members of any one group for no reason other than race or ethnic origin is discrimination for its own sake. This the Constitution forbids." *Regents of Univ. of Cal.* v. *Bakke* (1978) (opinion of Powell, J.). These equal protection maxims apply to all races.

In order to preserve these principles, the Supreme Court recently has required that any governmental action that expressly distinguishes between persons on the basis of race be held to the most exacting scrutiny. Furthermore, there is now absolutely no doubt that courts are to employ strict scrutiny when evaluating all racial classifications, including those characterized by their proponents as "benign" or "remedial."

Strict scrutiny is necessary because the mere labeling of a classification by the government as "benign" or "remedial" is meaningless. As Justice O'Connor indicated in *Croson*:

> Absent searching judicial inquiry into the justifications for such race-based measures, there is simply no way of determining what classifications are "benign" or "remedial" and what classifications are in fact motivated by illegitimate notions of racial inferiority or simple racial politics. Indeed, the purpose of strict scrutiny is to "smoke out" illegitimate uses of race by assuring that the legislative body is pursuing a goal important enough to warrant use of a highly suspect tool. The test also ensures that the means chosen "fit" this compelling goal so closely that there is little or no possibility that the motive for the classification was illegitimate racial prejudice or stereotype.

Under the strict scrutiny analysis, we ask two questions: (1) Does the racial classification serve a compelling government interest, and (2) is it narrowly tailored to the achievement of that goal? As the *Adarand* Court emphasized, strict scrutiny ensures that "courts will consistently give racial classifications . . . detailed examination both as to ends and as to means."

Finally, when evaluating the proffered governmental interest for the specific racial classification, to decide whether the program in question narrowly achieves that interest, we must recognize that "the rights created by . . . the Fourteenth Amendment are, by its terms, guaranteed to the individual. The rights established are personal rights." *Shelley* v. *Kraemer* (1948). Thus, the Court consistently has rejected arguments conferring benefits on a person based solely upon his membership in a specific class of persons.

With these general principles of equal protection in mind, we turn to the specific issue of whether the law school's consideration of race as a factor in admissions violates the Equal Protection Clause. The district court found both a compelling remedial and a non-remedial justification for the practice.

First, the court approved of the non-remedial goal of having a diverse student body, reasoning that "obtaining the educational benefits that flow from a racially and ethnically diverse student body remains a sufficiently compelling interest to support the use of racial classifications." Second, the court determined that the use of racial classifications could be justified as a remedy for the "present effects at the law school of past discrimination in both the University of Texas system and the Texas educational system as a whole."

A

. . .

2.

Here, the plaintiffs argue that diversity is not a compelling governmental interest under superseding Supreme Court precedent. Instead, they believe that the Court finally has recognized that only the *remedial* use of race is compelling. In the alternative, the plaintiffs assert that the district court misapplied Justice Powell's *Bakke* standard, as the law school program here uses race as a strong determinant rather than a mere "plus" factor and, in any case, the preference is not narrowly applied. The law school maintains, on the other hand, that Justice Powell's formulation in *Bakke* is law and must be followed—at least in the context of higher education.

We agree with the plaintiffs that any consideration of race or ethnicity by the law school for the purpose of achieving a diverse student body is not a compelling interest under the Fourteenth Amendment. Justice Powell's argument in *Bakke* garnered

only his own vote and has never represented the view of a majority of the Court in *Bakke* or any other case. Moreover, subsequent Supreme Court decisions regarding education state that non-remedial state interests will never justify racial classifications. Finally, the classification of persons on the basis of race for the purpose of diversity frustrates, rather than facilitates, the goals of equal protection.

Justice Powell's view in *Bakke* is not binding precedent on this issue. While he announced the judgment, no other Justice joined in that part of the opinion discussing the diversity rationale. In *Bakke,* the word "diversity" is mentioned nowhere except in Justice Powell's single-Justice opinion. In fact, the four-Justice opinion, which would have upheld the special admissions program under intermediate scrutiny, implicitly rejected Justice Powell's position. ("We also agree with Mr. Justice Powell that a plan like the 'Harvard' plan . . . is constitutional under our approach, *at least so long as the use of race to achieve an integrated student body is necessitated by the lingering effects of past discrimination.*") (emphasis added). Justice Stevens declined to discuss the constitutional issue.

Thus, only one Justice concluded that race could be used solely for the reason of obtaining a heterogeneous student body. As the *Adarand* Court states, the *Bakke* Court did not express a majority view and is questionable as binding precedent. ("The Court's failure in *Bakke* . . . left unresolved the proper analysis for remedial race-based government action.")

Since *Bakke,* the Court has accepted the diversity rationale only once in its cases dealing with race. Significantly, however, in that case, *Metro Broadcasting, Inc.* v. *Federal Communications Comm'n* (1990), the five-Justice majority relied upon an intermediate scrutiny standard of review to uphold the federal program seeking diversity in the ownership of broadcasting facilities. In *Adarand,* the Court squarely rejected intermediate scrutiny as the standard of review for racial classifications, and *Metro Broadcasting* is now specifically overruled to the extent that it was in conflict with this holding. No case since *Bakke* has accepted diversity as a compelling state interest under a strict scrutiny analysis.

Indeed, recent Supreme Court precedent shows that the diversity interest will not satisfy strict scrutiny. Foremost, the Court appears to have decided that there is essentially only one compelling state interest to justify racial classifications: remedying past wrongs. In *Croson,* the Court flatly stated that "[u]nless [racial classifications] are *strictly reserved for remedial settings,* they may in fact promote notions of racial inferiority and lead to a politics of racial hostility" (emphasis added).

Justice O'Connor, in her *Adarand*-vindicated dissent in *Metro Broadcasting,* joined by Justices Rehnquist, Scalia, and Kennedy, explained this position:

> Modern equal protection has recognized only one [compelling state] interest: remedying the effects of racial discrimination. The interest in increasing the diversity of broadcast viewpoints is clearly not a compelling interest. It is simply too amorphous, too insubstantial, and too unrelated to any legitimate basis for employing racial classifications.

Indeed, the majority in *Metro Broadcasting* had not claimed otherwise and decided only that such an interest was "important." Justice Thomas, who joined the Court after *Metro Broadcasting* was decided, roundly condemned "benign" discrimination in his recent *Adarand* opinion, in which he suggests that the diversity rationale is inadequate to meet strict scrutiny.

In short, there has been no indication from the Supreme Court, other than Justice Powell's lonely opinion in *Bakke,* that the state's interest in diversity constitutes a compelling justification for governmental race-based discrimination. Subsequent Supreme Court caselaw strongly suggests, in fact, that it is not.

Within the general principles of the Fourteenth Amendment, the use of race in admissions for diversity in higher education contradicts, rather than furthers, the aims of equal protection. Diversity fosters, rather than minimizes, the use of race. It treats minorities as a group, rather than as individuals. It may further remedial purposes but, just as likely, may promote improper racial stereotypes, thus fueling racial hostility.

The use of race, in and of itself, to choose students simply achieves a student body that looks different. Such a criterion is no more rational on its own terms than would be choices based upon the physical size or blood type of applicants. Thus, the Supreme Court has long held that governmental actors cannot justify their decisions solely because of race.

Accordingly, we see the caselaw as sufficiently established that the use of ethnic diversity simply to achieve racial heterogeneity, even as part of the consideration of a number of factors, is unconstitutional. Were we to decide otherwise, we would contravene precedent that we are not authorized to challenge.

While the use of race *per se* is proscribed, state-supported schools may reasonably consider a host of factors—some of which may have some correlation with race—in making admissions decisions. The federal courts have no warrant to intrude on those executive and legislative judgments unless the distinctions intrude on specific provisions of federal law or the Constitution. A university may properly favor one applicant over another because of his ability to play the cello, make a downfield tackle, or understand chaos theory. An admissions process may also consider an applicant's home state or relationship to school alumni. Law schools specifically may look at things such as unusual or substantial extracurricular activities in college, which may be atypical factors affecting undergraduate grades. Schools may even consider factors such as whether an applicant's parents attended college or the applicant's economic and social background.

For this reason, race often is said to be justified in the diversity context, not on its own terms, but as a proxy for other characteristics that institutions of higher education value but that do not raise similar constitutional concerns. Unfortunately, this approach simply replicates the very harm that the Fourteenth Amendment was designed to eliminate.

The assumption is that a certain individual possesses characteristics by virtue of being a member of a certain racial group. This assumption, however, does not withstand scrutiny. "[T]he use of a racial characteristic to establish a presumption that the individual also possesses other, and socially relevant, characteristics, exemplifies, encourages, and legitimizes the mode of thought and behavior that underlies most prejudice and bigotry in modern America." Richard A. Posner, *The DeFunis Case and the Constitutionality of Preferential Treatment of Racial Minorities,* 1974 Sup. Ct. Rev. 12 (1974).

To believe that a person's race controls his point of view is to stereotype him. The Supreme Court, however, "has remarked a number of times, in slightly different contexts, that it is incorrect and legally inappropriate to impute to women and minorities 'a different attitude about such issues as the federal budget, school prayer, voting, and foreign relations.'" Michael S. Paulsen, *Reverse Discrimination* and Law School Faculty Hiring: The Undiscovered Opinion, 71 Tex. L. Rev. 993, 1000 (1993) (quoting Roberts v. United States Jaycees [1984]). "Social scientists may debate how peoples' thoughts and behavior reflect their background, but the Constitution provides that the government may not allocate benefits or burdens among individuals based on the assumption that race or ethnicity determines how they act or think." *Metro Broadcasting* (O'Connor, J., dissenting).

Instead, individuals, with their own conceptions of life, further diversity of viewpoint. Plaintiff Hopwood is a fair example of an applicant with a unique background. She is the now-thirty-two-year-old wife of a member of the Armed Forces stationed in San Antonio and, more significantly, is raising a severely handicapped child. Her circumstance would bring a different perspective to the law school. The school might consider this an advantage to her in the application process, or it could decide that her family situation would be too much of a burden on her academic performance.

We do not opine on which way the law school should weigh Hopwood's qualifications; we only observe that "diversity" can take many forms. To foster such diversity, state universities and law schools and other governmental entities must scrutinize applicants individually, rather than resorting to the dangerous proxy of race.

The Court also has recognized that government's use of racial classifications serves to stigmatize. *See, e.g., Brown v. Board of Educ.* (1954) (observing that classification on the basis of race "generates a feeling of inferiority"). While one might argue that the stigmatization resulting from so-called "benign" racial classifications is not as harmful as that arising from invidious ones, the current Court has now retreated from the idea that so-called benign and invidious classifications may be distinguished. As the plurality in *Croson* warned, "[c]lassifications based on race carry the danger of stigmatic harm. Unless they are reserved for remedial settings, they may in fact promote notions of racial inferiority and lead to the politics of racial hostility."

Finally, the use of race to achieve diversity undercuts the ultimate goal of the Fourteenth Amendment: the end of racially motivated state action. Justice Powell's conception of race as a "plus" factor would allow race always to be a potential factor in admissions decisionmaking. While Justice Blackmun

recognized the tension inherent in using race-conscious remedies to achieve a race-neutral society, he nevertheless accepted it as necessary. Several Justices who, unlike Justices Powell and Blackmun, are still on the Court, have now renounced toleration of this tension, however. *See Croson* (plurality opinion of O'Connor, J.) ("The dissent's watered down version of equal protection review effectively assures that race will always be relevant in American life, and that the 'ultimate goal' of 'eliminat[ing] entirely from government decisionmaking such irrelevant factors as a human being's race . . . will never be achieved.") (quoting *Wygant* [Stevens, J., dissenting]).

In sum, the use of race to achieve a diverse student body, whether as a proxy for permissible characteristics, simply cannot be a state interest compelling enough to meet the steep standard of strict scrutiny. These latter factors may, in fact, turn out to be substantially correlated with race, but the key is that race itself not be taken into account. Thus, that portion of the district court's opinion upholding the diversity rationale is reversibly flawed.

B

We now turn to the district court's determination that "the remedial purpose of the law school's affirmative action program is a compelling government objective." The plaintiffs argue that the court erred by finding that the law school could employ racial criteria to remedy the present effects of past discrimination in Texas's primary and secondary schools. The plaintiffs contend that the proper unit for analysis is the law school, and the state has shown no recognizable present effects of the law school's past discrimination. The law school, in response, notes Texas's well-documented history of discrimination in education and argues that its effects continue today at the law school, both in the level of educational attainment of the average minority applicant and in the school's reputation.

In contrast to its approach to the diversity rationale, a majority of the Supreme Court has held that a state actor may racially classify where it has a "strong basis in the evidence for its conclusion that remedial action was necessary." *Croson* (quoting *Wygant*). Generally, "[i]n order to justify an affirmative action program, the State must show there are 'present effects of past discrimination.'" *Hopwood v. Texas*

("*Hopwood I*") (quoting *Podberesky v. Kirwan*); *see also Wygant* (opining that "in order to remedy the effects of prior discrimination, it may be necessary to take race into account") (opinion of Powell, J.).

Because a state does not have a compelling state interest in remedying the present effects of past *societal* discrimination, however, we must examine the district court's legal determination that the relevant governmental entity is the system of education within the state as a whole. Moreover, we also must review the court's identification of what types of present effects of past discrimination, if proven, would be sufficient under strict scrutiny review. Finally, where the state actor puts forth a remedial justification for its racial classifications, the district court must make a "factual determination" as to whether remedial action is necessary. *Wygant.* We review such factual rulings for clear error.

1.

The Supreme Court has "insisted upon some showing of prior discrimination by the governmental unit involved before allowing limited use of racial classifications in order to remedy such discrimination." *Wygant* (plurality opinion of Powell, J.) (citing *Hazelwood School Dist. v. United States*). In *Wygant,* the Court analyzed a collective bargaining agreement between a school board and a teacher's union that allowed the board to give minorities preferential treatment in the event of layoffs. A plurality rejected the theory that such a program was justified because it provided minority role models. Such a claim was based upon remedying "societal discrimination," a rationale the Court consistently has rejected as a basis for affirmative action. Accordingly, the state's use of remedial racial classifications is limited to the harm caused by a specific state actor.

Moreover, the plurality in *Wygant* held that before a state actor properly could implement such a plan, it "must ensure that . . . it has strong evidence that remedial action is warranted" (O'Connor, J., concurring in part and concurring in judgment). The plurality felt that "[i]n the absence of particularized findings, a court could uphold remedies that are ageless in their reach into the past, and timeless in their ability to affect the future."

The *Croson* Court further discussed how to identify the relevant past discriminator. Writing for the Court, Justice O'Connor struck down a minority business set-aside program implemented by the City of Richmond and justified on remedial grounds. While the district court opined that sufficient evidence had been found by the city to believe that such a program was necessary to remedy the present effects of past discrimination in the construction industry, the Court held:

> Like the "role model" theory employed in *Wygant,* a generalized assertion that there had been past discrimination in an entire industry provides no guidance for a legislative body to determine the precise scope of the injury it seeks to remedy. It 'has no logical stopping point.' *Wygant* (plurality opinion). 'Relief' for such an ill-defined wrong could extend until the percentage of public contracts awarded to [minority businesses] in Richmond mirrored the percentage of minorities in the population as a whole.

The Court refused to accept indicia of past discrimination in anything but "the Richmond construction industry."

In addition, in a passage of particular significance to the instant case, the Court analogized the employment contractor situation to that of higher education and noted that "[l]ike claims that discrimination in primary and secondary schooling justifies a rigid racial preference in medical school admissions, an amorphous claim that there has been past discrimination in a particular industry cannot justify the use of an unyielding quota." Such claims were based upon "sheer speculation" about how many minorities would be in the contracting business absent past discrimination.

Applying the teachings of *Croson* and *Wygant,* we conclude that the district court erred in expanding the remedial justification to reach all public education within the State of Texas. The Supreme Court repeatedly has warned that the use of racial remedies must be carefully limited, and a remedy reaching all education within a state addresses a putative injury that is vague and amorphous. It has "no logical stopping point."

The district court's holding employs no viable limiting principle. If a state can "remedy" the present effects of past discrimination in its primary and secondary schools, it also would be allowed to award broad-based preferences in hiring, government contracts, licensing, and any other state activity that in some way is affected by the educational attainment of the applicants. This very argument was made in *Croson* and rejected:

> The "evidence" relied upon by the dissent, history of school desegregation in Richmond and numerous congressional reports, does little to define the scope of any injury to minority contractors in Richmond or the necessary remedy. The factors relied upon by the dissent could justify a preference of any size or duration.

The defendants' argument here is equally expansive.

Strict scrutiny is meant to ensure that the purpose of a racial preference is remedial. Yet when one state actor begins to justify racial preferences based upon the actions of other state agencies, the remedial actor's competence to determine the existence and scope of the harm—and the appropriate reach of the remedy—is called into question. The school desegregation cases, for example, concentrate on school districts—singular government units—and the use of interdistrict remedies is strictly limited. Thus, one justification for limiting the remedial powers of a state actor is that the specific agency involved is best able to measure the harm of its past discrimination.

Here, however, the law school has no comparative advantage in measuring the present effects of discrimination in primary and secondary schools in Texas. Such a task becomes even more improbable where, as here, benefits are conferred on students who attended out-of-state or private schools for such education. Such boundless "remedies" raise a constitutional concern beyond mere competence. In this situation, an inference is raised that the program was the result of racial social engineering rather than a desire to implement a remedy.

No one disputes that in the past, Texas state actors have discriminated against some minorities in public schools. In this sense, some lingering effects of such discrimination is not "societal," if that term is meant to exclude all state action. But the very program at issue here shows how remedying such past wrongs may be expanded beyond any reasonable limits.

Even if, *arguendo,* the state is the proper government unit to scrutinize, the law school's admissions program would not withstand our review. For the admissions scheme to pass constitutional muster, the State of Texas, through its legislature, would have to find that past segregation has present effects; it would have to determine the magnitude of those present effects; and it would need to limit carefully the "plus" given to applicants to remedy that harm. A broad program that sweeps in all minorities with a remedy that is in no way related to past harms cannot survive constitutional scrutiny. Obviously, none of those predicates has been satisfied here.

We further reject the proposition that the University of Texas System, rather than the law school, is the appropriate governmental unit for measuring a constitutional remedy. The law school operates as a functionally separate unit within the system. As with all law schools, it maintains its own separate admissions program. The law school hires faculty members that meet the unique requirements of a law school and has its own deans for administrative purposes. Thus, for much the same reason that we rejected the educational system as the proper measure—generally ensuring that the legally-imposed racially discriminatory program is remedial—we conclude that the University of Texas System is itself too expansive an entity to scrutinize for past discrimination.

In sum, for purposes of determining whether the law school's admissions system properly can act as a remedy for the present effects of past discrimination, we must identify the law school as the relevant alleged past discriminator. The fact that the law school ultimately may be subject to the directives of others, such as the board of regents, the university president, or the legislature, does not change the fact that the relevant putative discriminator in this case is still the law school. In order for any of these entities to direct a racial preference program at the law school, it must be because of past wrongs at that school.

2.

Next, the relevant governmental discriminator must prove that there are present effects of past discrimination of the type that justify the racial classifications at issue:

> To have a present effect of past discrimination sufficient to justify the program, the party seeking to implement the program must, at a minimum, prove that the effect it proffers is caused by the past discrimination and that the effect is of sufficient magnitude to justify the program.

Podberesky v. Kirwan (4th Cir. 1994). Moreover, as part of showing that the alleged present effects of past discrimination in fact justify the racial preference program at issue, the law school must show that it adopted the program specifically to remedy the identified present effects of the past discrimination.

Here, according to the district court: "The evidence presented at trial indicates those effects include the law school's lingering reputation in the minority community, particularly with prospective students, as a "white" school; an underrepresentation of minorities in the student body; and some perception that the law school is a hostile environment for minorities." Plaintiffs now argue that these three alleged effects are at most examples of societal discrimination, which the Supreme Court has found not to be a valid remedial basis. "The effects must themselves be examined to see whether they were caused by the past discrimination and whether they are of a type that justifies the program." *Podberesky*.

As a legal matter, the district court erred in concluding that the first and third effects it identified—bad reputation and hostile environment—were sufficient to sustain the use of race in the admissions process. The Fourth Circuit examined similar arguments in *Podberesky*, a recent case that struck down the use of race-based scholarships. The university in that case sought, in part, to justify a separate scholarship program based solely upon race because of the university's "poor reputation within the African-American community" and because "the atmosphere on campus [was] perceived as being hostile to African-American students."

The *Podberesky* court rejected the notion that either of these rationales could support the single-race scholarship program. The court reasoned that any poor reputation by the school "is tied solely to knowledge of the University's discrimination before it admitted African-American students." The court found that "mere knowledge of historical fact is not the kind of present effect that can justify a race-exclusive remedy. If it were otherwise, as long as there are people who have access to history books, there will be programs such as this."

We concur in the Fourth Circuit's observation that knowledge of historical fact simply cannot justify current racial classifications. Even if, as the defendants argue, the law school may have a bad reputation in the minority community, "[t]he case

against race-based preferences does not rest on the sterile assumption that American society is untouched or unaffected by the tragic oppression of its past." *Maryland Troopers Ass'n v. Evans* (4th Cir. 1993). "Rather, it is the very enormity of that tragedy that lends resolve to the desire to never repeat it, and find a legal order in which distinctions based on race shall have no place." Moreover, we note that the law school's argument is even weaker than that of the university in *Podberesky,* as there is no dispute that the law school has never had an admissions policy that excluded Mexican Americans on the basis of race.

The *Podberesky* court rejected the hostile-environment claims by observing that the "effects"—that is, racial tensions—were the result of present societal discrimination. There was simply no showing of action by the university that contributed to any racial tension. Similarly, one cannot conclude that the law school's past discrimination has created any current hostile environment for minorities. While the school once did practice *de jure* discrimination in denying admission to blacks, the Court in *Sweatt v. Painter* (1950), struck down the law school's program. Any other discrimination by the law school ended in the 1960's.

By the late 1960's, the school had implemented its first program designed to recruit minorities, and it now engages in an extensive minority recruiting program that includes a significant amount of scholarship money. The vast majority of the faculty, staff, and students at the law school had absolutely nothing to do with any discrimination that the law school practiced in the past.

In such a case, one cannot conclude that a hostile environment is the present effect of past discrimination. Any racial tension at the law school is most certainly the result of present societal discrimination and, if anything, is contributed to, rather than alleviated by, the overt and prevalent consideration of race in admissions.

Even if the law school's alleged current lingering reputation in the minority community—and the perception that the school is a hostile environment for minorities—were considered to be the present effects of past discrimination, rather than the result of societal discrimination, they could not constitute compelling state interests justifying the use of racial classifications in admissions. A bad reputation within the minority community is alleviated not by the consideration of race in admissions, but by school action designed directly to enhance its reputation in that community.

Minority students who are aided by the law school's racial preferences have already made the decision to apply, despite the reputation. And, while prior knowledge that they will get a "plus" might make potential minorities more likely to apply, such an inducement does nothing, *per se,* to change any hostile environment. As we have noted, racial preferences, if anything, can compound the problem of a hostile environment.

The law school wisely concentrates only on the second effect the district court identified: underrepresentation of minorities because of past discrimination. The law school argues that we should consider the prior discrimination by the State of Texas and its educational system rather than of the law school. The school contends that this prior discrimination by the state had a direct effect on the educational attainment of the pool of minority applicants and that the discriminatory admissions program was implemented partially to discharge the school's duty of eliminating the vestiges of past segregation.

As we have noted, the district court accepted the law school's argument that past discrimination on the part of the Texas school system (including primary and secondary schools), reaching back perhaps as far as the education of the parents of today's students, justifies the current use of racial classifications.

No one disputes that Texas has a history of racial discrimination in education. We have already discussed, however, that the *Croson* Court unequivocally restricted the proper scope of the remedial interest to the state actor that had previously discriminated. The district court squarely found that "[i]n recent history, there is no evidence of overt officially sanctioned discrimination at the University of Texas." As a result, past discrimination in education, other than at the law school, cannot justify the present consideration of race in law school admissions.

The law school now attempts to circumvent this result by claiming that its racial preference program is really a "State of Texas" plan rather than a law school program. Under the law school's reading of the facts, its program was the direct result of the state's negotiations with what was then the United States Department of Health, Education and Welfare's Office for Civil Rights (OCR). To bring the Texas public higher education system into compliance with title VI, the state adopted the so-called "Texas Plan."

In light of our preceding discussion on the relevant governmental unit, this argument is inapposite. Even if the law school were specifically ordered to adopt a racial preference program, its implementation at the law school would have to meet the requirements of strict scrutiny.

Moreover, these alleged actions in the 1980's are largely irrelevant for purposes of this appeal. There is no indication that the Texas Plan imposed a direct obligation upon the law school. To the contrary, the law school's admissions program was self-initiated. Moreover, the current admissions program was formulated primarily in the 1990's, and the district court did not hold otherwise. ("Against this historical backdrop [including Texas's dealing with the OCR], the law school's commitment to affirmative action in the admissions process evolved.") Thus it is no more correct to say that the State of Texas implemented the program at issue than it is to assert that the Commonwealth of Virginia, not the City of Richmond, was responsible for the minority set-aside program in *Croson.*

The district court also sought to find a remedial justification for the use of race and, at the same time, attempted to distinguish *Croson* using *United States* v. *Fordice* (1992). The court held that the law school had a compelling interest to "desegregate" the school through affirmative action. The reliance upon *Fordice* is misplaced, however. The district court held that *Fordice*'s mandate to schools "to eliminate every vestige of racial segregation and discrimination" made *Croson* inapplicable, and reasoned that this mandate includes the effects of such prior practices or policies.

Fordice does not overrule *Croson.* The central holding of *Fordice* is that a state or one of its subdivisions must act to repudiate the continuing "policies or practices" of discrimination. In other words, a state has an affirmative duty to remove policies, tied to the past, by which it continues to discriminate. The *Fordice* Court did not address, in any way, a state actor's duty to counter the present effects of past discrimination that it did not cause.

In sum, the law school has failed to show a compelling state interest in remedying the present effects of past discrimination sufficient to maintain the use of race in its admissions system. Accordingly, it is unnecessary for us to examine the district court's determination that the law school's admissions program was not narrowly tailored to meet the compelling interests that the district court erroneously perceived. . . .

Wiener, Circuit Judge, specially concurring.

"We judge best when we judge least, particularly in controversial matters of high public interest." In this and every other appeal, we should decide only the case before us, and should do so on the narrowest possible basis. Mindful of this credo, I concur in part and, with respect, specially concur in part.

The sole substantive issue in this appeal is whether the admissions process employed by the law school for 1992 meets muster under the Equal Protection Clause of the Fourteenth Amendment. The law school offers alternative justifications for its race-based admissions process, each of which, it insists, is a compelling interest: (1) remedying the present effects of past discrimination (present effects) and (2) providing the educational benefits that can be obtained only when the student body is diverse (diversity). As to present effects, I concur in the panel opinion's analysis: Irrespective of whether the law school or the University of Texas system as a whole is deemed the relevant governmental unit to be tested, neither has established the existence of present effects of past discrimination sufficient to justify the use of a racial classification. As to diversity, however, I respectfully disagree with the panel opinion's conclusion that diversity can never be a compelling governmental interest in a public graduate school. Rather than attempt to decide that issue, I would take a considerably narrower path—and, I believe, a more appropriate one—to reach an equally narrow result: I would assume *arguendo* that diversity can be a compelling interest but conclude that the admissions process here under scrutiny was not narrowly tailored to achieve diversity. . . .

F. Test For Narrow Tailoring

When strictly scrutinizing a racial classification for narrow tailoring, the first question is "What is the purpose of this racial classification?" The present ef-

fects rationale having proven feckless in this case, today's answer to that first question is a given: The law school's purpose is diversity. Accordingly, I perceive the next question to be, "Was the law school's 1992 admissions process, with one TI range for blacks, another for Mexican Americans, and a third for other races, narrowly tailored to achieve diversity?" I conclude that it was not. Focusing as it does on blacks and Mexican Americans only, the law school's 1992 admissions process misconceived the concept of diversity, as did California's in the view of Justice Powell: Diversity which furthers a compelling state interest "encompasses a far broader array of qualifications and characteristics of which racial or ethnic origin is but a single though important element."

When the selective race-based preferences of the law school's 1992 admissions process are evaluated under Justice Powell's broad, multifaceted concept of diversity, that process fails to satisfy the requirements of the Constitution. The law school purported to accomplish diversity by ensuring an increase in the numbers of only blacks and Mexican Americans in each incoming class to produce percentages—virtually indistinguishable from quotas—of approximately five and ten percent, respectively. Yet blacks and Mexican Americans are but two among any number of racial or ethnic groups that could and presumably should contribute to genuine diversity. By singling out only those two ethnic groups, the initial stage of the law school's 1992 admissions process ignored altogether non-Mexican Hispanic Americans, Asian Americans, and Native Americans, to name but a few.

In this light, the limited racial effects of the law school's preferential admissions process, targeting exclusively blacks and Mexican Americans, more closely resembles a set aside or quota system for those two disadvantaged minorities than it does an academic admissions program narrowly tailored to achieve true diversity. I concede that the law school's 1992 admissions process would increase the percentages of black faces and brown faces in that year's entering class. But facial diversity is not true diversity, and a system thus conceived and implemented simply is not narrowly tailored to achieve diversity.

Accordingly, I would find that the law school's race-based 1992 admissions process was not narrowly tailored to achieve diversity and hold it constitutionally invalid on that basis. . . .

QUESTIONS FOR REFLECTION

1. Why, according to Judge Smith, is diversity not a compelling state interest?

2. Why does Judge Smith reject a remedial justification for the law school's admissions procedures?

3. Why does Judge Wiener contend that the admissions process was not narrowly tailored?

4. On which classical theories of justice is the *Hopwood* decision most readily justifiable? On which is it problematic?

ANTONIN SCALIA

The Disease as a Cure

Antonin Scalia is Justice of the United States Supreme Court. (Source: From the Washington University Law Quarterly, *1979, no. 1. Copyright © 1979. Reprinted by permission.)*

I have grave doubts about the wisdom of where we are going in affirmative action, and in equal protection generally. I find this area an embarrassment to teach. Here, as in some other fields of constitutional law, it is increasingly difficult to pretend to one's students that the decisions of the Supreme Court are tied together by threads of logic and analysis—as opposed to what seems to be the fact that the decisions of each of the justices on the court are tied together by threads of social preference and predisposition. Frankly, I do not have it in me to play the game of distinguishing and reconciling the cases in this utterly confused field.

The chaos in which we find ourselves is exemplified well enough by *Bakke* itself. Four of the justices tell us that both the Constitution and Title VI permit racial preference; four of the justices tell us that whatever the Constitution may permit, Title VI forbids it. And the law of the land, pronounced by the one remaining justice, apparently is that Title VI is no different from the Constitution; governmental racial distinctions of any sort are "odious to a free people" and their validity "inherently suspect"; they must pass "the most exacting judicial examination," and can only be justified by a "compelling" state interest. We later learn that the "compelling" interest at issue in *Bakke* is the enormously important goal of assuring that in medical school—where we are dealing with students in an age range of twenty-two to twenty-eight, or in Bakke's case, thirty-three to thirty-nine—we will expose these impressionable youngsters to a great diversity of people. We want

them to work and play with pianists, maybe flute players. We want people from the country, from the city. We want bespectacled chess champions and football players. And, oh yes, we may want some racial minorities, too. If that is all it takes to overcome the presumptions against discrimination by race, we have witnessed an historic trivialization of the Constitution. Justice Powell's opinion, which we must work with as the law of the land, strikes me as an excellent compromise between two committees of the American Bar Association on some insignificant legislative proposal. But it is thoroughly unconvincing as an honest, hard-minded, reasoned analysis of an important provision of the Constitution.

There is, of course, a lot of pretense or self-delusion (you can take your choice) in all that pertains to affirmative action. Does anyone really think, for example, that the situation has changed at Davis? So instead of reserving class places for minority students, the school will open all slots to all applicants, but in choosing among them, will take into account the need for diversity—piano players, football players, people from the country, minority students, etc. When it comes to choosing among these manifold diversities in God's creation, will being a piano player, do you suppose, be regarded as more important than having yellow skin? Or will coming from Oshkosh, Wisconsin, be regarded as more important than having a Spanish surname? It will be very difficult to tell.

Only two results of the *Bakke* decision are certain. First, the judgments that the Davis medical school makes in filling these 100 slots will be effectively un-appealable to the courts. (There is no way to estab-lish, for example, that the diversity value of New York City oboists has not been accorded its proper weight.) Second, when all is said and done, it is a safe bet that though there may not be a piano player in the class, there are going to be close to sixteen mi-nority students. And I suspect that Justice Powell's delightful compromise was drafted precisely to achieve these results—just as, it has been charged, the Harvard College "diversity admissions" program, which Mr. Justice Powell's opinion so generously praises, was designed to reduce as inconspicuously as possible the disproportionate number of New York Jewish students that a merit admissions system had produced.

Examples abound to support my suggestion that this area is full of pretense or self-delusion. Affirma-tive action requirements under Title VI and VII are said repeatedly "not to require the hiring of any un-qualified individuals." That gives one a great feeling of equal justice until it is analyzed. Unfortunately, the world of employment applicants does not divide itself merely into "qualified" and "unqualified" indi-viduals. There is a whole range of ability—from un-qualified, through minimally qualified, qualified, well qualified, to outstanding. If I cannot get Leon-tyne Price to sing a concert I have scheduled, I may have to settle for Erma Glatt. La Glatt has a pretty good voice, but not as good as Price. Is she unquali-fied? Not really—she has sung other concerts with modest success. But she is just not as good as Price. Any system that coerces me to hire her in preference to Price, because of her race, degrades the quality of my product and discriminates on racial grounds against Price. And it is no answer to either of these charges that Glatt is "qualified." To seek to assuage either the employer's demand for quality or the dis-favored applicant's demand for equal treatment by saying there is no need to hire any unqualified indi-viduals is a sort of intellectual shell game, which di-verts attention from the major issue by firmly responding to a minor one.

But, of course, even the disclaimer of compulsion to hire unqualified individuals loses something when it is translated into practice by the advocates of affir-mative action. Consider, for example, the following statement by Professor Edwards: "This is not to say that blacks or women must be thrust into positions for which they are not qualified; however, when the choice is between white males and other qualified or qualifiable individuals, we should open the available positions to those who formerly could not occupy them." Note that what begins with the ritualistic de-nial of any intent to foster hiring of the unqualified imperceptibly shifts to a call for hiring of the "quali-fiable," which surely must be a subcategory of the unqualified. It is typical of the confused level of de-bate that characterizes this field.

Another example of pretense or self-delusion is the Department of Labor's regulations concerning goals for hiring to overcome "underutilization": "The purpose of a contractor's establishment and use of goals is to insure that he meets his affirmative action obligation. It is not intended and should not be used to discriminate against any applicant or employee because of race, color, religion, sex, or national ori-gin." This is, quite literally, incredible. Once there is established a numerical figure, the failure to meet it will have material, adverse consequences; namely, the substantial risk of cutoff of government contracts and the substantial certainty of disruptive and ex-pensive government investigations. All that we know about human nature and human motivations indi-cates quite clearly that discrimination often will be produced in an effort to meet or exceed the magic number. I am a businessman who has, let us say, six more jobs to fill, and I am three short of my minority "goal." Reaching the goal will render my government contracts secure and will save thousands of dollars in the expenses necessary to comply with the demands of an equal employment investigation. If I consult my self-interest, which people tend to do, I will hire three minority applicants, even if they are somewhat less qualified than others. When the results that are inevitable are compared with the results that are said to be "intended," one must conclude that the drafter of the regulation is either fooling us or fooling him-self. I appreciate, of course, that any antidiscrimina-tion law with teeth in it will generate *some* pressures to favor minority groups. But that is worlds away from the "we-need-three-more-nonwhites" attitude that is the utterly predictable result of so-called "goals."

Judge Wisdom, dissenting in the *Weber* case, makes the following statement: "The Union's duty to bargain in good faith for all its members [an obliga-tion imposed by law] does not prevent it from fairly advancing the national policy against discrimination, even if that requires assisting some of its members more than others." One has to be reminded of the line from *Animal Farm,* to the effect that all animals are created equal but some are more equal than others. And one cannot help but think that a paraphrase of Judge Wisdom's statement would fit very nicely in the mouth of a good old-fashioned racist employer: "We favor all applicants, but we favor white applicants more than others." It is very difficult to take Judge Wisdom's argument as a serious attempt to identify and grapple with the real issue rather than as an elaborate intellectual word game.

Another pretense or self-delusion—perhaps the grandest of all—is the notion that what was involved in the *Weber* case is voluntary private discrimination against whites. As Judge Wisdom put it: "While the government might not be able to require that restorative justice be done, neither should it prevent it." Fancy that! To think that the real issue in *Weber,* and presumably all those "reverse discrimination" cases, is damnable federal regulation: whether the federal government should be able to *prevent* the discrimination against better-qualified employees, which Kaiser and thousands of other businesses throughout the country are champing at the bit to engage in! That is, of course, chimerical. Nobody really believes that Kaiser would have established the challenged program, or the union permitted it, without the "incentive" of federal administrative regulations, which in effect makes the application of what Judge Wisdom calls "restorative justice" a condition for the award of government contracts and for the avoidance of expensive litigation in and out of the courts. To discuss the issue in the fictitious context of voluntarism not only makes any intelligently reasoned decision impossible in the particular case, but poisons the well of legal discourse.

The Restorative Justice Handicapping System

That last quotation concerning "restorative justice" may explain why I feel a bit differently about these issues than, for example, Judge Wisdom or Justice Powell or Justice White. When John Minor Wisdom speaks of "restorative justice," I am reminded of the story about the Lone Ranger and his "faithful Indian companion" Tonto. If you recall the famous radio serial, you know that Tonto never said much, but what he did say was (disguised beneath a Hollywood-Indian dialect) wisdom of an absolutely Solomonic caliber. On one occasion, it seems that the Lone Ranger was galloping along with Tonto, heading eastward, when they saw coming towards them a large band of Mohawk Indians in full war dress. The Lone Ranger reigns in his horse, turns to Tonto, and asks, "Tonto, what should we do?" Tonto says, "Ugh, ride-um west." So they wheel around and gallop off to the west until suddenly they encounter a large band of Sioux heading straight toward them. The Lone Ranger asks, "Tonto, what should we do?" Tonto says, "Ugh, ride-um north." So, they turn around and ride north, and, sure enough, there's a whole tribe of Iroquois headed straight towards them. The Ranger asks, "Tonto, what should we do?" And Tonto says, "Ugh, ride-um south," which they do until they see a war party of Apaches coming right for them. The Lone Ranger says, "Tonto, what should we do?" And Tonto says, "Ugh, what you mean, 'we,' white man?"

I have somewhat the same feeling when John Minor Wisdom talks of the evils that "we" whites have done to blacks and that "we" must now make restoration for. My father came to this country when he was a teenager. Not only had he never profited from the sweat of any black man's brow, I don't think he had ever seen a black man. There are, of course, many white ethnic groups that came to this country in great numbers relatively late in its history—Italians, Jews, Irish, Poles—who not only took no part in, and derived no profit from, the major historic suppression of the currently acknowledged minority groups, but were, in fact, themselves the object of discrimination by the dominant Anglo-Saxon majority. If I can recall in my lifetime the obnoxious "White Trade Only" signs in shops in Washington, D.C., others can recall "Irish Need Not Apply" signs in Boston, three or four decades earlier. To be sure, in relatively recent years some or all of these groups have been the beneficiaries of discrimination against blacks, or have themselves practiced discrimination. But to compare their racial debt—I must use that term, since the concept of "restorative justice" implies it; there is no creditor without a debtor—with that of those who plied the slave trade, and who maintained a formal caste system for many years thereafter, is to confuse a mountain with a molehill. Yet curiously enough, we find that in the system of restorative justice established by the Wisdoms and the Powells and the Whites, it is precisely *these* groups that do most of the restoring. It is they who, to a disproportionate degree, are the competitors with the urban blacks and Hispanics for jobs, housing, education—all those things that enable one to scramble to the top of the social heap where one can speak eloquently (and quite safely) of restorative justice.

To remedy this inequity, I have developed a modest proposal, which I call RJHS—the Restorative Justice Handicapping System. I only have applied it thus far to restorative justice for the Negro, since obviously he has been the victim of the most widespread and systematic exploitation in this country; but a similar system could be devised for other creditor-races, creditor-sexes, or minority groups. Under my system each individual in society would be assigned at birth Restorative Justice Handicapping Points, determined on the basis of his or her ancestry. Obviously, the highest number of points must go to what we may loosely call the Aryans—the Powells, the Whites, the Stewarts, the Burgers, and, in fact (curiously enough), the entire composition of the present Supreme Court, with the exception of Justice Marshall. This grouping of north European races obviously played the greatest role in the suppression of the American black. But unfortunately, what was good enough for Nazi Germany is not good enough for our purposes. We must further divide the Aryans into subgroups. As I have suggested, the Irish (having arrived later) probably owe less of a racial debt than the Germans, who in turn surely owe less of a racial debt than the English. It will, to be sure, be difficult to draw precise lines and establish the correct number of handicapping points, but having reviewed the Supreme Court's jurisprudence on abortion, I am convinced that our justices would not shrink from the task.

Of course, the mere identification of the various degrees of debtor-races is only part of the job. One must in addition account for the dilution of bloodlines by establishing, for example, a half-Italian, half-Irish handicapping score. There are those who will scoff at this as a refinement impossible of achievement, but I am confident it can be done, and can even be extended to take account of dilution of

blood in creditor-races as well. Indeed, I am informed (though I have not had the stomach to check) that a system to achieve the latter objective is already in place in federal agencies—specifying, for example, how much dilution of blood deprives one of his racial-creditor status as a "Hispanic" under affirmative action programs. Moreover, it should not be forgotten that we have a rich body of statutory and case law from the Old South to which we can turn for guidance in this exacting task.

But I think it unnecessary to describe the Restorative Justice Handicapping System any further. I trust you find it thoroughly offensive, as I do. It, and the racist concept of restorative justice of which it is merely the concrete expression, is fundamentally contrary to the principles that govern, and should govern, our society. I owe no man anything, nor he me, because of the blood that flows in our veins. To go down that road (or I should say to return down that road), even behind a banner as gleaming as restorative justice, is to make a frightening mistake. This is not to say that I have no obligation to my fellow citizens who are black. I assuredly do—not because of their race or because of any special debt that my bloodline owes to theirs, but because they have (many of them) special needs, and they are (all of them) my countrymen and (as I believe) my brothers. This means that I am entirely in favor of according the poor inner-city child, who happens to be black, advantages and preferences not given to my own children because they do not need them. But I am not willing to prefer the son of a prosperous and well-educated black doctor or lawyer—solely because of his race—to the son of a recent refugee from Eastern Europe who is working as a manual laborer to get his family ahead. The affirmative action system now in place will produce the latter result because it is based upon concepts of racial indebtedness and racial entitlement rather than individual worth and individual need; that is to say, because it is racist.

Evil Fruits of a Bad Seed

But I not only question the principle upon which racial affirmative action is based; I even question its effectiveness in achieving the desired goal of advancing a particular race. Professor Edwards, for example, states in one of his pieces that: "The continued existence of long-standing myths about the inherent inability of blacks to perform certain work has also contributed to their exclusion from significant jobs in the employment market." That strikes me as true, but one may well wonder whether the prescribed solution of affirmative action based on race will eliminate the myths rather than assure their perpetuation. When one reads the *Bakke* case, the most striking factual data is the enormous divergence in the average college grades and average test scores of the regular admittees and the special (minority) admittees of the Davis medical school for the years Bakke was rejected. In 1973 they looked like this:

	Grade Point Average		Medical College Admission Test			
	Science	Overall	Verbal	Quanti-tative	Science	Gen'l Info.
Regular	3.51	3.49	81	76	83	69
Minority	2.62	2.88	46	24	35	33

Do you suppose the "image" of minority groups has been improved by this? I suggest that, to the contrary, the very ability of minority group members to distinguish themselves and their race has been dreadfully impaired. To put the issue to you in its starkest form: If you must select your brain surgeon from among recent graduates of Davis medical school and have nothing to go on but their names and pictures, would you not be well advised—playing the odds—to eliminate all minority group members? It is well known to the public that the outstanding institutions of higher education graduate the best and the brightest principally through the simple device of admitting only the best and the brightest. And it is obvious to the public that (to the extent these schools flunk *anyone* out) the same factor that produced special admissions will also tend to produce special retention and, ultimately, special graduation. Thus, insofar as "public image" is concerned, the immediate and predictable effect of affirmative action is to establish a second-class, "minority" degree, which is a less certain certificate of quality. In other words, we have established within our institutions of higher education (and wherever else racial affirmative action is applied) a regime reminiscent of major league baseball in the years before Jackie Robinson: a separate "league" for minority students, which makes it difficult for the true excellence of the minority star to receive his or her deserved acknowledgment. To be sure, the students' teachers, and those of us who have the opportunity of examining the students' transcripts, can tell who is or is not outstanding. But those members of the public about whom Professor Edwards is concerned—those who judge by generalities, or by "image," if you will—are they likely to think better or worse of minority graduates? The person who was so ignorant as to say "a Negro simply cannot become a truly outstanding doctor" can now plausibly add "—and the fact that he obtained a degree from one of the best medical schools in the country doesn't prove a thing."

In response to this, the advocates of racial affirmative action might say the following: "Even if, as you say, our system cannot give an increased number of minority students a first-class Davis degree—and indeed, even if it may, as you say, make it impossible for *any* minority student to obtain a first-class Davis degree—at least it gives more minority students the concrete benefits of a first-class Davis education." But that is questionable pedagogy. In grammar school, at least, where the politics of race do not yet seem to have permeated pupil assignment within schools, we do not "help" a disadvantaged student by admitting him into a faster group. Why should college and graduate school be different? During the guns-on-campus disturbances at Cornell, one-half of that school's black students were on academic probation. Why? They were neither stupid nor lazy. As a whole their test scores were in the *upper* 25 per cent of all students admitted to college. But the Cornell student body as a whole was in the upper one percent. Was it really "helping" these young men and women, either from the standpoint of their personal intellectual development or from the standpoint of their "image" as minority graduates in later life, to place them in an environment where it was quite probable (as probable as such things can ever be) that they did not belong? It solved the political problems of the school administrators, no doubt. And it may have given the administrators, faculty, and alumni the warm feeling that they were doing their part (at no expense, by and large, to their own children) for "restorative justice." But did it really help these young men and women? With few exceptions, I suspect not.

I could mention other harmful, practical effects of racial affirmative action. It has been suggested, for example, that one consequence is to encourage the location of industries in areas where affirmative action problems are likely to be reduced; that is, away from the inner cities where the game of racial percentages produces significantly higher quotas (or, if you prefer, goals). In any case, it is a fact that statistics show an increase in the economic status of blacks in the years immediately preceding affirmative action and a decline thereafter. Whatever else the program may be, it is not demonstrably effective.

Conclusion

I am, in short, opposed to racial affirmative action for reasons of both principle and practicality. Sex-based affirmative action presents somewhat different constitutional issues, but it seems to me an equally poor idea, for many of the reasons suggested above. I do not, on the other hand, oppose—indeed, I strongly favor—what might be called (but for the coloration that the term has acquired in the context of its past use) "affirmative action programs" of many types of help for the poor and disadvantaged. It may

well be that many, or even most, of these benefited by such programs would be members of minority races that the existing programs exclusively favor. I would not care if *all* of them were. The unacceptable vice is simply selecting or rejecting them *on the basis of their race.*

A person espousing the views I have expressed, of course, exposes himself to charges of, at best, insensitivity or, at worst, bigotry. That is one reason these views are not expressed more often, particularly in academia. Beyond an anticipatory denial, I must content myself with the observation that it must be a queer sort of bigotry indeed, since it is shared by many intelligent members of the alleged target group. Some of the most vocal opposition to racial affirmative action comes from minority group members who have seen the value of their accomplishments debased by the suspicion—no, to be frank, the reality—of a lower standard for their group in the universities and the professions. This new racial presumption, imposed upon those who have lifted themselves above the effects of old racial presumptions, is the most evil fruit of a fundamentally bad seed. From racist principles flow racist results.

QUESTIONS FOR REFLECTION

1. Scalia rejects the justification for affirmative action from rectification or compensation. Why? Do you find his arguments compelling?

2. What harms does affirmative action produce, according to Scalia?

BERNARD R. BOXILL

from *Blacks and Social Justice*

Professor Bernard R. Boxill is a Professor of Philosophy at the University of North Carolina at Chapel Hill. (Source: From Bernard R. Boxill, Blacks and Social Justice, *rev. ed., pp. 147–72. Footnotes have been omitted. Copyright 1984, 1992 by Roman and Littlefield Publishers. Reprinted by permission.)*

Liberals into Former Liberals

As Michael Kinsley has observed in *Harper's,* "No single development of the past fifteen years has turned more liberals into former liberals than affirmative action." This metamorphosis, if it is not merely an unmasking, is ostensibly due to the belief that affirmative action perverts the just goal of civil rights. That goal, protest the disillusioned liberals, is to guarantee that persons be treated as individuals and judged on their merits; but affirmative action, they complain, guarantees that individuals are treated as mere members of racial groups, and their merits disparaged and ignored.

These liberals are not appeased by Allan Bakke's victory in the Supreme Court in 1978. For although the court ruled that Bakke was wrongly denied admission to the medical school at the University of California at Davis, it allowed that race could be used as a factor in considering applicants. As *Time* announced on its cover: "What Bakke Means. Race: Yes. Quotas: No."

As with busing, the arguments for preferential treatment fell into two classes, backward-looking and forward-looking. Backward-looking arguments justify preferential treatment considered as compensation for past and present wrongs done to blacks and their effects. Forward-looking arguments justify preferential treatment considered as a means to present or future goods, particularly equality. Both the assumptions and the aims of these two kinds of argument must be carefully distinguished.

Backward-looking arguments assume that blacks have been, or are being, wronged. Forward-looking arguments assume that blacks are generally inferior to whites in status, education, and income. Backward-looking arguments aim at compensating blacks. Forward-looking arguments aim at improving the status, education, and income of blacks.

The Backward-Looking Argument

The fundamental backward-looking argument is simply stated: Black people have been and are being harmed by racist attitudes and practices. Those wronged deserve compensation. Therefore, black people deserve compensation. Preferential treatment is an appropriate form of compensation for black people. Therefore black people deserve preferential treatment.

Criticism of this argument falls into two main classes: on the one hand, critics charge that the claims to compensation of the black beneficiaries of preferential treatment are unfounded or vacuously satisfied; on the other hand, they charge that these claims are outweighed by other considerations.

The most common version of the first type always uttered by the critic with an air of having played a trump, is that, since those members of groups that have been discriminated against who benefit from preferential hiring must be minimally qualified, they are not the members of the group who deserve compensation. The philosopher Alan Goldman, for example, argues this way: "Since hiring within the preferred group still depends upon relative qualifications and hence upon past opportunities for acquiring qualifications, there is in fact a reverse ratio established between past discriminations and present benefits, so that those who most benefit from the program, those who actually get jobs, are those who least deserve to." But surely a conclusion that preferential hiring is unjustified based on the argument above is a non sequitur. Let us grant that qualified blacks are less deserving of compensation than unqualified blacks, that those who most deserve compensation should be compensated first, and finally that preferential hiring is a form of compensation. How does it follow that preferential hiring of qualified blacks is unjustified? Surely the assumption that unqualified blacks are more deserving of compensation than qualified blacks does not require us to conclude that qualified blacks deserve no compensation. Because I have lost only one leg, I may be less deserving of compensation than another who has lost two legs, but it does not follow that I deserve no compensation at all.

Even Thomas Nagel, one of the country's leading philosophers and a strong defender of preferential treatment on the basis of the forward-looking argument, resorts to this criticism of the backward-looking argument. Thus he labels a "bad" argument, one that maintains that the "beneficiaries of affirmative action deserve it as compensation for past discrimination," because, he says, "no effort is made to give preference to those who have suffered most from discrimination." Indeed, Nagel makes exactly the same point as Goldman: Because the blacks who benefit from preferential treatment are qualified, "they are not necessarily, or even probably the ones who especially deserve it. Women or blacks who don't have the qualifications even to be considered are likely to have been handicapped more by the effects of discrimination than those who receive preference." But for the reasons given, this criticism is bogus. Furthermore, since Nagel defends preferential treatment on forward-looking, egalitarian grounds, this puts him into deeper trouble than it does those who reject preferential treatment altogether.

For, if preferential treatment makes no effort to give preference to those who have suffered most, neither does it make an effort to give preference to those who are most unequal to whites. In other words, if the qualified have suffered least, they are also least unequal, and it seems a bad strategy, if one is aiming for equality, to prefer them. Nagel could object that preferring the qualified is a good egalitarian strategy because it will lead indirectly to equality. But a variant of the idea is open to the advocate of the backward-looking argument. He could argue that preferential treatment of the qualified also helps to compensate the unqualified insofar as it shows them that if one is qualified, being black is no longer a bar to promotion. . . .

To sum up to this point: The criticism of the backward-looking argument for preferential treatment under consideration is unsound in one of its forms, and irrelevant in the other. Insofar as it assumes that many blacks have escaped wrongful harm as a result of discrimination it is unsound. Even if some blacks have escaped harm this would not be sufficient to make preferential treatment unjustified, because the overwhelming majority it benefited would deserve compensation. Insofar as the criticism assumes the black preferred are less wronged or harmed than other blacks it is irrelevant. The backward-looking argument does not exclude compensating unqualified blacks, or deny that compensating unqualified blacks, or deny that they are more deserving of compensation. Neither does it say that qualified blacks must be compensated first. It asserts only that blacks deserve compensation for the wrongful harms of discrimination. Thus, it is unaffected by the claim that qualified blacks may be the least wronged and harmed of blacks. The fact that qualified blacks are wrongfully harmed at all, and that preferential treatment is appropriate compensation, is sufficient justification for it.

Now, I have admitted that it is a weak argument which tries to justify preferential treatment of qualified blacks applying for desirable places and positions on the grounds that, had there been no discrimination, these blacks would probably have qualified for such places and positions without preferential treatment. The key assumption in this argument is simply not plausible. But if we assume that compensation is owed to blacks as a group, then a stronger version of that argument can be advanced, which goes as follows: Blacks as a group have been wronged, and are disadvantaged, by slavery and discrimination. Consequently, blacks as a group deserve compensation. Furthermore, had it not been for slavery and discrimination, blacks as a group would be more nearly equal in income, education, and well-being to other groups who did not suffer from slavery or the extent and kind of discrimination from which blacks have suffered. Consequently, assuming that compensating a group for wrongful disadvantages requires bringing it to the condition it would have been in had it not been wrongfully disadvantaged, compensating blacks as a group requires making them, as a group, more nearly equal to those other groups. But if blacks as a group were more nearly equal in income, education, and well-being to such groups, some blacks would then fill desirable positions. Accordingly, compensating blacks as a group requires putting some blacks in desirable positions. However, only the blacks who are now most qualified can, fittingly, be placed in desirable positions. Hence, even if those blacks are *not* the very ones who would have filled such places and positions had there been no slavery and discrimination, compensating blacks as a group may specifically require preferential treatment of qualified blacks. . . .

. . . We can form some estimate of the assets blacks as a group had before slavery and discrimination. Consequently, we can apply the ideal conception of compensation, and reasonably propose to place blacks as a group in the position they would have occupied had there been no slavery and discrimination. . . .

. . . [I]t has seemed to many critics that preferential treatment, insofar as it involves preferential admissions and hiring, is unfair to young white males. For example, according to Robert K. Fullinwider, a research associate at the Center for Philosophy and Public Policy at the University of Maryland, the compensation argument for preferential treatment confuses the sound compensation principle—"he who wrongs another shall pay for the wrong"—with the "suspect" principle—"he who benefits from a wrong shall pay for the wrong." To clinch the point, Fullinwider asks us to consider the following ingenious example: A neighbor pays a construction company to pave his driveway, but someone maliciously directs the workmen to pave Fullinwider's driveway instead. Fullinwider admits that his neighbor has

been "wronged and damaged" and that he himself has "benefited from the wrong." However, since he is not responsible for the wrong, he denies that he is "morally required to compensate" his neighbor by "paying" him for it.

This example makes us see that not all cases where compensation may be due are straightforward, though one kind of case clearly is. If John steals Jeff's bicycle and "gives" it to me, however innocent I may be, I have no right to it and must return it to Jeff as soon as I discover the theft. Given that this example is unproblematic, in what way does it differ from Fullinwider's, which is problematic?

One difference is that, whereas I can simply hand over Jeff's bicycle to him, Fullinwider cannot simply hand over the pavement in his driveway. It will be objected that the proposal was not that Fullinwider should hand over the pavement, but that he should pay his neighbor for it. But this is a different case. I did not say that I had a duty to pay Jeff for his bicycle. I said that I had a duty to return the bicycle to Jeff. If Jeff told me to keep the bicycle but pay him for it, I do not admit that I would have a duty to do so. I could object fairly that when I accepted the bicycle I did not believe that I would have to pay for it, and if I had thought that I would have to, I might have not accepted it. Paying for the bicycle now would impose on me, because I might have preferred to spend my money in a different way and, being innocent of any wrongdoing, I see no reason why I should be penalized. The point is that though the beneficiary of an injustice has no right to his advantage, if he is innocent of the injustice, he does not deserve to be penalized. Thus, where compensation is concerned, the obligations of the innocent beneficiary of injustice and of the person responsible for the injustice are quite different. Though the former has no right to his benefits, the process of compensation cannot impose any losses on him over and above the loss of his unfair benefits. If compensation is impossible without such loss, it is unjustified. On the other hand, in the case of the person responsible for injustice, even if compensation requires him to give up more than he has unfairly gained, it is still justified.

But, though Fullinwider's example is cogent as far as it goes, it is irrelevant as an argument against preferential hiring. It is cogent as far as it goes because, as the above analysis shows, requiring young white males to pay women and minorities for all the unfair advantages they have enjoyed would indeed be unfair. The advantages cannot, as in my example of the bicycle, simply be transferred from their hands into those of the preferred group. Compensation of this kind would impose on young white males time and effort over and above the cost of the unfair advantages they are required to return. They could justly protest that they are being penalized, because they might not have accepted the advantages had they known what they would cost them—now they are "out" both the advantages and their time and effort. But preferential hiring does not require young white males to pay, at an additional cost to themselves, the price of their advantages. It proposes instead to compensate the injured with goods no one has yet established a right to and therefore in a way that imposes no unfair losses on anyone. And these goods are, of course, jobs.

It may be objected that, although a white male applicant may not have established a right to this or that job, he has a right to fair competition for it, and preferential hiring violates that right. But, on the contrary, by refusing to allow him to get the job because of an unfair advantage, preferential hiring makes the competition fairer. The white male applicant can still complain, of course, that, had he known that preferential hiring would be instituted, he would not have accepted his advantages in the first place. Since, if he knew that preferential hiring would be instituted, he would necessarily also have known that his advantages were unfair, his complaint would amount to his saying that, had he known his advantages were unfair, he would not have accepted them. But then, if he is concerned with fairness, and if preferential hiring makes the competition fairer, he should have no objections to it. Or to state the proposition somewhat less contentiously, preferential hiring imposes no unfair losses on him.

Thus, a fairer application of Fullinwider's example about the driveway to the case of preferential hiring would be as follows: Suppose an "improve-your-neighborhood group" offered a valuable prize for the best driveway on the block. Would Fullinwider be justified in insisting that he deserves to get the prize over his neighbor who has, at further cost to himself, built another, somewhat inferior driveway?

To sum up my discussion of forms of the backward-looking argument for preferential treatment, while I have insisted that all, or nearly all, blacks are victims of racial injustice, I have conceded that it has handicapped some blacks more than others, and that other kinds of injustice have handicapped some whites more than racial injustice has handicapped blacks. Consequently, although the backward-looking argument is the bedrock of the case for preferential treatment, to complete that case we must look forward.

The Forward-Looking Argument

Whereas the backward-looking argument tried to justify preferential treatment as compensation for past wrongful harms, the forward-looking argument tries to justify preferential treatment on the grounds that it may secure greater equality or increase total social utility. Moreover, the fact that blacks were slaves and the victims of discrimination is irrelevant to the forward-looking argument, which, its proponents imply, would not lose force even if blacks had never been slaves and never were discriminated against. All that is relevant to the argument is that blacks are often poor, generally less than equal to whites in education, influence, and income, and preferentially treating them will alleviate their poverty, reduce their inequality, and generally increase total utility.

The forward-looking argument has one very clear advantage over the backward-looking argument. As we have seen, a persistent criticism of the backward-looking argument is that, although some blacks deserve no compensation for discrimination because they have not been harmed by discrimination, they are precisely the ones benefiting from preferential treatment. I have tried to rebut this criticism, but this is unnecessary if the forward-looking argument is adopted. For that argument does not require the assumption that the beneficiaries of preferential treatment have been harmed by discrimination, or even that they have been harmed at all. Indeed, it does not require that they be less than equal to whites, and is consistent with their being relatively privileged. For it endorses a strategy of increasing the incomes and education even of blacks superior in those respects to most whites if, however indirectly, this will, in the long run, effectively increase blacks' equality and increase total social utility.

Now whether or not preferential treatment has such consequences is in the end an empirical question, but some critics, as I will show, insist on concocting specious *a priori* arguments to show that preferential treatment necessarily causes a loss in social utility.

Thus it has been argued that since, by definition, preferential treatment awards positions to the less qualified over the more qualified, and since the more qualified perform more efficiently than the less qualified, therefore preferential treatment causes a loss of utility. But suppose that less qualified blacks are admitted to medical school in preference to more qualified whites, and suppose the resulting black doctors practice in poor black neighborhoods treating serious illnesses, while if the whites they were preferred to had been admitted they would have practiced in affluent white neighborhoods, treating minor illnesses. In that sort of case, it is not at all necessarily true that preferential treatment causes a loss in utility. Some authors try to avoid the force of this argument by switching the basis of their criticism from the fact that preferential treatment may reward the less qualified to the false assertion that preferential treatment may reward the "unqualified." Thus, Goldman reminds us that "all will suffer when unqualified persons occupy many positions." This is criticism of a straw man.

It has also been claimed that the forward-looking argument that preferential treatment increases utility is open to a serious philosophical objection. Thus philosopher George Sher writes that the utilitarian, or forward-looking, defense of preferential treatment is "vulnerable" to the "simple but serious" objection that "if it is acceptable to discriminate in favor of minorities and women when doing so maximizes utility, then it is hard to see why it should not also be acceptable to discriminate against minorities and women when that policy maximizes welfare." And against Thomas Nagel who argues that racial discrimination, unlike reverse discrimination, "has no social advantages . . . and attaches a sense of reduced worth to a feature with which people are born," Sher makes a similar objection. He says that Nagel gives us no reason to believe that "there could never be alternative circumstances in which racial, ethnic, or sexual discrimination had social advantages which did outweigh the sense of reduced worth it produced," and maintains that Nagel still has not shown us that such discrimination is illegitimate under "any circumstances at all."

The serious utilitarian is likely to dismiss Sher's criticisms with the same impatience with which he dismisses the stock criticism that utilitarianism allows slavery. As R. M. Hare notes, it is the "strength" of the utilitarian doctrine that "the utilitarian cannot reason *a priori* that whatever the facts about the world and human nature, slavery is wrong. He has to show it is wrong by showing, through a study of history and other factual observation, that slavery does have the effects (namely the production of misery) that make it wrong." In particular, he is not undone by the arguments of the intuitionist who thinks up "fantastic" examples which show slavery to be right according to the principles of utilitarianism, because these show only that the intuitionist has "lost contact with the actual world." Much the same thing can be said about Sher's notion that there are circumstances in which racial discrimination would be legitimate according to utilitarian principles. . . .

. . . I have used more space in rebutting criticisms than in arguing positively for conclusions. This is because the main arguments for affirmative action are straightforward, and yet philosophers persist in concocting ever more desperately ingenious objections to it. Not that I believe that any one of the various backward- and forward-looking arguments is by itself sufficient to justify affirmative action. Affirmative action is justified by the combined force of these arguments and by the way they complement and support each other. The weaknesses in some are made up by the strengths of others. For example, the weakness in the case for compensation on an individual basis is made up for by the case for compensation on a group basis, and the weaknesses of both these cases are strengthened by considerations stemming from the forward-looking argument. A society which tries to be just tries to compensate the victims of its injustice, and when these victims are easily identified, either as individuals or as a group less than equal to others, the case for treating them preferentially is overwhelming.

QUESTIONS FOR REFLECTION

1. How does Boxill criticize the argument that affirmative action helps those who least need it?

2. How does Boxill justify compensating blacks as a group? Do you find his argument compelling? Why or why not?

3. Do you agree with Boxill that all blacks have been harmed by discrimination and deserve compensation—even Bill Cosby and Oprah Winfrey, for example?

4. How might Boxill respond to the argument that the social and economic position of blacks is due more to culture than to discrimination?

5. What is Boxill's forward-looking argument for affirmative action?

THOMAS SOWELL

"Affirmative Action": A Worldwide Disaster

Thomas Sowell is Senior Research Fellow at the Hoover Institution at Stanford University.
(Source: Reprinted from Commentary *[December 1989], by permission; all rights reserved.)*

Arguments for and against "affirmative action" have raged for about twenty years in the United States. Similar arguments have provoked controversy—and even bloodshed—for a longer or a shorter period, in the most disparate societies, scattered around the world. India, Nigeria, Australia, Guyana, Malaysia, Sri Lanka, Pakistan, and Indonesia are just some of the countries where some groups receive official, government-sanctioned preferences over others. While the American phrase "affirmative action" is used in Australia and Canada, other countries have used a variety of other phrases, such as "positive discrimination" (India), "sons of the soil" preferences (Indonesia, Malaysia), "standardization" (Sri Lanka), or "reflecting the federal character" of the country (Nigeria). The same general principle of government apportionment of coveted positions, to supersede the competition of the marketplace or of academia, was of course also embodied in the *numerus clausus* laws used to restrict the opportunities of Jews in pre-war Central and Eastern Europe.

The countries with preferential policies have varied enormously in cultural, political, economic, and other ways. The groups receiving preferences have likewise varied greatly, from locally or nationally dominant groups in some countries to the poorest and most abject groups, such as the untouchables of India. Such vast disparities in settings and people make it all the more striking that there are common patterns among these countries—patterns with serious implications for "affirmative-action" policies in the United States. Among these patterns are the following:

1. Preferential programs, even when explicitly and repeatedly defined as "temporary," have tended not only to persist but also to expand in scope, either embracing more groups or spreading to wider realms for the same groups, or both. Even preferential programs established with legally mandated cut-off dates, as in India and Pakistan, have continued far past those dates by subsequent extensions.

2. Within the groups designated by government as recipients of preferential treatment, the benefits have usually gone disproportionately to those members already more fortunate.

3. Group polarization has tended to increase in the wake of preferential programs, with nonpreferred groups reacting adversely, in ways ranging from political backlash to mob violence and civil war.

4. Fraudulent claims of belonging to the designated beneficiary groups have been widespread and have taken many forms in various countries.

In the United States, as in other countries around the world, the empirical consequences of preferential policies have received much less attention than the rationales and goals of such policies. Too often these rationales and goals have been sufficient unto themselves, both in the political arena and in courts of law. Without even an attempt at empirical assessment of costs versus benefits, with no attempt to pinpoint either losers or gainers, discussions of preferential policies are often exercises in assertion, counter-assertion, and accusation. Illusions flourish in such an atmosphere. So do the disappointments and bitterness to which illusions lead.

Foremost among these illusions is the belief that group "disparities" in "representation" are suspect anomalies that can be corrected by having the government temporarily apportion places on the basis of group membership. Every aspect of this belief fails the test of evidence, in country after country. The prime moral illusion is that preferential policies compensate for wrongs suffered. This belief has been supported only by a thin veneer of emotional rhetoric, seldom examined but often reiterated.

I. The Assumptions of "Affirmative Action"

"Temporary" Policies

When U.S. Supreme Court Justice William J. Brennan described the "affirmative-action" plan in the *Weber* case as "a temporary measure," he was echoing a view widely held, not only in the United States but also around the world. Britain's Lord Scarman likewise said:

> We can and for the present must accept the loading of the law in favor of one group at the expense of others, defending it as a temporary expedient in the balancing process which has to be undertaken when and where there is social and economic inequality.

The rhetoric of transience and the reality of persistence and proliferation are both international features of preferential policies. "Affirmative-action" plans initially justified in the United States by the unique historic sufferings of blacks have been successively extended, over the years, to groups that now add up to several times as many people as the black population—and more than half of the total American population. These include not only American Indians, Hispanics, and Asians, but also women. A very similar pattern emerged in India, where official preferences were established more than forty years ago for untouchables, for some tribal groups, and for unspecified "other backward classes." Since then, so many groups have managed to get themselves included under "other backward classes" that they now outnumber the untouchables and the tribal peoples put together.

Even where no new groups are added to those legally entitled to official preferences, new occupations, institutions, and sectors of the society can fall under the coverage of preferential policies. Malays were granted preferential employment in government back in colonial Malaya under the British. After Malaya became independent Malaysia, and especially after the "New Economic Policy" announced in 1969, preferences spread to university admissions, government loans, occupational licenses, and employment in private businesses, both local and foreign-owned. The island nation of Sri Lanka has followed a pattern much like that of Malaysia. Preferences for the Sinhalese have not spread to other groups but have simply become more pronounced and more widespread over time.

Perhaps the classic example of preferences that spread far beyond their initial group and their original rationale have been the preferences in Pakistan. The desperately poor Bengalis of East Pakistan were "underrepresented" in the civil service, the military, business, and the professions. Even the administration of East Pakistan was filled with West Pakistanis. Preferential policies to correct this were advocated in 1949 as "temporary" expedients to be phased out in five to ten years. In reality, however, these policies have lasted decades beyond this time and in 1984 were extended to 1994 by the late President Zia. Not only did preferential quotas spread well beyond people from the East Pakistan region; they persisted long after East Pakistan broke away in 1971 to form the independent nation of Bangladesh. In other words, those who provided the initial rationale for preferential policies have now disappeared by secession but the policies themselves have acquired a political life of their own.

Despite such patterns in these and other countries, the word "temporary" continues to be used in discussions of preferential policies—judicial and scholarly, as well as popular and political. No argument seems to be considered necessary to show that this transience can be enforced, so that the word "temporary" will be something more than political decoration. Indeed, few seem to feel a need to specify whether the dimensions of "temporary" are to be measured in actual units of time or by the attainment of some preconceived social results. If the latter, then the distinction between "temporary" and "eternal" can be wholly illusory in practice. In short, the nebulousness of the concept of "temporary" preference has matched its futility.

Statistical Disparities

Equally nebulous are the assumptions about the statistical "disparities" and "imbalances" that preferential policies are supposed to correct.

The idea that large statistical disparities between groups are unusual—and therefore suspicious—is commonplace, but only among those who have not bothered to study the history of racial, ethnic, and other groups in countries around the world. Among leading scholars who have in fact devoted years of research to such matters, a radically different picture emerges. Donald L. Horowitz of Duke University, at the end of a massive and masterful international study of ethnic groups—a study highly praised in scholarly journals—examined the idea of a society where groups are "proportionately represented" at different levels and in different sectors. He concluded that "few, if any, societies have ever approximated this description."

A worldwide study of military forces and police forces by Cynthia Enloe of Clark University likewise concluded that "militaries fall far short of mirroring, even roughly, the multi-ethnic societies" from which they come. Moreover, just "as one is unlikely to find a police force or a military that mirrors its plural society, so one is unlikely to find a representative bureaucracy." One reason is that "it is common for different groups to rely on different mobility ladders." Some choose the military, some the bureaucracy, and some various parts of the private sector. Even within the military, different branches tend to have very different racial or ethnic compositions—the Afrikaners, for example, being slightly underrepresented in the South African navy and greatly overrepresented in the South African army, though their utter dominance in the government ensures that they cannot be discriminated against in either branch. Powerless minorities have likewise been greatly overrepresented or even dominant in particular branches of the military or the police—the Chinese in Malaysia's air force and among detectives in the police force, for example.

In the private sector as well, it is commonplace for minorities to be overrepresented, or even dominant, in competitive industries where they have no power to prevent others from establishing rival businesses. Jewish prominence in the clothing industry, not only in the United States, but in Argentina and Chile as well, did not reflect any ability to prevent other Americans, Argentines, or Chileans from manufacturing garments, but simply the advantages of the Jews' having brought needle-trade skills and experience with them from Eastern Europe. The fact that Jews owned more than half the clothing stores in mid-19th-century Melbourne likewise reflected that same advantage, rather than any ability to forbid other Australians from selling clothes. In a similar way, German minorities have been dominant as pioneers in piano manufacturing in colonial America, czarist Russia, Australia, France, and England. Italian fishermen, Japanese farmers, and Irish politicians have been among many other minority groups with special success in special fields in various countries, without any ability to keep out others.

Another distinguished scholar who has studied multi-ethnic societies around the world, Myron Weiner of MIT, refers to "the universality of ethnic inequality." He points out that those inequalities are multidimensional:

> All multi-ethnic societies exhibit a tendency for ethnic groups to engage in different occupations, have different levels (and, often, types) of education, receive different incomes, and occupy a different place in the social hierarchy.

Yet the pattern Professor Weiner has seen, after years of research, as a "universality" is routinely assumed to be an *anomaly*, not only by preferential-policy advocates, but also by the intelligentsia, the media, legislators, and judges—all of whom tend to assume, as a *norm*, what Professor Horowitz has found to exist (or even to be approximated) in "few, if any, societies." That what exists widely across the planet is regarded as an anomaly, while what exists virtually nowhere is regarded as a norm, is a tribute to the effectiveness of sheer reiteration in establishing a vision—and of the difficulties of dispelling a prevailing vision by facts.

Some might try to salvage the statistical argument for discrimination by describing discrimination as also being universal. But, to repeat, groups who are in no position to discriminate against anybody have often been overrepresented in coveted positions—the Chinese in Malaysian universities, the Tamils in Sri Lankan universities, the southerners in Nigerian universities, all during the 1960's, and Asians in American universities today being just some of the minorities of whom this has been true. All sorts of other powerless minorities have dominated particular industries or sectors of the economy, the intellectual community, or government employment. Among businessmen, India's Gujaratis in East Africa, the Lebanese in West Africa, the Chinese in Southeast Asia, the Jews in Eastern Europe, and Koreans and Vietnamese in black ghettos across the United States are just some examples. Among high government officials, the Germans were greatly overrepresented in czarist Russia, as were Christians in the Ottoman empire. Among intellectuals, the Scots were as dominant in 18th- and 19th-century Britain as the Jews have been in other parts of Europe. In short, large statistical disparities have been commonplace, both in the presence of discrimination and in its absence. Indeed, large disparities have been commonplace in the utilization of preferential programs designed to reduce disparities.

The intellectual and political *coup* of those who promote the randomness assumption is to put the burden of proof entirely on others. It is not merely the individual employer, for example, who must disprove this assumption in his own particular case in order to escape a charge of discrimination. All who oppose the randomness assumption find themselves confronted with the task of disproving an elusive plausibility, for which no evidence is offered. As for counter-evidence, no enumeration of the myriad ways in which groups are grossly disparate—in age of marriage, alcohol consumption, immigration patterns, performance in sports, performance on tests—can ever be conclusive, even when extended past the point where the patience of the audience is exhausted.

Those viscerally convinced of the pervasiveness of discrimination and its potency as an explanation of social disparities—and convinced also of the effectiveness of preferential policies as a remedy—are lit-

tle troubled by the logical shakiness of the statistical evidence. That is all the more reason for others to be doubly troubled—not simply because an incorrect policy may be followed but also, and more importantly, because actions ostensibly based on the rule of law are in substance based on visceral convictions, the essence of lynch law. . . .

Assumptions as Law

Flaws in logic or evidence are unfortunate in intellectual speculation but they are far more serious in courts of law, where major penalties may be inflicted on those whose employees or students, for example, do not have a racial or ethnic composition that meets the preconceptions of other people. Some U.S. Supreme Court Justices have repeatedly treated statistical disparities as tantamount to discrimination and assumed the task of restoring groups to where they would have been otherwise. Even where group disparities in "representation" reflect demonstrable performance disparities, these performance disparities themselves have been taken as proof of societal discrimination. Thus, in the *Weber* case, Justice Harry Blackmun declared that there could be "little doubt that any lack of skill" on the part of minority workers competing with Brian Weber "has its roots in purposeful discrimination of the past." In the *Bakke* case, four Justices declared that the failure of minority medical-school applicants to perform as well as Allan Bakke "was due principally to the effects of past discrimination." The Court's task, therefore, was one of "putting minority applicants in the position they would have been in if not for the evil of racial discrimination."

All this presupposes a range of knowledge that no one has ever possessed. Ironically, this sweeping assumption of knowledge has been combined with an apparent ignorance of vast disparities in performance, disparities favoring groups with no power to discriminate against anybody. From such judicial speculation it is only a short step to the idea of restoring groups to where they would have been—and *what* they would have been—but for the offending discrimination.

What would the average Englishman be like today "but for" the Norman conquest? What would the average Japanese be like "but for" the enforced isolation of Japan for two-and-a-half centuries under the Tokugawa shoguns? What would the Middle East be like "but for" the emergence of Islam? In any other context besides preferential-policy issues, the presumption of knowing the answers to such questions would be regarded as ridiculous, even as intellectual speculation, much less as a basis for serious legal action.

To know how one group's employment, education, or other pattern differs statistically from another's is usually easy. What is difficult to know are the many variables determining the interest, skill, and performance of those individuals from various groups who are being considered for particular jobs, roles, or institutions. What is virtually impossible to know are the patterns that would exist in a non-discriminatory world—the deviations from which would indicate the existence and magnitude of discrimination.

Age distribution and geographic distribution are only two very simple factors which can play havoc with the assumption that groups would be evenly or randomly distributed in occupations and institutions, in the absence of discrimination. When one group's median age is a decade younger than another's—not at all uncommon—that alone may be enough to cause the younger group to be statistically "overrepresented" in sports, crime, and entry-level jobs, as well as in those kinds of diseases and accidents that are more prevalent among the young, while the older group is overrepresented in homes for the elderly, in the kinds of jobs requiring long years of experience, and in the kinds of diseases and accidents especially prevalent among older people.

Another very simple factor operating against an even "representation" of groups is that many ethnic groups are distributed geographically in patterns differing from one another. It would be unlikely that American ethnic groups concentrated in cold states like Minnesota and Wisconsin would be as well represented among citrus growers and tennis players as they are on hockey teams and among skiers. It is also unlikely that groups concentrated in land-locked states would be equally represented in maritime activities, or that groups from regions lacking mineral deposits would be as well-represented among miners or in other occupations associated with extractive industries as groups located in Pennsylvania or West Virginia.

Differences in geographic concentrations among racial and ethnic groups are by no means confined to the U.S. In Brazil, people of German and Japanese ancestry are concentrated in the south. In Switzerland, whole regions are predominantly French, German, or Italian. In countries around the world, an overwhelming majority of the Chinese or the Jewish population is heavily concentrated in a few major cities—often in just one city in a given country. Group differences in geographical distribution can reach right down to the neighborhood level or even to particular streets. In Buenos Aires, people of Italian ancestry have concentrated in particular neighborhoods or on particular streets, according to the places of their own or their ancestral origins in Italy. In Bombay, people from different parts of India are likewise concentrated in particular neighborhoods or on particular streets.

Lest the point be misunderstood, while these two simple and obvious factors—age and location—are capable of disrupting the even "representation" that many assume to exist in the absence of discrimination, there are also innumerable other factors, of varying degrees of complexity and influence, that can do the same. Moreover, differences in age and location may play a significant role in explaining *some* socioeconomic differences between *some* groups but not other socioeconomic differences between those groups, or among other groups. The purpose here is not to pinpoint the reasons for intergroup differences—or even to assume that they can all be pinpointed—but rather to show how arbitrary and unfounded is the assumption that groups would be evenly "represented," in the absence of discrimination. Precisely because the known differences among groups are large and multidimensional, the presumption of weighing these differences so comprehensively and accurately as to know where some group would be "but for" discrimination approaches hubris.

Even the more modest goal of knowing the *general direction* of the deviation of a group's position from where it would have been without discrimination is by no means necessarily achievable. What are the "effects" of centuries of injustice, punctuated by recurring outbursts of lethal mass violence, against the overseas Chinese in Southeast Asia or against the Jews in Europe? Both groups are generally more prosperous than their persecutors. Would they have been still more prosperous in the absence of such adversity? Perhaps—but many peoples with a long history of peace, and with prosperity supplied by nature itself, have quietly stagnated. This is not to say that the Jews and the Chinese would have done so. It is only to say that *we do not know and cannot know.* No amount of good intentions will make us omniscient. No fervent invocation of "social justice" will supply the missing knowledge.

Incentives and Results

"Affirmative-action" policies assume not only a level of knowledge that no one has ever possessed but also a degree of control that no one has ever exercised. Proponents of preferential policies have tended to reason in terms of the rationales and goals of such policies—not in terms of the *incentives* these policies create. Yet these incentives acquire a life of their own, independent of—and often counter to— the avowed goals of preferential policies. Nor are these simply isolated "mistakes" that can be "corrected." They are the fruition of fundamental misconceptions of the degree of control that can be maintained over a whole galaxy of complex social interactions.

At the individual level, the potential beneficiary and the potential loser are not mere blocks of wood passively placed where the policy dictates. Nor are they automatons who continue acting as before, except for modifications specified for them by others. Rather, they respond *in their own ways* to preferential policies. One of these ways was exemplified by a question raised by a group activist seeking preferential hiring in India's city of Hyderabad: "Are we not entitled to jobs just because we are not as qualified?" A Nigerian wrote of "the tyranny of skills." The sense of entitlement—independent of skills or performance—has long been an accompaniment of preferential policies, for the most disparate groups in the most disparate societies.

The late South African economist W. H. Hutt pointed out long ago that the most "virulent" white supporters of early racial-preferential policies in the mines were "those who had not troubled to qualify themselves for promotion," and who therefore relied on being white instead. Today, in the Virgin Islands, even schoolchildren excuse their own substandard academic and behavioral performance by pointing out that government jobs will be waiting for them as U.S. citizens—jobs for which their better-behaved and better-performing West Indian classmates are ineligible. In Malaysia, likewise, "Malay students, who sense that their future is assured, feel less pressure to perform," according to a study there. A study of black colleges in the United States similarly noted that even students planning postgraduate study often showed no sense of urgency about needing to be prepared "because they believed that certain rules would simply be set aside for them." In India, even a fervent advocate of the untouchables, and of preferential policies for them, has urged untouchable students in medical and engineering schools to abandon their "indifference."

The disincentives created by group preferences apply to both preferred and non-preferred groups. As W. H. Hutt wrote of the South African "color bar," these racial preferences "have vitiated the efficiency of the non-whites by destroying incentives" and have also "weakened incentives to efficiency on the part of the whites who have been featherbedded." A very similar principle is found in the very different setting of Jamaica, after it became independent and black-run. There it was the whites who faced the disincentives of the non-preferred. Many withdrew from the competition for public office because they "felt that the day of the black man had come and questioned why they had to make the effort if the coveted job or the national honor would go to the blacks, despite their qualifications." The upshot is that preferential policies represent not simply a transfer of benefits from one group to another, but can also represent a net loss, as both groups perform less well as a result.

Those who initiate preferential policies cannot sufficiently control the reactions of either preferred or non-preferred groups to ensure that such policies will have the desired effect, or even move in the desired direction: Counterproductive reactions that reduce national prosperity or social tranquility adversely affect even members of the preferred group, who are also members of the general society. Whether their gains in one role exceed their losses in the other role is an empirical question whose answer depends on the specifics of each situation. One of the clearly undesired and uncontrolled consequences of preferential policies has been a backlash by non-preferred groups. This backlash has ranged from campus racial incidents in the United States to a bloody civil war in Sri Lanka.

Honors

Nowhere is control more illusory than in the awarding of honors, whose very meaning and effect depend upon other people's opinions. Preferential honors for members of particular groups can easily render suspect not only those particular honors but also honors fully merited and awarded after free and open competition. If one-fifth of the honors received by preferred groups are awarded under double standards, the other four-fifths are almost certain to fall under a cloud of suspicion as well, if only because some of those who lost out in the competition would prefer to believe that they were not bested fairly. It is by no means clear that more real honors—which are ultimately other people's opinions—will come to a group preferentially given awards. Preferential honors can in practice mean a moratorium on recognition of the group's achievements, which can be confounded with patronage or pay-offs. This need not inevitably be so. The point is that the matter is out of the control of those who decide award policy, and in the hands of others observing the outcomes and deciding what to make of them.

Honor is more than a sop to personal vanity. It is a powerful incentive which accomplishes many social tasks, including tasks that are too arduous and dangerous to be compensated by money—even inducing individuals in crisis situations to sacrifice their lives for the greater good of others. In more mundane matters, honor and respect from one's colleagues and subordinates are important and sometimes indispensable aids, without which even the most talented and conscientious individuals sometimes cannot fulfill their promise. To jeopardize the respect and recognition of individuals from preferred groups by rewarding "honors" tainted with double standards is not only to downgrade their own achievements but also to downgrade their chances of accomplishing those achievements in the first place. For example, minority faculty members have often complained about a lack of intellectual and research interaction with their colleagues, and of being thought of as "affirmative-action" professors. After the media revealed that black students

were admitted to the Harvard Medical School with lower qualifications, white patients began to refuse to be examined by such students. The negative effects of tainted honors are by no means limited to academia.

Partial Preferences

The illusion of control includes the belief that preferential policies can be extended *partway* into a process while maintaining equal treatment in the remainder of the process. For example, in the early days of "affirmative action" in the United States, it was sometimes asserted that special efforts to recruit minority employees or minority students would be followed by equal treatment at the actual selection stage and afterward. Special concern for particular groups might also mean only special scrutiny to see that they were treated equally. President John F. Kennedy's Executive Order No. 10,925 required that employers who were government contractors "take affirmative action to ensure that the applicants are employed, and that employees are treated during employment without regard to race, creed, color, or national origin." That is virtually the antithesis of what "affirmative action" has come to mean today, either in the United States or in other countries where the term refers to statistical results viewed precisely *with regard* to race, color, creed, or national origin.

The concept of preferential concern stopping partway into a process is not confined to employment or to the United States. In India, a government minister has urged a small lowering of university admissions standards for students from scheduled castes (untouchables) and scheduled tribes, with the proviso that "he was recommending relaxation for admission and not for passing or grading." Similar views were once expressed in the United States, where special recruitment programs for minority students quickly led to lower admission standards for them—and this in turn sometimes led to "affirmative grading," to prevent excessive failures by minority students. Double standards in grading may originate with the individual professor or be a result of administrative pressures. Halfway around the world—in Soviet Central Asia—professors are also pressured to give preferential grading to Central Asian students. In Malaysia, preferential grading is virtually institutionalized. As Gordon P. Means puts it:

Although grading is supposed to be without reference to ethnicity, all grades must be submitted to an evaluation review committee having heavy Malay representation. Individual faculty members report various instances when grades were unilaterally raised, apparently for purposes of "ethnic balance."

Sometimes preferential grading takes the less direct form of creating special or easier subjects for particular groups, such as Maori Studies in New Zealand, Malay Studies in Singapore, or a variety of ethnic studies in the United States.

Whether in employment, education, or other areas, carefully limited or fine-tuned preferences have repeatedly proved to be illusory. Neither time limitations nor other limitations have in fact stopped their persistence and spread.

A wide variety of moral arguments has been used to justify preferential policies. Some of these arguments have little in common, except for being largely unexamined in the excitement of crusading zeal—and being successful politically. Among the reasons given for preferences are that (1) the group is indigenous; (2) the group has been historically wronged; and (3) the group happens to be less well represented in desirable institutions or occupations, for whatever reason, so that this "imbalance" must be "corrected."

Whatever the arguments for preferential policies, these preferences (as we have seen) can long outlive the validity of those arguments, whether the degree of validity be zero or 100 percent, or anywhere in between. A genuinely disadvantaged group can cling to preferences, or seek more, long after their disadvantages have been redressed. The moral question, therefore, is not simply whether particular groups deserve particular benefits for particular periods of time, or until particular social conditions are achieved. The real quesion is whether the *actual consequences of the particular processes* being initiated are likely to be justified, morally or otherwise. . . .

Historical Compensation

The wrongs of history have been invoked by many groups in many countries as a moral claim for contemporary compensation. Much emotional fervor goes into such claims but the question here is about their logic or morality. Assuming for the sake of argument that the historical claims are factually correct, which may not be the case in all countries, to transfer benefits between two groups of living contemporaries because of what happened between two sets of dead people is to raise the question whether any sufferer is in fact being compensated. Only where both wrongs and compensation are viewed as collectivized and inheritable does redressing the wrongs of history have a moral, or even a logical, basis.

The biological continuity of the generations lends plausibility to the notion of group compensation—but only if guilt can be inherited. Otherwise there are simply windfall gains and windfall losses among contemporaries, according to the accident of their antecedents. Moreover, few people would accept this as a general principle to be applied consistently, however much they may advocate it out of compassion (or guilt) over the fate of particular unfortunates. No one would advocate that today's Jews are morally entitled to put today's Germans in concentration camps, in compensation for the Nazi Holocaust. Most people would not only be horrified at any such suggestion but would also regard it as a second act of gross immorality, in no way compensating the first, but simply adding to the sum total of human sins.

Sometimes a more sociological, rather than moral, claim is made that living contemporaries are suffering from the *effects* of past wrongs and that it is these effects which must be offset by compensatory preferences. Tempting as it is to imagine that the contemporary troubles of historically wronged groups are due to those wrongs, this is confusing causation with morality. The contemporary socioeconomic position of groups in a given society often bears no relationship to the historic wrongs they have suffered. Both in Canada and in the United States, the Japanese have significantly higher incomes than the whites, who have a documented history of severe anti-Japanese discrimination in both countries. The same story could be told of the Chinese in Malaysia, Indonesia, and many other countries around the world, of the Jews in countries with virulent anti-Semitism, and a wide variety of other groups in a wide variety of other countries. Among poorer groups as well, the level of poverty often has little correlation with the degree of oppression. No one would claim that the historic wrongs suffered by

Puerto Ricans in the United States exceed those suffered by blacks, but the average Puerto Rican income is lower than the average income of blacks.

None of this proves that historic wrongs have no contemporary effects. Rather, it is a statement about the limitations of our knowledge, which is grossly inadequate to the task undertaken and likely to remain so. To pretend to disentangle the innumerable sources of intergroup differences is an exercise in hubris rather than morality.

As one contemporary example of how easy it is to go astray in such efforts, it was repeated for years that the high rate of single-parent, teenage pregnancy among blacks was "a legacy of slavery." Evidence was neither asked nor given. But when serious scholarly research was finally done on this subject, the evidence devastated this widely held belief. The vast majority of black children grew up in two-parent homes, even under slavery itself, and for generations thereafter. The current levels of single-parent, teenage pregnancy are a phenomenon of the last half of the 20th century and are a disaster that has also struck groups with wholly different histories from that of blacks. Passionate commitment to "social justice" can never be a substitute for knowing what you are talking about.

Those who attribute any part of the socioeconomic fate of any group to factors internal to that group are often accused of "blaming the victim." This may sometimes be part of an attempt to salvage the historical-compensation principle but it deserves separate treatment.

"Blame" and "Victims"

The illusion of morality is often confused with the reality of causation. If group A originates in a country where certain scientific and technological skills are widespread and group B originates in a country where they are not, then when they immigrate to the same third country, they are likely to be statistically "represented" to very different degrees in occupations and institutions requiring such skills. There is nothing mysterious about this, in causal terms. But those who wish to attribute this disparity to institutional discrimination are quick to respond to any mention of group B's lesser scientfic-technological background as a case of "blaming the victim." By

making the issue *who* is to blame, such arguments evade or preempt the more fundamental question— whether this is a matter of blame in the first place.

Clearly today's living generation—in any group— cannot be *blamed* for the centuries of cultural evolution that went on before they were born, often in lands that they have never seen. Nor can they be blamed for the fact that the accident of birth caused them to inherit one culture rather than another. In causal terms, it would be a staggering coincidence if cultures evolving in radically different historical circumstances were equally effective for all purposes when transplanted to a new society. Blame has nothing to do with it. . . .

"Underrepresentation" and "Life Chances"

Quite aside from claims of historic wrongs, the argument has often been made—on grounds of morality as well as political or social expediency—that the "underrepresentation" of particular groups in desirable roles is an "imbalance" to be "corrected." Majorities have pressed such claims as readily as minorities, in circumstances where their only disadvantages were their own lack of skills or interest, as well as where a plausible case could be made that imposed disabilities have handicapped them.

Among the many unexamined assumptions behind preferential policies is the belief that intergroup friction is a function of the magnitude of income gaps, so that more social harmony can be achieved by reducing these gaps. As with so much that has been said in this area, evidence has been neither asked nor given, while counter-evidence is plentiful, varied, and ignored.

In Bombay, the hosility of the Maharashtrians has been directed primarily at the South Indians, who are somewhat ahead of them economically, rather than against the Gujaratis, who are far ahead of them. Throughout sub-Saharan Africa, there has historically been far more hostility directed by Africans against Asians than against Europeans, who are economically far ahead of both. A similar pattern is found *within* African groups. In Nigeria, for example, the Yoruba were far ahead of the Ibo economically in 1940, while there was a much smaller gap at that time between the Hausa and the Ibo. Yet the hostility and violence between Hausa and Ibo in that era greatly exceeded any friction between either of these groups and the Yoruba. Later, as the Ibos rose, narrowing the gap between themselves and the Yoruba, it was precisely then that Ibo-Yoruba outbreaks of violence occurred.

Advocates of preferential policies often express a related belief, similarly unsupported by evidence, that an even distribution of groups across sectors of the economy tends to reduce social frictions and hostility. Much history suggests the opposite, that (in the words of Professor Horowitz) "the ethnic division of labor is more a shield than a sword."

The utter dominance of particular sectors by particular minority groups has been quietly accepted for generations in many countries—until a specific, organized campaign has been whipped up against the minority, often by members of the majority who are seeking to enter the minority-dominated sector and are finding their competition very formidable. Often majority-group customers or suppliers actually prefer dealing with the minority-run entrepreneurs. Even in the midst of ethnic riots against other groups certain middleman minorities have been spared— the Greeks in the Sudan, Hindus in Burma, Marwaris in Assam. Organized boycotts of minority businessmen have been spearheaded by majority-group business rivals, from Uganda and Kenya to the Philippines and the United States. Contrary to what is widely (and lightly) assumed, neither an even representation of groups nor mass resentment at unevenness is "natural."

Repeatedly, in countries scattered around the world, it has been precisely the rise of newly emerging ethnic competitors—whether in business, government, or the professions—which has produced not only friction with groups already dominant in the sectors concerned but also, and much more importantly, has led the newcomers to whip up their whole group emotionally against the already established group. A Sri Lankan legislator noted this pattern early in that country's interethnic troubles:

> University graduates and people like that are the cause of all the trouble—not the vast mass of the Sinhalese people. It is those men, these middle-class unemployed seeking employment, who are jealous of the fact that a few Tamils occupy seats of office in government—these are the people who have gone round the countryside, rousing the masses and creating this problem.

Halfway around the world a similar charge was made, that "the educated Nigerian is the worst peddler of tribalism." In the very different setting of Hungary in the 1880's, the promotion of anti-Semitism was largely the work of students, intellectuals, and sections of the middle classes, while the Hungarian peasant masses remained relatively unresponsive.

Advocates of preferential policies often see these policies as not only promoting social harmony by reducing gaps in income and "representation," but also as part of a more general attempt to "equalize life chances." Much effort is expended establishing the moral desirability of this goal and the extent to which we currently fall short of it, while little or no effort goes into establishing our *capability* to accomplish such a staggering task. One clue to the magnitude and difficulty of what is being attempted are the various ways in which first-born children excel their siblings. A completely disproportionate number of the famous individuals in history were either first-born or the only child. In more mundane achievements as well, the first-born tend to excel. A study of National Merit Scholarship finalists showed that, even in five-child families, the first-born became finalists more often than all the other siblings combined. The same was true in two-, three-, and four-child families. Such disparities, among people born of the same parents and raised under the same roof, mock presumptions of being able to equalize life chances across broader and deeper differences among people in a large, complex, and, especially, multi-ethnic society.

The abstract moral desirability of a goal cannot preempt the prior question of our capacity to achieve it. This is not even a question of falling short of all that might be hoped for. It is a question of risking counterproductive, disastrous, and even bloody results.

Beneficiaries and Losers

Part of the moral aura surrounding preferential policies is due to the belief that such policies benefit the less fortunate. The losers in this presumed redistribution are seldom specified, though the underlying assumption seems to be that they are the more fortunate.

Empirical evidence for such assumptions is largely lacking and the *a priori* case for believing them is unconvincing. For example, the effects of preferential policies depend on the costs of complementary factors required to use the preferences. These costs can obviously be borne more readily by those who are already more fortunate. Benefits set aside for businessmen of the preferred group are of no use to members of that group who do not happen to own a business, or possess the capital to start one. Preferential admission to medical school is a benefit only to those who have already gone to college. Because preferential benefits tend to be concentrated on more lucrative or prestigious things, they are often within striking distance only for the fortunate few who have already advanced well beyond most other members of the preferred group. In Third World countries, where the great demand is for clerical jobs in the government, the poorer groups in these countries often have difficulty reaching even the modest level of education required for such employment.

Preferential scholarships for Malays in Malaysia are a classic example. Students from families in the lower-income brackets—63 percent of the population—received 14 percent of the university scholarships, while students whose families were in the top 17 percent of the income distribution received more than half of the scholarships. In India, preferential programs for both untouchables and "other backward classes" show the same pattern. In the state of Haryana, 37 different untouchable castes were entitled to preferential scholarships but only 18 actually received any—and just one of these received 65 percent of the scholarships at the graduate levels and 80 percent at the undergraduate level. Similar patterns are found in other parts of the country. In the state of Tamil Nadu, the highest of the so-called "backward classes" (11 percent of the total) received nearly half of all jobs and all university admissions set aside for such classes. The bottom 12 percent received no more than 2 percent of the jobs and university admissions.

In some cases—including the United States—the less fortunate members of a preferred group may actually retrogress while the more fortunate advance under preferential policies. After "affirmative-action" policies took hold in the early 1970's, blacks with little education and little job experience fell further behind the general population—and indeed further behind whites with little education and little job experience. Meanwhile, blacks with college education or substantial job experience advanced economically, both absolutely and relative to whites with the same advantages. Yet another example of the benefits of "affirmative action" to those already more fortunate are the business "set-asides" that give minority entrepreneurs preferential access to government contracts under Section 8(a) of the Small Business Act. Minority businessmen who participate in this program have an average net worth of $160,000. This is not only far higher than the average net worth of the groups they come from, but also higher than the average net worth of Americans in general.

This pattern of simultaneous advance at the top and retrogression at the bottom is not confined to the United States. In India, the era of preferential policies has seen the proportion of untouchables increase significantly among high-level government officials, while the proportion of untouchables who work as landless agricultural laborers has also increased. In Malaysia, the representation of Malays on corporate boards of directors has increased significantly, while the proportion of Malays among the population living below the official poverty level has also increased.

Just as the advocates of preferential policies arbitrarily assume that such policies will benefit the "disadvantaged," so they arbitrarily assume that this will be at the expense of the "privileged." They neither offer evidence of this in advance nor are so impolitic as to collect data on this point after preferential programs have been inaugurated. Such evidence as exists points in the opposite direction. In Bombay, preferential policies to put Maharashtrians into the ranks of business executives had only minor effects on the Gujaratis who were dominant in that occupation, reducing the proportion of Gujarati executives from 52 percent to 44 percent. Among the South Indians, however, their 25-percent representation among Bombay executives was cut in half, to 12 percent. A similar pattern appeared in the very different setting of prewar Hungary, where policies favoring

Gentiles had relatively little effect on the Jewish financial and industrial elite but imposed real hardships on the Jewish middle class and lower middle class. In the United States, despite voluminous official statistics on all sorts of racial and ethnic matters, no one seems to have collected data on the actual losers under "affirmative action." It may be significant, however, that those who have protested their losses all the way up to the U.S. Supreme Court have not been named Adams, Cabot, or Rockefeller, but DeFunis, Bakke, and Weber.

II. The Illusion of Compensation

What makes compensation an illusion is not only that sufferers are not in fact compensated, or the effects of historic wrongs redressed—or even accurately identified and separated from innumerable other social factors at work simultaneously. Both the principle of compensation and the particular form of compensation via preferential policies require careful examination.

The Principle of Compensation

Given the mortality of human beings, often the only compensation for historic wrongs that is within the scope of our knowledge and control is purely symbolic compensation—taking from individuals who inflicted no harm and giving to individuals who suffered none. In addition to the moral shakiness and social dangers of such a policy, it also promotes a kind of social irredentism, a set of *a priori* grievances against living people, whether or not they have ever inflicted harm on those who feel aggrieved. In view of the futile but bitter and bloody struggles engendered by territorial irredentism, there is little good to hope for by applying this same principle in a new field.

The factual reality that actual benefits from compensatory preferences tend to be concentrated in the already more fortunate elites among the preferred groups makes the moral case for such policies weaker and the social dangers greater. The more educated, articulate, and more politically sophisticated elites have every incentive to whip up group emotions in favor of more and better preferences, despite the increasing group polarization this may produce, and to be intransigent against any suggestion that any such prefer-

ences should ever be reduced or ended. This has been a common pattern in the most disparate countries.

In principle, compensation can take many forms, beginning with a simple transfer of money from one group to another. In practice, however, preferential policies are the form taken in many countries around the world. The implications of that particular form, and of its alternatives, raise still more troubling questions.

The Form of Compensation

If, notwithstanding all philosophic objections to the principle of group compensation, such a policy is in fact chosen, then the particular form of the compensation can make a major difference in the costs and the consequences of compensatory policies. When resources, or the benefits they create, are transferred from group A to group B, this is not necessarily—or even likely—a zero-sum process, in which the value of what is lost by one is the same as the value of what is gained by the other. What is transferred may be subjectively valued differently by the losers and the recipients. There may also be objectively discernible differences in the use of the same resources by the two groups.

Compensatory policies may, in theory, take place through transfers of money, transfers of in-kind benefits, or through differential applications of rules and standards. In Australia, for example, various money and in-kind transfers to the aborigines add up to more than $2,000 annually for every aboriginal man, woman, and child. Such transfers arouse relatively little political opposition or social backlash. Similarly, in the United States, monetary compensation for Japanese Americans interned during World War II aroused relatively little controversy—and even that little controversy quickly subsided, once the decision was made.

Such monetary transfers are less costly to individual members of the majority population the more the majority outnumbers the minority receiving the transfer. Obviously, if group A is 100 times as large as group B, each member of group B can receive $100 at a cost of only one dollar to each member of group A. However, even where the losses sustained by one group are significant, monetary transfers may still be efficient, in the narrowly economic sense that what is lost by one group as a whole is gained by another group, with no direct net loss to society as a whole. Whatever the merits or demerits of the particular transfer on other grounds, it is not inefficient. Politically and socially, the opposition to such transfers is therefore unlikely to be as great as opposition to the same net transfers in forms that cost more to the losers than is gained by the gainers. Preferential policies often cost the losers more than is gained by the gainers. Preferential policies, by definition, involve a differential application of rules and standards to individuals originating in different groups. Even where the preferences are not stated in terms of differential rules or standards, but rather in terms of numerical quotas, "goals," or "targets," differences in the qualifications of the respective pools of applicants can readily make numerical similarities amount to differences in standards. This is a very common result in countries around the world. In Nigeria, programs to have college-student populations reflect "the federal character" of the country—i.e., tribal quotas under regional names—led to a situation where cut-off scores for admission to the same college varied substantially between students from different tribes or regions. In Sri Lanka, demographic "standardization" policies led to similar disparities in qualification requirements for individuals from different regions of the country. In India, attempts to meet quotas for untouchable students led to drastic reductions in the qualifications they needed for admission to various institutions. Where applicant pools in different groups are different in qualifications, numerical quotas are equivalent to different standards. Therefore preferential policies in general, however phrased, are essentially an application of different rules or standards to individuals from different groups. The question then is: what are the effects of transfers between groups in this particular form?

There are many ways in which intergroup transfers through differential standards can become negative-sum processes, in which what is lost by one group exceeds what is gained by another, thus representing a direct loss to society as a whole—as well as causing indirect losses, due to a larger resistance or backlash than if the recipient group had obtained the same value or benefit in some other form. An obvious example is when a particular group, in which 90 percent of the students admitted to college succeed in graduating, loses places

to another group in which only 30 percent of the students graduate. Group A must lose 900 graduates, in order for group B to gain 300 graduates. It might be objected that this overstates the net loss, since there may be some marginal benefit simply from having attended college, even without graduating. Offsetting this, however, is the fact that groups with lower qualifications tend to specialize in easier and less remunerative fields, whether in India, Malaysia, the Soviet Union, or the United States. Therefore group A may lose 900 graduates largely concentrated in mathematics, science, and engineering, while group B gains 300 graduates largely concentrated in sociology, education, and ethnic studies.

The *apparent* losses to one group under preferential policies may also far exceed the real losses, thereby further raising the indirect social costs of backlash and turmoil. For example, an observer of India's preferential policies for untouchables (known officially as "scheduled castes") has commented:

> . . . we hear innumerable tales of persons being deprived of appointments in favor of people who ranked lower than they did in the relevant examinations. No doubt this does happen, but if all these people were, in fact, paying the price for appointments to Scheduled Castes, there would be many more SC persons appointed than there actually are. To illustrate: supposing that 300 people qualify for ten posts available. The top nine are appointed on merit but the tenth is reserved, so the authorities go down the list to find an SC applicant. They find one at 140 and he is appointed. Whereupon all 131 between him and the merit list feel aggrieved. He has not taken 131 posts; he has taken one, yet 131 people believe they have paid the price for it. Moreover, the remaining 159 often also resent the situation, believing that their chances were, somehow, lessened by the existence of SC reservations.

Where certain opportunities are rigidly "set aside" for particular groups, in the sense that members of other groups cannot have them, even if these opportunities remain unused, then there is the potential for a maximum of grievance for a minimum of benefit transfer. Admission to medical school in India's state of Gujarat operates on this principle—and has led repeatedly to bloody riots in which many people have died. Reservations or "set-asides" in general tend to provoke strong objections. The first major setback for "affirmative action" in the U.S. Supreme Court was based on objections to reserved-admissions places for minority applicants in the 1978 *Bakke* case. A later major setback occurred in *City of Richmond v. Croson* (1989), where minority business set-asides were struck down by the Supreme Court. Similarly, in India, an exhaustive, scholarly legal study of preferential policies found: "Virtually all of the litigation about compensatory discrimination has involved reservations, even though preferences in the form of provisions of facilities, resources, and protections directly affect a much larger number of recipients." This litigation has been initiated mostly by non-preferred individuals who complain of being adversely affected. In some ultimate sense, non-preferred individuals are just as much adversely affected by preferences in other forms that direct resources away from them and toward preferred groups. But it is preference in the specific form of "reservation" or "set-aside" that seems most to provoke both violence and litigation.

By contrast, resource transfers designed to enable disadvantaged groups to meet standards are accepted while attempts to bring the standards down to them are overwhelmingly rejected. In the United States, preferential policies have repeatedly been rejected in public-opinion polls. However, the same American public has strongly supported "special educational or vocational courses, free of charge, to enable members of minority groups to do better on tests." More than three-fifths of all whites even support "requiring large companies to set up special training programs for members of minority groups." The issue is not simply whether one is for or against the advancement of particular groups or is willing to see transfers of resources for their betterment. The method by which their betterment is attempted matters greatly in terms of whether such efforts have the support or the opposition of others.

III. Replacing Illusions

With all the empirical weaknesses, logical flaws, and social dangers of preferential policies, why have they become so popular and spread so rapidly around the world? One reason is that their *political* attractions

are considerable. They offer an immediate response—a quick fix—at relatively little government expense, to the demands of vocal, aroused, and often organized elites, speaking in the name of restive masses. This restiveness of the masses is by no means incidental. Violence has frequently preceded preferences, from the American ghetto riots of the 1960's to the Malay and Indonesian riots against the Chinese at about the same time, to terrorism in India, and massive mob violence against the Tamils in Sri Lanka. This violence by the masses is typically used politically to promote elite purposes via preferential policies. An international study of ethnic conflicts concluded:

> Preferences tend to respond to middle-class aspirations almost entirely. They do little or nothing about the resentments of those who do not aspire to attend secondary school or university, to enter the modern private sector or the bureaucracy, or to become businessmen. Although lower-class resentments are often profound—it is not, after all, the middle class that typically participates in ethnic violence—the resentments may have nothing to do with occupational mobility and preferences do not address them.

Preferential policies, then, are politically attractive as a response, however socially ineffective or counterproductive such policies may later prove to be in practice. At a sufficiently superficial level, the moral attractions of preferential policies are considerable as well. Even in South Africa, moral appeals were made on behalf of a "civilized labor policy"—protecting European workers' customary standard of living from being undercut by Africans and Indians accustomed to living on less—and clergy, intellectuals, and others not personally benefiting joined in support of these policies on that basis. Preferential policies allow intellectuals as well as politicians to be on the side of the angels (as locally defined at the time) at low cost—or rather, at a low down payment, for the real costs come later, and have sometimes been paid in blood.

The last refuge of a failed policy is "the long run," in which it will supposedly be a success. In other words, those who predicted the short run wrongly ask to be trusted with the much harder task of predicting the long run rightly. This argument, used to defend the counterproductive effects of preferential policies, is far less defensible in an international perspective where older preferential policies (as in India or Sri Lanka) have progressed from intergroup political hostility to bloodshed in the streets and deaths by the thousands, while newer programs (as in the United States) are still in the process of increasing group polarization, and the even more recent preferential policies taking shape in Australia and New Zealand are still at the stage of optimistic predictions.

Even the most damning indictment of a policy is almost certain to be met with the response: "But what would you replace it with?" However effective as a political tactic, such a question confuses rather than clarifies. It is like an arbitrary prohibition against saying that the emperor has no clothes, until a complete wardrobe has been designed. The question misconceives policy, and human actions in general, in yet another way: no one who extinguishes a forest fire or removes a cancer has to "replace" it with anything. We are well rid of evils.

This is not to say that none of the aspects of social issues raised during "affirmative-action" controversies should ever be addressed by public policy. The case for public policy in general, or for a particular public policy, must be made on the individual merits of the particular issues raised—but not as a general "replacement" for some discredited policy.

What must be replaced are the social illusions and misconceptions underlying preferential policies, for any alternative policy based on the same illusions and misconceptions will have the same fatal weaknesses in its structure. In some countries and for some purposes social policy may wish to ameliorate the lot of the less fortunate or make it possible for individuals or groups to acquire the knowledge and skills necessary for their own advancement. It is infinitely more important that such efforts be based on facts and logic than that there be one particular scheme selected from innumerable possibilities as the uniquely designated "replacement" for existing policy.

We may or may not be able to agree on what the ideal, or even a viable, policy must be. What we can agree on is far more fundamental: We can agree to *talk sense*. That will mean abandoning a whole vocabulary of political rhetoric which preempts factual questions by arbitrarily calling statistical disparities "discrimination," "exclusion," "segregation," and the like. It will mean confronting issues instead of impugning motives. It will mean specifying goals and defending those specifics, rather than speaking in terms of seeking some nebulously unctuous "change" or "social justice." Perhaps more than anything else, talking sense will mean examining policies in terms of the incentives they create, and the results to which these incentives lead, rather than the hopes they embody. It will mean that evidence takes precedence over assertion and reiteration. . . .

VI. Politics versus Progress

. . . Could some judicious blend of preferential programs and programs designed to improve the performances of less educated groups work? Here the problem is that the two kinds of programs create incentives that work at cross-purposes, even if their goals are the same. Forcing students to meet higher standards—a painful process for them and their teachers alike—will be made all the more difficult if the students know that these standards are unnecessary for them to reach whatever educational or employment goals they have, or even to be promoted to the next grade. If group-representation statistics are the standard by which institutions will be judged, other standards will be sacrificed for the sake of body count. This is true not only of educational institutions but of other institutions as well.

Political feasibility is the greatest obstacle to new policies with an overriding goal of advancing the less fortunate because time is the key ingredient in such advancement on a large scale. Even in the extreme case of South Africa, where massive transfers of the nation's resources were focused on a small minority of its people, in *addition* to preferential policies pursued in utter disregard of the losses and even tragedies suffered by others as a result, it was decades before the Afrikaner "poor whites" became middle-class. Only in terms of political appearances are preferential policies a "quick fix." The dangers of an actual retrogression among the masses of the beneficiary group cannot be dismissed, either from an analytical or an empirical perspective. Even greater dangers have materialized in countries that have experienced bloodshed in the wake of group polarization brought on by preferential policies.

While current political feasibility may be the touchstone of the professional politician, it cannot be the last word for others. In many countries, what is most politically feasible are policies that further a continued drift in the direction of group polarization and the dangers and disasters this entails. Specific alternative policies will differ for different groups and different countries. What is crucial is that these alternatives be examined in terms of the incentives they create and the results to which such incentives can be expected to lead—regardless of the rationales, aspirations, or symbolism of these policies. Determining in this way what *should* be done is not an exercise in utopianism, for once there is a consensus on what needs to be done, that in itself changes what is politically feasible.

The starting point for rethinking and reform must be a recognition that "affirmative action" has been a failure in the United States and a disaster in other countries that have had such policies longer. Indeed, a growing polarization and increasing numbers of ugly racial incidents (especially on campuses that are strongholds of "affirmative action") may be early warnings that we too may be moving from the stage of mere failure to the stage of social disaster.

QUESTIONS FOR REFLECTION

1. What patterns does Sowell find in affirmative-action programs around the world?

2. What are Sowell's responses to arguments from compensation? Do you find them convincing?

3. To what incentives do affirmative-action policies give rise, according to Sowell? How are these incentives harmful, in his view?

4. Some advocates of affirmative action believe that race is a good proxy for disadvantage in general. Sowell disagrees. Why? What evidence does he present?

WILLIAM G. BOWEN AND DEREK BOK

from *The Shape of the River*

William G. Bowen is President of The Andrew W. Mellon Foundation and former President of Princeton University. Derek Bok is former President of Harvard University and former Dean of Harvard Law School. (Source: from The Shape of the River. *Princeton: Princeton University Press. Copyright © 1998 by Princeton University Press. Reprinted by permission of Princeton University Press.)*

. . . In our view, race is relevant in determining which candidates "merit" admission because taking account of race helps institutions achieve three objectives central to their mission—identifying individuals of high potential, permitting students to benefit educationally from diversity on campus, and addressing long-term societal needs.

Identifying Individuals of High Potential

An individual's race may reveal something about how that person arrived at where he or she is today—what barriers were overcome, and what the individual's prospects are for further growth. Not every member of a minority group will have had to surmount substantial obstacles. Moreover, other circumstances besides race can cause "disadvantage." Thus colleges and universities should and do give special consideration to the hard-working son of a family in Appalachia or the daughter of a recent immigrant from Russia who, while obviously bright, is still struggling with the English language. But race is an important factor in its own right, given this nation's history and the evidence presented in many studies of the continuing effects of discrimination and prejudice. Wishing it were otherwise does not make it otherwise. It would seem to us to be ironic

indeed—and wrong—if admissions officers were permitted to consider all other factors that help them identify individuals of high potential who have had to overcome obstacles, but were proscribed from looking at an applicant's race.

Benefiting Educationally from Diversity on the Campus

Race almost always affects an individual's life experiences and perspectives, and thus the person's capacity to contribute to the kinds of learning through diversity that occur on campuses. This form of learning will be even more important going forward than it has been in the past. Both the growing diversity of American society and the increasing interaction with other cultures worldwide make it evident that going to school only with "the likes of oneself" will be increasingly anachronistic. The advantages of being able to understand how others think and function, to cope across racial divides, and to lead groups composed of diverse individuals are certain to increase.

To be sure, not all members of a minority group may succeed in expanding the racial understanding of other students, any more than all those who grew up on a farm or came from a remote region of the United States can be expected to convey a special rural perspective. What does seem clear, however, is that a student body containing many different backgrounds, talents, and experiences will be a richer environment in which to develop. In this respect, minority students of all kinds can have something to offer their classmates. The black student with high grades from Andover may challenge the stereotypes of many classmates just as much as the black student from the South Bronx.

Until now, there has been little hard evidence to confirm the belief of educators in the value of diversity. Our survey data throw new light on the extent of interaction occurring on campuses today and of how positively the great majority of students regard opportunities to learn from those with different points of view, backgrounds, and experiences. Admission "on the merits" would be short-sighted if admissions officers were precluded from crediting this potential contribution to the education of all students.

Imposition of a race-neutral standard would produce very troubling results from this perspective: such a policy would reduce dramatically the proportion of black students on campus—probably shrinking their numbers to less than 2 percent of all matriculants at the most selective colleges and professional schools. Moreover, our examination of the application and admissions files indicates that such substantial reductions in the number of black matriculants, with attendant losses in educational opportunity for all students, would occur without leading to any appreciable improvement in the academic credentials of the remaining black students and would lead to only a modest change in the overall academic profile of the institutions.

Addressing Long-Term Societal Needs

Virtually all colleges and universities seek to educate students who seem likely to become leaders and contributing members of society. Identifying such students is another essential aspect of admitting "on the merits," and here again race is clearly relevant. There is widespread agreement that our country continues to need the help of its colleges and universities in building a society in which access to positions of leadership and responsibility is less limited by an individual's race than it is today.

The success of C&B* colleges and universities in meeting this objective has been documented extensively in this study. In this final chapter, it is helpful to "look back up the river" from a slightly different vantage point. Some of the consequences of mandating a race-neutral standard of admission can be better understood by constructing a rough profile of the approximately 700 black matriculants in the '76 entering cohort at the C&B schools whom we estimate would have been rejected had such a standard been in effect. Our analysis suggests that:

- Over 225 members of this group of retrospectively rejected black matriculants went on to attain professional degrees or doctorates.
- About 70 are now doctors, and roughly 60 are lawyers.
- Nearly 125 are business executives.
- Well over 300 are leaders of civic activities.
- The average earnings of the individuals in the group exceeds $71,000.
- Almost two-thirds of the group (65 percent) were *very* satisfied with their undergraduate experience.

Many of these students would have done well no matter where they went to school, and we cannot know in any precise way how their careers would have been affected as a result. But we do know that there is a statistically significant association, on an "other things equal" basis, between attendance at the most selective schools within the C&B universe and a variety of accomplishments during college and in later life. Generally speaking, the more selective the school, the more the student achieved subsequently. Also, we saw that C&B students as a group earned appreciably more money than did the subgroup of students in our national control with mostly As, which suggests that going to a C&B school conferred a considerable premium on all C&B students, and probably an especially high premium on black students. Black C&B students were also more likely than black college graduates in general to become leaders of community and social service organizations. These findings suggest that reducing the number of black matriculants at the C&B schools would

---

* "College and Beyond."

almost certainly have had a decidedly negative effect on the subsequent careers of many of these students and on their contributions to civic life as well.

Even more severe effects would result from insisting on race-neutral admissions policies in professional schools. In law and medicine, all schools are selective. As a consequence, the effect of barring any consideration of race would be the exclusion of more than half of the existing minority student population from these professions. Race-neutral admissions policies would reduce the number of black students in the most selective schools of law and medicine to less than 1 percent of all students. Since major law firms and medical centers often limit their recruitment to the most selective schools, this outcome would deal a heavy blow to efforts to prepare future black leaders for the professions.

But what about the other students (most of whom are presumably white) who would have taken the places of these retrospectively rejected black students in selective colleges and professional schools? There is every reason to believe that they, too, would have done well, in school and afterwards, though probably not as well as the regularly admitted white students (who were, after all, preferred to them in the admissions process). Still, on the basis of the evidence in this study, the excluded white male students might have done at least as well as their retrospectively rejected black classmates, and probably even better in terms of average earnings. On the other hand, fewer of the "retrospectively accepted" white women would have been employed, and those who were employed would have earned about the same amount of money as the retrospectively rejected black women. Fewer of the additional white students, women and men, would have been involved in volunteer activities, especially in leadership positions.

Would society have been better off if additional numbers of whites and Asian Americans had been substituted for minority students in this fashion? That is the central question, and it cannot be answered by data alone.

Fundamental judgments have to be made about societal needs, values, and objectives. When a distinguished black educator visited the Mellon Foundation, he noted, with understandable pride, that his son had done brilliantly in college and was being considered for a prestigious graduate award in neuroscience. "My son," the professor said, "needs no special consideration; he is so talented that he will make it on his own." His conclusion was that we should be indifferent to whether his son or any of the white competitors got the particular fellowship in question. We agreed that, in all likelihood, all of these candidates would benefit from going to the graduate school in question and, in time, become excellent scientists or doctors. Still, one can argue with the conclusion reached by the parent. "Your son will do fine," another person present at the meeting said, "but that isn't the issue. *He may not need us, but we need him!* Why? Because there is only one of him."

That mild exaggeration notwithstanding, the relative scarcity of talented black professionals is all too real. It seemed clear to a number of us that day, and it probably seems clear to many others, that American society needs the high-achieving black graduates who will provide leadership in every walk of life. This is the position of many top officials concerned with filling key positions in government, of CEOs who affirm that they would continue their minority recruitment programs whether or not there were a legal requirement to do so, and of bar associations, medical associations, and other professional organizations that have repeatedly stressed the importance of attracting more minority members into their fields. In view of these needs, we are not indifferent to which student gets the graduate fellowship.

Neither of the authors of this study has any sympathy with quotas or any belief in mandating the proportional representation of groups of people, defined by race or any other criterion, in positions of authority. Nor do we include ourselves among those who support race-sensitive admissions as compensation for a legacy of racial discrimination. We agree emphatically with the sentiment expressed by Mamphela Ramphele, vice chancellor of the University of Cape Town in South Africa, when she said: "Everyone deserves opportunity; no one deserves success." But we remain persuaded that present racial disparities in outcomes are dismayingly disproportionate. At the minimum, this country needs to maintain the progress now being made in educating larger numbers of black professionals and black leaders.

Selective colleges and universities have made impressive contributions at both undergraduate and graduate levels. To take but a single illustration: since starting to admit larger numbers of black students in the late 1960s, the Harvard Law School has numbered among its black graduates more than one hundred partners in law firms, more than ninety black alumni/ae with the title of Chief Executive Officer, Vice President, or General Counsel of a corporation, more than seventy professors, at least thirty judges, two members of Congress, the mayor of a major American city, the head of the Office of Management and Budget, and an Assistant US. Attorney General. In this study, we have documented more systematically the accomplishments of the nearly 1,900 black '76 matriculants at the twenty-eight C&B schools, and the evidence of high achievement is overwhelming—there is no other word for it. These individuals are still in their late thirties, having entered college just over twenty years ago. We shall be very surprised if their record of achievement is not magnified many times as they gain seniority and move up various institutional ladders. If, at the end of the day, the question is whether the most selective colleges and universities have succeeded in educating sizable numbers of minority students who have already achieved considerable success and seem likely in time to occupy positions of leadership throughout society, we have no problem in answering the question. Absolutely.

We commented earlier on the need to make clear choices. Here is perhaps the clearest choice. Let us suppose that rejecting, on race-neutral grounds, more than half of the black students who otherwise would attend these institutions would raise the probability of acceptance for another white student from 25 percent to, say, 27 percent at the most selective colleges and universities. Would we, as a society, be better off? Considering both the educational benefits of diversity and the need to include far larger numbers of black graduates in the top ranks of the business, professional, governmental, and not-for-profit institutions that shape our society, we do not think so.

How one responds to such questions depends very much, of course, on how important one thinks it is that progress continues to be made in narrowing black-white gaps in earnings and in representation in top-level positions. As the United States grows steadily more diverse, we believe that Nicholas Katzenbach and Burke Marshall are surely right in insisting that the country must continue to make determined efforts to "include blacks in the institutional framework that constitutes America's economic, political, educational and social life." This goal of greater inclusiveness is important for reasons, both moral and practical, that offer all Americans the prospect of living in a society marked by more equality and racial harmony than one might otherwise anticipate.

We recognize that many opponents of race-sensitive admissions will also agree with Katzenbach and Marshall, but will argue that there are better ways of promoting inclusiveness. There is everything to be said, in our view, for addressing the underlying problems in families, neighborhoods, and primary and secondary schools that many have identified so clearly. But this is desperately difficult work, which will, at best, produce results only over a very long period of time. Meanwhile, it is important, in our view, to do what can be done to make a difference at each educational level, including colleges and graduate and professional schools.

The alternative seems to us both stark and unworthy of our country's ideals. Turning aside from efforts to help larger numbers of well-qualified blacks gain the educational advantages they will need to move steadily and confidently into the mainstream of American life could have extremely serious consequences. Here in the United States, as elsewhere in the world, visible efforts by leading educational institutions to make things better will encourage others to press on with the hard work needed to overcome the continuing effects of a legacy of unfair treatment. Leon Higginbotham spoke from the heart when, commenting on the aftermath of the *Hopwood* decision, he said, "I sometimes feel as if I am watching justice die." To engender such feelings, and a consequent loss of hope on the part of many who have not attained Judge Higginbotham's status, seems a high price to pay for a tiny increase in the probability of admission for white applicants to academically selective colleges and universities. . . .

QUESTIONS FOR REFLECTION

1. Why, according to Bowen and Bok, is affirmative action compatible with admission according to merit?

2. What educational benefits do affirmative action programs produce, in their view?

3. What evidence do Bowen and Bok adduce for the societal benefits of affirmative action plans?

4. Critics sometimes charge that affirmative action is unfair to white students who are displaced. How do Bowen and Bok answer that charge?

5. How do they answer the objection that affirmative action harms society by channeling educational resources to less qualified students?

6. Do you think that Bowen and Bok would find similar patterns among students admitted to the average state university, for example? Why or why not?

SEXUAL EQUALITY

Discrimination, as we have seen, is unfair. It involves treating similar cases differently, and that contradicts the categorical imperative. For that reason, we have come to see racial discrimination as a form of injustice. We have struck down segregation as unconstitutional and have worked toward a society in which race will truly be a morally irrelevant consideration.

Discrimination on the basis of sex seems just as odious as discrimination on the basis of race. Women should not be denied opportunities available to men, just as blacks should not be denied opportunities available to whites. There has been a history of discrimination against women, which has limited women's educational and occupational opportunities. Eliminating that discrimination has become an important social goal.

The goal of sexual equality, however, is more controversial than the goal of racial equality, and the means to the goal, however it is defined, are similarly controversial. In *Brown* v. *Board of Education* (1954), the Supreme Court held that segregating students by race was inherently discriminatory. But not until *U.S. v. Virginia* (1997) did the Court make a similar ruling concerning segregation by sex. The Court found that Virginia could not legitimately restrict admission to Virginia Military Institute to men. That decision remains controversial in a way that *Brown* does not. No one alleges that racial segregation has educational benefits. But there is evidence that separating the sexes does help some young people learn. Moreover, the Court has not similarly forced women's colleges to open their doors to men.

The goal of sexual equality differs from that of racial equality in other ways. Having separate bathrooms for blacks and whites was one of the most objectionable features of segregation, but no one objects to having separate bathrooms for men and women. Minorities are thoroughly integrated into the armed forces, but placing women in combat units has ignited controversy in various countries. Many who would be appalled at racial restrictions on marriage object to same-sex marriage. There are also

important historical differences. Much discrimination against women has not been discrimination in the law but discrimination in private conduct—in parents refusing to pay for college educations for their daughters, for example, or in men and women alike believing that only men can perform certain kinds of jobs.

Alison Jaggar criticizes two common understandings of the goal of sexual equality. To some, sexual equality means blindness to sexual differences—treating men and women the same. (This is what Christine Littleton calls "the symmetrical approach.") But this may not always be fair; men and women differ in some morally relevant ways. Only women, for example, get pregnant, give birth, and nurse babies. A rule against pregnancy or breast-feeding in the workplace thus affects men and women differently, even if it applies to people of both sexes on its face. To some, consequently, sexual equality has meant responsiveness to such sexual differences. (This is what Littleton calls "the asymmetrical approach.") But admitting that men and women are different and deserve to be treated differently threatens to open the door to discrimination against women. Jaggar argues for a new, dynamic conception of sexual equality as requiring similarity of treatment in some circumstances and different treatment in others, depending on what best serves the long-term interests of women.

Littleton begins by distinguishing versions of the symmetrical and asymmetrical approaches. She, too, finds them unsatisfying and seeks to redefine sexual equality as acceptance. Her approach, like Jaggar's, focuses on the consequences of treating men and women alike or differently. But while Jaggar urges us to do whatever best promotes women's long-term interests, Littleton urges us to seek an equality of consequences.

Susan Okin focuses on a different aspect of sexual equality. Many of the roots of inequality are not in the law but in the family—in the division of household duties, in the different roles that men and women are expected to fulfill, and in the models for personal and social relationships that men and women are socialized to accept. Injustice in the family echoes throughout society as a whole. So, achieving sexual equality requires us to rethink and restructure family relationships.

Christina Hoff Sommers worries that feminists such as Jaggar, Littleton, and Okin fail to take the preferences of real women seriously. Women are free to choose what fields to study, what careers to pursue, whether or not to marry or have children, and what kinds of relationships to seek with others. Their choices differ from those of men in various ways. That has broad social, economic, and political consequences that often conflict with particular conceptions of sexual equality. Feminists thus face a dilemma: abandon those concepts of equality or seek to restrict women's freedom and alter their choices.

JUSTICES RUTH BADER GINSBURG AND ANTONIN SCALIA

Majority and Dissenting Opinions in *United States* v. *Virginia Et Al.* (1996)

Ruth Bader Ginsburg and Antonin Scalia are Justices of the United States Supreme Court. (Source: United States v. Virginia et al. 518 U.S. 515 [1996].)

Justice Ginsburg delivered the opinion of the Court.

Virginia's public institutions of higher learning include an incomparable military college, Virginia Military Institute (VMI). The United States maintains that the Constitution's equal protection guarantee precludes Virginia from reserving exclusively to men the unique educational opportunities VMI affords. We agree.

I.

Founded in 1839, VMI is today the sole single-sex school among Virginia's 15 public institutions of higher learning. VMI's distinctive mission is to produce "citizen-soldiers," men prepared for leadership in civilian life and in military service. VMI pursues this mission through pervasive training of a kind not available anywhere else in Virginia. Assigning prime place to character development, VMI uses an "adversative method" modeled on English public schools and once characteristic of military instruction. VMI constantly endeavors to instill physical and mental discipline in its cadets and impart to them a strong moral code. The school's graduates leave VMI with heightened comprehension of their capacity to deal with duress and stress, and a large sense of accomplishment for completing the hazardous course.

VMI has notably succeeded in its mission to produce leaders; among its alumni are military generals, Members of Congress, and business executives. The school's alumni overwhelmingly perceive that their VMI training helped them to realize their personal goals. VMI's endowment reflects the loyalty of its graduates; VMI has the largest per-student endowment of all undergraduate institutions in the Nation.

Neither the goal of producing citizen-soldiers nor VMI's implementing methodology is inherently unsuitable to women. And the school's impressive record in producing leaders has made admission desirable to some women. Nevertheless, Virginia has elected to preserve exclusively for men the advantages and opportunities a VMI education affords.

II.

A.

From its establishment in 1839 as one of the Nation's first state military colleges, see 1839 Va. Acts, ch. 20, VMI has remained financially supported by Virginia and "subject to the control of the [Virginia] General Assembly." First southern college to teach engineering and industrial chemistry, VMI once provided teachers for the State's schools. Civil War strife threatened the school's vitality, but a resourceful superintendent regained legislative support by highlighting "VMI's great potential[,] through its technical know-how," to advance Virginia's postwar recovery.

VMI today enrolls about 1,300 men as cadets. Its academic offerings in the liberal arts, sciences, and engineering are also available at other public colleges and universities in Virginia. But VMI's mission is special. It is the mission of the school

> to produce educated and honorable men, prepared for the varied work of civil life, imbued with love of learning, confident in the functions and attitudes of leadership, possessing a high sense of public service, advocates of the American democracy and free enterprise system, and ready as citizen-soldiers to defend their country in time of national peril.

In contrast to the federal service academies, institutions maintained "to prepare cadets for career service in the armed forces," VMI's program "is directed at preparation for both military and civilian life"; "[o]nly about 15% of VMI cadets enter career military service."

VMI produces its "citizen-soldiers" through "an adversative, or doubting, model of education" which features "[p]hysical rigor, mental stress, absolute equality of treatment, absence of privacy, minute regulation of behavior, and indoctrination in desirable values." As one Commandant of Cadets described it, the adversative method "dissects the young student," and makes him aware of his "limits and capabilities," so that he knows "how far he can go with his anger, . . . how much he can take under stress, . . . exactly what he can do when he is physically exhausted."

VMI cadets live in spartan barracks where surveillance is constant and privacy nonexistent; they wear uniforms, eat together in the mess hall, and regularly participate in drills. Entering students are incessantly exposed to the rat line, "an extreme form of the adversative model," comparable in intensity to Marine Corps boot camp. Tormenting and punishing, the rat line bonds new cadets to their fellow sufferers and, when they have completed the 7-month experience, to their former tormentors.

VMI's "adversative model" is further characterized by a hierarchical "class system" of privileges and responsibilities, a "dyke system" for assigning a senior class mentor to each entering class "rat," and a strin-

gently enforced "honor code," which prescribes that a cadet "does not lie, cheat, steal, or tolerate those who do."

VMI attracts some applicants because of its reputation as an extraordinarily challenging military school, and "because its alumni are exceptionally close to the school." "[W]omen have no opportunity anywhere to gain the benefits of [the system of education at VMI]."

III.

The cross-petitions in this case present two ultimate issues. First, does Virginia's exclusion of women from the educational opportunities provided by VMI —extraordinary opportunities for military training and civilian leadership development—deny to women "capable of all of the individual activities required of VMI cadets," the equal protection of the laws guaranteed by the Fourteenth Amendment? Second, if VMI's "unique" situation as Virginia's sole single-sex public institution of higher education offends the Constitution's equal protection principle, what is the remedial requirement?

IV.

Today's skeptical scrutiny of official action denying rights or opportunities based on sex responds to volumes of history. As a plurality of this Court acknowledged a generation ago, "our Nation has had a long and unfortunate history of sex discrimination." Through a century plus three decades and more of that history, women did not count among voters composing "We the People"; not until 1920 did women gain a constitutional right to the franchise. And for a half-century thereafter, it remained the prevailing doctrine that government, both federal and state, could withhold from women opportunities accorded men so long as any "basis in reason" could be conceived for the discrimination.

In 1971, for the first time in our Nation's history, this Court ruled in favor of a woman who complained that her State had denied her the equal protection of its laws. Since *Reed,* the Court has repeatedly recognized that neither federal nor state government acts compatibly with the equal protection principle when a law or official policy denies to women, simply because they are women, full citizenship stature—equal opportunity to aspire, achieve, participate in, and contribute to society based on their individual talents and capacities.

Without equating gender classifications, for all purposes, to classifications based on race or national origin, the Court, in post-*Reed* decisions, has carefully inspected official action that closes a door or denies opportunity to women (or to men). To summarize the Court's current directions for cases of official classification based on gender: Focusing on the differential treatment or denial of opportunity for which relief is sought, the reviewing court must determine whether the proffered justification is "exceedingly persuasive." The burden of justification is demanding, and it rests entirely on the State. The State must show "at least that the [challenged] classification serves 'important governmental objectives' and that the discriminatory means employed are substantially related to the achievement of those objectives.'" The justification must be genuine, not hypothesized or invented *post hoc* in response to litigation. And it must not rely on overbroad generalizations about the different talents, capacities, or preferences of males and females.

The heightened review standard our precedent establishes does not make sex a proscribed classification. Supposed "inherent differences" are no longer accepted as a ground for race or national origin classifications. Physical differences between men and women, however, are enduring: "[T]he two sexes are not fungible; a community made up exclusively of one [sex] is different from a community composed of both."

"Inherent differences" between men and women, we have come to appreciate, remain cause for celebration, but not for denigration of the members of either sex or for artificial constraints on an individual's opportunity. Sex classifications may be used to compensate women "for particular economic disabilities [they have] suffered," to "promot[e] equal employment opportunity," to advance full development of the talent and capacities of our Nation's people. But such classifications may not be used, as they once were, to create or perpetuate the legal, social, and economic inferiority of women.

Measuring the record in this case against the review standard just described, we conclude that Virginia has shown no "exceedingly persuasive justification" for excluding all women from the citizen-soldier training afforded by VMI.

Justice Scalia, dissenting.

Today the Court shuts down an institution that has served the people of the Commonwealth of Virginia with pride and distinction for over a century and a half. To achieve that desired result, it rejects (contrary to our established practice) the factual findings of two courts below, sweeps aside the precedents of this Court, and ignores the history of our people. As to facts: it explicitly rejects the finding that there exist "gender-based developmental differences" supporting Virginia's restriction of the "adversative" method to only a men's institution, and the finding that the all-male composition of the Virginia Military Institute (VMI) is essential to that institution's character. As to precedent: It drastically revises our established standards for reviewing sex-based classifications. And as to history: It counts for nothing the long tradition, enduring down to the present, of men's military colleges supported both by States and [by] the Federal Government.

Much of the Court's opinion is devoted to deprecating the closed-mindedness of our forebears with regard to women's education, and even with regard to the treatment of women in areas that have nothing to do with education. Closed-minded they were—as every age is, including our own, with regard to matters it cannot guess, because it simply does not consider them debatable. The virtue of a democratic system with a First Amendment is that it readily enables the people, over time, to be persuaded that what they took for granted is not so, and to change their laws accordingly. That system is destroyed if the smug assurances of each age are removed from the democratic process and written into the Constitution. So to counterbalance the Court's criticism of our ancestors, let me say a word in their praise: They left us free to change. The same cannot be said of this most illiberal Court, which has embarked on a course of inscribing one after another of the current preferences of the society (and in some cases only the counter-majoritarian preferences of the society's law-trained elite) into our Basic Law. Today it enshrines the notion that no substantial educational value is to be served by an all-men's military academy—so that the decision by the people of Virginia to maintain such an institution denies equal protection to women who cannot attend that institution but can attend others. Since it is entirely clear that the Constitution of the United States—the old one—takes no sides in this educational debate, I dissent.

I

The all-male constitution of VMI comes squarely within such a governing tradition. Founded by the Commonwealth of Virginia in 1839 and continuously maintained by it since, VMI has always admitted only men. And in that regard it has not been unusual. For almost all of VMI's more than a century and a half of existence, its single-sex status reflected the uniform practice for government-supported military colleges. Another famous Southern institution, The Citadel, has existed as a state-funded school of South Carolina since 1842. And all the federal military colleges—West Point, the Naval Academy at Annapolis, and even the Air Force Academy, which was not established until 1954—admitted only males for most of their history. Their admission of women in 1976 (upon which the Court today relies), came not by court decree, but because the people, through their elected representatives, decreed a change. In other words, the tradition of having government-funded military schools for men is as well rooted in the traditions of this country as the tradition of sending only men into military combat. The people may decide to change the one tradition, like the other, through democratic processes; but the assertion that either tradition has been unconstitutional through the centuries is not law, but politics-smuggled-into-law.

And the same applies, more broadly, to single-sex education in general, which, as I shall discuss, is threatened by today's decision with the cutoff of all state and federal support. Government-run nonmilitary educational institutions for the two sexes have until very recently also been part of our national tradition. "[It is] [c]oeducation, historically, [that] is a

novel educational theory. From grade school through high school, college, and graduate and professional training, much of the Nation's population during much of our history has been educated in sexually segregated classrooms." These traditions may of course be changed by the democratic decisions of the people, as they largely have been.

Today, however, change is forced upon Virginia, and reversion to single-sex education is prohibited nationwide, not by democratic processes but by order of this Court. Even while bemoaning the sorry, bygone days of "fixed notions" concerning women's education, the Court favors current notions so fixedly that it is willing to write them into the Constitution of the United States by application of custom-built "tests." This is not the interpretation of a Constitution, but the creation of one.

II.

It is hard to consider women a "discrete and insular minorit[y]" unable to employ the "political processes ordinarily to be relied upon," when they constitute a majority of the electorate. And the suggestion that they are incapable of exerting that political power smacks of the same paternalism that the Court so roundly condemns. Moreover, a long list of legislation proves the proposition false.

III.

A.

It is beyond question that Virginia has an important state interest in providing effective college education for its citizens. That single-sex instruction is an approach substantially related to that interest should be evident enough from the long and continuing history in this country of men's and women's colleges. But beyond that, as the Court of Appeals here stated: "That single-gender education at the college level is beneficial to both sexes is a fact established in this case."

The evidence establishing that fact was overwhelming—indeed, "virtually uncontradicted," in the words of the court that received the evidence. As an initial matter, Virginia demonstrated at trial that "[a] substantial body of contemporary scholarship and research supports the proposition that, although males and females have significant areas of developmental overlap, they also have differing developmental needs that are deep-seated." While no one questioned that for many students a coeducational environment was nonetheless not inappropriate, that could not obscure the demonstrated benefits of single-sex colleges. For example, the District Court stated as follows:

> One empirical study in evidence, not questioned by any expert, demonstrates that single-sex colleges provide better educational experiences than coeducational institutions. Students of both sexes become more academically involved, interact with faculty frequently, show larger increases in intellectual self-esteem and are more satisfied with practically all aspects of college experience (the sole exception is social life) compared with their counterparts in coeducational institutions. Attendance at an all-male college substantially increases the likelihood that a student will carry out career plans in law, business and college teaching, and also has a substantial positive effect on starting salaries in business. Women's colleges increase the chances that those who attend will obtain positions of leadership, complete the baccalaureate degree, and aspire to higher degrees.

"[I]n the light of this very substantial authority favoring single-sex education," the District Court concluded that "the VMI Board's decision to maintain an all-male institution is fully justified even without taking into consideration the other unique features of VMI's teaching and training." This finding alone, which even this Court cannot dispute, should be sufficient to demonstrate the constitutionality of VMI's all-male composition.

But besides its single-sex constitution, VMI is different from other colleges in another way. It employs a "distinctive educational method," sometimes referred to as the "adversative, or doubting, model of education." "Physical rigor, mental stress, absolute equality of treatment, absence of privacy, minute regulation of behavior, and indoctrination in desirable values are the salient attributes of the VMI educational experience." Id., at 1421. No one contends that this method is appropriate for all individuals; education is not a "one-size-fits-all" business. Just as

a State may wish to support junior colleges, vocational institutes, or a law school that emphasizes case practice instead of classroom study, so too a State's decision to maintain within its system one school that provides the adversative method is "substantially related" to its goal of good education. Moreover, it was uncontested that "if the state were to establish a women's VMI-type [i.e., adversative] program, the program would attract an insufficient number of participants to make the program work"; and it was found by the District Court that if Virginia were to include women in VMI, the school "would eventually find it necessary to drop the adversative system altogether." Thus, Virginia's options were an adversative method that excludes women or no adversative method at all.

There can be no serious dispute that, as the District Court found, single-sex education and a distinctive educational method "represent legitimate contributions to diversity in the Virginia higher education system." As a theoretical matter, Virginia's educational interest would have been best served (insofar as the two factors we have mentioned are concerned) by six different types of public colleges —an all-men's, an all-women's, and a coeducational college run in the "adversative method," and an all-men's, an all-women's, and a coeducational college run in the "traditional method." But as a practical matter, of course, Virginia's financial resources, like any State's, are not limitless, and the Commonwealth must select among the available options. Virginia thus has decided to fund, in addition to some 14 coeducational 4-year colleges, one college that is run as an all-male school on the adversative model: the Virginia Military Institute.

Virginia did not make this determination regarding the makeup of its public college system on the unrealistic assumption that no other colleges exist. Substantial evidence in the District Court demonstrated that the Commonwealth has long proceeded on the principle that "[h]igher education resources should be viewed as a whole—public and private—" because such an approach enhances diversity and because "it is academic and economic waste to permit unwarranted duplication." It is thus significant that, whereas there are "four all-female private [colleges] in Virginia," there is only "one private all-male college," which "indicates that the private sector is providing for th[e] [former] form of education to a much greater extent than it provides for all-male education." In these circumstances, Virginia's election to fund one public all-male institution and one on the adversative model—and to concentrate its resources in a single entity that serves both these interests in diversity—is substantially related to the State's important educational interests.

B.

IV.

As is frequently true, the Court's decision today will have consequences that extend far beyond the parties to the case. What I take to be the Court's unease with these consequences, and its resulting unwillingness to acknowledge them, cannot alter the reality.

A.

Under the constitutional principles announced and applied today, single-sex public education is unconstitutional. By going through the motions of applying a balancing test—asking whether the State has adduced an "exceedingly persuasive justification" for its sex-based classification—the Court creates the illusion that government officials in some future case will have a clear shot at justifying some sort of single-sex public education. Indeed, the Court seeks to create even a greater illusion than that: It purports to have said nothing of relevance to other public schools at all. "We address specifically and only an educational opportunity . . . as 'unique'. . . ."

The Supreme Court of the United States does not sit to announce "unique" dispositions. Its principal function is to establish precedent—that is, to set forth principles of law that every court in America must follow. As we said only this Term, we expect both ourselves and lower courts to adhere to the "rationale upon which the Court based the results of its earlier decisions." That is the principal reason we publish our opinions.

And the rationale of today's decision is sweeping: for sex-based classifications, a redefinition of intermediate scrutiny that makes it indistinguishable from strict scrutiny. Indeed, the Court indicates that

if any program restricted to one sex is "uniqu[e]," it must be opened to members of the opposite sex "who have the will and capacity" to participate in it. I suggest that the single-sex program that will not be capable of being characterized as "unique" is not only unique but nonexistent.

In any event, regardless of whether the Court's rationale leaves some small amount of room for lawyers to argue, it ensures that single-sex public education is functionally dead. The costs of litigating the constitutionality of a single-sex education program, and the risks of ultimately losing that litigation, are simply too high to be embraced by public officials. Any person with standing to challenge any sex-based classification can haul the State into federal court and compel it to establish by evidence (presumably in the form of expert testimony) that there is an "exceedingly persuasive justification" for the classification. Should the courts happen to interpret that vacuous phrase as establishing a standard that is not utterly impossible of achievement, there is considerable risk that whether the standard has been met will not be determined on the basis of the record evidence—indeed, that will necessarily be the approach of any court that seeks to walk the path the Court has trod today. No state official in his right mind will buy such a high-cost, high-risk lawsuit by commencing a single-sex program. The enemies of single-sex education have won; by persuading only seven Justices (five would have been enough) that their view of the world is enshrined in the Constitution, they have effectively imposed that view on all 50 States.

This is especially regrettable because, as the District Court here determined, educational experts in recent years have increasingly come to "suppor[t] [the] view that substantial educational benefits flow from a single-gender environment, be it male or female, that cannot be replicated in a coeducational setting." "The evidence in th[is] case," for example, "is virtually uncontradicted" to that effect. Until quite recently, some public officials have attempted to institute new single-sex programs, at least as experiments. In 1991, for example, the Detroit Board of Education announced a program to establish three boys-only schools for inner-city youth; it was met with a lawsuit, a preliminary injunction was swiftly entered by a District Court . . . and the Detroit Board of Education voted to abandon the litigation and thus abandon the plan. Today's opinion assures that no such experiment will be tried again.

B.

Justice Brandeis said it is "one of the happy incidents of the federal system that a single courageous State may, if its citizens choose, serve as a laboratory; and try novel social and economic experiments without risk to the rest of the country." But it is one of the unhappy incidents of the federal system that a self-righteous Supreme Court, acting on its Members' personal view of what would make a "more perfect Union," (a criterion only slightly more restrictive than a "more perfect world"), can impose its own favored social and economic dispositions nationwide. As today's disposition, and others this single Term, show, this places it beyond the power of a "single courageous State," not only to introduce novel dispositions that the Court frowns upon, but to reintroduce, or indeed even adhere to, disfavored dispositions that are centuries old. The sphere of self-government reserved to the people of the Republic is progressively narrowed.

. . . Today's decision does not leave VMI without honor; no court opinion can do that.

In an odd sort of way, it is precisely VMI's attachment to such old-fashioned concepts as manly "honor" that has made it, and the system it represents, the target of those who today succeed in abolishing public single-sex education. The record contains a booklet that all first-year VMI students (the so-called "rats") were required to keep in their possession at all times. Near the end there appears the following period-piece, entitled "The Code of a Gentleman":

> Without a strict observance of the fundamental Code of Honor, no man, no matter how "polished," can be considered a gentleman. The honor of a gentleman demands the inviolability of his word, and the incorruptibility of his principles. He is the descendant of the knight, the crusader; he is the defender of the

defenseless and the champion of justice . . . or he is not a Gentleman.

> A Gentleman . . .
>
> Does not discuss his family affairs in public or with acquaintances.
>
> Does not speak more than casually about his girlfriend.
>
> Does not go to a lady's house if he is affected by alcohol. He is temperate in the use of alcohol.
>
> Does not lose his temper; nor exhibit anger, fear, hate, embarrassment, ardor or hilarity in public.
>
> Does not hail a lady from a club window.
>
> A gentleman never discusses the merits or demerits of a lady.
>
> Does not mention names exactly as he avoids the mention of what things cost.
>
> Does not borrow money from a friend, except in dire need. Money borrowed is a debt of honor, and must be repaid as promptly as possible. Debts incurred by a deceased parent, brother, sister or grown child are assumed by honorable men as a debt of honor.
>
> Does not display his wealth, money or possessions.
>
> Does not put his manners on and off, whether in the club or in a ballroom. He treats people with courtesy, no matter what their social position may be.
>
> Does not slap strangers on the back nor so much as lay a finger on a lady.
>
> Does not 'lick the boots of those above' nor 'kick the face of those below him on the social ladder.'
>
> Does not take advantage of another's helplessness or ignorance and assumes that no gentleman will take advantage of him.
>
> A Gentleman respects the reserves of others, but demands that others respect those which are his.
>
> A Gentleman can become what he wills to be . . ."

I do not know whether the men of VMI lived by this Code; perhaps not. But it is powerfully impressive that a public institution of higher education still in existence sought to have them do so. I do not think any of us, women included, will be better off for its destruction.

QUESTIONS FOR REFLECTION

1. Is the history of discrimination against women important to the Court's decision? If so, why?

2. Under what circumstances may the State limit opportunities for women? Is there a philosophical rationale for that criterion?

3. How did Virginia try to justify restricting VMI to men? How does the Court respond?

4. Why, in Justice Scalia's view, does the Court's decision restrict freedom?

5. What is the role of tradition in Justice Scalia's argument? In what sense is his argument Burkean?

MARY WOLLSTONECRAFT

from *A Vindication of the Rights of Woman* (1792)

(*Source: from Mary Wollstonecraft,* A Vindication of the Rights of Woman [*London: J. Johnson, 1792].*)

Contending for the rights of woman, my main argument is built on this simple principle, that if she not be prepared by education to become the companion of man, she will stop the progress of knowledge and virtue; for truth must be common to all, or it will be inefficacious with respect to its influence on general practice. And how can woman be expected to cooperate unless she know why she ought to be virtuous? Unless freedom strengthen her reason till she comprehend her duty, and see in what manner it is connected with her real good? If children are to be educated to understand the true principle of patriotism, their mother must be a patriot; and the love of mankind, from which an orderly train of virtues spring, can only be produced by considering the moral and civil interest of mankind; but the education and situation of woman, at present, shuts her out from such investigations.

. . . [S]urely, Sir, you will not assert, that a duty can be binding which is not founded on reason? If indeed this be their destination, arguments may be drawn from reason: and thus augustly supported, the more understanding women acquire, the more they will be attached to their duty—comprehending it—for unless they comprehend it, unless their morals be fixed on the same immutable principle as those of man, no authority can make them discharge it in a virtuous manner. They may be convenient slaves, but slavery will have its constant effect, degrading the master and the abject dependent.

But, if women are to be excluded, without having a voice, from a participation of the natural rights of mankind, prove first, to ward off the charge of unjustice and inconsistency, that they want reason—else this flaw in your NEW CONSTITUTION will ever shew that man must, in some shape, act like a tyrant, and tyranny, in whatever part of society it rears its brazen front, will ever undermine morality. . . . if women are not permitted to enjoy legitimate rights, they will render both men and themselves vicious, to obtain illicit privileges. . . .

In what does man's pre-eminence over the brute creation consist? The answer is as clear as that a half is less than a whole; in Reason.

What acquirement exalts one being above another? Virtue; we spontaneously reply.

For what purpose were the passions implanted? That man by struggling with them might attain a degree of knowledge denied to the brutes; whispers Experience.

Consequently, the perfection of our nature and capability of happiness, must be estimated by the degree of reason, virtue, and knowledge, that distinguish the individual, and direct the laws which bind society; and that from the exercise of reason, knowledge and virtue naturally flow, is equally undeniable, if mankind be viewed collectively.

. . . [T]he society is formed in the wisest manner, whose constitution is founded on the nature of man. . . .

Rousseau exerts himself to prove that all *was* right originally; a crowd of authors that all *is* now right; and I, that all will *be* right.

QUESTIONS FOR REFLECTION

1. Wollstonecraft argues that women, as mothers, play an important role in transmitting culture and virtue to the young. What follows from this, in her view?

2. Discrimination against women harms both men and women, according to Wollstonecraft. How?

3. Wollstonecraft is in part arguing against Rousseau, who held that virtue for a man differs from virtue for a woman. What is her argument?

4. Wollstonecraft contends that sex is not a morally relevant consideration. What role does reason play in her argument?

ALISON M. JAGGAR

Sexual Difference and Sexual Equality

Alison Jaggar is Professor of Philosophy at the University of Colorado at Boulder. (Source: Reprinted by permission from Deborah Rhode (ed.) Theoretical Perspectives on Sexual Difference (New Haven: Yale University Press, 1990). Copyright © 1990 by Alison M. Jaggar.)

The persistence and intensity of the perennial interest in sexual difference is not sustained by simple curiosity. Instead, it derives from an urgent concern with issues of sexual justice. For almost two and a half millennia, . . . men and later women have debated the nature, extent, and even existence of the differences between the sexes and reflected on their relevance for the just organization of society. . . .

Equality is a contested ideal notoriously open to a variety of interpretations. In the first part of this paper, I outline two ways in which some contemporary feminists have construed equality in legal contexts, identifying some of the problems that accompany each construal. In the second, I argue that both these conceptions of sexual equality presuppose unacceptable interpretations of sexual difference, and I go on to sketch an approach to understanding sexual difference that is more adequate to recent feminist insights. I suggest that this alternative approach to sexual difference casts the initial construals of sexual equality in a new light, pointing to the need for rethinking and perhaps even moving beyond the traditional ideal of western feminism.

Equality

Sexual Equality as Blindness to Sexual Difference

Western feminists have not always been unanimous in demanding sexual equality. Even though this ideal inspired not only some of the earliest English feminists but also participants in the U.S. Seneca Falls Convention of 1848, most nineteenth-century feminists in the United States did not endorse such a radical demand, preferring instead to retain membership in women's separate sphere. Despite the ideology of separate spheres, however, feminist challenges to such inequities in the legal system as women's inability to vote or to control their own property on marriage developed eventually into demands for identity of legal rights for men and women or, as it came to be called, equality before the law. By the end of the 1960s, mainstream feminists in the United States had come to believe that the legal system should be sex-blind, that it should not differentiate in any way between women and men. This belief was expressed in the struggle for an Equal Rights Amendment to the U.S. Constitution, an amendment that, had it passed, would have made any sex-specific law unconstitutional.

Nineteenth-century feminist demands for the suffrage and for property rights drew on a variety of arguments, sometimes claiming that women possessed distinctive ethical insight and nurturant capacities. A persistent theme in the feminist argument, however, was insistence on women's capacity to reason, an insistence conditioned by the classical liberal assumption that the ability to reason was the only legitimate ground for the ascription of democratic rights. From the eighteenth century on, feminists have argued consistently that women's reasoning capacity is at least equal to men's (though not necessarily identical to it) and have attributed women's lesser intellectual attainments primarily to their inferior education. Such arguments obviously tend to minimize the significance of the physiological differences between the sexes, since those differences are construed as irrelevant to the ascription of political rights. By the late 1960s and early 1970s, at the beginning of the most recent wave of western feminism, a conspicuously rationalist approach to women's equality was shared widely, though not universally, by English-speaking feminists, and arguments for so-called androgyny were common. The androgyny recommended typically was not physical, but mental and moral.

Over the past two decades, . . . however, it has become apparent that strict equality before the law may not always benefit women, at least not in the short term. Differences between the sexes have emerged as sufficiently significant to motivate some feminists as well as nonfeminists to recall the second part of the Aristotelian dictum: justice consists not only in treating like cases alike but also in treating different cases differently.

Contemporary feminists have identified a wide variety of differences between the sexes as relevant to sexual justice, though it should be noted that they are not always unanimous either about the list of differences or about the significance of its various items. What follow are only a few examples of differences between the sexes that many feminists claim it is unjust to ignore. Some of the differences seem almost inseparable from female biology, while others are linked more obviously with women's social circumstances.

The apparently biologically based differences between the sexes generally are connected with women's procreative capacity. The most evident and most frequently debated of such differences is women's ability to become pregnant and to give birth. In the now notorious case of *Gilbert v. General Electric* (1976), most feminists argued that a disability plan excluding disabilities related to pregnancy and childbirth discriminated against women, or treated women unequally, despite the indisputable fact that such a plan would fail "equally" to cover any man who became pregnant. A structurally similar example was a purportedly sex-blind ordinance forbidding firefighters to breast-feed between calls, an ordinance that of course applied "equally" to male and female firefighters. . . .

In the domestic sphere . . . some feminists recently have come to question whether justice is served best by treating men and women exactly alike. For example, no-fault divorce settlements dividing family property equally between husband and wife almost invariably leave wives in a far worse economic situation than they do husbands. In one study, for instance, ex-husbands' standard of living was found to have risen by 42 percent a year after divorce, whereas ex-wives' standard of living was reduced by 78 percent. This huge discrepancy in the outcome of divorce results from a variety of factors, including the fact that women and men typically are differently situated in the job market, with women usually having much lower job qualifications and less work experience. Child custody is another aspect of family law in which feminists recently have questioned the justice of viewing men and women as indistinguishable. For example, some feminists have argued that the increasingly popular assignment of joint custody to mothers and fathers unfairly penalizes women because joint custody statutes increase the bargaining strength of men at divorce and thereby aggravate the dependence of women, threatening their economic rights, their ability to raise their children without interference, and their geographic mobility.

. . . We live in a society divided deeply by gender, in which differences between the sexes, whatever their cause, are pronounced and inescapable. When these differences are ignored in the name of formal equality between the sexes, continuing substantive inequalities between women and men may be either obscured or rationalized and legitimated. At least in the present social context, sexual equality in the procedure often may ensure rather than obliterate sexual *inequality* in outcome.

Sexual Equality as Responsiveness to Sexual Difference

Within the last ten or fifteen years, increasing numbers of feminists have been challenging the assumption that sexual equality always requires sex-blindness. The growing public recognition that equality in areas other than gender relations is compatible with and may even require substantive differences in practical treatment adds plausibility to this challenge. For instance, equality in education ordinarily is taken to be compatible with, and even to require, the provision of different educational programs and bilingual or otherwise specially qualified teachers to serve the needs of children with varying abilities and disabilities. Similarly, there is increasing public willingness to provide special resources for people who are disabled or differently abled: readers for the blind, interpreters for the deaf, and adequate work space and access for those confined to wheelchairs.

Commitment to affirmative action in hiring probably constituted the first contemporary feminist challenge to the traditional sex-blind understanding of sexual equality. Affirmative action programs are generally uncontroversial among feminists because they are conceived as temporary expedients, as means rather than as ends. Typically such programs are defended as special protections for women (and other "suspect categories"), necessary in the short term in order to counter existing inequality of opportunity, but as something that should be abandoned once opportunities have been equalized. Rather than challenging the ideal of deinstitutionalizing sexual difference, therefore, affirmative action ultimately presupposes that ideal.

Most of the other proposals for achieving sexual equality through the recognition of sexual difference are considerably more controversial than affirmative action, even among feminists. One such proposal is that employers should be forbidden to terminate or to refuse a reasonable leave of absence to workers disabled by pregnancy or childbirth even though such leaves may not be available to workers who are disabled for other reasons. The *Miller-Wohl* and *California Federal* cases, for instance, sharply divided the feminist legal community.

Even more controversial than special pregnancy and maternity leaves are proposals to loosen the standard criteria of legal responsibility for women in some circumstances. For instance, there have been moves to recognize so-called premenstrual syndrome, which by definition afflicts only women, as a periodically disabling condition during which women enjoy diminished legal responsibility. Other feminist lawyers have proposed that there should be special criteria for identifying self-defense, criteria that go beyond immediate life-threatening danger, in the cases of women who kill their abusive husbands . . .

It is easy to understand why most proposals for achieving sexual equality through the institutional recognition of sexual difference are controversial among feminists. The reason is that the supposed benefits of such recognition are bought only at a certain price to women. This price includes the danger that measures apparently designed for women's special protection may end up protecting them primarily from the benefits that men enjoy. This has happened frequently in the past. For instance, as one author remarks,

> The protective labor legislation that limited the hours that women could work, prohibited night work and barred them from certain dangerous occupations such as mining may have promoted their health and safety and guaranteed them more time with their families. But it also precluded them from certain occupations requiring overtime, barred them from others where the entry point was the night shift, and may have contributed to the downward pressure on women's wages by creating a surplus of women in the jobs they are permitted to hold.

. . .

A further problem with treating women differently from men is that it reinforces sexual stereotypes. Among the most familiar and pervasive of prevailing stereotypes are the correlative assumptions that men by nature are sexual aggressors and that women's very presence is sexually arousing and constitutes a temptation to aggression. In recent years these assumptions have been the basis of court decisions excluding women from the job of prison guard in Alabama maximum security prisons and even from the job of chaplain in a male juvenile institution. Such decisions have not only the direct consequence of "protecting" women from jobs that may be the best paid available to them (in the case of the prison guard) or to which they may even feel a religious calling (in the case of the chaplain); they also have far-reaching indirect consequences insofar as they perpetuate the dangerous and damaging stereotype that women by nature are the sexual prey of men. This cultural myth serves as an implicit legitimation for the prostitution, sexual harassment, and rape of women, because it implies that such activities are in some sense natural. Other legislation designed to draw attention to the need to protect women's sexuality, such as legislation defining the subjects in pornography paradigmatically as female, may well have similar consequences.

Legal recognition of women as a specially protected category may also encourage homogenization or "essentialism," the view that women are all alike. . . . As the present wave of feminism has rolled on, middle-class white feminists have been forced to recognize that their definitions of women's nature and women's political priorities too often have been biased by factors like race, class, age, and physical ability. Legislation that separates women into a single category inevitably will define that category in a way that makes a certain subgroup of women into the paradigm for the whole sex. One group of women may be penalized by being forced to accept protection that another genuinely may need. One example is insurance plans that require all female employees to pay premiums for coverage of disabilities arising out of pregnancy and childbirth but which do not require the same contributions from male employees. Such a requirement forces lesbians, infertile women, and women who are not sexually active to underwrite the costs of heterosexual activity by some women—and, of course, by some men.

When the risks involved in the sex-responsive approach to sexual equality become apparent, feminist theory arrives at an impasse. Both the sex-blind and the sex-responsive interpretations of equality seem to bear unacceptable threats to women's already vulnerable economic and social status. In the next section I suggest that each interpretation of sexual equality rests on a construal of sexual difference that is inadequate for feminism.

Difference

The sex-blind interpretation of sexual equality rests on an assumption that existing differences between women have relatively little social significance. The obvious defect of this denial is that it ignores the extent to which sex and gender affect every aspect of everyone's life. People's work and play, dress and diet, income level and even speech patterns are regulated by social expectations regarding the appropriate appearance and behavior of sexed individuals, so that on all these dimensions people vary systematically, though not solely, according to sex. Prevailing norms of gender may be and often are challenged by certain individuals in certain areas,

but for most people most of the time these norms are simply the given framework of daily life. Feminists cannot deal with sexual difference simply by closing their eyes to its social institutionalization and refusing to recognize existing social and political realities.

The sex-responsive conception of sexual equality by definition is sensitive to these realities, but there are others to which it is blind. These are the realities of the differences *among* women, differences of race, class, sexual preference, religion, age, ethnicity, marital status, physical ability, and so on. Increasingly, contemporary feminists are recognizing that there is no typical woman, no essence of womanhood that underlies these other characteristics—which often constitute additional vectors of domination. Any conception of sexual difference that ignores these features is inadequate for a feminism seeking to represent the interests of all women.

There is an additional problem with the conception of sexual difference that underlies the sex-responsive conception of sexual equality. This problem emerges when sex-responsiveness is justified, as it invariably is, in terms of "protection" or "compensation," terms suggesting that women are damaged or disabled in comparison with men. Sometimes women's disabilities are seen as resulting from social causes, war wounds sustained by women as a result of life in a male-dominated society; sometimes women's disabilities are seen as presocial in origin, akin to female birth defects. In either case, however, the sex-responsive interpretation of sexual equality usually rests on a conception of sexual difference according to which women are inferior to men at least in some ways.

A Dynamic Approach to Sexual Difference

In saying that a more deeply feminist understanding of sexual difference must be dynamic rather than static, I mean that it must reflect the continually expanding feminist awareness of the ways in which the history of women's subordination, especially as this intersects with the history of other subordinated groups, has shaped and continues to shape both existing differences between the sexes and the ways in which we perceive and evaluate those differences.

A more fully feminist understanding of sexual difference does not deny that deep differences may exist between the sexes, but it does not assume that these differences are presocial or biological givens, unambiguous causes of women's apparently universal inequality and subordination. Instead, feminists must be committed to exploring the ways in which not only women's cognitive and emotional capacities, but even our bodies and our physical abilities, have been marked by a history of inequality and domination. . . . The differences we perceive between men and women may be results as much as causes of sexual inequality. . . .

[T]he context of social inequality is likely . . . to condition the values assigned to perceived sexual differences, so that male attributes are interpreted as assets and female attributes as defects. Social inequality of the sexes may even force revision of the standards by which sexual difference is measured, if men do not measure up well by those standards. The early development of I.Q. tests provides a clear example of this: when females performed better than males on the tests, their superior performance was taken as an indicator of the tests' invalidity and the tests were revised until the males performed up to the female standard. One doubts that the tests would have been revised if females had performed worse than males. . . .

When sexual difference comes to be understood in ways that are dynamic and woman-affirming rather than static and woman-devaluing, a new light is thrown on the ideal of sexual equality.

A Different Feminism

A dynamic approach to understanding sexual difference helps to explain the inadequacy of both the sex-blind and the sex-responsive ways of construing sexual equality. Because it recognizes the reality of sexual difference, such an approach shows why a sex-blind procedure may be unjust if it makes sexual inequality in outcome more likely. Simultaneously, through its recognition both of differences between women and the social genesis of many inter- and intrasex differences, it shows the dangers of self-fulfilling prophecy that lurk in the sex-responsive approach to sexual equality. A dynamic understanding of sexual difference demonstrates why feminism

must rethink traditional interpretations of sexual equality.

. . . Feminists seem caught in the dilemma of simultaneously demanding and scorning equality with men.

My own view is that feminists should embrace both horns of this dilemma, abandoning neither our short-term determination to reform existing society not our long-term desire to transform it. We should develop both the pragmatic and the utopian strands in our thinking, in the hope that each may strengthen the other.

On the one hand, feminists should continue to struggle for women to receive a fair share of the pie, carcinogenic though it ultimately may be. They should use the rhetoric of equality in situations where women's interests clearly are being damaged by their being treated either differently from or identically with men. It seems likely that neither of the two prevailing interpretations of equality is best in all circumstances. Sometimes equality in outcome may be served best by sex-blindness, sometimes by sex-responsiveness—and sometimes by attention to factors additional to or other than sex. Because perceived sexual differences so often are the result of differences in treatment, it seems prudent to advocate only short-term rather than permanent protections for women. For example, affirmative action and special legal defenses for chronically abused women seem less dangerous to women's status than premenstrual exemptions from legal responsibility. Some questions that have been presented as issues of sexual equality, such as antipornography ordinances and moves to draft women, may be decided better by reference to considerations other than those of equality.

Throughout the battle for sexual equality, it is necessary to remain critical of the standards by which that equality is measured. In particular, feminists should be ready constantly to challenge norms that may be stated in gender-neutral language but that are established on the basis of male experience and so likely to be biased in favor of men. One example of such a norm is the ordinance forbidding firefighters to breast-feed between calls; another is the minimum height requirement for airline pilots, a requirement based on the seemingly sex-blind concern that pilots be able to reach the instrument panel. Feminist challenges to such norms should mitigate at least to some extent the concern that sexual equality simply will "masculinize" women by assimilating them to male standards. The need to redesign the organization of both paid work and of domestic responsibility in order to avoid this kind of male bias must surely modify the extremes of gender polarization.

Simultaneously with insisting on sexual equality in a world presently racked by scarcity and injustice, feminists should develop their long-term visions of a world in which equality is less a goal than a background condition, a world in which justice is not "the first virtue of social institutions," but in which justice and equality are overshadowed by the goods of mutual care. But this must be care in a new sense, not the feminized, sentimentalized, privatized care with which we are familiar; not care as a nonrational or even irrational feeling; not care as self-sacrifice (Noddings' "motivational displacement"), nor care as contrasted with justice. Feminists need to develop a distinctive conception of care, one that draws on but transcends women's traditional practice. Feminist care must be responsive both to our common humanity and our inevitable particularity. Neither narrowly personal nor blandly impersonal, it can consist neither in the mechanical application of abstract rules nor in an uncritical surge of feeling, but must transcend both rationalism and romanticism.

The development of such a conception of care is a practical and political as much as an intellectual project. It cannot take place in a world that is structured by domination, where the public sphere is separated sharply from the private, and where inequality is justified in terms of such familiar, gender-linked, western oppositions as culture/nature, mind/body, reason/emotion—dichotomies in which each of the first terms is associated with the masculine and considered superior to each of the second. Instead, experimentation with ways of transcending equality requires an enriched and in some ways protected environment, a consciously feminist community dedicated to discovering less rigid and less hierarchical ways of living and thinking. We need not fear that such an environment will be so sheltered as to produce a weakened, hothouse plant. Far from being sheltered from the cold winds of the larger world, alternative communities may be particularly vulnerable to them. It is stimulating but hardly comfortable to live daily with contradictions.

QUESTIONS FOR REFLECTION

1. What is sexual equality, according to Jaggar?

2. Why is strict equality before the law sometimes insufficient?

3. What is Jaggar's view of affirmative action for women?

4. What is the conception of sexual equality as responsiveness to sexual differences? Why does Jaggar find it problematic?

5. On what issues do the two usual conceptions of sexual equality disagree?

6. What is Jaggar's proposal for sexual equality?

7. Jaggar criticizes Rawls in seeking to substitute mutual care for justice. What is her proposal, and how does it constitute a criticism of Rawls?

8. Someone might object that Jaggar's proposal is arbitrary and offer the following counterproposal: "Let's treat men and women equally whenever that promotes the long-term interests of men, and differently when *that* promotes the long-term interests of men." How might Jaggar defend herself against the charge of arbitrariness?

CHRISTINE A. LITTLETON

Reconstructing Sexual Equality

Christine Littleton is Professor of Law at UCLA. (Source: from California Law Review 75 (1987). Copyright © 1987 by California Law Review, Inc. Reprinted by permission.)

Development of Feminist Legal Theory

Feminist Reponses

Feminist legal theory has been primarily reactive, responding to the development of legal racial equality theory. The form of response, however, has varied. One response has been to attempt to equate legal treatment of sex with that of race and deny that there are in fact any significant natural differences between women and men; in other words, to consider the two sexes symmetrically located with regard to *any* issue, norm, or rule. This response, which I term the "symmetrical" approach, classifies asymmetries as illusions, "overboard generalizations," or temporary glitches that will disappear with a little behavior modification. A competing response rejects this analogy, accepting that women and men are or may be "different," and that women and men are often asymmetrically located in society. This response, which I term the "asymmetrical" approach, rejects the notion that all gender differences are likely to disappear, or even that they should.

1. Symmetrical Models of Sexual Equality

. . . There are two models of the symmetrical vision —referred to here as "assimilation" and "androgyny." Assimilation, the model most often accepted by the courts, is based on the notion that women, given the chance, really are or could be just like men. Therefore, the argument runs, the law should require so-

cial institutions to treat women as they already treat men—requiring, for example, that the professions admit women to the extent they are "qualified," but also insisting that women who enter time-demanding professions such as the practice of law sacrifice relationships (especially with their children) to the same extent that male lawyers have been forced to do.

Androgyny, the second symmetrical model, also posits that women and men are, or at least could be, very much like each other, but argues that equality requires institutions to pick some golden mean between the two and treat both sexes as androgynous persons would be treated. However, given that all of our institutions, work habits, and pay scales were formulated without the benefit of substantial numbers of androgynous persons, androgynous symmetry is difficult to conceptualize, and might require very substantial restructuring of many public and private institutions. In order to be truly androgynous within a symmetrical framework, social institutions must find a single norm that works equally well for all gendered characteristics. Part of my discomfort with androgynous models is that they depend on "meeting in the middle," while I distrust the ability of any person, and especially of any court, to value women enough to find the "middle." Moreover, the problems involved in determining such a norm for even one institution are staggering. At what height should a conveyor belt be set in order to satisfy a symmetrical androgynous ideal?

Symmetry appears to have great appeal for the legal system, and this is not surprising. The hornbook definition of equal protection is "that those who are similarly situated be similarly treated". . . . Symmetrical analysis also has great appeal for liberal men, to whom it appears to offer a share in the feminist enterprise. If perceived difference between the sexes is only the result of overly rigid sex roles, then men's liberty is at stake too. Ending this form of sexual inequality could free men to express their "feminine" side, just as it frees women to express their "masculine" side.

2. Asymmetrical Models of Sexual Equality

Asymmetrical approaches to sexual equality take the position that difference should not be ignored or eradicated. Rather, they argue that any sexually equal society must somehow deal with difference, problematic as that may be. Asymmetrical approaches include "special rights," "accommodation," "acceptance," and "empowerment."

The special rights model affirms that women and men *are* different, and asserts that cultural differences, such as childrearing roles, are rooted in biological ones, such as reproduction. Therefore, it states, society must take account of these differences and ensure that women are not punished for them. This approach, sometimes referred to as a "bivalent" model, is closest to the "special treatment" pole of the asymmetrical/symmetrical equality debate. Elizabeth Wolgast, a major proponent of special rights, argues that women cannot be men's "equals" because equality by definition requires sameness. Instead of equality, she suggests seeking justice, claiming special rights for women based on their special needs.

The second asymmetrical model, accommodation, agrees that differential treatment of biological differences (such as pregnancy, and perhaps breastfeeding) is necessary, but argues that cultural or hard-to-classify differences (such as career interests and skills) should be treated under an equal treatment or androgynous model. Examples of accommodation models include Sylvia Law's approach to issues of reproductive biology and Herma Hill Kay's "episodic" approach to the condition of pregnancy. These approaches could also be characterized as "symmetry, with concessions to asymmetry where necessary." The accommodationists limit the asymmetry in their models to biological differences because, like

Williams, they fear a return to separate spheres ideology should asymmetrical theory go too far.

My own attempt to grapple with difference, which I call an "acceptance" model, is essentially asymmetrical. While not endorsing the notion that cultural differences between the sexes are biologically determined, it does recognize and attempt to deal with both biological and social differences. Acceptance does not view sex differences as problematic per se, but rather focuses on the ways in which differences are permitted to justify inequality. It asserts that eliminating the unequal consequences of sex differences is more important than debating whether such differences are "real," or even trying to eliminate them altogether.

Unlike the accommodationists, who would limit asymmetrical analysis to purely biological differences, my proposal also requires equal acceptance of cultural differences. The reasons for this are twofold. First, the distinction between biological and cultural, while useful analytically, is itself culturally based. Second, the inequality experienced by women is often presented as a necessary consequence of cultural rather than of biological difference. If, for instance, women do in fact "choose" to become nurses rather than real estate appraisers, it is not because of any biological imperative. Yet, regardless of the reasons for the choice, they certainly do not choose to be paid less. It is the *consequences* of gendered difference, and not its sources, that equal acceptance addresses. . . .

The foregoing asymmetrical models, including my own, share the notion that, regardless of their differences, women and men must be treated as full members of society. Each model acknowledges that women may need treatment different from that accorded to men in order to effectuate their membership in important spheres of social life; all would allow at least some such claims, although on very different bases, and probably in very different circumstances.

A final asymmetrical approach, "empowerment," rejects difference altogether as a relevant subject of inquiry. In its strongest form, empowerment claims that the subordination of women to men has itself constructed the sexes, and their differences. . . . A somewhat weaker version of the claim is that we simply do not and cannot know whether there are any important differences between the sexes that have not been created by the dynamic of domination and subordination. In either event, the argument runs, we should forget about the question of differences and focus directly on subordination and domination. If a law, practice, or policy contributes to the subordination of women or their domination by men, it violates equality. If it empowers women or contributes to the breakdown of male domination, it enhances equality.

The reconceptualization of equality as antidomination, like the model of equality as acceptance, attempts to respond directly to the concrete and lived-out experience of women. Like other asymmetrical models, it allows different treatment of women and men when necessary to effectuate its overall goal of ending women's subordination. However, it differs substantially from the acceptance model in its rejection of the membership, belonging, and participatory aspects of equality.

3. The Difference That Difference Makes

Each of the several models of equality discussed above, if adopted, would have a quite different impact on the structure of society. If this society wholeheartedly embraced the symmetrical approach of assimilation—the point of view that "women are just like men"—little would need to be changed in our economic or political institutions except to get rid of lingering traces of irrational prejudice, such as an occasional employer's preference for male employees. In contrast, if society adopted the androgyny model, which views both women and men as bent out of shape by current sex roles and requires both to conform to an androgynous model, it would have to alter radically its methods of resource distribution. In the employment context, this might mean wholesale revamping of methods for determining the "best person for the job." Thus, while assimilation would merely require law firms to hire women who have managed to get the same credentials as the men they have traditionally hired, androgyny might insist that the firm hire only those persons with credentials that would be possessed by someone neither "socially male" nor "socially female."

If society adopted an asymmetrical approach such as the accommodation model, no radical restructuring would be necessary. Government would need only insist that women be given what they need to resemble men, such as time off to have babies and the freedom to return to work on the same rung of the ladder as their male counterparts. If, however, society adopted the model of equality as acceptance, which seeks to make difference costless, it might additionally insist that women and men who opt for socially female occupations, such as child-rearing, be compensated at a rate similar to those women and men who opt for socially male occupations, such as legal practice. Alternatively, such occupations might be restructured to make them equally accessible to those whose behavior is culturally coded "male" or "female." . . .

Equality as Acceptance

The model of equality as acceptance . . . [insists] that equality can . . . be applied *across* difference. It is not, however, a "leveling" proposal. Rather, equality as acceptance calls for equalization across only those differences that the culture has encoded as gendered complements. The theory of comparable worth provides one example of this, and the field of athletics yields another.

Most proponents of comparable worth have defined the claim along the following lines: jobs that call for equally valuable skills, effort, and responsibility should be paid equally, even though they occur in different combinations of predominantly female and predominantly male occupations. Thus, when an employer has defined two classifications as gendered complements, the employer should pay the same to each. Equality as acceptance makes the broader claim that *all* behavioral forms that the culture (not just the employer) has encoded as "male" and "female" counterparts should be equally rewarded. Acceptance would thus support challenges to the overvaluation of "male" skills (and corresponding undervaluation of "female" ones) by employers, rather than limiting challenges to unequal application of an existing valuation or to the failure to make such a valuation.

In the sphere of athletics, equality as acceptance would support an argument that equal resources be allocated to male and female sports programs regardless of whether the sports themselves are "similar." In this way, women's equality in athletics would not depend on the ability of individual women to assimilate themselves to the particular sports activities traditionally engaged in by men.

Under the model of equality as acceptance, equality analysis does not end at the discovery of a "real" difference. Rather, it attempts to assess the "cultural meaning" of that difference, and to determine how to achieve equality despite it. This formulation . . . [locates] difference in the relationship between women and men rather than in women alone, as accommodation arguably does. Acceptance would thus provide little support for the claim that traditionally male sports (such as football) should be modified so as to accommodate women (or vice versa). Equality as acceptance does not prescribe the superiority of socially female categories, nor even the superiority of androgynous categories. It does, however, affirm the equal validity of men's and women's lives.

Finally, equality is acceptance . . . [acknowledges] that women and men frequently stand in asymmetrical positions to a particular social institution. It recognizes women are frequently disadvantaged by facially neutral practices and insists that such asymmetries be reflected in resource allocation. To carry forward the athletics example, equality as acceptance would support an equal division of resources between male and female programs rather than dividing up the available sports budget per capita. Since women and men do not stand symmetrically to the social institution of athletics, per capita distribution would simply serve to perpetuate the asymmetry, diverting more resources to male programs, where the participation rate has traditionally been high, and away from female programs, where the participation rate has been depressed both by women's exclusion from certain sports and by the subordination of those activities women have developed for themselves.

It may be apparent from the preceding paragraphs that equal acceptance as a legal norm does not automatically produce one and only one "right answer" to difficult questions of equality. Instead, it provides support for new remedial strategies as well as a method of uncovering deeper layers of inequality. . . .

QUESTIONS FOR REFLECTION

1. What is a symmetrical approach to sexual equality? How does Littleton object to it?

2. What is an asymmetrical approach? How do various asymmetrical approaches differ?

3. What practical difference does the choice of a model of sexual equality entail?

4. What is Littleton's model of sexual equality as acceptance?

5. How does Littleton's model differ from Jaggar's preferred model?

SUSAN OKIN

Justice and Gender

Susan Okin is Martha Sutton Weeks Professor of Ethics in Society at Stanford University. (Source: from Philosophy and Public Affairs 16 *(Winter 1987). Copyright © 1987 by Princeton University Press. Reprinted with permission of Princeton University Press.)*

We as a society pride ourselves on our democratic values. We don't believe people should be constrained by innate differences from being able to achieve desired positions of influence to improve their well-being; equality of opportunity is our professed aim. The Preamble to our Constitution stresses the importance of justice, as well as the general welfare and blessings of liberty. The Pledge of Allegiance asserts that our republic preserves "liberty and justice for all."

Yet substantial inequalities between the sexes still exist in our society. In economic terms, full-time working women (after some very recent improvement) earn on average 71 percent of the earnings of full-time working men. One-half of poor and three-fifths of chronically poor households with dependent children are maintained by a single female parent. The poverty rate for elderly women is nearly twice that for elderly men. . . .

Until there is justice within the family, women will not be able to gain equality in politics, at work, or in any other sphere.

. . . The typical current practices of family life, structured to a large extent by gender, are not just. Both the expectation and the experience of the division of labor by sex make women vulnerable. As I shall show, a cycle of power relations and decisions pervades both family and workplace, each reinforcing the inequalities between the sexes that already exist within the other. Not only women, but children of both sexes, too, are often made vulnerable by gender-structured marriage. One-quarter of children in the United States now live in families with only one parent—in almost 90 percent of cases, the mother. Contrary to common perceptions—in which the situation of never-married mothers looms largest—65 percent of single-parent families are a result of marital separation or divorce. Recent research in a number of states has shown that, in the average case, the standard of living of divorced women and the children who live with them plummets after divorce, whereas the economic situation of divorced men tends to be better than when they were married.

A central source of injustice for women these days is that the law, most noticeably in the event of divorce, treats more or less as equals those whom custom, workplace discrimination, and the still conventional division of labor within the family have made very unequal. Central to this socially created inequality are two commonly made but inconsistent presumptions: that women are primarily responsible for the rearing of children; and that serious and committed members of the work force (regardless of class) do not have primary responsibility, or even shared responsibility, for the rearing of children. The old assumption of the workplace, still implicit, is that workers have wives at home. It is built not only into the structure and expectations of the workplace but into other crucial social institutions, such as schools, which make no attempt to take account, in their scheduled hours or vacations, of the fact that parents are likely to hold jobs.

Now, of course, many wage workers do not have wives at home. Often, they *are* wives and mothers, or single, separated, or divorced mothers of small children. But neither the family nor the workplace has taken much account of this fact. Employed wives still do by far the greatest proportion of unpaid family work, such as child care and housework. Women are far more likely to take time out of the workplace or to work part-time because of family responsibilities than are their husbands or male partners. And they are much more likely to move because of their husbands' employment needs or opportunities than their own. All these tendencies, which are due to a number of factors, including the sex segregation and discrimination of the workplace itself, tend to be cyclical in their effects: wives advance more slowly than their husbands at work and thus gain less seniority, and the discrepancy between their wages increases over time. Then, because both the power structure of the family and what is regarded as consensual "rational" family decision-making reflect the fact that the husband usually earns more, it will become even less likely as time goes on that the unpaid work of the family will be shared between the spouses. Thus the cycle of inequality is perpetuated. Often hidden from view within a marriage, it is in the increasingly likely event of marital breakdown that the socially constructed inequality of married women is at its most visible.

This is what I mean when I say that gender-structured marriage *makes* women vulnerable. These are not matters of natural necessity, as some people would believe. Surely nothing in our natures dictates that men should not be equal participants in the rearing of their children. Nothing in the nature of work makes it impossible to adjust it to the fact the people are parents as well as workers. That these things have not happened is part of the historically, socially constructed differentiation between the sexes that feminists have come to call *gender*. We live in a society that has over the years regarded the innate characteristic of sex as one of the clearest legitimizers of different rights and restrictions, both formal and informal. While the legal sanctions that uphold male dominance have begun to be eroded in the past century, and more rapidly in the last twenty years, the heavy weight of tradition, combined with the effects of socialization, still works powerfully to reinforce sex roles that are commonly regarded as of unequal prestige and worth. The sexual division of labor has not only been a fundamental part of the marriage contract, but so deeply influences us in our formative years that feminists of both sexes who try to reject it can find themselves struggling against it with varying degrees of ambivalence. Based on this linchpin, "gender"—by which I mean *the deeply entrenched institutionalization of sexual difference*—still permeates our society. . . .

The combined effect of the omission of the family and the falsely gender-neutral language in recent political thought is that most theorists are continuing to ignore the highly political issue of gender. The language they use makes little difference to what they actually do, which is to write about men and about only those women who manage, in spite of the gendered structures and practices of the society in which they live, to adopt patterns of life that have been developed to suit the needs of men. The fact that human beings are born as helpless infants—not as the purportedly autonomous actors who populate political theories—is obscured by the implicit assumption of gendered families, operating outside the range of the theories. To a large extent, contemporary theories of justice, like those of the past, are about men with wives at home.

Gender as an Issue of Justice

For three major reasons, this state of affairs is unacceptable. The first is the obvious point that women must be fully included in any satisfactory theory of justice. The second is that equality of opportunity, not only for women but for children of both sexes, is seriously undermined by the current gender injustices of our society. And the third reason is that, as has already been suggested, the family—currently the linchpin of the gender structure—must be just if we are to have a just society, since it is within the family that we first come to have that sense of ourselves and our relations with others that is at the root of moral development. . . .

Gender and Equality of Opportunity

The family is a crucial determinant of our opportunities in life, of what we "become." It has frequently been acknowledged by those concerned with real equality of opportunity that the family presents a problem. But though they have discerned a serious problem, these theorists have underestimated it because they have seen only half of it. They have seen that the disparity among families in terms of the physical and emotional environment, motivation, and material advantages they can give their children has a tremendous effect upon children's opportunities in life. We are not born as isolated, equal individuals in our society, but into family situations: some in the social middle, some poor and homeless, and some superaffluent; some to a single or soon-to-be-separated parent, some to parents whose marriage is fraught with conflict, some to parents who will stay together in love and happiness. Any claims that equal opportunity exists are therefore completely unfounded. Decades of neglect of the poor, especially of poor black and Hispanic households, accentuated by the policies of the Reagan years, have brought us farther from the principles of equal opportunity. To come close to them would require, for example, a high and uniform standard of public education and the provision of equal social services—including health care, employment training, job opportunities, drug rehabilitation, and decent housing —for all who need them. In addition to redistributive taxation, only massive reallocations of resources from the military to social services could make these things possible.

But even if all these disparities were somehow eliminated, we would still not attain equal opportunity for all. This is because what has not been recognized as an equal opportunity problem, except in feminist literature and circles, is the disparity *within* the family, the fact that its gender structure is itself a major obstacle to equality of opportunity. This is very important in itself, since one of the factors with most influence on our opportunities in life is the social significance attributed to our sex. The opportunities of girls and women are centrally affected by the structure and practices of family life, particularly by the fact that women are almost invariably primary parents. What nonfeminists who see in the family an obstacle to equal opportunity have *not* seen is that the extent to which a family is gender-structured can make the sex we belong to a relatively insignificant aspect of our identity and our life prospects or an all-

pervading one. This is because so much of the social construction of gender takes place in the family, and particularly in the institution of female parenting.

Moreover, especially in recent years, with the increased rates of single motherhood, separation, and divorce, the inequalities between the sexes have *compounded* the first part of the problem. The disparity among families has grown largely because of the impoverishment of many women and children after separation or divorce. The division of labor in the typical family leaves most women far less capable than men of supporting themselves, and this disparity is accentuated by the fact that children of separated or divorced parents usually live with their mothers. The inadequacy—and frequent nonpayment—of child support has become recognized as a major social problem. Thus the inequalities of gender are now directly harming many children of both sexes as well as women themselves. Enhancing equal opportunity for women, important as it is in itself, is also a crucial way of improving the opportunities of many of the most disadvantaged children.

As there is a connection among the parts of this problem, so is there a connection among some of the solutions: much of what needs to be done to end the inequalities of gender, and to work in the direction of ending gender itself, will also help to equalize opportunity from one family to another. Subsidized, high-quality day care is obviously one such thing; another is the adaptation of the workplace to the needs of the parents. . . .

The Family as a School of Justice

One of the things that theorists who have argued that families need not or cannot be just, or who have simply neglected them, have failed to explain is how, within a formative social environment that is *not* founded upon principles of justice, children can learn to develop that sense of justice they will require as citizens of a just society. Rather than being one among many co-equal institutions of a just society, a just family is its essential foundation.

It may seem uncontroversial, even obvious, that families must be just because of the vast influence they have on the moral development of children. But this is clearly not the case. I shall argue that unless the first and most formative example of adult interaction usually experienced by children is one of justice and reciprocity, rather than one of domination and manipulation or of unequal altruism and one-sided self-sacrifice, and unless they themselves are treated with concern and respect, they are likely to be considerably hindered in becoming people who are guided by principles of justice. Moreover, I claim, the sharing of roles by men and women, rather than the division of roles between them, would have a further positive impact because the experience of *being* a physical and psychological nurturer—whether of a child or of another adult—would increase that capacity to identify with and fully comprehend the viewpoints of others that is important to a sense of justice. In a society that minimized gender this would be more likely to be the experience of all of us.

Almost every person in our society starts life in a family of some sort or other. Fewer of these families now fit the usual, though by no means universal, standard of previous generations, that is, wage-working father, homemaking mother, and children. More families these days are headed by a single parent; lesbian and gay parenting is no longer so rare; many children have two wage-working parents, and receive at least some of their early care outside the home. While its forms are varied, the family in which a child is raised, especially in the earliest years, is clearly a crucial place for early moral development and for the formation of our basic attitudes to others. It is, potentially, a place where we can *learn to be just.* It is especially important for the development of a sense of justice that grows from sharing the experiences of others and becoming aware of the points of view of others who are different in some respects from ourselves, but with whom we clearly have some interests in common.

The importance of the family for the moral development of individuals was far more often recognized by political theorists of the past than it is by those of the present. Hegel, Rousseau, Tocqueville, Mill, and Dewey are obvious examples that come to mind. Rousseau, for example, shocked by Plato's proposal to abolish the family, says that it is

> . . . as though there were no need for a natural base on which to form conventional ties; as though the love of

one's nearest were not the principle of the love one owes the state; as though it were not by means of the small fatherland which is the family that the heart attaches itself to the large one.

. . .

In a just society, the structure and practices of families must give women the same opportunities as men to develop their capacities, to participate in political power and influence social choices, and to be economically secure. But in addition to this, families must be just because of the vast influence that they have on the moral development of children. The family is the primary institution of formative moral development. And the structure and practices of the family must parallel those of the larger society if the sense of justice is to be fostered and maintained. While many theorists of justice, both past and present, appear to have denied the importance of at least one of these factors, my own view is that both are absolutely crucial. A society that is committed to equal respect for all its members, and to justice in social distributions of benefits and responsibilities, can neither neglect the family nor accept family structures and practices that violate these norms, as do current gender-based structures and practices. It is essential that children who are to develop into adults with a strong sense of justice and commitment to just institutions spend their earliest and most formative years in an environment in which they are loved and nurtured, *and* in which principles of justice are abided by and respected. What is a child of either sex to learn about fairness in the average household with two full-time working parents, where the mother does, at the very least, twice as much family work as the father? What is a child to learn about the value of nurturing and domestic work in a home with a traditional division of labor in which the father either subtly or not so subtly uses the fact that he is the wage earner to "pull rank" on or to abuse his wife? What is a child to learn about responsibility for others in a family in which, after many years of arranging her life around the needs of her husband and children, a woman is faced with having to provide for herself and her children but is totally ill-equipped for the task by the life she agreed to lead, has led, and expected to go on leading?

QUESTIONS FOR REFLECTION

1. What patterns of injustice does Okin find in family relationships?

2. How does injustice in the family lead to inequality in society at large?

3. What role does the family play in forming people's conceptions of justice?

4. What might be done to make family relationships more just?

5. Suppose that many people choose to live in family relationships that Okin considers unjust, even when they are aware of alternatives that are available to them. How might Okin react?

CHRISTINA HOFF SOMMERS

from *Who Stole Feminism?*

Christina Hoff Sommers is W. H. Brady Fellow at the American Enterprise Institute. (Source: from Who Stole Feminism? *New York: Simon and Schuster. Copyright © 1994 by Christina Hoff Sommers. Reprinted by permission of Simon & Schuster.)*

. . . That is the corrosive paradox of gender feminism's misandrist stance: no group of women can wage war on men without at the same time denigrating the women who respect those men. It is just not possible to incriminate men without implying that large numbers of women are fools or worse. Other groups have had their official enemies—workers against capitalists, whites against blacks, Hindus against Muslims—and for a while such enmities may be stable. But when women set themselves against men, they simultaneously set themselves against other women in a group antagonism that is untenable from the outset. In the end, the gender feminist is always forced to show her disappointment and annoyance with the women who are to be found in the camp of the enemy. Misandry moves on to misogyny.

Betty Friedan once told Simone de Beauvoir that she believed women should have the choice to stay home to raise their children if that is what they wish to do. Beauvoir answered: "No, we don't believe that any woman should have this choice. No woman should be authorized to stay at home to raise her children. Society should be totally different. Women should not have that choice, precisely because if there is such a choice, too many women will make that one."

De Beauvoir thought this drastic policy was needed to prevent women from leading blighted, conventional lives. Though she does not spell it out, she must have been aware that her "totally different" society would require a legion of Big Sisters endowed by the state with the power to prohibit any woman who wants to marry and stay home with children from carrying out her plans. She betrays the patronizing attitude typical of many gender feminists toward "uninitiated" women.

An illiberal authoritarianism is implicit in the doctrine that women are socialized to want the things the gender feminist believes they *should not want*. For those who believe that what women want and hope for is "constrained" or "coerced" by their upbringing in the patriarchy are led to dismiss the values and aspirations of most women. The next step may not be inevitable, but it is almost irresistible: to regard women as badly brought-up children whose harmful desires and immature choices must be discounted.

Gender feminists, such as Sandra Lee Bartky, argue for a "feminist reconstruction of self and society [that] must go far beyond anything now contemplated in the theory or politics of the mainstream women's movement." Bartky, who writes on "the phenomenology of feminist consciousness," is concerned with what a proper feminist consciousness should be like. In her book *Femininity and Domination,* she says, "A thorough overhaul of desire is clearly on the feminist agenda: the fantasy that we are overwhelmed by Rhett Butler should be traded in for one in which we seize state power and reeducate him." Bartky, however, does not advocate any authoritarian measures to protect women from incorrect values and preferences shaped by "the masters of patriarchal society." She points out that at present we do not know how to "decolonize the imagination." She cautions that "overhauling" desires and "trading in" popular fantasies may have to wait for the day when feminist theorists develop an "adequate theory of sexuality." In her apocalyptic feminist vision, women as well as men may one day be radically reconstructed. We will have learned to *prefer* the "right" way to live.

Although they may disagree politically about what measures to take with women who make the wrong choices, de Beauvoir and her latter-day descendants share a common posture: they condescend to, patronize, and pity the benighted females who, because they have been "socialized" in the sex/gender system, cannot help wanting the wrong things in life. Their disdain for the hapless victims of patriarchy is rarely acknowledged. When feminists talk of a new society and of how people must be changed, they invariably have in mind men who exploit and abuse women. But it is not difficult to see that they regard most women as men's dupes.

Consider how Naomi Wolf (in *The Beauty Myth*) regards the eight million American women members of Weight Watchers—as cultists in need of deprogramming. Most gender feminists may not be ready to advocate coercion of women of low feminist consciousness, but they are very much in favor of a massive and concerted effort to give the desires, aspirations, and values of American women a thorough makeover. As the feminist philosopher Alison Jaggar puts it, "If individual desires and interests are socially constituted . . . , the ultimate authority of individual judgment comes into question. Perhaps people may be mistaken about truth, morality or even their own interests; perhaps they may be systematically self-deceived." Note that Jaggar explicitly impugns the traditional liberal principle that the many individual judgments and preferences are the ultimate authority. I find that a chilling doctrine: when the people are systematically self-deceived, the ultimate authority is presumed to be vested in a vanguard that unmasks their self-deception. As Ms. Jaggar says, "Certain historical circumstances allow specific groups of women to transcend at least partially the perceptions and theoretical constructs of male dominance." It is these women of high feminist consciousness who "inspire and guide women in a struggle for social change."

Respect for people's preferences is generally thought to be fundamental for democracy. But ideologues find ways of denying this principle. The gender feminist who claims to represent the true interests of women is convinced that she profoundly understands their situation and so is in an exceptional position to know their true interests. In practice, this means she is prepared to dismiss popular preferences in an illiberal way. To justify this, feminist philosopher Marilyn Friedman argues that popular preferences are often "inauthentic" and that even liberals are aware of this:

> Liberal feminists can easily join with other feminists in recognizing that political democracy by itself is insufficient to ensure that preferences are formed without coercion, constraint, undue restriction of options, and so forth. Social, cultural, and economic conditions are as important as political conditions, if not more so, in ensuring that preferences are, in some important sense, authentic.

Friedman is quite wrong in her assumptions: anyone, liberal or conservative, who believes in democracy will sense danger in them. Who will "ensure" that preferences are "authentic"? What additions to political democracy does Friedman have in mind? A constitutional amendment to provide reeducation camps for men and women of false consciousness? Is she prepared to go the authoritarian route indicated by de Beauvoir?

The feminist who thinks that democracy is insufficient believes that seemingly free and enlightened American women have values and desires that, unbeknownst to them, are being manipulated by a system intent on keeping women subjugated to men. Romance, a major cause of defection from the gynocentric enclave, is ever a sticking point with gender feminists. Gloria Steinem, writing on the subject, engages in this kind of debunking "critique": "Romance itself serves a larger political purpose by offering at least a temporary reward for gender roles and threatening rebels with loneliness and rejection. . . . It privatizes our hopes and distracts us from making societal changes. The Roman 'bread and circuses' way of keeping the masses happy. . . . might now be updated." Jaggar, too, sees in romance a distraction from sexual politics: "The ideology of romantic love has now become so pervasive that most women in contemporary capitalism probably believe that they marry for love rather than for economic support."

For her authoritarian disdain, de Beauvoir deserves our liberal censure. But the less authoritarian feminists also deserve it. No intelligent and liberal person—no one who has read and appreciated the limpid political prose of George Orwell or who has learned from the savage history of twentieth-century totalitarianism—can accept the idea of a social agenda to "overhaul" the desires of large numbers of people to make them more "authentic."

In her defense, the gender feminist replies that effective teachers or political leaders must always try to help others overcome benightedness. When women are caught in a system designed to perpetuate male domination, they must be enlightened. There is nothing intrinsically illiberal about seeking to make them conscious of their subjugation. It is the very essence of a liberal education to open minds and enlighten consciousness. If that entails "reeducating" them and overhauling their desires, so be it.

This argument could easily be made in an earlier era when classically liberal principles were being applied to men but not to women. In the nineteenth century, the proposition that all men are created equal was taken to mean "all males." Women did not have the rights that men had, and, what is more, they were being taught that their subordinate status was fitting and natural. Feminist philosophers like John Stuart Mill and Harriet Taylor rightly feared that such teaching was helping to perpetuate inequities. Under the circumstances, political democracy applied only minimally to women. Because they did not vote, their preferences were not in play, and the question of how authentic their preferences were was of importance inasmuch as it affected their ability to agitate for the rights that were being withheld from them.

But women are no longer disenfranchised, and their preferences are being taken into account. Nor are they now taught that they are subordinate or that a subordinate role for them is fitting and proper. Have any women in history been better informed, more aware of their rights and options? Since women today can no longer be regarded as the victims of an undemocratic indoctrination, we must regard their preferences as "authentic." Any other attitude toward American women is unacceptably patronizing and profoundly illiberal. . . .

QUESTIONS FOR REFLECTION

1. Why must feminism disrespect women, according to Sommers?

2. Why do feminists often seek to restrict women's freedom, in Sommers's view?

3. Feminists often think of themselves as trying to "raise the consciousness" of other women. Why does Sommers object to that goal?

4. How might Jaggar, Littleton, or Okin respond to Sommers's objections?

5. Compare Sommers's conception of freedom to that of Mill.

GLOBAL EQUALITY

The central problem of distributive justice is how goods should be allotted to members of society. Ordinarily, this is a problem within a given society. Methods of allotment may leave some with very little, while others possess much. Some may not have enough to eat. Some may have inadequate housing or no housing at all. Some may lack basic medical care or education. The problem of distributive justice, from this perspective, is to determine which methods of allocating a society's goods to its members are just, or, to put it another way, respect the members' rights.

The same points arise, however, in contemplating global allocations of goods. Some societies are wealthy while others are poor. Some nations enjoy high living standards while others face starvation, malnutrition, and disease. The problem of distributive justice in a global setting is, in practical terms, to determine the extent to which richer societies have obligations to help less fortunate societies.

Garrett Hardin takes a global and pessimistic view of problems of poverty. He compares the world to a sea, with about one-third of the population in a lifeboat and the other two-thirds trying to avoid drowning and hoping to climb aboard. The lifeboat, he argues, has a limited capacity and cannot admit many more members. We have no obligation to admit anyone—and certainly no obligation to surrender our place. Hardin asserts further that aid to the poor does not help them; on the contrary, it damages the environment, leading to a "tragedy of the commons," and harms future generations.

Peter Singer, too, treats the problem on a global scale. People in wealthy countries enjoy a comfortable life, whereas many in poor countries suffer and starve. This, he contends, is not just unfair; it is tantamount to homicide. Inhabitants of wealthy countries could prevent the hungry from dying without large sacrifices. He rejects the theory of distributive justice proposed by Locke and Nozick, arguing that we have very serious moral obligations to help those in danger of starvation. He also contends that Hardin's lifeboat analogy is inappropriate.

Finally, Gerald P. O'Driscoll, Kim R. Holmes, and Melanie Kirkpatrick describe a paradox of foreign aid. A society's wealth correlates with the degree of economic freedom it allows. Poor societies, then, are typically not very free. They suffer from extensive government control of the economy, which keeps their citizens poor and their rulers rich. The rulers of such countries tend to subvert aid, redirecting it from its intended uses to their own pockets. The more a country needs our help, the less likely aid is to reach those we seek to help.

GARRETT HARDIN

The Case against Helping the Poor

Garrett Hardin is Professor of Biology at the University of California at Santa Barbara. (Source: Reprinted with permission from Psychology Today Magazine, *Copyright © 1974, Sussex Publishers, Inc.)*

Environmentalists use the metaphor of the earth as a "spaceship" in trying to persuade countries, industries and people to stop wasting and polluting our natural resources. Since we all share life on this planet, they argue, no single person or institution has the right to destroy, waste, or use more than a fair share of its resources.

But does everyone on earth have an equal right to an equal share of its resources? The spaceship metaphor can be dangerous when used by misguided idealists to justify suicidal policies for sharing our resources through uncontrolled immigration and foreign aid. In their enthusiastic but unrealistic generosity, they confuse the ethics of a spaceship with those of a lifeboat.

A true spaceship would have to be under the control of a captain, since no ship could possibly survive if its course were determined by committee. Spaceship Earth certainly has no captain; the United Nations is merely a toothless tiger with little power to enforce any policy upon its bickering members.

If we divide the world crudely into rich nations and poor nations, two-thirds of them are desperately poor, and only one-third comparatively rich, with the United States the wealthiest of all. Metaphorically each rich nation can be seen as a lifeboat full of comparatively rich people. In the ocean outside each lifeboat swim the poor of the world, who would like to get in, or at least to share some of the wealth. What should the lifeboat passengers do?

First, we must recognize the limited capacity of any lifeboat. For example, a nation's land has a limited capacity to support a population and, as the current energy crisis has shown us, in some ways we have already exceeded the carrying capacity of our land.

Adrift in a Moral Sea

So here we sit, say fifty people in our lifeboat. To be generous, let us assume it has room for ten more, making a total capacity of sixty. Suppose the fifty of us in the lifeboat see 100 others swimming in the water outside, begging for admission to our boat or for handouts. We have several options: we may be tempted to try to live by the Christian ideal of being "our brother's keeper," or by the Marxist ideal of "to each according to his needs." Since the needs of all in the water are the same, and since they can all be seen as "our brothers," we could take them all into our boat, making a total of 150 in a boat designed for sixty. The boat swamps, everyone drowns. Complete justice, complete catastrophe.

Since the boat has an unused excess capacity of ten more passengers, we could admit just ten more to it. But which ten do we let in? How do we choose? Do we pick the best ten, the neediest ten, "first come, first served"? And what do we say to the ninety we exclude? If we do let an extra ten into our lifeboat, we will have lost our "safety factor," an engineering principle of critical importance. For example, if we don't leave room for excess capacity as a safety factor in our country's agriculture, a new plant disease or a bad change in the weather could have disastrous consequences.

Suppose we decide to preserve our small safety factor and admit no more to the lifeboat. Our survival is then possible, although we shall have to be constantly on guard against boarding parties.

While this last solution clearly offers the only means of our survival, it is morally abhorrent to many people. Some say they feel guilty about their good luck. My reply is simple: "Get out and yield your place to others." This may solve the problem of the guilt-ridden person's conscience, but it does not change the ethics of the lifeboat. The needy person to whom the guilt-ridden person yields his place will not himself feel guilty about his good luck. If he did, he would not climb aboard. The net result of conscience-striken people giving up their unjustly held seats is the elimination of that sort of conscience from the lifeboat.

This is the basic metaphor within which we must work out our solutions. Let us now enrich the image, step by step, with substantive additions from the real world, a world that must solve real and pressing problems of overpopulation and hunger.

The harsh ethics of the lifeboat become even harsher when we consider the reproductive differences between the rich nations and the poor nations. The people inside the lifeboats are doubling in numbers every eighty-seven years; those swimming around outside are doubling, on the average, every thirty-five years, more than twice as fast as the rich. And since the world's resources are dwindling, the difference in prosperity between the rich and the poor can only increase.

As of 1973, the U.S. had a population of 210 million people, who were increasing by 0.8 percent per year. Outside our lifeboat, let us imagine another 210 million people (say the combined populations of Colombia, Ecuador, Venezuela, Morocco, Pakistan, Thailand, and the Philippines) who are increasing at a rate of 3.3 percent per year. Put differently, the doubling time for this aggregate population is twenty-one years, compared to eighty-seven years for the U.S.

Multiplying the Rich and the Poor

Now suppose the U.S. agreed to pool its resources with those seven countries, with everyone receiving an equal share. Initially the ratio of Americans to non-Americans in this model would be one-to-one. But consider what the ratio would be after eighty-seven years, by which time the Americans would have doubled to a population of 420 million. By then, doubling every twenty-one years, the other group would have swollen to 354 billion. Each American would have to share the available resources with more than eight people.

But, one could argue, this discussion assumes that current population trends will continue, and they may not. Quite so. Most likely the rate of population increase will decline much faster in the U.S. than it will in the other countries, and there does not seem to be much we can do about it. In sharing with "each according to his needs," we must recognize that needs are determined by population size, which is determined by the rate of reproduction, which at present is regarded as a sovereign right of every nation, poor or not. This being so, the philanthropic load created by the sharing ethic of the spaceship can only increase.

The Tragedy of the Commons

The fundamental error of spaceship ethics, and the sharing it requires, is that it leads to what I call "the tragedy of the commons." Under a system of private property, the men who own property recognize their responsibility to care for it, for if they don't they will eventually suffer. A farmer, for instance, will allow no more cattle in a pasture than its carrying capacity justifies. If he overloads it, erosion sets in, weeds take over, and he loses the use of the pasture.

If a pasture becomes a commons open to all, the right of each to use it may not be matched by a corresponding responsibility to protect it. Asking everyone to use it with discretion will hardly do, for the considerate herdsman who refrains from overloading the commons suffers more than a selfish one who says his needs are greater. If everyone would restrain himself, all would be well; but it takes only one less than everyone to ruin a system of voluntary restraint. In a crowded world of less-than-perfect human beings, mutual ruin is inevitable if there are no controls. This is the tragedy of the commons.

One of the major tasks of education today should be the creation of such an acute awareness of the dangers of the commons that people will recognize its many varieties. For example, the air and water have become polluted because they are treated as commons. Further growth in the population or per-capita conversion of natural resources into pollutants will only make the problem worse. The same holds true for the fish of the oceans. Fishing fleets have nearly disappeared in many parts of the world; technological improvements in the art of fishing are hastening the day of complete ruin. Only the replacement of the system of the commons with a responsible system of control will save the land, air, water, and oceanic fisheries.

The World Food Bank

In recent years there has been a push to create a new commons called a World Food Bank, an international depository of food reserves to which nations would contribute according to their abilities and from which they would draw according to their needs. This humanitarian proposal has received support from many liberal international groups and from such prominent citizens as Margaret Mead, U.N. Secretary General Kurt Waldheim, and Senators Edward Kennedy and George McGovern.

A world food bank appeals powerfully to our humanitarian impulses. But before we rush ahead with such a plan, let us recognize where the greatest political push comes from, lest we be disillusioned later. Our experience with the "Food for Peace program," or Public Law 480, gives us the answer. This program moved billions of dollars worth of U.S. surplus grain to food-short, population-long countries during the past two decades. But when P.L. 480 first became law, a headline in the business magazine *Forbes* revealed the real power behind it: "Feeding the World's Hungry Millions: How It Will Mean Billions for U.S. Business."

And indeed it did. In the years 1960 to 1970, U.S. taxpayers spent a total of $7.9 billion on the Food for Peace program. Between 1948 and 1970, they also paid an additional $50 billion for other economic-aid programs, some of which went for food and food-producing machinery and technology. Though all U.S. taxpayers were forced to contribute to the cost of P.L. 480, certain special interest groups gained handsomely under the program. Farmers did not have to contribute the grain; the Government, or rather the taxpayers, bought it from them at full market prices. The increased demand raised prices of farm products generally. The manufacturers of farm machinery, fertilizers and pesticides benefited by the farmers' extra efforts to grow more food. Grain elevators profited from storing the surplus until it could be shipped. Railroads made money hauling it to ports, and shipping lines profited from carrying it overseas. The implementation of P.L. 480 required the creation of a vast government bureaucracy, which then acquired its own vested interest in continuing the program regardless of its merits.

Extracting Dollars

Those who proposed and defended the Food for Peace program in public rarely mentioned its importance to any of these special interests. The public emphasis was always on its humanitarian effects. The combination of silent selfish interests and highly vocal humanitarian apologists made a powerful and successful lobby for extracting money from taxpayers. We can expect the same lobby to push now for the creation of a World Food Bank.

However great the potential benefit to selfish interests, it should not be a decisive argument against a truly humanitarian program. We must ask if such a program would actually do more good than harm, not only momentarily but also in the long run. Those who propose the food bank usually refer to a current "emergency" or "crisis" in terms of world food supply. But what is an emergency? Although they may be infrequent and sudden, everyone knows that emergencies will occur from time to time. A well-run family, company, organization or country prepares for the likelihood of accidents and emergencies. It expects them, it budgets for them, it saves for them.

Learning the Hard Way

What happens if some organizations or countries budget for accidents and others do not? If each country is solely responsible for its own well-being, poorly managed ones will suffer. But they can learn from experience. They may mend their ways and learn to budget for infrequent but certain emergencies. For example, the weather varies from year to year, and periodic crop failures are certain. A wise and competent government saves out of the production of the good years in anticipation of bad years to come. Joseph taught this policy to Pharaoh in Egypt more than 2,000 years ago. Yet the great majority of the governments in the world today do not follow such a policy. They lack either the wisdom or the competence, or both. Should those nations that do manage to put something aside be forced to come to the rescue each time an emergency occurs among the poor nations?

"But it isn't their fault!" some kindhearted liberals argue. "How can we blame the poor people who are caught in an emergency? Why must they suffer for the sins of their governments?" The concept of blame is simply not relevant here. The real question is, what are the operational consequences of establishing a world food bank? If it is open to every country every time a need develops, slovenly rulers will not be motivated to take Joseph's advice. Someone will always come to their aid. Some countries will deposit food in the world food bank, and others will withdraw it. There will be almost no overlap. As a result of such solutions to food shortage emergencies, the poor countries will not learn to mend their ways and will suffer progressively greater emergencies as their populations grow.

Population Control the Crude Way

On the average, poor countries undergo a 2.5 percent increase in population each year; rich countries, about 0.8 percent. Only rich countries have anything in the way of food reserves set aside, and even they do not have as much as they should. Poor countries have none. If poor countries received no food from the outside, the rate of their population growth would be periodically checked by crop failures and famines. But if they can always draw on a world food bank in time of need, their population can continue to grow unchecked, and so will their "need" for aid. In the short run, a world food bank may diminish that need, but in the long run it actually increases the need without limit.

Without some system of worldwide food sharing, the proportion of people in the rich and poor nations might eventually stabilize. The overpopulated poor countries would decrease in numbers, while the rich countries that had room for more people would increase. But with a well-meaning system of sharing, such as a world food bank, the growth differential between the rich and the poor countries will not only persist, it will increase. Because of the higher rate of population growth in the poor countries of the world, 88 percent of today's children are born poor, and only 12 percent rich. Year by year the ratio becomes worse, as the fast-reproducing poor outnumber the slow-reproducing rich.

A world food bank is thus a commons in disguise. People will have more motivation to draw from it than to add to any common store. The less provident and less able will multiply at the expense of the abler and more provident, bringing eventual ruin upon all who share in the commons. Besides, any system of "sharing" that amounts to foreign aid from the rich nations to the poor nations will carry the taint of charity, which will contribute little to the world peace so devoutly desired by those who support the idea of a world food bank.

As past U.S. foreign-aid programs have amply and depressingly demonstrated, international charity frequently inspires mistrust and antagonism rather than gratitude on the part of the recipient nation.

Chinese Fish and Miracle Rice

The modern approach to foreign aid stresses the export of technology and advice, rather than money and food. As an ancient Chinese proverb goes: "Give a man a fish and he will eat for a day; teach him how to fish and he will eat for the rest of his days." Acting on this advice, the Rockefeller and Ford Foundations have financed a number of programs for improving agriculture in the hungry nations. Known as the "Green Revolution," these programs have led to the development of "miracle rice" and "miracle wheat," new strains that offer bigger harvests and greater resistance to crop damage. Norman Borlaug, the Nobel Prize–winning agronomist who, supported by the Rockefeller Foundation, developed "miracle wheat," is one of the most prominent advocates of a world food bank.

Whether or not the Green Revolution can increase food production as much as its champions claim is a debatable but possibly irrelevant point.

Those who support this well-intended humanitarian effort should first consider some of the fundamentals of human ecology. Ironically, one man who did was the late Alan Gregg, a vice president of the Rockefeller Foundation. Two decades ago he expressed strong doubts about the wisdom of such attempts to increase food production. He likened the growth and spread of humanity over the surface of the earth to the spread of cancer in the human body, remarking that "cancerous growths demand food; but, as far as I know, they have never been cured by getting it."

Overloading the Environment

Every human born constitutes a draft on all aspects of the environment: food, air, water, forests, beaches, wildlife, scenery and solitude. Food can, perhaps, be significantly increased to meet a growing demand. But what about clean beaches, unspoiled forests, and solitude? If we satisfy a growing population's need for food, we necessarily decrease its per-capita supply of the other resources needed by men.

India, for example, now has a population of 600 million, which increases by 15 million each year. This population already puts a huge load on a relatively impoverished environment. The country's forests are now only a small fraction of what they were three centuries ago, and floods and erosion continually destroy the insufficient farmland that remains. Every one of the 15 million new lives added to India's population puts an additional burden on the environment, and increases the economic and social costs of crowding. However humanitarian our intent, every Indian life saved through medical or nutritional assistance from abroad diminishes the quality of life for those who remain, and for subsequent generations. If rich countries make it possible, through foreign aid, for 600 million Indians to swell to 1.2 billion in a mere twenty-eight years, as their current growth rate threatens, will future generations of Indians thank us for hastening the destruction of their environment? Will our good intentions be sufficient excuse for the consequences of our actions?

My final example of a commons in action is one for which the public has the least desire for rational discussion—immigration. Anyone who publicly questions the wisdom of current U.S. immigration policy is promptly charged with bigotry, prejudice, ethnocentrism, chauvinism, isolationism or selfishness. Rather than encounter such accusations, one would rather talk about other matters, leaving immigration policy to wallow in the crosscurrents of special interests that take no account of the good of the whole, or the interests of posterity.

Perhaps we still feel guilty about things we said in the past. Two generations ago the popular press frequently referred to Dagos, Wops, Polacks, Chinks and Krauts, in articles about how America was being "overrun" by foreigners of supposedly inferior genetic stock. But because the implied inferiority of foreigners was used then as justification for keeping them out, people now assume that restrictive policies could only be based on such misguided notions. There are other grounds.

A Nation of Immigrants

Just consider the numbers involved. Our government acknowledges a net inflow of 400,000 immigrants a year. While we have no hard data on the extent of illegal entries, educated guesses put the figure at about 600,000 a year. Since the natural increase (excess of births over deaths) of the resident population now runs about 1.7 million per year, the yearly gain from immigration amounts to at least 19 percent of the total annual increase and may be as much as 37 percent if we include the estimate for illegal immigrants. Considering the growing use of birth-control devices, the potential effect of educational campaigns by such organizations as Planned Parenthood Federation of America and Zero Population Growth, and the influence of inflation and the housing shortage, the fertility rate of American women may decline so much that immigration could account for all the yearly increase in population. Should we not at least ask if that is what we want?

For the sake of those who worry about whether the "quality" of the average immigrant compares favorably with the quality of the average resident, let us assume that immigrants and native-born citizens are of exactly equal quality, however one defines that term. We will focus here only on quantity; and since our conclusions will depend on nothing else, all charges of bigotry and chauvinism become irrelevant.

Immigration vs. Food Supply

World food banks *move food to the people,* hastening the exhaustion of the environment of the poor countries. Unrestricted immigration, on the other hand, *moves people to the food,* thus speeding up the destruction of the environment of the rich countries. We can easily understand why poor people should want to make this latter transfer, but why should rich hosts encourage it?

As in the case of foreign-aid programs, immigration receives support from selfish interests and humanitarian impulses. The primary selfish interest in unimpeded immigration is the desire of employers for cheap labor, particularly in industries and trades that offer degrading work. In the past, one wave of foreigners after another was brought into the U.S. to work at wretched jobs for wretched wages. In recent years the Cubans, Puerto Ricans, and Mexicans have had this dubious honor. The interests of the employers of cheap labor mesh well with the guilty silence of the country's liberal intelligentsia. White Anglo-Saxon Protestants are particularly reluctant to call for a closing of the doors to immigration for fear of being called bigots.

But not all countries have such reluctant leadership. Most educated Hawaiians, for example, are keenly aware of the limits of their environment, particularly in terms of population growth. There is only so much room on the islands, and the islanders know it. To Hawaiians, immigrants from the other forty-nine states present as great a threat as those from other nations. At a recent meeting of Hawaiian government officials in Honolulu, I had the ironic delight of hearing a speaker, who like most of his audience was of Japanese ancestry, ask how the country might practically and constitutionally close its doors to further immigration. One member of the audience countered: "How can we shut the doors now? We have many friends and relatives in Japan that we'd like to bring here some day so that they can enjoy Hawaii too." The Japanese-American speaker smiled sympathetically and answered: "Yes, but we have children now, and someday we'll have grandchildren too. We can bring more people here from Japan only by giving away some of the land that we hope to pass on to our grandchildren some day. What right do we have to do that?"

At this point, I can hear U.S. liberals asking: "How can you justify slamming the door once you're inside? You say that immigrants should be kept out. But aren't we all immigrants, or the descendants of immigrants? If we insist on staying, must we not admit all others?" Our craving for intellectual order leads us to seek and prefer symmetrical rules and morals: a single rule for me and everybody else; the same rule yesterday, today, and tomorrow. Justice, we feel, should not change with time and place.

We Americans of non-Indian ancestry can look upon ourselves as the descendants of thieves who are guilty morally, if not legally, of stealing this land from its Indian owners. Should we then give back the land to the now living American descendants of those Indians? However morally or logically sound this proposal may be, I, for one, am unwilling to live by it and I know no one else who is. Besides, the logical consequence would be absurd. Suppose that intoxicated with a sense of pure justice, we should decide to turn our land over to the Indians. Since all our wealth has also been derived from the land, wouldn't we be morally obliged to give that back to the Indians too?

Pure Justice vs. Reality

Clearly, the concept of pure justice produces an infinite regression to absurdity. Centuries ago, wise men invented statutes of limitations to justify the rejection of such pure justice, in the interest of preventing continual disorder. The law zealously defends property rights, but only relatively recent property rights. Drawing a line after an arbitrary time has elapsed may be unjust, but the alternatives are worse.

We are all the descendants of thieves, and the world's resources are inequitably distributed. But we must begin the journey to tomorrow from the point where we are today. We cannot remake the past. We cannot safely divide the wealth equitably among all peoples so long as people reproduce at different rates. To do so would guarantee that our grandchildren and everyone else's grandchildren would have only a ruined world to inhabit.

To be generous with one's own possessions is quite different from being generous with those of posterity. We should call this point to the attention of those who, from a commendable love of justice and equality, would institute a system of the commons, either in the form of a world food bank or of unrestricted immigration. We must convince them if we wish to save at least some parts of the world from environmental ruin.

Without a true world government to control reproduction and the use of available resources, the sharing ethic of the spaceship is impossible. For the foreseeable future, our survival demands that we govern our actions by the ethics of a lifeboat, harsh though they may be. Posterity will be satisfied with nothing less.

Addendum 1989

Can anyone watch children starve on television without wanting to help? Naturally sympathetic, a normal human being thinks that he can imagine what it is like to be starving. We all want to do unto others as we would have them do unto us.

But wanting is not doing. Forty years of activity by the U.S. Agency for International Development, as well as episodic nongovernmental attempts to feed the world's starving, have produced mixed results. Before we respond to the next appeal we should ask, "Does what we call 'aid' really help?"

Some of the shortcomings of food aid can be dealt with briefly. Waste is unavoidable: Because most poor countries have wretched transportation systems, food may sit on a dock until it rots. Then there are the corrupt politicians who take donated food away from the poor and give it to their political supporters. In Somalia in the 1980s, fully 70 percent of the donated food went to the army.

We can school ourselves to accept such losses. Panicky projects are always inefficient: Waste and corruption are par for the course. But there is another kind of loss that we cannot—in fact, we should not—accept, and that is the loss caused by the boomerang effects of philanthropy. Before we jump onto the next "feed-the-starving" bandwagon, we need to understand how well-intentioned efforts can be counterproductive.

Briefly put, it is a mistake to focus only on starving people while ignoring their surroundings. Where there is great starvation there is usually an impoverished environment: poor soil, scarce water and wildly fluctuating weather. As a result, the "carrying capacity" of the environment is low. The territory simply cannot support the population that is trying to live on it. Yet if the population were much smaller, and if it would stay smaller, the people would not need to starve.

Let us look at a particular example. Nigeria, like all the central African countries, has increased greatly in population in the last quarter-century. Over many generations, Nigerians learned that their farmlands would be most productive if crop-growing alternated with "fallow years"—years in which the land was left untilled to recover its fertility.

When modern medicine reduced the death rate, the population began to grow. More food was demanded from the same land. Responding to that need, Nigerians shortened the fallow periods. The result was counterproductive. In one carefully studied village, the average fallow period was shortened from 5.3 to 1.4 years. As a result, the yearly production (averaged over both fallow and crop years) fell by 30 percent.

Are Nigerian farmers stupid? Not at all! They know perfectly well what they are doing. But a farmer whose family has grown too large for his farm has to take care of next year's need before he can provide for the future. To fallow or not to fallow translates into this choice: zero production in a fallow year or a 30 percent shortfall over the long run. Starvation cannot wait. Long-term policies have to give way to short-term ones. So the farmer plows up his overstressed fields, thus diminishing long-term productivity.

QUESTIONS FOR REFLECTION

1. Explain Hardin's lifeboat analogy.

2. What role does population play in Hardin's argument? What are his factual premises about population? Do you find them plausible?

3. What is "the tragedy of the commons"?

4. What, in Hardin's view, would be the consequences of establishing a world food bank?

5. What, if anything, does Hardin assume about the nature of justice?

PETER SINGER

from *Practical Ethics*

Peter Singer is Professor of Philosophy and Director of the Center for Human Values at Princeton University. *(Source: Reprinted from Peter Singer,* Practical Ethics. *Copyright © 1979 by Cambridge University Press. Reprinted with the permission of Cambridge University Press.)*

Some Facts

Consider these facts: by the most cautious estimates, 400 million people lack the calories, protein, vitamins and minerals needed for a normally healthy life. Millions are constantly hungry; others suffer from deficiency diseases and from infections they would be able to resist on a better diet. Children are worst affected. According to one estimate, 15 million children under five die every year from the combined effects of malnutrition and infection. In some areas, half the children born can be expected to die before their fifth birthday.

Nor is lack of food the only hardship of the poor. To give a broader picture, Robert McNamara, President of the World Bank, has suggested the term "absolute poverty." The poverty we are familiar with in industrialized nations is relative poverty—meaning that some citizens are poor, relative to the wealth enjoyed by their neighbours. People living in relative poverty in Australia might be quite comfortably off by comparison with old-age pensioners in Britain, and British old-age pensioners are not poor in comparison with the poverty that exists in Mali or Ethiopia. Absolute poverty, on the other hand, is poverty by any standard. In McNamara's words:

> Poverty at the absolute level . . . is life at the very margin of existence.
>
> The absolute poor are severely deprived human beings struggling to survive in a set of squalid and de-

graded circumstances almost beyond the power of our sophisticated imaginations and privileged circumstances to conceive.

> Compared to those fortunate enough to live in developed countries individuals in the poorest nations have
>
> An infant mortality rate eight times higher
>
> A life expectancy one-third lower
>
> An adult literacy rate 60% less
>
> A nutritional level, for one out of every two in the population, below acceptable standards; and for millions of infants, less protein than is sufficient to permit optimum development of the brain.

And McNamara has summed up absolute poverty as:

> a condition of life so characterized by malnutrition, illiteracy, disease, squalid surroundings, high infant mortality and low life expectancy as to be beneath any reasonable definition of human decency.

Absolute poverty is, as McNamara has said, responsible for the loss of countless lives, especially among infants and young children. When absolute poverty does not cause death it still causes misery of a kind not often seen in the affluent nations. Malnutrition in young children stunts both physical and mental development. It has been estimated that the health, growth and learning capacity of nearly half the young children in developing countries are affected by malnutrition. Millions of people on poor diets suffer from deficiency diseases, like goitre, or blindness caused by a lack of vitamin A. The food value of what the poor eat is further reduced by parasites such as hookworm and ringworm, which are endemic in conditions of poor sanitation and health education.

Death and disease apart, absolute poverty remains a miserable condition of life, with inadequate food, shelter, clothing, sanitation, health services and education. According to World Bank estimates, which define absolute poverty in terms of income levels insufficient to provide adequate nutrition, something like 800 million people—almost 40% of the people of developing countries—live in absolute poverty. Absolute poverty is probably the principal cause of human misery today. . . .

The Obligation to Assist

The Argument for an Obligation to Assist

The path from the library at my university to the Humanities lecture theatre passes a shallow ornamental pond. Suppose that on my way to give a lecture I notice that a small child has fallen in and is in danger of drowning. Would anyone deny that I ought to wade in and pull the child out? This will mean getting my clothes muddy, and either cancelling my lecture or delaying it until I can find something dry to change into; but compared with the avoidable death of a child this is insignificant.

A plausible principle that would support the judgment that I ought to pull the child out is this: if it is in our power to prevent something very bad happening, without thereby sacrificing anything of comparable moral significance, we ought to do it. This principle seems uncontroversial. It will obviously win the assent of consequentialists; but non-consequentialists should accept it too, because the injunction to prevent what is bad applies only when nothing comparably significant is at stake. Thus the principle cannot lead to the kinds of actions of which non-consequentialists strongly disapprove—serious violations of individual rights, injustice, broken promises, and so on. If a non-consequentialist regards any of these as comparable in moral significance to the bad thing that is to be prevented, he will automatically regard the principle as not applying in those cases in which the bad thing can only be prevented by violating rights, doing injustice, breaking promises, or whatever else is at stake. Most non-consequentialists hold that we ought to prevent what is bad and promote what is good. Their dispute with consequentialists lies in their insistence that this is not the sole ultimate ethical principle; that it is *an* ethical principle is not denied by any plausible ethical theory.

Nevertheless the uncontroversial appearance of the principle that we ought to prevent what is bad when we can do so without sacrificing anything of comparable moral significance is deceptive. If it were taken seriously and acted upon, our lives and our world would be fundamentally changed. For the principle applies, not just to rare situations in which one can save a child from a pond, but to the everyday situation in which we can assist those living in absolute poverty. In saying this I assume that absolute poverty, with its hunger and malnutrition, lack of shelter, illiteracy, disease, high infant mortality and low life expectancy, is a bad thing. And I assume that it is within the power of the affluent to reduce absolute poverty, without sacrificing anything of comparable moral significance. If these two assumptions and the principle we have been discussing are correct, we have an obligation to help those in absolute poverty which is no less strong than our obligation to rescue a drowning child from a pond. Not to help would be wrong, whether or not it is intrinsically equivalent to killing. Helping is not, as conventionally thought, a charitable act which it is praiseworthy to do, but not wrong to omit; it is something that everyone ought to do.

This is the argument for an obligation to assist. Set out more formally, it would look like this.

First premise:	If we can prevent something bad without sacrificing anything of comparable significance, we ought to do it.
Second premise:	Absolute poverty is bad.
Third premise:	There is some absolute poverty we can prevent without sacrificing anything of comparable moral significance.
Conclusion:	We ought to prevent some absolute poverty.

The first premise is the substantive moral premise on which the argument rests, and I have tried to show that it can be accepted by people who hold a variety of ethical positions.

The second premise is unlikely to be challenged. Absolute poverty is, as McNamara put it, "beneath any reasonable definition of human decency" and it would be hard to find a plausible ethical view which did not regard it as a bad thing.

The third premise is more controversial, even though it is cautiously framed. It claims only that some absolute poverty can be prevented without the sacrifice of anything of comparable moral significance. It thus avoids the objection that any aid I can give is just "drops in the ocean," for the point is not whether my personal contribution will make any noticeable impression on world poverty as a whole (of course it won't) but whether it will prevent some poverty. This is all the argument needs to sustain its conclusion, since the second premise says that any absolute poverty is bad, and not merely the total amount of absolute poverty. If without sacrificing anything of comparable moral significance we can provide just one family with the means to raise itself out of absolute poverty, the third premise is vindicated. I have left the notion of moral significance unexamined in order to show that the argument does not depend on any specific values or ethical principles. I think the third premise is true for most people living in industrialized nations, on any defensible view of what is morally significant. Our affluence means that we have income we can dispose of without giving up the basic necessities of life, and we can use this income to reduce absolute poverty. Just how much we will think ourselves obliged to give up will depend on what we consider to be of comparable moral significance to the poverty we could prevent: color television, stylish clothes, expensive dinners, a sophisticated stereo system, overseas holidays, a (second?) car, a larger house, private schools for our childen. . . . For a utilitarian, none of these is likely to be of comparable significance to the reduction of absolute poverty; and those who are not utilitarians surely must, if they subscribe to the principle of universalizability, accept that at least *some* of these things are of far less moral significance than the absolute poverty that could be prevented by the money they cost. . . .

Objections to the Argument
Property Rights

Do people have a right to private property, a right which contradicts the view that they are under an obligation to give some of their wealth away to those in absolute poverty? According to some theories of rights (for instance, Robert Nozick's) provided one has acquired one's property without the use of unjust means like force and fraud, one may be entitled to enormous wealth while others starve. This individualistic conception of rights is in contrast to other views, like the early Christian doctrine to be found in the works of Thomas Aquinas, which holds that since property exists for the satisfaction of human needs, "whatever a man has in superabundance is owed, of natural right, to the poor for their sustenance." A socialist would also, of course, see wealth as belonging to the community rather than the individual, while utilitarians, whether socialist or not, would be prepared to override property rights to prevent great evils.

Does the argument for an obligation to assist others therefore presuppose one of these other theories of property rights, and not an individualistic theory like Nozick's? Not necessarily. A theory of property rights can insist on our *right* to retain wealth without pronouncing on whether the rich *ought* to give to the poor. Nozick, for example, rejects the use of compulsory means like taxation to redistribute income, but suggests that we can achieve the ends we deem morally desirable by voluntary means. So Nozick would reject the claim that rich people have an "obligation" to give to the poor, in so far as this implies that the poor have a right to our aid, but might accept that giving is something we ought to do and failing to give, though within one's rights, is wrong —for rights is not all there is to ethics.

The argument for an obligation to assist can survive, with only minor modifications, even if we accept an individualistic theory of property rights. In any case, however, I do not think we should accept such a theory. It leaves too much to chance to be an acceptable ethical view. For instance, those whose forefathers happened to inhabit some sandy wastes around the Persian Gulf are now fabulously wealthy, because oil lay under those sands; while those whose forefathers settled on better land south of the Sahara live in absolute poverty, because of drought and bad harvests. Can this distribution be acceptable from an impartial point of view? If we imagine ourselves about to begin life as a citizen of either Kuwait or Chad—but we do not know which—would we accept the principle that citizens of Kuwait are under no obligation to assist people living in Chad?

Population and the Ethics of Triage

Perhaps the most serious objection to the argument that we have an obligation to assist is that since the major cause of absolute poverty is overpopulation, helping those now in poverty will only ensure that yet more people are born to live in poverty in the future.

In its most extreme form, this objection is taken to show that we should adopt a policy of "triage." The term comes from medical policies adopted in wartime. With too few doctors to cope with all the casualties, the wounded were divided into three categories: those who would probably survive without medical assistance, those who might survive if they received assistance, but otherwise probably would not, and those who even with medical assistance probably would not survive. Only those in the middle category were given medical assistance. The idea, of course, was to use limited medical resources as effectively as possible. For those in the first category, medical treatment was not strictly necessary; for those in the third category, it was likely to be useless. It has been suggested that we should apply the same policies to countries, according to their prospects of becoming self-sustaining. We would not aid countries which even without our help will soon be able to feed their populations. We would not aid countries which, even with our help, will not be able to limit their population to a level they can feed. We would aid those countries where our help might make the difference between success and failure in bringing food and population into balance.

Advocates of this theory are understandably reluctant to give a complete list of the countries they would place into the "hopeless" category; but Bangladesh is often cited as an example. Adopting the policy of triage would, then, mean cutting off assistance to Bangladesh and allowing famine, disease and natural disasters to reduce the population of that country (now around 80 million) to the level at which it can provide adequately for all.

In support of this view Garrett Hardin has offered a metaphor: we in the rich nations are like the occupants of a crowded lifeboat adrift in a sea full of drowning people. If we try to save the drowning by bringing them aboard, our boat will be overloaded and we shall all drown. Since it is better that some survive than none, we should leave the others to drown. In the world today, according to Hardin, "lifeboat ethics" apply. The rich should leave the poor to starve, for otherwise the poor will drag the rich down with them.

Against this view, some writers have argued that overpopulation is a myth. The world produces ample food to feed its population, and could, according to some estimates, feed ten times as many. People are hungry not because there are too many but because of inequitable land distribution, the manipulation of Third World economies by the developed nations, wastage of food in the West, and so on.

Putting aside the controversial issue of the extent to which food production might one day be increased, it is true, as we have already seen, that the world now produces enough to feed its inhabitants—the amount lost by being fed to animals itself being enough to meet existing grain shortages. Nevertheless population growth cannot be ignored. Bangladesh could, with land reform and using better techniques, feed its present population of 80 million; but by the year 2000, according to World Bank estimates, its population will be 146 million. The enormous effort that will have to go into feeding an extra 66 million people, all added to the population within a quarter of a century, means that Bangladesh must develop at full speed to stay where she is. Other low-income countries are in similar situations. By the end of the century, Ethiopia's population is expected to rise from 29 to 54 million; Somalia's from 3 to 7 million, India's from 620 to 958 million, Zaire's from 25 to 47 million. What will happen then? Population cannot grow indefinitely. It will be checked by a decline in birth rates or a rise in death rates. Those who advocate triage are proposing that we allow the population growth of some countries to be checked by a rise in death rates—that is, by increased malnutrition and related diseases; by widespread famines; by increased infant mortality; and by epidemics of infectious diseases.

The consequences of triage on this scale are so horrible that we are inclined to reject it without further argument. How could we sit by our television sets, watching millions starve while we do nothing? Would not that be the end of all notions of human equality and respect for human life? Don't people have a right to our assistance, irrespective of the consequences?

Anyone whose initial reaction to triage was not one of repugnance would be an unpleasant sort of person. Yet initial reactions based on strong feelings are not always reliable guides. Advocates of triage are rightly concerned with the long-term consequences of our actions. They say that helping the poor and starving now merely ensures more poor and starving in the future. When our capacity to help is finally unable to cope—as one day it must be—the suffering will be greater than it would be if we stopped helping now. If this is correct, there is nothing we can do to prevent absolute starvation and poverty, in the long run, and so we have no obligation to assist. Nor does it seem reasonable to hold that under these circumstances people have a right to our assistance. If we do accept such a right, irrespective of the consequences, we are saying that, in Hardin's metaphor, we would continue to haul the drowning into our lifeboat until the boat sank and we all drowned.

If triage is to be rejected it must be tackled on its own ground, within the framework of consequentialist ethics. Here it is vulnerable. Any consequentialist ethics must take probability of outcome into account. A course of action that will certainly produce some benefit is to be preferred to an alternative course that may lead to a slightly larger benefit, but is equally likely to result in no benefit at all. Only if the greater magnitude of the uncertain benefit outweighs its uncertainty should we choose it. Better one certain unit of benefit than a 10% chance of 5 units; but better a 50% chance of 3 units than a single certain unit. The same principle applies when we are trying to avoid evils.

The policy of triage involves a certain, very great evil: population control by famine and disease. Tens of millions would die slowly. Hundreds of millions would continue to live in absolute poverty, at the very margin of existence. Against this prospect, advocates of the policy place a possible evil which is greater still: the same process of famine and disease, taking place in, say, fifty years' time, when the world's population may be three times its present level, and the number who will die from famine, or struggle on in absolute poverty, will be that much greater. The question is: how probable is this forecast that continued assistance now will lead to greater disasters in the future?

Forecasts of population growth are notoriously fallible, and theories about the factors which affect it remain speculative. One theory, at least as plausible as any other, is that countries pass through a "demographic transition" as their standard of living rises. When people are very poor and have no access to modern medicine their fertility is high, but population is kept in check by high death rates. The introduction of sanitation, modern medical techniques and other improvements reduces the death rate, but initially has little effect on the birth rate. Then population grows rapidly. Most poor countries are now in this phase. If standards of living continue to rise, however, couples begin to realize that to have the same number of children surviving to maturity as in the past, they do not need to give birth to as many children as their parents did. The need for children to provide economic support in old age diminishes. Improved education and the emancipation and employment of women also reduce the birthrate, and so population growth begins to level off. Most rich nations have reached this stage, and their populations are growing only very slowly.

If this theory is right, there is an alternative to the disasters accepted as inevitable by supporters of triage. We can assist poor countries to raise the living standards of the poorest members of their population. We can encourage the governments of these countries to enact land reform measures, improve education, and liberate women from a purely childbearing role. We can also help other countries to make contraception and sterilization widely available. There is a fair chance that these measures will hasten the onset of the demographic transition and bring population growth down to a manageable level. Success cannot be guaranteed; but the evidence that improved economic security and education reduce population growth is strong enough to make triage ethically unacceptable. We cannot allow millions to die from starvation and disease when there is a reasonable probability that population can be brought under control without such horrors.

Population growth is therefore not a reason against giving overseas aid, although it should make us think about the kind of aid to give. Instead of food handouts, it may be better to give aid that hastens the demographic transition. This may mean agricultural assistance for the rural poor, or assistance with education, or the provision of contraceptive services. Whatever kind of aid proves most effective in specific circumstances, the obligation to assist is not reduced.

One awkward question remains. What should we do about a poor and already overpopulated country which, for religious or nationalistic reasons, restricts the use of contraceptives and refuses to slow its population growth? Should we nevertheless offer development assistance? Or should we make our offer conditional on effective steps being taken to reduce the birthrate? To the latter course, some would object that putting conditions on aid is an attempt to impose our own ideas on independent sovereign nations. So it is—but is this imposition unjustifiable? If the argument for an obligation to assist is sound, we have an obligation to reduce absolute poverty: but we have no obligation to make sacrifices that, to the best of our knowledge, have no prospect of reducing poverty in the long run. Hence we have no obligation to assist countries whose governments have policies which will make our aid ineffective. This could be very harsh on poor citizens of these countries—for they may have no say in the government's policies—but we will help more people in the long run by using our resources where they are most effective. (The same principles may apply, incidentally, to countries that refuse to take other steps that could make assistance effective—like refusing to reform systems of land holding that impose intolerable burdens on poor tenant farmers.) . . .

Too High a Standard?

The final objection to the argument for an obligation to assist is that it sets a standard so high that none but a saint could attain it. How many people can we really expect to give away everything not comparable in moral significance to the poverty their donation could relieve? For most of us, with commonsense views about what is of moral significance, this would mean a life of real austerity. Might it not be counterproductive to demand so much? Might not people say: "As I can't do what is morally required anyway, I won't bother to give at all." If, however, we were to set a more realistic standard, people might make a genuine effort to reach it. Thus setting a lower standard might actually result in more aid being given.

It is important to get the status of this objection clear. Its accuracy as a prediction of human behaviour is quite compatible with the argument that we are obliged to give to the point at which by giving more we sacrifice something of comparable moral significance. What would follow from the objection is that public advocacy of this standard of giving is undesirable. It would mean that in order to do the maximum to reduce absolute poverty, we should advocate a standard lower than the amount we think people really ought to give. Of course we ourselves —those of us who accept the original argument, with its higher standard—would know that we ought to do more than we publicly propose people ought to do, and we might actually give more than we urge others to give. There is no inconsistency here, since in both our private and our public behaviour we are trying to do what will most reduce absolute poverty.

For a consequentialist, this apparent conflict between public and private morality is always a possibility, and not in itself an indication that the underlying principle is wrong. The consequences of a principle are one thing, the consequences of publicly advocating it another.

Is it true that the standard set by our argument is so high as to be counterproductive? There is not much evidence to go by, but discussions of the argument, with students and others have led me to think it might be. On the other hand the conventionally accepted standard—a few coins in a collection tin when one is waved under your nose—is obviously far too low. What level should we advocate? Any figure will be arbitrary, but there may be something to be said for a round percentage of one's income like, say, 10%—more than a token donation, yet not so high as to be beyond all but saints. (This figure has the additional advantage of being reminiscent of the ancient tithe, or tenth, which was traditionally given to the church, whose responsibilities included care of the poor in one's local community. Perhaps the idea can be revived and applied to the global community.) Some families, of course, will find 10% a considerable strain on their finances. Others may be able to give more without difficulty. No figure should be advocated as a rigid minimum or maximum; but it seems safe to advocate that those earning average or above average incomes in affluent societies, unless they have an unusually large number of dependents or other special needs, ought to give a tenth of their income to reducing absolute poverty. By any reasonable ethical standards this is the minimum we ought to do, and we do wrong if we do less.

QUESTIONS FOR REFLECTION

1. What is absolute poverty?

2. Can the world support its people, according to Singer? Why or why not?

3. Why, according to Singer, do some people go hungry?

4. Singer questions our intuitive moral sense that living affluently is different from murdering people. What are his arguments? Do you find them persuasive?

5. How does Singer criticize Locke's and Nozick's theories of rights?

6. Evaluate Singer's argument for our obligation to assist the absolutely poor.

7. How does Singer respond to Hardin's lifeboat argument?

GERALD P. O'DRISCOLL, JR., KIM R. HOLMES, AND MELANIE KIRKPATRICK

Who's Free, Who's Not

Gerald P. O'Driscoll, Jr., is Senior Fellow and Director of the Center for International Trade and Economics at the Heritage Foundation. Kim R. Holmes is Vice President and Director of the Kathryn and Shelby Cullom Davis Institute for International Studies at the Heritage Foundation. Melanie Kirkpatrick is Assistant Editor of the editorial page of The Wall Street Journal.

There is good news and bad news in the annual Index of Economic Freedom, to be published today by the Heritage Foundation and *The Wall Street Journal.*

The good news is that economic freedom continues to grow worldwide, continuing the amazing spread of the past decade. This is the seventh edition of the Index and the seventh year in a row that economic liberty has increased. This is heartening news indeed.

The bad news is that unfree economies still outnumber free ones. Most of the world's economies—81—remain mostly unfree or repressed, compared with 74 that are free or mostly free.

The best way to understand what this means for ordinary people, not just for traders or investors, is to compare average per-capita incomes. The average man, woman or child living in a repressed or mostly unfree economy lives a life of poverty on only about $2,800 a year. Compare this with the prosperous residents of the world's free economies, where the average per-capita income is $21,200, or nearly eight times greater. Put simply, the difference between poverty and prosperity is freedom.

The annual Index of Economic Freedom ranks the world's economies according to 50 economic variables in 10 broad categories: banking and finance, capital flows and foreign investment, monetary policy, fiscal burden of government, trade policy, wages and prices, government intervention in the economy, property rights, regulation, and black markets. Data from the seven years we've been ranking the world's economies are now online at www.index.heritage.org.

Here, region by region, are the principal findings of the 2001 Index of Economic Freedom:

North America and Europe

This is the most economically free region, and the richest. It also made the most progress toward economic freedom this year, with 24 countries improving their scores. The U.S., Britain, Ireland, Luxembourg, the Netherlands, and Switzerland are all in the top ten. Ireland, the Celtic tiger, has leapt into the #3 position.

Index of Economic Freedom
2001 Rankings

Free		

Free

1 Hong Kong
2 Singapore
3 Ireland
4 New Zealand
5 Luxembourg
U.S.
7 U.K.
8 Netherlands
9 Australia
Bahrain
Switzerland
12 El Salvador

Mostly Free

13 Chile
14 Austria
Canada
Denmark
Estonia
Japan
U.A.E.
20 Belgium
Germany
Taiwan
23 Bahamas
Cyprus
Finland
Iceland
27 Czech Rep.
Thailand
29 Argentina
South Korea
Sweden
32 Italy
Portugal
34 Uruguay
35 Barbados
Bolivia
Spain
38 Norway
39 France
Peru
Trinidad &
Tobago
42 Hungary
Kuwait
Lithuania
Panama
46 Costa Rica
Latvia
48 Belize
Greece
Guatemala
Morocco
Oman
Sri Lanka

54 Israel
Poland
56 Jamaica
Malta
Samoa
59 Cambodia
Dom. Rep.
Lebanon
Slovak Rep.
63 Benin
Jordan
Slovenia
Tunisia
Turkey
68 Armenia
Botswana
Colombia
Mali
Mauritius
Mexico
Namibia

Mostly Unfree

75 Ivory Coast
Malaysia
Mongolia
Saudi Arabia
Swaziland
Uganda
81 Philippines
Senegal
South Africa
84 Ghana
Guinea
Madagascar
87 Kenya
Qatar
Zambia
90 Algeria
Cameroon
Paraguay
93 Brazil
Gabon
95 Bulgaria
Burkina Faso
97 Cape Verde
Djibouti
Gambia
Guyana
Honduras
Mozambique
Nigeria
104 Fiji
Lesotho
106 Croatia
Ecuador
Nicaragua
Pakistan

110 Albania
Nepal
Niger
Tanzania
114 China
Georgia
Indonesia
Malawi
Papua New
Guinea
Venezuela
120 Chad
Egypt
Moldova
Rwanda
124 Ethiopia
Kyrgyz Rep.
Romania
127 Congo (Rep.)
Mauritania
Russia
130 Kazakstan
Togo
132 Bangladesh
133 India
Suriname
Ukraine
Yemen
137 Equatorial
Guinea
Haiti
139 Azerbaijan
Tajikistan

Repressed

141 Bosnia
Guinea-Bissau
Syria
144 Vietnam
145 Burma
146 Belarus
Zimbabwe
148 Turkmenistan
149 Uzbekistan
150 Laos
151 Iran
152 Cuba
153 Iraq
Libya
155 North Korea
Angola
Burundi
Congo (*Dem. Rep.*)
Sierra Leone
Somalia
Sudan

A star here is Lithuania, which catapulted to #42 from #61 last year after an ambitious program of private sector development and lower government spending. It is also the most improved economy in the history of the Index. Of the former communist countries, Estonia (#14) is the closest to becoming a fully free economy, with lower taxes and lower inflation raising its score this year.

Contrast these with Moldova, whose score declined more than any other country in the world. It's now way down the list at #120, due to growing inflation, higher government spending, more regulations and a not unconnected rise in black market activity. Russia, #127 this year, has seen its score drop year after year.

Western European countries bear the marks of the 1992 Maastricht Treaty, which set strict monetary standards and fiscal disciplinary requirements for would-be member states of the European Monetary Union. This commitment to monetary union, which took place last year, presented a policy challenge for signatories. Some have barely tried to adhere to these policies, but others, such as Luxembourg, seized the opportunity to enact structural reforms. All eleven countries in the EMU rate our highest possible monetary score.

Latin America and the Caribbean

El Salvador leads the region, improving enough to be labeled "free" for the first time. This is the "Hong Kong" of Latin America.

Many Latin American countries saw their scores rise because of their success at lowering inflation. The most dramatic example is Uruguay, whose inflation dropped to 5.6% in 1999 from 112.5% in 1990. Improvements were also seen in Brazil, Haiti, Barbados, Bolivia, Costa Rica, El Salvador, and Peru.

Paraguay fell into the mostly unfree category, tying Moldova for the biggest global drop in economic freedom this year. Argentina is still mostly free, but lost ground due to a decline in property rights. Economic liberty is waning in mostly unfree Venezuela, where tariff rates are up, regulations on business are growing, and protection of private property is declining. Venezuela's score not only worsened last year, but it has one of the worst records over the seven-year history of the Index.

North Africa and the Mideast

Economic freedom declined overall here this year. The big exception is Bahrain, still in the top ten even though its score fell this year; its high score is chiefly a result of the lack of taxation on personal income or corporate profits. Bahrain also has one of the world's lowest levels of inflation as well as a strong and efficient court system.

The United Arab Emirates has the second-freest economy in the region, followed by Kuwait, Morocco, Oman, Israel, and Jordan. Tunisia and Lebanon improved to mostly free this year, while Saudi Arabia became mostly unfree. Other mostly unfree economies are Qatar, Algeria, Egypt, and Yemen. The repressed economies—no surprise here—are Syria, Iran, Iraq, and Libya.

Sub-Saharan Africa

There is actually some good news to report this year from this poverty-stricken part of the world. For the first time in the history of the Index, Sub-Saharan Africa shows a net improvement in economic freedom, albeit from a dismal base.

That said, this remains the world's most economically unfree region—and by far the poorest. Of the 42 countries graded, none is free and only six are mostly free (Mauritius, Benin, Mali, Namibia, Zambia, and Botswana). This year we suspended grading of six countries because of the unreliability of data. Mozambique, still mostly unfree, is the second-most improved economy over the history of the Index. South Africa's score worsened this year, due in part to restrictive labor regulations, putting it in the mostly unfree category.

Asia-Pacific

Schizophrenia is the word to describe economic liberty in this region. Four of the world's freest economies are here—Hong Kong, Singapore, New Zealand, and Australia. But the Asia-Pacific is also home to six of the most repressed economies: Vietnam, Laos, Burma, Turkmenistan, Uzbekistan, and North Korea.

The world's single biggest improvement in economic freedom occurred in this region, with Thailand up to 27th place from 46. Its gain was thanks to lower inflation, less government spending, and lower tariffs.

Hong Kong is still Number One, but government spending rose, which isn't a good sign; in determining Hong Kong's score, that was offset by a decline in inflation. Singapore remains in second place, but its overall score declined due to increasing evidence of governmental interference in the economy.

QUESTIONS FOR REFLECTION

1. What evidence do the authors offer for their claim that "the difference between poverty and prosperity is freedom"?

2. What criteria do the authors use for determining the level of freedom in an economy? Why does freedom in these respects promote prosperity?

3. What implications does this study have for foreign aid? What, if anything, can richer countries do to promote greater global equality?